Archives of Maryland

Muster Rolls

and

Other Records of Service

of

Maryland Troops

in the

American Revolution

1775–1783

Published by Authority of the State, under the Direction
of the Maryland Historical Society

BALTIMORE
Maryland Historical Society
1900

Notice

In many older books, foxing (or discoloration) occurs and, in some instances, print lightens with wear and age. Reprinted books, such as this, often duplicate these flaws, notwithstanding efforts to reduce or eliminate them. The pages of this reprint have been digitally enhanced and, where possible, the flaws eliminated in order to provide clarity of content and a pleasant reading experience.

Muster Rolls and Other Records of Service
of
Maryland Troops in the American Revolution 1775-1783
(Volume Eighteen of the Maryland Archives)

Originally published
Baltimore, Maryland
1900

Reprinted by:

Janaway Publishing, Inc.
732 Kelsey Ct.
Santa Maria, California 93454
(805) 925-1038
www.janawaygenealogy.com

2017

ISBN: 978-1-59641-393-1

Made in the United States of America

PREFACE.

To THE MARYLAND HISTORICAL SOCIETY:

Gentlemen :—We have the honor to submit the Eighteenth Volume of the Maryland Archives, containing the Records of Maryland Troops in the Continental Service during the War of the American Revolution, 1775–1783.

This publication of the muster rolls and other records of service of Maryland men in the war of the American Revolution was undertaken in March, 1897. The bravery and excellent reputation of the troops of the Maryland Line were such that their names deserved to be rescued from oblivion, while the services rendered by men of this State in the Flying Camp, German Regiment and other commands were also noteworthy.

A large number of Revolutionary papers were found in the possession of the Johns Hopkins University, to which institution they had been presented by the late Col. J. Thomas Scharf, formerly Commissioner of the Land Office. The custody of these papers was given the Society with authorization to copy and print such of them as should seem desirable. All lists in this work, without indication of source, are to be understood as a part of this collection. In December, 1896, the Society had purchased at auction in New York City a number of muster rolls, some of which had at one time been in Col. Scharf's possession. These are indicated by the letter M. In the Land Office of the State at Annapolis are a number of valuable Revolutionary papers. Some of these contained information duplicating that elsewhere obtained; but one of them, a Record of the soldiers in the Maryland Line from 1776 to 1780, is the most important single list in this work. It comprises over 6,000 names and is contained in three manuscript volumes. A list of those who served in the two battalions of select militia called out in 1781, was also obtained from the Land Office. We are indebted to the courtesy of the Maryland Society of the Sons of the American Revolution for permission to print the copy of the pay-roll of the Maryland Line 1781–83, which they obtained from the Land Office.

There are two plans for the preparation of a work of this kind: one, adopted by the State of Connecticut, to print the lists as found and give a general index of names, the other, adopted by the State of

Massachusetts, to put together all the information concerning each man and arrange all names in alphabetical order. We have adopted the former plan for several reasons; first, because this is a volume of Maryland Archives and, as such, should contain the lists as they are found; secondly, because we have no sufficient means at hand to enable us to identify or differentiate the persons of the same name found in different lists; and, thirdly, because for certain purposes it is interesting and useful to know who were associated in any command.

Doubtless, it will be found that the records are not absolutely complete. The wonder is rather that so many lists have been preserved through so many vicissitudes and opportunities of loss. We have sufficient information from what has been preserved, to give us the record of most of the Continental soldiers. Unfortunately, we have not found the rolls of those two companies who marched from Frederick County to the siege of Boston, but many of the records of the Independent companies are in our possession. The muster rolls of the Flying Camp are preserved, but no record of their service can be found. The records of the Maryland Line are quite complete. A chronological arrangement of the muster and pay-rolls has been adopted as far as possible. The rolls of certain special commands, such as Lee's and Pulaski's Legions, which it is difficult to fit into any chronological arrangement, are placed at the end of the work. It should be noted that the term "deserter," when used without the addition "to the enemy," merely signifies that the soldier was absent from his command without leave. The discipline of the Revolutionary armies was not strict, and many left the ranks, when they were needed at home, returning to the service after a few months.

After most of the volume was in type, certain muster rolls were secured too late to be inserted in their proper place in the volume. These are contained in an appendix.

The Committee deems it proper to record its indebtedness to Dr. Steiner, the Junior member of the Committee, for the large amount of time and labor bestowed by him in the preparation of the present volume. Acknowledgments are also due to Dr. F. E. Sparks, the Society's Archivist, for careful work in superintending details of verification and arrangement. Respectfully,

CLAYTON C. HALL,
HENRY STOCKBRIDGE,
BERNARD C. STEINER,
Committee of Publication.

BALTIMORE, 1900.

TABLE OF CONTENTS.

	PAGE
Early and Independent Companies	4
Flying Camp Papers	29
Volume I of "Musters of Maryland Troops." (1st, 2nd, 3rd, 4th and Rawlings' Rgts.)	76
Volume II of "Musters of Maryland Troops." (5th, 6th, 7th and German Regiment.)	181
Supplementary German Regiment Papers	261
Volume III "Musters of Maryland Troops." (Names left out.)	273
Miscellaneous Maryland Line Papers	293
a. Muster and Pay Rolls for 1780	332
b. " " " " " 1781	361
c. " " " " " 1782	414
d. " " " " " 1783	476
e. Depreciation Certificates stopped 1784	514
f. Pay-roll of 1786	518
Artillery Rolls	563
Rolls of Maryland Men in Lee's Dragoons	585
" " " " " Pulaski's and Armand's Legions	591
" " " " " various other corps not belonging to Maryland	596
Miscellaneous Naval Rolls	606
Rolls of Escaped and Exchanged Prisoners	616
Return of Invalids	618
Appendix	637
Index	663

EARLY AND INDEPENDENT COMPANIES

RESOLVES OF THE MARYLAND CONVENTION OF DECEMBER, 1775.

1 January, 1776.

"Resolved, That this province be immediately put in the best state of defence.

Resolved, That a sufficient armed force be immediately raised and embodied under proper officers, for the defence and protection of this province.

Resolved, That 1444 men, with proper officers, be immediately raised in the pay and for the defence of this province.

Resolved, That 8 companies of the said troops, to consist of 68 privates each, under proper officers, be formed into a battalion.

Resolved, That the remainder of the said troops be divided into companies of 100 men each.

Resolved, That two companies of the said troops, to consist of 100 men each, be companies of matrosses, and trained as such."

14 January, 1776, Resolves were passed which authorized the troops to consist of a battalion of 9 companies, 7 independent companies, 2 companies of artillery and 1 company of marines. The officers were selected and their pay fixed. The Council of Safety was empowered to order these troops into Virginia, Delaware and Pennsylvania.

A Muster Roll of the Battalion of Regular Troops in the Service of the Province of Maryland and

First of that Part of the said Battalion stationed at Head Quarters at the City of Annapolis; to wit.

William Smallwood, Esquire,	Colonel.	present.
Thomas Price,	" Major.	"
Charles Wallace,	" Paymaster.	"
Christr. Richmond,	" Clerk to Colonel.	"
Dr. Michael Wallace,	1st Surgeon's Mate.	sick.
Joseph Marbury,	" Quarter Master.	present.
Mr. Jacob Brice,	Acting Adjutant.	"

and of the 1st, 2nd, 3rd, 6th, 7th and 9th Companies as follows. Also the 4th and part of the 8th, stationed at Baltimore Town.

First Company.

Commd. Jany. 3d, 1776.	John Hoskins Stone, Captain.	sick.	
" " " "	Daniel Bowie, 1st Lieut.	present.	
" " " "	John Kidd, 2nd "	"	[inst.
" " " "	Benjamin Chambers, Ensign.	resigned his comm. 3rd	

Rank.	Date of Enlistment.	Names.		Remarks.
Cadet		William Courts	present	
"		Henry Ridgely	"	
	Jan 30	James Fernandis		on detachment duty
	24	John Mitchell	"	
		Samuel Jones	"	
		Charles Smith	"	
		Thos. Simpson	"	
		James Sims, Sr.	absent	on furlough 23 May
		Samuel Hanson	present	
		Samuel McPherson	"	
Drum.	Mch 16	Henry Walworth	sick	in barracks
Fifer	Apl 15	Dennis Broderick	present	
Privates	Jan 24	Andrew Ross Lindsay		on detachment duty
	"	Andrew Green Sims		on guard
	"	Thomas Norris	"	
	"	Ignatius Doyglass	"	
	"	William Smoot		" "

Rank.	Date of Enlistment.	Names.		Remarks.
Privates	Jan 24	Edmund Cox	present	
	"	William Wheatly	"	
	"	John Boen	sick	in hospl
	"	John Hopson	present	
	"	John Adams	"	
	"	Thos. Way Connell	"	
	"	Joseph Cheatham	"	
	"	James Thompson	"	
	"	Samuel Thompson	"	
	"	John Plant	"	
	"	Thomas Smith	"	
	"	Jonathan Chunn	sick	and on furlough
	"	George Thomas	present	
	"	James Sims, Jr.	"	
	"	Samuel Wheatly	"	
	"	Bernard Nash	"	
	"	John Neal	"	
	"	Luke Matthew Sherburn	"	
	"	Samuel Luckitt	"	
	"	John Skipper	"	
	"	Thomas Burrows	"	
	"	Samuel Granger	"	
	"	Alban Smith	"	
	"	Edward Green	"	
	"	John Smith	"	
	"	John McPherson	"	
	"	Clement Edelen	"	
	"	Patrick Brady		on guard
	"	Francis Sherhard	"	
	"	Samuel Kurk	"	
	"	Francis Green Baggott		" "
	"	Charles Green	"	
	"	Charles Griffin		" "
	"	John Ward	"	
	"	Richard Sheake	"	
	"	Edward Edelen	"	
	"	Saml. Hamilton		" "
	"	Francis Ware Luckett	"	
	25	Matthew Garner	"	
	27	Nathaniel Downing	"	
	"	Josias Miller	"	
	"	John Shaw	"	
	"	Edward Smith	"	
	"	John Norris	"	
	"	Joseph Jason Jenkins	"	
	"	James Hoge		" "

Rank.	Date of Enlistment.	Names.	Remarks.	
Privates	Feb 1	Benjamin Gray	present	
	2	Richard Smith	"	
	3	John Smoot	"	
	4	William Clark	"	
	"	John Neary		on guard
	6	Saml. Vermillion	"	
	"	Truman Hilton	sick	in barracks
	7	Gilbert Garland		on guard
	Mch 6	Mark McPherson		" "

M

Second Company.

Commd.	Jan 20th, '76,	Patk. Sims, Captain.	present	
"	" " "	Benj. Ford, 1st Lieut.	"	
"	" 3rd, "	John Beans, 2nd "	"	
"	" " "	Henry Gaither, Ensign.	"	

Rank.	Date of Enlistment.	Names.	Remarks.	
Cadet		John Burgis	present	
"		Walter Cox	absent	on furlough 25 May
Serjt.	Feb 12	John Richardson	present	
"	Mch 7	Peter Clarke	"	
"	Feb 12	Edward Spurrier	"	
"	3	Alexius Conner	sick	in barracks
Corpl.	"	Michael Burgis	present	
"	Jan 29	Gazaway Watkins	"	
"	"	John Elson	"	
"	"	Henry Leek	"	
Drum.	"	Benj. Lewis	"	
Fifer	Feb 3	Thos. Horson	"	
Privates	Jan 28	Jonathan Robinson		on detachmt. duty
	Feb 7	John Lindsay		on guard
	17	Coxon Talbott		" "
	7	Lawrence Querney		" "
	Jan 29	James Mitchell	"	
	31	Peter Gallworth	"	
	Feb 17	Bozely Wright		" "
	3	Milburn Cox		" "
	"	John Willey	"	
	Apl 6	James Adams	"	
	"	Hugh Tomlin	"	
	8	Amos Green	"	
	9	Christr. Brumbargher	"	

Rank.	Date of Enlistment.	Names.	Remarks.
Privates	Mch 7	Thomas Simpkins	present
	11	Elisha Everit	"
	5	Willm. Skipper	"
	Feb 14	Willm. Heyder	"
	2	Philip King	"
	Mch 5	Richd. Johnson	"
	"	John Veach	"
	Feb 1	Patirck Nowlan	"
	9	Moses McNew	"
	29	Jacob Penn	"
	6	James Byzch	"
	3	Ben. Vermillion	"
	Mch 22	Richd. Lowe	"
	Feb 8	Robt. Nelson	"
	3	Basil Ridgly	"
	20	Michael Waltz	"
	23	Willm. Evans	"
	8	John Grant	"
	Mch 6	Thos. Connor	"
	Jan 26	John Russel	"
	Mch 6	John Edelin	"
	Feb 3	Danl. Rankins	"
	Jan 28	James Perry	"
	Feb 3	Richard Cox	"
	26	Joseph Steward	"
	7	Thomas Walsh	"
	3	John Walker	"
	Jan 31	Edwd. Caine	discharged 1 June
	Mch 11	Chas. Burroughs	"
	Jan 31	Philip Jinkins	"
	Mch 10	Ben. Burroughs	"
	Jan 28	Francis Thompson	"
	29	Francis Osburne	"
	Feb 5	Michael Barnitt	"
	13	Paul Hagarty	"
	3	Elias Perry	"
	29	Veach Burgis	"
	"	Jacob Holland	"
	3	Middleton Marlow	"
	"	John D. Lanham	"
	"	John Mills	"
	"	Thos. Perkins	"
	"	Henry Lanham	"
	10	Edward Blacklock	"
	6	John Rodery	"

RANK.	DATE OF ENLISTMENT.	NAMES.		REMARKS.
Privates	May 12	Robt. Sapp		present
	10	Thos. Daws		"
Also—				
Privates	Mch 6	Edmd. Carroll		sick
	Apl 19	Edwd. Jones		present
		M		

THIRD COMPANY.

Commd. Jan. 3d, 1776.		Barton Lucas, Capt.	present	
" " " "		Wm. Sterrett, 1 Lt.		on furlough
" " " "		Alex. Roxburgh, 2 Lt.	"	
" " " "		Wm. Ridgely, Ensign.	"	

RANK.	DATE OF ENLISTMENT.	NAMES.	REMARKS.	
Serjt.	Jan 20	Peter Brown	present	
"	21	James Burnes	"	
"	29	Zacha. Tannahill	"	
"	30	Levin Will Coxen	"	
Corpl.	31	Saml. Hamiltone	"	
"	Feb 3	Benedict Woodward	"	
"	Jan 29	Benjn. Warner	sick	in barracks
"	Feb 3	Zacha. Gray	"	" "
Drum.	Jan 22	Geo. Rex Leonard	present	
Fifer	Apl 19	Joshua Saffell	"	
Privates	Jan 20	John Cissell		at the magazine
"	"	Zacha. Tilly	"	
"	"	Christopher Beal		on guard
"	"	Leonard Watkins	"	
"	"	Thomas Scott	"	
"	"	Daniel McKay	"	
"	22	John Baker	"	
"	"	John Dunn	"	
"	"	Hugh Conn	"	
"	"	Robt. Lesache	"	
"	"	John Brown	"	
"	"	Benjn. Kelly	"	
"	"	Josias Connally	"	
"	23	Rhody Hously	"	
"	26	James Murphy	"	
"	27	George Knott	"	
"	"	John Enright	"	
"	"	Thos. Murray	"	

Rank.	Date of Enlistment.	Names.		Remarks.
Privates	Jan 29	William Pearce	present	
	"	Charles Jones	"	
	30	Josiah Hatton	"	
	31	Richard Stone	"	
	Feb 3	Samuel Ray		on guard
	Jan 31	George Hamiltone	"	
	Feb 3	John Fleming	sick	in barracks
	"	John Wood		deserted May 8th
	"	Richard Brookes		on guard
	5	Zacha. Willing	"	"
	"	Richard Wade	"	"
	7	John Owings	present	
	5	Alex. Jackson	"	
	8	John Murphy	"	
	"	John Jackson		dischd. 28th May
	6	John Flint	"	
	13	Abijah Buxtone	"	
	"	Nathan Peake	"	
	2	Timothy Collins	"	
	3	Jeremiah Owings	"	
	13	Joseph Barry	"	
	17	John Armstrong	"	
	Apl 11	George Wright	"	
	Mch 10	Philip Weller	"	
	Feb 8	Amos Allen	"	
	27	John Hughes	"	
	25	Thos. Forguson	"	
	7	Obediah Sumers	absent	on furlough 16 May
	"	Absolam Stevenson	present	
	20	John Halsey	"	
	16	Thos. Windom	"	
	Mch 2	James Smith	"	
	Jan 26	George Evauns	"	
	Mch 10	Thos. Shannen	"	
	Jan 22	George Leadbarn	"	
	27	Michl. Catons	sick	in barracks
	22	James Hurdle	present	
	Apl 2	Francis Cole	"	
	Feb 8	Alex. Allen	"	
	25	Wm. Baker	"	
	Apl 17	Garret Brinkenhoof	"	
	Jan 25	John Rex Leonard		
	Mch 10	Bazil Jenkins		
	Feb 2	Bartholomew Finn		
	"	Roddey Owings		

RANK.	DATE OF ENLISTMENT.	NAMES.	REMARKS.
Privates	Feb 17	George Read	disch 13 May
	May 14	James Gardiner	
	18	Patk. Collins	in the black hole
	June 9	Zachariah Hutchins (?)	present
		M	

FOURTH COMPANY.

Commd.	Jan. 3d, '76.	Thomas Ewing,	Captain.	present	
"	" " "	Joseph Butler,	1st Lieut.	"	
"	" " "	Vacant,	2nd "	Joseph Baxter was elected by the Convention 2 Jan., 1776. Probably resigned.	
"	" " "	Edward Pratt	Ensign.	present	

RANK.	DATE OF ENLISTMENT.	NAMES.	REMARKS.
Serjt.	Jan 8	John Smith, 1st Serjt.	present
"	"	John Toomy, 2d "	"
"	13	Thomas Cunningham, 3d Serjt.	"
"	23	Robert Morrow, 4th "	" discharged 3d May
Corpl.	May 3	George Hamelton, 1st Corpl.	"
"	"	Robert Harvey, 2d "	sick in hospital
"	26	Samuel McMellon, 3d "	" " "
"	"	William McMellon, 4th "	" " "
Drum.	23	Patrick Ivory	present
Fifer	"	—— Hired	"
	3	John McGlaughlin, Corpl.	"
	20	Vachel O'Legg	"
	18	Richard Watts	"
	24	Charles Pritchard	"
	"	Levi Vezey	discharged 31 May
	22	William Martin	"
	20	Leonard Lion	sick
	29	Nathaniel Cortland	present
	20	Samuel Glasgow	"
	29	William Baggott	"
	24	William McGinnis	"
	"	Thomas Hamelton	"
	27	James Bennett	discharged 29 April
	18	Edward Price	"
	27	Thomas Haynon	deserted 7th instant
	20	Robert Crafford	"
	Jan 27	Thomas Crafford	"

Rank.	Date of Enlistment.	Names.		Remarks.
Privates	Jan 18	William Grimes	present	
	24	Dennis Turley	"	
	29	Patrick Reed	"	
	24	James Matthews	"	
	"	Charles Rieley	sick	in the hospital
	"	John Rieley	"	" " "
	22	Matthew Murry	present	
	18	John Herron	"	
	22	Thomas Hill		discharged 26th April
	29	Michael Cady	"	
	20	Peter Burk	sick	in the hospital
	"	William Chaplin	present	
	29	John Price	"	
	20	John O'Neal	"	
	"	Richard Whealin	"	
	29	Thomas Holland	"	
	"	Thomas Mason	"	
	22	Neal Dearmond	"	
	"	William McCaulley	"	
	29	William Little	absent	on furlough
	"	Richard Carbury	present	
	8	Terrence Martin	"	
	29	John Gorden	"	
	24	Thomas Baker		discharged 3d June
	"	Samuel Wiltshire	"	
	29	Edward McKinzie	"	
	22	Valentine Smith	"	
	24	Edward Cosgrove	sick	in the hospital
	29	Thomas Wiseman	present	
	"	William Nixon	"	
	24	Edward Wright	sick	
	22	Andrew Warrick	present	
	24	Peter Smith	"	
	29	John Haney	absent	on furlough
	8	Thomas Donolan	present	
	29	Hugh Pugh		deserted 19th instant
	27	William Parr	"	
	24	Patrick Baxter	"	
	29	Richard Doyle	"	
	24	John Cavender	"	
	"	Thomas McGuire	"	
	27	Samuel Thomas	sick	in the hospital
	29	James O'Lary	"	" " "
	June 3	William McGlaughlin	present	
	May 31	Samuel Goslin	"	

Rank.	Date of Enlistment.	Names.	Remarks.
Privates	Apl 26	Joseph Mongomery	present
	May 3	James Reed	
	8	James Lamb	"
Also—			Signed
			Thos. Ewing Captain
		Cornelius Murphy	
Drum.		Thos. Roberts	
		Wm. Preston	deserted
		James Wills	
		Michael Davis	
		Thomas Jones	
		Hugh Munroe	
		Ralph Allison	
		William Hart	
		Wm. Luguard	
		John Purtle	
		Abraham Tennis	
		Edward Freeman	
		Francis Millner	
		James Wells	refused

Fifth Company.

Nathaniel Ramsey, Captn.
Levin Winder, 1st Lieut.
Alexander Murray, 2nd Lieut.
Walker Muse, Ensign.

Elected by the Convention of Maryland, Jan. 2nd, 1776.*

Sixth Company.

Commd. Jan. 3d, '76.	Peter Adams, Captain.	present	
" " " "	Nathl. Ewing, 1st Lieut.	"	
" " " "	Alex. Murray, 2d "		on furlough
" " " "	John Jordan, Ensign.	"	

Rank.	Date of Enlistment.	Names.	Remarks.
Serjt.	Jan 30	Joseph Elliott	present
"	Feb 15	Edward Edgerly	"
"	Jan 30	Thomas McKeel	"
"	"	Thomas Dwyer	"

*See Proceedings of the Conventions of Maryland, pp. 67, 68.

Rank.	Date of Enlistment.	Names.		Remarks.
Corpl.	Jan 22	Danl. Dwigens	present	
"	"	Saml. Dwigens	"	
"	30	Jas. Rogan	"	
"	23	Danl. Floyd	"	
Drum.	Feb 15	Robert Ross	"	
Fifer	Jan 22	Chas. McKeel		dischd. 7 June
Privates	"	John Clark	"	
	"	Zacha. Nicholson	"	
	"	Henry Covington	"	
	"	Wm. Laighton	"	
	"	Wm. McDaniel	"	
	"	George Jackson	"	
	23	John Hatton	"	
	"	Alex. Wright	"	
	"	John Floyd	"	
	"	Elijah Floyd	"	
	"	Moses Floyd	"	
	"	John McFadon	"	
	"	Carbry Burn	"	
	"	John McClain	absent	on furlough
	25	John Johnson	present	
	26	Jas. Kelly	"	
	30	Willm. McGreger	"	
	"	Thos. Fisher	"	
	"	John Powell	"	
	"	Joseph Pirkens	"	
	"	Joseph Bootman	"	
	"	Hugh Wallace	"	
	"	Willm. McDaniel, 2nd	"	
	"	James Bell	"	
	Feb 6	Henry Clift	"	
	"	Thos. Cooper		on guard
	15	Saml. McCubbin		" "
	"	Wm. Glover		" "
	"	John Bryan	"	
	"	Wm. Holms		" "
	"	Wm. Ray	"	
	"	Thos. Laffy	"	
	"	Jas. Kirk	"	
	"	Wm. Leeson	"	
	22	John Lowry	"	
	"	John McClain, of Harford	"	
	"	Alex. Fulton	"	
	"	Jas. Craig	"	
	"	Robert Man	"	

Rank.	Date of Enlistment.	Names.		Remarks.
Privates	Feb 22	Patk. Quigley		in the black hole
	24	Wm. Locke	present	
	"	Wm. Nagle	"	
	"	John Lynch	"	
	"	Hugh McClain	"	
	"	Jas. Carmichael	"	
	"	Thos. Williams		on guard
	"	John Kerby		" "
	"	Jas. Gibson	"	
	"	Jno. Galway	"	
	"	Robt. Ritchie	sick	in barracks
	May 7	Wm. Aitken	present	
	"	Hugh Galway	"	
	"	John Morrow	"	
	"	Geo. Dowling	"	
	"	Wm. Clark		on detach. duty
	"	Wm. Temple	"	
	20	John Phelps	"	
	7	James Barkley	"	
	15	Crisenberry Clift	"	
		M		

Seventh Company.

Commd.	Jan. 3d, '76.	John Day Scott, Capt.	present	
"	" " "	Thos. Harwood, 1 Lt.	"	
"	" " "	Thos. Goldsmith, 2 "	absent	on furlough
"	" " "	James Peale, Ensign.	present	

Rank.	Date of Enlistment.	Names.		Remarks.
Cadet		James Disney	absent	on furlough
Serjeant	Jan 20	Saml. Barber		disch. 23 May
"	"	Willm. Sands	"	on furlough recruit'g
"	Mch 9	John Smith Selby	present	
"	Feb 15	Thos. Gordon	"	
Corporal	26	Willm. Noyes	"	
"	15	Joshua Lamb	"	
"	"	Andw. Ferguson	"	
"	25	John Smith	absent	on furlough
Drummer	Jan 20	John Meek	present	
Fifer	Feb 3	Edward George	"	
Privates	Jan 20	James Low	"	
	"	John Babb	"	

Rank.	Date of Enlistment.	Names.		Remarks.
Privates	Jan 20	Joseph Green	present	
	"	Willm. Austin	"	
	"	Joseph Anglain	"	
	"	Anthony Ryan	"	
	"	Nicholas Watkins	"	
	22	Richard White	"	
	"	Thomas White	absent	on guard
	"	Joseph Bassil	"	" "
	24	Cephas Hoy		on detachment duty at the magazine
	"	Hugh Armstrong	present	
	27	Ignatius Boon	"	
	"	Joseph Mattingly	"	
	29	Dennis Howley	"	
	"	John Jasper	absent	on guard
	"	Burgess Howard	sick	boarded out
	"	Francis Fairbrother	"	" "
	"	Richard Rawlings		confined in guard-house, to be disch., disch. 21 April
	Feb 1	Henry Weedon	present	
	"	Charles Leech	sick	in barracks
	"	Thomas Mayo	present	
	5	John Ashton	"	
	10	Clement Barber	"	
	"	Joshua Naylor	sick	" "
	"	Edward Lloyd Wales		disch. 25 May
	"	Thomas Robinson	"	in barracks
	"	Thomas Weedon	present	
	14	Willm. Johnston	absent	on guard
	15	John Boothe	present	
	Mch 12	Thomas Hamilton	"	
	Feb 15	Joseph Matthews	"	
	26	Edward Murphy	"	
	25	Nicholas Gassaway	"	
	26	Charles O'Neale	sick	in barracks
	"	Peter Lawless	present	
	28	James Connery, (or Conway)		disch. 23 May
	Mch 1	Richd. Elwood	"	
	5	James Pope	"	
	"	Moses Paget	sick	in barracks
	8	Joseph Yater	"	" "
	9	Willm. Watts	present	
	11	Joseph Orme	sick	" "
	"	Dorset Hoy	present	

Rank.	Date of Enlistment.	Names.		Remarks.
Privates	Mch 11	John Harper		disch. 9 May
	"	Francis Mitchell	present	
	"	John Carr	"	
	8	John Majors	"	
	"	Edward Edwards	"	
	Jan 24	Dennis Kellis	"	
	Feb 12	James McGill	"	
	16	John Hooper		disch.
	Jan 29	James Murphy	"	
	Mch 12	James Ranter	"	
	Jan 21	Nicholas Watkins	"	
	Feb 28	Abraham Chapman		disch.
	Mch 11	Nathaniel O'Neale	"	
	"	James Devaun	"	
	"	William Sewell	"	
	Feb 15	Wm. McKinsey	absent	making cloaths for company
	Apl 14	John Nottingham	present	
		Wm. Kinnick	"	
		Elisha Richardson	sick	in barracks
		Nicholas Ridgely	present	
		John Swan	"	
		M		

Eighth Company.

Samuel Smith, Captain. Joseph Ford, 2nd Lieut.
James Campbell, 1st Lieut. Bryan Philpot, Ensign.

Elected by the Convention of Maryland, Jan. 2nd, 1776.*

A Copy of the Enlistment of the Eighth Company of the 1st Battalion of Maryland forces. We whose names are hereto Subscribed do voluntarily Enlist ourselves Soldiers to Serve as Such during the present dispute between Great Britain & America unless Sooner discharged by Order of the Convention or Council of Safety of Maryland for the Time being hereby Subjecting ourselves to Such Rules & Regulations as are or shall be made by the Convention of Maryland for Regulating & governing the forces in the Pay of this Province, Witness our hands

* See Proceedings of the Conventions of Maryland, pp. 67, 68.

18   Records of Maryland Troops in the Continental Service

1776		1776		Balto. Town, 1 Apl, 1776
Jan 11	Patrick Walsh	Jan 24	John Rowan	A Roll of this Com-
"	Festus Burke	"	Adam Cramer	pany was returned the
"	John Rashe	25	Ludo. Taylor	—day of——but not be-
"	Dyonisius Hargreaves	26	Philip Hawkins	ing made out properly
"	Christian Closs	27	Samuel Percival	was returned. Since
12	Samuel Clark	"	Thomas Nowlan	which I have chang'd
"	Laurence Hutin	"	Jacob Plumly	some of the men or find-
"	John Cain	"	Gasper Clutter	ing it difficult to train
13	Andrew Yaeter	"	John Offield	them.
"	William Hopkins	"	Matthew Ritchie	Sam. Smith
"	Robert Britt	"	Robert Ford	
"	Joseph Crosbie	"	Francis Petty	
		"	John Dill	
		"	Jerry Jones, deserted	

. [Torn off.]

NINTH COMPANY OF LIGHT INFANTRY.

Commd. Jan. 3rd, '76. George Stricker, Capt.   present.
   "   "   "   "   Thomas Smyth, Jr., 1st Lieut.   "
   "   "   "   "   James Ringgold, 2nd   "   resigned 3d inst.
   "   "   "   "   Hatch Dent, Jr., 3rd   "

RANK.	DATE OF ENLISTMENT.	NAMES.		REMARKS.
Cadet		Richard Dorsey	present	
"		Larkin Dorsey	"	
Serjt.	Jan 12	Peter McNaughton	"	
"	20	John Good	"	
"		David Giveny	"	
"	26	William Bruce	"	
Corpl.	Feb 4	William McPherson	"	
"	Jan 20	Adam Everly	"	
"		Jacob Alexander	"	
"	31	Robert Chandler	sick	in hosp'l
Drum.	28	John Row	present	
Fifer		Dennis May	"	
Privates	20	Jacob Gardner	"	
	21	Davall Stottlemeir		on detach. duty
	"	Henry Miller	"	
	"	Fredk. Keller	"	
	"	Alex. Nailor	"	
	"	Melcher Brobeck		" " "
	"	John Mugg		on guard
	"	Michael Hackethorn	"	
	"	Henry Young	"	

Rank.	Date of Enlistment.	Names.		Remarks.
Privates	Jan 22	Valentine Lynn		on guard
	"	James Miller		" "
	"	John Heywood		" "
	"	William Tarrance	present	
	"	Andrew Hardy	"	
	"	Adam Bromcord	"	
	"	John Gerrish	"	
	"	Martin Kipheart	"	
	"	Michl. Curtz	"	
	"	Michl. Mullen	sick	in hospital
	"	Isaac Rice	present	
	"	Robert Tune	"	
	"	William Lynn	"	
	"	Michael Miller	"	
	"	William Witner	sick	in barracks
	"	John Glatz	present	
	"	Andrew Conslean	"	
	"	Fredk. Miles	sick	in hospital
	"	Nicholas Nailor	present	
	25	Alexander Boston	"	
	26	Thomas Byrn		drafted for Artillery
	"	Samuel Price	absent	on furlough 27 May
	"	Samuel Denny	present	
	" .	Causamer Hill	"	
	"	John Hoofman	"	
	"	William Casbear	"	
	27	John McCabe		discharged from the service 11 May, '76
	28	George Hellmold	"	
	"	John Ross	"	
	"	Samuel Workman	"	
	"	Philip Kern	"	
	"	John Kasler	"	
	"	James Taylor	"	
	29	Jacob Grenewald	"	
	"	Frederick Myre	"	
	"	Jacob Harman	"	
	"	Peter Kline	"	
	"	Pacel Martin	"	
	"	Jacob Fisher	"	
	"	George Cretzinger	"	
	"	Willm. Smith	"	
	31	Stephen Fleehearty	"	
	"	George Morriner	"	
	"	George Kipheart	"	

Rank.	Date of Enlistment.	Names.		Remarks.
Privates	Jan 31	Henry Remsburg (?)	present	
	"	Peter Breat	"	
	"	Michael Deaver	"	
	Feb 8	John Hite	"	
	"	James Beale	"	
	10	Solomon Cretzinger	"	
	"	Peter Myre	"	
	12	Basil Holland	"	
	Mch 4	Levean Todd	"	
	10	Michael Haun	"	
	Apl 11	John Taylor	sick	in barracks
	17	John Cobeth		on guard
	June 7	Notley Davis	present	
			Signed,	W. Smallwood.

June 10th, 1776. M

Stationed at Baltimore Town—

Francis Ware, Lieutenant Colonel. — present.
Mordecai Gist, 2nd Major. — "
Dr. Charles Frederick Wiesenthal, Surgeon. — absent.
Dr. William Augustus Dashiell, 2nd Surgeon's Mate. — present.
And the 4th, 5th and 8th Companies.

M

1st INDEPENDENT MARYLAND COMPANY. [CHARLES AND CALVERT COUNTIES.]

Rezin Beall, Capt.
Bennet Bracco, 1st Lieut.
John Halkerston, 2nd "
Daniel Jenifer Adams, 3rd Lieut.

officers elected by the Convention of Maryland Jan. 2nd, 1776.*

Bennet Bracco, Capt.
John Halkerston, 1st Lieut.
Thomas Beale, 2nd "
Colmore Williams, 3rd "

later list given in McSherry's Hist. of Maryland.†

2nd INDEPENDENT MARYLAND COMPANY. [SOMERSET COUNTY.]

John Gunby, Capt.
Uriah Forrest, 1st Lieut.
William Bowie, 2nd "
Benjamin Brooks, 3rd "

officers elected by the Convention Jan. 2nd, 1776.‡

---

*Proceedings of the Conventions of Maryland, pp. 67, 68, 73, 93.
†McSherry's Hist. of Maryland, appendix A.
‡Proceedings of the Conventions of Maryland, pp. 67, 68, 73, 93.

Muster Roll of the 3d Md. Independent Company, Aug. 20th, 1776.
[Worcester County.]

John Watkins,	Captain.	Commd. Jan. 5th	present.
Moses Chaille,	1st Lt.	" " "	absent, gone to be married.
Solomon Long,	2nd "	" " "	present.
Ely Dorsey,	3rd "	" " "	"

Rank	Names.	Date of Enlistment.		Remarks.
Serjeant	Richard Grace	Jan 25	present	
"	Solomon Jarvis	"	"	
"	Dixon Quinton	Feb 2	absent	on furlough 12th inst
"	James Done	Apl 7	"	" " 29th June
Corpl.	Peter Hall	Jan 29	present	
"	John Purdy	25	sick	in barracks
"	Josiah Cathell	Feb 5	"	" "
"	Littleton Johnson	3	present	
Drum.	John Morgan Jones	June 16	"	
Fidler	William Jones	Mch 19	"	
Privates	Richard Ayres	Feb 10	"	
	Arthur McHenry	"	"	
	John McCormick	Apl 1	absent	on furlough 12th
	John Williams	Feb 27	present	
	Luke Lamb	10	sick	in the country
	James Truitt	18	"	at his mother's
	Joseph Johnson	9	present	
	Dennis Driskell	5	"	
	William Marchmont	3	sick	in the country
	Thos. Niember	10	present	
	James Cathell	13	"	
	John Brasher	2	absent	on furlough 10th
	Bennet Mason	Apl 29	present	
	Robert Shipley	Feb 15	"	
	Willm. Jarman	Mch 4	"	
	James Hall	Feb 12	"	
	Zadok Purnell	7	sick	at his mother's
	John Houston	2	present	
	James Crapper	9	"	
	John McQue	3	sick	in barracks
	Belitha Taylor	5	present	
	Levi Cathell	13	"	
	James Barber	Mch 11	"	
	George Bishop	Feb 18	sick	at his father's
	Philip Hall	3	present	
	John Shockley	Apl 8	sick	in barracks
	Randall Smulling	Feb 13	present	
	Solomon Taylor	9	"	
	Jesse Selby	Apl 28	"	

Rank.	Names.	Date of Enlistment.		Remarks.
Privates	Jesse Wright	Feb 21	present	
	Thomas Donaldson	24	"	
	Zadock Timmons	9	"	
	Ephraim Stilley	"		deserted 19 July
	Edward Coll	"	sick	in barracks
	John Freeman	Mch 12	"	" "
	Arthur Allen	Feb 9	absent	on furlough
	Stephen Allen	"	"	" "
	Kendall Hislup	2	present	
	Joseph Roan	3	"	
	Jas. White, (of Wm.)	6	"	
	Isaac Lone	3	"	
	Joshua Wheelton	24	"	
	Dunnick Dennis	Mch 9	sick	in the country
	Robert Jarman	28	present	
	James Ayres	Feb 28	sick	" " "
	Benj. Curtis	10	present	
	John Cottingham	3	"	
	Edwd. Maglamary	13	sick	" " "
	James White, (of J.)	10	present	
	Samuel Owings	13	"	
	Laban Teague	9	"	
	Laban Cathell	13	"	
	Kendall Smock	3	"	
	Francis Jester	"	"	
	Jacob Ardes	"	"	
	James Mason	2	"	
	Reuben Magee	21	"	
	Samuel Donaldson	Apl 15	sick	" " "
	William Davis	16	present	
	Levin Davis	May 6		deceased 20 July
	Thomas Hayward	Feb 3	absent	on furlough
	John Morris	Mch 12	present	
	Levi Morris	16	sick	in barracks
	Wm. ———ton	Apl 17	present	
	James Selby	30	"	
	Jarman Beatherd	Mch 18	absent	on furlough
	Thos. Williams	Apl 15	"	" "
	George Truitt	Feb 2	sick	at his father's
	Wm. Cowley	14	"	" " "
	John Franklin	8	present	
	Saml. Truitt	Apl 1	"	
	James Nelson	Feb 10	"	
	Wm. Cahoon	3	"	
	Zachariah Bishop	8	"	
	Walter Ives	17	"	

Rank.	Names.	Date of Enlistment.		Remarks.
Privates	Elisha Baker	Mch 16	absent	on furlough
	Thos. Lendall	Apl 21	present	
	Danl. Wheelton	Feb 24	"	
	Willm. Digman	3	"	
	George Jarman	Apl 5	"	
	Willm. Streets	Feb 9	"	
	Jesse Gray	May 16		deserted 30 June
	Lambert Purnell	7	sick	at his mother's
	Robert Holston	June 30	present	
	Thos. Newman	May 20	"	
	George Roberson	June 1	"	
	John Donaldson	Feb 3	"	
	Abram Smith	May 1	"	
	John Nicholson	June 9	"	
				Signed J. Watkins, Capt.

M

MUSTER ROLL OF THE 4TH INDEPENDENT MARYLAND COMPANY.
[TALBOT COUNTY.]

Muster Roll of the 4th Independent Company of Maryland Regular Troops, September, 1776.

Commissd. Jan. 5th, 1776.   James Hindman, Capt.
"   "   "   "   Archibald Anderson, 1st Lieut.
"   "   "   "   Edward Hindman, 2nd   "
"   Mch. 7th, "   William Frazier, 3rd   "

	Date of Enlistment.	Serjeants.	Date of Enlistment.	
Thomas Hall	Jan 20	deserted 28 July		
		Peter Hardcastle	Jan 26	
		John Miller	22	enlisted as corporal
James Morgan	"			
William Martindale	28			
		CORPORALS.		
Perdue Martindale	Jan 28	Clement Cannon	Jan 23	enlisted as a private
James Orrell	26			
Levin Frazier	Feb 11	enlisted as a private		
		DRUM AND FIFE.		
James Mead	Mch 16	John Williams		
		PRIVATES.		
Bryan Sinnett		William All	Feb 3	
John Emory	Jan 26	Richard Snook	"	

PRIVATES.

Name	Date of Enlistment	Notes	Name	Date of Enlistment	Notes
David Thatcher	Jan 28		James Coburn	Jan 31	
Nathan Harrington	"		Edward Welch	30	
Peregrine Evans	Feb 19		Benjamin Crisp	"	
Lawrence Connerley	Jan 25		Jonathan Valiant	Feb 5	
John Fleming			John Hopkins	2	
Joshua Chippey	28		Nathan Madding		
Humphry Spencer	Feb 2		John Ryan	6	
Henry Stapleford	15		Nathan Duling	Jan 25	
Solomon Harris	5		Daniel Richardson	Feb 12	
John Millington	15		Lambert Robinson	Jan 20	
Robert Ferguson	19		Job Barnes	"	
Thomas Brown	Jan 20		Thomas Colvert	25	
James Burgess	24		William Smith	29	
Henry Higgins	26	disch. 28 July	James Watts	20	
Richard Caton	29		David Priestley	23	
William Blanch	Feb 4		William Pitts	25	
Stephen Bryan			William Tarr	Feb 2	
Hambleton Warren	19		Delahay Duling	Jan 26	
Reuben Jeffers	Jan 28		Joseph Merchant	28	missing 27 Aug. Long Island
James Devereux	29				
James Todd	Feb 7				
John Hughes	Jan 25	missing 27 Aug. on Long Island	Thomas Davis	27	
			Russel Armstrong	25	
			Henry Gates		
Thomas Camper	26		John Foster Leverton	28	
Jacob Jeffers	28		Joseph Jackson	"	
James Robinson	Feb 6		Thomas Lumley	"	
John Humbey	8		Philemon Porter	25	
Charles Moore	12	deserted 3 Aug.	John Smith	28	
			William Beauver	Feb 2	
Henry Martin	Jan 20	enlisted as corporal	William Bratchee	12	
			Ben. Worthington	Jan 22	
Peter Bromwell	22		Thomas Buckley	24	
James Ray	23		Thomas Start	25	
Robert Ellis	"		Richard Sampson	Feb 8	
Francis Hazledine	25		William Jenkins	Jan 22	
Samuel Giles	28		James Jones	"	
Daniel Higgins	29		John O'Bryan	23	
Gilbert Burgess	Feb 12		William Woods	28	
Andrew Hughes	Jan 20		George McNamara	26	deserted 3 Aug.
Richard McDaniel	23				
Richard Besswick	25		William Kenney		
Peter Jeffers	27		Nicholas Farewell		
Thomas Barker	Feb 5	left on Long Island 29 Aug.	Thomas Burgess		
			Charles Cooper	25	

PRIVATES.

Name	Date of Enlistment		Name	Date of Enlistment	
Thomas ———			Ezekiel Abbott	Jan 23	deserted 3 Aug. taken again 5 Aug.
John Buckley	Jan 24				
John Masterson	28				
John Garrott	Feb 10				
Matthew Hardikin	Jan 23		John Dobson	31	dead
Thomas Connerly	25		John Sweeney	Feb 1	
William Burgess	"		Thomas Liles	2	
William Melony	"		Stephen Byram	6	
Robert Heffernon	30		John Murphy	7	
Josias Murdoch	31	deserted			

Names in the above list, without date of enlistment, are taken from a roll published in the "Pennsylvania Magazine of History and Biography," January, 1898, page 503. Stephen Bryan is, perhaps, Stephen Byram, and Thomas ——— is, perhaps, Thomas Connerly.

5TH INDEPENDENT MARYLAND COMPANY. [ST. MARY'S COUNTY.]

John Allen Thomas, Captain. officers elected by the Con-
John Steward, 1st Lieut. vention Jan. 2nd, 1776.*
John Davidson, 2nd "
Henry Neale, 3rd "

MUSTER ROLL OF THE 6TH INDEPENDENT MARYLAND COMPANY. [DORCHESTER COUNTY.]

Commissd. Jan. 5th, 1776.	Thomas Woolford, Capt.	present.
" " " "	John Eccleston, 1st Lieut.	"
" " " "	Hooper Hodson, 2nd "	"
" Mch. 2nd, 1776.	Lilburn Williams, 3rd "	"

Date of Enlistment.	Names.		Remarks.
Feb 20	John Gray	present	
"	Willm. Woolford	"	
Jan 20	Hugh McKinley	sick	in barracks
Apl 2	John Linch		dischd. 29th June
Feb 26	Hooper Hodson	present	
20	William Watts	"	
23	Jas. McCollester	"	
7	Edwd. McFading		dischd. 10th inst
Mch 15	Richd. Frazier	"	
4	Peter Taylor	"	

*Proceedings of the Conventions of Maryland, pp. 67, 68, 73, 93.

Date of Enlistment.	Names.		Remarks.
Aug 10	Hugh Walworth	present	
Feb 20	Thomas Howell	"	
Jan 25	Richard Wood	"	
"	John Martin	"	
26	John Callihorn	"	
"	Samuel Ash	sick	in the country
"	John Watkins	"	in barracks
27	Chris. Minges	absent	on furlough
28	Thomas Gaines	sick	in barracks
27	John Murphy	present	
29	Jacob Hustone	"	
"	Edward Flin	"	
"	Wm. Compton	"	
1	Patk. Farren	sick	" "
"	William Cole	present	
2	Lawrence Hughes	sick	" "
4	Lawrence Fitzpatrick	present	
"	Barney Maloy	sick	in the country
"	William Thom	present	
"	Samuel McCracking	sick	" " "
8	Daniel Norris	present	
"	Samuel Rones	sick	in barracks
Feb 15	George Nest	present	
"	William Lee	"	
26	John Malone	"	
"	Joseph Read	"	
Mch 2	Hugh Kelly	"	
"	Michl. Conner	"	
"	Daniel Brophy	"	
7	John Welsh	"	
Feb 21	Edward Hodson	"	
"	Nathan Wright	sick	in the country
"	Edmond Garoughty		dischd. 10th August
23	John Dunn	present	
"	Deweast Downing	"	
"	Jonathan Price	"	
Mch 21	Ephm. Wheelar	"	
11	Patrick Rach	sick	in barracks
12	John Basset	present	
Feb 20	Thos. Grayham	"	
"	Luke Cox	"	
"	Solomon Tylor	"	
"	Thomas Bayley	"	
"	Robert Ruarke	"	
"	William Smith	"	
"	Matthew Hayard	"	

during the War of the American Revolution, 1775–83.

Date of Enlistment.	Names.		Remarks.
Feb 20	Charles Foxwell	sick	in the country
"	Samuel North	present	
"	Miles Shehern	"	
"	Calib Joy	"	
"	Daniel Dinet	"	
"	William Mann	"	
"	Philip Hodge	"	
23	William Dingle	"	
"	Francis Noble	sick	in barracks
"	John Hayward	present	
"	John Caffey	"	
"	Edward Hardikin	"	
26	Matthew Colbert		deceased 8th June
Mch 3	J——— Sherren	"	
4	William ———lihay	"	
"	Thomas Harrison	"	
5	Edward Williams	"	
4	William Killinough	"	
9	Thomas Saunders	"	
14	Isaac Southard	"	
Feb 24	Levin Prichard	"	
"	Joseph Staplefort	"	
"	Spencer Saunders	"	
25	John Noble	"	
26	Richardson Gamble	"	
Mch 1	James Sulivain	"	
"	Patrick Caton	"	
7	John Keron	"	
4	Patrick Connorly	"	
15	Denniss ———	"	
19	William Hale	sick	in the country
21	Hooper Elliot	present	
28	John Martin, (of Dorset)	"	
"	Thomas Hayard	"	
"	James Andrew	absent	on furlough
Apl 1	Samuel Spencer	present	
8	William Hays	sick	in barracks
"	James Urey	present	
9	Jeremiah Andrew	"	
May 2	Robert Skinner	"	
7	James Haney	"	
9	Thomas Hart	"	
Apl 3	Richard Bush	"	
May 27	Absolum Comini	"	
July 20	Robert Henderson	"	
26	William Becks	"	

Date of Enlistment.	Names.		Remarks.
July 13	James Dolly	present	
20	John Stevens	absent	on furlough
"	Robert Smith	present	
"	Benjamin Deshield	sick	in barracks
Aug 10	William Andrew	present	

M

Signed, Thomas Woolford, Capt.
Aug. 19th, 1776.

7TH INDEPENDENT MARYLAND COMPANY. [QUEEN ANNE'S AND KENT COUNTIES.]

  Edward Veazy, Capt.   officers elected by the
  William Harrison, 1st Lieut.   Convention Jan. 2nd,
  Samuel Turbutt Wright, 2nd Lieut.   1776.*
  Edward DeCourcy, 3rd Lieut.

Officers of the two Rifle Companies that served before Boston in 1775.

  Capt. Michael Cresap   Capt. Thomas Price
  1st Lieut. Thomas Warren   1st Lieut. Otho Holland Williams
  2nd Lieut. Joseph Cresap   2nd Lieut. John Ross Key.†
  Ensign Richard Davis

NOTE.—Early artillery companies will be found under the heading of Artillery Rolls.

* Proceedings of the Conventions of Maryland, pp. 67, 68, 73, 93.
† McSherry's Hist. of Maryland, appendix A.

FLYING CAMP.

RESOLVES OF CONTINENTAL CONGRESS.

3 June, 1776.

"Resolved, That a flying camp be immediately established in the middle colonies; and that it consist of 10000 men; to complete which number,

Resolved, That the colony of Pennsylvania be requested to furnish of their militia 6000, Maryland, of their militia 3400, Delaware government, of their militia 600.

Resolved, That the militias be engaged to the first day of December next, unless sooner discharged by Congress."

RESOLVES OF THE MARYLAND CONVENTION OF JUNE, 1776.

25 June, 1776.

"Resolved unanimously, That this province will furnish 3405 of its militia, to form a flying camp, and to act with the militia of Pennsylvania and the Delaware government in the middle department; that is to say, from this province to New York inclusive, according to the request of the Congress in their resolutions of the 3d day of this instant June."

These companies were to serve within said limits until 1 December, 1776, unless sooner discharged by Congress. None were to be compelled to serve out of said limits or beyond 1 December. They were to be arranged in 4 battalions and 1 company, each battalion consisting of 9 companies. Warrants were to be issued, by the President of the Convention, to the persons appointed by the Convention, to enroll the non-commissioned officers and privates. A captain was to enroll 30, a lieutenant 20, and an ensign 16 men. Enrollments, even if not completed, were to be returned to the Convention, or Council of Safety, by July 20th. If any enrollments were not complete, the Convention, or Council of Safety, could commission the persons to whom the warrants were directed or any other persons, as would best promote the service. Enrollments were to be of those who voluntarily offered themselves. All who enrolled were to sign the following enrollment: "We the subscribers, do hereby enroll ourselves to serve as militia of Maryland in the middle department, that is to say, from this province to New York inclusive, until the first day of December next, unless sooner discharged by the honourable Congress according to the resolutions of the Convention of Maryland, held at Annapolis the 21st day of June, 1776."

The order adopted in arranging the Flying Camp Companies is that of the Convention of Maryland in the election of the officers of said companies, 29 June, 1776. After each County's name, the names of the officers of the companies for such County, elected by the Convention, are given. See Proceedings of the Conventions of Maryland, p. 176.

St. Mary's County.

Capt. Uriah Forrest
1 Lt. Wm. Bond
2 Lt. Moses Tabbs
Ensign Edward Mattinly *

A List of men enrolled by Capt. Uriah Forrest, Lieut. Wm. Bond, Lieut. Moses Tabbs and Ensign Mattingley, to compose one company in Col. Thomas Ewing's Battalion for the Flying Camp. Mustered, examined and passed July 28th, 1776, by Ign. Fenwick, Jr.

Geo. Armstrong
Chas. Lewellin
Ign. Simms, Jr.
Saml. H. Briscoe
Wm. J. Hager
John Maddox
John McKoy, (McKay)
Edw. Spalding
Geo. Elms
Edw. Marshall
Fran. Watkin
Edward White
John Bramhall
Auston Howard
Matthew Shanks
Charles Jones
Wm. Ennis
Thos. Bartcly
Elias Baily
Robert Shanks
Jesse Dennis
James Tear
James Melton
Jesse Tennison

Thos. Shircliff
Jo. Bradshaw
James Bramhall
Thos. Davie
Luke Cusick
Jesse Herbert
Thos. Martin
Richard Bullock
Jesse Jordan
Wm. Hebb
Joshua Ellis
Gabriel Williams
John Moore
Richard Gardiner
Saml. Jordan
James Jordan
Chas. Bond
Justinian Weeden, (Wheeden)
Wm. Cheseldine
Reubin Craig
Thos. Wood
Wm. Coode
Joseph Dailey

William Rock
Jere. Allstone, (Allstan)
Alex. Shanks
Ign. Knott
Thos. Bridgitt
Wm. Moles
Joseph Long
John Bond, Jr.
Moses Adams
John Baker
Enoch Sanders
John Price, Jr.
Henry Horn Carter
Wm. Howard
Wm. Burnett
Thos. Cook, Jr.
Enoch Adams
Richard Morris
Wm. Johnstone
Wm. Carpenter, Jr.
Richard Kerbey
Thos. Haywood
Thos. Files

Wm. Adams
Jo. Adams
Robt. McClannon, (McClelland)
Wm Hendry
John Christopher
Richard Hindmore
Joseph Alvey
Ign. Watkin, (Wathen)
John Fields
Richard Weakley, (Weaklin)
John C. Watkin, (Wathen)
John Hughs
Thos. Cahill
John Holland
John Compton
Thos. Biggs
Rich. E. Gatton, (Gadden)
Joseph Johnstone
John Graves

Enlisted by Lieut. Wm. Bond, July 3rd, 1776. Reviewed and passed by John H. Briscoe, July 12th, 1776.

Gerard Cheseldine.

*Proceedings of the Conventions of Maryland, p. 176.

CHARLES COUNTY.

Capt. Thomas Hanson
1 Lt. George Dent
2 Lt. Samuel Jones
Ensign William Adams

Capt. Belain Posey
1 Lt. Henry Boarman
2 Lt. John Forbes
Ensign Gerard Fowke*

Enrolled by Thos. Hanson. Passed by Saml. Hanson, Jr., July 19th, 1776.

Paul Parker	William Donnollon	Hezekiah Dunington
William Hanson	Samuel Leach	Richard Thompson
Joseph Simms	Thomas Gaugh	William Henry
Whorton Qualls	Thomas Milstead	Joseph Timms
John Nelson	Wilson Gray	Francis Wier
William Cox	Jesse Evans	Edward Pearson
David Dyal	Alexander Evans	Richard Fowke
Thomas Jordan	William Rippith	Thomas Harrison
Penner Nelson	Alexander Swan	Isaac Steuart
Edward Wilmon	John Worder	Henry Mudd

Townly Ratcliff   John Adlow Clements, of Joseph

Gentlemen :—The above is the enrollment of two men, one of which I was defective when I waited on you the 5th inst. and the other, Viz. John Adlow Clements, enrolled in the place of a certain Bayne Smallwood whom I have returned to you, by erasing whose name and adding the other you'll greatly Oblige
    Gentlemen Your Mt. Obt. St.
Sunday, 11th of August, 1776.   Geo. Dent, of John.

Enlisted by Samuel Jones. All, except John Hatchen and Samuel Chandler, passed by Will. Harrison July 27th, 1776.

Samuel Elgin	Thomas Goley, (Goaley)	John Franklin
Jacob Johnson	Elijah Clark	George Gray
Richard Clinscales, (Clinkscales)	James Scott	Charles Riggin
	Ignatius Luckett	William Wapels, (Waple)
John Brawner	Samuel Maddox	John Philops, (Phillips)
Joseph Manning	Noah Maddox	Samuel Chandler
George Speake	John Hatchen	William Franklin

* Proceedings of the Conventions of Maryland, p. 176.

Enrolled by Wm. Adams. Passed by Wm. Harrison, July 25th, 1776.

Joseph Mcant	Walter Sutherland	John Fitzgerald	Richard Elgin
Thos. Patterson	Thomas Ashford	Zachariah Davis	John Carvoll
Aaron Maddox	Antipas Coltart	Michael Notaire	Wm. Johnson
Samuel Adams	Thos. Perry	Walter Coomes	John C. Coomes

Enlisted by Capt. Belain Posey. Reviewed by John Marshall, July 8th, 1776.

Joseph Taylor, (Talor)	Henry Duggins	Samuel Hodskin, (Hodgkins)
John Posey	Baker Wathen	Hezekiah Cooksey
John Aushur	George Mountgomery	Clement Boarman
Thos. Andrew Dyson	John Williams	John Simmons
Richard Ferrell	Francis Edilen	Gilferd Minetree
John Mudd	Zeph. Swann	John Burnett
Thomas Maccan	Ledstone Smd. Cooksey	Jacob Dixson
Joseph Boarman	Gerrard Johnson	William Robertson
Daniel Barron	Gustavous Burch	John Wilder Wood
Thomas Barron	Thomas Suit, (Sute)	Joseph Thompson
Benjamin Mudd	Henry Boarman, Jr.	

ADDITIONAL MEN.

Alexander Weakling	Basill Swann	Paul Minitree
Wm. S. Compton	James Swann, Jr.	William Layman
Benj. Postin	St. Larence Posey	Ignatius Martin
Benjamin Cox	James Cox	Thomas Posey

Last man enrolled July 27th, 1776.

Enlisted by Henry Boarman. Mustered and passed by J. Hawkins, July 18th, 1776.

Henry Miles	Richard Blanford	Francis Wathan
Thomas Ozburn	Henry Miles, of Joseph	Ignatius Beaven
Samuel Daily	James Downing	James Montgomery
Leonard Smith	Joseph Philbert	Walter Glasgow
Charles Beaven	Francis Wathan, of Barton	Henry Luckett
James Keech	John Bowling	Richard Smith
Edward Miles Smith	Matthew Johnson	

Enlisted by Lieut. Forbes. Passed by J. Hawkins, July 20th, 1776.

William Burroughs	Gladden Hunt	John Dent
Richard Beavan	Thomas Tyser	Gerrard Davies

George Walls	Zeph. Burroughs	William Woodburn
William Walls	Perry Michall	Robert Spicknall
William Anderson	Richard Kinnick	James Greer
William Whitely	Jesse Edwards	Luke Gardiner
John Robertson	George Harrison	Leonard Hickey

CALVERT COUNTY.

Capt. John Brooke
1 Lt. Frederick Skinner
2 Lt. Nathaniel Wilson
Ensign James Somerville*

Enlisted by Captain John Brooke. Passed by Alex. Somervill, July 25th, 1776.

Richard Everitt	Richard Gray	Wm. Price
John McKenney	Wm. Brinkley	Stephen Hutchings
Absolam Games	William Gardener	Ellis Dixon
Thomas Gray	Basil Hellen, (drummer)	John Tucker
John Hungerford	John Baker	Walter Bowen, (Bawen)
Edward Denton		

Enlisted by Capt. John Brooke. Passed by Joseph Wilkinson, July 26th, 1776.

James Hellen	Richard Hudson	William Marques
Thomas Everett	Clement Hutchins	John Morris
Absolum Greaves	Nathaniel Simmons	Benjamin Parran
Nathl. Cullember	Benjamin Harvey •	George Ireland
Thomas Hardesty, (son of Jos.)	John Baptis Delafrany	

Enlisted by Frederick Skinner. Passed by Benjamin Mackall, 4th, August 23rd, 1776.

Ignatius Blanford	Kilman Lisby	John Younger
Joseph Blanford	Joseph Briant	James Lawrence
John Boon	Thomas Gwin	John Grimes
Henry Wood	James Clerke	John Stevens
William Wilson	Archibald Edmondson	John Ramsay, Jr.
Arthur Skinner	John Sanders	John Prout
Thomas Rice		

William McDaniel, a man enlisted by Frederick Skinner, is not present, but am of Opinion upon being examined will certainly pass as effective.   Benj. Mackall, 4th.

---

*Proceedings of the Conventions of Maryland, p. 176.

Enlisted by Nathaniel Wilson. Passed by Benj. Mackall, 4th, August 23rd, 1776.

George Young	Rich. Allen	John Cullenber	James Stewad
Robert Games	John King	Joseph Crook	Jono. Wedge
Arron Abell	Cuthbirt Abell	Leonard Moore	Adam King
Benson Biles	Jereh. Wood	Saml. Ashcom	William Evans

Enlisted by Nathaniel Wilson. Passed by Joseph Wilkinson, August 31st, 1776.

Samuel Day	Arthur Hall
Thomas Stone	Benjamin Johns

Enrolled by Ensign James Somervill. Passed by Alex. Somervill, July 25th, 1776.

George Gray	Bazil Newton	Joseph Davis
William Baker	Henry Newton	Joseph Bruden
James Greaves Avis		

Enrolled by Ensign James Somervill. Passed by Jos. Wilkinson, July 26th, '76.

Jesse Day	Richard Marshall	Roger Howard
James Simmons	Thomas Hardesty	Elisha Quarey
John Wells	John Burkett	Joseph Deale

PRINCE GEORGE'S COUNTY.

Capt. John Hawkins Lowe	Capt. Robert Bowie
1 Lt. John Magruder Burgess	1 Lt. Benjamin Brooks
2 Lt. William Duvall	2 Lt. William Dent Beall
Ensign Horatio Clagett	Ensign Colmore Beans, resigned and William Shircliff appointed July 6th, 1776, by the Convention
Capt. Alexander Howard Magruder	2 Lt. Benjamin Contee
1 Lt. William Sprigg Bowie	Ensign Alexander Truman*

Enrolled by Capt. John H. Lowe. Reviewed and passed by John Addison, July 13th, 1776.

Walter Bayne	Samuel McSwain	Willian Worren
Lenard Lacklin	Samuel Hambleton	Josias Bayne
Philip Locker	David Burtin	Thomas D. Marlow

* Proceedings of the Conventions of Maryland, pp. 176, 177.

during the War of the American Revolution, 1775–83.

James Penny	John Masters	Josua Sissill
John Willson	Osburn Talburt	John Hoggins
Henry Wade	Eli Lanham	David Bently
George Wade	Abraham Russill	John Sherwood
Thomas Jenkins	Darby Mullowny	Elias Lanham
John White	Benjamin Talburt	James Locker
Richard Pickrell	John Worren	James Lowe

Enrolled by Lieut. John M. Burgess. Reviewed and passed by John Addison, Lieut. Col. of the Lower Battalion, July 20th, 1776.

John Taylor	Andrew Ogden	John Williams
Thomas Mitchell	Richard B. Edelen	Solomon Write
James Hinds	William Orde	Jacob Miller
John Miller	Edward Longly	James Ball
Nathan Lowe	James Clemons	John Marlowe
Wm. Tuell	William Long	Walter Dyer
Samuel Warner	James Jarboe	

Enrolled by Lieut. William Duvall. Passed the 18th of July, 1776, by John Addison, Lieut. Col. of the Lower Battalion.

Benjamin Jonson	James Kidwell	John Conner
John Macdaniel	James Miles	Bassil Hatten
William Shugar	George Jinkens	Notly Ford
Joseph Hoppes	George Boswell	Walter Power
William Gilpin	Ignatious Gilpin	Bayne Smallwood
Ebenezar Athy	Ignatious Howard	George Daymond
Samuel Morris	Edward B. Smith	

Enrolled by Ensign Horatio Clagett. Reviewed and passed by John Addison, July 15th, 1776.

Butler Edelen Stonestreet	John Clements	Ledstone Smallwood
Zacharias Meek Wade	Thomas Willcoxon	James Johnson
Elijah Kidwell	Wm. Smallwood Wynn	Walter Dyar
Smallwood Aeton	Henry Aeton	William Berrey
Henry Hannon	John Vinson	John Marlow
John Lay	Peter Oard	George Newman
Ralph Clements	Jacob Miller	

A Return of Capt. Bowie's Muster Roll. Part of the Flying Camp. Made by Lt. Brooke, Lt. Beall and Ensign Shircliff.

Names	When enrolled	By whom	Place of nativity	Highth	No. guns	Ages	Remarks
Charles Mitchell	July 6	B. Brooks	Maryland	5.5	1	18	Brown hair, fair skin
William Berk	10	do	P. G. County	5.4		17	
Wm. Anderson	8	do	do	5.10	1	22	
Benj. Duvall	12	do	do	5.10½	1	16	
Andrew Millar	17	do	do	5.11	1	25	
Nathan Mitchell	"	do	do	6.	1	20	
Wm. Hutcheson	"	do	do	5.6	1	25	
James Hardie	"	do	do	5.10	1	24	
John Dew	25	do	do	5.9	1	20	
Edward Mitchell	20	do	do	5.6	1	22	
Thomas Johnson	Aug 8	do	England	5.10	1	35	
William Roberts	20	do	do	5.6		23	
Joseph Williams	"	do	P. G. County	5.8		48	
John James	July 25	do	do	5.4		25	
Thos. Simpson, Jr.	16	William Shircliff	Chas. County	6.	1	17	
Thomas Owen	"	do	do	6.¼	1	23	
Basil Bowman, (Bazil S. Boarman)	14	do	do	6.3	1	19	
John F. K. Sanders	16	do	do	5.11		20	
Walter Macatee	17	do	do	6.¼	1	21	
Thomas Sanders	"	do	do	5.8½	1	18	
John Wallace	16	do	do	5.8½		21	
Roger Simms	"	do	do	5.8½		21	
Mark Norriss	"	do	do	5.7¼	1	17	
James Deven	13	do	do	5.10		20	
William Spalding	17	do	do	5.6½		17	
Wm. Boomar, (Boarman)	12	do	do	5.4½	1	16	
John Fisher	17	do	Germany	5.6½	1	25	
Thos. Simpson, Sr.	16	do	Chas. Co.	6.	1	25	
Joseph Shutliff, (Shiercliff)	"	do	do	5.11	1	22	
Chas. Sewele, (Sewall)	12	do	do	5.10	1	22	
Leonard Edelen	15	do	P. G. County	5.8	1	22	
Jeremiah Atchuson, (Atchison)	27	Capt. Bowie	do	5.8	1	18	
George Edelen	"	do	do	5.7¼		17	
Thomas Roby	Aug 3	do	do	5.5¼		17	
Wiseman Clagett	July 17	do	do	5.9	1	23	
Greenbury Simpson	16	do	do	6.¼	1	27	
Saml. Busey	20	do	do	5.6	1	31	
William Mud	Aug 3	do	do	5.4	1	19	

Names	When enrolled	By whom	Place of nativity	Higthh	No. guns	Ages	Remarks
John Macclane	July 17	Capt. Bowie	P. G. County	5.8	1	31	
Thomas Webster	Aug 4	do	Scotland	5.5		42	
Edward Kaine	July 16	Wm. D. Beall	England	5.5		20	Fair complexion, brown hair
Thomas Drown	18	do	do	5.7		25	Dark hair, fair complexion, much pocked
John Hurley	19	do	Ireland	5.6		25	Well made with dark hair, fair complexion
Edward Jenkerson	"	do	England	5.11		40	Red hair, brown complexion
Peter Phealean	"	do	do	5.8		26	Black hair, fair complexion
John Mantle	20	do	do	5.6		20	Brown hair, fair complexion, very well made
James Phillips	22	do	do	5.6		22	Black hair, yellow complexion
William Harriss	"	do	do	5.7		21	Black hair, fair complexion
Jeremiah Cooke	29	do	Maryland	5.4		18	Black hair, brown complexion
John McDonnald	30	do	do	5.8		20	Brown hair, brown complexion
Thomas Fitzsimmons	Aug 4	do	England	5.3½		21	Black hair, brown complexion
Thomas Gordon	"	do	Scotland	5.2½		19	Brown hair, brown complexion
Joseph Coewn (?)	9	do	Maryland	5.5		25	ditto, ditto
James Olive	"	do	England	5.7		18	Brown hair, fair complexion
John McDonnald	18	do	do	5.6		33	Brown hair, brown complexion
Thomas Lann	4	Capt. Bowie	Maryland	5.4		16	
Basil Ray	July —	do	do	5.8	1	22	
George Older	21	do	do	5.10		24	
Elijah Coe	22	do	do	6.	1	25	
Philip Pindle, (Pindell)	Aug 1	do	do	5.9	1	18	

Enlisted by Alexander Howard Magruder. Reviewed by Jos. Sim, Col. of the 11th Battalion, Prince George's County, August 21st, 1776.

Names.	When Enrolled.	Names.	When Enrolled.
Robert Baden	July 3	Wm. T., (or F.), Greenfield, (Cadet)	July 18
Jeremiah Baden	"	William White	"
Thos. Wm. Sasser	"	William Sasser	"
Edward Mullan	4	Edwd. Stephens	"
Henry Bean	"	John White	"
John Sollers	"	Maryland Beaven	July 20
Isaac Barnett	9	John Watson	25
Randolph Marlow	10	Benjamin Rawlings	"
John Downing	"	John Rawlings	Aug. 1
Hugh Stephens	15	William Mayhew	"
John Young	18	Bryan Mayhew	5
Benj. Paggatt	"	Thomas Lane	19
Thomas Bean	"	Leonard White	"
Put on List after viewed by the Colonel			
Peter Dayley	July 23	Joseph Bumford, (Fifer)	July 12
Charles Leech	"	Blk. Boy Gim, (Drummer)	14

Raised by Alex. Trueman, Ensign, for Capt. Magruder's Company. Passed by Jos. Sim, Prince George's County, August 21st, 1776.

Names.	When Enrolled.	Names.	When Enrolled.
Thomas Baden	July 3	Wilson Cage, (or Caye)	July 8
Elijah Rawlings	4	Nevitt Rawlings	4
Thomas Cohoe	"	William Burnes	20
John Mills	5	John West	2
Benjamin Ellis	6	Samuel Grover	3
William Teanneclift	8	Jonathan Weeden	5
Leonard Hickey	7	John Bean	4
Richard Jones	"	George Naylor	"

ANNE ARUNDEL COUNTY.

Capt. Edward Norwood
1 Lt. Samuel Godman
2 Lt. John W. Dorsey
Ensign Richard Talbott
Capt. Edward Tillard
1 Lt. Samuel Lloyd Chew
2 Lt. John Sprigg Belt
Ensign John Gassaway, resigned and John Kilty appointed by the Convention, July 5th, 1776.

Capt. Daniel Dorsey
1 Lt. Joseph Burgess
2 Lt. John Lorah. Must be John O'Hara, who resigned and James Howard appointed by the Council of Safety, July 24th, 1776. It is printed Lorah in the Journal of the Convention, but it must be a mistake.
Ensign Michael Burgess
Capt. James Disney

during the War of the American Revolution, 1775–83.   39

1 Lt. Henry Ridgely	Capt. Thomas Hammond
2 Lt. Jonathan Sellman	1 Lt. Thomas Mayo
Ensign Edward Spurrier	2 Lt. Joshua Merriken
	Ensign Andrew Hammond*

Enlisted by John Worthington Dorsey. Passed by John Dorsey, July 22nd, 1776.

Jonas Smart	Patrick Robinson	Michael O'Conner
Richard Sparks	Moses Petcock	Joseph Tearn
Charles Harvey	Petticoat Earp	Dennis O'Hario
William Ridgway	Mathew Boys	Robert Archibald
George Bennette	Mark Halfpenny	Robert Burgoone
John Hood	James Logey	Lawrence Greyer
Samuel Partridge		

Enlisted by Rich. Talbot. Passed by John Dorsey, July 22nd, 1776

Ignatius Davis	Cornelius Mattox	Hanbury Jones
William Phelps	Edw. Bennette	Chas. Sewell
William Jones	Thomas Weston	Thos. Bland
Alex. Scott	Robert Gainer	James Fosh
Mich. Gladman	Charles Chapman	Ely Hyatt
Bartholemew MacDonald		

Capt. Tillard's Muster Roll, 1776.

Enrolled by Edw. Tillard. All of Maryland except Joseph Jee of England. Returned the Council of Safety, July 10th.

Soldiers' Names.	Hight.	Soldiers' Names.	Hight.	Soldiers' Names.	Hight.
Jacob McSeney, (Macceney)	5. 10	Richard Dennisson, (Denison)	5. 7½	Geo. Parker	5. 7½
Steph. Allingham, (Allenjem)	5. 11	Geo. Simmons	5. 5	Henry Powell	5. 8½
Caleb Conner	5. 9	Willm. Dove, Jr.	5. 8	John Battee	5. 4
John Miles	5. 9	Thomas Taylor	5. 9	Wm. Brashears	5. 5
Robert Day	5. 10	Saml. White	5. 6½	Richard Sansberry	5. 6
Willm. Simmons	5. 7	Charles Watkins	5. 7	James Frazier, (Fraser)	5. 7
John Stone	5. 6	Isaac ——— (Jones?)	5. 9		
Edwd. Cowley, (Crowley)	5. 6	Jacob Sollars	5. 3	Isaac Lansdale	5. 7
Willm. Parrett, (Parratt)	5. 6	Willm. Wells	5. 6½	Fardinan Battee	5. 5
				Joseph Jee	5. 6½
John Deale	5. 8	Philip Davis	5. 6½	Wm. Cowley	5. 6

*Proceedings of the Conventions of Maryland, p. 177.

Enrolled by S. Chew. All of Maryland. Enrolled the 25th July and returned the Council of Safety.

Soldiers' Names.	Hight.	Soldiers' Names.	Hight.	Soldiers' Names.	Hight.
David Furganson, (Ferguson)	5. 11	Willm. Roberts	5. 6	Benj. Childs	5. 6½
John Grames	5. 7	John Morgan	5. 4	Richard Camden, (Cambden)	5. 8
John Giddings	5. 8	Orrell, (Oriel), Marr	5. 8	Nathan Wells	
Peter Gardiner, (Gardner)	5. 2	Lovely, (Lovedy), Hinton	5. 6	James Bowie	
Joseph Crandle, (Cramdale)	5. 5	Solomon Tayler	5. 7	John Gardner, (Gardiner)	5. 9
Willm. Nowell	5. 10½	Henry Roberts	5. 10	Abraham Chapman	5. 4
Robert Sollars	5. 2½	John Souvener, (Scrivner)	6. 1		

Enrolled by J. Belt. All of Maryland except James Johnson of Scotland, and Thomas Tophouse of England.

Joseph Crasby	5. 8½	John Slack	5. 3½	Willm. Williams	5. 3½
Willm. Ray	5. 6	John Galwith	5. 4½	James Johnson	
John Smith	5. 5½	John White	5. 4½	Henry Lamboth	5. 7
Humphry Menchon	5. 2	Willm. McNorton	5. 7½	Thomas Tophouse	5. 2
Zadock Brashears	5. 8½	Willm. Collins	5. 6	Willm. Everett	5. 4½

Enrolled by J. Kilty. All of Maryland.

John Lavy	5. 6½	Zachariah Turner	5. 6½	John Everitt	5. 4
Thomas Stone					

Enlisted by Capt. Edward Tillard. Passed by Rich. Harwood, Jr., July 16th, '76.

Isaac Jones   Wm. Miles   Robert Welsh   Danl. Skelly

A List of men enlisted by Joseph Burgess for the Flying Camp. Passed July 20th, 1776.

Rich. Burgess	Wm. Edge	Ely Barnes	Joseph Hobbs
Philip Barnes	Joshua Burgess	John Leason	Samuel Stoner
Elijah Barnes	James Higgins	John Nuton	John Knock
Benj. Whips	George Sturt	John Rickords	Wm. Shedbolt
Jacob Jarvis	Wm. Wood	Edw. Purdy	Charles Dorsey

during the War of the American Revolution, 1775-83.

Enlisted by Michael Burgess. Passed by Col. Hyde, July 20th, 1776.

Vachel Dorsey	Jacob Lavely	Vachel Stevens, son of Benjamin	Joseph Webb
Richd. Johnson	Wm. James	John Jimson, (or Jenison)	Daniel Brown
James Carwin	Thos. Price		Henry Ireland
Patrick Stoaks	Thos. Gaither		John Frost
Math. Wilson		Aquilia Barnes	

Enrolled by Capt. James Disney, Jr. Passed by Col. Richard Harwood, July 13th, 1776.

Richard Ricketts	Gassaway Watkins	Isaac Jones	Isaiah Cheney
Stephen Watkins	John Watkins	Benjamin Jones	Benj. Phelps
Richard Disney, Jr.	Thomas Latten	Richard Jones	Basil Barry
Robert Davis	John Thomas	William Nicholason	Jacob Barry
Vincent Lusby	John Watts	Richard Jones, (barber)	Samuel Watts
William Holliday	Snowden Taylor		Chaney Williams
John Hopper	Richard Robinson	William Nichols	Joseph Williams, Jr.
Thomas King	William Williams	Thomas Baldwin	Willliam Rear

Enrolled under Henry Ridgely, Jr. Passed by Col. J. Carvil Hall, Aug. 26th, 1776.

Thomas Pattan	John Waters	Thomas Williames	George McIntoch
Edward Hearn	Edward Moyston	Patrick Burke	Benjamin Penn
Thomas Millard	Thomas Grinall	George Robinson	Joseph Bennett
Henry Hall	Jacob Ryan	John Molony	Samuel Levy
George Morfitt	Richard Harrison	John Graitwood	James Warwick

Enlisted by Edw. Spurrier. Passed by Thomas Dorsey, July 20th, 1776.

John Wells	Charles Hunt	James White	Charles Fenton
Robert Mark	Nathan Ryan	Mathew Daley	John Benson
Charles Ashmore	Wm. Reynolds	Thos. McCauley	Richard Page
Richard Biddle	Thos. Reynolds	Zachariah McCauley	John Linsey, (or Linday)

Enlisted by Thomas Mayo. Last man enlisted July 20th, 1776.

Edward Marshall	Nicho. Brewer	James Evans	Wm. Langly
Wm. Humphreys	Benjamin Miller	Thos. Moss	Joseph Jacobs
Nathaniel Shepherd	Jas. Davidson	Wm. Sally	Charles Mattox
Thos. Fairbrother	Wm. McCartin	Nathnl. Hall	Stephen Grymes
Wm. Grimes	Nathl. Grimes	Edward Jefferson	John Brown

FREDERICK COUNTY—LOWER DISTRICT. [MONTGOMERY COUNTY.]

Capt. Edward Burgess	Capt. Leonard Deakins	Capt. Benjamin Spyker
1 Lt. John Gaither	1 Lt. Thomas Nowland	1 Lt. Greenbury Gaither
2 Lt. Thaddeus Beall	2 Lt. Elisha Williams	2 Lt. Richard Anderson
Ensign Thomas Edmondson	Ensign John Griffith, resigned and Dennis Griffith appointed by the Council of Safety, Oct. 2nd, 1776.	Ensign Nicholas Scybert*

A List of Capt. Edward Burgess' Company of Militia in the Lower District of Frederick County, viz:

Edward Burgess, Capt.
Thomas Edmonston, 1st Lieut.
Alexander Estep, 2nd Lieut.
Zephaniah Beall, Ensign.

*Nathan Orme
*Richard Weaver Barnes
*Charles Gartrell
*Alexander Lazenby
Edward Harden
*Zachariah Aldridge
*Samuel Beall White
*Nathan Waters
*Benjamin Fitzjarrald
*Gilbert Bryan
*Nathan Musgrove
*James Burgess
*Benjamin Burgess
Arthur Legg
*Thomas Freeman
John Sheekels, (or Shukels)
*John Ray
*Shadrech Penn, (Peen)
*Zephaniah Browning
*George Fryback
*John Hanson Wheeler
*Samuel Wheeler
*Thomas Culver
*Henry Lazenby
*Jeremiah Beall
John Harding
*Samuel Taylor Orme
*Thomas Wallis
*John Lashyear, (Layzare)
Reson Hollon

Alexcious Simms
Thomas Nichols
Laurance Hurdle
William Crow
Lenard Wood
Saml. Carter
Thomas Beall
Kinsey Hanee
Joseph Gartrell
*John Geehan, (or Guhan)
James Hurvy
Edward Trout
Samuel Solamon
William Hopkins
*Miles Mitchell
*Thomas Wood
*Charles Maccubin Reynolds
*Joseph Estep
*John Tuckker
Jeremiah Ferrell
Samuel Purnal
Thomas Sheekels, (Shukels)
Thomas Gittings
Archibald Hoskinson
Alexander Barratt
Owen Haymon
Alexander Edmonston Beall
John Beaden
Alexander Tucker

John Wilcoxen
Richard Burgess
John Fryback
Daniel Lewis
John Ryan
Benj. Tucker
Wevour Waters
Morris Brashears
Obed Willson
Stephen Gatrell
James Beall, (of Roger)
John Elwood
James Carter
Josiah Harding, (Harden)
Henry Clark
John Nichols
Alexander Robert Beall
William Garten
Solomon Dickerson
William Young Conn
Marthew Lodgeade
Leaven, (Leven), Beall
John Ferrell
William Hicke
Dennis Marhay
John Crook
Samuel Taylor
William Blackburn
Richard Nicholasson

---

* Proceedings of the Conventions of Maryland, p. 177.

during the War of the American Revolution, 1775-83.   43

Lower District of Frederick County, to wit:—

I do hereby certify that I have at sundry times reviewed eighty-seven of the men as above enrolled by Capt. Edward Burgess, for the service of the Flying Camp; but that, two, to wit: Obed Wilson and Henry Clarke, who are on the said List, are reported by Capt. Burgess to be effective, able bodied men; and in my opinion and judgment the whole number so reviewed, is composed of effective men and fit for military duty.   Given under my hand this 7th Day of August, 1776.

John Murdock.

[Names with a star prefixed are those who were enlisted by Capt. Burgess, July 12th, 1776.]

Enrolled by Capt. Leonard Deakins. Reviewed and passed by Richard Crabb and Francis Deakins, Frederick County, July 13th, 1776.

Lloyd Beall	William Draper	Thomas Stewart
Zachariah Askey	Henry Allison	John Stewart
William Lanham	Leonard Hagon	William Walker
Richard O'Daniel	Charles Mahoney	James McCulloch
David Green	John Baptis Gauff	William Lovet
John Taylor	James Gauff	Jessee Woodward
Thomas Lightfoot	John Yates	Nathan Wilson
James McDeed	Jacob Veatch	Robert Wilson
Samuel Spycer	William Longley	Edward Jinkings
Bartholomew Edelin	Dennis Griffith	William Hays

Enrolled by Capt. Benj. Spyker. Reviewed and passed by Will. Deakins, Jr., Frederick Co., July 29th, 1776.

1 Zachariah Rily	11 John Smith	21 John Reynolds
2 John Gorman	12 Archibald Trail	22 William Holland
3 John McDavid	13 Nathan Green	23 Allan Mackabee,(Mockbee)
4 Edward Northcrafft	14 John Currington	24 Francis Downing
5 Neil Dogherty	15 William Murphy	25 James Wilson
6 Michael Stanly	16 Joseph Crawly	26 Thomas Love
7 William Carlin	17 Edward Goodwin	27 Thomas Knowlar
8 Peter Hoey, (Hoy)	18 Timothy Maclamary	28 Abraham Booker
9 Strutton Hazel	19 John Turner	29 Joseph Penny
10 Henry Burton	20 William Glory	30 John Wilson

Enlisted by Greenbury Gaither. Reviewed and passed by Will. Deakins, Jr., Fredk. Co., July 29th, 1776.

1 Nathan Trail
2 James Artis
3 Aaron Wood
4 John Keemer
5 William Leitch
6 William Baitson, (Bateson)
7 Charles Saffle
8 Nicholas Gaither
9 Lodowick Davis, (Davies)
10 Bennett Herd
11 Richard Short
12 Thomas Chattell, (Chattle)
13 John Haymond Nicholls
14 Richard Cooke
15 Lewis Mullican
16 James Pelly
17 Eli Smith
18 John Collins
19 William Lowry
20 Osborn West

Enrolled by Richd. Anderson. Passed by R. Crabb, Aug. 5th, 1776.

Henry Mackee, (Mackey, Makee)
Michael Rily, (Riley)
Walter Nichols, (Nicholl)
Edward Waker
Thomas Malloon
John Gaskin
Robert Drake

Patrick Carroll
Thomas Wise
William House
Leven Kersey
William Jerbo
John Lowry
John Langton

John Evans
Henry Atchison, (Atchingson, Hutchingson)
John Madding
Robert Rickets
Zachariah Evans
Benjamin Holland

Enrolled by Nich. Scybert. Passed by R. Crabb, Aug. 5th, 1776.

Geor. Sybert, (Scybert)
Nathan Roberts
Stephen Harper
John Cook
Joseph Ross
Patrick Murphy

George Heater
Dennis Clary
Richard Kisby
Michael Carter
Thomas Sheppart
William Pack

John Cavenor, (Caverner, Cavernor)
Philip Hindon
Stephen Warman
George Heathman

FREDERICK COUNTY—MIDDLE DISTRICT. [FREDERICK COUNTY.]

Capt. Philip Meroney
1 Lt. Elisha Beall
2 Lt. John Hellen
Ensign William Beatty, Jr
Capt. Jacob Good
1 Lt. John Baptist Thompson

2 Lt. John Ghiselin
Ensign John Smith
Capt. Peter Mantz
1 Lt. Adam Grosh
2 Lt. Peter Adams
Ensign John Richardson *

* Proceedings of the Conventions of Maryland, p. 177.

List of Capt. Philip Maroney's Company in the Flying Camp, Aug. 5th, 1776. Reviewed and passed by Charles E. Griffith, August, 1776.

Garah Harding
William Jacobs
John McCrery
Daniel Shehan
John Churchwell
George Holliday
George Hill
William Gilmour, (Gilmore), deserted
Patrick Murphy
Francis Quynn
Samuel Wheeler
John Shank
James McKinzie
Thomas Gill
William Calvert
John McClary
William Skaggs
John Marshall
Bennett Neall
John Test
Thomas Kirk, Jr
Ninion Nichols, (Nickols)
William Cash
James Burton
Thomas Bayman
Thomas Hillery
James Beall, (Ball)
John Brease, (Breeze)
Patrick Scott
William McKay, (McKoy)
Zadock Griffith
Henry Meroney

Henry Clements
Thomas Fenly, (Finley)
James McCormack Beall, deserted
Patrick Connan
Chas. Philpott Taylor
James Lowther
Henry Barkshire, deserted
John Maynard
James Beckett
James Tannehill
John Miller
James Bryant
Michael Arran
Jacob Barrack
John Donack
James Kelam
George McDonald
James Hutchcraft
Jacob Holtz
Henry Smith
Richard Wells
Elisha Rhodes
Paul Boyer
Samuel Busey
John Kenneday
William Chandler
William Hilton
Warran Philpot
Christopher Wheelen
James Buller
John Jones

James Carty
John Hutchinson
Luke Barnet
William Barnitt
Samuel Silvor
Edward Salmon
James McCoy
John Sehom
Robert McDonald
Richard Tongue
Herbert Shoemaker
John Myer
Richard Fletcher
Joseph McAllen
Thomas Harrison
John Alsop
Charles Dullis
Joshua Pearce
Jacob Rhodes
George Kelly
William Louden
Christian Smith
Frederick Beard
Henry Fisher
James Hudson
Michael Hale
John Rite, deserted
William Byer
Francis Freeman
John Cash
William Hollings
Jacob Burton

Frederick County, July the 27th, 1776.

I hereby certify that I have this day received Twenty Two men for the Flying Camp which were enrolled by Lieutenant Elisha Beall which appeared to me, to be able bodied men, Two of which he intended for Capt. Meroney, as Witness my hand the day abovesaid.

Jos. Wood, Jr.

Enrolled by Capt. Jacob Good, Lieut. John Battis Thompson, Lieut. John Ghiselin and Ensign John Smith. Reviewed and passed by Baker Johnson, July 20th, 1776.

Christeen Clisce	Henry Miller	Joseph McCracken
George Obalam	Ludwick Mober	William Linch
Tobias Hammer	Peter Giddy	John Toughman
George Rice	Jacob Horine	Edward Pegman
Philip Fletcher	Philip Pepple	John Wart
Martin Fletcher	Daniel Means	Michael Dodson
Christeen Gobble	Henry Brawner	Benj. Norris
Adam Keller	Patrick Money	George Bonagal
John Dwyre	John Money	George Ettleman
John Billow	Peter Penroad	James Vaughan
John Chamberlin	James Campbell	Wm. Brown
William Trace	Leonard Macalee	Geo. Spunogle
Jacob Freeman	Thomas Anderson	Peter Weaver
James Collins	Jacob Bearae	George Free
Thomas White	Philip Jacob	Daniel McTier
Charles Freind	William McClane,	Patric McIntire
James Estup	(McClame)	Danl. McIntire
John O'Bryan	Peter Havclay	Danl. Merfey
John Wimer	Philip Cenedey	Thomas Adams
George Gobble	Patrick Deneley	John Sill

The 16 men last above mentioned are enrolled by the above officers, but did not appear at the review. I am informed they are able bodied and effective.

B. Johnson.

Enrolled by Capt. Jacob Good, Lieut. John Baptis Thompson, Lieut. John Ghiselin and Ensign John Smith, for the Flying Camp. Reviewed and passed by Col. Charles Beatty, July 20th, 1776.

Anthony Thomas	John Duncan	Danl. Benning
Matthew King	Saml. Hamilton	John Robertson
Joseph McClaine	William Price	George Carroll
David Jones	Henry Fanslar	John Henderson
John Harrison	William Boe	Patrick White
Fettea Stuffle	Jacob Martin	John Test
Jacob Ridingour	Jonathan McDonall	Robert McLeod
George Benter	Zachariah Ward	Wm. Drome
Joseph Ray	John Slagel	Wm. Brinsford

The five men last above mentioned are enrolled by the above officers, but did not appear, at the review. I am informed they are able bodied and effective.

C. Beatty.

List of men enrolled in Capt. Mantz's Company. Passed by C. Beatty, July 13th, 1776.

William Richardson	John Bennett	George Tennaly
John Shelman	John Gisinger	Jonathan Jones
Andrew Loe	Peter Snowdenge,	Frederick Heeter
Henry Bear	(Snowdeigel)	Rudolph Morolf
Andrew Wolf	John Striser	John Redenour
John Kellar	Henry Myer	John Mouer, (Mourrer)
John Martin	John Shenk	John Dutterer
Andrew Speak	John Smith, dyer	Martin Heckentom
Charles Smith	Jos. Williams	Abraham Boucher, (Bucher)
John Newsanger,	Philip Flack	Philip Bowman
(Neswangher)	John Hendrickson	George Stoner
John Gombare, Jr	Peter Fine	Henry Hulsman
Jacob Bayer	Wm. Hendrickson	Henry Grose
George Siegfried	Dennis Realley	George Plummer
Jacob Stevens	Thomas Smith	Peter Wagoner
William Mills	Jacob Carnant	Thomas Tobiry
Mathias Overfelt	John Snider	Philip Aulpaugh
David Eley	John Lock	Jacob Shade
Henry Smith	Saml. Yaulet	Henry Teener
John Smith	James Adams	Henry Berreck
Peter Bell	Peter Walts	John Baker
John Twiner	Henry Huffman	Daniel Hinds
John Netsley	Jacob Crapell, (Creppell)	Henry Hinds
Geo. Mich. Hawk	Mathew Rudrieck	George Boyer
John Conrad	Christ. Stanley	Joseph Shame
Joseph Pinnall, (Pannell)	Thomas Stanley	Michael Baugh
Frederick Kallenberger	Chr. Kallenberger	Nicholas Beckelh,
Valentine Brunner	Jacob Kern	(Beckwith)
John Foster	George Hower	Jacob Bowman
Mich. Cramer	David Nail	Andrew Ringer
Laurence Myers		

We the subscribers, do hereby Certify that Capt. Peter Mantz had his Complyment of Men Inrolled for the Flying Camp on the 1st Day of July, 1776.
        Witnesseth

                        Adam Fischer,
                        Nicholas Tice,
                        Nicholas White.

I do hereby Certify that the Above Adam Fischer, Nicholas Tice and Nicholas White are men of Credit and may be depended on.
                                                    C. Beatty.

Frederick Town, July 13th, 1776.

Gentlemen:

Capt. Mantz informs me that his Company will be ready to march by the 20th of this Instant if he can be supplied with canteens, camp kettles and a few guns. Therefore I hope you will send up some money by the bearer hereof in order to purchase the guns and canteens for they may be had here for the cash. No camp kettles are to be had here, therefore hope you will give orders concerning them and to what place he is to march and you will greatly oblige

Yr Humble Servant,

C. Beatty.

To the Honourable Council of Safety for Maryland.

[Capt. Mantz' Company was ordered to Leonardtown and from there to Philadelphia where it arrived Aug. 23rd.*]

Frederick County.

At the request of Lt. John Hellen, I have this day Reviewed and Passed twelve able bodied effective men for the Flying Camp. I also Reviewed and Passed, on the 14th Instant, twenty four effective men for the Flying Camp for Ensign Wm. Beatty, Jr., eight of which he requests may be appropriated for Lt. John Hellen's Warrant. Given under my hand this 20th day of July, 1776.

Joseph Wood, Jr.

FREDERICK COUNTY—UPPER DISTRICT. [WASHINGTON COUNTY.]

Capt. Aeneas Campbell	Ensign Nathan Williams
1 Lt. Clement Hollyday	Capt. Henry Hardman
2 Lt. John Courts Jones	1 Lt. Daniel Stull
Ensign David Lynn	2 Lt. Peter Contee Hanson, re-
Capt. John Reynolds	signed and Jona. Morris appointed by the
1 Lt. Moses Chapline	Council of Safety, August 7th, 1776.
2 Lt. Christian Orndorff	Ensign John Rench †

Enrolled by Capt. Aeneas Campbell. Reviewed and passed by Major Francis Deakins, July 18th, 1776.

*Md. Archives XII, 239.   † Proceedings of the Conventions of Maryland, p. 177.

John Moxley
Levi Walters
George Hoskins
William Frankline
William Davis
John Gillam, (Gillum)
Henry Beeding, (Beading)
Michael Hagan
Daniel Moxley
George Gentile, (Gentle)
William Dixon
Mark Chillon

Martin Kiezer
Shedereck Locker
John Steel
James Williams
Samuel Lintridge, (Lentarage)
Benjamin Osburn, (Ozenburn)
William Veatch
William Lucas, (Luckas)
Charles Byrn, (Burn)
William Housley, (Owsley)

Notley Talbot, (Talbort)
John Martin, (Martain)
Charles Hoskins
Barton Lovelass, (Charles Lovless)
Grove Tomlin, (Tamlane)
William Stallings, (Stalion)
Thomas Gillam, (Gillum)
John Henry
Richard Lewis
Aeneas Campbell, Jr, cadet

Enrolled by Capt. Campbell. Passed by Maj. John Fulford.

James Raidy
John Williams

John Compton
Peter Boardy

William Poland
Cornelius Harling

Enrolled by 1st Lieut. Clement Hollyday. Passed by Maj. Francis Deakins, July 25th, 1776.

Josh. Harbin
Charles Lucas, (Luckas)
John Ellis

Stephen Gentile
Joseph Beeding
Philip Sulivane

John Ferrell
Patrick Rine
Benjamin Ellit

Enrolled by 1st Lieut. Clement Hollyday. Passed by Col. Wm. Lucket, Aug. 8th, 1776.

Ignatius Maddox
William Carroll
John Snowden Hooke
Richard Sarjeant, Jr.

James Weakley
George Kingston
John Simpson Aldridge
Charles Thomas Philpot

Jeremiah Fulsome
John Heart
Edward Cane

Enrolled by 2nd Lieut. John Courts Jones. Reviewed and passed by Thomas Johns, Frederick County, July 22nd, 1776.

Robert Beall Crafford
Philip Tracy
Henry Jones
Thomas Chappell
Jacob Mills
Hezekiah Speake
Walter Raley, (Raleigh)

Zephaniah Mockbee
John Higdon, Jr
William Lewis
Henry Allison
Nathan Thompson
James Glaze
Archibald Chappell

Hugh Elder
Arthur Carns
William Windham
Samuel Busey
Alexander Adams
Lewis Peak, (Speake)
Stephen West

Enrolled by Ens. David Lynn. Passed by Maj. Francis Deakins, July 25, 1776.

Thomas Owen	William Briggs	Daniel Ferguson
John Jeans	Francis Kitely	John Self
William Lamar	Nathaniel Glaze	William Oliver
William Thompson	Peter Hardesty	John White
Stephen West	Thomas Barrett	Abraham Chapman

Enlisted by Capt. John Reynolds, Frederick Co., July 18th, 1876. Passed by Joseph Smith.

William Walker	Wm. Patrick	Edward Brown
Moses Hobbins	Archibald Mullihan	Henry Coonse
John Ferguson	Edward Pain	George Deale
Wm. Bradford, volunteer	Wm. Coffeeroth	Benedict Eiginor
Jacob Hosler	John Wade	Edward Dumalt
Thomas Fowler	Thomas Stogdon	Daniel Murphey
John Been	Silus Tomkins	Ludowick Kiding
David Grove	John Class	Christopher Curts, (Cortz)
Thos. Bissett	John Hurley	Henry Knave
Wm. Messersmith	Thomas Pitcher	Thomas McKoy, D. S. T.

Enlisted by Moses Chapline, July 24th. Passed by Joseph Smith.

Henry Saftly	James Nowles, D. S. T.	William Baumgartner
John Berry	Edward Nowles	George Baumgartner
Rinear Bennett	Thomas Barrett, D. S. T.	Teeter Waltenback
Francis Thornbourgh	Christian France	James Thompson
Peter Seaburn	Jacob Weisong	George Reynolds
Thomas Sands	Joseph Finch	Philip Wyonge
James Cunningham	John Hood	Allexander Sparrow

Enlisted by Lieut. Christn. Orndorff, July 20th. Passed by Joseph Smith.

Christian Weirich	Joseph Emrich	Nicholas France
Nicholas Weirich	Jacob Brunner	Thomas Wilkins
Peter Loar	Edward Kerny	George Flick
Jacob Long	Nathaniel Linder	George Bowersmith
Nicholas Pinkely	Hermon Consella	Robert Wells
Mathias Wolf	Nicholas Hasselback	John Walker
John Randle	Philip Loar	Garrett Closson
Michael Edelman		

during the War of the American Revolution, 1775–83.   51

Enlisted by Ensign Nathan Williams. Passed by Joseph Smith, July 25th, 1776.

Basill Williams	Joseph Moor	Jacob Teeter
Simon McClane	Laurance Williams	William Fanner
Joseph Carrick	Bennett Madcalf	John Iden
John Peirce Welsh	Ephraim Skiles	William Kerney
John McKenny	John Powell	John Eove, (Cove?)
Benjamin Dye	Michael Cortz	Jacob Linder
Jacob Forsythe	Clement Howard	Rodger Dean
Edward Garner, D. S. T.	John Teeter	James Stewart

Capt. Henry Hardman's Return, made July 19th, 1776. Passed by Henry Shryock, July 19th, 1776.

Chs. White	James Duncan	Jno. Welsh
Francis Frumantle	Peter Haines	Jno. Moor
Daniel Matthews	Phil. Brugh	Jno. Aim
James Jordon	Peter Fiegley	Jno. Barry
George How	Chr. Neal	Stephen Preston
Thomas West	George Fiegley	Rhd. Noise
Jno. Kirk	Phil. Brener	Mathias Houks
Maurice Baker	Abm. Troxel	Stephen Rutlidge
Daniel Cline	Samuel Sprigg	William Davis
Jno. Newman	Barny Riely	Thomas Collins
Jno. Brown	John Closs	William Divers
Livie Jones	Peter Digman	Chr. Metts
Thomas Fish	Chn. Berringer	Danl. Wicks
John Lindsey	Thomas McGuyer	Jno. Dicks
Jno. Troxel	Paul Shley	Jacob Storam
Jno. Collins	Wm. Crale	Saml. Richardson
Thos. Smith	James Martin	Conomus Acre
Chas. Feely	Danl. Fisher	Daniel Carty
Abm. Miller	Phil. Flack	Rhd. Morgon
George Colley	James Green	Wm. Campian
Jno. Mowen	Isaac Hardey	Isaac Barnet
Martin Rickenbaugh	Wm. Casey	Chr. Fogely
Pat. Ryley	Saml. Smith	Michael Pote
Robert English	Wm. Wallis	George Rismel
James Crale	Thos. Jones	Chr. Alinger
Jno. Stoner	Danl. Henderson	Peter Splise
Jacob Hirsh	John Ward	Chr. Walker
Jno. Bemhart	George Morrison	John Hager
Jno. Grant	Chr. Hart	Jas. Munn
Thos. Robison		

BALTIMORE COUNTY.

Capt. Zachariah Maccubbin
   1 Lt. Thomas Yates, promoted to a Captaincy and John Christie appointed 1 Lt. by the Council of Safety, August 5th, 1776.
   2 Lt. John Christie, promoted 1 Lt. and Thomas Lingan appointed 2 Lt. by the Council of Safety.
   Ensign Thomas Lingan, promoted 2 Lt. and William Wilmot appointed Ensign by the Council of Safety.
Capt. John E. Howard

1 Lt. Thomas Lansdale
2 Lt. William Riley
Ensign Robert Morrow
Capt. James Young
1 Lt. James Bond
2 Lt. John Smith
Ensign James Toole
Capt. John Stevenson, resigned and Thomas Yates appointed Capt.
1 Lt. Edward Oldham
2 Lt. James Ogleby
Ensign Joseph Lewis *

Enlisted by Zachariah Maccubin. Reviewed and passed by Thos. Jones, July 20th, 1776.

Joseph Britten,	Charles Griffen, (Griffin)	William Limebarker
Basil Geoghegan	William Dunsyre	Mathew Skiffington
John Phinnimore	John Oaram	John Thompson
John Coale	Henry Young	Luke West
Thomas Robinson	Michael Carnee	Mathew Moore
John Cooke	Hugh Lynch	George Bailey
Thomas McDaniel	Thomas Cummins	Joseph Weston
Edward Puntany	Christopher Fells	Bartholomew Donohue
Isaac Hall	Hugh Paulton	James Howard
Thomas Griffen, (Griffin)	Jacob Wilderman	James Griffith

Enlisted by John Christie. Passed by Thos. Jones, July 25th, 1776.

John Tuder	Thomas Kenny	Lewis Wise
Thomas Fox	Benjamin Quine	Roberson Wood
John White	Peter Millar	Edward Smith
Edward Kersey	Thomas Mahany	William Bailey
Charles Burnett	Joshua Bond	Benjamin Furlong
George Price	Francis Ward	Nathan Biggs
Michael Martin	John Lennox	

Enlisted by William Wilmott. Passed by John Cradock, August 14th, 1776.

Edward Chenoweth	George Allen	Edward Traisey
William Harriman	James Lawrence	John Hosel
Henry Middleton	Jacob Knight	Edward Parrish
Joseph Welch, (Welsh)	Hugh Gainer	Richard Hood
Richard Cole, (Coale)	Charles Kelley	John Hood
Thomas Chenoweth	Daniel McIntire	

* Proceedings of the Conventions of Maryland, p. 177.

during the War of the American Revolution, 1775–83.   53

Enlisted by John E. Howard, of Baltimore County. Passed by William Hyde, Baltimore Town, July 17th, 1776.

John Caldwell	Nicholas Clark	George Fullum
Thomas Haley	John Davis	John Talbott
Nathan Griffith	George Pattington	John Neal
Barney McLaughlin	Malcolm McFee	Abraham Tennes
Patrick Welsh	Greenbury Griffith	Jacob Yater
George Griffith	Robert Smetherest	Gabril Wilson
John Hamilton	Nicholas Griffith	John Clark
Benj. Bank	Nicholas Rim	Joseph Muller
White Wilson	James Griffith	Thomas McLain
Darby Murphey	Thomas Murphey	Daniel Lacey

Enlisted by Thomas Lansdale, of Baltimore County. Passed by Thomas Jones, 2nd Major Baltimore Town Battalion, July 20th, 1776.

John Van Zandt	Patrick Newgin	James Wells
John Coleing	Jacob Rawlings	Lawrence Connelly
Thomas Murphey	Tobias Wilson	Daniel Smyth
William Marriott	Edward Holebrooke	Benjamin R. Talbot
William Adams	William Drewitt	Thomas Barney
Richard Clarke	Nehemiah Lunn	Hugh Moore
Richard Burke	Jacob Stowie	

Enlisted by Wm. Reily. Reviewed and passed by Thos. Jones, July 26th, 1776.

Knotliff Taylor	Timothy Mahony	Thomas Watson
Jacob Hooper	John Murphy	James Meloy
James Fitzgerald	Edward Parish	John McFall
Timothy Tate	John McMahon	Nicholas Corbley
Dennis Doyle	William Sollers	James Grey
Fergus Lee	Edward Reedy	

Enlisted by Wm. Reily. Reviewed and passed by Wm. Hyde.

Joseph Hoy	Edward Palfrey	Florence Mahony

Enlisted by Robert Morrow of Baltimore County. Passed by Thomas Jones, July 20th, 1776.

John Murphey	Job Lewis	Philip Norwood
John Noyes	David Fahay	Cornelius Conner
Thomas Stephens, (Stephen)	Stephen Shelmerdine	Samuel Adams
	Edward Young	Samuel Adams, 2d
Hugh Oneal	Jehu Bowen	William Schooling
Alexander Burke, (Burk)	James Bowen	

A List of Men Enrolled by Capt. Jas. Young, Lieut. Jas. Bond, Lieut. John Smith and Ensign James Tool. To Compose one Company in Col. Thos. Ewing's Battalion for the Flying Camp. August, 1776.

Names.	By Whom Enlisted.	Where Enlisted.	When Enlisted.	Size.	Age.	Place Nativity.	Remarks.
CADETS.				ft. in.			
Stephen Dorsey	Capt. Jas. Young	Harford Co.	July 7	5 9¾	18	America	dark hair
Joshua Brown	Lieut. Bond	“ “	9	5 9¼	20	“	light colored hair
John Allinder	“ “	“ “	7	5 6½	19	“	light colored hair
Wm. Osborne, (Osbourn)	“ “	“ “	“	5 2½	21	“	short black hair
Thos. Gouldsmith	“ “	“ “	“	5 3	18	“	short light hair
William Bunting	“ “	“ “	“	5 6¼	34	England	short black hair
SERGEANTS.							
John Poe, 1st	Capt. Jas. Young	Baltimore Co.	“	5 8	22	America	long black hair
Thomas Hill, 2nd	“ “	“ “	“	5 6¼	27	Ireland	long black hair
Benj. Hipwells, 3rd	Ensign Tool	“ “	5	5 9	23	“	long black hair
David Smith, 4th	Lieut. Smith	Harford Co.	15	5 8	20	America	light colored hair
CORPORALS.							
John Burk, (Bourk), 1st	Capt. Jas. Young	Baltimore Co.	6				
Jereh. Sullivan, (Swillivan), 2nd	“ “	“ “	5	5 7	32	Ireland	short black hair
Jas. Gordon, 3rd	“ “	“ “	7	5 9¼	19	“	short light hair
Thos. Sullivan, (Swillivan), 4th	“ “	“ “	“	5 7	27	“	much pock marked
DRUMMER.							
Thomas Cole	“ “	Harford Co.	“	5 2	25	England	short black hair
FIFER.							
Francis Herd, (a servant)	Lieut. Smith	“ “	15	5 6	20	America	short curled hair
PRIVATES.							
Edward Higman	Capt. Jas. Young	Baltimore Co.	July 5	5 3¼	18	England	black hair, scar on his cheek
William Ryan	“ “	“ “	“	5 7¼	26	America	black hair, sandy complexion
James McMaken, (Makin)	“ “	“ “	“	5 2½	34	Ireland	short light hair
John McCann	“ “	“ “	“	5 1¼	29		long black hair

Names.	By Whom Enlisted.	Where Enlisted.	When Enlisted.	Size.	Age.	Place Nativity.	Remarks.
PRIVATES.				ft. in.			
Robert Curtis	Capt. Jas. Young	Baltimore Co.	July 5	5 3¼	28	England	light hair
Nicholas McAvoy	" "	" "	"	5 0½	41	Ireland	short hair, full face
Henry Evans	" "	" "	"	5 1	20	"	short black hair, round face
John Damnitz	" "	" "	7	5 2	28	Germany	black hair, pock marked
William Collins	" "	" "	"	5 1½	26	Ireland	black hair
Anthony Grimes	" "	" "	5	5 5½	26	England	sandy hair, pock marked
William Gradey, (Gready)	" "	" "	7	5 4	30	Ireland	sandy complexion
Orrise Patty	" "	" "	5	5 8	25	America	short black hair
Abraham Jarman	" "	" "	7	5 5¼	21	"	short black hair
Thomas Proctor	" "	" "	"	5 5¼	20	"	sandy hair
Wm. Appleby	" "	" "	"	5 6¼	24	"	black curled hair
Wm. Price	" "	Harford Co.	"	5 3	26	England	full faced
Edward Murphey	" "	" "	"	5 8	25	Ireland	short black hair and stoppage [in his speech
Richard Hackett	" "	" "	"	5 4	28	England	black hair
Nicholas Rylie, (Reiley)	" "	" "	"	5 3½	27	Ireland	sandy complexion
David Galvin	" "	Baltimore Co.	"	5 5	25	"	black hair
Terrence Grimes	" "	" "	"	5 7½	30	"	black hair, scar on his left cheek
Benjamin Yarnall	" "	" "	"	5 10¼	28	England	pock marked
George Childs	" "	" "	"	5 3	21	Ireland	full faced
Rengard Jackson	" "	Annapolis	"	5 3	21	"	black hair
David Phillips	" "	Baltimore Co.	"	5 8	24	America	short hair, pock marked
George Berry	" "	" "	"	5 5	17	"	short hair
Wm. Swillivan	" "	" "	"	5 6	29	"	long hair
Wm. Goodson	" "	" "	"				
Benj. Wilson	Lieut. Bond	" "	"	5 6¾	21	"	sandy complexion
Saml. Quay, (Qua)	" "	" "	"	5 2½	18		short black hair
Anthony Potter	" "	" "	"				

Names.	By Whom Enlisted.	Where Enlisted.	When Enlisted.	Size.	Age.	Place Nativity.	Remarks.
PRIVATES.				ft. in.			
James Quay, (Qua)	Lieut. Bond	Baltimore Co.	July 7	5 6	18		sandy hair
John Gill	"	"	"	5 2½	31	Ireland	light colored hair
Jas. Mehaney, (Mahoney)	"	"	"	5 1	18	America	short black hair
James Barns	"	"	"	5 5	19		sandy complexion
James Groves	"	"	"	5 4	24		short curled hair
Hugh Deiver, (Devier)	Lieut. Smith	Harford Co.	July 15	6 1½	38	England	black hair
William Rice	"	"	"	5 9¾	26	Ireland	sandy hair
Michael Meloy	"	"	"	5 5	20	America	straight hair
Robert Stevenson	"	"	"	5 7¾	28	Ireland	sandy complexion
Lawrence Connoway, (Conaway)	"	"	"	5 3¾	21	"	black hair
Patrick Tiarny	"	"	"	5 4¼	23	"	sandy complexion, black hair
Patrick Fowler	"	"	"	5 4½	28	"	sandy hair
Jas. Hannah, (Hanna)	"	"	"	5 8½	31	America	thin visage
Peter Donnavon, (Donavan)	"	"	"	5 5	50	England	thin visage
William King	"	"	"	5 8	21	Ireland	sandy complexion
Joseph Whiteflatt	"	Baltimore Co.	"	5 4	25	"	curled hair
David Collins	"	"	"	5 2	23	"	full faced
John Carney	"	"	"	5 4	40	America	sandy complexion
Pat. McDonald	"	Harford Co.	"	5 7½	21	"	black hair
James Smith	"	"	"	5 5	26		
Chas. O'Neale	"	Baltimore Co.	July 5	5 7¼	20	America	short black hair
Wm. Jordon	Ensign Tool	"	"	5 6	38	"	sandy hair
Jas. Benny	"	"	"	5 3	29	Ireland	long black hair
John Blakney, (Blackney)	"	"	"	5 8¼	20	Germany	short black hair
John Carr	"	"	"	5 6		America	full faced, black hair
Wm. Vandike, (Vandyke)	"	"	"	5 6¼		Ireland	sandy complexion
James Currye, (Corry)	"	"	"				fair complexion

Names.	By Whom Enlisted.	Where Enlisted.	When Enlisted.	Size. ft.in.	Age.	Nativity.	Remarks.
PRIVATES.							
Geoge Stibbonds Comer, (Colman)	Ensign Tool	Baltimore Co.	July 5	5 6¼	35	England	short curled hair
Peter Daulton	"	"	"	5 6¼	29	Ireland	sandy complexion
Thomas Tallon	"	"	"	5 4	25	"	full faced, pitted with smallpox
Daniel Key, (Keay)	"	"	"	4 11	29	England	sandy complexion
Arthur Shane, (Shean)	"	"	"	5 5¼	20	America	long light colored hair
Hugh Gwin	"	"	"	5 5	20	Ireland	short curled hair, pitted with [smallpox
John Love	"	"	"	5 5	41	Scotland	sandy complexion
Thomas Moffitt, (Moffatt)	"	"	"	5 7	22	Ireland	black hair
John Smith	"	"	"	5 10	38	America	short hair
James Ryan	"	"	"	5 7¼	30	Ireland	fullfaced
George Betson, (Bettson)	"	"	"	5 7	16	America	short hair
Jacob Stroup, (Straup)	"	"	"	5 4¼	20	"	black hair
Michael Boyd	"	"	"	5 5	32	Ireland	sandy complexion
Joseph Smith	"	"	"	5 4¼	36	America	short curled hair
William Garrett	Capt. Jas. Young	"	"	5 5¼	40	England	black hair
Peter Jennett, (Jannett)	"	"	"	5 5	21	Ireland	long brown hair
Nicholas McGeaugh, (McGaw)	Lieut. Smith	"	15				
James Casey	Capt. James Young	"	7				
John Rodgers	"	"	"				
John Walters, (Watters)	"	"	"				
William Barns, (James Barnes?)	Lieut. Bond	"	"				
William Sandlant	"	"	"				
Bartholomew Downey, (Dawney), absent	Ensign Toole	"	5				
Michael Ulence, absent	"	"	"				
Thomas Stevenson	"	"	"				
John Waller							
John Brown							
James Bryan, (James Ryan?)							

[The last eleven names are on the Muster Roll of July, 1776, but not on that of August, 1776.]

Enlisted by Capt. Thomas Yates. Reviewed and passed by Thomas Jones, 2nd Major of the Baltimore Town Battalion, July 18th 1776.

*Patrick Sheehan	*Edward Dulany	William Green
*Valentine Kizer, (Kiser)	*Timothy Driskill	James Walker
*John Rieley	*William Saylers, absent	*William Peach
*Robert Gregory	Jeremiah Driskill	*Benjamin Heritage
*Richard Cumings, (Cummins)	Jacob Shanley	*Martin Hynes
	Michael Hart	Timothy Sheehan
*Joseph Fisher	Larrons Keenan	John McDearmett
*John Roach, (Reach)	Richard Mansel, (Mansal)	John Murrey
*John Lindiff	Charles Lovett	Roger Deland
*William Lawrence	Thomas Johnson	*John Barnett
*Thomas Crafford, (Crayford)	John Selly	*William Collins, absent
	*Francis Milner	*James Wright, "
*Edward Willson	Robert How	*Joseph Grey, "
*Daniel O'Brien, Serjt.	Joseph Darlington	

[Names with a star prefixed are those who were passed by M. Gist, July 5th, 1776.]

Enlisted by Lieut. Edward Oldham. Passed by Thomas Bond, July 19th, 1776.

John Jeffreys	Richard Smith	John Shipley
Nicholas Day	William Forgeson	John Miller
Charles Sweiney	William Eaton	Nathan Fitspartrick
Steven Torrell, (Forrell)	Stephen Body	James Ryant
John Dunnevan	John Hipkins	Henry Henderson
Henry Kagen	Isaac Hanson	Anthony Cummins

Enlisted by James Ogleby. Reviewed and passed by John Cradock, August 15th, 1776.

John Minney	Moses Rutter	Timothy Shawnesey
Isaac Willson	Robert Cowell	John Wills
Thomas Ward	Thomas Rutter	Philip Bailey
Robert Gilhampton	Timothy Carty	Richard Rollings
John Smith	Joseph Hown	Thomas Kelley
Charles Loud	David Harriman	John Smith
George Hinley	William Meadows	Samuel Baxter
John Kelly		

Enlisted by Ensign Lewis. Reviewed and passed by William Hyde.

Nathl. Twining	Roger Dellin	Thomas Ward
James Norris	Charles Kelley	John Smith
Toal McCollester	Samuel Baxter	Isaac Wilson
Rich. Donavan	John Mining	John Barnett
James Kemp	Robt. Gilhampton	Manna Roe
Joseph Smith		

HARFORD COUNTY.

Capt. Aquila Paca	Capt. Bennet Bussey
1 Lt. John Beedle Hall	1 Lt. Joshua Miles
2 Lt. Michael Gilbert	2 Lt. Azabel Hitchcock
Ensign John Patterson	Ensign Aquila Amos *

Enrolled by Capt. Paca. Reviewed and passed by Jas. Carvel Hall, July 24th, 1776.

Isaac Johnson	Reese Jones	Thomas McDaniel
James Thomas	Edward Morris	John Loney
Thomas Stevenson	William Saunders	Alexander Nolstone
Barney Haney	John Morris	Michael Barry
Jas. Allen	John Collins	William Duly
Job Bennington	Wm. Brucebanks	John O'Neal
Joseph Glyn	Cornelius Akins	Amatio Taylor
Aquila Lee Jones	Thomas Younger	William Durham
William Robinson	Isaac Giant	Alexander Admiston
Jacob Dozens	Jonathan Walker	Jas. Willson
Isaac Dozens	Thomas Welsh	Michael Morris
Wm. Gray Dozens	John Clarke	Matthew Snodey
Ephraim Collins	Thomas Dusft, (or Dufft)	

Enrolled by Lt. J. B. Hall. Passed by Aquilla Hall, Aug. 5th, 1776.

Joab Murphey	Charles Williams	Edward Low
William Hart	Isreal Combest	William Hassett
Stephen Crouch	Michael Mullen	James Hurley
William Logan	Nicholas Brady	John Walker
John Brackenridge	George Stewart	Phillip Peiken, (or Pictern)
James McKnight	Leven Dorsey	Alexander Edmonston
John Ryan	Thomas Harrod	

* Proceedings of the Conventions of Maryland, pp. 177, 178.

Enrolled by Capt. Bennet Bussey. Passed by Thos. Bond July 20th, 1776.

Grafton Preston	Thomas Hinks	Bartho. Finn, (Firm)
John Clayton, (Clyton)	James Moore	Arch. McNear
Robt. Ogle	Robt. Carlile, (Carlisle)	James Cox
Ewd. Johnson	Simon Howard, (Froward)	Godfrey Woolmore
Wm. Greenhill, (Green Hill)	John Steel	William Miles
Wm. Preston	Thos. Able	James Smith
Isaac Akeright, (Aksright)	Lawrence Hynds	Benj. Rhoads
James Mathews	Wm. Cooper	Edw. Freeman
Michael Carr	John Toole	Denis Clancey
Francis Williams	Wm. Howe	

Enrolled by Capt. Bennett Bussey. Reviewed and passed by Thos. Jones, 2d Major of the Balt. Town Battalion of Militia.

Ambrose Timmons	Thomas Lacy

Enrolled by 1st Lieut. Joshua Miles. Passed July 27th, '76.

James Nelson	James Moore	John Condron
Michael McNeile	Denis Clancy	Hugh McMillen
Thomas Slatry	Patrick Doran	John Dennis
James Mays	William Gaddis	Valentine Stratford
Bartholomew Downs	Laurence Hinds	John Tapler
Henry Shane	Thomas Godfrey	John Spencer
John Rogers	John Downey	

Enrolled by Lieut. Asell Hitchcock, Jr. Passed by Asell Hitchcock, July 25th, 1776.

Thos. James	Richard Hopkins	Saml. Hodgskins
Wm. Cunningham	Saml. Baxley	Martin Scary
Wm. Wright	John Garrett	Jonathan Cunningham
Asell Rockwell	Andrew Craven	John Lyon
Wm. Rutledge	Jos. Wood White	Noah Reaves
Wm. Night	Claudius Jamison	Patrick Norton
Wm. Condron	Chas. Porter	

Enrolled by Ensign Aquila Amos. Passed by Thos. Bond, July 25th, 1776.

Mordicai Amos	Winstone Smith	Samuel Peacock
Joshua Amos	Barney Devine	John Catherwood, (Carthwood)
William Gash	John Roberts	John O'Donel
Richard Burk	John Miles	Nathan Smith
George Gardner, (Garder)	Daniel Darby	John Long

during the War of the American Revolution, 1775-83.   61

CECIL COUNTY.

Capt. Joshua George	Capt. Walter Alexander
1 Lt. William Veazey	1 Lt. Andrew Porter
2 Lt. John Stockton	2 Lt. Harman Arrants
Ensign Richard Bird	Ensign George Hamilton *

CAPT. JOSHUA GEORGE'S COMPANY.

Reviewed and passed by John D. Thompson, Lieut. Col. 18th Battalion, Cecil County, 18th August, 1776.

John Etherington	James Lawrenson	George Boyce
James Hays	Joseph Veazey	John Dennis
Thomas Parsley	William Ford	James Kimble Price
Henry McGahan	John McCoole	William McWilliams
Isaac Money	Augusteen H. Ensor	Bassett McClarey
Joseph Kirk	Thomas Campbell	Tile Belew
Henry Maulden	Silvester Latham	Richard Hays
Jeremiah Lanchaster	James Brown	Charles Elexson
Ephraim Lee, (or See)	Aron Latham	Daniel Wilson
William Husler	Richard F. Elwood	Richard Harrison
James Conner	Noble Veazey	Robert Walmsley, (Walmley)
Joseph Hukins	Michael Morrison	John Hurley
William Patterson	Archibald Lemon	James Mansfield
Daniel Daley	William Richardson	John Pemberton
Jesse Comegys	Henry Campbell	Benomi Currier
Joseph Moss	Robert S. Scott	James Beverly
Garrett Othoson	John Baker	Andrew Mitchell
John Ryland	James Hussa	John Bailey
Augusteen Can	Slyter Bouchell	Daniel McCurdey
Jonathan Comegys	Nathl. Dawson	George McNamarr
John Cox	William Sears	John McCurdey
John Jaraliman	Samuel Money	David McCurdey
Ephraim Cooper	Ephraim Price	William Garrott
Benjamin Serverson	Noble Price	Joseph Haltham
William Hall	Edward Savin	Edward Furner
John Nowland	Marlow Taylor	David Marr
James Middlecut	Joseph Terry	Evin Hughes
James Smith	James Wroth	John McCoy
Gilbert Nowland	Johnson Braddock	

Cecil County, July 16th, 1776.

I have mustered Twenty men Enrolled by Mr. William Veazey, First Lieutenant of a Company of Militia to be raised in Cecil County to make part of the Flying Camp, and do hereby certify that they are a parcel of able bodied effective men. Given under my hand the day and year above.

Jno. D. Thompson,
Lieut. Col. 18th Batt.

---

* Proceedings of the Conventions of Maryland, p. 178.

Cecil County, July 20th, 1776.

I hereby certify that I have mustered Twenty men Enrolled by Mr. John Stockton, Jr., Second Lieutenant of a Company of Militia to be raised in Cecil County to make part of the Flying Camp, and that they are a parcel of able bodied effective men. Given under my hand the day and year above.

Jno. D. Thompson,
Lieut. Col. 18th Batt.

Cecil County, July 29th, 1776.

Sirs—Mr. Richard Bird has Enrolled Sixteen men, part of Capt. George's Company, Three of which did not appear at the time the others met to be mustered and passed. The other Thirteen are able bodied effective men. The whole of Mr. Bird's men will in a day or two be mustered and passed. As Capt. George is anxious to go to Annapolis to get Directions, it is thought not necessary to detain him for the few remaining. In a few days a Roll of the whole will be transmitted to you. I am Sirs Your very Humb. Servt.

Jno. D. Thompson.

To The Honourable The Council of Safety of Maryland.

Enrolled by Capt. Walter Alexander. Passed by Col. Charles Rumsey, July 24th, 1776.

William Alexander	Joseph Dawson	John McClintock
Christopher Rutledge	James Cavinder	Joseph Beath, (Bath)
Jonathan Mullins	Kenniday Bay	Stephen McConnel
William Kite	Alexander Work	Patrick Robison
Edward Martin, (Martain)	Robert Evans	John Denney
Robert Ray	James Cochran	James Smith
John Patterson	Abraham Holms	Thomas Quail
Thomas Doyl	Ezekiel Alexander	William Conway
Phineas Harvey	James Alexander	John Mills
Thomas Owens	Robert Longwill	John Davidson
Gregry Pearce		

Enrolled by 1st Lieut. Andrew Porter. Reviewed and passed by Elihu Hall, of Elisha, July 27th, 1776.

John Tibbs	James Conner, (Connor)	Stephen Right
Edward Gallinough	William Creaighton, (Creaghton, Creaton)	Daniel Linsey
William Mackey		Dinish Smith
Stephen Mahoney	John Tower	James Quigley
Roger Daugherty	Patrick McFaden	William Beard
John Barry	John Duffy	Solomon Collins
John Smith	John Campbell	Michael McCasker
George Carlin, (Carlon)	Frances Farrel	

during the War of the American Revolution, 1775-83. 63

Enrolled under Harman Arrants. Reviewed and passed by Charles Rumsey, August 3rd, 1776.

Richard Hodgson	Thomas Bricen	William Grace
Edward Donoly	Levi Veazey	Jonathan Richardson
Johnandrew Strikeingburg	William Beek	Thomas Citely, (Ceitly)
James Wallace	Samual Lewis	John Rickets
Jesse Price	Calab Donoly	William Jonson
Robert Hemphill	Henry Beedlee	Michael Smith
Nathan Phillips	James Sapington	

Enrolled by Ensign Hamilton. Reviewed and passed by Thomas Hughes, Lieut. Col. 30th Battalion, July 25th, 1776.

Names.	When enrolled.	Names.	When enrolled.
John Hamilton, Jr	July 1	Samuel Payenter	July 22
Thomas Baker	4	Thomas Halluran	"
Joseph Talen	9	David Emmitt	18
Simon Gibney	15	Patt Shiels	"
Patt Downey	17	John Emmitt	25
James Doogan	18	Thomas Dixson	"
Samuel Davis	"	John Cunningham	"
Hugh May	22	Nathan Bennett	"

KENT COUNTY.

Capt. Isaac Perkins	Capt. Thomas Smyth
1 Lt. Abraham Falconer	1 Lt. James Williamson
2 Lt. Jesse Cozden	2 Lt. Nathaniel Kinnard
Ensign James Henry	Ensign Josiah Johnson*

Enlisted by Capt. Isaac Perkins. Reviewed and passed by Wm. Henry, July 17th, 1776.

Benjamin Burchinall	Benjamin Everitt	Joseph Greenwood
John Williams	Conrod Whiteman	John Lynch
William Apsley	David Tulley	Richard Kennard
William Mann	Nathaniel Herring	John Pearce
John Phillips	Adam Laurence	David Crane
Abednegoe Jackson	Froggitt Tillard	Daniel Turner
John Rollison	Augusteen Spencer	Thomas Norman
William Dauherty	James Butcher	Edward Stewart
Denniss Hurley	John McKinney	William Jones
David Newell	Daniel Knock	Samuel Sinnett

* Proceedings of the Conventions of Maryland, p. 178.

Capt. Perkins assures me that he had his Company full on the 5th Day of this Inst.

William Henry.

Enlisted by Lieut. Abraham Falconer. Reviewed and passed by William Henry, July 19, 1776.

Daniel Ahern	James Ragan
Benj. Roberts	Michael Thomas
William Hunter	Daniel Mulcahy
George Burch	Nazareth Freeland
Benj. Pharow	Love Alley, (or Alby)
Benj. Garland, (or Gavland)	Wm. Herring
Joseph Morris	James Wise
Robert Little	Ebenezar Costillo
Danl. Toas Massy	John Walls, Jr.
Jeremiah Collins	Wm. Walls, Jr.

Enlisted by Lieut. Jesse Cosden, July 4th, 1776. Reviewed and Passed by Wm. Henry, July 13th, 1776.

Lambert Boyer	Daniel Sevell, (or Serell)
William Hammon	Edwd. Wm. Johnson
John Cosden	John Smith
Cornelius Comegys	Wm. Wiltshier
John Finley	James Reyley
John Woodall	William Hill
Matthew Smyth	James Green Wood
Hartley Sapington	Johnson Brooks
Wm. Smith	Joshua Vanzant
Saml. Eades	James Copper

Enrolled by Lieut. James Williamson, July 10th, 1776. Reviewed and passed by Edward Worrell, July 29th, 1776. Part of the Company of Capt. Thos. Smyth, Jr.

Thomas Punny	Charles Scoone	Anthony Dunn
James Wilson	Owen Whaland	Stephen Kindle
James Dunn, Jr	Thomas Rolph	James Saunders
William Hynson	Frogget Younger	Daniel McConnican
Charles Scott	John Hughes	John Phillips
John Holder	Caleb Catlin	James Carmichael
John Rolph	Thomas Ridiford	

Enlisted by Lieut. Nathaniel Kinnard, Jr. Reviewed and passed by William Henry, July 22nd, 1776.

William Foreman	Richard Lane
Francis Lamb	Phillip Reed
Joseph Howard	Wm. Foster
Charles Jones	Wm. Kinnard
John Punney	Francis Armstrong
John Sillivin	John Curtain
Wm. Giant	Benj. Connerwey
Stephin Giant	Isaac Smith
Anguish McDonnold	Thomas Knimptum
Benj. Jones	John Husselton

Enlisted by Ensign Josiah Johnson. Reviewed and passed by William Henry, July 27th, 1776.

George Tolson	Thomas Jones
George Foard	Morriss Marrah
William Meeks	John Rosse
Robert Meeks	Henry Truelock, Jr.
George Scone	Daniel Donnowin
Theophilius Lowmuth, (or Lowmuch)	William Jones
John Patten, (or Tatten)	William Dugan
George Connor	Nathan Brooks

QUEEN ANNE'S COUNTY.

Capt. John Dean	Capt. John Dames
1 Lt. John Hawkins	1 Lt. Thomas Lane Emory
2 Lt. John Neville	2 Lt. Sam'l Wright Thomas
Ensign Samuel Earle	Ensign John Jackson *

CAPT. JOHN DEAN'S COMPANY.

From 1 to 30, inclusive, enrolled by Capt. John Dean and passed by Jno. Seney July 13th, from 31 to 55, inclusive, enrolled by 1st Lt. John Hawkins and passed by James Kent July 8th, from 56 to 75, inclusive, enrolled by 2nd Lt. John Neville and passed by Jno. Seney July 17th, and from 76 to 86, inclusive, enrolled by Ensign Samuel Earle and passed by Th. Wright, Col. of the 20th Batt. of Militia, July 18th, 1776.

* Proceedings of the Conventions of Maryland, p. 178.

1 Joseph Foreacres
Joseph Turner
John Arno
William Knotts
John Delanaway
Matthew Peters
Samuel Connaway
John Holding
William Dudley
William Comegys
William Ascott, (Arscott)
John Wells
Solomon Price
Thomas Clymer,(Clymore)
Edward Coppage
William Spry
Solomon Phillips
James Ryan
Joseph Smyth, (Smith)
Robert Kenniford
James Lawrence
John Cole
Jacob Walters
Joseph Elliott
Samuel Green
Griffin, (Griffith), Oliver
John Clemmonds
Christr. Simmonds
Wm. Clark, of Wm.
Charles Bryne
31 Edward Pickering, (Pickorine)
Jonas Daugherty, (Dehorty)
Daniel Daugherty, (Dehorty)
James Gould Sparkes
James Hamilton, (Hambleton)
Wm. Deford
Charles Deford
Joseph Wright
Lodman Downes
James Lawrence
John Williams
Thomas Meredith, (Meradith)
Matthew Griffith
James Kersey, (Cearsey)
Thomas Tarr
William Parkes
James Meredith,(Meradith)
Wm. Caulker, (Corker)
James Burk
Benj. Moore, (More)
James Gould
Willson Boone
Wm. Rogers
Wm. Hendley, (Henley)
Edward Taylor
56 Wm. Price
Richard Wells
Wm. Wallace
George Bostick
Thomas Burchinall
John Rolph
Thomas Rolph
Wm. Rolph
John McHannah
James Hudson Greaves
John Clark
Claudius Sylvester
James Lawrence
Richard Nabb
John Cannon
John Emory Hall
Thomas Devorix
James Baggs
Thomas Holmes
Charles Keene
76 Edward Holdson,(Holson)
John Taylor
Wm. Morgan
James Williams
Thos. Meredith O'Bryon
James Reed
Nathaniel Tucker
Matt. Brown Chambers
Benj. Blunt
Elias McConakin, (McConnikin, McConnican)
Thos. Chambers

CAPT. JOHN DAMES' COMPANY.

Passed by John Seney, July 25th, 1776.

John Godwin
Charles Scrivner
Joseph Rediew
John Gormon
William Larey
John Smith
James Clayland, Jr
Thomas Davis, Jr
Christopher Yewell
Edward Loyd
Joseph Rigbey
John Laurence
James Macy Slaughter
William Holding
Rob't Hannah,(or Mannah)
Pay, (or Pery), Ashford
William Sevill
John Hargadine
James Butler, Sr.
John Bennett
Acquilla Downes
Samuel Bowlsover
James Tool
Daniel Saunders
Nathan Baker
Charles Jinkins
Thomas Yewell
Peter Cockey
John Yewell
John Weedon
Joseph Rodness
Samuel White
Thomas Murphy

during the War of the American Revolution, 1775–83.

Elisha Nabb	Thomas Jackson	Robert Scrivener
James Barnes	John Thorn	John Jonson
Samuel Blunt	Jacob Seth	James Cook
John Chace	Edward Thomas	George May
John Baxter	Samuel Legg	Thomas Dailey
John McConikin	Joseph Jackson	James Robinson
John Meridith	John Grimes	Thomas Malone, (or Malom)
John Bennett	John Newell	Charles Dimond
Benjamin Teakle	David Newell	Benjamin Blunt
John Sherwood	John Kemp	William Osburn
William Emory	Thomas Bailey	Thomas Felick
Nathan Emory Clements	John Crouch	Philip Kinnimon
Samuel Emory	William Robinson	James Harris
Elias Jeffers	James Brown	William Shields
John Mansfield	William Sillivant	John Phillips
William Greenwood	Benjamin Holdine	Aaron Sanders
Benjamin Tolson	Thomas Betts	Edward Williams
John Barnard	Thomas Parfit	

TALBOT COUNTY.

Capt. Greenbury Goldsborough   2 Lt. John Thomas
1 Lt. Woolman Gibson, son of John   Ensign Perry Benson*

CAPT. GREENBURY GOLDSBOROUGH'S COMPANY.

Reviewed and passed by Chris. Birckhead, Col. of the 4th Battalion of Militia, July 27th, 1776.

William Goldsborough	Robert Bond
Thomas Skinner	Thomas Knapp
James Bracco	Ephraim Small
Jonathan Gibson	Jonathan Small
Robert Newcomb	Roger Kelly
Joseph Newnam	Jonathan Woods
Risdon Newnam	John Sewell
Jarman, (or Jerman), Cade	John Warren
Isaac Lewis	Thos. Coleman
James Austin	Saml. Pritchet
Jonathan Floyd	William Bent
Peter Meagher	William Knight
John Crowder	John Mears
Wm. Ozbun, (Ozbon)	Thomas Simmons
Christopher Bruff	John Mills
Isaac Steuart, (Stuart)	John Holland

* Proceedings of the Conventions of Maryland, p. 178.

John Empson
Richard Pounder
William Shields
Andrew Steuart, (Stuart)
Hugh Sherwood
William Ray
Jacob North
William Ozbun, (Ozbon)
John Start
James Barber
Henry Winstandley
David Fitzpatrick
John Ray
George Parrott
John Parrott
James Ashcroft, (Ashcraft)
Stephen Harrison
William Powell
Thomas Hill
James Fairbanks
Philemon Ward
George Garey
Joseph Nowels
Richard Lunderkin, (Lundergin)
John Woolcutt
James Shields
Solomon Harris
John Shawhane
William Winstandley
Thomas Maquay
William Bryan
John Hewey
Joseph Sewell
Oakley Haddaway
Thomas Lambden Haddaway
Thomas Rolinson, (Rolingson)
Andrew Oram
John Samuels
Daniel Willis
John Dorgin
George Sanxton
Wm. Fitzpatrick
John Atkins
John Warner
Ephraim Maquay
James Farguson
Henry Oldfield
Solomon Horney
John Green
Robert Steuart, (Stuart)
Edward Jones
Henry Davis
Vachel Savere
John Tibby

My part of the Company was complete Friday the 19th July, 1776.
                                       Greenbury Goldsborough.

CAROLINE COUNTY.

Capt. Zabdiel Potter, unable to raise a company, resigned and was appointed Surgeon's Mate by the Council of Safety. As his successor the Council of Safety appointed Jos. Richardson.
1 Lt. Thomas Wyer Lockerman

2 Lt. Levin Handy
Ensign Philip Casson, resigned
Capt. Philip Fiddeman
1 Lt. Henry Downes
2 Lt. John Reynolds
Ensign Thomas Mason *

Enlisted by Capt. Richardson. Passed by Wm. Richardson, Aug. 31st, 1776.

* Proceedings of the Conventions of Maryland, p. 178.

Andrew Price
Thomas Comerford
Massy Fountain
John Webb
William Brown
John Kanahan
Edward Hardin
Perry Gannon
Alex. Robbs
Cornelius Morris
Hughett Conner
Wm. Walker
John Hobbs
Ellis Thomas
John Diragin, (Duregin)

John Needles
William Hobbs
John McKinney
Silah Parrott
Michal Walker
John Hughs
Robert Thomas
Zebdiah Billitor
Thomas Vaine
John Vaine
John Ford
James Tanner
Benj. Caulk
William Cook
Zadock Harvey

Enrolled by Thomas Wynn Loockerman. Last man enrolled July 17th, 1776.

Jarvus, (or Jervis), Willis
John Carter
John Turner
John Cohee
Robert Waddle
James McQuallity
Thomas Scoudrick

William Allcock
John Ritchee, (Richee)
William Sharp
William Cooper
Samuel Hopkins
Elijah Tylor, (Tyler)
Elijah Clark

John Thomas
William Clark
Henry Willis
Andrew Willis
Joseph Thomas
John Ryan

Enrolled by Lieut. Levin Handy. Reviewed and passed by William Hopewell, Aug. 4th, 1776.

William Foster
John Froume, sick
William Willin
George Handy
George Martin
Thomas Merrill

John Selby Martin
John Reed
James Haven
William Dorman
John Benston
Isaac Broughten

Isaac Duncan
Fradrick Barnicassle
Charles Roach
Jesse Parker
William Hosier
Charles Richardson, Aug. 2nd.

No enlistments of Capt. Philip Fiddeman's Company found. The company was raised, however, and marched to Philadelphia. See Md. Arch., XII, pp. 225, 234, 251, 258.

DORCHESTER COUNTY.

Capt. Thomas Burk
1 Lt. Berkit Falcon

2 Lt. John Lynch
Ensign James Woolford Gray *

Enrolled by Thomas Burke. Passed by Thom. Muse and Robt. Harrison, Aug. 8th, 1776.

Thos. Bourke, Capt.
Birket Falcon, 1st Lieut.

John Lynch, 2nd Lieut.
James W. Gray, 3rd Lieut.

James Ridgaway	George Procter	*Morris, (or Mores), Lane
Henry Pritchett	James Ingram	*Thomas Nowland, (Noland)
John Jones	Barnaby Current	*Martin Dorsey
Adam Smith	Michael Mullin	*James Murphy
Isaac Cordery	John Mitchell	*John Bailey
John McGraw	John Vinson	*John Talbott
John Hooper	Wm. Hubbard	*Daniel Coffee
Matthew Anderson	Charles Strong	*Wm. Morrane, (Moren)
James Kelly	Wm. Man	*Wm. O'Harr, (O'Harra)
Thomas Hill	John Wiley	*Henry Bright
Joseph Travers	Thomas Bartlet	*John Dick
Lewis Pickron	David Kirk	*Michael Berry, (Barry)
John Eliason	Wm. Sanders	John Priday
Matthew Handley	Elijah Bright	*Peter Laughlain,
Caste Williams	John Bourk	(Laughlanhon)
Valentine Arnett	Whittington Walace	*William Collins
Solomon Jones	Bryan Sweeny	*John Connley, (Conley)
Charles Ffooks	William Rogers	*Thos. Dawling, (Dowling)
Ezekiel Hooper	Thomas Cook	*Jeremiah Connell
Wm. Collins, Tay^r	Samuel Stanford	*John Shaw
Matthew Bright	Thompson Bright	*Geo. Burrell
Hooper Evans	William Moore	*Spencer Sibra, (Sebree)
Thomas Hooper	*Hugh Walworth	Thomas McCann
Wm. Wilson	Thomas Keene	John McGuyar
Thomas Watson	Wm. Mills	Thomas Nubry
George Branigan	Wm. G. Goutee	John Swan
John Redington	Caleb Busick	Hugh McCall
Emanuel Nicholson	James Fraizer	Abel Germier
John Brown	George Murphy	Thomas Marshall
John Clary	Levin Lane	Peter Marshall
Stephen Stubbs	John Cummins	Edward Ingram
Thomas Roberts	Henry Sutton	Joseph Insley, absent
David Cullin	Jos. Shehawn	Anthony Fleetwood, absent
John Burriss	*John Bradly, deserted	*Henry Harrington, deserted
James Dickson, deserted	*Robert Reynolds, deserted	*Geo. Childs, deserted
*Thomas Aires, (Ayres)	*John Penn, deserted	*Thomas Jones, deserted
Kimbral Follin		

* Proceedings of the Conventions of Maryland, p. 178.

I hereby certify that I enrolled the six men here last mentioned, and that they have since deserted. John Lynch.

[Names with a star prefixed are those who were enlisted by Lt. John Lynch, July 12th, 1776.]

A company in Cecil County, Capt. John Oglevie, 1st Lt. Joseph Tanner, 2nd Lt. Elisha Rodgers, Ensign James Boggs, enrolled July 25th, 1776, for the Flying Camp and offered to the Council of Safety. For the complete list of the names of the men in this company see Md. Arch., XII, 132.

PROCEEDINGS OF THE MARYLAND CONVENTION.

10 September, 1776.

"The president laid before the convention a letter and several resolutions from the honourable the president of the congress, of the third day of this instant, which was read and thereupon the convention taking the same into consideration,

Resolved, That the commanding officers of the several battalions of militia in Prince George's, Frederick, Anne Arundel, Baltimore, Harford, Cecil, Kent, Queen Anne's and Caroline Counties, be requested to call their battalions together as soon as possible, and that the field officers of the said Counties, respectively, select companies of volunteers as follows, to wit: Prince George's one, Frederick three, that is, one in each district thereof, Anne Arundel two, Baltimore two, Harford two, Cecil three, Kent two, Queen Anne's two, and Caroline one; that each company consist of 68 privates, 4 sergeants, 4 corporals, one drummer, and one fifer, under the command of a captain, two lieutenants and an ensign."

(Officers to be recommended by the field officers or the committee of observation of each county).

"That the said companies be enrolled until the first day of December next, unless sooner discharged by congress, and receive continental pay from the day of enrollment.

That the companies of militia so to be raised be enrolled in the counties and districts where they are directed to be raised as aforesaid, and not of inhabitants of other counties or districts.

That if any company of militia shall offer themselves, they shall be allowed to go into the service under their present officers; or if the present officers of any company, with a considerable number of their company, offer to go shall be able to fill up the number by enrollment of others, such company may march under such officers."

FREDERICK COUNTY—MIDDLE DISTRICT. [FREDERICK COUNTY.]

Vallentine Creager, Capt.
Phillip Smith, Jr., 1st Lieut.
George Need, (Neet), 2nd Lieut.
John Parkinson, (Pirkinson), Ensign

Serjeants.
Solomon Bentley, 1 Josiah Hedges, 3
Aquilla Carmack, 2 Christian Cumber, 4
Joseph Allsop, Drummer

Corporals.
John Brattle, 1 Charles Menix, 3
Solomon Rowlins, 2 John Link, 4
Peter Trux, (Trucks), Fifer

Thomas Edison
Christian Smith
George Dotts
Jacob Bostion
Matthias Andess
John Springer
Oliver Linsey
Ludwick Moser, (Mouser)
James Silver
Michael Fox
George Burrawl, (Burrol)
Jacob Barrick, (Barrack)
Jonothan Beard
Christopher Cooper
Patrick Daugherty, (Daugerty)
Jacob Holtzman
Peter Lickliter
John Mortt
William Slick
Thomas Tumbleson, (Tombleson)
Adam Russ
Jacob Weyant, (Wicant)

John Ciferd
James Cammell, (Campbell)
Henry Decamp
James Buckhannon, (Buchanan)
Peter Heveron
Jacob Rignall, (Rignell)
Edward Hossilton
John Smith
Laurence Stull
Samuel Hulse
William Weier
James Smith
Joseph Smith
Thomas Parkinson, (Pirkinson)
Henry Fogle
Henry Fox
Frederick Hardman
John Waggoner
Adam Waggoner
Adam Simmon, (Simon)
George McDonald
Henry Clice, (Clise)

Thomas Nailor, (Nalor)
George David
Henry Reich
Patrick Dayley
James Branwood
Thomas Cook
Philip Greenwood
Robert Sellers, (Sellors)
John White
David Barringer
Patrick Rowin
George Serjeant
Peter Dick
Cornelius Downey
William From
George Younger
Lodwick Woller, (Wooler)
Daniel Moore
Evan Morris
William Preston
Robert Parson
John Langley
Daniel Bryan
Jacob Ringer

We, the Subscribers, Delegates in Convention for Frederick County, do hereby certify that

Valentine Cregar was appointed Captain.
Philip Smith, 1st Lieut.
George Need, 2nd "
John Pirkinson, Ensign, of the

Company of Militia directed to be raised in Frederick County, and that they have embodied their Company and marched therewith to the Camp at New York, but that no Commissions have as yet issued.

October 3rd, 1776.   Upton Sheredine,
                                                      Chris. Edelen,
                                                      Adam Fischer.

A company in Montgomery County under Capt Richard Smith, 1st Lt. Walter White 2nd Lt. Thomas Hayes, Ensign Thomas Sprigg, enrolled for the Flying Camp Sept. 19th, 1776. For the complete list of the names of the men in this Company see Md. Arch. XII, 352.

A company from Harford County under Capt. Robert Harris, 1st Lt. William Cole, 2nd Lt. Benjamin Scott, Ensign James Steele, enrolled for the Flying Camp, arrived at Philadelphia Nov. 2nd, 1776. Warrant issued by the Council of Safety Sept. 23rd, 1776, to Harris to raise this company. For the complete list of the names of the men in this Company see Md. Arch. XII, 435.

Capt. Daniel Clapsaddle, 1st. Lt. Frederick Nicodemus, 2nd Lt. David Harvy, Ensign Matthias Hickman, were commissioned by the Council of Safety Sept. 26th, 1776, officers of a company enrolled for the Flying Camp in Washington County.

CAPT. CLAPSADLE'S RETURN. GUNS, ETC, 1776.

An Account What Was Taken By the Enemy at Fort Lee On the Armies Retreat from that Place, [Nov. 20th, 1776,] of the Continentle Property From Captn. Daniel Clapsadle's Company, viz. 14 Tents, 14 Camp Cittles, 30 Canteens, 49 Habersacks, 6 Blankets, 1 Rifle, 2 Muskes & 2 Bayonets, 8 Belts, 31 Tommehocks, 3 Bouches and 4 Horns.   Daniel Clapsadle, Capt.

A List Guns, &c delivered to Mr. Robert Gowers, Dec. 6, 1776. Per his receipt at Philadelphia, 47 Guns, 31 Bay^{ts}, 34 Belts, 19 Tomahawks, 53 Blankets, 24 Haversacks, 62 Pouches, 34 Powder-Horns, 9 Rifles, 1 Drum-Sticks & Sling.   Daniel Clapsadle, Capt.

A company in Cecil County, enrolled for the Flying Camp, under Capt. Samuel Evans, 1st. Lt. Henry Dobson, 2nd Lt. Thomas Ramsay,

Ensign Wm. Steuart, marched to Philadelphia Oct., 1776. The officers were commissioned by the Council of Safety Sept. 28th, 1776.

A company in Cecil County, enrolled for the Flying Camp, under Capt. James Maxwell, 1st Lt. John Hartshorne, 2nd Lt. William Johnstone, Ensign Adam Glascow, commissioned Oct. 3rd and ordered to Philadelphia Oct. 15th, 1776, by the Council of Safety.

A company in Frederick County, enrolled for the Flying Camp, under Capt. Andrew Hynes, 1st Lt. Isaac McCrackin, 2nd Lt. Ezekiel Cox, Ensign John Jacobs, commissioned Oct. 12th and ordered to Philadelphia Oct. 15th, 1776, by the Council of Safety.

A company in Harford County, the Harford Greens, enrolled for the Flying Camp, under Capt. Francis Holland, 1st Lt. John Carlile, 2nd Lt. William Young, Ensign Robert Morgan, commissioned Oct. 15th, 1776, by the Council of Safety. This company marched to Philadelphia Oct. 23rd, 1776.

Applications from Col. Richardson's Regiment.

1st Lt. Hawkins	Capt.	St. Jones
" " Porter	"	" Maslin
2nd " Cosden	"	" Ridgeway
Adjt. Robt. Campbell	"	" Skinner
1st Lt. Saml. Thomas	"	" Needles
2nd " Johnson	"	" Gibson
" " Handy	"	" Alexander
" " Burk	"	" Gold
" " Lynch	"	" Cole, a good officer and a prisoner
3rd " Gray	"	" Catlin, back
Ensign Henry	"	Privates James Hacket, a prisoner and good soldier
" Moore	Lt.	
" Mason	"	George Handy, to be promoted
" Benson	"	Oakly Haddaway, ditto
Qr. Mastr. Edmondson		John Reed, ditto, bad
		Benjamin Roberts, ditto, 2nd Lt.

Gentlemen:

I have acted sometime past as Ensign to Capt. Evans of the Maryland Flying Camp, and having an inclination of continuing in the Service co'd I be appointed to a First Lieutenancy in the same Company with Thomas Ramsay, for which I apply. Captain Evans will give you my Character and if it is such that you can intrust me with such an Office Shall gladly accept it and acknowledge it as a favor done.

Gentlemen,
Your obt. Hble. Servt.
Wm. Stewart,
4 December, 1776.

To the Gentlemen, Commissioners
from Maryland for appointing
Officers in the Standing Army.

Philadelphia, December 7th, 1776.

Gentlemen:

We beg Leave to Recommend to your Honours for an Ensign's Commission in the Company now Recruiting by Captain Andrew Hynes, Mr. Richard Donovan as he has served in said Company when in the service of the Last Maryland Flying Camp as first Serjeant, in which office he availed himself in his duty in such a sort as to Merit a more worthy Recommendation, We are Gentlemen

Your Honours Most Obedt. huml. servants,
Andrew Hynes.
Ezekiel Cox.

To the Honorable
The Commissioners
For the State of Maryland.

MUSTERS OF MARYLAND TROOPS.

"Maryland Line."

RESOLVES OF CONTINENTAL CONGRESS, 16 SEPTEMBER, 1776.

"Resolved, That 88 battalions be inlisted as soon as possible, to serve during the present war, and that each state furnish their respective quotas in the following proportions, ... Maryland 8 battalions."

RESOLVES OF MARYLAND CONVENTION, 9 OCTOBER, 1776.

"Resolved, That the 8 battalions required by congress to be raised by this state, exceeds its just quota, ... That this state, desirous of exerting the most strenuous efforts to support the liberties and independence of the United States, will therefore use its utmost endeavours to raise the 8 battalions required, (including the troops already raised and in the service of the United States), as soon as possible.

That four commissioners be appointed to repair to the camps in the Jerseys and New York, and there obtain a list of such of the officers in the regular troops and flying camp from this state, now in the service of the United States, as are willing to engage in the service during the war; and also to enlist or cause to be enlisted all or every of the said regular troops or flying camp militia in the service of the United States during the war, continuing the regular battalion and forming the independent companies into a battalion, and filling both up according to the continental establishment; and the said commissioners, or any three of them, may also fill up such of the blank commissions sent to this convention by congress, as may be immediately necessary for the officering of the said corps; but in filling up the said commissions they are required not to introduce into the corps of the now regulars, any officer other than such as are of those regulars, nor into the corps which may be formed of the flying camp militia, any officer not now an officer in the said regulars or flying camp."

RESOLVES OF MARYLAND CONVENTION, 11 NOVEMBER, 1776.

"Resolved, That this Convention adjourn . . . . And that the said Council of Safety be and are fully empowered to take and pursue all measures that they shall think necessary or proper for raising, completing, and equipping the 8 battalions resolved by this convention to be raised for the Continental service, agreeable to the resolves of this convention."

RESOLVES OF CONTINENTAL CONGRESS, 27 JUNE, 1776.

"Resolved, That six companies of riflemen, in addition to the three companies now at New York, be raised, and the whole regimented; and that a commission be granted to captain Stevenson, to be colonel of the said regiment of riflemen, which is to be enlisted for three years, unless sooner discharged by Congress; the men to be allowed a bounty of ten dollars; and that Moses Rawlins be lieutenant-colonel, and Otho Holland Williams, major of the said regiment: That four companies of riflemen, for the said regiment, be raised in Virginia, and two in Maryland."

(Rawlings became colonel about 1 January, 1777.)

RESOLVES OF CONTINENTAL CONGRESS, 9 OCTOBER, 1778.

"Resolved, That if any of the states in which col. Moses Rawlins shall recruit for his regiment shall give to persons enlisting in the same, for three years, or during the war, the bounty allowed by the state, in addition to the continental bounty, the men so furnished, not being inhabitants of any other of the United States, shall be credited to the quota of the State in which they shall be enlisted."

RESOLVES OF CONTINENTAL CONGRESS, 23 JANUARY, 1779.

"Resolved, That col. Rawlings and such of the officers of his corps as shall be appointed by the commander-in-chief, forthwith recruit three companies of that corps to the full complement: That the volunteers be inlisted for the war, and ordered to repair to Fort Pitt."

Colonel Moses Rawlings' Rifle Regiment was originally raised in Maryland and Virginia as Stephenson's Maryland and Virginia Rifle Regiment, and reorganized in 1777 as one of the 16 additional Regiments.

MUSTERS OF MARYLAND TROOPS, VOL. I.

Names.	Rank.	Time of Service. Enlisted.	Discharged.	Remarks.
\multicolumn{5}{c}{First Regiment.}				
Allen, Barna.	private	10 Dec 76	16 Augt 80	prisoner
Austin, Robt..	id	25 Mar 77	10 May 80	died
Adams, John	Copr	10 Dec 76		
	reduced	1 Jany 78	6 March 78	deserted
Allison, Thomas	private	10 Dec 78	16 Augt 80	prisoner
Allen, Alexander	id	id	27 Dec 79	discharged
Angleir, Joseph	id	id	9 March 77	dead
Armstrong, Hugh	id	10 id	2 July 77	deserted
Austin, James	id	21 May 77		never joined
Adams, James	Corpl	10 Dec 76	13 Sept 77	missing
Allen, William	private	20 May 78	3 Sept 78	died
Adams, Adam	id	16 May 78	1 Nov 80	present
Athey, Ebenezer	id	4 June 78	5 April 79	discharged
Adams, John	id	1 June 78	id	id
Allen, Jesse	id	18 May 78	20 Feby 79	id
Atchison, Jeremiah	id	30 May 77	23 Sept 78	died
Adams, Ignatius	id	9 May 79	1 Nov 80	present
Atchison, say Hutchinson, Wm.	id	31 May 79	see H. record Book	
Alvey, Josiah	id	24 May 79		
Arnold, Wm.	Drum	Joined 1 Jany 80		
			1 Nov 80	present
Adams, Peter	Lt. Col.			
	Lt. Col. Comt.		1 Augt 79	
Arvin, Ananias	private	10 June 79	8 Augt 80	deserted
\multicolumn{5}{c}{Second Regiment.—Beginning January 1778.}				
Andrew, Jeremiah	Corpl		2 Oct 78	dead, paid
Andrew, James	id	10 Jany 77	10 Jany 80	discharged, paid
Aspin, Thomas	private	15 Augt 77	1 Nov 80	serving in Armons as farrier, paid
Allender, John	id		do	discharged
Angles, John	id	not mustered since		
Allen, Solomon	private	do		
Anderson, Arc.	Corpl	10 Dec 76	promoted to 3 Regt.	
	Major		10 June 77	
Abbot, Geo., 9 mo.	private	20 May 78	1 Nov 80	present
Arnet, Thomas	id		time out	discharged
Alvey, John	id	10 June 79	1 Nov 80	present
Abdel, Jacob	id	9 May 79	in May 79	deserted
Austin, Henry	id	14 April 78	16 Augt 80	missing

MUSTERS OF MARYLAND TROOPS, VOL. I.

NAMES.	RANK.	TIME OF SERVICE. Enlisted.	Discharged.	REMARKS.
THIRD REGIMENT.—*Beginning* 77.				
Alexander, James	pt	22 Mar 77	29 Sept 80	discharged, off Rolls
Appleby, Wm.	pt		15 March 78	deserted
Appleby, Jno.	id			below joined
Armstrong, Geo.	Lieut Capt	10 Dec 76		
Armsworthy, Baptist	pt	22 April 77	16 Augt 80	missing
Adams, Wm.	pt	27 April 77	29 April 79	deserted
Allen, William	private Corporal Sergt	15 Feby 78 1 June 79	16 Aug 80	prisoner
Allison, James	Lieut			
Andrews, Joshua out July 78	private	2 May 77		deserted
Adams, Richard out July 78	id	22 Augt 77		id
Arnold, Thomas	id	2 June 77	Augt 77	died
Aschum, Samuel out Augt 80	Corpl private	10 March 77 1 June 78	Augt 78 10 March 80	off Rolls
Anderson, John reenlisted	id	20 Feby 77	28 Feby 80 18 Augt 80	time expired deserted
Adamisell, John	id		26 Oct 77	died
Allen, John	id	20 April 78	Dec 78	off Rolls
Allibon, Thomas	id	15 April 78	16 Augt 80	missing
Adams, John	id	3 Mar 78	1 Nov 80	present
Adams, Thomas	id	22 April do	9 Dec 78	
Alvey, Travers	id	28 April do	1 Nov 80	present
Assom, John	Corpl	19 Feby 78	28 Mar 79	discharged
Alvey, Thomas Green	private 1 Feb 79 Corpl	24 April 78	wounded	furlowed
Adams, Nathaniel	private	22 May 78	18 Oct 78	
Adams, Thomas	id	25 April 78		
Anderson, William	id	23 April 78		
Adams, James	id			
Armstrong, James July &c. must. 80	Drum		16 Augt 80	missing

Names.	Rank.	Time of Service. Enlisted.	Discharged.	Remarks.

Fourth Regiment.—Beginning Dec. 1777.

Names.	Rank.	Enlisted.	Discharged.	Remarks.
Adamson, George[1]	private	27 Dec 76	16 Augt 80	missing
Aaron, Moses	id		Jany 78	left out the rolls
Adams, Mark	id		Dec 77	drafted for sea
Adamson, Alexander[2]	Drum		16 Aug 80	missing
Anderson, Daniel[3]	private		1 Nov 80	present
Allender, Joshua[4]	id	paid June mus. 80		time expired
Adams, William[5]	Lieut	10 Dec 76	Augt 78	resigned
Allcock, Martin[6]	private		16 Aug 80	missing
Adams, Richard[3]	id	12 Feby 78	17 May 78	deserted
Allen, Richard[4]	id	11 Jany 78	1 May 78	do
Aldham, Danl[2]	id	21 Apl 78	July 80	do
Allman, William[4]	id / Corpl	19 May 78 / 1 Dec 79	} July 80	do
Austin, Isaac[1] joined May & June must. 80	private		16 Aug 80	missing
Arnold, Christopher	pt	paid		R. see Chr. Onnel

Rawlings' Regiment.

Names.	Rank.	Enlisted.	Discharged.	Remarks.
Austin, James	Drum	17 Augt 76	20 Dec 76	deserted
Allexander, Mathw.	Sergt	28 July do		
Andrews, William	private / Corpl	18 do do / 1777		paid
Arnot, T. D.	pt	17 Augt 76		
Alexander, John	id			
Allinger, Stepn.	id			
Aitzil, Jacob	id			
Adams, Jacob	id	5 Feby		
Adams, Jacob	id	9 June		

First Regiment.

Names.	Rank.	Enlisted.	Discharged.	Remarks.
Brown, Peter	Lieut	10 dec 76	10 July 77	resigned
Britt, Robert	Sergt 1 Jany 80, 2 m Sergt		1 Nov 80	present, forage [Dep.
Bennett, George	Corpl		missg.	11 Sept 77
Basil, John	pt		27 Dec 79	discharged
Brown, John	id	19 May 77	21 Jany 78	deserted
Bruce, William	Lieut / Capt	10 Dec 76 / 1 Augt 79	6 July 78	appd. Adjt.

[1] Oldham's. [2] Norwood's. [3] Godman's. [4] Selman's. [5] Bowie's. [6] Burgess'. (These are names of captains of companies.)

MUSTERS OF MARYLAND TROOPS, VOL. I.

NAMES.	RANK.	TIME OF SERVICE. Enlisted.	Discharged.	REMARKS.
Brady, Patrick	Sergt	10 Dec 76	12 Oct 78	reduced
			27 Dec 79	discharged
Broderick, Dennis	fifer	10 Dec 76		
fife major		1 Apl 77	deserted 78	Wilmington
Buxton, Abijah	private	10 Dec 76	27 Dec 79	discharged
re-enlisted	mustr.	June 80	1 Nov 80	present
Booth, John	pt	do	8 Sept 78	died
Burrows, Thomas	id	do	4 Apl 77	id
Bond, William	id	1 Feby 77	17 Apl 77	deserted
Beanes, J. H.	Capt	10 Dec 76	2 Dec 77	resigned
Brown, William	pt		24 June	deserted
Boon, John	Corpl	26 May 77		
	Sergt	1 July 79	26 Mar 80	discharged
	Ensign	14 March 80		
	Lieut			
Boon, Ignatius	pt	10 Dec 76		
	Sergt	1 Dec 77	27 Dec 79	discharged
Beall, Christopher	do	do	do	do
Brown, John	do	14 April 77		deserted
Bulley, William	do	10 June 77	16 Aug 80	prisoner
Blanford, Igs.	pt	21 June 77	time out	discharged
	Corpl	1 July 79		
	Sergt	12 Dec 79		June 80
Bailey, Robert	do	2 June 77	3 Augt 80	deserted
Basford, William	do	10 Dec 76	27 Dec 79	discharged
Booth, John	do	do	27 Nov 77	deserted
Bootman, Joseph	do	do	7 Feby 77	dead
Basil, Daniel	fife	10 Apl 77	1 Nov 80	present
Baker, William	pt	10 Dec 76		dead or deserted
Butler, Jacob	id	id	20 Mar 77	died
Babbs, John	id	id	13 Dec 79	discharged
Baker, John	id	3 May 77	10 Aug 80	deserted
Baker, Joseph	id	27 Mar 77	dead or deserted	
Bromgart, Adam	id	28 May 77	9 Oct 77	deserted
		joined 9 April 79		
Burgess, Vachl.	Corpl			
	Ensign	17 Apl 77		
	Lieut		22 Aug 79	resigned
Brown, William	pt	3 Apl 77		dead or deserted
	Sergt	10 May 77	May 80	discharged
Bartley, Thomas	Corpl	17 Mar 77	prisr. 12 May 79, joined Aug 79	
	Sergt	20 Oct 77	reduced 10 Feby 78, Sergt 7 Mar 78	
	pt	29 Mar 77	reduced 5 Nov 79, Sergt again, discharged 21 Mar 80	

MUSTERS OF MARYLAND TROOPS, VOL. I.

NAMES.	RANK.	Time of Service. Enlisted.	Discharged.	REMARKS.
Burch, Francis	pt	29 Mar 77	29 Mar 80	discharged
Barbar, Clemt.	id	10 dec 76	27 Dec 79	id
Barber, Saml.	Adjt	5 May 77	resigned July 6, 78	
Bell, Lawson	pt	4 Jany 78	27 Dec 79	transferred, discharged 1 Apl 80
Baker, John	pt	3 May 78	paid	Sickann's
Briscoe, Philip	id	3 June 78	5 April 79	discharged
Brissington, Abra.		17 May 78	dead or deserted	
Bivens, Luke	pt	4 May 78	May 80	invalids
Burnes, Michael	id	9 May 78	4 Dec 78	deserted
Barclay, James			June 78	deserted
Butler, John	id	4 June 78	1 Sept 78	died
Bateman, George	id	5 ditto	9 mo. out	
re-enlisted 5 April 79—8 Jany 80 discharged				
Burton, Francis		3 May 78		
Buchanan, John	Drum	9 May 79	1 Nov 80	present
Bassett, Peter	pt	20 June 79	30 June 80	deserted
Boarman, Thomas		15 June 79	16 Augt 80	prisoner
Bagley, Sam'l		5 July 79	do	missing
Button, Thomas		30 May 79	12 Dec 79	deserted
Brookbank, James		5 July 79	dead or deserted	
Berry William			27 July 80	do
Brookbank, Jno.		31 July 79	1 Nov 80	present
Bryant, James	Fife	24 Nov 78	do	do

SECOND REGIMENT.—*Beginning with the Muster Rolls for January,* 1778.

Briscoe, John H.	Sergt		1 Jany 78	resigned
Bostwick, Richard	Corpl	4 Mar 77	10 June 80	discharged
Brown, Thomas	pt	27 Jany 77	4 Nov 79	died
Burgess, Thomas	id	1 Jany 77	10 Aug 79	died of wounds received at Stony Point
Brewer, Richard	pt		23 Jany 78	deserted
Blades, John	id	10 Mar 77	28 Jany 80	prisoner war
Bush, Richard	id		12 Feby 79	died
Burk, Levy, (or Burch)	id	10 Dec 76		
	Corpl	June 80	1 Nov 80	present
Beaver, William	pt		10 Jany 80	discharged
Bradley, John	fifer	13 Jany 77	paid depreciation	
	pt	1 Jany 80	23 March 80	prisoner
Bettis, Jacob	id	29 Dec 76	29 Dec 79	discharged
Brewer, Thomas	Sergt	7 Aug 77		
add. to Corpl		1 June 78	1 June 80	discharged
	Sergt	1 Feby 80		

during the War of the American Revolution, 1775–83.   83

MUSTERS OF MARYLAND TROOPS, VOL. I.

NAMES.	RANK.	TIME OF SERVICE. Enlisted.	Discharged.	REMARKS.
Broughton, Joshua	pt		31 Dec 79	died
Bryan, Charles	id		10 Jany 80	time out while on furl.
Barret, James	id		ditto	discharged
Buckley, Daniel	id	28 Feby 76	1 Nov 80	present
Beall, Charles	id.		10 Jany 80	discharged
Boles, William			1 May 80	died
Boyles, Daniel	pt	10 Dec 76	Mar 79	transferred to Invalids
			5 May 80	discharged
Bayley, John	id			struck off
Brady, James	id		22 Jany	deserted
Baldwin, James	id			struck off
Belamy, John	id	Entered on the other side		
Beck, Osborne	id		10 Jany 80	discharged
Burgess, James	id	1 Jany 79	10 Jany 80	discharged
Buckley, Thomas	id	20 Feby 78	1 Nov 80	present
	Sergt	1 Feby 80		
Bandy, John	pt	25 Feby 78	78	died wounds
Bryan, John	pt	1 Aprl 78	78	died
Brookes, William	id	13 Feby 78	1 Nov 80	present
Burch, Joseph	id	28 Feby 78	Corpl 1 Feby 80	
	Corpl	15 May 78	private 25 Oct 80	
Corporal 1 April 79	pt	1 Mar 78	1 Nov 80	present
Brookshear, James	id	25 Aprl 78		time out, discharged
Bramble, Eton	id	1 May 78	1 July 78	deserted
Burnes, Zekiel	id	23 April 78	16 Aug 80	killed
Bramble, Hackett	id	4 May 78	1 Nov 80	present
Bellows, Isaac	id	15 May 78	dead or deserted	
Bishop, Thomas	id	4 Mar 78	1 Nov 80	present
Boarman, Daniel	id	20 Jany 78	July 80	deserted
Baldwin, John	id	19 Aprl 78	20 April 78	do
Ball, Richard	id	5 Aprl 78	15 April 78	do
Brathwait, Wm.	id	1 May 78	} 1 Nov 80	present
	Corpl	1 Mar 80		
Burns, John	pt	20 do do	Mar 80	died
Boon, Foster	id	28 May 78	8 Mar 79	discharged
Battingly, Stanley	id	31 May 78	3 April 79	do
Bell, Thomas	id	24 do	do	do
Biggs, Thomas	id	4 April 78	do	do
Barnes, James	id	29 May 78	do	do
Burris, Norm.	id	30 May 78	do	do
Brown, Thomas[1]	id		10 Jany 80	do

[1] Dent's

MUSTERS OF MARYLAND TROOPS, VOL. I.

Names.	Rank.	Time of Service. Enlisted.	Discharged.	Remarks.
Butt, Zachariah	id	28 Mar 78	16 Aug 80	missing
Butt, Baruch	id	3 April 78	1 Nov 80	present
Browning, William Priso. Mar 80	id	6 June do	Mar 80	prisoner war
Beck, Amos	id	10 do do	16 Augt 80	missing
Brannon, James	pt	8 Mar 77	8 Mar 80	discharged
Boyland, Andrew	id	20 May 78	3 Aprl 79	discharged
Batson, James	id	do do	July 79	time out, discharged
Byrne, Charles	id		16 Augt 80	killed
Boyes, Alexander	id	8 May 78	21 Jany 79	discharged
Baker, John	id	25 ditto	26 Dec 78	deserted
Butts, Thomas	Drum	8 April 78	1 Nov 80	present
Butts, Edward	fifer private	28 Mar do 1 July 79 }	1 Nov 80	present
Bennet, Frederick	Fifer	26 do do	1 Nov 80	do
Bramble, William	pt		3 April 79	do
Barrett, Danl. Joined 9 May 79	id Corpl	1 May 80 }	16 Aug 80	missing
Brown, Solomon 1st muster June 79	pt		19 June 79	deserted
Blanford, Richard	id	13 June 79	16 Augt 80	missing
Bramble, David	id	7 do	1 Nov 80	present
Brooks, Thomas	id	8 July 79	22 July 79	deserted
Brashears, Igns.	id	18 Jany 77	18 Jan 80	discharged
Boyd, Thomas	Ensn Lieut	27 Oct 79 June 80		
Brittenham, Solo.	fifer	1 April 80	16 Aug 80	missing
Bellemy, John	pt		1 Nov 80	present
Buttons, Levin	id	5 April 80	do	do
Bramble, Levin	id	16 July 80	do	do

Third Regiment.—*Beginning* 77.

Names	Rank	Enlisted	Discharged	Remarks
Baldwin, Henry	Ensn Sergt qr. mast.	27 May 78 26 Feby 77		
Bridges, Richard	pt	9 Mar 77	1 Nov 80	present
Bate, Thomas	id	21 June 77		not heard of,
Branwood, James	id		taken on S. Island 22 Augt	
Banney, James	id		2 Nov 78 5 Nov 79	to Invalids discharged }
Blakney, (or Blake), Jno.	id		19 July 80	deserted
Burnes, James	id Corpl Sergt	1 June 79 1 Sept 79 }	1 Nov 80 deserted about the 15 Mar 81	

MUSTERS OF MARYLAND TROOPS, VOL. I.

Names.	Rank.	Time of Service. Enlisted.	Discharged.	Remarks.
Brookes, Benja.	Capt	10 Dec 76		
Brown, Thomas	Corpl	1 Jany 77	1 Nov 80	present
Bennett, Jesse	pt	5 Apl 77	1 May 79	deserted
Butterworth, Jos.	id		16 Aug 80	missing
Bray, Joseph	id	28 do do	1 Feb 80	
Burnett, Thomas out May 78 Sergt July 80	id Sergt Nov 78 Corpl	13 May 77 15 Mar 78	16 Aug 80	prisoner Camden
Beard, William	pt	29 June 77	19 Dec 78	died, Invalid Corps Sept. 11, 78
Bloyds, Daniel	id	19 Aprl 77	4 July 80	deserted
Burris, William	id	18 Aug do	20 Dec 77	died
Barkers, James	id	18 Sept do	14 July 78	deserted
Barker, William	id	6 Augt do	16 Augt 80	missing
Burris, George	id	9 Sept do	2 Jan 78	died
Bailey, John	Lieut		18 Nov 79	resigned
Bailey, Joseph	Serg & pt	21 May 77 10 Oct do	furd. 5 Augt 78, never returned	
Byass, James	pt	1 Jany 77	1 Nov 80	present
Beaver, Martin	id	9 May 77	served time out	
Breakley, John	id	2 July 77	do do	do
Benn, Whidd'r	id Corpl	8 Aug 77 15 Feby 78	1 Nov 80	present
Bush, Francis	pt		Aug 80	deserted
Bryan, Daniel	id		7 Dec 77	died
Brice, Jacob	Capt B. Insp.	10 Dec 77 1 May 78		
Bronely, John	pt Sergt	3 April 77 3 Oct 77	16 Augt 80	prisoner
Brearly, George	pt	27 June do	not heard of	
Brown, James	id	21 July do	Dec 78	died
Brown, John	id		1 Nov 80	present
Burns, Hugh	id Corpl	4 May 77 20 May 78	16 Augt 80	prisoner
Barber, John	pt		do do	missing
Boston, John N.	id	28 April 77		deserted
Brady, Michael	id	27 July do	23 July 78	do
Butler, Richard	id	16 Nov 77	1 Nov 80	present
Baker, John	id	10 April 77	21 Feby 80	time expired
Bidgood, William	id		28 Feby 78	deserted
Bolton, Richard joined 27 April, 78	id		15 Oct 79	do
Best, James	id		27 Oct 78	died

MUSTERS OF MARYLAND TROOPS, VOL. I.

Names.	Rank.	Time of Service. Enlisted.	Discharged.	Remarks.
Burk, Peter	pt	1 Oct 78	1 Jan 80	off rolls
	Corpl			
Bicknall, Esau	pt			dead or deserted
Byars, John	id	Know nothing of him		
Bartholomew, Ben	Adjt		Mar 78	cashiered
Barrett, John	pt	25 April 78	18 Augt 80	deserted
Bartley, Thomas S.	id	do do	16 do do	missing
Bachilor, Thomas	id	26 do do	know nothing of him	
Burns, David	pt	25 April 78	16 Aug 80	missing
Bryan, John	id	taken by prior enlistment, re-enlisted in State Regt.		
Blissell, Edward	id	27 April 78	time out	discharged
Bullock, Jesten.	id	24 ditto		dead, time unknown
Blunderwill, John	id	30 ditto	18 Oct 78	dead
Bailey, John B.	id	24 ditto		
Brown, William	Sergt	24 Feby 78	4 June 78	deserted
Butler, George	do	28 April 78	20 June 78	ditto
Bradley, James	pt	3 April 78	14 Aug 78	ditto
Buttery, Thomas	id	16 May 78	16 Aug 80	killed
Brown, Basil	id	9 April 78	1 Nov 80	present
Brown, George	id	23 do do	do	do
Bowers, Thomas	id		12 Sept 78	died
Brett, John	id		21 Jan 80	deserted
Bray, Joseph	id		see the other side	
Bingley, Alexander	id	13 May 78	1 Nov 80	present
Barnhouse, Rodolph	id	1 June 78	4 Aug 79	discharged
Branson, Thomas	id	25 do do	30 Oct 78	do
Burch, Zacharh.	id	26 May 78	1 Nov 80	present
Bean, Leonard	id	29 do do	do	do
	1 Jany 80, Corpl			
Blake, George	pt	9 June 78	24 Nov 78	deserted
Brown, William	id	23 April 78	know nothing of him	
Barry, William[1]	id	do do	do	do
Bellwhight, Sam'l[2]	id	do do	1 Nov 80	present
Bachilor, William	id	27 do do	Sept	dead
Beaver, John	id	1 June 78	13 Feby 79	discharged
Boardman, Rob't	id	1 May 78	Dec 79	deserted
Brand, Gabriel	pt	5 June 78	1 Nov 80	present
Bean, John	id	do do	ditto	ditto
Bird, Thomas	id	do do	ditto	ditto
Boyd, Benjamin	id	8 May 78	ditto	ditto
Byalls, Peter	id	9 do do	23 Mar 80	prisoner

[1] Griffith's.   [2] Jones'.

during the War of the American Revolution, 1775-83.

MUSTERS OF MARYLAND TROOPS, VOL. I.

Names.	Rank.	Time of Service. Enlisted.	Discharged.	Remarks.
Bullock, John	pt		April and May	time expired
Blair, John	id	15 Jany 79	1 Nov 80	present
Berry, Isaac	fife	10 May 78		know nothing of him
Brickstake, Roger joined 17 June 79	pt		16 Augt 80	missing
Batson, George 1 muster May 79	id	1 Dec 76		time out 1 Dec 79
Bullen, John 1 muster May 79	id		Sept 79	deserted
Bowie, Matthew	id	18 May 79	Feby 80	id
Buccard, Peter	id	5 Sept 77	1 Oct 80	present
Barry, William[1]	id		16 Augt 80	missing
Bailey, Thomas joined 15 Sept 79[2]	id	3 May 77	1 Nov 80	present

From October Musters, 1780, and July, &c.

Names.	Rank.	Enlisted.	Discharged.	Remarks.
Bailey, James	Drum	7 Mar 80	1 Nov 80	present
Buckley, John	pt	7 Jan 80	do	do
Blower, James	id	3 Mar 80	do	do
Berry, William	fife		July 80	deserted
Busby, Christopher	pt		16 Augt 80	missing
Bolton, William	id		do do	killed

Fourth Regiment.—*Beginning December*, 1777.

Names.	Rank.	Enlisted.	Discharged.	Remarks.
Beach, John	Drum M.	1 May 77	1 Nov 80	present
Barrett, Joshua[3]	pt Sergt	18 Dec 76 } 1 June 79 }	16 Augt 80	missing
Bowen, Samuel	pt		10 Sept 78	discharged
Baulk, Benjamin	do	19 Dec 76	19 Dec 79	ditto
Branmon, Caleb[4]	do		25 May 80	time expired
Barrow, James	id		15 June 78	discharged
Bannerman, Jno.	id	1 May 77		
Bates, John[5]	id		1 Nov 80	present
Bostwick, Thomas	id	12 Jan 77	12 Jan 80	discharged
Bredding, John	id		16 Augt 80	missing
Bond, Joshua	id		——— 76	
Begley, George[6]	id	9 May 77	16 Augt 80	prisoner
Boyd, Edward	id		1 April 78	deserted
Brown, John	id		1 dec 77	discharged
Bidwell, Richard[7]	id	6 Dec 76	6 Dec 79	do

[1] Late Smith's. [2] Brooks'. [3] Oldham's. [4] Norwood's. [5] To Selman's, Godman's. [6] Lansdale's. [7] Sellman's.

MUSTERS OF MARYLAND TROOPS, VOL. I.

NAMES.	RANK.	TIME OF SERVICE. Enlisted.	Discharged.	REMARKS.
Bowen, Jehu[1]	Ensn		16 Oct 78	remov'd to Mary'd Dragoons
Banks, Charles	pt		21 May 79	died
Bransby, William	id		26 Feby 78	deserted
Brown, Christopher	id	19 July 77	July 80	ditto
Beach, John	Drum M.	1 May 77	see above	D. Major
Buttoridge, John	pt		Jan 78	left out the Rolls
Dec 77 sea service				
Bowie, Wm. Sprigg[2]	Capt			left out of Roll
Berry, John	pt	5 Aug. 77	July 80	discharged
Brown, James	id Drum Fife M.	{ 19 May 77 1 June 78 1 June 80 }	16 Augt 80	missing
Bradley, George	Corpl	29 May 77	1 Nov 80	present
Burgess, Joseph[3]	Capt	10 Dec 76	17 Nov 78	died
Belt, John Sprigg	Lieut Capt	do do 15 Dec 77		
Baker, William	pt	7 April 77	1 Nov 80	present, (deserted, so say Capt Belt)
Badham, Edward	id		15 April 78	deserted
Bardmore, John	id		Feby 78	left out Rolls
Bowdon, Arthur	id	17 April 77	17 April 80	time expired
Blackwell, Hugh	id	2 April 77	April&May 79	not heard of
Bloice, Abraham	id	11 Augt 77	Dec 79	deserted
Brown, Isaac,[4] joined from Sellman's		26 Dec 77	see Isaac Brown below	
Booth, William	pt	21 Jan 78	14 Sept 78	transd. 4 Pens. Regt.
Britt, Thomas[1]	id	19 Jan 78	19 May 80	deserted
Burn, Michael,[5] joined Oldham's 1 June 79	id	26 April 78	July 80	ditto
Bond, James	pt	27 April 78	9 Jan 80	ditto
Blower, John[6]	id	9 May 78	23 Jan 80	ditto
Brown, Isaac	pt Corpl	{ 26 Feby 77 1 Nov 78 }	26 Feby 80	time out
Barnett, John[7]	pt	5 May 78	16 Augt 80	missing
Bright, William From Capt. Brown's Ary.	id	1 April 78	1 Nov 80	present
Batteast, John	pt	25 April 78	May 79	deserted
Bardeu, William	id	2 May 78	April 80	left out

[1] Spurrier's.   [2] Bowie's.   [3] Burgess'.   [4] Lansdale's.   [5] Norwood's.   [6] To Sellman's, Lansdale's, April, 78.   [7] Sellman's.

MUSTERS OF MARYLAND TROOPS, VOL. I.

Names.	Rank.	Time of Service. Enlisted.	Discharged.	Remarks.
Bowler, Peter[1]	pt	27 April 78	1 Nov 80	present
Barraclift, John[2]	id	9 May 78	Sept 80	deserted
Bryan, Thomas	id	8 May 78	5 May 80 } July 80	ditto ditto
Bates, Roland[3]	id	15 May 78	July 80	ditto
Brown, John[2]	pt	21 April 78	Dec 21 1780	discharged
Brown, Thomas[4] prs'r 22 Augt, joined 23 June 78	id Corpl 1 Jan 80	6 Sept 77	1 May 80 } July 80	deserted ditto
Brown, Robert prs'r 22 Aug 77, joined 23 June 78	pt	23 Feby 78	{ 14 May 80 } { July 80 }	ditto ditto
Bermingham, Patrick[5]	id	20 May 78	16 Augt 80	missing
Boshibea, Joseph	id	22 Jan 78	1 Nov 80	present
Brisington, Philip[1]	id	1 April 78	see below	
Butler, Joseph[6]	id	28 May 78	16 Aug 80	missing
Bushell, Peter[7] pris'r 22 Aug 77, joined 10 Aug 80	id	18 April 77	18 April 80	discharged
Balff, Edward[1]	pt	1 Aug 78	9 June 80	deserted
Brown, Luke[7]	id	1 July 77	July 79	ditto
Brishington, Philip,[1] Enlisted in So. Caro. with the enemy	id	1 April 78	16 Augt 80	missing
Ballamy, John[7]	pt joined	27 May 79 } 24 Sept 80 }	1 Nov 80	present
Byrne, Michael Joined 1 June 79	pt	see Michael Burn, Norwood's Compy.		
Brown, Richard[8] Mus'd June 79	id		16 Augt 80	missing
Belford, Jeremiah[8]	id	8 May 79	Jan 80	deserted
Bowen, Robert	fifer	16 do do	16 Augt 80	missing
Bentley, Thomas[8] Late Godman's	pt	23 Oct 79	2 Jan 80	deserted
Bowser, Samuel Joined 1 Nov 79	id	18 May 77	18 Mar 80	discharged
Bailey, Joseph[7] Joined May & June mus. 80	id	left out Oct. 1780		
Bailey, Philip	pt	16 April 80	1 Nov 80	present
Burgess, Joshua	Ensign	14 Mar 80		

[1] Reily's, late Bowie's.   [2] Godman's.   [3] Norwood's.   [4] Lansdale's.   [5] Sellman's.
[6] Burgess', June, 78.   [7] Oldham's.   [8] Belt's.

MUSTERS OF MARYLAND TROOPS, VOL. I.

Names.	Rank.	Time of Service. Enlisted.	Time of Service. Discharged.	Remarks.
\multicolumn{5}{c}{RAWLINGS' REGIMENT.}				
Buller, Patrick	pt	18 Aug 76	27 Dec 76	deserted
Barnes, Richard	pt	8 do	18 do	ditto
Baker, Charles	pt	29 do	9 Aug 79	discharged
Burton, Joseph 3	pt	July 76,		
Batten, Wm. promd. to Sergt 79	Sergt	76		
Burton, Joshua	pt		1 July 79	discharged
Burk, John	pt			
Baker, Charles	pt			
Bush, Dennis 3	Sergt		21 July 79	do
Beatty, William	pt			
Becraft, John			1 July 79	do
Brown, George			9 Aug 79	do
Bean, Gilbert			4 Sept	deserted
Bedinger, Daniel	Corpl		9 Aug 79	discharged
Burch, Benjamin	Sergt			
Balman, Thomas	pt		9 Aug 79	do
Brown, John	do			
Brannan, George	do		do do	do
Barnes, James	do		do	do
Burgess, Edward 1 yr.	do		1 July 79	do
Berry, Zachariah	do	6 May 78		
Barnett, John	Sergt			
Bean, John	pt	4 April 78		
Blair, Samuel	do	1 do		
Bierley, Jacob	do	6 do		
Brooks, Benjamin	do	29 do		
Beall, William 6 mo.	do	8 Feby 79		
Burnsides, John 6 mo.	pt	19 May 79		
Brunt, Edward do	do	13 do 79		
Brown, William do	do	2 April 79		
Barnett, Robert do	do	24 Mar 79		
Bair, Peter do	do	7 Mar 76		
Beall, Thomas	Capt	25 July 76		
\multicolumn{5}{c}{FIRST REGIMENT.}				
Cosgrove, Edward	pt	10 Dec 76	23 Jan 80	joined
Cann, Ingram	do	do	27 Dec 79	discharged
Crosbey, Joseph	do	do	30 April 77	deserted
		joined 3 June 79	deserted	6 July 79
Clary, William	pt	17 Feby 77		
Clancy, John	do	5 Mar	April 80	prisoner

MUSTERS OF MARYLAND TROOPS, VOL. I.

NAMES.	RANK.	TIME OF SERVICE. Enlisted.	Discharged.	REMARKS.
Carvin, Thomas	pt	9 May	4 Oct 77	missing
Chaney, John	do	14 Feb	10 May	deserted
Chaney, Richard	do	10 Dec 76		
Chunn, Jonathan	do	do	6 Mar 77	died
Callahan, (or Cullanan) Jno.	do	do	22 Augt 77	prisoner
		joined 28 July 78	discharged 27 Dec 79	
Chaplin, William	pt	10 Dec 76	6 Mar 78	deserted
Clements, John	do	21 Feby 77	22 Feby 80	discharged
Coe, Richard	Sergt		22 Feby 79	appd. Q. M.
			27 Dec 79	discharged
Coe, Milburn	Corpl		do	do
Coe, Hezekiah	pt		31 Nov 77	died
Courts, William	Lieut	10 Dec 76	17 April	promd. 2d Regt.
Chapman, Henry	pt	11 Mar 77	June	died
Clark, William	do	10 Dec 76	July 77	deserted
Connor, Thomas	do	do	27 Dec 79	discharged
Carmichael, James	do	do	10 July 77	do
Cramphur, James	do	14 Feby 77	25 April 79	do
Capshort, Martin	do		not joined	
Corbett, Jacob	do	2 Mar 77	2 Mar 80	discharged
Chapman, William	do	29 do do	28 do do	ditto
Cox, Edmond	Sergt	10 Dec 76		
	Q. M.	19 July 77	dismissed 3 October 1778	
Connally, John	pt	10 July 76	17 Dec 77	deserted
Cullis, John	do	12 feby 77	prisoner	Jan 25 80
Callahan, John	do	10 April 77	18 July	deserted
Cronan, John	do	23 feb 77	23 feb 80	discharged
Clements, James	do	28 do do	28 do do	do
Clements, Henry	do	16 April 77	time out	discharged
Corbett, Patrick	do	13 Mar 78	25 feb 79	deserted
Currill, John	do	2 April 78	feb 79	died
Chapman, Thomas	do	3 May 78	1 Nov 80	present
Caile, David	do	10 June 78	do do	do
Coombs, William	do	6 do do	5 Aprl 79	discharged
Clark, Thomas	do	24 April 78	June 80, off rolls, left out June 80	
Connelly, John	do	2 Mar 78	3 Aprl 79	deserted
Casser, William		28 Apl 78	July 79	not heard of
Cheney, John	do	10 Feb 78	10 Sept	discharged
Chinn, Samuel			17 do 78	died
Cooley, Robert	do	20 May 78	6 Oct 78	do
Cooley, Joseph	do	8 Jan 79	1 Nov 80	present
Cooley, James	do	20 do	5 April 79	discharged
Carroll, John	do	12 May 78	July 79	deserted
Carroll, John, Jnr.		17 May 78 8 Jan 79 }	1 Nov 80	present

MUSTERS OF MARYLAND TROOPS, VOL. I.

Names.	Rank.	Time of Service. Enlisted.	Time of Service. Discharged.	Remarks.
Closs, Christian		10 Dec 76	16 Aug 80	deserted
Coleson, John		24 Jan 78	10 Feby 79	do
Collard, James	fife	1 Dec 78	1 Nov 80	sick Maryd.
Campton, Edward	Ensn	12 April 79 }		
	Lieut	1 Aug 80 }		
Cooley, Mordecai	private	26 April 79	16 Aug 80	missing
Cormine, John	pt	20 June 79	16 Aug 80	missing
Coombs, Nicholas	do	11 Sept 79	1 Nov 80	present
Clements, William	do	do do	do	do
Congleton, David	do		13 Jan 80	deserted
Cotting, Peter	do	30 June 80		do
Crist, John	do		30 June 80	do
Carpenter, Hump'y	do	June 80	16 Aug 80	prisoner
Cole, Michael	do	Mar 80	1 Nov 80	present
Cregan, Dennis		14 May 78	26 April 80	to Invalids
	joined 1st Regt.		14 July 81	per Invalid Ret.

Second Regiment.—*Beginning January*, 1778.

Names.	Rank.	Enlisted.	Discharged.	Remarks.
Crisps, Benjamin	pt	4 Mar 77	25 dec 79	discharged
Campher, Thomas	do	3 do do	1 Nov 80	present
Calvert, Eleakim	do	27 May 77	10 Jan 80	discharged
Cooksey, John	do	8 do do	do do	do
Connely, Laurence	do	4 Mar 77	May 80	do
Conner, John	Drum			out of Rolls 1777
Cavender, Patrick	pt		16 Aug 80	missing
Connally, Thomas	Corpl		15 May 78	deserted
Cunningham, Jno.	pt	30 dec 76	5 Jan 79	discharged
Carly, Lawrence	do	9 feb 77	16 Aug 80	missing
Carleton, Richard	do			out of Rolls Dec 77
Connally, Michael	do	{ 1 June 77 }	1 Nov 80	present
	Corpl	{ 1 May 80 }		
Campbell, Peter	Sergt		16 Mar 78	deserted
Crips, Nathaniel	pt	12 Jan 77	1 Nov 80	present
Cato, William	do		} 1 Nov 80	do
	Sergt	1 Jan 80		
	pt	15 Sept 80		
Christopher, John	pt	28 July 77	1 Nov 80	prisoner
must. Jan 78 left out Feby in. in April 78			16 Aug 80	prisoner
Cole, William	pt	} 1 Jan 79	10 Jan 80	discharged
	Corpl			
Cheshire, Thomas	pt			off Rolls Dec 77
Carr, Solomon	do			do do
Crawford, Jacob	Sergt			

MUSTERS OF MARYLAND TROOPS, VOL. I.

Names.	Rank.	Time of Service. Enlisted.	Discharged.	Remarks.
	q. mr.	11 Feb 79	} 10 Jan 80	discharged
	Ensign	26 Jan 80		
	Lieut			
Cross, Joseph	Sergt	11 Feby 77	do do	do
Cross, Samuel	pt	10 Jan 77	do do	do
Christian, John	do		12 feb 78	died
Cain, John	do			off Rolls Dec 77
Conner, Michael	Sergt		1 Feb 78	discharged
Cromey, Andrew	pt	3 April 77	1 Nov 80	present
Carroll, John	do		21 May 78	deserted
Cators, Patrick	Sergt			reduced to the ranks 15 Jan, 8 may 78, deserted
Courts, William	Lieut			
Carroll, Jeremiah	pt			struck off Jan 78
Cain, Hugh	do	18 Mar 78	16 Aug 80	missing
Carroll, Bryan	do	1 Mar 78	1 Nov 80	present
Cole, John	do	27 Dec 77	Mar 79	died
Cantewell, William	do	4 feb 78	Mar 80	deserted
Connegin, John	do		see McConnegan	
Cooksen, Peter	do		19 May 78	deserted
Cornish, John	do	27 April 78	79	dead
Collins, Jacob	do	12 May 78	1 Dec 79	transfd. to Invalids
Claridge, Henry	do	6 do do	Oct 80	
Chamberlain, Jonas	do	20 do do	16 Aug 80	missing, once a
Coatney, William	do	25 April 78	12 Jan 80	deserted [Corpl
Cairy, Patrick	do	20 May 78	1 Nov 80	present
Cosfield, Luke	pt	20 May 78	Jan 79	struck off
Conner, David	do	23 April do	sick Mary'd	Invalid war
Citizen, Morris	do	4 May 78	1 Nov 80	present
Crooke, Joseph	do	28 May 78	79 Feby	not heard of
Clark, Charles	do	30 May 78	3 April 79	discharged
Clark, Joseph	do		Jan 79	struck off
Conner, Patrick	do	Mar 77	1 Nov 80	present
Crating, John	do		Jan 79	struck off
Clark, Igns.	do	30 May 78	3 April 79	discharged
Compton, Alexd.	Sergt	1 Jan 77	10 Jan 80	do
Chard, John	pt	26 Jan 77	left out Aprl Rolls 80, time out	
Chatland, William	do	17 Mar 77	sick Maryd., 1 Nov 80	
Cook, Benjamin	do	1 May 78	} Jan 79	struck off
	Corpl	12 Oct 78		
Cutler, William	pt	5 June do	1 Nov 80	present
Cusick, Michael	do		18 Dec 78	deserted
Cope, John	do	20 May 78	10 Oct 78	died
Craft, James	do	do do	24 dec 78	discharged

Names.	Rank.	Time of Service. Enlisted.	Discharged.	Remarks.
Cornish, Constant	pt	do do	3 April 79	discharged
Code, William	do	do do	do do	do
Clarke, William	do	3 April 78	16 Aug 80	prisoner
Current, James	do	25 May 78	26 dec 78	deserted
Clark, William	do	do do	Jan 79	time out
Champhin, John	do	do do	26 Dec 78	deserted
see John Camphin on the other side				
Connely, Michael	do	do do	Mar 79	discharged
Cooper, Charles	do	4 Mar 77	returnd pd. by Denny	
prisr. 25 Mar 80				
Cowsway, Solomon	do	20 May 78	24 dec 78	discharged
Collins, James	Sergt	24 dec 76	10 Jan 80	discharged
Conway, James	pt		Feby 80	died
Cathel, James	do		12 dec 79	discharged
Cook, Benjamin	Corpl			
taken by prior Enlistment				off Rolls
Cox, Emund[1]	Sergt	15 Mar 79	1 Nov 80	present
	private	1 Jan 80		
	Sergt	1 April 80		
reduced again 1 Sept 80				
Chisley, Robert	Lieut			
	Capt			
Carnes, Benjamin	pt	11 June 79	1 Nov 80	do
Campin, John	do	19 do do	do do	do
Joined 25 Oct 80	Corpl	1 Jan 80		
Cooly, George	pt	April 80	ditto	ditto
Copeland, William	Drum		ditto	do
	June 80			
Corsey, Hampton	do pt	24 Mar 80	do do	do
Collings, William	do	6 April 80	16 Aug 80	missing
Collins, James	do			
left out June Rolls 79			June 79	left out Rolls
Conner, William	do		1 Nov 80	present

Third Regiment.—*Beginning* 77.

Names	Rank	Enlisted	Discharged	Remarks
Coomes, Richard	Sergt	10 May 77		
private 25 May 79	Sergt	18 June 78	May	discharged
Crismond, Leonard	fife	3 Feby 77	left out Mar 80, time expired	
Clarke, George, or Jno.	pt	16 do do	do do	
Clements, Henry	do	28 do do	time expired 28 feb 80	
	Corpl	1 Augt 77		
	Sergt	1 June 79	promoted to be Ensign	

[1] Williams's.

MUSTERS OF MARYLAND TROOPS, VOL. I.

NAMES.	RANK.	TIME OF SERVICE. Enlisted.	Discharged.	REMARKS.
Carr, John	Ensn			
Conn, Robert	pt / Corpl	10 Jan 78	1 June 79	deserted
Collins, Thomas	pt		16 Augt 80	missing
Carty, Martin	do		Dec 77	deserted
Joined June 79				
left out Nov 77				
Childs, George	do / Corpl	Jan 77 / 1 April 78	1 Nov 80	present
Callahan, John	pt	11 May 77	see Retahan	
Clark, Peter	Lieut		July 79	resigned
Cockran, George	pt		1 Nov 80	present
Coffer, James	do	28 Jan 77	1 Jan 80	deserted
Cullip, William	do		June 79	left out the Roll
Clinch, John	do			deserted
out April 78				
Cooenah, Thomas	do	20 Mar 77	16 Aug 80	missing
Collins, John	do	3 May do	3 May 80	dischd. by Maj.
Children, John, (or Wm.)	do	do do	do do	do [Anderson
Cummins, Ephram	do		10 Jan 78	deserted
Connally, Francis	do	18 Sept 77	4 Nov 77	do
Callahan, Daniel	do	6 Aug do	5 Mar 78	do
Cooender, Charles	do / Corpl / Sergt	15 feb 78	31 Dec 79	do
Conner, James	pt		16 Aug 80	missing
Carter, James	do	10 Jan 77	10 Jan 80	discharged
Campbell, William	do		July 78	struck off
Collins, Jno., (Griffith)	do		16 Aug 80	. missing
Cooper, Charles	Drum	20 Aprl 77	mustd. dead May 78	
			16 Nov 77	died Invalid corps
Cockran, Owen	pt	12 May 77		
Clancy, Daniel	do	15 June 77	1 Nov 80	present
Crouch, Joseph	do	10 April 77		
Crouch, John	pt	10 April 77	1 Feby 80	discharged
Connelly, Patrick	do	31 Aug 77	16 Aug 80	deserted
Conner, John	do	20 April do	20 do do	do
Crauford, Robert	do	2 July do	16 do do	missing
Callahan, Samuel	do	2 Jan 77		
Crosby, James	do	1 Mar 77	14 do do	deserted
Chaphey, John	do			do
mus. Nov 77				
Carr, John	do	24 Nov 77	1 Nov 80	present
Cockey, Peter	Ensn	10 April 77	Feby 79	died

MUSTERS OF MARYLAND TROOPS, VOL. I.

Names.	Rank.	Time of Service. Enlisted.	Discharged.	Remarks.
Clagett, Horatio	Lieut	10 Dec 76	Capt. 10 Oct 77	
Colter, Antipas	Sergt	2 April 77	2 April 80	time expired
Clark, John	pt	nothing known of him		
did not appear upon the Rolls till Dec 79 then mustd. deserted				
Carroll, William	pt		20 Jany 79	discharged
Cullomine, John	do	jd. 1 April 78	28 June 78	killed
Carney, Edward	do	28 April 78		
missing Monmouth 28 June 78, left out Jan & Feb 80, joined 26 July 79				
Clark, John	pt	6 Feb 78	Aug 78	struck off
out Aug 78				[sion
Cheser, Bennett	do	26 April 78	{ 10 July 83, discharged on pen- { Jan & Feb 80, transferred to In- valids
Collins, George	do	do do	15 June 81	discharged
Coyle, Samuel	do	3 April 78	1 Nov 80	present
Joined Oct 80				
Cheek, Nathaniel	do	12 feb 77	1 April 79	discharged
Cox, William	do	24 Jan 78	26 May 78	deserted
Craig, John	do	5 May 78	joined Oct Rolls 80	
Cassiday, Allen	do	1 April 78	18 Aug 80	deserted
Cassidy, Barney	do	20 ditto	16 Aug 80	killed
Cox, John	do	17 ditto	28 April 80	to Invalids, died 5 Sept 80
Cooley, Joseph	pt	16 April 78	16 Nov 78	deserted
Cissell, Barton	do	27 ditto	} 1 Nov 80	present
musd. Corpl July 1780	Corpl	15 Jan 79	}	
Chrispin, Alexander	pt	18 Feb 78	16 Aug 80	missing
Clements, Charles	do	17 April 78	1 Nov 80	present
Clemons, David .	do			}
joined Feby Mar 79			21 June 80	} deserted
Carter, Luke	do	19 May 78	1 Nov 80	present
Carpenter, John	do	23 ditto	4 April 79	discharged
Cushman, James	do	31 ditto	ditto	ditto
Carter, Justenian	do	25 ditto	11 Aug 78	died
Carter, Jesse	do	14 ditto	June 78	deserted
Carr, William	do	2 June 78	18 Aug 80	do
Cullinane, Dennis	do	28 ditto	1 Feby 79	discharged
Cook, Jeremiah	do	28 Feby 77	31 Jan 80	do
Culling, James	do	25 April 78	May 79	left out the Rolls
Carthew, Edmund	do	do do	3 feb 80	deserted
Clagett, John	do	do do	1 Nov 80	present
Cooke, Richard	do	24 May 78	16 Aug 80	missing
Cowen, Thomas	do	30 June 78	22 Jan 80	deserted
Cannum, William	do	1 June 78	13 Feby 79	discharged

during the War of the American Revolution, 1775–83.

MUSTERS OF MARYLAND TROOPS, VOL. I.

NAMES.	RANK.	TIME OF SERVICE. Enlisted.	Discharged.	REMARKS.
Conway, Laurence	pt	1 June 78	13 Feby 79	discharged
Clements, Mark	do	16 Mar 78	16 Aug 80	missing
Coonehan, Thomas	do	19 do do	5 Jan 80	deserted
Cavender, Charles	do	28 April 78	see Sergt. Cavender	
Clarke, Thomas[1]	do	4 June 78	1 May 79	died
Clark, Thomas[2] Jan 79 pt. reinlisted 5 Mar 79	do Sergt	}	1 Nov 80	present
Conner, John Clagett joined 5 May 79	pt	no account of him	last must. in 80	
Carrier, Thomas	do	11 May 79	16 Aug 80	missing
Chilmans, George	do	23 April 79	ditto	ditto
Carey, Richard 1st must. Oct 79	do	no account of him	musters in 80	
Collier, William 1st must. Oct 79	do	3 June 78	15 Sept 82	discharged
Carlton, Thomas must. Oct & Nov, left out Dec Roll 79	do		Dec 79	struck off
Cissill, John B.	Corpl	15 Jan 79	see the other side, Barton	

FROM OCTOBER ROLLS, 1780.

Carty, John	Drum		1 Nov 80	present
Carr, Hezeka.	fife	1 June 80	do	do
Clark, Zacha.	Drum		do	do
Cardiff, Thomas	pt	4 feb 80	do	do
Creamer, James	do		do	do
Crauford, James	do		do	do
Courts, John	do	7 feb 80	16 Aug 80	missing
Cunningham, Joseph	do		do	do
Cissall, Nicholas	do		do	do
Cooke, William			7 dec 78	discharged from Invalids

FOURTH REGIMENT.

Cromwell, Thomas[3]	Lieut	20 May 77	10 Dec 79	resigned
Clark, Richard	Sergt pt	6 dec 76 12 May 78	} 6 Dec 79	discharged
Clark, Michael	pt	7 Dec 76	16 Aug 80	missing
Cavanaugh, William	do		9 July 78	deserted
Cord, Roger[4]	Corpl		1 April 78	do
Craig, George	pt	3 April 77		joined
Clark, William	do		15 June 78	discharged

[1] Baly's.   [2] Brooke's.   [3] Oldham's.   [4] Norwood's.

MUSTERS OF MARYLAND TROOPS, VOL. I.

Names.	Rank.	Time of Service. Enlisted.	Discharged.	Remarks.
Cullimane, Jerema.	pt		28 July 79	dead
Craig, John[1]	Corpl		1 Nov 89	present
Oct 80, mustd. as	private			
Craine, Michael	Drum		June 78	musd. not heard of
	private	1 Aug 78		
Crutchley, Benjamin	do	Jan 77	12 Jan 80	discharged
Cypress, William	do	1 ditto	12 Jan 80	ditto
Crosby, John[2]	Corpl	6 April 77	1 Nov 80	present
	private	1 Sept 78		
Chew, Richard[3]	Sergt			
	Ensign			
Cantwell, Richard	pt		24 June 80	deserted
Coland, John[4]	Sergt	5 dec 76	1 Nov 80	present
Collins, Timothy[2]	Corpl	19 feb 77	12 feb 80	time expired
to Lansdale's 22 May 78	Sergt	11 feb 78		
Chatterton, John	pt	6 dec 76	6 dec 79	discharged
Corsey, Charles	do			dead or deserted
Cloney, John	do	20 Aug 77	13 dec 79	deserted
Carvin, James	do	4 dec 76	10 dec 79	discharged
Cooper, James[2]	do	19 ditto	5 feb 79	to Invalids
Cook, Henry	do	3 Jany 77	3 Jan 80	discharged
Cain, (or Kain), Michael	do	28 May 77	28 May 80	ditto for inability
Crabb, Jeremiah	Lieut		1 April 78	resigned
Chamberlain, Ben.	pt	27 April 77	1 Nov 80	present
Colegate, John[5]	Ensign		1 May 80	resigned
	Lieut	4 Aug 78		
Clark, James	Sergt	25 Mar 77		
	S. Major	10 feb 80	25 Mar 80	time expired
Carter, William	pt	29 July 77	1 Nov 80	present
Carroll, Joseph	pt	9 Aug 77	9 Aug 80	discharged
Clark, Richard	do	14 April 77	14 April 80	do
Callahan, William	do	24 Mar 77	1 April 79	deserted
Chadwick, William	do	5 April 77	5 April 80	discharged, same person, see Shadwick
Congleton, William[6]	do	17 Mar 78	Aug 78	died
Conner, William, (or Jas.)	do	21 April 78	25 Mar 79	deserted
Cregan, Lawrence[7]	do	26 do do	16 Aug 80	missing
Cathagin, Annanias[3]	do	22 Apl 78	1 Nov 80	present
Cross, Charles[3]	do	3 do do		
Reduced 13 Oct 80, (Sellman's)	Corpl	1 June 80	1 Nov 80	present

[1] Godman's.   [2] Lansdale's.   [3] Sellman's.   [4] Spurrier's.   [5] Burgess'.   [6] Oldham's.   [7] Norwood's.

MUSTERS OF MARYLAND TROOPS, VOL. I.

NAMES.	RANK.	TIME OF SERVICE. Enlisted.	Discharged.	REMARKS.
Cruell, John	pt	24 April 78	1 Sept 78	discharged
Cole, Joseph[1]	do	1 April 78	5 Jan 80	deserted
Smith's late Spurrier's.				
Craig, John	do	6 May 78	17 May 80	do
Catchsides, Abm.	do	do do	1 Nov 80	present
Crosby, George[2]	do	17 feb 78	1 April 80	deserted
(Riely's late				
Crosby, Richard	do	25 Mar 78	16 Aug 80	missing
Craig, John	do	6 May 78	1 Nov 80	present
Joined Oct 80				
Cain, Edward	do	1 do do	16 Aug 80	missing
Cummins, Richard[3]	Corpl	6 dec 76	6 dec 79	discharged
Cail, Robert	pt	11 May 78	dead or deserted	
Cappock, Simons[4]	do	14 do do	16 July 79	died
Clinton, Thomas[5]	do	1 July 78	1 Nov 80 present	to Godman's and promoted to fifer 1 Aug 78
Crampton, James[6]	do	19 May 78	15 Nov 78	to invalids
Chivers, Andrew	do	18 May 78	30 June 80	deserted
Cupit, John	do	13 May 78	3 Sept 79	do
Carroll, Dennis[1]	do	21 May 78	1 April 80	do
Coleman, Michael[2]	do	16 April 78	10 Jan 78	do
Callahan, Michael	do	5 do do	1 Nov 80	present
Chevick, John[7]	do	12 May 78	July 80	present
Burgess', June 78				
Clinton, Thomas[8]	fife	see above, Lansdale's Co.		
Godman's, July 78				
Cain, Robert[3]	pt	11 May 78	dec 79	deserted
Caton, William[3]	do	15 June 79	April 80	to invalids
Cheney, Richard[3]	do		Nov 79	deserted
Colegate, Asaph[8]	do	29 feb 80	1 Nov 80	present
	From Invalids' Return.			
Conner, Dennis	Sergt	4 Aug 80	27 May 79	discharged
	Rawlings' Regiment.			
Colman, John	pt	16 July 76		
Crockett, John	do	28 Aug 76		
Callender, John	do	17 July	11 July 79	discharged
Chinea, Adam S.	do	1 Aug 76		
Cooper, John	do	17 ditto	9 Aug 79	discharged
Corbett, Jesse	do	15 ditto		

[1] Lt. Smith's. [2] Riley's. [3] Oldham's. [4] Norwood's. [5] Lansdale's. [6] Sellman's.
[7] Burgess'. [8] Godman's.

MUSTERS OF MARYLAND TROOPS, VOL. I.

NAMES.	RANK.	TIME OF SERVICE. Enlisted.	Discharged.	REMARKS.
Cartrell, John	pt	8 Oct 76		
Cooper, William	do	15 July 76	15 July 79	discharged
Campbell, Pat.	do	10 Oct 76	20 Oct 76	deserted
Crawford, Jno.	Sergt		1 July 79	discharged
Cartrill, William	pt		9 Augt 79	do
Collins, John	do			
Collins, Patrick	do	9 Aug 76	9 Aug 79	do
Cardonis, Jno.	do	25 Mar		
Conwell, Arthur	do		9 Oct 79	do
Cockran, Jno.	do			
	Corpl	1 Sept		
Cockindall, Elijh.	pt	1 Oct 77		
Craig, Thomas	do	Aug 76		
Cravin, Jeremiah			9 Aug 79	do
Chinworth, Jno.	Sergt		9 Aug 79	discharged
Chinworth, Arthur	Corpl		do	do
Crumm, Adam	pt		1 July 79	do
Carly, Dennis	do			
Coone, Adam	do		15 July	killed
Crawford, Robt.	Corpl	2 Oct		
Connally, Wm.	pt	18 Mar		
Carmichael, Jno.	do	28 ditto	6 April	discharged
Connally, Philip	do	6 April		
Cunningham, Thos.	do	15 do		
Carpenter, Chrisn.	do	12 Aug		
Cooper, Jno., 6 Mo.	Sergt			
Clark, Jos., ditto	pt			
Christie, Jas., do	do			
Craig, Saml., do	do			

FIRST REGIMENT.

NAMES.	RANK.	Enlisted.	Discharged.	REMARKS.
Dignam, Christn.	pt	10 Dec 76	21 Jan 78	deserted
Devine, Dennis	do	do	1 Nov 80	present
Davis, William	do	29 April 77		
Davis, Richard	do	24 Jan 77		
Douglass, Igns.	Sergt	20 Feby 77	25 Dec 79	discharged
Downing, Natl.	pt	10 Dec 76	27 do do	ditto
Dyer, Jonathan	do	26 Mar 77	13 July 80	deserted
Daly, James	do	10 Dec 76	24 May 77	do
Dewell, Thomas	do	7 Apl 77		
Dutton, Notley	do	29 Mar 77	see below	
Devaun, James	do	10 Dec 76	27 dec 79	discharged
Donovan, Jeremh.	do	22 Apl 77	17 Dec 77	deserted

MUSTERS OF MARYLAND TROOPS, VOL. I.

Names.	Rank.		Time of Service. Enlisted.	Discharged.	Remarks.
Dugan, Danl.	pt		1 Apl 77		deserted
Downes, James	do		8 ditto		do
Davis, William	do		10 Mar 77	20 Apl 77	died
Downing, Saml.	do		16 do	16 Mar 80	discharged
Dunn, Dennis	do		18 Mar 78	3 dec 78	deserted
Dawkins, Charles	Sergt		25 April 78	1 Nov 80	present
Dodson, John	pt		5 feb 78	11 June 78	discharged
Davidson, James	do		20 April 78	25 Jan 80	prisoner
Dohorty, Jesse	do		7 May 78		
Denny, Peter	do		20 May 78	30 Aug 78	deserted
Davis, Enus	9 mos. do		21 ditto	5 Aprl 79	discharged
Dutton, Thomas	do	do	5 June 78	1 Nov 80	reinlisted
Dutton, Notley	3 yrs. do		29 Mar 78	24 May 79	discharged
Delozier, Wm.	9 mos. do		4 June 78	14 Feby 79	ditto
Dunning, Dennis	pt		17 dec 78	1 Nov 80	present
	Drum		1 April 79		
Davaun, Michael	pt			Feby 79	discharged
Donovan, (or Dennis), Paul	do		9 June 79	8 July 79	deserted
Dixon, John			28 Aprl 79	1 Nov 80	present
Denear, Francis			8 June 79	do	do
Ducey, William			do	July 79	deserted
Devorah, Butes			29 do	1 Nov 80	sick
Dortch, William			25 June 80	do	present
Dixon, Hanry			7 feb 80	do	do
Doyle, Martin	Corpl			3 Aug 80	deserted 8 feby 81 discharged

Second Regiment.

Names.	Rank.	Enlisted.	Discharged.	Remarks.
Devereaux, Jno.,(or James)	Sergt		10 Jan 80	discharged
Devinns, Emanl.	pt		12 dec 79	ditto
Dawson, William	do		10 Jan 80	ditto
Duel, Charles	do		14 June 80	deserted
Dent, Hatch	Capt	17 Apl 77		resigned
Duvall, Saml.	pt		10 Jan 80	discharged
Duvall, Joseph	do	4 feb 77	4 feb 80	ditto
Dowling, James	do		10 Jan 80	ditto
Dyer, Edward	Lieut B. Q. Master Capt	10 April 77 Jany 79		
Dyer, Thomas	pt Sergt	22 Jany 77 1 May 78	time elaps'd, Jany 80	left out Rolls
Drake, Richard	pt	27 April 77	Jan 79	left out
Davis, William	Corpl		9 Sept 78	died
Dayly, James	pt		29 dec 77	ditto

MUSTERS OF MARYLAND TROOPS, VOL. I.

Names.	Rank.	Time of Service. Enlisted.	Discharged.	Remarks.
Davidson, John	Capt } Major }	10 dec 76 }	}	
Duling, (or Duley), Nathl.	pt		10 Jan 80	discharged
Dean, Edward	do	16 May 78	feb 80	ditto
Dulany, James	do	24 Jan do	July 80	ditto
Deal, Noble	do	14 feb do	1 July 78	deserted
Dorsey, Elie	Capt	10 dec 76	left out of the musters Mar 79,	
	not having assigned any cause for his absence since Sept 78			
Day, John	pt	2 April 78	18 June 79	deserted
Draper, John	do	10 May 78	Jan 79	discharged, being
Daily, Thomas	do	16 ditto	27 Oct 79	died [a servant
Drury, Robt. B.	do		3 April 79	discharged
Dent, George	do	25 May 78	ditto	ditto
Drury, Joseph	do	24 ditto	ditto	ditto
Davidson, Geo.	do	6 July 78	23 feb 79	ditto
Dennis, Dunick	do		12 dec 79	ditto
Dent, John	do	20 May 78	78	died in Town
Devin, James	do	14 ditto	3 April 79	discharged
Debora, Jacobus	do			
	fife	1 Mar 79	}	
	private	1 Mar 80	} 1 Nov 80	present
Dailey, John	pt		17 June 79	deserted
1st mus. June 79				
Duvall, Edward	Lieut	17 Aprl 77 }		
	Capt		} 16 Augt 80	killed Camden
Dowes, William	pt	8 June 79	never joined	
. muster Nov 79, never appeared				
Denston, John June 80	pt		1 Nov 80	present
Dusky, Jonathn. June 80	do	sick Maryland, 1 Nov 80		

THIRD REGIMENT.—*Beginning* ———

Names.	Rank.	Enlisted.	Discharged.	Remarks.
Deale, John	pt	13 feb 77	1 Jan 78	deserted
Dolton, Peter	do		16 Augt 80	missing
Dunkin, John	do		19 July 80	deserted
Donovan, Peter	do	22 April 77	28 April 80	discharged
Donaldson, Phil.	do	3 May 77	8 Nov 79	deserted
Duvall, Isaac	Ensn } Lieut }			
Dudley, Joseph	pt		26 Sept 80	ditto
Dixon, George	do	27 April 77	1 Nov 80	present
Dillon, William	do	1 May 77 }	1 Nov 80 }	ditto
	Corpl	1 April 79 }	}	
Deaver, John	Lieut	10 Dec 76	8 April 79	resigned

MUSTERS OF MARYLAND TROOPS, VOL. I.

Names.	Rank.	Time of Service. Enlisted.	Discharged.	Remarks.
Dommit, William	pt	8 Sept 77	7 July 78	deserted
Downey, Dennis	do	13 Mar 77	Dec 79	struck off
left out Dec Roll 79	Sergt	10 Oct 77	April 80	discharged
Dyer, John	pt	Jan 77	1 Nov 80	present
Doyer, Peter	do		7 dec 79	died
Duvall, George	pt	12 Jan 77	12 Jan 80	discharged
Dollison, James	do		Augt 80	deserted
Draper, Thomas	do			do
Denshon, James	Corpl	30 Mar 77	Sept 78	discharged
private Sept 78	Sergt	1 Mar 80		
Denton, James	pt	30 June 77	18 Augt 80	deserted
Deaver, Aquilla	do	14 May 77	1 Nov 80	present
Dean, George	do	26 Nov 77	18 Oct 79	deserted
Dyer, Walter	Sergt	26 June 77	26 Jan 80	promoted
Dunnington, Wm.	pt	6 April 77	Re-enlisted again	
Daily, Philip	do		31 mar 78	discharged
Dashiell, Wm.	Surgn		5 dec 80	died at Baltimore
Denwood, Levin	Mate	(see 7th Regt. Surgeon)		
Dutton, George	pt	25 April 78	June 78	deserted
Ducater, Jno.	do	24 ditto	5 feb 79	died
Davis, Jno.	do	13 May 78	16 Aug 80	killed
Dolby, Daniel	do		12 July 80	deserted
Joined 22 July 78				
Dyer, James	do	22 May 78		
Davis, Jno., (Bailey)	do	28 April 78	16 dec 78	died
Dunn, Thomas	do	do	1 June 79	discharged
Dennis, Edward	do	27 do	1 Nov 80	prisoner
Dailey, Patk.	do	30 do	1 Jan 80	off the Rolls
Davis, Edward	do	28 May 78	16 Augt 80	missing
Dimsey, Luke	pt	19 May 78	1 Nov 80	present
Dennison, Jas.	do	3 June 78	May 79	time expired
Daken, James	do	29 May 78	not musterd. 1780	
Daniel, Jno. Natl.	do	20 ditto	16 Augt 80	missing
Dent, Jno.	do	1 May 77	not musterd. 1780	
Deaver, William	do	1 July 78	ditto ditto	
Day, Jacob	do	14 May 78	1 Nov 80	present
Driver, John	do	12 May 78	27 Jan 80	deserted
Dean, John	do	not mustered 1780		
first must. feb 79				
Downey, John	do		10 dec 79	deserted, (joined Sept 79)
Dorsey, Joshua	do	not mustered 1780		
1st must. July 79				

MUSTERS OF MARYLAND TROOPS, VOL. I.

Names.	Rank.	Time of Service. Enlisted.	Discharged.	Remarks.

From October Muster, 1780.

Names.	Rank.	Enlisted.	Discharged.	Remarks.
Derrington, Francis	pt	on the Roll for Oct 80, left out Nov 80		
Drudges, Thomas	do	2 feb 80	1 Nov 80	present
Dunnington, Jer.	do	left sick at Salsbury, Aug 80		
Demay, John	do		16 Aug 80	missing
Dunington, Wm.	do		1 Aug 80	deserted
Douglass, James	do		16 Aug 80	killed
Drury, John	do		do	missing
Davids, C. W.	Sergt	77	83 deserted from Invalids	
Dugan, Paul Md. list.		1 April 77	26 Aug 80 discharged, Invalids	
Dewire, James		26 April 80 to Invalids	1 Sept 82, retired on pension	

Fourth Regiment.—*Beginning December, 1777.*

Names.	Rank.	Enlisted.	Discharged.	Remarks.
Drishell, Jeremiah[1]	pt	6 Dec 76		
Dunnevan, (or Dunnegan), John Joined again Oct 80	do	28 June 77		
Delany, Edward	do	16 dec 76	16 dec 79	discharged
Dunster, John[2]	do		1 June 79	to Invalids
22 Aprl 80 musd. in Invalids to have joined his Regt., not so 1 Nov 80				
Dorsey, Nicholas	Lieut	17 April 77	10 Nov 78	resigned
Denbugh, Wm.[3]	pt			deserted
Dye, William	do	detained in Maryland March 1778		
Dodson, Michael[4]	do / Corpl / pt	20 April 77 / 1 Nov 78 / 15 June 79	20 April 80	discharged
Downes, William[5]	do	19 Aug 77	16 Aug 80	missing
Dorhorty, Francis	do		26 Feb 78	deserted
Davis, Thomas[6]	do	7 Mar 77	16 Aug 80	missing
Dawson, James	do	20 Aug 77	June 79	left out Roll, joined and discharged 23 Feby 81
Duffey, Michael	do	25 July 77	transfd. to Invalids 1 dec 78, 15 Sep 82 dischd.	
Doran, Barnaba[2]	do		16 Aug 80	missing
Doyall, Thomas[7]	do	4 feb 78	1 Nov 80	present
Dohorty, Arthur[2]	do	30 April 78	Sept 80	deserted
Deliazon, Peter[8] Smith's, late Spurrier's	do	21 do	1 Nov 80	present
Darling, Robert[9] to Belt's, joined June 79	do	25 do	do	do

[1] Oldham's. [2] Norwood's. [3] Godman's. [4] Lansdale's. [5] Spurrier's. [6] Burgess'. [7] Bowie's. [8] Lt. Smith's. [9] Belt's.

during the War of the American Revolution, 1775–83.   105

MUSTERS OF MARYLAND TROOPS, VOL. I.

NAMES.	RANK.	TIME OF SERVICE. Enlisted.	Discharged.	REMARKS.
Daffin, James	Sergt	8 April 78	1 Nov 80	present
Dwyer, Thomas[1]	Drum	16 Mar 78		
Riely's late Bowie's	private	1 June 78	3 July 80	deserted
Durnor, Thomas[2]	do	10 Jan 78	16 Aug 80	missing
Dennison, Patk.	do	4 June 78	20 Jan 80	deserted, joined
Dougherty, John[3]	do			
prisoner 22 Aug 77, joined 22 July 78			20 dec 78	do
Dougherty, Edward[4]	pt	13 May 78		
	Corpl	1 Aug 79		
	Sergt	1 Jan 80	1 Nov 80	present
Davis, John	pt	6 dec 76		
prisr. 22 Aug 77, joined 23 June 78, Corpl 6 dec 79, Sergt 1 Jan 80, July 80 deserted				
Dease, Michael[5]	pt	30 April 78	5 July 80	deserted
Dowen, Nicholas	do	11 May 78	23 June 79	ditto
Denmass, Wm.[4]	fifer	22 April 78	11 June 80	ditto
Burgess', June 78				
Derry, Michal[5]	pt			
Lt. Smith's, Sept 78				
from Col Stewart's Pennsa. Regt.		to Pennsa. Line, 28 July 79		[Regt.
Durbinn, John	pt	6 Sept 78	3 May 79	transfd. to Hazen's
Dorsey, Charles	do	19 feb 77		
	Corpl	1 July 79	19 Feby 80	discharged
Devire, Darby[1]	pt	3 May 78	16 Aug 80	missing
Deane, Francis[7]	fifer	2 Sept 79	dead or deserted	
Drowns, Robert[1]	Drum	28 Aug 79	left out after April 80	
	private	Mar 80		
Dean, John[2]	Major	11 Mar 78		
Douglass, William[8]	fife		1 Nov 80	present
mus. May & June 80				
	RAWLINGS' REGIMENT.			
Denniston, James	Drum	17 Aug 76		for war
Dytche, Peter	pt	27 July 76		
Devenport, Adam	do		9 Aug 79	discharged
Davis, Levi				
Davoir, Cornelius			9 Apr	deserted
Dewist, Francis				
Dowdon, James				
Debrular, John			9 Augt 79	discharged
Dennis, Henry				
Davis, Joseph	pt		ditto	ditto
Davis, David	do		6 July	do
Deacon, Pierce	do	13 April 79		
Denaho, John	do	7 May		
Davis, James	do	27 Mar		

[1] Riely's.   [2] Oldham's.   [3] Godman's.   [4] Lansdale's.   [5] Lt. Smith's.   [6] Burgess'.   [7] Selman's.   [8] Spurrier's.

8

MUSTERS OF MARYLAND TROOPS, VOL. I.

Names.	Rank.	Time of Service. Enlisted.	Discharged.	Remarks.
First Regiment.				
Elliott, Thomas	pt	10 dec 76	27 dec 79	discharged
Edwards, Edward	do	do	1 Nov 80	present
Eadlin, John	do	do	27 dec 79	discharged
Ewing, Nathanl.	Capt	do	16 Mar 79	resigned
Edelin, Clement	Sergt	do	27 Dec 79	discharged
Evans, William	pt	do	27 Nov 77	deserted
Enwright, John	do	do	15 April 77	ex. for A. Hughes
Eadlin, Edward	do	do	27 Dec 79	discharged
Eltham, John	do	28 feb 78	} 16 Aug 80	prisoner
	Corpl	27 feb 80		
Ellicott, Edward	pt	13 May 78	1 Nov 80	present [son
Everett, Elisha	do	12 Mar 78	18 Aprl 79	exchd. for Jeffer-
Ennis, George			10 June 78	deserted

Second Regiment.—*Beginning with the Muster Rolls for January, 1778.*

Ewing, Samuel	P. M.	17 April 77	1 July 80	deserted
Edgerly, Edward	Adjt	} 3 April 77 }		
	Lieut	27 May 78		
Emmory, John	pt	3 May 77	Mar 80	discharged
Ellis, Robert	do	4 Mar 77	14 April 79	deserted
Ellis, Barnard	do		Jan 78	left out
Evans, Peregrine	do	10 Jan 77		
Sergt 10 Jany 80	Corpl	1 May 78	} 1 Nov 80	present
Ewing, James	Lieut	17 April 77		
Eccleston, John	Capt	} 10 dec 76 }		
June 79 mustered pd.	Major	10 dec 77		
Easom, Bartholm.	pt	} 18 May 78 }	1 Nov 80	present
	Corpl	1 July 80		
Easom, Joseph	pt	ditto	1 July 78	deserted
Everitt, Joseph	do	28 May 78	18 Dec 78	discharged
Ellis, Michael	fife	3 Nov 78	1 Nov 80	present
Elbon, Mathew[1]	pt	4 May 79	16 Aug 80	missing
First must. July 79				
Elbon, Nathanl.	do	14 June 79	1 Nov 80	present
Eddy, James[2]	see James Ady			
First must. July 79				
Ervine, Abram	see Irvine			

Third Regiment.—*Beginning 1777.*

Edwards, John	Sergt			
	Sergt. Major	11 Aug 77	28 Aug 78	} Comy. Dept.
transfd. to Comy. dept.		28 Aug 78		

MUSTERS OF MARYLAND TROOPS, VOL. I.

NAMES.	RANK.	TIME OF SERVICE. Enlisted.	Discharged.	REMARKS.
Ecort, Godfrey	pt	9 May 77	dead or deserted	
Elliott, Robert	do	2 April 77	ditto ditto	
Evans, Thomas	do	1 Jan 77	1 Nov 80	present
English, William	do	8 Mar 78	6 Sept 79	deserted
Evans, William	do		16 May 78	dead
Elliott, Thomas	do	1 June 78	18 Aug 80	joined
Edelin, Basil	Corpl	27 May 78	discharged, time out	
Edelin, George	do	30 May 78	13 feb 79	discharged
Edelin, Henry rein. 12 feb 79, 14 feb 79	do furld.	ditto	} April and May 79, left out	
English, James	F. Major	1 May 79	16 Aug 80	prisoner
English, Samuel	pt	must. Oct and Nov 79.	Struck off Dec 79, left out Dec Roll 79	

FOURTH REGIMENT.—*Beginning Dec.*, 1777.

Eaton, William[1]	pt		April 78	left off the Rolls
Ellis, John[2]	do	23 Aug 77	3 Jan 79	deserted
Elliott, Samuel[3]	do	3 Oct 77	3 Oct 80	discharged
Ennis, Thomas[4]	do	14 May 77	14 Mar 80	ditto
Ellis, William[2]	pt	24 Jan 78	1 nov 80	present
Eyre, John[5]	do Corpl	} 18 April 78 1 June 78 }	14 May 80	deserted
Evins, Edward[2]	pt	24 feb 78	1 nov 80	present
Evins, William	do	26 ditto	ditto	ditto
Edwards, Thomas[6] out May and June 80	Sergt Q.M.Sergt	20 Jan 78 1 May 80	} 1 Nov 80	ditto
Eades, Thomas[7]	pt	6 may 78	16 Aug 80	missing
Ellwood, Richard	do	3 do	do	do
Easton, John[8]	do	12 do	do	do
Emanuel, Peters[8]	do	21 Aprl 78	4 Nov 78	deserted
Eyles, Samuel[6]	do	6 July 78	11 May 80 July 80	} do do
England, (or Ingle), Wm., or Ingle[2]	do	8 May 79	1 Nov 80	present

RAWLINGS' REGIMENT.

Eaton, William	pt		9 Aug 79	discharged
Evans, John	Corpl			
Earls, Richard	Drum			
Eakins, Archd. 6 mo.	pt	4 May 79		
Eakins, Solomon do	do	9 April 79		
Ellis, Thomas do	do	6 Mar 79	4 May 79	deserted

[1] Oldham's. [2] Lansdale's. [3] Sellman's. [4] Spurrier's. [5] Norwood's. [6] Burgess'. [7] Riely's. [8] Lt. Smith's.

MUSTERS OF MARYLAND TROOPS, VOL. I.

Names.	Rank.	Time of Service. Enlisted.	Discharged.	Remarks.

First Regiment.

Names.	Rank.	Enlisted.	Discharged.	Remarks.
Flora, Jacob	pt	10 Dec 76	1 Nov 80	present
Floharty, Stephen		10 Dec 76		
	Corpl	1 Aug 79	27 dec 79	} discharged
Fairbrother, Francis	do	10 Dec 76		hospital
Fitzsimmons, Henry		13 Mar 77	22 Aug	prisoner
		17 April 78, joined	13 Mar 80	discharged }
Fulton, Alexander	pt		27 dec 79	ditto
Flemming, Jno.	do	10 dec 76	20 Nov 77	died
Ford, Joseph	Capt	10 dec 76		resigned
Fernandis, Jas.	Lieut	do		
	Capt		15 July 79	resigned
Francois, John	pt	1 Jan 78	1 Nov 80	present
Franklin, Thos.	do	2 feb 78	1 Nov 80	sick Jersey
Fowler, Henry	do	23 May 78	5 April 79	discharged
Fresh, Stephen	do	20 do	6 July 79	deserted }
joined 20 Sept 79		1 Nov 80		present
Fowler, Joseph	pt	20 Jan 78	1 Nov 80	do
Ford, Archd.	do	30 May 78	14 Feby 79	discharged
Fisher, William	do	17 do	1 Nov 80	present
Flint, James	do	1 June 79	4 Jan 80	deserted
Fishwater, Ben.	Corpl	1 June 79		
	Sergt	June 80	} 1 Nov 80	present
Fowler, Jonathan	pt	22 April 79	16 Aug 80	missing, joined
Ford, John	Mu'n	June 80	12 Aug 80	deserted

Second Regiment.—*Beginning Jany., 1778.*

Names.	Rank.	Enlisted.	Discharged.	Remarks.
Finch, George	pt	8 Jan 77	10 Jan 80	discharged
Finlason, George	do	2 Aprl 77	1 Nov 80	present
Ferguson, Robt.	do	18 do	1 April 79	discharged
Fowler, William	do	nothing known of him 78 Jan		
French, Martin	do	10 Jan 77	10 Jan 80	discharged
Foumel, William	do		July 80	sick Jersey
Freeman, Jacob	do		10 Jan 80	discharged
Faulkner, Amos	do		25 June 78	deserted
Flynn, Edward	Corpl		22 Jan	ditto
Forman, Jacob	pt	} June 80	16 Aug 80	missing
	Corpl			
Ford, Hezekiah	Sergt			
	Ensign	} 1 Sept 77		
	Lieut	first muster June 79	Adj., 10 June 79	
Frazier, Hobart	pt	1 feb 78	1 July 78	deserted
Foxwell, Charles	do	do	do	do

MUSTERS OF MARYLAND TROOPS, VOL. I.

Names.	Rank.	Time of Service. Enlisted.	Discharged.	Remarks.
Fowler, John left out of must. for April 78	pt	4 April 78	April 78	struck off
Frederick, Bennet	fife	27 Mar 78		see B
Fipps, Thomas Phips in letter P	pt	6 May 78	1 Nov 80	present see
Farrill, James	pt	25 Mar 78	1 Nov 80	present
Farrill, Thomas	do	2 do	7 dec 79	deserted
Fricker, John	do	13 do	Corpl., 1 mar 79	dead or deserted
Fitzpatrick, Lawrce. private 1 Nov 78	do Corpl	29 Aprl 78	27 feb 79	deserted
Fitzgerald, Jas.	pt	3 do	1 Nov 80	present
Forly, William	do	13 May 78	do	do
Fenwick, Francis	do	29 do	3 Aprl 79	discharged
French, Stephen	do	25 do	do	do
Farrand, Patk.	do		10 Jan 80	do
Freeman, Francis	do	do	1 Nov 80	present
Flanegan, Henry	do		3 Aprl 79	discharged
Fulsom, John	do		1 Nov 80	sick Maryd.
Fergusson, Jno.	do	1 Aprl 79	16 Aug 80	prisoner
Franklin, Edwd.	do		10 Jan 80	dischd., joined 4 May 79

Third Regiment.—Beginning 1777.

Names.	Rank.	Enlisted.	Discharged.	Remarks.
Franklin, Francis	pt	23 April 77		dead or deserted
Florence, Lewis	do	17 do		do
Farmer, Samuel	Ensign Lieut		16 Aug 80	wounded prisoner
Farmer, Nathl.	Sergt		Mar 79	left out the Roll
Fleming, Richard	pt		15 Mar 78	deserted
Flanagan, Wm.	fifer private	6 April 77 5 May 79	2 April 80	time expired
Fuller, William	pt		20 Jan 79	discharged
Farence, Owen	do	6 April 77	7 May 80	died
Forrest, Uriah	Major	10 Dec 76	Lt. Col.	
Ferren, Philip	pt	20 April 78		off Rolls
French, Randolph	do	27 do	feb 79	discharged
Farding, John	do	do	Nov 78	struck off
Furnor, Edward	do	19 Jan 78	1 Nov 80	present
Fleeton, William	Sergt	30 Mar 78	29 May 78	taken prior En-
Fernand, Andrew	pt	10 do	1 Nov 80	present [list.
Forbus, John	do	2 Sept 77	16 Aug 80	missing
Fairburn, Wm.	do	76	do	prisoner
Fain, Michael	do	14 April 77	May 79	out the Roll
Fell, Christopher	do		July 78	to Invalids

MUSTERS OF MARYLAND TROOPS, VOL. I.

NAMES.	RANK.	TIME OF SERVICE. Enlisted.	Discharged.	REMARKS.
Foster, James	pt	28 May 78	1 Nov 80	present
Fields, Joseph	do	2 do	May 79	out the Rolls
Fields, George	do	20 April 78	23 Mar 80	prisoner
Francis, Alexander	do	26 May do	1 Nov 80	present
Fraim, John	do	8 June 78	June 79	left out the Rolls
Freeman, Richard	do	5 do	1 Nov 80	present
Farn, Patrick Joined 17 Jan 79	pt	3 May 78	27 Jan 80	deserted

From October Musters, 1780.

NAMES.	RANK.	Enlisted.	Discharged.	REMARKS.
Franklin, Wm. R.	pt	15 April 80	1 Nov 80	present
Ferril, John	do	2 feb 80	do	do
Freemoult, Robert		6 Oct 78	11 June 83	dismissed on furlough
Fagan, Charles		16 do 79	29 Oct 79	deserted

Fourth Regiment.—Beginning December, 1777.

NAMES.	RANK.	Enlisted.	Discharged.	REMARKS.
Fowler, James[1]	pt	28 Jan 77	10 Sept 78	discharged
Frisby, William	do		Oct 79	deserted
Finely, Coleman[2]	do		3 May 78	do
Feraby, Richard[3]	do	26 May 77	1 Nov 80	present
Fitzgerald, James[4]	Sergt / pt	12 Feby 77 / 1 Jan 79	12 feb 80	discharged
Flinn, Fredk.	do	4 May 77	16 Aug 80	missing
Flaharty, James	do	16 feb 77	16 feb 80	discharged
Ferrell, James[5]	Sergt / pt / Sergt	12 feb 77 / 15 Aug 78 / 30 Sept 78	12 feb 80	discharged
Fosh, James	pt		2 Aprl 78	deserted
Flannery, Christ.	pt	12 Aug 77	16 Aug 80	missing
Fell, Edward	do	26 do	5 Nov 78	discharged
Frazier, William	do	14 Mar 77	14 Mar 80	do
Frewen, Richard[6]	do	20 April 77	Jan 80	deserted
Fox, John	pt		10 April 78	deserted
Filley, William[7]	do	12 April 78	10 Jan 80	do
Fitzpatrick, Bryan[2]	do	6 May 78	16 Aug 80	missing
Flanagan, William[6]	do	7 May 78	18 Jan 80	prisoner
Farrell, James[3]	do	5 do	27 April 79	discharged
Ford, Robert[4]	Sergt / private	23 April 78 / 1 Jan 80	April 80	died
Fisher, Joseph[1] prisoner 22 Aug 77	Corpl Joined 16 July 78	16 dec 76	16 Dec 79	discharged

[1] Oldham's. [2] Norwood's. [3] Godman's. [4] Lansdale's. [5] Spurrier's. [6] Burgess'. [7] Bowie's. [8] Sellman's.

MUSTERS OF MARYLAND TROOPS, VOL. I.

NAMES.	RANK.	TIME OF SERVICE. Enlisted.	Discharged.	REMARKS.
Foy, John[1]	pt	10 May 78	16 Aug 80	missing
Foisdell, Stafford[2]	Drum	16 April 78	1 Nov 80	present
	pt	1 July 78		
Fountain, Peter[3]	do	15 May 78	do	do
French, John[4]	do	13 do 79	16 Aug 80	missing
	Corpl	1 June 80		
Fenwick, Richard[5]	pt	9 July 79	1 Nov 80	present
	Corpl	1 April 80		
Follet, Benjamin[2]	Drum	11 feb 80	do	do
Fitzgerald, Jno. Joined June mus. 80	pt		26 Oct 80	deserted
Folliott, Joseph	fifer	16 April 80	1 Nov 80	present
Fossett, Robert	pt		16 Aug 80	missing

RAWLINGS' REGIMENT.

NAMES.	RANK.	Enlisted.	Discharged.	REMARKS.
Farmer, John	pt	27 July 76		
Ford, John	Corpl	Aug 76	3 Aug 79	discharged
France, Peter	pt		9 do	do
Firth, Robert	Corpl	28 May 79		
Furguson, Jas.	do	Aug 76	19 Aug 79	discharged
Fleming, Thos.	pt	do		
Flinn, Thomas	Sergt	20 Mar		
Ferguson, Alex.	pt	4 Jany		
Finnegan, Paddy	do	12 Mar		
Forsyth, John	Sergt			
Fardo, Wm. L.	pt	Aug 76	9 do	do
Fox, Balser	do		30 Sept	deserted

FIRST REGIMENT.

NAMES.	RANK.	Enlisted.	Discharged.	REMARKS.
Gaither, Henry	Lieut	10 dec 76		
	Capt	17 April 77		
Georgehagan, John	Sergt	do	10 April 77	promoted
Griffith, James	pt	25 Mar 77	25 Mar 80	discharged
Grover, I. Mason	do	14 feb 77	1 July 78	Corpl 24 feb 80 discharged
Green, John	do	21 Mar 77	6 Mar 78	deserted
Green, William joined 6 May 79	do Corpl		11 Jan 80	discharged
Gibney, David	pt	10 dec 76		deserted
Gwynn, James	do	19 April 77	16 Aug 80	prisoner
Gassaway, Nicholas	Sergt	10 dec 76	17 April	promoted
Gray, Benjamin reinlisted for war	pt	do 80	27 dec 79 1 Nov 80	discharged present
Gosnell, Saml.	do	do		deserted

[1] Lansdale's.   [2] Riely's.   [3] Burgess'   [4] Belt's.   [5] Spurrier's.

MUSTERS OF MARYLAND TROOPS, VOL. I.

Names.	Rank.	Time of Service. Enlisted.	Discharged.	Remarks.
Gee, Joseph	Drum	7 April 77	April 80	time out
Glasgow, Saml.	Corpl	10 Dec 76	17 July 77	deserted
Green, Amos	pt	do		
Green, Richard	do	21 April 77	25 Dec 77	1 Nov 80, do
Gorman, John	do	3 June 77	Jan 80	prisoner
Gailand, Gilbert	do Sergt	} 10 dec 10 June 77	14 feb	Corpl 13 Sept
Greenwalt, James	pt Corpl Sergt	21 Mar 77 1 Aug 78	} Mar 80	discharged
Gough, Charles	pt	21 Mar 77	Jan 80	prisoner
Gutrick, William	do		dead or deserted	
Garner, Mathew	Sergt Ensign	10 dec 76	} 5 Mar 78	resigned
Garton, James	pt	12 May 78	15 July 80	deserted
Gordon, Thomas	Qt. Mr.	joined 5 July 78,	reduced 22 feb 79, discharged 18 dec 79	
Ganina, Abm.	pt	14 Mar 78	1 Nov 80	present
Gattau, Richard	do Corpl	10 June 78 1 July 80	} do	do
Gates, Leonard	pt		do	do
Gardiner, John	do	1 June 78	16 Aug 80	missing 5 April 79
Gates, William	do	4 do	5 April 79	discharged
Garner, Thomas	do	17 do		struck off
Garvey, William	do	28 Aprl 78	2 June 78	missing
Gatton, Sulvester		4 Oct 78	1 Nov 80	present
Green, Saml.	do	9 Jan 79	do	do
Green, John		do	do	do
Galloway, Hugh	do	10 dec 76	15 Mar 79	deserted
Griffin, William	fifer	19 Jan 79	16 aug 80	prisoner
Glashen, Hendry	pt Drum	25 feb 79 1 July 79	} 1 Nov 80	present
Gee, George		8 May 79	July 79	deserted
Grooms, Emanuel	pt	10 dec 76	27 dec 79	discharged
Gordon, George	Sergt	11 feb 80	16 Aug 80	prisoner
Glover, Thomas	pt	14 feb 80	1 Nov 80	present
SECOND REGIMENT.				
Garnett, Andrew	fifer	1 Jan 77	1 Nov 80	present
Gollihigh, Wm.	pt		3 Sept 79	deserted
Gallaway, Joseph	Corpl		10 Jan 80	discharged
Gorman, John	do		20 Jan 78	deserted
Gray, Jacob	do	4 Mar 77	1 Nov 80	present
Giles, Samuel	do	do	14 April 79	discharged

MUSTERS OF MARYLAND TROOPS, VOL. I.

Names.	Rank.	Time of Service. Enlisted.	Discharged.	Remarks.
Gray, Joseph	Corpl		28 feb 78	died
Gassaway, Jno.	Lieut Capt	17 April 77 2 April 80		
Guibard, Thomas	pt		16 July 80	
Musd. as Sergt between April and June Discharged as such				
Griffin, John	pt	1 Jan 77	10 Jan 80	discharged
Joined April Mus. Roll 78				
Gold, William	pt	20 feb 78	1 Nov 80	present
Griffin, Mack	do	1 Jan 78	do	do
Griffin, Nathan	do	do	do	do
Galloway, Charles	do	16 May 78	Nov 79	not heard of
Gray, Richard	do	28 Jan 78	15 dec 78	dead
Grinnel, Stephen	pt	29 May 78	3 April 79	discharged
Godthart, Barton	do	30 do	do	do
Goodyer, Edward	do	1 do	feb 80	not heard of
Garner, Henry	do	6 July do	4 April 79	discharged
Giles, John	do	9 May do	18 July 78	died
Garner, Abel	do	20 do	3 April 79	discharged
Grace, William	do	25 do	Mar 79	do
Grishill, Jno.	do	do	78	dead
Garish, William	do	do	26 Dec 78	deserted
Gooster, Reubin	do	27 dec 78	1 Nov 80	present
Gray, James	do	24 do 76		returned
Galworth, Gabl.	do		10 Jan 80	discharged
Gardiner, Richd.	Sergt		18 do	do
Gale, John	Lieut Capt	10 April 77 10 dec 77		
first mus. June 79				
Grace, Richard	Lieut Capt	never joined		
1 mus. June 79				
Green, Henry	pt	26 April 79	1 Nov 80	present
Galloway, James	do		Nov 79	not heard of
Gassaway, Henry[1]	Ensn	26 Jan 80		

Third Regiment.—*Beginning* 77.

Gordon, Thomas	pt	22 Jan 77	28 Jan 80	taken prisoner
Gladson, William	pt	28 May 77	28 Jan 80	discharged
Gilpin, William	do	do feb do	21 do	do
Glasgow, Walter	do	13 May 77	16 Aug 80	missing
Grant, Samuel	Sergt		15 May 78	deserted
Gouger, Joseph	pt		Mar 79	left out the Roll
Green, Henry	do	23 April 77	15 Mar 78	deserted
Gills, John	do	4 dec 76	1 Nov 78 4 dec 79	transfd. to Invalids discharged from do

[1] Gale's.

MUSTERS OF MARYLAND TROOPS, VOL. I.

Names.	Rank.	Time of Service. Enlisted.	Discharged.	Remarks.
Geary, Richard	pt		dead or deserted	
Garnett, Francis	do	10 Aug 77	April 78	struck off
Gassaway, Nich.	Ensn Lieut	} 17 April 77 {		
Gorsuch, Thomas	Drum	3 June 77	1 Nov 80	present
Griffith, Saml.	Capt		12 Aug 78	resigned
Griffith, Chas.	Lieut		19 May 77	do
Gavin, Michl.	pt	5 Jan 77	5 Jan 80	discharged
Galloway, Marsl.	Drum pt	27 June 77 4 May 78	} 1 nov 80	present
George, Edward Drum Major	} do {	} 1 Aug 78 {	} 16 Aug 80 April 85	prisoner returned
Gainer, Jno.	pt	11 May 77	16 Aug 80	missing
Garrett, John	do	28 feb 77	28 feb 80	time expired
Gilpin, Igs.	do		2 July 78	deserted
Garrett, Leonard	pt	25 feb 77	29 feb 80	time expired
Gorman, Hugh	do		July 78	struck off
Gist, Mordicai	Col	10 dec 76		
Gadrick, Philip	pt	28 Aprl 78	June 78	deserted
Graves, James	do	15 May 78	do	discharged
Gordan, William	do	20 Mar 78	1 Nov 80	present
Goodwin, James present Oct Roll 80	do	}	} 1 Nov 80 {	present
Greenwell, Robt.	Sergt		9 Jan 79	discharged
Gill, John Exchg. and joined 22 July 78	pt	21 May 77	1 feb 79	do
Gregory, William	pt	13 May 78	Corpl 1 Nov 79, 16 Aug missing	
Gordon, (or Jordon), William	do		do	do
Goldsbury, Henry[1] reinlisted 18th Nov 78	do	14 May 78 }	} 1 Nov 80	present
Goldsmith, Notley	pt	28 do	4 April 79	discharged
Geoghegan, Anthy.	Drum	20 Mar 78	1 Nov 80	present
Grace, Jesse	pt	25 April 78	do 17 April 81	do discharged
Gibson, John	do	20 do	do	do
Gardiner, Richd.	do	24 do	not mustd. in 80	
Griffiths, John	do	18 May 78	1 Nov 80	present
Gorrell, Abm.	do	1 June 78	time out, discharged	
Grant, Richard	do	11 Jan 78	13 feb 79	do
Green, Isaac	do	2 June 78	1 Nov 80	present
Gask, William	do		14 feb 79	discharged
Glascoe, William	do	12 April 78	1 Nov 80	present
Gordon, John	Drum	15 June 79	1 Nov 80	present

[1] Deaver's.

during the War of the American Revolution, 1775-83.   115

MUSTERS OF MARYLAND TROOPS, VOL. I.

Names.	Rank.	Time of Service. Enlisted.	Discharged.	Remarks.
	October Muster, 1780.			
Goldsborough ———		see Henry Goldsborough		
Goldsborough, Chs.	pt	2 feb 80	1 Nov 80	present
Goddard, John	do	do	do	do
Gates, William	do	13 Mar 80	do	do
Grant, James	do		16 Aug 80	missing
	Fourth Regiment.—*Beginning Dec'r*, 1777.			
Gregory, Robt.[1]	Corpl	7 dec 76	1 dec 79	dischd. pt. 20 feb 79
Godfrey, Thomas	pt		Dec 77	drafted for sea
Gilhamton, Robt.	do	do	16 Aug 80	missing, joined &
Godman, Saml.	Capt	10 dec 76	left out	[died 1 Oct 81
Gainer, Hugh[2]	pt	Dec 76	1 Nov 80	present
Gray, James	do	do	dec 79	discharged
Garth, James	do	5 Jan 77	1 Nov 80	present
Glorey, William	do		16 May 78	discharged
Garvin, John[3]	do	20 Nov 77	1 Nov 80	present
Goodall, Elias	do		April 78	left out
Gassaway, Henry[4]	Sergt		6 dec 79	discharged
promoted Ensign 2d Regiment				
Greenwell, Jesse	pt		feb 78	died of his wounds
Griffith, George[5]	Sergt	14 July 77	23 June 79	deserted
Gibson, Joseph[6]	do	1 April 77	7 dec 79	discharged
Gill, Hugh[7]	pt	19 Aug 77	19 Aug 80	do
Green, James[6]	do	27 Jan 78	16 Aug 80	missing
Guarn, Hugh[1]	do	28 dec 76	28 dec 79	discharged
Gray, Thomas	Drum pt	15 April 78 1 June 78 }	1 Nov 80	present
Gollier, John[8]	do	26 April 78	16 Aug 80	missing
Gentils, John[8]	do	5 feb 78	3 July 78	deserted
Gaiffin, Michael	do	18 May 78	16 Aug 80	missing
Gray, Robert[4]	do	2 do	1 Nov 80	present
Goldsborough, Jno.[9]	do	25 April 78	Sep 80	deserted
Smith's, late Spurrier's				
Glaswey, Pat.	do	25 April 78	Corpl 1 Apl 80, 16 Aug 80 mis-	
Gordon, Thomas[10]	do	27 do	14 Aug 79	deserted [sing
Rieley's, late Bowie's				
Getcomb, John	do	5 May 78	5 Sept 78	discharged
Gamble, William[1]	do	20 do		discharged, see below
Gardiner, Alexd.[8]	do	16 April 78	1 July 80	deserted
Gummy, Peter[9]	fifer	17 June 78	1 Jan 80	deserted

[1] Oldham's. [2] Godman's. [3] Lansdale's. [4] Selman's. [5] Lt. Spurrier's. [6] Bowie's. [7] Burgess'.
[8] Norwood's. [9] Lt. Smith's. [10] Riely's.

MUSTERS OF MARYLAND TROOPS, VOL. I.

NAMES.	RANK.	TIME OF SERVICE. Enlisted.	Discharged.	REMARKS.
Garrish, Francis[1]	pt	18 May 78	17 May 80	deserted
Gamble, William[2]	do	26 July 78	May 79	discharged
Gainford, Mathias	do	18 May 79	July 80	deserted
Gwinn, John[3] musd. Feby 78	Corpl Sergt	1 July 79	1 Nov 80	present
Gorman, John[1]	pt	27 Aug 79	16 Aug 80	missing
Glinn, James[2]	do		1 Nov 80	present
joined 17 Mar 80, transfd. from the Virginia Troops 1 dec 79				
Goff, Richard[4]	pt	2 feb 80	July 80	deserted
Gray, James[5]	do	17 April 80	1 Nov 80	present
			same person before mentioned, discharged and reinlisted supposed	

RAWLINGS' REGIMENT.

NAMES.		RANK.	Enlisted.	Discharged.	REMARKS.
Gratsinger, John		pt			
Gordon, John		do	27 May 79		
Grimes, David		do			
Gowarn, Brian		do	11 Mar		
Glass, Andrew		do	31 April		
Green, John		do	17 July		
Glass, Anthony		do	31 Mar		
Godfrey, Jno.	6 mo.	do	15 feb 79		
Guthrey, Wm.	do	do	2 Mar		
Gault, James	do	do	12 do		
Gibson, John	do	do	10 do		
Gullion, John	do	do	1 Mar		
Gullion, Jeremh.	do	do	23 do		
Germing, Wm.		do			
Guthry, William		Lieut	19 Feb 79		

FIRST REGIMENT.

NAMES.	RANK.	Enlisted.	Discharged.	REMARKS.
Hardy, Thos. Dent	Lieut	19 July	6 July 78	resigned
Heron, John	Corpl	10 dec 76	6 Mar 78	deserted
Horson, Thomas	Drum	do	27 dec 79	discharged
Hiltzhimer, Franz say Kelsimer	pt	do	do	do
Hannagan, Brian	do	do		exd. in 77
Hargraves, Dennis	do	do	10 feb 77	died
Higgins, Dennis	do	15 feb 77	11 Sept 77	missing
Howe, Walter	do	18 do	11 Jan 80	discharged
Helmes, John	do	1 feb	do	do
Howard, Joseph	do	9 May 77	1 Nov 80	present

[1] Riely's. [2] Oldham's. [3] Godman's. [4] Lansdale's. [5] Lt. Hanson's.

MUSTERS OF MARYLAND TROOPS, VOL. I.

NAMES.	RANK.	TIME OF SERVICE. Enlisted.	Discharged.	REMARKS.
Hoye, Cephas	pt	10 dec 76		never joined
Hanson, Saml.	Ensn		7 dec 77	resigned
Hamilton, Saml.	Sergt	do	11 July 78	joined Comy.
Harrod, John	pt	do	13 Mar 79	deserted [Dept.
Hartlove, John	do	do	16 Aug 80	missing
Hanson, Saml. Q. M.	Ensn Lieut	24 July 77 1 Aug 79	} 1 Aug 78	Qt. Mr.
Heywood, John	pt		25 July 77	deserted
Hughes, Henry	do		1 April 80	do
Harwood, Thomas	Capt	10 dec 76	10 June 77	resigned
Hilleary, Rignal	Ensn Lieut	do 27 May 78	}	
Hutchinson, R. G.	pt	18 feb 77		
Hutchinson, Saml.	do	do	11 feb 80	time expired, dis-
Hale, Thomas	do	11 Mar	16 Aug 80	missing [chgd.
Hopkins, A. H.	pt	6 Mar 77	Jan & feb 80,	left out musr.
Holmes, William	do	10 dec 76	27 dec 79	discharged
Hamilton, Thos.	do	do	6 Mar 78	deserted
Holsey, John	do	do		
Hughes, John	do	do		exchanged for R. Baily
Heldmole, Geo.	do	do	31 Oct 77	deserted
Hennen, Thos.	do	do		
Huling, Thos.	do	24 April 77	27 May	deserted
Hogg, James	do	10 Dec 76	27 dec 79	discharged
Howard, Benja.	do	3 Mar 77	2 Mar 80	do
Hubbard, Hanson	do	25 do	3 May 80	do
Hanan, Henry	do Corpl	27 May 77 1 June 79	} 1 Jan 80	promoted Sergt.
Hall, Elisha	Ensn Lieut	27 May 78	22 Aug 77	prisoner
Howby, Dennis	pt	10 Dec 76	28 May 77	deserted
Hamilton, Geo.		do	21 April	ex. R. Green
Howsman, Tho.		1 April 77	3 April 79	deserted
Harding, Robt.	do	10 May 77	Sept 79 18 Mar 80	transferred to Invalids discharged }
Hickey, Leond.	do Corpl	10 dec 76 3 June 78	} reduced 5 Nov 79	} 27 July 80 de- serted
Hughes, Andrew	pt	18 April 77	18 Aug 80	missing
Hebb, Jesse	Sergt	8 Mar 77	10 July 77	discharged
Hagarthy, Paul	pt	10 dec 77	27 dec	do
Horrill, Jas.	do	2 April 77		
Howard, Thos.	Surgn. Mate	1 April 78	79	resigned

MUSTERS OF MARYLAND TROOPS, VOL. I.

Names.	Rank.	Time of Service. Enlisted.	Discharged.	Remarks.
Havers, Jno.	pt	12 Jan 78	18 July 80	deserted
Humpton, Wm.	pt	Mar 78	16 Aug 80	missing
Hennesey, Edwd.	do	21 May 78	4 April 79	Ex. for Edwd. Jefferson
Hunter, Thos.	do	25 feb 78	10 Sept 80	discharged
Harrington, Wm.	do	8 May 78	1 Nov 80	present
Hanington, Richd.		5 June 78	5 April 79	discharged
Hanington, Levin		do	do	do
Howell, John		12 May 78	20 June 79	deserted
Hutton, Lance.		11 June 78	16 Aug 80	prisoner
	Corpl	1 Jan 80		
Hanson, Robt.		25 Mar 78		
Hynes, John	pt	5 June 78	15 Sept 79	deserted
Hudson, Thos.	do	16 May 78	28 feb 79	discharged
Hunt, James	do	20 do	14 do	do
Hickey, Fran.	do	2 do	do	do
Hardy, George	do	5 June 78	5 April 79	do
Higdon, Wm.	do	5 April 79	1 Nov 80	present
Harding, Jno.	do	30 Mar 79	1 Aug 80	deserted
Holland, Wm.	do	9 May 79	16 do	missing
Hughes, Wm.	do	17 do	1 Nov 80	present
Horrell, Jno.	do	17 June 79	do	do
Hall, Joseph	do	1 do	do	do
Hannon, Jno.	do	22 May 79	do	do
Harding, A.		10 June 79	see A. A. Arvin	
Howard, Stephen		21 do	16 Aug 80	missing
Harry, Thomas	do	20 feb 80	do	prisoner
Hoskins, Rand.	do	2 feb 79	1 Nov 80	present
Hagan, Raphael	Corpl		16 Aug 80	prisoner
Harris, Silvester	pt		10 do	deserted
Hart, William	do		16 do	prisoner

Second Regiment.—Beginning Jan., 1778.

Hopkins, John	pt	1 Jan 77	10 Jan 80	discharged
Hughes, Andrew	do	7 April 77	Jany 79	died in Hosptl.
Howard, James	do		Jan 78	struck off
Hardikin, Edward	Sergt		10 Jan 80	discharged
Holder, Kemp,	pt		do	do
Holder, John	do		do	do
Hazell, Philip	Sergt	22 Mar 77	9 Sept 78	died
Head, John	Drum	15 Jan 77		
Hasser, John	pt		15 Mar 78	discharged
Hamilton, George	do		3 April 79	deserted

MUSTERS OF MARYLAND TROOPS, VOL. I.

NAMES.	RANK.	TIME OF SERVICE. Enlisted.	Discharged.	REMARKS.
Hawkins, Philip	pt		10 Jan 80	discharged
Hill, Richard	Corpl		do	do
Hatcher, Igns.	pt		do	do
Hughes, John	Corpl	sick Maryd.		
reduced to	pt	1 June 78	1 Nov 80	present
Henly, Roger	do		10 Jan 80	discharged
Hardman, John	Lieut	10 April 77	died 31 Aug 1780 of wounds	
	Capt	2 April 80	recd. at Battle of Camden	
Hayward, Thomas	Corpl			
Harding, John	pt		16 Aug 80	prisoner
Howell, Thomas	fifer		15 May 78	deserted
Hart, Thomas	pt		16 Aug 80	killed
Hughs, Lawrence	do		8 feb 79	deserted
Harrison, Tho.	do	2 Mar 76	1 Nov 80	sick Maryd.
Harris, Solomon	do	14 Aug 79	16 Jan 80	discharged
Holeston, William	do		19 June 78	deserted
Henry, Adam	do	1 Jan 78	16 Aug 80	missing
Harper, William	do	19 Mar 78	9 Jan 79	died
Harper, Richard	do	do	1 Nov 89	present
Hays, Bartholo.	do	do	1 July 78	deserted
Hall, John	do	18 do	24 Jan 79	died
Hill, James	do	4 Jan 78	1 Nov 80	present
Heaney, John	do	3 April 78	do	do
Harmer, Jos.	do	12 May 78	15 Sept 80	deserted
Holliday, Geo.	do	9 Oct 77	9 Oct 80	discharged
Horsefield, Jos.	do	20 May 78	1 Nov 80	present
Hagarthy, Geo.	do	12 do		
	Sergt	1 Jan 80	do	do
Hobbs, Thomas	pt	28 May 78	do	do
Howard, John	do	25 feb 78	do	do
Howard, Leond.	do	23 May 78	3 April 79	discharged
Hill, Edward	do	29 do	2 dec 78	died
Howell, John	do		3 April 79	deserted
Hughston, Jacob	do		1 Nov 80	present
Hillyer, W. P.	do	30 do	16 Aug 80	prisoner
Hayle, Anthony	do	8 June 78	do	do
Hall, George	pt		4 June 79	deserted
Hughes, Samuel	do	19 May 78	1 Nov 80	sick in Maryd.
Hughes, Henry	do	20 do	21 feb 79	discharged
Hodibuck, Conrad	do	25 do	16 Aug 80	killed
Hugill, Joseph	do	do	1 Nov 80	present
Hill, Abner	do	20 do	78	died fishkill
Holmes, Thomas	do	do	time out, discharged	
Hubbard, Charles	do	do	78	died fishkill

MUSTERS OF MARYLAND TROOPS, VOL. I.

NAMES.	RANK.	TIME OF SERVICE. Enlisted.	Discharged.	REMARKS.
Haslip, William	do	24 May 79	18 Sept 79	discharged
Hooper, Abram	do	1 July 79	1 Nov 80	present
Haire, James	do	1 June 79	do	do
Hayes, Vachel	do Drum	30 July 79	killed at 16 Aug 80	missing
Hayes, Luke	pt	22 June 79	1 Nov 80	present
Haynie, Ezekiel	S. M. Surgn	1 Aug 79		
Horsfield, Luke	pt		16 Aug 80	prisoner
Harris, James	do	17 April 80	1 Nov 80	present
Hackett, Joshua	do		16 Aug 80	missing

THIRD REGIMENT.—Beginning 77.

NAMES.	RANK.	Enlisted.	Discharged.	REMARKS.
Hatkerston, Robt.	Sergt	5 feb 77	9 Jan 80	discharged
Hamilton, William	Drum	5 May 77	1 Nov 80	present

SMALLWOOD'S REGIMENT.

NAMES.	RANK.	Enlisted.	Discharged.	REMARKS.
Hewin, John	pt	2 feb 77	16 Aug 80	prisoner Camden
Musd. as Sergt. Aug 80, says he got from the British in feb 80, never joined afterwards				
Horner, Robt.	pt	5 feb 77	no acct. of him	
Hopewell, Jno.	do	19 do	21 feb 80	discharged
Hall, Fredk.	do	11 May 77	10 Jan 78	deserted
Harrison, Joseph	pt	14 April 77	14 April 80	discharged
Hardie, James	Sergt			
Hammond, Joseph	pt		28 Aug 78	deserted
Hood, (or Wood), John	do			
Head, William	do	3 May 77	April 78	struck off
Hall, William	do	3 June 77	1 Aug 78	deserted
Holder, John	do	8 Sept 77	9 Nov 79	do
Hudson, John	do	do	28 Jan 78	do
Hayley, John	do	20 May 77	16 April 80	discharged
pt 1 June 79	Corpl	October 78		
Hood, Edward	pt	1 Jan 77	1 Nov 80	present
Hazlewood, Jacob	do		Mar 79	left out the Roll
Hughes, John	do	5 dec 76	16 Aug 80	missing
Hart, Zacha.	Sergt	20 June 77		
Hoole, Joseph	pt	4 Sept 77	16 Aug 80	killed
Husey, James	do	1 do	July 78	deserted
Heney, Barna.	do Corpl private	1 April 77 20 May 78 1 July 79	16 Aug 80	do—joined
Holloway, Jno.	do		feb 78	died
Hannagin, Bri.			11 Sep 77	prisoner

MUSTERS OF MARYLAND TROOPS, VOL. I.

Names.	Rank.	Time of Service. Enlisted.	Discharged.	Remarks.
Hough, John	private	Nov 77 joined		
Howard, John	Corpl pt	} 1 June 78	Aug 78	struck off
Hughes, Saml. pt 15 July 79	do Corpl	} 23 May 78		
Howard, Thomas	pt		10 Jan 78	died
Hilton, Samuel	do		15 do	do
Hagarthy, Dennis	do		1 June 78	discharged
Harpur, Francis	do	5 April 78		
Hughes, James	pt	25 April 78	Aug absent wo. leave, never [joined
Haydon, John	do	do		
Hoskins, John	do	20 do	16 Aug 80	missing
Hart, William	do	6 feb 78		
Holmes, John	do	30 April 78	do	do
Howard, Austin	do	do	1 Nov 80	present
Hall, Richard	do	21 do	do	do
Harley, Henry	do	25 do	16 Aug 80	missing
Holt, William	do	23 do	14 Oct 78	discharged
Henry, Elias mustered ———	pt Sergt	} 4 May 78 1 Oct 80	1 Nov 80	present
Harley, Edward	pt	5 May 78	do	do
Howard, William	Corpl pt	24 feb 78 31 Oct 78	feb 79	discharged
Hatfield, Edward	do	27 April 78	1 Nov 80	present
Harris, William	do		do	do
Higdon, Thomas	do	7 Mar 78	do	do
Hines, Henry	do	do	do	do
Hopkins, Francis	do	9 do	do	do
Hood, Richard	do	9 May 78	16 Aug 80	missing
Hurst, Phineas	do Sergt	25 do 18 Jan 79	} 1 Jan 80	deserted
Hoskins, Zepha.	pt	30 May 78	14 April 79	discharged
Harris, Josias Joined 3 Aug 78 musd. Sergt 1 Oct 80	do Corpl	26 do 5 May 79	1 Nov 80	private
Hines, Peter	pt	2 June 78	18 Aug 80	deserted
Holloway, William	fifer		27 Oct 80	deserted
Harper, Stephen	pt	25 April 78	1 Nov 80	present
Holbrook, James	do	27 do	do	do
Hardey, Elias	do	25 do	do	do
Hackett, James	do	20 May 78	1 Jan 80	deserted
Hamilton, Jno.	do	22 Apl 78	1 Nov 80	present
Hair, Robert	do	1 June 78		
Hardman,(or Harding),Jno.	do	20 April 78	16 Aug 80	missing

MUSTERS OF MARYLAND TROOPS, VOL. I.

NAMES.	RANK.	TIME OF SERVICE. Enlisted.	Discharged.	REMARKS.
Harris, Joseph	pt			
Hennis, John	do	4 June 78	26 Sep 80	deserted
Hall, William	do	14 May 78	26 Nov 78	do
Harris, Thomas	do		31 dec 79	do
Hall, Frederick deserted 10 Jan 78, joined 25 Mar 79 and was on the Rolls to April 80	do	11 May 77	dead or deserted, Capt. Baldwin say he deserted on ye way to S. ward	
Hays, Levin	Sergt	10 dec 76		
Hines, Michael	pt		May 79	deserted
Handly, Thomas	do	4 Jan 78	16 Aug 80	missing
Howard, Peregrim	do	9 May 79	1 Nov 80	present
Howard, Charles	Sergt	do	do	do

FROM OCTOBER MUSTER, 1780.

Haslip, John	pt		do	do
Holland, Daniel	do	10 Mar 80	16 Aug 80	

FOURTH REGIMENT.—*Beginning Dec., '77.*

Hall, Josias C.	Col	10 Dec 76		
Hamilton, Jno.	P. M.	1 Aug 77		
	Ensn	27 May 78		
	Lieut	11 June 79		
Hanson, Isaac	Qr. M.	1 May 77		
	Ensn	8 Nov 79		
	Lieut. d Q. Mr.	15 Dec do		
Hood, James	Q. M. S.	1 May 77	20 Aug 78	assd. Comy. 2d B.
	Corpl	5 Mar 77		
Howard, J. E.	Major Lt. Col. Lieut. Col. Comd.	10 Dec 76		
Harding, Daniel [1] private Sept 79	pt Corpl	30 May 77 1 April 78	Jan 80	discharged
Harp, Reice	pt		1 Mar 78	died
Herwell, Thomas	do	8 dec	8 dec 79	discharged
Hinks, Thomas	do	6 do	6 do	do
Hood, John [2]	Sergt	24 April 77	24 April 80	time expired
Hanes, John	pt		June 80	deserted
Houspan, Jno. C. [3]	do		25 May 80	time expired
Hessey, John H.	do	13 May 77	do 13 May 80	do discharged
Holland, Thomas	do	19 Apl 77	1 Mar 80	struck off

[1] Oldham's.   [2] Norwood's.   [3] Belt's.

MUSTERS OF MARYLAND TROOPS, VOL. I.

NAMES.	RANK.	Enlisted.	Discharged.	REMARKS.
Hatfied, Edward[1]	pt		1 Jan 80	discharged
Harvey, Charles	do	1 Jan 77	1 Nov 80	present
	Sergt	1 dec 79		
Hamilton, J. A.[2]	Ensn	10 dec 76		
	Lieut	1 feb 78	}	
	Capt			
Hickory, Jno.	pt	25 May 77	16 Aug 80	missing
Hyde, John	do	13 feb 77	1 Nov 80	present
Hedge, William[3]	do	6 dec 76	2 Jan 80	deserted, joined
Harley, Jeremh.	pt		1 Jan 78	died [again
Hatton, Thomas	do	4 Aug 77	16 Aug 80	missing
Hall, William[4]	do	29 May 77	29 May 80	discharged
Hilland, Mark[5]	do		1 April 78	deserted
Harris, Richard[6]	do	13 Aug 77	13 Aug 80	discharged
Hitland, Henry	do	18 do	16 do	prisoner
	Corpl	1 July 79	}	
	Sergt	10 Feby 80		
Hipsley, Jos.	pt		25 Jan 78	deserted
Hinon, Nichs.	do	22 April 77	22 April 80	time expired
Heltinhead, Jno.	do	19 Aug 77	Dec 79	deserted
Hartshorn, Jno.	Adjt	25 Jan 78	}	
	Lieut	21 May 79		
Hoops, Adam	do	from Hazin's Regt., 15 dec 79	}	
exchanged with Lieut. Lewis 3 Nov 76				
Hull, William[7]	pt	8 Jan 78		
Howell, John	do	21 do	1 Nov 80	present
Harding, Thomas	do	25 do	June 79	discharged
Hagan, Andw.	do	12 feb 78	16 Aug 80	missing
Hickey, Thomas[8]	do	26 Aprl 78	2 Jan 80	deserted
	Corpl	1 do 79	}	
Hackett, John	pt	26 Apl 77	1 June 79	to Invalids
			11 July 83	or Furlough dismd.
Holden, Jos.	do	6 May 78	28 feb 80	deserted
Huddleston, Th.[7]	do	2 — 78	June 79	discharged
Howe, William	do	21 April 78	1 Nov 80	present
Hollyday, Isaac[9]	do	2 May 78	do	do
	fifer	1 Aug 78	}	
(Smith's, late Spurrier's)	private	31 July 79		
Hooper, Jeremh.	do	4 April 78	6 Oct 78	died
Hudson, William	pt	2 May 78	3 June 79	to Invalids, 17 Sept 79
Hennis, Joseph[8]	do	20 feb 78		[deserted

[1] Godman's. [2] Lansdale's. [3] Spurrier's. [4] Riely's. [5] Bowie's. [6] Burgess',
[7] Selman's. [8] Norwood's. [9] Lt. Smith's.

MUSTERS OF MARYLAND TROOPS, VOL. I.

Names.	Rank.	Time of Service. Enlisted.	Discharged.	Remarks.
Hamilton, Geo.[1]	pt	2 June 78	Dec 79	deserted
Hals, John	do	20 May 78	8 Nov 78	died
Hellam, Thomas[2]	do	16 do	1 April 79	deserted
Hynes, Isaac[3]	do	18 do	10 Nov 78	died
Hailey, Thomas[4]	do	6 dec 76	6 dec 79	discharged
prisoner 22 Aug 77, joined 23 June 78				
Horam, Saml.[5]	Drum	4 April 78	see Samuel Oram	
Hindes, Jacob	pt	30 do	1 Nov 80	present
Hodges, John[6]	do	14 May 78	16 Aug 80	missing
Harpham, Robt.	do	18 do	do	prisoner
	Corpl	1 Aug 79		
	Sergt	1 June 80		
Hyner, Joseph	pt	20 feb 78	20 Dec 78	deserted
Harvey, Richd.[7]	do	28 Aug 78	June 79	do
Hall, John[4]	do	19 Apil 79	11 Oct 80	do
	Corpl	1 April 80		
Handley, Philip[7]	pt	2 Sept 79	16 Aug 80	missing
Hatton, John[8]	do	26 Oct 79	July 80	deserted
Hay, John	do	5 do	16 Aug 80	missing
Hailey, Thomas[4]	do	11 feb 77	11 feb 80	discharged
to serve till 11 feb 80 in the room of Tobias Wilson discharged 6 Dec 79				
Hood, James[8]	Corpl	5 Mar 77	5 Mar 80	discharged
Hudson, Robt.[9]	pt		July 80	deserted
Joined June mus. 80				
Harris, Thomas[10]	pt		16 Aug 80	missing
Hull, Nathl.	do		1 Nov 80	present
Hall, Tobias		8 Oct 77	2 Mar 78	died

RAWLINGS' REGIMENT.

Names.	Rank.	Enlisted.	Discharged.	Remarks.
Harrison, Kinsey	pt		9 Aug 79	discharged
Howe, John	Corpl	22 July 76		
Howard, J. B.	pt	24 Sept 76	2 April 77	do
Hogans, Roger	do			
Helms, Geo.			9 Aug 79	do
Hains, Peter	do		do	do
Harkenson, Josiah	S. Maj.	1 feb 79	1 July 79	do
Hays, Gabriel	Q.M.Sergt.	6 May	10 July do	do
Hart, William	pt	18 April		
Horsfield, Thos.		28 May	Corpl	14 Dec
Hays, John 1 yr.			1 July 79	discharged

[1] Oldham's. [2] Norwood's. [3] Godman's. [4] Lansdale's. [5] Lt. Smith's. [6] Burgess'.
[7] Riely's. [8] Lt. Lee's. [9] To Oldham's, Belt's. [10] Selman's.

MUSTERS OF MARYLAND TROOPS, VOL. I.

NAMES.	RANK.	TIME OF SERVICE. Enlisted.	Discharged.	REMARKS.
Howe, Daniel	fife	6 Mar		
Hazlewood, Jacob	pt		9 Aug 79	do
Hill, Thomas	do	5 feb		
Haggarty, Nic.	Corpl	12 Mar		
Holland, Francis	pt	4 June		
Haney, Michael	do	15 April		
Herbert, William	pt	20 May		
Hansford, William	do	26 Oct		
Hannah, Jno.	6 mo.			
Harbeson, Wm.	do			
Hays, Alex.	do			
Hall, Sam.	do			
Hurn, Henry	do			
Harbeson, Rob.	do			
Hum, Daniel	do		8 April 79	killed
Halfpenny, Isaac	pt			

FIRST REGIMENT.

NAMES.	RANK.	Enlisted.	Discharged.	REMARKS.
Ivory, Patrick	Drum	10 Dec 76	12 feb 79	deserted 19 dec 79, joined 20 May 79
Johnson, Vincent	pt	10 do	11 Sep 77	killed
Jordon, John	Lieut Capt	10 do 1 June 79		
Jenkins, Jason	Corpl } Sergt	1 Mar 79	27 dec 79	discharged
Jenkins, George	pt	20 feb 77	20 feb 80	do
Jackson, John	do	not musd.	after July 79 (in Invalids, died 21 dec 79)	
Jenkins, Edward	pt	22 Mar 77	22 Mar 80	discharged
James, John	do	6 April do	16 Aug 80	missing
Jenkins, Phil.	do	10 dec 76	16 Sept 78	prisoner 27 dec 79 discharged
Jackson, Thomas	do	1 Mar 77	1 June 77	dead
Johnson, William reinlisted	Corpl	10 dec 76	27 dec 79	discharged
Jasper, John	pt	do	22 Jan 78	deserted
Jones, William	Drum	18 Mar 77	21 do	do, joined 22 March, from to by D. Major
Ingleton, Thomas	pt	do	18 Mar 80	discharged
Joyce, William	do	2 May 78	1 Nov 80	present,
Jacobs, Zachariah				see 3d Regt.
Jenkins, Thomas	do	20 do	5 April 79	discharged
Jeckett, William	do	15 Aug 78	7 dec 78	do

MUSTERS OF MARYLAND TROOPS, VOL I.

Names.	Rank.	Time of Service. Enlisted.	Discharged.	Remarks.
Jefferson, Edward	pt	4 April 79		
		left out June 80, 18 July deserted		
Johnson, Archd.	pt	23 May 79	1 Nov 80	present
Sergt 15 June 80	Corpl	1 Jan 80		
Irons, (or Iams), John	pt	3 June 79	do	do
Jenkins, Isaac	pt	5 May 79	16 Aug 80	missing
Irvine, Edward	do	11 July 79	1 Nov 80	present
Jenkins, Joseph	do	1 do	do	do
Jones, Isaac	do	1 Aug 79	do	

SECOND REGIMENT.—*Beginning with the Muster Rolls for Jany., 1778.*

Names.	Rank.	Enlisted.	Discharged.	Remarks.
Johnson, Robert			19 Mar 81	discharged
Iiames, Thomas	Sergt	10 Jan 77	1 Jan 80	discharged
Issabel, Robt.	Drum	10 feb 76		
	Sergt	10 Jan 80		
Jeffers, Reubin	pt	27 Jan 77	10 Jan 80	discharged
Jeffers, Jacob	do	11 Mar 77	do	do
Jeffers, Peter	do	15 do	do	do
Irvin, Abm.	do	17 feb 77	11 June 79	prisoner war
Jones, James	do		Mar 78	died
Jacobs, Henry	do	Dec 76	1 Nov 80	present
	fifer	1 Jan 80		
Jones, Neile	pt	16 Nov 77	do	do
Jones, Joseph	do	6 feb 77	do	do
Innis, John	do	28 July 77	16 Aug 80	prisoner
Johnson, Robt.	do	19 Mar 78	1 Nov 80	present
Jennings, Wm.	do	78	discharged from Hospital Dec 78	
Joel, John	do	21 Jan 78	Corpl	July deserted
Jones, John	do	5 April 78	16 Aug 80	prisoner
Jenkins, William	do	1 June 78	1 Nov 80	present
Jackson, Abed	do	25 May 78	3 April 79	discharged
Jackson, James	Corpl	29 Jan 77	Sergt 1 Aprl 80, 1 Nov 80 present	
Jones, David	pt	1 feby 78		do do
	Corpl	do 79		
Jones, Lewis	pt	6 July 79	23 feby 79	discharged
Jones, Aaron	do	20 May 78	17 feby 79	died
Insley, Robert	do 9 mo.		31 Jan 79	dead
Insly, Naboth	do		3 April 79	discharged
Insly, John	do		do	do
Insly, David	do		do	do
Insly, Abram	do	26 July 79	1 Nov 80	present
Johnson, John	do	9 June do	22 July 79	deserted
Johnson, William	do		1 Nov 80	present

during the War of the American Revolution, 1775–83.   127

MUSTERS OF MARYLAND TROOPS, VOL. I.

NAMES.	RANK.	TIME OF SERVICE. Enlisted.	Discharged.	REMARKS.

THIRD REGIMENT.—*Beginning* 77.

Jones, Samuel	Lieut	10 Dec 76 }		
	Capt	6 Aug 77	11 feb 80	resigned
Irvin, Mathias	pt	21 May 77	May 80	discharged
Jeffers, Thomas	Corpl		1 Oct 79	do
Jones, Lewis	pt	21 feb 77	21 feb 80	time expired
Jones, Cuthbert	Drum	4 Aprl 77 }	4 Aprl 80	discharged
	pt	4 June 78		
Jordon, Justian.	do	18 Apl 77		
red'd to pt 25 May 79	Sergt	2 April 78		
Jones, John	pt			[ex. for Jno. Pasgrove
Jones, Thomas	do	20 Jany 77	1 June 78	11 Virginia Regt.
Jones, William	do	8 Aug do	16 Aug 80	missing
James, John	Ensn	1 Jan 77 }		
	Lieut	10 April 77	11 Jan 80	resigned
Jones, Thomas	pt		1 Oct 80	present
Jones, Job	Drum			
Johnson, Richard	pt		27 April 78	discharged
Johnson, Benj.	Fife	10 June 78 }	1 Nov 80	present
	pt	1 feb 79		
Jones, Thomas	do	1 Mar 78	do	do
	Corpl	1 April 80		
Johnson, Benj.	pt		16 Aug 80	missing
James, Walter	do	30 June 78	time out, discharged	
Jones, Richard	do	5 do	do	do
Jones, Joseph	do	14 May 78	16 Aug 80	missing
Jones, Philip	do	20 May 78		
Jamison, John	Sergt	14 April 79	to Invalids, dischd. 7 Nov 80 }	
			June 79 left out the Roll	
Jeames, Walter	pt	30 June 78	time out, discharged	
Johnson, Barnard	fifer	18 feb 78		
Jackson, William	pt	25 Aprl 78		
Jacob, Zacha.	do	13 May 78	1 Nov 80	present
Johns, James	do	25 dec 76		
1 must. Mar 79 mustered discharged 28 Dec 79				
James, Walter	pt		time out, discharged	
Jordon, Jestenian	do	25 May 79	(see J. Jordon, Sergt.)	
Jones, Lewis	fife	5 Aprl 79	Dec 79	died

JULY, &c., MUSTERS, 1780.

Johnson, Henry	Sergt		26 July 80	deserted
Jones, James	Drum		16 Aug 80	missing
Jenkins, Richd.		1 Sept 77	12 feb 81	discharged

MUSTERS OF MARYLAND TROOPS, VOL. I.

Names.	Rank.	Time of Service. Enlisted.	Discharged.	Remarks.
Fourth Regiment.—*Beginning Dec., 77.*				
Johnson, Abm.[1]	pt		26 Sept 78	died
Inch, John	do		22 Dec 77	missing
Johnson, Jos.[2]	do	1 Mar 77	1 Nov 80	present
Johnson, Miles[3]	do	6 Jan 77	6 Jan 80	discharged
Jenkins, Jos.[4]	do	1 Jan 77	8 do	do
Jameson, Adam	do	25 July 77	1 Nov 80	present
Jefferies, David[5]	do		Jan 78	left out the Roll
James, William[6]	Corpl	11 April 77 }		
	pt	29 Mar 79 }	1 Nov 80	present
Jerriott, James	do	11 April 77	16 Aug 80	missing
Isaacs, Isaac	do	18 Aug 77	18 do	discharged
Jackson, Anth.	do	10 Mar 77	Sept 79 to Invalids, 25 Apl 80 [discharged	
Jones, Joseph	do		Jan 78	left out the Roll
Jacobs, Robinson[1] (Smith's, late Bowie's)	do	13 April 78	16 Aug 80	missing
Innis, Thomas[7] waited on Maj. Morris (with orders Jan 79)	do	12 Mar 77 }	feb 78 }	left the Roll
Jessup, Thomas (Riely's, late Bowie's)	pt	26 April 78	1 Nov 80	present
Jones, Joseph[8]	do	28 do	15 June 78	discharged
Jones, Samuel[1]	do	19 May 78	16 Aug 80	missing
Jacks, Richard[8] Joined 26 Sept 79	do	28 do	July 80	deserted
Johnson, John[7]	do	8 do	1 Oct 80	present
Joseph, John	pt	21 April 78	4 Nov 78	deserted
James, Francis[8]	do		26 feb 80	do
Joace, William	do		1 Nov 80	present
Johnson, John	do	1 Jan 80	16 Aug 80	missing
Rawlings' Regiment.				
Iron, John	pt	24 Aug 76	reinlisted into 1st M. R.	
Jones, Joshua	do	23 July do	12 Nov 76	ex. another
Johnson, Jno. M.	do	23 do		
Jeans, Joseph	Sergt	1 Oct 79		
Jordan, John	pt	3 May 79		
Jackson, John	do			
Jarmy, William	do	1 Mar		
Islman, Michl. 6 mo.		31 Mar 79		

[1] Norwood's.   [2] Godman's.   [3] Selman's.   [4] Spurrier's.   [5] Bowie's.   [6] Burgess'.
[7] Lt. Smith's.   [8] Riely's.

MUSTERS OF MARYLAND TROOPS, VOL. I.

Names.	Rank.	Time of Service. Enlisted.	Discharged.	Remarks.

First Regiment.

Names.	Rank.	Enlisted.	Discharged.	Remarks.
Kernan, Barna.	pt	10 Dec 76	19 July 77	died
Keen, John	do	28 Jan 77		deserted
King, Philip	do	10 dec 76	22 Jan 78	do
Kelly, James	do	do	22 Aug 77	prisoner, 27 dec 79 [discharged
Kelly, John	do	do		Riely, see R
Kennady, Tho.	do			deserted
Keener, Lawrce.	do	22 Mar 77		do
Kirby, John	do	10 dec 76	22 Aug	prisoner
Kelly, Dennis	do	1 April 77	28 Mar 80	} present
reinlisted 10 Apl 80	Corpl	June 80	1 Nov 80	
King, Adam	pt	27 Mar 77		
Keech, Saml.	do	10 dec 76	10 April 77	died
Kellow, William	do	1 June 78		} present
Sergt 1 Jan 80	Corpl	1 Aug 79	1 Nov 80	
Knott, James	pt	22 May 79	pris. Jan 80	struck off
Kephart, Martin	do		27 dec 79	discharged
King, Thomas	do	Aprl 79	1 Nov 80	present
Francis, Keltrimer	see letter H			

Second Regiment.—*Beginning Jan., 78.*

Names.	Rank.	Enlisted.	Discharged.	Remarks.
Knott, James	pt			
Knott, Jeremh.	do		}	dead or deserted
Kinsey, David	do			
Kersey, Daniel	do	24 Jan 78	16 Aug 80	missing
Kilby, Thomas	pt	20 Aprl 78		
Corpl 1 feb 80	Sergt	1 July 80	} 16 Aug 80	prisoner
Keephart, Ad.	pt	12 Jan 78	1 Nov 80	present
King, George	do	21 do		
Knight, Jacob	do	19 May 78	1 Nov 80	present
Kearnes, James	do	29 do	1 Oct 80	do
Killman, Edwd.	do	20 do	1 Nov 80	do
Killegan, Jas.	do	9 May 79	do	do
Knight, George	do		1 Oct 80	} do
left out June Roll 79				

Third Regiment.—*Beginning 77.*

Names.	Rank.	Enlisted.	Discharged.	Remarks.
King, Isaac	pt			
Kelly, William	do	15 May 77	15 Mar 78	deserted
Kersey, Brian	do			
Kelly, Hugh	do	18 July 78	to Invalids 16 Sept 78	died

MUSTERS OF MARYLAND TROOPS, VOL. I.

Names.	Rank.	Time of Service. Enlisted.	Discharged.	Remarks.
Kimble, Stephen	pt	1 April 77	June Muster 82	
Kelly, George	do	1 July 77	prior Enlistment	
Knight, Thos.	do	25 April 78 }		
	Fifer	1 July 78 }		
Kelly, Hugh	pt	18 April 78	see above	
Kennedy, Wm.	do	25 do	Sep 78	struck off
Kelly, Patrick	do	20 do	29 June 78	deserted
Kenedy, Michl.	do	23 do	6 feb 80	to Invalids
musd. in Invalids joined former Regt, not joined 1 Nov 80				
Kelly, James	pt	ditto	16 Aug 80	missing
King, Henry	Sergt	25 May 78 }		
Comy. Dept.		Oct 78 }	Comy. Dept.	
King, Jeremiah	pt	22 do }		
	Corpl	14 Aug 78 }	14 April 79	dischd.
Kidwell, Benj.	pt	26 May 78	1 Nov 80	present
Kelly, Michael	do	25 Apl 78	28 Sept 79	deserted
Kirk, William	do	20 do	May 79	left out the Roll
Keith, Duncan	do	} 1 July 79		
	Corpl	}		
Kennedy, Wm.	pt		1 Nov 80	present
Kiggan, Jno.	do	12 May 78 }		
	Corpl	1 July 79 }		
S. Major	Sergt	1 Jan 80 }	16 Aug 80	prisoner
Kennedy, Michael	pt	28 April 78		
Kendall, Sam.	do	26 May 79		
Kennedy, Thomas	do	4 June 79	1 Nov 80	present, see [Thomas Cannady

From October Muster, 1780.

Kernall, Wm.	pt		ditto ditto	

Fourth Regiment.—*Beginning Dec., 77.*

Kelly, Richard[1]	pt	4 June 77	4 Mar 79	deserted
Kelly, John	do	1 dec 76	15 Nov 78	do
Kenney, Thomas[2]	do		Dec 79	discharged
Kilty, John	Lieut			
Knox, Jno.[3] O. S.	pt	1 Jan 77	1 Nov 80	present
. Bowie's (see Jno. Knox 7 Regt.)				
Kenney, Jno.[4]	pt		Jan 78	left out
sent to shipping				
Kelly, Matthew[5]	do	4 May 77	22 Apl 80	time expired

[1] Oldham's. [2] Godman's. [3] Spurrier's. [4] Bowie's. [5] Burgess'.

MUSTERS OF MARYLAND TROOPS, VOL. I.

NAMES.	RANK.	TIME OF SERVICE. Enlisted.	Discharged.	REMARKS.
Kennedy, David	pt		Jan 78	left out the Roll
Kidd, John	do	25 Aug 77	1 Nov 80	present
Keats, Thomas[1]	do	28 Jan 78	do	do
	Corpl	1 Feb 80		
	Sergt	1 March 80		
Kelly, Mathew[2]	pt	29 Jan 78	16 Aug 80	missing
King, William[1]	do	25 April 78	1 Nov 80	present
Knight, John[3]	fife	26 May 78	do	do
King, John[4]	pt	18 do	25 Jan 80	prisoner
Knight, John[5]	do	23 feb 79	1 Oct 80	present
Kennedy, James[2]	do	22 May 79		
	Corpl	1 feb 80		
pt 1 Sept 80	Sergt	1 June 80	1 Nov 80	do
Kelly, Edward[6]	pt	18 Nov 79	April 80	discharged

RAWLINGS' REGIMENT.

NAMES.	RANK.	Enlisted.	Discharged.	REMARKS.
Kann, John	pt	July 76		
Kimboll, Josias	do	2 Oct		
Kirby, Patk.	do	76		
Kemp, James 3	do			
Knight, David			15 Sep 79	discharged
Kelly, James				
Kirk, Edward				
King, James	do	21 Mar		
Kerr, Robt. 6 mo.	Sergt			
Kean, Danl. do		Mar		
Kean, James do		do		
Kelly, Edward do		do		

FIRST REGIMENT.

NAMES.	RANK.	Enlisted.	Discharged.	REMARKS.
Leeke, Henry	Sergt	17 April 77	10 dec 79	discharged
pt 10 December 76				received a discharged afterwards
Logan, Charles	pt	10 Dec 76	6 Mar 77	deserted
Leaf, Robert	do	30 Jan 77		never joined
Lewis, Benjamin	do	10 dec 76	10 April 77	died
Lowden, Michael	do	do	16 Aug 80	prisoner
Lanham, Jno.	do	do	27 dec 79	discharged
Langley, William	do		3 June 77	deserted
Linn, Valen	do	do	27 dec 79	discharged
	Corpl	12 Apl 77	11 Oct 77	joined in July 78, reduced 15 Sept 78

[1] Selman's. [2] Bowie's. [3] Lansdale's. [4] Oldham's. [5] Riely's. [6] Belt's.

MUSTERS OF MARYLAND TROOPS, VOL. I.

Names.	Rank.	Time of Service. Enlisted.	Discharged.	Remarks.
Little, Richard	pt	19 Apl 77	12 Aug 77	prisoner
Leadburn, Geo.	do	10 dec 76	do	do prisr. 16 Aug 80
reinlisted 1 musr. June 80			27 dec 79	discharged
Lucus, William	pt	1 feb 77	21 Jan 78	deserted
			27 dec 79	discharged, re-[inlisted }
Luckett, Saml.	Sergt	10 dec 76	27 dec 79	discharged
Luckett, F. Ware	Corpl	do	16 April 78	died
Lomax, John	pt	6 June 77	Jan 80	prisoner
Long, Thomas	do	10 July 77	20 Aug 77	deserted
Layman, Wm.	Ensn Lieut	10 April 77	4 June 79	resigned
Lowe, James	Sergt	10 dec 76	3 Oct 77	reduced
Lowe, Richard	pt	do		never joined
Lidington, Peter	do	8 May 77	1 feb 79	transferred to Invalids
Lamb, Joshua	Corpl Sergt	10 dec 76 1 Aug 77	27 dec 79	discharged
Lowe, James	pt	10 do	1 Mar 80	deserted
Lewis, Jonathan	do	5 June 78	1 Nov 80	
Luffer, John	do	17 do	do	present
Lawrence, Joshua	do	19 feb 78		
Loveless, Elisha	do	22 May 78	16 Jan 79	dead
Lawson, Michl.	do	5 June 78	5 April 79	discharged
Lanham, Richard	do	do	do	do
Lynch, John	Corpl	10 dec 76	April 79	do
Lock, William		do	23 May 78	deserted
Land, William	pt	1 feb 77	May 80	transferred to Invalids }
			16 Oct 80	discharged
Lindsey, Theops.	do	2 June 79	pris. Jan 80	
Lasher, John	do	3 May 79	June 80	deserted
Luckett, David	Ensn	26 Jan 80		
Lewis, Joseph	Musn	June 80	16 Aug 80	missing

Second Regiment.—*Beginning Jany., 1778.*

Names.	Rank.	Enlisted.	Discharged.	Remarks.
Lowe, J. Tolson	Sergt Ensn	26 Jan 80	10 Jan 80	discharged
Langford, Elijaha	pt	1 Jan 77	do	do
Lloyd, Michl.	do	do	1 Nov 80	present
London, William	do		1 Mar 78	discharged
Long, Solomon	Capt	10 dec 76	4 June 78	resigned

MUSTERS OF MARYLAND TROOPS, VOL. I.

Names.	Rank.	Time of Service. Enlisted.	Discharged.	Remarks.
{ Summers, Obad.				see S
{ Smith, Robt.				do
Lettman, William	pt			killed Eutaw
Laws, William	do	18 May 77	1 Nov 80	present
Leonard, James	do	20 Jan 77	20 Jan 80	discharged
Lucas, John	Sergt	14 do	14 do	do
reduced to pt 27 Aug 78 reappd.	do	27 Sept 78		
Lindsay, James	Corpl	10 feb 77		
reduced to pt 16 feb 79	Corpl	3 Aprl 79	10 feb 80	do
Lane, Bartholw.	pt		10 Jan 80	do
Lynch, Barney	do		11 June 78	deserted
Lucas, Basil	Sergt		10 Jan 80	discharged
Launders, Geo.	pt	29 Aprl 78	1 Nov 80	present
Lucas, John	do	15 May do	do	do
Laws, George	do	2 June do	do	do
Lynch, John	do		4 June 79	deserted
Lord, Henry	do	4 May 78	1 Nov 80	present
Laine, Solomon	do	20 do	3 Apl 79	discharged
Laine, Levin	do	do	do	do
prisr. 8 Jan 80				
Levingston, Henry	do	10 June 78		
Langrell, Asquith	do		3 Aprl 79	do
Lucas, James	do	} 10 Jan 80		discharged
	Sergt	} 25 Dec 79		deserted
Lovelet, Benja.	pt		Apl & May 79	deserted
Lyles, Zacha.	pt	11 June 79	1 Nov 80	present
Lord, Levin	do	26 May 79	do	do
Lee, William	do	10 June do	do	do
Land, Richard	do	Aprl 80	do	do

Third Regiment.—*Beginning* 77.

Lawler, David	pt	5 feb 79	16 Aug. 80	missing
Lacey, Stephen	do	7 Aprl 77		
Lynch, William	do	1 Jan 77	1 Oct 80	present
Love, John	do	do	1 Nov do	do
Lilly, William	do	do		
not heard of since 4 June 78, joined Smith's Compy. May 79				
Lowe, John	Corpl	1 May 77	Sergt 2 feb 80	time expired
Lauglane, Mark	pt	see Mack MacLaughlin		
Lawler, John	Corpl	1 July 77	7 July 78	deserted
Lyon, Jacob	Sergt	1 June 79	to Invalids Sept 5 81	died
Lassell, Alex.	pt	2 May 77	April & May 79	left out the
Lyles, Henry	Lieut			[Roll

MUSTERS OF MARYLAND TROOPS, VOL. I.

NAMES.	RANK.	TIME OF SERVICE. Enlisted.	Discharged.	REMARKS.
Long, Thomas	Corpl pt	15 feb 78	1 Nov 80	present
Leach, James	do			
Lynch, John	do	7 April 78		
Lee, John[1]	do	25 do	20 July 80	deserted, joined
Luff, Thomas, (or Jno.)	pt	9 Mar 78	16 Aug 80	missing, sup-[posed killed
Lucast, Peter	fife	30 April do	do	do
Leonard, Hugh	do	3 do	17 May 78	deserted
Lynn, Thomas	do		8 June 78	do
Layman, Jeremh.	do	4 May 78		Corpl 5 June 79
Layman, Garliner	do	31 do	July 80	deserted, rein-[listed 10 Nov 78
Lee, John[1]	do	15 do	1 Nov 80	present
Lyon, Isaac	do	19 do	do	do
Looney, Thomas	do	1 Aprl 78	16 Aug 80	missing
Lee, Joseph	do	5 June 78	5 Dec 78	died
Lewis, Thomas	do	do	1 Nov 80	present
Longest, Danl.	do	20 Mar 78	14 April 80	to Invalids Sept 15 82 dischd.
Lowes, Henry	do	4 June 78	9 Sept 80	deserted
Larner, John joined feb 79	do			
Larey, Danl. joined feb 79	do			
Lavender, Jno.	do	19 May 79	feb 80	died
Lewton, Thomas	do	11 do	28 Sept 79	deserted

FROM OCTOBER MUSTERS, 1780.

| Lawler, Michael | pt | 1 Jan 80 | 1 Nov 80 | present |

FOURTH REGIMENT.—*Beginning Dec.*, 77.

Logie, James[2]	Sergt do M.	Dec 76 1 Aug 77	agrees to serve to the end of	
Oldham's Asst.	F. M.	10 Feby 80		[James Warder's time
Lewis, Charles	Corpl Sergt	18 dec 76 1 June 78	18 Jan 80	discharged
Lewis, Nicholas	pt	13 Jan 77	13 Jan 80	do
Lawler, David[3]	Corpl pt	12 April 77 29 Sept 78	12 April 80	do

[1] Smith's. [2] Oldham's. [3] Norwood's.

MUSTERS OF MARYLAND TROOPS, VOL. I.

NAMES.	RANK.	TIME OF SERVICE. Enlisted.	Discharged.	REMARKS.
Lewis, Joseph	Lieut	exchd. with Lieut. A. Hoops from Hazen's Regt.		
Lennox, John[1]	pt	Corpl 1 dec 79	Sept 80	deserted
Lynch, Hugh	pt	13 April 77	13 Aprl 80	discharged
Lansdale, Thomas	Capt	10 dec 76		
Lucas, John[2]	Major Sergt pt	9 dec 77	July 80	deserted
Leavley, Jacob[3]	Corpl pt	23 feb 77 13 Aug 80 }	23 feb 80	discharged
Lake, William	do	8 Jan 77	5 July 80	deserted
Lindsay, Jno.	do	23 dec 76	16 Aug 80	missing
Lilly, William[4]	do	see William Filly		
Lloyd, Thomas	do		Jan 78	left out the Roll
Leamon, William[5]	Sergt	22 April 77	22 Apl 80	time expired
Lynch, John	pt	5 Aug 77	1 Nov 80	present
Lucas, James	pt	18 Aug 77	Mar 79	deserted
Loveday, Thomas	fife M.	10 feb 78		do
Lee, Parker[6]	Ensn Lieut	1 Jan 78 16 Oct 78		
Lawler, John[2]	pt	16 Jan 78	June 78	transfd. to 10th Virga.
Lewis, Edward	do	7 feb 78	17 May 78	deserted [Regt.
Ludford, Henry[1]	do	24 Mar 78	1 June 80	do
Levie, Alexander[7]	do	22 April 78	1 Nov 80	present
Longdon, Thomas[8] Smith's, late Spurrier's	do	8 do	Sept 80	deserted
Lynch, Robt.	do	15 do	1 Nov 80	present
Lamal, (or Lamie), William	do	21 do	15 Sept 78	deserted
Lawrence, James	do	25 do	3 June 79	to Invalids, 5 Oct 80 deserted
Leary, Daniel	do	7 May 78	4 Jan 80	May & June 80
discharged by furlough, man in his place	Corpl 27 do, private 20 Oct 79			
Lindiff, John[9]	Sergt Sergt. M.	1 May 80		} 16 Aug 80 priso- [ner
prisr. 22 Aug 77, joined 16 July 78, Qr. M. Sergt. 20 Aug 78				
Lieuty, John	pt	19 May 78	Sep 80	deserted
Leary, Daniel[3]	do	11 do	4 Jan 80	do
Lyons, William[1]	do	2 Nov 78	20 dec 78	do
Leary, Michael[3] prisr. 27 Aug 77, joined 24 July 78	do Corpl	28 Jan 77 1 Nov 79 }	8 Jan 80	do
Lions, William[10]	pt	13 June 78	10 April 79	discharged

[1] Godman's. [2] Selman's. [3] Spurrier's. [4] Bowie's. [5] Burgess'.
[6] Norwood's. [7] Lansdale's. [8] Lt. Smith's. [9] Oldham's. [10] Riely's.

MUSTERS OF MARYLAND TROOPS, VOL. I.

NAMES.	RANK.	TIME OF SERVICE. Enlisted.	Discharged.	REMARKS.
Lister, Charles	pt	2 May 78	16 Aug 80	missing
Lunn, John[1]	do		July 80	deserted
London, John[2]	do	6 Oct 79	16 Aug 80	missing
Lester, John[3] to Oldham's	pt	14 Sept 79	July 80	deserted

RAWLINGS' REGIMENT.

NAMES.	RANK.	Enlisted.	Discharged.	REMARKS.
Lovely, Thomas	fife	21 Aug 76		
Lynch, Daniel	pt	2 July	28 Nov 76	deserted
Layard, George	do	16 Aug	12 dec 76	do
Livistone, John	do		9 Aug 79	discharged
Lemon, Patk.	do		13 May 79	do
Lacey, John	do		9 Aprl 79	deserted
Lewis, Lewis	do		do	do
Lewis, Lawrence	do		15 Mar	do
Lockhart, Jno.	do	10 Mar		
Linley, James 6 mo.	Corpl			
Larimore, David do	pt			
Lanham, Nehimh.				

FIRST REGIMENT.

NAMES.	RANK.	Enlisted.	Discharged.	REMARKS.
Mudd, Richard	Sergt		7 Jan 82	discharged
McKeel, Thomas	Ensn	10 dec 76		never served
McKoy, Alexander	fifer	4 Aprl 77	14 July 77	died
McGinnis, Willian	pt	14 dec 76	12 Aug 77	deserted
Mitchell, James	do	do	16 Aug 80	missing
McCain, ———	do	do	10 Aprl 77	Virga.
McDaniel, Roger	do	5 Mar 77	June 80	deserted
Mason, Thomas	do	23 do		never joined
Muse, Walker	Lieut	10 dec 76	Capt. 10 June 77	
Mitchell, Jno.	do	* do		
	Capt	15 July 77		
Marlow, Middlen.	Sergt		27 dec 79	discharged
Mitchell, Francis	pt	10 dec 76	27 do	do
Martin, Hezek.	do			never joined
Mills, John	do		10 June 77	discharged
McCallister, Arch.	Lieut	17 April 77	B. Capt.	24 Sept 79
Mattingly, Jos.	pt	10 dec 76		
	Sergt	24 May 77	27 dec 79	discharged
McKensey, Wm.	pt	10 dec	20 April 77	died
McDonough, Wm.	do	5 Apl 77		never joined
Monroe, Danl.	do	3 May 77	20 May 80	discharged
Mackay, Thos.	do	19 Aprl 77	11 Sept	taken prisoner

[1] Lt. Colgate's.   [2] Belt's.   [3] Oldham's.

MUSTERS OF MARYLAND TROOPS, VOL. I.

Names.	Rank.	Time of Service. Enlisted.	Discharged.	Remarks.
McCoy, John	Sergt	10 dec 76	Aug 78	joined forage
Miller, Michael	pt	do	22 Aug	[Dept.
		joined	15 Sept 78	present 1 Nov 80
McKean, MacMal.	do	do	24 feb	exchanged for J. Shout
Mathews, Jos.	pt	10 dec 76	13 Aug 78	deserted
McCarty, Jesse	do	do	24 May	do
McLane, Jno.	Corpl	O. S.	27 dec 79	discharged
McLane, Hugh	pt	10 dec 76	25 Aprl 79	do
Murray, Mathew	do	do	15 Apl 78	deserted
McNew, Moses	do	do	31 Aug 80	
		joined 18 Oct 80	1 Nov 80	present
Mire, Frederick	pt	10 dec 76	27 dec 79	discharged
May, Dennis	fifer	do	22 Aug 77	prisoner
McCormick, Richd.	pt	18 Mar 77	18 Sept 77	missing
McPherson, Sam.	Lieut	10 dec 76	Captain	7 April 80
McPherson, Mark	Sergt	do	27 dec 79	discharged
	Ensn	Lieut		
Mudd, Martin	Sergt	10 May 77	24 Sept 78	died
Martin, Ignatius	pt	18 Mar 77	27 Aug 77	do
Mudd, Thomas	do	14 Aug 77	18 Oct 77	discharged
Murray, Alexr.	Capt	10 Dec 76	10 June	resigned
Miller, Josiah	Corpl	do	27 dec 79	discharged
Mayhew, Thos.	pt	do		Exchd. for L. Hickey
Majors, Jno.	do	4 feb 78	16 Aug 80	prisoner
Mitchell, Jno.	do	28 do 77	17 dec 77	deserted
Meek, Jesse	do	4 Mar 77	June 80	left out, not heard of
Malcomb, Tho.	do	5 do	17 dec 77	deserted [Nov 80
		joined 1 April 78	7 Mar 80	discharged
McNamara, Benja.	pt	10 Mar 77	never joined	
McCarty, James	do	25 feb 77	26 feb	deserted
Mitchell, Igns.	do	16 May 77	16 May 80	discharged }
	Sergt	1 Aug 77	25 July 78	promoted }
Maynadier, Hy.	Surgn. Mate			
Millston, Barker	pt	9 Oct 77	1 Jan 78	deserted
Morrison, Wm.	do	17 Sept 77	17 Sept 80	discharged
Moire, Peter	do	3 May 78		
	Corpl	1 Mar 80	16 Aug 80	missing
McNamara, Darley	pt	7 May 78	do	do
Marsh, Benja.	do	10 June 78	23 Mar 80	prisoner
Mudd, Richard	do	6 Jan 79	6 Jan 80	discharged
	Corpl	1 Jan 80		
McCaul, Wm.	do	1 Sept 79	1 Nov 80	present
Martindale, Jno.	pt	4 May 78	16 Aug 80	missing }
	Fife Major	1 July 80		

MUSTERS OF MARYLAND TROOPS, VOL. I.

Names.	Rank.	Time of Service. Enlisted.	Discharged.	Remarks.
Miller, Jacob	pt	4 June 78	28 feb 79	discharged
Martin, Lond.	do	1 do	14 do	do
May, Richard	do	23 May 78	5 April 79	do
Mudd, Bent.	do	9 feb 79		
	Sergt	1 July 80	1 Nov 80	present
McNaughton, Peter	do	10 dec 76	do	do
Morrison, Jno.	fifer	9 April 78	do	do
McCormick, Jno.	do	1 Oct 77	do	do
Moore, Francis	pt	25 April 79		
Medcalf, Richd.	do	6 Mar 78		
McCoy, Hugh	pt	15 May 79	16 Aug 80	missing
Moran, Azell	do	14 June 79		
	Drum	1 Aug 79	21 Aug 80	do
Miles, Walter	pt	1 Sept 79	1 Nov 80	present
	Corpl	1 Jan 80	1 April 83	discharged
Medcaff, Robt.	pt	June 80	12 Aug 80	deserted
Millet, George	pt. mus'd	do	16 Aug 80	missing
Millstead, Jno.	do	1 feb 80	1 Nov 80	present
Menitry, Gueld'd		29 Jan 80	do	do

SECOND REGIMENT.—*Beging. with the Muster Rolls for January*, 1778.

Names	Rank	Enlisted	Discharged	Remarks
Marshall, Wm.	Surgn. Mate			removed to hospital
Moore, Hezekiah	Qr. M. S.	3 June 77		promoted
Mead, James	Drum M.	15 Aug 77	1 Nov 80	present
Miller, John O. S.	Sergt	4 Mar 77	10 Jan 80	discharged
Martin, Robt.	Corpl		do	do
Masterson, Jno.	pt	do	do	do
Murphy, James	do		1 June 78	died
McDonald, Stephn.	do		14 feb 78	deserted
McLaughlan, Wm.	do	1 Sept 77	1 Nov 80	present
Moser, Cruise,	pt	6 Jan 77	16 Aug 80	killed
McGraw, Christ.	Drum	1 Aprl 77	1 Nov 80	present
McAndrew, Pat.	pt		28 Jan 78	deserted
Mason, Caleb	Corpl		10 Jan 80	discharged
Miles, John	pt		do	do
Mahoney, Clemt.	do		22 Jan 78	in Hospt., time expired
Joined April Muster Roll 78			1 April 80	10 Jan 80 discharged
Mitchell, Henry 10 Jany 80 discharged	Corpl Sergt. 1 Aug 78, reducd to pt. 27 Aug 78, Sergt. 27 [Sept 78			
McNemara, Pat.	pt		10 Jan 80	discharged
Malone, Andrew	do corpl	1 Feb 78	do	do

MUSTERS OF MARYLAND TROOPS, VOL. I.

Names.	Rank.	Time of Service. Enlisted.	Time of Service. Discharged.	Remarks.
Mason, James	pt		12 dec 79	discharged
More, William	do	17 Mar 77	16 Aug 80	prisoner
Murphy, Anthy.	do Sergt	1 Jan 80	do	deserted
Magragh, Jno.	pt		1 April 80	do
McHendricks, James	do Corpl	20 July 78	10 Jan 80	discharged
Murphy, Michael	pt		7 do	deserted
Martin, John	do		22 Jan 78	do
Maloy, Michael	do		do	do
Maynard, Peter	do Corpl	1 feb 80	16 Aug 80	do
Marlow, Saml.	pt		29 Sept 79	discharged
Mentges, Chrisn.	do	18 feb 77	18 feb 80	do
Melvin, Peter	do	4 do	1 Nov 80	present
Mockbee, Wm.	pt		Nov 80	not heard of
Martin, John	do	12 feb 77	16 Aug 80	prisoner
Maloy, Barney	do		1 Nov 80	present
McCalmont, Jas.	Surgn	1 Jan 78	10 June 79	resigned
Moore, Reubin	pt	27 dec 77	1 Nov 80	present
Moore, William	do	do	do	do
Mann, William	do	30 Mar 78	joined again 12 Sept 79, 1 Nov 80 present	
McFarlen, James	do		19 May 78	deserted
Miller, James	do	10 April 78		
Murphey, James	do	18 Mar 78	20 July 78	died
McDugle, Jno.	do	21 April 78	1 July 78	died
McConneken, Jno.	do	6 do	do	do
Matthews, Saml.	do	28 do		
McAdams, Jno.	do	15 Jan 78	Sergt 10 Jan 80, 1 Nov 80 present	
McDonald, Alex.	do	11 Mar 78	17 July 80	deserted
McGee, John	do	29 Jan 78	8 Mar 79	discharged
Matthews, Thos.	do	26 feb 78	18 June 79	deserted
Magraugh, Jas.	do	18 do	1 Nov 80	present
McCay, Henry	do	16 do	15 Aprl 78	deserted
McGraw, John	do	2 May 78	18 Oct 78	died
Mulhulland, Arthur	do	13 do	1 Nov 80	present
Morgan, Johnson	do	22 April 78	25 July 78	died
McCarty, Thimothy	do	9 May 78	17 July 80	deserted
McCoy, William	do	30 April 78	16 Aug 80	prisoner
McKenney, Jno.	do		dec 78	deserted
Mattingley, Thos.	pt	31 May 78	3 April 79	discharged
Mattingley, Phil.	do	do	do	do
Mackey, Jacob	do	1 June 78	do	do
Metcalf, Jno.	do	do	15 July 78	died
Mansell, James	do		4 Aug 79	deserted

140 *Records of Maryland Troops in the Continental Service*

MUSTERS OF MARYLAND TROOPS, VOL. I.

Names.	Rank.	Time of Service. Enlisted.	Discharged.	Remarks.
Maxwell, Wm.	pt		12 Nov 78	deserted
Miles, Fredk.	do	25 April 78	1 May 81	discharged
	Corpl	10 Jan 80	1 Nov 80	present
Mason, James	pt	29 May do	1 Oct 80	ditto
Mathews, Wm.	do	1 June 78	Nov 80	not heard of, afterwards joined Invalids }
Murphy, Jno.	do	3 May 78	2 April 79	deserted
Manning, Hy.	do		1 Aprl 80	discharged
McKean, Levin	do	20 do	3 April 79	do
Mitchell, Levin	do	do	do	do
Moxey, Gregory	do	do	24 dec 78	do
Medlicutt, Jas.	do	25 do	26 do	deserted
Mahood, Jno.	do	do	Mar 79	discharged
McCurdy, Jno.	do	do	do	do
McClarey, Bassel	do	do	26 dec 78	deserted
McCallister, Jos.	do	28 do	24 do	discharged
Marlow, Butler	do		10 Jan 80	do
Malone, Jno.	do		20 June 79	deserted
Meglamery, Edwd.	do		1 do 80	discharged
McCormick, Mathew	do	30 do 79	16 Aug 80	prisoner
Moore, Richd.	pt		15 Nov 79	deserted
Morain, Jno.	do	3 Aug 79	1 Nov 80	present
Martin, Joseph	do	22 May 79	22 July 79	deserted
Mason, Caleb	Ensn	26 Jan 80	16 Aug 80	killed Camden
Mitchell, Richd.	pt	20 Mar 80	1 Nov 80	present
Mie, Thomas	do	May 78	do	do

Third Regiment.—*Beginning 77.*

Marbury, Jos.	Capt	10 dec 76		
Mudd, Henry	Corpl	21 May 79	}	
McCanh, Jos.	do	5 Aprl 77		
McNorton, Wm.	do	16 May 77	} all out November 77	
Maddox, Notly	do	18 feb 77		
McPherson, A.	do	9 May 77	} dec 77	died
Molohon, Wm.	Lieut	10 Dec 76	1 July 78	resigned
McMullen, Timo. or McMahon	Corp Sergt Sergt. Mt.	do 7 Sep 77 28 Aug 78	} joined in Carolina from Pennsylvania	
Mansfield, Jas.	fife		1 Mar 79	discharged
Manning, Wm.	pt		15 Mar 78	deserted
McLaughlin, Nic.	do	11 May 77	1 Nov 80	present
Morton, James	do	do	21 Sep 80	deserted
Mileter, Pat.	do	25 Mar 77	25 Mar 80	discharged

MUSTERS OF MARYLAND TROOPS, VOL. I.

NAMES.	RANK.	Enlisted.	Discharged.	REMARKS.
McDonald, Arch.	pt	6 May 77	28 Aug 80	deserted
Manger, Nic.	Lieut	20 feb 77	Capt.	
McCay, John	Corpl	1 Aprl 77	1 April 80	discharged
Mattehannan, Wm.	pt	2 Aug do		
Martin, Phil.	do	4 do		
Murray, James	Sergt pt	20 June 77	Aprl & May 79	left out the [Rolls
McGuire, Michl.	pt	1 April 77		
Menton, Danl.	do		1 Nov 80	present
Martin, Michl.	do	12 Jan 77	12 Jan 80	discharged
McLamar, Timoy.	do	do	do	do
Morris, Thomas	do		16 Aug 80	missing
McGuire, Jas.	do	10 do	5 Jan 80	discharged
McGuire, Jno.	Sergt	26 Mar 77	} promoted Ensign	
	Sergt. Major	26 Sept		
	Adjt	28 Mar 78		
Morris, Michl.	pt	7 July 77	25 Jan 78	died
Manfield, Robt.	do	15 April 77	1 May 78	to Invalids
Mercer, Jno.	do	10 Mar 77	10 Mar 80	discharged
Murphy, Danl.	do		June 79	left out the Roll
McDermot, Tho.	do	12 Jan 78		
McGee, Hugh	do	28 do	14 April 78	deserted
Morris, Jno.	Sergt		20 May 80	discharged
McDaniel, Elisha	Corpl		12 Dec 77	died
Minning, Jno.	pt	30 Oct 77	1 Dec 79	deserted
McCann, Jno.	do	21 July 77	dec 77	do
			20 Aug 80	do
McMullen, Jas.	do		April 78	struck off
Morrow, Wm.	do	25 April 78		
Murphy, Chs.	pt	17 April 78		
	Corpl	1 Sept 79		
	Sergt	1 Jan 80		
Maires, Saml.	pt	21 do	Sept 79	struck off
Morgan, Richd.	do	22 do	Oct 78	died
Mackey, Tho.	do	20 do	Jan 80	struck off
Magson, Mard.	do	do	do	do
McKim, Ben.	do		1 do	time expired
McGee, William	do	20 Apl 78	1 Nov 80	present
McGee, Charles	do	28 do	do	do
McAtee, Leond.	do	26 do	19 feb 79	discharged
McAtee, Thomas	do	do	do	do
Main, David	do	2 Mar 78		
	Corpl	1 July 78	16 Aug 80	prisoner
Mingo, Jos.	pt	22 April 78		
Mumford, Chs.	do		20 Jan 79	discharged

MUSTERS OF MARYLAND TROOPS, VOL. I.

NAMES.	RANK.	TIME OF SERVICE. Enlisted.	Discharged.	REMARKS.
Moyland, Dens.	pt		19 dec 79	deserted
Moses, Jacob	do		1 Oct 80	present
Morris, Jno.	do	14 do	1 Nov 80	do
Morgan, Jereh.	do	16 May 78	14 Oct 78	died
McCalley, Jno.	do	19 do	4 April 79	discharged
McCartney, Edwd.	do		June 78	do
McCummert, Michl.	pt	30 April 78		
McDonah, Michl.	do	30 May 78	30 Oct 79	deserted
McDonald, Wm. D.	Sergt		1 Nov 80	present
Matthews, Jno.	pt	11 June 78	do	do
McCarty, Wm.	do	30 do	16 Aug 80	missing
Mayhew, Thomas	do	20 July 78	23 Jan 79	discharged
Mayhew, Jona.	do	do	reinlisted	see below
Mullens, Timy.	do	19 May 78	16 Aug 80	missing
McMillion, Wm.	Sergt		June 79	out the Roll
Mahugh, Jona.	pt	9 Jan 79	1 Nov 80	present
May, Joseph	do	4 June 78	16 Aug 80	missing
Mobley, Thomas	do	5 do	12 April 79	discharged
McLaughlan, Mark	do	20 Mar 77	1 Nov 80	present
McCloud, Hugh	do	5 Jan 77	5 Jan 80	discharged
Murray, John	do	7 feb 79	to Invalids, dismissed or furlough July 11th, 1783	
Murnet, Michl.	do	30 April 78	do	do
Miller, John	do		6 feb 80	to Invalids
Moore, Matthew	do	18 May 78	1 Nov 80	present
Monghon, Pat.	do	23 April 79		
Matthews, Geo.	do	11 May 79		
Mandewitt, Phil.	do	28 Nov 79	4 Jan 80	deserted
Mills, John	Corpl	27 Mar 80	1 Nov 80	present
McFarlane, Alex.	pt		do	do

OCTOBER MUSTER, 1780.

NAMES.	RANK.	Enlisted.	Discharged.	REMARKS.
Mitchell, Wm.	pt	15 feb 80	1 Nov 80	present
Mattingly, Chs.	do		do	do
Mohan, Patk.	do		16 Aug 80	missing, see
Monghon, (or) Mahorn				[above

FOURTH REGIMENT.—*Beginning December*, 1777.

NAMES.	RANK.	Enlisted.	Discharged.	REMARKS.
McAllester, Joel[1]	Sergt	8 dec 76	8 dec 79	discharged
Mason, John	pt	6 do	do	deserted
McKenny, Robt.	do	30 Jan 77	30 Jan 80	discharged

[1] Oldham's.

MUSTERS OF MARYLAND TROOPS, VOL. I.

Names.	Rank.	Time of Service. Enlisted.	Discharged.	Remarks.
Murphey, Jno.	pt			deserted
McGain, Pat.	do		feb 78	do
Mansell, Richd.	do	7 dec 76		
pt 1 June 78	Sergt	1 Aprl 78	26 Oct 80	do
Merino, Charles	pt	19 Jan 77	19 Jan 80	discharged
McNeall, Jno.[1]	Corpl	Exchanged for Thomas Potts		
		20 May 77	20 May 80	dischd., reinlisted
Murphey, Cornes.	pt	7 Apl 77	1 Nov 80	present
Murphey, Tho.[2]	do	dec 76	Jan 80	deserted
Mumford, Robt.	do		15 June 78	discharged
Moore, Mathew[3]	do	76	1 Nov 80	present
Menchim, Humpry.	do	1 May 77	do	do
Moreton, Joshua	do	feb 77	July mus. 79	died Maryland
McDaniel, Thos.	do	8 Jan 77		
	Corpl	1 Aprl 80	July 80	deserted
Miller, William	pt			see the other side
McIntire, Danl.	pt		1 Nov 80	present
Martin, John	do			
Murphey, David[4]	do		3 May 78	deserted
Mathews, John, (or Wm.)	do	16 May 77	10 Jan 80	do
McDermot, Owen	do	19 do	1 Oct 80	present
reinlisted ——				
McCarty, Jere.	do	25 do	Apl & May 79	left out
McIntosh, Geo.[5]	do		10 Aprl 80	do the Roll
	Corpl	26 dec 77		
	private	31 Oct 78		discharged
McKenzie, Brice	pt	6 dec 76	6 dec 79	do
Murphey, Pat.	do	6 Jan 77	6 Jan 80	do
reind., entd. below				deserted Oct 80
Marshall, Edwd.	do			
Moyston, Edwd.	do	6 dec 76	6 dec 79	discharged
Marks, John[2]	do	30 May 77	14 May 80	do
Morton, Vachel	do	1 feb 77	1 feb 80	do
Murphey, Thos.	do	9 feb 77	1 Nov 80	present
Manwaring, Chs.	do		30 June 78	died
McAway, Chas.[6]	do	18 Aug 77	1 Nov 80	present.
Mattinson, Danl.	do	10 feb 77	13 feb 80	discharged
Mallows, Robert[7]	do	10 Apl 77	10 Apl 80	time expired, 20
Millions, (or Miller), Wm.[8]	pt	25 July 77		[Apl 80 dischd.
	Corpl	1 April 79	17 July 80	discharged
to Riely's Co. & promd. to	Sergt	1 July 79		

[1] Norwood's.   [2] Spurrier's.   [3] Godman's.   [4] Lansdale's.   [5] Sellman's.
[6] Bowie's.   [7] Burgess'.   [8] Riely's.

MUSTERS OF MARYLAND TROOPS, VOL. I.

Names.	Rank.	Time of Service. Enlisted.	Discharged.	Remarks.
Mustin, Richard	pt	27 Mar 77		
	Corpl	1 Apl 78	1 Mar 80	time expired
	pt	1 feb 79	1 April 80	discharged
McCormick, Jno.	do	1 Aug 77	April & May 79	not heard of
Malone, Conner	pt		Jan 78	left out the Roll
McAway, Thomas	do	18 Aug 77	dec 79	deserted, joined
Murphey, John[1]	do	17 Jan 78	16 Aug 80	missing
Miller, John[2]	do	12 feb 78	June 78	left out
Madden, Chris.[3]	do	27 Apl 78	7 Aug 79	deserted
Mathias, James[4]	do	3 do	1 Nov 80	present
McCormick, Thos.[1]	do	6 May 78	23 Jan 80	deserted
Maxwell, Richd.[5]	do	3 do	23 Oct 78	died
Smith's, late Spurrier's				
McGlachlan, Corns.	do	4 do	13 dec 79	deserted
McCarty, James[6]	do	31 Mar 78		
Riely's, late Bowie's	Corpl	1 Mar 80	16 Aug 80	prisoner
	Sergt	1 May 78		
Murry, John[7]	pt	1 May 80	dec 79	deserted
McKew, Thomas	do	19 do	1 June 79	discharged
Morton, Archl.	do	26 June 78	June 80	do
McDonald, Jos.[3]	do	11 May 78		
	Corpl	1 Oct 78		
	private	1 Mar 79	16 Aug 80	prisoner
	Corpl	1 Aug 79		
McGinity, Pat.[8]	pt	30 Mar 78	do	missing
McLone, James[4]	do	6 dec 76	do	do
prisoner 22 Aug 77, Joined 23 June 78				
Murphy, Timoy.	pt	16 May 78	1 Nov 80	present
Montgomery, Alex.[6]	Sergt	19 do		
	pt	21 feb 79	July 80	deserted
McKinley, Jas.	do	22 May 78	15 feb 80	do
McMillion, Hugh	do	13 do		
	Corpl	1 Sept 78	1 Nov 80	present
	Sergt	1 July 79		
Miles, John[9]	pt	17 May 78	July 80	deserted
May and June Roll 80, deserted time not known				
Morris, William	pt	28 May 78	16 Aug 80	missing
McAway, Stephen[10]	do	7 June 79	15 May 80	deserted
Merican, Edwd.[7]	do	11 Aug 79	28 dec 79	do
Murphy, Pat.[1]	do		14 Oct 80	do

[1] Sellman's.   [2] Bowie's.   [3] Norwood's.   [4] Lansdale's.   [5] Smith's.
[6] Riely's.   [7] Oldham's.   [8] Godman's.   [9] Burgess'.   [10] Belt's.

MUSTERS OF MARYLAND TROOPS, VOL. I.

Names.	Rank.	Time of Service. Enlisted.	Discharged.	Remarks.
McKenny, Lawr.[1]	pt		16 Aug 80	missing
Marwood, Andrew[2]	do		Oct 80	deserted
McKnight, Jno.	do	23 feb 79	1 do	present

RAWLINGS' REGIMENT.

Names.	Rank.	Enlisted.	Discharged.	Remarks.
McCartny, Jere.	pt	29 feb 79		
McKann, Jno.	Sergt	2 Aug 76		deserted
McGowan, Ben.	pt	22 do	12 Nov 76	do
McCulloch, Wm.	do	6 July		
McCann, Pat.	do	22 Aug		
Morton, Jos.	do	2 do	18 feb 77	died
McBride, Jno.	do			
McCreary, Thos.			17 Aug	deserted
Marlow, Wm.	do			
McMachen, Peter	do			
Mitchell, Conrad	do		6 July 79	discharged
McVay, James	do		10 June	deserted
Markwell, Wm.	do		8 Mar 80	discharged
McBride, Jno.	fife			
Magruder, Enoch 1 yr.	Sergt			
McAttee, Saml.	pt		1 Aug 79	do
Marlon, John 1 yr.	do			
Morgan, Jno.	pt		8 May	deserted
McKenny, Rodk.	do			
McCartny, Peter	do	11 April		
Mains, Francis	do	28 Mar		
McKinny, Felix	do	1 May		
McAdams, Alixd.	do	3 April		
Mains, George	do	10 do		
Miller, David	do	5 do		
McClean, Lackn.	do	7 do		
Murphy, Michl.	do	16 Oct		
McCoy, Eneas	do	8 April		
McDonald, Jno. 6 mo.		1 mar 79		
McMahan, Peter	do		10 June	do
McKinsie, Thos.	do			
McFarren, Walter	Drum			
McCord, Saml.	pt	30 mar		
McGuire, Pat. 6 mo.		12 mar		
McGlaughland, J. 6 mo.		30 do		

[1] Spurrier's.
[2] Hoop's.

MUSTERS OF MARYLAND TROOPS, VOL. I.

Names.	Rank.	Time of Service. Enlisted.	Time of Service. Discharged.	Remarks.
First Regiment.				
Nixon, William	pt	10 dec 76	16 Mar 78	deserted
Nicholls, Becket	do	24 Jan 77		never joined
Naylor, Alexr.	Sergt	10 dec 76		transferred
Nicholson, Nichl.	pt	do	27 dec 79	discharged }
reinlisted 15 Aprl	Sergt		1 Nov 80	present }
Naylor, Nicholas	do			
	Q. M. S.	Corpl 10 Dec 76		
Nayry, John	Sergt	10 June	1 Nov 80	present }
time out 1 Jan 80, reinlisted 11 Mar 80				}
Neagle, William	pt	10 Dec 76	4 feb 77	dead
Nash, Barnard	do	do	17 Mar 77	do [charged
Neale, John	do	do	Sergt 25 July 78, 27 dec 79 dis-	
Nithington, Jere.	do	28 feb 77	20 feb 80	discharged
Nolan, Patk.	do	10 dec 76	27 dec 79	do
Noyes, William	S. Major	do	do	do
Neale, Thomas	pt	4 May 78	1 Nov 80	present
Nelson, John	Ensn	26 Jan 80		
Second Regiment.—*Beginning Jany., 1778.*				
Noble, William	pt		29 Aprl 78	deserted
Norton, George	do	1 Mar 77	8 Mar 80	discharged
Nutt, George	do	10 Jan 77	10 Jan 80	do
Noble, John	do		1 do	do
	Sergt	1 June 78		
Nesbitt, Richd.	pt	11 May 78	7 Mar 79	deserted
Nickleson, Henry	pt	4 Aprl 78	}	
	Corpl	10 Jan 80	} 1 Nov 80	present
Nickleson, Steph.	pt	18 do	} 16 Aug 80	prisoner
	Corpl	1 feb 79	}	
	Sergt	10 Jan 80	} furlough	
Newton, William	pt	10 dec 76	1 Nov 80	present
Nienbar, Thomas	do A.S.		June 80	} discharged
			20 May 80	}
Noble, Martin	do	26 June 79	16 Aug 80	missing, died of wounds
Third Regiment.—*Beginning 77.*				
Newnan, Wm.	pt	18 Aprl 77	1 Jan 80	deserted
Nevill, Philip	do	12 May 77		
Nowland, John	do		26 Jan 79	to Invalids }
			18 July 81	deserted }
Neall, Charles	do	26 April 78		

MUSTERS OF MARYLAND TROOPS, VOL. I.

NAMES.	RANK.	Enlisted.	Discharged.	REMARKS.
Nailor, Joshua	pt	30 Mar 78	16 Aug 80	prisoner
	Sergt	24 Oct 78		
Norris, John	pt	29 May 78	4 April 79	discharged
Nunan, John	do	1 July 78	6 dec 78	deserted
Nisbet, Barney	do	25 April 78	16 Aug 80	missing
Nisbit, Charles	do	30 do	1 April 79	discharged
Nicholls, Sael	do	11 do	11 Aprl 81	do
Neagle, Morris	do		16 Aug 80	prisoner
		continued to the end of the war		
Nonan, William	do		see above	
Nott, Nathanl.	Corpl		16 Aug 80	prisoner

FOURTH REGIMENT.—*Beginning December, 77.*

NAMES.	RANK.	Enlisted.	Discharged.	REMARKS.
Nujant, Pat.[1]	pt	15 dec 76	16 dec 79	discharged
Norris, Philip[2]	do		31 Oct 78	died
Nelson, John	do		22 May 80	discharged
Norwood, Edwd.	Captain	10 do	29 Sept 78	left the service
Newton, Thomas[2]	pt		3 May 80	deserted
Noland, Patk.	do		25 dec 79	discharged
	reinlisted 15 Aug 80		29 Aug 80	died
Naylor, Joshua[4]	Corpl	1 Aug 77	20 May 80	discharged
Nash, Chrisn.	pt		Jan 78	left out the Roll
Nicholson, Anthy.[5]	do	6 Aug 77	feb 79	dead
Nicholl, Archd.[6]	do	10 feb 78	Aug 80	deserted
Nicholson, Geo.	do	7 Mar 78	16 Sept 79	died
Nuttall, Joseph[7]	do	14 Aprl 78	3 June 79	to Invalids
Smith's, late Spurrier's	Joined 17 April 81			discharged
Norton, Lawrence[8]	do	21 Aprl 78	July 80	deserted
Riely's, late Bowie's				
Noland, Thomas[2]	do	23 do	16 Aug 80	missing
Nelson, Richd.[9]	do	20 May 78		
Nason, Saml.[8]	do	20 Aprl 78	5 Sept 78	discharged
Nowland, James[2]	do	18 Nov 78	16 Aug 80	missing
	Corpl	1 July 79		
	Sergt	1 April 80		
Newcomb, Robt.[1]	pt	25 April 78	dec 79	deserted
Needham, Wm.	Sergt	3 June 79	1 Nov 80	present
Nicholls, Edward[10]	pt	21 May 79	20 May 80	deserted
			July 80	do
Nicholls, Jos.	do		1 Nov 80	present

[1] Oldham's.   [2] Norwood's.   [3] Godman's.   [4] Bowie's.   [5] Burgess'.   [6] Lansdale's
[7] Smith's.   [8] Riely's.   [9] Selman's.   [10] Belt's.

MUSTERS OF MARYLAND TROOPS, VOL. I.

Names.	Rank.	Time of Service. Enlisted.	Discharged.	Remarks.
\multicolumn{5}{c}{RAWLINGS' REGIMENT.}				
Norris, Ben.	Corpl	20 July 76		
Nailor, Isaac	pt		9 Aug 79	discharged
Neale, Joseph		5 feb		
\multicolumn{5}{c}{FIRST REGIMENT.}				
Ofield, John	pt	10 dec 76	1 Jan 80	discharged
Owings, John	do	do	6 Mar 78	deserted
Oneal, John	do	do	24 May 77	do
Ostrow, William	do	17 June 77	1 Oct 79	
did not return to his furlough, discharged by G. Smallwood 20 April 80				
Oneal, John	pt	11 April 78	23 Jan 80	deserted
Owings, Joseph	do	5 June 78	feb 79	discharged
Owings, Saml.	do	mustered	joined	1 April 80
\multicolumn{5}{c}{SECOND REGIMENT.—Beginning January Muster, 1778.}				
Ormond, Wm.	pt		13 June 78	discharged
O'Boyle		see Boyles		
Orm, William	Corpl		10 Jan 80	do
Orm, Moses	pt		do	do
Outterbridge, Leod.	do	1 May 78	1 Nov 80	present, 25 April 81 discharged
Oaster, (or Ostend), Henry	do	14 April do	see H. Austin	
O'Bryan, Jno.	do	4 Mar 77	16 Aug 80	deserted
Orme, Joseph	do			
Owings, Saml.	do			
	Corpl	3 Oct 78	10 Jan 80	discharged
\multicolumn{5}{c}{THIRD REGIMENT.—Beginning 77.}				
Owings, Arthur	Sergt	private	15 Aug 78	
Osmond, John	pt	17 May 77	1 Nov 80	present
Osborn, William	do	15 Aug 77	24 Jan 78	died
O'Connell, Wm.	do	21 April do	6 do	do
Ogden, James	do			
Owens, John	do	11 Mar 78	dec 78	do
Overcreek, Jos.	do	4 June 78	16 Aug 80	missing
Oram, Cooper	do	30 April 78		
Oliver, Nicholas	pt	May 79	struck off	

MUSTERS OF MARYLAND TROOPS, VOL. I.

Names.	Rank.	Time of Service. Enlisted.	Discharged.	Remarks.

Fourth Regiment.—*Beginning December, 77.*

Names.	Rank.	Enlisted.	Discharged.	Remarks.
Oneil, Hugh[1]	pt	1 dec 76	15 Nov 78	deserted
Owings, James	do	do	1 dec 79	discharged
O'Conner, Dennis[2]	Sergt		Aug 78	left out
O'Keiff, Constantine	pt		June 78	mustered not heard of
Oram, John[3]	do		13 April 80	discharged
Onnell, Christopr.	do		12 Jan 80	do
Oldham, Edward	Lieut	10 dec 76	Capt. 20 May 77	
O'Donnally, Thos., (or Timy.)[4]	pt		31 Jan 78	deserted
O'Quinn, Danl.[5]	do	2 April 77	1 Nov 80	present
O'Hara, George[6]	do	6 May 78	1 April 79	deserted
Riely's, late Bowie's				
Oram, Saml.[7]	Drum	7 April 78	1 Nov 80	present

Rawlings' Regiment.

Names.	Rank.	Enlisted.	Discharged.	Remarks.
O'Hara, Patk.	pt			

First Regiment.

Names.	Rank.	Enlisted.	Discharged.	Remarks.
Peake, Nathan		certified by Ensign B. Burgess that his time of service		[expired 17 Nov 82
Pearce, Ezekiel	pt	10 dec 76	12 May 79	prisr., dischd. 27 dec 79
Parr, William	pt	do	16 Sept	missing, deserted
Plant, John	Corpl	do	1 July 78	appd. a Sergt.
Pearce, Joshua	pt	do		
Paine, George	do	1 Mar 77	18 Mar 80	discharged
Phillips, William	do	8 do	12 Mar 77	deserted
Pearce, John	do		7 Sept 80	discharged
Pindall, Nicks.	do	3 feb 77	31 July 79	died
Parkinson, Jno.	do	7 Mar	16 Aug 80	prisoner
Phillips, John	do	15 Mar	do	missing
Porter, Charles	Sergt	10 dec 76	17 April	promoted
Powel, John	pt	do		
Peck, Nathl. reinlisted	do	do	1 Nov 80	present
Palmer, Anthy.	do	8 feb 77	27 dec 79	discharged
Peale, James	Lieut	10 dec 76		
	Capt		1 June 79	resigned 2 June 79
Price, Edward	pt	do	20 Mar 77	deserted
Posey, James	do	18 feb 77		
Posey, Benja.	do	9 Mar 77	7 Mar 80	discharged

[1] Oldham's. [2] Norwood's. [3] Godman's. [4] Spurrier's. [5] Burgess'. [6] Riely's. [7] Smith's.

MUSTERS OF MARYLAND TROOPS, VOL. I.

Names.	Rank.	Time of Service. Enlisted.	Discharged.	Remarks.
Pope, James	pt	10 dec 77	22 April 77	for J. Donovan 3 Regt.
Pike, James	do	21 Mar 77	21 Mar 80	discharged
Priest, John	do	27 April 77	11 Sept 77	missing
Paine, Jerem.	do	10 Mar 77	2 Aug 77	died
Pringle, John	do	6 feb 78	16 Aug 80	missing
Powell, Joseph	do	7 May 78	19 Aug 80	deserted
Phelps, Benja.		20 April 78	27 Oct 78	dead
Poling, William		21 May 78	1 Oct 80	present
Penn, John	pt	16 do	28 feb 79	discharged
Penn, Stephen	do	do	do	do
Posey, Bennett	do	5 June 78	5 April 79	do
Proctor, Charles	do	29 May 78	3 Nov 78	dead
Proctor, Walter	do	22 Aprl 78	10 Mar 79	do
Perrie, John	do		1 April 80	deserted
Perrie, Simon	do	12 May 78	1 Nov 80	present
Price, John	pt 1 July 80 Corpl	6 May 78 1 June 79 joined —	} 16 Aug 80	prisoner
Pennuwell, Chas.	pt	2 July 79	Sept 79	transfd. to 2 Regt.
Phearson, Jos.		5 July	Jan 80	prisoner
Parsons, William			29 Nov 79	deserted
Pain, John	1 musr.	June 80		Artillery
Pherson, William		22 June 79	1 Nov 80	present
Purdy, John	Sergt		see 2d Regt.	
Phillips, William	pt	1 May 78	do do	
Praul, Edward	Lieut Capt	1 Jany 77 10 June do	}	
Price, Benja.	pt		1 Nov 80	present

Second Regiment.

Price, Thomas	Col	10 dec 76	30 April 80	resigned
Price, John	Q. M. again Sergt	10 Jan 80		
Pitts, William joined feby musr. reduced to pt	Sergt. M.	15 Sept 77 27 Aug 78	} 1 Nov 80 left out of musr. for Sept 78	present
Porter, Philemon	do Corpl	1 Jan 78	10 Jan 80	discharged
Powers, Thomas	pt	8 Mar 77	17 July 80	deserted
Pallet, James	do	19 do	16 Aug 80	do
Price, Benja.	Lieut	10 Apl 77	Capt. 1 July 79	
Perkle, Jacob	pt			
Parrot, Chrisr.	Sergt		10 Jan 80	discharged }
reinlisted in service to take up deserts till Aug 80 by Col. Forrest				

MUSTERS OF MARYLAND TROOPS, VOL. I.

Names.	Rank.	Time of Service. Enlisted.	Discharged.	Remarks.
Payn, Benjamin	pt		10 Jan 80	discharged
Powell, William	do		do	do
Purdy, John	Sergt		4 Mar 78	deserted
Pickeron, John	pt	13 feb 78	1 Nov 80	present
Peters, Joseph	do	9 May 78	18 July 78	dead
Pritchard, James	do	15 do		do
Parker, John	do	18 April 78	April 80 transfd. to Invalids	
Preston, And.	do	19 May do	4 July 79	died
Philips, John	do	24 feb 78	15 April 78	deserted
Pennington, Jno.	do		Sept 78	died
Phillips, William	do / Corpl	1 May 78 / 1 Jan 80	} 16 Aug 80	deserted
Phillips, Henry	pt	16 do	1 Nov 80	present
Payne, Barny	do	29 do	3 April 79	discharged
Purtle, Robert	pt	25 May 78		time out, discharged
Prather, Zach.	do / Sergt	1 do / 10 Jan 80	} 1 Nov 80	present
Pagram, William	pt	2 June do	16 Aug 80	prisoner
Plummer, Cupid	do	1 Aprl do	1 Nov 80	present
Plummer, Obe.	do	do	do	do
Pierce, Aquilla	do	4 do	do	do
Pierce, Danl.	Drum pt	18 do	do	transferred
Parsley, Edwd.	do	25 May 78	26 dec 78	deserted
Pew, Humphrey	Corpl / Sergt	20 Sept 78	} 10 Jan 80	discharged
Phillips, David	pt	19 Mar 77	12 Sept 78	deserted
Pollard, Kinsey	do	20 May 78	78	died
Patton, John	do	do	3 April 79	discharged
Perry, Charles	do		Mar 79	do
Purchass, Wm.	do / Corpl / pt	15 Aug 79 / 1 May 80 / 31 Oct 80	} 1 Nov 80	present
Pennywell, Chas.	do	2 July 79	24 Nov 79	deserted
Penney, John	do	April 80	1 Nov 80	present
Phips, Thomas	do	6 May 78	4 May 81	discharged

Brought from letter F

THIRD REGIMENT.—*Beginning* 77.

Pearson, Edward	pt	13 May 77	8 May 80	discharged
Pratt, William	Corpl / Sergt	1 April 77 / 15 Mar 78	} 2 April 80	time expired
Phillips, David	pt		18 Aug 80	deserted
Price, William	do		Nov 77	do

Records of Maryland Troops in the Continental Service

MUSTERS OF MARYLAND TROOPS, VOL. I.

Names.	Rank.	Time of Service. Enlisted.	Discharged.	Remarks.
Paton, John	pt		15 Mar 78	deserted
Pepper, Josep	do	11 May 77	1 Nov 80	discharged
Purdie, Edwd.	do	5 Mar 77	16 Aug 80	missing
Procter, Richd.	do	4 June do	1 Nov 80	present
Peck, Joshua	do	6 Aprl do	dec 79	deserted
Pitman, John	do	10 Jan do	12 Jan 80	discharged
Parry, John	Corpl	4 Sept 77		
pt 1 Sept 78	Sergt	21 June 78	28 Aprl 79	deserted
Pope, James	pt	10 dec 76		
Parriott, Is.	do		4 Aug 77	died
Pike, Thomas	do	24 Nov 77	1 Sept 78	deserted
Parriott, Wm.	do			do
Price, Thomas	pay M.	Lieut	11 feb 80	
Patrick, George	pt	25 Mar 78	18 Aug 80	
Pickard, John	do	26 Aprl 78	1 Mar 79	discharged
Price, William	do	do	Jan 80	struck off
Parker, Danl.	do	20 do	June 78	deserted
Pasgrove, (or Pascoe), John	Sergt	6 feb 78	15 July 78	do
Poole, Benja.	pt	3 April 78	1 Nov 78	discharged
Prigg, Charles	pt	9 Aug 77	1 Oct 79	to Invalids
Petmore, Richd.	do	12 May 78	16 Aug 79	deserted
Pendergast, Jno.	do	27 April 78	1 Nov 80	present
Pendleberry, Marmd.	do	21 do	16 Aug 80	missing
Preston, Stephen	do	21 May 78	do	do
Powell, John	Drum	13 do	2 do	deserted
Pike, William	pt	5 June 78	16 do	missing
Pennock, Jona.	do	do	do	do
Pennington, Jno.	do	29 May 78	do	do
Peters, William	do	25 June 78	1 Nov 80	present
Perrin, Philip	do	20 April 78	16 Aug 80	missing
Pinnuch, Jona.	do	9 Jan 79	see above	
Peterkin, Philip	Sergt		20 Aug 80	deserted, pt.when
Preston, Saml.	pt			[deserted
Price, John	do	transferred to 1st Regt. by prior right		
Parmer, Thomas	do	21 May 79	22 dec 79	transferred to In-
			21 June 80	deserted [valids

Fourth Regiment.—*Beginning December, 77.*

Pindell, Richd.	Sergn. Mate			
	Sergn.	11 Nov 77		
Purcell, William[1]	pt	6 Aug 77	16 Aug 80	
Philips, John	do		24 feb 80	deserted

[1] Norwood's.

MUSTERS OF MARYLAND TROOPS, VOL. I.

NAMES.	RANK.	TIME OF SERVICE. Enlisted.	Discharged.	REMARKS.
Patterson, Wm.	pt	Jan 78		Excd. for P. Doran
Parrish, Edward[1]	Corpl			
	Sergt	1 June 79	8 dec 79	discharged
Penn, John	pt		10 dec 77	died
Prior, William[2]	do	30 May 77	1 Nov 80	present
Prudent, Thomas	do	4 Mar 77	11 June 80	deserted
Popham, Samuel[3]	do		1 April 78	transfd. to Artill-
Petterfer, William[4]	do		28 May 78	discharged [ery
Powell, John[5]	do		feb 78	left out the Roll
Potts, Thomas[6]	Corpl	⎫		Waggoner Wil-
Joined Lansdale's	private	⎬		[mington
Oldham's	private	⎭ 1 June 78	Sept 79 not heard of	
Price, Daniel[7]	pt		16 Aug 80	missing
Pringle, Thomas	do	15 April 78	6 May 80	deserted
	fife			[lough
Purnell, Stephen[8]	pt	3 do	25 do	destd. on fur-
Perry, Francis[9]	do	18 Mar 78	27 do	deserted
to Col. Hall's Co.				
Peach, William[9]	Sergt	2 Aug 77 ⎫		
	pt	31 Oct 79 ⎭	22 April. 80	deserted
Smith's, late Spurrier's, afterwards upon showing cause, discharged				
Powell, Peter[8]	pt	11 May 78	15 Aprl 79	deserted
Picker, William[9]	do	23 feb 78	1 Nov 80	present
Riely's, late Bowie's				
Page, John[1]	do	27 April 78	16 Aug 80	missing
Paine, Anthy.[8]	do	1 May 78	25 Jan 80	deserted
Patterson, Robt.[1]	do	10 do	10 dec 79	
Pheasant, Sam.[2]	do	8 Mar 78	June 80	dischd. finding
Pike, James[3]	Sergt	16 April 78 ⎫		[substitute
	pt	1 Aug 78 ⎭	22 dec 79	deserted
Pike, John	fifer	27 Jan 78 ⎫	July 80	do
	pt	12 May 80 ⎭		
Polston, Emanuel[8]	pt	29 April 78	30 July 78	died
Parker, Jerrold[9]	do	19 May 78	1 Nov 80	present
Preston, Grafton[9]	do	1 June 78	1 Mar 79	discharged
Prior, John[10]	do	3 April 80	1 Nov 80	present

RAWLINGS' REGIMENT.

Pritchard, Sam.	Corpl	23 July 76	10 Mar 77	died
Power, Saml.	pt	17 Aug 76	19 Aug 79	discharged
Pike, Hutchen	do	21 do	19 feb 77	do

[1] Godman's. [2] Lansdale's. [3] Sellman's. [4] Spurrier's. [5] Burgess'. [6] Norwood's.
[7] Oldham's. [8] Lt. Smith's. [9] Riely's. [10] Lt. Hanson's.

Names.	Rank.	Time of Service. Enlisted.	Discharged.	Remarks.
Pritchard, Wm.	pt	23 July		
Parker, George		16 April 79		
Palmer, Jacob		5 May		died Nov 80 per Certificate of Adamson Tannaker
Pierce, Edward	Corpl		22 Sept 79	discharged
Phillips, George	pt	20 Mar		
Proser, Danl.	do	10 May		
Pinks, Jas. 6 mo.	do	23 April		

First Regiment.

Quarney, Lawce.	pt	10 dec 76	27 dec 79	discharged
Quay, James	id		16 July 79	killed Stoney [Point
pay commences 15 feb 78				

Second Regiment.

Quick, Jno.	pt			
	Sergt	1 Jan 80	1 Nov 80	present

Third Regiment.—Beginning 77.

Quiggins, Henry	pt	30 May 77	16 Aug 77	killed
Quiggins, John	do	do	Corpl. 1 Aug 78	
Quinland, Jas.	do	5 April do	16 dec 78	deserted
Quynn, Joseph	do	20 May 78	1 Nov 80	present

Fourth Regiment.

Queen, Jno.[1]	Corpl			see Gwinn

Rawlings' Regiment.

Quinn, Patk.	pt	15 Oct 76	1 Jan 77	deserted

First Regiment.

Ritchie, Mathew	pt	10 dec 76	6 Mar 78	deserted
Rogers, William	do	do	16 Aug	prisoner
Ryan, Michael	do	4 feb 77	11 Jan 80	discharged
Rolls, William	do	7 June 77	June 77	deserted from Invalids
Reed, Thomas	do	10 dec 76	11 Sept 77	missing
Roxburgh, Alex.	Capt	do	1 April 80	Major of 7 Regt.
Read, John	pt	do	27 dec 79	discharged
Reese, Henry	do	14 April 77	July 80	to 7th Regt.
Rankin, Danl.	do	10 dec 76	27 dec 79	discharged

[1] Godman's.

during the War of the American Revolution, 1775–83.   155

MUSTERS OF MARYLAND TROOPS, VOL. I.

NAMES.	RANK.	TIME OF SERVICE. Enlisted.	Discharged.	REMARKS.
Roberts, Zacha.	Corpl	31 Mar 77 servg. Q. M. Dept.,	2 May 80 dis- [charged
Ridgely, William	Lieut	10 dec 76		
Ricketts, Vincent	pt	do	1 Nov 80	present
S. Major 10 Aug 1780	Corpl	1 Jan 80	Sergt. Sept 80	
Robertson, Thos.	pt	do	27 dec 79	discharged
Rash, John	do	do		
Ray, Samuel	do	do	Mar 10	dead
Ridgely, Bazil	Ensn 17 April Corpl from 10 dec 75, resigned 7 dec 77			
Ricketts, John	pt	22 Mar 77		
Reynolds, James	do	12 April 77	Oct 4	missing
Robertson, Michl.	do	26 Mar 77		
	Q. M. Sergt. 26 Mar 80			discharged
Rigg, Charles	pt	29 Mar 77	1 feb 79	Corpl. 28 Mar 80 [discharged
Ryan, Anthy.	do	10 dec 76	20 Mar 77	deserted
Robinson, Jno.	pt	10 dec 76	16 Aug 80	prisoner
Richardson, Elisha	do	23 April 77	27 dec 79	discharged
Riely, Charles	do	10 dec 76	3 May 77	ex. for J. Baker
Richmond, Chr.	pay M.	1 Jany 77		
	Lieut	27 May 78	Capt. Oct 81	
Riely, John	pt	10 dec 77	22 Jan 78	deserted
Roberts, Richd.	do	23 April 78	Aug 78	dead
Roberts, William	do	1 May 78	1 July 80	joined, 1 Nov 80 [present
Russell, Henry	do	29 do	1 feb 79	died
Roberson, Charles	do	10 June 78	1 Nov 80	present
Roby, John	do	13 May 78	reinlisted	
	prisoner	Jan 80	9 Jan 82	discharged
Roberts, William	fifer	4 May 78	16 Aug	prisoner
Rady, James	pt	3 Mar 78	8 July 79	deserted
Rady, Laurence	do	7 feb 78	do	do
Reynolds, Jno.	do	14 do	1 Nov 80	present
Riely, Patk.	do		16 Aug 80	prisoner
Rollins, Chs.	do	11 Aprl 79	31 Aug 80	deserted
Reynolds, Robt.	do	3 June 79	1 Nov 80	present
Robey, Joseph	do	14 June 79	25 Sept 80	died
	fifer	1 Oct 79		
Rose, William	pt	10 June 79		
	Sergt	14 Aug 79		
	S. M.	25 dec 79	1 Nov 80	present
Rowe, Robert	pt	see 2nd Regt.		
Ryan, Mathew	do	transferred to Invalids 15 Jan 78, see 2nd [Regt.		

MUSTERS OF MARYLAND TROOPS, VOL. I.

Names.	Rank.	Time of Service. Enlisted.	Discharged.	Remarks.

SECOND REGIMENT.

Names.	Rank.	Enlisted.	Discharged.	Remarks.
Robertson, Lambert	pt	4 Mar 77	10 June 80	discharged
Richardson, Danl.	do	27 Jan 77	do	do
Ray, James	do	4 Mar 77	do	do
Revell, Randall	Sergt		do	do
Read, Obadiah	pt		16 Jan 78	deserted
Rones, Samuel	do		17 do	do
Roly, Silvester	do			do
Riggan, Timy.	do			do
Ray, Joseph	do	24 dec 76	1 Nov 80	present
Rawlings, Jona.	do		16 Aug 80	prisoner
Rowe, Robert	do		12 dec 79	discharged
Ryan, Matthew	do		15 Jan 78	13 June 78 dis-[charged
Read, John	Ensn	10 Apl 77	12 April 79	resigned
Read, James	pt	4 do 78	May 80	deserted
Rigg, George	do	16 Mar 78	10 Jany 80	do, 16 Aug 80 [prisoner
Robinson, Nathl.	do	20 Aprl 78	29 Aprl 78	deserted
Richardson, Edwd.	fifer	6 May 78	20 feb 79	discharged
Rider, James	pt	15 May 78	24 dec 78	do
Richards, Thomas	do	23 feb 78	13 April 78	transferred to
Richy, William	do	22 Apr 78	know nothing	of him [Gist's Co.
Rawn, Patk.	do	5 May 78	1 Nov 80	present
Riswick, Jos.	do	30 do	3 April 79	discharged
Randall, David	do	24 do	do	do
Riely, (or Riney), Jonathan	pt	25 April 78	3 April 79	discharged
Ryan, John	do	1 Jan 77	feb 80	prisoner
Rolls, Richard	do	18 May 78		
	fifer	1 July 79	16 Aug 80	prisoner
Read, William	pt	20 May 78	79	discharged
Riggs, Andrew	do	10 feb 78	1 Nov 80	present
			10 feb 81	discharged
Runien, Henry	do		1 June 79	deserted
Ratcliff, Robt.	do	28 Aug 79		do
	Nov Roll 79, never appeared			
Robertson, Jno.	do	June 80	16 Aug 80	prisoner
Roberson, David	do		24 do	deserted

THIRD REGIMENT.

Names.	Rank.	Enlisted.	Discharged.	Remarks.
Reeder, Hezekiah	Lieut	14 Mar 77	9 feb 78	resigned
Roberts, Thomas	Corpl	2 June 77	18 June 78	died
Reynolds, Charles	pt	22 May 77	9 Jan 80	discharged

during the War of the American Revolution, 1775–83.

MUSTERS OF MARYLAND TROOPS, VOL. I.

NAMES.	RANK.	TIME OF SERVICE. Enlisted.	Discharged.	REMARKS.
Ridgely, Henry	Capt			
Roland, Patk.	pt		13 Mar 80	deserted, 19 Aug [80 deserted
Rock, Oliver	Sergt	23 feb 77	23 feb 80	discharged
Reed, James	pt	23 Aprl 77	June 78	dead
Richardson, Edwd.	do	1 feb 77	1 Nov 80	present
Rue, William	do	13 Sept 77	14 July 78	deserted, joined
Richardson, Wm.	do		1 Nov 80	present
Roberts, John	pt	10 Jan 77	10 Jan 80	discharged
Roberts, John	Sergt	3 Jan 77		time expired
left out Jan & feb 80, time expired				
Ridgely, Saml.	Corpl	17 April 77	16 Aug 80	prisoner
	Sergt			
Richards, John	pt	Jan 80		present, struck off
	Sergt	July 1780	10 feb 80	discharged
Rowe, William	pt	16 Aug 77		
private 1 July 78	Corpl	15 Mar 78		
do 1 June 79 again	do	1 April 79	1 Nov 80	present
Reveley, Francis	Lieut	15 April 77		
Richards, Paule	pt	1 Jan 78	do	do
Relahan, Jno.	do	11 May 77	do	do
Ramsey, Nathanl.	Lt. Col.	10 dec 76		
Riely, John	pt	25 April 78	28 Aug 80	deserted
Readon, Patk.	do	28 do	July 78	struck off
Robb, John	do	23 do	16 Aug 80	missing
Reewark, Jas.	do	25 do		joined
Rae, Barny	do	do		Nov 80 out
Richardson, Jno.	do	22 do		
Rock, Edward	Corpl			
	pt	1 April 78	June 78	struck off
Rock, John	do	26 April 78		present
Rock, William	pt	26 April 78	1 Nov 78	present
Rutter, Thomas	do	16 Jan 78	dec 78	died
Robertson, Wm.	do	3 feb 78	14 July 78	deserted
Roads, Jeremiah	do	31 May 78	1 Nov 80	present
reinlisted 17 feb 79			17 feb 82	discharged
Rains, Adam	do	May 78	1 Nov 80	present
joined 2 Aug 78				
Ragan, Morris	do	21 do	19 Oct 79	deserted
Russell, Thomas	do	16 do		
Roberson, Thomas	do	3 do	July 80	do
Ryan, Nathan	do	8 April 78		
Reidy, William	do		Oct 78	struck off
Riely, James	do	10 June 78	1 Nov 80	present
rein. 17 Nov 78				

MUSTERS OF MARYLAND TROOPS, VOL. I.

NAMES.	RANK.	TIME OF SERVICE. Enlisted.	Discharged.	REMARKS.
Reynolds, Benedt.	pt	28 July 78	time out, discharged	
Robertson, John	do	2 May 78	1 Nov 80	present
Roberts, Edward	do	10 June 78	16 Aug 80	missing
Reynolds, Richard	fifer	20 May 78	10 Dec 78	died
Redding, William	do			
Rowlings, Benedict Joined Sept 79	do	18 June 78	18 June 81	discharged

FOURTH REGIMENT.

NAMES.	RANK.	Enlisted.	Discharged.	REMARKS.
Ridgely, Revely	Sergt		11 Nov 77	resigned
Riely, John[1]	pt	1 dec 76	1 Nov 80	present
Ragan, James	do	17 dec 76	16 dec 79	discharged
Riding, Henry	do	1 April 78	1 Nov 80	present
Riding, Henry	do	11 Jany 77	June 80	deserted
Ramsey, Henry,[2]	do	3 April 77	1 Nov 80	present
Reynald, Tobias	do		24 May 80	discharged
Rolls, William	do		1 May 81	discharged
Riely, William[3]	Lieut	10 dec 76	Capt. 15 Oct 77	
Rowland, William[4]	pt	23 April 77	1 Mar 80	discharged
Reedy, Thomas	do		2 April 78	deserted
Rawlings, Jacob reduced 9 Dec 77	Sergt do	6 Mar 77 1 June 79 }	6 Mar 80	discharged
Rowley, John[6]	pt	7 June 77	14 May 80	do
Reading, John[1] to Oldham's	do Sergt	4 April 77 8 dec 79 }	16 Aug 80	prisoner
Ray, David[6]	pt	14 Mar 77	14 Mar 80	discharged
Rowe, James[7]	Sergt July 78 musd. sick Hospl., to be left out till joins			
Robinson, Hugh Corpl 1 April 79	pt Corpl pt	12 April 77 1 April 78 10 Oct 78 }	12 April 80	time expired
Rigney, Michl.	do	10 July 77	12 Sept 79	deserted
Ross, John	Surgn. Mate 7 Mar 78			
Robinson, Peter 30 Jany joined			April 78	left out
Richardson, Robt.[5]	pt	7 feb 78	1 Nov 80	present, joined [Oct 80
Roads, William[6] Norwood's	do Corpl private	2 feb 78 do 1 April 79 }	15 May 80 16 Aug 80	deserted missing
Raynard, Jno. C.	do	23 April 78	27 May 80	do
Roberts, Joseph[3]	do	1 Mar 77	1 Nov 80	present
Rogers, Joseph[4]	do	17 Mar 78	29 dec 79	deserted
Ringrose, James[5]	do	7 May 78		

[1] Oldham's. [2] Norwood's. [3] Godman's. [4] Lansdale's. [5] Selman's. [6] Bowie's. [7] Burgess'.

MUSTERS OF MARYLAND TROOPS, VOL. I.

NAMES.	RANK.	TIME OF SERVICE. Enlisted.	Discharged.	REMARKS.
Radley, John[1]	private	5 May 78		
	Corpl	1 April 79	1 Nov 80	present
	Sergt	1 Mar 80		
Rorke, Michl.[2]	pt	26 July 78	2 Mar 79	discharged
Redman, Thomas[3]	do	27 Aprl 78	1 Nov 80	present
Hoops', late Norwood's,				
Reynolds, Benedict[1]		1 Nov 80 prest., 28 July 78 enlisted		
Russell, John[4]	do	7 July 79	1 Nov 80	present
Rose, James	do	21 Aug 79	24 feb 80	deserted

RAWLINGS' REGIMENT.

NAMES.	RANK.	Enlisted.	Discharged.	REMARKS.
Rose, Isaac	Corpl	1 Aug 76		
	Sergt	Nov 77	9 Aug 79	discharged
Ross, Ruben	pt	20 July 76	11 July 79	do
Rowland, Henry	do	20 Sept	2 Sept 79	do
Rigdon, John	do	6 do		
Riely, James	do	do	17 dec 76	deserted
Russell, Nichs.	do		9 Aug 79	discharged
Rankins, Wm.	do	11 Aprl 79	26 July	do
Reed, John	Q. Mr.			
Richards, Wm.	Sergt		31 July 79	discharged
Roof, Peter 1 yr.	pt		9 Aug 79	do
Riely, John	do	21 Aprl 79		
Ryan, James	do	26 June		
Rock, John	do	26 Mar		
Rudolph, Jacob	do	23 Mar		

FIRST REGIMENT.

NAMES.	RANK.	Enlisted.	Discharged.	REMARKS.
Stillwell, Obadiah	Sergt	10 dec 76	27 dec 79	discharged
Splavin, Timothy	pt	do	6 Mar 78	deserted
Spillard, Mathew	do	do		do
Smith, Peter	do	do	27 dec 79	discharged
reinlisted			1 Nov 80	present
Smith, Joseph	do	6 April 77		
Sapp, Robert	do	16 do		deserted
Smoot, William	Sergt	10 dec 76	27 dec 79	discharged
Smith, Alvin	pt	do	5 Mar 77	died
Smith, Richard	do	do	27 dec 79	discharged
Shea, Daniel	do	do	do	do
Sergeant, William	do	do	6 Mar 78	deserted
Smith, William	do	do	1 Nov 80	present

[1] Riely's.   [2] Godman's.   [3] Hoops'.   [4] Oldham's.

MUSTERS OF MARYLAND TROOPS, VOL. I.

NAMES.	RANK.	TIME OF SERVICE. Enlisted.	Discharged.	REMARKS.
Smith, James	pt	22 feb 77	22 feb 80	discharged
	Corpl 1 Jan 78		Sergt July 79	
Shirvin, Charles	pt		29 Sept 78	dead
Smith, John	Sergt	10 dec 78	14 Aug 78	Forage Dept.
Skipper, William	pt	22 feb 77		deserted
Sullivan, John	do	8 Mar		never joined
	prisr.	Jany 80		
Simmes, James	Q. Lieut	17 April 77		
Sewel, William	pt	10 dec 76	27 dec 79	discharged
Smith, Valentine	do	do	May 80	transferred to In- [valids
Smith, John Dichd. the 27 dec 79	do	do	14 dec 82	discharged
Strap, Jacob	do	24 feby 77	24 Jan 80	do
Seward, David	do	21 May 77	11 Sept	missing
Slack, John	pt	22 Mar 77	23 Mar	deserted
Shepard, Francis	Sergt	10 dec 76	27 dec 79	discharged
Smith, John	Corpl	do	do	do
Sheridan, Thomas	pt	6 Mar 77		
Skepper, John	do	10 dec 76	Aug 77	died
Simms, Ignatius	do	19 May 77	17 July 79	do
Smith, Charles	Lieut	10 dec 76	10 feb 80	resigned
Sewall, Clement	Sergt	4 Mar 77	14 Sept	promoted
Shaw, John	pt	10 dec 76	1 feb 80	discharged
Simpson, Thomas	do	28 May 77		
	Corpl	1 Aug 77	5 Jan 80	discharged
Steel, Elisha	pt	24 feb 77		
	fifer	1 Aug 77	20 feb 80	do, as pt.
Stone, John H.	Col.		1 Aug 79	resigned
Sim, Patk.	Lt. Col.		20 June 77	do
Sterritt, William	Major		16 dec 77	do
Swann, Barton	pt	7 Sept 77	20 Sept 78	died
Sanders, Thomas	do	25 Oct 77	16 Aug 80	prisoner
Shaw, Alex.	O. Soldr., joined 4 dec 77, furloughed June 80			
Spykes, William	pt	3 Mar 78	1 Nov 80	present
Sutherland, Wm.	do	6 Jan 78	July 79	not heard of
Smith, William	do	9 Mar 78	1 Nov 80	present.
Simmons, Danl.	do	15 April 78	Corpl. 5 Nov 79, 16 Aug 80	
	Sergt	1 Jan 80		[prisr.
South, Alexander	pt	9 May 78	18 Aug 80	missing
Savoy, Philip		20 May 78	25 Jan 80	prisoner
Smith, Joseph		11 do		
Sherivenor, Jno.		1 do		
Salsbury, Thomas		14 feby 78	feb 79	died

MUSTERS OF MARYLAND TROOPS, VOL. I.

NAMES.	RANK.	TIME OF SERVICE. Enlisted.	Discharged.	REMARKS.
Smith, Nathl.		13 Mar 78	July 79 } May 80 }	died
Sheridan, John 3		6 Mar 77	2 Mar 80	discharged
Scott, Charles		28 May 78	1 Nov 80	present
Scott, Joshua		27 do	do	do
Saunders, Bennett		4 June 78	5 Aprl 79	discharged
Skiffington, Roger		19 Jan 78	16 Aug 80	missing
Spalding, Wm.	pt		26 Nov 78	dead
Snilling, John	do	1 Aprl 78	12 Sept 80	joined
Smith, John	do	24 do	1 Nov 80	present
Stallings, Thomas	do	1 May 79	1 Jan 80	transferred to In-
Simms, Edward	Ensn	11 Sept 79	7 feb 80	resigned [valids
Smoot, William	do	26 Jan 80		
Souther, Valenn.	Musn.	June 80	14 Aug 80	deserted
Smith, Anthy.			16 do	prisoner
Smith, John		24 Jan 80	16 Aug 80	missing
From 7th Regiment				

SECOND REGIMENT.

NAMES.	RANK.	Enlisted.	Discharged.	REMARKS.
Steward, John	Major	17 April 77		
Sampson, Richd.	Sergt	6 Sept 77	10 Jan 80	discharged
Sinnett, Bryan	Corpl	8 Jan 77 }		
	Sergt	1 Jan 78 }	10 Jan 80	discharged
Spencer, Humpy.	private	4 Mar 77 }		
Sergt 1 May 80	Corpl	10 Jan 80 }	1 Nov 80	present
Stevens, Levi	pt	8 Jan 77	10 Jan 80	discharged
Spencer, Jos.	do	10 April 77 }		
Q. M. S.	Sergt	10 Jan 80 }	1 Nov 80	present
Smook, Richd.	pt	10 dec 76	1 May 80	discharged
Shipley, Robt.	do	30 Jan 77	1 Nov 80	present
Sanders, Spencer	do	Aug 79	discharged having got a man in [his place	
Stevens, Benja.	do		10 Jan 80	discharged
Spicer, Levin	do		15 Mar 78	deserted
Scott, Charles	do	see the other side, C. Scott Corpl.		
Sharp, Henry	do			
Skinner, Robt.	do			
Sute, Jesse	Sergt	20 Jan 77 }		
Sergt June 80, reduced to pt 7 Oct 79 }			1 Nov 80	present
Shotten, James	do	18 May 77	entd. below on the other side	
Spicknall, Mathew	Sergt		10 Jan 80	discharged
Spalding, Aron	pt	1 Jan 77 }		
Musd. as Sergt for May & June 80		}	1 Nov 80	present
Sweeney, Richd.	pt	1 Sept 77	16 Aug 80	killed

MUSTERS OF MARYLAND TROOPS, VOL. I.

NAMES.	RANK.	Enlisted.	Discharged.	REMARKS.
Smith, John	pt		10 Jan 80	discharged
Summers, Oba.	Sergt		20 April 80	joined
Smith, Robert	pt	13 April 77	1 do	discharged
Sears, John	Sergt		10 Jan 80	do do
Sterling, Isaac	pt	10 Jan 77	do	do
Slocome, Solomon	do		27 May 78	deserted

Joined June musr. 78, joined 24 Sept 80, afterwards J. Davidson & deserted to [Enemy

Southerland, Alex.	pt		10 Jan 80	discharged
Saunders, Jno.	do		15 feb 78	died
Smith, John	do Sergt. 10 Jan 80, 16 Aug 80 killed			

reduced 8 Oct 79 to pt, Corpl 1 June 78, Sergt. 10 Sept 78

Spalding, Henry	pt	do 77	10 Jan 80	discharged
Summers, Thomas	do		do	do
Shoebrook, Philip	do	26 feb 78	13 June 78	do
Smith, Henry	do	17 Jan 78		
Smith, James	do	do	1 Nov 80	present
Scott, Charles	do	10 dec 76	Corpl. 15 May 78	
Swaney, James	do	78	2 June 79	died
Smoot, William	do	3 May 78	23 dec 78	deserted
Sergeant 10 July 78				
Sammon, John	pt	13 April 78	1 Nov 80	present
Sanders, James	do	24 do	Oct 80	deserted
Spicer, John	do	20 May 78	21 Aug 80	do
	Corpl	1 feb 80		
Scoot, Isaac	pt	20 April 78	1 Nov 80	present
Smith, Levi	do	26 feb 78	13 May 78	deserted
Schean, Daniel	do	10 do	15 April 78	do
Schean, James	do	29 April 78	,	sick Maryland
Shovell, John	do	9 do	1 Nov 80	present
Spraigh, (or Spray), John	Corpl	24 do	16 Aug 80	prisoner
	pt	1 Nov 78	fifer 1 June 79	
Sergeant, Thomas	do	24 April 78	20 Nov 78	died
Slone, Charles	do	13 May 78	1 Nov 80	present
Stone, Joseph	do	29 do	3 April 79	discharged
Stone, John	do	25 do	do	do
Smith, John	do	24 do	do	do
Senner, John	do	29 do	25 dec 78	died
Strickland, Jos.	do	24 do	3 April 79	discharged
Snow, Charles	do	16 do	Oct 80	died
Smee, Thomas	do	1 June do	see T. Mee	
Smith, Anthy.	do	15 April do	1 Nov 80	present
Joined June 79				
Scriviner, Robt.	do	4 ditto	do	do
	Sergt	1 feb 80		

MUSTERS OF MARYLAND TROOPS, VOL. I.

NAMES.	RANK.	TIME OF SERVICE. Enlisted.	Discharged.	REMARKS.
Saunders, Thomas	pt A. S.		10 Jan 80	discharged
Standley, Roger	pt	20 May 78	10 Oct 78	died
Stanton, Mathew	do	do	3 April 79	discharged
Smith, David	do	10 Mar 78	1 Nov 80	present
Savin, Edward	do	25 May 78	26 dec 78	deserted
Stanton, Mathew	do	20 do		
Shottin, James	pt		16 Aug 80	missing
Simpson, Charles	Corpl			
reduced to	pt	1 Jan 79	feb 80	died
Suite, Edward	do	8 July 79		
1 musr. Augt	Corpl	1 feby 80	1 Nov 80	present
Sullivan, Mark	pt	26 June 79	16 Aug 80	missing
Stokes, Thomas	do	21 do	1 Nov 80	present
Slade, John	do	16 May 79 musr. Nov Roll 79 never appeared		
Sappington, Thomas		3 Aug do	4 Sept 79	deserted
Sears, John	Ensn	26 Jan 80		
Stoaks, John	pt		16 Aug 80	missing
Sails, Gabriel	do	4 June 80	14 do	deserted
Saunders, Robt.	do			sick Maryland
Summers, Oba.	Sergt			see L
Smith, Robt.	pt			do.

THIRD REGIMENT.

Swann, Alexr.	pt	16 feb 77	16 Aug 80	missing
Swann, Basil	do	18 Mar 77	Jan 78	struck off
Smith, William	do	21 April 77	do	do
Sanders, John	do	10 June 77	15 July 79	to Invalids
Smith, John[1]	Lieut	10 Dec 76	Capt.	
Sheriden, Bartholm.	Sergt	exchanged into Congress Regt.		
Silk, William[2]	pt		Mar 79	left out the Rolls
Stainger, Fortunatus	do	11 June 77	16 Aug 80	missing
Stanley, William	do	11 May 77	1 April 79	transferred to Invalids
			May 80	discharged
Sears, Noah	do	3 Jany 77	1 Nov 80	present
Southall, Jos.	do	1 Aprl 77	do	do
Smith, James	do	16 do	16 Aug 80	missing
Sheridan, James	do	14 feb 77	Jan 79	transferred to Invalids, dismissed on Furlough 11 July 83
Skepper, Isaac	do	24 June 77	April 78	struck off
Smoot, Thomas	Sergt	23 April 77	29 Aug 78	discharged
Spry, Joseph	pt	9 Sept 77	Jan 78	struck off

[1] Marbury's.   [2] Smith's.

MUSTERS OF MARYLAND TROOPS, VOL. I.

NAMES.	RANK.	Enlisted.	Discharged.	REMARKS.
Swann, John	pt		1 April 79	discharged
Stevenson, Jno.	do		Aug 80	deserted
Stringer, Joseph	do	Jan 77	Dec 79	struck off
Dec Roll 79 left out			14 April 80	discharged
Stanley, Thomas	do		19 feby 79	deserted
Strong, John	do	3 April 77	Dec 78	do
Short, Edward	do	2 do	16 Aug 80	missing
Slade, John	do		3 feb 78	dead
Stallings, Thomas	do		15 Jan 78	discharged
Stallings, Jacob	do		do	do
Smith, Edwd. Miles	Q. M. S.		16 Mar 80	time expired
Smith, Leonard	pt	18 Mar 77	11 Mar 80	
Smith, John	do	1 Jan 77	16 Aug 80	prisoner
	Corpl	1 Jan 79		
Swain, John	pt	8 Sept 77		deserted
deserted 1 mus., joined feby 1778				
Sappington, Thomas	S. Mate			
Sutton, Edward	pt	25 Mar 78	3 July 80	do
Sanders, John	do	25 April 78	16 Aug 80	missing
Stroud, William[1]	do	15 do	18 do	deserted
Sullivan, James	do	4 Mar 78	21 Aug 79	do
Spalding, William	do	30 do	Feby 79	discharged
Shink, Joseph	do	2 May 78	24 feb 79	died
Scriables, Jeremh.	do	29 April 78	14 Oct 78	do
Spraggs, John	do	28 do	6 Mar 79	do
Spalding, George	do	1 May 78	19 feby 79	discharged
Sullivan, Patk.	Corpl	April 78	June 79	out the Roll
	private	1 Sept 78		
Scantling, Thomas	do	2 May 78	16 Aug 80	missing
Swann, Leonard	do	3 do	1 Nov 80	present
Suffolk, Richd.	do		do	do
Shell, Richard	do		27 Jan 80	deserted
Sadler, Humphy	do		30 Aug 78	died
Smith, Saml.	do		28 do	deserted
Shirley, George	do	31 May 78	24 do	died
Smart, Richd.	do	25 do	4 April 79	discharged
Sanders, John	fifer		16 Aug 80	missing
Speak, Thomas	pt	20 Aprl 78	April & May 79 left out Rolls	
Joined 22 Aug 78				
Smith, Josias	do	2 June 78	do	do
Joined 22 Aug 78				
Sears, James	pt	20 April 78		

[1] Smith's.

MUSTERS OF MARYLAND TROOPS, VOL. I.

Names.	Rank.	Time of Service. Enlisted.	Discharged.	Remarks.
Self, John	pt	25 April 78	28 Sept 79	discharged
Sugars, William	do	do		
Smith, Matthew	do	24 May 78		
Smith, Levin	do	5 June 78	20 Oct 78	died
Simms, James	Sergt	pt		
Joined Oct 78	pt	June 79	21 Sept 79	do
Steel, Joseph	do	10 June 78	16 Nov 78	do
Still, John	do	4 do	see below	
Smith, Henry	do	13 May 78	Nov 80	out
Smith, Joseph	do	3 June 78	16 Aug 80	missing
Joined and Discharged 13 Aug 81				
Swails, Robert	Sergt		feby 79	discharged
Still, James		18 Nov 78	1 Nov 80	present
Sullivan, Thomas	pt		2 feb 80	deserted
Joined 18 June 79				
Scott, John	do	Joined Sept 79		
Scoot, William	do	Musd. Oct & Nov, left out dec 79		

From October Muster, 1780.

Names.	Rank.	Enlisted.	Discharged.	Remarks.
Scott, John	Drum	13 Aprl 80	1 Nov 80	present
Swann, William	do	do	do	do
Simmes, Jesse	Corpl	20 Mar 80	1 Nov 80	present

Fourth Regiment.—*Beginning December, 77.*

Names.	Rank.	Enlisted.	Discharged.	Remarks.
Smith, Samuel	Lt. Col.	10 April 77		
Smith, William[1]	Sergt	28 Jan 77	feb 79	died
Spencer, William	pt	24 do	14 Jan 80	discharged
Shean, Patk.	do	1 dec 76	} 16 Aug 80	prisoner
	Corpl	1 Sept 79		
Smith, John	pt	6 dec 76	do	do
Smith, John, 2d	do		18 June 79	deserted
Shean, Timothy	do	7 do	16 Aug 80	missing
Smith, Joshua	do	14 Jan 77	14 Jan 80	discharged
Smith, James[2]	do		8 July 79	deserted
Smith, Daniel	do		3 May 78	do
Scott, Alexr.[3]	Sergt		dec 79	time expired
Skiffington, Mathias	do		16 Aug 80	missing
	private	28 April 78		
Sollers, William	do		10 April 80	deserted
Smith, Edward	do	1 April 77	1 do	discharged
Sansberry, Richd.	do		14 dec 79	do

[1] Oldham's.   [2] Norwood's.   [3] Godman's.

MUSTERS OF MARYLAND TROOPS, VOL I.

Names.	Rank.	Time of Service. Enlisted.	Discharged.	Remarks.
Stedds, Richd.	private		28 April 80	discharged
Smith, James[1]	Lieut		20 June 79	resigned
Sowall, Charles	do		17 Nov 77	do
Smothers, Robt.	Corpl	1 May 77	1 May 80	discharged
Smith, William	Drum	1 Mar 77	1 Nov 80	present
Sinklair, Andrew	pt		14 June 78	discharged
Sellman, Jona.[2]	Capt	10 dec 76		
Shercliff, Wm. of Field &c.	Lieut	do	feb 78	resigned by Roll signed by Sam. Smith, Lt. Col.
Skally, Danl.	Corpl	6 dec 76	6 dec 79	discharged
Stockett, Henry	fifer	6 dec 76		
	Fife Major	1 July 78	} 6 dec 79	discharged
Spurrier, Edward[3]	Lieut	10 dec 76		
	Capt	21 May 78	}	
Shelmerdine, Steph.	Lieut	ditto	10 Dec	resigned
Street, George	pt	6 dec 76	Sept 80	deserted
Simmons, John	do	1 feb 77	16 Aug 80	prisoner
Stewart, Robert	do	12 Jan 77	1 Nov 80	present
Sheain, Arthur	do		3 Aug 78	discharged
Sewell, John	do	5 do	5 Jan 80	time expired, discharged
Simms, Thomas Joined 19 feb 80	do	3 April 77	22 April 80	deserted
Smith, Thomas	do	26 July 77	} 1 Jan 80	supposed dis-[charged
		26 Jan 77	}	
Sprigg, Thomas[4]	do			
Stokes, Patk.[5]	do		April 78	left out the Roll
Sterne, John	do			
Stewart, Richd.[6]	do	23 feb 78	10 July 78	deserted
Steenson, John[1]	do	19 Jan 78	26 April 78	do
Smith, John[2]	do	22 do	10 July 78	do
Street, James	do	17 do	16 dec 79	do
Street, Samuel[7]	fifer	31 Mar 78	July 80	do, joined
Scroggy, Francis	pt	25 April 78	16 Aug 80	missing
Stacy, Robert[1] to Lansdale's Co., joined	do	27 do	1 Nov 80	present
Silver, James[1]	do	9 May 78	16 Aug 80	missing, joined
Smith, Labs. C.[2]	do	11 do	1 Nov 80	present
Simmons, Thomas[8] Smith's, late Spurrier's	do			
Salbott, William[9] Riely's, late Bowie's	do	27 April 78		

[1] Lansdale's. [2] Sellman's. [3] Spurrier's. [4] Bowie's. [5] Burgess'.
[6] Godman's. [7] Norwood's. [8] Lt. Smith's. [9] Riely's.

MUSTERS OF MARYLAND TROOPS, VOL. I.

Names.	Rank.	Time of Service.		Remarks.
		Enlisted.	Discharged.	
Staid, Thomas	pt	27 April 78	1 Nov 80	present
Smith, Humphy.	do	5 May 78	27 Aug 78	discharged
Simmons, John[1]	pt	20 May 78	Corpl. 10 Feby 80	} deserted
	pt	1 May 80		
Simmes, James	do	10 June 78	Dec 78	discharged
Smith, Thomas	do	16 May 78	1 Nov 80	present
Smith, Elijah	do	22 April 78	2 April 80	
		9 July 78		
Smith, John[2]	do	29 May 78	1 Mar 79	discharged
Stewart, James[3]	do	1 July 78	1 Oct 80	present
		deserted in Mar 81, Capt. Ewing		
Shoemaker, Jacob[4]	pt	9 Aug 78	} 26 Jan 80	promoted to be
	Sergt	1 Mar 79	} see forwd.	[Ensign
Stevens, William[1]	pt	6 May 78	feby 78	} left out the Roll
			July 79	} do
Stovely, James[4]	do	1 Mar 79	15 May 80	deserted
			July 80	do
Smith, Jno., (Tayler)[1]	do	14 do	Jan & feb 80	absent with leave
			Mar 80	left out
Slye, Robert[3]	do	7 July 79	17 Jan 80	deserted
Shulmear, Peter[6]	do	23 do	16 Aug 80	missing
Swiney, Dennis	do		do	do
Smith, Reubin[7]	do	24 Oct 79	1 Nov 80	present
Smith, Nathan[6]	Ensn	18 Nov 79	}	
	Lieut	14 feb 80	}	
Shoemaker, Jacob	Ensn	26 Jan 80	}	[wounds
	Lieut	14 feb 80	} 1780 prisoner and died of his	
Shadwick, William	pt	5 April 77	5 April 80	time expired
Stead, William[1]	do		16 Aug 80	missing
Joined June mus. 80				
Spilliard, Mathew	do		do	do
Joined June mus. 80				

RAWLINGS' REGIMENT.

Sanders, Joshua	Sergt	17 July 76		died
Smith, Thomas	pt	29 do	21 July 79	discharged
Scarriat, Thomas	do	22 do		
Scott, Joseph	do	18 do	20 dec 76	deserted
Stafford, John	do	17 Sept		
Sadler, John	do	13 Nov	do	do
Shephard, Jona.	do	July		
Shaw, Basil		5 April 79	Sergt. 27 July 79	

[1] Oldham's. [2] Lansdale's. [3] Lt. Smith's. [4] Riely's. [5] Hoops'. [6] Sellman's. [7] Belt's.

MUSTERS OF MARYLAND TROOPS, VOL. I.

Names.	Rank.	Time of Service. Enlisted.	Discharged.	Remarks.
Smith, Wm. 3			9 Aug 79	discharged
Soaker, James 3			21 July do	do
Stephens, John 1 yr.			9 Aug	do
Such, George	Sergt	14 do		
Shaw, William	pt	11 Mar		
Shocknesey, Thos.	do	15 Mar		
Stackpole, Jas.	do	24 April		
Shafer, Adam 6 mo.		25 Mar		
Stacks, John				
Starr, William	do	2 Sept 76	17 Jan 77	deserted

First Regiment.

Names.	Rank.	Enlisted.	Discharged.	Remarks.
Taylor, John	Sergt	10 dec 76	77	deserted
Taylor, John	pt	do	June 80	do
Taylor, Ludowk.	do	do	15 Mar 78	do
Timmons, William	do	4 Mar 77	10 Mar	do
Thomas, George	do	10 dec 76	7 Mar 77	died
Turner, Thomas	do	1 feb 77	22 Jan 78	deserted
Towzey, Thomas	do	12 April 77	12 April 80	discharged
Thompson, Saml.	do	10 dec 76	10 April 77	died
Tucker, William	do	18 feb 77	18 feb 80	do
25 Dec 79	Corpl	20 dec 79		
Taylor, James	pt	24 Mar		deserted same mo.
Taylor, Aquilla	do	10 dec 76	1 Jan 78	dead
Tomling, Hugh	do	do	27 dec 79	discharged
Thomson, James	Sergt	do	do	do
Talbot, Coxon	pt	do	23 May 77	died
Thomson, Francis	do	do	27 dec 79	discharged
reinlisted mustered		June 80	1 Nov 80	present
Timms, Joseph	pt	25 Oct 77		
	Corpl		14 Sept 80	discharged
Thackerel, Rezin	pt	27 April 78	16 Aug 80	missing, killed
Thomson, Charles	do	5 June 78	5 April 79	discharged
Timms, Edward	do	11 feb 78	1 Nov 80	present
Taylor, William	do	26 April 78	do	do
Thomson, Richd.	do	1 June 78	21 Oct 78	died
Taylor, John	do	9 mo.	5 April 79	dischd.
Timmons, Wm.	do	21 Sept 79	June 80	left out, deserted
Tucker, John	do	9 feb 80	left out	October 80
Tucker, John	pt	21 feb 80	1 Nov 80	present
Thomas, William	do June must. 1780		16 Augt	missing
Tippet, Notley	do		1 Nov 80	present

MUSTERS OF MARYLAND TROOPS, VOL. I.

NAMES.	RANK.	TIME OF SERVICE. Enlisted.	Discharged.	REMARKS.

SECOND REGIMENT.—*Beginning with the Muster Rolls for Jany., 1778.*

Thatcher, David	Corpl / pt	22 April 77 } 19 June 79	10 Jan 80	discharged
Thompson, Benja.	do	10 Jan 77	do	do
Tharp, Jacob	do	Apr & May 79 to Invalids, 31 May 80 died		
Tull, John	do / Corpl	} 12 Sept 78	10 Jan 80	discharged
Thomas, Hezeka.	Sergt	10 Jan 77	do	do
Tarleton, Jeremha.	pt / Corpl	do } 1 June 78	do	do
Thomas, Stanhope	pt	7 April 77	do	do
Taylor, William	do		do	do
Towland, William	do	1 Jan 77	1 Nov 80	present
Thompson, William			Jan 78	Lt. Dragoons
Thompson, William	Drum		July 80	Hosptl., supposed [dead
Taylor, Edward	pt			
Thoroughgood, Jno.	do / Corpl	} 1 July 78	1 Nov 80 / 1 Jan 80	present } discharged }
Tiler, Edward	pt / Corpl	10 Jan 78 } 15 May 78	10 Jan 80	do
Thompson, Bennitt	pt	20 July 77	1 July 78	dead
Thompson, Charles	do	do		deserted
Taylor, Thomas	do	19 Mar 78		
Thompson, Thomas	do	2 April 78	1 April 80	do
		joined & 4 dec 80		discharged
Tate, John	S. Mate	10 May 78		resigned
Trego, James	pt	20 April 78	78	died Dansbury
Thompson, Lambert	do	12 Jan 78	1 Nov 80	present
Tutton, William	do	30 do	1 Apri 79 transfd. to Invalids } 4 Jan 83 discharged on pen- }	
Turner, Abram	do	24 May 78	30 Sept 78	died [sion
Thomson, Barthola.	do		1 Nov 80	present
Turner, William	do	20 do	feb 80	deserted
Tayler, John	do	20 Mar do	1 Nov 80	present
Thomas, Joseph	do	25 May 78		discharged
Tayler, John	do	do	Mar 79	do
Thorougood, John	Sergt	1 Jan 80	1 Nov 80	present

THIRD REGIMENT.—*Beginning 77.*

Taylor, Snowden	pt		6 Dec 79	discharged
Thompson, Natha.	do	19 Aprl 77		
out April 78, joined May				

MUSTERS OF MARYLAND TROOPS, VOL. I.

NAMES.	RANK.	TIME OF SERVICE. Enlisted.	Discharged.	'REMARKS.
Tarance, Owen	pt	6 April 77		see Farance
Turner, Richd.	do	26 do		
	Corpl	16 Mar 78	16 Aug 80	prisoner
	Sergt	29 Augt 78		
Turbott, John	pt		23 feb 80	discharged
	Corpl	Oct 78		
Taylor, Robert	pt	15 Jan 77	15 Jan 80	do
reinlisted, see forward				
Taylor, Thomas	do	12 do	12 do	do
Tenfield, Richd.	do	do	do	do
Toole, Thomas	pt			
Twyford, Wm.	do	5 Nov 77	22 dec 77	died
Tippits, Peter	do	25 May 77	1 Nov 80	present
Tucker, Thomas	do	2 Sept 78	transferred to 11 feb 80	Invalids deserted
Tarry, James	do	25 April 78	22 Mar 80	prisoner
reinlisted			joined	
Truman, John	Sergt	30 do	promoted 80	
Thomas, James	pt	1 May do	1 Nov 80	present
	Drum	4 June 78		
	private	11 June 79		
Thompson, Ignats.	do	13 do		
or Athanatus	Corpl	14 Aug 78	do	do
Q. M. Sergt. 1 March 80	Sergt	1 Jan 80		
Turner, John	pt	23 May 78	do	do
reinlisted 15 Jan 79				
Tibbles, Robert	do	18 do	12 dec 78	deserted
Taylor, Griffith	do	20 April 78	1 Nov 80	present
Taylor, John	do	1 June 78	13 feby 79	discharged
Tarman, Henry	do	5 do	Aug 79	deserted
rein. 17 Nov 78			(Jesse Suits)	
Trigg, Samuel	do	6 Jan 78	1 Nov 80	present
Tasker, Richard	do	27 May 78	1 Nov 80	do
reinlisted				
Tawman, Henry	do	17 Nov 78		
Tillert, Samuel	do		20 Jan 79	discharged
Townley, Henry	do	4 June 78	16 Aug 80 joined	missing
Thomas, Thomas	do	13 May 78		
Tedford, John	do	12 do		
Tragasskiss, Jacob	pt		16 Aug 80	missing

MUSTERS OF MARYLAND TROOPS, VOL. I.

NAMES.	RANK.	TIME OF SERVICE. Enlisted.	Discharged.	REMARKS.

FROM OCTOBER MUSTER, 1780.

NAMES.	RANK.	Enlisted.	Discharged.	REMARKS.
Turner, Leonard	pt		1 Nov 80	present
Trusky, Samuel	do		do	do
Trusty, John	do		do	do
Taylor, Robert	do		do	do
Thomson, Joseph	do	1 April 80	do	do
Thomas, Thomas	do		do	do

FOURTH REGIMENT.—*Beginning Dec.*, 1777.

NAMES.	RANK.	Enlisted.	Discharged.	REMARKS.
Twineing, Natha.[1]	Ensn	29 feb 77	} 1 June 79	resigned
	Lieut	20 Nov 77		
Tood, Benjamin	Sergt		June Roll 78	left out
Townshend, Wm.[2]	pt		Jan 80	deserted
Tidings, Caleb[3]	do	1 July 77	} 1 July 80	time expired
	Corpl	31 Oct 78	} 16 May	discharged
	Sergt	1 dec 79		
Taylor, John[4]	pt		26 feb 78	deserted
Turner, Samson	do		1 Mar 78	discharged
Turner, Thomas[5]	do	14 Aug 77	1 Nov 80	present
Tracey, Thomas	do		25 Jan 78	deserted
Tompson, Lawce.	do	7 do	1 Nov 80	present
Troy, John[1]	do	23 Mar 78	9 July 78	deserted
Tiser, James[2]	do	26 April 78	Jan 80	do
Thomas, John[6]	pt	4 May 78	16 Aug 80	missing
Topping, Peter	do	do	1 Nov 80	present
Thornby, Joseph[7]	do	17 April 77	16 Aug 80	missing
prisr. 22 Aug 77, joined 23 June 78				
Taylor, John[8]	do	4 May 78	do	do
Tree, Thomas	do	12 July 79	do	do
Tumberson, Evan[1]	do	Dec 76	1 Nov 80	present
Tipling, Isaac			16 Aug 80	missing

RAWLINGS' REGIMENT.

NAMES.		RANK.	Enlisted.	Discharged.	REMARKS.
Thomson, John		Sergt	15 July 76		
Tress, Peter		pt	76		
Tracy, Charles	1 yr.	do		1 July	discharged
Trust, Peter	3	do			
Trotten, Lowden		Corpl			
Thomson, Chas.	1 yr.			do	do
Treviss, John		pt			
Taylor, William		do			

[1] Oldham's.　[2] Norwood's.　[3] Selman's.　[4] Spurrier's.　[5] Burgess'.
[6] Godman's.　[7] Lansdale's.　[8] Riely's.

MUSTERS OF MARYLAND TROOPS, VOL. I.

Names.	Rank.	Time of Service. Enlisted.	Discharged.	Remarks.
Thompson, Thomas	1 yr.		9 Aug	
Tryar, And.	Sergt		1 July 79	discharged
Twinch, George	Drum			
Terring, Wm. M.	Fifer		15 do	do
Tannehill, Josiah	Adjut	1st do		

Second Regiment.—*Beginning January,* 1778.

Uncles, Benja.	pt	11 April 77	11 April 80	discharged

Third Regiment.—*Beginning* 77.

Urquhart, Andw. Out Nov 77	pt	3 July 77		

First Regiment.

Vermillion, Saul	pt	10 dec 76	12 Mar 77	deserted, joined

Second Regiment.—*Beginning Jan.,* 78.

Vaughan, Wm.	pt		5 May 81	discharged
Valient, Jonathan	pt	11 Mar 77	10 Jan 80	discharged
Vaughan, William	do	6 May 78	1 Nov 80	present }
			6 May 81	discharged }
Vincent, John	do	1 ditto	do	do
Vautier, Danl.	do	2 April 78	do	do
Varlow, Stephen	do	10 June 78	do	do
Vickers, John	do		20 Mar 80	deserted

Third Regiment.—*Beginning* 77.

Fourth Regiment.—*Beginning Dec.,* 77.

Vansant, John[1]	pt	6 dec 76	1 Nov 80	present
Vergen, John[2]	Sergt			

First Regiment.

White, Jona.	wounded 25 April 81 Camden, 29 Sept furld. by Genl. Smallwood, 29 Sept 81 to be settled with to that time full pay			
Winder, Levin	Capt	10 dec 76	Major 17 April 77	
Wheelan, Martin	pt	do	24 May 77	deserted
Watkins, Leonard	do	do		
Wilson, John Fred.	do	4 feb 77		
Wilson, John, Jr.	do	21 do		

[1] Lansdale's.   [2] Burgess'.

during the War of the American Revolution, 1775-83.

MUSTERS OF MARYLAND TROOPS, VOL. I.

Names.	Rank.	Time of Service. Enlisted.	Discharged.	Remarks.
Wheatly, Samuel	Corpl	10 dec 76	22 Aug 77	prisr. war
Whilling, Thomas	pt	do	6 Mar 78	deserted
Ward, Ignatius	do	10 feb 77	11 feb 80	discharged
Welstead, William	do	10 dec 76	27 dec 79	do
Weller, Philip	do	do	do	do
Wheatley, William	Corpl	do	28 June 78	killed
Walker, John	pt			
	Corpl	1 Oct 77	27 dec 79	discharged
Wood, William	pt		19 Aug 77	died
Watkins, Nichs.	Corpl	10 dec 76	27 dec 79	discharged
	Sergt	18 April 77		
Walker, William	pt	14 Mar 77	27 Nov 77	deserted }
		joined and deserted again 6 Augt 78		}
Wise, Thomas	do	26 do	26 Mar 80	discharged
Wyndham, Thomas	Corpl	10 dec 76	27 dec 79	do }
reinlisted 10 Jan 80	Sergt	10 Jan 80	1 Nov 80	present }
Watts, Richard	pt	10 dec 76		
Willshire, Samuel	do	do	24 May 77	deserted
Watkins, Nicholas	Corpl	do	10 dec 79	discharged
Wiseman, Thomas	pt	do	17 Aug 80	deserted
Ward, Ignatius	do	11 feb 77		see above
Waters, Richard	Lieut	10 April 77	Capt. 7 April 80	
Wallace, Hugh	pt	10 dec 76		
Wellman, Jacob	do	7 Mar 77		
Wellman, William	do	do	22 Aug 77	prisoner
Whelen, Richard	do	10 dec 76	3 June 77	Exd. Jno. Gorman
Williams, Thomas	do	do		}
	Corpl	1 Aug 77	redd. 10 feb 78	} discharged
		left out of musr. taken in April 80		
Wallace, Michael	Surgeon	10 dec 76		resigned
Warfield, Walter	S. Mate	27 Nov 77	28 feb 79	
Williams, John	pt	11 May 78	16 Aug 80	missing
Weston, Thomas	do	9 do	1 Nov 80	present
Williams, Jno., Jr.	do	24 April 78	31 Aug 80	deserted
		Joined 10 Oct 80		
Williams, John	do	20 April 78 }		
musr. Oct 80		5 April 79 }	1 Nov 80	present
Wright, Alexr.	do	9 June 78		
Ward, George		10 June 78	1 Nov 80	present
Woodard, Jesse	do	6 do	5 April 79	discharged
Welch, George	do	16 do	do	do
Wade, Lanct.	do	4 do	do	do
Ward, Thomas	do	20 May 78	14 feb 79	do
Williams, John. Gist				

MUSTERS OF MARYLAND TROOPS, VOL. I.

Names.	Rank.	Time of Service. Enlisted.	Discharged.	Remarks.
Walker, John, Jr.	pt	12 Sept 79	1 Nov 80	present
Whitticer, Francis	do	15 May 80	16 Aug 80	prisoner
West, Alexr.	do	mr. June 80	1 Nov 80	present
West, John	fifer		16 Aug 80	missing
White, Jonathan	pt	12 dec 79	1 Nov 80	present
Willing, Littleton	pt		16 Aug 80	prisoner

SECOND REGIMENT.—*Beginning with the Musr. Rolls for Jan., 78.*

Names.	Rank.	Enlisted.	Discharged.	Remarks.
Woolford, Thomas	Lt. Col.	17 April 77		
Welch, John	pt		23 dec 78	discharged
Worthington, Ben.	do	Joined Mar 80 4 Mar 77	16 Aug 80	missing
			dec 78	deserted
joined musd. Mar 79		No Land	dec 79	do again
Wright, Nathan	Sergt	10 Jan 80		discharged
Walker, Thomas	Corpl		22 Jan 78	deserted
Worring, John	pt			
Wall, Patk.	do		24 do	do
Wright, John	do	24 dec 76	24 dec 79	discharged
White, James	Sergt		10 Jan 80	do
Waymore, Thomas	pt			
Joined 18 April 79			1 April 80	do
Wheeler, William	do		10 Jan 80	do
Winset, Raphl.	do		do	do
Wheatley, Henry	do	15 Mar 77	15 Mar 80	do
Wright, Jesse	do	1 Aug 77	1 Nov 80	present
Walker, Edward			22 Jan	deserted
Wisely, Benja.	do	4 feb 77	June 79	transferred to Invalids

4 Nov 79 joined again, 4 feb 80 discharged, memorandum, he deserted 25 Oct 79

Names.	Rank.	Enlisted.	Discharged.	Remarks.
Williams, Sullivan	Lieut	10 April 77	Capt. 17 April 77	
Wheeler, Nathl.	pt	1 Jan 77	16 Aug 80	prisoner
Welsh, John[1]	pt	5 April 78		
B. Price's Co.	fifer			
Welsh, John	pt		16 Aug 80	missing joined
Woolford, William	Ensn	17 April 77	Lieut. 11 April 79	
Webster, Thomas	pt	24 dec 76	16 Aug 80	killed
Waters, Richard	S. M.	7 May 78		
Williams, David	pt	12 April 78	1 Nov 80	present
	fifer	1 Nov 78		
Wheatley, Wm.	pt	20 April 78	do	do

[1] B. Price's.

MUSTERS OF MARYLAND TROOPS, VOL. I.

NAMES.	RANK.	TIME OF SERVICE. Enlisted.	Discharged.	REMARKS.
Wilson, William	pt	19 May 78	16 Aug 80	killed
Wingate, Andw.	do	1 do	1 Nov 80	present
Wall, William	do	15 do	1 July 78	deserted }
Joined and discharged by Col. Forrest 22 Aug 80				
Williams, Cassitee	do	16 do	16 Aug 80	missing
Joined Aug 79				
Welsh, James	pt	28 April 78	28 June 78	killed Battle Monmouth
Warlough, John	do	20 May 78	16 May 80	deserted
Winsett, James	do	29 do	3 April 79	discharged
Wheatly, John	do	do	do	do
Wise, Thomas	do	25 do	3 April 79	do
Wheatley, Sylvt.	do	16 do	16 Aug 80	missing
Woodbarn, Jona.	do	1 June 78	3 April 79	discharged
Wells, Martin	do	24 May 78		do
Williamson, Alex.	do	do	Sept 78	do
Williams, John	Corpl		10 Jan 80	do
Wood, Thomas	do	20 do	1 Nov 80	present
White, Edward	pt	18 Mar 78	} 1 Nov 80	present }
	Corpl	July 80	depreciation twice recd.	
Whood, John	pt	5 June do	16 Aug 80	missing
Woodward, John	do	20 May do	do	do
Wall, Jesse	do	20 do	3 April 79	discharged
Wall, David	do	do	do	do
Wilson, Danl.	do	9 feb 78	1 Nov 80	prisoner
Wills, George	do	25 May 78	26 dec 78	deserted
Wright, William	do	20 do	3 Aprl 79	discharged
Wright, Saml.	do	do	24 dec 78	do
Wallis, Thomas	do		do	do
Wood, John	fifer	2 June 78 }		
	private	1 Mar 79 }		
	fifer	1 Aprl 79 }	1 Nov 80	present
Warfield, Walter	Surgn	10 June 79 }		
Surgeon's Mate of 6 M. R.		1 April 78 }		
Welch, Thomas	pt	8 May 79	1 Nov 80	present
1 mus. July 79				
Wilkinson, Jno.	do		16 Aug 80	missing
do Aug 79				
Wake, Richd.	fifer	25 do }		
	pt	1 Oct 79 }	26 dec 79	deserted
Wilson, James	do	14 June 79	1 Nov 80	present
Wimberry, Thos.	do	10 Mar 80	do	do
1 mus. Jan 80				
Waters, York	do	June 80	do	do }
			4 June	discharged

Names.	Rank.	Time of Service. Enlisted.	Discharged.	Remarks.
Winn, John	pt		16 Aug 80	prisoner
Ward, Peter	do	20 Mar 80	do	killed
Wait, Thomas	pt	16 May 80	1 Nov 80	present
Willing, William	pt		1 Nov 80	present
Whitcomb, Notley	do	15 June 80	18 Aug 80	discharged

Third Regiment.—Beginning 77.

Names.	Rank.	Enlisted.	Discharged.	Remarks.
Wright, Richard Nov & Dec 78	Corpl Sergt	14 Aprl 77	24 Sept 79	died
Williams, Jeremiah	pt	15 Mar 77	15 Mar 80	discharged
Wildman, Edward	do	23 April 77	10 dec 79	deserted
Wright, William	do	15 do	20 Nov 77	died
Williams, David prisr. 11 Sep 77, joined 18 June 78	do	22 June 77	27 Sep 79	deserted & musd. deserted in Aug 1780
Welch, Patk. not heard of since 4 June 78, Joined	do			
Watkins, William said to be dead May musr. 78	do	May 79		
Wood, John Excd. & joined 22 July 78	do	28 April 77	28 April 80	discharged
Wells, Edmund	do	28 Aug 77	11 Mar 77	deserted
Wire, James	do	25 April 77		
Wilmot, William	Lieut	10 dec 76	Capt. 15 Oct 77	
Walker, Robert	pt	14 April 77	1 Nov 80	present
Whittaker, (or Whitcomb), Thos.	fifer	17 do musr. feb 78	16 Aug 80	missing
Wood, Thomas	do	10 July do	3 April 78	died
Williams, Osborn	Ensn	18 Mar 77		
Wright, Thomas	pt	13 May do	16 Aug 80	missing
Wayton, John	Sergt	7 May do	1 Jan 80	off the Roll
Watkins, Peter	pt	8 Sept 77	10 feb 78	died
Weathersby, Thos.	pt	9 Sept 77	Jan 78	off Roll
Walls, Sutton	do	do	6 Jan 78	died
Weathersby, Jas.	do	do	78 off Rolls	
Webb, John Jan 78 absent wth. leave pt 23 May, April Roll 78	do Sergt	was discharged 1 April 79 10 June 77		procuring a man in his place
Whittaker, Francis	pt	12 Jan 77	12 Jan 80	discharged
Woolford, Michl.	do	5 May 77	1 Nov 80	present
Wilson, James	do	12 Jan 77	12 Jan 80	discharged
Wade, James	do	2 June 77	16 Aug 80	missing
Wilmot, Fredk.	do	12 feb 77	1 Nov 80	present
Watson, Thomas	do	1 Jan 77	16 Aug 80	missing joined

MUSTERS OF MARYLAND TROOPS, VOL. I.

NAMES.	RANK.	TIME OF SERVICE. Enlisted.	Discharged.	REMARKS.
Walker, John	pt	1 Aprl 77	} 16 Aug 80	joined
	Corpl	5 Oct do		
	pt	8 April 78		
Wilder, Henry	do	12 Aug do	19 June 78	deserted
Woodthey, John	do	20 Aprl do	12 feb 78	died
Woodley, Jonathan	do	9 June 77	11 Mar 78	deserted
Whittle, Robert	Corpl			
Joined 5 May 79	pt			
White, John	do	28 Aprl 77	time expired 30 April 80	} discharged
Wilson, William	do	24 May 77	1 Nov 80	present
Whiteley, William	do	27 Mar 77	1 May 80	discharged
Whitmore, Stephen	do	off Rolls Jan 78		
by J. Lowe's certificate was enlisted 20 feb 77				
Wilcox, James			10 Mar 80	died
out Aug 78, Joined 5 May 79				
Wells, Jno.[1]	do	21 April 78	May 79	left out the Rolls
Welsh, John	pt	6 feb 78	16 Aug 80	missing }
			1 Nov 80	present
Joined 20 July 79, left sick at pluckemain, Jersey, in April 80				
Willingham, Jno. B.	pt	13 May 78	feb 79	discharged
Williams, Zepha.	do	2 do	16 Aug 80	killed
Wild, James	do	14 Apl 78	do	missing
Wort, (or Word), Richard	do		June 78	transferred to Invalids
Whitmore, Stephen	do			
out Aug 78				
Wedding, John	do	25 May 78	23 Sep 78	died
Warring, William	do	do	15 Mar 79	discharged
Windham, George	do	25 April 78	1 Nov 80	present
Wade, Edmund, (or) Edward	} do	24 do		Guard
Watkins, James	do	2 June 78	} 16 Aug 80	prisoner
	Corpl	1 July 79		
Wilder, Henry	pt		dec 78	deserted
Joined Oct 78				
West, William	do	5 June 78	1 Nov 80	present
rein. 9 Jan 79				
Williams, John	do	14 Aprl 78	do	do
Wood, Jno.[2]	do	26 Jan 77	do	do
Wilson, Barnaby	do	9 May 78	do	do
Windberry, George	do	5 June 78	May 79	time expired
Wood, Dorsey	do	11 May 78	24 dec 78	discharged
Wilkinson, Wm.	do	3 Mar 78	1 Nov 80	present

[1] Smith's. [2] Claggett's.

MUSTERS OF MARYLAND TROOPS, VOL. I.

Names.	Rank.	Time of Service. Enlisted.	Discharged.	Remarks.
Williams, John	pt	20 feb 79	3 Mar 79	deserted
Whight, Tarance 1st musr. June 79	do	3 Sept 78	1 Nov 80	present
Wilson, John	do	1 July 79	5 Jan 80	deserted

From October Muster, 1780, & July, &c.

Names.	Rank.	Enlisted.	Discharged.	Remarks.
Williams, Charles	pt	27 Mar 80	1 Nov 80	present
Windley, John	do			
Wilson, Barney	fifer		16 Aug 80	prisoner
Windley, Benja.	pt			
White, Saml. B. (from B. 3 Regt.)	do	2 April 78	1 Nov 80	present
Watson, Thomas			15 Nov 83	discharged

Fourth Regiment.—*Beginning Decr., 77.*

Names.	Rank.	Enlisted.	Discharged.	Remarks.
Winstanly, Francis[1]	pt	15 dec 76	29 June 78	deserted or gone to Invalids, deserted from Invalids 11 June 81
Williams, Thomas	do		10 Sept 78	discharged
Wells, John[2] joined private	Corpl	1 Aug 78	1 Nov 80	present
West, Fredk.[3]	pt		feb Roll 78	died Baltimore
Welsh, John	do		1 Aug 80	discharged
Wright, John joined 16 Aug 79	do	4 Aug 77	16 do	missing
Webster, John[3] do	do		July 80	deserted
Warden, James	do Sergt. 1 April 78 } pt 1 Mar 79 }		dec 79	dischd.
Ware, John	do		16 Aug 80	missing
Williamson, Robt.	do		June 78	not heard of
Williamson, Thos.	do		do	do
Wilderman, Jacob[4]	Corpl pt. 28 Aug 78 } Sergt 1 Jan 79 }		13 April 80	dischd.
Welch, Joseph	pt		16 Aug 80	missing
Wood, Robertson	pt	1 Jan 77	1 Nov 80	present
Welch, Thomas	do	3 Mar 77	3 Mar 80	discharged
Wilson, Tobias[5]	Sergt	11 feb 77	6 dec 79	dischd., Thos. Hailey to serve the remainder his time
Wood, Thomas	pt	13 do	1 Nov 80	present
Wright, Edward	do	26 July 77	do	do
Wallingsford, Jas.[6]	do	6 Jan 77	6 Jan 80	dischd.
Watkins, Stephen	do	15 July 77	20 May 80	do

[1] Oldham's. [2] Norwood's. [3] Spurrier's. [4] Godman's. [5] Lansdale's. [6] Selman's.

MUSTERS OF MARYLAND TROOPS, VOL. I.

Names.	Rank.	Time of Service. Enlisted.	Discharged.	Remarks.
Webb, Jos.[1]	Sergt		11 feb 78	died
Wood, William[2]	pt	20 dec 76	20 dec 79	dischd.
Wheland, Jno., or Geo.[1]	do	9 Aug 77	10 dec 79	deserted
Warwick, James[2]	do	6 Jan 77	6 Jan 80	dischd.
Warwick, Wm.[2]	do	20 May 77	20 April 80	do
	Corpl	20 feb 78		
	pt	1 April 78	1 Mar 80	time expired
Williams, Thomas	do	16 April 77	July 80	deserted
left out June 78, joined 1 June 78				
Walker, John[4]	do			see Riely's below
Bowie's, Mar 78				
Waldron, Joseph[5]	do	20 April 78	Sept 80	deserted
Williams, John	do	29 do	22 Nov 78	do
Wiggins, James[6]	do	20 Mar 78	16 Aug 80	prisoner
Lansdale's, Aprl 78				
Willis, John[7]	do	6 dec 76	6 dec 79	dischd.
Smith's, 78				
Williams, Wm.	do	13 May 78	16 Aug 80	missing
Wilkerson, John[8]	do	13 Mar 78		
Riely's, late Bowie's				
Walker, John[8]	do		16 Aug 80	do
Whitehouse, Jos.[9]	do	5 May 78	1 Nov 80	present
Wheeler, James[6]	pt	1 May 78	16 Aug 80	missing
Whitehouse, Sam.[9]	do		10 April 79	dischd.
Whitecotton, James[6]	do	29 do	4 Mar 79	deserted
Williams, Jereh.	do	3 do	16 Aug 80	missing
	Corpl	1 June 80		
Williams, John	pt	16 May 78	4 Oct 78	joined
Williams, Jarvis[9]	do	17 do	1 Nov 80	present
Walker, John[6]	do	29 Jan 78	June 78	left out
Welch, John[9]	do	6 July 78	11 May 80	deserted
			July 80	do
Wilmington, Jos.	do		1 Nov 80	present
Joined Oct 78				
Williams, John[9]	do	16	16 Aug 80	missing
mus. June 79				
Willshire, John[6]	do	18 June 79	15 Jan 80	deserted
Wood, Jacob[10]	do	25 May 78	2 July 80	do
Wood, James[11]	do	3 feb 80	1 Nov 80	present

[1] Spurrier's. [2] Burgess'. [3] Selman's. [4] Bowie's. [5] Norwood's. [6] Lansdale's. [7] Smith's. [8] Riely's. [9] Godman's. [10] Hoops'. [11] Lt. Hanson's.

MUSTERS OF MARYLAND TROOPS, VOL. I.

Names.	Rank.	Time of Service. Enlisted.	Discharged.	Remarks.

RAWLINGS' REGIMENT.

Names.	Rank.	Enlisted.	Discharged.	Remarks.
Watson, Abram	pt	26 Aug 76		
Wilson, William	do	20 April 79		
Williams, Alexr.	do		15 July 79	discharged
Whireley, David	1 yr. do		1 July 79	deserted
Wade, George	do		1 July	do
Wilson, Helbriath	do			
Weedon, Jonathan	do		15 May 79	do
		Joined 17 Nov 79		
Watts, James	pt		15 July 79	killed
Williams, Andrew	1 yr.		6 do	discharged
White, John	Corpl	11 April 79		
Whilmon, Jno.	Drum	17 Mar		
Wallenberg, F.	Corpl			
Willyard, Henry	Drum			
White, Jas.	6 mo. pt	11 Mar		
Wannaker, B.	6 mo.		8 April 79	killed
Woodman, Jno.	do	25 June		

FIRST MARYLAND REGIMENT.

Names.	Rank.	Enlisted.	Discharged.	Remarks.
Yeator, Joseph	pt	10 dec 76	16 Aug 80	prisoner

SECOND REGIMENT.

Names.	Rank.	Enlisted.	Discharged.	Remarks.
Yates, Richard	pt	17 Mar 78	15 Sept 78	died
Yates, James	do	29 do	3 April 79	dischd.

THIRD REGIMENT.

Names.	Rank.	Enlisted.	Discharged.	Remarks.
Young, John out July 78	pt	20 April 77		
Yarnall, Benja.	do	26 Jan 77		

FOURTH REGIMENT.—*Beginning Dec., 77.*

Names.	Rank.	Enlisted.	Discharged.	Remarks.
Young, Benja.[1] Joined Hoops' Co.	Sergt		8 dec 79	dischd.
Young, John[2]	pt	14 May 78	1 Nov 80	present

RAWLINGS' REGIMENT.

Names.	Rank.	Enlisted.	Discharged.	Remarks.
Young, Peter	1 yr.			
Young, John		19 Mar 79		no Land

[1] Godman's. [2] Norwood's.

MUSTERS OF MARYLAND TROOPS, VOL. II.

"MARYLAND LINE."

RESOLVES OF CONTINENTAL CONGRESS, 25 MAY, 1776.

" Resolved, That one battalion of Germans be raised for the service of the United Colonies."

RESOLVES OF CONTINENTAL CONGRESS, 27 JUNE, 1776.

"The committee to whom it was referred to devise a mode of raising the German battalion, voted on the 25th of May last, brought in their report, which was taken into consideration: Whereupon,

Resolved, That four companies of Germans be raised in Pennsylvania and four companies in Maryland, to compose the said regiment: That it be recommended to the convention, or in their recess, to the council of safety of Maryland, immediately to appoint proper officers for, and direct the inlistment of, the four companies to be raised in that colony:

That the said companies be inlisted to serve for three years, unless sooner discharged by Congress, and receive bounty, pay, rations, and all other allowances equal to any of the continental troops: That the said companies, when raised, be formed into a battalion, under the command of such field officers as Congress shall appoint: That the rank of the captains of the said companies be regulated as Congress shall hereafter direct."

RESOLVES OF THE MARYLAND CONVENTION OF JUNE, 1776.

6 July, 1776.

" Resolved, That this province will raise . . . . four companies of Germans, according to the requisitions of Congress in their resolutions of the 27th day of June last.

That . . . two of the said companies of Germans be raised in Baltimore county, ... and two of the companies of Germans be raised in Frederick county. That each of the companies of Germans consist of one captain, two lieutenants, one ensign, four sergeants, four corporals, one drummer, one fifer, and seventy-six privates."

RESOLVES OF CONTINENTAL CONGRESS, 17 JULY, 1776.

" Resolved, That Nicholas Hauseigger be colonel; George Stricker, lieutenant-colonel; Ludewick Wiltner, major of the German battalion.

Resolved, That another company be added to the German battalion: That David Welper be appointed captain of said company."

CONTINENTAL CONGRESS,

25 September, 1776.

"The committee appointed to settle the rank of the captains and subalterns in the German battalion, reported the same as follows, which was agreed to:

Captains, Daniel Burkhart, Philip Graybill, George Hubley, Henry Fister, Jacob Bonner, George Kaports, Benjamin Weiser, William Keyser, and David Woelpper.

First-lieutenants, Frederick Rolwagen, John Lora, Peter Boyer, Charles Bulsel, William Rice, Jacob Kotz, Jacob Bower, Samuel Gerock, and Bernard Hubley.

Second-lieutenants, George Hawbacker, Christian Meyers, John Landenberger, Michal Bayer, George Schaeffer, Adam Smith, Frederick Yeiser, William Ritter, and Philip Schrawder.

Ensigns, John Weidman, Martin Shugart, Christian Helm, Jacob Crummet, Jacob Cramer, Paul Christman, Christopher Godfrey Swartz, and John Landenberger."

The German Regiment was regarded as one of the additional 16 Regiments raised under Resolutions of Congress 27 December, 1776.

MUSTERS OF MARYLAND TROOPS, VOL. II.

Names.	Rank.	Time of Service. Enlisted.	Discharged.	Remarks.
5th Maryland Regiment.				
Ayres, John[1]	pt	22 Mar 1777	7 Mar 80	time expired
Anderson, James[2]	do	24 June 77	April 7—	left out
Allen, James	do	8 July 77	1 Nov 80	present, paid
Austin, Harris	fife	25 July	1 Jany private, left out of Rolls	
Ayres, Thomas[3]	pt	17 dec 76	1 Nov 80	present
Ayres, James[4]	do	10 dec 76	10 dec 79	time out
Q. M. Sergt. 1 Mar 79	Sergt	9 July 77		
Alexander, Wm.[5]	Lieut	10 dec 76	27 Augt 77	died
Allen, Gilbert	pt	20 Augt 77	16 Aug 80	missing
Armstrong, Jno.[6]	do	10 Mar 77	23 Mar 80	prisoner
Ayres, William[6]	do		June 78	left out
Abel, John[7]	do	8 June 78	Augt 78	not heard of

[1] Dean's. [2] Hawkins'. [3] Lynch's. [4] Handy's. [5] Johnson's. [6] Emory's. [7] Lt. Hamilton's.

MUSTERS OF MARYLAND TROOPS, VOL. II.

Names.	Rank.	Time of Service. Enlisted.	Discharged.	Remarks.
Allen, Emanual[1]	Lieut	6 May 78	16 Aug 80	missing, paid
Arnett, William[2]	do	6 June 78	Feby 79	died
Austin, Joseph[1]	do	10 June 78	Jany 80	prisoner war
Andrews, Jno.[3]	do	1 Jany 79	1 Nov 80	present
Adair, William[4]	do	27 May 79	16 Augt 80	missing

6TH MARYLAND REGIMENT.

Ahern, William[5]	pt	15 May 78	16 Aug 80	missing
Allen, Robert[6]	Sergt	25 Jany 77	10 Jany 80	discharged
Ashbox, Jacob	pt	30 April 78	April & May 79	mustd. not [heard of
Ambler, George[7]	do	4 April 77		
Ayers, Fredk.	do	19 May 78	16 Aug 80	killed
Allen, Jacob[8]	do	3 April 77	16 Aug 80	prisoner
Atkinson, Wm.	do	28 Aprl 77	16 Aug 80	missing
Arris, James[9]	do	1 July 78		
Armstrong, Alex.[6]	pt	9 June 78	14 March 79	discharged
Armstrong, Thomas	do	9 June 78	14 Mar 79	discharged
Armstrong, Robert[9]	do	2 May 78	16 Aug 80	prisoner
Andeton, William[10]	do	23 May 78	10 March 79	deserted
Askins, Zacha.	Sergt		13 Sept 80	deserted
Anderside, Wm.	pt	26 Mar 78	16 Aug 80	missing
Armstrong, John Mus. 1780	do		1 Nov 80	present.

SEVENTH REGIMENT MARYLAND TROOPS.

Adams, D. Jenifer	Major	10 dec 76	1 June 79	resigned
Anderson, Richard	pt	10 dec 76	5 July 78	discharged
Adams, Peter	Qr. Master Lt. Col.	27 June 77		
Annis, Benjamin[11]	pt	1 April 77	1 April 80	discharged
Anderson, Richd.[12]	do	10 dec 76	See Richd. Anderson above	
Anderson, Richd.	Lieut Capt	10 dec 76 28 dec 77		
Aaron, Michael[13]	pt	6 dec 76	13 dec 76	deserted
Acre, Cronamus	pt	7 dec 76	8 dec 79	discharged
Ash, or Nash, Edmund[14]	do	9 May 77	See Edward Nash	
Allsop, John	pt	4 Augt 77	1 Aug 80	discharged
Ainsworth, Robt.[15]	do	19 April 77		off Rolls 77
Armstrong, George	do	12 June 77	13 July 77	deserted
Anderson, John,[16] joined 10 Aug 78	} do		Augt 78	to invalids, from thence discharged 5 feby 80

[1] Handy's. [2] Ensign Jones'. [3] Johnson's. [4] Lynch's. [5] Ghiselin's.
[6] Dobson's. [7] Beall's. [8] Chapline's. [9] Williams'. [10] Miles'.
[11] Jones'. [12] Grosh's. [13] Morris'. [14] Bayly's. [15] Reynolds'. [16] Deam's.

MUSTERS OF MARYLAND TROOPS, VOL. II.

NAMES.	RANK.	TIME OF SERVICE. Enlisted.	Discharged.	REMARKS.
Asshwell, Wm.	pt		16 Augt 80	missing
Adams, Danl. Jen.	Major	10 Dec 76	See above	
Adams, William	Ensign	.		
	Lieut	14 April 78		
Adams, Nathaniel[1]	pt	23 feb 78	20 Aug 79	deserted
Ashmore, John[2]	do	6 June 78	1 Nov 80	present
Abbott, Thomas[3]	do	30 May 78	6 March 79	discharged
Allsop, Joseph[4]	do	8 June 78	30 March 79	discharged
Armond, Abell[5]	do	7 June 78	1 July 80	deserted
Able, Cuthbert[6]	Sergt	1 feb 80	1 Nov 80	present

GERMAN REGIMENT.

NAMES.		RANK.	Enlisted.	Discharged.	REMARKS.
Arrings, Levy to 1 Jany 81	3	pt		1 Aug 80	present
Ashly, James W. L. to 1 Jany 81		pt	25 April 78	do	do
Alexander, Jacob do	3	Sergt	1 feb 78	do	do
Armstrong, John	3			26 July 79	discharged
Abel, John	3			20 do	ditto
Arnold, George	9			22 March 79	ditto
Amersley, John		See John Hammersley			
Aberly, Leonard				2 dec 78	ditto

5TH REGIMENT MARYLAND TROOPS.

NAMES.	RANK.	Enlisted.	Discharged.	REMARKS.
Bennett, Thomas[7]	pt	30 Mar 77	3 April 80	discharged
Bromel, Robert	do	10 dec 76	16 Aug 80	missing
Boxly, David	do	9 July 77	1 Nov 80	present
	fifer	15 Aug 78		
Buckley, John	do	3 Nov 77	20 Nov 78	deserted
Benton, Mark[6]	Lieut	20 feb 77	1 June 79	resigned
Burk, James	pt	3 April 77	April 78	left out
	Corpl	1 Feby 78		
Brinsfield, George	pt	5 Aug 77	13 Oct 78	discharged
Brooks, Lawrence[9]	Sergt	4 July 77	13 Oct 78 off Rolls, to Invalids ⎫ 10 Aug 81 discharged ⎭	
Bright, James	pt	14 June 77	March 80	left out
		.	14 May 80	discharged by Col. Forrest
Benton, John	do	6 June 77	April 78	left out
Barrick, John	do	7 Mar 77	ditto	ditto

[1] Bayly's. [2] Jones'. [3] Spyker's. [4] Morris'. [5] Beatty's.
[6] Lamar's. [7] Dean's. [8] Hawkins'. [9] Lynch's.

MUSTERS OF MARYLAND TROOPS, VOL. II.

Names.	Rank.	Time of Service. Enlisted.	Discharged.	Remarks.
Branffield, John	pt	17 dec 76	16 Aug 80	missing
Barry, John	do	do	1 Nov 79	deserted
Baetts, Samuel	do	13 Nov 77	28 June 78	missing
Burns, William	do	19 Jan 78	April 78	left out
Benson, Perry[1]	Lieut / Capt	10 Dec 76 } 11 Mar 78 }		
Birk, Nathaniel	pt	14 Jan 77	10 Jan 80	discharged
Barrett, Nicholas	do	10 Feby 77	7 feb 80	do
Blades, James	do	31 Mar 77	16 Aug 80	missing
Barnes, George	do	20 May		off Rolls
Byron, Thomas[2]	do / Corpl / Sergt	13 feb 77 } 1 Oct 77 } ——— }	16 Aug 80	missing
Burnett, Charles[3]	do	27 Jany 77	17 July 78	died
Bernard, John[4]	do	28 do	15 July 78	died
Burnett, John	Corpl / pt	14 Aug 77 } 17 July 78 }	1 Nov 80	present
Bowser, Samuel	pt	18 Mar 77	1 June 79	transferred to 4th [Maryland Regt.
Burns, Thomas	pt / Corpl / pt	18 Mar 79 } 8 Nov 78 } 12 Jan 80 }	January 80	present
Bryan, Luke	pt	15 Mar 77	16 Mar 80	discharged
Bird, Richard	Lieut / Capt	10 May 77 } 1 June 79 }		
Bantham, Perie[5]	pt	23 Feby 79	1 Nov 80	present
Bay, Kennedy	pt	6 dec 76	6 Sept 80	deserted
Brown, James	pt	6 do 76	16 Aug 80	missing, see Depreciation account
Blanch, William[6]	Corpl pt.	15 Aug 78	Jany 80	present
Boyd, Samuel	private	23 April 78	15 June 78	discharged
Brinsfields, George[2]	do	see Brinsfield, Geo. Hawkins Co., the other [side
Benny, John	do	2 April 78	Aug 78	died
Burgan, Joshua[5]	do / Corpl	30 May 78 } 10 July 78 }	19 Oct 78	died
Bryan, John	pt	4 May 78	6 Sept 80	deserted
Bradley, James	do	29 May 78	May 79	died, time not [known
Bendon, Thomas	do			off Rolls
Barruch, James	do	6 June 78	18 Nov 78	died
Boone, John	do	8 June 78	Aug 78	not heard of
Birh, Nathaniel[7]	do	1 April 78	see N. Burk Hund	
Brent, John	do	14 May 78	16 Aug 80	missing

[1] Handy's. [2] Johnson's. [3] Emory's. [4] Gray's. [5] Lt. Hamilton's.
[6] Ensign Jones'. [7] Lynch's.

MUSTERS OF MARYLAND TROOPS, VOL. II.

Names.	Rank.	Time of Service. Enlisted.	Discharged.	Remarks.
	fifer	1 Oct 79		
Blackam, George[1]	pt	1 May 78	1 Nov 80	present
Bending, Thomas	do	6 June 78	Aug 78	not heard of
Brown, John	do	6 June 78	2 July 78	deserted
Barrow, James[2]	do	16 June 78	16 Aug 80	missing
Biles, William	pt	6 June 78	1 Mar 79	discharged
Bentley, Samuel	do	6 June 78	1 Aug 78	died
Beck, Alexander[3]	do	4 Mar 78	Nov 79	died
Burns, Michael	do	4 April 78	Nov 79	died
Blunt, Benjamin[1]	do	12 June 78	May 79	not heard of
Burrough, John	do	1 June 78	July 78	left out
Burrough, Zacha.	do	1 June 78	ditto	ditto
Birh, Jeremiah[4]	do	4 June 78	28 June 79	deserted
Bowser, Thomas	do	4 June 78	1 Nov 80	present
Bailey, James	pt	27 April 78	16 Aug 80	missing
	Corpl	12 June 79		
	Sergt			
Bowen, Abraham	pt	14 May 78	1 Nov 80	present
Bailey, Mark[5]	do	2 April 77	1 Jany 80	deserted
Bantham, John[6]	do	18 June 77	1 Nov 80	present
Barrett, Solomon[7]	do	19 June 79	1 Nov 80	present
Bateman, Nathl.[4]	do	May 79	1 Nov 80	present
Bryan, William[8]	do		last muster January 80	
Brown, Solomon	do		do	
Bradshaw, James	do		1 Nov 80	present
Beachbeach, Benja.	do		16 Aug 80	missing
Bryan, George[9]	pt		Sept 77	taken by prior [enlist.

Sixth Maryland Regiment.

Names.	Rank.	Enlisted.	Discharged.	Remarks.
Boyer, Lambert[10]	Lieut	7 Aprl 77	12 Oct 77	resigned
Buller, James	pt	23 Aug 77	15 Aug 80	discharged
Broughton, Wm.	do	20 Aug 78	last muster Jany 80	
Boyle, Robert	do	19 May 78	Mar 79	left out
Boward, Valentine	do	5 May 78	16 Aug 80	missing
Burk, James	pt	16 May 78	1 Nov 80	present
Boward, Leonard	do	17 May 78	1 Nov 80	present
Beanes, Colmore	Surg. Mate	25 June 77	12 Oct 77	resigned
Bradley, John[11]	pt	5 feb 77	5 feb 80	discharged
Brady, Thomas	do	16 April 77	last muster Jany 80	
Bithel, John	pt	1 June 77	} 1 Nov 80	present
	Corpl	1 Jany 79		

[1] Handy's. [2] Ensign Jones'. [3] Johnson's. [4] Hawkins'. [5] Emory's. [6] Lt. Hamilton's. [7] Benson's. [8] Lynch's. [9] Dean's. [10] Ghiselin's. [11] Dobson's.

MUSTERS OF MARYLAND TROOPS, VOL. II.

Names.	Rank.	Time of Service. Enlisted.	Discharged.	Remarks.
Bullin, Thomas	pt	18 May 77	last muster Jany 80	
Beavan, Charles[1]	Ensign	28 July 77		paid
	Lieut	26 Jany 78	July 80	resigned
Wales, Edward L.	Sergt	8 Mar 77	1 Jany 78	resigned
	Ensign	17 Mar 77		
Boulton, Richard	pt	24 Aug 77	24 Aug 80	discharged
Ballard, Richard	do	10 Jany 78	3 July 79	deserted
Beale, Wm. D.[2]	Capt	10 Dec 76		
Bruff, James	Lieut	20 feb 77	Capt. 8 Sept 81	
Buchan, William	Sergt	20 June 77	16 May 80	discharged
Bayley, Seth	Corpl	16 Aprl 77	16 Aug 80	prisoner
	pt	1 June 78		
Baldwin, Wm. J.	pt	5 feb 78	16 Aug 80	missing
	Sergt	5 feb 79	Sergt. Major	
Blake, Michael	pt	24 April 78	June mus. 78	left out the Roll
Batton, Hugh	do	20 May 78	Aug 79	died
Body, Robert	do	21 do	16 Aug 80	killed
	fifer	1 July 78		
Brown, John[3] 22 Mar 79 Sergt., reduced pt. 29 Mar 79, again Sergt. 25 April 79	Corpl	5 dec 76	30 Sept 80	to Invalids
Beveren, Thomas	pt	5 dec 76	16 Aug 80	prisoner
Buyers, James	do	30 do 76	30 dec 79	discharged
Booth, Edward[4]	Sergt	16 Jan 78	1 Nov 80	present
Sergt Oct do	pt	Jany 79		
Boyle, James	do	17 Jan 77	16 Aug 80	killed
Barker, William[5] now Miles'	do Sergt. 21 July 77, pt. 1 July 78, 16 May 80 discharged			
Boe, William	do	14 Mar 77	16 Aug 80	prisoner
	pt	12 May 78	1 April 79	discharged
Beall, John[6] 1 July 78 joined	do	1 July 78	1 April 79	discharged
Baker, Peter 1 July 78 joined	do	1 July 78	1 April 79	do
Binehart, Andrew 1 July 78 joined	do	1 July 78	see Richard, Andrew	
Bradley, Cornel[7] 1 must. June 78	do	10 June 78	14 Mar 79	discharged
Blackburn, Thos.[1]	do	1 June 78	3 Sept 78	discharged
Brown, John	do	1 June 78	1 April 79	do
Backett, Isaac[2] 1 must. Jany 78	do	22 May 78	1 Nov 80	present
Banfield, James[3] Joined June 78	do	28 dec 76	28 dec 79	discharged

[1] Trueman's. [2] Beall's. [3] Hynes'. [4] Harris'. [5] Chapline's. [6] Ghiselin's. [7] Dobson's.

MUSTERS OF MARYLAND TROOPS, VOL. II.

Names.	Rank.	Time of Service. Enlisted.	Discharged.	Remarks.
Bowers, George[1]	pt	1 May 78	1 Nov 80	present
Barrett, John rein. 23 dec 78	do	30 do	17 Aug 80	deserted
Batman, Thos.	do	4 June 78	4 feb 79	discharged
Birk, Richard	do	18 May 78	26 dec 79	deserted
Brannan, Timothy[2]	pt	see O'Brannon of Hynes' Company		
Burns, Simon[3]	do	7 May 78	20 dec 79	deserted
Burness, Benjamin	do	23 May 78	17 July 80	do
Burk, Garret	do	8 May 78	22 feb 79	do
Bradley, John	do	16 May 78	17 July 80	do
Brown, John[1]	do	15 June 78	25 June 78	do
Billop, Henry[3]	do	8 April 79	1 Nov 80	present
Bowler, Aaron[4] joined 21 Sep 79	do		last muster Jany 80	
Brazenton, Thos.[5]	do	25 Aug 79	16 Aug 80	missing
Bare, Thomas	do	2 Sept 79	1 Nov 80	present
Bome, Barthw.[4]	do		do	ditto
Bumgardner, George Oct Roll 1780	do	26 feb 80	do	ditto
Brockett, Richard	do		do	ditto
Burch, Benja.				see below
Buller, Thomas	do		21 Aug 80	deserted
Baker, Abram	do		17 July 80	ditto
Burch, Benja.	do	18 Jany 80	16 Aug 80	missing

SEVENTH MARYLAND REGIMENT.

Names.	Rank.	Enlisted.	Discharged.	Remarks.
Bryan, Richard[6]	Corpl / pt	16 Mar 77 / 31 May 78	16 Mar 80	discharged
Bush, John	pt	13 April 77	25 May 77	deserted
Barrett, Williams	pt / Corpl	17 Mar 77 / 30 Sept 78	17 Mar 80	discharged
Bowden, Thos.[7]	pt	16 feb 77	16 feb 80	discharged
Brown, Daniel	do	30 May 77	13 Sept 77	deserted
Brindley, Michael	do	2 April 77	4 Oct 77	killed G. Town
Brown, Zebulon[8]	do	5 June 77	March 78	off Rolls
Barnicloe, Thos.	do	1 Nov 77	Mar 78	off Rolls
Bryan, John[9] joined 11 Aug 78	do	10 June 77	1 Nov 80	present
Bryant, James[10]	do	13 April 77	13 April 80	discharged
Bernig, (or Bercning), Danl.	do	6 dec 76	1 Nov 80	present
Broderick, Dennis July 78 returned	do	6 feb 77	16 Aug 80	missing

[1] Lt. Williams'. [2] Harris'. [3] Miles'. [4] Trueman's. [5] Norris'.
[6] Jones'. [7] Grosh's. [8] Spyker's. [9] Stull's. [10] Morris'.

during the War of the American Revolution, 1775–83.

MUSTERS OF MARYLAND TROOPS, VOL. II.

NAMES.	RANK.	TIME OF SERVICE. Enlisted.	Discharged.	REMARKS.
Bailey, Patrick	pt	18 Mar 77	9 June 77	deserted
Bryant, John	do	20 Mar 77	22 Aug 77	prisoner
Birk, Michael	do	1 April 77	30 June 80	deserted
joined 11 Aug 78				
Bryant, Daniel	do		7 Jan 80	discharged
Berry, John	do	6 April 77	June 78	off Rolls
Brown, William	do	6 April 77	July 77	off Rolls
Bayley, Mountjoy	Capt	3 dec 76	14 Sept 78	resigned
Beatty, William	Lieut	10 dec 76		paid
	Capt	14 Sept 78		
Beall, Lloyd	do	10 April 77		paid
Baker, Joel[1]	pt	19 dec 76	1 June 79	Corpl. 26 Jany [dischd.
Birk, John	do	10 May 77	11 Sept 77	prisoner
Brady, James	do	5 May 77	Sept 78	deserted
Joined June 78				
Bleas, Joseph	do	28 May 77	16 Aug 80	missing
Bracco, James	Ensign	10 Feby 77	3 jan 80	resigned
	Lieut	28 dec 77		
Brooks, Jacob[2]	pt	1 April 77	3 May 79	deserted
Burges, John	do	12 April 79	April 80	discharged
Bomgardner, Wm.	pt	2 May 77	8 May 80	do
joined 4 June 78				
Botts, Joseph	do	11 May 77	1 Nov 80	present
Burrill, John	do	10 July 77	12 July 77	deserted
Barney, Moses[3]	Corpl	1 Aug 78	1 Nov 80	present
from Sergt reduced to pt 3 Sept 78		Sergt 1 April 80		
Benson,(or Penson), Edmund	pt		Feby 78	off Rolls
Boone, Richd.	do	8 feb 77	1 Nov 80	present
				claimed by R. B. Boone
Barnes, Benja.[4]	do	31 jany 78	} March 79	not heard of
from Hazen's in Room of Wm. Monk				
Brown, Joshua[5]	do	23 Aprl 78	1 Nov 80	present
Banks, James	do	23 April 78	May 78	off Rolls
Barlow, John[1]	do	4 Mar 78	18 May 78	deserted
Burgess, Josias[6]	do	20 April 78	1 Nov 80	present
Bedder, James	do	25 April 78	1 Nov 80	present
Beckett, Humpy.	do	24 May 78	1 Nov 80	present
Bulger, Danl.	do	5 June 78	March 79	discharged
Biggs, Benja.	do	11 April 78	16 Aug 80	missing
Bruff, Wm.	do	24 April 78	1 Nov 80	present
	Corpl	May 80		

[1] Bayly's.   [2] Reynolds'.   [3] Deams'.   [4] Spyker's.   [5] Grosh's.   [6] Jones'.

MUSTERS OF MARYLAND TROOPS, VOL. II.

Names.	Rank.	Time of Service. Enlisted.	Discharged.	Remarks.
Bryan, Richard	pt	See above		
Burn, Elijah[1]	pt	12 May 78	20 Aug 78	discharged
Beaven, Thos.	do		March 79	not heard of
Bower, Boston[2]	do	1 June 78	1 April 79	discharged
Baker, Boston	do	2 June 78	1 April 79	discharged
Barnett, Daniel[2]	do	11 Aprl 78	1 Nov 80	present
Brannan, Lawrce.[4]	do	22 Aprl 78	14 May 79	private
	Corpl	18 June 78		
	Sergt	1 Jany 80	16 Aug 80	missing
Burton, John	pt	20 April 78	16 Aug 80	missing
Briggs, Wm.[3]	do	6 June 78	30 Mar 79	discharged
Brown, George	do	21 April 78	16 Aug 80	missing
Broughton, Adam[5]	do	20 July 78	9 April 79	discharged
Blades, William	do	20 July 78	9 April 79	ditto
Bissill, Assa	do	20 July 78	9 April 79	do
Bizel, Abram[3]	do	12 Oct 78	16 Aug 80	
	fifer	1 Nov 78		missing
Buck, George[6] 8 Aug 79 exchanged	pt	19 May 78	26 April 79	prisoner, 1 Nov 80 present
Bowles, Martin in Provost Mar 79	do	30 April 78	26 Aug 80	deserted
Berry, James[2]	do	12 July 78	30 Mar 79	discharged
Bedford, Thomas[7]	do	14 Aug 79	16 Aug 80	missing
Bryant, Patrick[2] Morris', 10 Feby 80	do	not mustered since Feby 80		
Bryan, Thomas[8] Mason's, Mar 80	do		27 Aprl 80	deserted
Brown, Thomas[9] Beall's, Mar 80	do		19 June 80	ditto
Buxton, Abijah[7]	do	14 Jan 80	1 Nov 80	present
Black, Francis[6] Beatty's, Mar 80	do		16 Aug 80	missing
Blair, John[10]	pt	2 April 80	1 Nov 80	present
Blake, Martin[7]	pt	29 May 80	16 Aug 80	missing
Brooks, Charles[2]	pt		do	do
Barnett, Jesse[11]	fifer	24 April 80	1 Nov 80	present
Brooks, John[6]	pt		1 July 80	deserted

GERMAN REGIMENT.

Names.	Rank.	Enlisted.	Discharged.	Remarks.
Bough, (or Buck), Geo. to 1 Jan 81	pt		1 Aug 80	
Bauswell, Saml. did not appear on Rolls till 80			22 Nov 80	deserted, joined in 81

[1] Spyker's. [2] Stull's. [3] Morris'. [4] Bayly's. [5] Grosh's. [6] Beatty's. [7] Anderson's. [8] Mason's. [9] Beall's. [10] Lynn's. [11] Jones'.

MUSTERS OF MARYLAND TROOPS, VOL. II.

Names.	Rank.	Time of Service. Enlisted.	Time of Service. Discharged.	Remarks.
Backer, Peter[1]			15 July 79	discharged
Benner, Michael			17 do do	do
Bender, (or Painter), Henry			12 Oct 79	do
Bishop, Jacob			26 July 79	do
Betzhover, Jacob			do	do
Beam, Philip	Corpl	30 July 75	24 do	do
Baylor, Danl.		5 Aug 75	do	do
Bower, John		23 July 75	24 do	do
Brown, John	fifer	21 July 75	do	do
Brieger, John	Corpl		17 July	do
Brodbech, Michael to 1 Jany 81	pt	paid from 1 Nov 79 to 1 Aug 80 pst.		
Bantz, George			22 Mar 79	discharged
Burk, John, (or Jas.)	Corpl		24 July 79	do
Beam, Conrad		26 July 75	do	do
Bennett, John				
Bates, Philip			22 Mar 79	do
Bowerd, Michael			16 July 79	do

Fifth Maryland Regiment.

Names.	Rank.	Enlisted.	Discharged.	Remarks.
Crawford, James	Qr. Mr.	14 Oct 77	20 Sept 79	resigned
Cleary, John	Qr. Mr. Sergt.	10 Aprl 77	20 July 77	dead
Crawford, James	do / Qr. Mr.	20 July 77 / 14 Oct 77	} dismissed	served full 79
Carmick, Robert[2]	fifer	30 Mar 77	16 Aug 80	missing, joined R.
Colfield, Francis[3]	pt	3 May	1 Nov 80	present
Callahan, Thomas	pt	10 May	April 78	left out
Carroll, John	do	18 June	ditto	do, joined R.
Condon, William	do	10 May 77		last muster Jany 80 } discharged May 80 by Col. Forrest
Cross, Robert	fifer / pt / fifer	19 Mar 77 / 1 Jan 78 / 20 Aug 78 } R		paid
Clary, John	Sergt	4 dec 76	10 April 77	Q. M. Sergt., Apl 78 left out
See John Cleary above, quere if not the same person				
Craig, Michael[4]	Corpl	20 Jan 77	16 Aug 80	missing
Cannon, Thomas	pt	28 Aug 77	April 78	left out
Carroll, John	do	22 Jan 78	1 Nov 80	present
Carter, John[5]	Corpl	7 dec 76	1 April 77	private, 6 dec 79 dischd.
Catlin, Thomas[6]	Sergt / pt	8 feb 77 / 11 Aug 78	8 Jan 80	discharged as Sergt.

[1] Myers'.   [2] Dean's.   [3] Benson's.   [4] Lynch's.   [5] Handy's.   [6] Johnson's.

MUSTERS OF MARYLAND TROOPS, VOL. II.

Names.	Rank.	Time of Service. Enlisted.	Discharged.	Remarks.
Catlin, B. Caleb	Corpl	28 Jan 77	Sergt. 7 June 77,	out April 78
Connady, John	pt	20 feb 77	April 78	left out
Connel, Patrick	do	28 do	} 79	left out
	Sergt	4 May 79		
Connely, Daniel	Corpl	12 Jan 77	pt. 30 Sept	June 78 left out
Chaires, John[1]	Sergt	28 Jan 77	12 Jan 80	discharged
Collins, William[2]	pt	22 Sept	30 Dec 77	died
Covington, Henry	do	10 dec 76	} 12 Jan 80	discharged
	Corpl	1 July 79		
Cosden, Jesse	Capt	10 dec 76	7 dec 77	resigned
Couch, Charles[3]	Corpl	27 Jan 77	1 Nov 80	present
1 musr. April 78 must. Sergt Oct 80				
Conner, James, Sr.	pt	4 Dec 76	4 dec 79	time expired
Conner, James, Jr.	do	3 dec 76	5 dec 79	do [valids
Conner, James, the 3d	do	10 April 77	Oct mus. 80 transferred to In- }	
			1 Nov 83 discharged on pen- }	
Cann, Augustine	do	8 dec 76	1 Nov 80	present [sion
Carman, James	do	21 feb 77	16 Aug 80	missing
Chritchets, William[4]	do	21 July 77	14 Jan 78	deserted
Joined April 78				
Chritchets, Benja.	do	21 July 77	16 Aug 80	missing
Joined April 78	must. Sergt Oct Roll 80			
Coheall, James[5]	do	6 June 78	Augt 78	not heard of
Coffee, Daniel[6]	do	17 dec 76	16 Aug 80	missing
1 mustr. Jany 78				
Collins, James	do	18 Jan 77	} 16 Aug 80	missing
1 mustr. June 78	Corpl	1 April 79		
Cooke, Moses	pt	2 June 78	1 Mar 79	died
Clift, James[6]	do	14 May 78	May 79	died, time unknown
Camble, Dunk	do	6 June 78	1 Mar 79	discharged
Connolly, John	do	5 May 78	Feby 79	mustrd. not heard of
Cooke, Moses	do	29 May 78	July 79	left out
Connally, John	do	15 May 78	6 June 78	deserted
Conner, George[7]	do	1 Jan 77	16 Aug 80	missing
Caves, John	do	26 May 78	Nov 79	died
Conner, Hugh[8]	do	9 feb 77	16 Aug 80	missing
now Gray's	1 musr. June 78			
Casley, William	do	9 June 78	16 Aug 80	missing
Clarke, William	do		July 78	left out
Chandler, John[8]	pt	19 June 78	last muster Jany 80	
1 musr. June 78				
Carney, Thomas	do	13 May 78	1 Nov 80	present

[1] Emory's. [2] Gray's. [3] Lt. Hamilton's. [4] Ensign Jones'.
[5] Lynch's. [6] Handy's. [7] Johnson's. [8] Hawkins'.

MUSTERS OF MARYLAND TROOPS, VOL. II.

Names.	Rank.	Time of Service. Enlisted.	Discharged.	Remarks.
Carr, Mathew	pt	6 June 78	2 July 79	deserted
Callahan, Dennis[1]	do	6 June 78	19 Mar 79	discharged
Callahan, Cornelius	do	10 June 78	30 June 79	deserted
Collins, Benja.	do	20 May 78	6 July 78	deserted
Caldwell, Charles	do	16 May 78	June 79	left out, not heard of for 11 mo.
Corker, John[2] now Gray's	do Joined 12 June 78	15 Jan 77	16 Aug 80	missing
Cox, John[1] Joined 18 Aug 78	do	27 July 77	June muster 79	not heard of [for 11 mo.
Clancy, Michael[3] 1 mustr. June 79	do Sergt pt	4 June 79 1 Aug 79 13 Sept 79	} 15 Nov 79	died
Clancy, Michael, Sr. 1st muster June 79	fifer	14 June 79	16 Aug 80	missing, joined [Regt.
Clark, Richard[4] Joined in June 79	pt		5 dec 79	discharged
Crouch, Amos[5]	do drum	7 July 79 1 Sept 79	16 Aug 80	missing
Conydon, Edward	pt	1 Sept 79	last mustr. Jan 80	
Connolly, Thomas[4] joined 1 Oct 79	do		do do	
Civill, William[6] Benson's, late Dean's	do	4 April 79	1 Nov 80	present
Conner, Dennis			mustered Oct 80 Sept deserted	
Chairs, John	Ensign			

SIXTH REGIMENT.

Corkery, William[7]	pt	31 Mar 78	10 July 80	deserted
Coughlan, Michael	do	14 May 78	last muster Jany 80	
Carroll, John	do	18 May 78	22 dec 79	deserted
Chambers, William		5 May 78	1 Nov 80	present
Charlton, J. W.	Paymr	22 April 77	1 Oct 78	resigned
Cardiff, Patrick[8]	pt fifer	1 Aug 77 1 May 78	16 Aug 80 ditto	prisoner drum major 1 May 78 }
Conner, William	pt	2 feb 77	5 feb 1780	discharged
Cahoe, Thomas[9]	do	29 July 77	1 Nov 80	present
Conner, Cornelius	do	Dec 76	21 Jan 80	discharged
Coleman, William[10]	do	2 Aug 77	2 Aug 80	discharged
Carney, Patrick	do	11 May 77	16 Aug 80	missing
Cleaver, Benja.	do	14 feb 78	1 Nov 80	present

[1] Emory's. [2] Handy's. [3] Lynch's. [4] Gray's. [5] Hawkins',
[6] Benson's. [7] Ghiselin's. [8] Dobson's. [9] Trueman's. [10] Beall's.

MUSTERS OF MARYLAND TROOPS, VOL. II.

NAMES.	RANK.	Enlisted.	Discharged.	REMARKS.
Curwell, Peter	pt	12 May 78	16 Aug 80	killed
Coir, Michael	do	11 May 78	16 Aug 80	killed
Collins, Charles	do	1 May 78	16 Aug 80	prisoner
Crail, James[1]	do	6 dec 76	78 June mustr.	left out
deserted 30 April 77, joined 1 Sept 1777				
Carlin, Wm.	do	9 dec 76	9 dec 79	discharged
Claward, Abram	do	20 feb 77	last muster Jany 80.	
Collins, George	do	18 June 77	6 June 82	present
Cannon, Patrick[2]	do	6 Aug 77	16 Aug 80	missing
Connally, Michael[3]	do	28 May 77	1 Nov 80	present
Q. M. S. 3 July 78	Sergt	3 Nov 77		
delivd. to	as Sergt Oct 78, reduced to private 21 Sept 80			
Coyn, Donn	pt	21 May 77	last mustr. Jany 80	
discharged by G. Lineder, joined again ——				
Chaplain, Moses[4]	Capt do	10 Dec 76	} 7 Oct 77	resigned
now Miles'	Capt	20 feb 77		
Clarke, David	pt	7 Mar 77	16 Aug 80	missing
Crowder, Saml.	pt	7 May 77	3 July 79	deserted
Crozier, John[5]	do	10 June 78	16 Aug 80	killed
1 mustr. June 78				
rein. 23 dec 78	}			
Campbell, John	do	24 May 78	1 Nov 80	present
1 mustr. June 78				
rein. 23 dec 78	}			
Cachey, Hector	do	9 June 78	do	do
1 mustr. June 78				
rein. 23 dec 78	}			
Carroll, William	do	9 June 78	14 Mar 79	discharged
1 mustr. June 78				
Church, Abram[6]	do	12 May 78	1 Nov 80	present
Cusick, Christopher	do	30 May 78	do	do
Coyle, Michael[6]	do	28 April 78	16 Aug 80	missing
Collen, Michael	do	30 April 78	16 Aug 80	do
Clifford, William	do	10 June 78	1 April 79	discharged
Courts, Christopher	do	1 June 78	do	do
Coventree, Jacob	do	22 May 78	feb 79	mustered time expired
Callaghan, Joseph	do	29 May 78	30 May 79	deserted
Clanahan, Robert	do	30 May 78	1 Nov 80	present
Cray, John	do	22 May 78	29 June 78	deserted
Collins, Edward[7]	do	23 May 78	1 Nov 80	present
Connard, Thos.[1]	do	9 April 78	10 July 78	deserted

[1] Hynes'. [2] Laurence's. [3] Harris'. [4] Chapline's.
[5] Dobson's. [6] Lt. Williams'. [7] Miles'.

MUSTERS OF MARYLAND TROOPS, VOL. II.

Names.	Rank.	Time of Service. Enlisted.	Discharged.	Remarks.
Cooney, Laughlan	pt	20 April 78	26 April 78	deserted
Craven, Andrew[1]	do	23 June 78	22 Mar 79	discharged
Cooke, William[2] 1 mustr. Augt 78	do	1 June 78	16 Aug 80	missing
Condrone, John[1]	do	1 Aug 78	8 Jan 79	died
Collard, William[3] 1st muster July 79	do		16 Aug 80	prisoner
Crime, Michael[4] 1st muster July 79	do		1 Nov 80	present
	Fifer	14 Oct 79		
Class, Michael[5]	pt	27 Augt 79	17 Oct 79	deserted
Carter, Noah[6]	Drum	22 dec 79	1 Nov 80	present
Cahoe, Thos., Jr. Oct Muster 1780	do		do	do
Carey, Edward	pt		Sept 80	missing
Cole, William	do	3 Oct 80	1 Nov 80	present

SEVENTH REGIMENT.

Names.	Rank.	Enlisted.	Discharged.	Remarks.
Churchill, John[7]	pt	10 Jan 77	May 77	off Rolls
Crail, William Joined the 31 April 79	do	18 May 79	1 Nov 80	present
Carter, Timothy Joined 21 July 78	do	12 April 77	11 April 80	discharged
Carter, Michael[8]	do	14 April 77	4 Oct 77	missing
Calihart, Frederick	do	6 May 77	June 78	off Rolls
Crowley, Dennis	Drum	18 May 77	16 Aug 80	missing
	pt	1 Aug 77		
Cole, William	do	10 May 77	12 April 78	deserted
	Corpl	1 Oct 77		
Coleman, John	pt	18 June 77	16 Aug 80	missing
Clary, Dennis retd. 16 July 78	Corpl	1 April 77		
	Sergt	1 Jany 80	1 April 80	discharged
Christian, John[9]	Sergt	22 May 77	Oct 77	off Rolls
Conroy, Hugh	pt	10 June 77	22 Aug 77	prisoner
Collins, James[10] reinlisted	Sergt	6 dec 76	2 April 80	discharged
Connally, James	Drum	14 April 77	June 78	off Roll
Carroll, George	pt	6 dec 76	8 dec 79	discharged
Cooke, William	do	8 Jan 77	25 May 79	deserted
Carty, James	do	9 Jan 77	16 Aug 80	missing
Conner, Thomas	pt	3 feb 77	Jany 78	off Rolls
Cooke, Thomas	do	1 Mar 77	16 Aug 80	missing

[1] Miles'. [2] Hynes'. [3] Trueman's. [4] Lt. Williams'. [5] Norris'.
[6] Jacobs'. [7] Grosh's. [8] Spyker's. [9] Stull's. [10] Morris'.

MUSTERS OF MARYLAND TROOPS, VOL. II.

Names.	Rank.	Time of Service. Enlisted.	Discharged.	Remarks.
Casey, Peter[1]	pt	28 Mar 77	16 Aug 80	missing
	Corpl	19 Oct 78		
	pt	20 June 80		
Clacker, Ghehoikin	pt	6 April 77	9 June 77	deserted
Carter, Richard	do	5 Sept 77	16 Aug 80	missing
Carroll, Patrick[2] to Anderson's	do	4 dec 76	11 Sept 77	prisoner
Cunningham, Peter	do	5 dec 76	1 Oct 80	present
Carnant, Jacob	do	6 dec 76	1 Nov 80	present
Crosby, Joseph	do	6 dec 76	8 dec 76	deserted
Carroll, William	do	21 Jan 77	2 Feby 77	deserted
Connally, Patrick	do	28 May 77	2 April 80	discharged
	Sergt	20 Mar 77		
Cofforth, William[2] from Reynolds' Co.	Fifer	26 dec 77	1 Nov 80	discharged
	F. Major	27 Jan 78		
Cunningham, James[3]	Corpl	25 June 77	1 July 80	deserted
Cofforth, Conrad	Fifer	20 Mar 77	May 80	discharged
Cahill, David	pt	24 April 77	20 April 80	do
Connelly, William	do	18 April 77	Jany 80	prisoner War
Coatney, Anthony	do	20 May 77	May 80	deserted
Casey, William Joined 21 Nov 77	do	30 May 77		
Chamberlain, John	pt	6 June 77	6 June 77	deserted
Callahan, Barthw.[4]	do	7 dec 76	7 dec 79	discharged
		appeared at Annapolis 25 April 89		
Clarke, Arthur	do		1 Nov 80	present
Connally, Laurence	do		28 June 78	missing
Curran, Robert	do		Feby 78	off Rolls
Clarke, John[5]	pt	4 May 78	June 79	dead
Cross, James	pt	21 April 78	5 July 80	deserted
Copes, John	do	9 May 78	1 Mar 79	discharged
Can, Nicholas[2]	do	6 Jan 78	Nov 78	off Rolls
Cox, Mathew	do	4 Mar 78	16 April 78	deserted
Chesire, John[6]	Sergt	11 Jany 78		
	Joined again and on 18 June 81 killed at 96			
Coleby, John	pt	30 April 78	March 80	prisoner War
Coventry, Charles	do	6 June 78	16 Mar 79	discharged
Craine, Henry	do	6 June 78	16 Mar 79	dischd., joined
Corner, Thomas[7] June, Spyker's	do		1 Mar 79	do
Class, Martin[8]	do	9 June 78	do	do

[1] Anderson's. [2] Bayly's. [3] Reynolds'. [4] Deams'.
[5] Spyker's, Grosh's. [6] Jones'. [7] Spyker's. [8] Stull's.

MUSTERS OF MARYLAND TROOPS, VOL. II.

NAMES.	RANK.	TIME OF SERVICE. Enlisted.	Discharged.	REMARKS.
Crow, Adam	pt	28 April 78	1 Nov 80	present
Colgain, William	do	22 April 78	11 Sept 80	deserted
Campbell, Isaac	do	29 June 78	Dec 79	off Rolls
Carpenter, Mathew	do	18 April 78	1 April 79	deserted
Cummings, Wm. Joined 2 Aug 79	do	23 April 78	1 Nov 80	present
Clarke, Richd.[1]	do	24 April 78	Nov & Dec 78	dead
Campbell, Nichs.	do	21 April 78	Jany 79	dead
Crowley, Darby[2]	do	25 feb 78	22 June 80	joined
Carney, Thomas	do	3 April 78	20 May 80	deserted
	Corpl	18 June 78		
Cypher, John[1]	pt	5 June 78	30 Mar 79	discharged
Campbell, John	do	8 June 78	30 Mar 79	discharged
Cox, Clarkeson[3]	do	7 June 78	11 April 79	discharged
Clarke, William[4] 2d Nov 78 Grosh's	do		11 Jan 79	transd. to 2nd [Md. Brigade
Cassady, Mathew[1] Oct 78 Md. Morris'	pt		16 Aug 80	missing
Carey, William[2]	do	21 May 78	16 Aug 80	missing
Christopher, Thos. H.	do	20 May 78	1 Nov 80	present
Chitham, Aquilla	do	May 78	} do	do
	Sergt	1 May 80		
Cox, Ezaiah	pt	1 Mar 79	5 Mar 79	deserted
Chandler, James[6]	do	1 Mar 80	8 May 80	deserted
Cowling, George[1]	do	22 Jan 80	16 Aug 80	missing
Calbart, Simon[6]	do	24 Jan 80	1 Nov 80	present
Carey, Owen[7] Mch 80 Lamar's	Corpl	1 feb 80	80 do	do
Carey, Michael[7] do Lamar's	Drum	10 feb 80	do	do
Compton, Igns.[8]	do	1 April 80	do	do
Curren, James[9]	do	8 feb 80	do	do
Caton, William[10]	do	30 Mar 80	16 Aug 80	missing
Carr, Stephen[6]	do	12 April 80	Nov 80	present
Clancy, Edwd.[1]	fifer	4 April 80	do	do
Cochran, John[6]	pt		do	do
Clements, James	do		do	do
Clarke, Saml.	do		do	do

[1] Morris'. [2] Bayly's. [3] Beatly's. [4] Grosh's. [5] Jones'.
[6] Anderson's. [7] Lamar's. [8] L. Beall's. [9] Mason's. [10] Lynn's.

MUSTERS OF MARYLAND TROOPS, VOL. II.

Names.	Rank.	Time of Service. Enlisted.	Discharged.	Remarks.

German Regiment.

Names.	Rank.	Enlisted.	Discharged.	Remarks.
Cahill, Timothy to 1 Jan 81	pt	27 May 78	1 Aug 80	present
Caufman, Jacob to do	do	21 Aprl 78	do	do
Cole, Benjamin to 1 Jan 81	do	20 May 78	do	do
Crothorn, George to 1 Jan 81	do	2 April 77	do	do
Curley, Owen	mustrd. dest. Pay roll		1 Aug 80	deserted, joined again
Croft, (Kraft), William	Corpl		26 July 79	discharged
Cole, John	Sergt		24 do	do
Cronise, Henry			24 do	do
Croft, John			24 July 79	discharged
Clifton, Thomas			26 do	do
Cambler, (or Gambler,) Michael	pt		1 Aug 80	pst. & 1 Jany 81 paid
Casner, Christopher to 1 Jany 81	do		do	do
Crower, Rudolph			15 July 79	discharged
Cowley, Michael			14 Aug 79	do do
Champness, Chs.			1 Aug 80	to Invalids
Cromer, (or Cramer), Jacob			20 July 79	discharged
Crush, Michael	see Michael Grosh			
Cline, John	see Kline			

Fifth Regiment.

Names.	Rank.	Enlisted.	Discharged.	Remarks.
Dean, John[1]	Capt	10 dec 76	16 Nov 77	prisoner taken F. Washington
Downs, Lodman	Corpl	28 Jan 77	1 Sept 77	promoted Sergeant
	pt	11 Jan 78	}	
	Sergt	1 Jan 79	} 5 Feby 80	discharged
Dawson, Andrew	pt	11 July 77	16 Aug 80	missing
Dennison, William	do	10 dec 76	April 79	deserted
Davis, Griffith[2]	Sergt	4 May 77	}	
	pt	12 June 79	}	
	Q.M.Sergt.	24 dec 79	}	
Deford, Jesse	pt	24 June	last muster Jany 80	
Davis, (Daves or Davis), William	do	30 June	April 78	left out
Dyal, John[3]	do	4 June 77	July 78	off Rolls

[1] Dean's. [2] Hawkins'. [3] Lynch's.

during the War of the American Revolution, 1775–83.

MUSTERS OF MARYLAND TROOPS, VOL. II.

NAMES.	RANK.	Enlisted.	Discharged.	REMARKS.
Dawson, John[1]	Sergt	9 Mar 77	} 6 Mar 80	discharged
	pt	29 May 79		
Dean, Thomas[2]	do	22 Mar 77	15 July 78	died
Denson, Isaac	do	10 dec 76	22 May 78	died
Dorsey, John	Sergt	23 feb 78		
Dawson, Joseph[3]	pt	15 Jany 78		joined
1 mustr. April 78				
Doyle, James	do	2 Jan 77	Sept 80	joined
Davis, Philemon[4]	do	26 April 78	discharged 16 May 80	
to Hawkins', 1 mustr. April 78				
Deford, John[5]	do	8 Mar 78	10 Oct 79	died
Deford, Joseph[5]	do	8 Mar 78		
	Corpl Oct Muster 80			
Downey, Alex.[3]	do	28 May 78	1 Mar 79	discharged, } reinlisted again
Muster again Sept Roll 78				
Davy, Edward	do	30 May 78	Aug 78	not heard of
Doblin, Edward	do	6 June 78	Aug 78	not heard of
Danks, John[6]	do	28 April 78	25 June 78	deserted & Sept 1 deserted
1 mustr. Jany 78				
Dean, Elijah	pt	15 May 78		joined R.
Doran, Michael[1]	do	1 June 78	1 Nov 80	present
1 muster June 78				
Dun, Patrick	do	6 May 78	feb 79	not heard of
Dickeson, John[4]	do	12 May 78	last muster Jan 80	
Duhague, John[1]	do	5 May 78	1 Nov 80	present
1 mus. June 78				
Dyers, (or Duis), George[7]	do	28 April 78	last muster Jany 80	
Dimond, Charles	do	4 June 78	19 Mar 79	discharged
Dice, (or Dues), James	do	12 June 78	Jany 80	prisoner war
Downey, John[8]	do	25 April 78	1 Nov 80	present
Dapson, James[2]	do	4 May 78	6 July 78	deserted
Dohorty, Barney[8]	do	14 June 79	1 Sept 79	to Invalids
1 must. June 79				
Dee, (or Dean), Elijah	do	11 May 78	1 Nov 80	present
1 mus. July 79				
Durgan, Patrick[8]	do	13 June 79	21 Nov 79	died
Durgan, James	do	16 June 79	1 Nov 80	present
	Fifer	1 Aug 79		
Downey, Dennis	pt			
Darah, John[9]	pt	1 Nov 80		present
joined 7 April 79				
Dowling, Roger[10]	do	16 June 79	do	do
Dutch, Mathias[11]	do	30 April 79	last muster Jany 80	

[1] Handy's. [2] Emory's. [3] Lt. Hamilton's. [4] Johnson's. [5] Hawkins'. [6] Lynch's. [7] Bird's. [8] Benson's. [9] Beall's. [10] Lt. Williams'. [11] Norris'.

MUSTERS OF MARYLAND TROOPS, VOL. II.

Names.	Rank.	Time of Service. Enlisted.	Discharged.	Remarks.
		Sixth Regiment.		
Donnally, Patrick[1]	pt	22 July 77	22 July 80	discharged
Donovan, Richd.	Ensign	10 Dec 76	17 April 77	Adjutant
	Adjt	17 April 77		
	Lieut	1 April 78	16 Aug 80	killed
Dobson, Henry[2]	Capt	10 dec 76		
Donnelly, Caleb	pt	20 May 78	1 Nov 80	present
Day, Samuel[3]	pt	23 May 77		last muster Jan 80
		discharged by Col. Forrest 14 May 1780		
Delon, (or Dolon), Peter	do	14 Oct 77	16 Aug 80	prisoner
	Corpl	1 Aug 79		
	Sergt	22 dec 79		
Duvall, Benja.[4]	pt	4 dec 76	last muster Jany 80	
private 6 July 79	Sergt	1 Mar 78		
Dunster, Peter	pt	10 Jany 77	16 Aug 80	killed
Dickason, Wm.	do	27 feb 77	last muster Jany 80	
Duffy, Terrence	do	5 May 77		
Dominick, Benja.	do	19 May 78	1 Nov 80	present
Donovan, Danl.[5]	do	9 feb 77	last muster Jany 80	
Dennis, Basil[6]	do	22 April 77	do	do
Dougherty, Michael[7]	Lieut	14 June 77	12 April 79	cashiered
Delany, Nicholas	pt	24 Jany 78	16 Aug 80	missing
Durgan, Anthony[1]	pt	13 June 78	Dec 79	absent wt. Leave
Dugan, Edward[2]	do	25 May 78	10 Sept 78	died
1 muster June 78				
Delefraney, John B.[3]	do	1 June 78	30 Nov 78	died.
Davis, John[4]	do	19 feb 77	wounded and discharged by	
Joined June 78, mustered March Roll 79			Genl. Arnold 25 Aug 78.	
Davett, Henry[5]	pt	22 April 78	last muster Jany 80	
Davis, Robert	do	28 April 78	1 Nov 80	present, discharg-[ed 1 May 81
Dailey, Patrick	do	1 June 78	April 79	deserted
rein. 24 dec 78				
Duvall, Richd.[6]	do	30 Mar 78	1 Nov 80	present
Duley, Saml.[8]	do	20 April 78	20 May 78	deserted
Durham, William	do	28 April 78	1 Nov 80	present
Davis, Samuel[8]	do	27 Mar 78	April 78	deserted, joined R.
Doran, Patrick[9]	Corpl	4 April 78	1 Nov 80	present
1 mustr. Aug 78	Sergt	19 Nov 78		
Dorsey, Levin[10]	pt	31 Aug 79	17 Oct 79	deserted
Dunbar, Saml.	do		17 July 80	deserted
1 muster Sept 79				

[1] Ghiselin's. [2] Dobson's. [3] Trueman's. [4] Beall's. [5] Hynes'.
[6] Laurence. [7] Harris'. [8] Lt. Williams'. [9] Miles'. [10] Norris'.

MUSTERS OF MARYLAND TROOPS, VOL. II.

NAMES.	RANK.	TIME OF SERVICE. Enlisted.	Discharged.	REMARKS.
Denoon, John Oct Mus. 80	drum	1 Mar 80	1 Nov 80	present
Davis, Henry	pt		do	do
Devericks, James joined 16 Sept 80	do		do	do
Davis, Richard	do		1 Oct 80	do
Doyle, John	do		16 Aug 80	missing
Decorn, John	do		16 Aug 80	missing

SEVENTH REGIMENT.

NAMES.	RANK.	Enlisted.	Discharged.	REMARKS.
Denny, Robert	pt	10 dec 76		
	Qr. Master	30 April 77		
	Py. Master	27 June 77		
	Lieut	3 Jany 80		
Donnally, Patrick	Adjt	13 April 77		
	Ensign	28 May 78		
	Lieut	7 Oct 79		
Dixon, Richard[1]	pt	1 April 77	28 Mar 80	discharged
Dowling, James[2]	pt	26 Jany 77		
	Corpl	8 June 77		private 1 Nov 1780
1 Jany 80 Sergt	Sergt	1 Nov 77		
	pt	6 Aug 77		
Day, Francis	pt	8 April 77	27 Oct 78	died
	Corpl	1 May 77		
Denn, Edward	pt	14 April 77	8 Mar 78	decd.
Davis, Thomas[3]	Corpl	20 April 77	16 Aug 80	missing
	pt	25 dec 77		
Driver, James	pt	20 April 77	16 Aug 80	missing
	Corpl	1 Mar 80		
	pt	1 June 80		
Delanaway, John	pt	21 May 77	16 Aug 80	missing
Davis, William[4]	do	Q. M. 77	2 Mar 80	discharged
Dixon, William	do	10 June 77	1 Jany 80	deserted
Doyle, Hugh[5] 4 May 79 private	Sergt	6 dec 76	9 dec 79	discharged
Donovan, William	pt	7 Jany 77	Sept 77	off Rolls
Dillon, James Joined Jany 78	do	5 feb 77		feby 78 off Rolls
Duley, William	do	24 Mar 77	16 Aug 80	missing
Dixon, John	do	3 April 77	31 July 77	deserted
Darby, John[6]	do	8 Aug 77	Sept 77	off Rolls
Dailey, (or Delany), Jno.	do	1 Sept 77	6 July 80	deserted

[1] Jones'. [2] Grosh's. [3] Spykers'. [4] Stull's. [5] Morris'. [6] Miles'.

MUSTERS OF MARYLAND TROOPS, VOL. II.

Names.	Rank.	Time of Service. Enlisted.	Discharged.	Remarks.
Deane, Roger[1]	pt	5 dec 76	July 78	off Rolls
Devitt, George	do	11 Jan 77	1 Nov 80	present
Downey, Cornelius	do	15 Jan 77	28 June 78	killed at Monmouth
	Corpl	Sept 77		
Dorman, Thomas	pt	9 feb 77	28 Mar 80	prisoner War
Duffey, John	do	8 May 77	16 Aug 80	missing
Donent, John	do	28 April 77	28 April 80	discharged, appld. 26 May 1789
Duncan, Robert	do	7 Aug 77	1 Nov 80	present
Davis, John	do	4 Aug 77	16 Aug 80	missing
Dennison, John	do	26 Nov 77	16 Aug 80	missing
	Corpl	19 Oct 78		
	Sergt	1 Jan 80		
Denny, Saml.	Sergt		2 Mar 81	discharged
Dixon, John	pt	17 Nov 77	25 Oct 80	deserted
Donavan, Wm.[2]	do		17 Mar 77	do
Denny, Saml.[3]	do	27 Mar 78	1 Nov 80	present
	Corpl	1 Jan 80		
	Sergt	1 April 80	discharged 2 Mar 81	
Davidson, Allen[4]	fifer	24 dec 77	8 feb 78	deserted
Davidson, James[5] 1 muster April 78	Sergt		May 78	off Rolls
Davidson, Luke	pt	27 dec 77	8 feb 78	deserted
Downs, Richd.[6]	do	6 June 78	16 Mar 79	discharged, reinlisted July 80
Dodd, James[3]	do	6 June 78	15 feb 79	discharged
Dailey, John[7]	do	6 May 78	May 80	deserted
Davis, Evans[4]	do	18 May 78	16 Augt 80	missing
Davis, Samuel[1]	do	9 May 78	1 Nov 80	present
	Sergt	1 June 80		
Dodson, Wm.[4]	pt	13 June 78	30 Mar 79	discharged
Duncan, Jessee[3] 1st muster Joined 20 July 78	Sergt		5 Jan 79	discharged
Dove, John[5] Field & Staff Q. M. 16 April 80	Sergt	1 May 78		
Disheroon, Thos.	pt		10 feb 79	died
Delany, John[8]	do	7 feb 79	2 June 80	deserted
Denwood, Levin	Surgeon	3 Oct 79		
Donaldson, Wm.[4]	pt		Jany 80	prisoner War
Devenish, George[9]	do		16 Aug 80	missing
Dawson, (or Davison), John[10]	do		16 Aug 80	missing

[1] Bayly's. [2] Deams'. [3] Grosh's. [4] Morris'. [5] Beatty's.
[6] Jones'. [7] Stull's. [8] Hardman's. [9] Lamar's. [10] Mason's.

MUSTERS OF MARYLAND TROOPS, VOL. II.

Names.	Rank.	Time of Service. Enlisted.	Discharged.	Remarks.
		German Regiment.		
Dyer, James	Invalid	1 May 77		5 May paid
Dalton, John	pt	1 June 77	1 Aug 80	present
Dunkin, James			16 July 79	discharged
Dretch, John			20 July 79	do
Danruth, Godlb.			30 do 79	do
		Fifth Maryland Regiment.		
Edmondson, Sam.	Q. M.	10 dec 76	14 Oct 77	resigned
Ellis, Richard[1]	private	15 Mar 77	16 Aug 80	missing
Emory, Richard	Capt	10 dec 76	27 dec 77	resigned
Emory, Gideon[2]	1 Lieut	14 feb 77		
Evans, Thomas	pt	28 April 77	July 78	off Rolls
			6 Jan 81	discharged
Engram, Wm.	do	18 May 77	see William Ingram	
Elfry, Godfrey[3]	do	20 Jan 77	12 Jan 80	discharged
Eaton, Richard[4]	do	10 dec 76	10 dec 79	time expired
Ellery, Dennis[5]	do	30 May 78	Aug 78	not heard of
Edgerly, Wm.[1]	do	29 May 78	time out Mar 79	left out
Ewbanks, Jona.[6]	do	13 do do	2 July 78	deserted
Ewbanks, Richd.	do	9 May 78	do do	do
Edwards, Burton[7]	do	6 May 78	11 April 79	do
Evans, John[6]	do	27 April 79	1 Oct 80	present
Eccleston, Jervis[8]	do	16 June 79	do do	do
		Sixth Maryland Regiment.		
Evans, William[9]	pt	21 July 77	12 Oct 78	deserted
deserted 20 Aug 77, joined 25 May 78				
Evans, Benja.	pt	28 April 78	31 Oct 79	died
Elliott, Joseph[10]	do	11 May 78	1 Nov 80	present
Ellms, George[11]	fife	14 Oct 77	do do	do
	fife Major	18 feb 78		
Etheridge, Jno.	pt	2 Mar 78	16 Nov 79	died
Estep, Alexander[12]	Lieut	20 feb 77	13 Oct 77	resigned
Elleary, (or Hilleary), John	pt	10 Jan 77	1 Nov 80	present
Elliott, John[13]	do	21 April 77	do	do
Evans, Richard	do	1 May 77	Jan 80	present
			1 May 80	discharged

[1] Lynch's. [2] Emory's. [3] Cosden's. [4] Ensign Jones', Benson's. [5] Lt. Hamilton's.
[6] Handy's. [7] Hawkins'. [8] Benson's. [9] Ghiselin's. [10] Dobson's.
[11] Trueman's. [12] Beall's. [13] Laurence's.

MUSTERS OF MARYLAND TROOPS, VOL. II.

Names.	Rank.	Time of Service. Enlisted.	Discharged.	Remarks.
Egan, Patrick[1]	pt	21 do do	1 Nov 80	present
Elvin, John[2] 9	do	2 June 78	14 Mar 79	discharged
Everett, Richard[3] 9	do	1 June 78	1 April 79	do
English, Saml.[4] 9	do	3 do do	do	do
Eddleman, Michl.[5] 3	do	8 Mar 77	10 dec 77	9 Mar 80 discharged
Ellis, Thomas 9	do	3 June 78	22 Mar 79	dischd.
Ellis, Brion	do		16 Aug 80	prisoner

SEVENTH MARYLAND REGIMENT.

Evans, John[6]	pt	16 Jan 77	Mar 78	off Rolls
Evans, John[7]	Sergt 5 Jan 80 Sergt Major	1 April 77	2 Mar 80	resigned
Early, Benja.[8]	pt	6 June 78	16 Mar 79	discharged
Edwards, Saml.[9]	do	19 May 78	26 May	deserted
Ellison, Richard[9]	do	2 May 78	26 May 79	died
Easter, Nichs.	pt		26 April 81	dischd.

GERMAN REGIMENT.

Elliott, Benja.	1 mus. desd. P. R.		1 Aug 80	deserted
Eissell, John 3			11 Aug 79	discharged
Ellsperger, Wolfgn.			16 July 79	do
England, Benja.	Drum		do	do
Elsing, Paul			30 July 79	do
Etnier, John			26 do	do
Ensey, Jas.			10 Oct 79	do
Etter, Jacob	Corpl		15 July 79	do
Engellee, (or) Angel, Peter			14 Aug 79	do
Engle, Bartel			6 Aug 79	do, died

FIFTH MARYLAND REGIMENT.

Frazier, William[10]	1st Lieut	10 dec 76		
Foster, Rigby	pt	30 May 77	1 Nov 80	present
Friend, James	do	7 Aug 77	1 Jany 80	do discharged Augt 80
Freeland, (or Freeman), John[11]	do	3 May		
Joined 1 April 79	Joined again 20 March 80			
Foster, William[12]	Sergt	15 dec 76	pt. 1 April 77, Corpl. 1 Nov, Sergt. 1 Oct 79, 16 Augt 80 missing	

[1] Harris'. [2] Dobson's. [3] Trueman's. [4] Lt. Williams'. [5] Miles'. [6] Jones'.
[7] Spyker's. [8] Grosh's. [9] Beatty's. [10] Dean's. [11] Hawkins'. [12] Handy's.

MUSTERS OF MARYLAND TROOPS, VOL. II.

NAMES.	RANK.	TIME OF SERVICE. Enlisted.	Discharged.	REMARKS.
Ferguson, James	Corpl	7 April 77	10 Jan 80	discharged
Foreman, William[1]	Sergt	13 dec 76		
	Sergt. Major	1 Jan 79		
Flynn, Bryan	pt	13 Mar 77	16 Aug 80	missing
Foreman, Perry	do	3 feb 77	April 78	left out
Freely, Charles	do	8 dec 76	16 Aug 80	missing
to Hamilton's or Comd. feby 80				
Finoughty, Thomas[2]	do	10 March 77	5 April 78	deserted
Finley, George[3]	do	14 Jan 77	12 Jan 80	discharged
prvt 1 April 79, Corpl April 78				
Farrell, William[4]	pt	4 Mar 77	1 Nov 80	present
1st muster 78				
Floid, Joseph,[5]	do	13 Jany 78	drum. 15 Aug 78, 10 Jan 80 dischd.	
Joined April 78				
Fullom, John[1]	do	17 Mar 77	1 Nov 80	present
Hugou's, 1 muster April 78				
Flowers, Edward[6]	do	30 Mar 78	16 Aug 80	missing
1 muster April 78				
Fairbanks, Johns[4]	do	1 June 78	15 Aug 80	died
Fields, Michael[6]	do	23 April 78	12 Aug 78	deserted
Foster, Stephen	do	2 June 78	Inlisted with Genl. Palaskey	
Fountain, William[7]	pt	13 June 78	Oct 78	died
Forson, George	do	20 May 78	Feby 79	heard of
Farrowfield, John	do	20 May 78	July 78	off Rolls
Fitzgerald, Thomas	do	12 May 78	Feby 79	not heard of
Foster, Mark[5]	do	15 May 78	1 Nov 80	present
Foster, Nathaniel	do	30 May 78	Jan 80	present
Ford, George[1]	do	13 May 78	15 Aug 78	joined
Fremly, Thomas[7]	do	19 June 78	1 Nov 80	present
1st muster June 78				
Ford, Ash	do	25 May 78	April & May 79 not heard of	
1st muster June 78				
Freeland, John	do		July 78	off Rolls
1st muster June 78 and July 78				

SIXTH MARYLAND REGIMENT.

Fouts, Jacob	Corpl	15 Aug 77	Augt 78	off Rolls
Ford, Benja.	Major	20 Feby 77 ⎫		
	do Col.	17 April 77 ⎬		
	do Col. Comt.	⎭		

[1] Johnson's.   [2] Emory's.   [3] Cosden's.   [4] Lt. Hamilton's.   [5] Ensign Jones'.
[6] Lynch's.   [7] Handy's.

MUSTERS OF MARYLAND TROOPS, VOL. II.

NAMES.	RANK.	TIME OF SERVICE. Enlisted.	Discharged.	REMARKS.
Finlow, Daniel[1]	pt	12 May 78	Jany 80	present
Finton, Abram	do	18 May 78	Aug 78	off Rolls
Freeman, Jeremiah[2]	do	15 July 77	do	do
Felton, Thomas[3]	do	3 March 77	7 May	dischd. by Col. Forrest
Fitzsimmons, Thos.	do	10 Jan 77	10 Jan 80	discharged
Faup, Benja.		5 May 78	(see Phap, Benjamin)	
Fox, Anthony[4]	Sergt	20 April 77	Jany 80	present }
		21 April 80		dischd. by Col. Howard }
Fitzpatrick, Bars.[5]	pt	22 July 77	7 Mar 79	died
Chaplin's, now Miles'				
Finacy, William[6]	pt	1 July 78	Dec 79	absent without leave
78 1 July Joined				
Fullam, Michl.	do	1 July 78	1 April 79	discharged
78 1 July Joined				
Finacy, John	do	1 July 78	Dec 78	do
1 July 78 Joined				
Furwott, John Peter[7]	do	29 Aprl 78	1 Nov 80	present
	Sergt	1 June 78		
Flick, George	pt	June 78	1 April 79	discharged
Farrance, Nichs.	do	22 April 78	do	do
Foster, Jona.[8]	do	20 May 78	Jany 80	present
Ford, William	do	19 May 78	16 Aug 80	missing
Ford, John[9]	do	28 Aprl 78	16 Aug 80	prisoner
Fitzgerald, Timothy[1]	do	11 July 78	1 Nov 80	present
Joined for 3 years 23 dec 78				
Fairfield, Thomas	pt	12 June 78	10 July 78	deserted
Filbert, Joseph[2]	Corpl	30 May 78	1 Nov 80	present
(See the Letter P).				
Freely, William[10]	pt	17 June 77	1 Jany 80	present
Joined 2 Aug 78				
Force, Joseph[11]	do	1 June 79	1 Jan 80	do
Frost, Silvester[3]	do	15 Sept 77	1 Jan 80	do
1 muster Oct 79				
Flack, James[12]	Sergt	23 April 79	1 Nov 80	do
Fuller, William	pt		do	do

SEVENTH MARYLAND REGIMENT.

Ford, George[13]	Corpl	3 Mar 77	3 Mar 80	discharged
	Sergt	1 Nov 77	}	
	pt	21 Sept 78	}	

[1] Dobson's.   [2] Trueman's.   [3] Beall's.   [4] Laurence's.   [5] Chapline's.
[6] Ghiselin's.   [7] Lt. Williams'.   [8] Miles'.   [9] Hynes'.   [10] Harris'.
[11] Somerville's.   [12] Jacobs'.   [13] Jones'.

MUSTERS OF MARYLAND TROOPS, VOL. II.

Names.	Rank.	Time of Service. Enlisted.	Discharged.	Remarks.
Fitzgerald, Benja.[1]	pt	11 feb 77	1 Nov 80	present
	Corpl	30 Sept 78		
	Sergt	1 June 80		
Finch, Joseph	pt	28 Mar 77	28 Mar 80	discharged
Fogwell, George[2]	Sergt	16 Jan 77	23 Jan 78	deserted
	pt	26 July 78		[Comd.
Farran, John[2]	Sergt	20 April 77	Oct 78	deserted from
Fisher, Henry	pt	24 July 77	Feb 78	off Rolls
Fletcher, Richd.[4]	do	14 July 77	24 Oct 77	died
	Corpl	1 Sept 77		
Fletcher, Phillip[5]	fifer	20 dec 76	4 dec 79	discharged
4 June 78 Joined				
Fox, John	pt	21 Mar 77	Jany 80	prisoner War
Farrell, John[6]	pt	3 dec 76	5 Jan 80	discharged
Furguson, John	do	6 dec 76	Feby 78	off Rolls
Joined Sept 77				
Frogget, Richard	do	17 Mar 77	22 Mar 80	discharged
Fitzgerrald, Michael	do	28 May 77	16 Aug 80	missing
Joined 21 July 78				
Farado, Absolam	do	16 Nov 77	1 Nov 80	present
Fitzgerald, Jeremiah[7]	do	1 April 77	do	do
Fullam, George[8]	Sergt		6 dec 79	discharged
	Q.M.Sergt.	1 July 77		
Fowler, John	pt		22 Aug 77	prisoner
Fummer, John Mths.	pt	8 feb 77	1 Nov 80	present
Flannigan, Richd.[4]	do	27 Jan 78	May 78	off Rolls
Fren, Andrew[9]	do	30 dec 77	8 feb 78	deserted
Fillson, James[2]	do	25 May 78		deserted from Hospital time unknown
Fubbard, Francis[3]	do		July 78	off Rolls
Fitzgerald, William[4]	do	1 June 78	1 Mar 79	discharged
Fisher, Abram	do	1 June 78	1 April 79	discharged
Felmott, Dorus	do	21 April —	1 Nov 80	present
Fitzgerald, Nichs.	do	2 May 78	1 Nov 80	present
Fickle, Benja.[5]	Sergt	6 April 78		
	Ensign	26 Jan 80	} Promoted	
Foster, Moses[6]	pt	23 April 78	1 Nov 80	present
Filson, Saml.	do	18 Aprl 78	do	ditto
	Sergt	16 dec 79		
Fortune, William[10]	pt	3 June 78	Jan 80 absent without leave, 30 June deserted	

[1] Beall's. [2] Grosh's. [3] Spyker's. [4] Stull's. [5] Morris'.
[6] Bayly's. [7] Reynolds'. [8] Deams'. [9] Beatty's. [10] Anderson's.

MUSTERS OF MARYLAND TROOPS, VOL II.

NAMES.	RANK.	TIME OF SERVICE. Enlisted.	Discharged.	REMARKS.
Fitzgerald, Henry[1]	pt	20 July 78	9 Aprl 79	discharged
Fennel, Edward[2]	do	23 June 78	dec 79	died
Flanning, John[1]	fifer	26 July 79	6 July 80	deserted
Flaharty, Stephen from 1 Regt. Mustered Sergt July 80	pt	27 dec 79	1 Nov 80	present
Fernan, Dennis		See Dennis Fernan		

GERMAN REGIMENT.

Fennell, John	pt	21 May 78	1 Aug 80	present
Ferrins, Henry	fifer	16 May 78	do	do
Folliot, John		Joined 10 Oct 79	do	prst., stop. F. S.
Fisher, Henry	pt	1 April 78	do	prst.
Fulham, Charles		23 April 78	do	prst.
Fleming, Patrick			9 Aug 79	discharged
Franklin, John	do	4 Mar 78	1 Aug 80	prst., dischd. 4 Mar 80
Frymiller, Jacob			15 July 79	discharged
Frantz, Abram			19 ditto	ditto
Frey, Bernard	Corpl		26 do	do
Fleck, John			26 do	do
Fisher, Philip			26 do	do
Filler, Fredk.			26 do	do
Finch, David			7 Aug 79	do
Forney, James			26 July do	do
Fisher, Philip			24 do	do
Fitzpatrick, Philip 9 mo.			29 Mar 79	do

FIFTH MARYLAND REGIMENT.

Gould, James[3] Q. M. 20 Sept 79	Ensn Lieut	20 May 77 } 11 Mar 78 }		
Gilling, Thomas	pt	19 May		
Gorman, John	do	4 Sept	16 Aug 80	missing
Gray, W. James[4]	1 Lieut Capt	10 Dec 76 } 26 dec 77 }		
Gilby, Henry	pt	18 feb 77	1 Nov 80	present
Gother, John	do	23 feb 77	do	do
Gray, James	do	1 Sept 77	16 Aug 80	missing
Gibson, Jonathan[5] Capt 1 May 1780	Lieut P. M.	10 dec 76 } 25 feb 79 }		
Garey, George	Corpl. Sergt	4 feb 77 } 1 July 79 }	4 Feby 80	discharged

[1] Grosh's. [2] Morris'. [3] Hawkins'. [4] Lynch's. [5] Handy's.

MUSTERS OF MARYLAND TROOPS, VOL. II.

Names.	Rank.	Time of Service. Enlisted.	Discharged.	Remarks.
Gill, William[1]	pt	6 Mar 77	1 Jan 80	present
Gully, John	pt	9 do	21 Mar 78	died
Griffith, Saml.	do		16 Aug 80	missing
Joined 1 April 78	Sergt	1 Mar 80		
Garrett, William[2]	Corpl			June 78 left out
1st muster Aprl 78				
Geeting, John[3]	pt	1 Mar 78	1 Jan 80	present
1st muster April 78				
Griffin, Elisha[4]	pt		10 June 78	discharged
1st muster June 78				
Griffin, Moses	do		10 June 78	do
1st muster June 78				
Gow, William	do	29 May 78	16 Aug 80	missing
	Corpl	1 April 79		
Gibson, John[3]	pt	29 May 78	1 Mar 79	discharged
Grenage, William	pt	18 May 78	1 Jan 80	present
Goady, William	do	6 June 78	do	do
Gelon, John[5]	do	6 June 78		
Gray, William	do	21 Aug 77	1 Jan 80	present
Gaad, Robert	do	6 June 78		off Rolls, time out
Goldby, John	do	6 June 78	Feby 79	not heard of
Gannan, William	do	6 June 78		off Rolls
Rein. 19 feb 79				
Graves, Moses[6]	do	6 May 78	Nov 78	died
Grindage, James	do	25 May 78	1 Jan 80	present
Glaudstone, Nathl.	do	14 May 78	Augt 78 mustered	not heard of
Garrett, Enoch[2]	do	4 June 78	18 Aug 78	died
Goodburn, Francis[7]	do	25 May 78	16 Aug 80	missing
1st muster Jan 78	Sergt	1 Mar 80		
Gray, John	pt	19 June 78	dec 78	not heard of
1st muster June 78				since 18 June 78
Greenwood, William	do	4 June 78	1 Mar 79	discharged
Gothard, Thomas[8]	pt	4 May 78	16 Aug 80	missing
1st muster June 78	Corpl	1 July 79		
George, James	pt	18 May 78		28 June 79 deserted
1st muster June 78	Joined dec 78			
Gosgraves, Thomas	pt			June 78 transfd., never joined
1st muster June 78				
Goodburn, Francis	do			Transfd. to Handy's Co. see other side
1st muster June 78				
Graves, Jonas	pt			16 Aug 80 missing
1st muster June 78	Joined Sept 79			

[1] Emory's. [2] Lt. Hamilton's. [3] Handy's. [4] Lynch's.
[5] Ensign Jones'. [6] Johnson's. [7] Bird's. [8] Hawkins'.

MUSTERS OF MARYLAND TROOPS, VOL. II.

NAMES.	RANK.	Time of Service. Enlisted.	Discharged.	REMARKS.
Gouldsparks, Jas.	pt	4 June 78	24 dec 78	discharged
Garnett, Benja. dischd. 23 Sept 79	Ensn Lieut	13 Aug 78 13 Oct 78		
Gregory, James[1] Joined 17 Mar 80	pt	14 June 79		
Gamble, Abraham[2]	do	21 June 79	1 Nov 80	present
Games, Francis[3]		30 April 79	do	do
Gill, John	pt		16 Aug 80	missing

SIXTH MARYLAND REGIMENT.

NAMES.	RANK.	Enlisted.	Discharged.	REMARKS.
Ghiselin, John[4]	Capt	20 June 77	1 June 79	resigned
Greenwood, James	Drum	4 May 77	1 Nov 80	present
Gibson, John	pt	22 Aprl 77	16 Aug 80	prisoner
Grantham, Henry	do	5 May 77	16 Aug 80	missing
Gahagan, James	do	20 April 78	30 Oct 78	deserted
Geoghegan, John	Ensn	29 feb 77	20 Jan 78	resigned
Greaden, Robert[5]	pt	3 Mar 77	1 Jan 80	present
Greaves, Absalom[6]	Corpl Sergt	23 Mar 77 28 May 78	1 Jany 80	do
George, William	pt	25 Aug 77	1 Nov 80	present
Graham, Moses	do	4 June 77	do	do
Greaves, Isaac[7]	do	4 Apr 78	do	do
Garnett, Pero.	do	15 May 78	6 Oct 78	discharged
Griffith, Stephen[8]	do Corpl	6 dec 76 1 Nov 77	April & May 79	left out
Galliher, John	pt	8 July 77	1 Jan 80	present
Gregory, Benja.[9]	do	24 April 77 27 April 80	do discharged by Col. Howard	ditto
Gordon, John	pt	30 Sept 77	July 78	unfit for service
Gridley, Martin[4] 1 July 78 Joined		1 July 78	10 Oct 78	died
Greenwood, Milburn	pt	20 Aprl 77	July 78	supposed dead
German, Thomas[5] 1 must. June 78 15 Oct 79 Joined	do	25 May 78	16 Aug 80	prisoner
Garrish, Edward 1 mustr. June 78	do	2 June 78	16 Aug 80	do
Grover, John[6]	do Drum	1 Jan 78 26 Aug 78	16 Aug 80	prisoner
Gardner, William	pt	1 June 78	1 April 79	discharged
Games, Francis	do	1 June 78	feby 79	left out
Garrehan, James[8]	do	1 Jany 80		present

[1] Benson's. [2] Hugou's. [3] Bird's. [4] Ghiselin's. [5] Dobson's.
[6] Trueman's. [7] Beall's. [8] Hynes'. [9] Laurence's.

MUSTERS OF MARYLAND TROOPS, VOL. II.

NAMES.	RANK.	TIME OF SERVICE. Enlisted.	Discharged.	REMARKS.
Grinnard, Paul[1]	pt	4 May 78	16 Aug 80	missing
Gory, Daniel[2]	do	13 Sept 79	16 Aug 80	do

SEVENTH MARYLAND REGIMENT.

NAMES.	RANK.	Enlisted.	Discharged.	REMARKS.
Grunby, John	Col	10 dec 76		
Grosh, Adam[3]	Capt	10 dec 76	30 Mar 80	resigned
8 June 79	Major			
Griffith, Richard	pt	1 Aprl 77	Sept 77	out of the Rolls
Gee, Richard[4]	do	23 Aprl 77	1 Nov 80	present
Gordon, Peter	do	30 May 77	Mar 78	off Rolls
Gilmore, William[5]	do	6 dec 76	11 dec 76	deserted
Green, David[6]	Sergt	4 dec 76	5 Jan 80	discharged
	Sergt. M.	4 June 77		
	Ensign			
Green, Robert	Sergt	8 Jan 77	4 Jan 80	discharged
Green, Cuthbert	pt	8 Jan 77	17 feb 78	died
Gibbons, William	do	15 Jan 77	July 78	off Rolls
Gardner, George	do	26 Nov 77	28 Jan 80	deserted
Goodwin, Henry[7]	do	1 July 77	April 78	off Rolls
Green, George	do	11 July 77	15 July 77	deserted
Griffith, Danl.[8]	Corpl			
15 Mar 79	pt			
1 June 79	Sergt		16 Aug 80	missing
Goodfrey, Wm.	Drum		7 Sept 77	discharged
Gaskin, Wm.	pt		21 June 80	deserted
Green, Samuel[3]	do	28 Mar 78	June 78	off Rolls
Grant, John[6]	do	20 feb 78	Jany 80	prisoner. of War
1 mustr. April 78				
Gilligan, John[9]	do	6 April 78	16 Aug 80	missing
Depreciation issued to Gen. Williams formerly of the Rifle Corps				
Geary, Saml.	pt	27 April 78	1 Nov 80	present
Gordon, Joseph[9]	do	30 April 78	16 Aug 80	missing
Graham, John	do	26 April 78	13 Aug 78	deserted
Gearrish, Sampson[4]	do		1 Mar 79	discharged
Grieg, Harvy[10]	do	5 May 78	3 Oct 78	died
Gahort, Jacob	do	1 June 78	1 April 79	discharged
Gandy, Jacob[5]	do	4 June 78	Jan 80	deserted
	Corpl	27 Oct 78		
Guize, John	pt	8 June 78	30 Mar 79	discharged
Givens, Ezekiel[11]	do	11 June 78	11 April 79	discharged
Green, Joseph[3]	do	20 July 78	20 dec 78	do
Green, David	Ensn	26 Jan 80		
Green, Robert	do	do		

[1] Miles'. [2] Norris'. [3] Grosh's. [4] Spyker's. [5] Morris'. [6] Bayly's.
[7] Reynolds'. [8] Deams'. [9] Jones'. [10] Stull's. [11] Beatty's.

MUSTERS OF MARYLAND TROOPS, VOL. II.

Names.	Rank.	Time of Service. Enlisted.	Discharged.	Remarks.
German Regiment.				
Gaul, Richd.	Sergt	16 May 78	1 Aug 80	prst.
Grosh, Michael	pt	1 Jany 77	do	do
Grupp, John			26 July 79	discharged
Getig, George			do do	do
Gavan, Francis			do do	do
Gould, Edward	Mustd. sick		1 July 79	
Gantner, Adam			20 July 79	discharged
Grunlin, (or Quinlin), Corns.		Mustd. killed at New Town July 79		
Grice, Peter	see Peter Kruise			
Gambler, Michael	see Cambler			
5th Regiment.				
Hindman, James	Col	10 dec 76	4 April 77	resigned
Hollyday, Clement	Pay Mr.	do	25 feb 79	resigned
Hindman, John	Surgeon	do	13 Jan 78	do
Hooper, E. William	Mate	15 July 77	28 April 78	do
Harrington, Nathan[1]	pt	10 dec 76	}	
	Sergt	1 Sept 77	} 1 feb 80	discharged
Hill, William	pt	23 July 77	}	
	Sergt	26 Sept 77	}	
	pt	29 Sept 78	}	
Houlder, John	do	30 Mar 77	16 Aug 80	prisoner
Halfpenny, Andrew	do	27 April 77	April 78	left out
Harris, John[2]	do	20 July 77	1 Nov 80	present
Hawkins, John	Capt	20 feb 77		
Hussey, Saml.[3]	pt	19 May	1 June 80	present
			May 80	discharged
Holland, John	do	14 June	15 Aug 79	discharged by Capt. Hawkins
Joined dec 78				
Hall, James	do	19 May	1 Jan 80	present
Handy, Levin	Capt	10 dec 76		
Harrison, John[4]	pt	12 Mar 77	April 78	left out
Hugou, B. Thomas[5]	2d Lieut	10 dec 76		
Herron, William	pt	20 Jan 77	1 Oct 80	present
Herron, John	do	4 April 77	April 78	left out
Hanna, Robert[6]	do	22 Jan 77	12 Jan 80	discharged
Hillman, Wm.[7]	do	10 dec 76	do	do
Joined 20 Nov 78				
Hinds, James	do	13 April 77	1 Jan 80	present
Handy, George[8]	Ensn	17 April 77	28 Aug 78	resigned
	Lieut	10 May 77		

[1] Dean's, Benson's.   [2] Hamilton's.   [3] Hawkins'.   [4] Handy's.
[5] Johnson's.   [6] Emory's.   [7] Gray's.   [8] Cosden's, Bird's.

MUSTERS OF MARYLAND TROOPS, VOL. II.

NAMES.	RANK.	Enlisted.	Discharged.	REMARKS.
Hadley, James	pt	14 Jan 77	April 78	left out
Hindsley, Solomon	do	9 feb 77	1 Jan 80	present
Hamilton, George	Lieut	10 dec 76		
	Capt	25 Jan 78		
Hartley, John[1]	pt		June 78	left out
1st mustr. April 78, out June 78				
Hart, Richard	pt		June 78	taken prisoner
1st mustr. April 78				
Hailey, Daniel	do	9 Mar 78		
Harper, Hezekiah	do	28 feb 78	1 Jan 80	present
Hughes, Thomas[2]	do	7 July 77	6 July 78	deserted
Hall, John[3]	do	14 June 78		
Hobee, Thomas[4]	do	2 June 78	Augt 78 mustered	not heard of, see the other side
Hansfield, George[3]	do	19 June 78	Augt 78	not heard of
1st muster June 78				
Hurley, Josiah	do	6 June 78	feby 79	died some months [since
Harvey, Zadock[5]	do	5 May 78		
Horney, William[3]	do	12 May 78	Nov 80 present	
Hull, John	do	12 May 78		
	fifer	1 April 79		
Hughey, John, or Jona.	pt	12 May 78	Feby 79	not heard of
Horney, Thomas[6]	do	6 June 78	20 Mar 79	discharged
Hawkins, James	pt	12 May 78	Feby 79	died
Horney, John	pt	6 June 78	20 Mar 79	discharged
Harris, Perry	do	6 June 78	2 Sept 78	do
Harris, Joseph[1]	do	4 June 78	1 Mar 79	discharged
Hilton, Benjamin	do	22 May 78		deserted
Mustr. Sept 78				
Harper, Richard	pt	4 April 78	8 Aug 78	died
Harwood, Nathl.	do	22 April 78	10 June 78	to Invalids
Holland, John	do	4 June 78	8 June 78	deserted
Harper, Hezekiah[2]	do	18 April 78	1 Jan 80	present
1st muster June 78				
Hamthon, Thos.	do	25 May 78	1 Oct 80	present
1st muster June 78				
Harper, Anthony	do	July 78		left out the Rolls
1st mustr. June 78 & July 78				
Hayes, Thomas	pt		do	do
1st muster June 78, out July 78				
Hall, John[4]	pt	4 June 78	June 79	died
Hukins, John	do	5 May 78	16 June 78	deserted

[1] Johnson's.   [2] Handy's.   [3] Lt. Hamilton's.
[4] Hawkins'.   [5] Lynch's.   [6] Ensign Jones', Benson's.

MUSTERS OF MARYLAND TROOPS, VOL. II.

Names.	Rank.	Time of Service. Enlisted.	Discharged.	Remarks.
Hodgson, John 1st muster June 78 Joined 11 Oct 78	pt	28 April 77		dischd. 28 April 80
Hargedine, John[1] 1st muster June 78	pt fifer pt	28 feb 78 15 Aug 78 1 Sept 79 }	16 Aug 80	missing
Hines, Thomas	do	15 May 78	25 Feby 79	discharged
Heath, Charles	do	21 April 78	18 Aug 78	died
Hill, James[2] 1st muster Mar 79	do		16 Aug 80	missing
Hobbee, Thomas[3] Joined 20 Mar 80	pt	30 June 79	16 Aug 80	missing
Harris, Arthur	Ensn	27 Aug 79		paid
Hewit, Henry[3] 1st mustr. 12 dec 79	pt	17 April 79		
Hobbs, John[4]	do	12 Mar 80		
Hopkins, Thomas	do	13 feby 80	1 Nov 80	present
Higdon, George	do		1 Oct 80	do
Hanagan, Charles	do		1 Nov 80	do
Hadin, George	do	12 feb 80		paid
Hudson, Solomon	do		1 July 80	deserted
Hudson, Asariah	do		1 July 80	do
Sixth Regiment.				
Hailey, Michael[5]	pt	20 Apl 77	12 April 79	died
Hills, Charles	do Corpl	21 April 78 5 Feby 80	1 Nov 80	present
Hall, John	pt Corpl	15 May 78 Oct 80	16 Aug 80	prisoner
Holland, Gabriel	pt	30 Aprl 78	1 Jan 80	present
Hayes, William	do	15 Aprl 78	10 Aug 80	deserted
Hagarthy, Andrew[6]	Drum	13 Mar 77	1 Jany 80	present
Higgins, Saml.	pt	7 feby 77	June 78	to Invalids, full pay to 1 Aug 80 }
Harris, William[7] reinlisted	pt	10 Jany 77		
Hollyday, John, Sr.	pt	21 April 78	16 Aug 80	killed
Hollyday, John, Jr.	pt	21 April 78	1 Nov 80	present
Hart, Richard	do	10 Mar 78	Oct 78	deserted
Hynes, Andrew	Capt	10 dec 76	1 Mar 79	resigned
Harst, Jacob	pt	8 dec 76	16 Aug 80	prisoner
Hamilton, Mathew	do	10 dec 76	10 dec 79	discharged
Harris, Robert[8]	Capt	10 dec 76	9 Nov 77	quit the Service

[1] Emory's. [2] Handy's. [3] Hawkins'. [4] Lynch's.
[5] Ghiselin's. [6] Dobson's. [7] Beall's. [8] Harris'.

MUSTERS OF MARYLAND TROOPS, VOL. II.

NAMES.	RANK.	TIME OF SERVICE. Enlisted.	Discharged.	REMARKS.
Hooper, Abram	pt	18 feb 77	Jan 80	present
Haymond, Owen[1]	Ensn	19 April 78	28 June 78	killed
now Miles'	Lieut	10 dec 77		
Hodges, Richard	pt	1 July 77	Jan 80	present
Hannon, Patrick	do	9 Aug 77	1 Aug 80	deserted
Hanson, Rezin[2]	do	6 June 78	} 23 July 80	ditto
	Corpl	1 Sept 78		
Haisty, James	pt	19 June 78	28 June 78	left out
Joined 10 June 78				
Hart, John[3]	do	2 June 78	1 Jan 80	present
1st muster June 78				
Howe, James[4]	do	1 June 78	1 April 79	discharged
Hall, William[5]	do	13 May 78	16 Aug 80	prisoner
	Corpl	1 July 78		
Harvey, William	pt	3 June 78	1 April 79	discharged
Henny, Michael	do	4 June 78	do	do
Hawley, William[6]	do	31 dec 76	1 Jan 80	present
Joined Jan 79				
Hamilton, Saml.	Ensn	27 May 79	July 80	resigned
Halley, William	pt		16 Aug 80	missing
Oct Musters 1780				
Henry, Peter	pt		1 Nov 80	present
Hatwell, Henry	do		16 Aug 80	prisoner
Housely, John	do	10 April 80	1 Nov 80	present

SEVENTH REGIMENT.

NAMES.	RANK.	Enlisted.	Discharged.	REMARKS.
Housley, William[7]	Sergt	31 Jan 77	22 Aug 77	prisoner
Harrison, Richd.	Drum	9 Mar 77	1 Jan 80	present }
			22 feby 80	
Hart, Joseph	pt	1 Mar 77	1 Mar 80	discharged
	Corpl	1 June 78		
	Sergt	30 Sept 78		
Hutchinson, Nichs.[8]	pt	16 Jan 77	12 Jan 80	discharged
Holden, Thomas	do	1 April 77	22 Aug 77	prisoner
Hudson, John	do	3 April 77	3 April 80	discharged
Hall, John[9]	do	20 April 77	July 78	off Rolls
Hand, Thomas	do	23 April 77	11 Sept 77	missing
Hare, Thomas	do	21 April 77	27 Aprl 80	discharged
Hollyday, Robt., or Thos.	do	14 July 77	Aprl & May 80	left out of the
	Corpl	16 Nov 77 }		Rolls
Corpl 4 Oct 78	pt	20 Mar 78		

[1] Chapline's. [2] Ghiselin's. [3] Dobson's. [4] Trueman's. [5] Lt. Williams'.
[6] Daugherty's. [7] Jones'. [8] Grosh's. [9] Spykers'.

MUSTERS OF MARYLAND TROOPS, VOL. II.

NAMES.	RANK.	TIME OF SERVICE. Enlisted.	Discharged.	REMARKS.
Harvey, James	pt	16 June 77	1 July 80	deserted
Hardcastle, Peter	Sergt	10 dec 76		
	Ensn	10 feb 77		
	Lieut	30 Nov 77		
Heritage, Thomas[1]	pt	3 Aug 77	11 Sept 77	missing
Howe, George[2]	pt	5 dec 76	13 April 80	discharged
July 78 returned				
Hower, George	pt	6 Aprl 77	31 July 77	deserted
Harrison, William	do	1 Jan 77	Jan 78	off Rolls
Henderson, Danl.	do	7 Aprl 77	30 Mar 78	discharged
Helmn, Balss.[3]	do	6 dec 76	17 dec 76	deserted
Hays, Thomas	do	7 Jan 77	16 Aug 80	missing
Hoster, Jacob	do	21 Jan 77	Jan 79	deserted
Hall, Thomas	do	16 feb 77		off Rolls
Hewlet, John	pt	26 feb 77		do
Joined 10 Aug 78				
Hutchcraft, James	do	6 Jan 77	April 80	deserted
Horn, Patrick, or John,	do	28 May 77	22 May do	do
Hullet, William[4]	do	5 June 77	25 Oct 80	do
Hall, Joseph[5]	do	16 Aug 80		missing
Fifer Oct 77	F. Major	1 Sept 77		
Holden, Habikuk	pt		16 Aug 80	missing
Joined 10 Aug 78				
Heberly, Fredk.	do		Feby 78	off Rolls
Haynes, John	do		17 May 77	deserted
Hoy, Patrick	do		7 dec 79	discharged
Howard, William[6]	do	8 May 78	21 May 78	deserted
Head, George[7]	do	30 dec 77	8 feb 78	deserted
Ham, James[8]	do	3 May 78	8 July 80	do
Hurdle, Lawrence	do	11 May 78	1 Nov 80	present
Hooper, Robert	do	6 June 78	16 Mar 79	discharged
Holtzman, Henry[6]	Sergt	11 May 78	26 Mar 1780	discharged by
	pt	20 Sept 79		Genl. Smallwood
Hill, Ebenezer[9]	pt		July 78	off Rolls
Hutton, William[1]	do	23 Aprl 78	12 Sept 78	deserted
Howell, Thomas	do	25 Aprl 78	78	off Rolls
Heister, Nichs.	do	24 Aprl 78	1 Nov 80	present
Hartley, Robert	do	29 May 78	19 June 78	deserted
Hopkins, John[2]	do	16 May 78	19 dec 78	died
Hammond, William	do	11 May 78	April 79	ditto
Hutton, William	do	20 May 78	Nov & Dec 78	ditto

[1] Stull's. [2] Morris'. [3] Bayly's. [4] Reynolds'. [5] Deams'.
[6] Grosh's. [7] Beatty's. [8] Jones.' [9] Spyker's.

MUSTERS OF MARYLAND TROOPS, VOL. II.

NAMES.	RANK.	TIME OF SERVICE.		REMARKS.
		Enlisted.	Discharged.	
Hannagan, Patrick	pt	9 June 78	16 Aug 80	missing
Hill, John	do	8 June 78	30 Mar 79	discharged
Hunt, Jacob	do	13 June 78	1 Nov 80	present
Hearty, Fredk.	do	13 June 78	1 Nov 80	do
Hayes, Levin	do	30 June 78	30 Mar 79	discharged
Holloway, John[1]	Corpl	18 May 78	} 8 April 79	deserted
	pt	1 Jany 79		
Humphrys, Thos.[2]	do	20 July 78	22 feb 79	discharged
Hopkins, William	do	20 July 78	2 Mar 79	do
Hammond, Edward	do	do	9 April 79	do
Holt, William	do	29 June 78	9 April 79	do
Hutchins, Caleb[1]	do	11 May 78	18 April 79	deserted
Hovington, Thomas[3]	do	27 feb 79	11 April 79	do
Hardman, Henry	Capt	10 dec 76	}	
	Major	1 June 79		
Hillman, William	pt		Sept 80	
Heading, John	do	10 June 79	1 Nov 80	present
Hall, Daniel[2]	do	9 July 79	1 Nov 80	do
Hunt, Thomas	do	2 July 79	19 Mar 80	to Invalids
Holson, Edward[4]	See Oldstone		1 July 80	deserted
Hoye, Thomas[5]	pt	25 April 78	1 Nov 80	present
Hagan, Leonard[4]	do	2 feb 79	do	do
Joined 9 May 80				
Hurley, William	do	22 feb 80	do	do
Hill, Henry[6]	do			
Hampton, William[6]	do	31 Jan 80	1 Nov 80	present
Hagan, Walter[7]	do	1 feb 80	do	do
Hagan, Leonard	do	1 Jany 80	1 Oct 80	R. paid

GERMAN REGIMENT.

NAMES.	RANK.	Enlisted.	Discharged.	REMARKS.
Hutchcraft, Thos.	Drum	16 May 78	1 Aug 80	present
Hazelip, Richd.	pt	1 April 78	do	do
Halfpenny, Thos.	do	22 April 78	do	do
Hartman, Michael	do	15 May 78	do	do
Hammersly, (or Amersly), Jno. W.		mustrd. deserted on P. R.	1 Aug 80	
Haller, F. William			18 July 79	discharged
Harley, John			30 July do	do
Hook, Joseph 3	Corpl		do	do
Herring, Henry			24 do	do
Hull, Casimer			26 do	do
Haseligh, Jacob			1 Aug 80	present

[1] Beatty's. [2] Grosh's. [3] Dove's. [4] L. Beall's. [5] Lamar's. [6] Jones'. [7] Mason's.

MUSTERS OF MARYLAND TROOPS, VOL. II.

Names.	Rank.	Time of Service. Enlisted.	Discharged.	Remarks.
Hazlewood, Thos. 9 mo.			20 Mar 79*	discharged
Heffner, Jacob			12 Oct 79	do
Hose, Jacob	Sergt		26 July 78	do
Hochshield, John	Corpl		24 do	do
Hockett, Jonathan			25 Aug 79	deserted
Heron, John	Sergt	12 Aug 75	24 July 79	discharged
Hewer, or Hoover, Peter			12 Oct 79	do
Hemerick, (or Emerick), Peter			24 July 79	do
Hatfield, John			26 July 79	do
Hain, Henry	Ensn			resigned
Hile, Conrad	See Conrad Stoyle			
Hoover, Jacob			12 Oct 79	discharged
Hughes, James	pt		1 Aug 80	present
Hausman, Conrad			26 July 79	discharged
Haninghouse, Dedrick			do	do

FIFTH REGIMENT.

Jones, Thomas[1]	Ensn	20 feb 77	13 Oct 78	resigned
Joyse, Thomas	pt	22 Mar 77	Aug 78	off Rolls
Johnston, Jacob[2]	do	20 May	16 Aug 80	missing
Johnston, John	do	27 May	1 Oct 79	transferred to Major
Jordan, John	do	10 Augt	1 Oct 80	present [Lee's
Mustered Q. M. Oct 80				
Johnson, Thomas[3]	Corpl	2 Jan 77		
	pt	4 April 78	12 April 79	deserted
Jones, Benjamin[4]	do	26 dec 76	Aug 78	off Rolls
Jones, Aaron	do	1 Jan 77	1 Nov 80	present
Johnson, Josiah	Capt	10 dec 76	1 Nov 78	Invalids
Mustered Jan 79 absent, sick since Sept 1777			left out April & May muster 79	
Jones, Jacob[5]	Ensn	20 feby 77	27 Jan 78	resigned
Jordan, John	pt	15 feb 77	July 78	left out
Ingram, Abraham[6]	Sergt	25 Jan 77	16 Jan 80	discharged
Jenkins, Joseph	pt	16 Mar 77	16 Mar 80	do
Jenkins, Samuel	do	18 feb 77	1 Oct 79	transferred, not heard of since
Jeffers, Richard	do	2 Aug 77	7 Mar 79	deserted & 6 Jan. 80 discharged
Jeffers, William	do	5 Mar 77	16 feby 80	discharged
	fifer	1 Feby 79		
	pt	1 Sept 79		

[1] Dean's. [2] Hawkins'. [3] Lynch's. [4] Handy's. [5] Johnson's. [6] Emory's, Gray's.

during the War of the American Revolution, 1775–83.

MUSTERS OF MARYLAND TROOPS, VOL. II.

NAMES.	RANK.	TIME OF SERVICE. Enlisted.	Discharged.	REMARKS.
Ingram, William	pt	18 Mar 77	18 July 80	deserted
Joined 1 May 79				
Johnson, Nichols[1]	pt	27 May 77	27 Mar 80	discharged
Joined 20 May 78				
James, William[2]	do		17 Mar 78	deserted
1st muster April 78				
Jones, Thomas[3]	pt	10 Mar 78		
	Corpl	1 April 78		
	Sergt	1 June 78	1 Nov 80	present
Jones, Benjamin	pt	1 April 78	16 Aug 80	missing
	Drum	1 May 79		
	pt	1 June 79		
Jones, Richard[1]	do	2 June 78	1 Jan 80	present
rein. 19 Feby 79				
Jones, John[2]	do	2 June 78	16 June 78	deserted
Impy, Michael[4]	pt	4 June 78	19 Mar 79	discharged
Johnson, Robert	pt	8 June 78	Dec 78	mustrd. not heard of since 18 June 78
Johnson, Mason	pt	14 May 78	July 78	left out
Jones, James[5]	pt	4 June 78	5 Jan 80	deserted
Johnson, Abram[6]	pt		15 July 78	deserted
1st mustr. June 78				

SIXTH MARYLAND REGIMENT.

Jacob, Jesse	Sergt	23 July 77	1 Nov 80	present
Jacobs, George	Ensn	20 feb 77		
	Lieut	14 July 77		
Jackson, John[7]	pt	16 May 77	Sept 80	sick Virginia, pst.
Ireland, George[8]	Lieut	20 feb 77	3 Oct 78	resigned [Oct 80
Jenkins, Francis	Sergt	9 June 77	1 Jan 80	present
	pt	20 April 78	16 May 80	discharged
Johnston, Thomas[9]	Corpl	11 Jan 77	11 Jan 80	ditto
	pt	1 Oct 79		
Jones, Thomas	pt	24 April 77	16 Aug 80	deserted
Jacobs, Jno. Jeremh.[10]	Lt.			
	Pay Mr.	1 Oct 78		
Johnson, John[11]	pt	22 April 78	1 Jan 80	present
Jenkins, Jehu	do	20 May 78	Aprl & May 79	not heard of
1st must. June 78				
Javers, Daniel[12]	do	23 May 78	1 Nov 80	present
Johnson, George	do	19 May 78	16 Aug 80	missing
Johnson, John	do	4 June 78	16 Aug 80	do

[1] Ensign Jones'. [2] Johnson's. [3] Lynch's. [4] Handy's. [5] Hawkins'. [6] Emory's.
[7] Dobson's. [8] Trueman's. [9] Beall's. [10] Hynes'. [11] Lt. Williams'. [12] Miles'.

MUSTERS OF MARYLAND TROOPS, VOL. II.

Names.	Rank.	Time of Service. Enlisted.	Discharged.	Remarks.
		SEVENTH REGIMENT.		
Jones, Jno. Courts[1]	Lieut	10 dec 76	}	
	Capt	28 dec 77		
Johnson, James	pt	10 feb 77	} 11 feb 80	discharged
	Corpl	1 July 77		
James, John	pt	10 feb 77	May 78	off Rolls
Jenkins, Thomas[2]	do	15 dec 76	6 Jan 80	discharged
to Beatty's Co.	Sergt	24 feb 78		
Justice, Charles[3]	pt		17 May 77	deserted
Jones, James, or John[4]	do	16 May 78	1 Jany 80	present
Johns, John[5]	do	21 May 78	1 Nov 80	do
Jones, Dennis	do	5 May 78	13 June 79	deserted
Jones, William	do	28 April 78	1 April 79	do
Jones, William[6]	do	20 May 78	May 79	died
Jones, Samuel[2]	do	6 June 78	29 June 79	deserted
Johnson, Simon	do	13 April 78	25 June 78	do
Johns, James[6]	pt	30 June 78	30 Mar 79	discharged
Jarvis, Cato[4]	do	18 May 78	9 April 79	do
Isham, Joshua[7]	Drum		1 Nov 80	present
James, Thomas[8]	pt	13 May 78	16 Aug 80	prisoner
Jackson, John[4]	do	12 June 79	8 dec 79	discharged
		GERMAN REGIMENT.		
Jones, Charles	Sergt	7 June 78	1 Aug 80	present
Johnson, William	Sergt	16 May 78	1 do	do
Jacquett, Danl.	do		26 July 79	discharged
Johnston, James		no pay from Sep 79	1 Aug 80	mustrd. dest.
		FIFTH MARYLAND REGIMENT.		
Keach, Ebenezer[9]	pt	9 Sept 77	April 78	off Rolls
Kennedy, Saml[10]	Corpl	1 April 77	do	do
	Sergt	12 April 77	sick in Maryland pr. cert. Dep.	
Kelly, David	pt	20 feb 77	1 Nov 80	present [acct.
Kent, Stephen[11]	do	7 Mar 77	30 Mar 80	deserted
King, Levin[12]	Ensn	20 feb 77	8 Nov 77	resigned
Kelty, William	S. Mate	28 April 78	}	
	Surgeon	1 April 1780		
Kincaid, John[13] 1st muster April 78	pt		Aug 78	not heard of
Kincaid, Peter	do	4 May 78	1 Nov 80	present
Kidney, Michael[14]	pt	20 May 78	do	do

[1] Jones'. [2] Bayly's. [3] Deams'. [4] Grosh's. [5] Stull's.
[6] Morris'. [7] Lynn's. [8] Beatty's. [9] Hawkins'. [10] Lynch's.
[11] Johnson's. [12] Emory's. [13] Hamilton's. [14] Handy's.

during the War of the American Revolution, 1775–83.

MUSTERS OF MARYLAND TROOPS, VOL. II.

NAMES.	RANK.	TIME OF SERVICE. Enlisted.	Discharged.	REMARKS.
Kinnahan, John[1] Joined 2 Oct 80	pt	6 June 78	1 Nov 80	present
Kerby, Nathaniel	pt	6 June 78	feby 79	mustr. not heard
Knowland, Lucas[2]	do	22 May 79	Jan 80	present [of
Kelson, George[3]	do	2 April 79	1 Nov 80	present
Kelly, William	do	do	do	do
	Drum	Oct 80		
King, Charles	pt		16 Sept 80	deserted

SIXTH REGIMENT.

NAMES.	RANK.	Enlisted.	Discharged.	REMARKS.
Kennick, William[4]	Sergt	12 feb 77		
	Sergt Major	12 Sept 77	12 feb 80	discharged
Kach, John[5]	pt	16 July 77	16 May 80	discharged
Kersey, Edward	pt	21 April 78	1 Jan 80	present
Knight, Isaac	do	19 May 78	4 April 79	transferred to In-
Kerrick, Joseph[6] reduced 9 Aprl 79 Corpl 1 Sept 79	pt Corpl	21 Jan 77 3 Aug 78	24 Aug 80	deserted [valids
King, Francis	pt	26 feb 77	1 Jan 80	present
	Corpl	10 April 79		
Kattakan, Joseph[7]	pt	18 April 77	Mar 78	left out
Kearns, James	do	8 July 77	1 Jan 80	present
Kelly, Patrick[8]	Corpl	29 Mar 77		
	pt	Aug 78	Sept 78	left out
Kearns, Thomas Joined July 79	do	14 dec 76		
Keough, William	pt	20 Mar 77		
Kennedy, William[9]	do	11 June 78	15 Oct 78	died
Heidley, Henry[10] 1st muster June 78	do	8 June 78	8 Mar 79	time expired
Kirshaw, William[4]	do	1 June 78	1 April 79	time expired, mustr. Hospital 1 Nov 78
Kelly, Thomas[11]	pt	22 April 78	17 June 78	discharged
Kernan, Martin	do	22 May 78	3 Jan 79	do
Kernan, Michael[11]	pt	18 May 78	16 Aug 80	missing
Knave, Henry[12]	pt	16 feb 77	1 Jan 80	present, dischd. 12 feb 80
Kelly, Edward[4]	do	21 April 78	26 April 78	deserted
Koik, Benja. H.[13]	Fifer	6 Mar 77	24 Aug 80	do

[1] Ensign Jones'. [2] Lynch's. [3] Handy's. [4] Trueman's. [5] Beall's.
[6] Hynes'. [7] Harris'. [8] Chapline's. [9] Ghiselin's. [10] Dobson's.
[11] Lt. Williams'. [12] Miles'. [13] Jacobs'.

MUSTERS OF MARYLAND TROOPS, VOL. II.

Names.	Rank.	Time of Service. Enlisted.	Discharged.	Remarks.

Seventh Regiment.

Names.	Rank.	Enlisted.	Discharged.	Remarks.
Kinney, John[1]	Corpl	13 April 77	Aug 77	left out of the
Kelly, Thomas[2]	pt	30 dec 76	16 Aug 80	missing [Rolls
Joined 22 Mar 80				
Keefe, Thomas	pt	10 Jan 77	1 Nov 80	present
	drum	16 feb 79		
Knowland, Michael	pt	1 April 77	1 April 80	discharged
Kelly, Thomas[3]	do	15 Aug 77	7 Sept 78	deserted
Keland, James[4]	Corpl	7 dec 76	16 Aug 80	missing
	pt	2 dec 77		
Knox, John	do	2 Sept 77	joined from Pennsylvania Line	
Joined 1 May 78				[in 1782
Kelly, Daniel[5]	do	21 Jan 77	July 77	off Rolls
Kelly, George	do	14 Mar 77	April 80	discharged
Joined May 77				
Keys, Patrick	do	19 Jan 77	3 June 79	deserted
Joined June 78				
Kelly, George[6]	do	22 May 77	22 June 77	do
Kinsey, Samuel[7]	Lieut	8 dec 76		
Kennedy, Thomas	pt		16 July 77	discharged
Kinchley, Morgan[1]	do	6 June 78	16 Aug 80	missing
Kindle, William[8]	do	25 April 78	1 Nov 80	present
King, John	do	28 April 78	1 Nov 80	do
Keen, William[9]	do	17 April 78	25 June 78	deserted
Kinsee, George[4]	do	4 June 78	Nov 78	left off the Rolls
Keitley, Francis[9]	do	30 June 78	1 Nov 80	present
Kelly, James[10]	do	14 feb 80	do	do
	Corpl	1 May 80		
King, John	pt	25 April 78	25 April 81	discharged
Kenny, William[11]	do	22 Jan 80	9 July 80	deserted

German Regiment.

Names.	Rank.	Enlisted.	Discharged.	Remarks.
Kruise, Peter			24 July 79	discharged
Kuntz, Philip			15 do	do
Kibber, John			26 do	do
Keyer, Keiser, Mathias			26 do	do
Kelly, Patrick	Corpl	24 July 76	24 do	do
Kendrick, John			July 79	deserted
Kline, or Cline, John			12 Oct 79	discharged, appeared 5 May,
Keplinger, Chresn. 9 mo.			22 Mar 79	do [1789

[1] Jones'. [2] Grosh's. [3] Spyker's. [4] Morris'. [5] Bayly's. [6] Reynolds'.
[7] Deams'. [8] Stull's. [9] Lynn's. [10] Mason's. [11] L. Beall's.

MUSTERS OF MARYLAND TROOPS, VOL. II.

NAMES.	RANK.	Time of Service. Enlisted.	Discharged.	REMARKS.
Kettle, Abram	pt	3 April 79	1 Aug 80	prst.
Keyser, Jacob	Sergt	13 feb 79	do	do
Kettle, Daniel		1 Nov 79	do	do
Kerns, Francis	pt	1 June 78	1 Aug 80	present
Koons, Peter	do	do		do
Keephart, Geo.	pt	13 feb 78	do	do
Kershner, Michael		16 July 79		discharged
Kline, Jacob			26 do	do
Kentz, Jacob			30 do	do
Kaufman, Jacob		See John Caufman		

FIFTH MARYLAND REGIMENT.

NAMES.	RANK.	Enlisted.	Discharged.	REMARKS.
Lawrence, James[1]	pt	30 May 77	1 Nov 80	present
Lofman, Benjamin	do	6 Aug 77	1 Jan 80	do
Lyon, John	Corpl private	} 13 May	8 May 80	discharged
Lynch, John	Capt	10 dec 76		
Lord, Andrew[2]	pt	8 Aug 77	23 Mar 80	prisoner
Lomax, Theops.[3]	do	31 Mar 77	16 Aug 80	missing
Lucas, John[4]	do Corpl	7 Sept 77 Oct 80	1 Nov 80	present
Lloyd, Joseph	do	22 Sept 77	1 Jan 80	do
Linex, James[5] pt 2 Sept 78 Corpl 1 Nov 78	Sergt } pt 30 June 79, pt Sergt	13 Jan 77 19 April 78 1 June 78	12 Jany 80	private discharged as
Lewis, Richard[6] 1st mustr. April 78	pt Corpl	15 June 78	1 Feb 80	dead or deserted
Lawrence, William	pt]	Aug 78	16 Nov 79	to Invalids, discharged
Lawrence, David[7] 1st mustr. April 78	do	12 Jan 77	May 79	not heard of
Lowrey, James[7] 1st mustr. April 78	do	1 Mar 78	2 Jan 81	discharged
Loe, Henry 1st mustr. April 78	do	1 Mar 78		[with Genl. Palaskey }
	Nathan Duley of 2nd Regt. asserts that Low never enlisted }			
Lord, Henry[3]	pt	2 June 78		
Lowry, John[7]	do	6 June 78	1 Mar 79	discharged
Lee, Jeremiah	pt	19 May 78	See below	
Ledenham, Nathl.[8]	do	6 June 78	Feby 79	deserted
Layton, Jehu[3]	do	4 June 78	19 Oct 78	died

[1] Hawkins'.   [2] Lynch's.   [3] Johnson's.   [4] Emory's.
[5] Cosden's, Gray's.   [6] Lt. Hamilton's.   [7] Handy's.   [8] Ensign Jones'.

MUSTERS OF MARYLAND TROOPS, VOL. II.

Names.	Rank.	Time of Service. Enlisted.	Discharged.	Remarks.
Longfellow, Thos.[1]	pt	4 June 78	16 Aug 80	missing
Lee, Jeremiah[2]	do	19 May 78	1 Oct 80	present
1st mustr. July 79		died some short time after this says Capt. Benson		
Lahea, William[3]	pt		16 Aug 80	missing
Linthicum, Francis			16 Aug 80	missing
Lilly, Robert	pt		Sept 80	deserted

SIXTH MARYLAND REGIMENT.

Names.	Rank.	Enlisted.	Discharged.	Remarks.
Lowther, James[4]	pt	23 Aug 77	24 Nov 78	deserted
Lintridge, Saml.	pt	26 April 78	25 June 79	do
Laukin, John[5]	do	21 feb 77	1 July 79	deserted
Joined 15 April 79		Joined Aug 79		
Linian, Darby	pt	13 May 77	1 Jan 80	present
Lock, George	do	11 feby 78	do	do
Linsey, Oliver[6]	pt	5 dec 76	} 5 Dec 79	time expired
	Corpl	13 Aprl 77		
Lawrence, Levin	Capt	1 April 77	1 April 78	resigned
Long, Joseph[7]	pt	16 Aprl 77	1 Nov 80	present
Longden, Joseph[4]	do	13 June 78	17 Jan 80	deserted
Loud, George	do	1 July 78	1 June 79	do
1 July 78 Joined, rein.				
Lee, Dudley	pt	1 July 78	1 April 79	dischgd., reinlisted
1 July 78 Joined				
Litt, Daniel	pt	1 July 78	1 April 79	discharged
Love, John[8]	pt	28 May 78	1 Nov 80	present
1st muster June 78, rein. 22 dec 78				
Leonard, Adam[9]	pt	3 June 78	4 feb 79	discharged
Layzer, Adam	do	30 May 78	1 April 79	time out, discharged
1st muster June 78				
Lewis, William[10]	do	3 May 78	4 feb 79	discharged
Lawless, John[9]	do	11 May 78	May 78	deserted
Lincoln, John[11]	do	27 April 79	1 Nov 80	present
Loyce, Peter	do	9 May 79	1 Jan 80	do
Linn, John	Lieut	1 June 79	1 Nov 80	do
Longley, James	pt		16 Aug 80	prisoner

SEVENTH MARYLAND REGIMENT.

Names.	Rank.	Enlisted.	Discharged.	Remarks.
Love, William[12]	pt	11 feb 77	11 Feb 80	discharged
Lowe, William	do	17 feb 77	Mar 78	off Rolls
Lamar, William	Ensn	14 feb 77	}	
Acting Q. Mr. July 78	5 July Lt	28 dec 77		

[1] Handy's. [2] Benson's. [3] Hawkins'. [4] Ghiselin's. [5] Beall's. [6] Hynes'. [7] Chapline's. [8] Dobson's. [9] Lt. Williams'. [10] Trueman's. [11] Lt. Norris'. [12] Jones'.

MUSTERS OF MARYLAND TROOPS, VOL. II.

NAMES.	RANK.	TIME OF SERVICE. Enlisted.	Discharged.	REMARKS.
Linn, David[1]	Lt	10 dec 76	}	
	Capt	22 May 79		
Lewis, Basil	pt	6 dec 76	July 77	off Rolls
Lynch, Patrick	do	6 feb 77	1 Jan 80	present
Life, Robert[2]	do	6 dec 76	18 April 77	deserted
Lynch, Patrick	do	22 May 77	22 May 80	discharged
Joined 22 May 80				
Lochlin, Michael	pt	17 Nov 77	16 Aug 80	missing
Lee, Thomas[3]	pt	18 May 77	1 May 80	deserted
Lard, William	do	3 June 77	Dec 77	off Rolls
Lawson, Ralph[4]	do		feb 78	do
Lee, Timothy[5]	do	18 Jan 78	12 feb 78	deserted
Lingo, Thomas[6]	do		Aug 78	dead
1st muster June 78				
Lister, Joshua[7]	do	22 May 78	1 Nov 80	mustrd. Hosptl. Annapolis
Lieth, Alexander[7]	do		1 Mar 79	discharged
Longfellow, Andw.[8]	do	20 July 78	12 feb 79	do
Lowry, John[6]	do	28 April 78	16 Aug 80	missing
Leonard, Robert[9]	do	9 Aug 79	16 Aug 80	do
Leakins, William	do	20 Aug 79	1 Nov 80	present
Lee, Joseph[9]	do	21 feb 80	16 Aug 80	missing
Larry, William[10]	do	15 feb 80	11 Sept 80	deserted
Love, David[11]	Sergt	8 Sept 79	1 Nov 80	present
Loveday, John[10]	pt	20 April 80	do	do

GERMAN REGIMENT.

Lecrose, John	pt	12 Mar 80	1 Aug 80	present
Larmore, Thomas	do		7 Aug 79	} prst., dischgd.,
			1 Aug 80	} reinlisted 30 mar
Lago, Charles	pt	1 April 80	1 Aug 80	present [80, present
Lowe, Jacob	Sergt	Aug 76	1 Aug 80	prst., dischgd. 21
Leithusier, George			22 July 79	discharged [feb 81
Larantz, Fredk.			15 do	do
Lorantz, Vendel			20 July	do
Ladder, John	Sergt		9 Aug 79	discharged
Lewis, William	do		16 July 79	do
Locker, Fredk.			9 Aug 79	do
Lantz, Martin			15 July 79	do
Ludwick, Leonard			24 do	do
Lawrey, Galfried			1 Oct 79	do

[1] Morris'. [2] Bayly's. [3] Reynolds'. [4] Deams'. [5] Beatty's. [6] Jones'.
[7] Spyker's. [8] Grosh's. [9] Anderson's. [10] Lynn's. [11] Lamar's.

Names.	Rank.	Time of Service. Enlisted.	Discharged.	Remarks.
Fifth Maryland Regiment.				
McKey, William	Q. M. Sgt.	14 Oct 77	1 feb 79	to Hide department
			14 April 80	discharged
Mead, James	Drm. Major	10 dec 76	transffd. 11 June 77	
McQuay, Thomas[1]	pt	10 Mar 77	1 Jan 80	present }
			8 Mar 80	discharged }
Maddin, Nathan	do	10 dec 76	do	do
Murphy, John	Corpl	15 Sept 78		
	Sergt	1 April 79		
	pt	20 April 77		
	Sergt	24 feb 80		
McCone, Thomas	pt	13 Jan 77	April 78	left out
Moreland, Henry[2]	Corpl	22 May		
	pt	1 Aprl 79	was carried home by Lt. Benton and detained in May till time out	
Meconican, Elias	Corpl	6 June	1 Jan 80	present
	pt	1 feb 78	16 May 80	discharged
Mills, Edward	do	24 July	15 Aug 78	died
McBride, James[3]	pt	20 feb 77	22 May 78	discharged
Murray, Mathew	do	17 feb 77	25 June 78	deserted
Mills, John[4]	pt	11 Mar		
to Bird's	Sergt	10 May	July 79	Forage department
	pt	16 Aug 79	18 feb 80	discharged
McDaniel, John[5]	do	30 Jan 77	10 Jan 80	discharged
McDaniel, Anguish	Corpl	1 Jan 77	12 Jan 80	do
McHalsey, or Halfey, Ben. mustd. Sept 78	pt	6 Jan 77		
Morgan, William[6]	Sergt	23 Jany 77	April 78	left out
Markey, William	do	4 dec 76	14 Oct 77	Q. Mr., left out
Magee, Josiah	do	29 July 77	1 Jan 80	present [Aprl 78
	Corpl	12 Jan 80	16 May 80	discharged
Murphy, Thomas	do	16 Jan 77		
	Sergt	22 dec 77	12 Jan 80	discharged
Murphy, James	Corpl	16 Jan 77	dec 78	left out, unfit for duty
			16 Jan 80	dischgd. from Invalids
Miles, Thomas	pt	25 Aprl 77		
	Corpl	10 Sept 77	16 Aug 80	missing
	Sergt	1 Nov 78		
McDermot, Michael	pt	20 Mar 77		
	Corpl	22 dec 77	5 April 77	deserted
Melles, William	pt	18 July 77	29 feb 78	died

[1] Dean's. [2] Hawkins'. [3] Lynch's. [4] Handy's. [5] Johnson's.
[6] Emory's.

MUSTERS OF MARYLAND TROOPS, VOL. II.

NAMES.	RANK.	Enlisted.	Discharged.	REMARKS.
Moore, Robert	pt	9 Mar 77	Sept 78	not heard of
Mitchel, Saml.	do	10 dec 76		
	Corpl	22 Oct 78	12 Jan 80	discharged
McLane, John	pt	18 feb 77	3 April 80	do
Moore, Smith[1]	2d Lieut	10 dec 76	10 May 77	resigned
Murphy, Edward	pt	23 dec 76	20 dec 79	discharged
Marrough, James	do	14 Jan 77	13 dec 79	do
Morrindon, Michael[2]	Corpl	13 Mar 77	13 Mar 80	do
1st muster April 78	Joined as private 16 May 79			
Marr, David	Drum	8 dec 76		
McWilliams, Wm.[3]	pt	6 dec 76	6 dec 79	discharged
McKinsey, Wm.[3]	Drum		Aug 78	off Rolls, to Invalids
1st muster April 78, out Aug 78			16 May 79	discharged
McDonald, Danl.[4]	pt	30 June 78	15 Mar 79	deserted 21 Jan
1st muster April 78				80 desertd.
Maloney, Wm.[5]	pt	3 May 77	29 Aug 78	deserted
Joined April 78, to Emory's Co.				
Mason, Arthur[2]	pt	22 April 77	1 Jan 80	present
			25 Aprl 80	discharged
McIntosh, John[2]	do	4 June 78	30 Sept 78	died
Massey, Jesse	do	9 June 78	Aug 78	not heard of
McFarlin, Charles[6]	pt			never joined
1st muster June 78, out July 78				
Madding, Sampson	pt	20 May 78	1 Mar 79	discharged
Mooney, William	do	2 June 78		inlisted with Genl. Palaskey
McGinney, Solomon[2]	do	15 May 78	11 Aprl 79	deserted
McKernal, Thomas	do	5 feb 78	1 Oct 80	present
Mason, John	do	4 June 78	1 Mar 79	discharged
Mann, Jesse	do	16 May 78	1 Nov 80	present
McDonald, Charles	do	19 May 78	6 June 78	deserted
Murphey, Wm.	pt	15 May 78	Feby 79	not heard of
Murphey, John	do	10 June 78	1 July 78	deserted
McCarty, Thomas[4]	do	22 Aug 77	21 feb 80	deserted
Murray, James	pt	2 June 78	16 Aug 80	missing
rein. 16 dec 79				
McKay, Isaac	pt	4 June 78	26 Mar 79	discharged
McKay, John	do	4 April 78	1 Nov 80	present
			14 feb 82	discharged
Murray, William	pt	22 Apr 78	1 Jan 80	present
mustd. Sept 78, reinlisted Dec 79				
Morgan, Thomas[3]	pt	25 May 78	1 Nov 78	died
1st muster June 78				

[1] Cosden's.   [2] Hamilton's.   [3] Handy's.   [4] Johnson's.   [5] Hawkins'.   [6] Lynch's.

MUSTERS OF MARYLAND TROOPS, VOL. II.

Names.	Rank.	Time of Service. Enlisted.	Discharged.	Remarks.
Merryfield, Josiah[1] 1st mustr. June 78	pt	6 May 78	21 June 79	deserted
Mansfield, George[2] 1st mustr. dec 78	do	19 June 78	1 Mar 79	discharged
Medley, Thomas[3]	pt	10 dec 78	17 June 79	deserted
Moore, Benjamin[3] Joined 1 May 76	do	23 Jan 77	9 Jan 80	discharged
McQuay, Martin[4] 1st muster June 79	pt	2 June 79	1 Jan 80	present
Miorley, Dennis 1st mustr. June 79	pt	7 June 79	1 Nov 80	do
McLemare, Wm. Cooke	pt drum pt	6 July 79 1 Aug 79 1 Oct 79	1 Oct 80	present
Marshall, William	do	27 April 80		paid
Murphey, Thomas	pt		16 Aug 80	missing

Sixth Maryland Regiment.

Names.	Rank.	Enlisted.	Discharged.	Remarks.
Miller, Henry[5]	Sergt	30 July 77	1 Jan 80	present
Meeks, Thomas[6]	do	21 July 77	do	do
			4 April 80	discharged
McDonald, John	pt	4 Sept 77	17 Aug 80	deserted
Mondle, George	do	4 April 78	1 Nov 80	present
Mathews, Robert	do	15 May 78	do	do
McManis, Henry	do	12 May 78	16 July 78	deserted
McLeod, Robert	do	2 May 78	16 Aug 80	missing
McKinsey, Thomas	do	2 May 78	5 Mar 79	transferred, not [heard of
Miles, Joshua[7]	Lieut Capt	3 Aprl 77 10 Oct 77	18 May 79	resigned
Monks, James	pt	6 feb 77	21 Aug 80	deserted
Muldroh, Robert	do	3 feb 77	19 Oct 78	died
Mellone, William	pt	17 May 77	16 Aug 80	killed
McLiney, (or McLenchey), James	do	20 feb 77	1 Jan 80	was present
pt 1 Jan 79	Corpl	1 Nov 77	5 feb	discharged
Milburn, Nicholas	pt	22 Apil 78	1 Nov 80	present
Mason, John	do	9 May 78	10 Aug 80	deserted
Miles, John[8]	Corpl	2 June 77	1 Jan 80	was present
Mahanny, Thomas	pt	14 Oct 77	1 Nov 80	present
Martin, Michael	pt	14 Oct 77	1 Jan 80	was present
Moses, Francis Joined 30 Jan 79	pt	3 April 78		

[1] Hawkins'.   [2] Hamilton's.   [3] Johnson's.   [4] Lynch's.
[5] Ghiselin's.   [6] Afterwards Somerville's.   [7] Dobson's.   [8] Trueman's.

MUSTERS OF MARYLAND TROOPS, VOL. II.

NAMES.	RANK.	TIME OF SERVICE. Enlisted.	Discharged.	REMARKS.
Markell, John[1]	Lieut	17 April 77	15 Aug 77	resigned
Mantle, John reinlisted	Sergt	10 Jan 77		
Moren, William Joined 20 feb 79	pt	24 feb 77		
Moren, Patrick	pt	24 feb 77	1 Jan 80 24 feb 80	was present discharged
McKindly, Wm.	do	11 feb 78	16 Aug 80	killed
McCrackin, Isaac[2]	Lieut	10 dec 76	12 Nov 77	resigned
McCreary, John	Ensn	20 feb 77	7 Aug 77	discharged
Moran, Edmond	Sergt Q. Mr. Lieut	5 dec 76 17 April 77 21 May 79	} 15 July 80	dismissed the Service
Maxwell, John	pt Corpl Sergt	1 Jan 77 16 May 77 1 Aug 77	} 5 May 79	died
McKirk, Benja.	Drum	6 Mar 77	See B. H. Kirk	
McConnell, John	fifer	19 May 78	Nov dec 78	left out
Morgan, Richard	pt	5 dec 76	5 dec 79	discharged
Morgan, Benjamin	pt	4 Jan 77	1 Nov 80	present
Marshall, John	do	13 Jan 77	1 June 79	to Invalids
McCalleb, Patrick	do	13 Jan 77	17 Aug 80	deserted
Marshall, Robert[2]	do	5 Mar 77	1 Jan 80 5 Mar 80	was present } discharged }
McNaiton, Wm.	do	17 Aug 77	4 June 78	deserted
Maunders, Thos.	do Corpl	23 April 78 20 Jan 80	16 Aug 80	prisoner
McCray, Henry[3]	Sergt	22 Aug 77	10 June 80	discharged
McDonald, Martin	pt	10 Aug 77	April & May 79	mustrd. not heard of
Mong, Richard	do	22 April 77	1 Jan 80 22 April 80	present } discharged }
Mitchell, John[4] Mustd. 11 Sept 77	Sergt Joined pt	26 May 77 14 mar 78 4 July 78		
Moulan, Richd.	Corpl	26 April 77	1 Jan 80 25 April 80	present discharged
McCan, Michael	pt	5 June 77	1 Nov 80	present
Murray, Thomas[5]	pt Sergt pt	10 feb 77 1 May 77 20 Aug 77	} 16 Aug 80	prisoner
Martin, William	do Corpl	29 April 77 1 June 78	1 Nov 80	present }

[1] Beall's. [2] Hynes'. [3] Laurence's. [4] Harris'. [5] Chapline's.

MUSTERS OF MARYLAND TROOPS, VOL. II.

NAMES.	RANK.	TIME OF SERVICE. Enlisted.	Discharged.	REMARKS.
Mathews, Thomas	pt	22 Mar 77	1 Jan 80	was present
Mooney, Patrick	do	3 April 77	16 Aug 80	missing
Mahoney, Edward	do	8 Mar 77	1 Jan 80 8 Mar 80	was present discharged }
McDonehough, Jno.[1] 1 July 78 Joined	pt	1 July 78	24 Nov 78	deserted
Marr, Paul 1 July 78 Joined		1 July 78	9 Jan 79	do
McNeale, Wm. 1 July 78 Joined rein. 2 dec 78	pt Corpl	1 July 78 1 dec 78 }	1 Nov 80	present
McConnell, Saml.[2] Joined June 78 Sergt 1 July 79	Sergt pt	10 June 78 11 May 79	1 Nov 80 9 June 81	present discharged
McMullin, Danl. 1st mustr. June 78 rein. 22 dec 78	Sergt	10 June 78	1 April 79	deserted
Maxwell, James 1st mustr. June 78 rein. 22 dec 78	pt } Corpl	1 June 78 1 Aug 79	1 Nov 80	present }
McKenny, James[3]	pt	1 June 78	25 Oct 78	died
McKay, John Alexr.[4]	do Corpl	5 May 78 1 July 78 }	1 Nov 80	present
McDonald, Allen	pt	28 April 78	April & May 79	left out
McCoy, James	pt	3 June 78	17 dec 78	died
Myers, Adam	do	3 June 78	1 April 79	discharged
Mong, Adam	do	30 May 78	1 do	do
McKinley, Archibld.	do	3 June 78	1 May 79	deserted
McCullough, Saml. reinlisted 23 dec 78	do	4 June 78	1 April 79	do
Malcome, Hugh	pt	30 May 78	1 April 79	discharged
McFaddon, John	do	1 June 78	4 feb 79	do
McLaughlin, Hugh	do	30 May 78	4 feb 79	do
Marshall, John rein. 20 Dec 78	do	1 June 78	1 Nov 80	present
McLaughlin, Wm.	pt	18 May 78	27 June 79	deserted
May, George[5]	do	7 May 78	Feby 79	do
Murphy, Hugh	do	8 July 78	17 Mar 79	do
Moore, William[6]	pt	20 April 78	16 Aug 80	missing
Morris, James[6]	do	6 June 78	16 Aug 80	missing
Mills, Benjamin	do	1 May 78	1 Jan 80	present
Mathews, William	do	3 June 78	1 Oct 80	do [heard of
Murphy, William	do		10 Aug 80	transfd., not

[1] Ghiselin's. [2] Dobson's. [3] Trueman's. [4] Lt. Williams'. [5] Hynes'. [6] Miles'.

MUSTERS OF MARYLAND TROOPS, VOL. II.

Names.	Rank.	Time of Service. Enlisted.	Discharged.	Remarks.
McCleery, Patrick[1]	pt	9 May 78	May 78	deserted
Miles, Joshua[2]	do	16 June 78	1 April 79	discharged
Malone, Hugh[3]	do		1 Jan 80	present
1st muster July 79				
Murdock, William	Ensn	6 Sept 79		
McFadgin, Abram[4]	pt	11 Aug 79	17 Oct 79	deserted [Kill
May, John[3]	do	25 Sept 79	Sept 80	Hospital Fish
Mullin, Patrick[4]	do	21 May 77	1 Jan 80	was present
Martin, John	pt	10 feb 80	1 Nov 80	present
Oct mustr. 80				
Moorman, Thos.	do	28 Mar 80	16 Aug 80	prisoner

Seventh Regiment.

Names.	Rank.	Enlisted.	Discharged.	Remarks.
Maddox, Walter[5]	fifer	9 Mar 77	28 June 78	killed at Mon-
	pt	1 Mar 78		mouth
McGurck, James	do	6 April 77	6 April 80	discharged
Maybury, Benja.[6]	Sergt	10 dec 76	July 78	off Rolls
	pt	1 July 77		
Mahaney, Thos., (or James)	Corpl	30 dec 76	27 Mar 78	deserted
McMullin, James	pt	10 Jan 77	3 April 79	do
Mahoney, Danl.	pt	26 Jan 77	12 Jan 80	discharged
Murray, John	do	6 April 77	12 April 80	do
McManis, Thomas[7]	do	4 June 77	12 May 80	do
Marquis, William	pt	24 May 77	12 May 80	do
Miller, Joseph, (or Joshua)	do	31 May 77	4 May	deserted
McDonald, John	do	15 Aug 77	7 Sept 78	ditto
Monk, William	do	15 Aug 77	31 Jan 78	to Congress Regt. for Benjamin Barnes
Meek, Francis[8]	pt	10 dec 76	26 dec 79	discharged
	Sergt	6 May 77		
Mahoney, Saml.	Corpl	22 April 77	Oct 77	off Rolls
Joined Sept 77				
Mahoney, Michael	pt	22 April 77	22 Aug 77	missing
Medler, Boston	drum	2 feb 77	1 Nov 80	present
	drum Major 1 May 80			
Medler, Jacob	pt	12 April 77	May 78	off Rolls
Moore, John	do	22 Mar 77	May 79	to Invalids, joined
Murray, Laurence	pt	27 May 77	June 80	deserted
Mathews, William	do	25 April 77	Sept 77	off Rolls
Minn, John	do	3 May 77	4 Mar 79	deserted
	Corpl	1 Oct 77	Joined May	
	pt	10 Sept 78		

[1] Williams'. [2] Miles'. [3] Trueman's. [4] Norris', formerly Harris'. [5] Jones'.
[6] Grosh's. [7] Spyker's. [8] Stull's.

MUSTERS OF MARYLAND TROOPS, VOL. II.

Names.	Rank.	Time of Service. Enlisted.	Discharged.	Remarks.
Mans, William	pt	21 Aprl 77		
Joined July 78	Corpl	16 May 79		
Mails, John	pt	30 June 77		
Mason, Thomas	Lieut	10 May 77		
	Capt	8 June 79		
Morris, Jonathan	Lieut	2 dec 76		
	Capt	28 dec 77		
Maguire, Thomas[1]	Sergt	7 dec 76	7 dec 79	discharged
	pt	1 July 77		
Malm, Andrew	Corpl	5 Jan 77		
from Sergt	pt	7 Oct 78	6 Oct 80	joined
Murrough, John	Corpl	5 Jan 77	Aug 77	off Rolls
Morrison, George	pt	8 dec 76	4 April 77	died
Murphey, Patrick	do	5 Jan 77	22 Aug 77	prisoner, off Rolls June 78
Manyan, Patrick	do	18 feb 77	4 feb 80	discharged
Mahoney, Patrick	do	10 Mar 77	Nov 77	off Rolls
	Corpl	1 Sept 77		
Murray, Edward	pt	13 Mar 77	9 July 80	deserted
McCloud, Edwd.	do	18 Mar 77	31 July 77	do
Maloney, Thomas	do	23 Mar 77	16 Aug 80	missing retd. & Invalided
Miles, Murphey	do	6 Aprl 77	16 Aug 80	missing
Mitchell, Francis	do	7 Aprl 77	1 July 80 3 day of Aug 80 discharged	
Maguire, John	pt	8 Aprl 77	July 77	off Rolls
Mooney, Patrick	do	15 Aug 77	8 July 80	deserted
25 July 79 Joined				
Murdock, Benja.	Ensn	17 April 77	12 April 79	resigned
	Lieut	28 dec 77		
McDonald, George[2]	Sergt	21 Jan 77	11 June 78	deserted
McKinney, John	pt	6 dec 76	22 Mar 77	do
McDonald, Robert[2]	do	11 feb 77		
Moore, John	do	15 Aug 77	1 Nov 80	present
Myers, John George[3]	Sergt	9 May 77	4 Oct 77	missing
	pt	1 Sept 77		
Majors, Charles	do	12 April 77	June 80	deserted
Mullet, William	do	5 June 77	See William Hulet	
Myers, Christopher	pt	16 July 77	1 Nov 80	present
McGuire, Danl.	do	9 April 77	9 April 77	deserted
Merrit, William[4]	Corpl		19 June 79	discharged
Maloney, James	pt		dec 77	off Rolls

[1] Morris'. [2] Bayly's. [3] Reynolds'. [4] Deams'.

MUSTERS OF MARYLAND TROOPS, VOL. II.

NAMES.	RANK.	TIME OF SERVICE. Enlisted.	Discharged.	REMARKS.
Mooring, William	pt		9 dec 77	discharged
McLaughlin, John			1 Nov 80	present
McManis, Barney	pt		18 Aug 80	died
Mortimer, John	do		16 Aug 80	missing
	fifer	7 Sept 77		
McFaul, James	pt		8 dec 79	discharged
Miller, Thomas	do			
Murphey, Michael			16 Aug 80	missing
Miller, Thomas	pt			[leave
Miller, Philip	Ensn	17 Apr 77	19 Sept 77	left the Regt. wo.
Messar, John[1]	pt	15 Mar 78	April 78	off, exchd. for Jas.
15 Mar 78 in the place of James McMullin				McMullin
Mathews, James[2]	pt	13 April 78	Oct 78	dead
McGreary, Alex.[3]	pt		26 April 78	deserted
1st mustr. April 78				
McDonald, Michael[4]	pt	23 Mar 78	28 Jan 80	deserted
1 Sept present				
McNabb, Charles[5]	Sergt	7 June 78	1 Nov 80	present
Moore, Andrew	pt	29 Mar 78	do	ditto, died
				15 Mar 81
Moran, William	pt	6 June 78	10 dec 79	discharged
Monro, John	do	2 May 78	5 June 79	deserted
Mullen, Dennis[2]	pt	30 May 78	16 Aug 80	missing
Mullen, Michael[6]	Sergt	30 Aprl 78		
Joined 2 Oct 78	pt	12 Oct 78	13 dec 78	deserted
Mathews, Richd.	do	20 May 78	16 Aug 80	missing
Manage, James[6]	pt	1 May 78	9 Sept 80	joined
McCormick, Andrew	do	24 April 78	1 Mar 79	deserted
Monro, Barny	pt	20 April 78	1 Nov 80	present
McNally, John[3]	do	2 April 78	1 Nov 80	do
Morris, Evan[4]	do	12 Mar 78	17 Mar 78	deserted
Morris, Saml.[3]	do	3 June 78	20 feb 79	discharged
McDonald, John	do	30 June 78	do	do
Maddin, Nathl.[1]	Sergt	28 Oct 78	30 April 79	deserted
	pt	20 feb 79		
McLane, Enoch[7]	Sergt	6 May 78	1 Nov 80	present
Macum, John	pt	11 May 78	16 Aug 80	missing
Moad, William	do	2 April 78	Joined 26 Oct 80	
McVay, David[1]	do	26 April 79	5 July 80	deserted
McMurray, Jeremh.	pt	14 April 79	13 Sept 79	do
Maxwell, John	do	1 June 79	1 Nov 80	present

[1] Grosh's. [2] Spyker's. [3] Morris'. [4] Bayly's. [5] Jones'. [6] Stull's. [7] Beatty's.

MUSTERS OF MARYLAND TROOPS, VOL. II.

NAMES.	RANK.	TIME OF SERVICE. Enlisted.	Discharged.	REMARKS.
McDanald, James[1] Joined 2 Nov 79	pt	23 June 78	23 Mar 80	prisoner of the Guards
Murphey, Joseph[2]	pt	Mar 79	16 Aug 80	missing
McCulloch, John[1]	pt	15 feb 80	16 Aug 80	do
Mick, John[2]	pt	1 feb 80	1 Nov 80	present
McGuire, Peter	do		16 Augt 80	missing
Morris, Cornelius	do	8 feb 80	1 Nov 80	present
Mills, John[2]	pt	do	do	
Murray, Thomson[4]	do	12 feb 80	12 July 80	deserted
McLean, Arthur[5]	Sergt	10 feb 80	1 Nov 80	present
Mattingly, Joseph	pt	3 feb 80	do	do

GERMAN REGIMENT.

Michael, Henry		26 July 79		discharged
Michael, John	Corpl		16 do	do
Mongaul, Fredk.		21 do 75	24 do	do
Miller, John	mustr P.R. 28 do		1 Augt 80	deserted
Miely, Jacob			11 Aug 79	discharged
Miller, Jacob, Jr.			20 July 79	do
McColough, Lewis			24 do	do
Mummart, William	pt		1 Aug 80	present
Miller, Jacob, Sr.			20 July 79	discharged
Martin, Henry	pay drawn from 1 Nov 79			
Maunsel, Wm.	first muster Aug 80		22 Nov 80	deserted

FIFTH MARYLAND REGIMENT.

Nichols, Nicholas[6]	pt	18 Jan 77	10 Jan 80	discharged
North, Jacob[7]	Corpl Sergt	28 June 77 June 78	1 Jan 80	was present
Nabb, Richard[8] 1st muster April 78 to Bird's	Sergt	26 Jan 77	12 Jan 80	discharged
Nicholson, John[9] Hawkins & Joined 15 Aug 79	pt	25 feb 78	1 May 79	prisoner, transfd. to Invalids in 1780
Newcome, Robert[7] 1st muster Aprl 78	pt	1 Mar 78	1 Aug 78	deserted
Newman, Jesse[8]	pt	4 June 78	1 Mar 79	discharged
Newman, William	do	4 June 78	Aug 78	not heard of
Nabb, Joseph[10]	do	6 May 78	1 Nov 80	present
Nevell, Robt.	do	18 May 78	July 78	left out
Nailor, William	do	25 April 78	1 Nov 80	present

[1] Morris'. [2] Mason's. [3] Lamar's. [4] Anderson's. [5] Lynn's.
[6] Dean's. [7] Handy's. [8] Lt. Hamilton's. [9] Johnson's. [10] Handy's, Gray's.

MUSTERS OF MARYLAND TROOPS, VOL. II.

Names.	Rank.	Time of Service. Enlisted.	Discharged.	Remarks.
Nicks, John[1]	pt	18 feb 80	16 Aug 80	missing
Nevill, Saml.	do		20 July 80	deserted
1st muster Mar 80				

SIXTH MARYLAND REGIMENT.

Names.	Rank.	Enlisted.	Discharged.	Remarks.
Nelson, John	Sergt	10 May 77	July 78	mustered resigned
Noland, Michael[2]	pt	2 feb 77	1 Jan 80	was present
Made prisoner in Jan 80 and exchanged the last of same year				1 feb 80
Newton, Basil[3]	pt	17 Mar 77	do	do
Norris, Jacob[4]	Ensn	15 May 77		
	Lieut	26 Jan 78		
Nash, Joseph[5]	pt	3 May 77	16 Aug 80	prisoner
	drum	1 May 79		
Nave, Henry[6]	pt	16 feb 79	See Henry Knave, Miles' Co.	
Nash, Thomas[3]	pt	1 June 78	1 Aprl 79	discharged
Nowell, James	pt	1 June 78	1 Nov 80	present
	fifer	3 Sept 78		
Nicholls, John[6]	pt	16 June 78	16 Aug 80	missing
Neagle, James[7]	do	18 June 79	1 Jan 80	was present

SEVENTH MARYLAND REGIMENT.

Names.	Rank.	Enlisted.	Discharged.	Remarks.
Nicholls, Thomas[8]	pt	29 Mar 77	1 feb 78	discharged
Nabb, Charles[9]	pt	2 May 77	8 May 80	do
Norton, John[10]	pt	16 Nov 77	26 Aprl 79	prisoner
Newton, or Luton, Joseph[11]	do	2 May 77	1 Aug 77	dead
Nash, Edward	pt	9 May 77	Nov 77	off Rolls
Newell, William[12]	Sergt		4 Oct 77	killed
Nayse, Richard	pt		feb 78	off Rolls
Newman, John[10]	pt	1 June 78	1 April 79	discharged
Nick, William[11]	pt	5 May 78	16 Aug 80	missing
Norman, Basil[13]	pt	6 June 78	1 Nov 80	present
Niblet, William[14]	pt	15 May 78	do	do
Nicholas, John[15]	do	29 June 78	9 April 79	discharged
Nichols, John Mc.[14]	pt	28 June 78	15 Mar 79	do
Neighbours, John[16]	pt	28 Jan 80	16 Aug 80	missing
Nowland, Michael	pt	See Knowland		

GERMAN REGIMENT.

Names.	Rank.	Enlisted.	Discharged.	Remarks.
Neving, William			1 July 79	missing
Nevitt, John		musterd. deserted	13 Nov 80	deserted

[1] Handy's. [2] Dobson's. [3] Trueman's. [4] Laurence's. [5] Chapline's, now Miles'.
[6] Miles'. [7] Norris'. [8] Jones'. [9] Spyker's. [10] Stull's. [11] Bayly's.
[12] Deams'. [13] Anderson's. [14] Beatty's. [15] Grosh's. [16] Mason's.

MUSTERS OF MARYLAND TROOPS, VOL. II.

NAMES.	RANK.	TIME OF SERVICE. Enlisted.	Discharged.	REMARKS.
FIFTH MARYLAND REGIMENT.				
O'Bryan, M. Thos.[1]	Sergt	19 May 77	1 Jan 80	was present
	pt	21 May 78	3 May 80	discharged
	Sergt	1 June 78		
Owens, James[2]	pt	1 Jan 77	do	do
Oglesby, Charles[3]	pt	2 Aprl 77	1 Aprl 80	discharged
Olephant, Thomas[4]	pt	28 July 77	23 April 78	died
Outerbridge, Stephen[2]	do	15 May 78	Sept 80	deserted
O'Bryan, Joseph[1]	do	4 June 78	19 June 78	deserted
SIXTH MARYLAND REGIMENT.				
Oram, Peter[5]	pt	12 Jan 77	12 Jan 80	discharged
O'Mullen, Patrick[6]	pt	21 May 77	See Mullen, Patrick	
O'Branan, Timothy	pt	21 May 77	April & May 79 transfrd., not heard of Nov 80	
O'Hara, John	pt	29 Aug 77	15 June 78	deserted
Owens, Stephen[7] 1st muster June 78	pt	16 May 78	1 Nov 80	present
O'Hara, Arthur[8]	pt	6 May 78	1 Jan 80	was present
Orchard, William[9]	pt	17 May 79	16 Aug 80	missing
Owens, James Oct mustr. 80	do		14 Sept 80	deserted
SEVENTH MARYLAND REGIMENT.				
Osband, John[10] Joined 22 July 78	pt	14 Aprl 77	26 May	deserted
Owens, William[11]	pt	17 Jan 77	10 Mar 78	do
Oliver, John	pt	15 Nov 77	16 Aug 80	missing
O'Neale, Patrick[12]	do	5 Aprl 77	1 Jan 80	was present
	Sergt	1 Sept 77		
	pt	26 dec 77		
O'Neale, Patrick[13] Joined	do		June 80	deserted
Oldstone, Edward[10]	pt	13 April 78	1 July 80	do
Orme, Charles[14]	do	6 June 78	1 Nov 80	present
Osborn, William	pt	6 June 78	16 Aug 80	missing
O'Ph——, Stephen[15]	do	14 June 80	See Stephen Flaharty	
GERMAN REGIMENT.				
O'Quin, Richd.			1 Sept 82	dischd. Invalids [dispd.

[1] Hawkins'. [2] Handy's. [3] Johnson's. [4] Emory's. [5] Hynes'. [6] Harris'.
[7] Dobson's. [8] Lt. Williams'. [9] Norris'. [10] Grosh's. [11] Bayly's. [12] Reynolds'.
[13] Deams'. [14] Jones'. [15] Morris'.

MUSTERS OF MARYLAND TROOPS, VOL. II.

Names.	Rank.	Time of Service. Enlisted.	Discharged.	Remarks.
	FIFTH MARYLAND REGIMENT.			
Pierce, John	Surgeon	13 Jan 78		
Purdy, Joseph	drum Major	11 June 77	1 Nov 80	present
Powers, Charles[1]	pt	27 July 77	April 78	left out
Proctor, John	pt	30 Mar 77	16 Aug 80	missing
Price, Nicholas[2]	pt	4 Sept		
Pryday, John[3]	pt	17 dec 76	16 Aug 80	missing
Peters, Joseph	do	16 Jan 77	1 Mar 79	discharged
Porters, William	do	18 feb 77	1 Mar 80	deserted
Paul, Thomas[4]	Sergt	27 April 77	1 Aug 79	Commss. Department
			27 April 80	discharged
Pounder, Richard	Corpl	6 dec 76	pt. 1 April 77	
	Corpl	1 April 79	16 Aug 80	missing
Poole, James[5]	pt	1 feb 77	1 Nov 80	present
Philips, Elijah[6]	do	10 dec 76	12 Jan 80	discharged
Philips, Jacob	do	10 dec 76	do	do
Parkfield, Wm.	do	4 Sept 77	1 April 78	discharged
Philips, John[7]	do	5 feb 77	5 feb 80	do
	Corpl	1 April 79		
Philips, Stephen[8]	Sergt	25 April 77		
1st muster April 78, Sergt 1 April 79				
	pt	July 78	25 April 80	discharged
Pennington, Robert	pt	10 feb 77	1 Nov 80	present
Pennington, George	pt		22 feb 80	deserted
Powell, John[9]	pt	2 Mar 78		
Proctor, Daniel[3]	do	15 May 78	1 Mar 79	discharged
Pierce, George[4]	pt	28 April 78		
Joined 1 April 80	drum	1 Aug 78	16 Aug 80	missing
Peters, Gabriel	pt	8 April 78	1 Nov 80	present
Payne, John[9]	do	15 feb 77	do	do
Mustrd. Sergt. reduced 26 April 79 sick Braskinridge				
Pilkinton, Michael	pt	3 June 78	21 Jan 80	joined
Poney, Edward	do	2 June 78	1 Mar 79	discharged
Mustrd. again Sept 78				
Powell, John[4]	pt	19 June 78	1 Jan 80	was present
Price, John	do	1 June 78	May 79	discharged
Powell, James[2]	do	5 May 78	15 Aug 78	died
Poor, Philip[9]	pt	7 July 79	1 Nov 80	present
Pendergrast, William	Lieut	29 Oct 79		paid

[1] Dean's, Benson's. [2] Hawkins'. [3] Lynch's. [4] Handy's. [5] Johnson's.
[6] Emory's. [7] Cosden's. [8] Lt. Hamilton's. [9] Lynch's, or Dower's.

MUSTERS OF MARYLAND TROOPS, VOL. II.

Names.	Rank.	Time of Service. Enlisted.	Discharged.	Remarks.

SIXTH MARYLAND REGIMENT.

Names.	Rank.	Enlisted.	Discharged.	Remarks.
Parsons, William[1]	pt	20 April 77	16 Aug 80	missing
Parsons, John	pt	28 May 77	16 Aug 80	killed
deserted 20 dec 77	Joined 25 May 78			
Pack, James	pt	29 April 78	4 Oct 78	died
Philip, William[2]	Corpl	13 Mar 77	} 15 feb 78	died
	Sergt	1 Nov 77		
Palmer, Samuel[3]	Corpl	5 April 77	1 Jan 80	was present }
			5 April 80	discharged }
Pattron, William	pt	9 May 78	8 Aug 80	deserted
	fifer	1 June 78	.	
Price, Stephen[4]	pt	9 June 78	1 Nov 80	present
Q. Mr. Sergt. 1 July 80	Corpl	10 Nov 77		
Pinnox, Isaac	pt	29 June 77	} Mar 79	[not known diedTrenton,time
deserted 4 Nov 77 & Joined 1 May 78				
Palmer, Michael[5]	pt	31 May 77	16 Aug 80	missing
Phillips, Saml.[3]	Sergt	9 June 78	13 Sept 80	deserted
1st muster June 78, rein. 22 dec 78				
Price, Thomas[6]	pt	12 June 78	18 Aug 78	died
1st muster June 78				
Perry, John[7]	pt	16 May 78	16 Aug 80	missing
Pound, John	Corpl	4 May 78	18 Aug 80	deserted
Corpl Oct 80	pt	1 Nov 79		
Piper, Joseph[6]	do	27 Mar 78	April 78	deserted
Pome, Barthw.[9]	pt	probably never joined		
1st muster July 79				[lids
Phap, Benjamin[3]	do	5 May 78	30 Sept 80	transferd.to Inva-
Parran, Thomas	Surgeon	11 Aug 78	July 80	resigned
Purdy, Edward	pt	5 feb 80	1 Nov 80	present
Oct Muster 80				
Purdy, John		20 feb 80	do	do
Purdy, Henry		5 feb 80	do	do
Pierce, John			16 Aug 80	missing
Pierce, Saml.			16 Aug 80	do
Pindell, Philip			16 Aug 80	do
Philbert, Joseph	Corpl	30 May 78	1 Nov 80	present
Peny, William[9]	pt	6 July 77	} 6 Aug 80	do
	Corpl	10 Oct 77		
	pt	1 June 78		

[1] Ghiselin's.   [2] Dobson's.   [3] Beall's.   [4] Harris'.   [5] Chapline's, now Miles'.
[6] Lt. Williams'.   [7] Miles'.   [8] Trueman's.   [9] Laurence's.

MUSTERS OF MARYLAND TROOPS, VOL. II.

NAMES.	RANK.	TIME OF SERVICE. Enlisted.	Discharged.	REMARKS.
\multicolumn{5}{c}{SEVENTH MARYLAND REGIMENT.}				

SEVENTH MARYLAND REGIMENT.

NAMES.	RANK.	Enlisted.	Discharged.	REMARKS.
Parran, Thomas	S. Mate	18 April 77	11 Aug 78	Surgeon of 6 Regt.
Parker, William[1]	pt	16 Jan 77	12 Jan 80	discharged
Purnell, Saml.	do	11 feb 77	9 feb 80	do
Porter, Charles	Ensign	17 April 77		
	Lieut	28 dec 77		
Enlisted to be Second Lieut		7 July 77	19 feb 80	discharged
Philips, George[2]	pt	18 Mar 77	Joined 25 July 79	
Pinder, John	pt	4 April 77	April 78	off Rolls
Parker, John	pt	4 April 77	April 78	off Rolls
Pinctly, John[3]	fifer	2 feb 77	feb 78	off Rolls
Poke, William	pt	3 May 77	Oct 77	off Rolls
Peacock, Neale[4]	do	24 dec 76	1 Nov 80	present
Philpot, Charles[5]	Sergt	4 dec 76	4 dec 79	discharged
Powell, John	Corpl	5 dec 76	4 Oct 77	killed
Porter, John	pt	19 dec 76	22 dec 76	deserted
Pike, William	pt	22 feb 77	31 July 77	do
Parmer, Nathl.	pt	15 Nov 77	16 Aug 80	missing
Pinckley, Michael[6]	pt	2 May 77	1 May 80	discharged
Pumphry, John	pt		16 Aug 80	missing
Preston, Thomas	pt		1 June 80	deserted
Price, Robert	pt			Hospital Annapolis
Pasterfield, Thomas[2]	pt	16 May 78	July 78	off Rolls
Pollard, William[1]	pt	30 April 78	Sept 79	not heard of
Prangley, William	pt	19 May 78	1 Nov 80	present
Price, James	pt	29 Mar 78	30 Mar 79	deserted
Peace, John[2]	Corpl	28 April 78	1 Nov 80	present
Sergt. Major May 80, 16 May 79 Sergt. and M. S. 2 Mar 80				
Paine, George[4]	pt	13 June 78	30 Mar 79	discharged
Pennywell, Radcliffe[2]	pt	20 July 78	9 April 79	ditto
Parris, John	pt	20 July 78	20 dec 78	deserted
Pepper, Elijah[7]	pt	20 May 78	1 Nov 80	present
Peacock, Thomas	pt	16 Mar 79	do	do
Pugh, Thomas[2]	pt	2 July 79		
20 Sept 79 Transferred				
Penn, Michael[7]	pt		1 Nov 80	present
Mar 80 Lt. Beall's				

GERMAN REGIMENT.

NAMES.	RANK.	Enlisted.	Discharged.	REMARKS.
Polhouse, Thomas to 1 Jan 81	Corpl	1 Nov 78	1 Aug 80	present
Proctor, Thomas to 1 Jan 81		4 May 78	do	do

[1] Jones'. [2] Grosh's. [3] Stull's. [4] Morris'. [5] Bayly's. [6] Reynolds'. [7] Beall's.

MUSTERS OF MARYLAND TROOPS, VOL. II.

NAMES.	RANK.	TIME OF SERVICE. Enlisted.	Discharged.	REMARKS.
Pointer, William			13 Nov 80	deserted
Porter, Robert to 1 Jan 81	pt	May 78	Aug 80	present
Painter, Henry	See Henry Bender			

FIFTH MARYLAND REGIMENT.

Quain, John[1]	pt	15 May 77		

SEVENTH MARYLAND REGIMENT.

Quynn, Timothy[2] 21 July 78 Joined	pt	30 Mar 77	16 Aug 80	missing
Quinley, Levin[3]	pt	4 May 78	dec 79	deserted
Quinton, William 1 Oct 80 joined	pt		1 Nov 80	present

GERMAN REGIMENT.

Quier, Henry			26 July 79	discharged

FIFTH MARYLAND REGIMENT.

Richardson, William	Col	10 Dec 76		
Ryan, Gilbert[4]	pt	13 July 77		
Rogers, Robert[1]	pt	1 May 77		
Ried, Philip[5]	Ensn	20 feb 77		
	Lieut	13 Oct 78		
Ross, Bathw.	pt	30 June 77	May 79	not heard of
Ryan, Robert[6]	do	10 feb 77	7 feb 80	discharged
Ray, William	do	11 Mar	16 April 78	Sergt., 5 May dead, April 78 left out
Richardson, Charles	do	17 Mar	17 Mar 80	discharged
Raisin, William[7]	Corpl	10 Jan 77		
Reily, John[8]	pt	18 feb 77	2 Sept 78	died
Reancifer, John[9]	Sergt	8 Jan 77	July 78	left out
Roster, William	pt	13 Jan 77	April 78	do
Ryan, James[10] 1st muster April 78 to Bird's	pt		16 Aug 80	missing
Redding, Thomas	pt	5 June 77	1 Jan 80	was present
	Corpl	4 Nov 78		
	pt	18 June 79		
Richie, John[6] 1st muster 78	pt	5 dec 76	do	do
Reynolds, Thomas[5]	pt	15 June 78	Mar 79	discharged

[1] Hawkins'. [2] Grosh's. [3] Morris'. [4] Dean's. [5] Lynch's. [6] Handy's.
[7] Johnson's. [8] Emory's. [9] Cosden's. [10] Hamilton's.

MUSTERS OF MARYLAND TROOPS, VOL. II.

Names.	Rank.	Time of Service. Enlisted.	Discharged.	Remarks.
Richards, Stephen[1]	pt	13 May 78		
Sick at Annapolis				
Ryall, John[2]	pt	6 June 78	20 Mar 79	discharged
Rumford, William[3]	pt	5 June 78	16 Aug 80	missing
	Sergt	6 Mar 80		
Richardson, Thomas[4]	pt	28 May 78	16 Aug 80	missing
Joined 12 Aug 79				
Reordon, John	pt	4 June 78	28 June 79	deserted
Ryan, Michael[5]	pt	1 Aprl 79	10 Jan 80	discharged
Rankin, Robert[6]	pt	5 May 79	16 Aug 80	missing
1 muster June 79				
Reynolds, Thomas[4]	pt	10 May 79	16 Aug 80	do
Reynolds, James	pt	30 Mar 79	1 Nov 80	present
Ross, Thomas	pt			
Reason, William	Ensn	26 Jan 80		

SIXTH MARYLAND REGIMENT.

Names.	Rank.	Enlisted.	Discharged.	Remarks.
Riely, Patrick[7]	Corpl	3 May 78	15 Aug 80	deserted
	pt	6 Oct 78		
Rowen, Christopher	pt	15 Aug 77	2 July 79	deserted
Ridley, Drew	pt	25 Aprl 78	10 Aug 80	do
Rogers, Michael[6]	pt	18 May 77		
Robertson, Saml.	pt	27 May 78	Sept 80	missing
Rigby, William[8]	Sergt	29 April 77		
	Q.M.Sergt.	Jany 79	30 April 80	discharged
Rayne, William[10]	pt	24 feb 78	27 Sept 78	died
Reason, Jacob	pt	13 Aprl 78	29 Jan 79	died
Robinson, William[11]	pt	30 dec 76	30 dec 79	discharged
Rawlings, Solomon	pt	5 dec 76	5 dec 79	do
Reardon, John[12]	pt	27 dec 76	16 Aug 80	missing
Rochester, Abram[8]	do	10 June 78	dec 79	absent without leave
1st muster June 78, 23 dec 78 reinlisted				
Balston, Joseph	pt	9 June 78	1 Nov 80	present
1 muster June 78, rein. 23 dec 78				
Rawlings, Benja.[9]	pt	1 June 78	1 April 79	discharged
Ryan, Hugh	pt	1 June 78	15 dec 79	died
rein. 1 Jany 79				
Ralph, William[10]	pt	24 April 78	1 Jan 80	was present
1st mustr. June 78				
Battican, James[12]	pt	18 April 78	See Hattakan, Joseph	
Roach, James[13]	do	4 May 78	1 Aug 80	deserted

[1] Handy's.   [2] Ensign Jones'.   [3] Johnson's.   [4] Hawkins'.   [5] Dean's.
[6] Lynch's.   [7] Ghiselin's.   [8] Dobson's.   [9] Trueman's.   [10] Beall's.
[11] Hynes'.   [12] Harris'.   [13] Miles'.

MUSTERS OF MARYLAND TROOPS, VOL. II.

NAMES.	RANK.	TIME OF SERVICE. Enlisted.	Discharged.	REMARKS.
Rork, John	pt	19 May 78	30 June 79	deserted
Reynolds, William	do	3 May 78	3 Mar 79	discharged
Rinehart, Andrew[1]	do	1 July 78	1 April 79	do
Reason, John, or James[2] rein. 9 Nov 78	pt	24 June 78	1 Jan 80	was present
Robertson, Robert	pt	24 Aprl 78	16 Aug 80	missing
Rattican, Peter[3]	do	1 July 78	1 Jan 80	was present
Rockhole, Hasael[4]	pt	4 Nov 79	1 Nov 80	present
Rice, Robert	pt	30 April 78	do	do
Rowland, Jacob[3] Joined 19 Aug 78	pt	27 June 77	do	do
Beaves, Noah[4]	Corpl	27 July 78	1 May 79	discharged
Roe, William[6] 1st mustr. Aug 79	pt		14 Sept 80	deserted
Rice, William[6]	pt	14 Aug 79	1 Nov 80	present
Richardson, John Oct Roll 1780	drum		16 Aug 80	missing

SEVENTH REGIMENT.

NAMES.	RANK.	Enlisted.	Discharged.	REMARKS.
Ross, Alexander[7]	pt	11 feb 77	1 Nov 80	present
Ramsey, Charles	do	17 Mar 77	17 Mar 80	discharged
Read, Christopher[8]	do	15 May 77	July 78	off Rolls
See a certificate in Read's depreciation acct.			5 May 80	discharged
Rotherford, John	pt	15 May 77	15 May 80	do
	Corpl	1 April 78		
	Sergt	4 Oct 78		
Riely, Patrick[9]	Corpl	4 dec 76	1 Nov 80	present
	pt	15 July 78		
Riely, Barney	do	12 dec 76	22 Aug 77	killed
Ragan, Darby	do	1 April 77	4 Oct 77	missing
Riggs, John[10]	drum	5 dec 76	8 dec 79	discharged
	D. Major	4 June 77		reinlisted
Riley, Walter	pt	5 dec 76	4 Oct 77	killed
Ringer, Andrew Joined Sept 77	do	6 dec 76	1 July 80	deserted
Robertson, Isaac	pt	21 Nov 77	8 April 79	do
Reynolds, John	Capt	10 dec 76		
Rodwell, Godfrey[11]	Sergt		Sept 77	off Rolls
Reynolds, Francis	pt		1 Nov 80	present
Rowell, William[12] to Grosh's, reinlisted	do	24 Mar 78	4 May 79 16 Aug 80	missing

[1] Ghiselin's. [2] Hynes'. [3] Harris'. [4] Miles'. [5] Jacobs'. [6] Norris'.
[7] Jones'. [8] Spyker's. [9] Morris'. [10] Bayly's. [11] Deams'. [12] Anderson's.

MUSTERS OF MARYLAND TROOPS, VOL. II.

NAMES.	RANK.	TIME OF SERVICE. Enlisted.	Discharged.	REMARKS.
Roe, Obediah[1]	pt	9 May 78	July 78	off Rolls
Rosstell, Joseph[2]	do	12 Jan 78	8 feb 78	deserted
Riely, John[3]	do	25 April 78	20 feb 80	do
Russell, Aron	do	30 May 78	30 Sept 78	died
Rimington, John	do	6 June 78	16 Mar 79	discharged
Read, James[4]	do	19 May 78	Aug 79	not heard of
Ryan, Patrick Joined	do	22 Aprl 78	16 July 80	deserted
Read, William[5]	do	5 May 78	16 Aug 80	missing
Rochford, Edward	do	23 April 78	27 do	deserted
Riggs, William[1]	do		11 Jan 79	transferrd. to 2d Md. Brigade
Row, John	do	20 July 78	9 April 79	discharged
Ricketts, Andrew	do	13 May 79	16 Aug 80	missing
Roberts, Horatio[6]	do	2 feb 80	16 Aug 80	do
Roxburgh, Alexr.	Major	1 April 80		promoted from 1st Regt.
Riggs, John[5]	fifer	6 May 80	1 Nov 80	present, see J. Riggs of Bayley's
Reese, Henry	pt	14 Aprl 77	do	do

GERMAN REGIMENT.

NAMES.	RANK.	Enlisted.	Discharged.	REMARKS.
Roach, (or Rock), John	drum	2 Mar 78	1 Aug 80	present & 1 Jan 81
Rider, William to 1st Jan 81		12 May 78	do	do [paid
Ronenberger, Chas. to 1st Jan 81		6 June 80	do	do
Ritmire, Michael to 1st Jan 81	pt	1 feb 80	do	do
Riely, Conrad			24 July 79	discharged
Rummelson, Wm.	Sergt		16 do	do
Robinson, Edward			20 July do	do
Robinson, Andrew			do	do
Raybert, Chs., or Chrisr.			26 July 79	do
Ruppert, Jacob			15 July 79	discharged
Rittlemeyer, George			11 Aug do	do
Rumfell, Henry			28 July do	do
Regalman, George			12 Oct 79	do
Ricknagle, Jacob			26 July 79	do
Richards, John		Mustrd. sick at Windsor 1 July 79		
Raver, Christr.			26 July 79	discharged
Riely, Bernard			6 Nov 80	deserted

[1] Grosh's.   [2] Beatty's.   [3] Jones'.   [4] Morris'.
[5] Bayly's.   [6] Mason's.

MUSTERS OF MARYLAND TROOPS, VOL II.

Names.	Rank.	Time of Service. Enlisted.	Discharged.	Remarks.
Fifth Maryland Regiment.				
Smyth, Thomas	Major	10 Dec 76		
Spratbrow, Wm.[1]	Sergt.Major	10 April 77		[Forage Depart.
	Sergt.Major	1 Nov 77	1 feb 79	transferred to
Shaw, Dennis[2]	Sergt	21 July 77	Dec 78	not heard of
Start, Moses[3]	pt	18 Jan 77	16 Aug 80	missing
Mustd. Sergt. Oct. 80				
Saunders,(or Launders), John	do	30 Mar 77	22 Mar 80	discharged
St. Clair, William	do	13 Jan 77	16 Aug 80	missing, joined
Saunders, William[4]	do	30 Mar 77		
to Hamilton's	Corpl	21 feb 80	30 Mar 80	discharged
Scoudrick, Charles	do	20 July 77	16 Aug 80	missing
Mustd. Corpl Oct 80				
Slaughter, Philip	fifer	10 Jan 77	April 78	left out
Scoudrick, Thomas	pt	13 July 77	1 Nov 80	present
Mustd. Corpl Oct 80				[reason assigned
Swany, Thomas	do	30 Mar 77	feb 80	struck off, no
Skinner, Thomas[1]	Lieut	20 feb 77	10 dec 77	resigned
Smith, Jonathan	pt	10 dec 77	1 Jan 80	was present
	fifer	20 Aug 78	May 80	discharged
Stableford, Taylor[3]	pt	30 July	do	do
Smith, Levi	pt	19 July		
	Corpl	20 Oct 78		
	Sergt	1 Aprl 79	1 Nov 80	present
Seth, Jacob	Sergt	15 Aug 77		
	pt	1 July 78	20 Aug 80	discharged
Stoakes, Peter[5]	2d Lieut	13 June 77	24 Aug 78	resigned
Stevens, Robert	pt	12 April 77	16 Aug 80	missing
Sullivan, James	pt	10 Sept 77	Jan 79	not heard of for 8 mos.
Samuels, John[6]	do	10 feb 77	April 78	left out
Smyth, Daniel	do	2 April	1 Nov 80	present
Stephenson, John	do	20 May	April 78	left out
Sullivan, William	do	27 July	1 Nov 80	present
Swift, Gideon	do	4 Sept	April 78	left out
Sutton, Abram[7]	do fifer	10 dec 76		[of Lee's Division
	F. Major	10 feb 79	16 Aug 80	missing, afterwards
Stone, (or Scone), George	pt	14 Jan 77	1 Nov 80	present
	Corpl	80		
Strickenburgh, Andw. John	pt	23 April 77	dec 78	left out
Sturges, Thomas	do	5 July 77	July 78	do
Stinson, William[8]	2d Lieut	14 feb 77	1 Nov 77	resigned

[1] Hawkins'.   [2] Dean's.   [3] Benson's.   [4] Hamilton's.
[5] Lynch's.   [6] Handy's.   [7] Johnson's.   [8] Emory's.

MUSTERS OF MARYLAND TROOPS, VOL. II.

Names.	Rank.	Time of Service. Enlisted.	Discharged.	Remarks.
Sharpt, (or Tharp), Danl.	pt	18 feb 77	22 May 78	discharged
Stewart, Thomas	pt	16 July 77		
Sheavers, Danl.	pt	26 Mar 77 Joined again	desd. 26 Jany 80 and never joined	
Smith, John[1]	pt	23 Jan 77	1 Nov 80	present
pt 1st Nov 78	Corpl	27 July 78		
Sharon, Frederick	do	8 Jany 80	do, 8 Jany 80	discharged
Smith, James[2]	pt	5 dec 76	19 May 79	do
1st mustr. April 78				
Sinnett, Nicholas	pt		June 78	left out
Small, Jonathan[3]	pt	10 feb 77	14 feb 80	discharged
1st mustr. April 78				
Sullivan, Perry[4]	pt	2 April 77	1 Nov 80	present
1st mustr. April 78				
Sappington, Thos.[2]	pt	1 June 78	do	do
reinlisted	Sergt	19 June 78		
Stockett, Thomas	pt	9 May 78	10 April 79	deserted
rein. 16 Jan 79				
Swift, David	pt	6 June 78	1 Mar 79	discharged
pt Dec 78				
Sullivan, Darby	pt		Augt 78	not heard of, see Darby Sullivan below
Swain, John	pt	8 June 78	Aug 78	mustd. not heard of
Shorter, Roger[5]	pt	21 Apr 78	1 Nov 80	present
1st mustr. June 78				
Sharp, William[6]	pt	29 May 78	1 May 81	discharged
Oct mustr. 80	Corpl			
Silvester, Thomas[7]	pt	20 May 78	21 Aug 78	died
Stewart, Andrew	pt	20 May 78	16 Aug 80	missing, 1 Aug 81 dischgd.
Satchell, James	pt	8 May 78	Feby 79	not heard of
Summers, Solomon	do	6 May 78	1 Nov 80	present
Sullivan, Darby[2]	do	6 June 78	15 Sept 79	died
1 Sept 78 to Hamilton's Co.				
Sherwood, Hugh[8]	pt	6 June 78	July 78	discharged
Saunders, George[4]	do	23 May 78	1 Nov 80	present
Sidner, Joseph	pt	6 June 78	15 Jan 80	joined
Shove, John[7]	do	4 June 78	19 Mar 79	discharged
Samuel, William	do	4 June 78	do	do
Sevell, William	do	4 June 78	See William Sewell below	
reinlisted				

[1] Cosden's.   [2] Lt. Hamilton's.   [3] Ensign Jones', Benson's.   [4] Johnson's.
[5] Lynch's.   [6] Benson's.   [7] Handy's.   [8] Ensign Jones'.

MUSTERS OF MARYLAND TROOPS, VOL. II.

Names.	Rank.	Time of Service. Enlisted.	Discharged.	Remarks.
Scott, James	pt	4 June 78	July 78	left out
Scudder, Jesse[1]	do	17 Aprl 78	2 July 79	deserted
1st muster June 79				
Smith, William	pt	3 June 78		
Sewell, William[2]	do	4 April 79	See Civill, William, Letter G R	
Stallings, Thos.[3]	pt	1 May 79	11 Nov 79	transferred, not heard of since
1st muster June 79				
Surton, Robert[1]	pt	1 dec 79	30 Oct 80	died
Joined 1 dec 79	Mustr. Sergt Oct roll 80			
Stoddart, William	Lieut			

SIXTH MARYLAND REGIMENT.

Names.	Rank.	Enlisted.	Discharged.	Remarks.
Somerville, James[4]	Lieut / Capt	20 feb 77 / 1 June 79	16 Aug 80	wounded
Shean, Patrick	pt	19 May 78	1 Jan 80	was present
Speak, Nathaniel	do	23 Aprl 78	do	do
Smith, William[5]	do	10 feb 77	26 Aprl 79	prisoner war
Sappington, Thos.	do	3 feb —	12 June 78	deserted
Shehey, Edward	pt	17 May 77	1 Nov 80	present
Swift, John[6]	pt	12 Aug 77	Oct 80	discharged
Smith, Benjamin[7]	pt	16 July 77	1 Jan 80	was present
Stephens, William	pt	23 June 77	2 July 79	deserted
Sharpless, Robert	pt / Corpl	28 feb 78 / 5 feb 79	1 Nov 80	present
Simmons, Noble	pt	11 feb 78	2 July 78	died
Spyers, William[8]	pt	8 Mar 77	Dec 78	do
Sharer, Michael	do	10 July 77	1 Jan 80	was present
deserted 13 Oct & Joined 13 April 78			16 May 80	discharged by Col. Forrest
Scott, Benjamin[9]	Lieut	10 dec 76	21 Sept 78	resigned
Swanton, Peter	pt	8 July 77	16 Aug 80	missing
Stevenson, Alexr.	Drum	1 Jany 77	1 Nov 80	present
Smith, John[10]	Lieut / Capt	10 dec 76 / 9 Nov 77		
Sparrow, Alexr.	pt / Corpl	17 dec 76 / 6 April 79	20 dec 79	discharged
Smith, Thomas[4]	pt	1 July 78	1 June 79	deserted
1 July 78, rein. 3 Sept 78 pt				
Summers, John[5]	pt	10 June 78	1 Nov 80	present
1st mustr. June 78, rein. 6 Sept 78, Joined 15 Aug 79				
Scott, James	pt	10 June 78	14 Mar 79	discharged
1st mustr. June 78				

[1] Hawkins'. [2] Dean's, Benson's. [3] Lynch's. [4] Ghiselin's. [5] Dobson's.
[6] Trueman's. [7] Beall's. [8] Hynes'. [9] Harris'. [10] Chapline's, now Miles'.

MUSTERS OF MARYLAND TROOPS, VOL. II.

NAMES.	RANK.	TIME OF SERVICE. Enlisted.	Discharged.	REMARKS.
Stalcob, Henry	pt	10 June 78	14 Mar 79	deserted
1st mustr. June 78				
Stonestreet, William	pt	1 April 78	1 Nov 80	present
1st mustr. June 78				
Spencer, George[1]	do	6 June 78	1 Jan 80	was present
1st muster June 78				
Smith, John[2]	do	5 dec 76		
Joined June muster 78				
Sullivan, Lawrence[3]	pt	14 May 78		
Joined Oct 78				
Sloop, Joseph	pt	16 May 78	1 Nov 80	present
	drum	1 Aug 78		
	pt	Oct 80		
Sponk, Jacob	do	4 May 78	1 Jan 80	was present
Sloop, John	do	2 May 78	3 Aug 78	died
Simkins, William	pt	2 June 78	1 April 79	discharged
Slately, Michael	pt	11 May 78	time expd., discharged April 79	
Spoutman, Francis	pt	1 June 78	1 April 79	discharged
1st mustr. June 78				
Sweney, Owen[4]	pt	23 May 78	16 Aug 80	missing
Suel, James	pt	25 May 78	1 Nov 80	present
Smith, Elias[2]	pt	28 Apr 78	1 Jany 80	was present reinlisted
Shipley, Saml.[4]	pt	3 June 78	22 Mar 79	discharged
Stewart, Saml.	fifer	11 June 78	1 Jany 80	was present reinlisted
Smith, John	pt	4 June 78	do	do
Series, John[5]	pt	11 May 79	June 79	absent wo. Leave
Smith, Thomas[6]	pt	30 June 77	1 Nov 80	present
1st mustr. July 79				
Shugert, Peter[3]	pt	30 Aprl 79	1 Nov 80	do
Solomon, David[6]	pt		16 Aug 80	prisoner
1st mustr. 21 Sept 79				
Sevink, Abraham	pt		1 Nov 80	present
Joined 21 Sept 79				
Stanley, Michael[7]	pt	17 May 79	do	do
Joined Sept 79				
Sanders, Danl.[3]	pt	27 Aprl 79	16 Aug 80	missing
Smith, Thomas[7]	do	10 Aug 79	1 June 80	was present
Smith, William	Sergt. Mate	1 Feby 80		
Stern, George	pt		1 Nov 80	present
Oct mustr. 1780				

[1] Beall's. [2] Hynes'. [3] Lt. Williams'. [4] Miles'. [5] J. Jacobs'. [6] Trueman's. [7] Norris'.

MUSTERS OF MARYLAND TROOPS, VOL. II.

Names.	Rank.	Time of Service. Enlisted.	Discharged.	Remarks.
Stewart, James	pt	8 Jan 80	1 Nov 80	present
Slackhouse, John	pt	2 April 80	do	do
		2 April 83	discharged	
Sinester, Thomas	pt		do	do
Shoemaker, Michael	pt		do	do
Speake, Joseph	pt		16 Aug 80	prisoner
Sowers, Michael	pt	6 Mar 80	16 Aug 80	prisoner
Smith, William	pt		10 Aug 80	deserted

SEVENTH MARYLAND REGIMENT.

Names.	Rank.	Enlisted.	Discharged.	Remarks.
Shoulder, Nicholas[1]	Drum	7 dec 76	Sept 77	out of the Rolls
Seveny, James	pt	10 April 77	8 May 77	deserted
Smith, James	do	2 April 77	1 Nov 80	present
Skinner, James John	Lieut	7 July 77		
Spyker, Benjamin	Capt	10 Dec 76	12 May 79	resigned
Smith, Isaac[2] retd. 16 July 78	pt	20 April 77		
Stoops, Andrew retd. July 78	pt	29 May 77		
Satterfield, Wm. Joined 2 Feby.	pt	7 June 77		
	Corpl	25 dec 77		
	Sergt	1 Mar 80	16 Aug 80	missing
Smith, William	pt	7 May 77	16 Aug 80	do
Shean, Dennis	do	15 Aug 77	13 Sept 80	discharged
Shaw, John	do	15 Aug 77	July 78	Invalid
			18 June 1781	discharged
Stull, Daniel	Capt	10 dec 76	14 Sept 78	resigned
Seburn, John[3]	pt	26 April 77	May 80	discharged
Simms, James[4]	pt	7 dec 76	9 dec 76	deserted
Storrom, Jacob	do	8 dec 76	7 dec 79	discharged
Smith, John	do	24 Jany 77	Jany 80	do
			19 Jany	mustered
Swain, Richard	do	14 April 77	June 79	off Rolls
	Corpl	1 Jan 78		
Sullivan, John	pt	15 April 77	9 June 77	deserted
Simpkins, Charles	do	1 Sept 77	1 Nov 80	present
Sullivan, Philip[5] Joined April 78	Corpl	4 dec 76		
Stewart, John	pt	3 dec 76	22 Aug 77	prisoner, never [retd.
Shaver, John	do	3 dec 76		
	fifer	1 Sept 77	Sept 78	
	pt	26 dec 77		deserted

[1] Grosh's.   [2] Spyker's.   [3] Stull's.   [4] Morris'.   [5] Bayly's.

during the War of the American Revolution, 1775-83.

MUSTERS OF MARYLAND TROOPS, VOL. II.

NAMES.	RANK.	TIME OF SERVICE. Enlisted.	Discharged.	REMARKS.
Scott, Patrick	pt	5 dec 76	16 Aug 80	killed
Joined June 78				
Stricker, John	do	6 dec 76	6 dec 79	discharged
Joined 22 Aug 77				
Stewart, Thomas	do	6 dec 76	4 Oct 77	killed
Shaver, Andrew¹	pt	4 May 77	3 May 80	discharged
Scott, James	pt	30 May 77	June 77	deserted
Scofield, William	do	28 June 77	30 June 77	do
Stapleton, Richard²	Corpl			
	Sergt	1 June 78		[dischd.
Joined 23 July 78	pt	10 feb 79	Sergt 1 June 79, 8 dec 79	
Shanley, Jacob	pt	14 dec 76	}	
reduced to pt 8 Nov 78	Corpl	1 Oct 77	}	[Invalids
	Sergt	28 dec 77	} 31 Oct 79	transferred to
Stevens, John	pt	10 feb 77	Nov 77	off Rolls
Stewart, William	do	12 Jan 77	Jan 78	off Rolls
Smith, John³	do	28 Mar 78	12 Aug 78	deserted
Sheerlock, Salathiel⁴	do	24 dec 77	8 feb 78	do
Sanson, Luke⁵	do	21 April 78		
Joined Oct 80				
Spigman, John	do	30 April 78	16 Aug 80	missing
Sly, William	do	30 April 78	16 Aug 80	do }
mustd. Corpl July 80			30 April 81	discharged }
Satchwell, Thomas	pt	6 June 78	8 May 80	deserted
Sargood, John	do	22 April 78	8 May 80	do
Swanwick, Thos.	do	8 June 78	16 Aug 80	missing
Sullivan, Thos.⁶	do	11 May 78	6 July 80	deserted
Salegh, Nichs.⁷	do	18 May 78	16 Aug 80	missing
Stonbreak, Valen.	do	2 May 78		deserted
Shaver, Peter	do	1 June 78	1 April 79	discharged
Stallings, Abram.⁸	do	20 May 78	1 Nov 80	present
to Lynch's Co.	drum	26 July 78		
Shoemaker, Peter	pt	17 May 78	16 Aug 80	killed
Smith, Aquilla⁹	do	2 June 78	1 Nov 80	present }
			2 June 81	discharged }
Smith, William	do	19 May 78	24 Mar 78	deserted
Sewell, John⁹	do	8 June 78	}	
	Corpl	25 Aug 78	}	
	Sergt	27 dec 79	} 16 Aug 80	missing
Short, James	pt	30 June 78	Jan 80	deserted
Slater, Barthw.⁹	pt	20 July 78	20 dec 78	do

¹ Reynolds'. ² Deams'. ³ Bayly's. ⁴ Beatty's. ⁵ Jones'.
⁶ Spyker's. ⁷ Stull's. ⁸ Morris'. ⁹ Grosh's.

MUSTERS OF MARYLAND TROOPS, VOL. II.

NAMES.	RANK.	TIME OF SERVICE. Enlisted.	Discharged.	REMARKS.
Stockley, John	pt	20 July 78	6 Jan 79	discharged
Sanky, John[1]	do	16 May 78	13 May 79	died
Stevens, Peter[2]	do	19 May	1 Nov 80	present
	Corpl	1 dec 79		
Smith, Danl.	pt	27 Jan 80	do	do
Sizland, William[1]	pt	6 Aug 80		missing
Mar 80 Beatty's	retd. per Cert. of Major Brice & Genl. Gist			
Stone, Cuthbert[3]	pt		1 Nov 80	present
June 80 Jones'				

GERMAN REGIMENT.

NAMES.	RANK.	Enlisted.	Discharged.	REMARKS.
Smitherd, John	pt	24 April 78	1 Aug 80	present
Shively, John	pt	1 Mar 78	do	do
Smith, Michael	drum	28 April 78	do	do
Smith, James	Corpl	1 April 78	do	do
Silver, George	pt	30 March	do	do
Smith, Christion	Mustd. pt		1 Aug 80	deserted
Smith, Mathias	pt	19 May 78	1 Aug 80	present
Shoemaker, S. Fredk.	Corpl	8 May 78	do	do
Slite, (or Fite), James		13 Aprl 78	do	do and 1 Jany 81
Stanton, John		4 May 78	do	do [paid
Smith, Robert	Mustd. pt		1 Aug 80	deserted
Settlemeyer, Chr.			20 July 79	discharged
Stauffer, George	Sergt		29 do	do
Smith, John			12 Oct 79	do
Sealors, Alexander			9 Aug 79	do
Shrayock, John			20 July 79	discharged
Slreiter, Joseph			16 do	do
Slife, John			20 do	do
Stanly, Christr.	Sergt		do	do
Shotts, John			24 do	do
Shoemaker, Michael			do	do
Studer, Philip			do	do
Smith, (or Smithly), Philip			12 Oct 79	do
Smith, John			10 Aug 79	do
Strome, Henry			17 July 79	do
Shark, John				died
Sollers, Frederick	Sergt		28 July 79	discharged
Shutz, Jacob			14 Aug 79	do
Shrayer, Mathias			1 Oct 79	do
Smith, Henry			25 Aug 79	do
Shaffer, John			19 July	do

[1] Beatty's.   [2] Anderson's.   [3] Jones'.

MUSTERS OF MARYLAND TROOPS, VOL. II.

Names.	Rank.	Time of Service. Enlisted.	Discharged.	Remarks.
Snider, John			24 July	discharged
Stonebraker, Adam			26 do	do
Shaffer, Adam		21 July	20 do	do
Switzer, Fredk.			16 do	do
Smithly, (or Smith), John			12 Oct do	do
Statler, Henry			do	do
Stoner, Michael			do	do
Stoyle, Conrad	See Hoyle		20 July do	do
Selwood, William		15 April 80	1 Aug 80	present
Selas, Andrew		22 May 80	do	do

Fifth Maryland Regiment.

Names.	Rank.	Enlisted.	Discharged.	Remarks.
Taylor, William[1]	pt	29 June 77	April 78	left out
Thomas, Allen	do	22 July 77	1 Jany 80	was present
Tylea, Benjamin[2]	do	24 June 77	April 78	left out
Taft, Joseph	do	do	1 Jan 80	was present
	Corpl	1 June 78 }		
	Sergt	12 Jan 79 }	16 May 80	discharged
Townshend, Benja.[3]	do	4 feb 77 }	1 Nov 80	present
	pt	1 Aug 78 }		
Tullock, William	do	25 Mar	April 78	left out
Taylor, Joshua	do	7 July }		
	Corpl	Oct 80 }	1 Nov 80	present
Thompson, Henry	pt	5 Sept	April 78	left out
Thompson, Cornelius[4]	do	26 Mar 77	1 Nov 80	present
Tullis, Litchfield[6]	do	30 Jan 77	27 July 78	discharged
Toomey, John	do	6 April	1 Jan 80	was present
			8 May 80	discharged
Thompson, Benja.[6]	do	8 feb 77	20 June 79	deserted
Turner, John[7]	do	29 May 78	May 79	not heard of
Tucker, Anthony[3]	do	7 May 78	1 Nov 80	present
Thomas, Richard[4]	do	4 June 78	20 Mar 79	discharged
Tanner, John	do	24 April 78	Nov 78	died
Twiner, Spintlo[3]	do		July 78	left out
1st mustr. June 78, out July 78				
Terrett, William[2]	pt	5 Jany 78	1 Jany 80	was present
1st mustr. June 78				
Terrier, Charles	do	30 April 78	16 Aug 80	missing
1st mustr. June 78				
Thomas, Isaac[7]	do	5 May 78	1 Oct 79	deserted

[1] Dean's.   [2] Hawkins'.   [3] Handy's.   [4] Johnson's.
[5] Emory's.   [6] Cosden's.   [7] Lynch's.

MUSTERS OF MARYLAND TROOPS, VOL. II.

Names.	Rank.	Time of Service. Enlisted.	Discharged.	Remarks.
Sixth Maryland Regiment.				
Thompson, John[1]	pt	2 June 77	1 Jan 80	was present
			2 June 80	discharged
Trainer, Patrick	pt	20 May 78	16 Aug 80	prisoner
Tuff, John	do	5 May 78	10 May 79	died
Tillard, Edward	Major	20 feb 77		
	Col			
Tidley, Edward[2]	pt	12 Mar 77	} 1 Nov 80	present
	Corpl	1 Sept 78		
Truman, Alexr.	Capt	.10 dec 76		
Taylor, Robert[3]	pt	22 feb 78	}	
mustr. Sergt Oct 80	Corpl	1 June 78	1 Nov 80	present
Thomas, George	pt	16 May 78	July 80	deserted
Turner, Richd.[4]	pt	24 Aug 77	24 Aug 80	discharged
Taylor, Benjamin[5]	do	23 May 77	1 Nov 80	present
Turnbridge, Saml.	D. Q. M. Sergt	1 July 77	17 June 78	discharged
Taymon, Benja.[1]	pt	1 July 78		dead or deserted
1st July 78 Joined				
Taggart, John[2]	pt	10 June 78	14 Mar 79	discharged
1st mustr. June 78				
Tuhton, (or Tuchstone), Christopher	pt	24 May 78	1 Nov 80	present
1st mustr. June 78, rein. 22 dec 78				
Thompson, Nathl.[6]	pt	13 May 78	}	
	Corpl	1 July 78		
Taylor, James[7]	pt	20 May 78	1 Aug 80	deserted [valids
Tancard, Thomas[8]	do	28 April 78	8 April 79	transferrd to In-
Thomas, John[7]	do	28 April 78	feby muster 79	died at Fish Kill
Taylor, George[6]	pt	27 April 79	1 Nov 80	present
Tuyger, Danl.[9]	pt		1 Jan 80	was present
21 Sept 79 Joined				
Thomas, John[8]	pt	7 Aug 79	1 Nov 80	present
Seventh Regiment.				
Tabbs, Barton	Surgeon	10 April 77	3 Oct 79	resigned
Taylor, James[10]	pt	30 dec 76	13 Sept 77	deserted & 26
Joined again				May 78 dischgd
Turner, Nathl.	pt	30 dec 76	5 Jan 80	discharged
Taylor, Thomas	pt	13 Mar 77	3 May 80	do
Taylor, William[11]	do	17 April 77	26 April 80	to Invalids

[1] Ghiselin's. [2] Dobson's. [3] Beall's. [4] Lawrence's. [5] Harris'.
[6] Lt. Williams'. [7] Miles'. [8] Hynes'. [9] Trueman's.
[10] Grosh's. [11] Spyker's.

MUSTERS OF MARYLAND TROOPS, VOL. II.

Names.	Rank.	Time of Service. Enlisted.	Discharged.	Remarks.
Townshend, Joseph	pt	9 May 77	1 April 80	died
Tutwiller, Jonathan[1] Joined June 78	Sergt	4 dec 76	7 dec 79	discharged
Thoupe, Richard[2]	pt	20 May 77	4 Oct 77	died
Thompson, John	do	9 June 77	Dec	deserted
Thompson, Jeremiah[3]	Sergt	8 Aug 77		deserted
Taylor, William Joined Oct 80	pt		1 Nov 80	present
Townshend, Aaron[4]	do	20 April 78	9 Oct 78	died
Townshend, Wm.	do	2 May 78	1 Nov 80	present
			24 April 81	discharged
Thompson, Jeremiah[5]	pt	20 Jan 78	8 Feby 78	deserted
Thompson, William[6]	do	5 May 78	July 79	deserted
Tongue, Robert	pt	6 June 78	16 Aug 80	missing
Turner, Solomon			12 May 81	
Tucker, John[6]	pt	6 June 78	16 Aug 80	missing
Toomy, Dennis	do	29 April 78	8 May 80	deserted
Turner, John[7]	pt	6 May 78	1 Nov 80	present
Trendall, Michael[8]	pt	20 April 78	16 Aug 80	missing
Turner, John[1]	do	8 May 78	Nov & dec 78	dead
Taylor, Saml.	do	20 May 78	2 June 78	deserted
Turner, Solomon[9]	do	2 Mar 78	16 Aug 80	missing
			12 May 81	discharged
Tanner, Thomas	pt	22 April 78	16 Aug 80	missing
Tomlinson, Zadock[1]	pt	8 June 78	30 Mar 79	discharged
Taylor, Saml.[6] Joined Oct 80	Fifer	22 April 78		
Taylor, John[7]	pt	20 July 78	23 Nov 78	died
Thomason, Ezekiel[8]	do	3 June 78	16 Aug 80	missing
Townshend, James	pt	Left with Baron Stuben when the Troops marched Southward		
Tanckard, Wm.[10]	pt		16 Aug 80	missing
Turnon, Dennis[1]	pt	1 feb 80	16 Aug 80	missing, joined
Taylor, Richard	pt	6 feb 80	1 Nov 80	present

German Regiment.

Names.	Rank.	Enlisted.	Discharged.	Remarks.
Timblin, John	pt	28 Aprl 78	1 Aug 80	present
Tawney, Fredk.	not on any musters			
Truck, John	Sergt	24 July 79		discharged
Taylor, William			12 Oct 79	do
Tite, James	See James Stite			

[1] Morris'. [2] Reynolds'. [3] Deams'. [4] Spyker's, Grosh's. [5] Beatty's.
[6] Jones'. [7] Grosh's. [8] Stull's. [9] Bayly's. [10] Lynn's.

Names.	Rank.	Time of Service. Enlisted.	Discharged.	Remarks.
\multicolumn{5}{c}{FIFTH MARYLAND REGIMENT.}				

Names.	Rank.	Enlisted.	Discharged.	Remarks.
FIFTH MARYLAND REGIMENT.				
Valliant, James[1]	pt	14 Mar 77	14 Mar 80	discharged
Vallient, John	do	14 do	do	do
Vallow, John[2]	do	1 Mar 78	1 Oct 80	present
Vincent, Benjamin[3]	do	22 May 79	1 Oct 79	deserted
GERMAN REGIMENT.				
Vaughan, Cornelius	pt	21 May 78	1 Aug 80	present
Vincent, William	do	15 May 78	do	do
Vatchle, John			24 July 79	discharged
Veatch, Abram			22 Nov 80	deserted
FIFTH MARYLAND REGIMENT.				
Woulds, James	Adjt	16 Mar 77	} 23 Sept 79	resigned
	Ensn	27 May 78		
Warfield, John[4]	2d Lieut	10 May 77	7 Nov 77	do
Willis, Andrew	pt	17 feb 77	14 feb 80	discharged
Willis, Jarvis[5]	Corpl	do	14 feb 80	do
Woods, Zadock	pt	31 May 77	Aprl 78	left out
Warren, John	pt	28 April 77	12 Oct 79	discharged
Worner, William[6]	do	10 May	April 78	left out
Worner, Solomon	do	do	do	do
Williams, Henry	Corpl	3 May	2 April 78	discharged
Welch, John[5]	pt	25 feb 77	} reduced 10 Sept 77	
	Corpl	16 April 77		
	pt	1 Aprl 78	25 feb 80	discharged
Walls, M. John[7]	Ensn	20 feb 77	13 Oct 78	resigned
Williams, John	pt	21 Mar 77	Aprl 78	left out
Wilson, John	do	1 Jan 77	1 Jan 80	discharged
Ward, Mathew[2]	D. fife	20 Aprl 77	3 Nov 79	died
Warner, Arbuckle[1]	pt	21 feb 77	2 Sept 80	do
Willoughby, William	do	29 Jan 77	31 Mar 79	deserted
Wright, Nathanl.	pt	18 July 77	1 Jan 80	was present
			1 Aug 80	off the Rolls
Welsh, Patrick	pt	10 May 77	27 Oct 78	to Invalids }
			13 May 80	discharged
Williams, Thomas[8] to Bird's	pt	6 Aprl 77	5 feb 80	do
Woodfind, Thos.[9] 1st mustr. April 78	pt		1 Oct 78	to Invalids
			23 feb 79	discharged
Willis, Daniel[10] 1st mustr. April 78	Drum	9 feb 77	16 Aug 80	missing } joined

[1] Emory's. [2] Johnson's. [3] Lynch's. [4] Dean's. [5] Williams'.
[6] Hawkins'. [7] Handy's. [8] Cosden's, Birds. [9] Lt. Hamilton's. [10] Handy's, Bird's.

MUSTERS OF MARYLAND TROOPS, VOL. II.

NAMES.	RANK.	TIME OF SERVICE. Enlisted.	Discharged.	REMARKS.
Walsh, David[1]	pt		1 feb 79	deserted 24 May do
1st mustr. April 78				
White, Joseph	pt	6 April 78	16 Aug 80	missing
Williams, James[2]	pt	1 June 78	5 Nov 78	died
1st muster June 78				
Wilson, George[3]	pt	29 May 78		depreciation issued twice
			1 Oct 80	present
			5 May 81	discharged
Waters, Abraham	pt	20 May 78	29 July 78	died
Woolcott, William[4]	pt	7 May 78		
Wright, William	pt	4 May 78	1 June 79	discharged
Winterbottom, John[5]	pt	6 June 78	23 Mar 79	do
Williams, Simon	pt	15 May 78	feb 79	not heard of
Wilson, David[1]	pt	4 Mar 78	1 Nov 80	present
reinlisted 1 dec 79, mustered present 1 Oct 80				
Wittington, Benja.	pt	14 May 78	Augt 78	not heard of
Witeman, Conrod[1]	pt	14 April 78	1 Mar 79	discharged
White, Joseph[6]	pt	8 April 78	1 Jan 80	was present
1st muster June 78		1 feb 79		
	Sergt	16 Aug 79		
Whittington, Joseph	pt		July 78	left out
1st muster June 78				
Watts, Solomon[7]	pt	2 May 78	June 79	died
Williams, Thos.	pt	9 June 78	19 Mar 79	discharged
Wright, Coursey	pt	20 April 78	19 June 78	deserted
Ward, William[8]	pt	1 July 78	28 feb 79	discharged
Wilkinson, John[9]	pt	17 May 79	1 Nov 80	present
1st muster June 78	Sergt	1 Aug 79		
Wallis, John[9]	pt	4 July 79	1 Jan 80	was present
			8 May 80	discharged by Col. Forrest
Wheller, Philip			16 Aug 80	missing
Oct Muster 80				
Wilson, George			5 May 81	

SIXTH MARYLAND REGIMENT.

Warrior, Daniel[10]	fifer	5 May 78	1 Oct 80	present
reduced to fife 8 Aug 79	Drum M.	1 April 79		
drum Major 2 Sept 79				
Williams, O. H.	Col	10 dec 76		

[1] Johnson's. [2] Lt. Hamilton's. [3] Lynch's. [4] Handy's. [5] Ensign Jones'.
[6] Handy's, Bird's. [7] Hawkins'. [8] Emory's. [9] Benson's. [10] Ghiselin's.

MUSTERS OF MARYLAND TROOPS, VOL. II.

Names.	Rank.	Time of Service. Enlisted.	Discharged.	Remarks.
Wright, Benja.[1]	Ensn	14 June 77		
	Lieut	1 Jan 78	28 Nov 78	absent wo. Leave
Westwood, William	pt	26 June 77	1 Nov 80	present
Wailes, Edward[2]	Ensn	See Letter B		
Woodam, Robert[3]	pt	17 feb 77	16 Aug 80	killed
Windle, Jonathan	do	24 Aprl 78	1 Nov 80	present
Woods, David	do	4 May 78	16 Aug 80	killed
Watson, James	do	21 May 78	4 feb 79	discharged
Wright, James[4]	Sergt	5 dec 76	June must. 78	left out
	S. Major	28 June 77		
Wiltz, Benjamin	pt	30 dec 76	30 Dec 79	discharged
	Sergt	7 Sept 77		
Welch, William	Sergt	2 Aprl 77	10 Jan 80	do
reduced	pt	20 Oct 77		
Williams, Nathan[5]	Lieut	10 dec 77	16 Aug 80	killed
Ward, William	pt	22 Aug 77	16 Aug 80	missing
Woods, Joseph[6]	pt	6 Mar 77	16 Aug 80	killed
Walker, Saml.[7]		2 May 1777		
	Sergt	25 Nov 77		
	pt	19 Nov 78	16 Aug 80	missing
Williams, Thos.[8]	pt	1 July 78	Feby 79	left out
Joined 1 July 78				
Willis, John[9]	pt	3 April 78	1 Nov 80	present
1st muster June 78				
Wice, Peter[9]	pt	3 June 78	4 Aprl 79	discharged
Wolf, Peter	pt	3 June 78	1 Aprl 79	do
Watson, James	do	1 June 78		
Whelan, Laurence D.	do	13 June 78	Oct 78	deserted
rein. 12 feb 79			26 feb 79	do
Ward, Zachariah	pt	5 May 78	21 Jan 79	deserted
Welsh, William	pt	11 May 78	7 July 78	do
Waters, John	pt	3 April 78	23 Aug 78	died
Watkins, Leonard[10]	Sergt	2 May 78	1 Jan 80	present
			11 May 80	discharged
Walker, Edward	pt	16 May 78	16 Aug 80	missing
Welsh, David[4]	pt	4 June 78	1 April 79	discharged
Wooling, Richard	pt	4 June 78	1 April 79	do
Wooling, Mason	pt	4 June 78	23 Oct 78	died
Joined 9 Oct 78				
Welch, William[2]	pt		16 Aug 80	prisoner
1st mustr. July 79				

[1] Dobson's. [2] Trueman's. [3] Beall's. [4] Hynes'. [5] Laurence's.
[6] Harris'. [7] Chapline's, now Miles'. [8] Ghiselin's. [9] Lt. Williams'. [10] Miles'.

MUSTERS OF MARYLAND TROOPS, VOL. II.

Names.	Rank.	Time of Service. Enlisted.	Discharged.	Remarks.
Wood, Joseph 1st muster July 79	pt		13 Nov 79	deserted
Wirey, Michael[1]	Fifer	12 May 79	1 Nov 80	present
Williams, Benja. Oct mustr. 80	pt		do	do
Wright, Absolom	do	20 Mar 80	16 Aug 80	missing

Seventh Regiment.

Names.	Rank.	Enlisted.	Discharged.	Remarks.
Wright, Thomas[2]	pt	4 feb 77	3 feb 80	discharged
Winstanley, Francis	do	8 Aprl 77	9 Aprl 77	deserted
Warner, Samuel[3]	Sergt	25 Mar 77	feb 78	off Rolls
Watkins, Solomon	pt	29 Mar 77	July 78	off the Rolls
Ward, William[4]	pt	18 April 77	Mar 78 May 80	off Rolls time out
Williams, John	Sergt	19 May 77	8 May 80	discharged
Wright, Edward	Ensign Lieut	1 Mar 77 28 dec 77	7 Oct 79	resigned
Wells, Valentine[5]	pt	27 Mar 77	April 78	off Rolls March
Wilson, James	do	7 April 77	May 78	off Rolls
Williams, Elisha	Capt	10 dec 76	28 Nov 78	resigned
Webb, William[6]	pt	7 Jan 77	9 June 77	deserted
Walker, Edward[7]	do	19 dec 76	22 dec 76	do
Wright, Edward Joined again	do	20 Aprl 77	16 Aprl 80	time out, discharged
Watkins, Gassaway	Ensign Lieut	1 May 77		
Warner, John[8]	Corpl	13 July 77	20 Oct 77	died
Woods, James	pt	24 April 77	27 Aug 78	do
Welch, Mark	pt	2 June 77	July 78	off Rolls, transferred to Invalids
Warrent, James	pt	26 June 77	Mar 79	not heard of
Winkfield, James[9]	pt		16 Sept 77	deserted
Ward, Thomas	do		16 Aug 80	missing
Wood, William	do		17 May 77	deserted
Wykell, or Vycall, Adam[4] 1st muster June 78	do	2 July 77	2 July 80	discharged
Whalor, Ignatius Mitchell[2] Mustr. John Apl & May roll, Sergt May 80	pt	25 feb 78	1 Nov 80	present
Wheelor, Thomas[10]	pt	23 April 78	Oct 78	died
White, Thomas	do	17 Mar 78	16 Aug 80 1 Mar 81	missing discharged depreciation recd. twice

[1] Norris'.   [2] Jones'.   [3] Grosh's.   [4] Spyker's.   [5] Stull's.
[6] Williams'.   [7] Bayly's.   [8] Reynolds'.   [9] Deams'.   [10] Spyker's, Grosh's.

MUSTERS OF MARYLAND TROOPS, VOL. II.

Names.	Rank.	Time of Service. Enlisted.	Discharged.	Remarks.
Wedge, William[1]	pt	14 Mar 78	1 Nov 80	present
Walter, Mathew[2]	do	27 dec 77	8 feb 78	deserted
Wastfalling, Danl.	do	27 dec 77	8 feb 78	do
Whatmore, Robert[3]	do	19 May 78	8 July 80	deserted
White, James	do	20 May 78	1 Nov 80	present
Wizer, Michael	do	1 June 78	16 Aug 80	missing }
			1 June 81	discharged
Whaling, Lawrence[4]	pt	13 May 78	1 Sept 78	deserted
Walker, Charles[5]	pt		1 Mar 79	discharged
June Spyker's				
Wildman, William	do	2 May 78	1 June 78	deserted
Waltman, Michael[6]	do	16 April 78	1 Nov 80	present
to Morris'				
Wheatley, George	do	9 June 78		
Woltmon, Nicholas	do	26 April 78	10 July 78	deserted
Wharton, William[6]	do	28 May 78	16 Aug 80	missing
Wolters, Ephriam[7]	do	4 May 78	Dec 79	deserted
Wilson, Daniel[4]	do		11 Jan 79	transferrd. to 2 Md. Brigade
White, Peter	do	20 July 78	20 Dec 78	deserted
Wheley, Zadock	fifer	20 Oct 78	June 79	off Rolls
	pt	1 Mar 79	Joined 82	
Webb, John[2]	pt	4 May 78	1 Nov 80	present
Whipple, William	do		9 Sept 80	deserted
Williams, Benja.[4]	do	9 June 78	15 April 80	paid
to Grosh's	Fifer	11 feb 79	Joined 82	
Weagle, George[6]	pt	9 Jan 78	9 Mar 79	discharged
Weeks, Benjamin[8]	do	20 Aug 79	16 Aug 80	missing
Wilson, William[9]	do	6 feb 80	16 Aug 80	do
Wedge, Samuel[2]	do	2 feb 80	16 Aug 80	do
Williams, Gabriel[10]	Sergt	6 feb 80	1 Nov 80	present
Worslick, William	pt		16 Aug 80	missing

GERMAN REGIMENT.

Names.	Rank.	Enlisted.	Discharged.	Remarks.
Wilstock, Henry to 1 Jan 81	pt	1 Nov 79	1 Aug 80	present
Wade, John to 1 Jan 81	do	4 May 78	do	do
Williams, Danl. to 1 Jan 81	do	9 June 80	do	do
Welty, John		17 July 78	do	do

[1] Bayly's. [2] Beatty's. [3] Jones'. [4] Grosh's. [5] Spyker's.
[6] Stull's. [7] Morris'. [8] Anderson's. [9] Lynn's. [10] Mason's.

MUSTERS OF MARYLAND TROOPS, VOL. II.

NAMES.	RANK.	Time of Service. Enlisted.	Discharged.	REMARKS.
Wright, Saml.	pt	3 June 80	1 Aug 80	present
Walker, John	do	10 Aprl 80	do	do
Woolford, Thomas	do	15 May 78	do	do
Williams, Joseph			22 July 79	discharged
Weaver, Michael			26 do	do
Waggoner, Chrisr.			12 Oct 79	do
Witsinger, Ludk.			20 July	do
Wink, Jacob			1 June 80	present
Wilhelme, George			17 July 79	discharged
Wagoner, Jacob			24 do	do

FIFTH MARYLAND REGIMENT.

NAMES.	RANK.	Enlisted.	Discharged.	REMARKS.
Yoe, Thomas[1]	pt	4 June 78	19 Mar 79	discharged
Yoe, Joseph, (or Robert) pt 1st May 79	do Sergt	8 June 78 1 July 78	} 1 Oct 79	deserted
Yewell, C. Solomon[2]	pt	4 June 78		
Young, Thomas[1]	pt	6 June 79	1 Jan 80	now present

SIXTH MARYLAND REGIMENT.

NAMES.	RANK.	Enlisted.	Discharged.	REMARKS.
Young, Samuel[3]	pt	22 April 78	1 Nov 80	present
Young, John[4]	do Corpl	10 Mar 77 1 dec 79	do	do
Young, Henry[5] 1st July 78 joined	pt	1 July 78	feb 79	left out
Young, Daniel[4]	pt	1 June 78	21 Nov 78	died
Young, Godhed Joined 21 Sept 79	do	2 Aug 78	23 Aug 80	to Invalids

SEVENTH MARYLAND REGIMENT.

NAMES.	RANK.	Enlisted.	Discharged.	REMARKS.
Yates, John[6]	Corpl Sergt Q.M.Sergt.	15 Aprl 77 7 June 77 1 Aug 77	} 16 April 80	discharged
Young, Thomas[7]	pt	4 June 77	July 78	Invalids
Young, William	do	15 Aug 77	1 Nov 80	present
Yoe, Thomas	Drum	26 Sept 77	Sept 80	discharged
Younger, George[8]	pt	8 Mar 77		off Rolls
Yates, Robert[9]	Corpl Sergt	15 dec 76 1 April 78	6 Jan 80	discharged
Yost, George[10]	Drum	4 May 77	20 May 80	discharged
York, William[11]	pt	12 July 78	14 Sept 78	died

[1] Hawkins'.   [2] Emory's.   [3] Dobson's.   [4] Trueman's.
[5] Ghiselin's.   [6] Grosh's.   [7] Spyker's.   [8] Morris'.
[9] Bayly's.   [10] Reynold's.   [11] Stull's.

MUSTERS OF MARYLAND TROOPS, VOL. II.

NAMES.	RANK.	TIME OF SERVICE. Enlisted.	Discharged.	REMARKS.
	GERMAN REGIMENT.			
Yakely, Michael			17 July 79	discharged
	SEVENTH REGIMENT.			
Zacharius, Fredk.[1]	pt	4 June 78	30 Mar 79	discharged
	GERMAN REGIMENT.			
Zimmerman, John			12 Oct 79	discharged

SOLDIERS WHO HAVE NOT RECEIVED DEPRECIATION AND PAY UPON INSUFFICIENT CERTIFICATES.

Abel Ormond	Certificate of John Dove	
John Waller	pt 2nd Regt., recd. depreciation twice	
Thomas James	deserted, 5 mos. pay recd. by Dove	
Joseph Southall	twice depreciation	Mr. Rose
Joseph Bray	do do	
Chrisr. Beall	do do	Crawford

Settled for by Mr. Crawford in final Settlements

[1] Morris'.

SUPPLEMENTARY GERMAN REGIMENT PAPERS.

German Regiment.

Roll of Capt. Henry Fister's Company. In the German Battalion. Commd. by Col. Nicholas Hussecker. 1776.

Lieut. Charles Balzel
" Michael Bayer
Ensign Jacob Grommet
Serjt. John Balzel, recommended
    by the Major & Capt.
" Philip Shroop
" Philip Shopper

Sergt. George Wintz
Corpl. George Hoover
" Fredk. Wilhite
" Jacob Tudderow
" Jacob Low
Drummer John Heffner

Privates

Henry Delawter
Henry Hawk
Fredk. Mittag
Jacob Fantz
Peter Copple
Jacob Kuntz
John Ridenhour
Willm. Snider
Adam Froshour
Christn. Sheafer
Leonard Everley, absent
John Wachtel, Dis. 24 July
George Studdlemier
Philip Colour
Valentine Shotter
Henry Ziegler
Jacob Tabler
Mathias King
Jacob Miller
Philip Isingminger
John Leather
Henry Hildebrand
Anthony Miller
Jacob Farber
Michael Moser

Privates

Ludwick Visinger
Jacob Hammer
Martin Watkins
Nicholas Frye
Jacob Weaver
Jacob Eggman
John Beckerson
George Clinton
Christopher Slender
Michael Beiker
Anthony Hamilton
Jacob Sheafer
Adam Charles
Abraham Fettie
John Imfeld
George Shrantz
Adam Smeltzer
John Bird
Gottlieb Klein
Peter Graff
John Ringer, absent
Jacob Croumer
Philip Stouder
Peter Hoover

Privates

Peter Americk
Conrad Houseman
John Klein
Henry Hain
Jacob Kurtz
John Zimmerman
Henry Smith
Adam Gentner
Henry Cronies
Leonard Ludwick
John Snider
Henry Herring
Peter Kuntz
Justinius Hogshield
Edward Robertson
John Shatz
Michael Stiener
John Able
Michael Shoemaker
Frederick Henninghouse
Thomas Polehouse
Bartle Engel
John Klein
John Miller, absent

Pay Roll of Capt. Michael Bayer's Company in the German Regiment, Continental Troops in the United States. Commanded by Lt. Col. Ludwick Weltner. For the months of July, August, September and October, 1779.

NAMES.	REMARKS.	NAMES.	REMARKS.
		Privates	
Capt. Michael Bayer, (Boyer)		Ludwick Wesinger	Dischd. July 20
Sergt. —— ——.	Promoted Aug. 1st	Rudolph Marolf	" " "
" —— ——	Dischd. " 9th	Jacob Miller, Jr.	" " "
" —— —nley	" July 20th	John Abel	" " "
Corpl. —— Polehouse	Promoted Aug. 1st	Adam Gantner	" " "
" —k Shoemaker	" " "	Jacob Miller, Sr.	" " "
" —rew Robinson	Dischd. July 20th	Jacob Cramer	" " "
" John Hoshield	" " 24th	Leonard Ludwick	" " 24
" John Shotz	" " "	Michael Shoemaker	" " "
Drum. Thomas Hatchcraft		Peter Emerick	" " "
" Henry Ferrins		Henry Herring	" " "
Privates		Michael Moser	" " "
Thomas Mahony		Henry Cronise	" " "
George Kepphard		Phillip Fisher	" " "
Peter Kuntz		John Snider	" " "
Abraham Kettle		John Wachtel	" " "
Henry Fisher		Phillip Strider	" " "
John Foliott	Joined Oct 10th	Jacob Riggnagle	" " 26
Owen Curley		Casemar Hill	" " "
Charles Fullim		Conrad Housman -	" " "
James Johnson		Michael Stoner	" Oct 12
—— Wade		William Taylor	" " "
—— Mallady		John Zimmerman	" " "
—— ——rd		John Cline	" " "
—— ——	Deserted Augt 25th	Peter Hewer	" " "
Edward Robinson	Dischd. July 20	Bartle Engle	Died Aug 6

Muster Roll of Capt. Geo. P. Keeport's Compy. of the First German Battalion Continental Troops. Commanded by Colonel Nichs. Husacker. Philadelphia, Sept. 19th, 1776.

ENLISTED.	NAMES.	ENLISTED.	NAMES.
1776		1776	
July 8	George P. Keeports, Capt.	July 15	Jacob Smith, 1st Serjt.
12	Saml. Gerock, 1 Lt.	30	Henry Speck, 2nd "
"	Willm. Ritter, 2 "	Aug. 19	John Keener, 3rd Serjt.
"	John Lindenberger, Ensign	"	Christn. Kearns, 4th "

during the War of the American Revolution, 1775–83.

Enlisted.	Names.		Enlisted.	Names.
1776			1776	Privates
July 15	George Cole,	1st Corpl.	Aug 7	Jacob Stein
19	Fredk. Moppes,	2nd "	8	John Schorcht
21	Ulrich Linkenfetter,	3rd "	9	Christn. Lichte
"	Philip Bitting,	4th "	10	George Schesler
15	Benja. England, Drummer		"	Danl. Fuhrman
	Privates		11	Henry Traut
"	Michael Brubacher		"	Jacob Schütz,
"	Michael Grosh		14	Peter Hahn
17	Michael Dochterman		19	George Miller
"	Christn. Settlemires		25	Peter Anckle
20	Peter Kries		5	Jacob Wink
21	Jacob Koefflich		"	Danl. Boehler
"	Adam Markel		12	John Harring
"	David Streib		18	John Franken
"	Joseph Carrol		July 15	John Cole
"	David Levy		21	Adam Schaeffer
"	Willm. Trux		"	Mathias Schreier
"	John Capes		"	Conrad Reitz
"	John Trux		"	John Brown
28	Jacob Bigler		"	Fredk. Mongoal
Aug 1	Jacob Burk		23	John Bauer
3	John Weller		26	Conrad Boehm
5	Gotfried Loure		28	John Miller, sick
"	Jacob Wagner		30	Phillip Boehm
6	Peter Bast		"	John Smith

Roll of Capt. William Heyser's Company. Dated October 23rd, 1776.

William Heyser, (Keyser), Captain.   Adam Smith, 2nd Lieut.
Jacob Kottz, 1st Lieut.   Paul Christman Ensign.

Sergeants.	Corporals.	Drums. & Fifes.
David McCorgan, (recomd. by Maj. & Cap.)	Andrew Filler	George Gittin, Drum
Jacob Hose	Phillip Reevenach	Jacob Gittin, Fife
Daniel Taquet, (or Jaques)	Barnard Frey	
Jacob Miller	William Lewis	

Privates	Privates	Privates
Peter Sheese, Deserted	John Smith	James Duncan
Henry Stroam "	Michael Weaver	John Breecher
Adam Stonebreaker	Jacob Belsoover	Fredk. Switzer
John Fogle	John Rothe	Jacob Fowee, Deserted
Jacob Klien	Wentle Strayly	Thomas Burney, "
George Miller	John Flick	John Itnier
Phillip Fisher	John Mettz, Deserted	Phillip Greechbaum
Jonathan Hecket	Henry Michael	Jacob Bishop
Henry Tomm	George Riggleman, Deserted	Alex. Sailor
Jacob Hoover		Martin Pifer, Deserted
Michael Cambler	Nicholas Baird	Peter Gittin
George Harmony	John Hottfield, Deserted	Frances Myers
Thomas Clifton	Jacob Greathouse, "	Melcher Benter
Micgael Boward	George Buch	Tobias Friend, Deserted
Henry Wagner	Stuffle Reever	Jacob Heefner, "
John Crafft	George Wise	John Smithley, "
John Shoemaker, Deserted	John Michael	Everheart Smith
Mathias Gieser	John Robertson	Godfrey Young
Mathias Dunkle	Adam Lieser, Deserted	Frederick Locher
Frederick Filler	Robt. Hartness, "	Michael Yeakly
Christian Sides, Deserted	Henry Benter	James Furnier
John Kibler	John Armstrong	Henry Queer
Stuffle Wagner	Simon Fogler	Henry Statler, Deserted
Jacob Heefner	Jacob Grass	John Cropp
Conrod Hoyle	Phillip Smithly, Deserted	
Balsor Fisher	George Wilhelm	

Pay Roll of Lt. Col. Weltner's Company in the German Regt. of the Continental forces of the United States. Commanded by Lt. Col. Ludwick Weltner, for the months July, August, Sept and Oct, 1779.

Names.	Remarks.	Names.	Remarks.
Capt. Philip Shrawder			
Serjt. William Lewis	Disd. July 16th	Privates	
		Michael Gambler	
" Jno. Danl. Jacquet	" " 26th	James Ashley	
" Jacob Hose	" " "	William Pointer	
Corpl. James Smith	Promd. Aug 1st	Jacob Mosen	
" John Michael	Disd. July 16th	Jonathan Hackett	Deserted Aug 25th
" John Brucher	" " 17th	Henry Straam	Disd. July 17th
" Adam Stonebraker	" " 26th	James Duncan	" " 16th
" Bernard Fry	" " "	George Wilhelm	" " 17th
Drum. Moses McKinsey		Melcher Benner	" " "
" Joshua McKinsey		Fredrik. Schwidzer	" " 16th

Names.	Remarks.	Names.	Remarks.
Privates	Dischd. July 17th	Privates	Dischd. July 26
Michael Yockley	" "	John Etnier	" "
Conrod Hoyle	" 20th	Jacob Bishop	" "
John Fliet	" 26th	Chris. Raver	" "
Fredrik. Filter	" "	Philip Fisher	" "
Michl. Weaver	" "	Fredk. Locker	" Aug. 9
James Forney	" "	Alex. Taylor	" "
Jacob Beltzhoover	" "	Patrick Fliming	" ".
John Groop	" "	George Regliman	" Oct. 12
George Getting	" "	Henry Stalter	" "
John Hatfield	" "	Christopr. Waggoner	" "
Henry Michael	" "	John Smith	" "
Thomas Clifton	" "	Henry Benter	" "
John Craft	" "	Philip Smithly	" "
Francis Gavin	" "	Jacob Heefner	" "
Jacob Kline	" "	John Smithly	" "
John Kebler	" "	Jacob Haver	" "
Mathias Keiser	" "	Henry Quier	" July 29
John Armstrong	" "		

A Roll of Capt. Philip Graybell's Company. 1776.

Enlisted by Capt. Greybell.

Ferdinand Lorentz
Philip Miller
Henry Millberger, (Millburger)
Jacob Freymiller, (Frymiller)
James Cappelle, (Caple)
John Rick
Lorentz Kneary
Jacob Etter
Peter Baker
Rudolph Crower
Adam Rohrbach, (Rohrbaugh)
Rowland Smith
John Shriock, (Shryock)
William Rommelsem, Serjt.
Jacob Striter
Martin Lantz
John Hearly, (Harley)
Wilfgang Ettsperger
Christopher Regele, (Regle)
Frederick Wm. Haller
John Moore
Wendell Andrews, (Andreas)
Michael Kearshner
Wolfgang Ettzinger
John Shaffer
David Mumma, (Muma)
Abraham Frantz
Frederick Weger
Henry Hartman
Wendel Lorentz
Jacob Hartenstein, (Hardenstein)
William Altimus
Jacob Burke
Jacob Kintz, (Keintz)
George Rittlemyer
Philip Kautz
Jacob Myer, (Myers)
John Shlife
John Machenheimer, Sjt.
George Stauffer, Corpl.
Gottlieb Danroth
Lorentz Danroth
Henry Decker
Jacob Hoffman
Charles Zarrell
Charles Charles
Joseph Procter
Joseph Braeter
Christian Apple
George Myers, (Myer)
Henry Willsdaugh
George Lighthauser, (Leithauser)
Joseph Smith
Henry Wilstock
Henry Rumfeld
George Hyatt, Fifer

18

Enlisted by Lieut. John Lohra, (Lorah).

Thomas Kimmel, (Kemmell)
Anthony Miller
Joseph Hook
Jacob Miley
Jacob Miller

Frederick Heller, Serjt.
Andrew Gorr, (Gore)
William Speck, Corpl.
Henry Hargeroder, (Hergeroder)

Michael Growley
Frederick Sollers, Corpl.
Nicholas Frey

Enlisted by Lieut. Christian Myers.

Jacob Kerns, (Kearns)
Simon Rinehart, (Reinhart)
Mathias Boyer, (Byer), Corpl.
Jacob Ruppert
Nicholas Keyser

John Welty
John Summers
Michael Huling
John Eyssell
William Litzinger, Serjt.

Fredk. Downey, (Tawney)
William Cunius, (Cunnius)
James Smith
Peter Finley, Drummer

Enlisted by Ensign Martin Shugart.

John Smith
John Bartholomew Deitch, (Dych)

William Kraft
Joseph Williams
Henry Spengle

Henry Smith
John Stricker, Cadet
Peter Segman

A List of Recruits belonging to the German Regiment. Commanded by Lieut. Colonel Weltner. White Plains, Sept. 5th, 1778.

Names.	Time of Service.	Names.	Time of Service.
John Kendrick	3 yrs	Samuel Barts	War
James Champness	War	Mathias Smith	do
George Buch	3 yrs	William Rider	do
Adam Mussler	do	William Malinia	do
William Vincent	do	Benj. Cole	do
Stephen McGrough	do	Timothy Cahill	do
William Neving	War	Robert Smith	do
James Woolford	3 yrs	Cornelius Vaughan	do
James Stiles	War	James Murphy	do
Peter Batolomey	do	Christian Castner	do
Richard Hazlip	3 yrs	William Pope	do
Robert Porter	do	John Fennell	do
William Mummard	War	Jacob Kauffman	3 yrs
Hugh McKoy	do	Thomas Proctor	do
John Ammersley	do	Richard Gaul	do
John Stanton	do	John Shively	do
John Bennet	do	Thomas Halfpenny	do
John Roach	do	William Johnston	do
Benj. Elliott	do	John Richards	do
Cornelius Quinlin	3 yrs	Albert Hendricks	9 mos
Philip Fitzpatrick	9 mos	Philip Bates	do
Francis Carns	3 yrs	George Arnold	do
Charles Jones	War	Adam Mattrit, fifer	War

during the War of the American Revolution, 1775–83.   267

Names.	Time of Service.	Names.	Time of Service.
Michael Smith, drummer	War	James Dyer	3 yrs
John Malady	do	Henry Fisher	do
Thomas Mackall	do	Jacob Alexander	do
Charles Fulham	do	Christian Kepplinger	9 mos
John Hughmore	do	Philip Hinkel	do
Thomas Hutchcrofft	do	Thomas Polehouse	do
John Wade	do	Abraham Miller	do
Alexander Smith	do	Bernhard Ridenhour	do
Frederick Shoemaker	do	Levy Aaron	3 yrs
James Johnston	do	Moses McKinsey	do
Casimir Hill	3 yrs	Joshua McKinsey	do
Thomas Mahony	do	Jacob Moser	do
John Smadern	do	Richard O'Quin	War
Jacob Dolton	do	James Ashley	do
John Timhen	do	James Smith	do
Michael Hardman	do	Thomas Rowlands	9 mos
Henry Ferrins	do	George Bantz	do
		Remarks.	
Thomas Hazelwood	War	on Furlough	
Richard Hopkins	9 mos	died 7 July	
Christn. Mumma	do	Died July 27th, '78	
William White	War	Was a Deserter from Carolina	
James Connoway	3 yrs	Ditto of Col. Chambers	
Thomas Holdup	War	Ditto of Carolina	
Mathias Custgrove	3 yrs	Deserted	
John Waldon	do	ditto	
Andrew Shuler	War	ditto	
John Stout	do	ditto	
Robert Barnet	do	sick, absent	
George Kephard	3 yrs	Deserted	
Edward Connoly	do	Taken by the Virginia Artillery	
Frederick Stone	do	Given up to the Laboratory	
John Weeguel	do	Left at Frederick Town	

The number of Officers in the four Maryland Companies belonging to the German Regiment:

1 Lieut. Colonel
1 Captain
4 Lieutenants
2 Ensigns

Number of Sergeants and Rank and File:
13 Sergeants
8 Drums and fifes
221 Rank and file.

MISCELLANEOUS.

Jacob Myers, Discharged	20 July	Peter Bartholomay
Henry Smith, "	15 Aug	Albert Henricks
David Mumma, "	20 July	Thos. Mahoney
Corpl. Wm. Krofft, "	26 "	Chris. Mummard
John Emersly		Thos. Machall
Adam Musler		Jas. Tomey, Discharged July 26
John Henrick		John Viebler
Stephen McGraw		John Weegul
Hugh McCaw, (or Koy)		

ENLISTMENTS FOR 3 YEARS, ALL IN CAPT. MICHAEL BAYER'S COMPANY.

Edward Bairford, Enlisted June 19th, 1780. Joined the Regiment at Northumberland

Michael Rightmyer, (Right Myer), Enlisted Feb. 1st, 1780

Charles Lago, Enlisted April 1st, 1780

Dineas Doron, (Dinnis Dorah), Enlisted June 26th, 1780

George Silver, Enlisted March 31st, 1780

John Rogers,   "   April 10th, 1780

John Nevet,   "   April 13th, 1780

Annapolis, 1st April, 1785.

Copy, to Joseph Howell,

    I have now to Address you upon a very serious subject. When we were so earnest about obtaining the Muster Rolls of the German Regiment, it was on a suspicion that several frauds had been committed upon this State, with respect to Depreciation. The State of Maryland passed an Act of Assembly granting Depreciation to all Officers and Soldiers of the Quota of that State, who had served three years in the Continental Army, consequently, that part of the German Regiment which was called the four Companies of Maryland, having served faithfully; became entitled to receive the same.

    The event of an examination with the Muster Rolls of 1779 and 1780 has shewn that our suspicions were not without foundation, for, of two hundred and sixty who have received Depreciation, there are forty seven, as by the List enclosed; who are not upon the Maryland Musters. Twelve of the forty seven are upon the Pennsylvania Musters, and the other thirty five not found Mustered in 1779 in any of the Rolls of the Regiment. For the thirty five, however, Discharges were procured, purporting that the Person mentioned in each of them served three years faithfully, and were for the most part discharged by Capt. Bunner in the Month of July, 1779. I have enclosed one of the Discharges which has the appearance of having been written at a much later date than what is expressed in it. We can trace out the Persons who presented them here and obtained the Certificates, but we want to find out whether Capt. Bunner, whose signature is to the greatest part of them, really did sign them, or not—there has been a most villainous combination somewhere and it has been excited by a knowledge that the State, for want of regular Musters, generally issued upon Discharges.

Now if *Bunner* is within your reach, I shall esteem it a favor if you will take another Man of Credit along with you, and enquire of *him* whether the Signature on the Discharge, (Charles Kees), now sent, is *his*—if he avows it, I shall be obliged to you for your Deposition, and that of the person with you, that he acknowledged it, which Deposition, with all the forms of Office, please to transmit to me. If, on the Contrary, Bunner denies it to be his, please to inform him of so much of these transactions as you may chuse to disclose, and obtain his affidavit, setting forth that he did not sign the same, or any of the Discharges, in the names of those, or any of them, on the enclosed List. I need not caution you about using your utmost address in endeavouring to lay open this Scene of Iniquity. Your own love of Justice, and the public Station you fill; will, I dare say, be sufficient incentives to your exertion in this dark business.

Pray has the State of Pennsylvania granted Depreciation to their three year's Men Discharged before the 10th of April, 1780; if it has, and continues to issue, it will be proper that the Comptroller should see the list I send, to examine it with his issues. Be pleased to procure the favor of Mr. Nicholson to furnish such remarks as may be necessary and transmit them to me as soon as possible.

Yrs.

C. Richmond.

List of Certificates fraudulently obtained from State of Maryland in the names of Soldiers of the German Regiment.

Names.	Sums.	To Whom Delivered.	Remarks.
Vendel Andrews	56, 16, 9	John Miller, per order	Not on any musters, 1779
William Basht	57, 17, 0	John Randall, for Stauffer	ditto
Charles Charrell	57, 5, 3	Jacob Myers p. order	ditto
James Calhoun	62, 13, 11	ditto	ditto
Frederick Charrell	58, 10, 1	John Miller	P. Boyer's Pennsylva. Co.
Timothy Conn	56, 13, 11	J. Randall for Stauffer	Not on any musters, 1779
Thomas Cammell	56, 11, 0	ditto	ditto
Peter Finley	63, 5, 3	John Miller	ditto

Names.	Sums.	To Whom Delivered.	Remarks.
Andrew Goar	56, 19, 8	John Miller	Not on any musters, 1779
George Hensell	56, 18, 9	Jacob Myers	Hubley's Co., Pennsylva.
Henry Hargrader, (or Hergood)	58, 14, 5	John Miller	Shrawder's Co., ditto
George Hyatt	63, 18, 10	ditto	Not on any musters, 1779
John Hart	63, 16, 2	ditto	P. Boyer's Co., Pennsylva.
Philip Helter	58, 5, 9	ditto	Shrawder's Co., Pennsylva.
George Hartsell	56, 13, 11	J. Randall, for Stauffer	Not on any musters, 1779
Michael Hausman	57, 2, 5	ditto	ditto
Michael Jackell	56, 8, 2	William Lewis	ditto
Nicholas Johnson	57, 1, 0	J. Randall, for Stauffer	ditto
William Kumius	58, 1, 7	Jacob Myers	ditto
Nicholas Keyser	56, 13, 11	John Miller	ditto
Charles Keys, (or Kees)	56, 16, 9	J. Randall, for Stauffer	ditto
William Kemp	56, 19, 8	ditto	ditto
Jacob Levy	58, 11, 4	David Levy	Rice's Pennsylvania Co.
Nicholas Lines	56, 16, 9	J. Randall, for Stauffer	Not on any muster, 1779
Henry Lane	56, 13, 11	ditto	P. Boyer's Pennsylva.
Anthony Miller	57, 8, 3	George Stauffer	Not on any muster, 1779
Henry Mielberger	57, 5, 6	ditto	ditto
John Moore	56, 16, 9	John Miller	ditto
Joshua Procter	57, 2, 7	ditto	ditto
Peter Sigman	58, 5, 10	Jacob Myers	ditto
Joseph Smith	56, 13, 11	George Stauffer	ditto
John Shultz	56, 9, 7	John Miller	ditto
Nicholas Stover	62, 4, 5	ditto	Bunner's Co., Pennsylva.
Henry Spengel	56, 15, 4	ditto	Not on any musters, 1779
James Smith	56, 12, 6	ditto	ditto [nia
Peter Shrover	57, 8, 4	J. Randall, for Stauffer	Bunner's Co., Pennsylva-
Valentine Shultz	79, 11, 10	ditto	Not on any musters
George Shriver	58, 5, 9	ditto	ditto
Jacob Smith	77, 2, 2	Himself	ditto
Frederick Tawney	57, 10, 1	John Miller	ditto
Frederick Weiger	58, 14, 9	Jacob Myers	ditto
Michael Yewling	57, 19, 1	John Miller	ditto
John Zeigler	56, 16, 9	J. Randall, for Stauffer	ditto
John Miller	80, 5, 4	Himself	Mustered Deserted

Discharges.

John Zeigler, Corporal in Capt. Boyer's Company, German Regiment. Served 3 years. Discharged July 21st, 1779.

Wilhelm Kemp, Private in Capt. Myers' Company, German Regiment. Served 3 years. Discharged July 23rd, 1779.

Peter Shrover, Private in Capt. Christian Myers' Company, Served 3 yrs. Dis. July 29th, 1779.

during the War of the American Revolution, 1775-83.

Valentine Shultz, Serjt. in Capt Baltzel's Co. Served 3 yrs. Dis. Aug. 13th, 1779.
Michael Hatman, Private in Capt. Christian Myers' Co. 3 yrs. Dis. July 17th, 1779.
George Hartzell,   " in Capt. Baltzel's Co. 3 yrs. Dis. July 19th, 1779.
George Shriver,   "   "   "   "   " 3 yrs. Dis. Aug. 11th, 1779.
Thomas Cammell,   "   "   " Charles Baltzel's Co. 3 yrs. Dis. July 17th, 1779.
Henry Lane,   "   "   "   "   "   "   "   "   " July 19th, 1779.
William Basht,   " in Capt. Boyer's Co. 3 yrs. Dis. Aug. 5th, 1779.
Nickolas Johnson,   " in Capt. Charles Baltzel's Co. 3 yrs. Dis. July 24th, 1779.
Timothy Conn,   "   "   "   "   "   "   "   "   " July 19th, 1779.
Michael Hausman,   " in Capt. Boyer's Co. 3 yrs. Dis. July 25th, 1779.
Nickolas Limes,   " in Capt. Charles Baltzel's Co. 3 yrs. Dis. July 21st, 1779.
Charles Kees,   "   "   "   "   "   "   "   "   "   "

All the above discharges were given at Camp Wyoming, except Schultz's and Shriver's at Camp Tioga. Each is signed by Jacob Bunner, Capt, Commanding the German Regt. Depreciation certificates were issued Dec. 5th, 1783, to all the above.

Wyoming, July 21st, 1779.

This is to certify that the Bearer, Charles Kees, a Private in the German Regiment in Captain Charles Baltzel's Company, Served three years as a good Soldier from the time of his Inlistment he is hereby Discharged from the same.

Whome it may Concern
Depreciation Certificate issued the 5th Decem. 1783.
C. Richmond
Aud. Genl.

Depce. C. R.
Given under my hand the Day and Date above written
Jacob Bunner, Capt.
Commanding the German Regt.

Philadelphia.

Personally appeared before me, William Adcock Esq., one of the Justices for the City and County of Philadelphia, Joseph Howell, Jr., Asst. Commissioner of Accounts, and John Phelan, Asst. to the Commissr. of Accounts, and made solemn Oath, that the annexed Certificate and discharge of Charles Kees was presented by them to Jacob Bunner, late a Captain in the German Regiment, and Acknowledged by him, the said Jacob Bunner, to be his Signature, and they do further swear, that the said Jacob Bunner did acknowledge to have signed nearly all the discharges that were given to the Soldiers of said Regiment, which discharges were given them on, or about, the time that is expressed in the discharge of Charles Kees, and further sayeth not. Sworn and subscribed this tenth day of May, 1785.

Sworn this 10th day of May, 1785
Before Willm. Adcock. (Seal)

Joseph Howell, Jr.,
John Phelan.

Comptroller Genl.'s Office,
May 17th, 1785.

Sir:

I have received yours of the 5th Inst. and have examined and compared it with my Returns. This State, adhering to the recommendations of Congress, makes up depreciation for none of the Troops discharged before the 10th April, 1780; and, altho I find in your List of the German Regiment, that the State of Maryland hath settled with a number of the same name as those which have been settled with here, such as Nicholas Stover, John Hart, George Hensil and some others, yet they were not the same men, but have been imposters, (very probably), with discharges dated in 1779 in these men's names who continued in the Army until 1780, and some of them till the end of the war, there is, however, none of those who continued till after April, 1780, per your list, which have been settled here. I am much obliged by the list of Settlements with Hartley's Regiment, or, as we called it, the 11th Pennsylvania Regiment, for it was incorporated therewith in 1779. Of the list you gave me, the following persons had been previously settled with here and received their depreciation, viz—John Burgess, Corpl., John Barber, Sergt., James Beal, Private, Jeremiah Ferrall, Sergt., & Willm. Marquis, Private, the rest of them I have marked off in my Rolls as settled by the State of Maryland, and shall not adjust their Accounts here. Joseph Hyner, only, of Moylan's Regiment, had been settled with, by this State, of all those upon your list, the residue I shall take care not to settle with. If there is any other communication which I have here omitted to make, please let me know. I have the person, who I think is at the bottom of the nefarious proceeding you have been fortunate enough to detect, bound over for an attempt of almost a similar nature here.

I am with great respect
Sir
Your Most Obedt. Servant,
Jno. Nicholson.

C. Richmond Esq., Audt. Genl.
State of Maryland.

MUSTERS OF MARYLAND TROOPS, VOL. III.

"Muster Rolls."

NAMES LEFT OUT, &C.

MUSTERS OF MARYLAND TROOPS, VOL. III.

NAMES.	RANK.	TIME OF SERVICE.		REMARKS.
		Enlisted.	Discharged.	

THIRD REGIMENT.

Men left out of the Alphabet, being off the Rolls to the last of Oct., 77.

Adam, Argent			22 Augt	prisoner
Arnold, Thomas				died in Augt

Capt. Jones Comy. Muster for Octobr. & November, 79. Recruits entered and mustered Deserted &c. as follows:

Arding, Benja.			19 June	deserted

FOURTH REGIMENT.—*Dec. Roll*, 1777.

Allen, Robt.		8 July	17 Aug	deserted

FIFTH REGIMENT.

Non Commissioned Officers and Soldiers of the 5th Maryland Regiment left out of the Roll Feby., 1778.

Andrews, Joseph		17 Sept	4 Oct 77	missing
			22 July 78	joined
Akers, Michael		17 dec 76	10 June 77	deserted
Atkins, Jno.		16 Jan 77	15 April	died
Abbot, John		12 May 77	20 Sept 77	deserted
Alford, William		31 dec 76	25 Mar 77	do
Alexander, Jno.		14 Jan 77	24 Jan	do
Abbott, John		12 May 77	20 Sept 77	deserted

SIXTH REGIMENT.

Non Comd. Officers and Soldiers of the Sixth Regiment left out before the Muster 1 June, 1780.

Ashman, Charles		7 Mar 77	Hospital Oct 77, not heard of	
Anguish, Alexr.		19 May 77	30 May 77	
Ambross, Patk.		1 July 77	transferred to Col. Chambers	
Anderson, John		29 Aug 77	Hosptl. Oct 77, not heard of	
Adams, William	pt	28 June 77	19 May 78	deserted
Addlemon, Michael	do	8 Mar 77	10 Dec 77	do
Allen, William	do	3 May 79	25 July	do

MUSTERS OF MARYLAND TROOPS, VOL. III.

Names.	Rank.	Time of Service. Enlisted.	Discharged.	Remarks.
\multicolumn{5}{c}{Left Out of Musters Third Regiment.}			

Left Out of Musters Third Regiment.

Names.	Rank.	Enlisted.	Discharged.	Remarks.
Buzzard, Leighton		26 Jan	15 May	died
Baker, Thomas		19 June	11 Sept	missing
Branwood, Jas.		Taken Staten Island 22 Aug		
Bonoday, Jas.			17 May	deserted
Baker, James			11 June	do
Bajaint, Thos.			11 Sept	prisoner
Breslor, Edward[1]			12 dec	deserted
Bay, Charles			4 Oct	killed
Berry, William			do	missing
Brady, Michael returned & entered			11 Sept	taken
Beveridge, Jno.		3 April	21 April	deserted
Bryan, Danl.			28 July	do

Fourth Regiment.

Names.	Rank.	Enlisted.	Discharged.	Remarks.
Burk, Patk.		6 dec 76	1 feb 77	do
Bonnett, Thos.[2]		22 Mar 77	25 April 78	do
Bray, John[3]		6 feb 78	10 July 78	do
Bosick, Joseph		19 May	30 May	do
Burk, Thomas		1 Sept	12 Oct	deserted

Fifth Regiment.

Non Commissioned Officers and Soldiers of the Fifth Maryland Regiment, left out of the Rolls February, 1778.

Names.	Rank.	Enlisted.	Discharged.	Remarks.
Bassicks, Richd.		10 dec 76	22 Aprl 77	transferred
Bromell, Peter		do	26 June 77	died
Bryan, (or Byron), Stephen		do	22 Aprl 77	transferred
Buckly, Thomas		do	14 Jan 78	deserted
Brayly, William		13 Jan 77	22 Aug 77	prisoner
Burgess, Thomas		10 dec 76	22 April 77	transferred
Blanch, William		do	1 Sept 77	taken by prior Enlistment
Brown, Aaron		do	30 Aug 77	deserted
Bryan, O. John		1 Sept 77	27 Nov 77	do
Byrom, Michael		1 June 77	12 Sept 77	died
Benton, James		24 do	21 dec 77	do
Barry, Michael[4]	Sergt	17 dec 76	12 April 77	do
Bryan, John		22 feb 77	25 Aug 77	deserted
Brown, John		4 do	11 feb 77	do
Beldock, Edward		10 Jan 77	17 Mar 77	do

[1] Lt. Smith's.   [2] Norwood's.   [3] Riely's.   [4] Lynch's.

MUSTERS OF MARYLAND TROOPS, VOL. III.

Names.	Rank.	Time of Service. Enlisted.	Discharged.	Remarks.
Bennit, Robt.		1 Mar 77	4 Mar 77	deserted
Benston, John		18 Mar	20 April	dead
Bennett, Jno.		10 Jan 77	1 July 77	died
Brannon, Jno.		16 Mar	15 April	deserted
Burns, Thomas		7 Sept	20 Sept	missing
Bailey, Mark		2 April	10 July 77 Joined 21 June	deserted }
Brown, John		10 Mar 77	20 Mar 77	deserted

Sixth Regiment.

Names.	Rank.	Enlisted.	Discharged.	Remarks.
Brown, James		1 May 77	15 Oct 77	transferred
Buchan, William	Sergt	Error see Roll		
Brawton, Mathew		2 Mar 78	24 April 78	
Bruff, Edward		24 July 77	15 Oct 77	transferred to Marines
Beall, James	pt	6 dec 76	11 dec 76	deserted
Branfield, James	pt	28 dec 76	28 feb 78	deserted musd. joined June 78
Bates, Henry	do	11 dec 76	22 Aug 77	missing
Bradley, Thos.	do	14 Jan 77	prior Inlistment	
Brodericks, Richd.	do	21 do	13 April 77	deserted
Bramwood, Jas.	do	5 dec 76	17 Aug 77	transferred
Brawner, Jacob	do	7 do	5 Mar 77	do
Baker, James	Sergt	14 Oct 77	25 Jany 78	died
Bates, John	pt	do	1 April 78	do
Barlsom, Anthy.	do	28 April 79	6 May	deserted
Bryan, Peter	do	1 June 79	5 June 79	do

Left Out of Musters Third Regiment.

Names.	Rank.	Enlisted.	Discharged.	Remarks.
Clark, George			4 Oct	killed Ger. Town
Carey, Richard			23 Aug	deserted
Chambers, Wm.			11 Sept	missing
Coalman, Mathew[1]			prior Enlistment	
Coalman, Saml.			4 Oct	killed
Cole, J. B. 5th Compy.	Sergt		do	do
Clark, James 6th Compy.			7 May	deserted
Causins, Peter			4 October	killed
Cunningham, John			2 June	deserted
Croane, Timothy			8 July	died
Crosby, James returned & entered			4 Oct	taken

[1] Brooks'.

MUSTERS OF MARYLAND TROOPS, VOL. III.

Names.	Rank.	Time of Service. Enlisted.	Discharged.	Remarks.
Cork, Ralph			6 June	deserted
Cowan, William			6 Aug	do
Cluff, John			10 May	drowned
Cudwick, Lewis			13 Oct	deserted
Cassidy, Hugh			11 Aug	do
Crawford, Jno.			8 do	do

Collins, John, of the 3d Maryland Regt., discharged 3d May, 1780 by Major Anderson.

Fourth Regiment.

Names.	Rank.	Enlisted.	Discharged.	Remarks.
Cullen, John		22 Oct 77	28 Nov	died
Cain, John		13 Aug	20 Aug	deserted
Curtis, William		15 June	28 July	do
Campbell, James		17 Aug	27 Aug	do
Cole, Henry		3 feb	29 July	prisoner or deserted

Fifth Regiment.

Non Commissioned Officers and Soldiers of the Fifth Maryland Regiment, left out of the Rolls February, 1778.

Names.	Rank.	Enlisted.	Discharged.	Remarks.
Cleary, John		10 April 77	20 July 77	dead
Connelly, Laurence		10 dec 76	22 April 77	transferred
Cooper, William		10 June 77	20 dec 77	died
Chilton, William		13 July 77	4 Nov 77	do
Cooper, Charles		10 dec 76	22 April 77	transferred
Critchets, William		21 July 77	14 Jan 78	deserted
			April 78	joined
Critchet, Benja.		do	do	do do
Chisholm, William[1]	Sergt	18 May 77	20 July 77	deserted
Certain, William		1 do	18 June	discharged
Chambers, Mathew Brown		25 July 77	9 dec	died
Clarke, John		9 Sept	17 Jan 78	do
Crosby, Joseph	Corpl	15 Jan 77	reduced 16 April	
			3 May 77	deserted
Collins, James		18 do	22 Aug 77	prisoner
Craine, Lawrence		6 April 77	do	do
Coffee, Daniel		17 dec 76	11 Sep 77	do
Cousins, Edwd.		20 feb 77	21 Aug 77	died
Condon, William		13 do	4 Oct 77	missing
Connor, Ambrose		7 April 77	15 April 77	discharged
Connor, George		1 Jan 77	28 Jan 78	deserted
			8 June 78	joined
Crook, Martin		11 Mar 77	6 dec 77	died

[1] Hawkins'.

MUSTERS OF MARYLAND TROOPS, VOL. III.

NAMES.	RANK.	TIME OF SERVICE. Enlisted.	Discharged.	REMARKS.
Crouch, Arthur		22 May 77	20 July 77	died
Coombs, William		25	5 Aug 77	do
Clayland, James		18 feb	18 April	discharged
Cox, Mathew[1]		16 Jan 77	11 Sep 77	prisoner
Cox, John		27 July	1 do	deserted
			Joined Aug 78	
Corker, John		15 do	25 Mar	deserted
Clements, Jno.		20 Jan 77	1 Oct 77	taken by prior Enlistment
Conner, Hugh		9 feb 77	1 April 77	deserted
LEFT OUT OF SIXTH REGIMENT.				
Concella, Andw.	Corpl	30 July 77	20 Sept 77	deserted
Conner, Hugh		23 Aug 77	Mar 78	left out
Cole, Thomas	Sergt	15 June 77	2 April 78	died
Clark, Charles	Sergt	10 Jan 77	15 Oct 77	transferred to Marines
Carr, Nicholas		28 April 77	1 Sept 77	transferred to Invalids
Catlin, James		7 do	15 Oct 77	do to Marines
Collins, Thomas		5 dec 76	13 April 77	deserted
Crail, James	pt	7 do	30 do	do
			28 feb 78	joined
Clarss, Francis	do	30 do	27 Nov 77	deserted
Collins, John	do	28 June 77	28 July 77	do
Colon, John	do	9 May 78	29 May 78	deserted
Connally, Jno.	do	5 June 79	21 June	do
LEFT OUT OF MUSTERS THIRD REGIMENT.				
Doun, James	pt		28 Jan 81	discharged
Hartley's Regt.				
Dalziell, Thomas		28 feb	23 June	deserted
Dorsey, Martin		prior Enlistment		
Dearlove, James		3 June	22 Aug	killed or taken
Drury, Thomas			10 feb	discharged
Dalby, Daniel			4 Oct	missing
Joined 22 July				
Dowling, John			28 May	deserted
FOURTH REGIMENT.				
Davis, William		25 Mar	5 April 77	deserted
Douch, William		28 do	12 do	do
Donnavan, Jno.			25 Nov 77	deserted
Dick, Hart.		6 dec 76	1 feb 77	do

[1] Cosden's.

Names.	Rank.	Time of Service. Enlisted.	Discharged.	Remarks.
Dickett, Jno.		16 feb 78	13 Mar 78	deserted
Donald, George		27 May	2 June	do
Ducasy, John		26 May	30 May	do
Davey, Thomas		30 June	26 July	do

Fifth Regiment.

Non Commissioned Officers and Soldiers of the Fifth Maryland Regiment left out of the Rolls February, 1778.

Devereaux, James		10 dec 76	22 April 77	transferred
Dicks, George		30 Mar 77	4 Oct 77	missing
Dwer, William		10 dec 76	22 April 77	transferred
Davis, Philemon		27 July 77	wounded and gone home	
Dixon, John	Corpl	1 feb 77	24 Aug 77	deserted
Davise, John		16 May 77	1 July 77	do
Davise, Joseph		do	20 Oct 77	do
Deoran, James		14 Jan	23 dec 77	died
Dunn, Jno. (D. F.)		10 dec 76	15 April 77	discharged
Daniels, Jacob		10 Jan 77	29 Jan 78	do
Dellen, Theobald		3 feb 77	28 Sept 77	deserted

Sixth Regiment.

Delany, James	Corpl	21 April 77	21 Jan 78	deserted
Davis, John		19 feb 77 musd. again	7 Mar 78 June 78	
Darrough, Jno.		16 feb 78	24 April 78	
Davis, John	Corpl	5 dec 76	21 April 77	deserted
Davis, John	pt	12 feb 77	14 feb 77	do
Davis, William	do	22 July 77	1 Jan 78	Hospital, not heard
Dixon, Richard	pt	15 July 79	12 Aug	deserted [of

Fourth Regiment.

Evans, Thomas		9 Oct	21 Nov	deserted

Fifth Regiment.

Non Commissioned Officers and Soldiers of the Fifth Maryland Regiment left out of the Rolls Febry., 1778.

English, Danl.		10 Aug	17 Jan	died
Edwis, Richard		22 May 77	20 July 77	discharged

Left Out of the Sixth Regiment.

Edwards, Wm.		4 Aug 77	1 April 78	died
English, Wm.	pt	10 dec 76	28 feb 78	deserted
Ervine, David	do	8 May 79	8 July	do

MUSTERS OF MARYLAND TROOPS, VOL. III.

NAMES.	RANK.	TIME OF SERVICE.		REMARKS.
		Enlisted.	Discharged.	

LEFT OUT OF MUSTERS THIRD REGIMENT.

Ferrall, Jere Hartley's Regt.			28 Jan 81	discharged
Farwell, James Hartley's Regt.	pt		do	do
Flaid, James			11 Sept	missing
Frost, James			15 Oct	deserted
Farris, Francis			13 May 79	do

FOURTH REGIMENT.

| Fitzburn, James | | 8 April | 10 April 77 | deserted |

FIFTH REGIMENT.

Non Commissioned Officers and Soldiers of the Fifth Maryland Regiment left out of the Rolls February, 1778.

Floyd, Joseph	Corpl	13 Jan 78	14 Jan 78	deserted
			April 78	joined
Foard, John		5 dec 76	15 Jan 77	dead
Fromee, John		7 do	28 April	died
Floyd, Saml.		4 feb 77	2 do	do [Enlistment
Floyd, John		29 May 77	24 Sep 77	taken by prior

SIXTH REGIMENT.

Feely, William		17 June 77	4 Nov 77	
Fisher, Danl.	pt	7 dec 76	11 Sept 77	died
Flemming, Jno.	do	5 Mar 77	24 feb 78	do
Farthing, Robt.	do	10 July 77	27 May 78	died

LEFT OUT OF MUSTERS THIRD REGIMENT.

Glasgow, Walter		13 May	23 June	deserted
Gardner, John			19 June	do
Grantt, James			22 Aug	taken
Griffin, Darby			12 June	deserted
Goodwin, James Joined April 78			left out January Roll 78	
Griffith, Thomas[1]		26 Mar 78	27th	deserted
Gee, George			4 July	do

FOURTH REGIMENT.

| Grace, William | Drum | | 25 Nov 77 | deserted |
| Goodchild, Wm.[2] | | 12 feb 78 | 13 May 78 | do |

[1] Lt. Armstrong's.   [2] Lansdale's.

MUSTERS OF MARYLAND TROOPS, VOL. III.

Names.	Rank.	Time of Service.		Remarks.
		Enlisted.	Discharged.	
Gibbs, John		26 April	2 May	deserted
Granade, Jno.		18 May	24 do	do
Grilliot, Jos.		26 April	4 do	do
Girte, Chrisr.		4 July	14 Aug	do
Glenn, James		Joined 1 Jan 80	15 Jan 80	do

FIFTH REGIMENT.

Non Commissioned Officers and Soldiers of the Fifth Maryland Regiment left out of the Rolls February, 1778.

Gadd, Thomas		12 July 77	4 Oct 77	missing
Grace, John		30 Mar 77	25 June 77	died
Gray, William		21 Aug 77	4 Oct 77	missing
			Joined 22 July 78	
Gibney, Simon		24 dec 76	29 Jan 77	deserted
Gray, Joseph		12 do	12 Mar	discharged
Githin, Robt.		1 feb 77	never joined	Regt.
Gurney, (or Gumey), Jno.		29 May 77	2 Jan 78	died
Gormely, Joseph		22 do	the same day	deserted
Guist, George		24 Mar	23 April 77	transferred
Gill, William		13 Jan 77	1 feb 77	taken by Civic
Gray, Thomas		2 May 79	13 June 79	deserted [power
Glann, Saml.		18 Jan 77	15 May 77	discharged

SIXTH REGIMENT.

Greenwood, Michl.		20 April left sick in Phila.		not heard of
Garland, James		15 Aug 77	18 Oct 77	died
Gorman, Jno.		21 May 77	15 July 77	
Graham, Alexr.		12 July 77	2 feb 78	
Gallaspie, John		18 July 77	28 July 77	deserted
Gregory, Saml.		3 May 77	6 feb 78	died
Gatreen, John	pt	5 dec 76	21 Jan 77	do
Grosman, Sol.	do	6 do	9 Mar 77	deserted
Gallagan, Jno.	do	7 Jan 77	28 feb 78	do
Gannon, John	do	6 June 77	15 Nov 77	do

LEFT OUT OF MUSTERS THIRD REGIMENT.

Hanson, Saml.[1]	Sergt	10 May 77	promoted 24 July 1st Regt. 1777	
Horner, Robt.			10 Aug	died
Harrison, Thomas			4 Oct	killed
Hannah, Miles			do	do

[1] Marbury's.

MUSTERS OF MARYLAND TROOPS, VOL. III.

NAMES.	RANK.	TIME OF SERVICE. Enlisted.	Discharged.	REMARKS.
Heart, William			prior Enlistment	
Hay, John			9 Sept	deserted
Hindmore, Richd.			11 feb 77	died
Hollyday, Jno.			2 do	deserted
Hough, John returned & entered			19 June	do
Henis, James			12 do	do
Hulet, John			22 Aug	taken
Harris, William Joined April 78			left out January Roll 78	
Hois, Thomas			25 April	deserted

FOURTH REGIMENT.

Hunt, Charles[1]		6 dec 76	1 feb 77	died
Harris, William		19 Aug 79	27 Aug 77	deserted
Hall, Tobias		27 May 77	1 July 77	do
Haggerty, Peter[2]		30 Jan 78	19 Mar 78	do

FIFTH REGIMENT.

Non Commissioned Officers and Soldiers of the Fifth Maryland Regiment left out of the Rolls February, 1778.

Higgins, Danl.		10 dec 76	30 Aug 77	deserted
Hopkins, John[3]		do	22 April 77	transferred
Hodgdon, (or son), John		28 April 77	22 Sept 77	deserted
Hills, Edward		5 Aug	4 Oct	prisoner
Hughes, Jacob		14 July	5 Nov 77	died
Howell, John		17 feb 77	4 May 77	discharged
Harding, Edwd.		1 Sept 77	1 feb 78	died
Handy, George[4]	Sergt	4 dec 76	17 April 77	transferred
Hughes, John	do	7 do	not joined Regiment	
Harrison, Stephen		6 do	16 Aug 77	deserted
Hamilton, Robt.		12 do	12 Mar	discharged
Humphreys, Thos.		1 April 77	17 Aug	deserted
Hughes, Thos.		7 July	4 Oct	prisoner 5 May 1778 returned
Haynes, Joseph		Inlisted and discharged same day		
Hamilton, Jno.		6 June 79	13 June 79	deserted

SIXTH REGIMENT.

Hoffman, John[5]	Sergt	14 July 77	31 Mar 78	died
Hayes, John		15 Aug 77	Mar 78	left out

[1] Selman's. [2] Bowie's. [3] Dean's. [4] Handy's. [5] Ghiselin's.

MUSTERS OF MARYLAND TROOPS, VOL III.

Names.	Rank.	Time of Service. Enlisted.	Discharged.	Remarks.
Harris, Walter		6 Aug 77	Mar 78	left out
Haverin, Peter		9 do	deserted same day	
Herron, Charles[1]	Sergt	20 April 77	30 Sep 77	transferred
Hauge, John	pt	10 dec 76	15 Oct 77	do
Hawley, Wm.		1 Jan 77	13 Oct Hospital, not heard of Joined Jany 79	
Hennsey, Jno.		1 April 77	10 April 77	
Haynes, Lawce.		20 Jan 77	26 May 77	
Heath, John	do	12 July 77	2 feb 78	deserted
Hanson, Robt.		17 April 77	4 June 78	
Hannagan, Jno.		9 June 77	4 Oct 77	missing
Harmon, Geo.	Sergt	5 dec 76	11 Sept 77	do
Hewitt, Elijah		1 feb 77	22 Aug 77	prisoner
Harvey, James	Drum	5 dec 76	16 dec 77	died
Hickey, William	pt	5 dec 76	13 April 77	deserted
Henderson, Jno.	do	6 do	27 Nov 77	do
Hurley, John	do	14 Jan 77	13 April 77	do
Hunter, Nathl.	do	24 Jan 77	22 May 77	do
Hailey, Thomas	do	29 Jan 77	25 Aug 77	do
Hamilton, Thos.	do	27 June 77	27 July 77	do
Hardy, Isaac	do	5 dec 78	22 Aug 77	prisoner
Hunt, John	Sergt	15 May 77	15 dec 77	died
Hottle, Jacob	pt	10 July 77	26 Nov 77	discharged
Hurdle, Robt.	do	9 June 77	13 Mar 78	by Govr. Maryd. discharged

Left Out of Musters Third Regiment.

Jordan, William			4 Oct	killed
Johnston, John			22 Aug	taken

Fourth Regiment.

Joseph, John		19 May	25 May	deserted

Fifth Regiment.

Non Commissioned Officers and Soldiers of the Fifth Maryland Regiment left out of the Rolls Feby., 1778.

Johnson, Nichs.		27 May	3 Sept 77	deserted
			20 May 78	joined
Jenkins, William		10 dec 76	14 Jan 78	deserted
Jones, Edward		10 feb 77	13 Mar 77	died
Jenkins, Chas.		9 dec 76	22 Aug 77	prisoner

[1] Lawrence's.

MUSTERS OF MARYLAND TROOPS, VOL. III.

NAMES.	RANK.	TIME OF SERVICE. Enlisted.	Discharged.	REMARKS.
		LEFT OUT OF MUSTERS THIRD REGIMENT.		
King, William		3 feb 77		
Kelly, George		prior Enlistment		
Kingston, Geo.		left out January Roll 78		
		FOURTH REGIMENT.		
Kennady, Robt.		19 Aug —	27 Aug 77	deserted
Killing, Jno.[1]		19 Mar 78	9 May 78	do
Keiff, Patk.		October and November in Goal		
		FIFTH REGIMENT.		

Non Commissioned Officers and Soldiers of the Fifth Maryland Regiment left out of the Rolls Feby., 1778.

Kemper, Thomas		10 dec 76	22 April 77	transferred
Kelly, James	Sergt	2 Jany 77	16 May 77	died
Kempton, Thos.[2]		5 dec 76	25 Mar 77	deserted
		SIXTH REGIMENT.		
Kelly, William[3]	Sergt	26 April 77	11 Sept 77	missing
Kelly, John	pt	17 feb 77	24 April 77	died
		LEFT OUT OF MUSTERS THIRD REGIMENT.		
Lawler, James		4 feb	12 feby	died
Lockett, Richd.		10 April	11 Sept	deserted
Lattlemore, Anda.			19 June	do
Lewis, Richard[4]	Sergt		15 Jan 78	do
		FOURTH REGIMENT.		
Levermore, Peter		7 May	12 May	deserted
		FIFTH REGIMENT.		

Non Commissioned Officers and Soldiers of the Fifth Maryland Regiment left out of the Rolls Feby., 1778.

Lysought, Jno.		17 dec 76	3 Aug 77	deserted
Lastly, Joseph		do	10 June 77	do
Lowrey, Chrisn.		28 Jan 77	20 May 77	do
Lee, Thomas	Sergt	5 dec 76	28 dec 76	died
Laythrum, Sylvester		7 March	never joined	
Lawrence, Jno.		23 Jan	5 Aug 77	died

[1] Riely's, late Bowie's.   [2] Cosden's.   [3] Harris'.   [4] Brice's.

MUSTERS OF MARYLAND TROOPS, VOL. III.

Names.	Rank.	Time of Service. Enlisted.	Discharged.	Remarks.

Sixth Regiment.
Non Commissioned Officers and Soldiers Sixth Regiment.

Names.	Rank.	Enlisted.	Discharged.	Remarks.
Long, Chris.	Sergt	18 April 77	21 Nov 77	deserted
Lloyd, Thomas	do	8 May 77	14 Jan 78	do
Lockwood, Stephen		21 May 77	2 feb 78	do
Lewis, William		26 Aug 77	2 feb 78	do
Lancaster, John	pt	1 Jan 77	11 Sept 77	missing
Larkin, Anthy.	do	25 July 77	7 Aug 77	deserted
Lewes, James	do	8 Jan 77	15 dec 77	died
Letchworth, Jos.	Sergt	21 June 77	3 April 78	do
Lewis, Enoch	pt	2 Mar 77	15 Oct 77	deserted
Lukart, Fredk.	do	5 May 79	25 May	do
Land, Jas.	do	21 do	21 June	do

Left Out of Musters Third Regiment.

Names.	Rank.	Enlisted.	Discharged.	Remarks.
Magness, Wm. Hartley's Regt.			28 Jan 81	discharged
McCant, Jos.				taken Staten Island 22 Aug
Maddox, Notley			16 Sept	died of wounds
Miller, William[1]		10 April	10 June	deserted
Mullinoux, Wm.			22 Aug	prisoner
May, Peter			27 Aug	deserted
Moses, Jacob[2]				missing Staten Island 22 Augt
Missett, Lawrence				do Brandywine 11 Sept
McCloud, Hugh			4 Oct	missing
McNash, Mathw.			11 Sept	taken
McIntire, Alexr.				died in June
Million, John[2]			left out January Roll 78	
McDonald, Martin[2]			do do do	
McGinnis, Robt.			13 July	deserted
Miller, John			13 May 79	do

Fourth Regiment.

Names.	Rank.	Enlisted.	Discharged.	Remarks.
Marsh, Thomas[4]	Sergt	14 July 77	5 Jan 78	died
Martin, Wm.			25 Nov 77	deserted
Marfee, Michl.[5]			16 Sept	do
McGuire, Philemon[6]		22 Mar 77	4 April 77	died
Millard, Thomas		6 dec 76	12 April 77	do
Murphy, James		12 Nov 77	15 Nov 77	deserted
Missick, Lawrence		23 April 77	30 April 77	do
Mowberry, Geo.		6 Mar 78	15 May 78	do
Moore, Jno.[4]		19 May 79	15 June 79	do
May, Francis		24 April	30 May	do
Martin, James		1 July	3 Aug	do

[1] Ridgely's. [2] Griffith's. [3] Brice's. [4] Oldham's. [5] Spurrier's. [6] Lansdale's.

MUSTERS OF MARYLAND TROOPS, VOL. III.

Names.	Rank.	Time of Service. Enlisted.	Discharged.	Remarks.

Fifth Regiment.

Non Commissioned Officers and Soldiers of the Fifth Maryland Regiment left out of the Rolls Febry., 1778.

Names	Rank	Enlisted	Discharged	Remarks
McCarty, Danl.		30 Mar 77	17 June 77	died
Martin, Henry		4 Jan 77	14 feb 77	do
Malsny, William		3 May 77	28 June 77	deserted
			11 April 78	joined again
Masters, William		5 July 77	18 July 77	deserted
McMahon, Francis	Sergt	17 dec 76	14 June 77	do
McKinsey, John		2 Jany 77	29 Oct 77	died
Morsell, John		10 Mar 77	10 Aug 77	do
Morton, Benja.		20 dec 76	2 Oct 77	deserted
McGaw, Nichs.		2 Jan 77	17 feb 77	died
McCarson, Jno.		16 Jan 76	26 Jan 77	deserted
McMahon, Jno.		10 dec 76	10 feb 77	do
McLaughlin, Philip		4 feb 77	7 Mar 77	do
Mason, Arthur		22 April 77	absent without leave, returned	
McCarty, Thomas		13 feb	22 Aug	prisoner }
			22 July 78	joined }
McClarty, George		Damn him he deserted 15 April 77	7 Jan 77 Enlisted	
Moore, William		20 feb 77	10 May 77	transferred
Meredith, James		16 Jan	1 April 77	discharged
Malcolm, Thomas		1 feb	6 do	died
Meryfield, Josiah		Inlisted and Discharged same day		
Monroe, Finley		19 July	4 Oct 77	prisoner

Left out of Sixth Regiment.

Names	Rank	Enlisted	Discharged	Remarks
McCoy, John		15 Aug 77	1 June 78	discharged
McEvoy, Patk.		4 Sept	13 do	do
McDonald, Wm.		30 Augt	deserted same day	
McDonough, Thos.	pt	20 April 77	21 Jan 78	deserted
McDonald, Thos.		7 Mar 77	23 Sept 77	do
Martin, Charles		5 May 77	2 feb 78	do
Murphy, Thomas		21 April 77	10 July 77	
Moran, William		17 June 77	25 May 78	
Main, Henry		27 April 77	11 Sept 77	missing
Moland, James		1 Aug 77		killed German Town
Mitz, Chris.	Sergt	5 dec 76	3 July 77	deserted
Massey, William	pt	15 Jan 77	4 Oct 77	killed
Morgan, Richd.				
Moorcraft, Wm.	do	9 dec 76	9 Mar 77	deserted
Martin, Thomas	do	17 Jan 77	14 feb 77	do [heard of
McCarty, Florence	do	28 April 77	1 Jan 78	Hospital, not

MUSTERS OF MARYLAND TROOPS, VOL. III.

Names.	Rank.	Time of Service. Enlisted.	Discharged.	Remarks.
McKey, John	pt	3 April 77	12 dec 77	deserted
McDonald, James		1 June 77 to Oct 77		discharged
	reind.	12 May 78	1 June 78	deserted
Mitchell, Jno.	pt	25 June 79 to July 79		do
McDonald, Jno.	do	15 May 79	20 Nov 79	do

Left Out of Musters Third Regiment.

Neagle, Morrice			4 Oct	prisoner

Fourth Regiment.

Newthall, Thos.			15 dec 77	discharged
Nivin, Patk.		7 May	20 May	deserted
Neil, John		26 Oct	20 Nov	d

Fifth Regiment.

Non Commissioned Officers and Soldiers of the Fifth Maryland Regiment left out of the Rolls Feby., 1778.

Nixon, Robt.	pt	1 Sept 77	14 Jan 78	dead
Notts, John		12 dec 76	26 dec 76	deserted
Norman, Thomas		4 Jan 77	16 April 77	deserted
Norman, Richd.		26 feb 77	20 July 77	do

Sixth Regiment.

Noaksworth, John		30 Aug		deserted same day

Left Out of Musters Third Regiment.

Owens, John[1]			13 July	deserted

Fifth Regiment.

Non Commissioned Officers and Soldiers of the Fifth Maryland Regiment.

Ormond, William[2]		27 feb 77	1 July 77	deserted
O'Hara, William	fifer	4 dec 76	22 Nov 77	died
Oar, John		14 Jan 77	24 Jany	deserted

Left Out of Sixth Regiment.

Okey, John		11 April 78	4 June 78	

Left Out of Musters Third Regiment.

Prarey, John			4 Oct	prisoner
Primer, Henry			12 dec	deserted
Peggs, Henry			15 Mar 77	do
Peacock, Robert			4 Oct	missing
Potter, John			8 Aug	deserted

[1] Dorsey's.   [2] Lynch's.

MUSTERS OF MARYLAND TROOPS, VOL. III.

NAMES.	RANK.	TIME OF SERVICE. Enlisted.	Discharged.	REMARKS.
	FOURTH REGIMENT.			
Patterson, Levin Oct & Nov 79		18 May	25 June	deserted
Pascall, Peter		22 May	1 June	do
Pound, Edward		22 Aug	5 Sept	do
	FIFTH REGIMENT.			

Non Commissioned Officers and Soldiers of the Fifth Maryland Regiment left out of the Rolls Feb., 1778.

NAMES.	RANK.	Enlisted.	Discharged.	REMARKS.
Pitts, William[1]		10 dec 76	10 May 77	transferred
Pratt, Jno.	Corpl appd. 30 Mar 77		27 Nov 77	died
Paine, Robert		5 May 77	22 Sept 77	deserted
Paul, Lewis Griffith		9 July	7 dec	died
Payne, William		12 Jan 77	17 Jan 77	deserted
Plowman, Philemon		10 Sept 77	30 Jan 78	do
Pritchett, Peter		do	4 Oct 77	missing
Price, Levin		14 July	25 July	deserted
			5 May 78	returned
Payne, John[2]	Sergt	15 feb 77	7 June 77	detained by Civil
			8 June 78	joined [power
Pigman, John		10 Jan 77	22 April 77	deserted
Parfoot, Thomas		21 Jan	2 April	died
Parrumore, Thos.		1 Aug	13 Aug 77	deserted
Potster, Peter		19 dec 76	6 April 77	died
Paul, William		8 Jan 77	12 do	do
Payne, Saml.		10 May 79	13 June 79	deserted
	SIXTH REGIMENT.			
Plumly, Jacob	Corpl	20 July 77	20 Sept 77	deserted
Patterson, Peter		20 April 77	18 Mar 78	do
Philips, Abram		5 May 77	9 Aug 77	shot for desertion
Pennox, Isaac		27 June 77	4 Nov 77	
Page, George	pt	17 feb 77	17 Mar 77	sick Hospital, never joined
Phillips, William	Sergt	1 Nov 77	15 feb 78	died
Peters, William	Was in a Consperacy in So. Carolina and was sent off from the Army			
	SIXTH REGIMENT.			

Non Commissioned Officers and Soldiers Sixth Regt.

NAMES.	RANK.	Enlisted.	Discharged.	REMARKS.
Quixall, Thomas		15 Aug 77	19 dec 78	deserted

[1] Dean's.   [2] Johnson's.

MUSTERS OF MARYLAND TROOPS, VOL. III.

Names.	Rank.	Time of Service. Enlisted.	Discharged.	Remarks.

LEFT OUT OF MUSTERS THIRD REGIMENT.

Names	Rank	Enlisted	Discharged	Remarks
Reland, Mathew	Appears taken as a servant			
Ricketts, William			16 Mar	deserted
Rooker, James			22 Aug	missing
Ryan, James				deserted
Rockhold, T.[1]	Sergt		22 Aug	taken
Richmond, Nathl.			do	do
Rock, John		21 feb	19 May 78	deserted
Reevin, Stephen			12 June 79	do
Ryan, Timothy			15 Aug	do

FOURTH REGIMENT.

Names	Rank	Enlisted	Discharged	Remarks
Ridgely, Doctor Fredk.	appd. Surgeon 4th Regt. 1777 by Assembly			
Ringrose, James[2]		7 May 78	31 May 78	deserted
Rich, Samuel[3]			10 July 78	do
Redweads, Jos.		14 Sept	26 Sept	do
Reeves, Jos.[4]		20 May 79	2 June 79	do

FIFTH REGIMENT.

Non Commissioned Officers and Soldiers of the Fifth Maryland Regiment left out of the Rolls Feby., 1778.

Names	Rank	Enlisted	Discharged	Remarks
Reily, William		8 Aug 77	30 Aug 77	deserted
Reily, Patk.		7 feb 77	12 Mar 77	died
Ready, Michael		4 Jan 77	25 April 77	transferred
Ray, William	Sergt	16 April 77	5 May 77	died (11 Mar pt.)
Roberts, Henry		5 dec 76	5 dec 76	deserted
Ryan, John		7 do	7 April 77	died
Richardson, Geo.		13 feb 77	16 Aug	deserted
Roche, Thomas		23 April 77	30 July 77	died
Rea, William		8 Jan 77	11 Sept 77	missing
Roster, Thomas		12 do	30 April 77	died

LEFT OUT OF SIXTH REGIMENT.

Names	Rank	Enlisted	Discharged	Remarks
Reeves, John	pt	15 July 77	16 Mar 78	died
Rooks, John		31 do	deserted same day	
Railey, Hugh		24 April 77	31 May 78	deserted
Reah, John		5 May 77	17 June 77	
Rutherford, Jas.		23 Mar 78	4 June 78	
Raidy, Edmd.	pt	6 dec 76	9 feb 77	died
Reidy, Michael	do	5 do	1 Sept 77	deserted
Ronderberk, John	do	18 Jan 77	9 Mar 77	do
Robertson, John	do	15 feb 77	3 Aug 77	do
Reily, Miles	do	24 do	13 April 77	do
Rowland, Jacob	do	27 Jan 77	27 July 77	do

[1] Brice's.   [2] Selman's.   [3] Burgess'.   [4] Oldham's.

MUSTERS OF MARYLAND TROOPS, VOL. III.

Names.	Rank.	Time of Service. Enlisted.	Discharged.	Remarks.
		Left Out of Musters Third Regiment.		
Smith, Bagwell		Enlisted 30 April 81 for 3 yrs. by Cert. of J. Bordley of Waters' Co.		
Stewart, Chas.		Artillery, has lost his papers		
Swann, Basil			10 Aug	died
Smith, William			11 Sept	missing
Sockett, Richd.			do	deserted
Shields, William			10 May	do
Swain, John[1]			8 Sept 77 Joined feb 78	do
Sweeny, Edward	Sergt		17 April	do
Sherry, William			4 Oct	killed
Spence, John			4 Aug	deserted
Shell, Richd.[2]		7 feb 78	19 May 78	do
Smith, Joseph			25 June	do
Sappington, Thos.			5 do	do
Smith, John			24 Sept	do
		Fourth Regiment.		
Scott, William		19 May	26 May 77	deserted
Smith, William		7 Jan 78	1 April 78	do
Sothoren, Anthy.		26 April	1 May	do
Sicard, Anthy.		24 do	6 June	do
Soap, Jno.		2 Aug	18 Aug	do
		Fifth Regiment.		

Non Commissioned Officers and Soldiers of the Fifth Maryland Regiment left out of the Rolls February, 1778.

Names.	Rank.	Enlisted.	Discharged.	Remarks.
Sampson, Richd.		10 dec 76	11 June 77	transferred
Snooks, Richd.		do	do	do
Spencer, Humphrey		do	22 April 77	do
Small, Jona.		10 feb 77	14 Jan 78	deserted
Stuart, Thomas		17 do	do	do
Smyth, John		30 Mar 77	17 July 77	died
Sutton, Ab.		22 do	22 Mar	taken by M. Page
Shoudon, Thomas		10 Aug	10 Aug 77	discharged
Sutton, Richd.	Corpl	12 feb 77	reduced April 16 4 July 77	deserted
Sullivan, John		14 do	15 July 77	deserted
Smith, Thomas		2 Jan 77	18 Mar 77	do
Saxey, Geo.		16 May	19 July	discharged
Smith, John[3] (D. F.)		16 Jan 77	1 April 77	do

[1] Lt. J. Deaver's.   [2] Marbury's.   [3] Emory's.

Names.	Rank.	Time of Service. Enlisted.	Discharged.	Remarks.
Shelton, Jno.		17 Jan	10 April	died
Stewart, Charles		6 June 77	6 dec 77	do
Smyth, Joseph	Corpl	17 March	25 Aug 77	do
Smith, John[1]	fifer	16 Jan 77	See Smith, Jno., 1st man Emory's	
Slocum, Solomon		25 do	10 May 77	discharged
Simmond, Wm. Fitz.		10 May 77	20 July 77	do
Stevens, George		8 Mar	8 April 77	do
Southerland, David		14 feb 77	16 Sept 77	deserted
Shelly, John		1 Jan	28 Sept	discharged
Stevens, Geo.		8 Mar	8 April 77	do
Silvey, Jacob		14 Jan 77	4 Aug 77	died
Smyth, John		10 May 79	14 June 79	deserted

Sixth Regiment.

Names.	Rank.	Enlisted.	Discharged.	Remarks.
Steers, John		6 feb 77	1 April 77	
Sullivan, Owen		8 July 77	5 Mar 78	
Sullivan, Thomas		28 April 77	18 Sept 77	
Smith, John	pt	5 dec 76	24 do	deserted
			June 78	joined
Solomon, Saml.	pt	5 dec 76	13 April 77	deserted
Swainey, Roger	pt	9 do	21 do	do
Staunton, Peter	do	15 Jan 77	21 do	do
Swartzell, Henry	do	23 Jan 77	24 Sept 77	do
Story, Robert	do	22 feb 77	3 Mar 77	do
Sharer, Michael	do	11 July 77	13 Oct 77	do
Shokey, Abram	do	10 Mar 77	3 Sept 77	do
Stratton, Mack	do	10 July 77	11 Sept 77	missing
Sax, Richard	do	23 May 77	4 Oct 77	killed
Smith, Thomas	do	14 Oct 77	1 Nov 77	deserted to
Saund, Thomas	do	17 May 79	8 July 79	deserted [Enemy
Smith, Alex. Lawson	Capt	13 July 1776		

Fourth Regiment.

Names.	Rank.	Enlisted.	Discharged.	Remarks.
Torny, Patk.		6 Mar 78	15 May 78	deserted
Talbott, William[2]			2 Aug 78	died
Thompson, James		10 Nov	19 Nov	deserted
Tawson, James		26 Oct	8 Nov	do
Thompson, James		14 Aug 77	20 Aug 77	do

[1] Emory's. [2] Riely's.

MUSTERS OF MARYLAND TROOPS, VOL. III.

NAMES.	RANK.	TIME OF SERVICE.		REMARKS.
		Enlisted.	Discharged.	

FIFTH REGIMENT.

Non Commissioned Officers and Soldiers of the Fifth Maryland Regt. left out of the Rolls Feby., 1778.

Thornton, Harry		28 Jan 77	29 May 77	discharged
Thomas, Michael		26 May	24 Aug 77	died

SIXTH REGIMENT.

Taggart, Danl.		8 feb 77	9 Oct 77	deserted
Tipton, Francis		2 May 77	15 July 77	
Tugby, John		15 July 77	28 Oct 77	died
Tracy, William		26 feb 78	13 May 78	

SEVENTH REGIMENT.

Doctor Tabbs appd. Surgeon 7th Regt. the 29th Mar., 1777 by Assembly

FIFTH REGIMENT.

Usher, John		3 feb 77	15 Mar 77	died
Vandyke, Wm.			28 Jan 77	deserted
Vinestreet, Jno.		26 July	19 Dec	died

LEFT OUT OF MUSTERS THIRD REGIMENT.

Williams, David Joined 18 June 78			11 Sept	missing
Wattson, Edward			4 Oct	killed
Wallis, Richard		17 May	11 Sept	do or taken
Wilkes, Charles			19 June	deserted
Walker, William			left out January Roll 78	
Watts, Richard			do do	do do
Webber, William			do	do do
Wright, Danl.[1]		24 Mar 78	17 May 78	deserted

FOURTH REGIMENT.

Wright, Jno.[2]		Musd., deserted in the musr. for June 79		
Webb, John		14 May	10 June 79	deserted
Wright, Charles		17 April	2 June	do
Williams, Jno.		8 Nov	17 Nov	do
Wilton, Jno.		1 Oct	2 Nov	do
Williams, John		24 Aug	10 Sept	do [reason
Welch, Thomas Lee's Legion		Musd. feb 80	Mar 80	left with. assg. any

[1] Lt. Deaver's.   [2] Riely's.

Names.	Rank.	Time of Service. Enlisted.	Discharged.	Remarks.

Fifth Regiment.

Non Commissioned Officers and Soldiers of the Fifth Maryland Regiment left out of the Rolls February.

Names.	Rank.	Enlisted.	Discharged.	Remarks.
Willington, John		10 dec 76	22 April 77	transferred
Worthington, Benja.		do	do	do
White, John		18 June 77	23 Oct 77	deserted
Williams, James		3 May 77	20 May	discharged
Williams, Nathan		3 May	22 May	do
Welsh, Patk.		2 Jan 77	30 Mar 77	died
Wilson, Mathew		17 dec 76	16 feb 77	deserted
Williams, Morgan		9 feb 77	20 April 77	transferred
Williams, Jno.		10 feb	15 feb	deserted
Wilkerson, Geo.		7 April 77	11 Sept	killed
Williams, John		17 feb 77	15 April	deserted
Waggoner, Joseph		5 May 79	13 June 79	do
Williams, Thomas		11 June 79	do	do
Wood, John		8 do	do	do
Williams, George		6 do	do	do

Sixth Regiment.

Names.	Rank.	Enlisted.	Discharged.	Remarks.
Woodward, Richard		14 Sept 77	26 Jan 78	died
Woods, John		16 Jan 77	2 Mar 77	deserted
White, Wood Jos.		12 July 77	2 feb 78	
Webber, George		18 do	do	
Welch, Nichs.		14 April 77	24 April 77	
Withers, James		25 May 77	21 feb 78	died
Wilson, John	pt	6 dec 76	11 dec 76	deserted
Wilson, Richd.	do	4 Jan 77	5 Mar 77	do
Williamson, Ben.	do	8 do	3 Aug 77	do
Whitman, Henry	do	2 May 77	22 do	prisoner
Wade, Augustin	do	12 feb 77	13 June 78	discharged
Wright, Jas.	Sergt Maj.	21 June 77	22 Aug 77	prisoner

Left out of Musters Fifth Regiment.

Names.	Rank.	Enlisted.	Discharged.	Remarks.
Yoe, Thomas		18 Mar	10 May 77	discharged

MISCELLANEOUS MARYLAND LINE PAPERS.

First Regiment.

I hereby certify that Thomas Hutson was drafted in the year 1778 to serve nine months in Continental Army, which time he served in my Company in the First Maryland. Given at Annapolis Nov. 5th, 1783.

Henry Gaither, Capt.

Second Regiment.

A Roll of John Eccleston's Company in the 2nd Maryland Regiment. Commanded by Col. Thomas Price.

John Eccleston, Capt.   John Gale, 1 Lieut.
John Ridd, Ensign.

Nathan Wright	James Murphy	Hugh Caine
John F. Lowe	Spencer Sanders	Reuben Moore
James Collins	Patrick Cavender	John Bandy
Edward Hardikin	John Lynch	Adam Henry
Randle Revle	George Hall	John Bryan
Jeremiah Andrew	John Flanagan	Daniel Kersey
James Andrew	John Crockett	James Delaney
Samuel Owens	Thomas Sanders	John Sammon
Charles Scott	Richard Rollins	David Williams
Edward Armstrong	William Nuton	William Goald
Richard Isable	Jacob Tharp	William Hillman
John Conner	Charles Moore	William Moore
Nathan Duley	Robert Skinner	Bryan Carroll
Benjamin Stevens	Silvester Ryley	John Cole
Levin Spicer	Obidiah Read	Thomas Buckley
Soloman Harriss	William Beaver	Henry Smith
Kemp Holder	Daniel Haly	Charles Pennerwell
John Blades	Timothy Riggin	James Smith
Jeremiah Carroll	John Martin	Peter Cahoon
Levy Burke	Robert Smith	John McAdams
Elijah Lankford	Darby Carter (?)	William Brooks
Richard Bush	James Pritchard	Joseph Burch
Samuel Roans	Henry Sharpe	John Pickeron
Joseph Gray	Edward Dean (?)	William Man
John Holder	Wm. Cantwell	Thomas Colvert

Charles Foxwell	Philip Strobrook, (or Shobrook)	William West, (alias Gill)
Barthw. Cook Hays	Robert Johnson	Ezekiel Burnes
Thomas Thompson	Jonathan Wiltshire	John McDougle
James Read	James Donnelly	Edward Scott
John McConnakin.	Thomas Kelley, (or Kelby)	Henry Turner, Vagrant
James McFarrin	William Wheatley	John Cornish
William Harper	Isaac Scott	James Sanders
Richard Harper	James Trego	Noble Dean
Thomas Taylor	Nehemiah Ellensworth	

Return of Recruits and Substitutes received and inlisted in Frederick County for the Second Maryland Regiment. Commanded by Colonel Thomas Price. 1778.

RECRUITS.

John Hart	Feb 18	James Ferrell	Mch 24	John Haney	Apl 6
George King	" 28	Charles Parker	" 28	John Shovell	
John Joel	" "	Jas. Fitzgerald	Apl 3	Lawrence Fitzpatrick	" 29
Alex. McDonald	Mch 12				

SUBSTITUTES.

John Day	Wm. Courtney	Thomas Ferrell
John Holden	David Conner	John McGraw
Nicholas Moss	Henry Oyster	Patrick Raven
John Baldwin	Roger Landers	Timothy McKarty
John McKinney	Wm. McKoy	George Hegerty
John Parker	Wm. Braithwait	John Draper
Wm. Richey	James Shehan	James Henessey
Johnsey Morgan	Thomas Brown	James Harmer
John Spray	Wm. Phillips	Richard Nisbett
Daniel Vantier	James Eddy	John Fricker
Charles Stone	Wm. Stephens	Luke Horsefield
Thomas Daley	John Burns	Wm. Alinder
Arthur Mullholland	Wm. Forbey	James Welch
Jacob Knight	Patrick Carey	James Horsfield
Andrew Preston	Jones Chamberlin	John Waller
Thomas Sarjent		

OLD SOLDIERS.

John Wright	Hugh Kelly	Thomas Summers
Thomas Webster	John Martin	Bartley Laine

Revd. James Armstrong served in the 2nd Md. Brigade from Nov., 1778, to Apl. 1780.

COMPANIES IN THE THIRD MARYLAND REGIMENT.

Muster Roll of Capt. Horatio Claggett's Co. in the 3rd Md. Regt. Under Command of Major Anderson, for December, 1779.

FIFTH COMPANY.

Capt.	Horatio Claggett	Commd. Oct 10th, 1777	
1 Lieut.	Osburn Williams	Commd. Apl 12th, 1779	resigned
2 "	Nicholas Gassaway	" " 17th, 1777	sick, absent

RANK.	NAMES.	DATE OF ENLISTMENT.	TIME.	REMARKS.
Serjt.	Antipas Coltart	23 Apl 77	3 yrs	
"	Jno. Morriss		War	
Corpl.	Josias Harriss	26 May 78	3 yrs	
"	Duncan Keith		War	
Drum. & Fife	Jno. Sanders		"	
Privates	James Jones		"	
	Jno. Forbus		"	
	Edwd. Davis		"	
	William West	9 Jan 79	3 yrs	
	Jno. Garrett	28 Feb 77	"	
	Jno. McCann		War	
	Robt. Whittle		"	
	Alex. Crispin		"	
	Patk. Fane		"	
	Jno. Robertson		"	
	James Willcox		"	
	Benj. Johnson		"	
	Richd. Tasco		"	
	Thos. Evins		"	
	Jno. Anderson	25 Feb 77	3 yrs	
	Jno. Beam	9 Jan 79	"	
	Richd. Cook	8 " "	"	
	George Brown	28 Apl 78	"	
	Jona. Pemnick	9 Jan 79	"	
	Thos. Higdon		War	
	Isaac Lyan		"	
	Jno. Wood		"	
	Wm. Glasgow	16 May 78	"	
	Jno. Driver		"	sick, present
	Richd. Suffolk		"	" "
	Saml. Hughes		"	" "
	Francis Hopkins		. "	on Fatigue

Rank.	Names.	Date of Enlistment.	Time.	Remarks.
Privates	Zach. Burck, (or Burch)	26 May 78	3 yrs	on Command
	Jno. White	28 Apl 77	"	" "
	Mark McGlocklain		War	" "
	James Riley	17 Nov 78	3 yrs	" "
	Jona. Mahugh	9 Jan 79	"	" "
	Alex. Frances		War	" "
	Steph. Priston		"	" "
	Henry Homs,(or Horns)	7 Mch 78	3 yrs	" "
	Leo. Swann	3 May "	"	" "
	Wm. Fairburn		War	" "
	Richd. Shell, (or Stull)		"	" "
	Wm. Whitely	29 Mch 77	3 yrs	" "
	Wm. Flanagin	9 April 77	"	" "
	Esau Buknell		War	" "
	Peter Tippitts		"	" "
	Wm. Willson		"	" "
	Benj. Kidwell		"	furlough 4 Jan 80
	Basil Brown		"	" " "
	Chas. Clements		"	" " "
	Wm. Dunington		"	sick Hospl.
	Jno. Minning		3 yrs	deserted 1 Dec 79
	Jno. Conner		War	" 17 "
	Philip Mandwell		"	" 4 Jan 80

Jan. 19th, 1780. Mustered Capt. Clagett's Company as specified in the above Roll.   T. Brice, Maj. Brig.

Roll of Capt Wm. Wilmot's Company in the 3d Regt. December, 1779.

Sixth Company.

Wm. Wilmot, Captain		Comd. 15 Oct '79		
Isaac Duvall, Lieut.		" 12 Apl '79		on furlough

Rank.	Names.	Date of Enlistment.	Time.	Remarks.
Serjt.	Wm. Allen		War	
Corpl.	John Turbott	12 Feb 77	3 yrs	
"	John Keegan		War	
"	Whedon Benn		"	
Fifer	Isaac Barry		"	sick, absent
Drum.	John Gordon		"	
Privates	John Clegett	25 Apl 78	3 yrs	
	Jacob Moses		War	
	Wm. Sugars		"	
	Saml. Bellwhite		"	

Rank.	Names.	Date of Enlistment.	Time.	Remarks.
Privates	John Pendergrast		War	
	Danl. Martin		"	
	Thos. Watson		"	
	John Stephenson		"	
	Edmd. Carthew		"	
	John Williams		"	
	Mark Clements		"	
	Thos. Robinson		"	
	Wm. Browne		"	
	Wm. Jones		"	
	Thos. Russell		"	
	James Dollison		"	
	James Byass		"	
	George Windham	25 Apl 78	3 yrs	
	George Fields		War	on Command
	John Gibson	30 Apl 78	"	" "
	Michl. Mumner		"	" "
	Mar——————	5 May 77	3 yrs	" "
	Jesse Grace	25 Apl 78	"	" "
	John Roberts	10 Jan 77	"	" "
	Peter Byall		War	" "
	Michl. Woolford		"	" "
	James Connor		"	on Guard
	Mamd. Penderberry		"	" "
	John Hailey	3 May 77	3 yrs	sick, present
	James Sayers		War	on furlough
	Godfrey Acort		"	"
	Jas. Holebrooke		"	"
	Michl. Martin	10 Jany 77	3 yrs	dischd. 12 Jan 80
	Timy. McNemara		"	" "
	George Duvall		"	" "
	Thos. Taylor		"	" "
	John R——an		"	" "
	Richd. T——ield		"	" "
	Fras. Whitaker		"	" "
	James Wilson		"	" "
	James Johns	26 Dec 77	"	" 28 Dec 79
	Thos. Coonehan		War	deserted 5 Jan 80
	John Wilson		"	" "
	Thos. Adams	25 Apl 78	3 yrs	sick Hospl. Yellow Springs 11 Jan 79
	Edwd. Wade	"	"	" Albany 20 July 79
	Nathan Ryan		"	" " 16 Oct 79

19 Jan., 1780. Mustered Capt. Wilmot's Company as specified in the above Roll.

T. Brice, Major Brigade.

Muster Roll of Capt.-Lieut. Armstrong's Co. in the 3d Regt. December, 1779. Commanded by Major Archibald Anderson.

G. Armstrong, Capt.-Lieut.   Commd. 12 August, 1778.

RANK.	NAMES.	DATE OF ENLISTMENT.	TIME.	REMARKS.
Serjt.	John Trueman		War	
"	Richd. Turner		"	
"	Phinchas Hurst			deserted 1 Jan 80
"	Athantius Thomson	12 May 78	3 yrs	Corpl. until appt. as Serjt. 1 Jan 80
Corpl.	Thos. Alvey		War	on Command
"	Wm. Dillin		"	
Drum. & fife	Barney Johnson		"	recruiting
Privates	Thos. Luff		"	
	John Collins	3 May 77	3 yrs	
	Wm. Rock	7 May 78	War	
	Auston Howard		"	
	Travis Alvey		"	
	Edward Harley	17 May 78	3 yrs	
	Luke Carter		War	
	Henry Gouldsborou	18 Nov 78	3 yrs	
	Jeremiah Rhodes	10 Oct 78	War	
	Richard Hall		"	
	John Holmes		"	
	Perrygreen Howard		"	
	Mathew Moore		"	
	Justinian Jourdan	8 Apl 77	3 yrs	
	George Collins	26 Apl 78	"	
	William Children	— May 77	"	
	Bennett Chesser		War	
	Jacob Tragasskiss		"	
	Wm. Ridding		"	
	John Scott		"	
	Baptis Armesworthy		"	
	John Blair	15 Jan 77	3 yrs	
	James Foster		War	
	Wm. Magee		"	
	Chas. Magee		"	
	John Adams		"	
	Thos. Carrier		"	
	John Rock	20 Apl 78	3 yrs	
	James Thomas		War	on Command
	Richd. Aris		"	" "
	John B. Cissell	15 Jan 79	3 yrs	" "
	Cuthbert John,(or Jones)	4 Apl 77	"	" "

during the War of the American Revolution, 1775-83.

Rank.	Names.	Date of Enlistment.	Time.	Remarks.
Privates	Valentine Murray	14 May 78	3 yrs	on Command
	John Morriss	14 Apl 78	"	" "
	Mathew Bowie		War	" "
	Elias Henry	4 Apl 78	3 yrs	on furlough
	Gerbiner Lemmon	10 Nov 78	"	sick
	Thos. Lavender		War	sick Hospital

Kimbels Farm, 19 Jan., 1780. Mustered Capt.-Lieut. Armstrong's Company as specified in above Roll. T. Brice, Major Brigade.

Muster Roll of the Major's Co. in the 3d Regt. Commd. by Major Anderson, for December, 1779.

Ensign & Paymaster Thos. Price   Commissioned officer

Rank.	Names.	Date of Enlistment.	Time.	Remarks.
Serjt.	Jas. Burnes		War	Furloughed
Corpl.	Geo. Childes		"	
"	Chas. Murphy		"	
Drum. & fife	Thos. Knight		"	Furlough
Privates	John Lee		"	
	John Love		"	
	Wm. Strowd		"	
	Patk. Millater, (or Mittater)		"	
	Jos. Harrison	14 Apl 77	3 yrs	
	Robt. Haires	19 Jan 79	"	
	Wm. Anderson		War	
	Geo. Patrick		3 yrs	
	Peter Donovan	22 Apl 77	"	
	Forts. Stringer		War	
	Arthur Owens		"	
	Isaac King	19 Jan 77	3 yrs	
	John Barrett		War	
	John Harden		"	
	James Renark		"	on Furlough
	Wm. Jordan		"	
	Henry Towers	14 Jan 78	3 yrs	" "
	Thos. Barkly		War	" "
	Francis Harper		"	" "
	Nichs. McLaughlin		"	" "
	Philip Perrin		"	" "

Rank.	Names.	Date of Enlistment.	Time.	Remarks.
Privates	John Sanders		War	on Furlough
	Thos. Eliott		"	" "
	David Philips		"	" "
	Peter Dotton		"	" "
	James Terry		"	" "
	John Duncan		"	" "
	Wm. Lilly		"	" "
	Edwd. Carney		"	" "
	Thos. Collins	23 Mch 77	3 yrs	" "
	John Robb		War	" "
	Wm. Barry		"	" "
	Wm. Linch		"	" "
	Patk. Roland		"	" "
	Thos. Allibon		"	" "
	James Morton	9 May 77	3 yrs	" "
	Thos. Mackey		War	" "
	Nathl. Thompson	19 Apl 77	3 yrs	" "
	Dennis Moyland		War	deserted 19 Dec
	Wm. Price		"	on Command
	Duke Mayson, (or Magson)		"	" "
	Peter Hines	19 Jan 79	3 yrs	" "
	James King			" "
	Jno. Welch			sick, absent
	Jno. Richardson		War	absent
	John Wood	23 April 77	3 yrs	sick, absent
	James Alexander	22 Mch	"	" "
	Wm. Kennedy		War	on Command

19 Jan., 1780. Mustered Major Anderson's Company as specified in the above Roll.   T. Brice, Maj. B.   *

Fourth Regiment.

Muster Roll of Capt. Alexander Lawson Smith's Company, including part of the Companies belonging to the Regiment of Lt. Col. Moses Rawlings, being a part of the 11th Virginia Regiment commanded by Col. Daniel Morgan, Lt. Col. Febiger and Lt. Col. Nicholas, during 1777 and afterward being a part of the 4th Maryland Regiment commanded by Col. Josias Carvel Hall.

From Rolls for June, July, 1777, Col. Morgan, Sept., 1777, Lt. Col. Febiger, Oct., 1777, Lt. Col. Nicholas, Jan., 1778 to Jan., 1779 inclusive, Col. Hall.

    * Thomas Olvie, Corporal in 3rd Md. Regt., May 25th, 1779.

Capt.	Alex. Lawson Smith			Commissd. July 13th '76	on furlough June and July '77, Feb '78 and Nov 15th '78, Dec '78, Jan '79
Lieut.	Wm. Bradford				on furlough Jan and Feb '78, resigned April 3rd '78
"	Adamson Tannahill				(last appears on Roll of July '77)
"	Elijah Evans				(last appears on Roll of Oct '77)

RANK.	NAME.	TIME.	DATE OF ENLISTMENT.	REMARKS.
Serjt.	John Thompson	3 yrs		(last appears on Roll of July '77)
"	Matthew Alexander	"		deserted Oct 7th '77
"	Joshua Saunders	"		at Hospital Oct '77, (last appears on Roll of Oct '77)
"	Isaac Rose	"		appt. 1 June '77, sick at New Hackensack Oct '78
"	John Stafford	"		Corpl. until Jan '78, appt. Corpl. 1 June '77
"	John Chinneth, (Chineth)	"		(first appears on Roll of Jan '78), at Hospital Jan to March 15th '78, at Hospital at Peeks Kill June to July 18th '78
Corpl.	John Howe, (How)	"		(last appears on Roll of July '77)
"	Wm. Andrews	"		appt. 1 July '77, at Hospital June and July '77, with Gen. Scott Sept '78
"	John Ford	"		with Baggage at Chads Ford June 6th '78, sick at New Castle June to July 24th '78
"	James Ferguson	"		Capt. Thos. Bell's Company
"	Arthur Chinneth, (Chineth)	"		(first appears on Roll of Jan '78), at Hospital Jan to 15 March '78, on detach. with Capt. Lynch Apl '78
Fifer	Thos. Lovely	"		promoted to Fife Major 10 Feb '78, reduced from Fife Major 1 July '78
Drummer	John McBride	"		Capt. Richard Davis' Company
Privates	Reuben Ross	"		Hosp. Sept '77 Oct '77
	Thomas Smith	"		
	Samuel Power	"		fur. March '78, at Hosp. Peeks Kill July 18th and Aug '78
	Abraham Watson	"		fur. Jan '78, deserted when on furlough Feb 1st '78
	John Callender	"		
	James Dennison	"		Hosp. Sept '77 to Feb '78
	John Cooper	"		
	John Debruler	"		Hosp. June & July '77

Rank.	Names.	Time.	Date of Enlistment.	Remarks.
Privates	Chas. Baker	3 yrs		fur. March '78, detach. Col. Pope Apl '78
	Henry Rowland	"		fur. March '78, waiter Sept '78, fur. Nov 15th '78–Feb '79
	Wm. Cooper	"		Hosp. June & July '77
	Wm. Cattrill, (Cattrell)	"		
	John Irons	"		Hosp. June and July '77
	Josias Kimble, (Kimbal)	"		Black River Hosp. June & July '77, Hosp. Nov, Dec '78, died Jan 1st '79
	Patk. Quinn	"		sick and present July '78
	John Leviston	"		
	David Knight	"	28 Aug '77	Hosp. Sep & Oct '77, with Baggage Chad's Ford June 6th '78
	Thos. Harris	"	21 Aug '77	missing 11 Sept '77
	John Collins	"	25 Aug '77	Hosp. Jan '78, (last appears on Roll of Jan '78)
	John Cotman	"		(last appears on Roll of July '77)
	John Crockett	"		(last appears on Roll of July '77)
	Wm. McCullough	"		Waggoner, (last appears on Roll of July '77)
	Thos. Dearmott	"		(last appears on Roll of July '77)
	Patrick McCann	"		(last appears on Roll of July '77)
	Jesse Corbett, (Corbit)	"		at Hospital June and July '77, (last appears on Roll of July '77)
	John Wilson	"	20 Mch '78	Brunswick Hosp. July 6th '78–Feb '79
	Wm. Pritchard	"		dead June 18th '77

Capt. Philip Griffith's Company.

Rank.	Names.	Time.	Date of Enlistment.	Remarks.
Privates	Joshua Burton	3 yrs		
	Patk. Lemon	"		on Detachment with General Woodford Apl '78, Waiter Sept '78
	John Carr	"		(last appears on Roll of July '77)
	John Johnston	"		(last appears on Roll of July '77)
	Peter Dyche	"		(last appears on Roll of July '77)
	Joseph O'Neill			joined July '78

Capt. Richd. Davis' Company.

Rank.	Names.	Time.	Date of Enlistment.	Remarks.
Privates	John Bourke	3 yrs		on Detachment with Col. Pope Apl '78, died at Monmouth Plains June 28th '78
	Patk. Kerby, (Kirby)	"		(last appears on Roll of July '77)

during the War of the American Revolution, 1775–83.

Rank.	Names.	Time.	Date of Enlistment.	Remarks.
Privates	Jona. Shepperd, (Shephard)	3 yrs		on furlough June and July '77, (last appears on Roll of July '77)
	John Cochran	"		(first appears on Roll of Jan '78), sick in Quarters Jan '78, on furlough Jan 17th '79
	Henry Dennis	"		(first appears on Roll of Jan '78), on Detachment with Col. Pope Apl '78
	Elijah Cochindall	"		(first appears on Roll of Jan '78), at Hospital Feb to Mch 15th '78
	Wm. Markwell	"		(first appears on Roll of Jan '78), on Detachment with Capt. Lynch Apl '78.

Capt. Thos. Bell's Company.

Rank.	Names.	Time.	Date of Enlistment.	Remarks.
Privates	Adrian Devenport	3 yrs		at Peeks Kill Hospital June to July 18th '78
	Wm. Batten	"		
	Peter Trust	"		wagoner Oct '77, sick in Quarters Feb and Mch '78, absent with leave June 3rd '78, returned to service August '78
	Patk. Collins	"		under guard Sept '77
	John Hopwood	"		joined Mch 15th '78, transferred to Rollins' Regt. Nov 18th '78
	Robt. Parrs	"	Aug 28 '77	deserted Sept 1st '77

May 18th, 1778. Isaac Hind, of Ann Arundel County, a substitute, received by Saml. Godman, Capt. in 4th Md. Regt.

Fifth Regiment.

James Murphy—Queen Anne's County, enlisted in 1777 in the Fifth Maryland Regiment. He lost a leg in the Service.

Sixth Regiment.

Pay Roll of Capt. Andrew Hynes' Company for the extra Month's Pay.

Capt. Andrew Hynes   1st Lieut. John T. Jacobs

Rank.	Names.	Rank.	Names.
Serjt.	John Maxwell	Privates	Daniel Donovan
"	Benj. Wilk		Benj. Moran
Corpl.	John Brown		Patrick McCaleb
"	—liver Linday		John Marshall
"	Stephen Griffey		Abraham Cloward
Fifer	Benj. H. Kirk		James Bryers
Privates	William Welch		Francis King
	William Carlin		William Spyers
	Solomon Rollins		Joseph Kirk
	Jacob Hearse		Robert Marshall
	Richard Morgan		

M.

Pay Roll of Capt. Robert Harris' Company for the extra Month's Pay.

1st Lieut. Benj. Scott   2nd Lieut. Michael Dougherty

Rank.	Names.	Rank.	Names.
Serjt.	Michael Connelly	Privates	Timothy Brannon
Corpl.	Richard Moland		Joseph Woods
"	Stephen Price		Peter Swanton
Fifer	Alex. Stephenson		James Rattican
Privates	Nicholas Delany		Dominick Coyn
	Abraham Hooper		James Kearns
	Michael McCann		Charles Ashman
	James Boyle		Wm. Hawly
	John Reardon		Benj. Taylor
	Patk. O'Mullan		Wm. Anderson, deserted
	Patk. Eagon		

M.

Companies of the 7th Regiment.

Inlistment of Capt. Frederick Deam's Company, 7th Regt.

1776.
Dec. 10th Fredrick Hoperly
           Thomas Preston
           Mathew Turner
           Patrick Hay

1776.
Dec. 11th William Bune
           Jerimiah Thomson
           Godfrey Rodwall
           Habycuck Holden

during the War of the American Revolution, 1775–83.   305

1776.		1777.	
Dec. 14th	Thomas Miller	Jan. 1st	Joseph Miller
	Arther Clark		Jno. Chaterlon, (Chaterton?)
	Alexander Mubary		Jno. Stephens
	Patrick O'Neal		Jno. Tarings
	George Fullum		Wm. Ashwall
	Jno. Noice		Robert Price
15th	Richard Jackson	5th	Jno. Lee
	Richard Noice		Robert Calvert
	James Kelly		Jno. Pumphry
16th	Jessy McCarty		Wm. Dickman
17th	Wm. Moring		Edmund Godfrey
19th	Wm. Wood	7th	Peter Smith
	Daniel McQuire		Neal McCrue
	Jno. Fowler		Wm. Merritt
	James Murphy		Jno. Slyser
	Exicael Solomon	14th	Robt. Stewart
	Dennis Doice	16th	Robert Lawsin
21st	Richard Boone		Wm. Caskin
	Francis Reynolds		Wm. Godfrey
	Moses Barney		Wm. Dennerivay
23rd	Daniel Griffin		Charles Chester
24th	Jno. Duffy		Barney Keener
	Dennis Dougherly, (Dougherty?)	17th	Wm. Newvall
	Stephen Slups		James McFall
25th	Edward Benson	19th	Thos. Simmons
	Cornelius Sullivan		Jno. Jones
	Daniel Larry		Jno. Moran
	Barney McMannis	23rd	David Evans
26th	William Taylor		Jno. Keysey
27th	Jno. Mallimore	28th	Richd. Stepleton
	James Ringfield		Thos. Thomson
	John Hains, (or Hairs)		Danl. Rief
	Jacob Shadley		Jno. Anderson
27th	Thos. Ward	Feb 4th	Bradley Killyham
	John Melony		Joseph Hall
	John McClockling		Richard Viceman
	Michael Murphy		

Muster Rolls of Capt. Jona. Morris' Co. in the 7th Md. Regt. Commanded by Col. John Gunby, Apl 1778–July 1779.

Capt.	Jona. Morris	Commissd. Dec 28th 1777	on furlough 7 Feb '78, on command Oct '78, on furlough 27 Feb '79
1st Lieut.	Thos. Mason	Apl 17th 1777	on furlough 2 May '78, on command Jan '79
2nd "	Benj. Murdoch	July 4th 1777	on furlough 24 Dec '78, (last appears on Roll of Mch '79)

Rank.	Names.	Time.	When Enlisted.	Remarks.
Serjt.	James Collins	3 yrs		sick and absent June '78, absent on leave Feb '79, on command Mch '79, recruiting June & July '79. Light Corps
"	Jona. Tootwiler, (Tutwiller)	"		pris. 22 Aug '77, joined 23 July '78
"	*Andw. Mallen, (Mallon)	"		reduced 7 Oct '78, absent with leave Feb '79. Scout
"	Hugh Doyl	"		Orderly to the sick
"	Benj. Fickle	War	6 April, '78	
Corpl.	Richd. Swine	3 yrs		sick Sept 78–Mar 79, (last appears on Roll of Mch '79)
"	*Patk. Riley,(Reyley)	"		reduced to Priv. 15 July '78, under guard Sept and Oct '78, sick at Newinsor June and July '79
"	John Sewell	"		(first appears on Roll of Sept '78)
"	Peter Casey	"		enlisted as a private, promoted 19 Oct '78, absent 4 Nov '78, in service June '79
"	Jacob Gandy	9 mos	30 June '78	on furlough 17 Jan '79–Aug '79
Drum. & Fife	Philip Fletcher	3 yrs		desert. July 3d, '77, returned to the service 4 June '78
"	*Abraham Stallions	War	20 May '78	enlisted as a private, sick and present Sept '78, transferred 1 Nov '78, (last appears on Roll of Oct '78)
"	Allen Davidson		24 Dec '77	deserted 8 Feb '78
"	James Conoly	3 yrs		sick and absent Apl and May '78, (last appears on Roll of May '78)
"	Abram Bizel, (Bissel)	War	12 Oct '78	enlisted as a private, promoted 1 Nov '78, on furlough 17 Jan '79
Privates	*Richd. Carter	3 yrs		Orderly for the sick Sept '78 and Feb '79, absent without leave Oct '78 and Mch '79, sick at Middle Brook June '79
	Jacob Storm (Storum, Storrum)	"		wagoner Jan '79, absent July '79
	*Wm. Duly	"		Light Corps
	*Danl. Benning	"		sick F. Kills 16 Sept '78, in service Jan '79
	*James Carty	"		
	Thos. Maguire	"		sick at Fish Kills Jan '79, at Hospital Feb and Mch '79

RANK.	NAMES.	TIME.	WHEN ENLISTED.	REMARKS.
Privates	*Neal Peacock	3 yrs		Orderly to the sick Sept and Oct '78, absent with leave Feb '79, returned to the service Mch '79
	*Patk. Lynch	"		
	*Chas. Symkins	"		sick at Fish Kills 16 Sept '78, sick in camp Feb and Mch '79, in service June '79
	Cronomus Acre	"		
	George Carroll	"		Light Corps
	Danl. Bryant, (Bryan)	"		sick Valley Forge June '78, in service Oct '78
	*Ed. Murry	"		absent with leave Feb '79
	*Thos. Cook	"		Commissary's Guard Sept '78, sick and absent Jan '79, sick in quarters Feb '79, sick in camp Mch '79, sick June '79, sick at Pluckimin July '79
	*John Knox, (Nox)	"		prisoner 4 Oct '77, joined 1 May '78, sick at Middle Brooke June '79
	Patrick Mannan, (Manyan)	"		waiter, on furlough June and July '79
	*John Dailey	"		omitted Feb and Mch '78
	*Thos. Maloney	"		absent without leave Oct '78, returned to service Mch '79
	*James Keelan, (Keeland)	"		Light Corps
	*John Grant	"		omitted 20 Feb–1 Apl '78, sick and absent Apl '79, in service Oct '78, Light Troops July '79
	*John Fox	"		Scout, sick at Valley Forge June '78, in service Oct '78, sick in camp Jan '79, sick at Brunswick Feb–June '79
	Patk. Murphy	"		sick and absent May '78, (last appears on Roll of May '78)
	Patk. Mooney	"		absent without leave 25 May '78, returned to service 25 July '79
	John Smith	"		waiter
	*Miles Murphy	"		Scout, Light Corps
	*Wm. Donnalson, (Donoldson)	"		Scout, sick at Fish Kills 16 Sept '78, in Hospital Oct 78, in service July 79
	John Berry	"		sick and absent Apl and May '78, (last appears on Roll of May '78)

Rank.	Names.	Time.	When Enlisted.	Remarks.
Privates	*Daniel Barnett	3 yrs	11 Apl '78	Orderly to Flying Hospital Sept and Oct '78
	*Nichs. Cammel, (Cambell)	"	21	sick at Fish Kills 16 Sept and Oct 78, sick at Albany Jan '79, at Hospital Feb and Mch '79, sick June and July '79
	Wm. Jones	"	20 May '78	sick in Flying Hospital 4 Sept and Oct '78, dead May '79
	Levin Quinley	"	4	sick at Cossels or Kerrels Ferry June '78–Aug '79
	John Hopkins	"	16	sick at Prinstown June '78, sick at Fish Kills 16 Sept '78, in service Oct '78, sick at Brunswick Dec '78, dead 19 Dec '78
	Ephm. Wootters	War	4	sick in Flying Hospital 27 July '78, Oct '78 and Jan '79–Aug '79
	Jas. Thos. Read	3 yrs	19	wagoner, absent Sept and Oct '78, Feb '79–July '79, not heard of July 79
	*Even. Davis, (Davice)	"	18	sick in Flying Hospital 8 Aug '78– Apl '79, on command June '79
	Richd. Clark	"	24 April '78	sick at F. Kills 7 Sept and Oct '78, (last appears on Roll of Mch '79)
	John McNalley	War	2	
	Moses Foster	"	23	absent without leave Oct '78
	Saml. Filson, (Felson)	"	18	
	John Turner	"	8 May '78	sick in Flying Hospital Sept and Oct '78, (last appears on Roll of Oct '78)
	Wm. Hammon	"	11	waiter, sick at Fish Kills 8 Oct '78–Jan '79, in Hospital Feb and Mch '79, dead May '79
	*Peter Shoemaker	3 yrs	17	sick at camp Jan '79, sick at Brunswick Feb '79, in Hospital Mch '79
	Simon Taylor	"	20	deserted 2 June '78
	Wm. Hutton	"	"	sick 22 Aug, Sept and Oct '78, (last appears on Roll of Oct '78)
	George How, (Howe)	"		Light Corps, pris. 22 Aug '77, joined 23 July '78
	*Dennis Brodricks	"		pris. 22 Aug '77, joined 23 July '78

RANK.	NAMES.	TIME.	WHEN ENLISTED.	REMARKS.
Privates	Patk. Ryon, (Ryan)	3 yrs	22 Apl '78	deserted 17 Oct '78
	*Francis Mitchel	"		Apl, May and June '78 omitted, absent without leave Oct '78, returned to service Feb '79, sick at Summersett June '79, sick at Pluckimin July '79
	*James Bryan	"		(first appears on the Roll of Sept '78)
	*Michael Burk	"		sick at Fish Kills 5 Oct '78–Jan '79, in the Hospital Feb and Mch '79, in service July '79
	George Pain, (Peign, Payne)	9 mos	30 June '78	dischd. 30 Mch '79
	*Jacob Hunt	"	"	on furlough 17 Jan '79
	Zadoch Tombleson	"	"	sick in camp Feb '79, dischd. 30 Mch '79
	Wm. Briggs	"	6 June '78	dischd. 30 Mch '79
	Saml. Morris	"	30 June '78	dischd. 28 Feb '79
	Francis Keetley, (Kelley)	"	"	transferred 11 Oct '78
	Joseph Alsop	"	"	dischd. 30 Mch '79
	Fredk. Zacharias	"	"	absent without leave Oct '78, dischd. 30 Mch '79
	*Wm. Fortune, (Fourtune)	3 yrs	"	on furlough 17 Jan '79, returned to service July '79
	*George Brown	"	21 Apl '78	
	James Short	9 mos	30 June '78	on furlough 17 Jan–Aug '79
	Elisha McDonnald	"	"	dischd. 28 Feb '79
	James Johns	"	"	sick in camp Oct '78, in service Jan '79, dischd. 30 Mch 79
	Levin Hays	"	"	sick in camp Feb '79, dischd. 30 Mch '79
	John Hill	"	"	dischd. 30 Mch '79
	John Guise, (Guice)	"	"	" "
	*Patk. Hanagan, (Hennigan)	3 yrs	9 June '78	sick Fish Kills Sept '78, on furlough 17 Jan '79
	John Cypher, (Sypher)	9 mos	30 June '78	dischd. 30 Mch '79
	John Cammell, (Campbell)	"	"	" "
	Wm. Dodson	"	"	sick in Flying Hospital 7 Sept and Oct '78, dischd. 30 Mar '79
	*Fredk. Harty	"	"	sick at F. Kills 16 Sept '78, in service Oct '78, on furlough 17 Jan '79

Rank.	Names.	Time.	When Enlisted.	Remarks.
Privates	George Kinser	9 mos	30 June '78	joined Virginia, (only appears on Roll of Sept '78)
	*Matthew Casaday	3 yrs		(first appears on Roll of Oct '78), on furlough 17 Jan '79
	James Berry	9 mos		(first appears on Roll of Jan '79), dischd. 30 Mch '79
	Edward Fennel, (Finnell)	3 yrs	23 June '78	sick at Chester Jan–Aug '79
	Alex. McGrary			deserted 26 Apl '78

Mustered at Wilmington May 22nd, '78 at Valley Forge June 1st, '78, at White Plains July 26th, '78, at Fish Kills Oct. 4th and Nov. 2nd, '78, at Middle Brook Feb. 2nd, Mch. 3rd and Apl. 3rd, '79, at Smith's Clove July 3rd, '79, and at Buttermilk Falls Aug. 14th, '78.

[Unless otherwise stated the service was from March, '78 to Aug., '79.

A star prefixed to any name indicates re-enlistment for during the war.

Jacob Gandy and James Short re-enlisted for 3 yrs., Gandy re-enlisted Oct. 27th, '78.]

Muster Roll of Capt. Beatty's Co. in the 7th Regt. June to Dec., 1779.

Commissd. 14 Sept., 1778   Wm. Beatty, Capt.   Joined 11 June '79
                             David Lynn, 1st Lt.   Promoted 10 June '79
"   14 Sept., 1778   Gassaway Watkins, Lieut.

Rank.	Names.	Time.	When Enlisted.	Remarks.
Serjt.	Chas. Philpot	3 yrs	4 Dec '76	dischd. 5 Dec '79
"	Robt. Green	"	8 Jan '77	dischd. 4 Jan '80
"	Robt. Yates, (Yeats)	"	8 Jan '77	dischd. 6 Jan '80
Drum.	Josh. Eshome	War		
Corpl.	Thos. Carney	"		on furlough Dec
"	John Denison	"		
"	Joel Baker	3 yrs	19 Dec 76	
Fife.	Abm. Stallions	War		
Privates	John Alsop	3 yrs	4 Sept '77	
	Andw. Ringer	War		on commd.
	Jos. Hutchcraft	"		on furlough Dec

during the War of the American Revolution, 1775–83.   311

RANK.	NAMES.	TIME.	WHEN ENLISTED.	REMARKS.
Privates	John Stricer	3 yrs	2 Dec '76	dischd. 6 Jan, 1780
	Wm. Reed, (Read)	War		sick at Fish Kill
	Absalom Fardo	"		on commd.
	Aquila Smith	3 yrs	2 June '78	
	Saml. Jones	War		
	Saml. Davis	"		on furlough
	Thos. Dorman	"		on commd.
	Michl. McLochlin	"		on guard
	Michl. McDonnold	"		desert. 12 Aug '79, but present in Dec.
	Michl. Fitzjarld, (Fitzgerald)	"		on commd.
	Patt. Scott	"		
	John Olliver	"		
	Robt. Dunken	"		on commd.
	John Davis	"		sick, present
	Darby Crowley	"		on guard
	Nathl. Adams	"		on commd.
	John Dickson, (Dixon)	"		on furlough Dec, on commd.
	Peter Cunningham			on commd.
	John Duffey	"		
	John More, (Moor)	"		
	John Burton	"		sick Camp
	Patt. Hoarn, (Horan)	3 yrs	22 May '77	on furlough
	Sol. Turner	"	12 " '78	on commd.
	George Gardiner	War		on commd.
	Thos. Hays	"		
	Patt. Connelly	3 yrs	2 Apl '77	on guard
	George Kelley	"	14 Mch '77	on commd.
	Richd. Froggat	"	17 " '77	
	Wm. Wedge	"	2 May '78	sick Camp
	Francis Kitely	War		on commd.
	John Ferrel	3 yrs	6 Dec '76	dischd. 6 Jan, 1780
	Edwd. Wright	"	20 Apl '77	on commd.
	Jos. Blaze	War		sick Camp
	John Hulett	"		on commd.
	Jacob Carnant	"		on commd.
	George Devit	"		on commd., on furlough Dec
	Wm. Nick	"		on commd., on furlough Dec
	Nathl. Palmer, (Parmer)	"		on commd.
	Thos. Tanner	"		on commd., Dec sick, present
	Patt. Lynch	3 yrs	22 May '77	on commd.

Rank.	Names.	Time.	When Enlisted.	Remarks.
Privates	John Devorant, (Durrant)	3 yrs	21 Apl '77	on commd., waggoner
	Larry Brannan	War		hospl. 3 June '79
	Patt. Key	"		deserted " " "

Voluntary Enlistments in the 7th Md. Regt. To serve three years.

Names.	When Enlisted.	Names.	When Enlisted.
John Parsons	Feb 15 1780	John Dawson	Feb 29 1780.
Thomas Kelly	" 25 "	Baptiste Désormeaux	" 11 "
James McDonnold	" 13 "	Joseph Ferrol	June 8 "
Joseph Lee	" 21 "	Wm. Leary,(Larrey)	March 12 "
William Lislend	" 29 "	John Boulanger	Feb 11 "

Voluntary Enlistments for 3 years, Dec. 3rd, 1776.

    Darby McNamarra   Terrence Duffey

MARYLAND ACTS, OCT., 1777.

"An ACT for recruiting the quota of troops of this state in the American army, and furnishing them with cloathing and other necessaries.

Whereas an enlistment of volunteers on bounty is the most eligible mode to furnish two thousand men for recruiting our quota of the American army;

Be it enacted, by the General Assembly of Maryland, That the said two thousand men be apportioned amongst the several counties, according to the number of militia in each county . . . . . .

Be it enacted, That every recruit, at the time of his enlistment shall have his choice of the regiment or company in which he will serve, provided such regiment or company be not full, and if full, he may choose any other regiment or company, which shall be entered against his name, and returned to the officer appointed to receive such recruit.

And be it enacted, That the recruits aforesaid shall be carried by the recruiting officers respectively before the lieutenant of the county in which such recruits are raised, to pass muster," . . . . .

A List of Recruits passed by James Brice, Lieut. of Annl. County.

James Clark	Gifford Minitree	Antoine Pomairol
John McLane	Pheltr. Souther	John Cope
Benj. Gray	Nathan Peak	Andrew White
George Leadbourn	George Gordon	Peter Cutong
Francis Thompson	Joseph Ford	John Neary
Germain Poulain	Jean Laravier	Wm. Ferguson

A List of the Men recruited agreeable to an Act of the General Assembly Entitled, "An Act for recruiting the Quota of Troops of this State &ca," who have been passed by James Brice, Lieut. of Annl. County.

NAMES OF RECRUITS.	COUNTRY.	TIME WHEN PASSED.
Adam Henry	Scotland	31st Dec, 1777
Willm. Sutherland	America	8th Jan, 1778
Joseph Fowler	England	12th
Willm. Lund		
Willm. Parsons		
John Havers		
John Franceway	France	
Roger Skiffington	Ireland	
John McAdams	America	
John Galvin	Ireland	17th
Robert Purdell	America	19th
John Coulston	England	
John Hughs		9th Feby
Jonathan Wiltshire	England	10th
John Headwood	Ireland	12th
James Quay	America	14th
Daniel Colbert	Ireland	25th
John Dodson		27th
Lawrence Riley		
Philip Shobrook		
John Eltham		28th
John Baxter		
Richard Brannum		
James Riley		5th March, 1778
Robert Medcalfe	England	7th
William Smith	America	9th
Brian Carroll	do	12th
William Sykes	England	20th
John Williams	do	
Hugh Cain		24th
David Jones		30th

Names of Recruits.	Country.	Time when Passed.
John Steel		
Edward White		
James Millar	England	8th April
William Jennings	do	9th
John Neale	Ireland	11th
Samuel Smith	do	
Thomas Clark	England	
John Wilbey	Ireland	
Henry Nicholson	America	12th
Aquila Pearce	do	
Robert Scriviner	do	
Edward Hanasy	Ireland	22nd May
William Smith		9th
Nathan Smith		
Philip Savory		19th
Silvester Gaither		30th Sept
William Jenkins	France	"
John Stanton		18th Nov
Anthony Nowry		"

Voluntary enlistment of John Grover, Jan. 28th, 1778.

A Return of Recruits for the Continental Army. Passed by Charles Beatty, Esq., Lieut. of Fredk. Co. March 10th, 1778.

When Passed.	Names of the Respective Recruits.	When Passed.	Names of the Respective Recruits.
1778		1778	
Jan 6	Nicholas Karr	*Feb 19	John Holland
* 12	Lambert Thompson	20	John Grantt
* "	Adam Keepheart, (Kephart)	* 21	John Garvis, (Jarvis)
* 21	Daniel Bowman	* 23	Patrick Ofalvey, (Ofarling)
* 28	Thomas Gill	* "	Thomas Richards
	James Houston	"	Nathaniel Adams
* 29	George Holliday	* 24	John Philips
	William Tuten	* 25	Thomas Matthews
*Feb 3	John Magee, (McGee)	"	Darby Crowley
* "	Richard Gray	* "	John Howard
* 11	John Hildrop	27	George Gibhart
* "	Daniel Shahan, (Schean)	"	Cosomer Hill
* 16	Henry Mackey	* "	Levy Smith
17	John Hamilton	28	Rosalius Lett
* 18	James McGraw		James Lett
	John McDonald	Mar 2	Solomon Turner

When Passed.	Names of the Respective Recruits.	When Passed.	Names of the Respective Recruits.
1778		1778	
*Mar 2	William Tallawer, (Tollaver)	*Mar 4	Thomas Bishop
3	Matthew Cox	5	William Atkinson
"	Jacob Alexander	6	Michael McDonald
4	John Barlow	* 10	Thomas Roberts

[Names with a star prefixed are those who were enlisted for the Second Maryland Regiment.]

A List of Recruits passed by the Lieut. of Frederick County as Part of the Quota of said County.

Date.	Names.	Date.	Names.
1778		1778	
Mch 12	Evan Morris	Apl 9	James McCabe
24	Alexander McGarey	10	John Schevel
28	William Wedge	10	Frederick Stein
28	John Smith	14	Edward Connelly
Apl 2	Thomas Mahoney	17	Henry Jones
3	Thomas Carney	18	Samuel Filson
6	Benj. Fickle		

Chas. Beatty, Lieut. of Fredk. Co.

RESOLVES OF CONTINENTAL CONGRESS, 26 FEB., 1778.

"Resolved, That the several states hereafter named be required forthwith to fill up by draughts from their militia, or in any other way that shall be effectual, their respective battalions of continental troops.....

Maryland—8 battalions including the German Regiment."

MARYLAND ACTS, MARCH, 1778.

"An ACT to procure troops for the American army.

Whereas it has been represented by congress as absolutely necessary to use the most vigorous exertions to bring a powerful army into the field the ensuing campaign, and it appearing to this assembly to be the indispensable duty of this state to adopt the most effectual means to attain that end,

Be it therefore enacted, by the General Assembly of Maryland, That two thousand nine hundred and two men be raised, including the two artillery companies already marched to camp, and such volunteers as have been already obtained by recruiting; and that one hundred and sixty men being deducted for the said two artillery companies, the remaining two thousand seven hundred and forty-two men be apportioned among the several counties, according to the number of militia in each county.

Out of which number, so apportioned, each county shall have a deduction for all able bodied men heretofore enlisted in virtue of the act, entitled, An act for recruiting the quota of troops of this state, in the American army, and furnishing them with cloathing and other necessaries.

And be it enacted, That every idle person above eighteen years of age, who is able bodied and hath no fixed habitation, nor family, nor any visible method of getting an honest livelihood, and who may be adjudged by the lieutenant of the county, or any field officer, to come properly under the above description of a vagrant, shall from and after such adjudication, be considered as a soldier enlisted, and have it in his choice, whether he will serve for nine months, or enlist for three years or during the war.

Provided nevertheless, That the governor and council shall have full power and authority, ... to discharge any person adjudged a vagrant, if in their judgement such person does not answer the above description.

And be it enacted, That no British prisoner or deserter, nor any convict, until his original term of service is expired, shall be enlisted or deemed a proper recruit, nor any servant whatever, until emancipated and set at liberty

And be it enacted, That all recruits, in virtue of this or the before recited act, shall be carried before the lieutenant of the county or some field officer in which the recruits are or shall be raised, to pass muster"

DORSET COUNTY, 1778.

John Pennington—a substitute

A List of Substitutes furnished under the Act, entitled, "An Act to procure Troops for the American Army," passed in March Session, 1778. Anne Arundel County.

during the War of the American Revolution, 1775–83.

NAMES OF SUBSTITUTES.	COUNTRY.	WHEN PASSED.	TERM.	TO WHOM DELIVERED.
Daniel Simmons	America	15th Apl, 1778	3 yrs	Col. Stone
William Berry	England	16th	"	"
Jacob Myers	Ireland	16th	"	"
Joseph Cole	England		"	Col. Smith
Thomas Byfield	"	22nd	War	Col. Stone
Richard Roberts		24th	3 yrs	"
Rezin Thackarel	America	27th	War	"
William McCall	England		"	"
Robert Beard	Scotland	28th	3 yrs	John Enwright for Pulaski
Jesse Doltrey	America	11th May	"	Col. Stone
Joseph Smith	"		War	"
John Jenkins	Wales	25th April	"	"
Edward Tame	England	12th May	3 yrs	"
Michael Burn	"	13th	War	"
Edward Elliott	"		"	"
Alexander South	"		"	"
Abram Brissington	Free Negro	18th	3 yrs	"
Benjamin Ritchie	Scotland	18th	War	John Enwright for Pulaski
John Scott		2nd	3 yrs	
Luke Burn		6th	"	
Joseph Smith			"	
Thomas Chapman			"	
Charles Snow			"	
Thomas Weston		16th	"	
John Bannon		4th	War	
John Kahoe			"	Jno. Enwright for Pulaski
John Braithwaite			3 yrs	" "
Thos. Bennington		15th	War	" "
Negro Anthony		30th April	"	
Owen Brannon		3d May	3 yrs	" "
Peter Moore		6th	"	
Joseph Wedon			War	
John Williams		8th	3 yrs	
Wm. Harrington			"	
Joseph Powell			"	
Thos. Neil			"	
Darby Macnamara			War	Col. Stone
Wm. Hampton		9th	3 yrs	
George Richardson			War	Jno. Enwright for Pulaski
Patrick Burke			"	
John Scriviner		20th	3 yrs	
Wm. Robarts			"	
Thos. Robinson		3rd	"	
John Thomas		5th	War	
John Williams			"	

Names of Substitutes.	When Passed.	Term.	To Whom Delivered.
Wm. Stevens		War	
Peter Topping	15th May, 1778	"	
John Johnson	16th	"	
John Williams		"	
Isaac Hind	18th	"	
John Fox	19th	"	
John Parraclift	9th	"	
Wm. Bellison	11th	"	
Robert Patterson	12th	3 yrs	
John Eassen		War	
Edmund Crow	18th	3 yrs	
Samuel Dixon		War	
Gerrard Parker	19th	"	
Joseph Butler	20th	3 yrs	
Stepn. Nicholson	24th April	"	
Daniel Pearce	24th	3 yrs or War	Capt. L. Williams
Benjamin Phelps		"	Lt. James Peale
Benjamin Gravels		"	" "
William Taylor	2nd May	"	" "
Charles Ivory		"	Capt. L. Williams
Obed. Plummer		"	" "
Cupit Plummer		"	" "
Willm. Roberts	4th	"	
John Murphy	10th	"	
James Davidson	16th	"	Lt. James Peale
Francis Burton	19th	"	
Joseph Waldrum	20th April	3 yrs	
Edward Cooper	21st	War	
John Page		"	
Michael Burn	26th	"	
James Tiser		"	
Lawrence Cragon		"	
John Hackett		"	
John Gollicor		"	
Robert Stacey		"	
Thomas Hickey		"	
Christopher Madden		"	
Jacob Hynes	28th	"	Lt. Edward Spurrier
Michael Dace	30th		
John Sullivan	4th May	"	Lt. Edward Spurrier
Dennis Clancey		"	
Thomas Jesap	5th	"	
Cornelius McLaughlin	5th	"	
Thos. McCormack	6th	"	
Jesse Dority		3 yrs	

Names of Substitutes.	When Passed.	Term.	To Whom Delivered.
Abram Catcherside	7th May, 1778	War	
Richd. Maxwell		"	
Joseph Whitehouse		"	
Thomas Bryan		"	
John Wilson	9th	"	
Peter Powell	11th	"	
Joseph Roberts		"	
Joseph McDannell		"	
John Williams	13th	"	Capt. Saml. Griffith
Rolen Bates	14th	"	
Michael Monks		"	
John Young	15th	"	
Arthur Donaghey		"	
Richd. Jenkins	16th	"	
Daniel Leary	18th	"	Ben Todd, (Recruiting
Robert Harpham		"	[Serjt.)
John King		"	Lt. Edward Spurrier
Robert Derling		"	
Simon Cappock		"	
Jarvis Williams		"	
Samuel Rich		"	
Samuel Jones	19th	"	
Thomas Hillum		"	Ben Todd, (Recruiting
William Lee	20th	3 yrs	[Serjt.)
James Thomas		War	John Enwright for Pulaski
Dennis Carroll		"	
James McKenley		"	

A List of Substitutes furnished by the Companys Classed.

Names.	When Passed.	Term.	To Whom Delivered.
Joseph Follitt	30th May '78	3 yrs	Enwt. for Pulaski
William Hall		War	Serjt. Gordon
Joseph Quynn		3 yrs	same
Joseph Jones		do	same
Dorsey Wood		9 mos	same
Israel Strum	2nd June	3 yrs	same
Saml. Fowler		9 mos	same
Lewis Francis		3 yrs	same
Benj. Gundun		do	same
Lewis Luairn		do	same

Names.	When Passed.	Term.	To Whom Delivered.
Jona. Lewis		3 yrs	Serjt. Gordon
Easy Nichols	10th June '78	do	Lt. Clarke
William Joice		9 mos	Serjt. Gordon
David Caghill		3 yrs	same
Benj. Marsh		3 yrs	same
Abram Turner		9 mos	same

Thos. Weems, he expected to go as an offr. wth. the Draughts as there was no drats. he was sent on board one of the Galleys, first having paid the money he rec'd into the treasury.—by Governor and Council.

ANNE ARUNDEL COUNTY RECRUITS AND SUBSTITUTES.

Substitutes Under the Act to Procure Troops for the American Army	117
Recruits. The Act for Recruiting the Quota of Troops of this State	50
Substitutes furnished by the Companys	16
4 Substitutes passed by Col. Dorsey's certifs. not retd.	4

A List of Substitutes Passed by the Lieut. of Frederick County as Part of the Quota of Said County Agreeable to the Late Act of Assembly.

Date When Passed.	Names.	Time of Service.	Regiment.
1778			
April 2	John Day	3 yrs	Col. Thomas Price
13	Nicholas Myss	3 yrs	Ditto
18	John Baldwin	3 yrs	Ditto
18	John McKinney	War	Ditto
18	John Parker	War	Ditto
20	Michael Hardman	3 yrs	German Regt.
21	Henry Fisher	3 yrs	Ditto
21	Nicholas Cammel	3 yrs	Gunby's Regt.
21	George Brown	3 yrs	Ditto
22	John Dalton	3 yrs	German Regt.
22	John Houlden	War	Col. Thos. Price's
22	Patrick Wryon	War	Col. Gunby's
22	William Richey	War	Col. Thos. Price's
22	Thomas Halfpenny	3 yrs	German
22	Johnsey Morgan	3 yrs or War	Price's
23	Moses Foster	War	Gunby's
23	Charles Fulham	War	German
24	Richard Clark	3 yrs	Gunby's
24	Richard Haylip	3 yrs	German
24	John Hamilton	War	Ditto

Date When Passed.	Names.	Time of Service.	Regiment.
1778			
April 24	John Spray	War	Price's
24	John Smatter	3 yrs	German
24	Stephen McGraw	3 yrs	Ditto
25	Joseph Weigle	War	Ditto
25	Drue Reddley	War	Gunby's
25	James Ashley	War	German
25	John Walton	3 yrs	Ditto
25	William Mummert	3 yrs	Ditto
25	William Cartney	War	Price's
27	James Murphy	War	German
27	Henry Oyster	War	Price's
27	Timothy Cahill	War	German
27	John McNaley	War	Gunby's
27	John Hammersly	War	German
27	Richard Keen	3 yrs	Gunby's
27	Thomas Holdup	War	German
28	James Welch	War	Price's
28	Charles Hills	3 yrs	Col. Williams'
28	Moses McKinsey	3 yrs	German
28	Joshua McKinsey	3 yrs	Ditto
28	John Temblin	3 yrs	Ditto
28	William Molnix	War	Ditto
29	Roger Landers	War	Price's
29	James Pack	War	Col. Williams'
29	Steven Stevenson	3 yrs	Gunby's
30	Adam Mushler	3 yrs	German
30	Gabriel Holland	War	Williams'
30	Simon Johnson	War	Gunby's
30	William McCoy	War	Price's
30	Samuel Hottenstein	3 yrs	German
May 1	Wm. Braithwaite	War	Price's
1	John Shively	3 yrs	Williams'
1	Thomas Brown	War	Price's
1	William Philips	3 yrs	Ditto
1	Richard Quin	War	German
2	James Dyer	3 yrs	Ditto
2	Robert McCland	3 yrs	Williams'
2	Thomas Hazlewood	War	German
2	John Malady	War	Ditto
3	Patrick Riley	3 yrs	Williams'
4	James Eddy	War	Price's
4	George Boogher	3 yrs	German
4	William Norris	War	Ditto
5	John Megraw	War	Price's

Date When Passed.	Names.	Time of Service.	Regiment.
1778			
May 5	Thomas Ferrell	War	Price's
5	Patrick Rawen	War	Ditto
5	William Nicks	3 yrs	Gunby's
5	John Wade	War	German
5	Daniel Woriew	War	Williams'
5	John Tuff	War	Ditto
5	Henry Grantham	War	Ditto
5	William Whit	War	German
6	John Twiner	War	Gunby's
6	James Champnis	War	German
6	Andrew Shuler	War	Ditto
7	Robert Barnett	War	Ditto
7	John Stanton	War	Ditto
8	Jona. Cunningham	War	Gunby's
9	Timothy McCarty	War	Price's
10	Jacob Kaufman	3 yrs	German
11	William Hamon	War	Gunby's
11	Daniel Barnett	War	Ditto
11	James Hennisy	War	Price's
11	Henry Holtzman	War	Gunby's
12	Jacob Moser	3 yrs	German
12	Mathias Cosgrove	3 yrs	Ditto
12	Hugh Moore	War	Ditto
13	John Fricker	War	Price's
13	Charles Slone	War	Ditto
13	Thomas Macrell	War	German
14	Lawrence Whalin	War	Gunby's
14	Michael Coughlan	3 yrs	Williams'
14	James Stite	War	German
15	Robert Porter	3 yrs	Ditto
15	Robert Mathews	3 yrs	Williams'
15	James Connoway	3 yrs	German
15	John Drapier	War	Price's
15	Thomas Wolfred	3 yrs	German
16	Richard Gaul	3 yrs	Ditto
16	Thomas Daley	3 yrs	Price's
16	Wm. Ahearn	3 yrs	Williams'
16	Wm. Johnson	3 yrs	German
16	James Burk	3 yrs	Williams'
16	John Jones	3 yrs	Gunby's
17	George Hagerty	War	Price's
17	Adam Madern	War	German
17	George Gardner	3 yrs	Gunby's
17	Peter Shoemaker	3 yrs	Ditto

Date When Passed.	Names.	Time of Service.	Regiment.
1778			
May 18	Joseph Branner	3 yrs	German
18	John Carroll	War	Williams'
18	John Bennett	War	German
19	Thomas Hutchcraft	War	Ditto
19	Samuel Davis	War	Gunby's
19	Patrick Shean	War	Williams'
19	Robert Boyle	War	Ditto
19	Arthur Mulholland	War	Price's
19	Samuel Edwards	3 yrs	Gunby's
19	William Nevin	War	German
19	Andrew Preston	War	Price's
19	Jacob Knight	War	Ditto
19	Mathias Smith	War	German
19	William Forbey	War	Price's
19	Hugh McCoy	War	German
20	Peter Barttomew	War	Ditto
20	Robert Smith	War	Ditto
20	Christian Casner	War	Ditto
20	William Rider	War	Ditto
20	Cornelius Vaughan	War	Ditto
20	John Burns	War	Price's
20	James Smith	War	German
20	John Fannell	War	Ditto
20	Benjamin Cole	War	Ditto
20	Henry Ferrence	War	Ditto
20	William Vincent	3 yrs	Ditto
20	Patrick Trainer	War	Williams'
20	Luke Horsefield	War	Price's
20	William Allender	War	Ditto
20	Patrick Cary	War	Ditto
20	Jonas Chamberlin	War	Ditto
20	James Johnson	War	German
20	Abraham Stallings	War	Gunby's
20	William Pope	War	German
20	John Stout	War	Ditto
20	Joseph Horsefield	War	Price's
20	Michael Smith	War	German
20	John Woler	War	Price's
20	William Prangley	War	Gunby's
20	Alexander Smith	War	German
20	Benjamin Ellott	War	Ditto
20	Charles Jones	War	Ditto
20	John Richards	War	Ditto
20	Samuel Fletcher	War	Ditto

Date When Passed.	Names.	Time of Service.	Regiment.
1778			
May 20	Dennis Waylon	War	Gunby's
Apl 21	Saml. Lintridge	War	
23	D——— —onner	3 yrs	
24	Thomas —rejent	3 yrs	
May 11	Richard Misbett	War	
12	Joseph Harmor	War	
14	Isaac Bellows	War	
19	William Stevens	War	
Apl 29	James Shehon		
23	Benj. Evans	3 yrs	
27	William Chambers	3 yrs	
May 18	Thomas Burk	War	
Apl 20	William Broughton	3 yrs or War	
20	Daniel Vantire	War	
22	John Gibbons	War	
May 12	Henry McManis	War	
15	William Hays	War	
15	John Hall	War	
Apl 21	John Roach		

A List of Substitutes Furnished by the Different Battalions After their being Classed in Order for the Draught. Frederick County.

Date When Passed.	Names.	Time of Service.	Regiment.
1778			
May 29	James Obryan	War	German
June 1	George Loux	9 mo	Col. Williams'
1	Francis Kerns	3 yrs	German
1	Christopher Keplinger	9 mo	Ditto
2	Michael Fullam	9 mo	Williams'
2	Thomas Williams	9 mo	Ditto
2	Christian Mummaw	9 mo	German
2	George Arnold	9 mo	Ditto
2	Philip Hinkle	9 mo	Ditto
2	Thomas Polhouse	9 mo	Ditto
2	George Bontz	9 mo	Ditto
2	Acquila Smith	3 yrs	Gunby's
2	Henry Young	9 mo	Williams'
3	Barnard Ridenour	9 mo	German
3	Abraham Miller, Jr.	9 mo	Ditto

during the War of the American Revolution, 1775-83.   325

Date When Passed.	Names.	Time of Service.	Regiment.
1778			
June 3	Albert Hendrickson	9 mo	German
3	Philip Beattys	9 mo	Ditto
3	Nathan Speake	3 yrs	Williams'
3	William Fortune	9 mo	Gunby's
3	Samuel Morris	9 mo	Ditto
3	Charles McNabb	War	Ditto
3	Jacob Hommer	9 mo	Ditto
4	Jacob Gandy	9 mo	Ditto
4	George Kinser	9 mo	Ditto
4	Frederick Lokerias	9 mo	Ditto
4	William Todd	War	Ditto
5	John Sifer	9 mo	Ditto
6	Reson Hanson	3 yrs	Williams'
6	William Finacy	9 mo	Ditto
6	Daniel Lett	9 mo	Ditto
6	Thomas Rowlands	9 mo	German
6	John Finacy	9 mo	Williams'
6	Philip Fitzpatrick	9 mo	German
6	William Ridge, (Cooper)	9 mo	Gunby's
6	Samuel Jones	3 yrs	Ditto
6	James Dodd	9 mo	Ditto
8	Thomas Swannick	3 yrs	Ditto
8	John Newman	9 mo	Ditto
8	John Cammell	9 mo	Ditto
8	John Sewell	War	Ditto
8	Zadock Tomlinson	9 mo	Ditto
8	Joseph Alsop	9 mo	Ditto
8	John Hill	9 mo	Ditto
8	John ——ise	9 mo	Ditto
5	William Jones	9 mo	Williams'
6	William McNeal	9 mo	Ditto
6	David Boulton	9 mo	Ditto
6	James Heasty	9 mo	Ditto
6	Dudley Lee	9 mo	Ditto
6	Teter Baker	9 mo	Ditto
6	John Bell	9 mo	Ditto
8	Thomas Smith	9 mo	Ditto
8	Paul Marr	9 mo	Ditto
9	William Kennedy	War	Ditto
9	John McDonnagh	9 mo	Ditto
9	Richard Hobson	9 mo	German
May 28	John Kendrick	3 yrs	Ditto
June 9	Martin Gridler	9 mo	Williams'
12	William Mefford	9 mo	Gunby's

Date When Passed.	Names.	Time of Service.	Regiment.
1778			
June 9	Andrew Renhard	9 mo	Williams'
13	Joseph Lougdon	War	Ditto
13	Anthony Durgan	3 yrs	Ditto
13	Wm. Robt. Howe.	9 mo	Ditto
13	Frederick Harty	9 mo	Gunby's
13	George Pain	9 mo	Ditto
13	William Doddson	9 mo	Ditto
13	Jacob Hunt	9 mo	Ditto
13	Benjamin Tarman	9 mo	Williams'
13	James Aires	9 mo	Ditto

A List of the Men's Names Enlisted by the Officers Mentioned, and Passed by me.

Date.	Officers' Names.	Men's Names.	Time of Service.
1778			
May 27	Capt. Montjoy Baily	John Smith	3 yrs
June 9	Capt. Jon. Morriss	Peter Hangin	3 yrs
May 26	Capt. Adam Grosh	James Feilson	3 yrs
26	Lieut. Edwd. Dyer	Patrick Crawley	War
June 15	Capt. Jno. Ghiselin	John Brown	3 yrs
23	Ditto	John Timly	3 yrs
23	Capt. Jona. Morriss	Edwd. Fennell	War
23	Ditto	William Lyons	War
18	Ditto	James Mullings	War
23	Ditto	James McDonald	War

May 10 Thomas Porter taken up as a Vagrant by Serjt. Benj. Fickle, & Delivered to Capt. Jona. Morriss.

May 2 Thomas Bowl taken up as Ditto by Wm. Bently & Jno. Wood who was Enlisted by an Officer in Col. Hartley's Regt. Penna. & taken away.

A List of Deserters taken up and Brought before the Lieutenant of Frederick County who were Committed to the Public Goal of said County.

Date.	Names.	Regiment or Company.
1778		
Apl 19	Jacob Haifley	German Regiment
22	Peter Peterson	Williams' ditto
23	Adam Goodeberger	Capt. Weaver's Co., Penna. Troops
23	Lodowick Mackeman	" Westfield's " Va. "
23	Hugh Riley	6th Md. Regt.
25	William Smith	Col. Rawlings
25	Conrod Michael	Ditto
25	Lawrence Fitzpatrick	Col. Price's
25	John Johnson	6th Maryland Regt.
25	John Langly	Col. Hartley's Penna. Troops
26	John Malone	Col. Thompson's ditto
27	John Charles	" Thuston's Va. do
25	Samuel Barts	Georgia Regt.
25	William McNamara	Baltimore Fort
21	John Braswell	4th North Carolina Regiment
May 7	Robert Sapp	1st Md. Regt.
18	Samuel Brotner	Col. Thuston's Va. Troops
Apl 25	Forrest McCatchen	" Hartley's Penna. do

Chas. Beatty, Lieut. of Fredk. Co.

A List of Draughts and Substitutes under the Command of Capt. Charles Williamson.

DRAUGHTS.

Wm. Dare
James Weems, (of John), now at Camp
Thomas Man

Benj. Askew
John Smith
Benj. Johns, (of Benjamin)

SUBSTITUTES.

Benj. Johns, (of Absolum)
Martin Wells, (of Martin)
Recruit Randall Wright 3 years sent to Camp with Lt. Clark
  do   John Grover ditto with Capt. Truman's Sergt.
        Joseph Shukland 9 months
        John B. Dela'Franey James McKenny
        David Randall James Lawrence
        Richard Calbut Wm. Gardner
        Basil Hellen Thomas Nash
        Francis Games Hugh Ryon
        Richard Everit Wm. Thomas—Vagrant
        Wm. Kirshaw James Charlton
        Daniel Young John King } Deserters
        James Nowell Wm. Scott
        Thomas Blackburn

June 14th, 1778   Benjamin Mackall, Lieut. of Calvert Co.

Prince George's County, June 15th, 1778.

Lt.	George Dyer	a draft	Charles Jenings	a draft
Serjt.	Josiah Gordon	" "	John Wilson	" "
	Chrisr. Beall	a deserter from 2nd Md. Regt.		
	George Inness	a substitute to serve for three years		
	Thos. Beall, son of Thomas	" " " nine months		

Muster Roll of Capt. John Kershner's Compy. Guarding the Prisoners of War. Fort Frederick June 27th, 1778. (1777–1778.)

Capt.	John Kershner	Privates Michael Kernam,	Dischd. 17 May
Lieut.	Jno. McLaughlin	Danl. Kemmer	
"	Peter Backer	Adam Coon,	Dischd. 5 June
Ensign	Wm. Conrod	Jacob Adams	" 6 "
Serjt.	Luke Sholly	Jno. Fiche	
"	Martain Phipher	Goodhert Tressel,	Deserted 2 "
"	David Wolgamot	Christiain Kirgery	
"	George Fanglar	James Flack	
Drum.	John Oster	George May,	" 2 June
& Fife.	Peter Lighter	Chris. Shock,	Dischd. 19 "
Corpl.	Jacob Craver	Jno. Robinson	
"	Jacob Barnt	Jacob Geerhert,	" 5 "
"	Peter Conn	David Fosney	
"	John Conn, Dischd. 21 June	Richd. Menson	
Privates	Michael Harlly	Peter Oster	
	George Stuart	Thos. McCullim	
	George Hudson	Casper Snider	
	Jno. Shriber	Peter Rough	
	Elias Reeter	Mathw. Williams	
	George Carter	Wm. Allin	
	Abraham Bower	Abraham Feeter	
	Martain Harry, (or Narry)	John Augusteen,	Deserted 26 May
	Andrew Miller, Dischd. 8 June	Jacob Rorer,	Dischd. 20 May
	Peter Haflegh	Peter Sybert	
	Fredk. Craft	Michl. Spesser	
	Henry Tyce	Fredk. Deefhem, (or Deefherr)	
	Adam Sydey, Dischd. 8 June	Fredk. Shackler	
	Jacob Binkler	Phillip Criegh,	Dischd. 14 June
	Abraham Troxal, Jr.	David Wirley,	" 5 "
	Jacob Ridenour	Christiain Nockey, (or Hockey)	
	Peter Adams	Jacob Tysher	
	Abraham Leedy		
	Jno. Gable		

J. Kershner, Capt.

Return of Substitutes, Drafts and Vagrants from St. Mary's County. June 10th, 1778.

When Entered.	Name.	Time of Serving.	When Entered.	Name.	Time of Serving.
1778			1778		
Apl 20	Patrick Kelly	3 yrs	May 28	Notley Goldsmith	9 mo
30	Wm. Spalding, son of Jas.	9 mo	25	Stephen French	do
20	Wm. McGee	3 yrs	25	John Stone	do
28	Charles McGee	War	25	Robert Swales	do
24	John Duncaster	9 mo	29	Barnard Pane	do
27	Edmd. Barton Cissell	9 mo	29	Stephen Greenwell	do
26	John Rock	3 yrs	29	John Wheatley	do
30	John Holmes	3 yrs	29	Joseph Stone	do
30	Austin Howard	3 yrs	29	Thomas Jarboe	do
26	Benj. Chesher, run off	War	29	Robert Greenwell	do
May 4	Bennet Cox, vagrant, deserted	9 mo	29	John Senior	do
			29	James Wimseld	do
13	John Bapt. Willingham	9 mo	30	Edward Barton Godart	do
Apl 21	Thos. Green Alvey	3 yrs	25	Geo. Dent	do
24	Justinian Bullock	3 yrs	26	Notley Tippett	do
30	John Blundull	3 yrs	29	Peter Richie	do
May 4	Elias Henry	3 yrs	30	Norman Bouroughs	do
Apl 24	John Bapt. Baley	3 yrs	June 1	Jonathan Woodburn	do
21	Richard Hall	3 yrs	May 29	Edmund Hill	do
28	Travers Alvey	3 yrs	25	Thomas Branson	do
May 2	Joseph Shanks	War	28	Joseph Crook	do
2	Zephaniah Williams	War	28	Benj. Dailey	do
1	James Thomas	3 yrs	13	James Graves	do
Apl 25	Henry Harley	3 yrs	Apl 27	Rudolph French	do
26	George Collings	3 yrs	23	John Fields	do
23	Wm. Holt	3 yrs	26	Leod. McAtee } vagrants or	do
May 5	Edwd. Harley	3 yrs	26	John McAtee } deserters	do
Apl 27	John Farden	3 yrs	May 1	George Spalding	do
29	Jeremiah Scraher	3 yrs	Apl 26	Wm. Rock	3 yrs
22	Thos. Curtis	War	May 14	Justinian Carter	do
28	John Spragu	3 yrs	16	Henry Causey	do
May 13	Athas. Thomson	3 yrs	Apl 20	John Morris	do
Apl 30	John Truman	War	May 14	Henry Gouldsburry	9 mo
May 26	Jeremiah Morgan	9 mo	2	Silvester Wheatley	3 yrs
23	John Turner	do	19	Luke Carter	War
23	John Blair	do	Apl 4	Thos. Biggs	9 mo
23	John Carpentor	do	May 16	Henry Philips	3 yrs
25	Edward Smith	do	14	Ignatius Downs	do
25	Leonard Branson	do	19	John McCalley	9 mo
25	Abednigo Jackson	do	31	Garbiner Lemmon	do
27	Edward McKarteney	do	31	Geo. Shirley	do

22

When Entered.	Name.	Time of Serving.	When Entered.	Name.	Time of Serving.
1778			1778		
May 31	Jeremiah Rhoades	9 mo	May 30	Danl. Friend, a ship carpenter, a draft	9 mo
31	James Coachman	do			do
30	Jessee Chiveral	do	25	Jesse Carter	do
23	David Johns	do	June 1	Jacob McKey	do
29	John Norris	do	1	John Medcalf	do
28	James Foster	do	1	John Barton Drury	do
23	Bennett McLeland	do	May 31	Thos. Mattingley	
22	Nathan Adams	do	31	Philip Mattingley	
22	Jeremiah King	do	31	Stanley Battin	
22	James Dyer	do		Joseph Johnston	do
25	Henry King	do		Joseph Smith	do
25	Thomas Wise	do		John Jones	do
25	Richard Smart	do		James Barnes	do
28	Smith Mahoney	do		Jonathan Riney	do
25	Robert Turtle	do	June 10	Rudolph Barnchouse, (Barnhouse)	do
28	Thomas More	do			
30	James Yates	do	10	Joseph Moore	do
30	Zepheniah Hoskins	do	10	Phineas Hurst	do
30	Joseph Fields	do	10	Michael Fields	3 yrs
23	Leonard Howard	do		James McBride	do
30	Ignatius Clark	do	10	William Spalding, a draft	
30	Charles Clarke	do		Benj. Morgan, a draft	
30	Joseph Reswick	do		Benj. Thomson, a deserter from the Continental Army.	

A List of Recruits, Substitutes and Draughts Furnished in Charles County by Vertue of an Act of Assembly for procuring Troops for the Continental Army, &c., passed 1778. Sept 11th, 1778.

VOLUNTAIR.

Saml. Hanson, of Walter.

RECRUITS.

Thomas Franklin
Henry Dickson

Thomas Salsbury
Benj. Jon. Biggs

SUBSTITUTES FOR 3 YEARS.

William Garvey
Stephin Fresh
Peter Dennis
John Helmsley
Francis Coffer
Simon Perrie
Dennis Pearson
John Morrison

George Ward
John Martindale
Martin Doyal
Perry Patterson
Henry Russell
William Poland
Samuel Owings
Charles Scott

Charles Robertson
George Ennes
Leonard Gates
Thos. G. Hinds
Charles Clements
William Glasgoe
Leonard Bean
Isaac Lyon

Substitutes During the War.

John Perrie	Abraham Garceny	John Hardin
Dennis Cragain	John Hinds	

Substitutes for 9 Months.

Richard E. Gattin	Bennit Mudd	Adam Adams
Randolph Hoskins	Benjamin Green	Jeremiah Parsons
Hezekiah Patterson	William Lovless	Robert Coley
John Penn	Stephin Penn	Benjamin Tasker
William Higoon		

Furnished by Classes for 9 Months.

Emanuel Goomes	John Taylor	Samuel Green
Walter Procter	Isaac Rollings	Jesse Woodward
John Williams	John B. Mills	William Griffin
Michael Lawson	Joseph Owings	Joseph Bradshaw
Jacob Miller	Matthew Johnson	John Carroll
Thomas Mahew	Samuel Chinge	John Carroll, Jr.
Benjamin Pryor	Richard May	William Coombes
Elias Lovless	Levine Smith	Richard Mudd
Josias Smith	Joseph Drurey	William Gates
Hewit Johnson	Thomas Dutton	Ebinezer Athey
Francis Hicky	Philip Briscoe	Robert Tharlkill
James Murrey	George Bateman	John Wedding
William Killow	Henry Fouler	Joseph Philbert
John G. Gardiner	James Devin	James Coley
Acton Robey	Bennet Posey	Joseph Coley
Matthew Smith	Charles Procter	Basil Wheeler
Jonathan White	George Walker	Richard Thompson
James Hunt	Samuel Thompson	John Hughes
Benjamin Rollings	Thomas Hudson	Bennit Sanders
Raphael Hagan	Jesse Allin	

Draughted and Joined the Army.

Leonard Martin	Francis Posey	William Warrin
Enious Davice	Benj. Wright, (Fined by	Thomas Ward
Silvester Gatten	Court Martial)	John Adams
William Delozior	John Butler	George Welch
Lancelot Ward		

Draughts Who Have Not Joined the Army.

George Higgs	Ignatius Baggott	Matthew Kidwell
Edward Flurry	Philip Morland	Richard Carroll

Frans. Ware, Lieut. of Chas. Co.

MUSTER AND PAY ROLLS FOR 1780.

MARYLAND ACTS—NOV., 1779.

"An ACT for recruiting the quota of troops of this state in the American army.

Whereas an enlistment of volunteers on bounty is the most eligible mode to furnish fourteen hundred men for recruiting our quota of the American army;

Be it enacted, by the General Assembly of Maryland, That the said fourteen hundred men be apportioned amongst the several counties according to the number of militia in each county.

And be it enacted, That every recruit, at the time of his enlistment, shall have his choice of the regiment or company in which he will serve, provided such regiment or company be not full, and if full, he may chuse any other regiment or company not being full, which shall be entered against his name.

And be it enacted, That the recruits aforesaid shall be carried by the recruiting officers respectively before the lieutenant, or any field officer, of the county in which such recruits are raised, to pass muster."

Bladensburgh, February 22nd, 1780.

Sir:

Inclos'd you have certificates for Eleven men authenticated by Mr. Christopher Lowndes. The men comes under the command of Serjeant Mantle who makes the number mentioned. I have three or four others who, not being certify'd, is obliged to remain behind. If your Excellency thinks proper Serjeant Mantle & Wm. Harriss will return, as their presence with me is very essential. No doubt your Excellency will think proper to cloth the recruits immediatly, it being a part of their Bounty.

I have the Honor to be
Your Excellency's
Most Obedient
Humble Serviant
Wm. D. Beall.

N. B. The Serjeant brings 14 Men 1 of which is not Certify'd owing to the freshes. W. D. B.

To His Excellency
   Thomas Sim Lee, Esq.

A Return of Recruits Passed by Joshua Beall, Lieut. P. G. Cty.

WHEN PASSED.	NAMES.	WHERE BORN.	AGE.	TIME OF SERVICE.
1780				
Feb. 14th	John Dacorne	France	28	3 yrs or during War
"	John Dupre	"	36	" " "
March 15th	John Ballard	Mty. Co.	18	"
"	Saml. Gold	"	16	"

Passed by Col. John Addison.

John Hughes   during War

Passed by Col. Barton Lucas.

Jan. 7th	Richd. Harris			
27th	William Harris			3 yrs or during War

Passed by Lt. Col. Abraham Boyd

Feb. 19th	Joseph Sabolle			3 yrs or during War
"	John Armstrong, Jr.			" " "
"	Henry Purdy			" " "
"	Edward Purdy			" " "
Jan. 31st	John Mantle			
"	John Armstrong, Sr.			
Feb. 12th	John Martin, Jr.			" " "
"	John Purdy, son of Henry			" " "

Men enrolled in Charles County by Capt. Joseph Marbury and Lieut. Samuel Hamelton. Capt. Marbury's Company, 3rd Md. Regt. 1780.

Peter Sanquehart	John Hughs	Joseph Thompson
Michael Lavigne	Jesse Semms, (Simmes)	William Swann
Julius Mercer	Willm. Gates	Benj. Steuart
James Armstrong	Wm. Robertson Franklin	*James Steuart
John Scott	John Boucher Haislope	*John Richards
Francis Dunington	Thomas Thompson	*William Fuller
Wm. Hamelton	William Conner	*James Langly
Frederick Hall	John Bapt. Mills	*Samuel Clarben

[Names prefixed by a star are those who were enlisted by Lt. Hamelton.]

Baltimore, March 2nd, 1780.

Men recruited by Samuel Chester and delivered to Capt. Samuel Farmer of the 3rd Md. Regt.

James Douglass	John Smith	James O'Bryan
James Cromer	Thomas Cardof, (Cardiff)	John Buckley
Thomas Hoopper, (Hooper)	James Grant	Zachria Clark
Adam Sheets	James Ryan	Richard Walls
Barney McCarren	Lucas Ives	James Hilton } Deserted.
James Dunavan	Robert Gatting, (Gathing)	James Penman
	George Sawyer	

Samuel Chester's Recruits. Passed by Thos. Sollers.

James Steel	George Watson	William Bolton
Samuel True	James Robinson	Patrick Moran

Men Inlisted in Fredk. Town for the 7th Md. Regt. from Jan. until April, 1780.

Henry Jones	deserted	George Hiland	gone to Camp
John Cockran	now in Fredk.	Hugh Kelley	ditto
John Parsons	ditto	Stephen Flaherty	ditto
John Aghern	deserted	Thos. Brown	ditto
Wm. Cocks	now in Fredk.	Michl. Pinn	ditto
Baptiste Desormaux	deserted	Francis Black	ditto
Alex. Sterling	gone to Camp	John Ross	ditto
John Newland	ditto	John Williams	in Fredk.
Michael Ceary	ditto	Joseph Kelsey	gone to Camp
James Burns	ditto	Wm. Leary	ditto
James McDonnold	in Fredk.	John Boulonger	deserted
John Dawson	ditto	Francis Williams	ditto
Abijah Buxton	gone to Camp	Thos. Corter	deserted & in Balto. goal
Henry Ostwabt	ditto	John Smith	deserted
James Allen	in Fredk.	Wm. Chamberlain	ditto
John Reiley	gone to Camp	Wm. Mais	in Fredk.
George Cowland	ditto	James Clements	deserted
Thos. Burns	ditto	James Brooks	ditto
James Chandler	ditto	John Brooks	in Fredk.
Joseph Lee	ditto	Saml. Wedge	gone to Camp
Thos. Kelley	ditto	Joseph Murphy	{ in McCullum's place, gone to Camp
Wm. Leseland	ditto		
Wm. Kenney	ditto		
Simon Colibert	ditto	John Williams	
Nicholas Hutchinson	in Fredk.	Jessey Barnet	
James Kelley	gone to Camp	Peter Outhouse	
John Mick	ditto	John Riggs	
David McCulloch	ditto	John Murphy	
Owen Ceary	ditto		

List of Recruits enlisted for during the war and Deserters enlisted for during the war from Kent Co., Apl. 6th, 1780.

RECRUITS.

		ENLISTED BY ENSIGN SEARS.			
Ezekiel Clifton	John Riley	Peter Ward	Mch 20, '80		War
Wm. Simmons	Thos. Sappington	Richard Mitchel	"	"	"	"
Robert Streights	Philip Hustons	Richard Ballard	" 23,	"	3 yrs
Wm. Jones	John Mackay				
Jas. Richardson	Nathan Harper	DESERTERS.			
Benj. Gilbert	Solomon Askins	David Welch	not joined '82		
John Frawney	Wm. Smyth	Mark Bailey			
Robt. Redgrave	Emanuel Berry	Saml. Druley	"	'	"
Saml. Wilson	Nathan Teat	Henry Roberts			
James Clifton	Chas. Delany				
Thos. Johnson	Joseph Savory				
John McCay	Joseph Donohoo				
	Patk. Reding				

Sergeant John Lindiff's Recruits. Passed by Thos. Sollers. (April 11th, 1780)

Charles Thompson	Pharo Flinn	Daniel Lacey
Matthias Kees	Francis Anthony Stooncloser	Thomas Jones
Patrick Murphey	Matthias Spillard	James Simson
William Snow	Philip James	

Men passed by Thos. Rutter, Baltimore County. (April 11th, 1780)

James Carman	Robert Tayler	Dennis Heiggens
Barney McCarnan	James Killey	James McLaughlin
James Donovan	Daniel Holland	James Welsh
John Handley	William Ray	William Hall
James Waldon	Thos. Colen	Thos. Roynorld
Willm. Doughlas	John Hughs	Richard Waller
John Larance	John Smith	Joshua Rogers
James Bayliss (?)	James Duglas	George Duvaull (?)
Thos. Harrison	John Barkley	John Trustee
John Fuller	Andrew Marwood	Michel Noles
Thomas Ryon	William Joyce	James Croford
Richard Goffer	Robert Hutson	James Brannan
Barnett Francher (?)	James Wood	Thos. Gore
James O'Brian		

2 men passed for William Towson and lost their names.

A List of Recruits and Deserters Passed by Thomas Sprigg, Lieut. of Washington County, April 22nd, 1780.

Felix Snider	Daniel Cline	Josep Clay
Henry Shepherd	Thomas McDaniel	John Kennear
Charles Girdler	William Allin	Thos. Williamson
Saml. Richardson	Anthony Byrne	John Patterson
Volintine Claper	William Simson	Jno. Casper Merser
James M'Clain	John Sickley	Allener Ratherford
Jacob Gregory	Martin Smith	Patrick Mellan
Jno. Row	Gedeon Walker	James Waddle
Jno. Hood	Henry Ross	James Harvey
Richard Allsy	James Draden	Jno. Hackett
Thomas Gillham	John Snider	Richd. Brockle
James Acklin	Balser Borett	George Flack
Joseph Smith	Jno. Smith	Fredk. Snyder
Paul Lappin	Henry Shaw	Balser Fox
Martin Smith	Wm. McFaron	Reuben Tedre
John Chambers	Thomas Evans	Fredk. Ream
John Brown	Wm. McDonald	Michl. Gambler
John Kenny	John Tyler	Jeremiah Shehan
John Farrol	Timothy Troy	Indian George
Saml. Guilman	James Neale	James Paupin
Patrick Collins	Charles McKensley	

MARYLAND ACTS—JUNE, 1780.

"An ACT to procure recruits to complete the battalions of this state in the service of the United States, and to raise an additional regiment, if necessary.

Whereas it has been represented by congress, and by letters from general Washington and the committee of co-operation, that it is absolutely necessary to bring a powerful army into the field this campaign; and it appearing to this general assembly their indispensable duty to make the most vigorous exertions to recruit the quota of troops of this state :

Be it therefore enacted, by the General Assembly of Maryland, That fourteen hundred men be forthwith raised, and that the same be apportioned among the several counties. . . . Out of which number, so apportioned, each county shall have a deduction for all able bodied men heretofore enlisted in virtue of the act passed at November session, seventeen hundred and seventy-nine, entitled, An act for recruiting the quota of troops of this state in the American army.

And be it enacted, That the lieutenant of the county, and the several field officers, together with the commissioners of the tax in each county, are hereby required, to meet . . . on the fifteenth day of July next, to class all the property last assessed in their respective counties into as many equal classes as there may be men wanted for such county, and each class shall, within ten days thereafter, find an able bodied recruit to serve during the war, or take up a deserter enlisted to serve during the war.

And be it enacted, That all recruits, raised in virtue of this act, shall be carried before the lieutenant of the county, or some field officer in which the recruits are or shall be raised, to pass muster.

And, Whereas this assembly has proposed to the commander in chief to raise a regiment of five hundred and thirty one men, to join the army in lieu of the militia required from this state:

Be it enacted, That the governor and council shall have full power and authority, upon notice that the commander in chief accepts the proposal, to order the following proportions of the said number of five hundred and thirty one men, to be raised by the several counties (in addition to the number by the first part of this act apportioned) . . . . . and the governor and council shall appoint such officers as they may think proper and necessary to command such regiment, and the first five hundred and thirty one men which are raised shall be incorporated into a regiment and forthwith sent forward to join the army under the commander in chief."

"An ACT to expedite the raising an additional battalion of regulars.

Whereas his excellency general Washington and the committee of co-operation have thought proper to accept the proposal made by the legislature of this state, to raise an additional battalion of regulars in lieu of the two thousand two hundred and five militia, at first requested to be furnished by this state, provided the same be raised so as to reach the place of rendezvous by the last of July, and it is thereupon become necessary to expedite the raising the said battalion:

Be it enacted, by the General Assembly of Maryland, That the lieutenants and field officers of the respective counties, shall immediately on receipt of this act, and of the acts of assembly passed this session, entitled, An act to procure recruits to complete the battalions of this state in the service of the United States, and to raise an additional regiment, if necessary, and the supplement thereto, at furthest, on or before the fifteenth day of this instant July, proceed to class all property in their respective counties, agreeable to the directions of said acts, into as many classes as there are men wanted to complete said battalion or regiment, and shall forthwith give notice to each class; and if recruits be not procured or deserters taken up within eight days after such class hath notice, shall proceed to order out the militia, agreeable to the directions of this act, and the recruits obtained or the deserters taken up shall forthwith be sent forward to the head of Elk, or other place of rendezvous, and put under the care of proper officers to be appointed by the governor and council, who are to march them with all expedition to head quarters, or such other place of rendezvous as may be directed by the commander in chief."

John Clare, Jr., enlisted July 12th, 1780, by virtue of an "Act to procure Recruits to complete the Battalions &c."

A Roll of the Men Furnished by the Classes of Prince George's County for filling up the Old Regiments, 1780.

Substitutes' Names.	Age.	Where Born.	Substitutes' Names.	Age.	Where Born.
George Stephins	35	England	Banks Webb	16	Native
Walter Watson	19	Native	Roger Mulloy	22	England
Henry Conley	21	do	Dinnis Tramel	17	Native
Wilkerson Greegsby	20	do	Andrew McGinnis	21	Ireland
William Jones	16	do	John Auber	35	England
James Wilson	20	Scotland	Jonn. Chubb	18	Native
Robert Avery	28	England	Jessey Cole	18	do
Isaac Berry	19	do	John Spencer	40	Scotland
John Moore	20	do	George Ryan	19	England
John Rumbald	18	Native	Thos. Walls	35	Native
Thos. Pingston	31	England	John Gregory	29	England
John Deacon	21	do			

Recruit's Name.	Age.	Where Born.	Recruit's Name.	Age.	Where Born.
George Campbell	36	Ireland	Joseph Kellee	20	Native

during the War of the American Revolution, 1775-83.   339

Sir:

The above is a Roll of the men furnished by the Classes for filling up the Old Regiments, together with Two men I recruited, for which I was obliged to pay three thousand pounds each. As some of those classes neglected furnishing Substitutes, I had employed men to recruit, but finding that the extraordinary pay I was oblige to advance to them, and the exorbitant Bounty I should be oblige to give for recruits, (especially after the Virginians began to give such extravagant Bounties for men to serve only 18 Months), would far exceed the 15 pr. Ct., I therefore thought it most prudent to desist from employing persons to recruit, till I received your farther orders on that head. When, on receiving your letter relative to the peoples bringing in Wheat at Sixty Dollars pr. Bushell in Lieu of the Substitutes or money I advertised them thereof, and allowed them four weeks for so doing. The time is now expired, and neither wheat nor money brought in. I am therefore now about issuing warrants to the Sheriff for distressing all those who have not complied with the Law, or your orders respecting the grain.

I am Sir,
Your Most Obedient Servt, Jos. Beall.
Lt. P. G's. Cty.

His Excy. Thos. Sim Lee.

Dorchester County Recruits and Deserters.   July 25th, 1780.

RECRUITS FROM DORCHESTER COUNTY AS THEIR QUOTA OF THE REGIMENT EXTRAORDINARY TO BE RAISED BY THE STATE.

Pope Connon	Ephraim Game	Barton Edwards
Henry Flannagan	Alex. Hughs	Jesse Forough
James Murray	Joseph Button	John Mills, Jr.
John Hobb	Constantine Wright	Benton Harriss
George Still	Owen Day	Levin Culver
John Dunn	Isaac Henderson	Richard Bounds
Robinson Ross	James Lord	

DESERTERS FROM THE CONTINENTAL ARMY ENLISTED TO SERVE DURING THE WAR.

Thomas Thompson	not joined '82	James Dulany	not joined '82
William Noble	do	James Ruark	joined
Isaac Scott	do	Stephen Culver	not joined

340 *Records of Maryland Troops in the Continental Service*

RECRUITS ENROLLED AND PASSED IN CONSEQUENCE OF AN ACT OF ASSEMBLY PASSED NOV. SESSION, 1779.

Patrick Bryan
Thomas Wyatts, (Waytts)
James Harris } These sent forward to the Army some time past
Levin Button } by Capt. W. Woolford, Lt. 2nd Md. Regt.
William Willen
David Robson, (Robinson)

John Carter } Deserters sent with Capt. Woolford to appear be-
Henry Causey } fore the Governor and Council to determine whether
Daniel Oliver } they are to continue in the Army or be discharged.
Laban Bramble
Gabriel Sales   for three years.

Henry Hooper, Lt. Dr. Co.

Recruits and Deserters from Balto. County. Furnished under the Acts to procure Recruits &c. and for raising an Additional &c.

James McGill	Patk. Connelly	Joseph Ablewhite
Edwd. Hawkins	James Bickham	John Fallen
Jas. Breaman	Thos. Higgenbotham	Patrick Kelley
John Pratten	John Jones	John Casey
Emanuel Farrara	John Hedgely	John Bennitt
Peter Walkletts	Anthony Flan	John Kildray
John Bolton	George Lynton	Bartholony McDono
Edwd. Dews	George Vernon	James Brown
Chas. Bolchlob	Thos. Murphey	Giles Powell
Wm. Mason	Jeremiah Sullivan	Peter McGuire
John Adams	Anthony Jackson	James Adams
Marane Ore	Thos. Eckister	John Hartford
Isaac English	Thos. Arthus	Wm. Wheeler
John McKinney	Thos. Theston	Chas. Burchfield
John Fre-Ladner	George Orridge	Richd. Biddle
John Ryan	Wm. Watkins	Samuel Gray
John Anderson	Lazarus Higgs	Michl. Doren
Wm. Collis	Christr. Shubut	Thos. Smith
Edwd. Evans	Wm. Aggis	Wm. Hamilton
Francis Barbett	John Higgins	Wm. Murphey
David Brian	Jas. Robinson	Wm. Tolbott
Peter Jones	John West	Thos. Smith
Simon Mackanary	Thos. Hall	James Walter Honee
Daniel King	John Brown	Andrew Russell
Samuel Chappel	Chas. Hales	Thos. Fisher
John Hamilton	Chas. Byrne	Alex. Hamilton
Wm. Smith	Thos. Nuth	George Dawe
John Blackburn	Henry Crook	Wm. Worthington
John Johnson		

during the War of the American Revolution, 1775–83.

Wm. Snow	a deserter from the 4th Regt.
Josh. Nichols	" " " "
Lewis Martin	" " " Balt. Matrosses
Wm. Johnson	" " " 2nd Md. Regt.
John OBryan	" " " 12th Va. "
John Philips	" " " Balt. Matrosses
John Perry	"

A List of Recruits raised in Montgomery County to make good her quota in the Continental Army.

Recruited by Capt. Lloyd Beall.

Richd. Taylor	Thompson Murray	Peter McGuire	Andrew McMahone
Edwd. Clancey	Dennis Ternen	Igns. Crumpton	Henry Hughes
John Loveden	John Worsley	Wm. Quintum	Henry Hill
Wm. Hurley	James Amley	Richd. Downes	Wm. Lewden
Cornels. Morris	John Davis	Phil. Sullivain	Wm. Caton.

Passed by Col. Orme.

James Moland	Alex. West	Wm. Westlick	Stephen Carr
John West	Wm. Glover	John Crague	Joseph Ferrill

Recruited by Robt. Green.

John Nabers	Willm. Hempstone	Leonard Hagan

Recruited by David Green.

Walter Hagan	Joseph Mattanly	George Devonshire

Recruited by William Jenkins.

Horatio Roberts

Recruited by Capt. Basil Roberts.

Richd. Bond	John Walten	Michael Coale	John Tucker

Recruited by Capt. Beall.

Charles Brooke	John Toplin	Daniel Devine
Joseph Sucksberry	James Curren	John Blair

Recruited by Capt. Gaither.

Umphrey Carpenter	Thomas Jordan	Francis Whitekar

Passed by Major Owen.

Joseph Law	James Blower	John Ballett	Thomas ———
Wm. Mitchell	James Campbell	James Doncaster	Christopher Onerah

1st 30 for the Extra Regmt.

1 Thomas Pendor	19 Thomas McBride	Partrick Riley
2 James Bigwood	William Quinton,	John Butcher
3 George Clarke	a deserter	John Robins
4 John Higgins	21 Thomas Maddin	Robert Ferrell
5 John Pickering	22 John Buller	John Jones
6 William Stewart	23 Partrick Smith	Elijah Clarke
7 Daniel Bulger	24 Richard Downes	John Freeman
8 John McGuire	25 John Smith	Anthony Wedge
9 Edward Daw	26 Partrick Cavenough	William Groves
10 William Cox	27 Thomas Shears	Thomas Elliss
11 John Maginnis	28 John Ahair	Thomas Matthews
12 James Barrow	29 Thomas Pennifield	Stephen Fennell
13 Joseph Floyd	30 Richard Kisby	John Tucker, a deserter
14 John Harvey	20 John McCoune, in Place	Thomas Burch
15 Jesse McCarty	of Wm. Quinton	Charles Reynolds
16 Henry Crane	Richd. Whiley	Timothy McLamar
17 William Curtin	James North, dead	John Clayton
18 John Whealand		

A List of Recruits and Deserters procured by the Lieut. & Field Officers of Queen Ann's County for the Regiment Extraordinary raised by the State of Maryland, July, 1780. Nov. 4th, 1780.

Thomas Yewell	John West Tate	John West
George Duncan	Benjamin Lee	Joseph Paggat
Edward Legg	Richard Gemmeson	James Baver
Charles White	Edward Vickers	Lambert Phillips
Job Sylvester	Elijah Barn	John Hickins
Robert Legg	John Oliver	Richard Murphy
Thomas Gadd	William Carter	Timothy Connor
William Aller	John Moore	Edward Dominie
Daniel Dulany		

Thomas Fox, deserted before he joined the Regt.
David Willon ⎫ deserters taken up enlisted for 3 years but enlisted ⎧ Joined
Thomas Trew ⎭ during the war ⎩ not " 1782
Joseph Crouch, deserter enlisted during the War   do
James Chittendon, deserter taken up and deserted again   do
William Terrett ⎫ deserters enlisted during the War ⎧ Joined
Benj. Loftsman ⎭ ⎩ do
Valentine Saint Tee, deserted before he joined the Regt.

William Hemsley,
Lieut. of Queen Ann's County.

A Return of Recruits enlisted in Harford County. 1780

Date of Enlistment.	Names of Recruits.	In what Regt. Enlisted.	The Term of Enlistment.
	John McDonal	1st Md. Regt.	3 years
	Aaron Winfrey		3 years
July 17	Moses Williams	New Regt.	during the War
"	Thomas Blunder	" "	"
"	Christopher Seemer	" "	"
"	William Chapman	" "	"
24	William Wilson, (deserted since Enlistment)	" "	"
16	Edward Freeman	" "	"
13	James Scott	" "	"
"	Edward Burgess	1st Md. Regt.	"
17	Dennis Downs	New Regt.	"
25	Joseph McNamarra	" "	"
28	William Lytle	" "	"
"	Nathanl. Sullavin	" "	"
31	Andrew McCune	" "	"
29	James Jordon	" "	"
25	James McDonal	" "	"
31	John Lewin	" "	"
Aug. 1	James Sullavin	" "	"
"	Wm. Bowden	" "	"
"	James Phillips	" "	"
3	Daniel Darby	" "	3 years
28	John Park, (broke Goal and made his escape)	" "	during the War
	Thomas Beaver	" "	
	John Garreguies	8th Md. Regt.	during the War
	William Gloury	James Fitz Gerrald	
	Francis McClane	Thomas Smith	
	John Butler	John Cooley	
	Peter Scott	James Jackson	
	Michl. Daugherty	William Lowry	
	James O'Brian	Thomas Duff	

A Return of Deserters taken up in Harford County.

Deserters' Names.	Regt. Deserted from.	Term of Enlistment.
George Kelley	Cicil County	during the War.
James Neagle	6th Regt.	ditto
Adam Smith	Virginia Troops	ditto
Robert Hair	3d Md. Regt.	ditto

Deserters' Names.	Regt. Deserted From.	Term of Enlistment.
John Park	New Regt.	during the War.
Thos Hanan, (1st Desertion)	1st Md. Regt.	ditto
John Roberts	Capt. Chesney's Co., 7th Md.	ditto
Thomas Aval	Delaware Regt.	ditto
Solomon Watson	ditto	ditto
Thomas Bryan	ditto	ditto
John Connally, (Conoly)	the Artillery	
Thomas Knight	Pennsylvania Troops	
Samuel Wetheral	1st Md. Regt.	
Daniel King	Balto. Co.	
Thomas Night	3rd Md. Regt.	ditto
John Lynch	ditto	ditto
Roger Cord	4th ditto	
Edward Hawkins	New Regt.	
William Lock	1st Md. Regt.	
James Wilson	Congress Regt.	
John Sampson	Thos. Connoway	James O'Bryan, (2nd desertion)
Thomas Simmons	James Kirk	
David Grant	James Harris	John King
John Ofield	Wm. Wathington	John Cooney
Thos. Renalds	Thos. Hanan, (2nd desertion)	William Wilson
Thos. Archer	Edwd. Freeman	Peter Hammer
Thomas Jones	Thos. Hanan, (3rd desertion)	John White
Nathaniel Bass	James Fitz Gerrald, (1st desertion)	John Lampert
Jas. O'Bryan, (1st desertion)		James White

Aug. 4th, 1780.   Richd. Dallam, Lt. Harford County.

A List of Men from Frederick. Return of Men sent to Annapolis by Capt. William Beatty. Delivered by Col. Baker Johnson 28th Aug., 1780.

Date of Enlistment.	Men's Names.		Date of Enlistment.	Men's Names.	
July 18	Adam Shate	⎫	Aug 1	Edward Rylet	⎫
25	Philip Fisher	⎪	7	Henry Lancaster	⎪ Not marched
Aug 5	John Babbs, (followed the 1st Troops)	⎬ Marched.	14	Barnaby Kelly	⎬ for want of their pay.
			15	John White	⎪
			21	Edward Smith	⎭
8	William Elkins	⎪	July 25	Morris McMahon	⎫
10	John Wells	⎪	27	Walter Burk	⎬ Deserted.
16	Jacob Blyth	⎪	Aug 6	George Kinsey	⎪
21	John Saunders	⎭	9	Rowland Baker	⎭

during the War of the American Revolution, 1775-83.

A LIST OF RECRUITS NAMES WHOSE INLISTMENTS OR DATES THEREOF I NEVER OBTAIN'D.

James McLean	John Jackson	John Mills
John Patterson	Dudley Lee	Alliner Rutherford
Anthony Weaver	George Jennings	Cornelius Bulger
John Wooden	John Dayley	James Lee

W. Beatty, Lt. Fredk. Co.

A List of Deserters taken up in Frederick County, October 9th, 1780.

John McDaniel	Deserted from Annapolis, belonging to one of the old Regiments.
John Walton	Deserted from Annapolis, belonging to the ————
Thomas Ellis	Deserted from the New Regt. at Chester, past from Montg. Co.
William Simpson	Deserted from Annapolis, sent from Washington.
Thomas Hand	Known by several to belong to the Maryland Line and When first Taken Acknowledged it, but now Denies and Refuses to tell to what Regiment he belongs.
William Hays	Acknowledges he is a Deserter, it is known that he Enlisted in Baltimore County, when first Taken said he Marched with the Militia from Baltimore, then said he belonged to the Virginia Line and now says he belongs to the Pennsylvania Line.

List of Recruits and Deserters in Cecil Co. Oct. 16th, 1780.

RECRUITS SENT TO CHESTER TOWN.

John Banbury	Wm. Sterling	John Toole
John Hurley	Saml. Hamilton	David Garner
James Thomas	Peter Munford	Wm. Mahoney
James Hayes	Thomas Baker	Wm. Walker
John Toulson	Benj. Mayberry	Wm. Jefferson
Chas. Shirkey	Patk. McDonald	James Crozier
Joseph Neighbours	Amos Davis	John Shirley
Wm. Smith	Peter Carberry	James Needs, a recruit
George Plumley	James Brown	John Robinson, "
John Young	James Maffitt	Richard Gillespie, " sick
Nathl. Jones	Morris McMahon	in Cecil Co.
John Tunstill	Robert Clark	Ephraim Hendrickson, a recruit

George Keller } Delivered by James Creswell, a recruiting Officer of this Co., to
John Campbell } Lieut. John Hamilton.

Deserters Sent to Chester Town.

Wm. Arno
Wm. McGreagor
John Corlet, a deserter, deserted
Wm. Lock } deserters taken up in Harford Co. for two of the Classes
James Kelly } of this Co. and delivered to Col. Dallam
John Brown, a recruit, deserted same day he enlisted
John Boyd, "   "   few days after he enlisted
Wm. Tucker, a recruit, deserted
Felix O'Nail,   "   "

Return of the Recruits in Caroline County, Oct. 17th, 1780.

Charles Fitzgarral	Wm. Fitzgarral	William Earl Hill

William Whiteley, Lt.

A List of Recruits from and Deserters taken up in Somerset County. Oct. 20th, 1780.

John Carter
Saml. Furrow
James Huet
Levi Reese
Barnaby Case
Edwd. Blake
Salathiel Carmine

John Mitchel
Chas. Revel
Levin Abbet
Abel Amoss, deserter, not joined '82
Wm. Rhoads } deserters belonging to
John Stevens } the Delaware State
Wm. Evans }

Recruits, Washington County.

1780 October 19th James Smith   November 10th Elisha Robinson

---

Muster Roll of the late Sixth Maryland Regiment, now the Fourth Company of the Second Battalion of Colonel Williams' Regiment of Infantry, serving in the Southern Army of The United States for the Month of October, 1780.

Captain Dobson   Lieut. Lynn

during the War of the American Revolution, 1775–83.

NAMES.	DATE.	WAR.	3 YEARS.	REMARKS.
Serjeants				
Jesse Jacobs		1		
James Flack	28 April '79	1		
John Mantle		1		
Saml. McConnell	10 June '78		1	
Edward Booth			1	
Patrick Doran		1		Furlough
Peter Fervott		1		On Guard
Wm. McNeil		1		On Guard
Joseph Philbert	30 May '78		1	
John Alex. McKey		1		On Comd. Light Infantry
William Martin		1		On Furlough Maryland
Robert Taylor		1		Recruiting
Corporals				
Edward Teadly		1		
James Maxwell			1	
John Young		1		
Peter Sugars		1		
Robt. Sharpless		1		Sick Absent Hillsborough
John Bethell		1		Sick Monmouth N. Jersey
Charles Hill				Comd. Light Infantry
Drum. & Fifers				
Alex. Stephenson		1		
James Greenwood		1		
John Denoon		1		
Thos. Cahoe, Jr.		1		
George Stumm		1		
James Steward		1		
Edward Purdy		1 or	1	
Noah Carter		1		
Rank & File				
Thos. Simister		1		
Wm. Rice		1		
Harry Billop		1		
Benj. Williams		1		
Joseph Elliott		1		
John Summers		1		
Isaac Beckell, (or Beckett)		1		
Michl. McCann				
Wm. Westwood		1		
Patrick Egan		1		
Chris. Cusick		1		
Nich. Milburn		1		
Saml. Young		1		

Names.	Date.	War.	3 Years.	Remarks.
Rank & File				
Hecter Cackey		1		
Wm. Harris		1		
John Hously		1		
Caleb Donelly		1		
George Montle		1		
Stephan Owens		1		
Robt. Clenchan, (or Clenehan)		1		
Wm. Chambers		1		
Edmond Collins		1		
John Marshall	20 Dec '78		1	
Joseph Sloop	May '78		1	
Wm. George		1		
Michl. Crime		1		
Michl. Wirey		1		
James Devericks				
John Dorough		1		
John Campbell		1		
John Ellery		1		
John Holliday, Jr.		1		
Moses Graham		1		
Asel Rockhold		1		
John Purdy	20 Feb '80	1		
John Armstrong		1		
Jona. Windle	24 Apl '78		1	
Wm. Durham		1		
Timy. Fitzgerald	22 Dec '78		1	
John Elliott			1	
John Stackhouse			1	
Michl. Shoemaker		1		
Thomas Bare		1		
George Taylor		1		
John Wells		1		
Wm. Cole				Joined, Recruit 3 October '80
Robert Davis	28 April '78		1	
John Thomas		1		
John Lincoln		1		
James Nowell		1		
Benj. Dominick		1		
Henry Davis				
George Bowers	1 May '78		1	
John Jackson		1		
Abraham Church	30 May '78		1	
Wm. Moran				

during the War of the American Revolution, 1775-83.   349

NAMES.	DATE.	WAR.	3 YEARS.	REMARKS.
Rank & File				
Wm. Stonestreet		1		
James Burk		1		
George Bomgardner		1		
Peter Henecy			1	
Mich. Connelly		1		
Thos. Mahanny		1		
Thomas Smith		1		
Bartle Bome		1		On Guard
Henery Purdy	5 Feb '80	1 or	1	do do
John Love	22 Dec '78		1	do do
Robert Matthews	15 May '78		1	do do
Abraham Swink		1		do do
Richard Duvall		1		do do
Thomas Cahoe, Sr.		1		do do
John Martin	10 Feb '80		1	do do
John May		1		Hospital Fish Kills
Richard Brockell		1		do Annapolis
Edward Shehee		1		do Hillsborough
Benj. Taylor		1		do do
Chris. Touchstone		1		do do
Mich. Rogers		1		do do
Mich. Stanley		1		do do
James Sewell		1		do do
Joseph Ralston	23 Dec '78		1	On Command, Detach.
Joseph Long		1		On Command, Gen. Smallwood
Benj. Moran		1		do do Detach.
Leonard Boward		1		Fatigue
Benj. Cleaver		1		Artificer Roan Oak
Jacob Rowland		1		Waiter on Mr. J. Jacobs, Md.
Isaac Greaves		1		do do Capt. Somervile, do
Thomas Kearnes		1		do do Genl. Gates
Robert Rice			1	Waggoner
William Fuller		1 or 1		do
Daniel Javins		1		Furlough, Maryland
Godfrey Young		1		Transfd. to Invalids Corps 23 Oct '80
Roger Dowlin		1		Sick Albany

Camp Hillsborough, North Carolina, Nov. 1st, 1780. Mustered then the Late Sixth Maryland Regiment now the fourth Company in Second Battalion of Col Williams' Regiment.

John Davidson, B. Inspt.

Records of Maryland Troops in the Continental Service

Muster Roll of the Maryland Corps in the Service of the U. States, Commanded by Captain Thomas Beall for the Months of Jan., Feb., March, April, May, June, July, Aug., Sept. and Oct. 1780.

Commissd.	Thomas Beall, Capt., absent. Dismissed the Service Aug. 14th, 1780.*
"	Adamson Tannehill, Capt., April 1st, 1778.
"	Elijah Evans, Lieut., Aug. 8th, 1776, absent.

RANK.	NAMES.	TIME OF SERVICE.	REMARKS.
Serjt.	Joseph Jeanes	War	
"	Basil Shaw	"	
"	George Twinch	"	Appd. April 25th, '80
"	Jonathan Weden	"	" Aug. 10th, '80
"	Wm. Batten	"	Reduced June 22nd, '80
"	Benj. Burch	"	
Corpl.	Elisha Cockindall	"	Appd. Apl. 10th, '80
"	John Brown	"	" May 1st, 80
"	Thomas Horsfield	"	
"	Loudon Trotter	"	
Drum. & Fife.	George Twinch	"	Prom'd. Apl. 25th, '80
	Jno. McBryde	"	
"	Thos. Lovely	"	Absent with leave
"	Danl. Howe	"	
Privates	James Denniston	"	
	Patrick Quinn	"	
	Henry Dennis	"	
	Saml. Martin	3 yrs	Absent
	Elisha Cockindall	War	
	Patrick O'Harra	"	Deserted July 1st, '80
	John Stacks	"	
	Thomas McKinsy	"	
	Dennis Carty	"	
	James Kilty	"	On Command
	Jacob Aitzil	"	
	Edward Kirk	"	
	John Jordon	"	
	Roderick McKinney	"	
	Jonathan Weeden	"	Promoted Aug. 10th, '80
	William Hart	"	Absent
	John Riley	"	
	John Brown	"	Promoted May 1st, '80
	John McKann	3 yrs	Dischd. May 3rd, '80
	James Cunnigham	War	Joined July 15th, '80, absent

* Pennsylvania Archives, Vol. XI, Second Series, page 602.

during the War of the American Revolution, 1775-83.

RANK.	NAMES.	TIME OF SERVICE.	REMARKS.
Privates	Jonathan Shepherd	War	
	Thomas Craigg	"	
	Wm. Beatty	"	
	Richard Hoggins	"	
	Nehemiah Lanham	"	
	George Parker	"	
	Wm. Marlow	"	
	John Burk	"	
	Wm. Wilson	"	
	Levy Davis	"	Deserted Aug. 20th, '80
	Jacob Palmer	"	
	Francis Dewist	"	
	John Gordon	"	
	Robert Fyrth	"	
	Kilbreth Wilson	"	
	Thomas Fleming	"	
	John Treviss	"	
	Wm. Tayler	"	
	Jacob Adams	"	On Command
	John Gratsinger	"	
	Thomas Hill	"	
	Joseph Neale	"	
	Wm. Jarmey	"	Deserted Sept. 30th, '80
	Zachariah Berry	"	On Command
	Pierce Deacon	"	
	James Dowden	"	

Pittsburgh July 13th, 1781. Then Mustered the Mary'd. Corps as Specified in the Above Roll.

J. Crawford, Lt. & Adjt. 8th Pennsa. Regt.

I do Swear that the within Muster Roll is a true State of the three Companies of the Mary'd. Corps without fraud to the United States or any Individual According to the best of my Knowledge.

Sworn before me this 13th day of July, 1781.
Before me

Jno. Gibson, Col. Comdt. F. Pitt.

That Part of Capt. Joseph Marbury's Company of Infantry belonging to the Maryland Line, which is Ordered to Fort Pitt. Aug., Sept., Oct., Nov. and Dec., 1780.

Serjeants	Privates	Privates
Basil Shaw	John Gordon	James Dowden
George Twinch	Nicholas Welch	Edward Kirk
Corporal	Robert Firth	John Traviss
John Brown	Thomas McKinsey	George Parker
Drummer	William Wilson	Francis Dewist
John McBryde	Daniel How	William Batton
Privates	Zachariah Berry	Joseph Neal
Thomas Hill	Rhodk. McKinsey	William Marlow
Thomas Flemming		

Return of Officers and Men of the 1st Company who were in Service from the First of August, 1780 to the first January, 1781.

William Reiley, Capt.   Retired 1 Jan., '83.
Lieut. William Adams
Ensign Henry Clements

Serjts.	Corpls.
Levi Smith	Abraham Bowin
John Wilkerson	John Smith
James Collins	Fife.
Drum.	Joseph Nabb
William Ferrell	

Privates	Privates	Privates
James Holmes	James Doyl	Emanuel Allen
John Bantham	Solomon Summers	George Dyace
Thomas Carney	Anthony Weaver	Wm. Horney
Paul Lappin	Valentine Clapper	Saml. Richardson
Henry Gilby	Perrigrine Sullivan	John Mills
Aaron Jones, (or Jonas)	David Wilson	George Kelvin (?)
John Andrew	Roger Shorter	Cornelius Thompson
James Allen	Thomas Gilliam	Thomas Bowzer
John Downey	John Fulham	George Jinnings
James Owings	Stafford Fosdale	Danl. Brumiger
William Hill	William Sivill	Thomas Elliot
Jervis Eccleston	Augusten Cann	John Hurley
Wm. St. Clair	Benj. Loftman	John McKay
Thomas Ayers	Thomas Frimley	John Carrol
John Hull	Alexander Downey	James Bayless
Charles Girdler		

3d April.

W. Adams, Lt.

Return of the Names Commissioned and Non Commissioned Officers and Privates of the 2nd Company wch. have been in the Service from 1st Aug., Year '80 to the 1st Jan., '81.

during the War of the American Revolution, 1775–83.

Mark McPherson, Ensign

Serjts.	Serjts.
Thomas Edwards	John Gwinn
John Colein	Charles Harvy, Transferred
Hugh McMillan	to Maryland

John McNight, Fifer

Privates	Privates	Privates
Richard Farraby	William Hedge	William Pecker
Peter Topping	William Carter	Edward Evans
Emal. Cathajane	Michal Clark	Elijah Smith
James Gray	Joseph McAntee	Henry Reading
Joseph Johnson	Adam Jamison	Evan Tumbleston
Willm. Ingle	Thomas Slade	Matthew Moore
Jeriah William	John Lynch	Chrisr. McWay
Michael Calihorn	Daniel O'Quinn	Henry Ramden
Thomas Murphy	Asaph Colegate	Thos. Richardson
John Kidd	John King	John Blades
Hugh Gainor	John Hyde	John Lucas
Conrod Smith	John Berryman	James Due

M. McPherson, Lieut.

A Return of the Commd., Non Commissd. Officers & Privates Names of the 3rd Company who have Been in the Service since 1st of Aug., till 1st of Jan., 1781.

John Sprig Belt, Capt. Retired 1 Jan., '83
Henry Baldwin, Lieut.

Serjts.	Drummer
Fras. MaGauran	Daniel Warrier
Jesse Jacobs	Fifer
Jas. Deverex	Alex. Stevenson

Privates	Privates	Privates
John Carson, promoted Serjt. Mch., 1781	John Nicholson	James Erwin
	John Wade	Jno. Nevitt
James Ashly, promoted Corpl. since Augt., 1781	Chr. Cusack	Geo. Bowers
	Jas. Steward	Daniel Kettle
Nichs. Milburne, ditto	John Armstrong	Abm. Kettle
Saml. Young, ditto	Wm. Stonestreet	Joseph Eliott
Richard Dewall	Joshua McKinsey	Moses McKinsey
Benj. Williams	Paul Greenard	Wm. Cooke
Michl. McCann	Jno. Holloday	Corns. Vaughan
Wm. Silwood	Thos. Hutchcraft	Matthew Dyche

Privates	Privates	Privates
Michael Smith	Henry Billop	Moses Graham
Thos. Larmore	George Mauntle	John Stanton
Absolum Wright	Saml. Boswell	Michael Hardman
Fras. Karns	Elias Smith	Geo. Bumgardner
Wm. Ryder	Chas. Jones	Chrisr. Smith
John Hall	John Eliott	Benj. Clever
George Taylor		

Henry Baldwin, Lt.

1st Maryland Regt.

Return of Officers and Men in the 4th Company who were in Service from the first of August, 1780, to the first of January, 1781.

James Woolford Gray, Capt.
Regnal Hilleary, Lieut.

Serjts.
John Reeder
Larrance Branham
Corpl.
Walter Howe

Drum.
Anthony Gohegan
Fife.
Robert Cornick

Privates	Privates	Privates
John Moore	Joseph Jenkins	Levin Abbitt
Jas. Kelley	George Foard	Luke Carter
Humphry Beckell, (or Beckett)	Chas. McGee	John Appleby
	James Byus	Joseph Southall
John Hamilton	Matthew Moore	John Lewin
Samuel Gray	Zachariah Clark	John Buckley
George Dixon	John Dyar	Matthew Carty
Thomas Jones	Austen Howard	John Gorman
Wm. Derrington	Joshua Pierce	John Ashmore
Chas. Ormer	John Love	John Gorden
Richard Tasko	Willm. Mitchell	Emanuel Farrara
Wm. McGee	John Lee	Hezekiah Carr
John Wells	Francis Hopkins	John Jerviss
Neal Peacock	Edward Erving	John Onions
Travers Alvey	John Fransway	Andrew Russell
Dudley Lee	Luke Demsey	Edward Evans
Michl. Pilkoston	Christopher Semore	James Thomas
Michl. Woolford	John Craig	Charles Murphy
Phillip Savoy	Edward Furrener	

J. W. Gray, Capt.

Camp James Island, April 4th, 1783.

Return of Commissioned and Non Commissioned Officers & Privates of the 5th Company who were in Service from 1st Aug., '80, to 1st Jan., '81, now serving in the 5th Company, 1st Maryland Regiment.

Benj. Price, Capt.
Willm. Rasin, Lieut.
Saml. Edmiston, Ensign

Serjts.
Willm. A. Needham
John Quick
Patrick Doran
Thomas Buckley
Corpls.
Issachar Mason
Henry Nicholson

Drummer
Thomas Hawson
Fifers
Jas. Greenwood
Danl. Bassell
Thomas Butt
Fredk. Bennett

Privates
Thos. Pennifield
Jesse Wright
Richard Kisbey
Willm. Carter
Joseph Rhea
Bennet Shirley
Francis Lang
Willm. Toland
William Cox
George Craggs
Stephen Fennell
John Frawney
William Manley
Rhode Woodland
William Hope
John Ennis
John West
Henry Mansfield
Benjamin Kearns
Charles Fitzgerald

Privates
Levi Lord
John Moore
Thomas Ellis
Richard Wiley
Leonard Holt
Thomas Pendor
Jeremiah French
Francis Freeman
William Fitzgerald
Charles Fulham
James Baber
Alexander Levi
George Duncan
Willm. Moore
Willm. Nuton
Thomas Gadd
William Hicks
William Shirley
Peter Degazoone

Privates
William Jones
John Branson
John Ashberry
Lambert Philips
Charles White
Patrick Reilley
Thomas Wember
Edward Holland
Enoch Ennis
Abm. Catchesides
Jacob Blake
Joseph Barton
James Huett
James Knott
James Smith
Job Sylvester
Edward Kersey
Henry Jacobs
William Lee

Ben. Price, Capt.

6TH COMPANY, 1ST MD. REG'T.

A Return of the Officers and Soldiers who were in the Service From the 1st of Aug. '80 to the 1st of Jan. '81.

Loyd Beall, Lieut.
Philip Hill, "

Serjts.	Corpls.
Stephen Fluharty	William Bruff
Samuel Fillson	George Field
Charles McNabb	Pett. Stephens

Fifer Drum.
Benj. Williams Bosston Medler

Privates	Privates	Privates
George Devatt	Michael Curtis	William Casey
Saml. Clarke	Fredk. Harty	Pett. McGwire
Zedk. Whaylay	Willm. Mann	Theops. Lincey
Wm. Hillman	Jno. McA Nally	Benj. Massh
Alexander Ross	Wm. Quinton	Jno. Armstrong
George Buck	Jno. Twiner	Henry Townley
Josa. Lesster	Luke Sampson	Geor. Hamillton
Robert Duncan	Chas. Clements	Jno. Hullett
Absm. Fardo	Moses Foster	Paull Roan
Darly Crowley	Richard Gae	Edwd. Crossgrove
Wm. Linkins	Jno. Mansfield	Wm. Ellkins
Jno. Knox	Jno. Mills	Jno. Fullford
Jno. Ryan	Wm. Niblett	Wm. Taylor
Elijah Pepper	Saml. Wedge	Wm. Phearson
Neal Morris	Lar. Harman	Jos. Phearson
Jno. Loveday	Chas. Simpkins	
Joseph Blasse	Wm. Craill	

Thos. Beatty, Lt.

1st MARYLAND REGIMENT.

A Return of the Commissd., Non Commisd. Officers and Privates Names of the 7th Company who have been in Service Since the 1st of August, '80 till the 1st of January, '81.

Samuel McPherson, Capt. Lt. and Adjt.
Edmund Compton, Lieut.
John Brevitt, Ensign.   Promoted to Lieut. Sept. 20th, 1780.

Serjts.	Corpls.
William Collis	Wm. Braithwate
Humphrey Spencer, (dead)	Bartholomew Essom
Robert Scrivner	Drummer
Aaron Spaldin	John Head
	Fifer
	Andrew Garnett

during the War of the American Revolution, 1775–83.

Privates	Privates	Privates
John Bradey	John Robins	Joseph Donnoho
Daniel Bulger	John Buckhannan	William Moore
Isaac Grieves	James Ferrell	William Rice
Aquilla Pierce, deserter	Abram Irvin	William Mathews, deserter
Philip Fitzpatrick	David Bramble	Charles Sickle
John Haney	Thomas Campher	Thomas Bare
William Gould	William Purchase	Patrick Rowing
Hampton Coarsey	John Taylor, deserter	William Jones, deserted to the British
Henry Greene	Adam Kephart	
John Welch	Jacob Knight	Thomas Porters
Roger Launders	William Laws	Lambert Thompson
Michael Lloyd, deserter	Michael Casner	Joseph Hewkill
Charles Cooper	Richard Blansford	John Sammon
James Mason	James Harris, deserter 1781	William Groves
John Gregory	Solomon Brittinham	Cathael Carmile
Thomas Waite	John Dennison	Pat. Cavanough
John Alby	William Glorey	Richard Biddle
Peter Melvin	John Sommers	James Bigwood
Wm. Moore	Benj. Gaither, deserter 1781	Daniel Jervais
James Willson, deserter	Robert Streets	

Saml. McPherson, Capt.

A List of the Officers and Soldiers of the 8th Company of the Maryland Line who were in Service from the first of August, 1780, until the first of January, 1781.

James Winchester, Lieut. Nicholas Gassaway, Lieut.

Serjt.
Peter McNaughtan
Corpls.
Benjamin Prior
George Childes

Drummer
Thos. Gossage
Fifer
John Martindale

Privates	Privates	Privates
Peter Smith	Samuel Hambleton	Edward Hammon
John Kerr, (dead)	William Lilley	Barnard Wilson
Richard Hall	Patrick Molohon	Benj. Steward
John Adams	John Williams	Noah Sears, (dead)
John Bailey	Thomas Thomas	Frederick Wilmott
Peter Bocard	Charles Goldsbury	Thomas Clark
Michael Lawler	Alexander Francis	Benjamin Boid
Basil Brown	Peregrine Howard	James Thomas
Thomas Kennedy	Richard Procktor	Samuel Callehan
John Brown	Samuel Harper	John Osburn

Privates	Privates	Privates
Henry Lowers, (or Sowers)	William Sax	William Nailor
Richard Butler	Darby McNemar	William Joice, (or Joiel)
Josep Hall	David Cail	John Brookbank
Amas Green	Stephen Fresh	John Irons
Francis Demar, deserter	Michael Miller	Jacob Flora
Wm. Horrington	William Poland	William Clarey
Abijah Buxton	John Jackson	Francis Fairbrother
Abraham Gaseney	Ignatius Adams	John Anderson
	Jonathan Fowler	

J. Winchester, Capt.

A List of the Commissd. and Non Commissd. Officers and Privates who were in the Service of Maryland from the 1st of August, 1780, to the 1st of Jan., 1781, Light Infantry Company, 1st Maryland Regiment.

Frances Reveley, Lieut.
John T. Lowe, Ensign.

Serjts.	Corpl.
Stephen R. Price	John Folden
Chas. Runnenberg	D. and F.
Archibald Johnson	Benj. H. Kerrick
	Michael Clansey

Privates	Privates	Privates
John Lynch	Michael Wierey	James Collard
Andrew Crummy	Robert Clanahan	Richard Mitchell
John Thomas	William McGlouchlin	James Managee
Wm. Sullivan	Daniel Buckley	Joseph Jones
John Burnett	Patrick Dennison	James Jackson
George Pearce	Jacob Myers	Henry Fisher
Rigby Foster	Barrack Butt	Livey, (or Leiry), Burck
Daniel Smith	James Wood	Thomas Evans
Robinson Ross	Henry Crane	Jacob Moses
John McCan	John Harrell	James Keelan
Charles Scott	William Jinkins	Joseph Botchabey
Edward Roberts	Richard Haislip	Edward Vickers
Michael Waldman	Joseph Sloop	James Crozier
James Ruarck	Bartholomew Thompson	John Delany
William Roberts	Reubin Smith	George Saunders
John Roach	John Walker	John Smallwood
Joseph Long	John Haidon	

April 1st, 1783.   Frances Reveley, Capt.

A List of Men in Service 1 Aug., 1780 to 1 Jan., '81.

Rank.	Men's Names.	When Enlisted.	Term of Service.	When Discharged.	Regt.
	Henry Dixon	8 Feb '79	3 years	8 Feb '81	
	Leonard Swan		"	2 May '81	
	George Brown		"	24 Apl '81	
	Zadock Harvey, (or Haney)		"	1 May '81	
	Samuel Owens	1777	War		
	James Kelly		"		
	Thomas Baily		"		
	Jno. Snelling		3 years	2 Aug '81	
	Thos Hovington				Col. Ramsay
	Able Arman				" "
	Francis Thompson				" "
	John B. Haislope		"	died 11 Sept '82	
	Lazarus Higgs	26 July '80	"		
	Notley Whitcomb				
	Jno. Hurdle, (or Hundle)				Matross
	Matthew McMackin		"	1 Sept '81	Matross
	John Robertson			2 Apl '81	
	Andrew Lord				
	Randal Hoskins		"	8 Jan '82	
Corpl.	Richard Gadden		"	26 Apl '81	
	John Claggett		"	25 " "	
	Dennis Trammel		"	31 May '83	
Corpl.	Leonard Bean		"	12 Apl '81	
Serjt.	Josias Harris		"	25 " "	
	John Milstead		War		
	Jeremiah Rhodes	1 May '78	3 years and 9 months	17 Feb '82	3d Md. Regt.
	Wm. Dillon			2 May '82	
	John Howard			July '81	
Serjt.	Thos. Harrison			" "	
	Aaron Simmons			" "	
Corpl.	James Daffin	5 Apl '78	3 years	5 Apl '81	4th Md. Regt.
	Richard Taylor	26 Feb '80	"	6 May '83	
	John McDonald				Roxburgh's Detachment
Corpl.	Wm. Sharpe		"	1 May '81	5th Regt.
Pt.	Stephen Hancock	July '80	War		
Serjt.	Joseph Philbert	2 June '78	3 years	2 June '81	2d Regt.
Pt.	Elias Hardy		"	25 Apl '81	
Pt.	Wm. Wilkinson		"	3 Mch '81	

Rank.	Men's Names.	When Enlisted.	Term of Service.	When Discharged.	Regt.
Pt.	Henry Philips		3 years	1 May '81	
Pt.	Thomas Summers	1776	War		
Pt.	Michael McGuire (?)		"	1 Sept '82	at his request being unfit for duty
	Saml. Hamilton		"		Winchester's Company
Serjt.	Jas. Dyar			6 Jan '83	German Regiment
	John Kildee		"		
	Wm. Aggis	26 July '80	"		
	Ths. Arthus	25 "	"		
	Joseph Ablewhite	28 "	"		
	Jas. Adams	31 "	"		
	John Bolton	18 "	"		
	Jno. Butler	12 Sept "	"		
	Js. Brown	29 July "	"		
	Js. Brannon	15 "	"		
	John Blackburn	22 "	"		
	Francis Barbett	20 "	"		
	David Bryan	20 "	"		
	John Bennett	30 "	"		
	Chs. Byrne	28 "	"		
	Jas. Bickham, Jr.	24 "	"		
	Wm. Dunkin, (or Demkin)	29 Mch '81	3 years		
	John Casey	28 July '80	War		
	Pat. Connelly	24 "	"		
	Chs. Chinchfiell	2 Aug '80	"		
	Michael Doren	2 " "	"		
	Edwd. Dewes	15 July '80	"		
	George Daw	14 Aug '80	"		
	William Richardson				7th Md. Regt.

MUSTER AND PAY ROLLS FOR 1781.

RESOLVES OF CONTINENTAL CONGRESS, 3 OCTOBER, 1780.

"*Resolved*, That such of the sixteen additional regiments as have not been annexed to the line of some particular state, and all the separate light corps of the army, both of horse and foot, and also the German battalion, be reduced on the 1st day of January next: that the non-commissioned officers and privates in those several corps, be incorporated with the troops of their respective states, and that such of them as do not belong to any particular state, be annexed to such corps as the commander in chief shall direct.

That the regular army of the United States, from and after the 1st day of January next, consist of 4 regiments of cavalry or light dragoons; 4 regiments of artillery; 49 regiments of infantry, exclusive of colonel Hazen's regiment, hereafter mentioned; 1 regiment of artificers:

That the several states furnish the following quotas, viz. . . . . Maryland, 5 regiments of infantry:

That the states shall select from the line of the army a proper number of officers to command the several regiments to them respectively assigned, taking notice that no new appointment is to be made of a higher rank than that of a lieutenant-colonel commandant:

And whereas, by the foregoing arrangement, many deserving officers must become supernumerary, and it is proper that regard be had to them:

Resolved, That from the time the reform of the army takes place, they be entitled to half pay for seven years, in specie, or other current money equivalent, and also grants of land at the close of the war, agreeably to the resolution of the 16th of September, 1776."

MARYLAND ACTS, OCTOBER, 1780.

"An ACT to draught the non-commissioned officers and privates of the regiment extraordinary into the battalions of the quota of this state, and to recal the commissioned officers of the said regiment.

WHEREAS congress have recommended to this state to reduce the number of their regiments in the continental service, and the commander in chief has most earnestly called upon this state to complete the number of men in said battalions without delay: And whereas it is deemed impracticable to comply with said requisition, so as to have the quota of men in the field at the time required, without draughting the non-commissioned officers and privates of the regiment extraordinary.

Be it therefore enacted, by the General Assembly of Maryland, That the non-commissioned officers and privates of the regiment extraordinary be draughted into the old battalions of the quota of this state in the continental service, and that the field and commissioned officers of said regiment be recalled.

And be it enacted, That the said field and commissioned officers shall be reimbursed the extraordinary expence they may have incurred, and over and above the pay that may be due to them at the time of their discharge, shall receive one year's pay, deducting therefrom the money and value of the cloathing and other necessaries by them received; provided always, that lieutenant-colonel Alexander Lawson Smith, of the said regiment extraordinary, do hold the rank of lieutenant-colonel, as a supernumerary officer of this state in the continental service, he having resigned his commission in the continental service for the purpose of accepting the command of the said regiment, and being entitled in course to the rank of lieutenant-colonel."

Arrangement of the Maryland Line in 5 Regts., January 1st, 1781.

Rank.	Names.	When Commissioned.	Rank.	Names.	When Commissioned.

1st Regiment.

Rank.		Names.	When Commissioned.	Rank.		Names.	When Commissioned.
Col.		Otho H. Williams	1st Jan '77	16 Lieut.		James Ewing	27 May '78
Lt. Col.		Uriah Forrest		21	do	James J. Skinner	14 Sept do
Major		John Eccleston	10 Dec do	26	do	Isaac Duvall	12 Apl '79
1	Captain	Thomas Lansdale	1 Jan do	31	do	John Hamilton	1 June do
6	do	Jona. Sellman	do do	36	do	Willm. Woolford	11 Sept do
11	do	John Hawkins	20 Feb do	41	do	Patrick Danelly	7 Oct do
16	do	Edwd. Prall	10 June do	46	do	Willm. Raison	26 Jan '80
21	do	Willm. Riely	15 Oct do	51	do	Joshua Burgess	14 Mch do
26	do	John S. Belt	15 Dec do	56	do	Hezekiah Ford	16 Aug do
31	do	Christn. Orendorff	1 Apl '78	61	do	John Nelson	1 Jan '81
36	do	Richd. Bird	1 June '79	1 Ensign		John T. Lowe	26 Jan '80
41	do	Geo. Armstrong	11 Feb '80	6	do	Edward M. Smith	do do
1	Capt.Lt.	Lloyd Beall	8 June '79	11	do	Saml. Edmiston	1 June do
6	do	Jno. J. Jacobs	16 Aug '80	Surgeon		Richard Pindell	
11	Lieut.	William Lamar	15 Nov '77	Mate		Ezekiel Hayne	

during the War of the American Revolution, 1775–83.   363

Rank.	Names.	When Commissioned.	Rank.	Names.	When Commissioned.

2ND REGIMENT.

Rank	Name	Commissioned	Rank	Name	Commissioned
Col.	John Gunby	17 Apl '77	17 Lieut.	Christr. Richmond	27 May '78
Lt. Col.	John E. Howard	11 Mch '79	22 do	George Jacobs	14 Sept do
Major	John Dean	do do	27 do	John Carr	12 Apl '79
2 Capt.	Benj. Brookes	1 Jan '77	32 do	William Adams	8 June do
7 do	Alex. Trueman	do do	37 do	Nicholas Gassaway	
12 do	Jonathan Morris	14 Apl do	42 do	Arthur Harris	26 Oct do
17 do	Walker Muse	10 June do	47 do	Thomas Price	11 Feb '80
22 do	William Wilmot	15 Oct do	52 do	William Murdoch	1 Apl do
27 do	John Jordan	20 Dec do	57 do	Zedekiah Moore	10 Sept do
32 do	Wm. Beatty	14 Sept '78	62 do	Mark McPherson	1 Jan '81
37 do	Thomas Mason	8 June '79	2 Ensign	Jacob Crawford	26 Jan '80
42 do	John Gassaway	2 Apl '80	7 do	William Smoote	do do
2 Capt.Lt.	Adam Hoops	15 Dec '79	12 do	James Arthur	17 June do
7 do	Edward Dyer	10 Sept '80	Surgeon	Walter Warfield	
12 Lieut.	Jno. A. Hamilton	1 Feb '78			

3RD REGIMENT.

Rank	Name	Commissioned	Rank	Name	Commissioned
Lt. Col. Commd.	Peter Adams	1 Aug '79	13 Lieut.	James Gould	11 Mch '78
Major	John Steward	17 Apl '77	18 do	James Winchester	27 May do
do	Henry Hardman	22 May '79	23 do	Philip Read	13 Oct do
3 Capt.	Henry Dobson	1 Jan '77	28 do	John Hartshorne	21 May '79
8 do	Joseph Marbury	do do	33 do	Rignal Hillary	15 July do
13 do	Lilburne Williams	17 Apl do	38 do	Philip Hill	
18 do	Robert Chesley	10 June do	43 do	Wm. Pendergast	29 Oct '79
23 do	John Smith, (6th)	9 Nov do	48 do	Henry Baldwin	11 Feb '80
28 do	James W. Gray	26 Dec do	53 do	David Luckett	7 Apl do
33 do	Edward Spurrier	21 May '79	58 do	Walter Dyer	15 Sept do
38 do	Benj. Price	1 July do	63 do	Nathan Wright	1 Jan '81
43 do	Richd. Waters	7 Apl '80	3 Ensign	John Boone	26 Jan '80
3 Capt.Lt.	Henry Lyles	11 Feb '80	8 do	John Trueman	do do
8 Lieut.	Francis Revely	15 Apl '77	Surgeon	Levin Denwood	

4th Regiment.

Rank.	Names.	When Commissioned.	Rank.	Names.	When Commissioned.
Lt. Col. Commd.	Thos. Woolford		14 Lieut.	James Simmes	27 May '78
			19 do	Peter Hardcastle	14 Sept do
Major	Levin Winder	17 Apl '77	24 do	Benj. Garnett	13 Oct do
do	Alex. Roxburgh	7 Apl do	29 do	Wm. Trueman Stoddert	21 May '79
4 Capt.	John Lynch	1 Jan '77			
9 do	Jacob Brice	do do	34 do	Elihu Hall	1 Aug do
14 do	Henry Gaither	17 Apl do	39 do	Levache de Vaubrunne	
19 do	John C. Jones	20 Sept do	44 do	Nathan Smith	15 Dec '79
24 do	Richd. Anderson	15 Nov do	49 do	Edmd. Compton	18 Feb '80
29 do	George Hamilton	25 Jan '78	54 do	Joshua Rutledge	1 May do
34 do	David Lynn	22 May '79	59 do	John Brevett	20 Sept do
39 do	John Mitchell	15 July do	64 do	John McCoy	1 Jan '81
44 do	Jona. Gibson	1 May '80	4 Ensign	Robt. Halkerston	26 Jan '80
4 Capt.Lt.	Saml. McPherson	7 Apl '80	9 do	Henry Gassaway	do do
9 Lieut.	Nicholas Mangers	15 Apl '77	Surgeon	William Kilty	

5th Regiment.

Rank.	Names.	When Commissioned.	Rank.	Names.	When Commissioned.
Lt. Col. Commd.	Benj. Ford		15 Lieut.	Archd. McAllister	27 May '78
Major	Archd. Anderson		20 do	Gassaway Watkins	14 Sept do
do	John Davidson	1 Jan '81	25 do	Jacob Norris	26 Nov do
5 Capt.	Wm. Dent Beall	1 Jan '77	30 do	John Lynn	1 June '79
10 do	John Smith, (3rd)	do do	35 do	Saml. Hanson	1 Aug do
15 do	Edward Oldham	20 May do	40 do	Thomas Rowse	
20 do	Horatio Clagett	10 Oct do	45 do	Robert Denny	3 Jan '80
25 do	John Gale	10 Dec do	50 do	Benj. Fickle	19 Feb do
30 do	Perry Benson	11 Mch '78	55 do	Roger Nelson	15 July do
35 do	James Somervill	1 June '79	60 do	Thomas Boyd	1 Jan '81
40 do	William Bruce	1 Aug do	65 do	John Sears	do do
45 do	Edward Edgerly	10 Sept '80	5 Ensign	Henry Clements	26 Jan '80
5 Capt.Lt.	Thos. B. Hugou	1 May '80	10 do	Adam Jamison	1 June do
10 Lieut.	James Bruff	7 Oct '77			

Officers Entitled to Promotions in their own Regiments Previous to Jan. 1st, 1781.

Wm. Pendergast when Appd. a Vacancy 5th Regt.
Wm. Raison   do   do
Edmd. Compton 18 Feb, Smith's resignation
Benj. Fickle   19 do Porter's dismission
Jos. Burgess when 1st Appd. a Vacancy
David Lucket 7 Apl. Roxburgh's promotion
William Murdoch 1 Apl. Bevin's resignation
Jos. Ruttledge 1 May when 1st Appd. a Vacancy
Roger Nelson 15 July Moran's dismission
H. Ford 16 Aug. Duvall's death
Zed. Moore 10 Sept. Hardman's   do
John Brevett 20 Sept. Shoemaker's do
Walter Dyer 15 Sept. Farmer's   do

The above Officers have Ensigns Commissions on the 1st Jan., 1781, but entitled to Lieutenancy on the dates specified.

Supernumeraries in the Late 7 Regiments Jan. 1st, '81.

Col.	Josias Carvel Hall	1 Jan '77	late 4th Regt.
Lt. Col. Comd.	Nathl. Ramsey		do 3rd do
Lt. Col.	Edward Tillard		do 4th do

Officers of the Maryland Artillery Supernumerary.

Richard Dorsey, Captain   Jacques Baques, 1st Lieut.   James McFadon, 1st Lieut.
Wm. Brown,   do   Nicholas Rickets,   do   Isaac Rawlings, 2nd do
Ebenezer Finley, Capt. Lt. Young Wilkinson,   do   John Cheviar,   do
James Smith,   do   Clement Skerrett,   do   John Carson,   do
Robert Wilmot, Lieut.

Officers in the Maryland part of the Rifle Regiment Supernumerary Jany., 1st, 1781.

Capt.	Thomas H. Luckett	1 Jan '77	Capt. Reazin Davis	27 July '80
do	Adamson Tannehill	Dec '78	Lt. Elijah Evans, claims	
do	James Lingan	do	Captaincy	10 Apl '78

Officers in the Maryland part of the German Regiment Supernumerary Jany. 1st, 1781.

Lt. Col.	Lodwick Weltner	9 April '77	Capt. Michael Bayer	25 May '78
Capt.	Charles Baltzel	10 May do	Lt. Martin Shugart	
do	Christian, (or Christopher), Mayers	12 Mch '78	do Jacob Gromath	4 Jan '78
			do David Morgan	8 April do

Ensign Jacob Reybold, 24 July '78
Surgeon's Mate Alexr. Smith, August '78.

OFFICERS IN THE MARYLAND PART OF COL. NATHANIEL GIST'S REGT.

Maj. Nathaniel Mitchell	Capt. Joseph Smith
Capt. John Gist	do Joseph Britain

There are many other officers not included here who raised their Companies in & went from the State of Maryland into the Continental Line who come under the same description with those above enumerated therefore upon Application the expediency of admitting their Claims must necessarily come under Consideration.

W. Smallwood, M. G.

Capt. Murdoch's Company of the Md. State Regiment. 15 M. '81.

John Reader, Serjt.	George Stevens	John Carter
John Auber, D. Maj.	Walter Watson	Samuel Scott
Ezekiah Crowson, Fifer	William Jones	John Rumwill
Chas. Revelle, Drummer	Roger Maloy	John Jones
Joseph Greer	Wilkinson Gregsby	Henry Connolly
William Manly	George Ryon	Thomas Pingston
Edward Hinths	Richard Biddle	John Walker, Serjt.
Thomas Smith	Samuel Furrow	John Moore
Hugh Burns	Salithiel Carmin	Banks Webb
Jeaneth Crowd	Levy Reese	Abram Barker
Henry Mansfeld	James Hewitt	

MARYLAND ACTS—OCT., 1780.

"An ACT to procure recruits.

WHEREAS this general assembly are earnestly called upon by several requisitions from congress, and letters from general Washington, to recruit the quota of troops of this state:

Be it enacted, by the General Assembly of Maryland, That one thousand men be forthwith raised to serve in the regiments of this state in the continental service for three years, if not sooner discharged, by an equal assessment on all property within this state.

And be it enacted, That the lieutenant of each county shall, as soon as may be after notice of this act, divide and apportion all the property last assessed in his county, ... into classes of sixteen thousand pounds each, ... and each class shall, within twenty days after classing as aforesaid, find an able bodied recruit, between sixteen and forty-five years old, to serve for three years, if not sooner discharged, and the same recruit deliver to the lieutenant of the county, to be by him passed.

And be it enacted, That any able bodied slave, between sixteen and forty years of age, who voluntarily enters into the service, and is passed by the lieutenant, in the presence and with the consent, and agreement of his master, may be accepted as a recruit.

And be it enacted, That the lieutenants aforesaid, and the field and commissioned officers of the militia in each county, shall, within five days after the expiration of the said twenty days, meet . . . . and shall proceed to examine whether each class hath found a proper effective recruit according to this act, and if any class hath not found such recruit, ... they shall cause lots to be cast . . . . and the person to whose lot it shall fall shall be from thenceforth, to every intent and purpose, considered as an enlisted soldier, to serve until the tenth day of December seventeen hundred and eighty-one, in the quota of this state of the continental troops, ... but if such person shall, within twenty days thereafter, provide a good and sufficient recruit, to serve until the said tenth day of December in his stead, he shall be discharged; or if he shall at any time afterwards find a good and sufficient recruit in his stead, to serve for three years unless sooner discharged, he shall be discharged.

And be it enacted, That all recruits raised in virtue of this act shall be carried before the lieutenant of the county in which the recruits are or shall be raised, to pass muster, ... but no imported convict who hath not served his full term of seven years, or British deserter, shall be passed as a recruit within this act.

And, for the discovery of deserters, and the punishment of those who entertain, harbour, or conceal them,

Be it enacted, That if, after the first day of March next, any free male person shall entertain, harbour, or conceal, any deserter, knowing him to be such, such person shall, upon such conviction, be considered as an enlisted regular soldier for the term of three years, and may be taken as such by any officer of the Maryland line; and if any free male person, convicted as aforesaid, shall be the father of such deserter, or of or above forty-five years of age, or unfit for the service, he shall furnish an able-bodied recruit for the war, and deliver him to the lieutenant of his county within ten days after conviction, and in case of neglect shall be liable to pay thirty-five pounds in specie, or the value thereof, to the lieutenant of his county, ... and if any female, the mistress of any family, shall entertain, harbour, or conceal, any deserter, and shall be thereof convicted as aforesaid, she shall furnish and deliver an able bodied recruit as aforesaid, or be liable to the payment of the same penalty as aforesaid, ... and if any person, liable to such penalty for not procuring a recruit as aforesaid, shall be unable to pay the same, the lieutenant of the county may commit such person, for any time not exceeding six months, to the work-house or goal of his county, there to be kept to hard labour."

A List of Recruits furnished in Caroline County agreeable to an Act of Assembly passed Oct., 1780.

SUBSTITUTES.

Handy Handly	Henry Fisher	Jacob Branton
Tom Potts	James Fisher	Wm Miers.

DRAFTS.

Allemby Millington	Matthias Noland	Edmond Lunceford
Elijah Jump	Nathan Batchelor	Roger Connelly
John Jones	Hezekiah Wheelar	Jonathan Greenhugh
Richard Chance		

Wm. Whiteley, Lt. Caroline Co., Apr. 16th, 1781.

VOLUNTARY ENLISTMENTS OF

William Standley	Dorchester County	April 18th '81	three years
Nathan Ross	" "	" 11th '81	" "
Charles Dean	" "	" 23d '81	" "
John Riley for the 6th Regt., Col. O. H. Williams, Aug 26th '81			" "

A Return of the Recruits, Draughts and Substitutes in Ann Arundel County under the Act to procure Recruits passed October Session, 1780.

NAMES.	TIME.		TO WHOM DELIVERED.
Chas. Alexander	3 years	Recruit	Col. Adams
William Barry	until 10th Dec	Draught	
Samuel Fowler	do	do	
Willm. Potter	3 years	Recruit	Capt. Trueman
William Elliott	'til 10th Dec	Draught	
Wm. Woodward, Jr.	do	do	

Names.	Time.		To Whom Delivered.
John Newton	3 years	Recruit	Capt. Trueman
Adam Musler	do	do	Lt. John Sears
Levy Moody	do	do	Col. Adams
Richard Moss	'til 10th Dec	Draught	
Johns Meek	do	do	
John Winterburn	3 years	Recruit	same
John Britton	do	do	same
Thomas Horn	do	do	Capt. Trueman
James Wallingsfort	'til 10th Dec	Substitute	same
Benjamin Combly	do	Draught	
William Spicer	do	do	
William Lovitt	do	do	
Charles Pennington	do	do	
Isaac Jones	do	do	
Thomas Atkinson	do	do	
Willm. Palmour	do	Substitute	Col. Adams
Thomas Hannen	3 years	Recruit	Lt. Jas. Jno. Skinner
Nathan Moss	'til 10th Dec	Draught	
Paul Phillips	do	do	
Machael Mundus	3 years	Recruit	Capt. Trueman
John Fitgency	'til 10 Dec	Draught	
Aaron McKenzie	do	do	
John Davis	3 years	Recruit	same
Nichs. Selby	'til 10 Dec	Draught	
Alex. Cockburn	3 years	Recruit	same
Gideon Walker	do	do	Col. Adams
Thomas Hawkins	'til 10 Dec	Draught	
Robert Folger	3 years	Recruit	Capt. Trueman
Francis Read	do	do	same
Willm. Appingstall	do	do	same
James Humphries	do	do	same
Michael Smith	do	do	same
Charles Onion	'til 10 Dec	Draught	
Willm. Beachman	do	do	
Misail Deavour	do	do	
John Jordan	War	Recruit	same
Jno. Brown, (Shoem.)	'til 10 Dec	Draught	
Edwd. Dorsey, of Caleb	do	do	
James Portland	do	do	
James Beachgood	do	do	
Pascho Isleck	do	Substitute	same
Chas. Williams	3 years	Recruit	same
John Griffis, Jr.	'til 10 Dec	Draught	
Thos. Batterson, (Negro)	do	Substitute	Col. Adams
Adam Allen	do	Draught	
John Collins	do	do	

NAMES.	TIME.		TO WHOM DELIVERED.
Thomas Gordon	3 years	Recruit	Col. Adams
Thomas Tongue	'til 10 Dec	Draught	
Ferdinando Battee, Jr.	do	Substitute	same
Jono. Brashears	do	Draught	same
Andrew Hoofman	3 years	Recruit	Maj. Steward
Samuel Wood	'til 10 Dec	Draught	
Jno. Birkhead	do	do	
Nathnl. Robt. Harnsbury	3 years	Recruit	same
Thomas Hawkins	do	do	Col. Adams
Caleb Tydings	'til 10 Dec	Substitute	same
George Collins	do	Draught	
Richard Foggitt	do	Substitute	Capt. Mitchell
William French	do	Draught	
James Davidson	do	Substitute	Col. Adams
Aaron Stevenson	3 years	Recruit	same
John Dads	'til 10 Dec	Draught	
John Cowman	do	do	
Wm. Summerland	do	do	
Isaiah Williams	3 years	Recruit	Capt. Trueman
James West	do	do	same
David Stewart	'til 10 Dec	Draught	
Thomas Moffitt	do	Substitute	Col. Adams

No draughts for Classes 86 and 87, there not being any Militia in the Classes.

The Draughts are ordered to Annapolis.

James Brice,
Lieut. of A. A. Co.

Talbot County, to Wit—

A List of persons Draughted to serve until the tenth day of December, 1781, in the quota of this State of the Continental Troops. May 1st, 1781.

PERSONS' NAMES.	COMPANY.	BATTALION.	CLASS.
James Collison	Bayside	36	1
John Duling	Sword in Hand	4	2
Richd. Hopkins, Jr.	Hearts of Oak	38	3
Thomas Cooper	Bayside	38	4
Wm. Jones, Jr.	Broad Creek	38	5
George Townsend	United	38	6
Thomas Wrightson	do	38	7
Anthony Kerby	Hearts of Oak	38	9
Joseph Leonard	do	38	10

Persons' Names.	Company.	Battalion.	Class.
Henry Delahay, Jr.	Oxford	38	11
Richard Standfield	Miles River	38	12
Charles Sherwood	do	38	13
Solomon Plummer	Wye	4	14
James Kinnard	do	4	15
James Kendrick	Volunteer	4	16
Alex: Anderson	do	4	17
Nathan Foster	do	4	18
Thomas Ozmond	Hand in Hand	4	19
Robt. Frampton	do	4	20
James Price, Sr.	Sword in Hand	4	22
Greenberry Goldsborough	Oxford	38	23
William Mardary	2 Volunteer	4	24
Capt. Richd. Bruff	Union	4	25
George Poney	do	4	26
John Robt. Saml. Coffree	do	4	27
Robert Kemp	Third Haven	4	28
Samuel Jenkins	do	4	29
Jonathan Clash	do	4	30
John Harrison, Jr.	Oxford	38	31
James Plowman, Jr.	Hand in Hand	4	33
Wm. Rakes	2 Volunteer	4	34
Richard Easley	Oxford	38	35

(32 Draughts)   Chrisr. Birckhead, Lieut. T. County,

May 7th, 1781.

Talbot County, to Wit—

A List of Recruits who have enlisted to serve three years in the quota of this State of the Continental Troops.

Names of the Recruits.	When Enlisted.
Thomas Jones	March 20th 1781
John Brown	" 30th 1781
Allin Townsend	April 11th 1781

May 7th, 1781.   Christr. Birckhead, Lieut. Talbot County.

A Return of the Men Draughted in Worcester County, May the first, 1781.

Thomas Handley	William Conner	Kendal Taylor
Adkins Dennis	Isaac Boston	Elisha Long
Henry Corckwell	William Marshall	Edward Bishop
Alexander Porter	Henry Ayrs	Isaac Marshal
William Butler	William Cowley	Ruben Cropper
Daniel Eashom	Richard Sturgis	Isaac Brillingham
Edward Cropper	Midleton Harmon	Levi Powell
Jesey Brattan	John Ewens, of Jushua	Levi Cropper, of Natl.
John Gray	Elias Penewell	John Brevard
William Handy	John Johnson	Seth Hutson
William Jones	Levin Newton	James Mumford
George Turner		

Joseph Dashiell, Lieut.

KENT COUNTY RECRUITS. [ALL ENLISTED FOR THREE YEARS.]

Henry Williams	William Brada	John Gleen
Henry Harris	Daniel B. Bayley	Jacob Jefferies
James Bryne	James Reynolds	William Taylor
Reubin Elbon	William Grace	James Wilson
John Collins	Richard Green	Augustine Bryan
William Lynes	Abraham Reynolds	Thomas Farmer
William Wilson	Smyth Bagwell	Edward Chambers
James Shepperd	John Thomas	Shadrick Sap
George Finley	Ishmael Wroth	John Starkey
William Dunkin	John Harris	Absolom Scott
Richard Dolvin	William Guggon	Richard Demby
William Elbon	James Chambers	Class 18 drafted May 5
Thomas Wood	Timothy Conner	

Agreeable to the assessment we made out thirty-nine Classes of sixteen Thousand pounds each & every Class, (except one), has furnished a recruit for three years according to the above list. The deficient Class was drafted on the fifth day of May & I hope that a recruit for three years will be produced for that Class. Alexander Boys passed by Class No. 35, we discovered was subject to fits; who we have since discharged, the Class agreeing to pay their proportion to the State. The said Boys having received but a small sum.

W. Bordley.

May 16th, 1781.

RESOLVES OF CONTINENTAL CONGRESS—31 MAY, 1781.

" Whereas the British king, regardless of the rights of mankind, and of the United States in particular, continues the ravages of war with relentless fury; . . . . and whereas the deficiency of the continental regular lines, makes it absolutely necessary to call forth a respectable body of militia, till those lines be completed; . . . . It is also earnestly recommended to the state of Maryland, immediately to raise, arm, equip and accoutre for the field, two battalions of infantry, consisting of nine companies of 64 rank and file each; and a corps of cavalry of 64 troopers; . . . . And it is further recommended . . . . to cause the said troops, as soon as raised, ... to be marched . . . . to such place or places as the commander-in-chief shall direct, to remain in the service for and during the space of three months, ... unless sooner discharged by Congress or the commander-in-chief, and to be subject to the orders of the commander-in-chief."

MARYLAND ACTS—MAY, 1781

"An ACT to raise two battalions of militia for reinforcing the continental army and to complete the number of select militia.

WHEREAS it hath been earnestly recommended by congress to call forth two battalions of militia in this state, for the purpose of aiding and assisting our friends, now actually invaded, in the southern states, and this present general assembly have thought it reasonable and necessary to comply with the said recommendation:

Be it therefore enacted, by the General Assembly of Maryland, That thirteen hundred and forty effective men, to compose the non-commissioned officers and privates of two battalions of militia, to be officered according to the resolutions of congress of the third and twenty-first days of October last, be immediately raised in this state, in manner hereafter directed, to act in conjunction with the continental army until the tenth day of December next.

And be it enacted, That the said two battalions be apportioned upon and raised in the several counties, according to the number of militia in each county.

And be it enacted, That proper persons shall be appointed in each county by the governor and council, to procure the said number of militia men on or before the 16th of July next, by voluntary enrollment, ... and where several persons are appointed to recruit in any county, he that shall procure the highest number of recruits exceeding twenty, shall be entitled to a commission as lieutenant . . . . and he that shall procure the next highest number of recruits exceeding ten, shall be entitled to a commission of an ensign in one of the companies of said battalions.

And be it enacted, That the governor and council shall be and are hereby authorised and requested to appoint fit and proper officers out of the Maryland line, not engaged in actual service the present campaign, down to captains inclusive, to command the said battalions and companies, ... and if such officers cannot be had, then to appoint such officers as may be wanted out of those best qualified,

And, Whereas there are many idle and disorderly persons in the several counties in this state, who pursue no visible means to obtain an honest subsistence, but spend their time in such a manner as to render no service to the community by which they are protected :

Be it enacted, That every such free male idle person above sixteen years of age, and who is able bodied and effective, and hath no family, nor any visible method of getting an honest livelihood, and who may be adjudged by the lieutenant of the county to come under the above description of a vagrant, shall, from and after such adjudication, be considered as a soldier enlisted, and shall have it in his choice whether he will serve until the tenth of December, or enlist for three years or during the war ; . . . . provided that no person who hath served in the continental army as a regular soldier, and hath been discharged, shall be deemed a vagrant under this act.

And be it enacted, That in case the number of militia be not procured in the several counties by voluntary enrollment, or by enrolling vagrants in manner as above mentioned, on or before the sixteenth day of July next, it shall and may be lawful for the lieutenant of the county, ... to call together the field officers of each county respectively, and cause the militia in their respective counties . . . . to be distributed into as many classes as men may be wanted, and each class shall, within five days, find a recruit to serve until the tenth day of December next, or . . . . shall cause such class as doth not find a substitute . . . to be draughted, and two persons to be selected therefrom by lot, and such person of the two as the lieutenant . . . . shall direct and appoint, shall be deemed a militia man enrolled to serve until the tenth day of December next, and shall accordingly march, unless he find a substitute, to be approved by the lieutenant . . . . within five days after such appointment shall be notified unto him ; and any nonjuror who shall voluntarily enlist and serve, or if draughted or procured as a substitute shall serve during the time aforesaid, such nonjuror shall be restored to all the rights and privileges of a free citizen of this state without exception.

And be it enacted, That the said recruits and militia men, draughted or otherwise procured to go in the above battalions, shall be subject to the continental articles of war; and all freemen, although blacks or mulattoes, who are not deemed vagrants or enlisted as such, shall be taken into the militia and be subject to a draught as above directed.

And be it enacted, That where any three persons, to be appointed by the governor and council as herein before directed, shall enlist the whole number of men wanted for that county before the sixteenth of July next, if the number be equal to that of a full company, to consist of seventy-four non-commissioned officers and privates, such persons shall be entitled to commissions as captain, lieutenant, and ensign."

List of Recruits & Substitutes for Queen Ann's County procured under the Law for raising Recruits passed at the October Session, 1780.

Recruits.	Term of Enlistment.	Substitutes.	Term of Enlistment.
John Barnaby	3 years	Nathaniel Bailey	9 months
Edward Bartlett	do	James Cockrill	3 years
John Smallwood	do	John Harriss	do
Substitutes.			
Thomas Harriss	do	James Smith	do
Jacob Collins	do	John Holland	do
Samuel Hadley	10 December	Charles Nabb	10 December
James Harriss	do	George Penfold	do
Thomas Berry	do	George Belfast	3 years
Daniel Keitch	9 months	George Ellas	do
Thomas Burk	10 December	Philip Russell	do
Arnold Longfellow	do		
		Draughts.	
Thomas Long		Charles Devons, (subject to fits)	Samuel Osburne
Thos. Ford		Jonathan Briley	Sabret Huxter
Joseph Dobson		Thomas Chambers	William Clark,
William Hollingsworth		David Huxter, (subject to fits)	(shoe maker)
William Whitaker		John Jerman	John Cohee
Benj. Greenage		Jeremiah Davenport	William Tarbutton
Richard Ratcliff		Robert Cockleton, (servt. to Mr. Forman)	Joseph Badger

June 11th, 1781.

William Hemsley,
Lieut. of Queen Ann's County.

Port Tobacco, 2nd Sept., 1781.

Dear Col.

The enclosed are Exact Lists of the draughts and Substitutes draughted &c. for this County the present year. I Judge you Will be amazed to See Such a number Discharged, therefore have Noted against their Respective Names, the Causes that Rendered it Necessary. There are Also Several that are So debilitated by Sickness that they are Not able to March at present, and a few Sculkers that I have Not been able as yet to git hold off, tho have made use of the most probable means for that purpose, and hope in a few days to accomplish it. Please Lay the Lists Before the Honorable the Governor and Council and Oblige

Dr. Sir

Your Respectfull Huml. Servt.,

Frans. Ware.

To Col. John H. Stone, Annapolis.

Return of the drafts from Charles County who were drafted the 11th and 12th June, 1781.

Names of Drafts.	In Service or Not.	Names of Drafts.	In Service or Not.
Charles Willett	Service	Levi Clinkscales	Service
Benjamin Shaw	do	Nellson Johnson	do
Jese Warder	do	William Glassgow	do
Joseph Newberry	do	Charles Athey	do
John Ensy Clements	do	William Lary	do
Lawrence Simpson	do	Notley Whitcombe	do
James Wright	do	Gerrard Wood	do
Roger Posey	do	Thomas James	do
Francis McCann	do	Benj. Calbert Johnson	do
Walter Brooke	do	Chas. Beavin, (sick)	
Allison Maddox	do	Caleb Thomas, (small pox)	
James Dunning	do	Thomas Hill, (Flux)	
James Anderson	do	Joseph Pagett, (Lame)	
John Lowrie	do	Alex. Wallace	
John Stone Hunt, enlisted for 3 years	do	Jediah Waters, (Lame)	
		Elias Rawlings	
Barton Wathen	do	Wm. Boarman, (small pox)	

Return of the drafts from Charles County who were drafted the 27th July, 1781.

* Names of draughts excused or discharged are not printed.

Names of Drafts.	In Service or Not.	Names of Drafts.	In Service or Not.
Thomas Gillsim	Service	Ignatius Montgomery	Service
Walter Warren Hannon	do	Barton Beall	do
Nicholas Miles	do	Charles King	do
Matthew Smoot	do	James Taylor	do
William Lovelin	do	Benedict Clements	do
Matthew Brooke		Henry Proctor	do
David Davis	do	Ignatius Stuart	do
John Boswell	do	Thomas Elliott	do
John Butler	do	James McDaniel	do
Henry Butler	do	Richard Robey	do
William Oliver	do	Thomas Davis	do
Hezekiah Elgin	do	Zechariah Posey	do
Lancelot Chunn	do	William Neale	do
Jese Davis	do	James Warrington	do
Harrison Elgin	do	John Huntington, (sick)	
George Maddox	do	Richard Meeke, (at sea)	
Charles McDonald	do	John Newberry, (sick)	
Samuel Dent	do	Joseph Owens, (sick)	
George Hudson	do	Richard Brown	
William Coombe	do	Joseph Beavin, (sick)	
Joshua Steuart	do	Edward Miles	
George McNess	do	Nicholas Hagan	
Hezekiah Mudd	do	Samuel Wright, (sick)	
William Clinkscales	do	Henry Clements	since enrolled himself
William Dorton	do		a Substitute in P. G. Co. & joined the
John Clements	do		Army

Dorchester County, June 28th, 1781.

Sir:

I have sent fourteen draughted Militia Men under the Care of Lieut. Hugh McGuire, procured under a late Act of Assembly, to serve in the Continental Army untill the 10th Day of December next. A List of their Names you have inserted below—several of them have been Waterman & seem very desirous of serving on board some of our Barges, particularly Peter Harrington, Job Hubbert, Roger Tregoe & Anthony Tall, Jr. I have desired Mr. McGuire to apply to your Board to satisfy him for transporting the draughted Men to Annapolis

I have the Honour to be
Sir yr. very hble. Servt.,
Henry Hooper.

His Excellency the Governor—Dorchester County in Council.

John Wheeler
Nehemiah Lingard
John Dicks
Samuel Hurst
Levin Thomas

Ezekiel Whitchocks
Job Hubbert
Willm. Procter, Jr.
Nathan Busick
Anthony Tall, Jr.

Roger Trego
Peter Herrington
John Booth
Willm. Dickinson

Arrangement of the Maryland Line July, 1781.

Rank.	Names.	When Commissioned.	Promotions Since Jany. 1st, '81.
	1st Regiment.		
1 Col.	Otho H. Williams	1 Jan '77	
2 Lt. Col.	John Steward	19 Feb '81	vice Forrest, resigned
2 Major	John Eccleston	10 Dec '77	
4 Capt.	Jonathan Sellman	1 Jan do	
13 do	Edward Prall	10 June do	
18 do	William Reily	15 Oct do	
23 do	John S. Belt	15 Dec do	
28 do	Christn. Orendorff	1 Apl '78	
32 do	Richd. Bird	1 June '79	
37 do	Geo. Armstrong	11 Feb '80	
42 do	Lloyd Beall	19 Feb '81	vice Lansdale, promoted
45 do	Thos. B. Hugou	1 June do	do Hawkins, resigned
5 Lieut.	William Lamar	15 Nov '77	
9 do	James Ewing	27 May '78	
14 do	Jas. Jno. Skinner	14 Sept do	
18 do	Isaac Duvall	12 Apl '79	
22 do	John Hamilton	1 June do	
26 do	William Woolford	11 Sept do	
35 do	William Raison	26 Jan '80	
40 do	Joshua Burgess	14 Mch do	
45 do	Hezekiah Ford	16 Aug do	
54 do	John T. Lowe	20 Jan '81	vice Jacobs, resigned
55 do	Edward M. Smith	19 Feb do	do Beall, promoted
57 do	Samuel Edmiston	14 Mch do	do Danelly, resigned
59 do	John Trueman	16 do do	do Nelson, killed
1 Surgeon	Richard Pindell		
1 Mate	Ezekiel Hayne		
	2nd Regiment.		
2 Col.	John Gunby	17 Apl '77	
1 Lt. Col.	John E. Howard	11 Mch '79	
3 Major	John Dean	do do	
5 Capt.	Alex. Trueman	1 Jan '77	
9 do	Jonathan Morris	14 Apl '77	

Rank.	Names.	When Commissioned.	Promotions Since Jany. 1st, '81.
14 Capt.	Walker Muse	10 June '77	
19 do	William Wilmot	15 Oct do	
24 do	John Jordan	20 Dec do	
33 do	Thomas Mason	8 June '79	
38 do	John Gassaway	2 Apl '80	
43 do	Adam Hoops	16 Mch '81	vice Brooks, promoted
44 do	Samuel McPherson	25 Apl '81	do Beatty, killed
1 Capt. Lt.	Edward Dyer	10 Sept '80	
6 Lieut.	John A. Hamilton	1 Feb '78	
10 do	Christopher Richmond	27 May do	
23 do	William Adams	8 June '79	
27 do	Nicholas Gassaway		
31 do	Arthur Harris	26 Oct '79	
36 do	Thomas Price	11 Feb '80	
41 do	William Murdoch	1 Apl do	
46 do	Zedekiah Moore	10 Sept do	
50 do	Mark McPherson	1 Jan '81	
56 do	Jacob Crawford	20 Feb do	vice Jacobs, resigned
58 do	Willm. Smoote	16 Mch do	do Hoops, promoted
65 do	James Arthur		do Carr, resigned
2 Surgeon	Walter Warfield		

3rd Regiment.

Rank.	Names.	When Commissioned.	Promotions Since Jany. 1st, '81.
1 Lt. Col. Comd.	Peter Adams	1 Aug 79	
4 Major	Henry Hardman	22 May do	
7 do	Thomas Lansdale	19 Feb '81	vice Steward, promoted
1 Capt.	Henry Dobson	1 Jan '77	
6 do	Joseph Marbury	do do	
10 do	Lilburn Williams	17 Apl do	
15 do	Robert Chesley	10 June do	
20 do	John Smith, (6th)	9 Nov do	
25 do	James W. Gray	26 Dec do	
29 do	Edward Spurrier	21 May '79	
34 do	Benjm. Price	1 July do	
39 do	Richd. Waters	7 Apl '80	
2 Lieut.	Francis Revely	15 Apl '77	
7 do	James Gould	11 Mch '78	
11 do	James Winchester	27 May do	
15 do	Philip Reed	13 Oct do	
20 do	John Hartshorne	21 May '79	
24 do	Rignal Hillary	15 July do	
28 do	Philip Hill		
32 do	William Pendergast	29 Oct '79	
37 do	Henry Baldwin	11 Feb '80	

Rank.	Names.	When Commissioned.	Promotions Since Jany. 1st, '81.
42 Lieut.	David Lucket	7 Apl '80	
47 do	Walter Dyer	15 Sept do	
51 do	Nathan Wright	1 Jan '81	
60 do	John Boone	12 Apl do	vice Lyles, resigned
3 Surgeon	Levin Denwood		

4th Regiment.

Rank.	Names.	When Commissioned.	Promotions Since Jany. 1st, '81.
2 Lt. Col. Comd.	Thomas Woolford		
1 Major	Levin Winder	17 Apl '77	
5 do	Alex. Roxburgh	7 do '80	
2 Capt.	John Lynch	1 Jan '77	
7 do	Jacob Brice	do do	
11 do	Henry Gaither	17 Apl do	
16 do	John Courts Jones	20 Sept do	
21 do	Richd. Anderson	15 Nov do	
26 do	George Hamilton	25 Jan '78	
30 do	David Lynn	22 May 79	
35 do	John Mitchell	15 July do	
40 do	Jonathan Gibson	1 May '80	
3 Lieut.	Nichs. Mangers	15 Apl '77	
8 do	James Simmes	27 May '78	
12 do	Peter Hardcastle	14 Sept do	
16 do	Benjm. Garnett	13 Oct do	
19 do	Wm. Truman Stoddert	21 May '79	
29 do	Levache de Vaubrunne		
33 do	Nathan Smith	15 Dec '79	
38 do	Edmd. Compton	18 Feb '80	
43 do	Joshua Rutledge	1 May '80	
48 do	John Brevett	20 Sept do	
52 do	John McCoy	1 Jan '81	
61 do	Robert Halkerston	25 Apl do	vice McPherson, promoted into 2nd Regt.
63 do	Henry Gassaway	12 May do	vice Hall, resigned
4 Surgeon	William Kelty		

5th Regiment.

Rank.	Names.	When Commissioned.	Promotions Since Jany. 1st, '81.
3 Lt. Col. Comd.	Benj. Ford		
6 Major	John Davidson	1 Jan '81	
8 do	Benj. Brookes	16 Mch do	vice Anderson, killed
3 Capt.	Wm. Dent Beall	1 Jan '77	
8 do	John Smith, (3rd)	do do	
12 do	Edwd. Oldham	20 May do	
17 do	Horatio Clagett	10 Oct do	
22 do	John Gale	10 Dec do	

Rank.	Names.	When Commissioned.	Promotions Since Jany. 1st, '81.
27 Capt.	Perry Benson	11 Mch '78	
31 do	James Somervill	1 June '79	
36 do	William Bruce	1 Aug do	
41 do	Edward Edgerly	10 Sept '80	
4 Lieut.	James Bruff	7 Oct '77	
13 do	Gassaway Watkins	14 Sept '78	
17 do	Jacob Norris	26 Nov do	
21 do	John Lynn	1 June '79	
25 do	Saml. Hanson	1 Aug do	
30 do	Thomas Rowse		
34 do	Robert Denny	3 Jan '80	
39 do	Benj. Fickle	19 Feb do	
44 do	Roger Nelson	15 July do	
49 do	Thomas Boyd	1 Jan '81	
53 do	John Sears	do do	
62 do	Henry Clements	25 Apl do	vice McAllister, resigned
64 do	Adam Jamison	1 June do	do Hugou, promoted into 1st Regt.

Recruits from Prince George's County, July 13th, 1781.

Names of Recruits.	Country.	Age.	When Enlisted.	Time of Service.	Remarks.
Terence Duffe	Ireland	40	Feb 23	3 years	Pennsylvania, sent to Annapolis
Chas. Hickie	ditto	44	23	ditto	ditto ditto
Thos. Hammond	Native	16	Apl 28	ditto	ditto
Allen Burrell	England	38	May 25	ditto	ditto
Aquilla Clements	Native	16	14	ditto	ditto
James Lyles	ditto	18		during war	At Annapolis as per Certificate from Col. Adams
Richard Jones	England	24	May 9	3 years	
Robert Robinson	Native	36	19	ditto	Sent to Annapolis
John Jones	England	27	21	ditto	ditto
Wm. McPherson	Native	16	23	ditto	ditto
James Clements	ditto	21	25	ditto	ditto
Wm. Marlow	ditto	16	25	during war	ditto
Alexander Steel	ditto	18	26	3 years	ditto
James Jackson	ditto	21	28	ditto	ditto
Philip Grahame	ditto	32	28	ditto	ditto

Names of Recruits.	Country.	Age.	When Enlisted.	Time of Service.	Remarks.
James Kelly	Native	28	May 29	3 years	Deserted
Wm. Harrison	ditto	44	30	ditto	Sent to Annapolis
Thomas Felton	England	39	June 4	ditto	Maryland, sent to Annapolis on furlough
Walter Bean Smallwood	Native	18	5	ditto	Sent to Annapolis on furlough
John Merry	ditto	23	May 28	ditto	Sent to Annapolis
John Connely	ditto	18	June 5	ditto	ditto on furlough
John Hickson	ditto	16	5	ditto	ditto " "
John Keitch	ditto	44	5	ditto	ditto " "
John Smith	ditto	16	18	ditto	
John Anderson	Scotland	44	9	ditto	
Willm. Allbright	German	33	12	during war	

DRAFTS FROM THE CLASSES FOR FILLING UP THE QUOTA OF MEN FROM PRINCE GEORGE'S COUNTY.

PERSONS DRAFTED.

William Hardacre
William Fraser
James Card
John Ryon, of Joseph
Thos. Mobberly
Edward Atchinson
Thomas Swain
John Ranter
William Walker
John Mitchell
Thomas Sadler
Saml. Hutchinson

Joseph Mockbee
Josias Beanes
Thomas Wood
Mathew Clubb
Isaac Jones
William Clarkson
Nicholas Lowe
John King
James Tannihill
James Smith
Zacha. Tilley

John Letman
Saml. Evans
Thomas Whitehead
Zachariah Wilson
Negro Absolom
Daniel Brodie
William Turnor
Charles Shaw
Jacob Aldridge
Ninian Edmonson
Thomas King

SUBSTITUTES.

Jereh. Leitch
Caleb Davis
Butler Marlow
James Wood

Thos. Keadle
John Spires
Zadock Riston

James Jones
Benj. Duvall, of Elisha
Richard Tyler

Recruits raised in Dorchester County pursuant to a late Act of Assembly for raising Two Battalions in this State.

Recruits' Names.	Date of Enrollment.	Recruits' Names.	Date of Enrollment.
Upper Battalion			
Wm. Harrington, (absent)	9 July '81	Elisha Stack, (absent, not sworn)	14 July '81
Aaron Perry, (during War, absent)	12 "	Andrew Kerven, (absent)	18 " "
John Huffington, (3 years, with Capt. Gray)	" "	David Foxwell	23 " "
		Wm. Valient, (absent, adjudged)	11 " "
Foster Hooper	" "		
Wm. Pritchett	" "	Elijah Lyons, (absent, adjudged)	12 " "
John Willen	" "		
John Stinnett	" "	Potter Shehee, (absent, not sworn)	" " "
John Watkins	" "		
Thomas Smith	" "	George Buly, (sick, absent, not sworn, no enrollment)	
David Murray Stewart	" "		
Philemon Timmons	13 "	David Meddiss	12 July '81
John Briley	12 "	Salady Standley	" " "
John Greenwood	" "	Frederick Johnson	" " "
James Taylor	" "	John Dean	13 " "
Andrew Bramble	" "	John Hambleton	" " "
Joseph Rose	" "	John White	" " "
Levin Collins	" "	Amos Griffith	" " "
Moses Morelake	" "	William Covey	16 " "
Lower Battalion.			
John Dobson	9 July '81	Richard Harrington, 3 yrs.	16 July '81
Robert Burress	" " "	Levin Harrington, "	" " "
James Driver	10 " "	George Williams	23 " "
Abel Garner		Godfrey Sullener	16 " "
Aaron Vinson	9 " "	William Harper	11 July '81
Matthew Navey	10 " "	Joseph Harper	" " "
Jacob Tucker	" " "	Richard Hayes	" " "
Thomas Morgan	" " "	John Willis	" " "
Benjamin Fletcher	" " "	William Procter	14 " "
William Roberts	" " "	David Davis	" " "
Henry Harper	" " "	Levin Ross	16 " "
Timothy Langrell	Robert Meekins	John Stevens	
Aaron Mitchell, (als. Newberry)	John Matkins	James Busick	
	David Jones	Thomas Owens	
Absolom Goostree			
For the Corps.			
Charles Sickle, (3 yrs.)	16 July '81	Robert Johnson	14 July, '81
Daniel Blake	17 " "	Wm. Murphy	16 " "
Levi Johnson, (absent, adjudged)	14 " "	Joseph Insley	" " "
		Levin McGraw	" " "
Charles Horner	23 " "	Adams Foxwell	" " "
Francis Insley	14 " "		

July 24th, '81.　　　　　　　　　　John Goldsborough, Dor. Co.

A Return of Draughts and Substitutes sent from St Mary's Co. under the Act of May Session to join the Troops at Annapolis.

SUBSTITUTES.

James Adams	Substituted 28 July '81	Edward Harley	Substituted 1 Aug '81
John Jennings	31 " "	Igns. Griffin	2 " "
Joseph Kerby	31 " "	Walter Buckler	5 " "
Igns. Adams	23 " "	Barnard Pain	31 July '81
William Kirkpartrick	26 " "	Moses Adams	31 " "
Thos. Curtis	26 " "	Peter Jarboe	31 " "
Joseph Wimsott	27 " "	Edwd. Hasil	1 Aug.'81
Igns. Pain	28 " "	Joseph Brown	2 " "
John Madox	28 " "	William Pike	2 " "
Joseph Reswick	28 " "	John Norris	2 " "
John Dent Suit	28 " "	John Greenwell	2 " "
Baptis Gough	29 " "	Thos. Wise	5 " "
Elisha Burrowes	30 " "	Cuthb. Jones	12 " "
Charles Gough	31 " "		

DRAUGHTS.—All draughted 27 July, '81.

Joseph Newton	Charles Attwood	Nicholas Goldsbury
Henry Briscoe	Jeremiah Hazel	Igns. Brion
Edward Monark	Solomon Dixon	William Adams
Jeremiah Herbert	Henry Norris	Bennet Anderson
Struton Edwards	Robert Jarboe	Igns. Mattingly
Igns. Howard	John King	William Pratt
Arnold Norris	Charles Tawney	Nathaniel Kahil
Zacha. Newton	Charles Cole	

Caroline County, 13th Aug., 1781.

Your Excellency & Honours:

Inclosed you have a list of our Recruits and Drafts those that are excused are marked and likewise those that have run, which I shall send forward as soon as we can Ketch them: I thought it most expedient to send these forward and not to wait for those that have deserted. There is five enlisted for three years which Compleats our Quota of the last Springs Drafts, whose inlistments I have sent forward.

I am your Excellency & Honours
Most Obedt. Humble Servt.
William Whiteley.

P. S.

If you are in want of Officers for the Drafts, there is a young man amongst them by the name of George Dawson, if you think him Capable

Shou'd be glad you would give him an Ensign's Commission. There is a man by the name of Gideon Longfellow who is a Recruit for this County and has since gone to Queen Ann's County and there entered as a Substitute for a Class, therefore beg you'll please to have him entered for this County.   W. W.

A List of Recruits and Drafts belonging to Caroline County.

Recruits to the 10th Dec.

James Darnell	Thoms. Baxter	Negro Dick, (run)
James Williams	John Baxter	John DeRoachbroom
Leven Minner	William Wales	Aaron Jester
Charles Cornish	Charles Wheelar	Gidian Longfellow
William Jones	William Barcoss	

Drafts to the 10th Dec. next.

Richard Browning	Thomas Clarkson, (run)	John Manning
Henry Harnaman	John Blades, (sick)	George Jewell, (sick)
Thomas Lane	William Eagle	Levy Chance, (run)
John Prouce	John Smith, (sick)	Wm. Hutson, (run)
Daniel Conner	Rich. Smith, of Ralph,(run)	Nathan Smith, (run)
Ansell Vallient	Thos. Matthews, (run)	George Dawson
Thomas Jackson, (run)	Garey Leverton	Roger Connelly
John Brown	Barth. Jadwin, (sick)	Nathan Batchelor, (run)
Hooper Hutson	John Hutson	Allemby Millington, (run)
John Fowler	Henry Emmerton	Robert Hobbs, (run)
Walter Edgell		

A List of the Recruits for Three Years.

George Carney	Solomon Sulivane	Robert Blood	Cornish Friend
	Thomas Crompton		

Wm. Whiteley,
14th August, 1781.

Chester Town, Kent County, Aug. 23rd, 1781.

Sir :

I have lately received several Letters from you, two of which relate to the forwarding the recruits to Annapolis, those raised in consequence of the Law passed last October, have been long since at Annapolis, & that part of the Law empowering the Lieutenants to excuse any indigent person drafted, who has a wife & children, we have nothing to do with, having hired recruits for three years. Your appointment as purchaser of cloathing I have received with an enclosed Law to seize all articles suitable for that purpose. The dificulty of purchasing without anything to purchase with, must be very apparent to your Excellency & to seize those articles from merchants, who have very few goods, and nothing else to depend on, will prove their ruin; yet I am fully convinced of the necessity of supplying the Soldiery with cloathing; & was it in my power to forward this business with any degree of propriety, I would undertake it, notwithstanding I am of opinion that Lieutenants of Counties are very improper persons to execute Laws of this Nature. Should you think it necessary to have seized, the few goods in our Town, you will please to appoint some other person for that purpose, as I am already fully employed. I have enclosed a list of the recruits obtained by virtue of the Law passed last Session, & have engaged Capt. Kemp to carry them to Annapolis in his Vessel from our Town, the drafted men are endeavouring to procure substitutes which I will send with all possible dispatch, those who do not get recruits may be very dificult to collect, a few of them are poor men with Families. The 27th battalion have furnished their proportion of select militia, the 13th battalion is Classed for the purpose of Drafting. Mr. George Hanson who was appointed collector of horses refused to Act, he being Lieut. in the troop of Light Horse, had not time to execute the Law. On his refusal, I appointed Capt. George Hartshorn who has been very unsuccessful, he has brought for examination about six horses, & tells me that the nonjurors have not horses fit for the purpose. I have done all in my power to spur him to execute the Law with dispatch & have requested him to call on the commissioners for their direction. I am apprehensive that I shall not be able to send all the recruits agreeable to my list, some of them being in the Country without permission.

     I am Sir with respect yr.
          hble. Servt.
To His Excellency   W. Bordley.
  Thos. Sim Lee, Esq.

  Kent County. A List of Recruits. [Enlisted for 3 yrs.]

Charles Ogilsby	William Grant, (during the War)	Samuel Whitehouse, (dead)
John Pearce		Nicholas Smith
William Caulk, (during the War)	Daniel Norris	Peregrine Reed
	John Kelly	Beal Thomas

Samuel Binn	William Paul	Edward Kelly
Hugh Pearce	Nathan Basnett	George Jones
Daniel Herrin	William Hall	George Thomas
Starling Thomas	James Kelly	James Hininbottom
Thomas Frasier	Henry Thomas	Wm. John Lessenby
James McDoal	Simon Beck	James Griffith
John Perkins	John Lesley	Daniel Ashley
	William Bogue	

Talbot County. August 30th, 1781.

A List of Persons draughted to raise two Battalions of Militia to reinforce the American Army, to serve 'till the 10th of December, 1781.

William Willoby	Richd. Smith	William Whittocks
William Harrisson, of James T. P.	Wm. Lane	Wm. Catrop
	Richd. Beswick	Joseph Neal
Wm. Lambden	Thomas Chapman	Richard Adley
Wm. Haddaway	Francis Baker	James Kearse
Wm. Higgins	Jonathan Cheesley	Isaac Cox, Jr.
Danl. Winterbottom	Isaac Faulkner, Jr.	James Berry, Jr.
John Blades	Levy Faulkner	John Cooper
Thomas Blades	Robert Hefferson	Bristol, (a free negro)
John Kerby	Hynson Faulkner	Wm. Brinn
Joseph Robinson	James Morris	James Akers
Richd. Spencer	George Brown	John Merrick
Joseph Hopkins, of Benja.	John Morgan	Thos. Hilsby, of Wm.
John Sewell	John Watson, of Benona	Saml. White
Edward Markland	Cloudsberry Austin	Wm. Chaplin
Joseph Norwood	Thos. Nilghbours, of Saml.	
Richard Start	Charles Allen	John Holt
Robert Robinson	Wm. Troth, Jr.	John Crowder
Robert Hopkins	James Tilghman	Spindilow, (a free negro)

Chrisr. Birckhead, Lieut. T. County.

A List of Recruits, Vagrants and Draughts raised in Washington County under the Act for raising two Battalions of Militia, &c.

WHEN ENLISTED.	RECRUITS.	WHEN ENLISTED.	RECRUITS.
Aug 24	John Fisher	Aug 18	William Newell
" 14	Philip Mustersbaugh	" "	Francis Gavin
" "	Jacob Keeson	" "	Tiller Younger

When Enlisted.	Recruits.	When Enlisted.	Recruits.
Aug 14	William Mount	Aug 20	Joseph Martin
" 15	Balser Young	" 18	Philip Nogle
" "	William Clifford	" 20	Elijah Wright
" "	Samuel Larrymor	" "	Patrick Owens
" 16	Peter Boret	" "	Basil Lakin
" 17	Wm. Allen	" 21	Peter Fry
" 15	Wm. Allen, (deserted)	" 22	George Shaver
" 17	Thomas Wright	" "	Nathl. Prutzman
" "	Peter Cramer	" 23	Christr. Ninor
" 18	Peter Aley	" 24	Adam Miller
" "	William Elkison	" "	John Bumgardner
" 10	Melchor Wickart	" 18	Joseph Hoskins
" 12	Simon Liedy	" 21	William Lewis
" 10	Danl. Hoover	" 22	Martin Bringman
" 14	Michl. Leatherman	" 24	John Long
" 15	Geo. Valentine	" "	Lodowk. Smith
" 18	Frederick Snyder	" 25	Hugh McGlaughlan
" "	Nicholas Cline	" 27	Wm. Haney
" 24	Jacob Weaver	Sept 5	John Russell
" "	Richard Higgins	" "	Samuel Wycoff, Jr.
" "	Andrew Barranger	" "	Andrew Rude
" 27	John Beard	" "	Isaac Dobson
Sept 5	William Rugles	" "	Benj. Howard, (deserted)
" "	John McNiel		
" "	Philip Anthony		Vagrants.
" "	John Flat	Aug 17	Casper Reed
" "	Henry Bray		
" "	Philip Ward		Draughts.
" "	Cornelius Cock, (or Coch)	Aug 18	Frederick Kinstry
" "	Daniel Pearce	" "	Michael Hammon
	Arthur Boyes, a Recruit for during the War		

Muster Roll of the late Capt. Beatty's Company under command of Lt. W. Lamar, in the 1st Maryland Regiment Serving in the Southern Army of the United States, made this — Day of August, '81. [For Jan., Feb., Mch., Apl., May, June and July, '81.]

Names.	Date of Enlistment.	Present in July.	Remarks.
Serjeants			
Enoch McLean		present	
Samuel Denney	2 March '78		Dischd. 2 Mch '81
Arthur McLean	10 Feb '80	"	

during the War of the American Revolution, 1775–83.

NAMES.	DATE OF ENLISTMENT.	PRESENT IN JULY.	REMARKS.
Serjeants			
Cuthbert Able	1 Feb '80		A. F. M. Jan–July
Stephen Flaharty			In Hospital 19 June and July
David Love	8 Sept '80		Lt. Infantry, transfd. 12 Mch
Benjamin Fitzgerald	Oct '79	absent	Recruiting in Md. Jan–July
Samuel Filson		"	" " " "
Moses Barney		"	" " " "
Gabl. Williams	6 Feb '80	"	" " " "
Igns. Wheeler		"	" " " "
Aquilla Cheatham		"	" " " "
Samuel Davis		"	" " " "
Ch. McNabb		"	" " " "
Owen Carey	1 Feb '80		Light Infantry, dead Mch '81
John Scott	9 July '80	present	State Regt., joined 12 Mch '81
Corpls.			
Wm. Bruff			
Peter Stephans			On guard.
James Kelley			Light Infantry, transferred 12 Mch '81
John Falling		"	State Regt., joined 12 Mch '81
Drum. & Fifes			
John Riggs	6 May '80		Light Infantry, transferred
Jesse Barnett, (or Barrett)		"	[12 Mch '81
Abram Stallings		"	
Saml. Taylor			Dead, June '81
Edward Clancey		"	
Joshua Ishome		absent	Recruiting in Md. Jan–July
Michael Carey		"	ditto ditto
Thos. Wingate	26 Oct '80		P. War, 25 April
Privates			
Zadock Whaley		present	On guard
Peter Outhouse		"	
Michl. Curtis		"	
Alexander Ross		"	
Jos. Mattingly		"	On guard
Jon. Hadan		"	
Robt. Dunkin		"	
Chas. Simpkins		"	Sick, July
John Loveday		"	
Richd. Taylor		"	On guard
Danl. Smith		"	
Jon. Maxfield		"	
Igns. Cumpton		"	Sick, July
George Devit		"	Sick, July
Thos. Peacock		"	

Names	Date of Enlistment.	Present in July.	Remarks.
Privates			
Absolum Fardo		present	
Leonard Hagan	1 Jany '80	"	
Elijah Pepper		"	On guard
Wm. Hurly		"	
Luke Simpson		"	
Stephen Carr		"	
Jacob Hunt		"	
Walter Hagan	1 Feby '80	"	
Wm. Leakin		"	
George Buck		"	
Christian Myers		"	
John Twiner		"	
William Young		"	
Wm. Quinton		"	On guard
Wm. Hamston	31 Jany '80	"	On guard
Saml. Clark		"	
James Managa		"	Deserted Jan, returned to Service 14 May
Lawre. Hurdle			Genl. Smallwood, July
Henery Reese			Waiter Major Roxburgh, July
Wm. Crail			Waiter Capt. Mason, July
Jacob Carnant			Lt. Infantry Jan, transfd. 12 Mch
John Ashmore		do	do
James White		do	do
Humphry Beckett		do	do
Michl. Waltman		do	do
Neal Peacock		do	do
John More		do	do
John W. Loclen		do	dead March
Chas. Ormes		do	transfd. 12 Mch
Bazel Norman		do	transfd. 12 Mch
Wm. Mann			Waiter to Capt. Anderson Deserted Feb, returned to Service 17 May. In Hospl. 19 June and July
Fredk. Harty			Lt. Infantry Jan, transfd. 12 Mch
Saml. Garcy	27 Apl '78	do	do
John O'Bryan		do	dead 25 April
Josiah Burgess	19 Apl '78	do	transfd. 12 Mch
Simon Colbert		do	deserted Feb
James McDonnel		present	Waggoner Jan–July
Cornelius Morris		"	do July
John Mills		"	do Jan–July
James Smith		"	do July
Partrick Riley		"	do do

during the War of the American Revolution, 1775–83. 391

NAMES.	DATE OF ENLISTMENT.	PRESENT IN JULY.	REMARKS.
Privates			
Willm. Niblet		present	Waggoner July
Dorest Felmot	5th May '78	do	Dischd. 5 May
Moses Foster		B. Smith, July	
Richard Gee		Orderly Hosptl. July	
Daniel Hall		ditto	ditto
Joshua Lester		ditto	ditto
Barney Munrow		Hosptl. 16 June and July	
Andrew Mallen		do 15 March and July	
Cuthbert Stone		Lt. Infantry. Hosptl. July	
Wm. Kindle	25 Apl '78	Discharged 25 April	
Nichls. Fitzjarold	2 May '78	Lt. Infantry, dischd. 2 May	
Joseph Gordan	1 do '78	do	do 1 do
Soloman Turner	12 do '78	do	transfd. 12 March
John King	25 Apl '78	do	do do
Nichls. Hearty	24 do '78	Discharged 24 April	
Willm. Townsend		do	May
Aquilla Smith	2 June	do	2 June
Adam Crow	28 Apl '78	Discharged 28 April	
Thomas Hay	25 do '78	do	25 do
Joshua Brown	23 do '78	do	23 do
John McNalley		P. War, 25 April	
James Current		do	do
John M. Funner		do	do
Willm. Prangley		do	do
Willm. Comming		do	do
John Webb		do	Feby
James Dowlen		do	25 April
Richd. Boon		Killed 15 March	
John Cockran		do	do
Geo. Phillips		Dead March	
Andrew More		Killed 15 March	
John Meeks		do	do
Francis Kitely		do	25 April
Willm. Wedge		Dead March	
Michael Penn		Deserted April	
Thos. Christopher		do	March
John Jones		do	15 do
James Brooke		do	January
Thos. Keeff		do	15 March
Willm. Mode		do	February
Daniel Barnet		do	January
James Clemonts		do	22 June
William Taylor		do	
Daniel Benning		do	January

Names.	Date of Enlistment.	Present in July.	Remarks.
Privates			
Philip Sulivan		Orderly in Hosptl. July	
William Casey		In Hospital July	
Francis Reynolds		do	do
Joseph Botts		do	do
—ar'y. Fitzjarold		do	do
Jon. Blair		do	Wounded March
David McVey		present	
Willm. Hellman		"	

I do swear that the within Muster Roll is a true State of the Company under my Command.   W. Lamar, Lt.

The following members of the 3rd, 4th and 5th Maryland Regiments received from Robert Denny, in Bills of Credit and in Specie, pay due them for the present Campaign. 3rd Regt., Augt. 28th, 1781.

1st Company, 3rd Regiment.

Serjts.
George Fields
Jno. Coolin
Jesse Suite
Robt. Scrivener
Chas. Jones

Corpls.
Peter Byall
Jos. Phearson
Joel Baker
Theo. Lindsay
Jona. Foster

Drummers
Wm. Stewart
Wm. Smith
Moses McKinsey
Joshua McKinsey

Privates
Benj. Smith
Jno. Holder
Jno. Hullett
Wm. Jefferies

Privates
Jno. Connolly
Elijah Neall
Jno. Jones
James West
Nath. Hawthorn
Jno. Newton, Sr.
Jno. Newton, Jr.
John Robey
W. B. Smallwood
Aqa. Clements
James Nott
Mattw. Kelly
Jno. Fullford
Wm. Newbury
Jno. Overman
Saml. Smith
John Brown
Patk. Mallone
Thos. Archer
Robt. Hornsbury
Jno. Beaumont
Basset McCleary
Richd. Hayes
Jno. Welsh

Privates
James Lowry
Andw. Lord
Handy Handley
James Russell
James Evans
Thos. Larramore
Henry Wilstock, (or Witstock)
Jesse McKinsey
Alex. Cockburn
Luke Merryman
Richd. Haslip
Francis Purcell
Jos. Austin
George Bough
Thos. Sheridan
Jos. Crouch
Patt. McKinsey
Levy Moody
Jacob Doyne
Christr. Smith
Robt. Robertson
Wm. Harrison
Matthias Sipher

Privates	Privates	Privates
Garrett Welsh	Jas. Kirk	Elijah Oakley
Jas. Erwin	Jno. Wilson	James Capell, (or Caple)
Tim. Cahill	Solomon Askins	Ewill Evans
Jesse Powers	Thos. Gordon	James Sappington
Jno. Armstrong	Richd. Dixon	Edward Wade

2ND COMPANY, 3RD REGIMENT.

Q. M. S.
William Forman

Serjts.
John H. Dorsey
Jno. Reeder
Jno. Lynch

Corpls.
William Lytle
Wm. Chatlin

Drummers
Jos. Follet
Jas. Collard
Thos. Atkinson
Aaron Perry

Privates
Peter Quidowney, (Equidoroney)
Silas Frost
Jno. McLane
Peter French
Jno. Bowdy
Stephen Kimble
Wm. Bowden

Privates
Levin Thomas
Francis Reed
Wm. Simmonds
Saml. Chapple
Jno. Gorman
Charles Lego
Jno. McCall
Danl. McFetteridge
Oliver Denny
James Waddell
Richard Todd
Abraham Shockey
David Hatton
Andrew Flood
Matthias Dytch
Jery Fitzgerald
James Hayes
William Roe
Barney Dougherty
James Lynch
James Chard
James Hall
Teagle Tigner
James Tigner
Saml. Hurst
Robert Jones

Privates
Edwd. Tanner
James Cromwell
Archd. Kersey
Jas. Anderson
Neal McCowan
Feolix Snyder
James Crayton
Edward Evans
Andrew Travis
Lewis White
Michl. Pilkington
Wm. Broughton
John Kildare
Philip McDonald
John McDonald
Jno. Young
Francis Matthews
John Hudson
James Hudson
Richard Miles
John Hicken
Jos. McLane
Patrick Fleming
John Graham
John Boady

3RD COMPANY, 3RD REGIMENT.

Serjts.
Terrence Duffey
James Jackson
Saml. Filson, (Philson)
Bennett Mudd
Archd. Johnson

Corpls.
Thos. Polehouse
James Ashley

Privates
Jno. Deakins
Thos. Pinfold
Jno. Spyers
Timothy Lynch
Jno. Nicholson
Henry Evitt
Michl. Smith
Arthur Coffin
Willm. Mason

Privates
Jesse Furrow
Clement Harwood
Henry Lane
Elijah Hutt
George Diz
Leonard Holt
Richard Lane
Henry Reese
Jno. Shockles

Corpls.
Lazarus Higgs
Geo. Hamilton
Wm. Browning
Danl. Birmingham
Saml. Evans

Drummers
Jno. Jordan
Isaac Hill
Isaac Young
Richd. Jamison
Jno. Jones.
Michl. Smith

Privates
George Credo
Charles Hickey
Danl. Buckley
Jno. Durant
Francis Rogers
William Potter
Michael Downs
Richard Spyers
Benjamin Smith
Benjamin Gaither
Michael Madden
Jno. Anderson
Alex. Hughes
James Due
Philip Savoy
Francis Carnes
Stephen Fennell
John Hughes
Saml. Hussey
Jno. Turner
Thomas James
Thomas Berry
Charles Cooper
Charles Williams
Wm. Moorecraft
John Campbell
John Powell
James Jackson
Thomas Pattison
Saml. Harrison
Willm. Hamilton
John Haynes
Jacob Flowers
Francis McCann
John Thompson
Willm. Hancock

4th Company, 3rd Regiment.

Serjts.
Willm. Collis
Jno. Walker
Jno. Carson
Francis Duffey
Jacob Keyser

Corpls.
Jacob Knight
James Clements
Jno. Davis

Drummers
Edwd. Armstrong
Jno. Roach
Archd. Butt
Thos. Hutchcraft
Jno. McKay

Privates
Wm. Chapman
Jno. Wade
Jno. Blades
Dennis Downes
William Glory
Michael Doring
Thomas Jones
Thomas Woodland

Privates
Thomas Arthurs
John Malady
Benjamin Baulk
Zach. Robertson
Saml. Gray
Thomas Potts
Philip Graham
Thomas Hammond
William Turner
Jno. Smith
Jno. Davies Tulley
Jno. Ryon
Thomas Porter
Samuel Boswell
Patrick Reading
James Crisbury
Peter Richards
Allen Townsend
Wm. Marlow
Lucas Ives
William Newton
Alex. Steele
Jno. Hicks
Jos. Turner
Momus Leary
Wm. Whitmore

Privates
Jno. Johnson
Henry Tarman
Joseph Isaacs
Henry Frazier
James Steward
Wm. McPherson
James Lyles
Jno. Stonehunt
Abm. Manning
Roger Landers
Thos. B. Allum
George Linton
James Jones
Willm. Preator
Saml. Silk
Thos. Hickenbottom
Wm. Maddux
Wm. Stanley
Francis McGurrow
Dennis Disman
William Berry
Peter Carbury
Robt. Campbell
Edward Walter
George Campbell
Thomas Neall

5TH COMPANY, 3RD REGIMENT.

Serjts.
Saml. Shoemaker
Nichls. Nicholson
John Brady
James Brown

Corpls.
Jno. Moore
Jno. Clancey
Ralph Hagen
Charles Fullam

Drummers
Jno. Hannon
Jno. Morrison
Henry Ferns
Jno. Onions

Privates
Benj. Marsh
Charles Dean
Jno. Willin
William Wilson
Abraham Kettle
George Silver
Henry Fisher, Sr.
Adam Mushler
Jacob Caufman
Danl. Williams
Peter Coons

Privates
George Fleck
Jno. Eppinstall, (Eppinstoole)
Jno. Flowers
Wm. Artman
Jos. Lewis
William Goodey
Henry Fisher, Jr.
Michl. Ritmire
Jno. Fennell
Jno. Holdson
Nichs. Hyner
Jno. Welty
Richard Jones
William Clover
Corns. Vaughan
William Craill
William Rider
Jos. Cox
Samuel Young
Nathl. Aldridge
Jno. McGlenn
Willm. Wheland
Thomas Tanner
John Follet
John Merry
Jos. Ferroll
Robert Eaton
Danl. Mann

Privates
James Wilson
Jno. Stoffell
Fredk. Stoffell
Jacob Detrow
Willm. Dawson
Lambert Goodey
James Hales
Dennis Creagon
Robert Folger
James Terry
Thomas Cullumber
Frederick Hioms
Henry Lynn
Robert Anderson
Charles Willett
John Gee
Jno. Wright
James Fisher
Jno. Flanagan
William Dytch
Jno. Curll
Andrew Rearside
Jno. Winslow
John Thompson
Dennis Tramell
William Taylor
John Fransey
Edward Mahawney, (Mahoney)

6TH COMPANY, 3RD REGIMENT.

Serjts.
George Holton
George Finlay
James Wood
Benjamin Ward

Corpls.
William Elburn
William Doncan
James Wilson
Isaac Henderson

Drummers
Henry Harris
Daniel Willis

Drummers
Thomas Clinton
William Copeland
James Bryan

Privates
William Aggis
Henry Emmes
William Harrison
Edward Scantlum
Levin Abott
Luke Osborne
William Taylor
Jacob Jefferies
Edward Bartlet

Privates
William Gudgeon
Smith Bragwell
James Chambers
Bennet George
Thomas Harris
Jno. Harris
Shadrach Sapp
Peter Hollowburn
Patrick Sullivan, (belonging to the Eastern Troops)
Peter Surkey, (belonging to the Eastern Troops)
James Sheppard
Jno. Burke

Privates
Richard Green
John Steward
John Cole
Philip McGlaskey
Jno. Smallwood
Jno. Anderson
Stephen Hancock
James Smith
David Wilton
Peter Cinquiad, (Cincuid, Kincade)

Privates
Thomas Johns
Abraham Reynolds
Jno. Starkey
Banks Webb
Isaac Davis
James Brannon
Absalom Scott
William Lyons
James Reynolds

Privates
Jno. Collins
Jacob Collins
Lawrence Simpson
Robert Carnes
Henry Burns
Notley Whitcomb
Edward Chambers
George Belfast

7TH COMPANY, 3RD REGIMENT.

Serjts.
John Newman
Wm. Needham
Jno. Neary
Wm. Martin
James Collins
Alex. Mackey

Corpls.
Jno. Biggs
Wm. Clements
Jno. Matthews

Drummers
Jno. McCauliff
Nichs. Elliott
Henry Burns
Philip Huston

Privates
Daniel Doncan
Jno. Harris, Sr.
Jas. Cockrall
James Evans
Jno. Thomas
William Brady
Thomas Wood
William Coe

Aquilla Deaver
John Milstead
John Young
Paul Richards
Thos. Bailey
Wm. Lynch
Benj. Gray, Serjt.
John Noble
Joseph Fowler

Privates
Joseph White
Richard Price
Thomas Adams
Kindall Cobb
Matthew Stainton
Richard Dalvin, (Delvin)
Richard Dimby
Jno. Pinder
Henry Williams
James Powell
Jos. McNamara
Andrew Haufman
Edwd. Appleton
Joshua Atkins
Jno. King
Emanuel Ebbs
John Walker
James Blancher
James Humphreys
Jno. Willis
William Porter
Jno. Lesley
James Needs
Solomon Green
James Scott
Thomas Clarke

Stafford Foysdoyle, (Foysdale)
Wm. Cutler
John Smith
Alex. Robertson
Benj. Williams
Charles McNabb, Serjt.
Richd. Fenwick, "

Privates
John Collins
Nathan Ross
Wm. Mansfield
Michael Mondis
Edward Edes
Richard Farraby
Prestly Brewington
Thomas Jones
John Hurley
Wm. Guantley
Oliver Stephens
William Correll
James Bailey
John Keetch
Thos. Clements
Thos. Matthews
Isaac Graves
John Ranson
Jno. McNeall
Henry Hughes
Francis Burton
James Lawrence
James Davidson
Abm. Dougan
Francis Taylor
John Brewington

John Willin, Serjt.
Gabriel Williams, "
Peter McNaughton, "
Aquilla Chittham, "
B. Fitzgerald, "
Saml. Davis, "
William Pitts
Wm. Rose, Serj. M.

during the War of the American Revolution, 1775–83. 397

4TH REGT. 10 SEPT., 1781.

Thos. Duffee	Aliad Melville	John Stephens
John Betsey	Moses Morleck	John Willin
George Leseh	Robt. Blood	Wm. Cork
Nathl. Baley	Thomas Davis	Wm. Whiticoe
Chas. Nabb	John Hudson	Thos. Long
Thomas Elliott	Heithcote Edwards	John Dobson
Luke Griffith	Geo. Carney	John Nelson
Robt. Mitchell	Cornish Friend	Thos. Burke
Saml. Lynch	Cato Snowden	Walter Pruit
Thos. Foxall	Andrew Bramble	George Jones
Edw. Fincham	Wm. Paul	Martin Rohrer
Wm. Lee	Philip Knight	Fredk. Meyers
John Briley	John A. Mildorph	John Gothard
John O'Conner	Wm. Burgis	Hanry Rorer
John Charles	John Cleverdence	Thomas James
John Taylor	James Darnell	Wm. Grant
Aaron Mitchell	Edward Henesy	Benj. Belcher
Michael Hennessy	John Paxman	Robt. Smith
David Meadows	Daniel Murphey	Jesse Locker
Timothy Donlon	Adam Weatherholt	Pompey Hollis
Philip Welsh	Peter Hammond	Wm. Absalom
Melby Christopher	Jacob Yeast	Igns. Smith
Isaac Christopher	Wm. Tillwood	James Green
Wm. Bacchus	Chas. Wheeler	James McDaniel
Chas. Gordon	Godfrey Sullender	Humphrey Wells
John Watkins	Wm. Donoho	Wm. Welsh
John Dean	John Loaness	

John Dove, Serjt., Aug. 28th.   Wm. Stewart, Fifer, Aug. 28th.
Wm. Smith, Drum. "   "   Thos. Clinton, "   "   "

5TH REGT. 13 OCT., '81.

John Riley	Smart Green	John McBryde, Drum.
George Parker	Jacob Keller	John Murrant, "
Edwd. Kirk	Thomas Calpin	Danl. Howe, Fifer
Thos. Fleming	Thomas Smith	John Brown, Corpl.
Patk. Quinn	James Driver	Elijah Cockendale, "
Joseph Fisher	Jeremiah Dillen	Robt. Firth, "
Edwd. Riley	Nehemiah Lingrell	Wm. Marlow
Jacob Adams	George Welsh	Dennis Carty
Roderick McKenny	Wm. Harper	Basil Shaw, Serjt.
Nehemiah Lanham	Fredk. Smith	Benj. Johnson, Aug 28th
Zacha. Berry	John Morris	Geo. Williams, Serjt.
Richard Hoggin	Richd. Peplow	Robt. Mahill, (or Hukell), Serjt.
Jona. Sheppard		

Annapolis, 13th October, 1781. Received of Robt. Denny the sum of one pound two shillings & sixpence by each of us subscribers, of the

Bills of Credit emitted for defraying the expences of the present Campaign, in part of pay due us.

William Cox, late 2nd Regt.	
William George, late 6th Regt.	
Daniel O'Neall	
William Moore	
Richard Blandford	These were prisoners and received £5 previous to this date.
Thomas Richardson, late 5th Regt.	
Emanuel Allen, late 5th Regt.	
Joseph Blaize, late 7th Regt.	
Thomas Bird	
Michaél Clancey, late 5th Regt.	

The following received from Robt. Denny such sums as were due them, October 13th, 1781.

Joseph Harper	Southard George	John Parks
Charles Horner	Thomas Jones	Richard Clarke
David Foxwell	Vincent Molen	James Underhill
William Justice	Walter Ferroll	John Armond
Christian Boss	William Camm	Benjamin Reed
John Faucett	Daniel Harden	Charles Syckle
Charles Davis	Thomas McKouff,(or McBruff)	Thomas Pettit
William Corsey	James Creighton	James Bowen
James Halloran	John Gordan	John Cannon
Edwd. Jackson	Wm. Batten	John Cole
Zachariah Mills	Franciss Dewiss	Joseph Neall
Isaac Nichols	John Gorman	Joseph McClain
John McDaniel	William Smith	Joseph Crouch
James McDaniel		

The following received from Robt. Denny pay due them.

Aug 13 '81 Lowrence Hurdle, 3rd Regt.	Oct 6 '81 James French
Jan 8 '82 Henry Lynn	Mch 5 '82 Nelce Jones, 2nd Regt.
18 " Wm. Kaugh	23 " Robt. Taylor
18 " Wm. Douglass	

The following received from Robert Denny pay due them.

LT. CLEMONS' CO. NOV. 2ND, 1781.

John Connelly	Amis Griffith	John Wilson
John Burn	John Toole	Harris Austin
Christr. Lambert	Jesse King	Timothy Langrell
Andw. Mullane	Nathl. Price	

Lieut. Batte	from Capt. Hall's Company.
Ensign Inglehart	from Capt. Sanders.
John Knighton } Stephen Beard } Richard Jones } Jnothan Weeden } William Onion } Austin Atwell } John Taymon } Jeremiah Wells }	from Capt. Sanders.
William Davis } Aquila Linthicum } Sabrit Journey } Cephas Benson } John Elliott } James Elliott }	from Capt. Mulliken.
Walter Dent } Israel Pearce } —— Sweney }	from Capt. Watkins.
Richard Butler } Notley Sweeney }	from Capt. Hall.

The Above list is handed to the Accotnt. by Major Higgins as of the Men for whom Dinner was furnished by M. Smith in April. They were draughts from Major Higgin's Battalion in Service of U. States.

Harford County, 11th December, 1781.

Sir:

Agreeable to Directions from the Lieut. Enclosed I transmit your Excellency, A Return of Recruits, Draughts &c, Agreeable to an Act Entitled an Act to procure Recruits, Also a Return of Substitutes & Draughts, Agreeable to an Act Entitled an Act to Raise Two Battalions of Militia—I should also have sent your Excellency an Account of the Balance due the State of the four Shilling Tax, but there is not yet as much Collected as has been paid to Recruits—and the Lieut. has thought it unnecessary to grant more Executions, as the Sheriff has not settled for, nor paid, what has been Already Granted, tho a long time in his hands. I am your Excellency's very Humble Servant

A. Crawford, Secy. L. H. County.

To his Excellency Thos. Sim Lee, Esq.

Return of Recruits, Substitutes & Draughts, raised in Harford County for the Two Battalions of Militia, Agreeable to an Act of Assembly in the Year 1781.

Names of Substitutes.	Names of Substitutes.	Names of Substitutes.
John Gordon	William Butler	Alex. Christie
Nathan Strong	James Keys	Thos. Monahon
John Usher	Wm. Truss	John Miles
John Morris	James Bond	Anguis McCreary
John Curl	George Todd	James Condren
Saml. Hodgkins	Peter Ratagan	Wm. Payne
Barachius Coop	John Sullivan	John Willard
William Bently	Samuel Scarborough, deserted	Thos. Ask
Edward Fincham	William Smith	James Silk
William Wright	Jeremiah Williamson	John Norris
Griffith Evans	John Shields	Robert Mitchell

Names of Draughts.		Remarks.
William Condron		
George O'Keil		
Horatio Coop		
Nathan Price		
John Offield		
John Dearmott		taken ill with the Flux
Aaron Grace		dischd., being poor & having a Wife & 5 [Children
David Deaver		id same having Wife & 7 Children
Negroe Tower		id same having Wife & Children
Nathan Gallion		Infirm and Sickly
Edward Prigg		id
Richd. Greenland		id
Richard Kenly		id
Jona. West		poor, a Wife & Children to support
Joseph Johnson		id
Thos. Rhoads		id
Wm. Grafton		id
Nathan Johns		a Quaker & id but did not appear
Richd. Johns		id son to the above
Isaac Henry		id did not appear
Robt. Jones		never taken up
Nathan Brownly		id
Henry Russ		id
James McGaw		id
John McGaw		id
Wm. Major		id
James Bevard		id
Joseph Aikens		id
Henry Harrod		id
Thos. Ely		Quaker id
Wm. Judd		kept out of the way
Michael Rook		run
James Andrews		id
Wm. Gash		id

A. Crawford, Secy. L. H. County.   11 Dec., 1781.

Return of Recruits, Substitutes and Draughts, raised in Harford County, Agreeable to an Act Entitled, An Act to procure Recruits, in the Year 1781.

NAMES OF SUBSTITUTES.	TERM OF ENLISTMENT.	NAMES OF SUBSTITUTES.	TERM OF ENLISTMENT.
Oliver Denny	three years	John Overman	three years
Edward Appleton	" "	John Hutson	" "
John Oldham White	a very great imposter	Lawrence Hines	" "
		William Newberry	" "
George Gardners	three years	John McCall	" "
John Pendall	" "	John Ranson	" "
John McClain	" "	Evan Thomas	" "
John Fulfit	" "	Patrick Mullen	" "
Thos. Sheredin	" "	James Hutson	" "
John Finnch	" "	James Cromwell	to the 10th Dec.
Philip McDonald	" "	Robert Jones	" " "
Neal McOwen	" "	John H. Dorsey	" " "
Wm. Coe	" "	Peter Wedoney	" " "
James Caple	" "	John O'Neal	" " "
Peter French	" "	John Thompson	" " "
John Willson	" "		

DRAUGHTS.	TERM OF ENLISTMENT.	DRAUGHTS.	TERM OF ENLISTMENT.
James McNabb	to the 10th Dec.	Wm. Carlen	lame and unfit for duty
Benj. Culver	dischd. by Gov. & Council	Daniel Davey	not to be found
Wm. Cantlin	lame and unfit for duty	Danl. Douglas	not to be taken
		Saml. McComas	run away

A. Crawford, Secy. L. H. County.
11 Dec., 1781.

Dates and Terms of Enlistments of men inlisted in the 4th and 5th Regts. in 1781.

NAMES.	WHEN ENLISTED.	REGIMENT.	TERM.	BY WHOM ENLISTED.
John Briley	July 29 '81	Md. Line	War	Captain Lynn
Benj. Belcher	Aug 7	4th Regt.	do	do
John Betsworth	11	Md. Line	3 years	do
Thos. Burke	12	4th Regt.	do	do
Nathl. Bailey	12	do	do	do
Thos. Berry	14	do	do	do
Andrew Bramble	17	Md. Line	do	do

Names.	When Enlisted.	Regiment.	Term.	By Whom Enlisted.
John Baxter	Aug 23	Md. Line	3 years	Captain Lynn
Christian Boss	28	5th Regt.	War	Lt. Sears
John Balor	Sept 1	do	3 years	do
Wm. Covey	Aug 3	4th Regt.	do	Lt. Crawford
Richd. Clarke	11	do	War	Capt. Lynn
John O'Connor	17	Md. Line	do	do
John Curll	18	do	3 years	do
Thos. Calpin	24	do	do	do
John Cleverdence	28	do	do	do
Milbey Christopher	29	do	do	do
Isaac Christopher	29	do	do	do
John Callahan	Sept 1	do	do	do
William Courcey	Oct 3	5th Regt.	do	Lt. Sears
John Cannon	Sept 1	do	do	do
Arthur Coffin	May 5	3d Regt.	War	Capt. Trueman
Alex. Cockburne	2	do	3 years	Col. Brice, Lt. A. A. Co.
John Deane	July 29	Md. Line	War	Capt. Lynn
John Dobson	Aug 2	4th Regt.	do	do
James Driver	4	do	do	do
Thos. Duffee	7	Md. Line	3 years	do
Timothy Donlan	17	do	do	do
Thos. Davis	18	4th Regt.	do	do
Geo. Dawson	21	Md. Line	do	do
Jeremiah Dillon	Sept 10	5th Regt.	do	Lt. Sears
Walter Evans	Aug 15	Md. Line	do	Capt. Lynn
Hethesale, (Hethcoat), Edwards	25	do	do	do
Jacob Flowers	11	do	do	do
Thomas Foxall	14	3d Regt.	do	do
Edward Fincham	15	Md. Line	do	do
John Frazier	31	do	do	do
John Fawcitt, (Fosset)	Sept 1	do	do	do
John Frederick	11	do	do	do
David Foxwell	6	do	do	do
Benj. Foard	9	5th Regt.	do	Lt. Sears
Walter Ferroll	12	do	do	do
Wm. Frazier	10	do	do	do
John Gothard	Aug 6	4th Regt.	War	Capt. Lynn
Luke Griffith, (or Griffen)	9	Md. Line	do	do .
Amos, (or Moses), Griffith	26	do	3 years	do
Francis Gavon	Sept 11	5th Regt.	do	Lt. Sears
John Huffington	July 12	Md. Line	do or War	Lt. Dorchester County
Richd. Herrington	16	do	3 years	do

during the War of the American Revolution, 1775–83.

Names.	When Enlisted.	Regiment.	Term.	By Whom Enlisted.
Levin Herrington	July 16	Md. Line	3 years	Lt. Dorchester County
Edwd. Hennessy	29	4th Regt.	War	Capt. Lynn
Michael Hennessy	Aug 8	do	do	do
William Hamilton	9	Md. Line	3 years	Lt. Crawford
James Hayes	15	do	do	Capt. Lynn
Pompey Hollis	16	do	do	do
Joseph Harper	26	do	do	do
William Harper	26	do	do	do
Foster Hooper	26	do	do	do
Charles Horner	Sept 6	do	do	do
James Holloren, (Halloran)	9	5th Regt.	do	Lt. Sears
John Jennings	Aug 17	Md. Line	do	Capt. Lynn
Edwd. Jackson	18	do	do	do
Aaron Jester	22	do	do	do
Wm. Justice	24	do	do	do
Robt. Johnson	26	do	do	do
William Jones	Sept 14	5th Regt.	do	Lt. Sears
Philip Knight	Aug 15	4th Regt.	do	Capt. Lynn
Thomas Kelly	Sept 6	Md. Line	War	do
Anthony Lewitz	Aug 9	do	3 years	do
Thomas Long	12	4th Regt.	do	do
William Leary	14	Md. Line	do	do
Thomas Lane	20	do	do	do
Timothy Langrell	26	do	do	do
David Meadows	July 29	do	do	do
Aaron Mitchell	29	4th Regt.	War	do
Moses Morelake, (Morleck)	30	do	do	do
Aliad Melville	Aug 4	do	do	do
Michael McKnight	4	do	3 years	do
Alex. McCoy	8	do	War	do
John Mifford, (Mofford)	11	Md. Line	3 years	do
Wm. Murphey	14	do	do	do
John A. Mildorph	14	do	War	do
Robert Mitchell	15	do	3 years	do
Daniel Murphey	16	do	War	do
Martin Madden	21	do	3 years	do
Francis McCann	24	do	do	do
John Morris	Sept 1	do	do	do
Hezekiah Massey.	1	do	do	do
Andrew Mullen	Dec 10	5th Regt.	do	Lt. Sears
Vincent Molen	Sept 10	do	do	do
John McAffee	1	do	do	do

Names.	When Enlisted.	Regiment.	Term.	By Whom Enlisted.
Aaron Perry	July 10	4th Regt.	War	Capt. Lynn
John Parks	Aug 1	do	do	do
Lodwick Pole	11	do	do	do
John Paxman	25	Md. Line	3 years	do
Walter Prewitt, (Pruett)	29	do	do	do
Nathan Price	30	do	do	do
Thos. Pattison	June 1	3d Regt.	War	Lt. Denny
Chas. Nabb	Aug 12	4th Regt.	3 years	Capt. Lynn
John Nelson	15	do	do	do
John Riley	Sept 8	5th Regt.	do	Lt. Sears
Benj. Ried, (Read)	6	do	do	do
Charles Syckle, (Sickle)	July 16	Md. Line	do	Lt. Dorchester County
Thomas Smith	30	4th Regt.	War	Capt. Lynn
John Stennett	Aug 4	do	3 years	do
William Scott	10	Md. Line	do	do
John Sheffer, (Shiffer)	11	4th Regt.	do	do
Robt. Smith	13	do	War	do
John Stephens	25	Md. Line	3 years	do
Godfrey Sullender	26	do	do	do
Salady Stanley	Sept 4	do	do	do
Patrick Shields	25	5th Regt.	do	Lt. Sears
John Sloan	10	do	do	do
John Taylor	Aug 1	4th Regt.	War	Capt. Lynn
John Thompson	9	do	do	do
Edwd. Tanner	13	3d Regt.	3 years	do
Henry Tucker	17	Md. Line	War	do
Wm. Tillwood	25	do	3 years	do
John Toole	Oct 11	5th Regt.	War	Lt. Sears
James Underhill	Aug 9	4th Regt.	3 years	Capt. Lynn
John Watkins	3	Md. Line	do	do
John Willin	4	4th Regt.	War	do
Philip Welsh	5	do	3 years	do
William Whitticoe, (Whittacar)	12	Md. Line	do	do
John Winstanley	18	do	do	do
James Williams	19	do	do	do
Charles Wheeler	19	do	do	do
Geo. Williams	27	do	do	do
Humphrey Wells	27	do	War	do
Richd. Williams	Sept 4	4th Regt.	3 years	do

Additional Names to the above List From a Return of Men Inlisted in the Md. Line in 1781.

NAMES.	WHEN ENLISTED.	REGT.	TERM.
Wm. Allen	15 Aug		Term not mentioned in
Peter Boughan	1 "		War [Inlistment
Robt. Blood	20 July	5th	3 yrs.
John Bailey	29 "		War
Peter Collins	21 "		3 yrs.
John Campbell	24 "		"
Thos. Crampton	14 Aug	5th	"
James Collins	2 May		"
Wm. Cock	13 July		War
Wm. Dannahugh	10 Aug		3 yrs.
Abraham Dogan	19 July		War
Thos. Dickenson	23 "		3 yrs.
John Davis	15 Nov	5th	"
James French	1 May		" Waggoner
Cornish Frend	17 July		War
Edward Fitcham	15 Aug		3 yrs.
Wm. Grant	22 "		War
Vincent Gray	11 Dec		3 yrs.
Peter Hammon	9 Aug		"
Danl. Holdman	9 "		"
Jesse Johnson	18 July		"
Geo. Karney	18 "	5th	"
Henry Korer	9 Aug		"
Martin Korer	——		"
Jesse Locker	7 Sept		"
Willm. Lee	8 Aug		"
Anthony Lewis	9 "	4th	"
John Lownas	13 "		"
Thomas Lam	20 "		"
Patrick Mellon	12 July		"
Fredk. Moyer	8 Aug		"
Alex. Montgomery	8 "		"
David Medes, (Meddis)	29 July		"
And. Mallone	4 Sept	5th	"
Henry Ritch	18 July		"
Geo. Roach	6 Aug		"
Willm. Roberts	14 Dec		"
Wm. Robertson	14 "		"
Wm. Smith	1 Sept		"
Wm. Smith	3 Aug		"
John Showman	8 "		"
Solomon Sullivant	20 June	5th	"

Names.	When Enlisted.	Regt.	Term.
Lewis White	12 Feb	5th	War
Adam Weatherhold	8 Aug		3 yrs.
Jacob Yeast	11 "		"
Aaron Jester, (or Tester)	22 "	4th	"

"An Alphabetical List of discharged Soldiers of the two Battalions of Militia raised to serve in the Continental Army in the year 1781."

County.	Names.	County.	Names.
	Adams, John		Austin, Harris
St Mary's	Anderson, Bennett	St Mary's	Adams, Moses
	Alsey, William	St Mary's	Adams, William
Charles	Anderson, James		Alsop, John
St Mary's	Adams, Ignatius		Alsop, Joseph
	Anthony, John		Atwell, Joseph
	Allender, Perry		Alexander, John
	Arbor, or Auburgh, John		Abbott, John
Charles	Brookes, Walter		Baun, John
Charles	Beall, Barton		Bussey, Samuel
	*Baker, George	St Mary's	Burris, Elisha
	*Baker, George		Beggarly, David
	Beard, Frederick	Kent	Basnett, Nathaniel
	Bryan, Edward	Charles	Boswell, John
Charles	Brookes, Matthew	Charles	Butler, John
	Baldwin, Samuel		Butler, Walter
	Bennett, Joshua	St Mary's	Brown, Joseph
	Beard, Richard		Beswick, Joseph, voucher lost
	Bridewell, Theodore		
	Beans, Joseph		Barneclow, Charles
Worcester	Butler, William		Barneclow, John
	Black, Aaron	Dorchester	Bramble, Andrew, Upper Battalion
	Baker, Nathan		
Charles	Butler, Henry	Caroline	Baxter, John, voucher lost
St Mary's	Briscoe, Henry		Bryan, Daniel
St Mary's	Bryan, Ignatius	Caroline	Baxter, Thomas
	Beard, Thomas		Beaven, Thomas
	Burris, Robert	Dorchester	Briley, John, Upper Battalion
	Benyan, Alexander		
	Brashears, John	Washington	Bringman, Martin
	Barnes, Thomas		Bozeman, William

* Probably different persons, as the amounts paid were not the same.

during the War of the American Revolution, 1775–83.   407

County.	Names.	County.	Names.
St Mary's	Black, Moses	Washington	Bowen, James
	Burns, Timothy		Brereton, William
	Bentley, William		
	Chard, William		Cheesely, James
	Cassady, James		Cummings, Nathaniel
Washington	Cline, Nicholas		Clash, Richard
Charles	Combes, William	Dorchester	Collins, Levy, or Levin, Upper Battalion
Pr. George's	*Connolly, John		
	*Connolly, John		Coop, Borachiah
	Coachman, John	Charles	Clements, Henry
	Curtis, Samuel		Clements, John H.
	Crawford, Hugh	Charles	Clinckscales, Levy, voucher lost
	Condon, William		
Caroline	Connor, Daniel		Clarke, George, voucher lost
Caroline	Connolly, Roger		
	Cheesely, Robert		Coops, Horatio
Talbot	Chapman, Thomas	Charles	Clinckscales, William
Charles	Chunn, Launcelot	St Mary's	Curtis, Thomas
St Mary's	†Cole, Charles		Canfield, Thomas
	†Cole, Charles		Coves, William
	Croney, William		Cregar, Michael
	Cruckley, Benjamin		Carlile, Basil
	Carter, Edward		Cromwell, James
Charles	Clements, John		Clements, Henry
	Clements, Bennett		Campbell, Allen
St Mary's	Dixon, Solomon	Anne Arundel	Davidson, James
	Dilman, John		Deaver, Samuel
Charles	Davis, Jesse		Dorsey, Henry
	Dunn, William		David, Valentine
	Dobson, William	Charles	Davis, David
	Duvall, Samuel		Dawson, Thomas
	Davis, Cornelius	Pr. George's	Duvall, Benjamin
	Duvall, Richard	Dorchester	Deane, John Upper Battalion
	Deale, Henry		
Charles	Dunning, James	Caroline	Derochbroom, John
Charles	Dent, Samuel		Dobson, Samuel
	Davis, Peter		Devitt, Valentine
Dorchester	Dicks, John		Duffey, Thomas
Dorchester	Davis, David, Lower Battalion		Donnelly, Patrick
			Dorman, Major
Pr. George's	Davis, Caleb		
	Eack, Adam		Elliott, Mark
	Edge, Peter	Charles	Elgin, Harrison

* See previous note.   † See previous note.

County.	Names.	County.	Names.
Caroline	Emerton, Henry	Charles	Elgin, Hezekiah
St Mary's	Edwards, Stratton		Everett, Elihu
			Eubanks, Thomas
	*Franklin, John		Farding, Aaron
	*Franklin, John		Fream, William
	Ford, William	Talbot	Faulkner, Isaac
	Frogget, Richard	Dorchester	Foxwell, Adam,
	Flechinger, Michael		For the Corps
	Fitzgerald, John	Talbot	Foster, Nathan
	Fulton, James P.		Fighter, George
Dorchester	Fetcher, Benjamin,		Fitzgerald, Clement
	Lower Battalion		Fickle, Isaac
	Fields, Charles	Kent	Frazier, Thomas
	†Finch, George		Frazier, Henry
	†Finch, George		Farr, Nicholas
	Febus, George	Talbot	Faulkner, Hynson
	Griffith, William	Queen Anne's	Greenage, Benjamin
Dorchester	Garner, Abell,	Dorchester	Goosetree, Absalom,
	Lower Battalion		Lower Battalion
	Gearey, Samuel		Green, Clement
Charles	Glasco, William		Gentle, Stephen
St Mary's	Gough, Baptist	Kent	Griffith, James
St Mary's	Greenwell, John		Gough, John Sparks
St Mary's	Gough, Charles		Grant, Thomas
	Gilpin, Benjamin		Gingle, George
	Gatton, Azariah		Gillis, William
	Gillum, Thomas		Gillis, Joseph
Dorchester	Greenwood, John,		Grimes, Greenbury
	Upper Battalion		Graham, George
Queen Anne's	Holland, John	Kent	Hall, William
	Hill, or Hall, James	Kent	Hickenbottom, James
	Hartshorne, Jonathan		Henwick, or Hancock,
Washington	Hover, Daniel		Elie
Washington	Hoskins, Joseph		Hasley, Stephen
	Hecketon, Martin		Hickman, Joshua
Queen Anne's	Harris, James		Harey, or Harvey, Richard
Washington	Haney, William		
	Heck, Daniel		Hogins, Jere
	Holtzman, Henry		Hardy, Kinsey
	Hurd, Bennett		Hunter, James
Kent	Herring, Daniel	St Mary's	Hazle, Edward
	Horne, George		Hall, Thomas

* See previous note.   † See previous note.

County.	Names.	County.	Names.
Dorchester	Hubbard, Job	St Mary's	Howard, Ignatious
Talbot	Holt, John	Dorchester	Harper, Joseph,
Charles	Hudson, George		Lower Battalion
St Mary's	Hubbard, or Herbert, Jere	Dorchester	Harper, William, Lower Battalion
St Mary's	Hazle, Jere	Dorchester	Horner, Charles, For the Corps
	Haycock, Solomon		Higden, Joseph
	Hamilton, John		Hagan, Michael
Dorchester	Harper, Henry, Lower Battalion	Charles	Hannon, Walter Warren
Dorchester	Hays, Richard, Lower Battalion		Hunter, William
			Henninger, George
Caroline	Hudson, Hooper		Holland, Charles
Queen Anne's	Hadley, Samuel		Hamilton, Edward
	Hooper, Abraham	Dorchester	Hurst, Samuel
	Hughes, William		
	Ijams, Vachel	Anne Arundel	Isleck, Pasco
Dorchester	Insley, Francis, For the Corps	Dorchester	Insley, Joseph, For the Corps
St Mary's	Jones, Cuthbert		Jenkins, Edward
	Jenkins, Edward		Jenkins, Joseph
Talbot	Jones, Thomas	St Mary's	Jarber, Peter
	Jones, Michael	St Mary's	Jarboe, Robert
Dorchester	Johnson, Frederick, Upper Battalion		Jefferson, Jestinian
		Dorchester	Johnson, Robert, For the Corps
	Jackson, John		
	Jones, Samuel		Jackson, Edward
Charles	Johnson, Nelson		Jenkins, Philip
Charles	Johnson, Benjamin		
	King, John	St Mary's	Kahill, Nathaniel
	Knowell, John	Kent	Kelly, Edward
	Knap, Nero	Kent	Kelly, John
Charles	King, Charles		Kelly, James
St Mary's	Kirkpatrick, William		Kettle, Thomas Gibson
	Kent, Isaac		Kinnard, Benjamin
	Kibley, Joseph		
Washington	Leatherman, Michael	Caroline	Longfellow, Gideon
Washington	Lyday, Simon		Lee, William
	Leath, Alexander		Lyons, John
	Long, Jonathan		Lewis, Isaac
Caroline	Lavington, Garey, or George	Kent	Lazenby, William John
			Laceman, Lodwick
	Latham, Aaron	Pr. George's	Letman, John

County.	Names.	County.	Names.
	Lancaster, Samuel		Linnington, John,
Queen Anne's	Longfellow, Arnold		voucher lost
	Lockyer, Philip	Washington	Lewis, William
Charles	Lovely, or Lovelin, Wm.		Long, Jacob
	Leath, John	Dorchester	Lingard, Nehemiah
	*Miller, John		Muser, Francis
	*Miller, John		McGuire, Nicholas
	McIlvaine, Benjamin	Dorchester	Morgan, Thomas,
St Mary's	Mattingley, Ignatious		Lower Battalion
Washington	McLaughlin, Hugh		Merrick, William
	Mahoney, Daniel		McCann, Marmaduke
	Moore, William	Charles	Maddux, George
	Myers, Philip	Charles	McNess, George
Dorchester	Madkin, John	Charles	McDonald, Charles
Anne Arundel	Moffitt, Thomas	Dorchester	Meadows, David,
Charles	Montgomery, Ignatius		Upper Battalion
	McGill, Thomas	Talbot	Morris, James
Talbot	Merrick, John		Miles, Jacob
St Mary's	Maddux, John		Massey, Hezekiah
	†Morgan, Thomas,	St Mary's	Monarch, Edward
	voucher lost		Meyer, John
	†Morgan, Thomas	Charles	Maddux, Allison
Dorchester	McGraw, Leonard, (Levin),		McGraw, James,
	For the Corps		voucher lost
Dorchester	‡Murphey, William,		Moser, Michael
	For the Corps	Frederick	McCray, James,
	‡Murphey, William		served from 7 Aug to
Dorchester	Meekins, Robert,		10 Dec '81
	Lower Battalion		Murphey, Hezekiah
Caroline	Minor, or Minie, Levin		§ Miller, George
Pr. George's	Marlow, Butler		§ Miller, George
	Mauledge, Samuel		McDonald, John
	Marr, William		McDonald, James
	McCartey, James	Dorchester	Morelake, Moses,
	Manspiker, Henry		Upper Battalion
	Morris, John		McConnell, Matthew
Charles	Miles, Nicholas		Malachi, Daniel
	Murphey, William		McKim, Benjamin
Charles	Mudd, Hezekiah ·		Murray, Matthias
	McGlamory, Elijah		McGlamory, John
	Mure, Thomas		Matthiot, John
	Martin, George		Morelache, Moses
St Mary's	Newton, Zachariah	St Mary's	Norris, Arnold

* See previous note. † See previous note. ‡ See previous note. § See previous note.

COUNTY.	NAMES.	COUNTY.	NAMES.
St Mary's	Norris, Henry		Nichols, Ace
	Nelson, John	Kent	Norris, Daniel
St Mary's	Norris, John		Nagle, Richard
Dorchester	Navey, Matthew, Lower Battalion	St Mary's	Norris, John
		Charles	Neale, William
	Needham, Michael		
Dorchester	Owens, Thomas, Lower Battalion		Owens, Isaac
			Onstrutt, George
Charles	Oliver, William		Ogden, John
	Offutt, Nathaniel		O'Neale, John
	Ogden, John		O'Connor, John
	Odle, Rigden		O'Neale, John
	O'Bryan, Joseph		O'Kell, George
Kent	Ogelsby, Charles		
Dorchester	Proctor, William, Lower Battalion	St Mary's	Pike, William
		St Mary's	Payne, Ignatious
	Polston, Joseph		Philpot, Thomas
Charles	Proctor, Henry	Charles	Posey, Zachariah
Queen Anne's	Penfold, George	Charles	Posey, Roger
	Paine, William		Pugh, Humphrey
	Popham, Benjamin		Platford, Edward
Kent	Perkins, John	St Mary's	Pratt, William
Kent	Pearce, John		Proctor, Thomas
Kent	Pearce, Hugh		Pronso, Jacob
	Pinter, Thomas		Perkinson, Thomas
St Mary's	Payne, Barney		Pardo, Benjamin
	Queener, John		Queake, Manasses
	Robertson, Edward	Dorchester	Ross, Levin, Lower Battalion
St Mary's	Risswick, Joseph		
Charles	Rollins, Elias		Ross, George
	Right, or Wright, Elijah		Rich, Vilet
	Roberts, Archibald		Ratiken, Peter
	Richardson, Jonathan	Kent	Read, Peregrine
Dorchester	Roberts, William, Lower Battalion	Dorchester	Rose, Joseph, Upper Battalion
	Richards, Samuel		Ridgely, Zephaniah
	Roberts, William		Richards, Clement
	Robinson, Charles		Rawlings, Solomon
	Ray, Benjamin		Ridge, William
	Roberts, William	Pr. George's	Reston, Zedock
			Richardson, William
	Sax, Henry	Caroline	Smith, Nathan

County.	Names.	County.	Names.
	Seabrooke, Richard		Scott, William
	Simmons, John		Shepherd, John
Washington	Snyder, Frederick		Smith, Emory
	Stitely, Frederick		Souther, William
	Scott, Robert	Charles	Smoote, Matthew
Talbot	Start, Richard		Smith, Ignatious
	Shine, or Shrine, Adam	Charles	Steward, Joshua
	Sadler, Thomas	St Mary's	Sute, John
	Snowden, Ned		Sparks, Nimrod
	Starr, Obediah		Shiffer, John
	Syass, James	Caroline	Smith, Richard
Charles	Steward, Ignatious	Talbot	Sherwood, Charles
Dorchester	Steward, David, Upper Battalion	Washington	Smith, Lodwick
			Silk, James
	Scott, Samuel		Sollers, William
	Steele, John	Dorchester	Stanley, Salady, Upper Battalion
	Skelly, John		
	Smith, John		
St Mary's	Taney, Charles	Dorchester	†Taylor, James, Upper Battalion
Talbot	Townsend, George		
	Tarman, Senr., Richard		Tucker, George
	Tarman, Junr., Richard		Tomlinson, Grove
	Taylor, Richard		Tarr, Thomas
	Tennant, James		Troy, Jeremiah
	*Taylor, Thomas		Thompson, James
	*Taylor, Thomas	Kent	Thomas, Beal
Anne Arundel	Tidings, Caleb	Dorchester	Toll, Anthony
Kent	Thomas, Starling		Turner, Junr., Solomon
Pr. George's	Tilley, Zachariah		Taylor, Jacob
Dorchester	Tucker, Jacob, Lower Battalion		Tyler, Robert Bradley
		Dorchester	Thomas, Levin
Charles	†Taylor, James		Taylor, Jason
Washington	Valentine, George	Dorchester	Vincent, Aaron, Lower Battalion
	Valiant, Aaron		
	Weems, David		Ward, John
	Willen, Charles		Wright, Benjamin
Charles	Warrington, James		Wallace, John
Charles	Wathen, Barton		Woodward, James
	Wickert, Michael		Welast, John
Washington	Wright, Thomas	St Mary's	Wise, Thomas
	Waggoner, Christopher	St Mary's	Winsett, Joseph
	Wood, Jeremiah		Willard, John
	Wilson, Acquila		Walls, George

* See previous note.   † See previous note.

COUNTY.	NAMES.	COUNTY.	NAMES.
Dorchester	Willis, John, Lower Battalion	Pr. George's	Wood, James Woodringer, Daniel
	Whitehook, Ezekiel	Pr. George's	Wood, Thomas
Charles	Wright, James	Charles	Warder, Jesse
Dorchester	Wheeler, John		Wilson, Tobias
Dorchester	White, John, Upper Battalion	Caroline Charles	Williams, James Whitcombe, Notley
	Wilson, Joseph Crawford		White, Henry
	Yeates, Thomas		Young, William
	Yeates, Benjamin		Young, Peter

Received this 21st day of July, 1787, of the State of Maryland, Sundry Accounts for Pay of Militia serving in the Continental Army, in the year 1781, agreeable to the foregoing list, amounting to five thousand, five hundred and twenty-three pounds, seven shillings and four pence currency of the State of Maryland, which amounts I am to forward to the Commissioner of Army Accounts to be settled, agreeably to the Ordinance of Congress of the seventh of May last.

John White,
Commissioner of Accounts for the States of
Pennsylvania, Delaware and Maryland.

Maryd. Currency,
£5523 ·· 7 ·· 4
Equal to 14,728 88-90 dollars.

NOTE.—Names of Counties are inserted from other Rolls.

MUSTER AND PAY ROLLS FOR 1782.

LIST OF DEFECTIVES FROM THE MARYLAND LINE, FROM JUNE, 1780, TO FEBY., 1782.

Names.	Dates.	Counties of Residence.	Names.	Dates.
Zachariah Askey	21 Sept '80	Frederick	John Riding	16 Aug '80
Samuel Philips	" "	Cicil	James Nowland	" "
Edmund Collins	6 Nov "	Frederick	John Hall	15 Mch '81
John McDaniel	18 Aug "	do	Charles Close	" "
John Pound	" "	Harford	Joseph McDonald	Aug '80
Robert Harmon	10 July "	N. Carolina	Thomas Brown	
William Dixon	5 " "	Prince Georges	Wm. Allman	July "
James Munks	2 Oct "	Scicell	John Simmons	
Thomas Bulling	" "	Harford	John Eyre	May "
Francis King	June "	Washington	John Lenox	Oct "
Elias Smith	" "	Frederick	Thos. McDonald	
Reason Hanson	Aug "	Montgomery	Alex. Adamson	
Patrick Mullen		Baltimore	John Pike	
Richard Ballod		Annarundel	John Licety (?)	
William Roe	June "	Frederick	Patk. Murphy	" "
Michael Standley	"	do	Richd. Jacks	
Michael Rogers	"	Harford	John Lucas	Aug "
William Chambers	14 Feb '81	Frederick	John Simmons	" "
Benjamin Taylor	10 Mch "	Harford	John Donovan	" "
William Moran	6 " "	Prince Georges	Michl. Byrne	" "
Thomas Smith	14 Feb "	Baltimore	Jno. Lester	" "
William Fuller	26 Jan "	do	Robert Hudson	" "
Timo. Fitzgerald	1 April "	do	John Heaton	" "
Thomas Simister	4 May "	do	Michl. Gainsford	
Jno. Peter Fevott	" "	Frederick	Richard Goff	
William Pattern	" "	do	Francis Garrish	
William Durham	7 " "	Harford	Edward Balf	
Leonard Boward	" "	Washington	Thomas Longdon	Oct '80
Caleb Donnolly	8 June "	Scicill	George Streett	Sept "
William Dunn	" "	do	James Stonely	July "
Michael Connolly	2 July "	Baltimore	George Crosby	" "
Michael Connolly	" "	Annarundel	Thos. Williams	" "
James McDonald	7 " "	Harford	Henry McAway	" "
Bartle Boome	1 " "	Frederick	Edwd. Nichols	" "
Edward Purdy	1 March "	Prince Georges	John Welsh	" "
James Kennedy	15 " "		Saml. Eyles	" "
Joshua Barrett	16 Aug '80		John Miles	" "

Names.	Dates.	Names.	Dates.	Counties of Residence.
Alex. Montgomery	July '80	Thomas Hatton		
Michael Dease	" "	Willm. Rhodes		
John Webster	" "	John Craig		
Danl. Oldham	" "	John Hodges		
John Church	" '81	James Jarrett		
Rowland Bates	Sept '80	Joseph Butler		
Joseph Walldram	" "	Chrisr. Flanery		
Thos. Bryant	July "	Wm. Williams	Aug '80	
Jno. Bartliff	Sept "	Willm. Downes	" "	
Jno. Lunn	July "	Laurence Craigen		
Archibald Nichols		Barnabas Doling		
John Goldsborough	Sept "	Samuel Jones		
John Fitzgerald	" "	Frs. Scroggy	" "	
Robert Gray	Mch '81	Thos. Newland	" "	
Richd. Mansell	Oct '80	John Brading	" "	
Joseph Wilmington	Mch '81	Math. Skivington	July "	
Thos. Turner	Aug "	John Page		
Joseph Nichols	" "	Pat. McGenalty	Aug "	
Robert Darling	Mch "	John Wills	15 Mch '81	
Danl. McIntire	Feb "	And. Marwood	Oct "	
James Glynn	" "	James Stuart	Feb "	
Jno. Pryor	" "	James Wigans		
Timo. Murphey	15 Mch "	Geo. Adamson		
Robert Stewart	Feb "	Robt. Brown	May '80	
Fredk. Flynn	16 Aug '80	Thos. Prudent	June "	
Michl. Griffin	June "	Jno. Thoroughgood		Prince Georges
John Easton		Thos. Pinkston	Sept '81	Annarundle
Patk. Bermingham	16 Aug "	Barnabas Maloy	May "	do
John Murphy	" "	Lawrence Carty	" "	Frederick
Matth. Spilliards	" "	John Bellamy	15 Mch "	Baltimore
Timo. Shean	" "	Edwd. Hinks	Aug "	Annarundel
Thomas Dwier	June "	Peter Eamick		Frederick
James Wheeler		John Higgins		Eastern Shore
Phil. Brissillton		Andrew Bramble	10 Oct "	
Thomas Eddis		Moses Morelake	" "	
James Greene		Godfrey Sollinder	" "	
John Taylor	16 Aug '80	Isaac Christopher	15 " "	
Darby Dwyer	" "	Milby Christopher	" "	
Richd. Ellwood	" "	John Millford	20 " "	
Peter Humman	3 Nov '81	Alex. Hughs		
Robert Smith	" "	Jacob Flowers		
Jno. Fincey (?)	" "	Benj. Smith		
James Hays	" "	Willm. Baker	'81	Baltimore
John Mildurph	" "	Michl. Connolly	2 July '81	Annarundle
James Greene	6 " "	Jno. Alex. Mackey	20 May "	Washington

Names.	Dates.	Names.	Dates.	Counties of Residence.
John Brittain	20 Nov '81	Isaac Beckett	26 June '81	Kent
Chas. Wheeler	29 " "	John Slight	15 Mch "	Annarundle
Willm. Tillwood	" "	Jas. Saunders	" "	Queen Anne's
John Frederick		Saml. Furrough	" "	Dorcet
Robert Blood		Jno. Holliday	" "	Kent
Adam Weatherholt		Jacob Allen	" "	Frederick
James Gillin		Thos. Collior	25 April "	Annarundle
John Jessup		John Reilly	" "	Queen Anne's
James Wilson		James Hughs		
Dennis Dolan		Benj. Elliott		
Michl. Ramler		Wm. Pointer		
John Dalton		Alex. Scalls, (or Sealls)		
John English		Thos. Helphery		
And. Humberry		James Brown		
Jerremiah Dilling		James Smith		
John Harmon		Jno. Larose		
Jas. Underhill		Jno. Hackett		
Willm. Stuart		Robert Smith		
Thos. Killpin		Thos. Makrell		
Jas. McDonald		Jno. Amorsley		
Vincent Molling		Abraham Welsh		
Richd. Paplow		Wm. Mansfield		
George Welsh		Bernard Reilly		
John McDonald		Jno. Campbell		
Danl. Buckley		Jno. Powell		
Jno. Arber		Thos. James		
Saml. Evans		Thos. Berry		
Willm. Mason		John Dycus		

Names of the Deserters from the First Regiment.

James Shepperd	Deserted 11 Nov '81	Isaac Henderson	Deserted 13 Dec '81
Thomas Harris	do do	Ben. Thompson	do 23 do
Richd. Jeffers	do 18 do		

Regiments and Dates of Desertion not Known.

James Fennel	John Brown	Richard Miles
Willm. Mattock	James Kisk	Robt. Jones, (or Johes)
James Wilson	John Welch	Thos. Atkinson
Robt. Robertson	Wm. Jefferies	Wm. Brawton
Willm. English	James Navy	James Waddle
James Anderson	James Gardner	Richd. Todd.
Andrew Lloyd	Geo. Gardner	Henry Fisher
Jonathan Foster	Lewis White	James Fisher
John Avelman	Danl. McPatridge	Wm. Goody
St. Leger Neal		

VOLUNTARY ENLISTMENTS OF

NAMES.	REGT.	TERM.	WHEN ENLISTED.	SWORN.
Zachariah Berry	2nd Md. Regt.	three years	March 6th, 1782	Mch 29th
Leavin Claridge	3rd "	do	May 21st, "	"
Daniel Howe	4th "	do	Feb 23rd, "	Feb 23rd
Benjamin Burch	4th "	do	Feb 14th, "	25th
Jonathan Weaden	4th "	do	April 3rd, "	25th
William Marlow	4th "	do	April 10th, "	25th
John Brown	4th "	do	May 18th, "	23rd
John Riley	6th "	do	Aug 26th, 1781	Aug 26th '81

BACON'S BRIDGE, APL. 19TH, 1782. PERSONS IN THE PROVOST.

NAMES.			CONFINED BY
Murphey Shee	Md. Brigade	plundering	Capt. Trueman
Arthur Corbin	Q. M. Dept.	thief	Maj. Roxburgh
Fed. Smith	Md. Brigade	thief	Capt. Mills

(From the Gist Papers.)

RETURN OF MEN OF THE MARYLAND LINE INLISTED IN 1782.

NAMES.	WHEN INLISTED.	TERM.	REMARKS.
Benj. Popham		3 years	recruited by Cap. D. Lynn in
James Murphy	6 Feb '82	War	deserted 8 March [FrederickTown
Isaac McFadden	16	do	
Laurence Mushter	16	do	
Godfrey Wolfe	18	3 years	deserted 8 March
Chas. Blundel	21	War	
Thos. Grant	25	do	deserted 15 March
Richd. Collins	25	do	deserted 20 March
Jesse Carter	25	do	
Richd. Jacks	26	3 years	deserted 10 March
Elijah Smith	28	do	deserted 10 March
John Wilmore	12 March	War	
Isaac Holland	12	do	
John Green	15	3 years	time out 9 Jan '82, reinlisted
Thos., (or John), Philips	1 April	do	
Benj. MaCall	1	do	
Wm. Dunn	11	do	
Chas. Love	17	War	
John Mifford	18	do	
Wm. Laurence	20	do	

NAMES.	WHEN INLISTED.	TERM.	REMARKS.
James Morris	11 May	3 years	
Isaac Date, (Deale)	19	do	
John Long	26	War	
Sylvester Gatton	3 July	3 years	
David McCullam	20	War	
Thomas Reynolds	5	3 years	
Wm. Smith	9 Aug	———	
Wm. Holland	23	3 years	
Thos. Barber	20	War	
James Dawson		do	
Edwd. Cantwell	1 Sept	3 years	
James Hunt	11	War	
Benj. Daniel	7	3 years	
Jos. Pully	15	War	
John Brireck	19	do	
John Walker	27 Aug	3 years	reinlisted
James Burk	13	do	deserted 14 August
John Abraham	22 Sept	do	do returned 25 Dec
Wm. Cawood	30	do	
Francis Orbough, (or Osbough)	1 Oct	do	
William Coleman	7	War	
Pat. Mayher	8	3 years	
James Murray	10	do	
John McElroy	10	do	
Josiah Burgiss	16	do	
Joseph Overcreek	1 Jan	War	recruited by Capt. John Agner [Hamilton, 2 Regt.
Patrick Nugent	16 Feb	do	
Joseph Sharp	25	do	
John McDonald	25	do	
Thos. Glenn	25	do	deserted
James Veal	28	do	
Timo. Campbell	1 March	do	
Thos. Wild	2	do	deserted
David Johnston	5	do	
Tobias Randles	6	do	
Edwd. Stone, (or Rone)	6	do	
Fredk. Wolveram	6	do	
John Bevard	13	do	
Wm. Norris	13	do	deserted
Saml. Powers	13	do	
Wm. Biddle	13	do	

during the War of the American Revolution, 1775–83.   419

Names.	When Inlisted.	Term.	Remarks.
Timo. Burns	16 March	War	
Benj. Houghton	16	do	
John Rogers	18	3 years	
John Watson	18	War	deserted
Andw. Potter	18	do	
John Smith	18	do	
Saml. Hardcastle	18	3 years	
Josiah Bay	19	do	deserted
John Merryman	19	do	deserted
John Donnald	20	War	
George McDonald	20	do	
James Brown	20	3 years	
David Banks	26	War	
Richd. Burrows	28	do	
Wm. Harris	26	do	
James Carven	25	do	
Joseph Ward	2 April	do	
Donald Cameron	3	do	
John Smith	3	do	
John Davis	3	do	
Jacob Scrivener	3	do	
Lewis Flash	6	do	
Isaac Carr	6	do	
Robert Deane	7	do	
Thos. Simmonds	7	do	
James Karnes	10	do	
John Underwood	10	do	
John Adams	10	do	
George Adams	10	do	
Isaac Burton	11	do	
Wm. Commott	11	do	

Alex. Wallace	4 March	3 years	recruited by Capt. Anderson, [4 Regt.
Abraham Stoner	13	War	
John Reid	14	do	
Joshua Cutmare	20	do	
Chrisr. Coye	20	do	
John Turner	10 April	do	
John Pope	11	do	
Ezekiel Kidwell	17	3 years	
John Cosby	21	War	

Names.	When Inlisted.	Term.	Remarks.
Basil Newton	16 March	3 years	recruited by Capt. Jas. Sumervill
Wm. Dervin, (or Duvin)	29	do	
Benj. Asgurth	14 April	do	
Wm. Dyke	14 Aug	do	deserted a few days after Inlistment
Wm. Smith	20 Feb	War	prov'd a Servt., claimed by his [Master and delivered
Paul Gilmore	1 March	3 years	
Thos. Billingham	6	do	
Wm. T. Bowling	12	do	
Roderick McKenny	16 Feb	do	
Stephen Nicholson	27	do	
John McBride	28	do	
Wm. Batton	10 March	do	
Wm. Marlow	10 April	do	
Geo. Partner	12	do	
Danl. Howe	14	do	
Nicholas Walsh	25	do	
John Brown	18 May	do	
John Gordon	25	do	
Francis Dewiss	20 June	do	
Richd. Hogan	15 Feb	do	
Thos. Carroll	3 April	War	
Robt. Firth	28 May	3 years	
Edwd. Kirk	12 April	do	
Dennis Carty	14 Feb	War	
Joseph Neal	14	3 years	
Wm. Johnston	26 April	do	
Geo. Twinch	2	do	
Peirce Deacon	10	do	
Thos. Craig	3 May	do	
Thos. Hill	27 March	do	
John Trevis	28	do	
Wm. Wilson	15 April	do	
James Dowden	10 May	do	
Wm. Taylor	2 April	do	
Isaac Johnson	29 May	do	
Basil Shaw	5 April	do	
Patrick Quynn	27 Feb	do	
Thos. Fleming	20 April	do	
Thos. McKinsey	23	do	
Jonath. Weedon	3	do	
Benj. Burch	14 Feb	do	reinlisted.
Thos. Loveday	17 March	3 years	inlisted by Capt. R. Denny
Jacob Sheets	19 June	War	
John Graham	24	3 years	

Names.	When Inlisted.	Term.	Remarks.
Zachariah Berry	6 March	3 years	inlisted by Major Roxburgh in Carolina
Joseph Jones	23 July	3 years	Denny
John Connolly	29	do	do
John Alsop	26 Feb	3 years	inlisted by Lt. Roger Nelson, [5 Regt.
Elisha Onsborn	27	do	
George Rhodes	10 March	do	
Martin Murphy	14	War	deserted 17 March
John Allen	18	3 years	
Thos. Jones	18	do	deserted
Geo. Dadisman	24	do	
Wm. Fields	18	do	deserted
Thos. Hawkes	1 April	War	
Jas. Murray	1	do	
Henry Barnes	27	3 years	
Rob. Jones	4 May	War	
Michael Griffith	11	do	
John Reese	18	do	deserted
Isaac Dall	19	do	
John Barrett	12 July	do	
Jacob Mifford	1 March	3 years	inlisted by Capt. W. Lamar, 1 Regt.
David Love	11	War	
Nichos. Fitzgerald	26	do	
George Hoggert	1 April	do	
James Smith	6	3 years	deserted 7 Apl.
James McCray	15	do	
Joseph Clancey	24 July	War	
John Johnson	15 Aug	3 years	
John McElroy	9 Oct	do	
Wm. Layland	14	do	
Jacob Gibson	17	do	
James Gelmore	19	do	
Robt. Eaton	19	War	
Henry Philips	19	do	

Names.	When Inlisted.	Term.	Remarks.
Alex. McGreger	17 March	War	inlisted by Capt. Thos. B. Hugou
James Burk	25	3 years	
James Scott	29	War	deserted
John Adams	29	do	
Phinehas Hervey	3 April	do	
John Williams, 2d.	6	do	
John Pennington	6	do	
John Paul	9	do	deserted at Head of Elk
James Williams	10	do	
John Nicholson	12	do	
Thos. Quinney	26	3 years	
James Morrison	5 May	War	
Henry Clawson	12 April	do	
Wm. Kent	3 May	3 years	
Alex. McCoy	6	War	
James Waters	6	do	
Michl. Dougherty	5	—	taken
John Gorman	11	War	
Robert Wright	6 June	do	
John Torrey	19 May	do	
Wm. Johnson	12 June	do	
Danl. Newman	23	do	
Richd. Scotton	24	do	
Joseph Harper		do	
Alex. Garrett		do	
Jas. Middleton	28 Aug	do	
Peter Dawson	11 Sept	3 years	

Barthw. Roche	23 March	3 years	by Capt. Clagget, 5 Regt.
Wm. Harrison	8 May	do	

Basil J. Dorsey	17 April	War	by Capt. J. A. Hamilton
Wm. Balentine	22	do	deserted
Randel Skly	22	do	
John Wilson, 2d.	22	do	
Chas. Davis	23	do	
Christn. Hanson	25	do	
John Bond	1 May	do	
James Green	1	do	inl. by Capt. J. A. Hamilton, de-[serted
Thos. Wilson	2	do	
John Hanna	3	do	deserted, taken 23 Oct.
Wm. Hart	7	do	

Names.	When Inlisted.	Term.	Remarks.
Christr. Reynor	9 May	War	
Richd. Perkins	9	do	
Geo. Shingleborrough	13	do	
Christian Ernest	14	do	
Wm. Matthews	19	do	
John Ballast, (or Ballart)	20	do	
James Thompson	21	do	
John McDonald	22	do	
John Fairweather	1 June	do	
Richd. Franklin	1	do	
Richd. Nabell	4	do	
James Loveless	4	3 years	deserted
John Burgess	12	War	
John Lowe	12	do	
John McFarlin	13	do	
Thos. Hand	15	do	
Thos. Gritchard	2 July	do	
John Sheppardson	2	do	
George Tate	11	3 years	
John Bluefield	30	War	
Richd. Jennings	13 Aug	do	
John Dougherty	—	do	
Saml. Mahew	14	do	
Richd. Burk	16	do	
Thos. Reynolds		do	
John Ward	20	do	
John Welsh		do	
John McDonald		do	deserted
Peter Sprangle	21	do	
Thomas Channon	24	do	
Basil Wheeler	4 Sept	do	
John Gray	10	do	
Philip Fraizer		do	
Geo. Findleston		do	

Arthur Boyes	30 March	3 years	inl. by Capt. J. Marbery, 3 Regt.
Geo. Tomlinson	30 May	do	
Joseph Moseley	19 Apl	War	
Roger Hagan	29	do	
Dyer Waters	6 May	do	
Zachariah Moore	18 June	do	
Danl. Skinner	26	do	
Isaac Jenkins	12 Sept	do	

Names.	When Inlisted.	Term.	Remarks.
Hillary Lanham	13 Sept	War	
Hezekiah Moore	15	do	
Thomas Sturgis	16	do	
John Garrick	21	do	deserted
Geo. Chambers	26	do	
Rezin Lowe	30	do	
Danl. Hurley	14 Oct	do	
Thos. McDowell	5 Apl	War	inlisted by Lt. J. Hartshorn, 3 Regt.
Rob. McCleary	25	do	
John Maxwell	13	do	
John Smallwood	29	3 years	
John Wilson	6 May	War	
John Connolly	9	do	
Hugh Weer	21	do	
Wm. Selley	21	do	
Wm. Utie	19 July	do	deserted 30 July
Alex. Christie	14 May	3 years	
Matthew Norris	17	do	
Alex. Boyes	1 April	3 years	inlisted by Lt. J. Sears, 5 Regt.
Peter Jackson	2	War	
John Crockett	4 May	do	
Wm. Hutchman	4	do	never recd. nor chargd. in accts.
Michl. Stanley	21	3 years	
John Hukill	8 June	do	
Danl. Hukill	8	do	
John Nelson	4 Aug	do	
John Moran	8	do	supposed reinlisted
Saml. Brady	12 Sept	do	
Job Buley	8 April	War	inl. by Capt. Lilburn Williams, 3 Regt.
John Applead	14	do	
John White	15	do	
Thos. Alford	15	do	
Geo. Trice	15	3 years	
John Vain	15	do	
Jeremiah Carter	16	do	
Danl. Campbell	27	War	
Brannick Meakins	29 March	do	
Evan Willings	27 April	do	

during the War of the American Revolution, 1775–83.

NAMES.	WHEN INLISTED.	TERM.	REMARKS.
Wm. Smallwood	27 April	War	
John Greenwood	27	do	
Thos. Keyes	24	3 years	
Joseph Rose	8	do	
Elijah Lyons	24	War	
Bennet Valient	27	3 years	
Isaac Kent	29	War	
John Husk	3 May	do	
Henry Winder	3	do	
Thos. Harding	3	do	
Arthur Pritchard	3	3 years	
Danl. Sullinger		do	
Thos. Hooper		do	
John Elliot		do	
Wm. Connelly		War	
Levin Cleridge		3 years	
Wm. Powell		War	
Joseph McCallister		do	Capt. L. Williams
Wm. Henderson		do	
Wm. Carey		do	
James Coleman		3 years	
Francis Irsley		do	
Chas. Missick		do	
Willis Cotter	7 Sept	War	
John Cotter	7	do	
Chas. Beachamp	5 Aug	do	
Paris Owens	14 Sept	3 years	
Chas. Griffiths	14	do	
Edwd. Paul	15 Aug	do	
Wm. Eagill	22 Sept	do	
John Acock	3 April	War	inl. by Lt. S. Hanson, 5 Regt.
Saml. Parramore, (or Palmore)	10	3 years	inl. by Capt. R. Waters, 3 Regt.
Ephraim Marshall	10	do	deserted
Chas. Hall	10	do	
Chas. Parramore, (or Palmore)	7 May	do	
Kemp Holder	20	War	
Cutler Jones	31	do	
John Wilson	30 June	do	
Edwd. Edwards	10	do	
Oliver Blake	7 May	3 years	

Names.	When Inlisted.	Term.	Remarks.
Thos. Whaley		War	inl. by Capt. Perry Benson, 5 Regt.
John Murray	17 May	3 years	
John Beale	15 April	3 years	inl. by Lt. Fickle, 5 Regt.
Michl. McDevitt	16	do	
James Beale	22	do	
Wm. Hunter	8 June	do	
Francis Reynard	22 Aug	War	
John Williams	3 Nov	3 years	
Lewis McCuttough	18 Aug	do	
John Steele	2 Sept	War	
Jonas Crawford	11 Nov	3 years	
John Lee	1 Dec	do	
James Roe	22 June	3 years	inlisted by Lt. Nathan Wright 3rd Regt.
Wm. Hill	6 July	do	
Edwd. Shebrick, (or Shelrick)	7	do	
Whittington Guild	9	do	
Wm. Madden	13	War	
Durden O'Neil	19	3 years	
Henry Gilpin	20	do	deserted
John Green	12	do	
Wm. Watkins	1 June	do	
John Wilson	1 Aug	do	
Wm. Deveraue	9 April	3 years	Capt. Jas. Ewing, 1 Regt.
Wm. Callaghan	12 June	3 years	Lt. Adam Jameson, 5 Regt.
Thos. Countess	12	do	
Thos. Hale	15	do	
Saml. Fisher	1 July	War	
Isaac Doncan	1	do	
Thos. Leagar	22	do	
Henry Bradley	23	3 years	
John Callaghan	23	War	
Danl. Stephens	24	do	
Richd. Reaves	24	do	
James Countess			Quere is not the Thos. Countess?
John Coulter	15 Oct	do	

Names.	When Enlisted.	Term.	Remarks.
Randolph Booth	10 March	3 years	Capt. Wm. Bruce, 5 Regt.
Edmund Wheatly	12	do	
Bennet Thompson	1 April	do	
Elisha Sullivan			
Jas. Crosingbury, (or Coosingbury)	17 March	do	
Wm. Caldwell	8 April	War	
John Sewell	11 Aug	War	Lt. R. Denny, 5 Regt.
Thos. Richardson	11	do	
Henry Tibbett	5 Sept	do	
Danl. Wilkins	5 Oct	do	
Joseph Norman	5	War	
Hugh Roney	17 June	do	
John Swails	28 Sept	3 years	
Geo. Warner	28 Oct	War	
John Jordine	12 Dec	do	
Thos. Wyndham	14 Jan '83	3 years	
Wm. Gray	9 Sept	3 years	inl. by Lt. J. Lynn, 5 Regt.
Wm. Carlton	7	War	
Peter Fletcher	9	do	
Isaac Loyder	28 Oct	3 years	deserted
John Shields	29	War	
James Stephens	8	do	
Nicholas McCarlin, (or McCaslin)	11	do	
John Stuart	11	do	
John Cooper	1	do	
Jeremiah Cypher	30 Sept	War	inl. by Capt. John A. Hamilton
Michl. Kaine	1 Oct	do	
Joseph Hudson	1	do	
Nichs. Perker	1	do	
Chas. Brutzill	1	do	
Wm. Laylan	1	do	deserted in Baltm.
John Layton	3	do	do 5 Oct
Jesse Wrinsile	3	do	do do
John Messer	3	3 years	
Wm. Belcher	5	War	
Jas. Poole	5	do	suppos'd reinlisted
Thos. Evans	10	do	ditto

Names.	When Enlisted.	Term.	Remarks.
Lodwick Chezloe	10 Oct	War	
Wm. Frazier	12	do	
John Rigan	12	do	
Michl. Burns	12	do	
Thos. Lawyer	14	do	
James Morris	14	do	
Lewis Davis	17	do	
John Kelner	18	3 years	
John Tully	19	War	
Patrick McDonough		do	
John Adamson		do	
Wm. Sowder		do	
Peter Francis		3 years	
Thomas Hand		War	supposed reinlisted
Saml. Crowell		do	
Thos. Blake			
John Miller		do	
James Reese	21 Feb '82	War	inl. by Maj. John Davidson, 5 Regt.
John Cleanscrote	21	3 years	
Thos. Gordon	25 March	do	
John Maxwell	5 April	do	
Bennet Heard	16	do	
Thos. Wood	25	do	suppos'd reinlisted
Daniel Harris	28 May	do	
John Smith	10 July	do	
Michael Scott	2 Nov	War	
Benj. Wright	20	do	
Geo. Baker	29 Oct	3 years	
James Barber	30 Dec	War	
Saml. Davis	8 Jan '83	do	
James Sengo			
Wm. Watkins	1 —		
John Green	12 July		
John Wilson	1 Aug	3 years	
Wm. McNeue		do	supposed reinlisted
John Hillam	23 Nov	3 years	Capt. D. Lynn, 4 Regt.
Dennis Bryan	10 Dec	do	
Stephen Erlinger	20	War	
Colvert Mason, (alias Woodyard)	30 Oct	3 years	inl. by Gen. Smallwood
Wm. Harris	2 Jan	War	

LIST OF SUNDRY SOLDIERS ENLISTMENTS FOR DURING THE WAR.

NAMES.	WHEN ENLISTED.	TERM.	NAMES.	WHEN ENLISTED.	TERM.
Wm. Powell	23 May '82	War	Saml. Smith	10 Apl '81	3 years
Parris Owens	7 Sept "	3 years	John Connally	5 June "	"
Evan Willing	27 Apl "	War	Wm. Harrison	30 May "	"
Jno. Vaine		3 years	Nathan Homersly	22 May "	"
Thos. Harding	3 May "	War	Garett Welch	15 March "	"
John Hursk	3 May "	3 years	Jas. Capels	4 May "	"
Jere. Carter	16 Apl "	"	Handy Handly	7 March "	"
Thos. Hooper	22 May "	"	Robert Robertson	19 May "	"
Wm. Cary	22 June "	"	Jacob Doyne	10 Apl "	"
Jno. Pritchard	8 March "	"	Aquilla Clements	16 May "	"
Sammerset Downed, deserted 5 Oct '82	5 Oct "	War	Jas. Kirk	19 May "	
			Elijah Oakly	28 Apl "	"
Chs. Griffith	14 Sept "	"	John Newberry	7 Apl "	"
Jno. Cotter	7 Sept "	"	Jas. Lowry	14 June "	War
Willis Cotter	7 Sept "	"	Chs. Beachem	5 Aug '82	"
Joseph McCallester	28 May "	3 years	James Coen	26 March "	"
Job Bewley	8 Apl "	War	Saml. Crowell	6 Dec "	"
Wm. Connally	7 May "	"	Wm. Hand	12 Dec "	"
Danl. Sellinger	26 June "	"	John Smith	18 Feb "	"
Wm. Henderson	28 May "	3 years	John Smith	3 Apl "	"
Walter B. Smallwood	5 June '81	"	Christr. Raynor	9 May "	"
Nathl. Hawthorn	20 July "	"	John Tulley	19 Oct "	"
John Baneworth	20 July "	"	John Welch	20 Aug "	"
Thos. Gordon	2 March "	"			

An Acct. of Pay due the Non Commis'd Officers and Privates of the Maryland Line, from Jan'y 1st, 1782, to Jan'y 1st, 1783.

NAME AND RANK.	WHEN COMMENCED.	WHEN LEFT SERVICE AND THE REASONS.	REMARKS.

1 Co., 1 B. Capt. Jona. Sellman. Lt. Nich. Gassaway. Ensign Henry Baker.

Jesse Simms	S.	All on	
George Childs	C.	1 Jan '82	
John Mills, 1st	C.	unless	
Wm. Dillon	C.	otherwise noted	furlough Maryd. dischd. 2nd May
Thomas Gossage	D.		
*James Bailey	D.		not heard of since June muster
*Wm. Hamilton, 1st	D.	do	waiter in Md.
*Wm. Swan	D.	do	do
John Carr	P.		

Name and Rank.		When Commenced.	When Left Service and the Reasons.	Remarks.
Richard Hall	P.	All on		
John Adams, 1st	P.	1 Jan '82		
John Baley, 1st	P.	unless		
Peter Bocard	P.	otherwise		
Michl. Lollar	P.	noted		
Daniel Clancey	P.			
John Ferrall	P.			
Basil Brown	P.			
*Andrew Fernen	P.		on June muster not heard of since surplus roll	
Thos. Canada	P.			
John Brown	P.			
Saml. Hamilton	P.			
Nehemiah Hadder	P.			
Wm. Lilley	P.			
Patk. Mollihan	P.			
John Goddard	P.			
John Williams, 1st	P.			
Robertson Ross	P.			
Wm. Sterling	P.			
Barney Lemmon	P.			
Thomas Drudge	P.			
Wm. Franklin	P.			
Thomas Thomas	P.			
James Crozier	P.			
John B. Haislip	P.		died 11 Sept '82	
Chas. Goldsbury	P.			
*Benj. Stuard	P.	1 Feb '82		
Alex. Francis	P.			
Peregrine Howard	P.			
Richard Procter	P.			
*Robert Taylor	P.		not heard from since June muster	
Saml. Harper	P.			
Wm. Gates	P.			
Edwd. Hammond	P.			
Barney Wilson	P.			
Noah Sayres, or Sears	P.			
Thos. Thompson	P.			waiter on Capt. Mr., Md.
William Peters	P.			
Joseph Thompson	P.			
Cornelius McLochlin	P.			
Edwd. Richardson	P.		dischd. 14 July '82	
*——nce White	P.		not heard of since June muster	
Willm. Lynch	P.			waiter, Maryd.
Aquilla Diver	P.			ditto

during the War of the American Revolution, 1775-83.   431

NAME AND RANK.	WHEN COMMENCED.	WHEN LEFT SERVICE AND THE REASONS.	REMARKS.
—— Richards	P.	All on	waiter, Maryd.
Thos. Baley	P.	1 Jan '82	ditto
*Isaac Henderson	P.	unless otherwise	not heard of since June muster	ditto
Jacob Blake, 1st	P.	noted	ditto	ditto
John Hancock	P.			
Frederick Wilmott	P.			
——as Clark, 1st	P.			
——el Calahan	P.			
John Osban	P.			
*Willm. Butler	P.		not heard of since March muster	furlough, Md.
*Thos. Cardiff	P.		do	do
*Saml. Trig	P.		do	do
Jas. Thomas, Jr.	P.			
Jas. Thomas, Sr.	P.			sick, Camden
*Benton Harris	P.		do	furlough, Md
Benj. Boyd	P.			
*John Turner	P.		discharged	
*John Beal	P.		ditto	
Wm. Kernal	P.	1 Feb '82	deserted 20 June '82	

2 Co., 1 B. Capt. Edward Prall.   Lt. Wm. Raisin.   Ensign Basil Burgess.

Thos. Windham	S.		furlough, Md
Peter McNorton	S.		
Wm. Martin	S.	died 30 Dec '82	
Dennis Kelly	S.		
Benj. Prior	C.		
*Walter, or Martin, Mills	C.		
Peter Smith	P., C. & S.		promoted Corpl. 15 Mch '82, made [Serjt. 1 Oct '82
John Martindale	D.		
Dennis Dunning	D.		waiter in Maryland
John McDonald	F.		
*John McCormick	F.	not heard of since March muster	waiter in Maryland
Michael Clansey	F.		
Joseph Hall	P.		
Amos Green	P.		
Francis Demar	P.		
Chas. Scott	P.		
Wm. Herrington	P.		
Thos. Lewis	P.	dischd. 13 Jan '82	
Abijah Buxton	P.		
John Harrell	P.		

Name and Rank.		When Commenced.	When Left Service and the Reasons.	Remarks.
Abraham Garsener	P.	All on		
Wm. Silkes	P.	1 Jan '82		
Darby McLamar	P.	unless		
David Cale	P.	otherwise		
Alexander West	P.	noted	died 1 Nov '82	
Thomas Glover	P.			
Wm. Clements	P.			
Stephen Fresh	P.			
Wm. Poling	P.			
Michael Miller	P.			
John Jackson	P.			
Ignatius Adams	P.			
Notley Tippet	P.			
Jonathan Fowler	P.			
Buto, (or Brito), Devo	P.		transferred to Invalids 4 Apl '82	
William Nailor	P.			
John Tucker	P.			[Guard
Benj. Gray	P.			on Gen. Small.'s
*Jonathan Millstead	P.			do do
Wm. Dorch	P.			
Wm. Kews, or Hews	P.		died 6 Dec '82	
Wm. Joice, 1st	P.			
John Brookbank	P.			
John Irons				
Jacob Flora	P.			
*Dennis Devine	P.		not heard of since June muster	
Thos. Bird	P.		discharged 13 Jan '82	
John Bean	P.		do 22 Jan '82	
Nathan Peeke	P.		disch'd 14 Nov '82	
Wm. Clary	P.			
Francis Fairbrother	P.			
John Dyxson	P.			waiter in Maryland
Joseph Fowler	P.			waiter in Maryland
Francis Thompson	P.			
Edward Elliott	P.			waiter in Maryland
Thos. Evins	P.			
*John Luffer	P.		not heard of since March muster	then furlough Maryland
Chas. Robinson	P.			do do
Simon Perry	P.			furlough Maryland
*James Harris, 1st	P.		ditto	then do
Banks Webb	P.			furlough Maryland
Stephen Preston	P.			do
John Anderson	P.			

Name and Rank.	When Commenced.	When Left Service and the Reasons.	Remarks.
Wm. Gughan, or Gudgeon	P.	All on 1 Jan '82	Annapolis waiter
Michael Clarke, 1st	P.	unless	
Christopher Lamberts	P.	otherwise	
Joseph Isaacs, 1st	P.	noted	sick in W'm'sb'gh, N.C. March '82
*John Nevitt, 1st	P.	not heard of since March muster	then sick in Wm's-burgh, N. Carolina
Laurence Simpson	P.		sick in Virginia
Notley Witcomb	P.		do
*Peter Richards	P.	not heard of since March muster	then sick as above

3 Co., 1 B. Capt. Wm. Rieley. Lt. Henry Clements.

Name and Rank.	When Commenced.	When Left Service and the Reasons.	Remarks.
Levi Smith	S.		
Abram Bowen	S.		
George Haydon	S.		
Thos. Sappington	S.	dischd. 12 Feb '82	
John Wilkinson	S.		
George Bateman	P.	dischd. 8 Jan '82	
William Forman	S.		
John Smith, 1st	C.		
*John Lucas, 2d	C.	on June muster & surplus roll	
*George Scone	C.	not heard of since March muster	then furlough Maryland
*Joshua Taylor	C.	ditto	then prisoner War
John Hull	D.		
Wm. Ferroll	D.		
James Reynolds	D.		reduced to private Jan '81
Joseph Nabb	F.		
*William Kelly	F.	not heard of since June muster	
Aaron Jones	P.		
John Andrew	P.		
Henry Gilby	P.		
Jas. Allen	P.		
Jas. Owens	P.		
John Downy	P.		
Perry Sullivan	P.		
Wm. St. Clair	P.		
Thos. Ayres	P.		
Jas. Doyle	P.		
Rigby Forster	P.		
Thos. Gilham	P.		

Name and Rank.		When Commenced.	When Left Service and the Reasons.	Remarks.
William Hill	P.	All on		
Benj. Loffman	P.	1 Jan '82		
John Burnett	P.	unless		
John Bantham	P.	otherwise		
James Holmes	P.	noted		promoted Corpl 1 Oct '82
Paul Lappine	P.			
John Johnston, 3rd	P.			
John Hughes, 1st	P.			
John McCay, 2nd	P.			
Thomas Carney,	P.			
Anthony Wearver	P.			
Thos. Feimley	P.			
John Fullam	P.			
Alex. Downy	P.			
David Wilson	P.			
William Horney	P.			
John Mills	P.			
Cornelius Thompson	P.			
Thos. Bowser	P.			
John Gother	P.		transferred Invalids, 25 Feb '82	
John Hood	P.		died 20 Dec '82	
Jarvis Eccleston	P.			
Augustin Cann	P.			
Chas. Girdler	P.			
Wm. Civil	P.			
Solomon Summers	P.			
Stafford Fosdale	P.			
Samuel Richardson	P.			
George Jurnings, (or Jennings)	P.			
Wm. Sullivan	P.			
Mark Forster	P.			
Alex. Rutherford	P.		dischd. 4 Jan '83	made up to 31 Dec
*Jonas Graves	P.		not heard of since June muster.	[and no longer
Anthony Burn	P.		on June muster and surplus roll	
Roger Shorter	P.			
John Harris	P.			
Joseph Geier	P.			
*Dennis Murley	P.		not heard of since June muster	
*Joseph Sidney	P.			
*George Saunders	P.			
*John Vallow	P.			waiter Col. Howard

during the War of the American Revolution, 1775-83.   435

Name and Rank.	When Commenced.	When Left Service and the Reasons.	Remarks.
*George Blackam	P.	All on	waiter Capt. Gibbons
*Abram Gamble	P.	1 Jan '82	furlough Mary'd
*Daniel Smith, 1st	P.	unless	ditto
*Robt. Pennington	P.	otherwise noted	not heard of since March muster	then ditto
*Thomas Ross	P.		not heard of since March muster	then furlough Mary'd
*John Canahan	P.		ditto	then taken prisoner 8 Sept '81
*Basley Barrett	P.		ditto	do taken prisoner 8 Sept '81
*Timothy Conner	P.		ditto	do do
James Pool	P.			do
*Wm. Woolcot	P.		ditto	do do 10 Feb '81
*Wm. Terrot	P.		ditto	do do 25 Apl '81
John Carroll, 2nd	P.			do
*James Bradshaw	P.		ditto	do do
John Duhague	P.		died 1 Dec '82	
Valentine Clapper	P.			
Emanual Allen	P.			
George Dyce	P.			
*Samuel Griffith	S.		not heard of since June muster	

4 Co., 1 B.   Capt. John S. Belt.   Lt. Hezekiah Ford.
              Ensign Francis Ware.

Name and Rank.	When Commenced.	When Left Service and the Reasons.	Remarks.
Leonard Smith	S.		
John Moore, 2nd	S.		
Lawrence Brannan	S.		
Humphry Becket	S.		
James Kelly, 1st	S.		
John Hamilton	C.		
*Griffin Taylor	C.	not heard of since June muster.	wounded at Eautaw
Walter Howe	C.		
Anthony Gohogan	D.		
Hezekiah Carr	D.		reduced 1 July '82
John Scott	D.		waiter in Maryland
Hezekiah, or Zachariah, Clark	F.		reduced 1 July '82
John Riggs	D.		
John Ashmore	P.		
*John Wood	P.	not heard of since June muster	
Willm. McGee	P.		
Emanuel Farara	P.		
Chas. McGee	P.		

Name and Rank.		When Commenced.	When Left Service and the Reasons.	Remarks.
George Foard	P.	All on		
Austin Howard	P.	1 Jan '82		
Christr. Seemore	P.	unless		
Francis Hopkins	P.	otherwise		
Michael Waltman	P.	noted		
James Ruark	P.			
Edward Roberts	P.			
Dudley Lee	P.			
John Cragg	P.			
John Appleby	P.			
Luke Dempsey	P.			
Thos. Jones	P.			
Jacob Moses	P.			
Luke Carter	P.			
John Fransway, or Francois,	P.			
John McCay, 1st	P.		dischd. 14 Feb '82	
Wm. Derrington	P.			
Edward Irvine	P.			
John Gordan	P.			
Neal Peacock	P.			
John Lee, 1st	P.			
Thomas Evans, 2nd	P.			pro'd C. 1 Oct '82
Richard Tasco	P.			
Travis Alby	P.			
Wm. Mitchell	P.			
*Alex. Bingley	P.		not heard of since June muster	
John Lewin	P.			
John Wells	P.			
Joshua Pearce	P.			
Henry Crooke	P.		Invalids 9 Apl '82	
Michael Woolford	P.			
James Byass	P.			
John Jarvis	P.			
Perry Bantham	P.			Com'd Maryland
Benj. Johnson	P.		not heard of since March muster	then ditto
Joseph Jenkins	P.			
John Buckley	P.			
John Love	P.			
*James Bluer	P.		do	then furlough Maryland
John Walker, 1st	P.			
Nathaniel Sullivan	P.		not heard of since June muster	
*James Sullivan	P.			

during the War of the American Revolution, 1775-83.   437

Name and Rank.	When Commenced.	When Left Service and the Reasons.	Remarks.
George Dixon	P.	All on	
Thomas King	P.	1 Jan '82	furlough Maryland
Francis Dunnington	P.	unless	
Samuel B. White	P.	otherwise	dischd. 24 Aug '82 furlough Md.
Philip Fisher	P.	noted	do
Lazarus Higgs	P.		do
*William Snow	P.	not heard of since March muster	then furlough Md.
*Jas. McNamara	P.	ditto	ditto ditto
Joseph Southall	P.		
John Dyer	P.		
Andrew Russell	P.		
*Thomas Weston	P.	do	ditto ditto
Chas. Bucklep	P.		furlough Maryland
John Jones	P.		ditto
Matthew Moore, 1st	P.		
Joseph Quinn	P.		ditto
James White	P.		
*Andrew Miller	P.	not heard of since June muster	
Edward Evans	P.		

5 Co., 1 B.   Capt. Lloyd Beall.   Lt. Edward M. Smith.

Name and Rank.	When Commenced.	When Left Service and the Reasons.	Remarks.
Stephen Fluharty	S.		
Arthur McClain	S.		
David Love	S.		furlough
*James Scott	S.	not heard of since March muster	then ditto
Samuel Fillson	S.		
Cuthbert Able	S.		
Chas. McNabb	S.		Asst. Forge Master
Samuel Davies, 1st	S.	dischd. by Col. Adams 1 Aug '82	sick in Va. March muster
Wm. Bruff	C.		promoted Sjt. 1 May '82
Peter Stephens	C.		Pris. 10 Apl '80
John Falling	C.		
Boston Medler	D.		
Benj. Williams	D.		
Edwd. Clancey	D.		
Jesse Barnett	F.		
Abram Stallions	F.		
*Thos. Wingate	F.	not heard of since then Mch muster	Pris. War
Saml. Clarke	P.		
Daniel Smith, 2d	P.		

Name and Rank.		When Commenced.	When Left Service and the Reasons.	Remarks.
Zadock Whaley	P.	All on		
Wm. Quinton	P.	1 Jan '82		
Wm. Harnston	P.	unless otherwise noted	on June muster and surplus roll	found and disch'd Jan '83
John Loveday	P.			
Wm. Casey	P.			
Alex. Ross	P.			
Joseph Mattingby	P.			
John Hadan	P.			
Richard Taylor	P.			
George Buck	P.			
Peter Maguire	P.			
Walter Hagan	P.			
*Wm. Young	P.		not heard of since March muster	then Com'd
John Twiner	P.			
Joshua Leister	P.			
James Keiland	P.			
Luke Sampson	P.			
Fredk. Harty	P.			
Leonard Hagan	P.			time expired Jan '83
John Blair	P.			
Neal Morris	P.			
Darby Crowley	P.			
Joseph Blaze	P.			
Michael Curtis	P.			
John Ryan	P.			
Robert Dunkin	P.			
John Neighbours	P.		on June muster and surplus roll	
Absalom Fardo	P.			
William Leakins	P.			
George Devitt	P.			
Elijah Pepper	P.			
*Laurence Hurdle	P.		not heard of since March muster	then Com'd Maryland
John Mills	P.			
Jacob Hunt	P.			
Jas. McDonald	P.			
Partrick Reiley	P.			furlough
*Jas. Smith, 1st	P.			waggoner in Md.
Wm. Niblett	P.			
Richd. Gee	P.			
*Danl. Hall	P.		ditto	transfer'd 23 March '82
*Philip Sullivan	P.		ditto since June muster	
Wm. Taylor, 1st	P.			

Name and Rank.	When Commenced.	When Left Service and the Reasons.	Remarks.
Wm. Mann	P.	All on	
Moses Foster	P.	1 Jan '82	
Willm. Cummings	P.	unless	Com'd Md
Peter Outhouse	P.	otherwise	do
Basil Norman	P.	noted	do
Chas. Simpkins	P.		
Wm. Crail	P.		
John Maxwell	P.		
1 Co., 2 B. Capt. Alex. Trueman.		Lt. Jacob Crawford.	Ensign Skirvins.
Stephen Price	S.		
Jesse Jacobs	S.		
Wm. Rose	S.		
Robt. Taylor, 2nd	S.		furlough in Md. Feb '82
Peter Shugart	C.	deserted 2 July '82	
John Thomas, 1st	C.		
Robt. Sharpless	C.		furlough Md. Feb '82
James Maxwell	C.		ditto
Danl. Warrior	D.		
Alex. Stevenson	D.		
James Greenwood	D.		
Benj. H. Kerrick	F.		
John Denoone	F.		waiter to Lt. Rutledge, Md.
Thos. Cahoe, Jr.	F.		ditto Lt. Lynn, ditto
Benj. Williams, 2nd	P.		
Absalom Wright	P.		
Michael Sours	P.	on June muster and surplus roll	
Saml. Young	P.		promoted Corpl. 1 Apl '82
Thomas McHandy	P.	died 28 Aug '82	
Jas. Steward, 1st	P.	ditto 1 Dec '82	
Joseph Kerrick	P.	ditto 27 do '82	
Adam Rider	P.		
George Mauntle	P.		
Wm. Harris, 1st	P.		
Darby Leneham	P.		
John Mantle	P.		
Michael McCann	P.		
Thos. Sheridan	P.		
Wm. George	P.	died 24 July '82	
Mathias Dytch	P.		
John Purdy	P.		
Henry Purdy	P.		

Name and Rank.		When Commenced.	When Left Service and the Reasons.	Remarks.
John Hillary	P.	All on	died 27 Dec '82	
Paul Grinnard	P.	1 Jan '82		
George Taylor	P.	unless		
Christopher Cusick	P.	otherwise		
Wm. Stonestreet	P.	noted		
Joseph Elliott	P.			
Michael Wiery	P.			
Isaac Grieves	P.			
Joseph Long	P.			
John Armstrong, 1st	P.			
Richd. Duvall	P.			
Nicholas Milburn	P.			promoted Corp. 1 [Apl '82
Joseph Sloop	P.			
Harry Billip	P.			
John Stackhouse	P.			furlough Md. June ['82
John Holliday	P.			
Jas. Devericks	P.			promoted S. 1 Oct ['82
Walter B. Smallwood	P.			
*Henry David	P.		not heard of since March muster	then sick in Virginia
*Jas. Neagle	P.		ditto	ditto ditto
*Richard Brockhill	P.		ditto	ditto at Annapolis
*Asel Rockhold	P.		ditto	ditto Artificer
Benj. Cleaver	P.			
George Bomgardner	P.			
Moses Graham	P.			
*Jacob Rowland	P.		ditto	then waiter Lt. Jacobs Mary'd
*Thos. Kearnes	P.		not heard of since March muster	then waiter to Gen. Gates
George Kelson	P.			
Jas. Nowell	P.			waiter Maj. Hardman, Md
Thos. Smith, 1st	P.			do do
Stephen Owens	P.			do Lt. Lynn
John Lincoln	P.			do Capt. Smith
John Elliott	P.			
Nathan Speak	P.		died 6 Oct	furlough Md. 2 Nov '80
Jas. Burck	P.			do 24 Aug '81
Thos. Cahoe, Senr.	P.			do 29 Dec '81
Nicholas Welch	P.			do 20 Feb '82
Jas. Sewell	P.			[8 Sept '81
*Patrick Eagen	P.		ditto	then prisoner War
*John Durough	P.		ditto	then do 15 Mch '81
John Hall	P.			
Benj. Mooren	P.		died 2 Feb '82	

Name and Rank.	When Commenced.	When Left Service and the Reasons.	Remarks.
2 Co., 2 B.	Capt. Thos. Mason. Lt. Zedekiah Moore. Ensign Malachi Bonham.		
Patrick Doran	S.	All on	
John Quick	S.	1 Jan '82	
Humphry Spencer	S.	unless	
Richd. Smith	S.	otherwise	['82
Wm. McNeal	S.	noted	furlough Md. Feb
*Saml. Wilson	S.	not heard of since March muster	then furlough Md. Feb '82
Edwd. Suite	C.	died 24 July	
Bennet H. Clements	C.		
Isaccher Mason	C.		
Henry Nicholson	C. & P.		reduced 19 Mch '82
Thos. Hawson	D.		ditto to private 1 July
Christopher McGraw	D.		['82
Edward Holland	D.		ditto
Daniel Bassett	F.		reduced 1 Oct '82
Fredk. Bennett	F.		do 1 Feb '82
Josias Alvey	P.	discharged 24 May	
John Ashberry	P.		
Jas. Barber	P.		
Jeremiah Brown	P.		
John Branson	P.		
Andrew Crummy	P.		promoted Corpl. 1 Oct '82
*Jacobus Debore	P.	not heard of since June muster	
George Dunkin	P.		
*William Day	P.	on June muster & surplus roll	time expires in July '83
John Ennis	P.		
Enoch Ennis	P.		
Willm. Fitzgerald	P.		
Chas. Fitzgerald	P.		
John Henly	P.		deserted 4 Aug '82
Peter Howard	P.		
Willm. Hope	P.		
Leonard Holt	P.		
Benj. Kearns	P.		
Levi Lord	P.		
Francis Lang	P.		
John Lee, 2nd	P.		deserted 4 Aug '82
Wm. Moore, 1st	P.		
John Moore, 1st	P.		
Richard Mitchell	P.		

Name and Rank.	When Commenced.	When Left Service and the Reasons.	Remarks.
Joseph Ray	P.	All on	
Wm. Shirley	P.	1 Jan '82	
Bennit Shirley	P.	unless	
Bartholomew Thompson	P.	otherwise	
Giles Thomas	P.	noted	
Daniel Votier	P.		deserted 1 July '82
Gabriel Williams	S.		disch'd 6 Feb '83
5 Co., 1 B.			
Willm. Hurly	P.		
*Cuthbert Stone	P.		not heard of since March muster
*Barney Munro	P.		ditto	then furlough Oct '81
*Jeremiah Fitzgerald	P.		ditto	then sick in Virginia
*Wm. Pringle	P.		ditto	then prisoner War
Robt. Walker	P.		
Lazarus Harmar	P.		
Thos. Baker	P.			sick Maryland
*John Plumary	P.		ditto	then ditto
*Laurence Whaland	P.	1 Apl '82	ditto
Wm. Hillman	P.		
2 Co., 2 B.			
Walter Watson	P.		
Jesse Wright	P.		
Wm. Carter	P.		
Rhode Woodland	P.		
Job Sylvester	P.		
Thos. Cooper	P.		died 1 Apl '82
John Smallwood, 1st	P.		
Francis Rogers	P.		deserted 13 July '82	Mch sick at George Town
*Richard Laine	P.		not heard of since March muster	then sick at Wm's-burgh
Chas. White	P.		
Jacob Blake	P.		
Francis Freeman	P.		
Peter Bushell	P.		
Gabriel Brand	P.		disch'd 12 Jan '82
Jeremiah French	P.		
James Corsey	P.		deserted 10 Dec '82
William Jones, 1st	P.		
*John Anderson, 2nd	P.		not heard of since March muster	then Gardner Gen. Smallwood, Md.
*Edward Laigg	P.		ditto	then Waggoner Clot. Genl.

Name and Rank.	When Commenced.	When Left Service and the Reasons.	Remarks.
*Jas. Isaacs	P.	All on 1 Jan '82 unless otherwise noted	not heard of since June muster	then transferred to the Corps of Invalids about Sept., 1781. Col. Tootal has his papers
George Dyer	P.		Mr. Randall has discharge	
John Frawney	P.			
Thos. Gadd	P.			
Benj. Gilbert	P.			
Wm. Hicks	P.			
John Moore, 3rd	P.		disch'd 12 Jan '83	furlough Md., Oct '81
*Caleb Hailey	P.		not heard of since March muster	furlough Md., Feb '82
Leonard Ennis	P.			do
Lewis Cunningham	P.			do
Walter Keech	P.			do
John Matthews, 1st	P.			do
James Smith, 2nd	P.			
Henry Tucker	P.		transfer'd 29 March	

3 Co., 2 B.   Capt. Saml. McPherson.   Lt. Wm. Smoot.

Name and Rank.	When Commenced.	When Left Service and the Reasons.	Remarks.
Wm. Collis	S.		
John Brady	S.		
Richd. Wheelor	S.		
*Luke Barnwell	S.	not heard of since March muster	then on furlough
Wm. Brathwaite	C.		
Bartholomew Eshum	C.		
John Head	D.		
John Peany	D.		
Andrew Garnett	F.		
*Walter Little	F.	on June muster and surplus roll	
Equilla Pearse	P.		
Philip Fitzpatrick	P.		
Robert Shipley	P.	died 20 July '82	
John Haney	P.		
John Mick	P.		
Wm. Goold	P.		
Jas. Hair	P.	died 6 July '82	
Hampton Coarsey	P.		
Henry Green	P.		
John Welch, 1st	P.		
*Jas. Shotten	P.	not heard of since June muster	

Name and Rank.		When Commenced.	When Left Service and the Reasons.	Remarks.
Jas. Jackson	P.	All on		
Roger Landers	P.	1 Jan '82		
Michael Lloyd	P.	unless		
Chas. Cooper	P.	otherwise		
Wm. Jenkins	P.	noted		
Jas. Meason	P.			
John Gregory	P.			
Thos. Waite	P.			
Levi Burck	P.			
John Alby	P.			
Peter Melvin	P.			
Wm. Moore, 2nd	P.			
James Wilson, 1st	P.			
Danl. Bulgar	P.			
Jacob Game	P.			
John Robbins	P.			
John Buckhannan	P.			
Jas. Farrell	P.			
Abram Irvin	P.			
David Bramble	P.			
*George Riggs	P.		not heard of since June muster	
Thos. Camphire	P.			
Wm. Purchace	P.			
Wm. Lee, 2nd	P.			
John Taylor, 1st	P.			
Adam Kipart	P.			
Jacob Knight	P.			
Wm. Laws	P.			
Michl. Casner	P.			
Richd. Blamford	P.			
Wm. Groves	P.			
*Nathan Cripps	P.		not heard of since June muster	
Joseph Jones	P.			
Lambert Thompson	P.			
*Wm. Lucas	P.			killed Oct '82
Callothil Carmile	P.			
Partrick Cavenough	P.			
Joseph Horsefield	P.			
Joseph Huskill	P.			
Richd. Biddle	P.			
James Shane	P.			sick in Maryland
Robt. Farrell	P.			with Capt Smith, Charles Town
John Romills	P.			waiter to Col. Williams

Name and Rank.	When Commenced.	When Left Service and the Reasons.	Remarks.
*John Moran	P.	All on 1 Jan '82 unless otherwise noted.	not heard of since March muster	then waiter to Lt. Jamison
Jas. Harris, 2nd	P.		
Thos. Ashell, or Aspell	P.		waiter to Lt. Armstrong
Wm. Cutler	P.		
Stephen Varlow	P.		waiter to Maj. Davidson
Levin Button	P.		ditto Dr. Haney
*Richard Lloyd	P.	ditto	then pris. War
*Chas. Burns	P.	ditto	ditto
*Richd. Downes	P.	ditto	ditto
*John McCowan	P.	ditto	ditto
*George Stevens	P.	not heard of since March muster	then pris. War
Solomon Britanham	P.		
4 Co., 2 B.	Lt. Wm. Adams.	Ensign John D. Carey.	
Terrence Duffee	S.		
Francis Duffee	S.		
Jesse Boswell	S.		
Robert Scribner	S.		
*Jas. Flack	S.		furlough Maryland
Jas. Hagen	C.		
*Edward White	C.	not heard of since March muster	then furlough Md. Jan '82
Wm. Steward	D.		
Wm. Prater	D.		
George Steem	F.		waiter in Md.
Wm. Moore, 3d	P.		
John Summers	P.		
Robert Clenehan	P.		
*Abram Shockee	P.	on June muster & surplus roll	
Thos. Baire	P.		
Wm. Rice	P.		
*Dennis Downes	P.	not heard of since June muster	time expires 10 June '83
William Glory	P.		
Thos. Arthurs	P.		
Jesse Powers	P.		
*Alex. Steel	P.	not heard of since June muster	
Thos. Patterson	P.		
Henry Evans	P.		
Wm. McLochlin	P.		
Aron Rawlings	P.		furlough Md. Jan '82
Benj. Gaither	P.		
*Joseph Adams	P.	on June muster & surplus roll	

Name and Rank.	When Commenced.	When Left Service and the Reasons.	Remarks.
Robert Straights	P.	All on	
*Chas. Hickey	P.	1 Jan '82	on June muster & surplus roll
*Edwd. Sheehee	P.	unless	not heard of since June muster
Jas. Crasberry	P.	otherwise	
John Newton, 1st	P.	noted	
Thos. Porters	P		
Richd. Hays	P.		
John Brewer	P.	died 7 July '82	
Joseph Donohoo	P.		
Saml. Scott	P.		furlough Md '82
Patrick Rowan	P.		
Wm. Jones, 2nd	P.		
*Joseph Martin	P.	not heard of since June muster	
Edwd. Kearsy	P.		
John Lucas, 1st	P.		
*Joseph Points	P.	not heard of since March muster	then waiter Maj. Giles, Md
John C. Harwood	P.		do Lt. Skinner, Va.
John Deakins	P.		
Jesse Furroughs	P.	deserted 1 Apl '82	
Edwd. Vickers	P.		
*Jeremiah Reed	P.	not heard of since June muster	
John Sammon	P.		
*John Fulsom	P.	ditto	
John Denson	P.		sick Camden
*Zachariah Prather	P.	ditto	
Wm. Matthews	P.		
*John Butcher	P.	ditto since March muster	then furlough Md. Jan '82. On pension
*Wm. Scaggs	P.	ditto since June muster	
James Bigwood	P.		
James Barrow	P.	trans'd Inv. 1 Apl '82	
Richd. Kisby	P.		
Danl. Jarvis	P.		
John Housely	P.		
*Peter Henesy	P.	not heard of since June muster	
John Shovell	P.		furlough Md. Jan '82
*John Deskey	P.	not heard of since March muster	then do
*George Holliday	P.	ditto	do do
Wm. Chatland	P.		do
*Wm. Allender	P.	ditto	then do
Thos. Bishop	P.		do
*George Collins	P.	not heard of since June muster	
Zachariah Mills	P.		
Chas. Sickle	P.		

Name and Rank.	When Commenced.	When Left Service and the Reasons.	Remarks.
5 Co., 2 B.	Lt. Thos. Price.	Ensign Thos. Beatty.	
Saml. F. Shoemaker	S.	All on	
Francis MaGauran	S.	1 Jan '82	Qr. Mr. Serjt.
Chas. Ronenberger	S.	unless	
Jacob Keyser	S.	otherwise disch'd 13 Feb '82	
Moses McKinsey	C.	noted	reduced 10 Nov '82
Joshua McKinsey	C.		ditto
John Roach	C.		reduced 1 May '82
Jas. Ashley	C.		
Benj. Cole	C.		
George Silver	P.		
Henry Fisher, 1st	P.		
Adam Mushler	P.		
Michl. Rhydmyer	P.		
George Bough	P.		
Owen Curly	P.	deserted 22 June '82	
John Wade	P.		
*John Malady	P.	not heard of since June muster	
Wm. Ryder	P.		
Thos. Larmore	P.		
Danl. Williams	P.		
John Follet	P.	deserted 30 June '82	
Cornelius Vaughan	P.		
Michl. Hardman	P.		
Chas. Jones	P.		
*Jas. Tite	P.	not heard of since June muster	
Francis Karns	P.		Inlisted in '78 in the German Regt. and was drafted in the line in '81 for the War
John Walker, 2nd	P.		
John Shively	P.	deserted 19 Apl '82	
Wm. Sillwood	P.		promoted C. 1 Oct '82, reduced 27 Dec
Jas. Johnston	P.	deserted 19 Apl '82	
Christopher Smith	P.		
Nathan Aldridge	P.		
John Stanton	P.		
*Edwd. Wade	P.	not heard of since June muster	
Alex. Robinson	P.		
Jas. Erwin	P.		
Thos. Jones, 2nd	P.		
Joseph McAtlee	P.		

Name and Rank.	When Commenced.	When Left Service and the Reasons.	Remarks.
Saml. Harrison	P.	All on	died 2 Aug '82
Mathias Cyphert	P.	1 Jan '82	
Peter Cones	P.	unless	deserted 11 Feb '82
Thos. Hutchcroft	P.	otherwise	
Richd. Haislip	P.	noted	
Nathan Hoursbury	P.		deserted 20 July '82
Luke Merryman	P.		
John Wilson, 1st	P.		
John Thompson	P.		
Wm. Hancock	P.		deserted 1 June '82
John Nicholson	P.		
*Henry Wilstock	P.		not heard of since March muster	then on Com'd Va.
Jacob Coffman	P.		deserted 1 July '82
Danl. Kettle	P.		
Samual Wright	P.		died 20 Jan '82	sick Fred'sburgh
Chas. Williams	P.		
John Nevitt, 2nd	P.		
Saml. Boswell	P.		
Jesse McKinsey	P.		
Abraham Kettle	P.		
*Timothy Cahill	P.		not heard of since June muster
Chas. Leago	P.			furloughed to Mary'd
Handy Handly	P.		deserted 6 Nov '81
*Michl. Downs	P.		not heard of since March muster	then sick Wm's-burg, Va.
*Wm. Hamilton, 2nd	P.		ditto	ditto ditto
Arthur Coffins	P.		
*Henry Ferns	P.		ditto	then Hosp'l George Town, Md.
Francis Purcell	P.		
John Haines	P.		died 2 Feb '83
John Fennell, 1st	P.			sick Annapolis
John Turner, 2nd	P.			do Baltimore
*Wm. Newberry	P.		on June muster and surplus roll

1 Co., 3 B.   Capt. Christian Orendorf.   Lt. John T. Lowe.
Ensign Saml. B. Beall.

Name and Rank.	When Commenced.	When Left Service and the Reasons.	Remarks.
Michael Smith, 1st	S.		
*Jacob Doyne	S.	16 June '82	
Benj. Ward	S.		
George Finlay	S.		
George Holton	S.		
James Wood	S.		on Command

during the War of the American Revolution, 1775–83.   449

NAME AND RANK.		WHEN COMMENCED.	WHEN LEFT SERVICE AND THE REASONS.	REMARKS.
*James Clement	C.	All on	not heard of since June muster	
Bennit George	C.	1 Jan '82	dead 1 Oct '82	
Saml. Gray	C.	unless		
John D. Tulley	C.	otherwise		reduced 1 Oct '82
Archibald Butt	D.	noted		transferred to N. C. Line 28 Apl '82
*Henry Harris	D.		not heard of since March muster	then sick at Wm's- burgh
Daniel Willis	F.			on furlough
*John Burke	P.		not heard of since June muster	
Thos. Gordon, 1st	P.		deserted 16 Apl '82	
*Henry Connelly	P.		not heard of since June muster	
Levin Abbott	P.			
Wm. Harrison, 1st	P.			
Richard Ariss	P.		deserted 16 Apl '82	
*Edwd. Scantlin	P.		not heard of since June muster	
Matthew Carty	P.			
*Henry Enniss	P.		ditto	
Jacob Collins	P.			
James Jones	P.			
*George Belfast	P.		ditto	
John Starkey	P.			
Garrett Welch	P.			
John Smith, 2nd	P.		on June muster and surplus roll	
Wm. Aggas	P.		deserted 29 Apl '82	
Barton Cecil	S.		disch'd 13 Jan '82	
Walter C. Davids	S.		deserted 1 Jan '83	
Jas. Chambers	P.			
Edwd. Furrener	P.			
John Cole	P.			
Thomas John	P.			
Oliver Stephens	P.			
Wm. Standley	P.			
Jas. Smith, 3d	P.			sick Annapolis
*Eccabut Golden	P.		not heard of since March muster	then ditto
Wm. Smith, 1st	P.			ditto
*John Steward, 1st	P.		ditto	then ditto
*Edwd. Bartlett	P.		ditto	
Stephen Hancock	P.			then sick Wm'sburgh ditto
Jas. Reynolds, 2nd	P.			
Jas. Brannin	P.			ditto
Robt. Carns	P.			ditto
Edwd. Mahoney	P.			ditto

Name and Rank.		When Commenced.	When Left Service and the Reasons.	Remarks.
*John Holston	P.	All on 1 Jan '82 unless otherwise noted	not heard of since March muster	then sick Wm'sburgh
*Peter Hollaby	P.		ditto	ditto ditto
*Abraham Reynolds	P.		ditto	ditto ditto
Chas. Murphy	P.			
James Wilson, 2d	P.			
*Wm. Dunkin	P.		ditto	ditto ditto
Thos. Perry	P.			
John Smallwood, 2d	P.			
Jacob Jeffers	P.			
Wm. Taylor, 2d	P.			
Benj. Baulk	P.			
Wm. McPherson	P.			
*Wm. Elbom	P.		not heard of since March muster	then sick Wm'sburg
*Leonard Turner	P.		deserted	
*Ephraim Ganes	P.		ditto	

2 Co., 3 B.   Capt. Jas. W. Gray. Lt. Rignal Hillary. Lt. Philip Hill. Ensign Basil Waring.

Name and Rank.			Remarks.
John Reeder	S.		
John Lynch, 1st	S.		
John Hamond Dorsey	S.	deserted 1 Jan '82	
John Moore, 4th	C.		
Wm. Little	C.		
Peter French	C.		
Wm. Willson, 1st	C.		promoted Sergt. 1 Oct '82
John Morrison	D.		
John Onians	D.		
Jas. Cholard	F.& P.		reduced 1 Apl '82
John Graham	F.		prisoner 1 May '82
Michael Pilkerton	P.		
Jacob Dudderow	P.		
*John Flowers	P.	not heard of since June muster	
Wm. Dawson	P.		
Frederick Jams	P.		
Dennis Trammell	P.		
John Gorman	P.		
David Hatten'	P.		
*Charles Willet	P.	not heard of since June muster	
Levin Thomas	P.		
Edward Chambers	P.		
Edward Tanner	P.		
Joseph Lewis	P.		

during the War of the American Revolution, 1775-83.   451

Name and Rank.	When Commenced.	When Left Service and the Reasons.	Remarks.
Joshua Cox	P.	All on	
Wm. Glaver	P.	1 Jan '82	
*Wm. Roe, 3rd	P.	unless	not heard of since June muster
John Spears	P.	otherwise	
John Francis	P.	noted	
Wm. Taylor, 3rd	P.		
John McCall	P.		
*John Appingstall	P.		not heard of since June muster
Chas. Dean	P.		
Saml. Rudolph	P.		deserted 15 Apl '82
Barnaby Doherty	P.		
Francis Reed	P.		
Nehemiah Lingard	P.		
James Tigner	P.		
Wm. Simonds	P.		
Wm. Goody	P.		deserted 1 Jan '82
Lambert Goody	P.		
Saml. Hurst	P.		
Philip Savoy	P.		
John Bowdy	P.		
*Henry Ferrence	P.		not heard of since March muster then sick at Hospital Georgetown
Aaron Perry	P.		deserted 1 Feb '82 [6 Sept '81
Dennis Cragon	P.		
*Archibald Kersey	P.		not heard of since June muster
John Young, 2nd	P.		Com'd Maryland
*Joseph McLain	P.		not heard of since March muster then Hospital Annapolis Aug '81
*Philip McDonald	P.		ditto then ditto
James Carey	P.		
Nicholas Free	P.	18 Dec '82	
James Hudson	P.		Hospital Annapolis Aug '81
John Hudson, 1st	P.		ditto
John Murray, 1st	P.		ditto
*Robert Tolgan	P.		not heard of since March muster then ditto
John Clancey	P.		made Corporal ditto Georgetown 6 Sept '81
*Robert Eaton	P.		not heard of since March muster then ditto
*Jas. Crumwell	P.		ditto then ditto Wm'sburgh Oct '81
Jas. Chard	P.		ditto
*Jas. Lynch	P.		ditto then ditto

Name and Rank.	When Commenced.	When Left Service and the Reasons.	Remarks.
*Andrew Flood	P.	All on 1 Jan '82 unless otherwise noted	not heard of since June muster	
*Patrick Fleming	P.		not heard of since March muster	then Wm'sburgh Oct '81
*Oliver Denny	P.		ditto	ditto ditto
*Wm. Bowden	P.		ditto	ditto ditto in Nov '81
Jas. Creighton, Craighton	P.			ditto
John Gee	P.			ditto
*Peter Baker	P.		ditto	then ditto
John McLain	P.			ditto
*John Thompson	P.		not heard of since June muster	
Henry Fisher, 2nd	P.			
Wm. Hartman	P.			

3 Co., 3 B.   Capt. Benj. Price.   Lt. Jas. Winchester.

Name and Rank.	Rank	When Left Service and the Reasons.	Remarks.
Archibald Johnston	S.		
George Fields	S.		
Nicholas Nicholson	S.		
Theophilus Linsey	C.		
Joseph Pherson	C.		
John Cooper, 1st	P.		
Wm. Potter	C.		
George Hamilton	C.		reduced 1 Oct '82
Peter Boyall	C.	died 15 Jan '82	sick W'msburg
John Hannon	F.		
Isaac Hill	F.		
Isaac Young	D.		
John Jones, 2d	D. & P.		reduced 1 Feb '82
Benj. Smith	P.		
Joseph Austin	P.	deserted 17 May '82	
Wm. Wheylin	P.		
Nicholas Hyner	P.		
*Stephen Kimble	P.	not heard of since June muster	
John McGlin	P.		
Henry Hughes	P.	deserted 17 May '82	
Zachariah Robertson	P.		
Thomas Clark, 2d	P.		
Jas. Knott	P.		
Benj. Marsh	P.		
John Armstrong, 2d	P.		
Levi Moody	P.	died 15 Oct '82	
Henry Townley	P.		
Patrick Kelly	P.	deserted 17 May '82	
Wm. Elkins	P.		

during the War of the American Revolution, 1775–83.

Name and Rank.		When Commenced.	When Left Service and the Reasons.	Remarks.
Jas. Philips	P.	All on		
Jeremiah Sullivan	P.	1 Jan '82		
Jas. Shepherd	P.	unless		
Joseph Cooley	P.	otherwise	disch'd 9 Jan '82	
Chas. Clements	P.	noted		promoted C. 1 Oct '82
Richd. Spires	P.			
Patrick Reed	P.		deserted 17 May '82	
John Newton, 2d	P.			
Richd. Dickson	P.		died 27 Dec '82	
Patrick McKinsey	P.			
John Smith, 3d	P.			
*Thos. Allen	P.		not heard of since March muster	then sick Annapolis 1 Jan '82
Peter Carbury	P.			ditto
George Linton	P.			ditto
Jas. Stewart, 2d	P.			Mch ditto
Jas. Terry	P.			do at Georgetown
John Lesley	P.			ditto
John Holder	P.			ditto
Thos. Tanner	P.		died 3 Jan '82	do at W'msburgh
*John Durant	P.		not heard of since June muster	ditto
*Benj. Shaw	P.		not heard of since March muster	then ditto
*Wm. Turner	P.		ditto	then ditto
*John Keech	P.		ditto	then ditto
Thos. Jones, 3d	P.		discharged 13 March '82	then ditto
Wm. Marlow	P.			do prod. X Serjt. 1 Nov '82
*Abraham Manhan, or Manning	P.			Mch sick at W'msburgh to be made up
*Michael Downes	P.		not heard of since March muster	then ditto
*James Lyles	P.		ditto	then ditto
John Stoffle	P.			ditto
Robert Campbell	P.			ditto
Jonathan Lewis	P.			
Randolph Hoskins	P.		disch'd 8 Jan '82	
*John Flanagan	P.		not heard of since June muster	sick Petersburgh
David Relly	P.			do Charlotte
John Smyth, 4th	P.			ditto
John Brown, 2d	P.			ditto
*John Patterson	P.		ditto	ditto

Name and Rank.	When Commenced.	When Left Service and the Reasons.	Remarks.
*Patrick Reading	P.	All on 1 Jan '82 unless otherwise noted	not heard of since March muster	then Smith at Annapolis
*Saml. Silk	P.		ditto	then Armourer, do
John McNeal	P.			Waggoner
*Wm. Dych	P.		not heard of since June muster	Artificer
John Fulford	P.			
*Henry Clark	P.		ditto	
Edward Cosgrove	P.			
John Wise	P.		deserted 4 May '82	Boon's Hospl. 4 March '82
Andrew Rereside	P.		died 16 Dec '82	ditto
John Hewlett	P.			ditto
Paul Rowwen	P.			look Genl. Gist

4 Co., 3 B.   Capt. Francis Revelley.   Lt. Henry Baldwin.

Name and Rank.	Rank	When Left Service and the Reasons.	Remarks.
Timothy McMahon	S.		promoted S. Major 10 Jan '82
James Collins	S.		
John Neary	S.		
John Newman	S.		
Wm. Clements	C.		
Danl. Brimugum	C.		reduced 1 Oct '82
John McCaliff	D.		do 1 Apl '82
Philip Huston	D.		
John Biggs	P.		
Joseph White	P.		
Thomas Matthews, 1st	P.		
Wm. Downes	P.		
John Carroll, 1st	P.	disch'd 13 Jan '82	
Richd. Dolvin	P.		
Henry Williams	P.		
Jas. Humphries	P.		
Wm. Porter	P.		
John Collins	P.		
Nathaniel Ross	P.		
John Hurly	P.		
Francis Taylor	P.		
Wm. Mansfield	P.		
William Brady	P.		
*Danl. Duncan	P.		pris. 11 Apl '82
Elijah Hutt	P.		
Thomas Shortwill	P.	deserted 9 Apl '82	
*Thos. Crofford	P.		pris. 11 Apl '82
Francis Burton	P.	do 15 May '82	

NAME AND RANK.		WHEN COMMENCED.	WHEN LEFT SERVICE AND THE REASONS.	REMARKS.
John Matthews, 2d	P.	All on	disch'd 16 Feb '82	
*John McRhea	P.	1 Jan '82		
Ebram, Abram, Doogan	P.	unless		
Nicholas Elliott	P.	otherwise		pro. Fifer 1 Apl '82
Christian Clore, (or Close)	P.	noted	died 1 Mch '82	
Benj. Williams, 3d	P.			
Peter Equed Downey	P.			
John Carll, 1st	P.			
Jas. Bailess	P.			
Jeremiah Owens	P.			
Wm. Coe	P.			Waggoner
Guilford Miniky	P.			
Richd. Dunby	P.			
Thos. Adams	P.			Waggoner
Thos. Matthews	P.			Waggoner
Thos. B. Clements	P.			
John Harris, 2d	P.			
James Cougherin, or Cockerile	P.			
Jas. Evans	P.			
Thos. Jones, 4th	P.			
John Thomas, 2nd	P.			
Thos. Wood, 2nd	P.			
*Edward Appleton	P.		not heard of since March muster	then on furlough Md., Jan '82
*Emanual Eabbs	P.		ditto	then on Comd. Annapolis, Jan '82
*Edward Blake	P.		ditto	then on Clothl. Genl. Guard
John King	P.			transf. 2 Regt. 4 Apl '82
John Jordan	P.		deserted 19 Apl '82	
*George Cougheren	P.		not heard of since March muster	then sick Petersburg
Solomon Green	P.			
Pressley Bruenton	P.			sick Peterbourough
Joseph McNamara	P.			Mch sick W'msburgh
*Wm. Gantley	P.		ditto	ditto ditto
Jas. Davidson	P.			
*Jas. Hays	P.		ditto	ditto
Saml. Chappel	P.			sick W'msburgh
*Neal McCowen	P.		not heard of since March muster	then ditto
John Kildare	P.			Mch do Georgetown
*Matthew Stanton	P.		ditto	then do Annapolis

Name and Rank.		When Commenced.	When Left Service and the Reasons.	Remarks.
*John Nolen	P.	21 Dec '82		
John Pendar	P.		died 10 Nov '81	sick W'msburgh
Alex. Steward	P.	All on		Mch sick W'msburgh
*Thos. Blansher	P.	1 Jan '82	not heard of since Mch muster	then do Annapolis
		unless		
John Willis	P.	otherwise		ditto
John Ransom	P.	noted		ditto
*Ezekial Taylor	P.		ditto	then ditto
John Hickins	P.			ditto
*Francis Matthews	P.		ditto	then ditto
Thos. Ellitt, 1st	P.	10 Feb '82		
1 Co., 4 B.	Capt. Wm. Wilmot.		Lt. Mark McPherson.	
Thos. Edwards	S.			
Hugh McMillan	S.			
John Gwin	S.			
Wm. Needham	S.			on Command, Jan '82
John Colein	S.			
Chas. Harvey	S.		trans. Invalids 10 Jan '83	
George Bradley	C.		died 31 Nov '82	
*Richd. Fenwick	C.		not heard of since March muster	then on furlough Md., and he must produce a Certificate of his doing duty after being furloughed or he will be Considered a deserter
Richd. Ferraby	C.			
Wm. Smyth, 2d	D.			pris. War in Charlestown 10 Dec '82
John McKnight	D.			
Thos. Clinton	F.			
John Beach	D.		died 15 Dec '82	
Joseph Follett	F.		died 25 July '82	
Wm. Douglass	P.		deserted 20 Nov '82	Waiter Dr. [Brown, Md.
Peter Topping	P.			
Michael Callihorne	P.			
Jeremiah Rhodes	P.		disch'd 17 Feb '82	
John Hyde	P.			
Emmanuel Carthagena	P.			
John Crosby, 1st	P.		died 24 July '82	
Robinson Wood	P.			
Rueben Smith	P.			
John Kidd	P.			

during the War of the American Revolution, 1775-83. 457

Name and Rank.	When Commenced.	When Left Service and the Reasons.	Remarks.
James Gray	P.	All on	
Hugh Gaynor	P.	1 Jan '82	
Wm. Carter, 2d	P.	unless	Flying Hospl. N. Army
Joseph Johnson	P.	otherwise	
Jas. Wood	P.	noted	
Wm. Ingle	P.		
*Robert Lynch	P.	not heard of since November muster	
Jeremiah Williams	P.		
*John Young, 1st	P.	not heard of since June muster	
Adam Jamieson	P.		
Thos. Murphy	P.		
Isaac Holliday	P.		
*John Bellamy	P.	ditto	
*Edward Freeman	P.	ditto	
Elijah Smith	P.		
*Jas. Silver	P.	ditto	
Daniel O'Quinn	P.		
John Berryman	P.		
Thos. Slade	P.		
Joseph Batts	P.		
Dennis Flannigan	P.	Private, Artillery	
Henry Ramsden, Ramsey	P.		
John Vanzant	P.		furlough Md.
John Dunnigan	P.		Hospl. Camden
John Lynch, 2d	P.		
*Cornelius Murphy	P.	not heard of since June muster	
Wm. Evans	P.		furlough Md.
Conrad Smith	P.		
*Joseph Whitehouse	P.	not heard of since March muster	then prisoner War
Edward Evans	P.		Hospl. Camden
*John Linday	P.	ditto	then furlough Md.
James Gath	P.		do
Matthew Moore, 2d	P.		Waggoner
Henry Redding	P.		do
*Jarvis Williams	P.	ditto	then in Md.
*Robert Stacey	P.	not heard of since June muster	
Joseph Roberts	P.		Mch waiter in Md.
Philip Bailey	P.		waiter Genl. Gist
Wm. Purcell	P.	not heard of since March	then waiter to Col. Wms.
Edward Wright	P.		do to Dr. Smith, Savannah
Joseph Bautcheby	P.		Taylor, Charlotte
Wm. Pecker	P.		

Name and Rank.		When Commenced.	When Left Service and the Reasons.	Remarks.
Evan Tumbleston	P.	All on		
Thos. Wood, 1st	P.	1 Jan '82		furlough Maryland
Christopher McAway	P.	unless		Artificer
Michael Smith, 2d	P.	otherwise		
*Edward Walter	P.	noted.		
*Wm. Morecraft	P.	15 Feb '82	not heard of since March muster	?
Philip Graham	P.			
Asaph Colegate	P.			
Wm. Hedge	P.			
Michael Clark, 2d	P.			
Ralph Hope	P.			
*Henry Matthews	P.		not heard of since March muster	then on Guard

2 Co., 4 B. Capt. John Mitchell. Lt. John McCoy. Ensign Joseph Cross.

Name and Rank.		When Commenced.	When Left Service and the Reasons.	Remarks.
Thos. Duffee	S.			
John Willing	S.			
George Lash	S.		deserted 11 Apl '82	
Kinsey Lanham	C.		died 20 Dec '82	
Nathaniel, or Nathan, Price	C.			promoted S. 1 March '83
Chas. Nabb	C.			sick W'msburg North Carolina
*Walter Evans	C.		not heard of since March muster	then ditto Virginia
Edward Henesy	P.			
Frederick Myers, Myirs	P.		deserted 11 Apl '82	
Cato Snowden	P.			
Ignatius Smith	P.		died 20 Apl '82	
Wm. Absalom	P.			
*Richard Clark	P.		not heard of since June muster	then Armour Artificers
Thomas Long	P.			
Aaron Mitchell	P.			
Humphry Wells	P.			
Joseph Jeans	S.			
Levi Scott	F.			
John Burns	P.			
Timothy Langrel	P.			
John Hudson, 2d	P.			
George Jones	P.			
Wm. Cork	P.			
Daniel Mann	P.			
Walter Prewit	P.			

during the War of the American Revolution 1775-83.   459

Name and Rank.		When Commenced.	When left Service and the Reasons.	Remarks.
Smart Greor	P.	All on		
John Taylor, 2d	P.	1 Jan '82		
Jas. Bowen	P.	unless		
Edward Fincham	P.	otherwise	not heard of since June muster	
*Wm. Grant	P.	noted.		
John Dobson	P.			
Amos Griffin	P.			
Wm. Paul	P.			
Francis McCann	P.			
John Lonass	P.		died 2 Oct '82	Waggoner
Alyard Melvin	P.			
*Wm. Richardson	P.		time expires 1 Apl '82	June do
John Briley, or Bailey	P.			
Thos. Elliott, 2d	P.			
Thos. Davies	P.			
John Watkins	P.			
Wm. Whittico	P.			
Michael McKnight	P.		deserted 25 Apl '82	
Saml. Green	P.		disch'd 9 Jan '82	
John Nelson	P.			Waggoner
Wm. Lee, 1st	P.			do
Thos. Foxall	P.			do
Heath C. Edwards	P.			do
Jacob Yeast	P.			do
Pompey Hollis	P.		died in 1783	do
*John Charles	P.		disch'd 15 Mch '83	
*John O'Conner	P.		not heard of since March muster	then sick Hospl. Virginia
*John Cuthart	P.		ditto	then do
John Cleverdence	P.			do
*Wm. Bercus	P.		not heard of since June muster	do
*Wm. Donoho	P.		not heard of since March muster	then do
David Meadows	P.			do W'msburg
George Carney	P.			do
Wm. Burgess	P.			
Timothy Donnelly	P.		deserted 15 Apl '82	
Robt. Michael	P.			
*John Stephens	P.		not heard of since March muster	then sick Hospl. in Virginia
*Jas. Darnell	P.		ditto	then do
Danl. Murphy	P.			do
*Cornish Freind	P.		ditto	then do

Name and Rank.		When Commenced.	When Left Service and the Reasons.	Remarks.
*John Poxman	P.	All on 1 Jan '82 unless otherwise noted.	not heard of since March muster	then sick Hospl. Virginia
*Thos. Lane	P.		ditto	then Petersburg
*Charles Gordon	P.		ditto	do do
*Martin Rosah	P.		not heard of since June muster	then sick Hospl.
John Edwards	P.			N. Carolina
Wm. Fairburne	P.		died 16 Mch '82	refer to Gray for his death
Thos. Burk	P.			sick N. Carolina
John Betsworth	P.		deserted 5 Apl '82	
Luke Griffin	P.			sick S. Carolina

3 Co., 4 B.   Lt. Edmond Compton.   Ensign Wm. Hanson.

Name and Rank.		When Commenced.	When Left Service and the Reasons.	Remarks.
Chas. Fulham	S.			
George Williams	S.			reduced 7 Apl '82
John Walker, 3rd	S.			sick Maryland
Basil Shaw	S.			
Saml. Evans	C.			promoted Serjt. 7 Apl '82
Wm. Browning	C.		deserted 2 July '82	
Nathan Harper	D.			
John T. West	F.		on June muster & surplus roll	waited of Major Winder
Alex. Levi	P.			
Peter Degazoone	P.			
Patrick Dennison	P.			
Thos. Crampton	P.			
*Thos. Gray	P.		on June muster not heard of since	promoted Corpl. 1 Apl '82
Abraham Catchsides	P.			
Wm. Manly	P.			
Thos. Pender	P.			
Stephen Fennell	P.			
Thos. Pennifield	P.			
Henry Crane	P.			
Jacob Myers	P.			
John West	P.			
Jonathan Chubb,	P.			
Richard Wiley	P.			
Lambert Philips	P.			
John Blair	P.		disch'd 15 Jan '82	
Thos. Ellis	P.			
Wm. Cox	P.			

during the War of the American Revolution, 1775-83.

Name and Rank.	When Commenced.	When Left Service and the Reasons.	Remarks.
John McGinnis	P.	All on	
Thos. Wember	P.	1 Jan '82	
Thos. Butt	P.	unless	
Wm. Toland	P.	otherwise	
Henry Ostin	P.	noted.	
Patrick Reiley, 2d	P.		
Thos. Buckley	P.		
George Cragg	P.		
Henry Mansfield	P.		
Patrick Nowlan	P.	not heard of since June muster	died last of Aug '82
Henry Rice, (or Reec)	P.		
David Crady	P.	on June muster & surplus roll	waiter Col. Gunby Md.
Jas. Huitt	P.		artificer
Joseph Burch	P.		furlough Md.
Wm. Newton	P.		
Danl. Bulkley	P.		
*Danl. Crosby	P.	not heard of since June muster	furlough Maryland
Baruck Butt	P.		waiter Md.
Wm. Conner	P.		do
George Clark	P.		furlough Md.
Thos. Wood, 3d	P.		do
Wm. Priest	P.		
John Jones, Senr., 3d	P.		
*Nathan Wheelor	P.	ditto	
*George F—— (?)	P.		ditto
Wm. King	P.		
Thos. Harrison, 1st	P.		June sick in Va.
John Whitcomb	P.		
*Jas. Killegan	P.	not heard of since June muster	
Edward Dominick	P.		
Jeremiah Mudd	P.	not heard of since March muster	then furlough '81
John Shanks	P.		do
*Thos. Smee	P.	ditto	then do
John Green, 2d	P.		furlough, may be another of the same name
John Conaly	P.		
Jas. West	P.		
Aquilla Clements	P.		
Elijah Oakley	P.		Waggoner
*James Smith, 4th	P.	on June muster & surplus roll	do
Jas. Sappington	P.		do

Name and Rank.		When Commenced.	When Left Service and the Reasons.	Remarks.
4 Co., 4 B. Capt. George, Richard, Bird. Lt. John Brevet. Ensign Thos. A. Dyson.				
Aaron Spalding	S.	All on		
John Carson	S.	1 Jan '82		
Elijah Cockendall	C.	unless	died 18 July '82	
Joseph Harper	P. & C.	otherwise		promoted Corpl.
Joseph Fisher	P.	noted.	died 20 Nov '82	[9 May
Christian Boss	P.			
Wm. Dickerson	P.		deserted 14 July '82	
Southy George	P.			
Jacob Kelly	P.			
John Blades	P.			
Walter Ferrall	P.			
Edward Jackson	P.			
Henry T——?	P.			
Thos. Gillon, (Gauser)	P.			
John Morant	P.		deserted 14 July '82	
John Nave	P.			
Wm. Harper	P.			
Frederick Smith	P.			
*Benj. Reed	P.		not heard of since March muster	
Danl. Harding	P.		deserted 14 July '82	
Thos. Smith, 2d	P.			
Jas. Driver	P.			
Danl. Foxwell	P.			
Wm. Chapman	P.			
Isaac Nicholls	P.			
John Morriss	P.			
John Fossett	P.			
James Halleron	P.		died 16 Dec '82	
Edward Reiley	P.			
Wm. H. Savage	P.			
Murphy Shee	P.			
John Johnson, 1st	P.			
Jacob Adams, or Adamson	P.			
Thos. Richardson	P.			
Wm. Corsey	P.			
*Wm. Justice	P.		not heard of since March muster	
*Charles Horner	P.		not heard of since June muster	
Wm. Camm	P.			
*Basset McClary	P.		not heard of since June muster	
Thos. Watson	P.			of Capt. Sellman's Co.
Wm. Inglis	P.		deserted previous to 1782	
Wm. West	P.		disch'd 13 Jan '82	

during the War of the American Revolution, 1775-83. 463

Name and Rank.		When Commenced.	When Left Service and the Reasons.	Remarks.
Benj. Fitzgerald	S.	All on		
Wm. Pherson	P.	1 Jan '82	prisoner 1 May '82	Capt. Prall's Co.
Solomon Barrett	P.	unless		Rieley's Co.
*Joseph Turner	P.	otherwise		
*John Hicks	P.	noted.		
*Ralph Tawney	P.		not heard of since March muster	said to be transferred from Sellman's Co. to 2d Regt.
Thos. Hammond	P.			
*Thos. Pott	P.		ditto	
Allen Townshend	P.			
Wm. Willson, 2d	P.			Gray's Co.
Fredk. Stoffel	P.		died 16 Jan '82	Price
Benj. Belcher	F.			Mitchell
Jas. McDonald	D.			do
Robt. Bowen	D.			do
*George Kelty	P.			
*Wm. Holt	P.		not mustered since	
*Wm. Roberts, 3d	P.			
Chas. Orms	P.			
John Wright	P.			
*Lawrence Simpson	P.			
*James Anderson	P.	26 March '82		
John Knox	P.	1 Apl '82	transfd. from Pa. Line	
James Managa	P.			
*John Lashley	P.			
Elias Smith	P.			
James Dyer, 2d	P.		disch'd 1 Sept '82	
*Wm. Cook	P.			
*Chas. Wheelor	P.			
*Robt. Cornick	D.			
*Henry Jacobs	P.			
*Joseph Barton	P.			
*John McNally	P.			
*Saml. Wedge	P.			
*John Wiley	C.	(not stated)		
*Henry Lawers	P.	(not stated)		
Richd. Butler	P.	(not stated)		served 12 months
Saml. Vermillion	P.			
*Richd. Price	S.	(not stated)		
*George Pearce	P.	(not stated)		
*John McCann	P.			
*John Delany	P.	(not stated)		
James Due	P.			
*Henry Bradley	P.	23 July '82		

Name and Rank.		When Commenced.	When Left Service and the Reasons.	Remarks.
*Joshua Barrett	S.	All on		
Lawrence Mesler	P.	1 Jan '82		
*Danl. Holdman	P.	unless		
*James Dawer		otherwise noted	must produce a certificate	on Surplus Roll
Elijah Sullivan		3 May	to the end	do ⎡ not on any
*Danl. Stephens		24 July	ditto	do ⎢ previous
George Patrick				do ⎢ roll
*Wm. Walker				do ⎣

Muse' Co.

Name and Rank.		When Commenced.	When Left Service and the Reasons.	Remarks.
Nathaniel Bailey	S.			on detacht. Nd.
John McDonald	S.			do
Wm. Smith	P.	9 Aug '82		do
*Wm. Keough	P.		deserted 23 Nov '82	do
*John Cole	P.		do 20 do	do
*John Sewall	F.	11 Aug	do 20 do	do
*George Plumly	P.		disch'd 31 Dec '82	do
Benj. Burck	C.		do 19 Jan '83	do
Hezekiah Massey	P.		do 31 Dec '82	do
*Elijah Lyons	P.	24 Apl	deserted from Head of Elk, 14 Nov '82	do
*John Gardner	P.		ditto 1 Jan '83	
*Wm. Johnson, 1st	S.			
Robt. Harpin	S.			
Isaac Johnson	C.			
Evan Thomas	C.			
*Jas. Barron	C.			
Robt. Firth	P.			
*John Reed	P.	14 March		
*Danl. McCollum	P.	20 July		
*Lewis Flash	P.	6 Apl		
*John Rodgers	P.	18 March		
*Jeremiah Carter	P.	16 Apl		
*Roger Hogan	P.	29 Apl		
*Thos. McQuinney		28 Apl		
*Francis Dewist				
*Wm. Batton		10 Mch		
*Thos. McKinsie		23 Apl		
Wm. Griffin	F.		disch'd 15 May '82 2d	
John Waller				
*Binneck Meakins	P.	29 Mch		
*Chas. Love	P.	17 April		
*John Pope	P.	11 do		
Wm. Devine	P.	reinlisted		

during the War of the American Revolution, 1775-83.

Name and Rank.	When Commenced.	When Left Service and the Reasons.	Remarks.
*Thos. Hall	P.	15 June	
*Patrick Quinn	P.	27 Feb '82	
Daniel Howe	P.	1 Jan '82	
Jas. Dowden	P.	1 Jan '82	
John Traverse	P.	1 Jan '82	
*Zachariah Berry	P.	6 March	
*George Trice	P.	15 April	
Edward Kirk	P.	1 Jan '82	
*Thos. Houseman	P.	(not stated)	
*Zadock Risden	P.	(not stated)	
*John Welch, 2d	P.	1 Aug	
*Joseph Ward	P.	2 April	
*John Gray	P.	10 Sept	
*Wm. Patterson	P.	30 May	
*Wm. Senah	P.	26 July	
*Matthew Kelly	P.	(not stated)	
*George Tate	P.	10 July	
Roderick McKinsie	P.	16 Feb	
*Thos. Richardson, 2d	P.	11 Aug	
Michael Standley	P.	1 Jan '82	
*Joseph Allen	S.	18 March	
*Joseph Neal	S.	1 Jan '82	
*Basil Newton	P.	16 March	
*Joseph Clancey	F.	24 July	
*Thos. Ellison	C.	(not stated)	
*Christopher Hinson	C.	(not stated)	
*Isaac Dunkin	P.	1 July	disch'd proper in '83
Thos. Harris, 1st	P.	1 Jan '82	
Sylvester Gatten	P.	2 July	
Wm. Hutchinson	P.	1 Jan '82	
Andrew Bramble	P.	do	
Selladay Standley	P.	do	
John Boody	P.	do	
John Baxter	P.	do	
*Wm. Powell	P.	not known	
*Jas. Williams	P.	10 Apl	
*John Vane	P.	5 do	
*John Lowe	P.	12 June	
Levin Harrington	P.	1 Jan '82	
*Wm. Rice, or Rue	P.	do	
*Richd. Jennings	P.	13 Aug	
*Jesse Locker	P.	1 Jan '82	
*Danl. Harness	P.	28 May	
*John Swales	P.	28 Sept	
*Wm. Madan	P.	13 July	

Name and Rank.		When Commenced.	When Left Service and the Reasons.	Remarks.
Solomon Sullivan	P.	1 Jan '82		
Jas. Hunt	P.	11 Sept		
*Chas. Griffith	P.	14 do		
*John Conner	P.	(not stated)		
*Peter Jackson	P.	2 April		
*Paris Owens	P.	14 Sept		
*Thomas Baxter	P.	21 Aug		
John Moore, 5th	P.	1 Jan '82		
*Alex. McGregor	P.	17 March		
*Edward Paul		15 Aug		
Jonathan Mahugh	P.	1 Jan '82		disch'd 9 Jan '82, reinlisted
*John Willman	P.	(not stated)		
*Jacob Mifford	P.	1 March		
*Whittington Gild	P.	9 July		
Richd. Harrington	P.	1 Jan '82		
John Clineslaught	P.	do		
*John Fairweather	P.	1 June '82		
John Courts	P.	1 Jan '82		
*Hugh Ware	P.	21 May		
*Wm. Cotter	P.	7 Sept		
Thos. Dickenson	P.	1 Jan '82		
Isom Coleman	P.	do		
*Wm. Holland	P.	23 Aug		
*James Kirk	P.	(not stated)		
*Thos. Channon	P.	24 Aug		
*John Williams, 2d	P.	6 Apl		

3RD COMPANY.

Name and Rank.		When Commenced.	When Left Service and the Reasons.	Remarks.
Richd. Huggins	S.	1 Jan '82		
Aquilla Chitham	S.	do		
*Thos. Craig	S.	3 May		
Stephen Nicholson	S.	1 Jan '82		reinlisted in the field
Benj. Burch	S.	do		
*Wm. Watkins	D.	do		
*John Burgess	C.	12 June		
*Kemp Holden	C.	20 May		
Thos. White	C.	1 Jan '82		
Benj. McCall	C.	1 April		
William Ayhun	P.	1 Jan '82		
*James Bell	P.	22 April		
*Wm. Hunter	P.	8 June		
*Danl. Hukill	P.	8 June		
John White, 2d	P.	15 April	to the end	
John Cannon	P.	1 Jan '82		
*Chas. Palmore	P.	7 May		

during the War of the American Revolution, 1775–83. 467

Name and Rank.		When Commenced.	When Left Service and the Reasons.	Remarks.
*Saml. Palmore	P.	10 April		
*Thos. Seego	P.	22 July		
*John Hukill	P.	8 June		
*George Daddisman	P.	24 March		
*John Beall, 2d	P.	15 April		
*Henry Barns	P.	27 do		
*Joseph Rose	P.	8 do		
*Chas. Mearick	P.	not known		
John Shafer	P.	1 Jan '82		
*Basil Dorsey	P.	17 March		
*Wm. Harris, 2d	P.	2 Jan		found as per discharge, dated 20 June, '83, from [Genl. Lincoln
*Thos. Harding	P.	3 May		
*Thos. McDowell	P.	5 Apl		
Robert Johnson	P.	1 Jan '82		
*George Miller	P.	(not stated)		
*Evans Willing	P.	27 April		
*Edward Roan	P.	6 March		
*John Greenwood	P.	27 April		
*Isaac Kent	P.	29 do		
*Wm. Smallwood	P.	27 do		
*Robert Dean	P.	7 do		
John Britton	P.	1 Jan '82		
Richard Freeman	P.	do	disch'd 12 Jan '82	
*Henry Windows	P.	3 May		
*Isaac Mitchell	P.	(not stated)		
*Frederick Flinn	P.	(not stated)		
*Wm. Connelly	P.	not known		
*Matthew Daley	P.	(not stated)		
*Edwd. Cantwell	P.	1 Sept '82		
*John Willson, 2d	P.	22 April		
John Turner, 3d	P.	1 Jan '82		
Isaac McFadon	P.	16 Feb		

4TH COMPANY.

Perry Evans	S.	1 Jan '82		
Harris Austin	S.	do		
*John Brown, 3d	S.	18 May		
*John Bond	S.	1 do		
John Davies, 1st	C.	1 Jan '82	promoted Corpl. 1 July '82	
*Isaac Deale	C.	19 May		
Wm. Dunn	C.	11 April		
Isaac Holland	D.	12 March		
Joel Baker	P.	1 Jan '82		

Name and Rank.		When Commenced.	When Left Service and the Reasons.	Remarks.
*John Long	P.	26 May		
*Martin Bowles	P.	1 Jan '82		
*Saml. Fisher	P.	1 July		
*Leonard Nable	P.	(not stated)		
*Robert McClary	P.	25 April		
Benj. Donnelly, (or Daniel)	P.	7 Sept		
John Richardson	P.	1 Jan '82		
Wm. Matthews, 2d	P.	19 May		
*Lawrence Pines	P.	(not stated)		
*Jas. Silk	P.	(not stated)		
John Bailey, 2d	P.	1 Jan '82		
John Campbell, 2d	P.	do		
*Joseph Cluley	P.	5 April '82		
*John Cotter	P.	7 Sept		
Herculus Hutchings	P.	1 Jan '82		
*Richd. Rivers	P.	24 July		
*John Nicholson	P.	12 May		
*Edward Burns	P.	26 Sept		
*Henry Frazer	P.	(not stated)		
*Wm. Deverix	P.	9 April		
Wm. Marshall	P.	1 Jan '82		
*Michael Keene	P.	1 Oct		
*Richard Burck	P.	16 Aug		
*Wm. Colin	P.	(not stated)		disch'd properly
*Darden Orrell	P.	(not stated)		[in 1783
*Wm. Watkins, 2d	P.	1 June		
*Edward Shoebrook	P.	1 July		
*Danl. Wilkins	P.	5 Oct		
*Wm. Eagle	P.	22 Sept		
*Joseph McCollister	P.	not known		
*Levin Claridge	P.	ditto		
Robert Folger	P.	1 Jan '82		
George Filleston	P.	do		
*Thos. Countess	P.	12 June		
Jas. Kelly, 2d	P.	1 Jan '82		
Benj. Worthington	P.	do		17 months service
*Richd. McDonald	P.	(not stated)		
Barney Haney	P.	1 Jan '82		
Jas. Hudson, 2d	P.	do		
*Godfrey Fletcher	P.	(not stated)	died 1 Jan 1783	
*John Acock	P.	3 April		
FREDERICK DETACHMENT.				
John Philips	P.	1 April '82		
John Barlow	P.	1 April	to the end	

during the War of the American Revolution, 1775–83.

Name and Rank.		When Commenced.	When Left Service and the Reasons.	Remarks.
Thos. Kettle	C.	All on	to the end, reduced 22 Feb '82	
Domini Coines	P.	1 Jan '82		
Neelee Jones	P.	unless		
Enoch McClain	S.	otherwise		
John Jordan, 2d, Clerk	P.	noted		
P. Joseph Purdy	D. M.			
Jonathan Short	S. M.		died 26 Oct '82	
James Mead	D. M.			
*George Elms	F. M.			
*Chas. Blundell	P.	21 Feb '82		
*Jesse Carter	P.	25 do		
*John Wilmore	P.	12 March		
*Wm. Lawrence	F.	20 April		
*James Morris	P.	11 May		
*Thos. Reynolds	P.	5 July		
*Thos. Barber	P.	20 Aug		
*James Dawson	P.	1 Sept	to the end	
*Joseph Pully	P.	15 do		
*John Briruk	P.	19 do		
*Jas Burck, 2d	P.	13 Aug		
*John Abraham	P.	22 Sept		
*Wm. Caywood	P.	30 do		
*Francis Orbough	P.	1 Oct		
*Wm. Coleman	P.	7 Oct		
*Patrick Mayhorne	P.			
*Jas. Murray, 1st	P.	10 Oct		
*John McElroy	P.	10 Oct		
*Joseph Overcreek	P.			
*Patrick Nugent	P.	16 Feb		
*Joseph Sharp	P.	25 Feb '82		
*J. Thos. Glinn	P.	25 Feb		
*James Neale	P.	28 Feb		
*Timothy Campbell	P.	1 March		
*David Johnson	P.	5 March		
*Tobyas Randalls	P.	6 March		
*Edward Stone	P.	6 March		
*Fredk. Wolveram	P.	6 March		
*John Bevard	P.	13 March		
*Saml. Powers	P.	13 March		
*Wm. Biddle	P.	13 March		
*Timothy Burns	P.	16 March		
*Benj. Houghton	P.	16 March		
*Andrew Potter	P.	18 March		
Jonathan Weedon	P.		to the end	
*Saml. Hardcastle	P.	18 March		

Name and Rank.		When Commenced.	When Left Service and the Reasons.	Remarks.
*John Donnold	P.	20 March		
*George McDonnald	P.	20 March		
*James Brown	P.	20 March		
*David Banks	P.	26 March		
*Richd. Burrows	P.	28 March		
*Jas. Carven	P.	25 April		
*Donald Cameron	P.	3 April		
*Jacob Scrivenor	P.	3 April		
*Isaac Carr	P.	6 April		
*Thos. Simonds	P.	7 April		
Robt. Legg	P.	1 Jan		
John Hackett	P.	1 Jan	supposed to be settled with. In the Invalid Regt.	
Isaac Green	P.	1 Jan	disch'd 15 Jan '82	
*James Karns	P.	10 April		
*John Underwood	P.	10 April		
John Adams, No. 2	P.	1 Jan		
*George Adams	P.	10 Jan		
*Isaac Burton	P.	11 Jan		
*Wm. Commett	P.	11 Jan		
*Alex. Wallace	P.	4 March		
*Abraham Stoner	P.	13 March		
*Joshua Cutmore	P.	20 March		
*Christopher Coy	P.	20 March		
*Ezekial Kidwell	P.	17 April		
*John Crosby, 2d	P.	21 April		
*Benj. Askew	P.	14 April		
*Paul Gilmore	P.	1 March		
*Thos. Billingham	P.	6 March		
*Wm. Bowling	S.	12 March		
*John McBride	P.	1 Jan		
*John Gordon, 2d	C.	1 Jan	promoted Corpl. 22 Dec '82	
*Thos. Carroll	P.	3 April		
*Dennis Carty	P.	14 Feb		
George Twinch	S.	1 Jan		
*Pierce Deacon	P.	10 April	not heard of since	
Thos. Hill	C.	1 Jan		
Thos. Fleming	P.	1 Jan		
*Jas. Morrison	P.	5 May		
*Alex. McCoy	P.	6 May		
*Jas. Middleton	P.	28 Aug		
*John Adams, 3d	P.	29 March		
*Phineas Hervey, (or Hewey)	P.	3 April		
*John Pennington	P.	6 April		

during the War of the American Revolution, 1775-83.   471

Name and Rank.		When Commenced.	When Left Service and the Reasons.	Remarks.
*Jas. Waters	P.	6 April		
*Robert Wright	P.	6 June		
*Henry Clawson	P.	12 Apl		
*Wm. Kent	P.	3 May		
*Michael Dougherty	P.	5 May		
*Peter Dawson	P.	11 Sept		[plus Roll
*Chas. Davis	P.	23 April	must produce a certificate	on Sur-
*John German	P.	11 May		
*Alex. Garrett	P.	not known		
*John Torrey	P.	19 May		
*Wm. Johnston, 2d	P.	12 June		
*Danl. Newman	P.	23 June		
*Richd. Scotten	P.	24 June		
*Wm. Harrison, 2d	P.	8 May		
*Christian Hanson	P.	25 April		
*Bartholomew Roach	P.	23 March		
*Randall Skly	P.	22 April		
*Thos. Wilsen	P.	2 May		
*John Hoina	P.	3 May		
*Wm. Hart	P.	7 May	not heard of since	
*Thos. Hand	P.	5 June		
*Christian Reynor	P.	9 May		
*Richd. Perkins	P.	9 May		
*George Singleborough	P.	13 May		
*Christian Ernest	P.	14 May		
*John McDonald, 3d	P.	22 May		
Raphael Hagan	C.	1 Jan	disch'd 30 April '82 by Col. Adams	
*John Ballast	P.	20 May		
*Josiah Burgess	P.	16 Oct		
*John Bluefield	P.	30 July		
*Richard Franklin	P.	1 June		
*Richard Nable	P.	4 June		
*John McFarlin	P.	13 June		
*Saml. Mahew	P.	14 Aug		
*Thos. Gritchard	P.	2 July		
*John Shephardson	P.	2 July		
*John Dougherty	P.	not known		
*John Waid, 2d	P.	20 Aug		
*Peter Sprangle	P.	21 Aug		
*George Chambers	P.	26 Sept		
*John Connelly, 2d	P.	9 May		
*Alex. Christie	P.	14 May		
*Basil Wheelor	P.	4 Sept		
*Philip Frazier	P.	not known		
*Arthur Boyes	P.	30 March		

Name and Rank.		When Commenced.	When Left Service and the Reasons.	Remarks.
*George Tomlinson	P.	30 May		
*Joseph Moseley	P.	19 April		
*Dyer Waters	P.	6 May		
*Zachariah Moore	P.	18 June		
*Hezekiah Moore	P.	15 Sept		
*John Matwell, 2d	P.	13 April		
*Rezin Lowe	P.	30 Sept		
*Daniel Hurly	P.	14 Oct		
*John Wilson, 3d	P.	6 May		
*Daniel Skinner	P.	26 June		
*Thos. Sturges	P.	16 Sept		
*William Solley	P.	21 May		
*Isaac Jenkins	P.	12 Sept		
*John Wilson, 4th	P.	30 June		
*Thos. Wood, 4th	S.	1 April		
*Hillary Lanham	P.	13 Sept		
*Matthew Norris	P.	17 May		
*Thos. Loveday	P.	17 March	not since heard of	
*Thos. Sheets	P.	19 June		
*Joseph Jones, 2d	P.	23 July		
*John Connelly, 3d	P.	29 July		
*John Alsop	P.	26 Feb		
*John Allen	P.	18 March		
*Elisha Osborn	P.	27 Feb		
*George Rhodes	P.	10 March		
*Thos. Hawkes	P.	1 April		
*Jas. Murray	P.	1 April		
*Robt. Jones	P.	4 May		
*Michael Griffith	P.	11 May		
*John Barrett, 1st	P.	12 July		
*Nicholas Fitzgerald	P.	26 March		
*John McElroy	P.	9 Oct		
*James McCray	P.	15 April		
*Wm. Layland	P.	14 Oct		
*Jas. Gilmore, 2d	P.	19 Oct		
*Jacob Gibson	P.	17 Oct		
*Henry Philips	P.	19 Oct		
*George Hoggart	P.	1 April		
*Jas. Thompson	P.	21 May		
*Wm. Henderson	P.	{ not known 28 May '82 }	Col. Tootal	
*Jas. Coleman	P.	do		
*Francis Irsley	P.	do		
*Chas. Beauchamp	P.	5 Aug		
*Ephraim Marshall	P.	deserted		

Name and Rank.	When Commenced.	When Left Service and the Reasons.	Remarks.
*Chas. Hall	P.	10 April	
*Cotter Jones	P.	31 May	
*John Johnston, 2d	P.	15 Aug	
*Wm. Mead	P.	1 Jan	
*Thos. Whaley	P.	not known	
*John Williams, 3d	P.	3 Nov	
*Edward Edwards	P.	10 June	
*Oliver Blake	P.	7 May	
*John Murray, 2d	P.	17 May	
*Michael McDevitt	P.	16 Apl	
*Lewis McCuttough, (or McCulloch)	P.	18 Aug	
*Francis Raynard	P.	22 Aug	
*John Steele	P.	2 Sept	
*John Lee, 3d	P.	1 Dec	
*Jonas Crawford	P.	11 Nov	
*Jas. Rowe	P.	22 June	
*Wm. Hill, 2d	P.	6 July	
*Henry Gilpin	P.	20 July	deserted
John Green, 1st	P.	1 Jan	disch'd 9 Jan, reinlisted 12 July
*Darden O'Neil	P.	19 July	
*John Wilson, 5th	P.	1 Aug	
*John Calahan	P.	23 July	
*Wm. Calahan	P.	12 June	
*Wm. Caldwell	P.	8 April	
*James Coosingbury	P.	17 March	
*Thos. Leagor	P.	22 July	
*Randolph Booth	P.	10 March	
*Edward Wheatly	P.	12 March	
*George Warner	P.	28 Oct	
*James Countess	P.	20 Sept	
*Benj., or Bennet, Thompson	P.	1 April	
*Henry Tibbett	P.	5 Sept	
*John Tordine	P.	12 Dec	
*Joseph Norman	P.	5 Oct	
*Hugh Roney	P.	17 June	
David Connor	P.	1 Jan	
*William Gray	P.	9 Sept	
*Wm. Carleton, or Carlin	P.	7 Sept	
*Peter Fletcher	P.	9 Sept	
*Wm. Frazier	P.	12 Oct	
*Peter Francis	P.	(not stated)	
*John Shields	P.	29 Oct	
*Jas. Stephens	P.	8 Oct	

Name and Rank.		When Commenced.	When Left Service and the Reasons.	Remarks.
*John Stuart, 2d	P.	11 Oct		
*Wm. Sowden	P.	1 Oct		
*Nicholos McFarlin	P.	11 Oct		
*John Messer	P.	3 Oct		
*Jas. Morris, 2d	P.	14 Oct		
*Patrick McDonough	P.	(not stated)		
John Miller	P.	1 Jan		
*John Cooper, 2d	P.	1 Oct		
*Jeremiah Cyphert	P.	30 Sept		
*John Kelner	P.	18 Oct		
*Joseph Hudson	P.	1 Oct		
*Nicholas Pecker	P.	1 Oct		
*Chas. Brutzill	P.	1 Oct		
*Wm. Belcher	P.	5 Oct		
*Michael Burns	P.	12 Oct		
*Thos. Blake	P.	(not stated)		
*Chezloe Lodwick	P.	10 Oct		
*Saml. Crowell	P.	(not stated)		
*John Rigan	P.	12 Oct		
*Thos. Lawyers	P.	14 Oct		
*Lewis Davies	P.	17 Oct		
*John Tully, 2d	P.	19 Oct		
*John Adamson	P.	(not stated)		
*John Crotchett	P.	4 May		
*Danl. Campbell	P.	27 April		
*Danl. Sullinger	P.	not known		
*John Husk	P.	3 May		
*Thos. Hooper	P.	(not stated)		
*John Nelson, 2d	P.	4 Aug		
Jeremiah Driskell	P.	1 Jan '82		
John Ferguson	P.	1 Jan	disch'd 1 April	
Jas. Curren	P.	1 Jan		
*Saml. Brady	P.	12 Sept		
*Job Buley	P.	8 April		
*John Applead	P.	14 April		
*John Alford	P.	15 April		
*Thos. Keys	P.	24 April		
*Bennet Valient	P.	27 April		
*Arthur Pritchard	P.	3 May		
*John Elliott	P.	not known		
*James Rose	P.	21 Feb		
*Thos. Gorden	P.	25 March		
*Bennet Heard	P.	16 April		
*John Hillam	P.	23 Nov		
*Michael Scott	P.	2 Nov		

during the War of the American Revolution, 1775-83. 475

Name and Rank.	When Commenced.	When Left Service and the Reasons.	Remarks.
*Benj. Wright	P.	20 Nov	
*Colvert Mason, alias Woodyard		(not stated)	
*George Baker	P.	1 Aug	
*Jas. Barber, 2d	P.	30 Dec	
*Dennis Bryan	P.	10 Dec	
*Stephen Erlinger	P.	20 Dec	
*Dennis O'Bryan	P.	11 Dec	
*George Bowers	P.	12 June	
Henry Young	P.	1 Jan	
George Parker	P.	1 Jan	
James Lowry	P.	1 Jan	
Jesse Suite (?)	S.	1 Jan	
John Cusber (?)	D.	1 Jan	
James Dyer, 1st	P.	1 Jan	
John Martin		1 Jan	
Thos. Summers		1 Jan	
John M. Funner	P.	1 Jan	
Isom, (or Asa), Moore		15 Sept	[old 7th Regt.
Joseph Murphy	P.	1 Jan	prisoner 16 Aug '80 and returned, of the
Michael Casey	P.	1 Jan	
James Grary	P.	1 Jan	
Edwd. Gearish	P.	1 Jan	disch'd 8 Aug
Richd. Mud	S.	1 Jan	do 9 Jan '82
Michael McGuire			do 9 Sept
Morris Neagle	P.	1 Jan	
*Wm. Rodgers	P.	1 Jan	entd. Gratuity
Saml. Street	F.	1 Jan	
John Williams, 4th	P.	1 Jan	disch'd 9 Jan '82
Edwd. Wade	P.	1 Jan	Genl. Guard
Wm. Robinson	P.	14 Dec	
James Fisher	P.	1 Jan	deserted 1 Jan '82
Jesse Grace	P.	(not stated)	discharged previous to '82
Peter Kincaid	P.	1 Jan	died January '82

[A star prefixed to any name indicates that the length of service is not known. In all other cases it is to be understood that service was from date of enlistment to Dec. 31st, 1782, or to an earlier date given after the date of enlistment.]

MUSTER AND PAY ROLLS FOR 1783.

Arrangement of the Maryland Line, January 1st, 1783.

NAMES.		WHEN COMMISSIONED.	NAMES.		WHEN COMMISSIONED.

FIRST REGIMENT.

Col.	John Gunby	17 April '77	Lieut.	Nicholas Gassaway	1 Jan '80
Lt. Col.	Levin Winder	3 June '81		Phillip Hill	9 May '78
Major	John Eccleston	10 Dec '77		Hezekiah Ford	16 Aug '80
Capt.	Joseph Marbury	1 Jan '77		Arthur Harris	26 Oct '79
	Jacob Brice	do		William Pendergast	29 do do
	John Smith,(late 6th)	do		William Raisin	26 Jan '80
	Henry Gaither	17 April do		Nathan Wright	1 Jan '81
	Edward Oldham	20 May do		John Sears	1 do do
	Walker Muse	10 June do		John F. Lowe	20 Jan '81
	John C. Jones	20 Sept do		Samuel Edminston	14 Mch do
	Horatio Claggett	10 Oct do		Robert Halkerston	12 April do
	Richard Anderson	15 Nov do		Henry Clements	25 do do
Lieut.	John Lynn	1 June '79		Henry Gassaway	25 do do
	Wm. Adams	8 do do		Francis Ware	Aug
	Regnal Hillery, died			Basil Burgess	18 June '81
	11 Aug '83	13 July do	Surg'on	Richard Pendell	
	Samuel Hanson	1 Aug do	Mate	Alexander Smith	

SECOND REGIMENT.

Lt. Col. Commd.	Peter Adams	1 Aug '79	Lt.	Joshua Rutledge	1 May
				Thos. Rouse	
Major	Henry Hardman	22 May do		Walter Dyer	15 Sept
	Alexander Rox-			John Brevill	20 do
	burgh	7 April '80		Thomas Boyd	1 Jan '81
Capt.	John Gale	10 Dec '77		Mark McPherson	1 do do
	James W. Gray	26 do do		Thos. A. Dyson	8 Sept '81
	George Hamilton	25 Jan '78		Basil Warring	25 Oct do
	Percey Benson	11 March		Malakiah Bonham	12 Sept do
	John Mitchell	15 July '79		John D. Carry	16 Oct do
	William Bruce	1 Aug '79		William Hanson	25 do do
	John Gassaway	2 April '80		Thomas Beatty	8 Sept do
	Lloyd Beal	19 Feb '81		Joseph Cross	6 Nov do
	Francis Reveley	18 June		*Wm Goldsborough	'82
Lt.	Henry Baldwin	11 Feb '81		William Telson	9 May do
	Edmond Compton	18 do	†Surg.	Walter Warfield	
	Benjamin Fickle	19 do	Mate	Wm. Watts	15 Aug '81
	David Luckett	7 April			

*On Arthur's resignation Spring of '82.   † To be found in Council Office.

during the War of the American Revolution, 1775–83.

NAMES.		WHEN COMMISSIONED.	REMARKS.
	ARTILLERY.		
Capt.	William Brown	22 Nov '77	Promoted Major 31 Jan '81
	Richard Dorsey	24 Nov '77	
	James Smith	1 Nov '79	
Capt. Lt.	Ebenezer Finly	24 Nov '77	
	James McFadden	1 Nov '79	
1 Lt.	James Bagus	3 Sept '79	
2nd Lt.	Clement Skerret	Feb '78	
	Nicholas Ricketts	Dec '77	
	Isaac Rawlins	3 Sept '79	
1 Lt.	Robert Wilmot	24 Nov '77	deranged in '80 for want of men.
2nd Lt.	Young Wilkinson	Mch '78	Furloughed by Genl. Greene Apl '82, deranged for want of Command
	John Cheevers	3 Sept '78	Furloughed by Genl. Greene 1780, deranged for want of Command

Copy   J. Howell, Jr.

Arrangement of the Maryland Line in Five Regiments; promotions filled to January 1st, 1783.

NAMES.	RANK.	WHEN COMMISSIONED.	PROMOTIONS.	CONTINUE OR RETIRE.
	FIRST REGIMENT.			
John Steward	Lt.Col.Comd.	9 May '82	Gen. Williamson's promotion, dead	continue
John Eccleston	Major	10 Dec '77		do
Jona. Sillman	do	9 May '82	Col. Steward's promotion	retire
Edwd. Prall	Captain	10 June '77		do
Wm. Riely	do	15 Oct do	cont'e on Duty So. Army 'til Aug '83	do
John S. Belt	do	15 Dec do		do
John Smith, (old 6th)	do	1 April '78	He took Capt. Orendorff's Rank and Orendorff his as settled by a board of Officers at the Southward	do
Lloyd Beal	do	19 Feb '81		do
Thos. B. Hugou	do	1 June do		do
Francis Revelly	do	18 do do	Capt. Armstrong's death	continue

Names.	Rank.	When Commissioned.	Promotions.	Continue or Retire.
James Winchester	Captain	9 Feb '82	Capt. Sillman's promotion, on duty with So. Army till Aug '83	retire
Philip Reed	do	do	Capt. Bird's death Aug or Sept '82, not known which. Prisoner War	prisoner
John Hamilton	Lieut.	1 June '79	continued with Army to end of War	retire
Wm. Raison	do	26 Jan '80		continue
Joshua Burgess	do	14 Mch do	Prisoner War	retire
Hezh. Foard	do	16 Aug do		do
John T. Lowe	do	20 Jan '81		do
Edwd. Miles Smith	do	19 Feb do		do
Saml. Edmiston	do	14 Mch do		do
John Trueman	do	16 do do	Invalid, Prisoner War	do
Geo. Winchester	do	1 June do	Lt. Carr's resignation, retire 1 Jan '83	
Henry Hawkins	do	Ensn. 1 Aug do	Appt. Ensn. 1 Aug '81, a vacancy for Lt. 1 Sept '82 on Lt. Manger's promotion	do
Malakh. Bonham	do	do 4 Sept do	do Hardcastle's resignation 12 Sept '82, with Detachment 'til dismissed Main Army	
Chas. Skerving	do		App. by G. Greene, vacancy 20 Nov '81 Lt. Richmond's prom.	
Richd. Pindell	Surgeon		his Appt. to be found in Council Chamber	
Alex. Smith	Mate		do	continue
Saml. Y. Keene	do		Appt. by G. Greene tho' there is no vacancy. His appointment never confirmed by the State but continued on duty till 31 Mch '83 in ye S. Army	

Second Regiment.

Names.	Rank.	When Commissioned.	Promotions.	Continue or Retire.
John Gunby	Colonel	17 Apl '77		
Levin Winder	Lt. Col.	3 June '81	Col. Howard's promotion	

during the War of the American Revolution, 1775–83.

Names.	Rank.	When Commissioned.	Promotions.	Continue or Retire.
Wm. D. Beal	Major	6 Nov do	Major Dean's death	retire
Alex. Trueman	Captain	1 Jan '77		do
Jona. Morris	do	14 Apl do	Prisoner War	do
Walker Muse	do	10 June do		continue
Thos. Mason	do	8 June '79		retire
John Gassaway	do	2 Apl '80		continue
Adam Hoops	do	16 Mch '81	to receive pay to 4 Oct '81, entitled to Commutation. Prisoner of War	retire
Saml. McPherson	do	25 Apl do	on duty in So. Army until June '83	do
Christ. Richmond	do	20 Nov do	Capt. Manger's death. Aid to G. Gates. On duty in the N. Army	do
Jacob Norris	do	14 Nov '82	Capt. Wilmot's death	do
Wm. Adams	Lieut.	8 June '79		
Nich. Gassaway	do	1 Jan '80		continue
Arthur Harris	do	26 Oct '79		
Thos. Price	do	11 Feb '80		retire*
Zedekiah Moore	do	10 Sept do	Dead	do
Mark McPherson	do	1 Jan '81		do
Jacob Crawford	do	20 Feb do		do
Wm. Smoote	do	16 Mar do		do
Henry Baker	do	Ensn. 1 Aug do	A vacancy from 3 June '81 Lt. Dyer's prom. Duty So. Army 31 Mch '83	
Edwd. Hamilton	do	do do	Vacancy 8 Sept '81 Bruff's promotion	do
John Carey	do	do 4 Sept do	do 16 Oct Woolford's death	
*George Browne	do			
Walter Warfield	Surgeon		to be found in Council Office	
Gerard Wood	Mate	1 Aug '81	on duty S. Army till 31 March '83	do
		Third Regiment.		
Peter Adams	Lt. Col. Com.	1 Aug '79		
Henry Hardman	Major	22 May do		continue
Thos. Lansdale	do	19 Feb '81	on Detacht. No. Army 30 June	retire

* G. Brown appointed by Genl. Greene, a vacancy in the spring of '82 on Lt. Murdock's resignation—the date of Brown's appointm't not known.

Names.	Rank.	When Commissioned.	Promotions.	Continue or Retire.
Joseph Marbury	Captain	1 Jan '77		continue
Lilburn Williams	do	17 April do		retire
James W. Gray	do	26 Dec do		continue
Edward Spurrier	do	21 May '79	on Duty No. Detacht.	retire
Benjn. Price	do	1 July do	on do So. Army, and arrived with troops from C. Town	do
Richard Waters	do	7 April '80		do
Edward Dyer	do	3 June '81	Capt. Dobson's promotion	do
John A. Hamilton	do	25 Oct do	Capt. Chesley's resignation	do
Gassaway Watkins	do	15 May '82	Capt. Orendorff's do	do
John Hartshorne	Lieut.	21 May '79	on Detachmt. No. Army, Adjt.	do
Rignal Hillary	do	13 July do		continue
Philip Hill	do	May '78	Prisoner	do
Wm. Pendergrast	do	29 Oct '79		
Henry Baldwin	do	11 Feb '80		do
David Luckett	do	7 April do		
Walter Dyer	do	15 Sept do		
Nathan Wright	do	1 Jan '81		
Basil Burgess	do	Ensn. 1 Aug '81	Vacancy 18 June Revelly promoted	
Thomas Dyson	do	do do	do 8 Sept Lamar prom.	continue
Basil Waring	do	do do	do 25 Oct Hamilton prom.	
Wm. Goldsborough	do	'82	do Spring of '82, Arthur's resign. date of Goldsborough's appmt. not known	
Levin Denwood	Surgeon		in Council Office, on Duty So. Army	retire
Wm. Watts	Mate	15 Aug '81		
Fourth Regiment.				
Thomas Woolford	Lt. Col. Com.	23 Oct '79	Prisoner of War	retire
Alex. Roxburgh	Major	7 April '80		continue
John Lynch	do	8 Sept '81	Major Dobson's death, Prisoner of War	retire
Jacob Brice	Captain	1 Jan '77		
Henry Gaither	do	17 April do		
John C. Jones	do	20 Sept do		continue
Richd. Anderson	do	15 Nov do		
Geo. Hamilton	do	25 Jan '78		do
David Lynn	do	22 May '79		retire
John Mitchel	do	15 July do		continue
Jona. Gibson	do	1 May '80	Dead	retire

during the War of the American Revolution, 1775–83. 481

Names.	Rank.	When Commissioned.	Promotions.	Continue or Retire.
James Bruff	Captain	8 Sept '81	Capt. Lynch's promotion, Prisoner of War	half pay
Wm. P. Stoddart	Lieut.	21 May '79		retire
Lavacher DeVauburn	do	Ensn. 10 Mch '77	Date of promotion not known, gone to France	
*Isaac Hanson	do	15 Dec '79	Prisoner of War	do
Edward Compton	do	18 Feb '80		continue
Joshua Rutledge	do	1 May do		do
John Brevet	do	20 Sept do		retire
John McCoy	do	1 Jan '81		do
Rob. Halkerson	do	12 Apl '81		
Henry Gassaway	do	25 do do		continue
Saml. B. Beal	do	Ensn. 1 Aug do	Vacancy Nath. Smith's resignation 4 July '81	retire
Henly Chapman	do	do 4 Sept do	Vacancy 8 Sept Duval killed	
William Hanson	do	do do	do 25 Oct Boones resigned	continue
†William Tolson	do		do 9 May '82 Winchester promoted	
William Kelty	Surgeon		Prisoner of War	
Elisha Harrison	Mate	15 Oct '81		

Fifth Regiment.

John E. Howard	Lt. Col. Com.	3 June 1781	Col. Foard's death.	
John Davidson	Major	1 Jan do		retire
Benj. Brookes	do	16 March do		continue
John Smith, 3d	Captain	1 Jan '77		do
Edward Oldham	do	20 May do		do
Horatio Clagget	do	10 Oct do		do
John Gale	do	10 Dec do		do
Perry Benson	do	11 March '78		do
James Sumervill	do	1 June '79		retire
Wm. Bruce	do	1 Aug do		continue
Wm. Lamar	do	8 Sept '81	Capt. Edgerly's death	
James Ewing	do	6 Nov do	Capt. Beall's promotion	
John Lynn	Lieut.	1 June '79		
Samuel Hanson	do	1 Aug do		continue
Thomas Rowse	do	15 Sept do		
Robt. Denny	do	3 Jan '80		retire
Benj. Fickle	do	19 Feb do		

* Omitted in arrangement of 1781 by being reported dead of his wounds in captivity—Cambden.

† Never received his appointment but was promised one and acted on the recruiting service, his situation is similar to Goldsborough's who was appointed.

Names.	Rank.	When Commissioned.	Promotions.	Continue or Retire.
Thos. Boyd	Lieut.	1 Jan '81		
John Sears	do	do do		continue
Henry Clements	do	25 Apl do		retire
Adam Jamison	do	1 June do		do
Francis Ware, Jr.	do	Ensn. · 1 Aug do	Vacancy some time in Aug on Lt. Lynn's resignation	
Thos. Beaty	do	do 4 Sept do	Vacancy 8 Sept Lt. Goud killed	
Joseph Cross	do	6 Nov 81	do 6 Nov '81 Ewing promoted	
Ezekiel Haynie	Surgeon	17 Jan '82		retire
John L. Elbert	Mate	1 Jan do		do

A List of Officers deranged in the Maryland Line 1 Jan., 1783.

Rank.	Names.	When Commissioned.	Remarks.
Lt. Col.	John Stewart		Dead
Major	Jonathan Silman	9 May '82	
Captain	Edward Prall	10 June '77	
do	William Reiley	15 Oct '77	continued on duty in S. Army till Aug
do	John S. Belt	15 Dec '77	
do	John Smith, (late 6th)	1 Apl '78	
do	Thomas B. Hugou	1 June '81	
do	James Winchester	9 Feb '82	Continued on duty with ye S. Troops till Aug. When ye arrived at Annapolis, recd. pay for Feb, Mch & Apl
do	Phillip Reed	do do	Prisoner of War
Lieut.	John Hamilton	1 June '79	
do	Henry Baker	Apd. Ens. 1 Aug '81	on duty till 31 Mch '83, S Army, entitd. to promtn. 3 June '81
do	Edward Hamilton	do 8 Sept do	entitd. to promtn. 8 Sept '81
S. Mate	Gerard Wood	1 Aug '81	on duty 31 Mch S. Army
Major	Thomas Lansdale	19 Feb '81	on duty Northern Army, paid
Captain	Lilbourne Williams	17 Apl '77	
do	Edward Spurrier	21 May '79	on duty Northn. Detachmt., paid
do	Benj. Price*	1 July '79	on duty and arriv'd with Troops from C. Town, paid for Feb, Mch & Apl

*Paid for Feb. Mch. & Apl.

Rank.	Names.	When Commissioned.	Remarks.
Captain	Richard Waters	7 Apl '80	
do	Edward Dyer	3 June '81	
do	John A. Hamilton	25 Oct '81	
do	Gassaway Watkins	13 May '82	Promoted Capt. 13 May '82
do	John Hartshorne	21 May '79	
Surgeon	Leven Denwood		
Lt. Col.	Thomas Woolford		Prisoner of war
Major	John Lynch	8 Sept '81	ditto
Captain	David Lynn	22 May '79	
do	John Gibson	1 May '80	Dead
do	James Bruff	8 Sept '81	Prisoner of War
Lieut.	Wm. T. Stoddard	21 May '79	
do	Levachee De Vaubrunn		
do	Isaac Hanson	15 Dec '79	Prisoner of War
do	John McCoy	1 Jan '81	
do	Saml. B. Beal	1 Aug '81	
do	Henly Chapman	4 Oct '81	entitled to Lt.
Surgeon	William Kelty		Prisoner of War
Mate	Elisha Harrison		
Lt. Col. Comt.	John E. Howard	3 June 81	
Major	John Davidson	1 Jan '81	Subsisten—
do	Benjm. Brookes		
Captain	James Summerville		
do	William Lamar		
do	James Ewing		
Lieut.	Robert Denny		
do	Adam Jameson		
Surgeon	Ezekiel Haynie		
Mate	John L. Elbert		

Copy   J. Howell, Jr.

Defective, the names of a Major, 7 Captains, 9 Lieutenants and a Surgeon being torn off.

Agreeable to a resolution of Congress bearing Date the 26th Day of May, 1783, the Bearer hereof, John Cole, private of the 1st Maryland Regiment, has leave of Absence until called upon by proper authority to join his Corps, or is finally discharged. Given at Annapolis, 31st day of July, 1783.

Registered & Attested,   J. Gunby, Col.
M. McPherson, Adjt.

Mathias Cyphert, private 1st Md. Regt., received the same leave as above, Aug 6th, 1783.

Prisoners in the Provost, May 9th, 1783.

Names.	Regt.	Crimes.	By Whom Conf'd.	When Conf'd.
Wm. Potter, Corpl.	Md.	neglect of Duty	Capt. Paskie	
John Summers	"	desertion		2 May
John Sammon	"	ditto		do
Wm. Harper	"	susp. of break'g in Q. M. Stores	} Capt. Price	7 do
Aaron Mitchell	"	ditto		do

J. W. Gray, Capt. Guard

[from the Gist Papers]

PAY ROLL OF THE MARYLAND LINE FOR 1783.

[Imperfect, pages 1 and 2 missing.]

Unless otherwise stated service is from Jan. 1st to Nov. 15th, 1783.

Names and Rank.		When Left Service and the Reasons.	Remarks.
John McKay	P.		
John Harris, 1st	P.		
Daniel Brumigen	P.	deserted 2 May '83	pardoned
John Hurley	P.		
Peter Equedoroney	P.		
Solomon Green	P.		
James Evans	P.		
Richard Dolvin	P.		
James Humphries	P.		
Thomas Elliott, 1st	P.	deserted 2 May '83	pardoned
John Carrell, 2nd	P.		
Samuel Richardson	P.		
Nicholas Elliot	P.		
George Jennings	P.		
George Kelson	P.		
Thomas Wood, 2nd	P.		
Thomas Jones, 5th	P.		
Thomas Carney	P.		
Cornelius Thompson	P.		
Joseph Sidney	P.	deserted 2 May '83	Waggoner Artificers, pardoned
Paul Lapping	P.		
James Bayless	P.		
John Duhague	P.	dead previous to '83	
John Lesslie	P.		Artificers
John McCaliff	P.		
James Davidson	P.		
Francis Taylor	P.		
John Hull	P.		
John Fullham	P.		
John Hood	P.	died 20 Dec '82	
Charles Girdler	P.		
William Brady	P.		
John Bamtham	P.		
2ND COMPANY. CAPT. WILMOT.			
Thomas Edwards	S.		
Hugh McMillan	S.		

Names and Rank.		When Left Service and the Reasons.	Remarks.
John Gwyne	S.		
John Colein	S.		
Charles Harvey	S.		
Nathan Price	C.		promd. Serjt. 1 Mch '83
Charles Nabb	C.	dischd. 14 Oct '83	
Richard Ferreby	C.		
Kirney Lahnnum	C.	died 20 Dec '82	
John McKnight	F.		
Peter Topping	P.		
Emanuel Carthagene	P.		
John T. West	P.		
James Gray, 1st	P.		
John Briley	P.		
Joseph Johnson	P.		
William Ingle	P.		
Jeremiah Williams	P.		
Joseph McAntee	P.		
Adam Jamieson	P.		
Thomas Slade	P.		
John Lynch, 2nd	P.		
Daniel O'Quinn	P.		
Asaph Colegate	P.		
John King	P.		
Michael Callihorne	P.		
Thomas Murphey	P.		
John Kidd	P.		
Hugh Gaynor	P.		
Conrod Smith	P.		
William Hedge	P.		
William Carter	P.		
Isaac Holliday	P.	died 30 Jan '83	
John Dunnagan	P.	died 25 Jan '83	
Michael Clark, 2nd	P.		
John Hide	P.		
John Berryman	P.		
David Crady	P.		
William Pecker	P.	deserted 2 May '83	pardoned
Edward Evans	P.		
Elijah Smith	P.		
Henry Reeding	P.		
Evans Tumblestone	P.		
Matthew Moore	P.		
Ralph Hope	P.		
Christopher McCaway	P.		Artificer
Henry Ramsey	P.		
Edward Wright	P.	died 4 Mch '83	

Names and Rank.		When Left Service and the Reasons.	Remarks.
Philip Bailey	P.	died 20 Feb '83	
Aaron Mitchell	P.		
William Cork	P.		
Daniel Mann	P.	deserted 30 Apl '83	pardoned
Daniel Murphy	P.		
Alyand Melvin	P.		
Edward Henecy	P.	died 28 Apl '83	
Southern George	P.		
Thomas Richardson, 1st	P.		
John Blades	P.		
Jacob Adamson	P.	died 24 Mch '83	
Walter Ferrill	P.		
John Nave	P.		
William Harper	P.		
Daniel Foxwell	P.		
John Morris	P.		
John Fossett	P.		
Murphy Shee	P.	died 28 Jan '83	
William Camm	P.		
Cato Snowden	P.		
William Absalom	P.		
Thomas Long	P.		
Timothy Langrill	P.		
John Lucas	P.		
Thomas Matthews, 2nd	P.		
James Due	P.		

3RD COMPANY.   CAPT. JOHN S. BELT.

Names and Rank.		When Left Service and the Reasons.	Remarks.
Francis Magauran	S.		
Jesse Jacobs	S.		
John Carson	S.		
James Deverex	S.		
William Rose	S.	deserted 29 Mch '83	pardoned
James Ashley	C.		
Nicholas Milbourne	C.		
Samuel Young	C.		
William Sillwood	P.		
Daniel Warrier	D.	deserted 27 Apl '83	pardoned
Alexander Stevenson	F.		
Richard Dewall	P.		
Benjm. Williams	P.		
Michael McCann	P.		
John Nicholson	P.		
Thomas Davies, 1st	P.		
John Wade	P.	deserted 15 Apl '83	pardoned
Christopher Cusack	P.		

NAMES AND RANK.		WHEN LEFT SERVICE AND THE REASONS.	REMARKS.
James Steward	P.	died 3 June '83	
Willm. Stonestreet	P.		
Joshua McKinsay	P.		
Paul Greenard	P.		
John Holloday	P.		
Thomas Hutchcraft	P.		
Edward Fincham	P.		
Thomas Burke	P.		
James Erwin	P.		
John Nevitt, 2nd	P.		
John Wilson	P.		
Charles Wheelor	P.		
George Jones	P.		
George Bough	P.		
Daniel Kettle	P.		
Abraham Kettle	P.		
Moses McKinsey	P.		
Wm. Cooke	P.		
Cornelius Vaughan	P.		
Matthias Dyche	P.	deserted 15 Apl '83	pardoned
Michael Smith, 1st	P.		
Francis McCann	P.		
Thomas Larymore	P.	deserted 15 Apl '83	pardoned
Absalom Wright	P.	ditto	pardoned
Francis Karns	P.		
William Ryder	P.		
William Whittico	P.		
John Hall	P.		
Thomas Foxall	P.		
Walter B. Smallwood	P.		
William Paul	P.		
Robert Mitchell	P.		
George Taylor	P.		
Henry Billop	P.		
John Thompson	P.		
George Mauntle	P.	deserted 15 Apl '83	pardoned
Samuel Baswell	P.		
Elias Smith	P.		
Charles Jones	P.		
Arthur Coffins	P.		
Richard Denby	P.	died 8 May '83	
John Elcott, 1st	P.	deserted 29 Apl '83	pardoned
Thomas Jones, 2nd	P.		
John Stanton	P.		
James Bowen	P.		
Smart Greer	P.		

during the War of the American Revolution, 1775–83.

Names and Rank.		When Left Service and the Reasons.	Remarks.
Michael Hartman	P.		
Benjm. Clever	P.		Artificer
Joseph Elliott	P.		
Thomas Elliotte, 2nd	P.		
George Bomgardner	P.		
Christopher Smith	P.		
Moses Graham	P.		
John Nelson, 1st	P.		

4TH COMPANY.   CAPT. JAMES W. GRAY.

John Reeder	S. & P.	deserted 29 Apl '83	reduced 15 Jan '83, pardoned
John Moore, 2nd	S.		
Humphrey Beckett	S.	deserted 29 Apl '83	pardoned
James Kelley	S. & P.		reduced 22 Feb '83
Lawrence Bromham	S. & P.		ditto 22 Feb '83
John Hamilton	C. & S.		promoted Sjt. 1 Mch '83
Walter Howe	C. & S.		do do 1 Mch '83
George Dixon	P. & C.		do Corpl. 1 Mch '83
Wm. Derrington	P. & C.		do do 1 Mch '83
Thomas Jones, 1st	P. & C.		do do 1 Mch '83
William Lytle	C.		
Samuel Gray	C.		
Anthony Gohegan	D.	deserted 30 Apl '83	pardoned
Robert Cornick	F.		
Luke Carter	P.		
John Ashmore	P.		
John Craig	P.		
William McGee	P.		
George Ford	P.		
Christopher Seymore	P.		
Francis Hopkins	P.		
John Gordon, 1st	P.		
Neal Peacock	P.		
John Love	P.		
William Mitchell	P.		
Emanuel Farrara	P.		
Richard Tascow	P.		
Matthew Moore, 1st	P.		
Joseph Jenkins	P.	deserted 29 Apl '83	pardoned
John Dyer	P.		
Joseph Southall	P.		
Hezekiah Carr	P.		
Zachariah Clark	P.		
John Fransway	P.		
John Lee	P.		
Richard Taylor	P.	dischd. 6 May	

490 *Records of Maryland Troops in the Continental Service*

Names and Rank.		When Left Service and the Reasons.	Remarks.
John Wells	P.		
Edward Irvin	P.		
John Jarvis	P.		
James Byas	P.		
John Lewin	P.		
Charles Ormes	P.		
Charles McGee	P.		
John Bulkley	P.		
Dudley Lee	P.		
Andrew Russell	P.		
Edward Evins	P.		
Luke Dempsey	P.		
John Onians	P.		
John Gorman	P.		
Francis Reed	P.		
Willm. Hartman	P.		
Philip Savoy	P.		
Edward Chambers	P.		
Michael Pilkerton	P.		
James Tigner	P.		
Lambert Goody	P.		
John Graham	P.	deserted 2 May '83	pardoned
Matthew Carty	P.		
Lewin Abbott	P.	deserted 29 Apl '83	pardoned
Edward Forreignner	P.		
Lawrence Simpson	P.		
Thomas Johns	P.	deserted 29 Apl '83	pardoned
William McPherson	P.		
Thomas Perry	P.		
James, or Jesse, Chambers	P.		
Jacob Jeffers	P.		
Charles Murphy	P.		
John Cole	P.		
*John D. Tally	P.		prisoner 20 Dec '82
Austin Howard	P.		
John Appleby	P.		
Michael Woolford	P.		
Traverse Alvey	P.	deserted 29 Apl '83	pardoned
Joshua Pierce	P.		
James Thomas	P.	deserted 29 Apl '83	pardoned
5th Company. Capt. B. Price.			
Wm. A. Needham	S.		
John Quick	S.		
George Williams	S.		
Charles Fulham	S.		

Names and Rank.	When Left Service and the Reasons.	Remarks.
Patrick Doran	S. & P.	reduced to private 20 Jan '83
James Greenwood	D.	
Thomas Hawson	F.	
Issachar Mason	P.	
Frederick Bennet	P.	
William Moore, 1st	P.	
John Ashbury	P.	
James Barber	P.	
John Branson	P.	
Daniel Bassett	P.	
William Carter	P.	
George Craggs	P.	
James Driver	P.	
Peter Degazoone	P.	
Stephen Fennell	P.	
John Frawney	P.	
Thomas Gadd	P.	
William Hope	P.	
Edward Holland	P.	
Benjamin Kearns	P.	deserted 30 Apl '83	pardoned
James Knott	P.	
Levi Lord	P.	
Alexander Levi	P.	
Francis Lang	P.	
Henry Mansfield	P.	
William Nuton	P.	
Thomas Pendor	P.	
Lambert Philips	P.	
Joseph Rhea	P.	
Partrick Reiley	P.	
William Shirley	P.	
Bennet Shirley	P.	
Jesse Wright	P.	
John West	P.	
Thomas Wember	P.	
Thomas Pennefield	P.	
Richard Kisby	P.	
George Duncan	P.	
Henry Jacobs	P.		drafted Artificer
William Hicks	P.	
William Cox	P.	
John Ennis	P.	
Henry Nicholson	P.	
John Moore, 1st	P.	
Rhode Woodland	P.	
Leonard Holt	P.	

Names and Rank.		When Left Service and the Reasons.	Remarks.
Enoch Ennis	P.		
Thomas Ellis	P.		
Abraham Catchsides	P.		
Richard Wiley	P.		
William Fitzgerald	P.		
Charles Fitzgerald	P.		
William Toland	P.		
Joseph Fowler	P.		
William Manley	P.		
William Jones, 1st	P.		
Thomas Butt	P.		
Jacob Blake	P.		
Francis Freeman	P.		
Job Sylvester	P.		
Charles White	P.		
Edward Kersey	P.		
Joseph Barton	P.		
William Lee, 1st	P.		
James Hewitt	P.		drafted Artificer
Jeremiah French	P.		
James Smith	P.		
John Whitcomb	P.	discharged for inability 30 Apl '83	
Peter Howard	P.	died 4 Feb '83	
6TH COMPANY. CAPT. LLOYD BEALL.			
William Bruff	S.		
Stephen Fluherty	S.		
George Fields	S.		
Charles McKnabb	S.		
Samuel Filson	S.		
Boston Medler	D.		
Benjm. Williams	F.		
Peter Stephens	C.		
William Potter	C.		
Robert Sharpless	C.		
John Scott	D.		
Charles Clements	C.	deserted 26 Apl '83	pardoned
Joseph Pherson	C.	ditto	pardoned
Theophilus Linsday	C.		
George Devit	P.		
Samuel Clark	P.		
Zedekiah, or Zadock, Whaley	P.		
Alexander Ross	P.		
George Buck	P.		
Joshua Leister	P.		

during the War of the American Revolution, 1775-83.   493

NAMES AND RANK.		WHEN LEFT SERVICE AND THE REASONS.	REMARKS.
Robert Duncan	P.		
Absalom Fardo	P.		
Darby Crowley	P.		
William Leakins	P.		
John Knox	P.		
John Ryan	P.		
Elijah Pepper	P.		
Neil Morriss	P.		
John Loveday	P.		
Joseph Blaze	P.		
Michael Curtis	P.		
Frederick Harty	P.		
William Mann	P.		
John McNelly	P.		
William Quinton	P.		
John Twiner	P.		
Luke Sampson	P.		
Moses Foster	P.		Artificer
Richard Gee	P.		
John Maxwell	P.		
John Miles, or Mills	P.		
Samuel Wedge	P.		
Lazarus Harmer	P.		
Charles Simpkins	P.		
William Crail	P.		
William Casey	P.		
Peter McGuire	P.		
Benjamin Mash	P.		
Robert Campbell	P.	deserted 29 Apl '83	pardoned
John Armstrong	P.		
Henry Townley	P.		
Richard Spires	P.		
George Hamilton	P.		promoted Corpl. 1 Mch '83
John Hewlett	P.		
Paul Rowan	P.		
Edward Cosgrove	P.		
William Elkins	P.		
John Fulford	P.		
John Jones, 2nd	P.		
Andrew Rauside	P.	died previous to '83	
John Smith, 4th	P.		
William Whaling	P.		
Richard Dixon	P.	died previous to '83	
Thomas Clarke, 2nd	P.		
Nicholas Hiner	P.		
John McGlin	P.		

Names and Rank.		When Left Service and the Reasons.	Remarks.
John McNeal	P.		
John Bowdy	P.	deserted 2 May '83	pardoned
Nehemiah Lingard	P.		
Samuel Hurst	P.		
John Spires	P.		
William Glover	P.		
John Wrighte	P.		
William Taylor, 1st	P.		
Zachariah Robinson	P.	mustered in the 8th Company	
William Niblet	P.		
William Hillman	P.		

7TH COMPANY. CAPT. SAMUEL McPHERSON.

Names and Rank.		When Left Service and the Reasons.	Remarks.
William Collis	S.		
John Brady	S.		
Robert Scrivenor, or Scribner	S.	died 15 Feb '83	
Humphry Spencer	S.		
Aaron Spalding	S.		
William Braithwaite	C.		
Bartholomew Essom	C.		
John Head	D.		
Andrew Garnett	F.		
Richard Hayes	P.		
Isaac Greaves	P.		
Aquilla Pierce	P.	deserted 29 Apl '83	pardoned
Philip Fitzpatrick	P.		
John Haney	P.		
William Goold	P.		
Hampton Coarsey	P.		
Henry Green	P.		
Roger Landers	P.		
John Welch, 1st	P.		
Michael Lloyd	P.		
Charles Cooper	P.		
James Meason, Mason	P.		
John Gregory	P.		
Thomas Waite	P.		
John Alby	P.		
William Moore, 2nd	P.		
Jacob Games	P.		
John Robins	P.		
John Buckhannan	P.		
James Farrell	P.		
David Bramble	P.		
Luke Merryman	P.		

Names and Rank.		When Left Service and the Reasons.	Remarks.
Thomas Camphor	P.		
William Purchace	P.		
Adam Kiphart	P.		
Jacob Knight	P.		
William Laws	P.		
Michael Casnor	P.		
Richard Blansford	P.		
James Harris	P.	deserted 1 May '83	pardoned
John Dennison, or Denion	P.		
William Glory	P.		
John Summers	P.		
Henry Ostin	P.		
Henry Evans, or Evis	P.		
Benjamin Gaither	P.	deserted 1 May '83	pardoned
Robert Streets	P.		
Joseph Donoho	P.		
William Rice	P.		
William Matthews	P.	deserted 1 May '83	pardoned
Thomas Patterson	P.	ditto	pardoned
Thomas Bear	P.		
John Sammon	P.		
James Cresbury	P.		
James Wilson, 1st	P.	deserted 17 April '83	pardoned
Charles Siekle	P.		
Abraham Irwine	P.		
John Taylor	P.	deserted 17 Apl '83	pardoned
Matthias Cyphert	P.		
Peter Melvin	P.		
Patrick Conavough	P.	to be altered name	
Daniel Bulger	P.		
William Moore, 3d	P.		
Thomas Porter	P.		
Richard Biddle	P.		
James Bigwood	P.		
Daniel Jarvis	P.		
Joseph Hewkill	P.	deserted 1 May '83	pardoned
Solomon Brittenham	P.		
Joseph Horsefield	P.		Artificer
William Groves	P.		
William Jones, 2nd	P.		
Lambert Thompson	P.		
Cathoel Carmile	P.		
Patrick Rowing, or Rowan	P.		

8TH COMPANY. CAPT. JAMES WINCHESTER.

Peter McNortin	S.		
Peter Smith	S.		

Names and Rank.		When Left Service and the Reasons.	Remarks.
Samuel Evans	S.		
John Willing	S.		
Benjm. Prior	C.		
George Childs	C.		
John Willey	C.		
Thomas Gossage	F.		
John Martindale	D		
Richard Hall	P.		
John Adams	P.		
John Baley	P.		
Peter Bocard	P.		
Michael Lawler, or Loller	P.		
Basil Brown	P.		
Thomas Canady	P.		
John Brown	P.		
Samuel Hamilton	P.		
William Lilley	P.		
Patrick Molohon	P.		
John Williams	P.		
Thomas Thomas	P.		
James Thomas, 2nd	P.		
Charles Goldsbury	P.		
Benjamin Steward	P.		
Alexander Francis	P.		
Peregrine Howard	P.		
Richard Proctor	P.		
Samuel Harper	P.		
Edward Hammond	P.		
Barney Wilson	P.		
Samuel Calahan	P.		
Henry Loyers, or Lawers	P.		
William Pherson	P.	{ mustered deserted 26 Apl in 7th Co. }	pardoned
Joseph Hall	P.		
Amos Green	P.		
Francis Demar	P.	deserted 27 Apl '83	pardoned
William Herrington	P.		
Abijah Buckstone	P.		
Abraham Garsene	P.		
William Sax, or Sikes	P.		
Darby McLamar	P.		
David Cale	P.		
Stephen Fresh	P.		
William Poland	P.		
Michael Miller	P.		
John Jackson	P.		

during the War of the American Revolution, 1775–83.

Names and Rank.		When Left Service and the Reasons.	Remarks.
Ignatius Adams	P.		
Jonathan Fowler	P.		
William Nailor	P.		
William Joice	P.		
John Brookbank	P.		
John Irons	P.		
Jacob Flora	P.		
William Clary	P.		
Samuel Vermillion	P.		
John Anderson, 1st	P.		
Garrard Welch	P.		
Joshua Cox	P.		
Charles Dean	P.		
David Hatten	P.	died 9 Mch '83	
Jacob Drudo, or Duddero	P.		
William Dawson	P.		
William Harrison	P.		
William Stanley	P.		
Noah Sears	P.	died 3 Apl '83	
Frederick Wilmot	P.		Artificer
Thomas Clark, 1st	P.		
Benjamin Boyd	P.		
John Osburn, or Osban	P.		
Richard Butler	P.		in Maryland
Francis Fairbrother	P.		
John Carr	P.	died 25 Feb '83	
Henry Bradley	P.		

9th Company. Capt. Francis Revelly.

Stephen R. Price	S.		
Chas. Runenberger	S.		
John Lynch	S.		
Archibald Johnson	S.		
Samuel F. Shoemaker	S.	deserted 12 Jan '83	
John Foldier, or Falling	C.		
Andrew Crummy	C.		
Thomas Evans, 2nd	P.		
Benj. H. Kerrick	D.		
Michael Clansey	F.		
William Sullivan	P.		
John Burnett	P.	deserted 26 Apl '83	pardoned
George Pearce	P.	ditto	pardoned
Rigby Foster	P.		
John McCall	P.		
John Gee	P.		
Daniel Smith, 2nd	P.		

Names and Rank.		When Left Service and the Reasons.	Remarks.
Edward Tanner	P.	deserted 26 Apl '83	pardoned
*Edward Roberts	P.		promoted Corpl. 1 Apl ['83
Michael Waltman	P.		
*James Ruarck	P.		promoted Corpl. 1 Apl ['83
William Roberts	P.		
Charles Scott	P.		
Robinson Ross	P.		
John McCann	P.	deserted 2 May '83	pardoned
John Harrell	P.		
John Roach	P.		
Joseph Long	P.		
Joseph Sloop	P.	deserted 27 Apl '83	pardoned
John Walker, 1st	P.		
Nathan Aldridge	P.		
Robert Clanahan	P.		
William McGloughlin, or McLochlin	P.		
James Sewall	P.		
Zachariah Mills	P.		
William Jenkins	P.	deserted 26 Apl '83	pardoned
Daniel Buckley	P.		
Patrick Dennison	P.		
Jacob Myers	P.		
Barrack Butt	P.		
Henry Crane	P.	deserted 26 Apl '83	pardoned
Richard Mitchell	P.		
Bartholomew Thompson	P.		
Amos Griffin	P.		
James Wood, 2nd	P.		
John Burns	P.	deserted 26 Apl '83	pardoned
Isaac Nichols	P.		
Joseph Botchabay	P.		
Rueben Smith	P.	died 9 May '83	
Richard Haislip	P.		
John Taylor	P.		
Henry Williams	P.		
Benj. Williams, 3rd	P.		
Abraham Dougan, or Doogan,"	P.		
Edward Vickers	P.		
James Collierd, or Cholard	P.		
James Crozier	P.		
John Delany	P.		
John Haiden, or Hadan	P.		
James Jones	P.		
Michael Weirey	P.	deserted 26 Apl '83	pardoned

during the War of the American Revolution, 1775-83. 499

Names and Rank.		When Left Service and the Reasons.	Remarks.
George Saunders	P.		
Robert Taylor	S.		
George Steem	F.		
James Managa			
Thomas Gillon			
*James Keelan	P.		
*Jacob Collins	P.		
*Jacob Moses	P.		
*Nehemiah Hader	P.		
Henry Fisher, 2nd	P.	German Regiment	
Levi Burck	P.	drum'd out & dischd. 3 May '83	
*James Jackson	P.		
*Joseph Jones, 1st	P.		
Alex. Rutherford	P.	dischd. 4 Jan '83	
*Joshua Barrett	S.		
John Armstrong, 1st	P.	formerly of the 5th Regt.	
*Daniel Holdman	P.		
Thomas Bulkley	P.		
Laurence Mesler	P.		
*Thomas Windham	S.		
David Middis	P.		
*Thomas Smith, 1st	P.		
Peter Outhouse	P.		
*John Newton, 1st	P.		
Thomas Crompton	P.		
Simon Perry	P.		
Jonathan Weedon	P.	died 13 Feb '83	
Thomas Wood, 4th	S.		
Charles Robinson	P.		
Thomas Summers			

NORTHERN DETACHMENT.

1.—Capt. Walker Muse. Lieut. Henry Chapman.

*Nathaniel Bailey	S.		
*John McDonald	S.		
William Johnson	S.	dischd. 22 Oct '83	
Robert Harpin	S.		
Daniel Willis	D.		
Samuel Street	F.	deserted 29 Apl '83	
Isaac Johnston	C.	dischd. 1 Oct '83	
*Evan Thomas	C.		
James Barron	C.		
John Hudson	P.		
Robert Firth	P.		
*James Hudson	P.		
*John Reed	P.		

Names and Rank.		When left Service and the Reasons.	Remarks.
*David McCollum	P.		
John Smallwood	P.	deserted 20 June '83	
*Lewis Flash	P.		
John Turner	P.		
John Rogers	P.		
Jeremiah Carter	P.		
James Brannon	P.		
William Smith, 3rd	P.		
Roger Hogan	P.		
John Stackhouse	P.	dischd. 4 May '83	
Thos. McQuinney	P.		
Francis De Wist	P.		
William Batton	P.		
Thomas McKinzie	P.		
*Samuel Chapel	P.		
Edward Ellicott	P.		
William Willion	P.		
John Purdy	P.	dischd. 27 Jan '83	
Benj. Burch	C.	do 19 do do	
Enoch McClain	S.		
*Birnnick Meakins	P.		
Charles Leago	P.	dischd. 1 Apl '83	
*Charles Love	P.		
*John Pope	P.		
William Devin	P.		
John Murray, 1st	P.		
*Notley Tippet	P.		
Thomas Hall	P.		
Patrick Quinn	P.		
Daniel Howe	P.		
James Dowden	P.		
John Traverse	P.		
John Housely	P.		
Zachariah Berry	P.		
George Trice	P.		
Edward Kirk	P.		
*Thomas Houseman	P.		
Zadock Risden	P.		
John Welch, 2nd	P.		
*Joseph Ward	P.		
*John Gray	P.		
William Patterson	P.		
John Ransom	P.		
*Banks Webb	P.		
John Walker, 2nd	P.		
Nicholas Welch	P.		

Names and Rank.		When Left Service and the Reasons.	Remarks.
William Senah	P.		
Matthew Kelly	P.		
George Tate	P.		
Roderick McKinsie	P.		
Thomas Richardson, 2nd	P.	not heard of 2 months past	
Michael Standley	P.		

2.—CAPT. HORATIO CLAGGETT.   LT. WALTER DYER.   ENSIGN HENRY HAWKINS

David Love	S.		
William Marlow	S.	to the End	
*Joseph Allen	S.		
Joseph Neal	S.	reduced to Private 15 Nov '83	
Dennis Dunning	D.		
*Joseph Clancey	F.		
*Thomas Ellison	C.		
John Fennel, 1st	C.		
*Christopher Hinson	C.		
William Gudgeon	P.		
*Preistly Bruington	P.		
Isaac Dunkin	P.	dischd. 15 Nov	
Thomas Harris	P.		
Sylvester Gatten	P.		
John McClain	P.		
William Hutchinson	P.		
Andrew Bramble	P.		
Selladay Standley	P.		
John Boody	P.		
Basil Newton	P.		
William Conner	P.		
John Baxter	P.		
*William Powell	P.		
James Newell	P.		
*James Williams	P.		
John Vane	P.		
John Lowe	P.		
*Levin Harrington	P.		
William Rue	P.	to the End	
*Richard Jennings	P.		
Jesse Locker	P.		
*Aron Rawlings	P.		
*Daniel Harness	P.		
John Swales	P.		
*William Madan	P.		
*Solomon Sullivan	P.		
*James Hunt	P.		
Charles Griffith	P.	dischd. 1 May '83	

Names and Rank.		When Left Service and the Reasons.	Remarks.
John Hickings	P.		
John Cleverdence	P.		
*Peter Jackson	P.		
Paris Owens	P.		
*John Conner	P.		
Thomas Baxter	P.	dischd. 24 Sept '83	
John Moore, 5th	P.		
*Alexander McGregor	P.		
*John Willman	P.		
Jacob Mifford	P.		
*Whittington Gild	P.		
Richard Harrington	P.		
John Climeslaught	P.		
*John Fairweather	P.		
John Courts	P.	time expired 16 Apl '83	
*Hugh Ware	P.		
*Willan Colter	P.		
*Thomas Dickerson	P.		
*Samuel Scott	P.	dischd. 20 June '83	
*Isom Coleman	P.		
William Holland	P.		
*James Kirk	P.		
*James Pool	P.		
*Thomas Channon	P.		
John Williams, 2nd	P.		

3.—Capt. Edward Spurrier. Lt. Joshua Rutledge.
Lt. Robert Halkerston.

Names and Rank.		When Left Service and the Reasons.	Remarks.
William McNeal	S.		
Richard Hogins	S.		
Aquilla Chitham	S.		
Thomas Craig	S.		
Stephen Nicholson	S.		
Benjamin Burch	S.	dischd. 3 Nov '83	
*William Watkins	D.		
John Denoone	F.		
*John Burgess	C.		
*Kemp Holden	C.		
Thomas White	C.		
Benjamin McCall	C.		
Thomas King	P.		
William Ayhun	P.		
*James Bell	P.		
William Hunter	P.		
*John Bell	P.		

Names and Rank.		When Left Service and the Reasons.	Remarks.
Daniel Hukell	P.		
John Jones, Jr.	P.		
John White	P.		
John Cannon	P.		
Charles Palmore	P.		
*Thomas Scego	P.		
John Hukill	P.		
George Dadisman	P.		
*Henry Barns	P.		
Joseph Rose	P.		
John Jones, Sr.	P.		
John Smith, 3rd	P.		
Charles Masseck	P.	dischd. 22 Oct '83	
*John Stoffel	P.		
John Shefar	P.		
*Bassell Dorsey	P.		
*Thomas Hardin	P.		
*Thomas McDowell	P.		
John Johnson, 1st	P.		prom. Corpl. 1 May '83
Robert Johnson	P.		
*Henry Windows	P.		
George Miller	P.		
*Evans Willing	P.		
*Edward Roan	P.		
*John Greenwood	P.		
*Isaac Kent	P.		
*William Smallwood	P.		
*Robert Dean	P.		
John Britton	P.		
*Isaac Mitchell	P.		
Frederick Flinn	P.		
William Connelly	P.	dischd. 16 July '83	
Matthew Daley	P.		
Edward Cantwell	P.	dischd. 24 Sept '83	
John Willson, 2nd	P.		
James Creighton	P.		
John Dixson	P.		
*Thomas Wood, 3rd	P.		
John Turner, 3rd	P.		
Christopher Rayner	P.	dischd. 10 Apl '83	
*Isaac McFadon	P.		
Edward Mahony	P.	not heard of	

4.—Capt. Wm. Bruce.   Lieut. Thomas Rowse.

Perry Evans	S.		Certd. Lt. Gassaway.
John Walker, 3rd	S.		

NAMES AND RANK.		WHEN LEFT SERVICE AND THE REASONS.	REMARKS.
Harris Austin	S.		
John Browne, 3rd	S.	Rawlings' Regt.	
*John Bond	S.		reduced 1 Feb '82
William Chatlin	C.		
*John Davis	C.		
James Maxwell	C.		
Isaack Deal	C.		
William Dunn	C.		
*Isaac Holland	D.		
Joel Baker	P.		
*John Long	P.		
Martin Bowles	P.		
*Samuel Fisher	P.		
Solomon Barret	P.		
*Leonard Nable	P.		
*Robert McClary	P.		
Benj. Donelly	P.		
John Richardson	P.		
*John Green, 2nd	P.		
William Matthews, 2nd	P.		
*Lawrence Pines	P.		
James Silk	P.		
*John Bailey	P.		
Joseph Cluley	P.		
John Cotter	P.		
Perry Bantham	P.		
Herculus Hutchins	P.		
Richard Rivers	P.		
*John Nicholson	P.		
*Edward Burns	P.		
*Henry Frazer	P.		
William Deveraux	P.		
Stephen Owens	P.		
William Marshall	P.	dischd. 3 Mch '83	
Stephen Hancock	P.		
*Michael Keen	P.		
*Richard Burck	P.		
*William Coulin	P.		
Dorden Orrell	P.		
James Burck, 1st	P.		
George Carney	P.		
William Watkins	P.		
Edward Shoebrook	P.		
*Lewis Cunningham	P.	time expired 22 July '83	
John Smith, 2nd			
*Daniel Wilkins	P.		

Names and Rank.		When Left Service and the Reasons.	Remarks.
John Harris, 2nd	P.		
Robert Ferrall	P.		
William Eagle	P.		
Joseph McCalister	P.	died 24 Mch '83	
Levin Clarage	P.		
*Robert Folger	P.		
George Filliston	P.		
*George Linton	P.		
Thomas Countess	P.		
James Kelly, 2nd	P.	dischd. 10 Apl '83	
Benjm. Worthington	P.		
*Richard McDonald	P.		
Barney Haney	P.	War	
James Hudson	P.		
James Terry	P.		
*John Philips	P.	commenced 8 Mch	
*James Sullivan	P.		
John Barlow	P.		
Thomas Kettle	C.		reduced 22 Feb '83
Domini Coines,(or Conies)	P.	(when commenced not stated)	
George Bowers	P.		
Thomas Baker	P.		
Samuel Crowell	P.		
James Gilmore	P.		
Daniel Sullinger	P.		

INVALID COMPANY.

Arthur McClain	S.	dischd. 10 Feb '83	
John Auber	D.		
Dennis Flanagan	P.	Private of Artillery	
Matthias Funner	P.		
Joseph Batts	P.		
John Cooper, 1st	P.		
John Mick	P.		
John Alsop	P.		
Jonathan Lewis	P.		
Giffard Miniky	P.	dischd. 16 Jan '83	
John Martin	P.		
Robert Carns	S.		
John Brown, 2nd	S.		
Abram Gamble	S.		
John Matthews, 1st	C.		
*Daniel Smith	C.		
Henry Crooke	P.		
*Christopher Lambert	P.		
David Kelly	P.		

Names and Rank.		When Left Service and the Reasons.	Remarks.
James Smith, 3rd	P.		promoted Corpl. 1 Oct '83
Joseph Quinn	P.		
John Shovell	P.		
James Shane	P.		
Patrick Reiley	P.	dischd. 3 Oct '83	
William Evans	P.		
John Shanks	P.		
James Gath	P.		
John Vanzant	P.		
John Neighbours	P.	dischd. 1 Feb '83	
Philip Fisher	P.		
James Burck, 2nd	P.		
Thomas Bishop	P.		
John C. Harwood	P.		waiting to Lt. Skinner, Virginia
Walter Keech	P.	dischd. 1 Aug '83	
William Hurly	P.		
Charles Bucklep	P.		
Thomas Watson	P.		
Joseph Burch	P.		
David Conner	P.		Joined 1 Oct '83

Lieut. Boham's Company.

Benj. Ward	S.	dischd. 1 July '83	
Terrence Duffee	S.		
George Finlay	S.		
Jesse Boswell	S.	time expired 1 June '83	
Leonard Smith	S.	dischd. 26 July '83	
Benjm. Fitzgerald	S.		
Richard Smith	S.	time expires 1 June '83	
Richard Wheelor	S.	dischd. 23 July '83	
Jesse Simms	S.	dischd. 20 Mch '83	
Thomas Duffee	S.		
William Preist	S.		
George Holton	S.		reduced 1 June
John Moore, 4th	C.		
James Hagan	C.	time expires 1 June '83	
Joseph Harper	C.		
Bennet Clements	C.	dischd. 23 July '83	
James Mead	D.		
John Riggs	D.	dischd. 6 May '83	
Abram Stallions	D.		
Alexander Stewart	P.	dischd. 1 Aug '83	
Joseph Greir	P.		
Christopher McGraw	D.		
Philip Hueston	D.		
Samuel Davies	F.		

during the War of the American Revolution, 1775-83.   507

Names and Rank.		When Left Service and the Reasons.	Remarks.
Isaac Young	F.		
Edward Clancey	F.		
John Peany	F.		
William Chapman	P.	dischd. 17 July '83	
Benjamin Smith	P.	do 1 Aug '83	
John Newton, 2nd	P.	do 31 Jan '83	
Elijah Hutt	P.		
John McGinnis	P.		
Jesse McKinsey	P.	dischd. 7 Aug '83	
Thomas Matthews, 1st	P.		
William Burgess	P.	dischd. 16 Aug '83	
Alexander Robinson	P.		
James Dawson	P.		
James West	P.		
Peter Bushell	P.	dischd. 1 May '83	
John Young, 2nd	P.		
Jacob Kelly	P.		
John Barrett	P.		
John Campbell, 2nd	P.		
Daniel Clancey	P.		
Adam Musler	P.		
Levin Button	P.		
Dennis Cragon	P.	Settled part in Invalids, dischd. 1 July '83	
Philip Graham	P.		
Richard Franklin	P.		
Cuthbert Able	S.	dischd. 1 Feb '83	
Edward Dominick	P.	do 1 July '83	
Benj. Gilbert	P.		
Thomas Smith, 2d	P.		
James Cockerill, or Cougherin	P.		
Levin Thomas	P.		
James McDonald	P.		
Barney Dougherty	P.		
John Deakins	P.		
John Edwards	P.		
William Stirling, 1st	P.		
Michael Smith, 2nd	P.		
William Cummings	P.		
William Cutler	P.		
Robert Bowen	P.		
Thomas Bailey	P.		
William Lee, 2nd	P.		
Adam Rider	P.		
Isom, or Asa, Moore	P.		
Wm. Taylor, 2nd, Sr.	P.		

Names and Rank.		When Left Service and the Reasons.	Remarks.
John Conley, 2nd	P.		
Christian Boss	P.		
Joseph White	P.	dischd. July '83	
John Haycock, or Hancock	P.		
Elisha Oakley	P.		
Henry Rees, or ——	P.		
William Mansfield	P.		
William Taylor, 3rd, Jr.	P.		
Patrick McKinsie	P.		
Daniel Williams	P.	time expires 1 Apl '83	
Frederick Iams	P.	dischd. 1 July '83	
George Silver	P.	do 5 Sept '83	
Giles Thomas	P.	do 25 July '83	
John Tucker	P.	do 21 Feb '83	
James Sappington	P.		
William Franklin	P.	dischd. 28 July '83	
John Nolan	P.		
James Procter	P.		
James Willson, 2d	P.		
James Philips	P.	dischd. 1 Aug '83	
Mark Foster	P.		
Jacob Yeast	P.	to the End	
Edward Jackson	P.		
Michael Clark	P.		
William Prater	P.		

Lieut. Lynn's Company.

Names and Rank.		When Left Service and the Reasons.	Remarks.
Joseph Jeanes	S.		
Dennis Kelly	S.	dischd. 1 Apl '83	
Jeremiah Brown	S.	do 1 May '83	
John Clancy	C.	Served 7 months and 16 days	
Wm. Clements	C.	dischd. 1 Aug '83	
John Gorden, 2nd	C.		
Benj. Belcher	F.		
William Stewart	F.		
Henry Fisher, 1st	P.		
John Starkey	P.		
James Greavy	P.		
Daniel Stephens	P.	to the End	
Gabriel Williams	S.	dischd. 6 Feb '83	
William Simonds	P.	do 1 July '83	
Thomas Newman	P.		
James Carey	P.		
Nicholas Free	P.		
James Reynolds	D.		
George Clarke	P.		

during the War of the American Revolution, 1775-83.   509

NAMES AND RANK.		WHEN LEFT SERVICE AND THE REASONS.	REMARKS.
Joseph Lewis	P.		
Charles Williams	P.	dischd. 27 Mch '83	
Notley Whitcomb	P.	time expires 1 April '83	
Benjm. Thompson	P.		
William Downes	P.		
James Shepherd	P.		
Isaac Hill	P.	dischd. 11 Aug '83	
Lazarus Higgs	P.	time expires 1 June '83	
Allen Townshend	P.		
Patrick Mayhorn	P.		
William Snowden	P.		
William Dorch	P.	dischd. 6 Aug '83	
George Baker	P.		
Thomas Sheridan	P.		
Benjm. Askew	P.		
John Mumford	P.		
William Hand	P.		
Nathan Harper	P.		
Thomas Thompson	P.		
John Abrams	P.		
James Barber	P.		
Thomas Wood, 1st	P.		
Basil Shaw	S.		
Thomas Clements	P.	dischd. 1 Aug '83	
James Roe	P.		
Nicholas Farr	P.		
Thomas Evans, 1st	P.		
Jesse Suite	S.		
Jacob Doyne	S.		
William Bowling	S.		
Zachariah Moore	S.		
Elisha Osborne	S.		
Thomas Hill	C.		
Thomas Fleming	C.		
Christopher Coy	C.		
Thomas Clinton	F.		
William Lawrence	F.		
Hugh Roney	P.		
Stephen Preston	P.		
Henry Tippett	P.		
John Calahan	P.		
Thomas Hammond	P.		
George Chambers	P.		
Thomas Sturges	P.		
James Countess	P.		
Peter Carberry	P.		

Names and Rank.		When Left Service and the Reasons.	Remarks.
Robert Walker	P.		
John Cooper, 2nd	P.		
Francis Purly	P.		
Francis Ensly	P.		
John Romills	P.		
John Moore, 3rd	P.	dischd. 12 Jan '83	
Thomas Billingham	P.		
John Willis	P.		
Leonard Ennis	P.		
James Cowen	P.		
William Coleman	P.		
Cotter Jones	P.		
Humphrey Wells	P.		
Edward Wheatley	P.		
Robert Wright	P.		
Lewis McCullough	P.		
Joseph Murphy	P.		
John Johnson, 2nd	P.		
James Morris	P.		
Dennis O'Bryan	P.		
George Blackham	P.		
John McElroy	P.		
Robinson Wood	P.		
*Samuel Neville	P.	(when commenced not stated), deserted in 1780 and must produce a certificate from an Officer of his Service	
*John Hicks	P.	(when commenced not stated)	
John Connelly, 1st	P.	dischd. 1 Apl '83	
James Wood	S.		
*William Helmes	P.	(when commenced not stated)	
*Joseph Procter	P.	(when commenced not stated)	
*Peter Ryan	P.	commenced 24 Sept '83	
*Thomas Petit	P.	(when commenced not stated)	
Jonathan Mayhugh	P.		
William Howe	P.	commenced 1 Oct '83	
Neilee Jones	P.		
*John Johnston, 3rd	P.	dischd. 11 Aug '83	
Michael Rhydmyer	P.	do 13 Feb '83	
William Forman	S.		
*Thomas Twinch	Q. M. S.		
George Elms	F. M.		
Timothy McMahon	S.		
Joseph Purdy	D. M.		
Barney Lemon	P.	dischd. 14 Apl '83	
Abraham Manning	P.		
Henry Young	P.		

Names and Rank.		When Left Service and the Reasons.	Remarks.
John McBride	P.		
George Parker	P.		
John Green, 1st	P.		
Joseph McNamara		dischd. 25 July '83	
*John Clancy, 2nd	P.		
James Lowry	P.	dischd. at Frederick in Nov '83	
Jacob Hunt	P.		
John Lincoln	P.		
Lawrence Simpson	P.		
John Wright	P.		
William Harris, 1st	P.	time expires 2 Feb '83	
George Twinch	S.		
Robert Legg	P.		
Joseph Overcreek	P.		
John Haynes	P.	died 2 Feb '83	
Edward Reiley	P.	dischd. 3 June '83	
Jesse Powers	P.	do 29 May '83	
Dennis Trammile	P.	do 31 do do	
Thomas Drudge	P.	died 10 Apl '83	
Francis Dunnington	P.	do 23 do do	
John Watkins	P.	do 26 do do	
Pompey Hollis	P.	do 28 do do	
Benjamin Cole	P.	dischd. 1 Apl '83	
James Reynolds, 2nd	P.		
James Rose	P.		
John Missell	P.		
*Stephen Olingan	·P.		
*John Charles	P.		
Michael Sours	P.	dischd. 5 May '83	
Jeremiah Mudd	P.	do 1 Aug '83	
Benjamin Gray	P.		
John Christr. Miller	P.		
William King	P.		
Levi Scott	D.		
John Vallow	P.		
Walter Watson	P.	dischd. 1 Aug '83	
Benjm. Johnston	P.		
Jeremiah Driskill			
William Gates	P.	dischd. 30 Mch '83	
William Moad	P.		
John Curl, 1st	P.		
Stephen Varlow	P.		
James White	P.	Invalided by the State 10 June '83	
Thomas Glover	P.	dischd. 14 Feb '83	
James Curren	P.	do 1 Mch '83	
Wm. Lynch	P.		

Names and Rank.		When Left Service and the Reasons.	Remarks.
John Blair, 1st	P.	Invalided by the State 10 June '83	
Aquilla Dever	P.		
William Clements, 1st		dischd. 31 July '83	
Thomas Harrison, 1st	P.		
John Waller	P.		
James Dyer, 1st	P.		
Basil Norman	P.		
Thomas Cahoe, Sr.			
Thomas Cahoe, Jr.			
William Peters	P.		
John Morrison	F.		
John Ferral	P.	dischd. 14 Feb '83	
John Mantle	P.	do do do	
Francis Thompson	P.	do 18 Apl do	
John Hughes	P.	do 10 May do	
John Goddart	P.	do 26 Feb do	
Walter Miles	C.	do 1 Apl do	
Joseph Mattingley	P.	do 1 Feb do	
John Mills	C.	do 14 Feb do	
Henry Purdy	P.	do do do	
George Haydon	P.	do 23 do do	
William Carlin	P.	do 15 Nov do	enlisted for War
Wm. Hamston	P.	do 31 Jan do	
John Holder	P.		
Walter Hagan	P.	dischd. 23 Feb '83	
John Nary	P.	do 23 Mch do	time expires
Nicholas Nicholson		do 1 Apl do	ditto in April
Morris Neagle			
George Patrick		dischd. 23 Mch '83	
William Purcell			
William Rodgers	P.		
Paul Richards	P.		
Jos. Roberts	P.		
Jeremiah Sullivan		dischd. 12 Mch '83	
Wm. Smith	D.		
Ed. Wade, 2nd	P.		
Jesse Barnet	F.	dischd. 1 Apl '83	
John McDonald	F.	do 1 June '83	
John Thomas, 2nd			
William Coe	P.		
Thomas Adams	P.		
John Biggs	P.	dischd. 1 July '83	
John Francis	P.		
James Chard	P.	dischd. 1 Aug '83	
Oliver Stephens	P.		
Benj. Baulk			

Names and Rank.		When Left Service and the Reasons.	Remarks.
John Smallwood, 1st			
Wm. Corsey	P.		
Jonathan Chubb		dischd. 1 July '83	
Joseph Isaacks			
Darby Lenehan		dischd. 1 Feb '83	time expires
Thomas Arthurs		time expires 1 Apl '83	
Elijah Sullivan	P.		
John Kildee			
John Adams, 2nd			
George Dyer	P.		
John Hannor	F.		
William Robinson	P.		

M.

[A star prefixed to any name indicates that the length of service is not known. In all such cases, however, service began 1 Jan., '83, unless otherwise stated. Deserters, when pardoned, are credited with 10 months and 15 days service, the same as the other soldiers in this roll.]

MARYLAND ACTS—OCTOBER, 1780.

An ACT to settle and adjust the accounts of the troops of this state in the service of the United States, and for other purposes therein mentioned.

WHEREAS, from a variety of causes, the United States have not complied with their engagements heretofore made with their officers and soldiers (which has occasioned great and unavoidable difficulties and distresses in the service) to whose virtuous and disinterested exertions America is much indebted:

Be it therefore enacted, by the General Assembly of Maryland, That Zephaniah Turner be and is hereby appointed commissioner to settle and adjust the pay due to the officers and soldiers of the troops of this state, and the said commissioner is hereby empowered and directed to estimate, in specie, all sums of paper money received by the said officers and soldiers, on account of their pay or otherways, ... according to the value thereof at the time of the money received.

And be it enacted, That the said commissioner is hereby empowered and directed to give to the officers and soldiers aforesaid, to whom pay as aforesaid may be found due, ... one certificate or more, bearing interest from the date thereof, and specifying the sum due in specie.

And be it enacted, That the said commissioner shall in like manner settle and adjust the pay and accounts of all officers and soldiers who have fallen or died in the service, and their widows and children shall be entitled to such certificates.

Be it enacted, That the lands commonly called Talbot's, or New Connought Manor, in Caecil county, My Lady's Manor in Baltimore or Baltimore and Harford counties, and Monococy Manor in Frederick county, being British property, and seized and confiscated as such, ... shall be and are hereby set apart and burthened and charged with the payment of the money and interest aforesaid due on the said certificates, and the same shall be raised out of the said lands, by sales thereof, in such manner as the general assembly shall hereafter direct.

Depreciation Certificates, stopped at the Treasuries agreeable to Act of Assembly passed November Session, 1784.

NAMES.	REGT.	FOR WHAT REASONS STOPPED.
Abel Arman	7th	obtained by John Dove, in 1783, although Arman had deserted in July, 1780, order for the receipt supposed to be forged.
Edward Bailey	1st	not mustered before Aug, 1780, therefore not entitled to Depreciation.
William Bramble	2nd	was enlisted for nine months only, therefore not entitled to Depreciation.
John Burgess	Hartley's	received his Depreciation in Pennsylvania, see the letter of Mr. Nicholson, Comptroller of that State.
John Barbar	do	do do do
James Beall	do	do do do
John Coomy	Hazen's	obtained twice, first upon a Certificate in the Name John Kuny, the second on a discharge John Coomy, the same person meant.
Patrick Connally	5th	was left out of the Rolls in the Year 1779, and never served afterwards, therefore not entitled to Depreciation.
John Cheshire	2nd	obtained by perjury and forgery, some person unknown having sworn himself to be Cheshire, and signed his name as such in June, 1783, the real John Cheshire was killed in June, 1781.
John Callahan	1st	he Deserted in the year 1778, therefore not entitled.
Michl. Connell	2nd	obtained upon his own Oath in June, 1783, his Wife as supposing him dead, had obtained his Depreciation before.
William Dye	4th	after serving one Year, was stopped in Maryland by his former Master, this part of his pay therefore stopped payment.

NAMES.	REGT.	FOR WHAT REASONS STOPPED.
John Edwards	2nd	no such Man on any Musters.
Patk. Flemon	German	issued twice, the name being spelled differently in the Certificates by which Depreciation was issued.
Nathan Forster	5th	issued twice, as supposing there were two of that name, but upon comparing with the Muster Rolls, there was but one of the Name.
John Francis	1st	was not in Service until the year 1781, therefore not entitled to Depreciation.
Jereh. Farrell	Hartley's	see John Burgess and others of Hartley's Regt.
Alex. Grim	Rawlings'	is not upon the Musters of Rawlings' Regiment or any others of the Maryland Quota.
Joseph Hyner	Moylan's	he received his Depreciation in Pennsylvania, before his Application to this State, his final Settlement, which is Stopped, will however discharge part of this Depreciation.
Charles Howard	3rd	obtained by Perjury and Forgery in 1783 by some person assuming the Name, Charles Howard having died in October, 1781.
Charles Hickey	2nd	he does not appear by the Musters to have enlisted before the year 1781, therefore not entitled to Depreciation.
Th. Hewington	7th	obtained by John Dove as Abel Arman's was, and stopped for the same reason.
Henry Ijams	5th	is not on any Musters therefore not entitled.
Willm. Jones	Artillery	he deserted by Information of Major Brown, therefore not entitled.
Wm. Johnson	5th	there is no such person on the Musters of the 5th Regt., there is a Wm. Johnson on the Rolls of the 2nd Regt. but neither of them entitled.
Patk. Lynch	7th	issued twice by mistake.
Wm. Marquis	Hartley's	see John Burgess and others.
Dennis McCarty	Rawlings'	not upon the Musters of Rawlings' Regiment.
James McGuire	3rd	received his Depreciation twice.
John Macam	7th	rec'd by John Dove in 1783, Macam has not been in the army since Augt. 16th, 1780, is supposed to be dead, and his Father has administered and now claims the Pay, &c.
Timothy Mullen	3rd	not regularly discharged not having appeared since August 1780, probably received by a person who assumed his name.
John Malcom	2nd	no such Man on the Musters of the 2nd Regt., probably received by a person who assumed his name.
Alex. Mackay	Artillery	he deserted, therefore not entitled.
Nichs. Nicholls	5th	stopped for the reasons given in the Auditor's Rept.

Names.	Regt.	For what reasons Stopped.
George Phillips	7th	George Phillips died in April, 1781, some person, assuming the name, received this in 1783.
Thos. Peacock	7th	he was killed the 8th Sept., 1781, John Dove received his Depreciation as if alive, in June, 1783.
John Pennington	3rd	not regularly mustered or discharged.
John Radley	4th	he was hanged for exciting a Mutiny, this was rec'd in 1783 by some person assuming his name, the Widow of Radley now claims what was due to her husband.
Robt. Smith	German	he was a Recruit after August, 1780, and deserted in 1781.
Jas. Stillwell	5th	not found on any of the Musters of the Maryland Quota of Continental Troops.
Jereh. Sullivan	6th	not on any of the Musters of the Maryland Line.
Wm. Townsend	7th	delivered to John Dove—another Wm. Townsend who was entitled had rec'd Depreciation, this man was not entitled.
Wm. Whipple	7th	received by John Dove in the manner described in the case of Abel Arman.
George Wilson	5th	issued twice, as supposing there were two of the same name, which, upon examination with the Musters did not turn out to be the Case.
Edward White	2nd	ditto. ditto. ditto.
Richd. White	1st	not found on any Musters.

C. Richmond, Aud. Genl.

List of Certificates for Depreciation of Pay fraudulently obtained by Soldiers of the Seven Maryland Regiments.

List of Depreciation Certificates which have been fraudulently obtained, the payment of which is stopped at the Treasuries agreeable to an Act of the last Session of Assembly. Auditor's Office, May 25th, 1785.

Date of Issue.	Names.	Date of Issue.	Names.
27 Oct '83	Vendel Andrews	27 Oct '83	George Hyatt
5 Dec "	William Basht	27 Oct "	Philip Helter
15 Oct "	James Calhoun	27 Oct "	John Hart
5 Dec "	Thomas Cammell	5 Dec "	George Hartsell
5 Dec "	Timothy Conn	5 Dec "	Michael Hausman
15 Oct "	Charles Charell	8 Aug "	Michael Jackell
27 Oct "	Frederick Charell	5 Dec "	Nicholas Johnson

Date of Issue.	Names.	Date of Issue.	Names.
27 Oct '83	Peter Finley	27 Oct '83	Jacob Kaufman
27 Oct "	Andrew Goar	15 Oct "	William Kumius
18 June "	John Hammersly	27 Oct "	Nicholas Keyser
18 June "	Henry Harris	5 Dec "	Charles Kees
22 Sept '81	John Hickens, stoppage taken off	5 Dec "	William Kemp
		11 Sept '81	Dennis McCarty
7 Aug '83	Jacob Levy	21 Oct '83	Anthony Miller
5 Dec "	Nicholas Lines	27 Oct "	John Miller
5 Dec "	Henry Lane	27 Oct "	Henry Mielberger
11 Aug "	Thomas Peacock	27 Oct "	John Moore
23 June "	John Pickeron, stoppage taken off Certificate of Service having been produced	15 Oct "	Fredk. Weiger
		27 Oct "	Michael Yewling
		5 Dec "	John Ziegler
		13 June "	Charles Hickey
		15 Oct "	George Hensell
27 Oct "	Joshua Procter	27 Oct "	Henry Hargrader
15 Oct "	Peter Sigman	5 Dec "	Valentine Shultz
21 Oct "	Joseph Smith	5 Dec "	George Shriver
27 Oct "	Henry Spengell	6 Mch '84	Jacob Smith
27 Oct "	John Shultz	27 Oct '81	Samuel Tindel, stoppage off
27 Oct "	James Smith		
27 Oct "	Nicholas Stover	27 Oct '83	Frederick Tawney
5 Dec "	Peter Shrover		

C. Richmond, Aud. Genl.

AN ACCOUNT OF ALL CERTIFICATES RECEIVED FROM JOHN WHITE, AJT. COMSR., BY OFFICERS AND SOLDIERS OF THE MARYLAND LINE.

Rank.	Names.	Served between 1 Aug 1780 and 1 Jan 1782	Served between 1 Jan 1782 and 1 Jan 1783	Served between 1 Jan and 15 Nov 1783	Served between 15 Nov 1783 and 10 July 1784
[Major]	Alex'd'r Roxburgh	"	"	"	
[Surg. Mate]	Alexander Smith	"	"	"	
[Lieut.]	Thomas Boyd	"	"	"	"
[Lieut.]	Henry Hawkins		"		
[Lieut.]	John McCoy	"	"		
[Capt.]	Thomas B. Hugon	"	"		
[Lieut.]	Jacob Gramoth				
Capt.	Edwd. Dyer	"	"		
Major	Henry Dobson	"			
Capt.	John Hardman				
Genl.	Mordecai Gist	"	"	"	
Lieut.	John G. Lowe	"	"	"	
"	Peter Hardcastle	"			
"					
"	Jacob R. Shoemaker				
Surg. Mate	Wm. J. Smith				
Lieut.	James Simms	"			
Surgeon	Richard Sappington				
Surg. Mate	John Ross				
Surgeon	Thomas Parren				
Lieut.	Edwd. Moran				
Ensign	Caleb Mason	"			
Surg. Mate	Elisha Hamson	"			
Ensign	Saml. Hamilton				
"	David Greene	"			
Lieut.	Samuel Farmer	"			
"	Richd. Donovan	"			
"	John Carr	"			
"	John Boon	'			
"	Charles Beaven				
Capt.	Joseph Marbury	"	"	"	
Lieut.	Martin Shugart	"			
"	Nathan Smith	'			
Capt.	Jonathan Gibson	"	"		
"	John Hawkins	"			
"	George Hamilton	"	"	"	

Rank.	Names.	Served between 1 Aug 1780 and 1 Jan 1782	Served between 1 Jan 1782 and 1 Jan 1783	Served between 1 Jan and 15 Nov 1783	Served between 15 Nov 1783 and 10 July 1784
	Officers Whose Accounts Were Settled.				
Capt.	George Armstrong	"			
"	Richard Anderson	"	"	"	"
Lieut.	William Adams	"	"	"	
"	William Bruff		"	"	
"	Thos. Beatty		"	"	
"	Henry Baldwin	"	"	"	
Capt.	John Sprig Belt	"	"		
Lieut.	Joshua Burgess		"		
Capt.	Lloyd Beall	"	"	"	
"	Joseph Burgess				
Maj.	Benj. Brooks	"	"		
Capt.	Richard Bird	"	"		
Lieut.	Basil Burgess	"	"	"	
Capt.	Michael Boyer	"			
"	Charles Baltzell	"			
"	Jacob Brice	"		"	
Lieut.	John Brevett	"	"	"	
Maj.	Wm. Dent Beall	"	"		
Lieut.	Joseph Britten				
Capt.	William Beatty	"			
Lieut.	Henry Baker	"	"		
"	Malachi Bonham	"	"	"	
"	Saml. B. Beall		"		
Capt.	Perry Benson		"	"	
Lieut.	William Bruce	"	"	"	
"	Henry Clements	"	"	"	
"	Joseph Cross	"	"	"	
"	Edmond Compton	"	"	"	
"	John Carey	"	"		
"	Henry H. Chapman		"	"	
"	Jacob Crawford	"	"		
Capt.	Robert Chesley	"			
Lieut.	John Colegate				
"	Walter Dyer		"	"	
Surgeon	Willm. A. Dashiell				
Maj.	John Davidson	"	"		
"	John Deane	"			
Lieut.	Thomas A. Dyson		"	"	
Capt.	Rezin Davis			"	
Lieut.	Isaac Duval	"			
Surgeon	Levin Denwood	"	"	"	
Lieut.	Robert Denny	"	"		

Rank.	Names.	Served between 1 Aug 1780, and 1 Jan 1782	Served between 1 Jan 1782 and 1 Jan 1783	Served between 1 Jan and 15 Nov 1783	Served between 15 Nov 1783 and 10 July 1784
Lieut.	Saml. Edminston	"	"	"	
Lt. Col.	John Eccleston	"	"	"	
Lieut.	Elijah Evans	"			
Capt.	James Ewing	"	"		
Dr.	John L. Elbert		"		
Capt.	Edward Edgerly	"			
Lieut.	Benj. Fickle	"	"	"	
"	Hezekiah Foard	"	"	"	
Lt. Col.	Uriah Forrest	"			
" "	Benj. Foard	"			
Lieut.	James Gould	"			
"	Nicholas Gassaway	"	"	"	
Capt.	John Gist				
"	James W. Gray	"	"	"	
"	John Gale	"	"	"	
Col.	John Gunby	"	"	"	
Lieut.	Wm. Goldsborough			"	
"	Henry Gassaway			"	
Capt.	John Gassaway			"	
"	Henry Gaither	"	"		
Lt. Col.	J. E. Howard	"	"		
Maj.	Henry Hardman	"	"		
Capt.	John A. Hamilton	"	"		
Lieut.	Edward Hamilton		"		
"	Robt. Halkerson	"	"	"	
Capt.	Levin Handy				
Lieut.	John Hartshorn	"	"	"	
"	Elihu Hall	"			
"	Arthur Harris	"		"	
"	Rignal Hillary		"	'	
"	Philip Hill	"	"	"	
"	Samuel Hanson	"	"	"	
"	Willm. Hanson		"	'	
"	John Hamilton	"	"		
"	Isaac Hanson	"	"		
Col.	Josias C. Hall	"			
Doct.	Ezekiel Haynie	"	"	"	
Capt.	Adam Hoops	"			
Lieut.	George Jacobs	"			
"	Adam Jamison				
Capt.	John C. Jones	"	"	"	
Surgeon	William Kilty	"	"	"	
"	Saml. Y. Keene	"	"	"	
Lieut.	John Lynn		"	"	"

during the War of the American Revolution, 1775–83.

Rank.	Names.	Served between 1 Aug 1780 and 1 Jan 1782.	Served between 1 Jan 1782 and 1 Jan 1783.	Served between 1 Jan and 15 Nov 1783.	Served between 15 Nov 1783 and 10 July 1784.
Capt.	Henry Lyles	"			
"	Thos. H. Luckett	"			
Lieut.	David Luckett		"	"	
Maj.	John Lynch		"		
Lieut.	Willm. Lemar	"	"		
Capt.	David Lynn	"	"	"	
Maj.	Thos. Lansdale	"	"	"	
Capt.	James M. Lingan	"	"		
"	Walker Muse	"	"	"	
"	Thos. Mason	"	"		
Lieut.	John Maguire				
"	David Morgan				
Capt.	Christian Myers				
Lieut.	Zedk. Moore	"	"	"	
"	Nicholas Mangers	"			
"	Lawrence Myers				
"	Mark McPherson	"	"	"	
Capt.	Jonathan Morris		"	"	
"	John Mitchell	"	"	"	
"	Saml. McPherson	"	"	"	
"	Jacob Norris		"	"	
Ensign	John Nelson	"			
Capt.	Edward Oldham	"	"	"	
"	Christn. Orendorff		"		
"	Benj. Price	"	"	"	
Col.	Thomas Price				
Lieut.	Thomas Price	"	"	"	
Surg.	Richard Pindell	"	"	"	
Lieut.	Willm. Pendergast			"	
Capt.	Edward Prall	"	"		
Ensign	Jacob Reybold				
Lieut.	Willm. Rasin	"	"	"	
Capt.	Willm. Reiley	"	"	"	
Lieut.	Joshua Rutledge				
Capt.	Christr. Richmond	"	"	"	
Lieut.	Thomas Rown	"	"	"	
Capt.	Francis Revelly	"	"	"	
"	Phillip Reed		"	"	
Lt. Col.	Nathl. Ramsey				
Lieut.	Jas. Jno. Skinner	"	"		
"	Edwd. M. Smith	"	"		
Capt.	John Smith		"	"	
"	James Somervill	"	"		
"	Jonathan Sellman	"	"		

Rank.	Names.	Served between 1 Aug 1780 and 1 Jan 1782.	Served between 1 Jan 1782 and 1 Jan 1783.	Served between 1 Jan and 15 Nov 1783.	Served between 15 Nov 1783 and 10 July 1784.
Lieut.	John Sears	"	"	"	
Capt.	Edward Spurrier	"	"		
Lieut.	Willm. Smoot	"	"		
Genl.	Willm. Smallwood	"	"	"	
Lieut.	Willm. Stoddard	"	"		
Capt.	Joseph Smith	"			
"	John Smith, (6 Regt.)	"	"		
"	Alex. Truman	"	"		
Lt. Col.	Edward Tillard				
Lieut.	James Toole				
"	John Trueman	"	"		
Capt.	A. Tannehill				
Lieut.	Willm. Towson		"	"	
Surg. Mate	William Watts	"	"	"	
Capt.	William Wilmott	"	"		
Lieut.	William Woolford	"			
Capt.	Saml. T. Wright				
Lt. Col.	Lodwick Weltner	"	"		
Brig. Gen.	O. H. Williams		"		
Lieut.	Francis Ware	"	"	"	
Lt. Col.	Thos. Woolford	"	"		
Lieut.	Nathan Wright	"	"	"	
Surgn.	Walter Warfield	"	"	"	
Lieut.	Basil Waring		"	"	
"	George Winchester	"	"		
Surg.	Gerard Wood	"	"		
Capt.	James Winchester	"	"	"	
"	Richard Waters	"	"		
Lt. Col.	Levin Winder	"	"	"	
Lieut.	Gassaway Watkins		"		
Capt.	Lilburn Williams		"		

PRIVATES.

Rank.	Names.	Remarks.	Served between 1 Aug '80 and 1 Jan '82.	Served between 1 Jan '82 and 1 Jan '83.	Served between 1 Jan '83 and 15 Nov '83.	Served between 15 Nov '83 and 10 July '84.
Private	Adam Adams	Dischd. 16 May '81	"			
"	Ignatius Adams			"	"	"
"	George Abbott	" 24 May '81	"			
"	John Alvey			"	"	"
"	Thos. G. Alvey	" 24 Apl '81	"			
"	John Appleby			"	"	"
"	Danl. Anderson	Died 15 Apl '81	"			

during the War of the American Revolution, 1775-83.

Rank.	Names.	Remarks.	Served between 1 Aug '80 and 1 Jan '82.	Served between 1 Jan '82 and 1 Jan '83.	Served between 1 Jan '83 and 15 Nov '83.	Served between 15 Nov '83 and 10 July '84.
Private	James Allen		"	"	"	
"	Thos. Ayres		"	"	"	
"	Emanuel Allen		"	"	"	
"	John Andrews		"	"	"	
"	William Aythur		"	"	"	
"	John Armstrong		"	"	"	
"	John Ashmow		"	"	"	
Serjt.	Cuthburt Able	Dischd. 1 Feb '83	"	"		
Corpl.	John Adams		"	"	"	
Private	Thomas Arthur	Time expires 1 Apl '83	"	"		
Drum.	John Auber	Invalided	"	"	"	
Private	John Ashbury		"	"	"	
"	John Armstrong, 2nd		"	"	"	
"	Harris Austen		"	"	"	
"	Thomas Adams		"	"	"	
"	Josias Alvey	Dischd. 24 May '82	"	"		
"	James Ashley		"	"	"	
"	Jacob Adams	Died 24 Mch '83	"	"		
"	William Absolom	[Dischd. 29 Nov '83]	"	"	"	
"	John Anderson		"	"	"	
"	Traverse Alvey			"	"	
"	Nathan Aldridge			"	"	
"	Levin Abbott		"	"	"	
"	John Adams, 2nd			"	"	
"	John Abrahams			"	"	
"	Benjamin Askew			"	"	"
"	John Alsop	[Dischd. 29 Nov '83]		"	"	
Serjt.	Joseph Allen			"	"	
Private	James Anderson					
"	James Anderson					
"	John Anderson				"	
Fifer	Daniel Basil		"	"	"	
Private	John Baker	Dischd. 3 May '81	"			
"	George Bateman	" 8 Jan '82	"	"		
"	John Brookbank		"	"	"	
"	Levi Burk	" May '83	"	"		
Serjt.	Thos. Buckley		"	"	"	
Private	William Brooks	" 18 June '81	"			
"	Joseph Burch		"	"	"	
"	Thos. Bishop	[Dischd. 29 Nov'83]	"	"	"	
Corpl.	Wm. Braithwait		"	"	"	
Private	Barrock Butt		"	"	"	
"	Thomas Butt		"	"	"	
"	Edward Butt	Died 15 Mch '81	"			

Rank.	Names.	Remarks.	Served between 1 Aug '80 and 1 Jan '82.	Served between 1 Jan '82 and 1 Jan '83.	Served between 1 Jan '83 and 15 Nov '83.	Served between 15 Nov '83 and 10 July '84.
Fifer	Frederick Bennet		"	"	"	
Private	Richd. Blansford		"	"	"	
Fifer	Solomon Brittenham		"	"	"	
Private	Levi Buttons	[Disch. 18 Sept '83]	"	"	"	
"	Levin Bramble	Died 13 July '81	"			
"	John Blades		"	"	"	
Corpl.	Thomas Brown	Killed 8 Sept '81	"			
Private	John Brown, 1st		"	"	"	
"	Richard Butler		"	"	"	
"	John Barret, 1st	Dischd. 1 May '81	"			
"	Thomas Barcklay		"	"	"	
"	Basil Brown		"	"	"	
"	George Brown	Dischd. 24 Apl '81	"			
"	Zachariah Burck	" 12 " '81	"			
Corpl.	Leonard Bean	" 12 " '81	"			
Private	Gabriel Brand	" 12 Jan '82	"	"		
"	John Beane	" 22 " '82	"	"		
"	Thomas Bird	" 13 " '82	"	"		
"	Benjamin Boyd		"	"	"	
"	John Blair	Dischd. 15 Jan '82	"	"		
"	Peter Bochard		"	"	"	
"	Thomas Bailey	[Dischd. 11 Aug '83]	"	"	"	
"	John Buckley		"	"	"	
"	Joshua Barret		"	"	"	
Corpl.	George Bradley	Died 31 Nov '82	"	"		
"	William Bruff		"	"	"	
Private	Peter Bowler	Dischd. 1 May '81	"			
"	Joseph Bautcheby		"	"	"	
Fifer	Robert Bowen		"	"	"	
Private	Philip Bailey	Died 20 Feb '83	"	"		
Drum.	John Beach	" 15 Dec '82	"	"		
"	John Buchanon		"	"	"	
Private	Daniel Buckley		"	"	"	
"	David Bramble		"	"	"	
"	James L. Brass		"	"	"	
"	John Burnet		"	"	"	
"	Perry Bantham		"	"	"	
Fifer	John Brent	Died 14 May '81	"			
Private	George Blackham	[Disch. 11 Aug '83]	"	"	"	
"	James Barron		"	"	"	
Serjt.	James Bailey	Died 27 Apl '81	"			
Private	Abraham Bowen		"	"	"	
"	John Bantham		"	"	"	
"	Solomon Barrett		"	"	"	
"	James Burk, 1st	[Dischd. 29 Nov '83]	"	"	"	

during the War of the American Revolution, 1775-83.

RANK.	NAMES.	REMARKS.	SERVED BETWEEN 1 AUG '80 AND 1 JAN '82.	SERVED BETWEEN 1 JAN '82 AND 1 JAN '83.	SERVED BETWEEN 1 JAN '83 AND 15 NOV '83.	SERVED BETWEEN 15 NOV '83 AND 10 JULY '84.
Serjt.	John Brown, 2nd	[Dischd. 29 Nov '83]	"	"	"	
Private	George Bowers	Died 1 May '81				
"	Henry Billup		"	"	"	
"	Thomas Bear		"	"	"	
"	George Bombgardiner		"	"	"	
Corpl.	Benj. Burch, 2nd	Dischd. 19 Jan '83	"	"		
Private	Thomas Brady	" 24 June '81	"			
"	Joseph Blaze		"	"	"	
"	Joseph Botts	[Dischd. 29 Nov '81]	"	"	"	
Serjt.	Moses Barney	Dischd. 1 Aug '81	"			
Private	Richard Boone	Died 15 Mch '81	"			
"	Joshua Brown	Dischd. 23 Apl '81	"			
"	Josiah Burgess	" 19 Apl '81	"			
"	Humphrey Becket		"	"	"	
"	Lawrence Bronham		"	"	"	
"	George Brown	Dischd. 23 Apl '81	"			
"	George Buck		"	"	"	
"	Martin Bowles		"	"	"	
"	Abijah Buxton		"	"	"	
Fifer	Jesse Barnett	Dischd. 5 Aug '83	"	"	"	
Private	Thomas Bowser		"	"	"	
"	James Barber	[Dischd. 29 Nov '83]	"	"	"	
"	Daniel Bulger		"	"	"	
Corpl.	Jesse Boswell	Time expires 5 Aug '83	"	"	"	
Private	Joseph Barton		"	"		
"	John Brewer	Died 17 July '82	"	"		
"	John Branson		"	"	"	
"	Jeremiah Brown	Dischd. 1 Aug '83	"	"	"	
"	Richard Biddle		"	"	"	
"	James Bigwood		"	"	"	
"	Peter Bushell	Dischd. 6 Sept '83	"	"	"	
"	Thomas Baker		"	"	"	
"	James Bailess		"	"	"	
	John Berriman		"	"	"	
	James Brannon		"	"	"	
	John Brion	Transd. Inv'ds Aug '81	"			
	John Biggs	Died 1 July '83	"	"	"	
	Jacob Blake		"	"	"	
Corpl.	John Brown, 3rd		"	"	"	
Serjt.	Benjamin Burch	Died 3 Nov '83	"	"	"	
Private	Gassaway Braziers	Dischd. 28 Jan '81	"			
"	George Bough		"	"	"	
"	Samuel Boswell		"	"	"	
"	William Battin		"	"	"	
"	Zachariah Berry	Died 6 Mch '84	"	"	"	"

Rank.	Names.	Remarks.	Served between 1 Aug '80 and 1 Jan '82.	Served between 1 Jan '82 and 1 Jan '83.	Served between 1 Jan '83 and 15 Nov '83.	Served between 15 Nov '83 and 10 July '84.
Private	John Burns		"	"	"	
"	Benjamin Bough		"	"	"	
"	James Bryan	Killed 15 Sept '81	"			
"	John Bowdy		"	"	"	
"	John Boody	[Dischd. 18 Sept '83]	"	"	"	
"	John Britton	[Dischd. 29 Nov '83]	"	"	"	
"	Christian Boss		"	"	"	
"	John Briley		"	"	"	
"	Benjamin Belcher		"	"	"	
"	Thomas Burck, 2nd	[Dischd. 29 Nov '83]	"	"	"	
Serjt.	Nathaniel Bailey		"	"	"	"
Private	Andrew Bramble		"	"	"	
"	John Baxter		"	"	"	
"	John Bailey		"	"	"	
"	William Burgess	Time expires 16 [Aug '83	"	"	"	
"	Joel Baker		"	"	"	
"	James Bowen		"	"	"	
"	William Brady		"	"	"	
"	George Belfast		"	"	"	
"	Charles Buckley	[Dischd. 29 Nov' 83]	"	"	"	
Serjt.	John Brady		"	"	"	
Private	James Barrow	Trans. Inv'ds 1 Apl '82				
"	Archibald Butt	" to N. C. Line 28 [Apl '82		"		
Corpl.	Peter Boyer	Died 15 Jan '82		"		
"	Danl. Brumagum					
Private	Presstly Bruington				"	"
"	John Blair, 1st	Invd. 10 June '83			"	"
"	Henry Bradly				"	"
Corpl.	John Burgess				"	"
Private	James Bell	[Dischd. 31 Aug '83]			"	"
"	John Bell, 2nd				"	"
"	Henry Barnes				"	"
Serjt.	John Bond				"	"
Private	Edward Burns				"	"
"	Richard Burk				"	"
"	John Barlow				"	"
"	James Burk, 2nd	Invd. 15 Nov '83			"	"
	Thos. Bilingham	[Dischd. 29 Nov '83]			"	"
"	Wm. Boling				"	"
"	John Barret, 1st	[Dischd. 15 Aug '83]			"	"
"	John Bailey, 2nd				"	"
"	George Baker				"	"
"	George Bowers	see back	"	"	"	

Rank.	Names.	Remarks.	Served between 1 Aug '80 and 1 Jan '82.	Served between 1 Jan '82 and 1 Jan '83.	Served between 1 Jan '83 and 15 Nov '83.	Served between 15 Nov '83 and 10 July '84
Private	Thomas Baxter	Died 24 Sept '83	"	"	"	
"	James Barber, 2nd				"	
"	James Blewer	Invd. 1 Mch '82	"	"		
"	John Butcher	" 1 Aug '82	"	"		
Drum.	James Bailey	Died 1 Aug '82		"		
Private	Nathan Bateman	Killed 18 June '81	"			
"	John Bennet	Invd. 15 Nov '82			"	
Private	William Clary		"	"	"	
"	David Cole		"	"	"	
"	John Carroll	Died 13 Jan '82	"	"		
Fifer	James Cholard		"	"	"	
	Wm. Clements, 2nd		"	"	"	
Private	Michael Cole	Died 16 Aug '81	"			
"	Thomas Campher		"	"	"	
"	Patk. Cavenough		"	"	"	
Serjt.	William Cata	Died 18 June '81	"			
Private	Hugh Cane	" 19 March '81	"			
"	David Conner	[Dischd. 29 Nov '83]	"	"	"	
"	Morris Citizen	Died 15 May '81	"			
"	Wm. Chatland		"	"	"	
"	Wm. Cutler	[Dischd. 18 Sept '83]	"	"	"	
Corpl.	John Campher	Killed 8 Sept '81	"			
Private	Hampton Coursey		"	"	"	
"	Wm. Conner, 1st		"	"	"	
Corpl.	George Childs		"	"	"	
Private	Daniel Clancy	[Dischd. 18 Sept '83]	"	"	"	
"	John Craig		"	"	"	
Corpl.	Bartin Cicil	Died 13 Jan '82	"	"		
Private	Charles Clements		"	"	"	
"	Luke Carter		"	"	"	
"	John Clegget	Died 25 Apl '81	"			
"	Thos. Clark, 1st		"	"	"	
Drum.	Hezekiah Carr		"	"	"	
Private	John Courts	Time expires 16 Apl ['83	"	"		
"	Michael Clark, 2nd		"	"	"	
Serjt.	John Colin		"	"	"	
Private	Thos. B. Clements	Died 1 Aug '83	"	"	"	
"	Wm. Carter, 2nd		"	"	"	
"	Emanl. Carthagene		"	"	"	
	Abrahm. Catchsides		"	"	"	
Fifer	Thomas Clinton	[Dischd. 29 Nov '83]	"	"	"	
Private	Michael Callahan		"	"	"	
"	Asaph Colegate		"	"	"	

Rank.	Names.	Remarks.	Served between 1 Aug '80 and 1 Jan '82.	Served between 1 Jan '82 and 1 Jan '83.	Served between 1 Jan '83 and 15 Nov '83.	Served between 15 Nov '83 and 10 July '84.
Private	Andrew Crummy		"	"	"	
"	John Carr	Died 25 Feb '83	"	"		
Fifer	Robert Cormick		"	"	"	
Private	John Carroll, 2nd		"	"	"	
"	Charles Couch	Died 24 Aug '81	"			
"	Augustin Cann		"	"	"	
"	Thomas Carney		"	"	"	
Fifer	Michael Clancey		"	"	"	
Private	Thomas Cahoe, Sr.		"	"	"	
Fifer	Thomas Cahoe, Jr.		"	"	"	
Private	Benjamin Cleaver		"	"	"	
"	Christopher Cusick		"	"	"	
"	Robert Clanahan		"	"	"	
"	William Cook		"	"	"	
"	William Crail		"	"	"	
"	Darby Crowley		"	"	"	
Serjt.	John Cheshire	Killed 18 June '81	"			
Private	William Casey		"	"	"	
"	Adam Crow	Dischd. 28 Apl '81	"			
"	Willm. Cummings		"	"	"	
Serjt.	Aquilla Chitham		"	"	"	
Corpl.	Owen Cavey	Died 16 Feb '81	"			
Private	Ignatius Cumpton	" 13 Oct '81	"			
"	James Curren	Dischd. 1 Mch '83	"	"		
"	Stephen Carr	Died 13 Oct '81	"			
Fifer	Edward Clancey	[Dischd. 10 Sept '83]	"	"	"	
Private	John Cochren	Killed 15 Mch '81	"			
Serjt.	William Collis		"	"	"	
Private	Jonathan Chub	Dischd. 1 July '83	"	"	"	
"	Wm. Chapman	[Dischd. 11 Sept '83] Time expires 1 May '83	"	"		
"	Henry Crook	Invalided	"	"	"	
"	William Cox		"	"	"	
"	Henry Craine		"	"	"	
"	George Clark	[Dischd. 7 Sept '83]	"	"	"	
"	Thomas Cooper	Died 1 April '82	"	"		
Corpl.	Bennet H. Clements	Dischd. 23 July '83	"	"	"	
Private	James Casey		"	"	"	"
"	Lewis Cuningham		"	"	"	
"	Calothel Carmile		"	"	"	
Fifer	David Crady		"	"	"	
Private	Michael Casner		"	"	"	
"	Samuel Callahan		"	"	"	
"	John Cooper, 1st	[Dischd. 11 Aug '83]	"	"	"	
"	Wm. Clements, 1st	Dischd. 31 July '83	"	"	"	

during the War of the American Revolution, 1775-83.   529

Rank.	Names.	Remarks.	Served between 1 Aug '80 and 1 Jan '82.	Served between 1 Jan '82 and 1 Jan '83.	Served between 1 Jan '83 and 15 Nov '83.	Served between 15 Nov '83 and 10 July '84.
Private	Kendel Cobb	Died 10 Nov '81	"			
"	Thomas Cannady			"	"	"
"	John Clancy, 2nd	[Dischd. 11 Aug '83]			"	
"	Valentine Clapper			"	"	"
"	Charles Cooper			"	"	"
"	George Coins			"	"	"
"	Benjamin Cole	Dischd. 1 Apl '83		"	"	
"	John Connelly, 1st	" 1 Apl '83		"	"	
"	Isom Coleman			"	"	"
"	Wm. Carter, 1st			"	"	"
"	James Crozier			"	"	"
"	Peter Carberry	Invalided 15 Nov '83		"	"	"
"	Saml. Chappell			"	"	"
"	Michael Curtis			"	"	"
"	John Cole, 1st			"	"	"
"	Jacob Collins			"	"	"
"	James Chambers	[Dischd. 29 Nov '83]		"	"	"
"	John Carson			"	"	"
"	John Collins			"	"	"
"	Thomas Clark, 2nd			"	"	"
"	John Curl			"	"	"
"	John Cleverdence			"	"	"
"	Arthur Coffins			"	"	"
"	Joshua Cox	[Dischd. 29 Nov '83]		"	"	"
"	Edward Chambers	[Dischd. 29 Nov '83]		"	"	"
"	James Chard	Dischd. 1 Aug '83		"	"	"
"	James Cochran	[Dischd. 29 Nov '83]		"	"	"
"	John Cannon			"	"	"
"	Thomas Compton			"	"	"
Serjt.	James Collins	[Dischd. 29 Nov '83]		"	"	"
Private	William Cork			"	"	"
"	George Carney	[Dischd. 29 Nov '83]		"	"	"
"	Robert Carns	[Dischd. 29 Nov '83]		"	"	"
"	Mathias Cyphart			"	"	"
Corpl.	James Clements			"	"	"
Private	William Coe			"	"	"
Corpl.	Elijah Cockendall	Died 18 July '82		"	"	
Private	John Crosby, 1st	" 24 July '83		"	"	
"	James Crasberry			"	"	"
"	William Camm			"	"	"
Fifer	Zachariah Clark				"	"
Private	Samuel Clark			"		"
"	Matthew Carty				"	"
"	Michael Clark, 1st	[Dischd. 18 Sept '83]			"	"
"	Dennis Cragan	[Dischd. 18 Sept '83]	"	"	"	

Rank.	Names.	Remarks.	Served between 1 Aug '80 and 1 Jan '82.	Served between 1 Jan '82 and 1 Jan '83.	Served between 1 Jan '83 and 15 Nov '83.	Served between 15 Nov '83 and 10 July '84.
Private	James Craighton	[Dischd. 29 Nov '83]		"	"	
"	Robert Campbell		"	"	"	
"	Edward Cosgrove		"	"	"	
"	Joseph Cooley	Dischd. 9 Jan '82	"	"		
"	Jeremiah Carter			"	"	"
Fifer	Joseph Clancey			"	"	
Private	William Cotter			"	"	
"	Thomas Channon			"	"	
Serjt.	Thomas Craig		"	"	"	
Private	Edward Cantwell	Dischd. 24 Sept '83		"	"	
"	John Campbell, 2nd	[Dischd. 7 Sept '83]	"	"	"	
"	Joseph Cluly	[Dischd. 29 Nov '83]		"	"	
"	John Cotter	[Dischd. 7 Sept '83]		"	"	
"	Thomas Countiss			"	"	
"	William Coleman	[Dischd. 23 Sept '83]		"	"	
"	George Chambers	[Dischd. 7 Sept '83]		"	"	
"	John Connelly, 2nd		"	"	"	
"	John Callahan			"	"	
"	James Countiss			"	"	
"	Willm. Carlin			"	"	
"	John Cooper, 2nd			"	"	
"	Christopher Coy	[Corpl., Dischd. 12 Aug '83]		"	"	
"	Michael Cary			"		
"	John Clineslought			"	"	"
"	John Conner				"	
"	Wm. Connelly				"	"
"	Levin Clarage				"	"
"	Samuel Crowell				"	
Corpl.	John Clancey, 2nd	[Dischd. 16 Aug '83]	"	"	"	
Private	James Coen	[Dischd. 12 Aug '83]			"	
"	John Charles	Dischd. 15 Mch '83	"	"		
"	William Colin				"	
"	William Coursey		"	"	"	
"	Patrick Connor	Invalided 1 Oct '81	"			
"	James Crawford		"	"	"	
"	Willm. Civill	Died on 15 June '83 on Jas. Isld.	"	"	"	
"	Timothy Cahill			"	"	
"	Christian Close	Died 1 Mch '82		"		
"	Jacob Carnant	" 15 Sept 81	"			
"	John Carter	Killed 8 Sept '81	"			
"	Owen Coffield				"	
"	George Collins	Dischd. 15 June '81	"			
"	Byan Carroll	" 1 June '83			"	
"	Michael Coyle	" 1 June '81	"			

during the War of the American Revolution, 1775-83.

Rank.	Names.	Remarks.	Served between 1 Aug '80 and 1 Jan '82.	Served between 1 Jan '82 and 1 Jan '83.	Served between 1 Jan '83 and 15 Nov '83.	Served between 15 Nov '83 and 10 July '84.
Private	Edward Cain	Invalided 15 Nov '83			"	
"	Joseph Crouch				"	
"	Thomas Cardiff	Invalided			"	
Serjt.	Charles Dawkins	Dischd. 5 Apl '81	"			
Drum.	Dennis Dunning		"	"	"	
Private	John Dixon		"	"	"	
"	Francis Demar		"	"	"	
"	William Dorch	Dischd. 6 Aug '83	"	"	"	
"	Henry Dixon	" 8 Feb '81	"			
"	John Denson		"	"	"	
"	George Dixon		"	"	"	
Corpl.	Willm. Dillon	Dischd. 2 May '82	"	"		
Private	John Dyer		"	"	"	
"	Aquilla Deaver		"	"	"	
"	Luke Dimpsey		"	"	"	
"	Thomas Drudge	Died 10 Apl '83	"	"		
"	John Donovan		"			
"	William Downs	[Dischd. 9 Sept '83]	"	"	"	
"	Thomas Doyle	Dischd. 4 Feb '81	"		.	
"	Peter Degagoone		"	"	"	
Corpl.	James Daffin	Dischd. 5 Apl '81	"			
Serjt.	Edmund Dougherty	Died 15 Jan '81	"			
Private	Francis Dunnington	" 23 Apl '83	"	"		
"	James Doyle		"	"		
"	John Duhague	Died 1 Dec '82	"	"		
"	John Downey		"	"	"	
"	Elijah Deane	Dischd. 31 May '81	"			
"	Robert Davis	" 1 May '81	"			
"	Richard Duvall		"	"	"	
Serjt.	Patrick Doran		"	"	"	
Drum.	John Denoon		"	"	"	
Private	James Devericks		"	"	"	
"	George Dewitt		"	"	"	
"	Robert Dunken		"	"	"	
Serjt.	Samuel Denny	Dischd. 2 Mch '81	"			
"	Samuel Davis		"	"	"	
Private	James Dyer		"	"	"	
"	John Delany, (or Delanaway)		"	"	"	
"	Mathias Dyche		"	"	"	
"	John Deakins	[Dischd. 12 Aug '83]	"	"	"	
"	Edward Domonick	Dischd. 1 July '83	"	"	"	
"	Joseph Donoho		"	"	"	
"	James Davidson		"	"	"	
"	William Deaver	Dischd. 7 Mch '82	"	"		

532   *Records of Maryland Troops in the Continental Service*

Rank.	Names.	Remarks.	Served between 1 Aug '80 and 1 Jan '82	Served between 1 Jan '82 and 1 Jan '83	Served between 1 Jan '83 and 15 Nov '83	Served between 15 Nov '83 and 10 July '84
Private	James Due		"	"	"	
"	William Devine		"	"	"	
"	James Dyer, 2nd	Dischd. 1 Sept '82	"	"		
"	John Donogan	Died 25 Jan '83	"	"		
"	John Davis, 1st		"	"	"	
"	William Dawson	[Dischd. 29 Nov '83]	"	"	"	
"	Barnaba Dougharty	Invalided 3 Nov '83	"	"	"	
"	Jacob Duddera	[Dischd. 29 Nov '83]	"	"	"	
"	Terrance Duffee	[Serjt., Dischd. 29 Nov '83]	"	"	"	
"	John Deane	Died 15 Dec '81	"			
"	John Dobson		"	"	"	
"	James Driver		"	"	"	
Serjt.	Thomas Duffee		"	"	"	
Private	Thomas Davis, 1st	[Dischd. 29 Nov '83]	"	"	"	
"	Abraham Dugan		"	"	"	
"	Thomas Dickeson		"	"	"	
"	Charles Deane		"	"	"	
"	Richard Dolvin		"	"	"	
"	Richard Dunby	Died 8 May '83	"	"	"	
"	Willm. Derrington		"	"	"	
"	James Dawson	[Dischd. 18 Sept '83]	"	"	"	
"	George Dunken				"	
"	Patrick Dennison		"	"	"	
"	Joseph Deford	Dischd. 8 Mch '81	"			
"	George Dice		"	"	"	
"	Alexander Downey		"	"	"	
"	Richard Dixon	Died 27 Dec '82	"	"		
"	Francis Dewist	[Dischd. 1 Sept '83]	"	"	"	"
"	James Dowden		"	"	"	"
"	Buto Devo	Invd. 4 Apl '82	"	"		
Serjt.	Francis Duffee			"		
"	Jacob Doyle, (or Doyne)			"	"	
Private	Isaac Dunken			"	"	
"	George Dadisman			"	"	
"	Basil Dorsey			"	"	
"	Robert Dean			"	"	
Corpl.	Isaac Deale	[Dischd. 29 Nov '83]		"	"	
"	William Dunn			"	"	
Private	Benj. Donnelly	[Dischd. 29 Nov '83]		"	"	
"	Wm. Devericks				"	"
"	Matthew Doley				"	
Fifer	Samuel Davis				"	
Private	Jeremiah Driscoll					
"	George Dyer		"	"	"	
"	John Dent	Invalided 1 Apl '83	"	"		

during the War of the American Revolution, 1775–83.

Rank.	Names.	Remarks.	Served between 1 Aug '80 and 1 Jan '82.	Served between 1 Jan '82 and 1 Jan '83.	Served between 1 Jan '83 and 15 Nov '83.	Served between 15 Nov '83 and 10 July '84.
Serjt.	John Dove	Dischd. 31 Jan '83	"	"		
Private	Benj. Dominick	Killed 8 Sept '81	"			
"	James Dennison	Dischd. 26 July '82		"		
"	Richard Downs	Dischd. 25 Apl '81	"			
"	Pearce Deacon	Died 1 Nov '82		"		
"	William Day	Dischd. 22 July '83			"	
"	John Davis	Died 12 Aug '82		"		
"	James Davidson	Dischd. 20 Apl '81	"			
"	Thomas Dutton	Killed 8 Sept '81	"			
"	Charles Davis				"	
Private	Henry Evis		"	"	"	
"	Edward Ellicot		"	"	"	
Serjt.	Peregrine Evins		"	"	"	
Corpl.	Bartholomew Esom		"	"	"	
Fifer	Michael Ellis	Dischd. 6 June '81	"			
Private	Thomas Evans, 2nd			"	"	
"	Thomas Ellicot, 2nd		"	"	"	
"	William Ellis	Killed 26 June '81	"			
"	Edward Evans, 1st		"	"	"	
"	William Evans	Invalided 15 Nov '83	"	"	"	
Serjt.	Thomas Edwards		"	"	"	
Private	Jarvis Eccleston		"	"	"	
"	Joseph Ellicot		"	"	"	
F. M.	George Elins		"	"	"	
Private	John Elliot, 1st		"	"	"	
Serjt.	Edward Evans, 2nd		"	"	"	
Private	William Elkins		"	"	"	
"	Thomas Ellis, 1st		"	"	"	
"	Enoch Ennis		"	"	"	
"	Leonard Ennis		"	"	"	
"	John Ennis		"	"	"	
"	John Edwards	[Dischd. 18 Sept '83]	"	"	"	
"	Peter Equidowney	[Dischd. 29 Nov '83]	"	"	"	
"	James Evans		"	"	"	
"	Thomas Elliott, 1st	[Dischd. 29 Nov '83]	"	"	"	
Corpl.	Samuel Evans		"	"	"	
Private	Thomas Evans, 1st	[Dischd. 24 Sept '83]	"	"	"	
"	James Ervine			"	"	
Fifer	Nicholas Ellicott			"	"	
Private	William Eagle			"	"	
Corpl.	Thos. Ellison, (or Allison)				"	
Private	Francis Ensley				"	
"	Heathcoat Edward				"	
"	Emanuel Ebbs		"	"	"	

Rank.	Names.	Remarks.	Served between 1 Aug '80 and 1 Jan '82.	Served between 1 Jan '82 and 1 Jan '83.	Served between 1 Jan '83 and 15 Nov '83.	Served between 15 Nov '83 and 10 July '84.
Private	Mcl. Evans	Dischd. 25 Oct '81	"			
"	Thomas Ellison	" 1 Jan '83			"	
Serjt.	John Edwards	" 1 June '81	"			
Private	Jacob Flora		"	"	"	
"	Francis Fairbrother		"	"	"	
"	John Fransway		"	"	"	
"	Stephen Fresh		"	"	"	
"	Joseph Fowler		"	"	"	
"	William Fisher	Dischd. 21 May '81	"			
"	Jonathan Fowler	Died Sept '83	"	"	"	
"	George Filleson	Invalided 6 June '83	"	"	"	
"	Henry Fisher, 2nd		"	"	"	
"	James Farrell		"	"	"	
"	James Fitzgerald	Dischd. 3 Apl '81	"			
"	Francis Freeman		"		"	
"	John Ferguson	Dischd. 1 Apl '82	"	"		
"	Edward Furrener		"	"	"	
"	James Foster	Died 30 June '81	"			
"	Alexander Francis		"	"	"	
"	Richard Freemane	Dischd. 12 Jan '82	"	"		
"	William R. Franklin	" 28 July '83	"	"	"	
"	John Farrell	" 14 Feb '83	"	"		
"	Richard Farraby		"	"	"	
"	Frederick Flinn		"	"	"	
"	Stafford Fosdale		"	"	"	
"	Peter Fountain	Dischd. 15 May '81	"			
Drum.	Benjamin Folliot	Died 17 June '81	"			
Private	Rigby Foster		"	"	"	
Serjt.	William Foreman		"	"	"	
Drum.	William Farrell		"	"	"	
Private	John Fulham		"	"	"	
"	Edward Flowers	Died 1 June '81	"			
"	Mark Foster	[Dischd. 7 Sept '83]	"	"	"	
Serjt.	Benj. Fitzgerald	[Dischd. 11 Sept '83]	"	"	"	
Private	Absalom Fardo		"	"	"	
"	John M. Funner	Invalided 15 Nov '83	"	"	"	
"	Doras Filmot	Dischd. 5 May '81	"			
"	Nicholas Fitzgerald	" 2 May '81	"			
"	Moses Foster		"	"	"	
Serjt.	Saml. Filson		"	"	"	
"	Stephen Fluharty		"	"	"	
Private	Dennis Flanagan	[Dischd. 29 Nov '83]	"	"	"	
"	Emanl. Farrara					
"	Philip Fisher	Invalided. [Dischd. 29 Nov '83]	"	"	"	

Rank.	Names.	Remarks.	Served between 1 Aug '80 and 1 Jan '82.	Served between 1 Jan '82 and 1 Jan '83.	Served between 1 Jan '83 and 15 Nov '83.	Served between 15 Nov '83 and 10 July '84.
Private	John Folling		"	"	"	
"	Robert Farrell		"	"	"	
Corpl.	Peter Farrell	Died 18 June '81	"			
Private	Jeremiah French		"	"	"	
"	Philip Fitzpatrick	[Dischd. 29 Nov '83]	"	"	"	
"	Charles Fitzgerald		"	"	"	
"	Willm. Fitzgerald		"	"	"	
"	John Frawney		"	"	"	
Serjt.	George Finlay		"	"	"	
Private	John Francis				"	
"	Robert Folger		"	"	"	
Corpl.	Peter French		"	"		
Private	Thomas Foxall		"	"	"	
"	Edward Fincham		"	"	"	
"	John Fosset	[Dischd. 29 Nov '83]	"	"	"	
"	Walter Ferrall		"	"	"	
"	Daniel, (David), Foxall		"	"	"	
"	Stephen Fennell		"	"	"	
"	George Ford		"	"	"	
"	John Fulford		"	"	"	
Serjt.	George Fields		"	"	"	
Private	Robert Firth		"	"	"	
"	Thomas Fleming		"	"	"	"
"	Joseph Fisher	Died 20 Nov '82	"	"		
"	John Fennel		"	"	"	
Corpl.	Charles Fulham		"	"	"	
Private	John Franklin	Dischd. 4 Mch '81	"			
"	Joseph Folliet	Died 25 July '82	"	"		
"	Thomas Frumley		"	"	"	
"	Lewis Flash				"	"
"	John Fairweather				"	"
"	Samuel Fisher				"	"
"	Richard Franklin	[Dischd. 18 Sept '83]			"	"
"	Nicholas Free	[Dischd. 29 Nov '83]			"	"
"	Henry Frazier				"	
"	Henry Fisher, 1st		"	"	"	
"	Nicholas Farr				"	
"	William Fairbourn	Died 16 Mch '82	"	"		
Serjt.	James Flack	Dischd. 28 Apl '82	"	"		
Private	Jeremiah Fitzgerald	Died 1 Aug '82		"		
"	Richard Fenwick				"	"
"	Andrew Ferneen				"	
"	James French	Enlisted in '82			"	
Serjt.	Benjamin Gray		"	"	"	
Private	Amos Green		"	"	"	

Rank.	Names.	Remarks.	Served between 1 Aug '80 and 1 Jan '82.	Served between 1 Jan '82 and 1 Jan '83.	Served between 1 Jan '83 and 15 Nov '83.	Served between 15 Nov '83 and 10 July '84.
Private	Abraham Garsene		"	"	"	
"	Sylvester Gatting	Dischd. 4 Sept '81				
"	Samuel Green,	" 9 Jan '82	"	"		
"	John Greene, 1st		"	"	"	
Fifer	William Griffin	Dischd. 15 May '82	"	"		
Private	Thomas Glover	" 14 Feb '83	"	"		
Fifer	Andrew Garnet	[Dischd. 29 Nov '83]	"	"	"	
Private	William Gold		"	"	"	
"	Mark Griffin	Dischd. 15 Jan '81	"			
"	Nathan Griffin	" 15 Jan '81	"			
"	Reuben Gooster	" 27 Dec '81	"			
"	Henry Green		"	"	"	
Drum.	Thomas Gossage		"	"	"	
"	Anthony Geohagan		"	"	"	
Private	Jesse Grace	Dischd. 17 April '81	"			
"	John Gibson	" 25 April '81	"			
"	Isaac Green	" 15 Jan '82	"	"		
"	William Glascow	" 12 April '81	"			
"	Charles Goldsborough		"	"	"	
Drum.	John Gorden, 1st		"	"	"	
Private	William Gates	Dischd. 30 Mch '83	"	"		
"	John Goddard	" 26 Feb '83	"	"		
"	Hugh Gainor		"	"	"	
"	James Garth		"	"	"	
Serjt.	John Given		"	"	"	
Private	James Gray, 1st		"	"	"	"
"	John Gorman, 1st		"	"	"	"
"	Thomas Gillen		"	"	"	"
"	Henry Gilby		"	"	"	
"	Abraham Gamble		"	"	"	
Drum.	James Greenwood		"	"	"	
Private	Moses Graham		"	"	"	
"	Isaac Graves		"	"	"	
"	Edward Garish	Dischd. 8 Aug '82	"	"		
"	Paul Grinard		"	"	"	
"	Richard Gee		"	"	"	
"	Samuel Gerry	Dischd. 28 April '81	"			
"	Joseph Gorden	" 1 May '81	"			
"	Henry Goldsborough	Died 17 June '81	"			
"	John Gordon, 2nd		"	"	"	
"	William Glory		"	"	"	
"	William Groves		"	"	"	
Serjt.	John Green, 2nd		"	"	"	
Private	Benj. Gilbert		"	"	"	
"	Thomas Gadd		"	"	"	

during the War of the American Revolution, 1775–83.   537

RANK.	NAMES.	REMARKS.	SERVED BETWEEN 1 AUG '80 AND 1 JAN '82.	SERVED BETWEEN 1 JAN '82 AND 1 JAN '83.	SERVED BETWEEN 1 JAN '83 AND 15 NOV '83.	SERVED BETWEEN 15 NOV '83 AND 10 JULY '84.
Private	Philip Graham	[Dischd. 29 Nov '83]	"	"	"	
"	Bennet George	Died 1 Oct '82	"	"		
"	Lambert Goody		"	"	"	
"	John Gee		"	"	"	
"	Amos Griffith			"	"	
Fifer	John Graham		"	"	"	
Private	Charles Girdler		"	"	"	
"	Thomas Gilham		"	"	"	
"	William Glover	[Dischd. 29 Nov '83]				
"	Solomon Green		"	"	"	
"	Charles Goff	Dischd. 21 Jan '81	"			
"	John Gregory		"	"	"	
"	James Gravey	[Dischd. 7 Sept '83]	"	"	"	
"	William Greenage	Dischd. 18 May '81, reinlisted			"	
"	Smart Greer		"	"	"	
"	Samuel Gray		"	"	"	
"	William George	Died 24 July '82	"	"		
"	Southy George		"	"	"	
"	Joseph Greer		"	"	"	
"	William Gudgeon	[Dischd. 29 Nov '83]	"	"	"	
"	John Gother	Invd. 25 Feb '82	"	"		
"	Jacob Games			"	"	
"	Benjamin Gater			"	"	
"	John Gray			"	"	
"	Sylvester Gatting		"	"	"	
"	Chas. Griffith			"	"	
"	Whittington Gild			"	"	
"	John Greenwood			"	"	
"	James Gilmore, 2nd			"	"	
"	William Gallispie	Dischd. 1 Oct '83	"			
"	John Gnatzinger	" 29 Mch '81	"			
"	Marshall Galloway		"	"	"	
"	James Goodwin		"	"	"	
"	William Grant		"	"	"	
"	Vincent Gray					"
"	Michael Grosh	Dischd. 4 Mch '81	"			
"	Robert Gilhampton	Died 1 Oct '81	"			
	Thomas Gray	" 15 Oct '82		"		
Private	William Harrington		"	"	"	
Corpl.	Ralph Hagan	Dischd. 30 April '82	"	"		
Drum.	John Head		"	"	"	
Private	John Hughs, 1st	Dischd. 10 May '83	"	"	"	
"	Richard Harper	" 19 Mch '81	"			

35

Rank.	Names.	Remarks.	Served between 1 Aug '80 and 1 Jan '82.	Served between 1 Jan '82 and 1 Jan '83.	Served between 1 Jan '83 and 15 Nov '83.	Served between 15 Nov '83 and 10 July '84.
Private	Thomas Harrison		"	"	"	
"	James Hill	Dischd. 15 Jan '81	"			
"	John Haney		"	"	"	
"	Joseph Horsfield		"	"	"	
Serjt.	George Hagarthy	Killed 15 Mch '81	"			
Private	John Howard	Dischd. 25 Feb '81	"			
"	Joseph Huckell		"	"	"	
"	James Hare	Died 6 July '82	"	"		
Drum.	Vachel Hays	Killed 8 Sept '81	"			
Private	John Hood	Killed 15 Mch '81	"			
"	Barney Haney	[Dischd. 11 Sept '83]	"	"	"	
"	Samuel Hughs	Killed 15 Mch '81	"			
"	John Homes	Dischd. 30 Apl '81	"			
"	Henry Horley	" 23 Apl '81, reinlisted	"		"	
"	Austin Howard		"	"	"	
"	Richard Hall		"	"	"	
"	Edward Harley	Dischd. 25 Apl '81	"			
"	William Harris	" 22 Jan '81	"			
Corpl.	Josias Harris	" 25 Apl '81	"			
Private	Elias Hardy	" 25 Apl '81	"			
"	John Hamilton		"	"	"	
"	Peregrine Howard		"	"	"	
Serjt.	Cornelius Howard	Died 1 Oct '81	"			
Private	John B. Haislip	" 11 Sept '82	"	"		
Drum.	Isaac Hill	Dischd. 11 Aug '83	"	"	"	
Serjt.	Charles Harvey		"	"	"	
Private	John Hide		"	"	"	
"	John Howell	Dischd. 21 Jan '81	"			
"	William Howe	" 2 July '81	"			
"	Isaac Holliday	Died 30 Jan '83	"	"		
"	Jacob Hines	Dischd. 1 May '81	"			
"	Nathaniel Hull	" 15 Jan '81	"			
Serjt.	Robert Harpham		"	"	"	
Private	Thomas Harris, 1st	[Dischd. 29 Nov '83]	"	"	"	
"	Henry Hines	Dischd. 30 Apl '81	"			
"	Francis Hopkins		"	"	"	
"	John Holder		"	"	"	
"	John Harris, 1st		"	"	"	
"	Zadock Harvey	Dischd. 1 May '81	"			
"	William Horney		"	"	"	
Drum.	John Hull		"	"	"	
Private	Charles Hill	Dischd. 21 Apl '81	"			
"	John Holliday		"	"	"	
"	John Housley		"	"	"	

during the War of the American Revolution, 1775-83. 539

Rank.	Names.	Remarks.	Served between 1 Aug '80 and 1 Jan '82.	Served between 1 Jan '82 and 1 Jan '83.	Served between 1 Jan '83 and 15 Nov '83.	Served between 15 Nov '83 and 10 July '84.
Corpl.	John Hall, 2nd		"	"	"	
Private	William Harris, 1st	Time expires 2 Feb '83	"	"		
"	Nicholas Heisler	Dischd. 24 Apl '81	"			
"	Jacob Hunt	[Dischd. 11 Sept '83]	"	"	"	
"	Frederick Harty		"	"	"	
"	Thomas Hoy	Dischd. 25 Apl '81	"			
"	William Hurley	[Dischd. 29 Nov '83]	"	"	"	
"	Leonard Hagan	Died 17 Dec '82	"	"		
"	Walter Hagan	Dischd. 23 Feb '83	"	"		
"	Randolph Hoskins	" 8 Jan '82	"	"		
"	John Hulet		"		"	
"	William Hughes	Died 6 Dec '82	"	"		
"	John Harrell		"		"	
"	Joseph Hall		"	"	"	
"	John Haden		"	"	"	
"	William Hillman		"	"	"	
"	John Higgins	Killed 14 June '81	"			
Corpl.	Lazerous Higgs	Time expires 1 June '83	"	"	"	
Private	Walter Howe		"	"	"	
"	John Hare	Died 27 May '81	"			
Drum.	Edward Holland		"	"	"	
Corpl.	James Hagan	Time expires 1 June '83	"	"	"	
Private	Peter Howard	Died 4 Feb '83	"	"		
"	William Hicks		"	"	"	
"	George Hamilton		"	"	"	
Drum.	Philip Huston	[Dischd. 12 Aug '83]	"	"	"	
Private	Nathan Harper	[Dischd. 11 Aug '83]	"	"	"	
"	Samuel Hamilton		"	"	"	
"	Samuel Harper		"	"	"	
"	Lazarous Harman		"	"	"	
"	Nehemiah Hadder		"	"	"	
"	Edward Hammond		"	"	"	
"	John Hancock		"	"	"	
"	Elijah Hutt	[Dischd. 29 Nov '83]	"	"	"	
"	Ralph Hope		"	"	"	
"	William Hill, 1st		"	"	"	
"	John Hood, 2nd	Died 20 Dec '82	"	"		
"	James Hewitt		"	"	"	
"	John Hillary	Died 27 Dec '82	"	"		
"	John S. Hunt	" 3 Dec '81	"			
"	James Harris, 2nd		"	"	"	
Corpl.	George Hadan	Dischd. 23 Feb '83	"	"		

Rank.	Names.	Remarks.	Served between 1 Aug '80 and 1 Jan '82.	Served between 1 Jan '82 and 1 Jan '83.	Served between 1 Jan '83 and 15 Nov '83.	Served between 15 Nov '83 and 10 July '84.
Private	Thomas Hawson		"	"	"	
"	Stephen Hancock		"	"	"	
"	John Hickens		"	"	"	
"	Daniel Howe		"	"	"	"
Serjt.	Richard Huggins	[Dischd. 29 Nov '83]	"	"	"	
Private	Thomas Hill		"	"	"	"
"	William Hope		"	"	"	
"	John Hurley		"	"	"	
"	Leonard Holt		"	"	"	
"	Nicholas Hiner		"	"	"	
	Richard Harrington		"	"	"	
"	Levin Harrington		"	"	"	
"	Edward Henesee	Died 28 Apl '83	"	"		
"	Pompey Hollis	" 28 Apl '83	"	"		
"	James Homes	1st Regt.				
"	Joseph Harper			"	"	
"	William Harper	[Dischd. 29 Nov '83]	"	"	"	
"	James Halloron	Died 16 Dec '82	"	"		
"	Daniel Holoman		"	"	"	
"	John Hudson, 1st		"	"	"	
"	Samuel Hurst	[Dischd. 29 Nov '83]	"	"	"	
"	James Hudson, 1st		"	"	"	
"	John Hawes	Died 2 Feb '83	"	"		
"	David Hatten	" 9 Mch '83	"	"		
"	William Hamston	" 31 Jan '83	"	"		
Serjt.	Thomas Harrison, 2nd	Dischd. 1 July '81	"			
Private	William Hedge		"	"	"	
"	William Hutcheson		"	"	"	
"	William Harrison, 1st		"	"	"	
"	Michael Hartman		"	"	"	
"	Richard B. Haselip		"	"	"	
"	Thomas Hutchcroft		"	"	"	
"	Richard Hays		"	"	"	
Serjt.	George Holton	Dischd. 5 Apl '84	"	"	"	"
Private	William Hartman	[Dischd. 29 Nov '83]	"	"	"	
"	James Humphrys	[Dischd. 29 Nov '83]	"	"	"	
"	Samuel Harrison	Died 2 Aug '82	"	"		
"	John C. Harwood			"	"	
"	John Harris, 2nd		"	"	"	
"	John Hicks			"	"	
"	Thomas Hammond	[Dischd. 29 Nov '83]	"	"	"	
"	Roger Hogan	[Dischd. 29 Nov '83]		"	"	
"	Thomas Hall			"	"	
"	Daniel Harness			"	"	
"	James Hunt			"	"	

during the War of the American Revolution, 1775-83.

Rank.	Names.	Remarks.	Served between 1 Aug '80 and 1 Jan '82.	Served between 1 Jan '82 and 1 Jan '83.	Served between 1 Jan '83 and 15 Nov '83.	Served between 15 Nov '83 and 10 July '84.
Private	William Holland			"	"	
Corpl.	Kemp Holden			"	"	
Private	William Hunter			"	"	
"	Daniel Hukill			"	"	
"	John Hukill			"	"	
"	Thomas Harding			"	"	
Drum.	Isaac Holland			"	"	
Private	Herculas Hutchings	[Dischd. 29 Nov '83]	"	"	"	
"	James Hudson			"	"	"
"	Thomas Houseman				"	
Corpl.	Christopher Hinson			"	"	
Private	William Hand				"	
Fifer	Benjamin Harrison					
Private	John Hannon		"	"	"	
"	Charles Hickey		"	"	"	
"	John Hutson, 2nd		"	"	"	
"	Caleb Hailey	Invalided 15 Nov '83	"	"	"	
"	John Holston		"	"	"	
"	Samuel Hughes	Invalided 1 Apl '81	"			
"	William Harris, 2nd	6 Regt.		"	"	
Drum.	William Hamilton		"	"	"	"
Private	Daniel Hall	Invalided 1 Mch '82	"	"		
Drum.	Henry Harris	Depreciation wrong	"	"	"	
Private	Lawrence Hurdle				"	"
"	Peter Hammond	Dischd. 5 July '82		"		
"	Burton Harris	Died of his wounds '84			"	
Private	William Joice, 1st		"	"	"	
Serjt.	Archibald Johnson		"	"	"	
Private	Edward Irvine	[James (?) Dischd. 29 Nov '83]	"	"	"	
"	Joseph Jenkins		"	"	"	
"	Henry Jacobs		"	"	"	
"	Nealy Jones		"	"	"	
"	Joseph Jones, 1st		"	"	"	
"	Robert Joshson	Dischd. 19 Mch '81	"			
Serjt.	James Jackson		"	"	"	
Corpl.	David Jones	Died 15 Jan '81	"			
Fifer	Benj. Johnson		"	"	"	
Private	Thomas Jones, 1st		"	"	"	
"	Thomas Jones	Dischd. 25 Apl '81	"			
"	Zachariah Jacobs	" 1 June '81	"			
"	Joseph Johnson		"	"	"	
"	Adam Jenison		"	"	"	
"	John Johnson	Died 15 Jan '81	"			

Rank.	Names.	Remarks.	Served between 1 Aug '80 and 1 Jan '82.	Served between 1 Jan '82 and 1 Jan '83.	Served between 1 Jan '83 and 15 Nov '83.	Served between 15 Nov '83 and 10 July '84.
Private	William Joice, 2d	Killed 8 Sept '81	"			
"	John Johnson, 1st	[Dischd. 29 Nov '83]	"	"	"	
"	William Ingles	Engle	"	"	"	
"	Aaron Jones		"	"	"	
Serjt.	Thomas Jones, 3d	Dischd. 13 Mch '82	"	"		
"	Jesse Jacobs		"	"	"	
Private	Daniel Jarvis	quere if not Danl. Javins	"	"	"	
Serjt.	Joseph Jeans		"	"	"	
Private	John Jones, Sr., 3rd		"	"	"	
"	John Johnson, 3rd	Dischd. 11 Aug '83	"	"	"	
"	William Jones, 1st		"	"	"	
"	William Jones, 2nd		"	"	"	
"	Jacob Jeffers	[Dischd. 29 Nov '83]	"	"	"	
"	Thomas John		"	"	"	
"	Robert Johnson		"	"	"	
"	John Jones, 2nd		"	"	"	
"	Edward Jackson		"	"	"	
"	Frederick Iiams		"	"	"	
"	William Jenkins		"	"	"	
"	John Jones, 1st		"	"	"	
"	George Jenings		"	"	"	
"	John Jackson		"	"	"	
"	Joseph Isaacs		"	"	"	
"	Abraham Irvine		"	"	"	
"	John Jarvis				"	
"	Isaac Johnson	Dischd. 1 Oct '83	"	"	"	
"	Thomas Jones, 2nd		"	"	"	
Serjt.	William Johnson	Dischd. 22 Oct '83	"	"	"	
Private	Charles Jones		"	"	"	
"	George Jones	[Dischd. 29 Nov '83]	"	"	"	
"	Thomas Jones, 4th		"	"	"	
"	John Irons		"	"	"	
"	James Jones				"	
"	John Jorden, 2nd					
"	Richard Jenings				"	"
"	Peter Jackson				"	"
"	John Johnson				"	"
"	Cotter Jones	[Dischd. 12 Aug '83]			"	"
"	James Isaacs	Invalided 15 Sept '83	"	"	"	
Serjt.	William Johnston	Dischd. 16 May '81	"			
"	Robert Isabel	" 4 July '82		"		
Private	William Justice					"
Serjt.	Dennis Kelly	Dischd. 1 Apl '83	"	"		
Private	Thomas King		"	"	"	

during the War of the American Revolution, 1775–83.   543

Rank.	Names.	Remarks.	Served between 1 Aug '80 and 1 Jan '82.	Served between 1 Jan '82 and 1 Jan '83.	Served between 1 Jan '83 and 15 Nov '83.	Served between 15 Nov '83 and 10 July '84.
Private	Adam Keephart		"	"	"	
"	Jacob Knight		"	"	"	
"	Edward Killman	Dischd. 24 May '81	"			
"	James Kelly, 2nd	" 10 Apl '83	"	"		
"	John Knoc, 1st	Died in '82	"			
"	John Kidd		"	"	"	
"	John King		"	"	"	
"	William King		"	"	"	
"	David Kelly		"	"	"	
"	John King	Dischd. 25 Apl '81	"			
Corpl.	Joseph Kerrick	Died 27 Dec '82	"	"		
Private	George Kelson		"	"	"	
"	Michael Kernon	Dischd. 18 May '81	"			
"	Benj. H. Kerrick		"	"	"	
"	William Kindle	Dischd. 25 Apl '81	"			
"	Francis Kitely	Died 25 Apl '81	"			
Corpl.	James Kelly, 1st		"	"	"	
Private	James Keeland		"	"	"	
"	John Kildee		"	"	"	
"	Richard Kisby				"	
"	Walter Keech	Dischd. 1 Aug '83	"	"	"	
" .	Jacob Kelly	[Dischd. 21 Aug '83]	"	"	"	
"	Thomas P. Kettle		"	"	"	
"	Benjamin Karns		"	"	"	
"	Edward Kearsey		"	"	"	
"	James Knot		"	"	"	
"	Edward Kirk		"	"	"	"
"	Francis Kearns		"	"	"	
"	Daniel Kettle		"	"	"	
"	Jacob Kiser	Dischd. 13 Feb '82	"	"		
"	Abraham Kettle		"	"	"	
"	Peter Kincade	Died 1 Jan '82	"			
"	George Kelty			"		
"	Matthew Kelly		"	"	"	
"	Isaac Kent			"	"	
"	Michael Keene			"	"	
"	James Kirk				"	
"	John Knox, 2nd			"	"	
"	Stephen Kamble	Died 1 Sept '82	"	"		
Serjt.	William Kello	Killed 15 Mch '81	"			
Private	James Killegan				"	
"	Nathaniel Knott				"	
Private	Jonathan Lewis		"	"	"	
"	Michael Lloyd	[Dischd. 29 Nov '83]	"	"	"	

Rank.	Names.	Remarks.	Served between 1 Aug '80 and 1 Jan '82.	Served between 1 Jan '82 and 1 Jan '83.	Served between 1 Jan '83 and 15 Nov '83.	Served between 15 Nov '83 and 10 July '84.
Private	William Letman	Killed 8 Sept '81	"			
"	William Laws		"	"	"	
"	Roger Landers, (Sanders?)		"	"	"	
"	John Lucas, 1st		"	"	. "	
"	George Laws	Died 22 Jan '81	"			
"	Benj. Loffman		"	"	"	
"	Levi Lord		"	"	"	
"	William Lee	Died 15 Sept '81	"			
"	Henry Laws		"	"	"	
"	William Little	Died 1 Aug '83	"	"	"	
"	William Linch		"	"	"	
"	John Love, 1st		"	"	"	
"	John Lee, 1st		"	"	"	
"	Thomas Lewis	Dischd. 13 Jan '82	"	"		
"	Michael Loller		"	"	"	
"	John Linday		"			
"	John Lynch, 2nd		"	"	"	
"	Alexander Levi		"	"	"	
"	Robert Legg	[Dischd. 29 Nov '83]	"	"	"	
"	Barney Lemmon	Dischd. 14 Apl '83		"		
"	John Linken	[Dischd. 26 Oct '83]	"	"	"	
"	Joseph Long		"	"	"	
"	John Lowry	Dischd. 28 Apl '81	"			
"	Joshua Liester		"	"	"	
"	William Leakins		"	"	"	
Serjt.	David Love		"	"	"	
Private	John Loveday	Died Aug '83	"	"	"	
"	John Lewin		"	"	"	
"	Francis Lang		"	"	"	
"	Christopher Lambert		"	"	"	
"	George Linton		"	"	"	
"	Paul Lapine		"	"	"	
"	Dudley Lee		"	"	"	
"	William Lucas	Killed 1 Oct '82	"	"		
"	Theopilus Lindsay		"	"	"	
Serjt.	John Lomax	Dischd. 6 Jan '81	"			
Private	Darby Lanahan	" 1 Feb '83	"	"		
"	Thomas Laramore		"	"	"	
"	Charles Leago	Dischd. 1 Apl '83	"	"		
Serjt.	Jacob Lowe	" 21 Feb '81	"			
Private	Kinsey Lanham	Died 20 Dec '82	"	"		
"	Joseph Lewis, 2nd	[Dischd. 29 Nov '83]	"	"	"	
"	John Lynch, 3rd		"	"	"	
"	John Lestley	lives in Georgetown	"	"	"	
"	William Lee, 2nd	[Dischd. 7 Sept '83]	"	"	"	

during the War of the American Revolution, 1775–83.

Rank.	Names.	Remarks.	Served between 1 Aug '80 and 1 Jan '82.	Served between 1 Jan '82 and 1 Jan '83.	Served between 1 Jan '83 and 15 Nov '83.	Served between 15 Nov '83 and 10 July '84.
Private	Thomas Long	[Dischd. 29 Nov '83]	"	"	"	
"	John Lonass	Died 2 Oct '82	"	"		
"	Nehemiah Lingard	[Dischd. 29 Nov '83]	"	"	"	
"	Timothy Langrill		"	"	"	
"	Jesse Locker		"	"	"	
"	William Little		"			
"	William Lee, 1st			"	"	
"	John Lashly	supposed John Lessley		"		
"	Charles Love			"	"	
"	John Lowe			"	"	
"	John Long			"	"	
Fifer	William Lawrence	[Dischd. 23 Sept '83]		"	"	
Private	James Lowrey	[Dischd. 9 Sept '83]		"	"	
Serjt.	Theophilus Lomax		"	"	"	"
Private	Edward Legg				"	
Drum.	Thomas Loveday				"	
Private	Zachariah Lyles	Died 18 June '81	"			
"	Dennis Leary				"	
Private	Michael Miller		"	"	"	
"	John Majors	Dischd. 15 Feb '81	"			
"	Darby Maclamar		"	"	"	
Serjt.	Richard Mudd	Dischd. 9 Jan '82	"	"		
F. M.	John Martindale		"	"	"	
Serjt.	Peter McNorton	[Dischd. 29 Nov '83]	"	"	"	
Fifer	John Morrison		"	"	"	
Corpl.	Walter Miles	Dischd. 1 Apl '83	"	"		
Private	Gilford Minike	" 16 Jan '83	"	"		
"	William Maglocklin		"	"	"	
Drum.	Christopher Magraw		"	"	"	
Private	James Mason		"	"	"	
"	William Moore, 1st		"	"	"	
"	William Mann, 2nd	Dischd. 19 Mch '81	"			
"	James Magraw	" 15 Feb '81	"			
Corpl.	Frederick C. Miles	" 1 May '81	"			
Private	Richard Mitchell		"	"	"	
"	William Moore, 2nd		"	"	"	
"	John Martin, 1st		"	"	"	
"	Cornelius Maglocklin		"	"	"	
Serjt.	Charles Murphy		"	"	"	
Private	William Macall		"	"	"	
"	Charles McGee		"	"	"	
"	John Morris	Dischd. 10 June '81	"			
"	Valentine Murray	" 19 June '81	"			
"	John Matthews, 1st	Invalided 15 Nov '83	"	"	"	

Rank.	Names.	Remarks.	Served between 1 Aug '80 and 1 Jan '82.	Served between 1 Jan '82 and 1 Jan '83.	Served between 1 Jan '83 and 15 Nov '83.	Served between 15 Nov '83 and 10 July '84.
Private	Jonathan Mahugh	Dischd. 9 Jan '82	"	"		
"	Matthew Moore, 1st		"	"	"	
Corpl.	John Mills, 1st	Dischd. 14 Apl '83	"	"		
Private	William Mitchell		"	"	"	
"	John McCann		"	"	"	
"	Jacob Moses, 1st					"
"	Patrick Mahorn		"	"	"	
"	Matthew Moore, 2nd		"	"	"	
"	Humphrey Menchen	Died 15 July '81	"			
"	Thomas Murphy		"	"	"	
"	Christopher McAway		"	"	"	
"	James Mathias	Dischd. 3 Apl '81	"			
Serjt.	Hugh McMillen		"	"	"	
D. M.	James Mead		"	"	"	
Private	Benj. McHaffe	Killed 18 June '81	"			
"	John McCay		"	"	"	
"	William Marshall	Dischd. 3 Mch '83	"	"		
"	George Mantle		"	"	"	
"	Robert Matthews	Dischd. 10 May '81	"			
"	Thomas McCernon	" 1 Feb '81	"			
Serjt.	John Mantle	" 14 Feb '83	"	"		
Private	Benj. Moran	Died 2 Feb '82	"	"		
"	Michael McCann		"	"	"	
Corpl.	James Maxwell		"	"	"	
Private	William Moore, 3rd		"	"	"	
"	John Martin, 2nd	Killed 15 Feb '81	"			
"	William Matthews, 1st					"
Drum.	Boston Medler		"	"	"	
Private	William Mann, 1st		"	"	"	
"	John Moore, 1st	[Dischd. 29 Nov '83]	"	"	"	
"	Christopher Miers	Died 13 Oct '81	"			
"	John McGlochlin	" 1 Mch '81	"			
"	Andrew Moore	" 15 Mch '81	"			
Serjt.	Charles McNabb		"	"	"	
Private	James Managa		"	"	"	
"	Joseph Murphy		"	"	"	
"	Peter McGuire		"	"	"	
"	John McNelley		"	"	"	
Serjt.	Enoch McLane		"	"	"	
Private	John Maxwell, 1st		"	"	"	
"	William Moad		"	"	"	
"	John Mick, (Meek)	[Dischd. 29 Nov '83]	"	"	"	
"	Neale Morris		"	"	"	
"	John Mills, 2nd		"	"	"	
"	Joseph Mattingly	Dischd. 1 Feb '83	"	"		

Rank.	Names.	Remarks.	Served between 1 Aug '80 and 1 Jan '82.	Served between 1 Jan '82 and 1 Jan '83.	Served between 1 Jan '83 and 15 Nov '83.	Served between 15 Nov '83 and 10 July '84.
Serjt.	Arthur McLain	Dischd. 10 Feb '83	"	"		
Private	Nicholas Milburn		"	"	"	
Corpl.	William Martin	Died 31 Dec '82	"	"		
"	William McNeal		"	"	"	
Serjt.	Samuel McConnel	Dischd. 9 June '81	"			
Private	Joseph McNamara	Dischd. 25 July '83	"	"	"	
"	James McDonnald	[Dischd. 9 Sept '83]	"	"	"	
Corpl.	Thomas Matthews, 1st		"	"	"	
Private	Timothy McLamar	Killed 18 June '81	"			
"	John McGinnis	[Dischd. 29 Nov '83]	"	"	"	
Serjt.	Jeremiah Mudd	Dischd. 1 Aug '83	"	"	"	
Corpl.	Issacher Mason		"	"	"	
Private	John Matthews, 2nd	Dischd. 16 Feb '82	"	"		
"	William Manley		"	"	"	
"	Henry Mansfield		"	"	"	
"	John Moore, 2nd		"	"	"	
"	John C. Miller		"	"	"	
"	Michael McGower	Killed 8 Sept '81	"			
"	Jacob Myers			"	"	"
"	Joseph McAtlee	Died Aug '83	"	"	"	
"	Jesse McKinsey	[Dischd. 9 Aug '83]	"	"	"	
"	Roderick McKinsey		"	"	"	"
"	John McNeal	[Dischd. 29 Nov '83]	"	"	"	
"	John Moore, 4th		"	"	"	
"	Adam Musler		"	"	"	"
"	John McCall		"	"	"	
"	David Meadows		"	"	"	"
"	Aaron Mitchell		"	"	"	
"	Aliard Melvin		"	"	"	
"	Robert Mitchell	[Corpl., Dischd. 29 Nov '83]	"	"	"	
"	Daniel Murphy		"	"	"	
"	Francis McCann	[Dischd. 29 Nov '83]	"	"	"	
"	John Morris, 2nd		"	"	"	
"	John Mills, 3rd		"	"	"	
"	John Moore, 3rd	Dischd. 12 Jan '83	"	"		
"	John Murray, 1st		"	"	"	
Serjt.	John McDonald		"	"	"	
Fifer	John McNight		"	"	"	
Private	Edward Mahony		"	"	"	
Corpl.	James Murphy	Invalided 10 July '81	"	was dischd. from Invalids 16 Jan '80		
Private	George McCauley	Dischd. 28 Jan '81	"			
"	Thomas McCauley	" 28 Jan '81	"			
"	Hezekiah Massey	" 31 Dec '82	"	"		

Rank.	Names.	Remarks.	Served between 1 Aug '80 and 1 Jan '82.	Served between 1 Jan '82 and 1 Jan '83.	Served between 1 Jan '83 and 15 Nov '83.	Served between 15 Nov '83 and 10 July '84.
Private	Benjamin Marsh		"	"	"	
"	John McCoy, 1st	Dischd. 14 Feb '82	"	"		
Serjt.	William Marlow		"	"	"	
"	Timothy McMahon	Died June '83		"	"	
Fifer	John McDonald	Dischd. 1 June '83	"	"	"	
Private	Luke Merryman		"	"	"	
Drum.	John McCaliff	[Dischd. 29 Nov '83]	"	"	"	
Private	William Mansfield	[Dischd. 29 Nov '83]	"	"	"	
"	Michael McGuire	Dischd. 9 Sept '82	"	"		
"	John Maglin	[Dischd. 29 Nov '83]	"	"	"	
"	Daniel Mann		"	"	"	
"	Peter Melvin		"	"		
"	John McClaine	[Dischd. 7 Sept '83]	"	"		
"	John Moore, 5th		"	"		
"	Thomas Matthews, 2nd	[Dischd. 11 Sept '83]	"	"	"	
"	Joshua McKinsey		"	"	"	
"	Moses McKinsey		"	"	"	
Serjt.	Francis McGauran		"	"	"	
Private	Thomas Mahony	Died 3 Apl '81	"			
"	Stephen McGraw	" 19 Mch '81	"			
"	Jacob Moses, 2nd	" 15 Mch '81	"			
"	Patrick McKinsey		"	"	"	
"	John McBride		"	"	"	
"	Thomas McKinsey		"	"	"	
"	Thomas Mahoney	Died 28 Aug '82	"	"		
"	Zachariah Mills		"	"	"	
"	Abraham Maning		"	"	"	
"	Patrick Molohon			"	"	
"	William McPherson			"	"	
"	Levi Moody	Died 15 Oct '82	"			
"	Lawrence Mesler			"	"	
"	Thomas McHandy	Died 28 Aug '82	"			
"	Daniel McCollom		"	"	"	
"	Thomas McQuinny		"	"	"	
"	Bennet Meakins		"	"	"	
"	William Madden		"	"	"	
"	Alexander McGrigger		"	"	"	
"	Jacob Mifford		"	"	"	
Corpl.	Benjamin McCaull		"	"	"	
Private	Thomas McDowell		"	"	"	
"	Isaac McFaddon		"	"	"	
"	Robert McClary		"	"	"	
"	William Mathews, 2nd		"	"	"	
"	James Morris, 1st	[Dischd. 29 Nov '83]	"	"	"	
"	John McElroy	[Dischd. 29 Nov '83]	"	"	"	

during the War of the American Revolution, 1775-83.   549

Rank.	Names.	Remarks.	Served between 1 Aug '80 and 1 Jan '82.	Served between 1 Jan '82 and 1 Jan '83.	Served between 1 Jan '83 and 15 Nov '83.	Served between 15 Nov '83 and 10 July '84.
Private	Zachariah Moore	[Serjt., Dischd. 7 Sept '83]		"	"	
"	Lewis McCullough			"	"	
"	Isom Moore			"	"	
"	Charles Messick	Died 22 Oct '83			"	
"	George Miller			"	"	
"	Isaac Mitchell			"	"	"
"	Joseph McCollester	Died 24 Mch '83			"	
"	Richard McDonald				"	
"	John Munford				"	
"	John Misseral				"	
"	John Moran					
"	Thomas Mec		"	"	"	
"	John Milstead		"	"	"	"
"	Thomas Maloney	Wounded 15 Mch '81	"			
"	Nicholas McNamara				"	
Serjt.	Bennet Mudd	Dischd. 6 Nov '81	"			
Serjt.	Nicholas Nicholson	Dischd. 1 Apl '83	"	"		
"	John Navey	" 23 Mch '83		"		
Corpl.	Henry Nicholson		"	"	"	
Serjt.	Stephen Nicholson		"	"	"	
Private	William Newton		"	"	"	
"	Morris Neigle		"	"	"	
"	Asabel Nichols	Dischd. 10 Apl '81	"			
"	Richard Neilson	Died 15 Mch '81	"			
Serjt.	William A. Needham		"	"	"	
Fifer	Joseph Nabb		"	"	"	
Private	William Nailor		"	"	"	
Fifer	James Newell		"	"	"	
Private	Isaac Nichols		"	"	"	
"	John Neighbours	Dischd. 1 Feb '83	"	"		
"	Basil Norman		"	"	"	
"	William Niblet		"	"	"	
"	John Newton, 1st		"	"	"	
"	Charles Nabb		"	"	"	
"	John Nelson		"	"	"	
"	John Newton, 2nd	Dischd. 1 Feb '83	"	"		
"	Patrick Noland	Died 1 Sept '82	"	"		
"	Michael Noland	Dischd. 1 Mch '81	"			
"	John Nevit, 2nd	[Corpl., Dischd. 29 Nov '83]	"	"	"	
"	Joseph Neal	[Dischd. 29 Nov '83	"	"	"	
"	John Nicholson		"	"	"	
"	John Nave		"	"	"	
"	John Noland			"	"	

Rank.	Names.	Remarks.	Served Between 1 Aug '80 and 1 Jan '82.	Served Between 1 Jan '82 and 1 Jan '83.	Served Between 1 Jan '83 and 15 Nov '83.	Served Between 15 Nov '83 and 10 July '84.
Private	Basil Newman	[Newton, Dischd. 29 Nov '83]			"	"
"	John Nicholson				"	"
"	Leonard Nable				"	"
"	Thomas Newman	[Dischd. 9 Sept '83]			"	
"	Thomas Neale	Died 15 Mch '81	"			
Private	Leonard Outerbridge	Dischd. 25 Apl '81	"			
"	John Osborn		"	"	"	
"	Joseph Overcreek	[Dischd. 29 Nov '83]	"	"	"	
"	Daniel O'Quinn		"	"	"	
"	Samuel Oram	Died 1 Sept '81	"			
"	Stephen Owens		"	"	"	
"	James Owens		"	"	"	
"	Charles Orms		"	"	"	
"	Henry Osten		"	"	"	
"	John O'Bryan	Died 25 April '81	"			
Fifer	John Onions		"	"	"	
Private	Peter Outhouse	[Dischd. 29 Nov '83]	"	"	"	"
"	Elijah Oakley			"	"	
"	Dennis O'Bryan			"	"	
"	Paris Owens			"	"	
"	Elisha Osborn	[Dischd. 29 Nov '83]		"	"	
"	Dorden Orrell				"	
"	Stephen Olinger				"	
"	Samuel Owens				"	"
Private	George Parker		"	"	"	
Serjt.	Nathan Peak	Dischd. 14 Nov '82	"	"		
Private	William Poland		"	"	"	
"	Simon Perry		"	"	"	
"	William Pherson		"	"	"	
"	John Pickering	Killed 18 June '81	"			
"	Henry Phillips	Dischd. 1 May '81	"			
	Cupid Plummer	" 27 May '81	"			
	Obediah Plummer	" 27 May '81	"			
Drum.	Aquilla Pierce		"	"	"	
Corpl.	William Purchase		"	"	"	
Drum.	John Peany	[Dischd. 29 Nov '83]	"	"		
Private	George Patrick	Dischd. 23 Feb '83	"	"		
"	Stephen Preston	[Dischd. 11 Aug '83]	"	"	"	
"	Richard Proctor		"	"	"	
"	William Peters		"	"	"	
"	William Pursell		"	"	"	
"	William Prior	Died 15 Feb '81	"			

during the War of the American Revolution, 1775–83.   551

Rank.	Names.	Remarks.	Served between 1 Aug '80 and 1 Jan '82.	Served between 1 Jan '82 and 1 Jan '83.	Served between 1 Jan '83 and 15 Nov '83.	Served between 15 Nov '83 and 10 July '84.
Private	William Pecker		"	"	"	
Drum.	Joseph Purdy		"	"	"	
Private	James Pool		"	"	"	
"	Gabriel Peters	Dischd. 8 Apl '81	"			
"	George Pierce		"	"	"	
Serjt.	Stephen Price		"	"	"	
Private	John Purdy	Dischd. 22 Jan '83	"	"		
"	Henry Purdy	" 14 Feb '83	"	"		
"	George Philips	Died 15 Apl '81	"			
"	Neale Peacock		"	"	"	
Serjt.	John Peace	Dischd. 28 Apl '81	"			
Private	Elijah Pepper		"	"	"	
"	Thomas Peacock	Killed 8 Sept '81	"			
"	Jesse Powers	Dischd. 19 July '83	"	"	"	
"	Thomas Phipps.	" 4 May '81	"			
"	Samuel Pheasent	" 8 Mch '81	"			
"	John Pope			"	"	
"	James Philips	Dischd. 1 Aug '83	"	"	"	
"	Thomas Pender		"	"	"	
"	Thomas Pennyfield		"	"	"	
"	Lambert Philips		"	"	"	
"	George Plumley	Dischd. 31 Dec '82	"	"		
"	Thomas Patterson		"	"	"	
"	Nathaniel Price [Serjt]	[Dischd. 29 Nov '83]	"	"	"	
"	Thomas Perry		"	"	"	
Corpl.	William Priest	[Dischd. 29 Nov '83]			"	
Private	Joshua Pierce		"	"	"	
	Michael Pilkerton		"	"	"	
Corpl.	Joseph Pherson		"	"	"	
Fifer	William Prater	[Dischd. 29 Nov '83]	"	"	"	
Private	William Paul		"	"	"	
"	Thomas Porter		"	"	"	
"	Robert Pennington		"	"	"	
"	William Patterson			"	"	
"	Charles Palmore			"	"	"
"	Samuel Palmer			"	"	"
"	John Philips			"	"	
Corpl.	Benjamin Prior			"	"	"
"	William Potter			"	"	
Private	William Porter		"	"	"	
"	William Powell			"	"	
"	Lawrence Pines				"	
"	Joseph } James } Proctor	[Dischd. 29 Nov '83]		"	"	
"	Francis Pursley	[Dischd. 29 Nov '83]		"	"	

Rank.	Names.	Remarks.	Served between 1 Aug '80 and 1 Jan '82.	Served between 1 Jan '82 and 1 Jan '83.	Served between 1 Jan '83 and 15 Nov '83.	Served between 15 Nov '83 and 10 July '84.
Corpl.	Samuel Perry					
Private	Thomas Proctor					
"	William Pagram		"	"	"	
"	Thomas Pettit	[Dischd. 29 Nov '83]	"	"	"	"
"	Arthur Pritchet				"	
"	Thomas Polhouse	Dischd. 4 Nov '81	"			
Serjt.	John Quick		"	"	"	
Private	Joseph Quinn	Invalided 15 Nov '83	"	"	"	
"	William Quinton		"	"	"	
Private	Patrick Quynn	[Dischd. 29 Nov '83]	"	"	"	
"	William Rowles	Dischd. 1 May '81	"			
"	William Rogers	Invalided 15 Nov '83	"	"	"	
"	William Roberts, 1st	Dischd. 15 May '81	"			
"	Charles Robinson	Invalided 15 Nov '83	"	"	"	
Drum.	William Roberts, 3rd		"	"	"	
Private	Joseph Rhea		"	"	"	
"	Patrick Rowan		"	"	"	
"	Andrew Riggs	Dischd. 10 Feb '81	"			
"	Edward Richardson	" 14 July '82	"	"		
"	Paul Richards		"	"	"	
"	John Rock	Dischd. 2 May '81	"			
"	William Rock	" 2 May '81	"			
"	Jeremiah Rhodes	" 17 Feb '81	"	"		
"	Adam Rains	" 24 May '81	"			
"	James Reily	Killed 17 Jan '81	"			
"	John Robinson	Dischd. 1 May '81	"			
"	Edward Roberts		"	"	"	
"	James Ruark		"	"	"	
"	John Richardson		"	"	"	
"	Henry Redding, Sr.		"	"	"	
"	Henry Ramsey		"	"	"	
"	Robart Richardson	Dischd. 15 Feb '81	"			
"	Joseph Roberts		"	"	"	
"	Thomas Redman	Dischd. 1 Apl '81	"			
"	Benedict Reynolds	" 28 July '81	"			
"	Bennet Rawlings	" 18 June '81	"			
Drum.	James Reynolds, 1st		"	"	"	
	Thomas Richardson, 1st		"	"	"	
Private	Robert Rice	Dischd. 26 Apl '81	"			
"	William Rice		"	"	"	
"	Alexander Ross		"	"	"	
"	Patrick Riely, 1st	[Dischd. 3 Oct '83]	"	"	"	
Fifer	John Riggs	[Dischd. 18 Sept '83]	"	"	"	
Private	Henry Reese		"	"	"	

during the War of the American Revolution, 1775-83.

Rank.	Names.	Remarks.	Served between 1 Aug '80 and 1 Jan '82.	Served between 1 Jan '82 and 1 Jan '83.	Served between 1 Jan '83 and 15 Nov '83.	Served between 15 Nov '83 and 10 July '84.
Private	Andrew Russell		"	"	"	
Serjt.	Charles Reynolds	Died 15 July '81	"			
Private	Patrick Reily, 2nd		"	"	"	
"	John Robins		"	"	"	
"	Aaron Rawlings		"	"	"	
Serjt.	John Reeder		"	"	"	
Private	Charles Riddle	Died 15 June '81	"			
"	John Romills		"	"	"	
"	Robinson Ross		"	"	"	
"	James Reynolds, 2nd	[Dischd. 9 Sept '83]	"	"	"	
"	Francis Reed		"	"	"	
"	Alexander Robinson		"	"	"	
"	Zachariah Robinson		"	"	"	
"	Samuel Richardson		"	"	"	
"	John Ryan		"	"	"	
"	Adam Rider				"	
"	Christopher Ronemberger		"	"	"	
"	Michael Rhydmyer	Dischd. 13 Feb '83	"	"		
"	John Roach		"	"	"	
"	William Rider		"	"	"	
"	John Ransom		"	"	"	
"	Paul Roan		"	"	"	
"	William Rue		"	"	"	
"	Horatio Roberts	Died 1 Mch '81	"			
"	Edward Riely	Dischd. 3 June '83	"	"	"	
"	Alex. Rutherford	" 1 Jan '83	"	"		
"	William Richardson	" 1 Apl '82	"	"		
Serjt.	William Rose			"	"	
Private	Andrew Reveside	Died 16 Dec '82		"		
"	Nathaniel Ross			"	"	
"	John Reed			"	"	
"	John Rodgers			"	"	
"	Thomas Richardson, 2nd			"	"	
"	Joseph Rose			"	"	
"	Richard Rivers			"	"	
"	James Roe	[Dischd. 29 Nov '83]		"	"	
"	Hugh Roney	[Dischd. 11 Aug '83]		"	"	
"	James Rose			"	"	
"	Christopher Raynor	Dischd. 10 Apl '83		"		
"	Zadock Risden	[Dischd. 18 Sept '83]		"	"	
"	Edward Rowan			"	"	"
"	Christopher Reed	Dischd. 1 Jan '81				
"	William Robinson			"	"	"
"	George Riggs				"	
"	Michael Redman				"	

Rank.	Names.	Remarks.	Served between 1 Aug '80 and 1 Jan '82.	Served between 1 Jan '82 and 1 Jan '83.	Served between 1 Jan '83 and 15 Nov '83.	Served between 15 Nov '83 and 10 July '84.
Private	James Ryan, (Peter?)	[Dischd. 29 Nov '83]	"	"	"	
Serjt.	John Radery	Shot 1 Sept '81	"			
Serjt.	Peter Smith		"	"	"	
Private	William Smith	Dischd. 18 June '81	"			
"	Thomas Saunders	" 1 Aug '81	"			
"	William Sikes		"	"	"	
"	William Smith	Dischd. 8 Feb '81	"			
"	Charles Scott		"	"	"	
"	John Snelling	Dischd. 2 Aug '81	"			
"	John Smith, 2nd		"	"	"	
Serjt.	Humphry Spencer		"	"	"	
"	Jesse Suit	[Dischd. 11 Sept '83]	"	"	"	
Private	John Salmon		"	"	"	
"	James Shane	[Dischd. 29 Nov '83]	"	"	"	
"	John Shovel		"	"	"	
	Anthony Smith	Dischd. 1 Apl '81	"			
Serjt.	Robert Scribner	Died 15 Feb '83	"	"		
Private	David Smith	Dischd. 1 Mch '81	"			
Serjt.	Aaron Spalding		"	"	"	
Private	Thomas Stokes	Killed 8 Sept '81	"			
"	Noah Sears	Died 3 Apl '83	"	"		
"	James Smith, 2nd	3rd Regt.	"	"	"	
Corpl.	John Smith, 4th		"	"	"	
Private	Leonard Swan	Dischd. 1 May '81	"			
Drum.	John Scott		"	"	"	
Corpl.	Jesse Simms	Dischd. 20 Mch '83	"	"	"	
Drum.	William Smith, 2nd		"	"	"	
Private	Conrod Smith		"	"	"	
"	Thomas Slade		"	"	"	
"	Thomas Smith	Dischd. 13 May '81	"			
"	James Stewart, 2nd	Died June '83	"	"	"	
"	Reubin Smith	Died 9 May '83	"	"	"	
"	Elijah Smith		"	"	"	
"	William Sinclair		"	"	"	
"	Andrew Stewart	Dischd. 1 Aug '81	"			
Serjt.	Levi Smith		"	"	"	
Private	Daniel Smith, 1st		"	"	"	
"	William Sullivan		"	"	"	
Corpl.	John Smith, 1st		"	"	"	
Private	Perry Sullivan		"	"	"	
Serjt.	Thomas Sappington	Dischd. 12 Feb '82	"	"		
Private	Roger Shorter		"	"	"	
Corpl.	William Sharp	Dischd. 1 Mch '81	"			
Private	Solomon Summers		"	"	"	

during the War of the American Revolution, 1775-83.

RANK.	NAMES.	REMARKS.	SERVED BETWEEN 1 AUG '80 AND 1 JAN '82.	SERVED BETWEEN 1 JAN '82 AND 1 JAN '83.	SERVED BETWEEN 1 JAN '83 AND 15 NOV '83.	SERVED BETWEEN 15 NOV '83 AND 10 JULY '84.
Private	George Saunders		"	"	"	
Corpl.	Robert Sharpless		"	"	"	
Drum.	Alexander Stevenson		"	"	"	
Private	John Summers		"	"	"	
"	William Stonestreet		"	"	"	
"	William Simmonds	Dischd. 1 July '83	"	"	"	
"	Joseph Sloop		"	"	"	
"	James Sewall	[Dischd. 29 Nov '83]	"	"	"	
"	Thomas Smith, 1st		"	"	"	
"	Michael Standley		"	"	"	
"	George Steem		"	"	"	
"	John Stackhouse	Dischd. 4 May '83	"	"		
"	Michael Sours	" 6 May '83	"	"		
"	James Smith, 3rd	7th Regt.	"	"	"	
"	Charles Simpkins		"	"	"	
Drum.	Abraham Stallions		"	"	"	
Private	Aquilla Smith	Dischd. 2 June '81	"			
Corpl.	Peter Stephens		"	"	"	
"	Daniel Smith, 2nd		"	"	"	
"	William Sly	Dischd. 1 May '81	"			
Private	Jeremiah Sullivan	" 12 Mch '83	"	"		
"	Christopher Seymore		"	"	"	
"	James Sullivan		"	"	"	
"	John Smith, 3rd	[Dischd. 29 Nov '83]	"	"	"	
"	Leonard Smith	Dischd. 26 July '83	"	"	"	
"	John Shanks	Invalided 15 Nov '83	"	"	"	
"	Bennet Shirley		"	"	"	
"	John Smallwood, 2nd		"	"	"	
Serjt.	Richard Smith	Dischd. 1 June '83	"	"	"	
Private	Alexander Stewart	" 1 Aug '83	"	"	"	
"	Samuel Scott	" 20 June '83	"	"	"	
"	Job Sylvester		"	"	"	
Drum.	Levi Scott		"	"	"	
Private	Robert Streets		"	"	"	
"	William Stirling	[Dischd. 11 Aug '83]	"	"	"	
"	Benjamin Smith	Dischd. 1 Aug '83	"	"	"	
"	John Smallwood, 1st		"	"	"	
"	John Starkey	[Dischd. 18 Sept '83]	"	"	"	
"	James Shepherd		"	"	"	
"	James Stewart, 1st	Died 1 Dec '82	"	"		
"	John Spires	[Dischd. 29 Nov '83]	"	"	"	
"	Charles Sickle		"	"	"	
"	Solomon Sollovan		"	"	"	
"	Richard Spires		"	"	"	
"	John Shefer		"	"	"	

Rank.	Names.	Remarks.	Served between 1 Aug '80 and 1 Jan '82.	Served between 1 Jan '82 and 1 Jan '83.	Served between 1 Jan '83 and 15 Nov '83.	Served between 15 Nov '83 and 10 July '84.
Private	Thomas Smith, 2nd		"	"	"	
"	Salady Standly	[Dischd. 29 Nov '83]	"	"	"	
"	Luke Samson		"	"	"	
"	John Smith	Died 15 July '81	"			
"	Thomas Summers		"	"	"	
"	Nathan Speake	Died 6 Oct '82	"	"		
"	William Silwood		"	"	"	
"	Benj. Steward		"	"	"	
"	Lawrence Simpson	[Dischd. 29 Nov '83]	"	"	"	
Drum.	William Steward	[Fifer, Dischd. 9 Sept '83]	"	"	"	
Private	George Silver	Dischd. 8 Mch '83	"	"		
"	John Stoffee		"	"	"	
"	Frederick Stoffee	Died 16 Jan '82	"	"		
"	Joseph Smith	Dischd. 13 Aug '81	"			
"	Philip Savoy		"	"	"	
Fifer	Samuel Street		"	"	"	
Private	Joseph Sidney		"	"	"	
"	Elias Smith		"	"	"	
"	Michael Smith, 2nd		"	"	"	
"	Christopher Smith		"	"	"	
"	Michael Smith, 1st		"	"	"	
"	Samuel F. Shomaker	[Dischd. 15 Aug '83]	"	"	"	
"	John Stanton		"	"	"	
"	Oliver Stephens		"	"	"	
"	Cato Snowden	[Dischd. 29 Nov '83]	"	"	"	
Serjt.	Basil Shaw	[Dischd. 29 Nov '83]	"	"	"	
Corpl.	Edward Suit	Died 24 July '82	"	"		
Private	Murphy Shee	" 28 Jan '83	"	"		
"	Thomas Seondrick		"	"	"	
"	Robert Shipley	Died 20 July '82	"	"		
"	Joseph Southall					
"	Thomas Sheriden	Time expires 26 Mch '84, to serve out for Thos. Duffy				
	Walter B. Smallwood		"	"	"	
"	William Shirley	Died 12 June '83	"	"	"	
"	William Standly		"	"	"	
"	Ignatius Smith	Died 20 Apl '82	"			
	James Sappington	[Dischd. 29 Nov '83]	"	"	"	
Serjt.	Jonathan Short	Died 26 Mch '82	"	"		
Private	Elijah Sullivan				"	"
"	Daniel Stevens	[Dischd. 7 Sept '83]			"	"
	William Smith, 3rd				"	"

Rank.	Names.	Remarks.	Served between 1 Aug '80 and 1 Jan '82.	Served between 1 Jan '82 and 1 Jan '83.	Served between 1 Jan '83 and 15 Nov '83.	Served between 15 Nov '83 and 10 July '84.
Private	William Sena			"	"	
"	John Swails			"	"	
"	Thomas Sergo			"	"	
"	William Smallwood			"	"	
"	Thomas Sturgess	[Dischd. 11 Aug '83]		"	"	
"	William Sewell				"	
"	James, or Saml., Silk				"	
"	Daniel Sullinger				"	"
Serjt.	Josiah Smith	Died 15 July '81	"			
Private	James Smith, 1st	Invalided 15 July '82	"	"		
"	Jacob Standley	" 1 Nov '83	"	"	"	
"	William H. Savage		"	"	"	
"	James Scott		"	"	"	"
Corpl.	Charles Scondrick	Died 1 July '81	"			
	Frederick Smith			"	"	
Private	Abraham Stockee	Died 1 Nov '82	"	"		
Corpl.	George Scone		"	"	"	
Private	William Sizeland				"	
"	Edward Shoebrook	Invalided 3 Nov '83		"	"	
"	William Snowden	[Dischd. 7 Sept '83]		"	"	
Serjt.	Joseph H. Spencer				"	"
Private	John Smithird	Dischd. 20 Apl '81	"			
	William Smith	Killed 3 June '83			"	
Private	Edward Timms	Dischd. 10 July '81	"			
"	William Taylor, 1st	[Dischd. 18 Sept '83]	"	"	"	
"	John Tucker	Dischd. 21 Feb '83	"	"		
"	Notley Tippet		"	"	"	
"	William Toland		"	"	"	
"	Lambert Thompson		"	"	"	
"	Bartholomew Thompson		"	"	"	
"	John Taylor, 1st		"	"	"	
"	Peter Tippet	Died 15 Dec '81	"			
"	James Thomas, Jr., 2nd		"	"	"	
"	John Turner, 3rd		"	"	"	
"	Richard Tasco		"	"	"	
"	Henry Townley		"	"	"	
"	Thomas Thompson		"	"	"	
"	John Trusty	Died 17 July '81	"			
"	Peter Topping		"	"	"	
"	Dennis Trammill	Dischd. 31 May '83	"	"	"	
"	John Taylor, 2nd		"	"	"	
"	Evan Tumbleston		"	"	"	
"	Cornelius Thompson		"	"	"	

Rank.	Names.	Remarks.	Served between 1 Aug '80 and 1 Jan '82.	Served between 1 Jan '82 and 1 Jan '83.	Served between 1 Jan '83 and 15 Nov '83.	Served between 15 Nov '83 and 10 July '84.
Serjt.	Robert Taylor, 2nd		"	"	"	
Private	George Taylor		"	"	"	
"	William Taylor, 2nd		"	"	"	
"	William Townsend	Dischd. 24 Apl '81	"			
"	John Twiner		"	"	"	
"	Samuel Taylor	Died 15 June '81	"			
"	Richard Taylor	Dischd. 6 May '83	"	"	"	
"	Francis Thompson	" 18 Apl '83			"	
"	Solomon Turner	" 12 May '81	"			
"	Thomas Tanner	Died 3 Jan '82	"			
"	James Terry	[Dischd. 23 Sept '83]	"	"	"	
"	Giles Thomas	Dischd. 25 July '83	"	"	"	
"	William Taylor, Jr., 3rd		"	"	"	
Serjt.	James Thomas, Sr.		"	"	"	
"	Allen Townsend		"	"	"	
"	Levin Thomas		"	"	"	"
"	James Tigner		"	"	"	
	John Thompson, 1st		"	"	"	
"	Edward Tanner		"	"	"	
"	Thomas Thomas		"	"	"	
"	John D. Tully		"	"		
"	John Thomas, 2nd		"	"	"	
Serjt.	George Twinch	[Dischd. 29 Nov '83]	"	"	"	
Private	John Traverse	Deserted in '84	"	"	"	"
Corpl.	Peter Teban					"
Private	Henry Tucker	Invalided 29 Mch '82	"	"		
"	John Turner, 2nd			"	"	
"	Francis Taylor			"	"	
	Benjamin Thompson			"	"	
"	Evan Thomas			"	"	
"	George Trice			"	"	
"	George Tate			"	"	"
"	Henry Tippet	[Dischd. 11 Aug '83]		"	"	
M. S.	Thomas Twinch, 2nd				"	•
Private	Samuel Taylor					
"	John Thomas, 1st		"	"	"	
"	James Tite	Died 1 Oct '82	"	"		
"	Samuel Tindell	Invalided 15 Aug '83	"	"	"	
	Samuel Trig	Dischd. 18 Mch '82		"		
"	John Timlon	" 28 Apl '81	"			
"	Dennis Terney				"	"
"	Joseph Thompson				"	
"	Christopher Touchstone	Died 8 Sept '81	"			
"	Anthony Tucker	Killed 8 Sept '81	"			

during the War of the American Revolution, 1775–83.   559

Rank.	Names.	Remarks.	Served between 1 Aug '80 and 1 Jan '82.	Served between 1 Jan '82 and 1 Jan '83.	Served between 1 Jan '83 and 15 Nov '83.	Served between 15 Nov '83 and 10 July '84.
Private	John Vane			"	"	"
"	Cornelius Vaughan		"	"	"	
"	William Vaughan	Dischd. 8 May '81	"			
"	John Vincent	Died 25 Apl '81	"			
"	Stephen Varlow		"	"	"	
"	Samuel Vermillion		"	"	"	
"	George Vernon	Killed 8 Mch '81	"			
"	Edward Vickers		"	"	"	
"	John Vanzant	Invalided 15 Nov '83	"	"	"	
"	John Varlow		"	"	"	
Private	John Willing		"	"	"	
"	John Wade, 1st		"	"	"	
"	Thomas Woolford	Dischd. 9 Nov '81	"			
"	Edward Wade, 2nd		"	"	"	
"	William Whaland		"	"	"	
"	John Willis	[Dischd. 29 Nov '83]	"	"	"	
"	John Waller					
"	Jonathan Weedon	Died 13 Feb '83	"	"		
"	Thomas Wood	Dischd. 28 Jan '81	"			
	Daniel Williams	" 1 Apl '83	"	"		
"	Nicholas Welch		"	"	"	
	Benjamin Williams, 3rd		"	"	"	
"	Thomas Wood, 3rd		"	"	"	
Serjt.	Thomas Windham		"	"	"	
Private	Henry Williams					
"	John Williams	Dischd. 9 Jan '82	"	"		
"	George Ward	" 10 May '81	"			
"	John Walker, Jr., 2nd			"	"	
Fifer	John T. West		"	"	"	
Private	Alexander West	Died 1 Nov '82	"	"		
"	Jonathan White	Invalided 13 Sept '81	"			
"	Jesse Wright		"	"	"	
"	John Welsh, 1st	[Dischd. 18 Sept '83]	"	"	"	
Fifer	David Williams	Dischd. 12 Apl '81	"			
Private	William Wheatly	" 20 Apl '81	"			
	Andrew Windgate	" 1 May '81	"			
"	Thomas Wood, 1st		"	"	"	
"	James Wilson, 1st		"	"	"	
"	Thomas Wimber		"	"	"	
"	York Waters	Dischd. 4 June '81	"			
"	Thomas Wate		"	"	"	
"	Robert Walker	[Dischd. 9 Sept '83]	"	"	"	
"	Michael Woolford		"	"	"	
"	Frederick Willmott		"	"	"	

Rank.	Names.	Remarks.	Served between 1 Aug '80 and 1 Jan '82.	Served between 1 Jan '82 and 1 Jan '83.	Served between 1 Jan '83 and 15 Nov '83.	Served between 15 Nov '83 and 10 July '84.
Private	Thomas Watson	[Dischd. 29 Nov '83]	"	"	"	
"	Samuel B. White	Dischd. 24 Aug '82	"	"		
"	William Wilson	Died 15 Mch '81	"			
	George Windham	Dischd. 25 Apl '81	"			
"	William West	" 13 Jan '82	"	"		
"	John Williams, 1st		"	"	"	
"	Barney Wilson		"	"	"	
"	William Wilkeson	Dischd. 1 Mch '81	"			
"	Charles Williams, 1st	" 20 Aug '83	"	"	"	
"	Robertson Wood		"	"	"	
"	Thomas Wood, 2nd	[Dischd. 29 Nov '83]	"	"	"	
"	Edward Wright	Died 4 Mch '83	"	"		
Corpl.	Jeremiah Williams		"	"	"	
Private	James Wood, 2nd		"	"	"	
Drum.	Daniel Willis		"	"	"	
Private	George Wilson	Dischd. 5 May '81	"			
"	David Wilson		"	"	"	
Serjt.	John Wilkeson		"	"	"	
Drum.	Daniel Warrior		"	"	"	
Private	Jonathan Windal	Dischd. 1 Apl '81	"			
Fifer	Michael Wiery		"	"	"	
	Benj. Williams, 2nd		"	"	"	
"	Absalom Wright		"	"	"	
"	Michael Wiser	Dischd. 1 June '81	"			
Private	William Wilson, 2nd		"	"	"	
"	Notley Whitcomb	Dischd. 1 Apl '81	"	"		
"	Samuel Wedge		"	"	"	
"	William Wedge	Dischd. 15 Mch '81	"			
"	James White	Invd. 10 June '83	"	"	"	
"	Michael Waltman		"	"	"	
Serjt.	Gabriel Williams	Dischd. 6 Feb '83	"	"		
Private	John Wells		"	"	"	
"	Richard Wiley		"	"	"	
"	John Wilson, 1st	[Dischd. 29 Nov '83]	"	"	"	
Corpl.	Richard Wheeler	Dischd. 23 July '83	"	"	"	
Private	Rhode Woodland		"	"	"	
"	John Whitcomb	Dischd. 7 Jan '83	"	"		
"	Walter Watson	" 1 Aug '83	"	"	"	
Serjt.	John Walker, 3rd		"	"	"	
Private	Banks Webb		"	"	"	
"	John West, 2nd		"	"	"	
Drum.	William Watkins	[Dischd. 29 Nov '83]	"	"	"	
Private	James Wilson, 2nd	[Dischd. 29 Nov '83]	"	"	"	
"	Charles Wheeler [Corpl., Dischd. 29 Nov '83]		"	"	"	
Serjt.	George Williams		"	"	"	

Rank.	Names.	Remarks.	Served between 1 Aug '80 and 1 Jan '82.	Served between 1 Jan '82 and 1 Jan '83.	Served between 1 Jan '83 and 15 Nov '83.	Served between 15 Nov '83 and 10 July '84.
Private	Humphry Wells	[Dischd. 11 Aug '83]	"	"	"	
"	William Wilson, 1st	[Serjt., Dischd. 29 Nov '83]	"	"	"	
"	James West	[Dischd. 29 Nov '83]	"	"	"	
Serjt.	James Wood, 1st		"	"	"	
"	Benjamin Ward	Dischd. 1 July '83	"	"	"	
Private	John Willing	Died 15 Dec '81	"			
"	Philip Welch	" 1 Dec '81	"			
"	John Wright	[Dischd. 29 Nov '83]	"	"	"	
"	Joseph White	Dischd. 1 July '83	"	"	"	
"	Zadock Whaley		"	"	"	
"	Anthony Weaver		"	"	"	
Drum.	Benj. Williams, 1st		"	"	"	
Private	John Wilkeson	Died 15 Jan '81	"			
"	William Whitteco		"	"	"	
"	Samuel Wright	Died 20 Jan '82	"	"		
"	Charles White			"	"	
"	John Walker, 1st	[Dischd. 29 Nov '83]	"	"	"	
"	Garret Welch			"	"	
"	John Welch, 2nd		"	"	"	
"	Joseph Ward			"	"	
"	James Williams		"	"	"	
"	Hugh Ware			"	"	
"	John Williams, 2nd			"	"	
"	John White, 2nd			"	"	
"	Henry Windows			"	"	
"	Evan Willing			"	"	
"	John Wilson, 2nd			"	"	
	William Watkins, 2nd			"	"	
"	Daniel Wilkins			"	"	
"	Benjamin Worthington			"	"	
"	Robert Wright	[Dischd. 11 Aug '83]		"	"	
"	Edward Wheatly			"	"	
"	Thomas Wood, 4th			"	"	
"	John Wilmore				"	
Corpl.	John Wiley				"	
Private	John Wilman				"	
"	Thomas White				"	
"	John Watkins	Died 26 Apl '83	"			
"	George Watson	" 4 July '81	"			
Serjt.	Samuel Wilson	Invalided 12 Oct '82	"	"		
Private	Edward Walter		"	"	"	
"	Calvert Woodward, (Mason)			"	"	
"	Sylvester Wheatley	Dischd. 1 July '81	"			
"	Charles Willet	Died 19 Sept '82	"	"		
"	Jarvis Williams		"	"	"	"

Rank.	Names.	Remarks.	Served between 1 Aug '80 and 1 Jan '82.	Served between 1 Jan '82 and 1 Jan '83.	Served between 1 Jan '83 and 15 Nov '83.	Served between 15 Nov '83 and 10 July '84.
Private	Samuel Young		"	"	"	
Corpl.	John Young, 2nd		"	"	"	
Private	Godfrey Young	Invd. 23 Oct '80	"			
"	Jacob Yeast		"	"	"	
"	Henry Young		"	"	"	"
"	Isaac Young	[Dischd. 2 Aug '83]		"	"	"
"	John Young	[Dischd. 18 Sept '83			"	

HAZENS.

	John Ryan		"	"	"	"
	Charles March		"	"	"	"
	Harvey Burns		"	"	"	"
	John Dugan		"			
	James McEntire		"	"	"	"
	Thomas Deavond		"	"	"	"
	William Dooley		"			
	Benjamin Willson		"			
	William Deacon		"	"	"	"
	Nehemiah Barns		"	"	"	"
	William Duly		"	"	"	"
	William Perkins		"	"	"	"
	John Crany		"	"	"	
	Joseph Lewis		"	"	"	
	Michael Fitzgerald		"	"	"	

INVALIDS.

	James Dyer		"			
	James Dwire		"			
	John Smith		"			
	Michael McGuire		"	"		
	John Saunders		"	"		
	Valentine Smith		"	"		
	John Willis		"	"	"	
	Paul Dugan		"			
	Michael Duffee		"			
	John O'Brion		"			
	Robert Poneston		"			
	John Howard		"			
	Jacob Lyons		"			
	John Brown		"			
	Thomas Evans		"			

Note.—Information in brackets is taken from a Register of Maryland Troops Discharged at the Post of Frederick Town.

ARTILLERY ROLLS.

The Enrolment of the First Company of Matrosses In the Province of Maryland, Commanded by Capt. Nathaniel Smith, Lt. Wm. Woolsey, Lt. Alex. Fornivall, Lt. George Keepott.*

DATE OF ENLISTMENT.	NAMES.	WHERE BORN.	HEIGHT.	OCCUPATION.	AGE.
	Serjeants				
Jan 24th '76	Wm. Cornwall	In the parish Armagh, Ireland	5.10	Joyner	30
	Samuel Chester	Shrewsbury, Eng.	5.6	Breeches Maker	26
	John Lemon	North of Ireland	5.7¾	Brick Maker	26
	John Hall	Pennsylvania	5.6	Brick Layer	22
	Corporals				
	Wm. Godman	Fredk. Co., Md.	5.8	Labourer	21
	Geo. Litzinger	Maryland	5.8¼	Brick Layer	21
	Isaac James	Philadelphia	5.9½	Taylor	27
	Alex. Craig	Ireland	6.0	Labourer	20
	Fifer				
	Marmadk. Grant	Dublin	5.4	Cane Maker	20
	Drummer.				
	Henry Kelleher	Cork, Ireland	5.8	Taylor	18
	John Power	Ireland	5.8	Brick Layer	36
	John Clarke	North Ireland	5.8	Glover	21
	Hugh Martin	Pennsylvania	5.7¾	Tanner & Currier	23
	Robt. Tool	County Kerry, Ireland	6.1½	Labourer	28
	David Garrison	West New Jersey	5.5	Brick Layer	30
	George Rees	Germany	5.7	Rope Maker	23
	Philip Sitzley	Pennsylvania	5.7	Breeches Maker	30
	Henry Rees	Germany	5.11	Wever	38
	Samuel Thompson	Nanticoke, Md.	5.8½	Shoe Maker	21
	Thos. Conner	Ireland	5.8¼	Hatter	19
	Nathl. Aldrich	Elk Ridge, Md.	5.8¼		21
	John Houlton	Philadelphia	6.0½	Plasterer	19
	Jno. Cunningham	Charles Town, Md.	6.0	Labourer	23
	Robert Mitchel	Charles Town, "	5.6	Sadler	22
	Joel Bennett	West New Jersey	5.7½	Shoe Maker	22
	Freeman Newman	Dublin, Ireland	5.5	Labourer	21

* This Company was raised in accordance with the Resolves of the Maryland Convention of December, 1775, see page 4.

Date of Enlistment.	Names.	Where Born.	Height.	Occupation.	Age.
Jan 24th '76	Alex. McMullen	North Ireland	5.6¾	Tanner	23
	John Schley	Bucks Co., Penna.	5.10¼	Brick Maker	26
	Barney Quinn	Dublin, Ireland	5.8	Labourer	21
	James Badley	Dublin, "	5.5½	Gardner	22
	James Roney	Leinst'r, "	5.7	Breeches Maker	23
	Willm. Forbes	Ireland	5.4	Wever	25
	Hugh McDowell	Newry, Ireland	5.5¼	Black Smith	28
	Roger O'Donnald	Donegal, "	5.7	Labourer	28
	Richd. Wilkinson	Dublin, "	5.6¾	Sailor	30
	John Gormon	Munster, "	5.7¼	Pump Borer	22
Jan 25th	Philip Jones	Maryland	5.7	Brick Layer	21
	Robert Brett	Maryland	5.6½	Taylor	24
	John Videon	Kent, England	5.7¾	Baker	23
	James Jack	Glasgo	5.4	Wever	24
	Edward Barrey	Ireland	5.5½	Silk Wever	33
Jan 25th	John Burke	County Kerry, Ireland	5.6½	Labourer	30
	John Pearson	Pennsylvania	6.0	Brick Layer	30
	John Turner	Nottingham, England	5.7	Sawyer	28
	Luke Gardiner	Killarney, Ireland	5.9	Barber	22
	David Walsh	Cork, Ireland	5.8	Cooper	23
	Danl. Donoghue	Cork, "	5.7	Plaisterer	22
Jan 27th	George Cooper	England	5.8¼	Labourer	20
	John Curties	Bucks Co., Pa	5.5	"	33
	Martin Gutro	Nova Scotia	5.8¾	"	28
	John Howard	Maryland	5.11	"	27
	Thos. Mahoney	Ireland	5.7	"	25
	James Barrey		5.10¼		33
	John Carroll	Limer'k, Ireland	5.6¼	Butcher	30
	Heart Dick	Scotland	5.7½	Baker	23
Jan 27th	Thos. Smith	Maryland	5.6¾	Carpenter	20
	Richd. Bourk, (Burke)	Ireland	5.7¼	Butcher	22
Jan 28th	David White	Dublin, Ireland	5.5¼	Wever	30
	Thos. Pearson	Philadelphia	5.5½	Brick Layer	28
	Robt. Thompson	Maryland	5.9	Labourer	33
	James Mathies	W. New Jersey	5.8½	"	24
	Andrew Shrike	Pennsylvania	5.6¾	Turner	17
	John Bradey	Dublin, Ireland	5.6½	Plaisterer	21
	Edmund Walsh	Cork, "	5.6½	Labourer	25
	Wm. Colbertson	Cork, "	5.5	"	30
	Wm. Ellis	Portsmouth, England	5.5½	"	36
	Peter Richards	Nova Scotia	5.9	"	23
	Henry Carroll	West of Ireland	5.5	Breeches Maker	21
	Willm. Read	Warwickshire, Eng.	5.7½	Stocking Wever	30
	Robert Foster	England	5.7¼	Brick Layer	23
Jan 30th	Benj. Spencer	Pennsylvania	5.5½	Brick Layer	30

during the War of the American Revolution, 1775-83.

DATE OF ENLISTMENT.	NAMES.	WHERE BORN.	HEIGHT.	OCCUPATION.	AGE.
Jan 30th '76	Joseph Bear	Nova Scotia	5.6½	Labourer	28
	Joseph Wilkes	England	5.6½	"	32
	Benj. Jones	Maryland	5.6¾	Brick Layer	30
Jan 31st	David Thomas	Gloucestershire, Eng.	5.7¼	Brick Layer	37
	Jacob Boger, (Booger)	Pennsylvania	5.5¾	Carpenter	20
	Felix Branagin	Armagh, Ireland	5.6¾	Labourer	33
	James Scott	Antrim, "	5.9¼	Shoe Maker	35
	Timothy Donnovin	Cork, "	5.4¼	Labourer	26
	Thomas Neilson	Tyrone, "	5.7½	Carpenter	24
	Jas. Henrickson	Maryland	5.6¼	Labourer	26
	Martin Cunden	Waterf'd, Ireland	5.7½	Drayman	21
	Patk. Shaughness	Dublin, "	5.7	Breeches Maker	21
	William Foard	Cecil Co., Md.	5.7½	Labourer	18
	Jas. McFadon	Ireland	6.1	"	20
	Timo. Murphey	Dublin, Ireland	5.4½	"	20
	Anthony Barns	Virginia	5.6	Shoe Maker	21
	David Moroney	Cork, Ireland	5.9	Brick Layer	22
Feb 1st	John Handlen	Dublin, "	5.5	Taylor	28
	Anthony Selister	Nova Scotia	5.4	Labourer	37
	John Philips	Dublin, Ireland	5.6½	"	20
Feb 3rd	John Conly, (Connolly)	Athlone, "	5 6½	Shoe Maker	26
	John Wilkins	South Carolina	5.9	Labourer	33
	James Brooks	North of England	5.5½	Weaver	23
	Richard Pitsland	South Carolina	5.7	Labourer	27
	Jno. Richardson	Pennsylvania	5.8¼	Carpenter	23
	Thos. Robinson	Harford Co., Md.	6.0	Black Smith	21
	Chas. Cloes	Antrim, Ireland	5.7	Labourer	19
	Francis Dushield	Nova Scotia	5.9¾	Brick Layer	23
	John Forrester	Maryland	5.8½	Labourer	28
	Alex. Forrester	Maryland	5.5	"	30
	Cornelius Forrester	Maryland	5.10¾	"	21

Baltimore, 19 February, 1776.
   the above Company Examined and passed by
                                                   M. Gist
                M.

NATHAN SMITH'S COMPANY.

June 29th, 1776.

RANK.	NAMES.	REMARKS.
Serjts.	Wm. Cornwall	present
	―― el Chester	"
	John Hall	"
	James McFadon	"

Rank.	Names.	Remarks.
Corpls.	Wm. Godman	present
	George Littsinger	"
	Alex. Craige	"
	Young Wilkinson	"
Fifer	Marmaduke Grant	"
Drum.	Henry Keleher	"
	David Garritson	"
	John Houlton	absent on Guard
	John Cunningham	present
	John Pearson	absent on Guard
	Thomas Robinson	present
	Nicholas Ricketts	"
	John Howard	"
	Saml. Thompson	"
	Corns. Forrester	"
	James Barry	"
	James Rice	"
	John Shley	"
	Fran. DeShields	"
	Robert Thompson	"
	Luke Gardiner	"
	Peter Richards	"
	David Moroney	"
	John Wilkins	"
	Martin Gutro	sick in Barracks
	Thomas Connor	present
	James Mathias	"
	John Forrester	"
	Nathaniel Aldridge	"
	George Cooper	"
	John Power	"
	John Clarke	"
	Barney Quinn	"
	David Walsh	"
	Hugh Martin	"
	John Vidon	"
	Martin Conden	"
	——el Bennett	"
	Thomas Nelson	"
	Richard Burke	"
	——m Reed	"
	—— Dick	"
	——vid Thomas	"
	John Gorman	"
	Thomas Mahony	"
	John Turner	"

during the War of the American Revolution, 1775–83.

Rank.	Names.	Remarks.
	Henry Rees	present
	Richd. Pitsland	"
	———oney	"
	R—— ODonnell	"
	—— Cloes	"
	—— Sitsler	"
	—— Jones	"
	Ro—— Toole	"
	Da—— Donahue	"
	P——k Shaughness	"
	Richd. Wilkinson	"
	Alex. McMullen	"
	Phelix Branagan	"
	Thomas Smith	"
	Andrew Shriek	"
	Benj. Jones	"
	John Troy	"
	John Connolly	sick in the Hospital
	John Philips	present
	Joseph Wilkes	"
	Edward Walsh	"
	John Brady	"
	John Carroll	"
	Robert Britt	"
	James Henrickson	"
	Anthony Barnes	"
	Robert Mitchell	"
	Jacob Boager	"
	William Ellis	"
	Benj. Spencer	dead or deserted, 18th Inst
	Edward Barry	present
	Hugh McDowell	"
	Thomas Pearson	"
	James Bradley	"
	David Whyte	"
	George Rees	"
	Alex. Forrester	"
	John Hanlon	"
	John Curtis	"
	Freeman Newman	"
	Wm. Culbertston	"
	Henry Carroll	"
	Timothy Murphy	"
	Anthony Silister	sick in barracks
	Timothy Donovan	present
	Ja——es Jack	"

Rank.	Names.	Remarks.
	William Forbes	present
	Frans. MaGauran	"
	James Scott	dead or deserted, 13th Inst
	Benjamin Todd	present
	Fredk. Pine	"
	William Delany	"

Whetstone Point, Sept. 7th, 1776.

First Company of Matrosses.

Capt. Nathaniel Smith.	Present.	
Lieutenant Alex. Furnivall.	"	
Lieutenant N. Ruxton Moore.	"	
Lieutenant Richd. Dorsey.	"	

Rank.	Day of Inlistment.	Names.	Remarks.	
Serjeants	Jan 26	Wm. Cornwall	Present	
		Saml. Chester	Absent	On Furlough 7th
		Jno. Hall	Present	
		Jas. McFadon	"	
Corporals		Wm. Godman	"	
		Geo. Litsinger	"	
		Alex. Craige	"	
		Young Wilkinson	"	
Drum		Henry Kelliher	"	
Fife		Marmaduke Grant	"	
		David Garrison	"	
		Jno. Holton	"	
		Jno. Pearson	"	
	May 29	Benj. Todd	Absent	On furlough 5th
	Jan 26	Thos. Robinson	Sick	In the Hospital
		Nichs. Ricketts	Present	
		John Howard	"	
		Saml. Thompson	"	
		Corns. Forrester	"	
		Jas. Barry	"	
	Apl 3	Jas. Rice	"	
	Jan 26	Jno. Shly	Sick	In Hospital
		Frans. deShields	Prest.	
	May 29	Wm. Delany	"	
	Jan 26	Robt. Thompson	"	
		Luke Gardiner	"	
		Peter Richards	"	

during the War of the American Revolution, 1775–83. 569

Rank.	Day of Inlistment.	Names.	Remarks.
		David Maroney	Sick In Town
		Jno. Wilkins	Present
	May 29	Fredk. Pine	"
	Jan 26	Martin Gutro	"
		Thos. Connor	"
		Jas. Mathias	"
		Jno. Forrester	"
		Nathan Aldridge	"
		Geo. Cooper	"
		Jno. Power	"
		Jno. Clarke	"
		Barny Quinn	"
		David Welsh	"
		Hugh Martin	"
	Aug 5	Jno. Vidon	"
	Jan 26	Leaven Dorsey	"
		Martin Condon	"
		Thos. Nelson	"
		Richd. Burke	"
		Wm. Read	"
	Aug 5	Jno. Ring	"
	Jan 26	Davd. Thomas	"
		Jno. Gorman	"
	Aug 31	Matthew Kelly	"
	Jan 26	Jno. Turner	"
		Richd. Pitsland	"
		Jas. Roney	"
		Roger O'Donnald	"
		Charles Cloes	"
		Philip Sitzler	"
		Philip Jones	"
		Robert Toole	"
		Danl. Donohou	"
		Patrick Shockness	"
	July 2	Stephen Fennell	"
	Jan 26	Richd. Wilkinson	"
		Alex. McMullon	"
		Felix Branagan	"
		Thos. Smith	"
		Andw. Shrake	"
		Benj. Jones	"
		Jno. Phillips	Sick In Hospital
		Joseph Wilkes	Present
		Edmund Welsh	"
		Jno. Brady	"

Rank.	Day of Inlistment.	Names.	Remarks.	
		Jno. Carroll	Absent	In Town
		Robt. Brett	"	On Guard
	June 20	Thos. Wilson	"	
	May 16	Fras. MaGauran	Present	
	Jan 26	Anthy. Barnes	"	
		Robt. Mitchell	"	
		Jacob Boger	"	
		Wm. Ellis	"	
		Hugh McDole	"	
		Thos. Pearson	"	
		Jno. Curtis	Absent	On Guard
		Jas. Bradley	Present	
		Davd. White	"	
		Geo. Rees	Absent	On furlough Aug 31st
		Alex. Forrester	Present	
		Jno. Handlen	"	
		Jno. Curtis	"	
		Freeman Newman	"	
		Wm. Culbertson	"	
		Henry Carroll	"	
		Tim Murphy	Sick	In Hospital
		Anthy. Selister	Present	
		Tim Donnavan	"	
	July 23	Bartho. Donohou	"	
	Jan 26	Jas. Jack	"	
		Wm. Forbes	"	
		Jas. Fox	Absent	On Guard
		Ed. Barry	Present	

Return of Capt. Nathaniel Smith's Matross Company.

Nathl. Smith.

Company of Matrosses Stationed at Annapolis.

Capt. John Fulford, commissioned Feb. 9th, 1776*
1st Lt. Thomas Goldsmith*
    William Brown, commissioned July 5th, 1776*
2nd Lt. Felix Lewis Baron Massenbach, commissioned Feb. 20th, 1776*
    Nicholas Ruxton Moore, commissioned March 23rd, 1776,* vice Massenbach resigned
    William Campbell, commissioned July 15th, 1776*
3rd Lt. Nicholas Ruxton Moore, commissioned March 1st, 1776*
    William Campbell, commissioned March 23rd, 1776*
    Adam Berthaud, commissioned July 17th, 1776*

* See Md. Archives vol. XI, pgs. 145, 169, 550, 173, 279, 196 and vol. XII, pgs. 47, 62.

RESOLVES OF THE MARYLAND CONVENTION 23 OCTOBER, 1776.

"*Resolved*, That three companies of artillery, each company to consist of ninety-two privates, four serjeants, four corporals, one drummer, and one fifer, commanded by one captain, one captain-lieutenant, and two lieutenants, be immediately raised; one of the said companies to be stationed at Baltimore town, and the remaining two companies to be stationed at the city of Annapolis. That the non-commissioned officers and privates be enlisted in the service of this state for the war: ..... and they shall not be compelled to march to any place out of this state."

MARYLAND ACTS—JUNE, 1777.

"An ACT to reinforce the *American* army.

And be it enacted, That the governor and the council be empowered to order any part of any of the artillery companies raised for the immediate defence of this state, not exceeding sixty-six privates, under officers proper for such a number of artillerists, to march with all expedition to the city of *Philadelphia*, there to obey the orders of congress, or of his excellency general *Washington*, and to remain in the continental service during this campaign, or so long as the commander in chief shall require their service, unless the exigencies of this state should require their recal by the governor and the council."

RESOLVES OF CONTINENTAL CONGRESS, 20 OCTOBER, 1777.

"*Resolved*, That the governor and council of Maryland be informed that the artillery regiments in the service of the United States have suffered so much in the late engagements, that there are not a sufficient number to do the duty of artillery-men in the army, and therefore that the government of that state be earnestly requested to order the companies of matrosses in the service of the state of Maryland to join the army immediately, and that the said companies shall be ordered to return whenever the government of that state shall require it."

A COMPANY OF MATROSSES AT ANNAPOLIS.

Capt. Thomas Watkins	Officers elected
1st Lt. Levin Lawrence	by the Convention
2nd Lt. Thomas Todd	of Maryland
3rd Lt. John Iiams, Jr.	Oct. 26th, 1776.*

* See Proceedings of the Convention, pg. 288.

Annapolis, December 12th, 1776.

A Return of Sundries wanting for the Recruits for the Artillery at Annapolis.

John Fitzjarrold	Joseph Tucker	John Carrall
James Simmons	Elisha Talbott	John Orber
Timothy Kennedy	William Nichols	Henry Scott
Partrick Coursey	John Folks	John Boyle
Anthony Murphy	James Clarke	John Saunders
Thomas Condram	James Cole	John King, Jr.
Wm. Pritchett	William Powell	Phillip Obrian
Joseph Duvall	William Poland	John Burgess
Thomas Fanning	Joseph Bryan	James Lawson
Andrew Keith	Joseph Deale	John Reynolds
William Brady	William Hoharo	Joseph Smith
Michael Clansey	Denniss Myhan	Robert Moree
Saml. Q. Winser	John Wells	James Moree
Zekiel Harris	John Lamb	

41 blankets, 41 coats, 41 vests, 35 breeches, 39 hats, 34 pair of shoes and 38 pair of stockings wanted for the above recruits.

James John Skinner,

Serjt. Captn. Fulford.

MUSTER ROLL OF CAPT. FURNIVAL'S COMPANY OF ARTILLERY.

3D COMPY. OF MATROSSES.

Date of Commission { Nov. 5th, 1776 Alex. Furnival, Capt.
Saml. Gerock, 1st Lieut.   Fever
Robt. Willmott, 2nd "   On Furlow
Saml. Sadler, 3rd "

RANK.	NAMES.		CAUSE OF ABSENCE.
Serjt.	Willm. Cornwall	sick	
"	Willm. Day	present	Reduced to a priv. Sent.
"	Richd. Lewis	sick	
"	Nath. Thomas	absent	On Furlow
Corpl.	Jno. Mahoney	present	
"	Jno. Wheeler	absent	On Furlow till 19th Ins.
"	Jeremh. Sullivan	present	
"	Danl. Rodden	sick	Putrid Fever
Drum.	Thos. Williams	present	
	Dennis Flanagan	"	
	Jno. Taylor	"	
	Jno. Yellum	sick	Convalescent

during the War of the American Revolution, 1775–83.

RANK.	NAMES.		CAUSE OF ABSENCE.
	Jno. Quin	present	
	Jno. Sandle	"	
	Howell Lewis	"	
	Bryan Farral	"	
	Corns. Carney	sick	Agae Fever
	Richd. Wheelen	present	
	Jno. Fitzpatrick	"	
	Jno. Fitzgerrald	deceased	Oct 15th
	Robert Craig	present	
	Danl. Neal	"	
	John Kendercline	sick	Shoulder bruised by Accident at [Camp
	Thos. Glessin	present	
	Phillip Masterson	"	
	Adam Myers	"	
	Saml. Lambart	"	
	Michael O'Conner	"	
	Robert Karr	sick	Burnt Arm at Camp
	John O'Donnell	present	
	Mathew McMahone	"	
	Saml. Coyl	absent	Prisoner in Balto. Goal
	Thomas York	present	
	Jno. Garrity	"	
	Thos. Yates	sick	Sore leg
	Jno. White	present	
	Thos. Price	"	
	Zephaniah White	"	
	Wm. Grimes	"	
	Thos. Randle	"	
	Jno. Ginnivan	"	
	Willm. Wade	sick	Flux
	Willm. Richardson	absent	Wounded by Accident
	John Stonehouse	deserted	Sept 20th
	John Bryan	present	
	Willm. McNamarra	deserted	Sept 29th

The Above is an Exact Return of my Company taken Nov. 17th, 1777.

Alex. Furnival, Captn. Artillery.

A REPORT OF CAPT. RICHARD DORSEY'S COMPANY OF ARTILLERY.

Richard Dorsey, Capt.   Ebenezar Finley, 1st Lt.   Wm. Judah, 2nd Lt.

Young Wilkinson, Serjt.	on furlow	Andrew Shrink	present
Nicholas Ricketts	do	present	Benj. Jones	"
Alex. Craige	do	"	Joseph Wilks	"
John Curtis	do	"	Edmd. Walsh	"

Ths. Pearson	Corpl.	present	John Brady		present
Sam. Thomson	"	"	Robert Britt		"
Jas. Hendrickson	"	"	Alex. Blake		"
Henry Kelliher	Drum.	"	Anthony Barnes		"
John Pearson		"	Robert Mitchell, in Goal for House Breaking		
Ths. Robinson		sick			
Cornelius Forrester		"	Edwd. Barry		"
James Barry		present	James Bradly, in Goal for House Breaking		
James Rid		"			
Edwd. Coughlan		"	David White		"
John Sly		sick	Alex. Forrester, sick in the Country with Fevers		
Wm. Delany, in Gaol on Susspion of House Breaking					
			John Handlen		"
Robt. Thompson		"	Freeman Newman		"
Peter Richards		"	Wm. Culbertson		"
David Marony		"	Henry Carrol		"
John Wilkins		"	Timothy Murphy		"
Fred. Pine		"	Timothy Dunnavin		"
Ths. Connor		"	[One, No. 57, torn off]		
James Mathias, in Gaol for House Breaking			Will (?) Forbes		"
			Hugh McDowell		sick
George Cooper		"	Saml. Chester		present
John Power		sick	John Curtis		"
John Clark		present	Ths. Nelson		"
David Walsh		"	Wm. Whittom		"
Martin Condon		"	John Akerly		sick
Richard Burke		"	John Cockerton		present
Wm. Reed		"	Thos. Grainger		"
Mathew Kelly		"	Wm. Clark, in Goal for House Breaking		
John Turner		"			
Joel Bennett		"	John Jarvis		"
Richd. Pitsland, sick in the Country with Bilious Fever			John Howard		"
			George Letzinger		"
R—— O'D——l,		"			
[Nos. 28 to 32 are torn off and Nos. 27 and 33 are partly torn off.]			1 Captain		
			2 Lieutenants		
			4 Serjeants		
—— Shoughnesey (?)		present	3 Corporals		
Stephen Fennell		"	1 Drummer		
Richard Wilkinson		"	56 Effective Privates		
Alex. McMullain		"	8 Sick		
Thomas Smith		"	1 On Furlow		

Nov. 17th, 1777.

The Above is a True State of my Company.

Richd. Dorsey, Capt. Artillery.

during the War of the American Revolution, 1775-83.

A Return of Capt. William Marbury's Company of Artillery.

Thomas McNear	Hezekiah Wayman	John T. Shaaff
John Sands	William James	James P. Maynard
John Bond	William Johnson	Daniel Murray
Christopher Hohne	Henry Smith	Francis T. Clemments
Edward Roberts	John Barber	Arthur Shaaff
Patrick Dunn	Jesse Lewis	Isaac Holland
William Grant	Francis Welsh	John Welsh
Danl. Wells, Jr.	Robert Lusby	Edward Pryse
William Glover	Richard Dorsey	Henry Johnson
William Taylor	Jonathan Rawlings	Henry Syble
Thomas Hewitt	William Robertson	Edward Holland
Jesse Ray	Andrew Williams	James Bright
John Thompson	John Williams	Robert Parker
Thomas Chalmers	John Callahan	John Sullivan, Jr.
John Keith	Richard Harwood, of Thomas	Richard Dawes

Muster Roll of Capt. William Brown's Company in the Regt. of Artillery in the Service of the United States of America, Commanded by Col. Charles Harrison, for November, 1778.

Commissioned,
- William Brown, Captain. Absent with Leave of Gen. Knox.
- James Smith, Capt. Lieut.
- James McFadon, 1st Lieut.
- Clement Skerritt, 2nd Lieut.
- Alex. Neilson, 2nd Lieut.

APPOINTED.	NAMES.	APPOINTED.	NAMES.
	Serjeants		
1777, Nov 22	John Stapples	1777, Nov 22	Thomas Barber
"	James Adams	"	Patrick Corcoran
"	Henry Slack	"	Charles Stewart
	Bombardiers		
"	Michael Hawk		William Jones
	Thomas Conderall		William Heany
	Michael O'Brian		
	Drummer		
"	James Brooks		
	Corporals		
"	Arthur Carnes		John Ratcliff
	Tamlin Spencer		Thomas Fanning
	Matthew Adams		

Appointed.	Names.	Remarks.
	Gunners	
1777, Nov 22	Phillip O'Brian	On Comd. with Capt. Brown
"	John Vaughan	
"	John Connelly	
"	Benj. Patman	Reduced to Matross, 1 Dec
	James Royston	
	Fifer	
	David Younge	

Inlisted.	Names.	Remarks.
	Matrosses	
1777, Nov 22	John Burke	Joined 7 Nov
	Isaac Burton	
	George Baker	
	William Connelly	
	Robt. Campbell	
	Timothy Connelly	Joined 5 Dec
	Patrick Coursey	
	John Carrell	
	Thomas Carter	
	James Coale	
	James Clarke	
	Hugh Champlin	
	James Compton	Joined 21 Dec
	William Davis	
	John Evans	
	John Fitzgerald, Sr.	
	John Fitzgerald, Jr.	Sick Bedford, 30 Aug
	John Foalks	
	James Ford	
	Charles Groom	
	Mark Goldsbury	
	Jonathan Gill	
	Ignatius Griffin	
	Danl. Heavey	
	Henry Higgs	
	John Head	
	Michael Hughs	[23 Nov
	Wm. Hickinson	Joined 15 Nov. Sent to Hosptl. N. Windsor,
1777, Nov 22	Edward Jeffirson	Sick Bedford, 30 Aug
	William Johnston	On Comd. with Artificers
	Francis Johnston	
	Petter Lawrence	Comd. for Col. Duply
	Joh ———	

Inlisted.	Names.	Remarks.
	Matrosses	
	John Lynch	
	James Moree	
	Charles Murritt	Sick Yellow Springs, 26 May
1778, May 8	Henry Magen	
1777, Nov 22	Chas. McGloghlan	
	Mays Nevin	
	Benj. Patman	Joined as Matross, 1 Dec
	Joseph Poague	
	Francis Popham	
	Saml. Popham	
	John Rhoads	
	Petter Robinson	
	John Reynolds	
	Darbey Spilcey	
1778, Jan 5	Thomas Smith	
1777, Nov 22	Charles Sutton	
	Robert Smith	
	John Slack	
	John Saunders	
	Reuben Scott	
	James Tayler	
	James Whailing	
	James Walsh	

[All in the above Roll enlisted for 3 years.]

Pluckimin, 23rd December, 1778. Mustered then Capt. Wm. Brown's Company as Specified in the Above Roll.

        Samuel F. Parker, D. C. M.

Proof of Effectives.

	Capt.	Cn. Lt.	1st Lt.	2 Lts.	Sgts.	Cpls.	Bomds.	Gunners.	Drummer.	Fifer.	Matrosses.
Present		1	1	2	6	5	5	3	1	1	50
Absent	1							1			6
Totals	1	1	1	2	6	5	5	4	1	1	56

We do swear that the within Muster Roll is a True State of the Company without fraud to these United States or to any Individual, According to the Best of Our Knowledge.

       James Smith, Capt. Lieut.
       Clement Skerrett, Lieut.

Sworn Before me at Pluckemin this 23rd day of December, 1778.
       T. Knox, M. G. Artillery.

MARYLAND ACTS—JULY, 1779.

"An ACT relating to the officers and soldiers of this state in the American army, and other purposes therein mentioned.

. . . .

And be it enacted, That the matrosses in the city of Annapolis and Baltimore-town, who are effective, shall be incorporated into one company, and sent as soon as may be to camp, and shall hereafter be considered as part of the quota to be found by this state, ... and the governor and council may select and appoint a proper number of officers to command such company, out of the most capable of the present officers, ... and the governor and council are requested to recommend such of them as remain to his excellency general Washington, to be provided for, and they shall continue in the pay of this state until they shall be taken into the continental service."

RESOLVES OF THE MARYLAND ASSEMBLY 9 MAY, 1780.

"*Resolved*, That the three companies of artillery belonging to this state in the continental army, commanded by Captains Brown, Dorsey and the late Captain Gale, be incorporated with and annexed to the regiment commanded by colonel Harrison, of the Virginia corps of artillery, or to some other in the continental Army.

Resolved, That the same be formed into four companies, with proper officers belonging to this state to command them, and that the governor and council be requested to communicate the above resolutions to congress as soon as may be, that the same may be carried into immediate effect and execution."*

Pay Roll of the 2nd & 3d Companies of Maryland Artillery, Incorporated, for Aug., Sept., Oct., Nov. & Dec., 1780.

NAMES.	REMARKS.	NAMES.	REMARKS.
Capt. James Smith	promoted from a Capt. Lt. and rec'd 4 mos. pay as such	Fifers Thos. Tyack Elisha Redman Peter Davis Thomas Potter	returned from No. Caro. Regt.

* For the results of the incorporation of the Maryland Artillery Companies with Harrison's Virginia Artillery see page 596.

Names.	Remarks.	Names.	Remarks.
Capt. Lt.			
Ebenr. Finley		Matrosses	
		William Hutton	
1st Lts.		Andrew Shrink	
Robt. Willmott		John Sandall	
James Baques		Thomas Bowler	
		Edward Berry	
2nd Lts.		Bennit Railey	
Nichs. Ricketts		Thos. Redman	
Young Wilkinson		Daniel Rodden	
Isaac Rawlings		Willm. Grimes	
John Cheever		John Prout	
		Jacob Owings	deceased 19 Nov '81, paid widow 1 mo.
Sergeants			
Jesse Thompson			
Wm. Rawlings		Thomas Randall	
David Welsh		John Ireland	
Wm. Cornwall		Danl. Neale	
Saml. Carter		John Clarke	
		Thomas Gleeson	
Corpls.		Peregrine Askew	
James Hutton		Hugh McDowell	
Rawleyh Spinks	deceased 28 Nov '81	Benedict Johnson	lost his leg
		Michael Connor	
Bombrs.		Philip Martuson	
James Hammond		John Brady	
Willm. Allen		James Neale	discharged Sept '82
		John Smith	" " "
Gunners		John Stanley	deceased 24 Apl '83
Philip Jones			
Willm. Dixon		John Compton	" 1 July '83
Dennis McCormack	discharged Sept '82	Cornelius Harling	" 8 June '83
		Michael O'Ferrell	" 23 Feb '83
Drummer		John Payne	" 22 May '83
Thos. Williams			

For the Arrangement of the Artillery Jan. 1st, 1781, and Jan. 1st, 1783, see pages 365 and 477.

Roll and Muster of the 1st Company of Maryland Artillery from Jan. 1st to Mch. 31st, 1782. [All Enlisted for the War.]

Names.	Remarks.	Names.	Remarks.
Capt. William Browne			
1st Lieut. James McFadon		Matrosses Isaac Burton Arthur Carnes Hugh Champlin John Fitzgerrald	
Serjeants Henry Slack Charles Stewart John Slack	Commd. Military Stores	Jonathan Gill Henry Higgs	Commd. Light Infantry
John Vaughan Charles Sutton		Daniel Heavey Francis Johnston Robert Livingston Joshua Lovley	
Corporals Michael Hawke Thomas Condran James Royston John Ratcliffe	Commd. Military Stores	John Sellman William Stalker Robert Smith David Young Mark Goldsbury Reuben Scott	Commd. Light Infantry
Thomas Fanning Thomas Browne		Timothy Connelly William Davis	
Bombardiers Michael O'Brian Phillip O'Brian		Charles Groome John Head	Commd. Forage Waggon
Gunners James Walsh James Moree	Comd. Light Infantry	Charles Murritt John Reynolds Peter Lawrence John Evans	Commd. Military Stores
James Whailing Peter Mayner		Joseph Poague Thomas Smith Charles Sutton	Promoted to Serjt. 1 Jan
Matrosses Thomas Browne	Promoted Corpl. 1 Jan	James Symonds Robert Myers	Sick Camden 6 Dec

I certifie the above Roll to be the true state of said Company, Camp near Bacon's Bridge, So. Carolina, 5th April, 1782.

W. Brown, Capt. Artillery.

Frederick German Artillery.

Serjt.	Bomb.	Bomb.
Fredk. Grammer	James McDonnall	Francis Welsh
Jona. Pinkney	Gideon Kent	John Gordon
Thos. McNier	Henry Johnson	Robert Lusby
John Sands	Samuel Lusby	Richd. Dorsey
	John May	Jona. Raullings
Corpl.	Elijah Pennington	Willm. Robeson
John Bond	Richard Flimming	Willm. Madcafe
Alex. Thompson	Jesse Ray	John Edwill
Chrs. Hohne	James Sears	W. Barns
Edwd. Roberts	John Thompson	Jos. Burneston
	David Biggs	Edwd. Lusby
Gunrs.	Thomas Lusby	Andrew Williams
Edward Roper	Thomas Chalmers	John McNier
John Kerr	John Keith	John Williams
Patrick Dunn	Hezekiah Wayman	John Callahan
James Elliott	Willm. Phelps	Richd. Harwood, of Thos.
Willm. Grant	Willm. Perdue	John T. Shaaff
Willm. Sifton	Willm. James	James P. Maynard
	John Barry	Daniel Murray
Bomb.	Willm. Johnson	Francs. T. Clements
Caleb Marriott	Robert Nicols	Arthur Shaaff
Danl. Wells, Jr.	Henry Smeth	John Keeth
Willm. Glover	John Barber	John Thompson
Willm. Tayler	Joseph Gest	Joseph Gist
Thomas Hewit	Jesse Lewis	
John Woolfit	Henry Wood	
	M.	

Artillery Men.

James Welch	Peregrine Askew	Joseph Poogue
Henry Higgs	Thomas Bowler	Robert Campbell
Hugh Champlin	Charles Groome	Thomas Larymore

Infantry.

Steven Hancock	Robert Statia	John McDaniel
Thomas Clarke	Richd. Haslip	Peter McGuire
Joshua Lister	Emanuel Carthegene	J. Smith

December 23rd, 1783. A Sargent and Corpral and Six Men.

I Hope that you Will Generrel Smallwood that you Wood Be So Good has to Be Stoo a Litel monney.

Han. Hus.

             Decem ....
  Account of Expences of Seventeen ....
  Great Guns, by order of the Governor ....
  the Entertainment given to Gen ....
   17 Men per List, to be paid by .. ..
  Auditors Office 12th January, 1784
    Passed for Four pounds f ....
   Receipt for 17 soldiers, Guards

[Entertainment of General Washington at Annapolis at the time he resigned his Commission.]

RESOLVES OF CONTINENTAL CONGRESS 15 MAY, 1778.

"*Resolved, unanimously*, That every non-commissioned military officer and soldier, who hath inlisted, or shall inlist, into the service of these states, for and during the war, and shall continue therein to the end thereof, shall be entitled to receive the further reward of 80 dollars at the expiration of the war."

A List of the Noncommissioned and Privates of the Maryland Artillery, who were entitled to the Gratuity of Eighty Dollars as allowed by Act of Congress of May 15th, 1778, and settled by Jno. White, Esquire, late Commissr.'s Assistant for Settling the Accounts of the Army for Maryland.

Henry Slack, Serjt	Robert Smith	Elisha Redman
Charles Stewart "	David Young	Thomas Potter
John Slack "	Mark Goldsbury	Michael Conner
John Vaughan "	Reuben Scott	William Grimes
Charles Sutton "	Timothy Connelly	John Ireland
Thomas Brown "	Charles Groom	Philip Masterson
Michael Hawke, Corpl.	John Head	John Prout
Thomas Condran "	Charles Muirett	Daniel Neal
James Roystan "	Peter Lawrence	Bennit Rieley
Philip O'Bryan "	John Evans	Andrew Sprink
Michael O'Bryan	Thomas Smith	Thomas Bowler
James Welch	James Simonds	John Brady
James Moree	Robert Myers	Danl. Rawdon
James Whaling	Jesse Thompson, Serjt.	Thomas Gleeson
Peter Maynor	William Rawlings "	Edward Berry
Isaac Burton	James Hutton "	Perry Askey
Arthur Carnes	William Cornwell "	Samuel Carter, Serjt.
Hugh Champlin	David Welch	Benedict Johnson

during the War of the American Revolution, 1775–83.

John Fitzgerald	James Hammond, Corpl	Thomas Redman
Jonathan Gill	William Hutton "	Thomas Randall
Henry Higgs	William Dixon	John Sandall
Daniel Havey	William Allen	Hugh McDowell
Robert Levingston	John Clark	Francis Johnston
Joseph Pogue	Thomas Williams	Richard Lewis, Serjt.
John Stillman	Thomas Tyack	William Davies
William Stalker	Peter Davies	Philip Jones

List of Non Commissioned Officers and Privates of the Maryland Artillery who received the Gratuity of Congress for serving to the End of the War   rec'd from
                                    J. Howell, Esq., Paymr. Genl.
Dec. 5th, 1788.

Return of Certificates issued to the NonCommissioned Officers &c, of the Corps of Maryland Artillery late commanded by Major Brown, taken from the Register of John White, Esquire, Asst. Commissr. of Army Accounts for the State of Maryland.

Henry Slack	Serjt.	John Sandall	M.	Rawling Spinks	M.
Charles Stewart	"	Edward Berry	"	William Hellin	"
John Slack	"	Isaac Burton	"	Thomas Redman	"
John Vaughan	"	Arthur Carnes, Corpl. & M.		James McGowen	"
Charles Sutton	"	Hugh Champlin, Jr.	M.	Timothy Donovan	"
Michael Hawke	Corpl.	John Fitzgereld, Jr.	"	John Wheeler	"
Thomas Condron	"	Jonathan Gill	"	Frederick Eyen	"
James Roystan	"	Henry Higgs	"	John Howard	"
John Ratcliffe	"	Daniel Havey	"	Jonas Philips	"
Thomas Fanning	"	Francis Johnston	"	William Davies	"
Thomas Brown	Serjt.	Robert Livingston	"	Charles Groom	"
Michael O'Bryan	B.	Joshua Lovely	"	John Head	"
James Welch	"	John Sillman	"	Charles Muiret	"
Phillip O'Bryan	Corpl.	William Stalker	"	John Reynolds	"
James Moore	Gun.	Robert Smith	"	Peter Laurence	"
James Whaling	"	David Young	"	John Evans	"
Peter Maynor	Fifer	Mark Goldsbury	"	Joseph Pogue	"
Samuel Carter	Serjt.	Reuben Scott	"	Thomas Smith	"
Richard Lewis	"	Timothy Conolly	"	James Simonds	"
James Hammond	Corpl.	Benedict Johnson	"	Robert Myers	"
William Hutton	"	John Paine	."	Thomas Brown	"
Dennis McCormick	"	Thomas Bowler	"	James Welch	"
William Hallin	B.	John Compton	"	Jesse Thompson	Serjt.
William Dixon	"	John Standley, Jr.	"	William Rawlings	"
John Clark	G.	John Brady	"	James Hutton	"

Thomas Williams	D.	Philip Jones	M.	William Cornwall	Serjt.
Elisha Redman	"	Hugh McDowell	"	James Hendrickson	M.
Thomas Potter	F.	John Smith	"	William Willthon	"
Peter Davies	D.	Daniel Rawdon	"	John Pearson	"
Perry Askey	M.	Thomas Tyack	F.	John Turner	"
Michael Conner	"	David Welch	Serjt.	James Berry	"
Thomas Gleeson	"	Thomas Barber,	"	David White	"
William Grimes	"	died in Virginia		Jacob Owens,	"
Cornelius Harling	"	John Connelly,	M.	died	
John Ireland	"	dischd. at Pow Pow		John Quinn,	"
Philip Masterson	"	Robert Campbell	"	dischd. in 1781	
James Neil	"	Michael Hughes	"	James Clark	"
Michael O'Farol	"	Edward Henesey,	"	William Allen	"
Daniel Neil	"	infantry afterwards			
John Prout	"	Peter Maynor, Sr.,	"		
John Redman	"	died			
Thomas Randall	"	Francis Popham,	"		
Bennet Reily	"	killed			
Andrew Shrink	"	Thomas Stanley	"		

```
Amount of pay for the Year 1782.........................Dols.   9189.83
    "    from 1 Aug to 1 Jan '82 ...... ........ ..............    9750.80
    "    for Gratuity ............. . .................... ...........   6240.00
    "    for 1783 . .................................................   4489.20
                                                                       ─────────
                                                                       29,670.03
```

Total amount received by Major W. Brown for the Non Commissd. & Privates of the Artillery late under his command, twenty nine thousand six hundred & seventy dollars & $\frac{3}{90}$ pts., which agrees with his Receipts.

                                                      Joseph Howell, Jr., Comiss.

Chrisr. Richmond, Esquire,
      Aud. General for Maryland
Entered in List of those entitled to Land.

ROLLS OF MARYLAND MEN IN LEE'S DRAGOONS.

CAPT.-MAJOR-LT. COL. HENRY LEE

Henry Lee was commissioned Captain of a Company of Virginia Dragoons June 18th, 1776. This Company was attached to the 1st Continental Dragoons March 31st, 1777.

RESOLVES OF CONTINENTAL CONGRESS 7 APRIL, 1778.

"*Resolved*, That captain H. Lee be promoted to the rank of major-commandant; that he be empowered to augment his present corps by inlistment to two troops of horse, to act as a separate corps."

RESOLVES OF CONTINENTAL CONGRESS 28 MAY, 1778.

"*Resolved*, That major Henry Lee's corps of partizan light dragoons consist of three, instead of two, troops."

RESOLVES OF CONTINENTAL CONGRESS 13 JULY, 1779.

"*Resolved*, That capt. M'Lane's company, now attached to the Delaware regiment, and the dismounted dragoons belonging to major Lee's partizan corps, be formed into a fourth troop and added to the corps: this troop to be commanded by capt. M'Lane, and to serve on foot."

RESOLVES OF CONTINENTAL CONGRESS 14 FEBRUARY, 1780.

"*Resolved*, That recruiting money be furnished to major Lee, to enable him to inlist seventy privates, to serve as dismounted dragoons in addition to those now in the corps; the whole to be formed into three troops."

RESOLVES OF THE MARYLAND ASSEMBLY 11 APRIL, 1780.

"*Resolved*, That the officers and soldiers raised in this state, and now in colonels Hazen's, Spencer's, Gist's and major Lee's corps, be entitled to receive the same privileges, bounties, and cloathing, that the officers in the line have or are entitled to receive under the resolution of the 4th of December, 1778, and the act of assembly, entitled, An act relating to the officers and soldiers of this state, in the American army, and other purposes therein mentioned, passed at a session of assembly, begun and held at the city of Annapolis, on Thursday the 22d day of July, in the year 1779."*

* Also see pages 596 and 597.

RESOLVES OF CONTINENTAL CONGRESS 21 OCTOBER, 1780.

"Resolved, ... That there be 2 partizan corps, consisting of 3 troops of mounted and 3 of dismounted dragoons, of 50 each, one of which corps to be commanded by col. Armand, and the other by major Lee, and officered by appointment of the commander in chief, with the approbation of Congress: and that the commander in chief be authorized to direct a mode for completing, recruiting and supplying the said corps."

RESOLVES OF CONTINENTAL CONGRESS 6 NOVEMBER, 1780.

"*Resolved*, That the partizan corps commanded by major Lee in future have two field officers, a lieutenant-colonel and a major.

Resolved, That major Lee be, and hereby is, promoted to the rank of lieutenant-colonel of cavalry in the army of the United States, retaining the command of his present corps."

A Roll of Men enlisted in the Partizan Cavalry under the command of Major Henry Lee, out of Cecil County, June, 1778.

John Germain Thomas	Jesse Crasby
James Wallace	Thomas Owins
Thomas Manly	Jos. Owins
Daniel Williamson	Christopher Rutledge
William Richardson	George Hill
John Ward	John Cummins
William Richardson, (miller)	Jos. Hemphill
Michael Rudulph	Jnonath Short
Thomas Broom	Abiah Hukill
Robert Crouch	George Boice

Sir :—Above you have a return of Men enlisted by me in the Partizan Cavalry, it has not been in my power owing to the absence of some of our Non Comd. Officers, to make a return e'er this, all the above men were enlisted out of yr. County.

I am, Sr. yr. very hbl. srvt.

John Rudulph,
L. P. L. D.

A Pay Roll for a Detachmt. of Dragoons of Lt. Col. Henry Lee's Legion, belonging to the State of Maryland, for the months of Aug., Sept., Oct., Nov. and Dec., 1780. [All paid for five months, except

Arch. Gordon, 2 months, and John Manly, not paid, being advanced and the time uncertain when.]

NAMES.	RANK.	NAMES.	RANK.
Michael Rudulph	Capt.	John J. Thomas	Privates
David Henderson	Serjt.	George Hill	
John Manly		Robert Crouch	
		Abiah Hukill	
William French	Beuglers	John Bennet	
Jesse Crasbey		Samuel Tenkins	
		John Kinard	
Samuel Thompson	Privates	James Arrants	
Christ. Rutledge		James Veazey	
Joseph Owens		William Dowdle	
Joseph Hemphill		John Towlin	
Richard Basset		George Boice	
James McCracken		John Howard	
Joshua Harvey		Arch. Gorden	
Willm. Chesnut		Abrahm. Sutton	Fife Major.

Michl. Rudulph,
Capt. Lee's Legion.
Oct 4th, 1783.

A Return of Dragoons who have served in Lieut. Col. Henry Lee's Legion, belonging to the State of Maryland.

NAMES.	COMMENCEMENT OF PAY.	NAMES.	COMMENCEMENT OF PAY.
Thomas Broom	7th Aprril, 1778	William French	7th Apl., '78 Bugler
George Hill	"	Jessee Crasby	" "
John Manly	"	David Henderson,	1st Jan., 1779
Christopher Rutledge	"	Promoted Serjeant, 1st Apl., '80	
Joseph Owens	"	Johsua Harvey	1st Jan., 1779
Joseph Hemphill	"	William Chisnut	"
Richard Bassett	"	Samuel Tenkins	
James McCracken	"	James Arrants	8th March, 1780
John Jerman Thomas	"	James Veazey	"
Robert Crouch	"	William Dowdle	12th March, 1780
Abiah Hukill	"	John Towlin	16th March, "
John Kinard	"	John Howard	1st April, "
John Bennet	"	John Johnson	10th July, 1780
George Boice	"		

There are several Men, who are entitled to have their Depreciation Accts. settled, whose Names are not entered above.

M. Rudulph

Return of Sundry Soldiers of Lee's Legion by Capt. Michl. Rudolph in October, 1783.

I do hereby certify that the bearer hereof John McColla Served three years in the 4th regt. Light Dragoons, as a private, and that he was a Citizen of the State of Maryland, and has been returned as one of its Soldiers. Nor has he received any consideration for the depreciation of his pay during the term of his Service, which commenced 10th April, 1777.

28th Sept., 1785.
David Hopkins,
Late Major Light Dragoons.*

I do certify that the bearer hereof, James McCrackin, (McCracking), a dragoon of the Partizan Legion, Commanded by Lieut. Col. Henry Lee, belonging to the State of Maryland has pay due him for his service in the Legion, from the first day of April, 1780, to this date, deducting one Months pay rec'd in cloathing.
Given this 20th Aug., 1783
Michl. Rudulph,
Capt., Lee's Legion.

Same to John Kinkead, (Kincaid), of Delaware.

By Virtue of the Orders of the Honble. Major Genl. Green, John Wisham, the Bearer hereof, Belonging to the Third Troop of the Partizan Legion, Commanded by Lieut. Col. Henry Lee, has Leave of Absence till called for, and then to repair to such rendezvous as shall be appointed in the State of Maryland, under pain of being considered and treated as a Deserter, the said Summons being published in the Maryland Newspapers three Weeks successively, to be considered as sufficient Notice. Given under my Hand this 17th Day of June, 1783.
Jos. Eggleston,
Ma. Comg., Lee's Legion.

Same to John Manly, George Boice and Robert Crouch of the Second Troop June 12th, 1783, George Hill of the Second Troop June 19th, 1783, and Jessey Cosby of the First Troop and William French of the Third Troop June 28th, 1783. Also the same to Thomas Broom of the First Troop March 20th, 1784, and William Dowdle of the Second Troop March 30th, 1784, signed by James Armstrong, Capt. 1st Troop.

---

* This has been accidentally misplaced. John McColla belonged to Moylan's (see page 599).

Agreeable to a resolution of Congress, bearing date the 26th day of May, 1783, the bearer hereof Archibald Gordon a Soldier (Was of Lt. Col. Henry Lee's Legion) belonging to the State of Maryland has leave of absence untill called upon by proper authority to join his Corps, or is finally discharged.

Given at the Head of Elk in Mary Ld. this 26th Aug., 1783.
        Michael Rudulph,
         Capt., Lee's Legion.

Sir—Please pay to Archibal Gordan my pay Due me as a Soldier in the Partizan Legion, and his Receipt Shall be good for the Same.
      Sir I am yours
         Abiah Hukill
         Christopher Rutledge
         Robert Crouch

I do authorize and appoint David Henderson to receive and settle the above Order from Abih. Hukill in favour of me. Given this 12th Sept., 1783   Archibald Gordon.

Michl. Rudulph, Capt., Lee's Legion.

        Cecil County 7th Novem., 1785.

Sir—Please to Settle with the Bearer, Mr Tobias Rudulph, what's Due to me On your Books for my Services as a Soldier in Col. Henry Lee's Legion as my furlow will shew and Remit it to me by him
    and you will Oblige Sr. yours &c
         Archibald Gordon.

Capt. White Or any Other
 Officer that hath the
 Settling said Accts.
      Called John Gordon

Power of Attorney from Abiah Hukins to David Henderson to collect all sums due from the United States to Hukins for his services in Lt. Col. Lee's Partizan Legion.

Same from William Dowdle to Thomas Broom, April 10th, 1784.

Sir:—Please Pay Unto Mr. Henry Robinson the Sum or Sums of money wich may Be Due on finall Setlement with John Kinkead and his Receipt Shall Be your Discharge for the same from Sir your
Humble Servt.

Elk, May 31st, 1785.   Wm. Hugg.

To the Agent for Col. Lee's Legion for State Maryland.

Same for pay due William Dowdle, assigned by him to Thomas Broom, signed T. Broom, May 30th, 1785.

Auditor's Office, 23rd April, '87.

I do certify That there is due from the State of Maryland to James Gillis' Admor. £18. 15s. due to the said Gillis as Trumpeter in Col. Lee's Legion, from Aug. 1st, 1780, to Jan. 1st, 1781.
C. Richmond, Aud. Genl.

Auditor's Office, 23rd April, '87.

I do certify That there is due from the State of Maryland to William Crookshank's Admix. £15. 12s. and sixpence for pay as Trooper in Col. Lee's Legion, from Aug. 1st, 1780, to Jan. 1st, 1781.
C. Richmond, Aud. Genl.

Same to the Administrator of Jonathan Short's estate.

ROLLS OF MARYLAND MEN IN PULASKI'S AND ARMAND'S LEGIONS.

Brigadier General Count Pulaski

RESOLVES OF CONTINENTAL CONGRESS 15 SEPTEMBER, 1777.

"*Resolved*, That a commander of the horse be appointed with the rank of a brigadier; the ballots being taken, count Pulaski was elected."

RESOLVES OF CONTINENTAL CONGRESS 28 MARCH, 1778.

"*Resolved*, That count Pulaski retain his rank of brigadier in the army of the United States, and that he raise and have the command of an independent corps to consist of 68 horse, and 200 foot, the horse to be armed with lances, and the foot to be equipped in the manner of light infantry: the corps to be raised in such way and composed of such men as general Washington shall think expedient and proper; and if it shall be thought by general Washington that it will not be injurious to the service, that he have liberty to dispense, in this particular instance, with the resolve of Congress against enlisting deserters."

RESOLVES OF CONTINENTAL CONGRESS 6 APRIL, 1778.

"*Resolved*, ... That, if any of the states in which brigadier Pulaski shall recruit for his legion, shall give to persons inlisting in the same for three years, or during the war, the bounty allowed by the state in addition to the continental bounty, the men so furnished not being the inhabitants of any other of the United States, shall be credited to the quota of the state in which they shall be inlisted."

RESOLVES OF THE ASSEMBLY OF MARYLAND 21 APRIL, 1778.

"*Resolved*, That the governor and council be authorized and empowered to assist brigadier-general Pulaski in recruiting for his legion; and that all persons enlisting in the same (not being inhabitants of any other of the United States) for three years or during the war, shall be allowed the bounty given by act of assembly to soldiers enlisting for three years or during the war, and shall be credited to the proportion of the county where such recruits shall have last resided; and such recruits shall not be subject to be draughted under the late act for procuring troops for the American army. That the said recruits be passed by the lieutenant of the county wherein they shall be enlisted, who shall keep an account of all such recruits."

RESOLVES OF CONTINENTAL CONGRESS 13 FEBRUARY, 1779.

"*Resolved*, That all the men, inhabitants of these states, who shall be recruited in the corps of gen. Pulaski, and colonel Armand, in any of the United States, shall be credited to the quota of the state in which they shall be inlisted, they not being inhabitants of any other of the United States.

Resolved, That brigadier general Pulaski and col. Armand, make returns to the board of war of the recruits they shall inlist; and in such returns the places of nativity and settlement, and the state wherein they were inlisted shall be particularly mentioned; and the board are hereby directed to transmit to the respective states, the names and numbers of such persons, inhabitants thereof, as shall be so inlisted."

RESOLVES OF CONTINENTAL CONGRESS 14 NOVEMBER, 1780.

"*Resolved*, That Congress approve the mode suggested by the commander in chief, of incorporating the remainder of the men of the late brigadier general Pulaski's legion, and as many of the officers as there are vacancies for, into colonel Armand's corps; and that a return be made to the board of war of the deficiency of that corps, that measures may be taken to complete it according to the late establishment; and that lieutenant-colonel Lee make a return of the deficiency of his corps, for the same purpose."

A List of Recruits Enlisted in Pulaski's Legion, Balto.

Edward Dannally	William Rolph	William Trugard
Roger Owings	John Collins	
Henry Kent	Bryan Dallam (?)	

This is to Certifie that I have Pas'd the Seven recruits & Substitutes above mentioned Enlisted by Capt. De Segond. General Polaskie's Legion, April 29th, 1778.

And. Buchanan, Lt. Col.

To the Counceal

I should have sent to you the certificat of the other men if Mr. Buckanon your lieutenant, was came in town since the 29 of April that he hath pas'd the seven above. I call for him many times I never met him, as soon as he will make his appeareance in town I'll present them and I'll send you his pass.

De Segond deLaplan.

Thomas Bond, enlisted in Baltimore May 8th, 1778, by Capt. Siggond for Count Pulaski's Legion.

Money advanced for General Pulaski's Legion since the 10th day of April til the 12th of May, 1778.

Names.	When Enlisted.	Names.	When Enlisted.
Edward Dannaly	April 10	Nicholas Ryland	May 8
Roger Owings	27	Thomas Hoult	9
John Cain	May 4	Charles Daemon	10
John Collins	April 28	James Carter	11
Henry Kent	22	Philop Beaty	11
William Rolph	22	John Tedford	12
John Price	May 6	William Trugard, deserter	22
Peter Neguire	8	William Herlity	6
Thomas Bond	8		
	£201.5.0.		

Affidavits of Benjamin Prior and Notley Tippett that they, in the company of Joseph Smith, enlisted in Count Pulaski's Legion, sometime in the month of July, 1779, being then in Charles Town, S. C. Said Smith is now before Richard Barnes, Lt. of St. Mary's County, taken up as a deserter.

Sworn to before Jeremiah Jordon.

St. Mary's County, July 26th, 1780.

ARMAND'S LEGION

Colonel Armand, Marquis De La Rouerie, commissioned 10 May, 1777.

RESOLVES OF CONTINENTAL CONGRESS 10 MAY, 1777

"*Resolved*, That Mons. Armand have a commission, with the rank of colonel, and that he be directed to repair to general Washington."

RESOLVES OF CONTINENTAL CONGRESS 25 JUNE, 1778.

"*Resolved*, That the independent corps raised by col. Armand, in consequence of general Washington's permission, be taken into continental pay. That general Washington be authorised to officer this corps with such foreign and other officers of merit as at present hold commissions, and who are not already and can not be annexed to other corps on the proposed arrangement of the army:

That if any of the States shall think proper to allow the non-commissioned officers and privates, who have or shall enlist in col. Armand's corps, the bounty allowed by them respectively, in addition to the continental bounty, the men so engaged shall be credited as part of the quota of the state who shall allow the additional bounty."

RESOLVES OF CONTINENTAL CONGRESS 21 JUNE, 1779.

"*Resolved*, That the non-commissioned officers and privates of the intended corps of German volunteers be transferred to the corps commanded by colonel Armand."

RESOLVES OF CONTINENTAL CONGRESS 23 FEBRUARY, 1780.

"*Resolved*, That the remains of the legion of the late count Pulaski be incorporated with the corps of colonel Armand, marquis de la Rouerie, in such manner as the commander in chief of the southern army shall think proper : the united corps to be formed into a legion to be commanded by colonel Armand."

RESOLVES OF CONTINENTAL CONGRESS 26 MARCH, 1783.

"*Resolved*, That in consideration of the merit and services of colonel Armand, he be promoted to the rank of brigadier-general, retaining the command of his present corps."

A Return of the Men belonging to the State of Maryland, who served in the First Partizan Legion, commanded by Brigadier General Armand, Marquis de la Rouerie, discharged Nov. the 15th, 1783.

Names and Rank.	What Year Enlisted.	Names and Rank.	What Year Enlisted.
Serjeant.		Privates.	
William Seth	1778	Dennis Lowe	1782
Corporals.		Benjamin Carlisle	1782
Joseph Higdon	1781	Benjamin Gilpin	1782
John Higdon	1782	Edward Jenkins	1782
Trumpeter.		George Tucker	1782
Joseph Herold	1782	Farrier.	
Privates.		Thomas Aspell, Draughted	1780
Edward Donnally	1779	Privates.	
William Bennister	1782	Bernard Thompson	1782
Farrieres.		Philip McDad	1782
Nathaniel Mason	1782	Jacob Ortner	1782
Peter Teams	1778	Michael Eckhart	1782
Corporal.		Frederick Stein	1782
Bazil Lowe	1782	Joseph Chalupetzky	1782

Names and Rank.	What Year Enlisted.	Names and Rank.	What Year Enlisted.
Privates.		Privates.	
Matthias Murray	1781	Jasper Shomig	1782
Bazil Carlisle	1781	Anthony Ulrich	1782
William Davis	1781	Jacob Bartling	1782
John Steel	1782	John Mate	1782
Robert Henwood	1782	George Young	1782
James Lowman	1778	Frederick Klein	1782
Clement Green	1781	John Fair	1782
		James McDonald	1778

Godfried Swartz, Adjutant of the Legion.
Armand, Mqis. de la Rouerie.

ROLLS OF MARYLAND MEN IN VARIOUS OTHER CORPS NOT BELONGING TO MARYLAND.

RESOLVES OF CONTINENTAL CONGRESS 27 DECEMBER, 1776.

"*Resolved*, That general Washington shall be, and he is hereby, vested with full, ample, and complete powers to raise and collect together, in the most speedy and effectual manner, from any or all of these United States, 16 battalions of infantry, in addition to those already voted by Congress; to appoint officers for the said battalions of infantry; to raise, officer, and equip 3000 light horse; three regiments of artillery, and a corps of engineers, and to establish their pay; to apply to any of the states for such aid of the militia as he shall judge necessary; . . . to displace and appoint all officers under the rank of brigadier-general, and to fill up all vacancies in every other department in the American army."

HOUSE OF DELEGATES, ASSEMBLY OF MARYLAND, 7 JANUARY, 1782.

COMMITTEE REPORT.

" THE committee, appointed to enquire the number of recruits wanting to complete the quota of this state, &c. beg leave to report . . . . . . that three companies of artillery (nearly full) belonging to this state, have been incorporated with colonel Harrison's regiment of Virginia artillery; and your committee are of opinion, that the said companies, in justice to this state, ought to have been attached to her line of infantry, and that the said regiment ought to be kept up by Virginia and this state, and that the promotion to vacancies ought to be extended in common to the officers so incorporated, agreeable to their rank and pretentions; but your committee are informed that although the said regiment now consists almost entirely of the men of the companies of this state, yet they are commanded by Virginia officers, and the former officers of the said companies belonging to this state are forced to retire from the service on half pay. Your committee are of opinion, that this matter ought to be represented to congress.

Your committee beg leave further to report as their opinion, that this state has been materially injured, by permitting corps of other lines, and of the additional sixteen regiments, to recruit within this state, as will appear by the following list of companies enlisted in this state, for the following corps of artillery, cavalry, and infantry, to wit: Colonel Hazen's regiment, 2 companies; Hartley's, 3; Gist's, 2; Grayson's, 2 or 3; Rifle, 4; officers discharged by colonel Brodhead at Fort Pit, and the men incorporated with Brodhead's regiment of Pennsylvania troops, but some of them have since deserted and joined the Maryland line; German, 4, now attached to the Maryland line about one company, desertion and term of service expiring must account for the remainder; Foreman's, 2 or 3, attached to the Jersey troops; Patten's, 2, attached to the Pennsylvania line; artillery, 3, incorporated with Harrison's Virginia regiment; Moylan's horse, 3; Baylor's horse, 1; Pulaski's, 1 or 2; Lee's, 1 or 2. In all 30 or 34 companies.

Your committee are informed, that many of the men in the said companies were enlisted for the war, and now remain in such of the above corps as have been continued on the establishment, and others of the reduced corps are now attached to the line of the state in which they have respectively served; and your committee are of opinion, that congress should be requested to order, that all the men, now in service, raised in this state for any of the above companies, be returned and annexed to the line of this state."

2ND CANADIAN OR HAZEN'S

COL. MOSES HAZEN, COMMISSIONED 22 JANUARY, 1776.

This Regiment was intended to be raised in Canada and for some time was called the 2nd Canadian. Later it was recruited in the United States. It was also called 'Congress Own.'

RESOLVES OF CONTINENTAL CONGRESS 19 APRIL, 1781

"*Resolved*, That it be, and hereby is recommended to the states of Rhode-Island and Providence Plantations, New-York, New-Jersey, Pennsylvania, Delaware, Maryland and Virginia, to make good the depreciation of the monthly pay of the officers and soldiers belonging to colonel Moses Hazen's regiment that are considered as a part of the quota of the respective states aforesaid, in the same manner they have made good the depreciation to the officers and soldiers in the battalion belonging to the lines of those states respectively."

Non-commissioned Officers and Privates of Col. Hazen's Regiment, belonging to the State of Maryland.

Capt. Popham's Company.
Daniel Keith, Private

Capt. Heron's Company.

Harvey Burnes, Private	David Kennedy, Private
James Hayton do	Thomas McGee do

Late Capt. Burnes's Company.

John McColgain, Drum.	Massy Fluart, Private
Willm. Brown, Private	John Kuny, (Coony) do
James Duncan do	Chas. March do
John Dugan do	Edward White do

Capt. Carlile's Company.

John Ryan, Serjt.	James Hopkins, Private
Thomas Capen (assigned his depreciation money March 23rd, 1781)	Martin Mulloy do
	James M'Intire, (McIntier) do
Wm. Douly, Corpl.	George Somerville, do
Geo. McDonald, Drum.	(assigned his depreciation money March 12th, 1781)
Nehemiah Barnes, Private	
John Batten do	William Smith, Private
William Deacons do	Francis Tycont do
Thomas Deavour do	Edward Wall do
Samuel Frazer do	

Capt. White's Company.
Christopher Nash

Capt. Munson's Company.
Bartholomew Sheridan, Serjt.

Capt. Pry's Company.

James Edes, Private	James Flood, Private	Wm. Perkins, Private

Capt. Taylor's Company.

Michael Anderson, Private	Hugh Conolly, Private
John Collins, do —Carlile	Saml. Richardson, do
(assigned his depreciation money March 15th, 1781)	Benjamin Wilson do

N. B.—John Durbin (from Capt. Carlile's Co.) Prisoner of War, not mentioned in the Body of this List.

Return of Hazen's Regiment, 1783.

Hartley's.
Resolves of Continental Congress 16 December, 1778.

"*Resolved*, That col. Hartley's regiment and the four independent companies raised in the state of Pennsylvania, commanded by captains

during the War of the American Revolution, 1775-83.   599

Doyle, Wilkie, Steel and Calkerwood, and also the remains of col. Patton's regiment, except capt. M'Lane's company, be incorporated into one regiment, and added to the Pennsylvania line, as an eleventh regiment, and that capt. M'Lane's company be annexed to the Delaware regiment."

COL. THOMAS HARTLEY, COMMISSIONED 1 JANUARY, 1777.
COL. JOHN PATTON, COMMISSIONED 11 JANUARY, 1777.

These were 2 of the Additional 16 Regiments. Hartley's was transferred to the Pennsylvania Line and designated the Eleventh Pennsylvania, the original Eleventh Pennsylvania having been disbanded 1 July, 1778. Patton's was broken up 13 January, 1779, and attached to Hartley's, except capt. McClean's Company, which was attached to the Delaware Line.

HARTLEY's REGIMENT, Aug. 1st, 1780–Jan. 1st, 1781.

Corpl.	John Burgess, no five months Pay	Pt.	George Miller
	Gassaway Brashears	Pt.	Thomas McCallo
Serjt.	John Barber	Pt.	George McCallo
	James Beall		Ben Marshall, no 5 mos.
	James Doren		Wm. Marquess
Serjt.	Jeremiah Ferrall	Corpl.	Matthew Pearson
Pt.	James Farwell	Pt.	Thomas Wood
Serjt.	John McDaniel		

MOYLAN'S.

COL. STEPHEN MOYLAN, COMMISSIONED 8 JANUARY, 1777.

4th Regiment of Light Dragoons, raised in Pennsylvania in 1777.

Aug. 1st, 1780–Jan. 1st, 1781.
Joseph Hyner, 5 mos.*

COL. NATHL. GIST'S REGT. OF RANGERS.

Col. Nathaniel Gist, commissioned 11 January, 1777.
Col. William Grayson, commissioned 11 January, 1777.
Col. Charles M. Thruston, commissioned January, 1777.

These were 3 of the Additional 16 Regiments and were consolidated as Gist's, 22 April, 1779.

* Also see John McColla, page 588.

Muster Roll of Capt. John Gist's Co., in Col. Nathl. Gist's Regt. of Rangers in the Service of the United States of America, Attached to the Third Maryland Regt., Commanded by Col. Mordicai Gist, for the Month of February, 1778.

Capt. John Gist,	Commissioned	March 9th, 1777.	
1 Lieut. John Toomy,	"	April 10th, 1777.	
2 Lieut. Richard Chinowith,	"	April 6th, 1777,	{ absent Contrary to Orders, gone to Maryland
Ensign George Winchester	"	April 8th, 1777,	{ on Command in Md. Since Sept. last

Names and Rank.	Time.	Remarks.	Names and Rank.	Time.	Remarks.
Serjt.			Privates		
Matthew McHugh	3 yrs.	Confin'd M. Guard	Paul Duggan	3 yrs	Sick in Hospl.
Corpl.					
Edward Joice	War		Danl. Brion	"	" "
Drum. & Fife.		Sick in Hospl.			
Michl. Smith	3 yrs.		James Ward	"	" "
			Jerry Coholen	"	" "
Privates			John Sponsellor	War	" "
John Connelly	War		David Dean	3 yrs	" "
William Rian	3 yrs		Nathan Chambers	"	" "
John Lewin	"		James Homes	"	" "
Thomas Watson	"		David Norton	"	" "
William Knowles	"		William Mays	War	" "
Walter Hartley	War	On Picquet	Michael Madden	3 yrs	" "
William Welch	"		Nicholas Shire	War	
Joseph Lovett	"		John Dobson	3 yrs	Deserted 29 Jan
Thomas Carroll	3 yrs				
Archd. Bartlett	"		Christr. Hughs	"	" "
William Harris	War		John Loyd	"	" "
Daniel Spratt	"	On Furlough	Isaac Bush	"	" "
			Timothy Sulivan	"	" "

Wilmington, March 17th, 1778, Mustered Capt. John Gist's Company, as Specified in the Above Roll.

A. Horton, D. M. M.

Capt. Joseph Smith, N. Gist's Regt.

Pay due from August 1st, 1780, to January 1st, 1781   £75.
Dec. 6th, 1784, Contents Rec'd.

Joseph Smith, Capt.

during the War of the American Revolution, 1775–83.

List of Non Commissioned Officers & Privates of Col. Grayson's Regiment.

Names and Rank.	When Enlisted.	Names and Rank.	When Enlisted.
	LATE CAPT. MOORE'S COMPANY.		
Serjts.		Privates	
Thomas Snead	Mch 4 '77	James Johnston	Apl 3
Sherwood Vaughan	4	George Tombleson	Mch 8
Edward Harvie	June 5	John Swepston	4
Corpl.		Joseph Wilson	6
John Robertson		Daniel White	
Drum.		John Woster, (or Woter)	14
Hazle Williams	Mch 18	Robt. McAdams	30
Corpls.		Peter Carberry	10
John Sale	4	John Winn	Apl 25
Robt. Oglesby	10	Elisha Derenton	Mch 7
Fifer		Thomas Curtis	Feb 8
Thomas Griffin	10	Christr. Obrion	Apl 9
Privates		George Lambert	Mch 29
John Tinsley	4	Charles George	Sept 30
Thomas Gordon	May 11	John Turnbull	
Thomas Carroll	Feb 14	Thomas Miller	Apl 23
Wm. Hitchcox	Jan 7	Charles Ward	
	LIEUT. DREW.		
Serjts.		Privates	
Edward Rinker	Mch 10	Luke Metheny	Mch 7
John Spitsfathom	Feb 14	John Gratage	July 23
Durit Cary	July 20	Timothy Kelley	14
Corpls.		William Crosby	Feb 27
Gilbert Been	Mch 10	Thomps. Flood	Mch 7
Luke Oneal	July 22	John Maruny	May 26
Chas. Melton	Jan 17	Jesse Rinker	July 16
Privates		Peter Kittare, or (Kintare)	May 20
Isaac Artes	May 8	Willm. Nurse	June 6
Caleb Balden	Mch 14	Henry Orum	Apl 4
Thomas Hopewell	Apl 5	Saml. Johnston	
John Kirk	Oct 11	Daniel Gilder	Sept 15
William Haley	Apl 1	Francis Ravenscroft	Apl 5
Saml. Batterton	July 13	Waitman Reenals	Mch 26
Richd. Perrell	May 13	John McDonnell	May
Jas. Thompson	25		

Names and Rank.	When Enlisted.	Names and Rank.	When Enlisted.

Late Grant.

Serjts.		Privates	
Hezekiah Bready		Anderson Briant	
Perigrine Bready		Morris Minisham	
Corpl.		William Foster	
Joseph Bready		William Knighton	
Privates		James Rains	
Benjamin Dawson		Joseph West	
Jesse Davis		Andrew Killgrest	
Jaby Friar		Michael Moody	
Henry Rains			

Ensign Kirk.

Serjts.		Privates	
Alexander Ratrey, (or Ratsey)		Smith Tompson	
Corpl.		Owen Kelley	
Joseph Smith		Patrick Boyd	
Privates		Andrew Laiswell	
William Gillaspy		Richard Spindles	
Hugh McGlochlin		John Williams	
Ambrose Jones			

Lieut. Bell.

Serjts.		Privates	
Patrick Shannon		Thomas Conway	Apl 5
James Tate	Mch 8	Abel Armstrong	Mch 28
Thomas Chapman		William Kingors	
Sampson Archer	May 1	James Shields	22
Corpls.		George Weefield	Apl 5
David Chambers	Mch 17	James Obrien	
John Stevens	Apl 4	Jos. Lee Bullock	Mch 17
John Mitchell	Mch 17	Ronsey Merritt	
Drums.		James Lockhart	July 25
Wm. McGowen		Bartho. Reagon	
Fifer		John Lock	May 4
John Brown		Ludwick Miller	
Privates		Thomas Foster	Mch 17
James Wilson	Mch 22	Gordon Kelley	Apl 3
William Shull	June 4	Martin Sutton	July 25
John Forchano	July 25	James Strickland	Mch 17
Dennis McKinnis		Joseph Kenny	17
Joseph Hood		Joseph Hays	17
John Monday	Mch 10	George Jones	July 30
Michael McMasters	28		

ENSIGN TRIPLETT.

Names and Rank.	When Enlisted.	Names and Rank.	When Enlisted.
Serjts.		Privates	
Patrick Coleman		Dennis Shea	June 30
Alex. Munroe	Feb 13	Wm. I. Conner	Apl 19
Corpls.		William Jacoe	Mch 15
John Hillard	Mch 21	John Jacoe	Apl 1
Wm. Mitchell	1	Thomas Johnson	
Privates		Benj. Atthea	Mch 11
James Taylor	8	Jeffery Basdill	1
Francis Rogers	Feb 25	John Parrot	July 4
Daniel Chumley	Apl 15	James Solomon	May 13
Charles Hagan	Feb 20	Peter Pool	Apl 16
George Gordon	June 24	Thomas Atthea	14

A List of Officers and Soldiers of Col. Grayson's Regt. to whom Depreciation and other Advances have been paid by the State of Maryland on Account of the United States.

Issued.	To Whom.	Depreciation Sums.	Pay from 1 Aug. '80 to 1 Jan. '81.	Time to which Depreciation was Paid.
15 Aug '82	Peter Carbury, Pt., reinlisted in the Maryland Line	£74.12.16	£12.8.4	18 May '80
7 Nov '82	Matw. Coffer	78.18.1	12.10.0	1 Aug '80
6 Oct '83	Nehemiah Crawford, Sergt.	88.2.4		10 Mch '80
20 Nov '83	Owen Coffield, Pt.	81.15.4	12.10.0	1 Aug '80
14 Aug '83	Wilson Gray	74.17.8		1 June '80
22 Aug '82	Thomas Harrison, Sergt.	103.3.11	18.15.0	20 Apl '80
6 Oct '83	John Howard, Pt.	80.15.0	18.15.0	1 Aug '80
26 May '83	Jacob Johnson, Corpl.	83.19.6		1 Aug '80
20 July '82	Joshua Power, Pt.	77.14.10		8 June '80
12 Feb '82	George Speak, Corpl.	88.8.11	13.15.0	1 Aug '80
23 Aug '82	Aaron Simmons, Pt.	77.1.5	12.10.0	18 July '80
6 Oct '83	Hezekiah Speake	72.3.2		10 Mch '80
9 Oct '83	William Speake	77.5.2		1 Aug '80
27 Apl '84	John Willis	73.9.0	12.10.0	11 Apl '80

BAYLOR'S DRAGOONS

COL. GEORGE BAYLOR, COMMISSIONED 8 JANUARY, 1777.
LT. COL. WILL. WASHINGTON, COMMISSIONED 20 NOVEMBER, 1778.

3rd Regiment of Light Dragoons, raised in Virginia in 1777. Consolidated, as Baylor's, with Bland's 1st Regt. 9 November, 1782.

FORMAN'S

COL. DAVID FORMAN, COMMISSIONED 12 JANUARY, 1777.

One of the Additional 16 Regiments. It was never fully completed and 1 July, 1778, was disbanded and officers and men transferred mainly to the New Jersey Line.

SPENCER'S

COL. OLIVER SPENCER, COMMISSIONED 15 JANUARY, 1777.
COL. WILLIAM MALCOLM, COMMISSIONED 30 APRIL, 1777.

These were 2 of the Additional 16 Regiments. They were consolidated as Spencer's, 22 April, 1779.

8TH PENNSYLVANIA

RESOLVES OF CONTINENTAL CONGRESS—15 JULY, 1776.

"*Resolved*, That the battalion for the defense of the western frontiers, be raised in the counties of Westmoreland and Bedford, in the following proportions, to wit: seven companies in Westmoreland, and one company in Bedford."

COL. DANIEL BRODHEAD, COMMISSIONED 29 SEPTEMBER, 1776.

This Regiment was raised for the defence of the frontier. Capt. Moorhead's Independent Company was attached to this Regiment.

Some Maryland troops were sent to Fort Pitt and Col. Brodhead tried to increase his Regiment, at Maryland expense, by discharging Maryland officers and enrolling the men in his own Regiment. Many of these men deserted him and returned to the Maryland Line.

WASHINGTON'S GUARDS

Circular Letter sent to Col. Alexander Spottswood and three other Colonels by General Washington.*

Morristown, 30 April, 1777.

Sir,

I want to form a company for my guard. In doing this I wish to be extremely cautious, because it is more than probable, that, in the

---

* Sparks' Writings of George Washington, Vol. IV, pg. 407.

course of the campaign, my baggage, papers, and other matters of great public import, may be committed to the sole care of these men. This being premised, in order to impress you with proper attention in the choice, I have to request, that you will immediately furnish me with four men of your regiment; and, as it is my farther wish, that this company should look well and be nearly of a size, I desire that none of the men may exceed in stature five feet ten inches, nor fall short of five feet nine inches, sober, young, active, and well made. When I recommend care in your choice, I would be understood to mean men of good character in the regiment, that possess the pride of appearing clean and soldier like. I am satisfied there can be no absolute security for the fidelity of this class of people, but yet I think it most likely to be found in those who have family connexions in the country. You will therefore send me none but natives, and men of some property, if you have them. I must insist, that, in making this choice, you give no intimation of my preference of natives, as I do not want to create any invidious distinction between them and the foreigners. I am, yours &c.

CALEB GIBBS, COMMISSIONED CAPTAIN AND COMMANDER OF WASHINGTON'S GUARDS 12 MARCH, 1777, COMMISSIONED MAJOR 29 JULY, 1778.

I hereby Certify that the after mentioned men joined the Commander in Chief's Guard at the different periods rit against their Names & that they have not drawn any pay in said Corps since their joining.

James McDonald,	Formerly of 7th Md. Regt.	Jan 1st, '81.
Edward Wade, (Weed)	" " 3rd " "	May 15th, '81.
John Dent,	" " 3rd " "	Apl 11th, '80.
Jere. Driskill,	" " 4th " "	Apl 11th, '80.
Thomas Gillen,	" " 5th " "	July, '80.

        W. Colfax, Lt. Comt.,
         Commd. in Chief's Guard.

Hd. Qurs., Head of Elk, 7th Sept., 1781.

MISCELLANEOUS NAVAL ROLLS.

A List of the Officers and Men on Board the Ship Defence the 19th of September, Anno Dom. 1776, George Cook, Commander.

1st Lieut.	Able Seamen	Surgeon's Mate
Henry Auchentick	James Hagan	Samuel Church
2nd Lieut.	Joseph Walpole	Purser
John Burnell	James Giffard	Francis Muir
Master	James Allen	Capt. Marines
James Cordray	Wm. Partus	Garret Brown
Chief Mate	Colin Brown	1st Lieut.
John Hale	John Valiant	Thomas Walker
2nd Mate	Wm. Gaggen	2nd Lieut.
Nathnl. Cooper	Dennis Larkins	Joseph Smith
3rd Mate	Thomas Howard	3rd Lieut.
Levin Langle	William Hurburt	William Morris
Midshipmen	Christr. Short	Sergeants
Peter Sharp	Alex. Nicholson	William Radford
James Rownds	David Primrose	Vachel Yates
Archibald Douglass	Willm. King	Michael Craig
William Carter	John Knight	Wm. DeCourcey
Capt. Clerk	Henry Carberry	Drummer
Francis Muir	Wm. Fleming	Thomas Roberts
Quartermasters	John Crapper	Corporals
James Hasty, Disrated	Ordinary Seamen	William Matthews
Oct. 23rd	Joseph Jones	Alexander Stanton
John Wright	Hoshier Cole	Privates
James Falconer	Henry Gilbert	Ezekiel Disney
Chas. Chamberlane	Thomas Gilbert	Robert Conner
Boatswains	Robert Fosset	Michael Conway
Anthony Hanson	Dennis Foloue	William Bishop
Benjamin Simpson	Richard Sutton	William Grantham
John Barr	Patrick Cole	John Schea
Yeoman	Charles Blunt	Charles McNealis
James Hawkins	Daniel Nevin	Simon Trainer
Gunner	Robert Hope	William Askins
John Berryman	Thomas Green	John Squible
Gunner's Mate	James Barry	William Judges
Henry Rentford	John McIntyre	John Power
Yeoman	Samuel Wolf	Benjamin Sutton
William Piercey	James Bradford	John Garvey
Qr. Gunner	William Trott	Morgan Murphy
James Arne	Joshua Ozier	James Cadey
Armourer	Lynn Sarmer	Conrad McGuire
Mathew Murray	James Collins	John Grant

Master at Arms	Ordinary Seamen	Privates
George Rowen	James Green	Barth. Deloray
Carpenter	Thomas Moore	Thomas Crow
Wm. Beauchamp	Abel Mason	John Donavin
Carpenter's Mate	Richard Cockey	Moses Greer
William Prince	Samuel Wilson	Robert Wilmott
Carpenter's Crew	Joseph Dennis	Henry Carr
Alex. Cummings	John McKennie	William Porter
Wm. Howard	Benjamin Thompson	John Lemmon
Nathan Ross	Jacob Sutton	Edward Gibbons
Cooper	John Vaughan	William Sohan
Joseph Dunbar	Abram Strong	James Armstrong
Ship Steward	Moses Scott	John Wilson
Joseph Burge	Timothy Kelly	William Huggard
Cabin Steward	John Smyley	James McGill
Fran. Jackquelin	Bazil Smith	Philip Handly
Cook	Robert McDonald	Waltely Masters
James Gaggen	John Davis	Barny McManus
Armourer's Mate	William Adair	William Davis
James Greer	Cabin Boys	James Smith
Able Seamen	Thomas Buckley	Loblolly Boy
Fran. Hurburt	James Brown	Clement Tossuir
Alex. Duffey, Rated Qr.	Surgeon	
Master Oct. 23rd	Nathan Dorsey	

May 2nd, 1777.

William Paddison, Captain of the armed Schooner Dolphin.

Pay Roll of Capt. Robert Conway's Crew of Sailors on Board the Sloop Molly belonging to the State of Maryland, untill the 15th June, 1777.

Men's Names.	Time of Entry.	When Discharged.
Robert Conway, Capt.	Feb 1	
Joseph Conway, Lieut.	Mar 9	
Wm. Thomas, Pilot	4	June 4
Levi Thomas, Midshipman	5	5
Francis Boatswain, Boatswain	Apl 11	
John Kelly, Gunner	Feb 19	June 10
Manuel Anthony, Mate	Apl 24	
William Culpepper, Carpr.	26	
Jas. McDonald, Steward	Feb 24	June 7
Tobias Zimmerman, Master at Arms	28	4
John Lamond	5	

Men's Names.	Time of Entry.	When Discharged.
John Traner	Feb 5	
Peter Packman	24	June 5
Henry Grimfeild	24	8
Darby Melony	25	9
Jeremiah Clifford	26	3
William Burnhouse	Mar 3	15
William Brown	3	3
John Price	3	3
Joseph Wheatcock	4	4
Joseph Bullock	5	10
John Hurst	11	
William Tignor	12	June 4
Augustine Auger	Apl 11	
Michael Anthony	22	
Manl. Davis	22	
Manl. Anthony	22	
Manl. Dicamon	24	
John Hicnarl	24	
John Jones	26	
John Johns	30	
John Ecloes	30	
Jacob Gonsac	30	
Mather Tindar	30	
Manl. Firnano	May 2	
Bravo Bilbo	13	

Oct. 18th, 1777.

Geo. Keith Elphinstone, Captain of the Perseus.

MARYLAND ACTS—OCT., 1780.

An ACT for the defence of the bay

"*Be it enacted, by the General Assembly of Maryland*, That the governor and council be authorised and requested to purchase (or cause to be built) and fitted with sails and oars, and manned as soon as possible, four large barges or row-boats, capable of carrying swivels and twenty five men at least; and that the governor and council be also authorised and requested to purchase (or cause to be built) as soon as possible, one galley, capable of carrying two eighteen and two nine pounders, with swivels; and one sloop or schooner, capable of carrying ten four pounders, and procure them to be well found, fitted, armed, and manned.

And be it enacted, That the governor and council be authorised and requested to appoint and commission a proper number of brave, experienced, and able seamen and officers, to command the said galley and sloop or schooner

And be it enacted, That a company of one hundred men be immediately raised to serve as marines on board the said galley and sloop or schooner, and occasionally on board the said barges or row-boats; and that the governor and council be authorised and requested to appoint and commission one captain and two lieutenants to command the said company of marines, and to direct such officers to procure by enlistment as soon as possible, the said number of healthy able bodied men, including two sergeants and two corporals, to serve in such company for the term of three years, unless sooner discharged.

And be it enacted, That if any officer, soldier, or marine, shall lose a limb, or be otherwise maimed or hurt, so as to be rendered incapable of procuring a livelihood, such officer, soldier, or marine, shall be entitled to receive the same provision and support as is or shall hereafter be established by this state for its officers and soldiers in the service of the United States."

MARYLAND ACTS—MAY, 1781.

A Supplement to the act for the defense of the bay.

"*Be it enacted, by the General Assembly of Maryland*, That for the immediate defense of the bay, ... the governor and council be authorised and empowered to purchase, at such price as they may think reasonable, the galley now in Baltimore-town, ... if on examination by such proper person as they may appoint, she shall be found to be sound and fit for the service, ... and that they have power to contract for the building another galley, agreeable to the act of assembly of the last session, and cause her to be completely fitted and manned at the public expense; both of which gallies to be employed in such manner as the governor and council shall from time to time direct, for the defense of our bay and the protection of the trade thereof;

Be it enacted, That the Governor and Council be authorised and empowered to contract for any number of barges, not exceeding eight, that they may think necessary for the defense of this bay, and to cause them to be completely fitted and manned."

A Pay List for the Barge Intreped, 1781.

Month of Entry.	Day.	Mens Names.	Quality.	Time payed up to.
June	1	Wm. Barns	Lieut.	July 14
	14	Oakely Haddaway	"	" "

Pay Roll of Part of the Crew Belonging to the Barge Intrepid in 1781.

Waterman	Chas. Price	Philem. Horney
Jos. Dawson	Peter Pickering	Robt. Spedding
Gunner	Nicholas Sherwood	Robt. Burch
Richard Eaton	David Robinson	Jesse Burkett
Watermen	Solo. Holmes	Alex. Cray
John Cook	Danl. M'Giney	Danl. Cork
John Sommers	Spedden Oram	David Robinson
Thomas Laruden	Jas. Holt	2nd Lt.
Henry Powell	Levin Jacobs	Elliott Shanahan

[3 months pay due to all except Cook and Laruden 1 month's pay. Shanahan's time is not given.]

July 14th, 1781. A Pay Roll for the Barge Terable.

Month of Entry.	Day.	Mens Names.	Quality.	Time pay'd up to.		Wages in Hard Money.	
June	1	John Ball	Lieut.	July 14	7.	6.	8.
	1	Danl. Caulk	Seaman	14	4.	8.	0.
	7	Nathan Porter	Gunner	14	4.	8.	8.
	13	Joseph Reddish	Seaman	14	2.	11.	8.

Errors Excepted, John Ball.

July 10th, 1782—August 2nd, 1782.
Oakley Haddaway, Lieutenant of the Barge Terrible

1782. Dr. The State of Maryland
In Acct. with Joseph Handy.

May 1st. To my pay as Lieut on board the Barge Protector from June 12th, '81, to this day, 10 mo. 18 days @ £13. 10 pr. mo. £143. 2. 0
Nov. 12th. By Cash £33. 15. 0
By Balance £109. 7. 0

Annapolis, August 5th, 1782. £143. 2. 0

Excepted   Joseph Handy.

The State of Maryland to Edward Spedden, Gentleman, Greeting.

Be it known that We reposing especial trust and Confidence in your Patriotism valour Conduct and Fidelity, do by these presents constitute and appoint you to be Second Lieutenant of the Barge Fearnought in the Service of this State, fitted out for repelling every hostile invasion thereof, and for the Defence of our Liberties. You are therefore carefully and diligently to discharge the Duty of Second Lieutenant of the said Barge by doing and performing all manner of things thereunto belonging, according to the rules and Discipline of War, and the usage of the Sea, and the Instructions which may from Time to Time be given you. And we do strictly charge and require all Officers, Seamen, Marines, and others under your Command, to be Obedient to your Orders as Second Lieutenant of the said Barge and you are to observe and follow all such Orders and Directions which you shall receive from the Supreme Executive Power of this State. This Commission to be in force until Lawfully revoked. Given at Annapolis in Council this 23rd Day of May, A. D. 1782.

ROLL OF THE BARGE FEARNOUGHT. CAPT. SPEDDING.

The Names of Men Enlisted for the Barge "Fearnought."	Time of Inlistment.	Last Place of Residence and Place of Their Birth.		Stature.	Complection.
Robert Burch	27 May	Talbot County		5.5	Dark
Wm. L. Merrick	27	"	"	5.5	"
George Willson	27	Caroline County		5.8	Fair
Thomas Moore	27	"	"	5.11	"
John Shipperd	28	Talbot	"	5.6	"
Thos. Shenin	28	"	"	5.8	"
John Stuart	28	"	"	5.6	Dark
Henry Buckly	28	"	"	5.9	Fair
Levi Neighbours	28	"	"	5.7	"
Thos. Ewbanks	28	"	"	6.0	"
John Jacobs, Jr.	28	"	"	5.6	Dark
Thos. Chapman		"	"		"
James Fleming	28	"	"	5.11	Fair
Zadok Harvey	29	Caroline	"	5.10	Dark
Chas. Price	29	Talbot	"	5.10	Fair
Richard Eaton	29	"	"	6.0	Dark
Wm. Lee	29	"	"	6.2	Fair
Wm. Low	30	"	"	5.7	"
Thos. Perry	1 June	Caroline	"	5.6	"
Henry Perry	1	"	"	5.6	"

The Names of Men Enlisted for the Barge "Fearnought."	Time of Inlistment.	Last Place of Residence and Place of Their Birth.	Stature.	Complection.
Joseph Bush	1 June	Talbot County	5.10½	Dark
Nehemiah Beckwith	1	Dorset "	5.7	"
David Davis	1	" "	5.11	"
James Frazier	1	" "	5.9	"
Wm. Frazier	1	" "	5.10	"
John Thomas, Jr.	1	" "	5.5½	"
Saml. Abbet	1	Talbot "	5.11	Fair
George Price	1	" "	5.5	"
Sails Canner	1	" "	5.10	Dark
Thos. Richardson	2	" "	5.10	Fair
Emmory Collins	2	Caroline "	5.6	Dark
Saml. Farrow	4	" "	5.8	Fair
Jacob Jackson	4	Queen Ann's County	5.5	Dark
Henry Powel	4	Caroline "	5.8½	"
James Neighbours	4	Talbot "	5.5	Fair
James Crouch	5	" "	5.5	Dark
Rich. Ewbanks	11	" "	5.10	Fair
James Collins	11	Caroline "	6.1	"
William Murphy	12	" "	5.9	Dark
William Rumble	15	" "	5.9	"
John Thomas	16	Dorset "	5.7	"
John Wheelor	1	" "	5.10	"
William Willby	30	" "	6.4	Fair
William Navy	10	" "	5.8	Dark
John Frazier	7 July	" "	6.1	"
Rich. Smith	22	{ Baltimore Town, born in Balto. County	5.8	Fair
Gideon Gambrel	15 June	Caroline County	5.7	"
Daniel Oneal	26 July	{ Annapolis, born in New England	5.10	Dark
George Gore	26	{ Annapolis, born in New England	5.8	"
John Faris, (or Fanis)	29	Talbot County		

[Each was paid £3 bounty except Richard Eaton, John Thomas and George Gore, who were paid £3.15.

Each enlisted for one year except William Navy and George Gore, who enlisted to Jan. 1st, 1783.]

A Pay Roll of the Officers and Men of the Barge Fearnought, Capt. Levin Spedden.

Officers' and Men's Names and Station.	Pay Per Month.	Officers' and Men's Names and Station.	Pay Per Month.
Captain Levin Spedden	£15	Boatswn. George Wilson	5. 12. 6
1st Lieut. Zadock Botfield	10	Gunner Jacob Jackson	5. 12. 6
2nd Lieut. Edward Spedden	10	Steward Samuel Abbot	3. 15. 0
Privates, £3 each per month	Privates		Privates
John Frazier, (for 1 year, Furld.)	Joseph Valliant, (absent)		Nehem. Beckwith, (absent)
William Lee, (absent)	John Jacobs		Henry Powel, (in Flying Fish)
William Frazier	Thomas Chapman		Thos. Perry, (in Flying Fish)
Thomas Moore	William Rumble		
Zadock Harvey	Thomas Ewbanks		John Thomas, Jr., (in Flying Fish)
William Merrick	James Collins		
Gideon Gambrel	Emory Collins		Richd. Eaton, (absent)
William Willowby	Henry Perry, (in Flying Fish)		John Thomas
George Price	John Steward		James Neighbours
Charles Price	Joseph Bush		David Davis
John Shepherd	William Low		James Frazier
Samuel Farrow	William Navy		Joseph Christian
John Weaver	John Wheeler		
Thos. Richardson	James Barnes, (paid off)		

[Pay commenced 21st Sept. '82, for all except Joseph Christian, whose pay commenced Nov. 15th, '82.

Each was paid for 2 Months and pay was due to Jan. 1st, 1783.]

Annapolis, Saturday, Dec., 1782.

Gentlemen

As you have suspended me from officiating the duty of Lt. on board the Barge Fearnought, I think It a hard case that I have not had a hearing in my own defence, as there is so many false reports propogated to my prejudice, in respect of my Conduct on that day in the action with the British Barges, Sincerely was this. I was Stationed at the bow Gun a 6lber. when we came into Action the first fire bursted, as much as Two feet of the uper part of the Muzzle blew of. I immediatly acquainted the Capt. of the Misfortune his answer was try her again my Answer was here is at It then and accordingly fired two rounds Shot & Two rounds Grape before the Comodore's Barge had blew up & It's said that I Contradicted his Orders when he gave Orders to board the British Barge then Nearly Along side the Comodore's Barge. I affirm on the word of a man that I did not hear the Orders given being at too great a distance & the men in Confusion but Expected as the men had their Oars out that we was to try to board the British Barge & try to save some of the Comodore's men if possible that was blown Overboard. I saw our men Confused in rowing some giving way a Head & Others backing water I called to them & told them to give way all together & not to be so Confused and as for leaving my Station I never left It till we where Oblidged to make our retreat & all Sails Set. Then I went Aft & told the boy at the Helmn to let me have the Helmn as I thought I could Steer better myself. & If Capt. Speddin wanted me forward I would gone at the first word.

    I am, Gentlemen
      Yr. Hble. Servt. tho' in Disgrace.
        Zadok Botfield.

         November the 26th Day, 1783.

Pleas to pay untow John Dawson Six Dolors being Dew me for Sarvis in the Barge ferenot Comemand by Captan Speden is Recat Shal be Good a Genst yours Umbel Servent

          Zadock + Herey.
          (his mark)

to Mist. Jonson.

1782. Pay Roll to the Schooner Flying Fish from Sept. 19th to Dec. 19th, '82.

Time Commenced.	Name and Station.	Amount Due.
Sept. 19th	Daniel Bryan, (Brian), Captain	£45. 0.0
Oct. 19th	George Grason, Lieut.	20. 0.0
Sept. 19th	James Joiner, Private	9. 0.0
ditto	William House, ditto	9. 0.0
ditto	William Dixon, ditto	9. 0.0
Oct. 4th	Wm. Bud, ditto	7.10 0
		£99.10.0
	E. Excepted.	
		Daniel Bryan.

Sailors enlisted by Capt. Bryan.

William Wood, Lt.	Robert Collins	Owen Cunningham
Thomas Birch, Lt.	Benito Losada	Edward Connolly
John Smith, Gunner	Modesto d Asoan	William House
William Warner, Steward	Antonio Cadenay	Solomon Boone
John Hudson, Carpenter	John Mitchell	David Wallace
Luke Young, Gun.Capt.Fr.	John Maxwell	William Swan
Wm. Dyer, Private	Andrew Boyd	Ebin Brown
Barney Casey	Edward Russum	Michael Fischer
Charles Jones	David Lowny	Henry Shepherd
John Hardy, Boatswain	Charles Riggs	Michael Sullivane
James Downing, Private	James McGwin,	James Pennington
John Anthony	(or McGwire)	Blagdon Abbutt
Emanual Roduger	Peter Hardy	John Armstrong
Antonio Cocoanat, (or	John Caine	Lawrence Simons
Coroanat)	John White	John Robins
Alexander McMullen	John Peters	Joseph Valliant
Joseph Ganney	John Robinson	William Dunn
Joseph Ramon		

Capt. Frazier.

Lieut. Botfield	Philn. Caldwell	William Frazier
Lt. Wm. Byus	John Wheeler	Thomas Walker
John Frazier	Nehem. Beckwith	

Capt. O. Delisle's Crew.

Lt. George Mignot	James Kerr	Joshua Nicholas
Lt. John Yeaton	James McConn	Antony Argers
Gasper Low	Silas Coolidge	Samuel Phill
Thomas Johnson	Thomas English	Charles Stoker
Richard Murray, (or	William Roiley	John Thomas
Munay)	Henry Simpson	Richard Johnson
Emanual Antony	Richard Turner	John Hergrears
John Gellard	Thomas Flint	Anthony Dyes
William Heyton		

A List of Men Blown up in the Barges.

William Lowe, Lieut.	George Brumwell	John Scott
Patrick Long, Gunner,	Joseph Sewull	Nathl. Grace
died of his wounds.	William Sewell	Joseph Riddish
James Raynolds	William Blake	James Spencer
John Kirby,	John Raynolds	Ralph Dawson
died of his wounds.	Charles Spencer	Robt. Harrison

ROLLS OF ESCAPED AND EXCHANGED PRISONERS.

Return of Maryland Officers exchanged from the 24th March, 1777.

Ensign	James Fernandez	1st Md. Regt.	March 24th 1777
	William Coats	1st Md. Regt.	ditto
Lieut.	D. Courcy	Smallwood's Regt.	Sept 27th '77
	Ely Dorsey	2nd Md.	ditto
Major	Otho H. Williams	Rifle Regt.	Jan 16th '78
Lieut.	Edward Duvall	2d Md.	April 20th '78
	Hatch Dent	1st Md.	ditto
	Walter Muse	1st Md.	ditto
	Saml. Wright	2nd Md.	ditto
	Edward Prall	1st Md.	ditto
Capt.	John Dean	5th Md.	Aug 26th '78
	Abraham Shepherd	Md. Cont'l	ditto
	Henry Hardman	6th Md.	ditto
Lieut.	John Gale	Md. Cont'l, 2nd Regt.	Oct 12th '78
Lt. Col.	Ramsey	Md. Cont'l	Oct 25th 1780
Major	Edward Tillard	Md. Cont'l	ditto
Lieut.	Thos. H. Lucket	Md., Rawlings	ditto
Cornet	Peregrine Fitzhugh	Baylor's	ditto
Lieut.	James Lingan	Rawlings'	ditto
	Thomas Warman	Rawlings'	ditto
	Christian Orendorff	Flying Camp	ditto
Ensign	Reg. Hillery	Cont'l	ditto
	John Levash	Cont'l	ditto
	Thomas Rouse	Cont'l	ditto
	Elihu Hall	1st Md.	ditto
Lieut.	Kelly		ditto
Col.	Luke Mabury	Militia	Sept 3rd 1781
Ensign	H. Beddinger	Rawlings'	Oct 25th 1780
	Rezin Davies	Rawlings'	ditto
	Edward Smith	Rawlings'	ditto

We whose Names are hereto Subscribed, being exchanged Prisoners from Charles Town, do acknowledge to have received of Lt. Robert Denny 5 Pounds Specie each, on Account.   September 3rd, 1781.

Law. Brennan	7th Regt.	Thomas Allison	1st Regt.
Jesse Jacobs	6th "	Roger O'Donald	Artillery
Robt. Harpham	4th "	John Ferguson	2nd Regt.
Matthew McMahon	Artillery	John Jones	2nd "
Benj. Peirce Beech	5th Regt.	John Smith	3rd "
Benj. Burch	6th "	Peter Caldwell	6th "
William Moore	2nd "	Danl. O'Neal	Artillery
Thomas Bird	3rd "		

during the War of the American Revolution, 1775-83.

The following Exchanged Prisoners each received the sum of 5 pounds from Robert Denny. 1781-1782.

Dec 3 1781	Henry Flannagan, exchanged prisoner from South Carolina	Jan 17 1782	John Linday, exchanged prisoner from Charles Town
Nov 26	Thomas Wood, ditto from Charles Town	Aug 24 1781	Stephen Preston, 3d Regt. ditto
Mch 13 1782	Nathl. Wheeler, ditto and in distress	Feb 4 1782	George Findleson ditto
"	"	"	Patrick Connor ditto
Dec 19 1781	James Garth	Oct 8 1781	Thomas Cardiff ditto
Aug 1	James Barren, 5th Regt.	10	John Wills ditto
"	Jos. Overcreek, 3d Regt.	9	Saml. Carter ditto
Sept 18	William Griffin, 1st Regt.	Feb 21 1782	Thomas Smee, exchanged prisoner & badly wounded
25	Thomas James, 7th Regt.		
26	Daniel Willis, 5th Regt.	Aug 1 1781	Benton Harris, 1st Regt.
28	Robt. Pennington, 1st Regt.	"	George Scone, 5th Regt.
"	Abraham Gamble, 1st Regt.	"	James Currin, 7th Regt.
"	"	"	John Brent, 5th Regt.
"	"	"	John Lowry, 7th Regt.
29	Thos. King, 1st Regt.	"	Willm. Deaver, 3d Regt.
"	Jona. White, 1st Regt.	"	Joseph Smith, 1st Regt.
"	Michael Cole, 1st Regt.	"	Willm. Sly, 7th Regt.
"	James Clark, Brown's Artly.	"	Dennis Tearnan, 7th Regt.
"	"	"	Emanuel Allen, 5th Regt.
Oct 2	Silvester Gatton, 1st Regt.	"	Edward Kain, 4th Regt.
24	Aaron Winfrey, Extra Regt., exchanged prisoner from Charles Town	"	Willm. Pegrim, 2nd Regt.
"	"	"	John Martin, 2nd Regt.
"	"	"	Thos. Saunders, 1st Regt.
"	William King, 4th Regt., exchanged prisoner from Charles Town	"	John Holmes, 3rd Regt.
"	"	"	Wm. Ashwell, 7th Regt.
"	"	"	Wm. Fairbairn, 3rd Regt.
Aug 2	Dennis Flanagan, Dorsey's Artly.	"	Wm. Marshall, 5th Regt.
"	"	20	Joseph Blaize, 7th Regt.
"	Rich. Wilkinson, Dorsey's Artly.	Nov 2	Thomas Barkley, exchanged prisoner from Charles Town
Dec 5	Mathias Funner, (Fanner)		
20	Thomas Bishop	Aug 15	Saml. Tindale, 3rd Regt. ditto
Aug 29	Wm. Wallkird, exchanged prisoner from Charles Town	Oct 6	John Howard, Artillery ditto
1	Robt. Ferroll, 2nd Regt.	11	Rich. Blandford, 2nd Regt. ditto
"	Robert Rankin, 5th Regt.		
20	John Courts, 3rd Regt.	17	James Smith, prisoner from Chs. Town
"	Michael Clancey, 5th Regt.		
"	Thos. Richardson, 5th Regt.	25	John Chivel, received £21.00.
		Apl 15 1782	Robert Sharpless, exchanged prisoner and wounded.
"	William George, 6th Regt.		
"	William Cox, 2nd Regt.		

RETURN OF INVALIDS.

A Sick Return, November 17th, 1777.

Men's Names.	Company.	Disorder.
Stephen Fennell	Capt. Dorsey	Convalescent
Hugh McDowell	do	Bilious Fever
John Poore	do	Sore Leg
John Sly	do	Peupneumony
Sargt. Cornwall	do	Convalescent
John Ackerly	do	Convalescent
Cornelius Forester	do	Rheumatism
Thomas Robertson	do	Intermittent Fever
Robert Carr	Furnavil	Sore Arm
Thomas Yates	do	Sore Leg
Daniel Rodden	do	Putrid Fever
John Jellom	do	Convalescent

G. Gale, Surgeon.

CONTINENTAL HOSPITAL RETURNS, 1777-1778.*

A List of the Soldiers in the Court House Hospital at Reading Nov. 17, 1777.*

Wm. Jeffries	5th Maryland	William Cofferoth	7th Maryland
John Barber	3rd Maryland	Charles Major	do
Henry Tom	Col. Weltner's	Coonrod Cofferoth	do
Nicholas Nichols	5th Maryland	Christopher Reed	do
Wm. Donaldson	7th Maryland	Thomas Young	do
Francis Mitchel	do	Wm. Markwelch	do

A List of Soldiers in the Brick House Hospital at Reading, Nov. 17th, 1777.*

John Hunt	6th Maryland	Samuel Huggins	6th Maryland

"A List of the Sick in the Potter's Shop at Reading, Nov. 17."*

Gilber Allen	5th Maryland	Wm. Pinkfield & wife	5th Maryland
Zadock Woods	do	Thomas Oliphant	do
Saml. Kennedy	do	David Kelly & wife	do
Thos. Fenitree & wife	do		

*Taken from the Pennsylvania Magazine of History and Biography, April, 1899, pages 38-50.

A Return of the Sick sent from Robinson's to New Windsor.*

| John Danster | 4th Maryland | Norwood's Co. |

Sir.

Please to receive into Hospital Richard Stids of Capt. Godman's Company belonging to the 4th Maryland Regt. & John Cornish of Capt. Eccleston's Company belonging to the 2d Maryland Regiment.

         John Ross, Asst. Surg.
           25th Novem., 1778.*

To Dr. Allison
 Superintending the Hospitals
 New Windsor

A Return of Sick of the 6th Maryland Regt. commanded by Col. Otho H. Williams.*

Robert Body	Capt. Beall's Co.	Fever	
John Holiday	do	do	
George Thomas	do	do	Putrid

Sir

Please to receive to ye Hospital the above sick.
          W. Warfield, A. S.
           6th M. Regt.
To the Hospital Surgeon   Nov. 25, 1778.
 at Newburg.

         Newburgh, 28th Nov., 1778.

Sir

You'l be kind enough to Receive into the Hospital the Following Soldiers of a Detachmt. under my Command, who for want of a Doctor are likely to Continue in a bad Situation if not Received. Your Compliance will be highly Acknowledged by Sir
     Your Most Hhble. Servt.
      J. Brice, Capt. Comdt. of a Detachmt.
         of the 1st Maryland Bg.*

To the Superintendt. of the Hospital
 at New Windsor.

John Sullivan	Capt. Brooks' Co.	3rd Regt. Md.
James Foster	do	do
John Owens	late C. Hindman's	do
Owen Corkran	Capt. Brice	do
Daniel Claney	do	do

* See note on page 618.

Newburgh, 1st Decmbr., 1778

Sir
Be kind enough to Receive into the Hospital William Ross of the 6th Maryland Regiment.

I am Sir your most Hhble. Servt.

J. Brice, Capt. Comdt. of a
Detachment of Maryd. Bg.*

To the Superindt.
of New Windsor.

Newburgh December 1, 1778.

Sir
Be pleased to Receive into the Hospital Benj. Moore of the Sixth Maryland Regiment whose situation requires Assistance.

I am Sir your Most Humble Servt.

Lud. Weltner, Lt. Col.*

To the Superindt. of the Hospital
at New Windsor.

A Return of Sick of the 6th Maryland Regt. Commanded by Col. Williams, Dec. the 7th, 1778.*

Samuel English	Lieut. Williams' Co.	Putrid Fever
Peter Woolf	do do	Intert. Fever
Pat. Trainer	Capt. Ghireliu's do	Infat.
Willm. Chambers	do do	do

W. Warfield, A. S.

Hospital Surgeon at New Windsor.

A Return of the Sick of the Second Maryland Regiment sent to the Hospital at New Windsor commanded by Lieut Col. Woolford, December 7, 1778.*

John Wall	Capt. Anderson's Co.	Fever Inflam.
Patrick Fenesick	Capt. Davidson's do	Fever Remit.
Saml. Hughes	do	Rheumat.

James McCallmont, Surgn.

* See note on page 618.

A Return of the Sick 7th Maryland Regiment Col. Gunby, Gen. Smallwood's Brig.*

Nichs. Carr	Capt. Bayle's Co.	Putrid Fever
Darby Crowley	do	do
Wm. Hopkins	Capt. Grosh	Interm. Fever
Ed. Fennile	Capt. Morris	do

H. Tabbs, Surgn.

F. Allison, Esq.
   Senr. Surgeon G. Hospital New Windsor.

A Return of the Sick in the 5th Maryland Regiment Commanded by Col. William Richardson, to be sent to the Hospital at New Windsor.*

Moses Cook	Lynch's Co.	Diarrhea
Robert Bromwell	Dean's do	Bilious fever
William Arnett	do do	Int. fever
James Hawkins	do do	do
Thos. Hinds	Emory's do	Jaundice
Thos. Greenwich	do do	Cough
Wm. Samuel	Richardson's do	Convalescent
Peter Kincaid	Hamilton's do	Bilious fever
Joseph Peters	Lynch's Orderly	

William Kilty, Surgeon
5th Maryland Regt.

Chester, Dec. 8, 1778.

A Return of Cloaths etc, 3rd Maryland.*

Daniel Lingist	Capt. Bailey	David Lawler	Capt. Marborough
Joseph Cronch	do Brice	Thos. Wright	do Hindman
Thos. Cowin	do do	Michl. Gownan	do Smith

Jacob Lyon,
Sergeant.

Dec. 10, 1778.

*See note on page 618.

A List of the Sick of the 2nd Maryland Brigade April 21st, 1779.

NAMES.	REGT.	HOSPITAL.
John Taylor	4th Md.	
Jas. Fitzgerald	ditto	
Dennis Carroll	ditto	
Thos. Davis	2nd Md.	Summerset Court-House
Nathl. Griffin	ditto	
John Holladay	6th Md.	
Wm. Merl	ditto	
John Toof	ditto	
Mark Griffin	2nd Md.	

Chas. Dabney, Lieut-Col.

[From the Gist Papers.]

RESOLVES OF CONTINENTAL CONGRESS 20 JUNE, 1777.

"*Resolved*, That a corps of invalids be formed, consisting of eight companies, each company to have one captain, two lieutenants, two ensigns, five serjeants, six corporals, two drummers, two fifers, and one hundred men. This corps to be employed in garrison, and for guards in cities and other places, where magazines or arsenals, or hospitals are placed; as also to serve as a military school for young gentlemen, previous to their being appointed to marching regiments; for which purpose, all the subaltern officers, when off duty, shall be obliged to attend a mathematical school, appointed for the purpose, to learn geometry, arithmetic, vulgar and decimal fractions, and the extraction of roots; and that the officers of this corps shall be obliged to contribute one day's pay in every month, and stoppages shall be made of it accordingly, for the purpose of purchasing a regimental library of the most approved authors on tactics and the petite guerre: That some officers from this corps be constantly employed in the recruiting service in the neighborhood of the places they shall be stationed in; that all recruits so raised shall be brought into the corps and drilled, and afterwards draughted into other regiments as occasion shall require.

Congress proceeded to the election of a colonel of the said corps of invalids; and, the ballots being taken,

Lewis Nicola, esq. was elected."

A Return of Invalids belonging to the Maryland Line, now in the Service at the Garrison of Philadelphia, June 19th, 1781.

Names.	Regiment.	Transferrments.
Thomas Adams	3d Maryland	27 July 1780
Lawrance Brooks, Serjt.	5th "	13 October 1778
Timothy Brennan	6th "	5 May 1779
Benjamin Cheshire	3d "	7 February 1780
William Collier	3d "	25 April 1780
James Connor	5th "	24 July 1780
Micheal Duffey	3d "	1 August 1778
Walter Chas. Davids, Serjt.	3d "	30 September 1778
Barns. Dougherty	5th "	8 September 1779
James Desire	3d "	22 April 1780
Robert Freemoult	3d "	6 October 1778
Edward Franklin	2nd "	24 July 1777
John Hackett	4th "	2 June 1779
Richard Jenkins	3d "	2 September 1778
William Keymer	3d "	19 October 1778
James Lipscomb, Serjt.	3d "	19 October 1778
Jacob Lyons, Serjt.	3d "	1 June 1779
Daniel Longist	3d "	24 April 1780
John McDonald	3d "	21 June 1779
John Murray	3d "	7 February 1780
John Nulan	3d "	26 January 1779
Joseph Polemus	4th "	27 May 1778
James Sherridan	3d "	27 October 1778
John Schwager, Serjt.	3d "	13 October 1778
Jacob Shandley	7th "	2 November 1779
John Saunders	3d "	14 July 1779
Valentine Smith	1st "	22 April 1780
William Tutone	2nd "	8 May 1779
Godfrey Young	6th "	23 October 1780
Luke Burns	1st "	22 April 1780
Dennis Cregannon	1st "	22 April 1780
Thomas Hunt	7th "	15 March 1780
Thomas Bond, Serjt.	Pulaski's	25 February 1779. Promoted Serjt. 15 Feb., 1780

Serjt. Brooks was discharged from the 5th, the 13th October, '78, but his discharge being contrary to Genl. Washington's order it was taken from him and he ordered to do duty in the Invalid Regt. by the Board of War, in which station he still continues & is returned as belonging to the quota of the State of Maryland.

Lewis Nicola, Col. Inv.

I certify that the men mentioned in within list were all transferred from the line of the State of Maryland State into the Invalid Regt. under my command and still continue therein & are returned as belonging to the quota of that State.   Philadelphia, 3 July, 1781.

Lewis Nicola, Col. Inv.

I certify that Thomas Bond of Count Pulaski's Legion joined the Invalid Regt. the 25th day of February, 1779, was appointed a Corporal therein 1st June, 1779, & promoted to a Serjeant 15th January, 1781, in which station he has continued ever since.

Lewis Nicola, Col. Inv.

Philadela. 28th June, 1781.

I do Certify that Thomas Bond was inlisted a Soldier by Capt. Siggond in Baltimore for Genl. Count Pulaski's Legion, May 8th, 1778, & was transfered to join the Invalid Regiment Feby. 25th, 1779, not being fit for Camp duty.   Henry Becker, Capt.

June 28th, 1781.   Light Dragoons.

James Murphy, of Queen Ann's County, enlisted in the 5th Md. Regt. in 1777, and was transferred to the Invalid Regt., (having lost a leg), from which he was discharged by Col. Lewis Nicola, Jan. 17th, 1780. He was referred by the Council of Maryland Oct 14th, 1785, as a pensioner under the Act of Oct., 1778, to the Orphans' Court of Queen Ann's County.

MARYLAND ACTS—OCTOBER, 1778.

An ACT for the relief of disabled and maimed officers, soldiers, marines, and seamen.

"*Be it enacted, by the General Assembly of Maryland*, That every commissioned officer, non-commissioned officer, and private soldier, who have or shall lose a limb, or have been or shall be so disabled in the service of the United States of America, as to render him incapable of getting a livelihood, and who, at the time of entering into the service of the said United States, was or shall be enlisted or recruited by this state, shall receive during his life, or the continuance of such disability, the one half of his monthly pay, from and after the time that his pay as an officer or soldier ceases.   And that every commander of any ship of war or armed vessel, commissioned officer, warrant officer, marine, or seaman, belonging to the United States of America, who have or shall lose a limb, or have been or shall be otherwise so disabled in the service of the said States, as to be rendered incapable of getting a livelihood, and who, at the time of engaging in the said service, was or shall be enlisted or recruited by this state, shall receive during his life, or continuance of such disability, the one half of his monthly pay, from and after the time that his pay as an officer, or marine, or seaman, ceases.

And be it further enacted, That every commissioned officer, non-commissioned officer, and private soldier, in the army, and every commander, commissioned officer, warrant officer, marine, or seaman, of any of the ships of war or armed vessels belonging to the United States of America, who have been or shall be wounded in any engagement, so as to be rendered incapable of serving in the army or navy, though not totally disabled from getting a livelihood, and who at the time of entering into the service of the said States, was or shall be enlisted or recruited by this state, shall receive such monthly sum as shall be adjudged adequate by the justices of the orphans court of the county in which such commissioned officer or private soldier of the army, or commander, commissioned officer, warrant officer, or seaman, of the navy, shall reside ; provided the same doth not exceed his half pay.

And be it enacted, That . . . . . the justices of the said courts are hereby enjoined to cause due entries to be made in their proceedings, of the name or names of all persons to whom drafts or orders shall be given in pursuance of this act ; also of their places of residence, in what regiment or company they served, the engagement or action in which they received their wound, and the sums alloted them ; also of the death of such disabled person, or ceasing of such allowance.

And be it further enacted, That all such officers and soldiers, who may be entitled to the provisions under this act, and shall be found to be capable of doing guard or garrison duty, may be formed into a corps of invalids, and subject to the said duty ; and all officers, marines, and seamen, of the navy, who shall be entitled to the same provision, and shall be found capable of doing any duty on board the navy, or any department thereof, shall be liable to be so employed."

A Muster Roll of the Invalids and Recruits of the Garrison At Fort Whetstone Point.

Mens Names.	Time of Appointment & Inlistment.	Remarks.
Saml. Swan, Serjt.	Appointed Oct 6th 1779	Discharged Nov 19th 1780
Benjamin Jones	Left as Inv. Sept 15th 1779	" May 8th 1781
William Richardson	" " " " " "	" " " "
Joseph Wilks	Left Sick Sept 15th 1779	Claimed by Lieut. Saml. Saddler as Fit for Duty Dec 23rd 1779
William Robinson	Inlisted Sept 23rd 1779	Discharged Jan 27th 1780
Peter Decamp	" " 28th 1779	Deserted from Recruiting Officer
Dominick Sara	" " " "	ditto ditto
Peter Laci	" " " "	ditto ditto
John Granada	" " " "	Deserted Dec 1st 1779
Samuel Powell	" Oct 2nd 1779	" Abt. the Last of Nov 1779
Thomas Acres	" " 4th "	Discharged Jan 27th 1780
Daniel Mathews	" " " "	Deserted Oct 12th 1779
Thomas Hooper	" " 21st "	Discharged Jan 27th 1780
Thomas Gillard	" Nov 15th 1779	" " " " "
Samuel True	" Dec 7th 1779	" " " " "

Proof of the Above Muster Roll.

   Present.
Deserted and one taken away by Lt. S. Saddler   7 privates
Discharged by Order of the Governor & Council   1 serjt.   7 "
         Total   1 serjt.   14 "

      Geo. P. Vreeportz.
        Baltimore, May 8th, 1781.

Detachment of Md. Troops at the Garrison of Whetstone Point.

Regt.	Names.	Regt.	Names.
2nd	Jas. Jackson, Serjt.	Extra	John Deakins
4th	Peter McNaughton	"	John Anderson
4th	John Colin, Serjt.	"	Thos. Pennifield
"	Jos. Fawlit, Fifer	"	Wm. Glorey
"	Wm. Smith, Drum.	"	Dennis Donans
"	John Moore	"	John Turnstil
"	Peter Blang	"	Wm. Chapmon
"	Henry Hughes	"	David Brien
Extra	Lazaris Higgs	"	Jesse O'Furra
"	James Brown	"	Jessey King

Regt.	Names.	Regt.	Names.
Extra	John Jones	4th	Mathew Kelley
"	Patrick Smith	Extra	Wm. Masson
"	George Daw	"	James Woodword
"	James Wilson	"	Thos. Porter
"	Elexander Steward	"	Edwd. Taylor
"	John Johnston	"	George Gilword
"	Joseph McItee	"	Jessey McCarty
"	Steaven Fennil	"	Mitchal Doring
"	Thos. Artis	"	James White

Jno. Hamilton, Capt. Lt.

[From the Gist Papers.]

The following wounded soldiers each received the sum of 5 pounds from Robert Denny, 1782.

Mch 5 Nelce Jones, a wounded soldier of the 2nd Md. Regt.
Mch 23 Robert Taylor, a wounded soldier in distress from the Southward.

Annapolis, June 25th, 1790.

Sir

I enclose returns of the invalid pensioners paid by this State, and I regret that they have been so long delayed which was owing to many of the returns being imperfect; indeed, although we have sent to many of the Counties to get the returns more perfect, they are not so complete as I would wish.

I think proper to make some remarks on the return of officers, and request that you will inform me which of them, (if any) are excluded from the half pay of the United States by the Acts of the late or present Congress, that I may communicate it to the legislature of this State, for them to determine whether they will continue the pensions to those who are rejected by the United States.

Perry Benson, James Bruff, Richard Anderson, John Trueman, John Lynn, James Ewing and James Somervill, have received their 5 years commutation from the United States, and under a particular law of this State made expressly for their relief have received half pay.

Jehu Bowen was wounded at German Town and afterwards resigned, but as the disability occasioned by his wounds still continued, the Legislature upon application passed a law putting him on a footing, as to his half pay, with other officers. He has not received commutation.

Rignal Hillary and John Levasche died in the service, their widows have received pensions equal to the half pay of their husbands, under the laws of this State which I believe is provided for by Acts of the late Congress.

John Hoskin Stone was wounded and resigned, but was afterwards put on the half pay establishment by a law of this State.

Uriah Forrest lost his leg in the action of German Town and resigned the 23rd of Feb., 1781, as will appear by the votes and proceedings of Congress. The State of Maryland advanced him a sum of money equal to seven years half pay of a Lt. . . . .

[Torn off.]

Return of Invalid Pensioners in Charles County.

Names.	Rank.	Age.	Corps.	Commanders' Names.	Cause of Disability.	When Disabled.	Where Disabled.	Place of Residence. Town & County.	When Pension Commenced.	When Pension Ceased and Reasons.	Allowance Per Month.	Whole Amount Paid.	Exact Time to Which the Pension Has Been Paid.
Wm. Morrison	Soldier	44	1 Md. Regt.		Wounded in the hand & head	16 Aug 1780	Camden	Charles Co.	17 Nov 1780		1.5.4¼	136.17.6	17 Sept 1789
John Martindale	Fifer	27	do		Burn on his left hand	28 Feb 1783	James Island	do	15 Nov 1783		1.7.6	94.18.6	15 Aug 1789
James Tillard	Soldier	26	do		Lost his left Arm		Little York	do	10 Dec 1781		1.5.4¼	116.6.2	10 Aug 1789
Thos. Sanders	do	52	do	John H. Stone, Col.	Wound on the hand & head	16 Aug 1780	Camden	do	29 July 1781		1.5.4¼	122.8.11½	29 Aug 1789
Simon Perry	do		do		Cause of disability unknown			do	15 Nov 1783	Removed out of the State Oct 1786	1.5.4¼	41.16.5½	15 Aug 1786
John Buckannan	Drummer		do		Wound on the knee	Sometime in 1782	North Carolina	do	15 Nov 1783	Died sometime in 1785	1.7.6	24.15.0	15 May 1785
William Green	Soldier	50	do		Rheumatic pains	Can't get information when nor where disabled		do	11 Jan 1780		1.5.4¼	148.5.7¼	11 Oct 1789
Jeremiah Mudd	Sergeant	30	2 Md. Regt.	John Gunby, Col.	Lost his left Arm	17 June 1781	96th South Carolina	Pr. Geo. Co.	5 Aug 1783		1.17.6	131.5.0	5 June 1789

John Muschett, Regr. of Wills, Charles County.

Return of Invalid Pensioners

Names.	Rank.	Age.	Corps.		Cause of Disability.	When Disabled and Where.
Abraham Gambell	Private	Abt. 30 yrs.	1st Md. Regt. Commander unknown	As appears per Capt. Perry Benson's Cert.	Wounded through the shoulder	25 April 178 at battle o Camden
Henry Clarage	do	Unknown	2nd Md. Regt. Col. Otho Williams	Per Col. William's Certificate	Wounded in the left arm & discharged from the Genl. Hosptl. of the Southern Army	

Return of Invalid Pensioners

Pensioners Names.	Rank.	Militia.	Continental.	Where Disabled.
John Snider	Corporal	Flying Camp		White Plains
Samuel Hennis	Private	Militia		White Horse
" "	"	"		" "
John Brown	Sergeant		6 Regt.	Camden
John Meek	Private		7 "	Guilford Ct. House
Philip Fisher	"		1 "	Guilford Ct. House
Henry Crook	"		1 "	Guilford Ct. House
James Shean	"		2 "	Monmouth
David Conner	"		2 "	Disabled by Sicknes
Charles Buchlup	"		1 "	Eutaw Springs
Thos. Bishop	"		2 "	Guilford Ct. House
John Auber	Sergeant		2 "	Eutaw Springs
James Smith	Private		2 "	Camden
John Alsop	"		7 "	Barges
Robert Kerns	Sergeant		2 "	York
James Burk	Private		2 "	Cowpens
James Garth	"		4 "	Ninety Six
Michael Waltman	"		1 "	Guilford Ct. House
Christr. Lambert	"		3 "	Disabled by Fire
Luke Sanson	"		1 "	Guilford Ct. House
Peter Cunningham	"		7 "	South Carolina
Paul Hagarty	"		1 "	Brandy Wine
John Trisner	"		7 "	German Town
Edward Rose	"	Militia		Jersey
John Shovell	"		6 "	Camden
John Gombare	"	Flying Camp		York Island

in Dorchester County.

Place of Residence.	When Pension Commenced.	When Pension Ceased and Reasons.	Allowance per Month.	Whole Amount Paid.	Exact Time to which the Pension has been paid up.
Dorchester County	13 Apl 1785	Ceased 13 Oct 1785 no further application being made	Ten Shillings	Three Pounds	to the 13th October 1785
Dorchester County	23 June 1785 Ceased 23 Sept 1785		Ten Shillings	Thirty Shillings	to the 23rd Sept 1785

Certified per Jno. Goldsborough,
Regr. Wills for Dorchester County.
Dec. 1st, 1789.

in Frederick County.

When Pension Commenced.	Allowance per Month.	When Pension Ceased.	Cause of Pension Ceasing.	Amount.
Dec 1 1776	27/6	Nov 1 1789		213 2 6
Sept 20 1777	25/	Sept 20 1782		75 0 0
Sept 20 1782	12/6	Nov 1 1789		53 6 8
Nov 29 1783	37/6	Mch 29 1786	removed or dead	52 10 0
" " "	25/	Nov 1 1789		88 16 6
" " "	25/	" " "		88 16 6
" " "	25/	Mch 29 1784	removed or supposed dead	5 0 0
" " "	25/	April 29 1787	dead	51 5 0
" " "	25/	Mch 29 1784	dead	5 0 0
" " "	25/	Nov 1 1789		88 16 6
" " "	25/	" " "		88 16 6
" " "	37/6	Mch 6 1788	dead	96 1 10½
" " "	25/	Nov 1 1789		88 16 6
" " "	25/	" " "		88 16 6
" " "	37/6	" " "		133 3 4
Feb 10 1784	25/	Mch 10 1788	dead	61 5 0
Nov 29 1783	25/	Nov 1 1789		88 16 6
Mch 29 1784	25/	" " "		83 16 6
Nov 29 1783	25/	" " "		88 16 6
Nov 16 1783	25/	Oct 16 1785	dead	28 15 0
Sept 29 1784	25/	Mch 29 1789	removed or supposed dead	67 10 0
Dec 27 1784	25/	Nov 1 1789		72 12 6
April 12 1785	25/	" " "		68 5 0
April 24 1786	12/6	Oct 24 1788	removed or supposed dead	18 15 0
Mch 29 1786	25/	Nov 1 1789		53 16 6
June 9 1788	25/	" " "		20 18 9
				1870 15 7½

George Murdoch, Regr. Wills,
Frederick County.

Return of Invalid Pensioners

Names.	Rank.	Corps.	Place of Residence.	When Pension Commenced
John Davis, (down County)	Private	Continental	Chester Town	in 1781
James Carmicheal	"	1 Md Regt. "	Kent Co.	in 1781
Robert Sharpless	Corporal	"	Chester Town	in 1785
John Davis, (up County)	Private	6 " " "	Chester Town at this time	in 1785
Hugh McClean	"	1 " " "		in 1785
George Second	Corporal	"	Kent Co.	in 1786
Daniel Smith	Private	"	" "	in 1786
John Lynch	Corporal	"	" "	in 1786

Return of Invalid Pensioners

Names.	Age.	Corps.	Cause of Disability.	When Disabled.	Where Disabled.
James Murphey	35	1 Md. Regt.	Lost one Legg	Aug 27, 1776	Long Island
James White					
John Blair					
James Current					
Christr. Reed					
William Hurley					
Saml. B. White	30	1 Md. Regt.	Disabled in the body	April 25, 1781	Camden

in Kent County.

When Pension Ceased and Reasons.	Allowance Per Month.	Whole Amount Paid.	Exact Time to Which the Pension Has Been Paid.
died in 1790	25/	£300 curry. & £114 10 specie	22 Oct 1789
died in 1785	25/	£56 5 0 currency & £52 10 specie	
struck off Nov. 9th, 1789, Court thinking him able to labor and a great Drunkard	27/6	£72 3 9 specie	
	25/	£67 10 specie	22 Oct 1789
struck off Oct. 22nd, 1789. Court thought him able bodied at this Time	25/	£67 10 specie	22 Oct 1789
allowed only £8.5 the last Order and were of opinion he ought not be allowed in future	27/6	£53 12 6 specie	Aug 1789
	25/	£45 specie	18 Jan 1789
	27/6	£33 specie	28 Aug 1789

John Nicholson, Regr. of Wills for Kent County.

in Montgomery County.

Place of Residence.	When Pension Commenced.	When & Why Pension Ceased.	Allowance Per Month.	Whole Amount Paid.	Exact Time to Which the Pension Has Been Paid Up.
Montgomery County	April 10, 1781	died Aug, 1789	25/	£123 15 0	10 July 1789 8 yrs 3 mos
	June 10, 1783		25/	95 16 8	1 Nov 1789 6 yrs 4 mos 21 days
	June 10, 1783		25/	95 16 8	1 Nov 1789 6 yrs 4 mos 21 days
	Dec 20, 1783		25/	87 18 4	1 Nov 1789 5 yrs 10 mos 10 days
	Aug 20, 1784		25/	77 18 4	1 Nov 1789 5 yrs 2 mos 10 days
	Dec 14, 1784		25/	73 2 6	1 Nov 1789 4 yrs 10 mos 17 days
Montgomery County	June 9, 1789		25/	5 18 4	1 Nov 1789 4 mos 22 days

Samuel Turner, Regr. Wills, Montgomery County.

Return of Invalid Pensioners

Names.	Rank.	Corps.	Commander.	Cause of Disability.	When Disabled.	Where Disabled.
Jonathan White	Private	1 Md. Regt.	Genl. Wm. Smallwood		25 April 1781	Cambden
Owen Coffield	ditto		Col. Grayson			
Joseph Greer				Lost a leg at the Siege of 96		
John Bean		3 Md. Regt.				Cambden
Wm. Tuel, per his widow	ditto		Capt. Horatio Clagett	Killed	4 Oct 1777	German Tow
Joseph Shirtley, per his widow	ditto		Col. Thos. Williams	Killed	4 Oct 1777	German Tow

Prince Georges County, to wit,

I Samuel Tyler, Register of the Orphans Court in and for the County aforesaid, d
Books of the Orphans' Court, in and for said County, concerning the Invalid Soldiers allowe
In Testimony whereof I have hereunto set my hand & Affixed the public seal of sai

[Seal.]

Return of Disabled Soldiers who have been Allowed by the

Names.	Rank.	Regiment.
John Lowrie	Private Soldier	Seventh
Nathaniel Wheeler	Private Soldier	Second

during the War of the American Revolution, 1775–83.   635

in Prince George's County.

Place of Residence, Town and County.	When Pension Commenced.	When Pension Ceased and Reasons.	Struck Off the List and Reasons.	Allowance Per Month.	Whole Amount Paid.	Exact Time to Which the Pension Has Been Paid.
near Uper Marlboro, Prince Georges Co.	29 Sept 1781			25/	£117 10	
do do	15 Nov 1783			25/	56 5	
	15 Nov 1783	dead		25/	52 10	15 May 1787
					40 0	in full for his wounds
					415 0 curry. & 68 5 real	31 July 1784
	6 June 1778		14 Aug 1781		320 0 curry. & 110 0 real	Oct 1781

hereby Certify that the within is a true Abstract of the proceedings, taken from the Minute pension by the worshipfull Justices of said Court.
Office this Twentieth day of January, Anno Domini Seventeen Hundred and Ninety.

   Samuel Tyler,
     Register of Wills for Prince G. County.

Orphans Court of Somerset County on Account their half pay etc.

Action they were Wounded.	Time of Beginning their Half Pay.	To What Time Settled With.	Whole Amount.
Camden	From the time his full pay ceased	13 July 1784	
Eutaw Spring	1 Jan 1783	1 Dec 1784	£43 2 6

   Somerset County, December 20th, 1784.
     Esme Bayly, Regr. Wills, S. C.

APPENDIX

APPENDIX.

After the most of the volume was in type, certain muster rolls were secured by the Maryland Historical Society at an auction sale of manuscripts in New York City. These are printed in an appendix, as they were procured too late to be inserted in their proper chronological order. In addition to these, the appendix contains a list of militia who served in 1777, which was found among the papers deposited by the Johns Hopkins University, a list of the Select Militia of 1781, enlisted from Frederick County, and a roll of the crew of the Ship Defence, compiled by Mr. Philip D. Laird, from papers in the Land Office. It has seemed best to include all available rolls in this volume, so the muster rolls of the Flying Camp Companies, and the Eastern Shore Militia Companies ordered to Virginia, first printed in Volume XII of the Archives of Maryland, are reprinted in this appendix.

EARLY AND INDEPENDENT COMPANIES.

Fifth Company of the First Battalion.*
Captain Nathaniel Ramsey.

| Capt. Nathl. Ramsey | present | 2nd Lieut. Daviot Plunket | present |
| 1st Lieut. Levin Winder | do | Ensign Walker Muse | do |

Rank.	Date of Enlistment.	Names.	Cause of Absence.	
Serjt.		John Gassaway	present	
do		Francis Revely	do	
do		Edward Sinclair	do	
do		John Brady	sick	in Hospital
Corpl.		Joseph Dixon	present	
do		John Bruce	do	
do		Alex. McConaughey	do	
do		Edwd. Ford	absent	on Furlough 8th Inst.
Drum		James Murphey	present	
Fife		John Harris, (hired)	do	

*See page 13.

Rank.	Date of Enlistment.	Names.	Cause of Absence.	
Privates		David Congleton	absent	on Guard
		Thomas Brewer	present	
		George Horner	do	
	May 18th '76	John Callenan	do	
		Ezekiel Pearce	do	
	May 29th	John Burgess	absent	on Guard
		Charles Turner	present	
		John Marr	dischd.	18th Inst.
		Thomas Hunter	present	
		Richard Cheaney	do	
		Godfrey Gash	do	
		James Hogg	do	
		Willm. Basford	sick	in Hospital
		Willm. Marr	present	
		Isaac Buttrim	absent	on Guard
		Mathew Neeley	present	
		James Mutton	do	
		Thomas Reed	do	
		Alex. McMunn	do	
		Nicholas Marr	do	
		Saml. Elliott	do	
		Philip Harley	do	
		[Torn off.]		

Present on Duty		Sick	Discharged
1 Captain	3 Corporals	1 Serjeant	6 Privates
2 Lieutenants	1 Drummer	4 Privates	Absent
1 Ensign	1 Fifer	Deserted	1 Corporal
3 Serjeants	54 Privates	1 Private	

M

Eighth Company of the First Battalion.*
Captain Samuel Smith.

1776			1776	
Jan 13	John Fletcher		Jan 23	Alexander Shaw
	Francis Hiltrhimer			John Snyder
15	William Arnold			Patrick Costigin
18	James Kelly			Obadiah Stillwill
	William Corbin			Aquilla Taylor
	Charles Simms		24	Nathan Bleak

* See page 17.

1776		1776	
Jan 20	James Daly	Jan 24	George Bennett
23	Geo. Edmondstone		Martin Wheelan
	William Wetstet, (or Welstet)		David Smith
	John Lorah		Michael Casy
	Joseph Grey		John Edwards
	Robert Westbay		Jacob Flori
	Fredk. Hambright		[Torn off.]

M

2ND INDEPENDENT COMPANY. [Somerset County.]*
CAPTAIN JOHN GUNBY.

DATE.	NAME.	REMARKS.
	[A large number of names torn off.]	
Mch	Wm. Matthews	sick in Barracks
2nd	John Tull	present
4th	Pressly Brewenton	sick in Barracks
	Thomas Parramore	present
	Wm. Craig	do
8th	John Cooksey	do
9th	Henry Chessey	sick in Barracks
	John Reed	present
	Nehemiah Knight	do
12th	Patrick Philips	sick at Princess Anne
14th	James Holder	deserted 24th June
20th	Abraham Ervin	sick in Barracks
Apl 5th	Solomon Tull	present
8th	George Finch	do
	Henry Clarke	do
9th	John Holder	do
	John Chittam	do
	Wm. Williams	do
	Philip King	do
15th	Joshua Gordey	do
19th	Francis Figgen	do
May 1st	Thomas Adams	deserted 24th June
14th	Jonathan Brown	present
15th	Wm. North	sick at Princess Anne
22nd	Elisha Taylor	present
28th	Richd. Trane Weatherly	do
29th	Willy Clarke	do
June 12th	John Mitchell	sick at Princess Anne
26th	Obadiah Summers	present

*See page 20.

Date.	Name.	Remarks.
July 4th	Wm. Jones	deserted 9th Inst.
15th	James Townsend	dischd. 21st Inst.
26th	William Stockwell	present
Aug 1st	John Dowse	sick in Barracks
6th	Richardson Moss	present
13th	Thomas Power	do

		Privates	
1 Captain	4 Corporals		
3 Lieutenants	1 Drummer	62 On Duty	16 Sick
4 Serjeants	1 Fifer	10 Deserted	1 Discharged

G. Duvall, Muster Master

Cambridge, Aug. 21st, 1776.

I hereby certify that the Second Independent Company under my Command was this Day Mustered by Charles Wallace Howard. The above is a true Copy of the Muster Roll of said Company.

The persons who were not present at said Muster were absent for the Causes mentioned opposite to their respective Names in said Muster Roll and no other.

Jno. Gunby.

M

6th Independent Company. [Dorchester County.]*
Captain Thos. Woolford.

Date.	Name.	Remarks.
	[A few names torn off.]	
Jan 27th	John Murphy	present
29th	Jacob Hustone	do
do	Edward Flin	do
do	William Kimplin	do
Feb 1st	Patrick Farren	do
do	William Cole	do
2nd	Laurence Hughes	do
4th	Laurence Fitzpatrick	do
do	Barney Maloy	do
do	William Thom	do
do	Samuel McCracking	do
8th	Daniel Norriss	do
do	Samuel Roans	do

*See page 25.

DATE.	NAME.	REMARKS.
Feb 15th	George Nut	present
do	William Lee	do
26th	John Malone	do
do	Joseph Read	do
Mch 2nd	Hugh Kelly	do
do	Michael Connar	do
do	Daniel Brophy	do
7th	John Welsh	do
Feb 20th	Edward Hodson	do
do	Nathan Wright	do
do	Edmund Garoughty	sick up at his Mothers
23rd	John Dunn	present
	Deweast Downing	do
	Jonathan Price	sick at John Greenwood's
Mch 21st	Ephraim Wheelar	present
11th	Patrick Rack	do
12th	John Basset	do
Feb 20th	Thomas Grayham	do
do	Luke Cox	do
do	Solomon Tylor	do
do	Thomas Bayley	do
do	Robert Ruarke	do
do	William Smith	do
do	Matthew Hayward	do
do	Charles Foxwell	do
do	Samuel North	do
do	Miles Shehern	do
do	Caleb Joy	do
do	Daniel Linch	do
do	William Man	do
do	Phillip Hodge	do
23rd	William Dingle	do
do	Francis Noble	do
do	John Hayward	do
do	John Caffey	do
do	Edward Hardekin	do
26th	Matthew Colbert	do
Mch 2nd	James Sherren	do
4th	William Delihay	do
do	Peter Taylor	do
do	Thomas Harrison	do
5th	Edward Williams	do
4th	William Kellinough	do
9th	Thomas Saunders	sick at his Father's
14th	Isaac Southard	present
Feb 24th	Levin Prichard	do

Date.	Name.	Remarks.	
Feb 24th	Joseph Staplefort	present	
do	Spencer Saunders	do	
do	Perry Harrison	dischd. by M. Gist 25th Inst.	
25th	John Noble	present	
26th	Richardson Gamble	do	
Mch 1st	James Sulivan	do	
do	Patrick Caton	do	
7th	John Heron	do	
14th	Patrick Connerly	do	
15th	Richard Frazier	do	
do	Dennis Devine	do	
19th	William Hale	do	
21st	Hooper Elliot	do	
28th	John Martin, D. C.	do	
do	Thomas Hayard	do	
do	James Andrew	do	
Apl 1st	Saml. Spencer	do	
8th	William Hays	do	Total
do	James Urey	do	1 Captain
10th	Jeremiah Andrew	do	3 Lieutenants
May 2nd	Robert Skinner	do	4 Serjeants
do	James Haney	do	4 Corporals
9th	Thomas Hart	do	1 Fifer
Apl 4th	Richard Burt	do	89 Privates

True Copy from the original Muster Roll of my Company.

Thos. Woolford.

M   G. Duvall, Muster Master.

EASTERN SHORE MILITIA COMPANIES ORDERED TO VIRGINIA.

RESOLVES OF CONTINENTAL CONGRESS—8 JANUARY, 1776.

"*Resolved*, That the convention or committee of safety of Maryland, be requested to order three companies of the minute-men in the service of that colony, to march immediately from thence to the counties of Accomack and Northhampton, in Virginia, instead of the forces that were directed to go thither from Pennsylvania, and to lay before Congress the accounts of their subsistence and pay, which shall be paid out of the continental treasury."

RESOLVES OF THE MARYLAND CONVENTION—15 JANUARY, 1776.

"*Resolved*, That the minute company in Dorchester county commanded by captain Joseph Robson, and the minute company in Queen Anne's county commanded by captain James Kent, and the minute company in Kent county commanded by captain William Henry, immediately march to Accomac and Northampton counties in Virginia, to the assistance of the inhabitants there; and that if any of the men belonging to either of the said companies cannot go on this occasion, then the full number to be made up of such volunteers as may offer for this particular service."

From the records of the Council of Safety, see Md. Archives, Vol. XI, it does not appear that Capt. Robson's Company marched.

A List of the Minute Company that march'd from Queen Anns County, Maryland the 3d Feby., 1776.*

James Kent, Capt.
Thomas Tillotson, 1st Lieut.
John Charris 2nd Lieut.

John Dames, Ensign
James Browne, Surgeon

Sergts.
George Findley
Ephraim Wyn Story
Philemon Davis
Samuel Copper

Corporals
John Jackson
Thomas Meridith Bryon
Thomas Freshwater, Drumr.
John Findley, Fifer.

William Stinson	Samuel Earle	James Browne
Matthew Mason	Edward Taylor	Edward Tryall
Edward Wright	Perigrine Ashford	William Tarr
John Hawkins	William Briggs	Samuel White
James Clayland	Edward Downes	James Harriss
Solomon Pratt	Robert Dawson	Nathl. Tucker
Samuel Seeney	William Morgan	William Bruff
John Hargadine	Richard Emory	John Smith
Barnaba Sinnott	Robert Love	Thomas Lane Emory
Joseph Elliott	John Lloyd	Christopher Jackson
John Godwin	Henry Coursey	William Scott
Charles Scrivenor	John Carman	Robert Russum
Christopher Yewell	Edward Harriss	John Burnett
John Keene	John Thomas	Richard Wickes
Thomas Meridith	Saml. Wright Thomas	William Deford
Jonathan Gibson	Robert Wright	James Gould Sparks
Joseph Wright	William Wilson Emory	John Emory Hall
John Kent	Thomas Mayson	Samuel Boulsover
Thomas Harriss	William Robinson	James Clayland, Jr.
William Middleton	Benj. Blunt	Jacob Gibson
William Holding	Walter Meeds	Richard Bruff
William Roe	William Larry	Gideon Emory

N. B.—John Kent was wounded the 6th Feby. and has not been able to join the Company since, William Middleton, William Roe, and John Findley, left the Compy. 1st March.

James Kent.

*Archives of Md., Vol. XI, page 194.

A List of the Minute Company from Kent County under the Command of William Henry, who marched from said County 29th January, 1776, and now stationed in Northampton County, Verginia.*

William Henry, Capt.	Serjts.	Corpls.	Drumr.
John Hyland } Lieuts.	Enos Reves	John Day	Joseph Purden
G. W. Forester }	Wm. Sprot	Robt. Gay	
William Clarke, Ensign	Geo. Vansant	Jas. Henry	Fifer
William Tillotson, Surgeon	Chas. Irons	Garret Vansant	Wm. ———
Robert Campbell, Adjutant			

John Bond	William Haley	Benedict Penington
Stephen Boddy	John Hurt	Matthew Richardson
Benj. Brockson	James Hurt	Sampson Redgrave
Henry Bostick	Peter Justice	Thos. Read
Lambert Boyer	William Johnson	John Richardson
John Burnsides	Nathl. Knock	Jacob Richardson
Henry Clarke	David Keain	Thos. Sewell
Edward Clayton	Francis Lemon	Thos. Sapington
James Campher	Geo. Littles, Sr.	John Stephenson
John Cole	Geo. Littles, Jr.	Benj. Stoops
John Cry	John Miller	John Stoops
Isaac Cornelius	John McGowan	Marlow Taylor
William Davis	William Miers	Wm. Peregr. Thrift
Samuel Davis	Enoch Massy	John Vansant
Samuel Eades	Nathl. McClelland	Christr. Vansant
Isaac Freeman	John Massey	Benj. Vansant
Daniel Fergusson	Saml. Money	Jas. Wilson, Sr
Abraham Freeman	Joseph Newsom	John Wilson
Salethiel Freeland	John Nowland	Jas. Wilson, Jr.
Lambert Flowers	Richd. Nab	William Wilson
Benj. Garland	Wm. Petegrew	John Wilmer
James Greedy	Chas. Phillipshill	James Woodland
Oliver Gallop	Andw. Park	Robert Young
William Gray		

Given under my hand at Head Quarters,
29th Feby., 1776.
William Henry.

FLYING CAMP MILITIA.

Capt. John Oglevee's Company.†

We the Subscribers, do hereby Enroll our Selves to serve, as Militia of Maryland, in the Middle Department, that is to say, from this Province to New York inclusive, untill the first day of December next, unless sooner discharged by the

*Archives of Md., Vol. XI, pages 298-9. †Archives of Md., Vol. XII, page 132. See page 71.

during the War of the American Revolution, 1775-83.

Honorable Congress, according to the Resolution of the Convention of Maryland held at Annapolis the 21st day of June, 1776.

Capt. John Oglevee	James Hasson	Daniel Robinson
1st Lieut. Joseph Tanner	Daniel McGuffin	George McClelland
2nd Lieut. Elisha' Rodgers	Alex. Thompson	David Morrison
Ensign James Boggs	John Sands	William Mullen
Wm. Tilyard	James Connor	Hugh McDowell
Thomas Ramsey	William Duffield	James Perry
Eliot Williams	John Johnson	John Minor
Oliver Bing	Matthew McDowell	Thomas King
William Smith	Benj. Hasson	Elisha Gatchel
Benj. McMahon	Michael Askin	James Hindman
James McKibbin	James Clendenin, (a lad),	Benj. Moody
John Jameson	Drummer	George Robinson
George Glass	Alexander Armstrong	Saml. Thompson
William Strean	Pattrick Donneley	Alex. Simpson
George Cunningham	Matthew Morgan	Josiah Porterfield
William Brisland	John Phillips	William Jameson
James M. Clenshey	James Wright	James Stevenson
William Brison	George Day	Thomas Newell
Andrew Thompson	William Bean	William Johnson
James Morrow	Carbery Cuningham	James Welch
Samuel Bing		

July the 25th, 1776: The within and above men were viewed and are able bodied effective men.

Charles Rumsey.

CAPT. RICHARD SMITH'S COMPANY.*

List of non commissioned officers and privates enrolled into a company of Militia for the service of the Flying Camp, under Captain Richard Smith, Lieuts. Walter White and Thomas Hayes and Ensign Thomas Sprigg, commencing the 19th of Sept., 1776, to each of whom the bounty money and one month's pay has been advanced at that time and at several dates since, as pr. List now in possession of

Oct. 15th, 1776.   Richd. Smith, Capt.

Levi Hayes	Jacob Irissler	Robert Muckleroy
Henry Clagett	William Veal Steuart	William Pollard
John Patrick	Michael Clancy	Jacob Hesse
Matthias Hemstone	James Long	William Preston
Andrew Hughes	Charles Steuart	Thomas Fanning
Jesse Harris	John Nolland	Ezekiel Harris
William Summers	Nicholas Rodes	John Gibson
Joseph Lewis	Alex. Mason	William Sutton
John Davies	John Hennes	John Harriss

*Archives of Md., Vol. XII, pages 352-3. See page 74.

John Smith
Alexander Read
Matthew Read
William Norris, (son of Benj.)
William Wallace
Levin Hayes
John Raynolds
Herbert Alex. Wallace
Robert Moore
Henry Kuhnes
Anthony Murphy

Thos. Hays
George Windom
Peter Night
William Madden
Henry Atcheson
Andrew Keath
Samuel Queen Windsor
John Bennett
John Hinton
William Johnston
John Bowen

John Fitzgerrald
John Carroll
John Burgess
Jeremiah Leitch
Dennias Mannan
Nicholas Rodes, Jr.
Zepheniah Wallace
William Pruett
James Jordan
Robert Robinson

CAPT. ROBT. HARRIS' COMPANY OF FLYING CAMP MILITIA.*

Philadelphia, 9th Nov., 1776.

Date 1776.	Men's Names.	Date 1776.	Men's Names.
Sept 16th	James Coop	Sept 21st	Richd. Hopkins
"	Mathw. McElhany	"	Wm. Chambers
"	Joshua James	"	Patrick Nowlan
"	Jno. Chance	Oct 4th	Wm. Crook
"	James Trene	"	Jas. Watson
"	Levi Low	"	Robt. Armstrong
"	Wm. Feely	"	Michael Daugherty
"	Alex. Stevenson	5th	Jas. Donnaly
"	Robt. Hannah	"	Matthew Criswell
"	Gregory White	16th	Edmd. Daugharty
18th	Robert Gordon	19th	Jonn. Smith
21st	James Bull	Sept 16th	Zebedee Hicks
"	James Harris	"	Horatio Coop
"	Wm. Hall	25th	Richard Jordan
28th	Jas. Blaney	Oct 4th	Jno. Haig
"	Christopher Fort	"	Gyks Hodges
Oct 15th	Wm. Lattimore	16th	James Rigden
"	Francis Gibson	17th	Jas. Witgurs
"	Jno. Davidson	18th	Benj. Wailey
16th	Davd. Armstrong	20th	Thos. Capen
"	Barnet Rain	"	David McCullough
"	Thos. Roads	Sept 27th	Able Green
"	Jno. Cook	Oct 1st	Mathw. Skel
"	Jno. Bush	2nd	Chas. Anderson
17th	Wm. Cook	3rd	David Campbell
"	Alex. Thomson	"	Thomas Stewart
19th	Hugh Hutson	"	Wm. Kirk Patrick
"	Wm. Jordan	6th	Joseph Steel

*Archives of Md., Vol. XII, pages 435-6. See page 74.

Date 1776.	Men's Names.	Date 1776.	Men's Names.
Sept 26th	Wm. Cuthbert	Oct 6th	Jno. Orr
"	Jas. Munday	"	Jno. Patrick
"	Joseph Sanders	"	Jno. Pain
25th	Jno. Armstrong	7th	Jno. Taylor
28th	Jona. Eddy	9th	Joseph Dueberry
29th	John Baker	7th	Jas. Miller
"	Jno. Laitimore	"	Jessy Logan
"	Aquilla Dunham	"	Robt. Spencer
Oct 1st	Edwd. Morgan	"	Griffith Evans
"	David Wary		

MARYLAND MILITIA IN CONTINENTAL SERVICE IN 1777.

RESOLVES OF CONTINENTAL CONGRESS 9 DECEMBER, 1776.

"*Resolved*, That expresses be immediately sent to the committees of the counties of Cœcil, Baltimore, Hartford, and Frederick, in Maryland, requesting that they apply, without delay, to the militia of their respective counties, and send forward, immediately, for the defence of the city of Philadelphia, and the reinforcement of general Washington's army, as many troops as possible, informing the said committees that some assistance, in the way of arms, may be furnished here, to such as have no arms to bring with them."

RESOLVES OF CONTINENTAL CONGRESS 21 JANUARY, 1777.

"*Resolved*, That it be recommended to the council of safety of Maryland, to request the militia of Hartford, Baltimore, Cœcil, and such other counties of their state as they shall think proper, to march, as soon as possible, to reinforce general Washington, giving directions that each company consist of not less than 36 privates, under the command of two commissioned officers, and that a field-officer take the command of every four companies."

A large number of men marched under the Resolves of Dec. 9th, 1776, especially from Frederick, Baltimore and Harford Counties, but no rolls of these companies, giving date of service, can be found. Johnson's and Buchanan's entire divisions were ordered out.

650 *Records of Maryland Troops in the Continental Service*

RESOLVES OF CONTINENTAL CONGRESS 19 APRIL, 1777.

"*Resolved*, That the gov. of the state of Maryland be authorized to detain the weakest continental battalion raised in the state of Maryland, till a further order of Congress; and that it be recommended to the executive authority of the state of Maryland, forthwith, to embody 300 of the militia of the said state, and to the executive authority of the state of Delaware, 100 of their militia, the said militia to co-operte with the battalion of continental troops, to obey the officer commanding the same, and to continue in service so long as the joint executive authorities of the states of Delaware and Maryland shall think necessary."

RESOLVES OF CONTINENTAL CONGRESS 1 MAY, 1777.

" Congress being informed, that governor Johnson has, in pursuance of the resolution of Congress, of April 19th, for the purposes therein expressed, detained colonel Richardson's battalion, two companies of which are now in Philadelphia on their way to general Washington:

Resolved, That the said companies proceed to the army, and that governor Johnson be empowered to replace them, by detaining two companies of the weakest Maryland battalion remaining in that state."

Roll of Capt. Robert Wrights Company of Militia, in the Service of the United States by a Resolution of Congress, under the command of Col. Wm. Richardson. Aug. and Sept., 1777.

Commissioned	July 7th '77 June 19th '77 July 7th '77	Warranted	May 27th Capt. Robert Wright 29th Lieut. John Kent, Jr., resigned Oct 10th 29th Lieut. Edward Thomas 27th Ensign Thomas Clymer

RANK.	APPOINTED.	NAMES.	REMARKS.
Serjeant	June 4th '77	Nathl. Wright	Sick in Hospital Sept
"	May 31st	Wm. Roe	
"	June 31st	Thos. Jackson	Sick in Quarters Aug. Deserted Sept 3rd
"	July 19th	John Cairey	
Corporal	May 31st	John Burnett	Enlisted in another Company Sept
"	June 1st	Thos. Covington	
"	May 31st	John Lloyd	
"	June 17th	Jas. Meredith	Sick in Quarters Aug

Rank.	Appointed.	Names.	Remarks.
Drum & Fife	July 19th	Thomas Yoe	Enlisted in another Company Sept
Privates	Enlisted June 7th	Jacob Seth	Dischd. Aug 15th
	7th	Charles Seth	
	May 31st	John Gormon	Enlisted in another Company Sept
	June 7th	John Davis	
	7th	John Jeffers, (Geffers)	Sick in Hospital Aug and Sept
	7th	Christr. Green	Dischd. Sept 1st '77
	7th	Peter Green	Dischd. Sept 1st '77
	7th	John Thom, (or Thorn)	Missing Oct 4th '77
	8th	Wm. Davis	Dischd. Sept 1st '77
	30th	Thos. Delanaway	Dischd. Sept 1st '77
	30th	Elias Jeffers	Deserted July 23rd
	30th	Wm. Morgan	Dischd. Sept 1st
	6th	Chas. Hands	Never joined Company. Dischd. Oct 7th
	July 7th	John Chase	Dischd. by Civil power
	June 10th	Chas. Walker	
	17th	Thos. Griffith	
	21st	Wm. Gray	Enlisted in another Company Sept
	16th	John Collins	Deserted Aug 5th, brought back 14th, Sick. Discharged [Sept 29th
	July 21st	Moses Ashford	
	June 26th	Nathaniel Baley, (Bailey)	
	July 6th	Bazil Jeffers	
	June 30th	Henry Weeden	Dischd. by Civil power
	July 1st	Wm. Price	Deserted Sept 12th
	4th	Thos. Roe	Dischd. Aug 10th
	June 2nd	Wm. Pinfield	Enlisted in another Company Sept
	2nd	Thos. Hall	Enlisted in another Company Sept
	July 19th	Saml. Wilkinson, (Wilkerson)	Deserted Sept 12th
	June 12th	Simon Rice	Deserted July 27th
	July 30th	Matthew B. Chambers	Enlisted in another Company Sept
	June 11th	Solo. Scott	Deserted Sept 12th
	July 3d	Philn. Davis	Enlisted in another Company Sept

Mustered Sept. 1st by Robt. Harrison, D. M. Master.
Mustered Oct. 15th by A. Horton, D. M. M.

RESOLVES OF CONTINENTAL CONGRESS 22 AUGUST, 1777.

"*Resolved*, That it be earnestly recommended to the state of Maryland, immediately to call out not less than 2000 select militia, to repel the expected invasion of the states of Pennsylvania, Delaware and Maryland; and that 1250 of the militia on the Western-shore of Maryland, repair, as soon as possible, to Baltimore and Hartford towns; that 750 of the militia on the Eastern-shore, repair as soon as possible, to Georgetown, on Sassafras, there to await the directions of general Washington:

That the militia requested from the states aforesaid, be in the pay of the continent to the 30th November next, unless sooner discharged by Congress, or the commander in chief:

That general Washington be directed to order brigadier-general Smallwood and colonel Gist, to repair immediately to the state of Maryland, to arrange, march and command the militia required of that state."

A large number of men marched under these Resolves, especially from Baltimore County, but no rolls can be obtained showing date of service. These troops were present at Paoli and Germantown. Capt. Cox, captain of a Baltimore militia company, was killed at Germantown. Maryland furnished more than 4000 militia during the years 1776 and 1777. They numbered about 1900 at Paoli and more than 1000 at Germantown.

It is, perhaps, not saying too much to state that almost the entire militia of Frederick and Baltimore Counties were in service at sometime during this year. The loss of these rolls causes the most serious gap in the Maryland records.

SELECT MILITIA OF 1781.

A List of Substitutes and Draughts raised in Frederick County under An Act to raise two Battalions of Militia, passed May Session, 1781.*

SUBSTITUTES.

William Dunn	Stephen Haffley	Frederick Stiteley
John Deilman	Nicholas Maguire	Christian Waggoner

* This Roll was presented to the Maryland Historical Society by Mr. Douglas H. Thomas, May 8th, 1899.

Aaron Farthing
Henry Clements
James Bowen
Adam Eck
Thomas Burch
Gilbert Smith
Pompey Colless
Robert Johnson
James Morris
Thedy Donlon
William Hamilton
John Shiffer
Thomas Canfield
John Oneill
Peter Edge
John Allsop
William Fream
Geo. Lodo. Fitcher
William Richardson
Valentine Dewitt
Benjamin Yeates
Menasses Queah
George Becker
John Ogdon
John Betsworth
Jacob Flower
George Miller
Richard Nagle
Jacob Ligamire

John Baum
John Haynes
Lodowick Pole
John Mefford
George Lesh
Henry White
John Frederick
Archibald Roberts
Francis Moser
Michael Moser
Solomon Rawlings
John Lenegen
Joseph Alsop
William Hunter
Gilbert Hunt
John Alexander
John Wilhite
George Hyringer
James Hamilton, Jr.
James Stokes
John Harbough
Henry McGarey
George Dytch
John Casey
William Burgess
Walter Farrell
Thomas Houston
John Morriss
Frederick Beard

John Franklin
Martin Hecketorn
William Ridge
Edward Robinson
Henry Young
John Neave
John Moore
John Miller
Shadrick West
Daniel Hack
Thomas Parkinson
William Dobson
Solomon Turner, Jr.
John Helmes, dischd. by
  Gen. Smallwood
Henry Holtzman
Peter Butler
John Miller
Philip Koontz
Murphy Shee
John Brown
John Qu——
John Neav——
Charles Hammond
Daniel Mehoney
James Bu——
Thomas Da——
Henry Hardman
Patrick Don——

DRAUGHTS.

Richard Seebrucks
Samuel Dobson
Edward Bryan
James Ogle
Adam Strine

Adam Souder
John Miller, (Major)
Peter Hartsoke
Christopher Scaggs

William Forquer
Michael Fleckinger
William Moore
Philip Myer

Benjn. Rice, appeared ready to march after Siege of York
William Scaggs, marched with Cattle to Fredericksburg

                       P. Thomas, Lt. Frederick County.

[All in the above Roll enlisted until the 10th of December, 1781. All marched to Annapolis unless otherwise noted.]

NAVAL ROLLS.

THE SHIP DEFENCE.

THE SHIP'S COMPANY.

	Adair, William, Armorer, Jan 11 to Oct 22, 1777; Armorer's Mate, Oct 22 to Dec 31, 1777.
B.	Allen, James, Quartermaster Jan 11 to May 18, 1777.
B.	Allen, Richard, Marine, March 30 to Dec 31, 1777.
+	Arm, ———, Quartermaster.
+	Arm, James, Ordinary Seaman.
+	Armstrong, James, Marine.
+	Askins, William, Marine.
B. +	Aubre, John, ——— Apl 1 to July 25, 1777.
	Auchenleck, ———, Lieutenant.
B.	Barnes, Henry, May 29 to July 27, 1777.
+	Barr, John, Coxswain.
	Barrance, James, ——— July 5 to Sept 22, 1777.
	Barrett, John, ——— Jan 25 to Dec 31, 1777.
+	Beachum, Wm., Carpenter's Mate.
B.	Bennett, George, ——— May 19 to July 23, 1777.
B.	Benton, Thomas, Carpenter, Feb 11 to July 26, 1777.
+	Berry, James, Marine.
	Berryman, John, Gunner, Jan 13 to Dec 31, 1777.
B.	Bird, Samuel, Marine, Apl 2 to Nov 7, 1777.
+	Birmingham, Christopher, Captain of Tender.
B.	Biscoe, Mackie, ——— May 19 to June 1, 1777.
+	Bishop, William, Marine.
	Blake, John, Boatswain, Jan 13 to June 17, 1777; Quartermaster, June 17 to Dec 31, 1777.
	Blackman, Stephen, Seaman, Jan 11 to Dec 31, 1777.
B.	Blithen, John, Corporal of Marines, May 12 to Aug 31, 1777.
+	Blunt, Charles, Marine.
	Bond, Nathaniel, Midshipman ———; Purser, Apl 15 to Dec 31, 1777.
+	Bradford, James, Ordinary Seaman.
+	Bradford, William, Sergeant of Marines.
B.	Brady, Michael, ——— June 20 to July 25, 1777.
B.	Braithwaite, John, Marine, Apl 28 to Dec 11, 1777.
	Briscoe, James, Marine, Oct 23 to Dec 31, 1777.
	Bromfield, Thomas, Captain of Marines, Apl 25 to Oct 15, 1777.
B.	Brooks, Thomas, ——— May 21 to June 28, 1777.
+	Brown, Colin, Sailor.
+	Brown, Garrett, Captain of Marines.
B.	Brown, Joseph, ——— Feb 17 to March 16, 1777.

B.	Brumicum, John, Seaman, May 29 to June 7, 1777.
+	Buckley, Thomas, Marine.
B.	Bunyan, John, Mate, May 24 to Aug 15, 1777; Chief Mate, Aug 15 to Dec 31, 1777.
	Burge, Joseph, Steward, Jan 11 to Apl 21, 1777.
+	Burnell, John, Master.
B.	Butler, James, ——— March 6 to June 1, 1777.
	Campbell, James, ——— Jan 28 to July 15, 1777.
	Campbell, John, ——— Jan 28 to Dec 31, 1777.
+	Carr, Henry, Marine.
B.	Carmen, John, Sergeant of Marines, June 1 to Nov 22, 1777.
	Carter, William, ——— May 1 to Aug 15, 1777.
+	Chamborlam, Charles, Sailor.
B.	Champion, George, Boatswain's Yeoman, Feb 26 to Dec 31, 1777.
B.	Cheshire, Benjamin, Marine, May 25 to Dec 31, 1777.
	Chevier, John, Midshipman, Nov 1 to Dec 31, 1777.
	Childs, Cud., Marine, June 1 to Dec 31, 1777.
B.	Clark, James, Marine, July 1 to Dec 31, 1777.
	Clegness, John Francis, Surgeon's Mate, Feb 10 to Dec 31, 1777.
B.	Cockerton, Robert, Cabin Steward, April 28 to Dec 31, 1777.
+	Cockey, Richard, Marine.
+	Cody, James, Marine.
	Coe, Job, Corporal of Marines, Jan 29 to Dec 31, 1777.
+	Cole, Patrick, Marine.
+	Colins, James, Marine.
B.	Colson, (or Coulston), John, Marine, Jan 30 to Dec 31, 1777.
B.	Compton, John, Marine, March 3 to Dec 31, 1777.
+	Conner, Robert, Marine.
	Cook, George, Lieut., Sept 12 to Nov 15, 1776. Captain, Nov 15, 1776, to Dec 31, 1777.
+	Cookson, John, Sailmaker.
	Cooper, Nathaniel, Second Mate, Jan 11 to June 1, 1777.
	Corbet, Patrick, Yeoman, Jan 13 to June 1, 1777; Marine, June 1 to Oct 15, 1777.
	Cordray, James, Second Mate.
	Cornaflean, William, Midshipman, Sept 4 to Sept 22, 1777; Clerk, Sept 22 to Dec 31, 1777.
+	Costillo, Thomas, Marine.
+	Crapper, John, Sergeant of Marines.
B.	Cratcher, Matthew, Marine, July 28 to Oct 1, 1777.
	Crawley, James, Marine, Oct 23 to Dec 31, 1777.
+	Cron, Thomas, Marine.
B.	Crosley, (or Crossley), William, Marine, Mch 16 to Dec 31, 1777.
B.	Cummings, Alexander, Marine ———; Carpenter's Yeoman, Feb 17 to Dec 31, 1777.
B.	Cunningham, Thompson, Boatswain's Mate, July 31 to Dec 31, 1777.
B.	Daefney, John, Seaman, Aug 9 to Sept 6, 1777.
+	Davis, John, Corporal of Marines.
+	Davis, William, Marine.

+	Delong, Bartholomew, Marine.
	Dennis, Joseph, —— Jan 25 to April 9, 1777.
	Dicks, Daniel, —— Jan 18 to April 12, 1777.
	Dickson, John, Seaman, Sept 1 to Dec 26, 1777.
+	Disney, Ezekiel, Sr., Ordinary Seaman.
+	Disney, Ezekiel, Jr., Marine.
+	Donavin, John, Marine.
	Dorsey, Joseph, Marine, Oct 23 to Dec 31, 1777.
+	Dorsey, Richard, Midshipman.
+	Douglas, Archibald, Tender's Crew.
	Douglass, William, Midshipman, Mch 13 to Apl 3, 1777.
	Driskill, John, Seaman.
B.	Dunbar, Joseph, Cooper, Jan 11 to Dec 31, 1777.
B.	Durdin, Thomas, —— Mch 6 to Dec 31, 1777.
	Evans, Robert, —— Aug 1 to Oct 31, 1777.
B.	Fall, Patrick, —— Jan 11 to May 18, 1777.
B.	Farrajara, John, Midshipman, Aug 9 to Sept 8, 1777.
B.	Fear, Ignatius, Gunner's Mate, May 28 to Sept 20, 1777.
B.	Fenton, Cornelius, Marine, April 1 to Dec 31, 1777.
	Fenwick, Richard, Marine, Oct 23 to Dec 31, 1777.
B.	FitzJeffrys, Aaron, —— June 21 to July 15, 1777.
B.	Flannagan, John, —— June 17 to June 29, 1777.
+	Flemming, John, Sergeant of Marines.
+	Flemming, William, Sergeant of Marines.
	Foster, William, —— March 27 to June 1, 1777.
B.	Fowler, Joseph, Boy, May 19 to Dec 31, 1777.
	Franceway, John, Marine, Jan 25 to Dec 31, 1777.
B.	Gagan, (Gaggen, Glagging), James, Cook, Feb 20 to Dec 31, 1777.
+	Gaggen, William, Ordinary Sailor.
	Gaither, Joseph, Clerk, Mch 18 to June 1, 1777.
B.	Gardner, (or Garner), Clement, Marine, May 22 to Dec 31, 1777.
B.	Gardner, Thomas, —— May 22 to July 7 1777.
B.	Garey, John, Marine, May 26 to Aug 15, 1777.
	Gibson, Joshua, Marine, May 22 to Dec 31, 1777.
+	Gibbons, Edward, Marine.
+	Gilby, Henry, Ordinary Sailor.
+	Gilby, Thomas, Ordinary Sailor.
+	Gilford, James, Ordinary Sailor.
B.	Gillis, Thomas, Third Mate, June 3 to Nov 25, 1777.
	Goldsbury, John, Marine, Oct 23 to Nov 15, 1777.
	Goldsbury, Stephen, Marine, Oct 23 to Nov 15, 1777. " Disch'd, being unfit for duty."
+	Gordon, Isaac Mount, Sergeant of Marines.
	Grant, John, Carpenter's Mate, Jan 14 to Dec 31, 1777.
+	Grantham, William, Marine.
B.	Green, James, Midshipman, June 24 to July 29, 1777.
+	Greer, James, Marine.
+	Greer, Moses, Marine.
B.	Gullehan, John, —— Mch 31 to July 15, 1777.

B.	Hagan, (Hagans), Charles, Cooper's Mate, Feb 12 to Dec 31, 1777.
+	Hall, John, Third Mate.
+	Hall, Stephen, Mate.
B.	Hall, William, ——— May 26 to July 28, 1777.
+	Haly, Oliver, Marine.
+	Hambleton, Charles, Sergeant of Marines.
	Hamer, (Harmer), John, "Taylor," Oct 10 to Dec 31, 1777.
+	Hanson, John, Midshipman.
B.	Harbest, (Harbert), Thomas, Marine, Jan 15 to Nov 15, 1777.
+	Harbert, William, Sailor.
B.	Harding, Richard,——— June 18 to June 29, 1777.
B.	Harper, Daniel, Boatswain, June 1 to Nov 24, 1777.
	Harris, William, Armorer, Feb 15 to Apl 13, 1777.
+	Hartie, James, Quarter Master.
B.	Havard, William, Seaman, Mch 6 to Dec 31, 1777.
B.	Havers, John, Cooper's Crew, June 19 to Dec 31, 1777.
B.	Hawkins, James, Midshipman, Mch 1 to Aug 15, 1777; with Ship's Tender, Aug 15 to Nov 15, 1777; Skipper, Nov 15 to Nov 24, 1777.
+	Henry, James, Marine.
+	High, George, Ordinary Sailor.
+	Hogan, James, Ordinary Sailor.
+	Hope, Robert, Ordinary Sailor.
B.	Hopewell, Thomas, Midshipman, May 15 to Dec 31, 1777.
B.	Hopkins, Roger, ——— Apl 28 to July 21, 1777.
	Hosier, Joshua, Seaman, Jan 23 to Dec 31, 1777.
B.	Howard, Thomas, Midshipman, Feb 2 to Dec 31, 1777.
	Howard, William, Carpenter's Mate, Aug 15 to Dec 31, 1777.
+	Howard, William, Marine.
B.	Hudson, William, Seaman, June 24 to Dec 31, 1777.
+	Huggard, William, Marine.
	Huggins, William, Marine, Sept 6 to Dec 31, 1777.
B.	Humphreys, Lewis, ——— June 25 to July 15, 1777.
+	Hurbert, Francis, Boatswain's Mate.
	Hurst, Cuthbert, (or Hurst, Catwood), ——— June 27 to Dec 31, 1777.
+	Hyndson, Anthony, Boatswain.
+	Jackelen, Francis, Marine.
+	Jennett, Green, Marine.
	Jerrial, John, Marine, June 8 to Aug 4, 1777.
	Johns, Aquilla, Lieutenant.
B.	Johnson, Horsford, Marine, Apl 28 to Dec 16, 1777.
	Johnson, John, Seaman, Jan 11 to March 3, 1777.
+	Jones, Joseph, Marine.
	Jones, Nathan, ——— Jan 25 to May 13, 1777.
	Jordan, Samuel, Corporal of Marines, Oct 22 to Dec 31, 1777.
	Jourdan, (Jorden), Jeremiah, ——— Jan 23 to Dec 31, 1777.
	Jourdan, (Jorden), John, Sergeant of Marines, Jan 23 to Dec 31, 1777.
+	Judges, William, Ordinary Sailor.
+	Kenderdine, John, Marine.
+	King, William, Ordinary Sailor.

B.	Kinsey, Thomas, Midshipman, Apl 9 to Dec 31, 1777.
B.	Kirk, Daniel, Marine, May 28 to Dec 31, 1777.
+	Knight, John, Marine.
B.	Land, William, Marine, Apl 2 to Dec 21, 1777.
+	Langrale, Levin, Sailor.
	Larkan, Dennis, Seaman.
B.	Lawrence, Joshua, Seaman, July 2 to Dec 31, 1777.
B.	Lee, (Leigh), Christopher, Marine, May 20 to Dec 31, 1777.
B.	Leigh, William, Surgeon's Mate.
+	Lemmon, John, Marine.
B.+	Leury, John, ——.
B.	Lilburn, (Lilbon), Walter, Midshipman, May 22 to Nov 24, 1777.
	Little, John, Seaman, Sept 20 to Dec 31, 1777.
+	Loyal, John, Marine.
	Luke, Folius, —— Jan 25 to Mch 31, 1777.
+	Lux, Robert, Midshipman.
	Lusby, Henry, Midshipman, Oct 15 to Nov 13, 1777; Lieutenant of Marines, Nov 13 to Dec 31, 1777.
	McAdams, John, Armorer, Oct 22 to Dec 31, 1777.
B.	McCarty, Florence, Seaman, June 25 to Dec 16, 1777.
B.	McClenan, (McCleland), Robert, Marine, June 26 to Dec 31, 1777.
B.	McCoy, George, —— April 1 to Dec 31, 1777.
+	McDonald, Robert, Ordinary Sailor.
+	McGill, James, Marine.
	McLaughlan, Mark, Carpenter, Aug 5 to Dec 31, 1777.
+	McNealis, Charles, Marine.
B.	Maddox, John, Marine, June 3 to Oct 15, 1777.
+	Mason, Abel, Ordinary Sailor.
B.	Massey, Henry Lee, Midshipman, May 10 to Dec 31, 1777.
+	Masters, Watterly, Marine.
	Matthews, John, Sweeper, Jan 25 to Dec 31, 1777.
+	Matthews, Wm., Corporal of Marines.
	Medley, Enoch, Seaman, Oct 23 to Dec 31, 1777.
	Mercer, Stephen, —— Jan 13 to April 21, 1777.
B.	Miller, Philip, Seaman, Jan 15 to Oct 1, 1777.
B.	Miller, William, Ship's Steward, June 2 to July 11, 1777; Seaman, July 11 to Oct 15, 1777; Gunner's Yeoman, Oct 15 to Dec 31, 1777.
B.	Mills, Jonathan, —— May 22 to July 23, 1777.
B.	Montgomery, John, Ship's Tender, June 7 to Dec 31, 1777.
B.	Moore, Thomas, Ordinary Sailor.
	Moore, John, Marine, May 10 to Dec 31, 1777.
+	Moores, James R., Purser.
+	Morris, Wm., Lieutenant of Marines.
+	Murphy, Samuel, Marine.
+	Murray, Matthew, Marine.
	Murphy, Morgan, Marine, Jan 13 to Mch 23, 1777.
	Nagill, (Nagale), Michael, Marine, Oct 8 to Nov 26, 1777.
B.	Nash, Thomas, Boatswain's Mate, Apl 28 to Aug 15, 1777; Marine, Aug 15 to Dec 11, 1777.

during the War of the American Revolution, 1775-83.   659

      Nesbit, Thomas, Seaman, Nov 15 to Dec 31, 1777.
      Neven, Daniel, Ordinary Seaman.
      Nichols, Walter, ———— Jan 16 to Aug 15, 1777; Quarter Gunner, Aug 15 to Dec 31, 1777.
      Nicholson, Alex., Sailor, Jan 11 to Aug 15, 1777; Quarter Master, Aug 15 to Dec 11, 1777.
+   Nicholson, James, Captain.
+   Nicholson, John, Lieutenant.
B.   Palmer, Thomas, Marine, May 29 to Dec 31, 1777.
B.   Parsons, William, Marine, Apl 28 to Dec 31, 1777.
B.   Peres, Anthony, Seaman, Aug 9 to Sept 6, 1777.
      Peters, Nicholas, Marine.
      Piercy, William, Midshipman, Jan 13 to Dec 31, 1777.
      Pike, John, Marine, Jan 21 to Dec 31, 1777.
      Poland, (Polland), William, Marine, Apl 1 to Dec 31, 1777.
+   Porter, William, Marine.
+   Porter, William, Sailor.
+   Power, John, Marine.
B   Powlet, Severn, ———— June 3 to July 23, 1777.
      Prew, William, Ship's Steward, July 9 to Dec 31, 1777.
B.   Price, Henry, Marine, May 21 to Dec 31, 1777.
+   Primrose, David, Sailor.
+   Prince, William, Marine.
B.   Quay, James, Ordinary Seaman, April 1 to Dec 31, 1777.
      Ragan, Roderick, Marine, Aug 12 to Oct 7, 1777.
B.   Ready, James, Marine, May 10 to Dec 17, 1777.
B.   Ready, Lawrence, Marine, May 10 to Dec 17, 1777.
      Rentford, Henry, Sailor, Feb 1 to Mch 11, 1777.
B.   Richardson, Alexander, ———— Feb 15 to May 15, 1777.
+   Riley, Michael, Marine.
+   Riley, Tim, Ordinary Sailor.
+   Roberts, Thomas, Marine.
      Robertson, George, Surgeon, May 20 to Dec 31, 1777.
      Robertson, William, Captain's Clerk, Feb 10 to Mch 26, 1777.
      Rogers, John, 2nd Lieut. of Marines, Mch 11 to Dec 31, 1777.
      Ross, George, 1st Lieut. of Marines, Mch 18 to Dec 31, 1777.
+   Ross, Nathan, ————.
      Rowe, John, ———— Jan 16 to July 23, 1777.
+   Rowen, George, Master at Arms.
+   Rowns, James, Midshipman.
B.   Scone, Charles, ———— March 6 to June 30, 1777.
+   Scott, Mores, Marine.
B.   Seagreave, Patrick, ———— May 21 to July 28, 1777.
      Seea, John, Marine.
B.   Sency, William, ———— Apl 28 to Aug 15, 1777.
      Sermon, Leonard, ———— Jan 23 to Apl 11, 1777.
+   Sharp, Peter, Midshipman.
+   Short, Christopher, Sailor.
+   Simpson, Benj., Boatswain's Mate.

	Skiffington, Roger, Marine, Jan 20 to Dec 31, 1777.
+	Slaymaker, John, Lieutenant.
	Skinner, Francis, Prize Master, Sept 15 to Dec 31, 1777.
	Smith, James, Marine, Oct 22 to Dec 31, 1777.
+	Smith, John Addison, Gunner.
+	Smith, Joseph, Lieutenant of Marines.
+	Sohan, William, Marine.
B.	Sommers, Jacob, ——— April 3 to Oct 15, 1777.
B.	Sommers, John, Quarter Master, Feb 15 to Dec 11, 1777.
+	Squib, John, Marine.
B.	Stanton, Alexander, Armorer, Jan 11 to Aug 15, 1777; Master at Arms, Aug 15 to Dec 31, 1777.
B.	Stiles, Solomon, Pilot, May 22 to Dec 31, 1777.
+	Strong, Abram, Marine.
B.	Sullivan, Bright, Sailmaker, July 15 to Dec 31, 1777.
+	Sutton, Benjamin, Marine.
+	Sutton, Jacob, Marine.
+	Sutton, Richard, Marine.
	Swailes, Robert, Marine, Oct 23 to Dec 31, 1777.
+	Thompson, George, Sailor.
	Thompson, John, ——— Jan 11 to Mch 1, 1777.
+	Tooloe, Dennis, Marine.
+	Topet, Robert, Marine.
+	Trainer, Simon, Marine.
+	Tregashes, Jacob, Armorer.
+	Trot, William, Ordinary Sailor.
+	Turnbull, C. George, Captain.
+	Tyler, Littleton, Carpenter.
	Vansickle, Gilbert, Seaman, Jan 28 to June 1, 1777.
B.	Vaughan, Abraham, Marine, Aug 3 to Nov 19, 1777.
+	Vaun, John, Marine.
	Walker, Samuel, Master, Apl 22 to Dec 31, 1777.
+	Walker, Thomas, Lieutenant of Marines.
	Walter, Levin, ——— Jan 21 to June 1, 1777.
+	Ward, John, Marine.
+	Watpole, Joseph, Sailor.
B.	Watson, James, ——— June 23 to Aug 15, 1777; Capt. After Guard, Aug 15 to Nov 23, 1777.
B.+	Wharton, Revel, ———.
B.	Wheeler, Benj., Marine, June 7 to Dec 31, 1777.
	White, Benj., Seaman, Sept 20 to Dec 31, 1777.
B.	White, Peter, Seaman, Aug 9 to Nov 2, 1777.
B.	Williams, Francis, Cook's Mate, Feb 11 to Dec 31, 1777.
B.	Williams, John, Marine, Apl 28 to Dec 31, 1777.
B.	Williams, Marshall, Seaman, Jan 21 to Mch 21, 1777.
+	Wilson, John, Corporal of Marines.
B.	Woods, Benj., Mate, June 20 to Aug 15, 1777; 2nd Mate, Aug 15 to Dec 28, 1777.
+	Wright, John, Seaman.

+	Wright, John, Quarter Master.
B.	Yates, Richard, Boatswain's Mate, Apl 28 to Dec 8, 1777.
	Yates, Vachel, Sergeant of Marines, ———; Lieut. of Marines, Feb 15 to Oct 15, 1777; Capt. of Marines, Oct 15 to Dec 15, 1777.

Compiled from Papers in the Land Office of Maryland by Philip D. Laird, 1896, and presented by him to the Maryland Historical Society.

It is compiled alphabetically from four Accounts of Seamen's Wages,—one from September 12, 1776, to August 15, 1777; one from August 15 to October 15, 1777; one from October 15 to November 15, 1777; one from November 15 to December 31, 1777—and from a List of Officers and Men, without date, which is manifestly prior to the dates of the pay accounts. The names in the list, where they are in addition to those in the pay accounts, are indicated by the mark +. The letter B., in the margin, indicates those who received bounty, the information being derived from two accounts of "Bounties paid by the Ship Defence," amounting, in the aggregate, to £630. The time of service is not given in all cases, in the pay accounts, and in a number of instances the rank is omitted. As far as possible dates of promotion are given.

HARFORD COUNTY PENSIONERS.*

List of the names of maimed Soldiers entitled to half pay under the Act of October Session, 1778.

Joseph Botts.
James Burk.
James Brewer.
John Butcher.
John Dent, Corpl.
James Dyre.
Michael Duffy.
William Evans.
George Finleyson.
Caleb Hazel.
John Howard.
James Scott.

Frederick Ire.
James Isaacs.
Daniel Keith.
Macnamara, (sic.)
Thomas McGee.
John Mathews, Corpl.
James O'Hara.
James Pope.
Christopher Reynol.
Valentine Smith.

James Smith.
William Ely.
John Shaw, Sergt.
Samuel Tyndall.
William Fulton.
Samuel Wilson, Sergt.
John Vanzant.
Richard Wilkinson.
Joseph Quinn.
John Lowery.
Edward Cain.

Allowances for the support of the families of Soldiers enlisted in the Continental Army, 1777–1780.

Richard Crosby.
James McCarty.
Wm. Murphy.

Edward Evans.
James Kelly.
Wm. Lytle.

Michael Coaleman.
Wm. Hendersides.

Sept. 1778, a commission was appointed 'to take the deposition of Joseph Barnes, a Soldier' in a suit pending.

*Extracts, from the 'Proceedings of the Orphans Court of Harford County, 1784–1803' and the 'Records of the County Court of Harford County, 1777–1780' made by Dr. G. W. Archer.

INDEX.

Aaron, Levy, 267.
Aaron (Arran), Michael, 45, 183.
Aaron, Moses, 80.
Abbot (Abbet), Saml., 612, 613.
Abbott, Ezekiel, 25.
Abbott (Abbot), George, 78, 522.
Abbott (Abbot), John, 273, 406.
Abbott (Abbitt, Abbet, Abbott), Levin (Lewin), 346, 354, 395, 449, 490, 523.
Abbott, Thomas, 184.
Abbutt, Blagdon, 615.
Abdel, Jacob, 78.
Abel (Able), John, 182, 184, 261.
Abell, Aaron, 34.
Abell (Able), Cuthbert (Cuthbirt, Cuthburt), 34, 184, 389, 437, 507, 523.
Aberly, Leonard, 184.
Able, Thomas, 60.
Ablewhite, Joseph, 340, 360.
Abraham (Abrahams), John, 418, 469, 523.
Abrams, John, 509.
Absalom (Absolom), William, 397, 458, 487, 523.
Absolom, Negro, 382.
Ackerly (Akerly), John, 574, 618.
Acklin, James, 336.
Acock, John, 425, 468.
Acort, Godfrey, 297.
Acre, Conomus (Cronamus, Cronomus), 51, 183, 307.
Acres, Thomas, 626.
Acton, Henry, 35.
Acton, Smallwood, 35.
Adair, William, 183, 607, 654.
Adam, Argent, 273.
Adamisell, John, 79.
Adams, Adam, 78, 331, 622.
Adams, Alexander, 49.
Adams, Daniel Jenifer, 20, 183, 184.
Adams, Enoch, 30.
Adams, George, 419, 470.
Adams, Ignatius, 78, 358, 384, 406, 432, 497, 522.

Adams (Adamson), Jacob, 80, 328, 351, 307, 462, 487, 523.
Adams, James, 7, 47, 78, 79, 340, 360, 384, 575.
Adams, John, 6, 30, 78, 79, 298, 331, 340, 357, 406, 419, 421, 430, 470, 496, 513, 523.
Adams, Joseph, 445.
Adams, Mark, 80.
Adams, Matthew, 675.
Adams, Moses, 30, 384, 406.
Adams, Nathan, 330.
Adams, Nathaniel, 79, 184, 311, 314.
Adams, Peter, 13, 44, 78, 183, 328, 363, 368, 369, 370, 379, 381, 471, 476, 479.
Adams, Richard, 79, 80.
Adams, Samuel, 32, 53.
Adams, Samuel, 2nd, 53.
Adams, Thomas, 46, 79, 297, 396, 455, 612, 523, 623, 641.
Adams, William (W.), 30, 31, 53, 79, 80, 184, 273, 352, 363, 379, 384, 406, 445, 476, 479, 519.
Adamson, Alexander, 80, 414.
Adamson, George, 80, 415.
Adamson, Jacob (see Adams), 462, 487.
Adamson, John, 428, 474.
Adcock, William, 271, 272.
Addison, John, 34, 35, 333.
Addlemon, Michael, 273.
Adley, Richard, 387.
Admiston, Alexander, 59.
Aggis (Aggas), William, 340, 360, 396, 449.
Aghern, John, 334.
Ahair, John, 342.
Ahearn (Ahern, Aybun), Wm., 183, 322, 466, 502.
Ahern, Daniel, 64.
Aikens, Joseph, 400.
Aim, Jno., 51.
Ainsworth, Robt., 183.
Aires (see Ayres).
Aitkin, William, 15.
Aitzil, Jacob, 80, 350.
Akeright (or Aksright), Isaac, 60.

Akerly (see Ackerly).
Akers, James, 387.
Akers, Michael, 273.
Akins, Cornelius, 59.
Aksright (see Akeright).
Alby, John (see Alvey), 357, 444, 494.
Alby, Love (see Alley).
Alby, Travers (see Alvey).
Aldham, Danl., 80.
Aldrich (see Aldridge).
Aldridge, Jacob, 382.
Aldridge, John Simpson, 49.
Aldridge, Nathan, 447, 498, 523, 569.
Aldridge (Aldrich), Nathaniel, 395, 563, 566.
Aldridge, Zachariah, 42.
Alexander, Chas., 368.
Alexander, Ezekiel, 62.
Alexander, Jacob, 18, 184, 267, 315.
Alexander, James, 62, 79, 300.
Alexander, John, 80, 273, 406, 653.
Alexander (Allexander), Matthew, 80, 301.
Alexander, Walter, 61, 62.
Alexander, William (——), 62, 74, 182.
Aley, Peter, 388.
Alford, John, 474.
Alford, Thos., 424.
Alford, William, 273.
Alinder (see Allender).
Alinger, Chr., 51.
All, William, 23.
Allbright, Willm, 382.
Allcock, Martin, 80.
Allcock, William, 69.
Allen, Adam, 369.
Allen, Alexander, 10, 78.
Allen, Amos, 10.
Allen, Arthur, 22.
Allen, Barna, 78.
Allen, Charles, 387.
Allen, Emanuel, 183, 352, 398, 435, 523, 617.
Allen, George, 52.
Allen, Gilbert, 182, 618.
Allen, Jacob, 183, 416.
Allen, James, 59, 182, 334, 352, 433, 523, 606, 654.

Allen (Allin), Jesse, 78, 331.
Allen, John, 79, 421, 472.
Allen, Joseph, 465, 501, 523.
Allen, Richard, 34, 80, 654.
Allen, Robert, 183, 273.
Allen, Solomon, 78.
Allen, Stephen, 22.
Allen, Thos., 453.
Allen (Allin), William, 78, 79, 273, 296, 328, 336, 388, 405, 579, 583, 584.
Allender (Allinder), John, 54, 78.
Allender, Joshua, 80.
Allender, Perry, 406.
Allender (Alinder), William, 294, 323, 446.
Allenjem (see Allingham).
Aller, William, 342.
Alley (or Alby), Love, 64.
Allibon, Thomas, 79, 300.
Allin (see Allen).
Allinger, Stepn. (see Erlinger), 80.
Allingham (or Allenjem), Steph., 39.
Allison, Dr. F., 619, 621.
Allison, Henry, 43, 49.
Allison, James, 79.
Allison, Ralph, 13.
Allison, Thomas (see Ellison), 78, 533, 616.
Allman, William, 80, 414.
Allstone (or Allstan), Jere., 30.
Allay, Richard, 336.
Allum, Thos. B., 394.
Alsey, William, 406.
Alsop (Allsop), John, 45, 183, 310, 406, 421, 472, 505, 523, 630, 653.
Alsop (Allsop), Joseph, 72, 184, 309, 325, 406, 653.
Altimus, William, 265.
Alvey (Alby), John, 78, 357, 444, 494, 522.
Alvey, Joseph, 30.
Alvey, Josiah, 78.
Alvey, Josias, 441, 523.
Alvey, Thos., 298.
Alvey, Thomas Green, 79, 329, 522.

Index.

Alvey (Alby), Travers (Traverse, Travis), 79, 298, 329, 354, 436, 400, 523.
Ambler, George, 183.
Ambross, Patk., 273.
Americk, Peter, 261.
Amley, James, 341.
Ammersley (Amersley, Amorsley), John (see Hammersly), 184, 266, 416.
Ammersly (see Hammersly).
Amoss, Abel, 346.
Amos, Aquila, 59, 60.
Amos, Joshua, 60.
Amos, Mordicai, 60.
Anckle, Peter, 263.
Anderside, Wm., 183.
Anderson, Alex., 371.
Anderson, Archibald (Major, ——), 23, 78, 295, 298, 299, 300, 364, 380.
Anderson, Bennett (Bennet), 384, 406.
Anderson, Chas., 648.
Anderson, Daniel, 80, 522.
Anderson, James, 182, 376, 393, 406, 416, 463, 523.
Anderson, John, 79, 183, 273, 295, 305, 340, 382, 394, 396, 432, 442, 497, 523, 626.
Anderson, Matthew, 70.
Anderson, Michael, 508.
Anderson, Richard (Capt.), 42, 44, 183, 364, 380, 390, 419, 476, 480, 519, 620, 627.
Anderson, Robt., 395.
Anderson, Thomas, 46.
Anderson, William, 33, 36, 79, 299, 304.
Anderton, William, 183.
Andess, Mathias, 72.
Andreas (see Andrews).
Andrew, James, 27, 78, 293, 644.
Andrew, Jeremiah, 27, 78, 293, 644.
Andrew, John, 352, 433.
Andrew, William, 28.
Andrews, James, 400.
Andrews, John, 183, 523.
Andrews, Joseph, 273.
Andrews, Joshua, 79.
Andrews (Andreas), Wendell (Vendel), 265, 269, 516.
Andrews, William, 80, 301.
Angel (see Engellee).
Anglain, Joseph, 16.
Angleir, Joseph, 78.
Angles, John, 28.
Anguish, Alexr., 273.
Annis, Benjm., 183.
Anthony, Emanuel, 615.
Anthony, John, 406, 615.
Anthony, Manuel, 607, 608.
Anthony, Michael, 608.
Anthony (Negro), 317.

Anthony, Philip, 388.
Appingstall, John, 451.
Appingstall, Willm., 369.
Apple, Christian, 265.
Applead, John, 424, 474.
Appleby, John, 79, 354, 436, 490, 522.
Appleby, Wm., 55, 79.
Appleton, Edward, 396, 401, 455.
Apsley, William, 63.
Arbor (Arber, or Auburgh) John (see Auber), 406, 416.
Archer, Sampson, 602.
Archer, Thos., 344, 392.
Archibald, Robert, 39.
Ardes, Jacob, 22.
Arding, Benj., 273.
Argers, Anthony, 615.
Aris (Ariss), Richard (see Ayres), 298, 449.
Arm, ——, 654.
Arm, James, 654.
Arman (Armond), Abel (Abell, Able), 184, 359, 514, 515, 516.
Armand, Col., 586, 591, 502, 503, 594, 595.
Armond, Abell (see Arman).
Armond, John, 398.
Armstrong, Abel, 602.
Armstrong, Alexander, 183, 647.
Armstrong, David, 648.
Armstrong, Edward, 293, 394.
Armstrong, Francis, 65.
Armstrong, George (G., Lieut., Capt.), 30, 79, 183, 298, 290, 362, 378, 477, 519.
Armstrong, Hugh, 16, 78.
Armstrong, James, 79, 294, 333, 588, 607, 654.
Armstrong, John, 10, 182, 183, 184, 264, 265, 333, 348, 353, 356, 393, 440, 452, 493, 499, 523, 615, 649.
Armstrong, Robert, 183, 648.
Armstrong, Russel, 24.
Armstrong, Thomas, 183.
Armsworthy (Armesworthy), Baptist (Baptis), 79, 298.
Arne, James, 606.
Arnelt, William, 183.
Arnet, Thomas, 78.
Arnett, Valentine, 70.
Arnett, William, 621.
Arno, John, 66.
Arno, Wm., 346.
Arnold (or Onnel), Christopher, 80, 149.
Arnold, George, 184, 260, 324.
Arnold, Thomas, 79, 273.
Arnold, William, 78, 640.

Arnot, T. D., 80.
Arrants, Harman, 61, 63.
Arrants, James, 587.
Arrings, Levy, 184.
Arris (see Ayres).
Arron (see Aaron).
Arscott (see Ascott).
Artes, Isaac, 601.
Arthur, James, 363, 379.
Arthur, Thomas (see Arthurs).
Arthurs (Arthur), Thomas, 394, 445, 513, 523.
Arthus, Thos., 340, 360.
Artis, James, 44.
Artis, Thos., 627.
Artman, Wm., 305.
Arvin, Ananias, 78.
Aschum, Samuel, 79.
Ascott (or Arscott), William, 66.
Asgurth, Benj., 420.
Ash, Edmund (see Nash, Edward).
Ash, Samuel, 26.
Ashbox, Jacob, 183.
Ashbury (Ashberry), John, 355, 441, 491, 523.
Ashcom, Samuel, 34.
Ashcroft (or Ashcraft), James, 68.
Ashell (or Aspell), Thos., 445.
Ashford, Moses, 651.
Ashford, Perigrine (Pay or Pery), 66, 645.
Ashford, Thomas, 32.
Ashley, Daniel, 387.
Ashley (Ashly), James, 264, 267, 321, 353, 393, 447, 487, 523.
Ashly, James W. L., 184.
Ashman, Charles, 273, 304.
Ashmore, Charles, 41.
Ashmore (Ashmow), John, 184, 354, 390, 435, 489, 523.
Ashton, John, 16.
Ashwell (Asswell), Wm., 184, 305, 617.
Ask, Thos., 400.
Askew, Benjamin, 327, 470, 509, 523.
Askew (Askey), Peregrine (Perry), 579, 581, 582, 584.
Askey, Zachariah, 43, 414.
Askin, Michael, 647.
Askins, Solomon, 335, 393.
Askins, William, 606, 654.
Askins, Zacha., 183.
Asoan (see d'Asoan).
Aspell (see Ashell).
Aspin, Thomas, 78.
Assom, John, 79.
Asswell (see Ashwell).
Atchinson, Edward, 382.
Atchinson (Atcheson, Atchingson or Hutchingson), Henry, 44, 618.

Atchison (Atchuson), Jeremiah, 36, 78.
Atchison, Wm. (see Hutchinson), 78.
Athey, Charles, 376.
Athey (Athy), Ebenezer (Ebinezer), 35, 78, 331.
Atkins, John, 68, 273.
Atkins, Joshua, 396.
Atkinson, Thomas, 360, 393, 416.
Atkinson, Willm., 183, 315.
Atthea, Benj., 603.
Atthea, Thomas, 603.
Atwell, Austin, 390.
Atwell, Joseph, 406.
Attwood, Charles, 384.
Auber (Arber, Arbor, Aubre, or Auburgh), John (see Harbough and Orber), 338, 366, 406, 416, 505, 523, 630, 654.
Auchentick (Auchenleck), Henry (——), 606, 654.
Auger, Augustine, 608.
Augusteen, John, 328.
Aulpaugh, Philip, 47.
Aushur, John, 32.
Austin, Cloudsberry, 387.
Austin (Austen), Harris, 182, 398, 406, 467, 523.
Austin, Henry (see Osten), 78.
Austin, Isaac, 80.
Austin, James, 67, 78, 80.
Austin, Joseph, 183, 392, 452.
Austin, Robert, 78.
Austin, Willm., 16.
Aval, Thomas, 344.
Avelman, John, 416.
Avery, Robert, 338.
Avis, James Greaves, 34.
Ayers, Fredk., 183.
Ayhun (see Ahearn).
Ayres (Aires, Arris), James, 22, 182, 183, 326.
Ayres, John, 182.
Ayres (Aris, Ariss), Richard, 21, 298, 449.
Ayres (Ayers, Aires), Thomas, 70, 182, 352, 433, 523.
Ayres, William, 182.
Ayrs, Henry, 372.
Aythur, William, 523.

Babbs (Babb), John, 15, 81, 344.
Baber, James, 355.
Bacchus, Wm., 307.
Bachilor, Thomas, 86.
Bachilor, William, 86.
Backer, Peter, 191, 328.
Backett (see Beckett).
Baden, Jeremiah, 38.
Baden, Rohert, 38.
Baden, Thomas, 38.
Badger, Joseph, 375.
Badham, Edward, 88.
Badley, James, 564.

Index. 665

Baetts, Samuel, 185.
Baggott, Francis Green, 6.
Baggott, Ignatius, 331.
Baggott, William, 11.
Baggs, James, 66.
Bagley, Saml., 82.
Bagus (see Baques).
Bagwell, Smyth (see Bragwell), 372.
Bailess (see Bayless).
Bailey, Edward, 514.
Bailey, George, 52.
Bailey, James, 87, 186, 396, 420, 524, 527.
Bailey (Baley, Bayley), John, 61, 70, 83, 85, 357, 405, 430, 459, 468, 496, 504, 526.
Bailey (Balcy), John B. (Bapt.), 86, 329.
Bailey, Joseph, 85, 89.
Bailey, Mark, 186, 275, 335.
Bailey (Baily, Bayley), Mountjoy (Montjoy), 189, 326, 621.
Bailey (Baley), Nathaniel, 375, 397, 401, 464, 490, 526, 651.
Bailey, Patrick, 180.
Bailey, Philip, 58, 80, 457, 487, 524.
Bailey, R., 117.
Bailey, Robert, 81.
Bailey (Baily, Baley), Thomas, 26, 67, 87, 359, 396, 431, 507, 524, 643.
Bailey, William, 52.
Baily, Elias, 30.
Bair, Peter, 90.
Baird, Nicholas, 264.
Bairford, Edward, 268.
Baitson (see Bateson).
Bajaint, Thos., 274.
Baker, Abram, 188.
Baker, Boston, 190.
Baker, Charles, 90, 302.
Baker, Elisha, 23.
Baker, Francis, 387.
Baker, George, 406, 428, 475, 509, 526, 576.
Baker, Henry, 429, 479, 482, 519.
Baker, J., 155.
Baker, James, 274, 275.
Baker, John, 9, 30, 33, 47, 61, 81, 82, 84, 85, 523, 640.
Baker, Joel, 189, 310, 392, 467, 504, 526.
Baker, Joseph, 81.
Baker, Maurice, 51.
Baker, Nathan, 66, 406.
Baker, Peter (Teter), 187, 265, 325, 452.
Baker, Rowland, 344.
Baker, Thomas, 12, 63, 274, 345, 442, 505, 525.
Baker, William, 10, 34, 88, 415.
Balden, Caleb, 601.

Baldwin, Henry, 84, 353, 354, 363, 379, 454, 476, 480, 519.
Baldwin, James, 83.
Baldwin, John, 83, 294, 320.
Baldwin, Samuel, 406.
Baldwin, Thomas, 41.
Baldwin, Wm. J., 187.
Balentine, Wm., 422.
Baley (see Bailey).
Balff (Balf), Edward, 89, 414.
Ball, James (see Beall), 35, 45.
Ball, John, 610.
Ball, Richard, 83.
Ballamy (see Bellamy).
Ballard (Ballett), John, 333, 342.
Ballard (Ballod), Richard, 187, 335, 414.
Ballast (Ballart), John, 423, 471.
Balman, Thomas, 90.
Balor, John, 402.
Balston, Joseph (see Ralston), 241.
Baltzell (Baltzel, Balzel), Charles, 261, 271, 365, 519.
Balzel, John, 261.
Banbury, John, 345.
Bandy, John, 83, 293.
Baneworth, John, 429.
Banfield, James, 187.
Bank, Benjamin, 53.
Banks, Charles, 88.
Banks, David, 419, 470.
Banks, James, 189.
Bannerman, Jno., 87.
Banney, James, 84.
Bannon, John, 317.
Bantham (Bamtham), John, 186, 352, 434, 485, 524.
Bantham, Perry (Perie), 185, 436, 504, 524.
Bantz (Bontz), George, 191, 267, 324.
Baques (Bagus), Jacques (James), 365, 477, 579.
Barber (Barbar), Clement, 16, 82.
Barber, James, 21, 68, 428, 441, 475, 491, 509, 525, 527.
Barber, John, 85, 272, 514, 575, 581, 599, 618.
Barber (Barbar), Samuel, 15, 82.
Barber, Thomas, 418, 460, 575, 584.
Barbett, Francis, 340, 360.
Barclay (see Barkley).
Barcklay (see Barkley).
Barcoss, William, 385.
Barden, William, 88.
Bardmore, John, 88.
Barker, Abram, 366.
Barker, Thomas, 24.
Barker, William, 85, 187.

Barkers, James, 85.
Barkley (Barclay), James, 15, 82.
Barkley, John, 335.
Barkley (Barkly, Barcklay, Bartcly), Thomas (see Bartley), 30, 290, 524, 617.
Barkshire, Henry, 45.
Barlow, John, 189, 315, 468, 505, 526.
Barlsom, Anthy., 275.
Barn, Elijah, 342.
Barnaby, John, 375.
Barnard, John, 67.
Barnchouse (see Barnhouse).
Barneclow, Charles, 406.
Barneclow, John, 406.
Barnes (Barns), Anthony, 565, 567, 570, 574.
Barnes, Aquilia, 41.
Barnes, Benja., 189.
Barnes, Elijah, 40.
Barnes, Ely, 40.
Barnes, George, 185.
Barnes (Barns), Henry, 421, 467, 503, 526, 654.
Barnes (Barns), James, 56, 57, 67, 83, 90, 330, 613.
Barnes, Job, 24.
Barnes, Joseph, 661.
Barnes (Barns), Nehemiah, 562, 590.
Barnes, Philip, 40.
Barnes, Richard, 90, 503.
Barnes, Richard Weaver, 42.
Barnes, Thomas, 406.
Barnet, Luke, 45.
Barnett (Barnet), Daniel, 190, 308, 322, 391.
Barnett (Barnet), Isaac, 38, 51.
Barnett (Barnet, Barrett), Jesse, 190, 334, 389, 437, 512, 525.
Barnett, John, 58, 59, 88, 90.
Barnett (Barnet), Robert, 90, 267, 322.
Barney, Moses, 189, 305, 380, 525.
Barney, Thomas, 53.
Barnhouse (Barnchouse), Rodolph (Rudolph), 86, 330.
Barnicassle, Frederick, 60.
Barnicloe, Thos., 188.
Barnitt, Michael, 8.
Barnitt, William, 45.
Barns, W., 581.
Barns, William, 57, 609.
Barnt, Jacob, 328.
Barnwell, Luke, 443.
Barr, John, 606, 654.
Barrack (Barrick), Jacob, 45, 72.
Barraclift (Bartliff), John, 89, 415.
Barrance, James, 654.

Barranger, Andrew, 388.
Barratt, Alexander, 42.
Barren, James, 617.
Barret, James, 83.
Barrett, Basley, 435.
Barrett, Danl., 84.
Barrett, Jesse (see Barnett), 389.
Barrett (Barret), John, 86, 188, 290, 421, 472, 507, 524, 526, 654.
Barrett (Barret), Joshua, 87, 414, 464, 490, 524.
Barrett, Nicholas, 185.
Barrett (Barret), Solomon, 186, 463, 504, 524.
Barrett, Thomas, 50.
Barrett, Williams, 188.
Barrick, Jacob (see Barrack).
Barrick, John, 184.
Barringer, David, 72.
Barron, Daniel, 32.
Barron, James, 464, 499, 524.
Barron, Thomas, 32.
Barrow, James, 87, 186, 342, 446, 526.
Barruch, James, 185.
Barry, Basil, 41.
Barry (Barrey), Edward (see Berry), 564, 567, 570, 574.
Barry, Isaac (see Berry), 296.
Barry, Jacob, 41.
Barry (Barrey), James (see Berry), 564, 566, 568, 574, 606.
Barry, John (see Berry), 51, 62, 185, 581.
Barry, Joseph, 10.
Barry (Berry), Michael, 50, 70, 274.
Barry, William (see Berry), 86, 87, 300, 368.
Bartcly. Thomas (see Barkley), 30.
Bartholomay (Barttomew, Batolomey), Peter, 266, 268, 323.
Bartholomew, Ben, 86.
Bartlet, Thomas, 70.
Bartlett, Archd., 600.
Bartlett (Bartlet), Edward, 375, 395, 449.
Bartley, Thomas, 81.
Bartley, Thomas S. (see Barkley), 86.
Bartliff (see Barraclift).
Bartling, Jacob, 595.
Barton, Joseph, 355, 463, 492, 523.
Barts, Samuel, 266, 327.
Basdill, Jeffery, 603.
Basford, William, 81, 640.
Basht, Henry, 271.
Basht, William, 269, 516.
Basil (Bassell), Daniel, 81, 355, 523.
Basil, John, 80.

666 Index.

Basnett, Nathan, 387.
Basnett, Nathaniel, 406.
Bass, Nathaniel, 344.
Basset, John, 26, 643.
Basset, Richard, 587.
Bassett, Daniel, 441, 491.
Bassett, Peter, 82.
Bassicks, Richd., 274.
Bassil, Joseph, 16.
Bast, Peter, 263.
Batchelor, Nathan, 368, 385.
Bate, Thomas, 84.
Bateman, George, 82, 331, 433, 523.
Bateman, Nathan, 527.
Bateman, Nathl., 186.
Bates, Henry, 275.
Bates, John, 87, 275.
Bates, Philip, 191, 266.
Bates, Roland (Rowland, Rolen), 89, 319, 415.
Bateson (Baitson), William, 44.
Bath (see Beath).
Batman, Thos., 188.
Batson, George, 87.
Batson, James, 84.
Batte, Lieut., 399.
Batteast, John, 88.
Battee, Ferdinando (Ferdinan), 39, 370.
Battee, John, 39.
Batten, John, 590.
Batten (Battin, Batton), William, 90, 303, 350, 352, 398, 420, 464, 500, 525.
Batterson, Thos., 369.
Batterton, Saml., 601.
Battican, James (see Rattican), 241.
Battin, Stanley, 330.
Battingly, Stanley, 83.
Batton, Hugh, 187.
Batts, Joseph, 457, 505.
Bauer, John, 191, 263.
Baugh, Michael, 47.
Baulk, Benjamin, 87, 394, 450, 512.
Baum (Baun), John, 406, 653.
Baumgartner (Bomgardner, Bombgardiner, Bumgardner), George, 50, 188, 349, 354, 440, 489, 525.
Baumgartner (Bomgardner), William, 50, 189.
Baun (see Baum).
Bauswell (Baswell) (see Boswell).
Bautcheby, Joseph, 457, 524.
Baver, James, 342.
Bawen (see Bowen).
Baxley, Saml., 60.
Baxter, John, 67, 313, 385, 402, 406, 465, 501, 526.
Baxter, Joseph, 11.
Baxter, Patrick, 12.

Baxter, Samuel, 58, 59.
Baxter, Thomas, 385, 406, 466, 502, 527.
Bay, Charles, 274.
Bay, Josiah, 419.
Bay, Kennedy (Kenniday), 62, 185.
Bayer, Jacob, 47.
Bayer, Michael (Michal) (see Boyer).
Bayle, Capt., 621.
Bayless (Bailess, Bayliss), James, 335, 352, 455, 485, 525.
Bayley, Daniel B., 372.
Bayley, John (see Bailey).
Bayley, Montjoy (see Bailey).
Bayley, Seth, 187.
Bayley, Thomas (see Bailey).
Baylor, Danl., 191.
Baylor, George, 603.
Bayly, Esme, 635.
Bayman, Thomas, 45.
Bayne, Josias, 34.
Bayne, Walter, 34.
Beach, John, 87, 88, 456, 524.
Beachamp (Beachem) (see Beauchamp).
Beachbeach, Benja., 186.
Beachgood, James, 369.
Beachman, Willm., 369.
Beachum (see Beauchamp).
Beaden, John (see Reading), 42.
Beading (Beeding), Henry (see Reading), 49.
Beall, ———, 378.
Beall, Alexander Edmondston, 42.
Beall, Alexander Robert, 42.
Beall, Barton, 377, 406.
Beall, Charles, 83.
Beall (Beal), Christopher, 9, 81, 260, 328.
Beall, Edward, 275.
Beall, Elisha, 44, 45.
Beall (Beal, Beale), James (see Ball), 20, 45, 272, 426, 514, 599.
Beall, James (of Roger), 42.
Beall, James McCormack, 45.
Beall, Jeremiah, 42.
Beall (Beal, Beale), John, 187, 426, 431, 467.
Beall, Jos., 333, 339.
Beall, Leaven (or Leven), 42.
Beall (Beal), Lloyd (—), 43, 189, 341, 356, 362, 378, 437, 476, 477, 492, 519.
Beall, Rezin, 20.
Beall (Beal), Saml. B., 448, 481, 483, 519.
Beall, Thaddeus, 42.

Beall (Beale), Thomas, 20, 42, 90, 328, 350.
Beall, William, 90.
Beall (Beal, Beale), Wm. Dent (Lt., Capt.), 34, 36, 37, 187, 332, 364, 380, 479, 481, 519, 619.
Beall, Zephaniah, 42.
Beam, Conrad (see Boehm), 191.
Beam, Jno. (see Bean), 295.
Beam, Philip (see Boehm), 191.
Bean (Been), Gilbert, 90, 601.
Bean, Henry, 38.
Bean (Beane, Been), John (see Beam), 38, 50, 86, 90, 432, 524, 634.
Bean, Leonard, 86, 330, 359, 524.
Bean, Thomas, 38.
Bean, William, 647.
Beanes (Beans), Colmore, 34, 186.
Beanes, J. H., 81.
Beanes, Josias, 382.
Beans, John, 7.
Beans, Joseph, 406.
Bear, Henry, 47.
Bear, Joseph, 565.
Bear (Bare, Baire), Thos., 188, 348, 357, 445, 495, 525.
Bearae, Jacob, 46.
Beard, Frederick, 45, 406, 653.
Beard, John, 388.
Beard, Jonathan, 72.
Beard, Richard, 406.
Beard, Robert, 317.
Beard, Stephen, 399.
Beard, Thomas, 406.
Beard, William, 62, 85.
Beath (Bath), Joseph, 62.
Beatherd, Jarman, 22.
Beatty, Charles, 46, 47, 48, 314, 315, 327.
Beatty (Beaty), Thomas, 356, 447, 476, 482, 519.
Beatty, William, 44, 48, 90, 189, 310, 344, 345, 350, 363, 379, 388, 519.
Beattys (Beaty) Philip (Philop), 325, 593.
Beauchamp (Beachamp, Beachem), Chas., 425, 429, 472.
Beauchamp (Beachum), Wm., 607, 654.
Beaumont, Jno., 392.
Beauver (see Beaver).
Beaven (Beavan, Beavin), Charles, 32, 187, 376, 518.
Beaven, Ignatius, 32.
Beaven, Maryland, 38.
Beaven, Richard, 32.
Beaven, Thomas, 190, 406.
Beaver, John, 86.
Beaver, Martin, 85.

Beaver, Thomas, 343.
Beaver (Beauver), William, 24, 82, 203.
Beaves, Noah (see Reaves), 242.
Beavin, Joseph, 377.
Beck, Alexander, 186.
Beck, Amos, 84.
Beck, Osborne, 83.
Beck, Simon, 387.
Beck, William, 63.
Beckell (see Beckett).
Becker, George, 653.
Becker, Henry, 624.
Beckerson, John, 261.
Becketh (see Beckwith).
Beckett (Becket, Beckell), Humphrey, 189, 354, 390, 435, 489, 525.
Beckett (Backett, Beckell), Isaac, 187, 347, 416.
Beckett, James, 45.
Becks, William, 27.
Beckwith, Nehemiah, 612, 613, 615.
Beckwith (Becketh), Nicholas, 47.
Becraf, John, 90.
Bedder, James, 189.
Beddinger, H., 616.
Bedford, Thomas, 190.
Bedinger, Daniel, 90.
Beech, Benj. Pierce, 616.
Beeding, Henry (see Beading).
Beeding, Joseph, 49.
Beedlee, Henry, 63.
Beggarly, David, 406.
Begley, George, 87.
Beiker, Michael, 261.
Belcher, Benjamin, 397, 401, 463, 508, 526.
Belcher, Wm., 427, 474.
Beldock, Edward, 274.
Belew, Tile, 61.
Belfast, George, 375, 396, 449, 526.
Belford, Jeremiah, 89.
Bell, James, 14, 466, 502, 526.
Bell, John, 325, 502, 526.
Bell, Lawson, 82.
Bell, Lieut., 602.
Bell, Peter, 47.
Bell, Thomas, 83, 301, 303.
Bellamy (Ballamy, Belamy, Bellemy), John, 83, 84, 89, 415, 457.
Bellison, Wm., 318.
Bellows, Isaac, 83, 324.
Bellwhite (Bellwhight), Saml., 86, 296.
Belt, John Sprig (J.), 38, 40, 88, 353, 362, 378, 435, 477, 482, 487, 519.
Beltzhoover (Belsoover, Bentzhover), Jacob, 191, 264, 265.
Bemhart, Jno., 51.
Bender (or Painter), Henry, 191.

Bending, Thomas, 186.
Bendon, Thomas, 185.
Benn, Whedon (Whiddr.), 85, 296.
Benner, Michael (Melcher), (see Benter), 191, 264.
Bennett (Bennet), Frederick, 84, 355, 441, 401, 524.
Bennett (Bennette, Bennit) George, 39, 80, 449, 641, 654.
Bennett, James, 11.
Bennett, Jesse, 85.
Bennett (Bennet), Joel (—el), 563, 566, 574.
Bennett (Bennet, Bennitt), John, 47, 66, 67, 191, 266, 275, 323, 340, 360, 527, 587, 648.
Bennett, Joseph, 41.
Bennett, Joshua, 406.
Bennett, Nathan, 63.
Bennett, Rinear, 50.
Bennett (Bonnett), Thos., 184, 274.
Bennette, Edw., 39.
Benning, Daniel, 46, 306, 391.
Bennington, Job, 59.
Bennington, Thos., 317.
Bennister, William, 594.
Bennit, Robt., 275.
Benny, Jas., 56.
Benny, John, 185.
Benson, Cephas, 390.
Benson (or Penson), Edmund (Edward), 189, 305.
Benson, John, 41.
Benson (Penson), Perry (Percey), 67, 74, 185, 364, 381, 426, 476, 481, 519, 627, 630.
Benston, John, 69, 275.
Bent, William, 67.
Benter, George, 46.
Benter (Bentner), Henry, 264, 265.
Benter, Melcher, 264.
Bentley, Samuel, 186.
Bentley, Solomon, 72.
Bentley, Thomas, 89.
Bently, David, 35.
Bently, William, 326, 400, 407.
Benton, James, 274.
Benton, John, 184.
Benton, Mark, 184.
Benton, Thomas, 654.
Bentzhover (see Beltzhoover).
Benyan, Alexander, 406.
Bercning (see Bernig).
Bercus, Wm., 450.
Berk, William, 36.
Bermingham, Patrick, 89, 415.
Bernard, John, 185.
Bernig (or Bercning), Dan'l, 188.
Berreck, Henry, 47.

Berriman, John (see Berryman).
Berringer, Chn., 51.
Berry, Edward (see Barry), 570, 582, 583.
Berry, Emanuel, 335.
Berry, George, 55.
Berry, Isaac (see Barry), 87, 338.
Berry, James (see Barry), 190, 310, 387, 584, 654.
Berry, John (see Barry), 50, 88, 189, 307.
Berry, Michael (see Barry), 70.
Berry, Thomas, 375, 394, 401, 416.
Berry (Berrey), William (see Barry), 35, 82, 87, 274, 317, 394.
Berry, Zachariah, 90, 351, 352, 397, 417, 421, 465, 500, 525.
Berryman (Berriman),John, 353, 457, 486, 525, 606, 654.
Berthaud, Adam, 570.
Best, James, 85.
Beswick, Joseph (see Riswick), 406.
Beswick (Besswick), Richard, 24, 185.
Bethell, John (see Bithel), 347.
Betsey, John, 397.
Betson (or Bettson), George, 57.
Betsworth, John, 401, 460, 653.
Bettis, Jacob, 82.
Betts, Thomas, 67.
Bevard, James, 400.
Bevard (Brevard), John, 372, 418, 469.
Beveren, Thomas, 187.
Beveridge, Jno., 274.
Beverly, James, 61.
Bewley, Job, 429.
Bickham, James, 340, 360.
Bicknall, Esau, 86.
Biddle, Richard, 41, 340, 357, 366, 444, 495, 525.
Biddle, Wm., 418, 469.
Bidgood, William, 85.
Bidwell, Richard, 87.
Bierley, Jacob, 90.
Biggs, Benja., 189.
Biggs, Benj. Jon., 330.
Biggs, David, 581.
Biggs, John, 396, 454, 512, 525.
Biggs, Nathan, 52.
Biggs, Thomas, 30, 83, 329.
Bigler, Jacob, 263.
Bigwood, James, 342, 357, 446, 495, 525.
Bilbo, Bravo, 608.
Biles, Benson, 34.
Biles, William, 186.
Billingham, Thomas, 420, 470, 510, 526.

Billiton, Zebdiah, 60.
Billop (Billip, Billup), Henry, 188, 347, 354, 440, 488, 525.
Billow, John, 46.
Binehart, Andrew (see Rinehart), 187.
Bing, Oliver, 647.
Bing, Samuel, 647.
Bingley, Alexander, 86, 436.
Binkler, Jacob, 328.
Binn, Samuel, 387.
Birch, Thomas, 615.
Birckhead, Chrisr., 67, 371, 387.
Bird, George Richard, 462.
Bird, John, 261.
Bird, Richard (Capt., George Richard), 61, 62, 185, 362, 378, 462, 478, 519.
Bird, Samuel, 654.
Bird, Thomas, 86, 398, 432, 524, 616.
Birh, Jeremiah, 186.
Birh, Nathaniel, 185.
Birk (Birh), Nathaniel, 185.
Birk, John (see Burke).
Birk, Michael (see Burk).
Birk, Richard (see Burke).
Birkhead, Jno., 370.
Birmingham, Christopher, 654.
Birmingham, Dan'l, 394.
Biscoe, Mackie, 654.
Bishop, Edward, 372.
Bishop, George, 21.
Bishop, Jacob, 191, 264, 265.
Bishop, Thomas, 83, 315, 446, 506, 523, 617, 630.
Bishop, William, 606, 654.
Bishop, Zachariah, 22.
Bissel (see Bizel).
Bissett, Thomas, 50.
Bissill, Assa, 190.
Bithel, John (see Bethell), 186.
Bitting, Philip, 263.
Bivens, Luke, 82.
Bizel (Bissel), Abram, 190, 306.
Black, Aaron, 406.
Black, Francis, 190, 334.
Black, Moses, 407.
Blackburn, John, 340, 360.
Blackburn, Thomas, 187, 327.
Blackburn, William, 42.
Blackham (Blackam), Geo., 186, 435, 510, 524.
Blacklock, Edward, 8.
Blackman, Stephen, 654.
Blackney (see Blakney).
Blackwell, Hugh, 88.
Blades, James, 185.
Blades, John, 82, 293, 353, 385, 387, 394, 462, 487, 524.

Blades, Thomas, 387.
Blades, William, 190.
Blair, John, 87, 190, 208, 329, 341, 302, 438, 460, 512, 524, 526, 632.
Blair, Samuel, 90.
Blaize (Blaze, Blasse, Bleas), Joseph, 189, 311, 356, 398, 438, 493, 525, 617.
Blake, Alex., 574.
Blake, Daniel, 383.
Blake, Edward, 346, 455.
Blake, George, 86.
Blake, Jacob, 355, 431, 442, 492, 525.
Blake (Blakney), John, 84, 654.
Blake, Martin, 190.
Blake, Michael, 187.
Blake, Oliver, 425, 473.
Blake, Thos., 428, 474.
Blake, William, 615.
Blakney (or Blackney), John (see Blake), 56.
Blanch, William, 24, 185, 274.
Blancher, James, 396.
Bland, Thos., 39.
Blaney, Jas., 648.
Blanford, Ignatius, 33, 81.
Blanford, Joseph, 33.
Blanford (Blansford, Blamford), Richard, 32, 84, 357, 398, 444, 495, 524, 617.
Blang, Peter, 626.
Blansher, Thos., 456.
Blaze (Blasse, Bleas), (see Blaize).
Bleak, Nathan, 640.
Blewer (see Blower).
Blissell, Edward, 86.
Blithen, John, 654.
Bloice, Abraham, 88.
Blood, Robert, 385, 397, 405, 416.
Blower (Blewer, Bluer), James, 87, 342, 436, 527.
Blower, John, 88.
Bloyds, Daniel, 85.
Bluefield, John, 423, 471.
Bluer (see Blower).
Blundell (Blundel), Chas., 417, 469.
Blunder, Thomas, 343.
Blunderwill, John, 86.
Blundull, John, 329.
Blunt, Benjamin, 66, 67, 186, 645.
Blunt, Charles, 606, 654.
Blunt, Samuel, 67.
Blyth, John, 344.
Boady (see Boody).
Boager (see Boger).
Boardman, Robt., 86.
Boardy, Peter, 49.
Boarman, Bazil S., 36.
Boarman, Clement, 32.
Boarman, Daniel, 83.
Boarman, Henry, 31, 32.

Boarman, Henry, Jr., 32.
Boarman, Joseph, 32.
Boarman, Thomas, 82.
Boarman, William, 36, 376.
Boatswain, Francis, 607.
Boeard (Bochard), Peter, 357, 430, 406, 524.
Body, Robert, 187, 619.
Body, Stephen (see Boody).
Boe, William (see Roe), 46, 187.
Boehler, Danl., 263.
Boehm (Beam), Conrad, 191, 263.
Boehm (Beam), Phillip, 191, 263.
Boen (see Bowen).
Boger (Boager, Booger), Jacob, 565, 567, 570.
Boggs, James, 71, 647.
Bogue, William, 387.
Boham (see Bonham).
Boice (see Boyce).
Bold (see Boyd).
Bolchlob, Chas., 340.
Boles, William, 83.
Boling (Bowling), Wm., 420, 470, 509, 526.
Bolton, John, 340, 360.
Bolton (Boulton), Richard, 85, 187.
Bolton, William, 87, 334.
Bome (Boome), Bartle (Barthw.), 188, 349, 414.
Bomgardner (Bombgardiner) (see Baumgartner).
Bonagal, George, 46.
Bond, Chas., 30.
Bond, James, 52, 54, 55, 56, 57, 88, 400.
Bond, John, 30, 422, 467, 504, 526, 575, 581, 646.
Bond, Joshua, 62, 87.
Bond, Nathaniel, 654.
Bond, Richd., 341.
Bond, Robert, 67.
Bond, Thomas, 58, 60, 593, 623, 624.
Bond, William, 30, 81.
Bonham (Boham), Malachi (Malakiah, Lt.), 441, 476, 478, 506, 519.
Bonner (see Bunner).
Bonnett (see Bennett).
Bonoday, James, 274.
Bontz (see Bantz).
Boody (Boady), John, 393, 465, 501, 526.
Boody (Body), Stephen, 58, 646.
Booger (see Boger).
Boogher, George, 321.
Booker, Abraham (see Boucher), 43.
Boomar (see Boarman).
Boome (see Bome).
Boon, Foster, 83.
Boon, Ignatius, 16, 81.
Boone (Boon, Boones), John (——), 33, 81, 185, 363, 380, 481, 518.

Boone (Boon), Richard, 189, 305, 391, 525.
Boone, Solomon, 615.
Boone, Willson, 66.
Booth, Edward, 187, 347.
Booth (Boothe), John, 16, 81, 378.
Booth, Randolph, 427, 473.
Booth, William, 88.
Bootman, Joseph, 14, 81.
Bordley, W., 372, 386.
Boret, Peter, 388.
Borett, Balser, 336.
Borroughs, Charles, 8.
Boshibea, Joseph, 89.
Bosick, Joseph, 274.
Boss, Christian, 398, 402, 462, 508, 526.
Bostick, George, 66.
Bostick, Henry, 646.
Bostion, Jacob, 72.
Boston, Alex., 19.
Boston, Isaac, 372.
Boston, John U., 85.
Bostwick, Richard, 82.
Bostwick, Thomas, 87.
Boswell, George, 35.
Boswell, Jesse, 445, 506, 525.
Boswell, John, 377, 406.
Boswell (Baswell, Bauswell), Samuel, 190, 354, 394, 443, 488, 525.
Botchabay (Botchabey), Joseph, 358, 408.
Botfield, Zadock (Lieut.), 613, 614, 615.
Botta, Joseph, 189, 392, 525, 661.
Bouchell, Slyter, 61.
Boucher (or Bucher), Abraham (see Booker), 47.
Bough, Benjamin, 526.
Bough, George (see Buck), 190, 392, 447, 488, 525.
Boughan, Peter, 405.
Boulonger (Boulange), John, 312, 334.
Boulsover (see Bowlsover).
Boulton, David, 325.
Boulton, Richard (see Bolton).
Bounds, Richard, 330.
Bourk (Bourke) (see Burke).
Bouroughs (Burris), Norman, 83, 329.
Boward, Leonard (see Howard), 186, 349, 414.
Boward (Bowerd), Micgael (Michael), 191, 264.
Boward, Valentine, 186.
Bowden, Thos., 188.
Bowden, Wm., 343, 393, 452.
Bowdon, Arthur, 88.
Bowdy, John, 393, 451, 494, 526.

Bowen (Bowin), Abraham (Abram), 186, 352, 433, 524.
Bowen, James, 53, 398, 467, 459, 488, 526, 653.
Bowen, Jehu, 53, 88, 627.
Bowen (Boen), John, 6, 648.
Bowen, Robert, 89, 463, 507, 524.
Bowen, Samuel, 87.
Bowen (or Bawen), Walter, 33.
Bower, Abraham, 328.
Bower, Boston, 190.
Bower, Jacob, 182.
Bower, John (see Bauer).
Bowers, George, 188, 348, 353, 475, 505, 525, 526.
Bowers, Thomas, 86.
Bowersmith George, 50.
Bowie, Daniel, 5.
Bowie, James, 40.
Bowie, Mathew, 87, 299.
Bowie, Robert (Capt.), 34, 36, 37.
Bowie, William, 20.
Bowie, Wm. Sprigg, 34, 88.
Bowl, Thomas, 326.
Bowler, Aaron, 188.
Bowler, Peter, 89, 524.
Bowler, Thomas, 579, 581, 582, 583.
Bowles, Martin, 190, 468, 504, 525.
Bowling, John, 32.
Bowling, William (see Boling).
Bowlsover (Boulsover), Samuel, 66, 645.
Bowman, Basil (see Boarman), 36.
Bowman, Daniel, 314.
Bowman, Jacob, 47.
Bowman, Philip, 47.
Bowser, Samuel, 89, 185.
Bowser (Bowzer), Thomas, 186, 352, 434, 525.
Boxly, David, 184.
Boyall (Byall, Byalls), Peter, 86, 297, 392, 452.
Boyce (Boice), George, 61, 586, 587, 588.
Boyd, Abraham, 333.
Boyd, Andrew, 615.
Boyd (Boid), Benjamin, 86, 357, 431, 497, 524.
Boyd, Edward, 87.
Boyd, John, 346.
Boyd, Michael, 57.
Boyd, Patrick, 602.
Boyd, Samuel, 185.
Boyd, Thomas, 84, 364, 381, 476, 482, 518.
Boyer (Capt.), 270, 271.
Boyer, George, 47.
Boyer, Lambert, 64, 186, 646.
Boyer (Byer), Mathias, 266.

Boyer (Bayer), Michael (Michal), 182, 261, 262, 268, 365, 519.
Boyer, P——, 269, 270.
Boyer, Paul, 45.
Boyer, Peter, 182, 526.
Boyes (Boys), Alexander, 84, 372, 424.
Boyes, Anthony, 388.
Boyes, Arthur, 423, 471.
Boyland, Andrew, 84.
Boyle, James, 187, 304.
Boyle, John, 572.
Boyle, Robert, 186, 323.
Boyles (O'Boyle), 148.
Boyles, Daniel, 83.
Boys, Matthew, 39.
Bozeman, William, 406.
Bracco, Bennet, 20.
Bracco, James, 67, 189.
Brackenridge, John, 59.
Brada, William (see Brady), 372.
Braddock, Johnson, 61.
Bradford, James, 606, 654.
Bradford, William, 50, 301, 654.
Bradley, Cornel, 187.
Bradley, George, 88, 456, 524.
Bradley (Bradly), Henry, 426, 463, 497, 526.
Bradley (Bradly), James, 86, 185, 567, 570, 574.
Bradley (Bradly), John, 70, 82, 186, 188, 275.
Bradshaw, James, 186, 435.
Bradshaw, Jo., 30.
Bradshaw, Joseph, 331.
Brady, James, 83, 189.
Brady (Bradey), John, 357, 395, 443, 494, 526, 564, 567, 569, 574, 579, 582, 583, 639.
Brady, Michael, 85, 274, 654.
Brady, Nicholas, 59.
Brady, Patrick, 6, 81.
Brady, Saml., 424, 474.
Brady, Thomas, 186, 525.
Brady, William (see Brada), 396, 454, 485, 526, 572.
Braeter, Joseph, 265.
Bragwell, Smith (see Bagwell), 305.
Braiding, John, 415.
Braithwaite, John, 317, 654.
Braithwaite (Braithwait, Braithwate), William, 83, 294, 321, 356, 443, 494, 523.
Bramble, Andrew, 383, 397, 401, 406, 415, 465, 501, 526.
Bramble, David, 84, 357, 444, 494, 524.
Bramble, Eton, 83.
Bramble, Hackett, 83.
Bramble, Laban, 340.

Index. 669

Bramble, Levin, 84, 524.
Bramble, William, 84, 514.
Bramhall, John, 30.
Bramhill, James, 30.
Bramwood (see Branwood).
Branagan (Branagin), Felix (Phelix), 565, 567, 569.
Brand, Gabriel, 86, 442, 524.
Branfield, John, 185.
Branfield, James, 275.
Branham (Bronham, Bromham), Lawrence (Larrance), 354, 489, 525.
Branigan, George, 70.
Branmon, Caleb, 87.
Brannan, George, 90.
Brannan (Brennan), Lawrence (Larry), 190, 312, 435, 616.
Branner, Joseph, 323.
Brannon (Brannan, Brannin), James, 84, 335, 396, 449, 500, 525.
Brannon, Jno., 275.
Brannon, Js., 360.
Brannon, Owen, 317.
Brannon (Brannan, Brennan), Timothy, 188, 304, 623.
Bransby, William, 88.
Branson, John, 355, 441, 491, 525.
Branson, Leonard, 329.
Branson, Thomas, 86, 329.
Branton, Jacob, 368.
Branwood (Bramwood), James, 72, 84, 274, 275.
Brashears (Braziers), Gassaway, 525, 599.
Brashears, Igns., 84.
Brashears, John, 406.
Brashears, Jono., 370.
Brashears, Morris, 42.
Brashears, Wm., 39.
Brashears, Zadock, 40.
Brasher, John, 21.
Brass, James L——, 524.
Braswell, John, 327.
Bratchee, William, 24.
Brattan, Jesey, 372.
Brattle, John, 72.
Brawner, Henry, 46.
Brawner, Jacob, 275.
Brawner, John, 31.
Brawton, Mathew, 275.
Brawton, Wm., 416.
Bray, Henry, 388.
Bray, John, 274.
Bray, Joseph, 85, 86, 260.
Brayly, Willm., 274.
Brazenton, Thomas, 188.
Braziers (see Brashears).
Bready, Hezekiah, 602.
Bready, Joseph, 602.
Bready, Perigrine, 602.
Breakley, John, 85.
Breaman, Jas., 340.
Brearly, George, 85.
Brease (Breeze), John, 45.
Breat, Peter, 20.

Bredding, John, 87.
Breecher, John (see Brucher).
Breiger, John, 191.
Brener, Phil., 51.
Brennan (see Brannan and Brannon).
Brent, John, 185, 524, 617.
Brereton, William, 407.
Breslor, Edward, 274.
Brett, John, 86.
Brett, Robert (see Britt).
Brevard, John (see Bevard).
Brevett, John, 356, 364, 365, 380, 462, 481, 519.
Brevill, John, 476.
Brewer, James, 661.
Brewer, John, 446, 525.
Brewer, Nicho., 41.
Brewer, Richard, 82.
Brewer, Thomas, 82, 640.
Brewington, John, 396.
Brewington (Brewenton, Bruenton, Bruington), Prestly (Pressly, Pressley, Presstly, Preistly), 396, 455, 501, 526, 641.
Brian (see Bryan).
Briant, Anderson, 602.
Briant, Joseph, 33.
Brice, Jacob (J., Capt.), 5, 85, 364, 380, 476, 480, 519, 619, 620, 621.
Brice, James (Col.), 313, 370, 402.
Brice, T., 296, 297, 299, 300.
Bricen, Thomas, 63.
Brickstake, Roger, 87.
Bridewell, Theodore, 406.
Bridges, Richard, 84.
Bridgitt, Thomas, 30.
Brien (see Bryan).
Briggs, William, 50, 190, 309, 645.
Bright, Elijah, 70.
Bright, Henry, 70.
Bright, James, 184, 575.
Bright, Matthew, 70.
Bright, Thompson, 70.
Bright, William, 88.
Briley, John, 383, 397, 401, 406, 459, 486, 526.
Briley, Jonathan, 375.
Brillingham, Isaac, 372.
Brindley, Michael, 188.
Bringman, Martin, 388, 406.
Brinkenhoof, Garret, 10.
Brinkley, Wm., 33.
Brinn, Wm., 387.
Brinsfields (Brinsfield), George, 184, 185.
Brinsford, Wm., 46.
Brion (see Bryan).
Brireck (Briruk), John, 418, 469.
Briscoe, Henry, 384, 406.
Briscoe, James, 654.
Briscoe, John H., 30, 82.
Briscoe, Philip, 82, 331.

Briscoe, Samuel H., 30.
Brisington (Brishington, Brissillton), Philip, 89, 415.
Brisland, William, 647.
Brison, William, 647.
Brissington, Abram (free negro), 82, 317.
Bristol (free negro), 387.
Britt (Brett), Robert, 18, 80, 564, 567, 574.
Britt, Thomas, 88.
Britten (Britain), Joseph, 52, 360, 519.
Brittenham (Britanham, Brittinham), Solomon, 84, 357, 445, 495, 524.
Britton (Brittain), John, 369, 416, 467, 503, 526.
Brobeck, Melcher, 18.
Brockell (Brockle, Brockett, Brockhill), Richard, 188, 336, 349, 440.
Brockson, Benj., 646.
Brodbech, Michael, 191.
Broderick (Brodericks), Dennis, 5, 81, 188, 308.
Brodericks, Richd., 275.
Brodhead, Daniel, 604.
Brodie, Daniel, 382.
Bromcord, Adam, 19.
Bromfield, Thomas, 654.
Bromgart, Adam, 81.
Bromwell (Bromell), Peter, 24, 274.
Bromwell (Bromel), Robert, 184, 621.
Bronely, John, 85.
Bronham (Bromham) (see Branham).
Brookbank, James, 82.
Brookbank, John, 82, 358, 432, 497, 523.
Brooke, Charles, 341.
Brooke, James, 391.
Brooke, John, 33.
Brooke, Matthew (see Brookes), 377.
Brooke, Walter (see Brookes), 376.
Brookes (Brooks, Brooke), Benjamin (Lt., Capt., ——), 20, 34, 36, 85, 90, 363, 379, 380, 481, 483, 519, 619.
Brookes (Brooke), Matthew, 377, 406.
Brookes, Richard, 10.
Brookes (Brooke), Walter, 376, 406.
Brookes, (Brooks), William, 83, 293, 523.
Brooks, Charles, 190.
Brooks, Jacob, 189.
Brooks, James, 334, 565, 575.
Brooks, John, 190, 334.
Brooks, Johnson, 64.
Brooks, Lawrence, 184, 623.
Brooks, Nathan, 65.

Brooks, Thomas, 84, 654.
Brookshear, James, 83.
Broom, Thomas, 586, 587, 588, 589, 590.
Brophy, Daniel, 26, 643.
Brotner, Samuel, 327.
Broughton, Adam, 190.
Broughton, Isaac, 69.
Broughton, Joshua, 83.
Broughton, William, 186, 324, 393.
Brown, Aaron, 274.
Brown, Basil, 86, 296, 357, 430, 496, 524.
Brown, Christopher, 88.
Brown, Colin, 606, 654.
Brown, Daniel, 41, 188.
Brown, Dr., 456.
Brown, Ebin, 615.
Brown, Edward, 50.
Brown, Garrett, (Garret), 606, 654.
Brown (Browne), George, 86, 90, 190, 295, 309, 320, 359, 387, 479, 524, 525.
Brown, Isaac, 88.
Brown (Browne), James, 61, 67, 85, 88, 185, 275, 340, 345, 395, 416, 419, 470, 607, 626, 645.
Brown, Jeremiah, 441, 508, 525.
Brown (Browne), John, 9, 41, 51, 57, 70, 80, 81, 85, 87, 89, 90, 186, 187, 188, 191, 263, 274, 275, 304, 326, 336, 340, 346, 350, 352, 357, 369, 371, 385, 392, 397, 416, 417, 420, 430, 453, 467, 496, 504, 505, 524, 525, 562, 602, 630, 653.
Brown, Jonathan, 641.
Brown, Joseph, 384, 406, 654.
Brown, Joshua, 54, 189, 391, 525.
Brown, Js., 360.
Brown, Luke, 89.
Brown, Peter, 9, 80.
Brown, Richard, 89, 377.
Brown, Robert, 89, 415.
Brown, Solomon, 84, 186.
Brown (Browne), Thomas, 24, 82, 83, 85, 89, 190, 294, 321, 334, 414, 524, 580, 582, 583.
Brown (Browne), William (W., Capt., Major), 46, 69, 81, 86, 90, 189, 297, 365, 477, 515, 570, 575, 576, 577, 578, 583, 584, 598, 608.
Brown, Zebulon, 188.
Browne, George (see Brown), 479.
Browne, James (see Brown), 645.
Browne, John (see Brown), 504.

Browne, Thomas (see Brown), 580.
Browne, William (see Brown), 297, 580.
Browning, Richard, 385.
Browning, William, 84, 394, 460.
Browning, Zephaniah, 42.
Brownly, Nathan, 400.
Brubacher, Michael, 263.
Bruce, John, 639.
Bruce, William, 18, 80, 364, 381, 427, 476, 481, 503, 519.
Brucebanks, Wm., 59.
Brucher (Breecher), John, 264.
Bruenton (see Brewington).
Bruff, Christopher, 67.
Bruff, Edward, 275.
Bruff, James (———), 187, 364, 381, 479, 481, 483, 627.
Bruff, Richard, 371, 645.
Bruff, William, 189, 356, 389, 437, 492, 519, 524, 645.
Brugh, Phil., 51.
Bruington (see Brewington).
Brumagum (Brumigen, Brumiger, Brumugum), Daniel, 352, 454, 485, 526.
Brumbargher, Christr., 7.
Brumicum, John, 655.
Brumwell, George 615.
Brunner, Jacob, 50.
Brunner, Valentine, 47.
Brunnum, Richard, 313.
Brunt, Edward, 90.
Brutzill, Chas., 427, 474.
Bryan, Augustine, 372.
Bryan, Charles, 83.
Bryan (Brian, Brion), Daniel (Capt.), 72, 85, 274, 307, 406, 600, 614, 615.
Bryan (Brian, Brien) David, 340, 360, 626.
Bryan, Dennis, 428, 475.
Bryan, Edward, 406, 653.
Bryan, George, 186.
Bryan, Gilbert, 42.
Bryan (Brion) Ignatius, 384, 406.
Bryan, James, 57, 309, 395, 526.
Bryan (Brion), John, 14, 83, 86, 185, 188, 274, 293, 525, 573.
Bryan, Joseph, 572.
Bryan, Luke, 185.
Bryan, Patrick, 340.
Bryan, Peter, 275.
Bryan, Richard, 188, 190.
Bryan (Byron, Byram), Stephen, 24, 25, 274.
Bryan (Bryant), Thomas, 89, 190, 319, 344, 415.
Bryan, William, 68, 186.

Bryant, Daniel, 189, 307.
Bryant, James, 45, 82, 188.
Bryant, John, 189.
Bryant, Patrick, 190.
Bryant, Thomas (see Bryan), 415.
Bryne, Charles, 66.
Bryne, James, 372.
Bryon, Thomas Meridith (see O'Bryon), 645.
Bu——, James, 653.
Buccard, Peter, 87.
Buch, George (see Buck), 264, 266.
Buchan, William, 187, 275.
Buchanan, And., 592.
Buchanan (Buchanon, Buckhannan, Buckannan), John, 82, 357, 444, 494, 524, 629.
Bucher, Abraham (see Boucher).
Buck, George (see Bough, Buch), 190, 356, 390, 438, 492, 525.
Buckhannon (or Buchanan), James, 72.
Bucklep (Buchlip), Charles 437, 506, 630.
Buckler, Walter, 384.
Buckley, Charles, 526.
Buckley (Bulkley), Daniel, 83, 358, 394, 416, 461, 498, 524.
Buckley (Bulkley), John, 25, 87, 184, 334, 354, 436, 490, 524.
Buckley (Buckly, Bulkley) Thomas, 24, 83, 274, 293, 355, 461, 499, 523, 607, 655.
Buckly, Henry, 611.
Buckstone, Abijah, 496.
Bud——, Wm., 614.
Buknell, Esau, 296.
Buley, Job, 424, 474.
Bulger, Cornelius, 345.
Bulger, Daniel, 189, 342, 357, 444, 495, 525.
Bull, James, 648.
Bullen, John, 87.
Buller, James, 45, 186.
Buller, John, 342.
Buller, Patrick, 90.
Buller, Thomas, 188.
Bulley, William, 81.
Bullin (Bulling), Thomas, 187, 414.
Bullock, John, 87.
Bullock, Joseph, 608.
Bullock, Jos. Lee, 602.
Bullock, Justinian (Jesten), 86, 329.
Bullock, Richard, 30.
Bulsel, Charles, 182.
Buly, George, 383.
Bumgardner, George, (see Baumgartner).
Bumgardner, John, 388.
Bumford, Joseph, 38.
Bune, Wm., 304.

Bunner (Bonner), Capt. Jacob, 182, 268, 269, 270, 271.
Bunting, William, 54.
Bunyan, John, 655.
Burch, Benjamin, 90, 188, 350, 417, 420, 466, 500, 502, 525, 616.
Burch, Francis, 82.
Burch, George, 64.
Burch, Gustavous, 32.
Burch, Joseph, 83, 293, 406, 461, 523.
Burch, Levy (see Burk).
Burch, Robert, 610, 611.
Burch, Thomas, 342, 653.
Burch, Zachariah (see Burck), 86, 296.
Burchfield, Chas., 340.
Burchinall, Benjamin, 63.
Burchinall, Thomas, 66.
Burck, Benj., 464.
Burck, Zachariah (see Burch), 296, 524.
Burden, Joseph, 34.
Burgan, Joshua, 185.
Burge, Joseph, 607, 655.
Burgess, Basil, 431, 476, 480, 519.
Burgess (Burness), Benj., 42, 188.
Burgess, Edward, 42, 43, 90, 343.
Burgess, Gilbert, 24.
Burgess, James, 24, 42, 83.
Burgess (Burges, Burgis), John, 7, 189, 272, 423, 466, 502, 514, 515, 526, 572, 599, 540, 648.
Burgess, John Magruder, 34, 35.
Burgess, Joseph, 38, 40, 88, 365, 519.
Burgess, Joshua, 40, 89, 362, 378, 478, 519.
Burgess (Burgiss), Josiah, 390, 418, 471, 525.
Burgess, Josias, 189.
Burgess (Burgis), Michael, 7, 38.
Burgess, Richard, 40, 42.
Burgess, Thomas, 24, 82, 274.
Burgess, Vachl., 81.
Burgess (Burgis), William, 25, 397, 450, 507, 526, 653.
Burgis, Veach, 8.
Burgoone, Robert, 39.
Burk, ——, 74.
Burk, Garret, 188.
Burk (Burck), James, 66, 184, 186, 191, 322, 349, 418, 422, 440, 469, 504, 506, 524, 526, 630, 661.
Burk (Birk), Michael, 189, 309.
Burk, Peter, 12, 86.
Burk, Walter, 344.
Burke (or Burk), Alexander, 53.

Burke, Festus, 18.
Burke (Burk), Jacob, 263, 265.
Burke (Burk, Bourk, Bourke, Birk), John, 54, 70, 90, 189, 191, 302, 351, 395, 449, 564, 576.
Burke (Burk, Burck, Burch), Levy (Levi, Livey, Leiry), 82, 293, 358, 444, 499, 523.
Burke (Burk), Patrick, 41, 274, 317.
Burke (Burk, Burck, Bourk, Birk), Richard, 53, 60, 188, 423, 468, 504, 526, 564, 566, 569, 574.
Burke (Burk, Burck), Thomas, 70, 324, 375, 397, 401, 460, 488, 526.
Burkett, Jesse, 610.
Burkett, John, 34.
Burkhart, Daniel, 182.
Burn, Anthony (see Byrne).
Burn, Carbury, 14.
Burn, Charles (see Byrne).
Burn, Elijah, 190.
Burn, John, 398.
Burn, Luke, 317.
Burn, Michael (see Byrne).
Burnell, John, 606, 655.
Burnes, Capt., 598.
Burnes, Ezekiel (Zekiel), 83, 294.
Burness, Benjm. (see Burgess), 188.
Burneston, Jos., 581.
Burnett (Burnet), Charles, 52, 185.
Burnett (Burnet), John, 32, 185, 358, 434, 497, 524, 645, 650.
Burnett, Thomas, 85.
Burnett, William, 30.
Burney, Thomas, 264.
Burnhouse, William, 608.
Burns, Chas., 445.
Burns, David, 86.
Burns, Edward, 468, 504, 526.
Burns (Burnes), Harvey, 582, 598.
Burns, Henry, 396.
Burns, Hugh, 85, 366.
Burns (Burnes), James, 9, 84, 299, 334.
Burns, John, 83, 294, 323, 458, 498, 526.
Burns, Luke, 623.
Burns (Burnes), Michael, 82, 186, 428, 474.
Burns, Simon, 188.
Burns, Timothy, 407, 419, 469.
Burns, Thomas, 185, 275, 334.
Burns (Burnes), William, 38, 185.
Burnsides, John, 90, 646.
Burrell, Allen, 381.

Index. 671

Burrell (Burrawl, Burrol), George, 70, 72.
Burrill, John, 189.
Burris, Elisha (see Burrowes).
Burris, George, 85.
Burris, Norm. (see Bouroughs).
Burris (Burress), Robert, 383, 406.
Burris, William (see Burroughs).
Burriss, John, 70.
Burrough, John, 186.
Burrough, Zacha., 186.
Burroughs, Ben., 8.
Burroughs (Burris), William, 32, 85.
Burroughs, Zeph., 33.
Burrowes (Burris), Elisha, 384, 406.
Burrows, Richd., 419, 470.
Burrows, Thomas, 6, 81.
Burt, Richard, 644.
Burtin, David, 34.
Burton, Francis, 82, 318, 396, 454.
Burton, Henry, 43.
Burton, Isaac, 419, 470, 576, 580, 582, 583.
Burton, Jacob, 45.
Burton, James, 45.
Burton, John, 190, 311.
Burton, Joseph, 90.
Burton, Joshua, 302.
Busby, Christopher, 87.
Busey, Samuel, 36, 45, 49.
Bush, Dennis, 90.
Bush, Francis, 85.
Bush, Isaac, 600.
Bush, John, 188, 648.
Busb, Joseph, 612, 613.
Bush, Richard, 27, 82, 293.
Bushell, Peter, 89, 442, 507, 525.
Busick, Caleb, 70.
Busick, James, 383.
Busick, Nathan, 378.
Bussey, Bennet, 59, 60.
Bussey, Samuel, 406.
Butcher, James, 63.
Butcher, John, 342, 446, 527, 661.
Butler, George, 86.
Butler, Henry, 377, 406.
Butler, Jacob, 81.
Butler, James, 66, 655.
Butler, John, 82, 331, 343, 360, 377, 406.
Butler, Joseph, 11, 89, 318, 415.
Butler, Peter, 653.
Butler, Richard, 85, 358, 399, 463, 497, 524.
Butler, Walter, 406.
Butler, William, 372, 400, 406, 431.
Butt, Archibald, 394, 449, 526.

Butt, Barrack (Barrock, Baruck, Baruch), 84, 358, 461, 498, 523.
Butt (Butts), Edward, 84, 523.
Butt (Butts), Thomas, 84, 355, 461, 492, 523.
Butt, Zachariah, 84.
Butterworth, Jos., 85.
Buttery, Thomas, 86.
Button, Joseph, 339.
Button (Buttons), Levin (Levi), 84, 340, 445, 507, 524.
Button, Thomas, 82.
Buttoridge, John, 88.
Buttrim, Isaac, 640.
Buxton (Buxtone), Abijah, 10, 81, 190, 334, 358, 431, 525.
Buyers (see Byers).
Buzzard, Leighton, 274.
Byall (Byalls) (see Boyall).
Byars, John, 86.
Byass (Byas, Byus), James, 85, 297, 354, 436, 490.
Byer, Mathias (see Boyer).
Byer, William, 45.
Byers (Buyers), James, 187, 304.
Byfield, Thomas, 317.
Byram, Stephen (see Bryan), 25.
Byrn, Thomas, 19.
Byrne, Anthony, 336, 434.
Byrne (Byrn, Burn), Charles, 49, 84, 340, 360.
Byrne (Burn), Michael, 88, 89, 317, 318, 414.
Byrom, Michael, 274.
Byron, Stephen (see Bryan).
Byron, Thomas, 185.
Byus, James (see Byass).
Byus, Wm., 615.
Byzch, James, 8.

Cachey (Cackey), Hector (Hecter), 194, 348.
Cade, Jarman (or Jerman), 67.
Cadenay, Antonio, 615.
Cadey (Cody), James, 600, 655.
Cady, Michael, 12.
Caffey, John, 27, 643.
Cage (see Caye).
Cahill (Caghill), David, 196, 320.
Cahill, Thos., 30.
Cahill, Timothy, 198, 266, 321, 393, 448, 530.
Cahoe, Thomas, 193, 195, 347, 349, 439, 440, 512, 528.
Cahoon, Peter, 293.
Cahoon, Wm., 22.
Cail (Caile, Cale), David, 91, 358, 432, 496.
Cail, Robert, 99.

Cain (Cane, Kain, Kaine), Edward, 8, 37, 49, 99, 531, 617, 661.
Cain (Caine, Cane), Hugh, 93, 293, 313, 527.
Cain (Caine), John, 18, 93, 276, 593, 615.
Cain (Kain, Kaine), Michael, 98, 427.
Cain, Robert, 99.
Cairey (Cairy) (see Carey).
Calahan, ——el, 431.
Calanahan, Robert, 498.
Calbert (see Colbert).
Calbut, Richard, 327.
Caldwell, Charles, 193.
Caldwell, John, 53.
Caldwell, Peter, 616.
Caldwell, Philm., 615.
Caldwell, Wm., 427, 473.
Cale (see Cail).
Calhoun, James, 269, 516.
Calihart, Frederick, 195.
Calkerwood, Capt., 599.
Callaghan, Joseph, 194.
Callahan, Barthw., 196.
Callahan, Cornelius, 193.
Callahan, Daniel, 95.
Callahan, Dennis, 193.
Callahan (Calahan, Callaghan, Callenan, Cullanan, Relahan, Retahan), John, 91, 95, 157, 402, 426, 473, 509, 514, 530, 575, 581, 640.
Callahan, Michael 99, 527.
Callahan (Calahan, Calléhan), Samuel, 95, 357, 496, 528.
Callahan, Thomas, 191.
Callahan (Calahan, Callaghan), William, 98, 426, 473.
Callender (Cullenber), John, 34, 99, 301.
Callihorn, John, 26.
Callihorne (Calihorn), Michael, 353, 456, 486.
Calpin (Killpin), Thomas, 397, 402, 416.
Calvert, Eleakim, 92.
Calvert, Robert, 305.
Calvert, William, 45.
Camble, Dunk, 192.
Cambler, Michael (see Gambler), 198, 264.
Camden (or Cambden), Richard, 40.
Cameron, Donald, 419, 470.
Camm, William, 398, 462, 487, 529.
Campbell, Capt. Aeneas, 49.
Campbell, Aeneas, Jr., 49.
Campbell, Allen, 407.
Campbell, Danl., 424, 474.
Campbell, David, 648.
Campbell, George, 338, 394.
Campbell, Henry, 61.
Campbell, Isaac, 197.

Campbell (Cammell), Jas., 17, 46, 72, 276, 342, 655.
Campbell (Cammell), Jno., 62, 194, 197, 309, 325, 345, 348, 394, 405, 416, 468, 507, 530, 655.
Campbell (Cambell, Cammel), Nicholas, 197, 308, 320.
Campbell, Pat., 100.
Campbell, Peter, 92.
Campbell, Robert, 74, 304, 453, 493, 530, 576, 581, 584, 646.
Campbell (Cammell, Kemmel, Kimmel), Thos., 61, 266, 269, 271, 516.
Campbell, Timothy, 418, 469.
Campbell, William, 95, 570.
Camper, Thomas (see Kemper), 24.
Campher, James, 646.
Campher, John, 527.
Campher (Camphor, Camphire), Thomas, 92, 357, 444, 495, 527.
Campian, Wm., 51.
Campin, John (see Champhin), 94.
Campton (see Compton).
Can, Nicholas, 196.
Canada, Thos. (see Cannady), 430.
Canahan (Kanahan, Kinnahan), John, 60, 221, 435.
Cane (see Cain).
Canfield, Thomas, 407, 653.
Cann (Can), Augustine (Augustin, Augusten, Augusteen), 61, 192, 352, 434, 528.
Cann, Ingram, 90.
Cannady (Canady, Canada), Thomas (see Kennedy), 430, 496, 529.
Canner, Sails, 612.
Cannon, Clement, 23.
Cannon, John, 66, 398, 402, 466, 503, 529.
Cannon, Patrick, 194.
Cannon, Thomas, 191.
Cannum, William, 96.
Cantlin, Wm., 401.
Cantwell, Edward, 418, 467, 503, 530.
Cantwell, Richard, 98.
Cantwell (Cantewell), William, 93, 293.
Capen, Thomas, 598, 648.
Capes, John, 263.
Caple (Capell, Capelle, Capels), James, 265, 393, 401, 429.
Cappock, Simon (Simons), 99, 319.
Capshort, Martin, 91.
Carberry, Henry, 606.
Carbury (Carberry), Peter, 345, 394, 453, 509, 529, 601, 603.

Carbury, Richard, 12.
Card (see Chard).
Cardiff, Patrick, 193.
Cardiff (Cardof), Thomas, 97, 334, 431, 531, 617.
Cardonis, Jno., 100.
Carey, Edward, 195.
Carey, James, 451, 508.
Carey (Cairey), John, 479, 519, 650.
Carey (Carry), John D., 445, 476.
Carey (Cary, Ceary), Michael, 197, 334, 389, 530.
Carey (Ceary), Owen, 197, 334, 389.
Carey (Cairy, Cary), Patrick, 93, 294, 323.
Carey, Richard, 97, 275.
Carey (Cary), William, 197, 425, 429.
Carleton, Richard, 92.
Carleton (Carlton), Wm. (see Carlin), 427, 473.
Carlile, Capt., 598.
Carlile, John, 74.
Carlile (or Carlisle), Robt., 60.
Carlin (or Carlon), George, 62.
Carlin (Carlen, Carleton), William, 43, 194, 304, 401, 427, 473, 512, 530.
Carlisle (Carlile), Bazil (Basil), 407, 505.
Carlisle, Benjamin, 594.
Carll, John (see Curll), 455.
Carlton, Thomas, 97.
Carlton, Wm. (see Carleton), 427.
Carly, Dennis, 100.
Carly, Lawrence, 92.
Carmack, Aquilla, 72.
Carman, James, 192, 335.
Carmen, John, 645, 655.
Carmichael, James, 15, 64, 91, 632.
Carmichael, Jno., 100.
Carmick, Robert (see Cornick), 191.
Carmile, Cathoel (Cathael, Calothel, Callothil), 357, 444, 495, 528.
Carmine (Carmin), Salathiel (Salithiel), 346, 366.
Carnant, Jacob, 47, 196, 311, 390, 530.
Carnee, Michael, 52.
Carnes, Arthur, 49, 575, 580, 582, 583.
Carnes, Benjamin (see Kearns), 94.
Carnes (Carns), Francis (see Kearns), 266, 394.
Carnes (Carns, Kerns), Robert, 396, 449, 505, 529, 630.
Carney, Corns, 573.

Carney, Edward (see Kerny), 96, 300.
Carney (Karney), George, 385, 397, 405, 459, 504, 529.
Carney, John, 56.
Carney, Patrick, 193.
Carney, Thomas, 192, 197, 310, 315, 352, 434, 485, 528.
Carpenter Chrisn., 100.
Carpenter, Humpy. (Umphrey), 92, 341.
Carpenter (Carpentor), John, 96, 329.
Carpenter, Mathew, 197.
Carpenter, Wm., 30.
Carr, Henry, 007, 655.
Carr, Hezekiah (Hezeka), 97, 354, 435, 489, 527.
Carr, Isaac, 419, 470.
Carr, John (Lt., ———), 17, 56, 95, 302, 363, 379, 429, 478, 497, 518, 528.
Carr, Mathew, 193.
Carr, Michael, 60.
Carr (Karr), Nicholas (see Farr), 277, 314, 621.
Carr (Karr), Robert, 573, 618.
Carr, Solomon, 92.
Carr, Stephen, 197, 341, 390, 528.
Carr, William, 96.
Carrick, Joseph (see Kerrick), 51.
Carrier, Thomas, 97, 298.
Carroll, Bryan (Brian, Ryan), 93, 293, 313, 530.
Carroll, Dennis, 99, 319, 622.
Carroll, Edmd., 9.
Carroll, George, 46, 195, 307.
Carroll (Carrol), Henry, 564, 567, 570, 574.
Carroll, Jeremiah, 93, 293.
Carroll (Carrol, Carrall, Carrell), John, 91, 93, 191, 193, 323, 331, 352, 435, 454, 485, 527, 528, 564, 567, 570, 572, 576, 648.
Carroll, John, Jr., 91.
Carroll, Joseph, 98, 263.
Carroll, Patrick, 44, 196.
Carroll, Richard, 331.
Carroll, Thomas, 420, 470, 600, 601.
Carroll, William, 49, 96, 194, 196.
Carson, John, 353, 365, 394, 462, 487, 529.
Carter, Darby, 293.
Carter, Edward, 407.
Carter, George, 328.
Carter, Henry Horn, 30.
Carter, James, 42, 95, 593.
Carter, Jeremiah, 424, 429, 464, 500, 530.

Carter, Jesse, 96, 330, 417, 469.
Carter, John, 69, 191, 340, 346, 366, 530.
Carter, Justinian (Justenian), 96, 329.
Carter, Luke, 96, 298, 329, 354, 436, 489, 527.
Carter, Michael, 44, 195.
Carter, Noah, 195, 347.
Carter, Richard, 196, 306.
Carter, Samuel, 42, 579, 582, 583, 617.
Carter, Thomas, 576.
Carter, Timothy, 195.
Carter, William, 98, 342, 353, 355, 442, 457, 486, 491, 527, 529, 600, 655.
Carthagene (Carthagena, Carthegene, Carthajane), Emanuel (Emmanuel), 353, 456, 486, 527, 581.
Carthew, Edmund, 96, 297.
Carthwood (see Catherwood).
Cartney (see Courtney).
Cartrell (see Cattrell).
Carty, Daniel, 51.
Carty, Dennis, 350, 397, 420, 470.
Carty, James, 45, 195, 306.
Carty, John, 97.
Carty, Lawrence, 415.
Carty, Martin, 95.
Carty, Matthew, 354, 449, 490, 529.
Carty, Timothy, 58.
Carvin (Carven, Carwin), James, 41, 98, 419, 470.
Carvin, Thomas, 91.
Carvoll, John, 32.
Cary, Durit, 601.
Cary, Michael (see Carey), 530.
Cary, Patrick (see Carey), 323.
Cary, Wm. (see Carey), 429.
Casbear, William, 19.
Case, Barnaby, 346.
Casey, Barney, 615.
Casey, James, 57, 528.
Casey, John, 340, 360, 653.
Casey (Casy), Michael, 475, 641.
Casey, Peter, 196, 306.
Casey, William, 51, 196, 350, 392, 438, 493, 528.
Cash, John, 45.
Cash, William, 45.
Caskin, Wm., 305.
Casley, William, 192.
Casner (Castner), Christian, 266, 323.
Casner, Christopher, 198.
Casner (Casnor), Michael, 357, 444, 495, 528.
Cassady, James, 407.
Cassady (Cassaday), Matthew, 197, 310.
Casser, William, 91.

Cassiday, Allen, 96.
Cassiday, Barney, 96.
Cassidy, Hugh, 276.
Casson, Philip, 68.
Castner (see Casner).
Casy (see Casey).
Cata (see Cato).
Catchsides (Catchesides, Catcherside), Abraham (Abram), 99, 319, 355, 400, 492, 527.
Cathagin, Annanias, 98.
Cathajane (see Carthagene).
Cathell (Cathel), James, 21, 94.
Cathell, Josiah, 21.
Cathell, Laban, 22.
Cathell, Levi, 21.
Catherwood (Carthwood), John, 60.
Catlin, ———, 74.
Catlin, B. Caleb, 192.
Catlin, Caleb, 64.
Catlin, James, 277.
Catlin, Thomas, 191.
Cato (Cata), William, 92, 527.
Caton, Patrick, 27, 644.
Caton, Richard, 24.
Caton, William, 99, 197, 341.
Catons, Michael, 10.
Cators, Patrick, 93.
Catrop, Wm., 387.
Cattrell (Cattril, Cartrell), Wm., 100, 302.
Caufman (Coffman) (see Kaufman).
Caulk, Benj., 60.
Caulk, Danl., 610.
Caulk, William, 386.
Caulker (or Corker), Wm., 66.
Causey, Henry, 329, 340.
Causins, Peter, 275.
Cavanaugh, William, 97.
Cavender, Charles, 97.
Cavender, John, 12.
Cavender, Patrick, 92, 293.
Cavenor (Caverner or Cavernor), John, 44.
Cavenough (Cavanough, Conavough), Patrick (Partrick), 342, 357, 444, 495, 527.
Caves, John, 192.
Cavey, Owen, 528.
Cavinder, James, 62.
Cawood (Caywood), Wm., 418, 400.
Caye (Cage), Wilson, 38.
Ccarsey (see Kersey).
Ceary, Michael (see Carey), 334.
Ceary, Owen (see Carey), 334.
Cecil (Cicil, Cissell), Barton (see Cissell), 96, 449, 527.
Ceitly (see Citely).

Cenedey, Philip, 46.
Certain, William, 276.
Chace, John (see Chase), 67.
Chadwick, William, 98.
Chaille, Moses, 21.
Chaires (Chairs), John, 192, 193.
Chalmers, Thomas, 575, 581.
Chalupetzky, Joseph, 594.
Chamberlain, Ben., 98.
Chamberlain (Chamberlin), John, 46, 196.
Chamberlain (Chamberlin), Jonas, 93, 323.
Chamberlain, Wm., 334.
Chamberlane (Chamberlam), Charles, 006, 655.
Chamberlin, Jones, 294.
Chambers, Benjamin, 5.
Chambers, Col., 267.
Chambers, David, 602.
Chambers, Edward, 372, 396, 450, 490, 529.
Chambers, George, 424, 471, 509, 530.
Chambers, James, 372, 395, 449, 490, 529.
Chambers, Jesse, 490.
Chambers, John, 336.
Chambers, Matthew Brown, 66, 276, 651.
Chambers, Nathan, 600.
Chambers, Thomas, 66, 375.
Chambers, William, 193, 275, 324, 348, 414, 620, 648.
Champlin, John (see Campin), 94.
Champion, George, 655.
Champlin, Hugh, 576, 580, 581, 582, 583.
Champness, Chs., 198.
Champness (Champnis), James, 266, 322.
Chance, Jno., 648.
Chance, Levy, 385.
Chance, Richard, 308.
Chandler, James, 197, 334.
Chandler, John, 192.
Chandler, Robert, 18.
Chandler, Samuel, 31.
Chandler, William, 45.
Chaney, John (see Cheney), 91.
Chaney, Richard (see Cheney), 91.
Channon, Thomas (see Shannen), 423, 466, 502, 530.
Chaphey, John, 95.
Chaplin, William, 12, 91, 387.
Chapline (Chaplain), Moses, 48, 50, 194.
Chapman, Abraham, 17, 40, 50.
Chapman, Charles, 39.
Chapman, Henry (Henry H., Henly), 91, 481, 483, 499, 519.

Chapman, Thomas, 91, 317, 387, 407, 602, 611, 613.
Chapman, William, 91, 343, 394, 402, 507, 528, 626.
Chappell, Archibald, 49.
Chappell (Chappel, Chapel, Chapple), Samuel, 340, 393, 455, 500, 529.
Chappell, Thomas, 49.
Chard (Card), James, 382, 393, 451, 512, 529.
Chard, John, 93.
Chard, William, 407.
Charles, Adam, 261.
Charles, Charles, 205.
Charles, John, 327, 397, 459, 511, 530.
Charlton, James, 327.
Charlton, J. W., 193.
Charrell (Charell), Charles, 269, 516.
Charrell (Charell), Frederick, 209, 516.
Charris, John, 645.
Chase, John (see Chace), 651.
Chatland, William, 93, 446, 527.
Chattell (or Chattle), Thomas, 44.
Chatlin, William, 393, 504.
Chatterton (Chaterton, Chaterlon), John, 98, 305.
Cheatham (Chitham, Chittham), Aquilla, 197, 389, 396, 406, 502, 528.
Cheatham, Joseph, 6.
Cheek, Nathaniel, 96.
Cheesely, James, 407.
Cheesely, Robert (see Chesley).
Cheesley, Jonathan, 387.
Cheever (Cheevers), John (see Chevier), 477, 579.
Cheney, Isaiah, 41.
Cheney, John (see Chaney), 91.
Cheney (Cheaney), Richard (see Chancy), 90, 640.
Chenoweth, Edward, 52.
Chenoweth, Thomas, 52.
Cheseldine, Gerard, 30.
Cheseldine, William, 30.
Cheshire, Benjamin, 329, 623, 655.
Cheshire (Chesire), John, 196, 514, 528.
Cheshire, Thomas, 92.
Chesley (Cheesely, Chisley), Robert (Capt.), 94, 363, 379, 407, 480, 519.
Chesnut, Willm., 587.
Chesser (Cheser), Bennett, 96, 298.
Chessey, Henry, 641.
Chester, Charles, 305.
Chester, Samuel (——el), 334, 503, 505, 568, 574.
Chevick, John, 99.

Chevier (Cheviar), John (see Cheevers), 365, 655.
Chew, Richard, 98.
Chew, Samuel Lloyd (S.), 38, 40.
Chezloe, Lodwick, 428.
Children, John, 95.
Children, William, 95, 298.
Childs, Benj., 40.
Childs, Cud, 655.
Childs (Childes), George, 55, 70, 95, 299, 357, 429, 496, 527.
Chillon, Mark, 49.
Chilmans, George, 97.
Chilton, William, 276.
Chinchfield, Chs., 360.
Chinea, Adam S., 99.
Chinge, Samuel, 331.
Chinn, Samuel, 91.
Chinneth (Chineth, Chinworth), Arthur, 100, 301.
Chinneth (Chineth, Chinworth), John, 100, 301.
Chinowith, Richard, 600.
Chippey, Joshua, 24.
Chisholm, William, 276.
Chisley (see Chesley).
Chitham (Chittham) (see Cheatham).
Chittain, John, 641.
Chittendon, James, 342.
Chivel, John (see Shovell), 617.
Chiveral, Jessee, 330.
Chivers, Andrew, 99.
Cholard (Collard, Collierd), James, 92, 358, 393, 450, 498, 527.
Chrispin (see Crispin).
Christian, John, 93, 195.
Christian, Joseph, 613.
Christie, Alex., 400, 424, 471.
Christie, Jas., 100.
Christie, John, 52.
Christman, Paul, 182, 263.
Christopher, Isaac, 397, 402, 415.
Christopher, John, 30, 92.
Christopher, Milbey (Milby, Melby), 397, 402, 415.
Christopher, Thos., 391.
Christopher, Thos. H., 197.
Chritchets (Critchet), Benjamin, 192, 276.
Chritchets (Critchets), William, 192, 276.
Chubb (Chub), Jonathan, 338, 460, 513, 528.
Chumley, Daniel, 603.
Chunn, Jonathan, 6, 91.
Chunn, Lancelot, 377, 406.
Church, Abram (Abraham), 194, 348.
Church, John, 415.
Church, Samuel, 606.
Churchill, John, 195.
Churchwell, John, 45.
Ciferd (see Cypher).

Cinquaid (Cincuid) (see Kincaid).
Cissall, Nicholas, 97.
Cissell (Cecil, Cicil), Barton, 96, 449, 527.
Cissell, Edmd. Barton, 329.
Cissell, John, 9.
Cissell (Cissill), John B., 97, 298.
Citely (or Ceitly), Thomas, 63.
Citizen, Morris, 93, 527.
Civill (Civil), William (see Sevill), 193, 434, 530.
Clacker, Chehoikin, 196.
Clagett, Henry, 647.
Clagett, Wiseman, 36.
Claggett (Clagget, Claggett), Horatio, 34, 35, 96, 295, 296, 304, 380, 422, 476, 481, 501, 634.
Claggett (Clagett, Clegett, Clegget), John, 96, 296, 359, 527.
Clanahan (Clenehan, Clenchan), Robert, 194, 348, 358, 445, 528.
Clancey (Clancy, Claney), Daniel, 95, 430, 507, 527, 619.
Clancey (Clancy), Dennis (Denis), 60, 318.
Clancey (Clancy), Edward, 197, 341, 389, 437, 507, 528.
Clancey (Clancy), John, 90, 305, 451, 508, 511, 529, 530.
Clancey, Joseph, 421, 465, 501, 530.
Clancey (Clancy, Clansey), Michael, 193, 358, 398, 431, 497, 528, 572, 617, 647.
Clap, Josep, 336.
Clapper (Claper), Valentine (Volintine), 336, 352, 435, 529.
Clapsaddle, Daniel, 73.
Clarben, Samuel, 333.
Clare, John, 338.
Clarey (see Clary).
Claridge (Clarage), Henry, 93, 630.
Claridge (Clarage, Cleridge), Levin (Leavin), 417, 425, 408, 505, 530.
Clark, ——as, 431.
Clark, Arthur (see Clarke), 305.
Clark, Charles (see Clarke), 93, 277.
Clark, Elijah, 31, 69.
Clark, George (see Clarke), 275, 407, 461, 528.
Clark, Henry, 42, 43, 454.
Clark, Hezekiah, 435.
Clark, Ignatius, 93, 330.
Clark, James (see Clarke), 98, 275, 313, 584, 617, 655.

Clark, John (see Clarke), 14, 53, 66, 96, 574, 583.
Clark, Joseph, 93, 100.
Clark, Michael (Michal) (see Clarke), 97, 353, 458, 486, 508, 527, 529.
Clark, Nicholas, 53.
Clark (Clarke), Peter (Lt.), 95, 320, 327.
Clark, Richard (see Clarke), 97, 98, 193, 308, 320, 458.
Clark, Robert, 345.
Clark, Samuel (see Clarke), 18, 390, 492, 529.
Clark, Thomas (see Clarke), 91, 97, 314, 357, 452, 497, 527, 529.
Clark, William (see Clarke), 7, 15, 69, 91, 94, 97, 375, 574.
Clark, Wm. (of Wm.), 66.
Clark, Zachariah (Zachria), 97, 334, 354, 435, 489, 529.
Clarke, Arthur (see Clark), 196.
Clarke, Charles (see Clark), 330.
Clarke, David, 194.
Clarke, Elijah, 342.
Clarke, George (see Clark), 94, 342, 508.
Clarke, Henry, 641, 646.
Clarke (Clerke), James (see Clark), 33, 572, 576.
Clarke, John (see Clark), 59, 94, 196, 276, 563, 566, 569, 579.
Clarke, Michael (see Clark), 433.
Clarke, Peter, 7.
Clarke, Richard (see Clark), 53, 197, 398, 402.
Clarke, Saml. (see Clark), 197, 356, 437.
Clarke, Thomas (see Clark), 97, 396, 493, 581.
Clarke, William (see Clark), 94, 192, 197, 641, 646.
Clarkson, Thomas, 385.
Clarkson, William, 382.
Claress, Francis, 277.
Clary, Dennis, 44, 195.
Clary (Cleary), John, 70, 191, 276.
Clary (Clarey), William, 90, 388, 432, 497, 527.
Clash, Jonathan, 371.
Clash, Richard, 407.
Class, John (see Closs), 50.
Class, Martin, 196.
Class, Michael, 195.
Claward (Cloward), Abram (Abraham), 194, 304.
Clawson, Henry, 422, 471.
Clayland, James, 66, 277, 645.

Clayton, Edward, 646.
Clayton (Clyton), John, 60, 342.
Cleanscrote, John, 428.
Cleary (see Clary).
Cleaver (Clever), Benjamin, 193, 349, 354, 440, 489, 528.
Clegget (Clegett) (see Claggett).
Clegness, John Francis, 655.
Clement (see Clements).
Clements, Aquilla, 381, 392, 429, 461.
Clements, Benedict, 377.
Clements, Bennett (Bennet, Bennet H.), 407, 441, 506, 528.
Clements, Charles, 96, 296, 330, 356, 453, 492, 527.
Clements (Clemments), Francis T., 575, 581.
Clements (Clemons), Henry (Lt.), 45, 91, 94, 352, 364, 377, 381, 398, 407, 433, 476, 482, 519, 653.
Clements (Clemonts, Clement), James, 91, 197, 334, 381, 391, 394, 449, 529.
Clements (Clemmonds), John, 35, 66, 91, 277, 377, 407.
Clements, John Adlow, of Joseph, 31.
Clements, John Ensy, 376.
Clements, John H., 407.
Clements, Mark, 97, 297.
Clements, Nathan Emory, 67.
Clements, Ralph, 35.
Clements, Thomas (Thos. B.), 396, 455, 509, 527.
Clements, William, 92, 396, 432, 454, 508, 512, 527, 528.
Clemmonds, John (see Clements), 66.
Clemons, David, 96.
Clemons, James, 35.
Clendenin, James, 647.
Clenehan (Clenchan) (see Clanahan).
Clenshey, James M., 647.
Cleridge (see Claridge).
Clerke (see Clarke).
Clever (see Cleaver).
Cleverdence, John, 397, 402, 450, 502, 529.
Clice (see Clise).
Clifford, Jeremiah, 608.
Clifford, William, 194, 388.
Clift, Crisenberry, 15.
Clift, Henry, 14.
Clift, James, 192.
Clifton, Ezekiel, 335.
Clifton, James, 335.
Clifton, Thomas, 198, 264, 265.

Climeslaught (Clineslought), John, 466, 502, 530.
Clinch, John, 95.
Cline, Daniel, 51, 336.
Cline, John (see Kline).
Cline, Nicholas, 388, 407.
Clinkscales, Levi (Levy), 376, 407.
Clinkscales, (Clinscales), Richard, 31.
Clinkscales, William, 377, 407.
Clinton, George, 261.
Clinton, Thomas, 99, 395, 397, 456, 509, 527.
Clisce, Christeen, 46.
Clise (Clice), Henry, 72.
Cloes (Close), Charles (—), 414, 565, 567, 569.
Cloney, John, 98.
Closs (Close, Clore), Christian, 18, 92, 455, 530.
Closs, John (see Class), 51.
Closson, Garrett, 50.
Clover, William, 395.
Cloward (see Claward).
Clubb, Mathew, 382.
Cluff, John, 276.
Cluley (Cluly), Joseph, 468, 504, 530.
Clutter, Gasper, 18.
Clymer (Clymore), Thomas, 66, 650.
Clyton (see Clayton).
Coachman, James, 330.
Coachman, John, 407.
Coale, James (see Cole), 572.
Coale, John (see Cole), 52.
Coale, Michael (see Cole), 341.
Coale, Richard (see Cole), 52.
Coaleman (see Coleman).
Coalman, Mathew, 275.
Coalman, Saml., 275.
Coarsey (see Coursey).
Coatney, Anthony, 196.
Coatney, William (see Courtney).
Coats, William, 616.
Cobb, Kendel (Kindall), 396, 529.
Cobeth, John, 20.
Coburn, James, 24.
Coehran, James, 62, 529.
Cochran (Cochren, Cockran), John, 100, 197, 303, 334, 391, 528.
Cock (or Coch), Cornelius, 388.
Cock, Wm., 405.
Cockburn (Cockburne), Alex., 369, 392, 402.
Cockerill (Cockerile, Cockrill, Cockrall, Cougherin), James, 375, 396, 455, 507.
Cockerton, John, 574.

Cockerton, Robert, 655.
Cockey, Peter, 66, 95.
Cockey, Richard, 607, 655.
Cockindall (Cochindall, Cockendall, Cockendale), Elijah (Elisha), 100, 303, 350, 397, 462, 529.
Cockleton, Robert, 375.
Cockran, George, 95.
Cockran, John (see Cochran), 100, 334, 391.
Cockran (Corkran), Owen, 95, 619.
Cocks (see Cox).
Cocoanat (or Coroanat), Antonio, 615.
Code (see Coode).
Cody, James (see Cadey), 655.
Coe, Elijah, 37.
Coe, Hezekiah, 91.
Coe, Job, 655.
Coe, Milburn, 91.
Coe, Richard, 91.
Coe, William, 396, 401, 455, 512, 529.
Coen (see Cowen).
Coewn, Joseph, 37.
Coffee, Daniel, 70, 192, 276.
Coffer, Francis, 330.
Coffer, James, 95.
Coffer, Matw., 603.
Cofferoth (Cofforth), Coonrod (Conrad), 196, 618.
Cofferoth (Coffeeroth, Cofforth), William, 50, 196, 618.
Coffield, Owen, 530, 603, 634.
Coffin, Arthur, 393, 402, 448, 488, 529.
Coffman (see Kaufman).
Coffree, John Robt. Saml., 371.
Coheall, James, 192.
Cohee, John, 69, 375.
Cohoe, Thomas, 38.
Coholen, Jerey, 600.
Coines (Conies, Coyn), Domini (Dominick, Donn), 194, 304, 469, 505.
Coins, George, 529.
Coir, Michael, 194.
Coland, John, 98.
Colbert, Daniel, 313.
Colbert, Matthew, 27, 643.
Colbert (Calbart, Colibert), Simon, 197, 334, 390.
Colbertson (see Culbertson).
Cole, ——, 74.
Cole, Benjamin, 198, 266, 323, 447, 511, 529.
Cole, Charles, 384, 406.
Cole, David, 527.
Cole, Francis, 10.
Cole, George, 263.
Cole, Henry, 276.
Cole, Hoshier, 606.

Index.   675

Cole (Coale), James, 572, 576.
Cole, J. B., 275.
Cole, Jessey, 338.
Cole (Coale), John, 52, 66, 93, 198, 263, 293, 396, 398, 449, 464, 483, 490, 529, 646.
Cole, Joseph, 99, 317.
Cole (Coale), Michael, 92, 341, 527, 617.
Cole, Patrick, 606, 655.
Cole (or Coale), Richard, 52.
Cole, Thomas, 54, 277.
Cole, William, 26, 73, 92, 195, 348, 642.
Coleby John, 196.
Colegate, Asaph., 99, 353, 458, 486, 527.
Colegate, John, 98, 519.
Colein (Coleing), John (see Colin), 53, 353, 450, 480.
Coleman, Isom, 466, 602, 529.
Coleman, James, 425, 472.
Coleman, John, 99, 195.
Coleman (Coaleman), Michael, 99, 661.
Coleman, Patrick, 603.
Coleman, Thos., 67.
Coleman, William, 193, 418, 469, 510, 530.
Colen, Thos., 335.
Coleson, John, 92.
Coley, James, 331.
Coley, Joseph, 331.
Coley, Robert, 331.
Colfax, W., 605.
Colfield, Francis, 191.
Colgain, William, 197.
Colibert (see Colbert).
Colin, John (see Colein), 527, 626.
Colin (Coulin), William, 468, 504, 530.
Coll, Edward, 22.
Collard, James (see Chollard), 92, 358, 393.
Collard, William, 195.
Collen, Michael, 194.
Colless, Pompey, 653.
Colley, George, 51.
Collier, William, 97, 623.
Collierd (see Cholard).
Collior, Thos., 416.
Collings, George (see Collins), 329.
Collings, William, 94.
Collins, Benja., 193.
Collins, Charles, 194.
Collins, David, 56.
Collins, Edward (Edmund, Edmond), 194, 348, 414.
Collins, Emory (Emmory), 612, 613.
Collins, Ephraim, 59.
Collins (Collings), George, 96, 194, 298, 329, 370, 446, 530.

Collins, Jacob, 93, 375, 449, 490, 529.
Collins (Colins), James, 46, 94, 192, 195, 276, 293, 306, 352, 396, 405, 454, 529, 606, 612, 613, 655.
Collins, Jeremiah, 64.
Collins, John, 44, 51, 59, 95, 100, 276, 277, 298, 302, 369, 372, 396, 454, 529, 592, 593, 598, 651.
Collins, Levin (Levy), 383, 407.
Collins, Patk., 11, 100, 303, 336.
Collins, Peter, 405.
Collins, Richd., 417.
Collins, Robert, 615.
Collins, Solomon, 62.
Collins, Thomas, 51, 95, 277.
Collins, Timothy, 10, 98.
Collins, William, 40, 55, 58, 70, 192.
Collis, William, 340, 356, 394, 443, 494, 528.
Collison, James, 370.
Colman (see Comer).
Colon, John, 277.
Colour, Philip, 261.
Colson (see Coulston).
Colter (Coltart), Antipas, 32, 96, 295.
Colter, Willan, 502.
Colvert, Thomas, 24, 293.
Combes (see Coombes).
Combest, Isreal, 59.
Combly, Benjamin, 369.
Comegys, Cornelius, 64.
Comegys, Jesse, 61.
Comegys, Jonathan, 61.
Comegys, William, 66.
Comer (or Colman), Geo., Stibbonds, 57.
Comerford, Thomas, 69.
Comini, Absolum, 27.
Comming, Willm. (see Cummings), 391.
Commott (Commett), Wm. 419, 470.
Compton, Alexd., 93.
Compton (Cumpton), Igns. (see Crumpton), 197, 389, 528.
Compton (Campton), Edmond, 92, 356, 364, 365, 380, 460, 476, 481, 519.
Compton, James, 576.
Compton, John, 30, 49, 579, 583, 655.
Compton, Thomas, 529.
Compton, Wm. 26.
Compton, Wm., S., 32.
Conavough (see Cavenough).
Conaway (see Conway).
Concella, Andw., 277.
Conderall, Thomas, 575.
Condon (Conden, Cunden), Martin, 565, 566, 569, 574.

Condon, William (see Condron), 191, 276, 407.
Condren, James, 400.
Condron (Condrone), John, 60, 195.
Condron (Condran, Condram), Thomas, 572, 580, 582, 583.
Condron, William (see Condon), 60, 400.
Cones, Peter, 448.
Congleton, David, 92, 640.
Congleton, William, 98.
Conies (see Coines).
Conley, Henry, 338.
Conley (Connley), John, 70, 508, 565.
Conn, Hugh, 9.
Conn, John, 328.
Conn, Peter, 328.
Conn, Robert, 95.
Conn, Timothy, 209, 271, 510.
Conn, William Young, 42.
Connady, John (see Kenneday), 192.
Connally, Francis, 95.
Connally, James, 195.
Connally (Conaly), John, 344, 429, 461.
Connally, Josias, 9.
Connally, Laurence, 196.
Connally, Michael, 92, 194.
Connally, Patrick, 196, 514.
Connally, Philip, 100.
Connally, Thomas, 92.
Connally, Wm., 100, 429.
Connan, Patrick, 45.
Connar (see Connor).
Connard, Thos., 194.
Connaway, Samuel, 66.
Connegin, John, 93.
Connel, Patrick, 192.
Connell, Jeremiah, 70.
Connell, Michl., 514.
Connell, Thomas Way, 6.
Connelly, Edward (see Connolly), 315.
Connelly, Henry (see Connolly), 449.
Connelly (Connely, Conoly, Connally), John, 91, 192, 277, 382, 398, 471, 472, 510, 529, 530, 576, 584, 600.
Connelly (Connely, Connerley), Laurence (Lawrence), 24, 53, 92, 276.
Connelly (Connely), Michael, 94, 304, 349.
Connelly (Connerly, Connorly), Patrick, 27, 95, 311, 340, 360, 644.
Connelly, Roger (see Connolly), 368, 385.
Connelly (Conolly), Timothy, 576, 580, 582, 583.
Connelly, William, 196, 425, 467, 508, 530, 576.
Connely, Daniel, 192.

Conner, Alexius, 7.
Conner, Caleb, 39.
Conner, Cornelius, 53, 193.
Conner, Daniel (see Connor), 385.
Conner, David (see Connor), 93, 294, 506, 527, 630.
Conner, Dennis, 99, 193.
Conner, George (see Connor), 192.
Conner, Hugh, 192, 277.
Conner, Hughett, 69.
Conner, Jas. (see Connor), 61, 62, 95, 98, 192.
Conner, John, 35, 92, 95, 293, 296, 466, 502, 530.
Conner, John Claggett, 97.
Conner, Michael (see Connor), 26, 93, 582.
Conner, Patrick, 93.
Conner, Robert, 606, 655.
Conner, Thomas (see Connor), 8, 195, 563.
Conner, Timothy, 372, 435.
Conner, William, 94, 98, 193, 333, 372, 461, 501, 527.
Conner, Wm. I., 603.
Connerwey, Benj., 65.
Connery, James (see Conway), 16.
Connley (see Conley).
Connolly (Connoly), Edward (see Connelly), 267, 615.
Connolly, Henry (see Connelly), 366.
Connolly (Conoly, Conly), John, 192, 344, 392, 407, 421, 424, 565, 567.
Connolly, Michael, 414, 415.
Connolly, Roger (see Connelly), 407.
Connolly (Connerly), Thomas, 25, 193.
Connon, Pope, 339.
Connor, Ambrose, 276.
Connor, Daniel (see Conner), 407.
Connor, David (see Conner), 473.
Connor, George (see Conner), 65, 276.
Connor, James (see Conner), 62, 297, 623, 647.
Connor (Connar) (see Conner), Michael, 579, 584, 643.
Connor, Patrick, 530, 617.
Connor, Thomas (see Conner), 91, 566, 569, 574.
Connor, Timothy, 342.
Connoway (Conaway), Lawrence (see Conway).
Conolly, Hugh, 508.
Conolly, Timothy (see Connelly).
Conoly, James, 306.
Conrad, John, 47.
Conrod, Wm., 328.

676   Index.

Conroy, Hugh, 195.
Consella, Hermon, 50.
Conslean, Andrew, 19.
Contee, Benj., 34.
Contess (see Countess).
Conway (Connoway, Connery), James, 16, 94, 267, 322.
Conway, Joseph, 607.
Conway (Conaway, Connoway), Laurence (Lawrence), 56, 97.
Conway, Michael, 606.
Conway, Robert, 607.
Conway (Connoway), Thomas, 344, 602.
Conway, William, 62.
Conwell, Arthur, 100.
Conydon, Edward, 193.
Coode (Code), William, 30, 94.
Cooenah, Thomas, 95.
Cooender, Charles, 95.
Cook, Benjamin, 93, 94.
Cook, George, 606, 655.
Cook, Henry, 98.
Cook, James, 67.
Cook, Jeremiah, 96.
Cook, John, 44, 610, 648.
Cook, Moses (see Cooke), 621.
Cook, Richard (see Cooke), 295.
Cook, Thomas (see Cooke), 30, 70, 72, 307.
Cook, William (see Cooke), 69, 463, 528, 648.
Cooke, Jeremiah, 37.
Cooke, John, 52.
Cooke, Moses (see Cook), 192.
Cooke, Richard (see Cook), 44, 96.
Cooke, Thomas (see Cook), 195.
Cooke, William (see Cook), 97, 195, 353, 488.
Cooksen, Peter, 93.
Cooksey, Hezekiah, 32.
Cooksey, John, 92, 641.
Cooksey, Ledstone Smd.,32.
Cookson, John, 655.
Cooley, James, 91.
Cooley, John, 343.
Cooley, Joseph, 91, 96, 453, 530.
Cooley, Mordecai, 92.
Cooley, Robert, 91.
Coolidge, Silas, 615.
Coolin, Jno., 392.
Cooly, George, 94.
Coombes (Coombs, Combes, Coombe), William, 91, 277, 331, 377, 407.
Coombs, Nicholas, 92.
Coomes, John C., 32.
Coomes, Richard, 94.
Coomes, Walter, 32.

Coomy, John (see Coony). 514.
Coon (Coone), Adam, 100, 328.
Coonehan, Thomas, 97, 297.
Cooney, Laughlan, 195.
Coons, Peter (see Kuntz), 395.
Coonse, Henry, 50.
Coony (Cooney, Coomy), John (see Kuny), 344, 514, 598.
Coop, Borachiah (Barachius), 400, 407.
Coop (Coops), Horatio, 400, 407, 648.
Coop, James, 648.
Cooper, Charles, 24, 94, 95, 276, 357, 394, 444, 494, 529.
Cooper, Christopher, 72.
Cooper, Edward, 318.
Cooper, Ephraim, 61.
Cooper, George, 564, 566, 569, 574.
Cooper, James, 98.
Cooper, John, 99, 100, 301, 387, 427, 452, 474, 505, 510, 528, 530.
Cooper, Nathaniel, 606, 655.
Cooper, Thomas, 14, 370, 442, 528.
Cooper, William, 60, 69, 100, 276, 302.
Coops (see Coop).
Coosingbury (Crosingbury), James, 427, 473.
Cope, John, 93, 313.
Copeland, William, 94, 395.
Copes, John, 196.
Coppage, Edward, 66.
Copper, James, 64.
Copper, Samuel, 645.
Copple, Peter, 261.
Corbett, Jacob, 91.
Corbett (Corbit), Jesse, 99, 302.
Corbett (Corbet), Patrick, 91, 655.
Corbin, Arthur, 417.
Corbin, Willm., 640.
Corbley, Nicholas, 53.
Corckwell, Henry, 872.
Corcoran, Patrick, 575.
Cord, Roger, 97, 344.
Cordery, Isaac, 70.
Cordray, James, 606, 655.
Cork, Danl., 610.
Cork, Ralph, 276.
Cork, William (see Caulk), 397, 458, 487, 529.
Corker, John, 193, 277.
Corker (see Caulker).
Corkery, William, 193.
Corkran, Owen (see Cockran), 619.
Corlet, John, 346.
Cormick (see Cornick).
Cormine, John, 92.
Cornaflean, William, 655.

Cornelius, Isaac, 646.
Corner, Thomas, 196.
Cornick (Cormick, Carmick), Robert, 191, 354, 463, 489, 528.
Cornish, Charles, 385.
Cornish, Constant, 94.
Cornish, John, 93, 294, 619.
Cornwall (Cornwell), William (Sargt.), 563, 565, 568, 572, 579, 582, 584, 618.
Correll, William, 396.
Corry (see Currye).
Corsey, Charles, 98.
Corsey, Hampton (see Coursey).
Corsey, James (see Kersey), 442.
Corsey, William (see Coursey).
Corter, Thos., 334.
Cortland, Nathaniel, 11.
Cortz (see Curts and Curtz).
Cosby, Jessey (see Crasby), 588.
Cosby, John, 419.
Cosden (Cozden), Jesse (—), 63, 64, 74, 192.
Cosden, John, 64.
Cosfield, Luke, 93.
Cosgrove (Crossgrove), Edward, 12, 90, 356, 454, 493, 530.
Cosgrove (Custgrove), Matthias, 267, 322.
Costigin, Patrick, 640.
Costillo, Ebenezer, 64.
Costillo, Thomas, 655.
Cotman, John, 302.
Cotter, John, 425, 429, 468, 504, 530.
Cotter, William (Willis), 425, 429, 466, 530.
Cotting, Peter, 92.
Cottingham, John, 22.
Couch, Charles, 192, 528.
Cougheren, George, 455.
Cougherin, James (see Cockerill), 455, 507.
Coughlan, Edwd., 574.
Coughlan, Michael, 193, 322.
Coulin, William (see Colin), 504.
Coulston (Colson), John, 313, 655.
Coulter, John, 426.
Countess (Contèss), James, 426, 473, 509, 530.
Countess (Countiss), Thos., 426, 468, 505, 530.
Courcey (see Coursey).
Courcy (see DeCourcy).
Coursey (Coarsey, Corsey), Hampton, 94, 357, 443, 494, 527.
Coursey, Henry, 645.
Coursey, Patrick, 572, 576.

Coursey (Courcey, Corsey), William, 398, 402, 462, 513, 530.
Courtney (Cartney, Coatney), William, 93, 294, 321.
Courts, Christopher (see Curts), 194.
Courts, John, 97, 460, 502, 527, 617.
Courts, William, 5, 91, 93.
Cousins, Edwd., 276.
Cove (see Eove).
Coventree, Jacob, 194.
Coventry, Charles, 196.
Coves, William, 407.
Covey, William, 383, 402.
Covington, Henry, 14, 192.
Covington, Thos., 650.
Cowan, William, 276.
Cowell, Robert, 58.
Cowen (Coen), James, 96, 429, 510, 530.
Cowin, Thomas, 621.
Cowland, George, 334.
Cowley (or Crowley), Edwd., 39.
Cowley, Michael, 198.
Cowley, William, 22, 39, 372.
Cowling, George, 197.
Cowman, John, 370.
Cowsway, Solomen, 94.
Cox, Benjamin, 32.
Cox, Bennet, 329.
Cox, Capt., 652.
Cox, Clarkeson, 197.
Cox, Edmund, 6, 94.
Cox, Edmond, 91.
Cox, Ezaiah, 197.
Cox, Ezekiel, 74, 75.
Cox, Isaac, 387.
Cox, James, 32, 60.
Cox, John, 61, 96, 193, 277.
Cox, Jos., 395.
Cox, Joshua, 451, 497, 529.
Cox, Luke, 26, 643.
Cox, Matthew, 196, 277, 315.
Cox, Milburn, 7.
Cox, Walter, 7.
Cox, Richard, 8.
Cox (Cocks), William, 31, 96, 334, 342, 355, 398, 491, 528, 617.
Coxen, Levin Will, 9.
Coy (Coye), Christopher, 419, 470, 509, 530.
Coyle, Michael, 194, 530.
Coyle (Coyl), Samuel, 96, 573.
Coyn, Dominick (Donn) (see Coines), 194, 304.
Cozden (see Cosden).
Crabb, Jeremiah, 98.
Crabb, Richard (R.), 43, 44.
Cradock, John, 52, 58.
Crady, David, 461, 486, 528.
Crafford, Robert (see Crawford).

Index. 677

Crafford, Robert Beall, 49.
Crafford (Crayford), Thos., 11, 68.
Craft, Fredk., 328.
Craft, James, 93.
Craft (Crafft, Croft), John, 198, 264, 265.
Cragan (Cragain) (see Cragon).
Cragg, George (see Craig), 461.
Cragg, John (see Craig), 436.
Craggs, George (see Cragg), 355, 491.
Cragon (Cragan, Cragain), Dennis (see Cregan), 331, 451, 507, 529.
Cragon (Craigen), Lawrence (see Cregan), 318, 415.
Crague (see Craig).
Craig, Alex., 563, 566, 568, 573.
Craig, George (see Cragg), 97.
Craig, Jas., 14.
Craig (Crague), John (see Cragg), 96, 98, 99, 341, 354, 415, 489, 527.
Craig, Michael, 191, 606.
Craig, Reubin, 30.
Craig, Robert, 573.
Craig, Saml., 100.
Craig (Craigg), Thomas, 100, 351, 420, 466, 502, 530.
Craig, Wm., 641.
Craigen (see Cragon).
Craighton (see Creighton).
Crail (Crale), James, 51, 194, 277.
Crail (Craill, Crale), William, 51, 195, 356, 390, 395, 439, 493, 528.
Craine, Henry (see Crane).
Craine, Lawrence, 276.
Craine, Michael, 98.
Cramdale (see Crandle).
Cramer, Adam, 18.
Cramer, Jacob (see Cromer).
Cramer, Mich., 47.
Cramer, Peter, 388.
Cramphur, James, 91.
Crampton, James, 99.
Crampton (Crompton), Thomas, 385, 405, 460, 499.
Crandle (or Cramdale), Joseph, 40.
Crane, David, 63.
Crane (Craine), Henry, 196, 342, 358, 460, 498, 528.
Crany, John, 562.
Crapell (or Creppell), Jacob, 47.
Crapper, James, 21.
Crapper, John, 606, 655.
Crasberry (see Cresbury).

Crasby (Cosby), Jesse (Jessee, Jessey), 586, 587, 588.
Crasby, Joseph (see Crosby), 40.
Cratcher, Matthew, 655.
Crating, John, 93.
Craven, Andrew, 60, 195.
Craver, Jacob, 328.
Cravin, Jeremiah, 100.
Crawford, A., 399, 400, 401.
Crawford, Hugh, 407.
Crawford, J., 351.
Crawford, Jacob (Lt.), 92, 363, 379, 402, 403, 439, 479, 519.
Crawford (Crauford, Croford), Jas., 97, 191, 335, 530.
Crawford, Jno., 100, 276.
Crawford, Jonas, 426, 473.
Crawford, Nehemiah, 603.
Crawford (Crauford, Crafford), Robert, 11, 95, 100.
Crawley, James, 655.
Crawley, Patrick, 326.
Crawly, Joseph, 43.
Cray, Alex., 610.
Cray, John, 194.
Crayton (see Creighton).
Creager, Valentine, 72.
Creagon (see Cregan).
Creaighton (Creaghton or Creaton), William, 62.
Creamer, James (see Cromer), 97.
Creaton (see Creaighton).
Credo, George, 394.
Cregan (Creagon), Dennis (see Cragon), 92, 395.
Cregan, Lawrence (see Cragon), 98.
Cregannon, Dennis, 623.
Cregar, Michael, 407.
Creighton (Craighton, Crayton), James, 393, 398, 452, 503, 530.
Creppell (see Crapell).
Cresap, Joseph, 28.
Cresap, Michael, 28.
Cresbury (Crasberry, Crisbury), James, 394, 446, 495, 529.
Creswell, James, 345.
Cretzinger, George, 19.
Cretzinger, Solomon, 20.
Criegh, Philip, 328.
Crime, Michael, 195, 348.
Cripps, Nathan, 444.
Crips, Nathaniel, 92.
Crisbury (see Cresbury).
Crismond, Leonard, 94.
Crisp, Benj., 24.
Crispin (Chrispin), Alexander, 96, 295.
Crisps, Benjamin, 92.
Crist, John, 92.
Criswell, Matthew, 648.
Critchet (Critchets) (see Chritchets).
Croane, Timothy, 275.

Crockett, John, 99, 293, 302, 424.
Crofford, Thos., 454.
Croford (see Crawford).
Croft, John (see Craft), 198.
Croft, William (see Kraft), 198.
Cromer (Cramer, Croumer), Jacob, 182, 198, 261, 262.
Cromer (Creamer), James, 97, 334.
Cromey, Andrew, 93.
Crompton (see Crampton).
Cromwell (Crumwell), Jas., 393, 401, 407, 451.
Cromwell, Thomas, 97.
Cron, Thomas, 655.
Cronan, John, 91.
Croney, William, 406.
Cronise (Cronies), Henry, 198, 261, 262.
Crook (Crooke), Henry, 340, 436, 505, 528, 630.
Crook, John, 42.
Crook (Crooke), Joseph, 34, 93, 329.
Crook, Martin, 276.
Crook, Wm., 648.
Crookshank, William, 590.
Cropp, John, 264.
Cropper, Edward, 372.
Cropper, Levi, 372.
Cropper, Ruben, 372.
Crosby, Danl., 461.
Crosby, George, 99, 414.
Crosby, James, 95, 275.
Crosby, John, 98, 456, 470, 529.
Crosby (Crosbey, Crosbie, Crasby), Joseph, 18, 40, 90, 196, 276.
Crosby, Richard, 99, 661.
Crosby, William, 601.
Crosingbury (see Coosingbury).
Crosley (or Crossley), William, 655.
Cross, Charles, 98.
Cross, James, 196.
Cross, Joseph, 93, 458, 476, 482, 519.
Cross, Robert, 191.
Cross, Samuel, 93.
Crossgrove, Edwd. (see Cosgrove), 356.
Crossley (see Crosley).
Crotchett, John, 474.
Crothorn, George, 198.
Crouch, Amos, 193.
Crouch, Arthur, 277.
Crouch, James, 612.
Crouch, John, 67, 95.
Crouch, Joseph, 95, 342, 392, 398, 531, 621.
Crouch, Robert, 586, 587, 588, 589.
Crouch, Stephen, 59.
Croumer, Jacob (see Cromer), 261.

Crow, Adam, 197, 391, 528.
Crow, Edmund, 318.
Crow, Thomas, 607.
Crow, William, 42.
Crowd, Jeaneth, 366.
Crowder, John, 67, 387.
Crowder, Saml., 194.
Crowell, Samuel, 428, 429, 474, 505, 530.
Crower, Rudolph, 198, 265.
Crowley, Darby (Darly), 197, 311, 314, 356, 438, 493, 528, 621.
Crowley, Dennis, 195.
Crowley, Edwd. (see Cowley).
Crowson, Ezekiah, 366.
Crozier, James, 345, 358, 430, 498, 529.
Crozier, John, 194.
Cruckley (see Crutchley).
Cruell, John, 99.
Crumm, Adam, 100.
Crummet, Jacob, 182.
Crummy, Andrew, 358, 441, 497, 528.
Crumpton, Igns. (see Compton), 341.
Crumwell (see Cromwell).
Crush (see Grosh).
Crutchley (Cruckley), Benjamin, 98, 407.
Cry, John, 646.
Cudwick, Lewis, 276.
Culbertson (Colberston, Culbertston), Wm., 664, 667, 570, 674.
Cullanan (see Callahan).
Cullember, Natbl., 33.
Cullen, John, 276.
Cullenber, John (see Callender), 34.
Cullimane, Jerema., 98.
Cullin, David, 70.
Cullinane, Dennis, 96.
Culling, James, 96.
Cullip, William, 95.
Cullis, John, 91.
Cullomine, John, 96.
Cullumber, Thomas, 395.
Culpepper, William, 607.
Culver, Benj., 401.
Culver, Levin, 339.
Culver, Stephen, 339.
Culver, Thomas, 42.
Cumber, Christian, 72.
Cumings (see Cummins).
Cummings, Alexander, 607, 655.
Cummings, Nathaniel, 407.
Cummings (Comming), William, 197, 391, 439, 507, 528.
Cummins, Anthony, 58.
Cummins, Ephram, 95.
Cummins, John, 70, 586.
Cummins (Cumings), Richard, 58, 507, 528.
Cummins, Thomas, 52.
Cumpton (see Compton).
Cunden (see Condon).

678   Index.

Cuningham, Carbery, 647.
Cunius (Cunnius), William (see Kunius), 266.
Cunningham, George, 647.
Cunningham (Cunnigham), James, 50, 196, 350.
Cunningham, John, 63, 92, 275, 563, 566.
Cunningham, Jonathan, 60, 322.
Cunningham, Joseph, 97.
Cunningham, Lewis, 443, 504, 528.
Cunningham, Owen, 615.
Cunningham, Peter, 196, 311, 630.
Cunningham, Thomas, 11, 100.
Cunningham, Thompson, 655.
Cunningham, Wm., 60.
Cupit, John, 99.
Curley (Curly), Owen, 198, 262, 447.
Curll (Curl, Carll), John, 395, 400, 402, 455, 511, 529.
Curran, Robert, 196.
Curren, James, 197, 341, 474, 511, 528, 617.
Current, Barnaby, 70.
Current, James, 94, 391, 632.
Currier, Benomi, 61.
Currill, John, 91.
Currington, John, 43.
Currye (or Corry), James, 56.
Curtain, John, 65.
Curties (see Curtis).
Curtin, William, 342.
Curtis, Benj., 22.
Curtis (Curties), John, 564, 567, 570, 573, 574.
Curtis, Michael, 356, 380, 438, 493, 529.
Curtis, Robert, 55.
Curtis, Samuel, 407.
Curtis, Thomas, 320, 384, 407, 601.
Curtis, William, 276.
Curts (Cortz, Courts), Christopher, 50, 194.
Curtz (Cortz), Michl., 19, 51.
Curwell, Peter, 194.
Cusber, John, 475.
Cushman, James, 96.
Cusick (Cusack), Christopher, 194, 347, 353, 440, 487, 528.
Cusick, Luke, 30.
Cusick, Michael, 93.
Custgrove, Mathias (see Cosgrove), 267.
Cuthart, John, 459.
Cuthbert, Wm., 649.
Cutler, William, 93, 396, 445, 507, 527.
Cutmore (Outmare), Joshua, 419, 470.

Cutong, Peter, 313.
Cypher (Cyphert), Jeremiah, 427, 474.
Cypher (Ciferd, Sypher, Sifer), John, 2, 197, 309, 325.
Cyphert, Mathias (Matthias) (see Sipher), 448, 483, 495, 529.
Cypress, William, 98.

Da——, Thomas, 653.
Dabney, Chas., 622.
Dace, Michael, 318.
Dacorne (Decorn), John, 201, 333.
Dadisman (Daddisman), George, 421, 467, 503, 532.
Dads, John, 370.
Daefney, John, 655.
Daemon, Charles, 593.
Daffin, James, 105, 359, 531.
Dailey, Benj., 329.
Dailey (Dayley, Delany), John, 102, 201, 202, 307, 345.
Dailey, Joseph, 30.
Dailey (Dayley), Patrick, 72, 103, 200.
Dailey (Daily), Thomas (see Daley), 67, 102.
Daily, Philip, 103.
Daily, Samuel, 32.
Daken, James, 103.
Dalby (Dolby), Daniel, 103, 277.
Daley, Daniel, 61.
Daley, Matthew, 41, 467, 503.
Daley, Thomas (see Dailey), 294, 322.
Dallam, Bryan, 592.
Dallam Richd., 344.
Dalton, John, 203, 320, 416.
Dalvin (or Delvin), Richard (see Dolvin), 396.
Daly, James (see Dayly), 100, 641.
Dalziell, Thomas, 277.
Dames, John, 65, 66, 645.
Damnitz, John, 55.
Danelly (see Donnelly).
Daniel, Benj. (see Donnelly), 418, 468.
Daniel, Jno. Natl., 103.
Daniels, Jacob, 278.
Danks, John, 109.
Dannahugh, Wm., 405.
Dannally (Dannaly) (see Donnally).
Danroth (Danruth), Gottlieb (Godlib), 203, 265.
Danroth, Lorentz, 265.
Danster (see Dunster).
Dapson, James, 199.
Darah, John, 199.
Darby, Daniel, 60, 343.
Darby, John, 201.
Dare, Willm., 327.
Darling, Robert, 104, 415.

Darlington, Joseph, 58.
Darnall (Darnell), James, 385, 397, 459.
Darrough (Dorough, Durough), John, 278, 348, 440.
Dashiell, Joseph, 372.
Dashiell, Wm., 103.
Dashiell, Wm. Augustus, 20, 519.
D'Ascan, Modesto, 615.
Date (or Deale), Isaac, 418.
Daugharty, Edmd. (see Dougherty), 648.
Daugherty (Dehorty), Daniel, 66.
Daugherty (Dehorty), Jonas, 66.
Daugherty, Michael (see Dougherty), 343, 648.
Daugherty (or Daugerty), Patrick, 72.
Daugherty, Roger, 62.
Dauherty, William, 63.
Daulton (see Dolton).
Davaun, Michael, 101.
Davenport, Adrian (see Devenport), 303.
Davenport, Jeremiah, 375.
Daves, William (see Davis), 198.
Davett, Henry, 200.
Davey, Daniel, 401.
Davey (Davie), Thomas, 30, 278.
Davice, Enious (see Davis).
David, George, 72.
David, Henry, 440.
David, Valentine, 407.
Davids, Walter C. (Walter Chas., C. W.), 104, 449, 623.
Davidson, Allen, 202, 306.
Davidson, Geo., 102.
Davidson, J. (see Slocum), 162.
Davidson, James, 41, 101, 202, 318, 370, 396, 407, 455, 485, 531, 533.
Davidson, John (Capt., Maj.), 25, 62, 102, 349, 364, 380, 428, 445, 481, 483, 519, 620, 648.
Davidson, Luke, 202.
Davie (see Davey).
Davies, Gerrard, 32.
Davies, John (see Davis), 467, 647.
Davies, Lewis (see Davis), 474.
Davies, Lodowick (see Davis), 44.
Davies, Peter (see Davis), 583, 584.
Davies, Rezin (see Davis), 616.
Davies, Samuel (see Davis), 437, 506.
Davies, Thos. (see Davis), 450, 487.

Davies, William (see Davis), 583.
Davis, Amos, 345.
Davis, Caleb, 382, 407.
Davis, Charles, 398, 422, 471, 533.
Davis, Cornelius, 407.
Davis, David, 105, 377, 383, 407, 612, 613.
Davis, Edward, 103, 295.
Davis, (Davice), Enus (Enious), 101, 331.
Davis (Davice), Evans (Even), 202, 308.
Davis, Griffith, 108.
Davis, Henry, 68, 201, 348.
Davis, Ignatius, 39.
Davis, Isaac, 396.
Davis, James, 105.
Davis, Jesse (Jese), 377, 407, 602.
Davis (Davise), John (see Davies), 53, 103, 105, 200, 202, 278, 311, 341, 369, 394, 405, 419, 504, 532, 533, 607, 632, 651, 655.
Davis (Davise), Joseph, 34, 105, 278.
Davis, Levi (Levy), 105, 351.
Davis, Levin, 22.
Davis, Lewis (see Davies), 428.
Davis (or Davies), Lodowick, 44.
Davis, Manl., 608.
Davis, Michael, 13.
Davis, Notley, 20.
Davis, Peter (see Davies), 407, 578.
Davis, Philemon, 199, 278, 645, 651.
Davis, Philip, 39.
Davis, Reazin (see Davies), 365, 519.
Davis, Richard, 28, 100, 201, 301, 302.
Davis, Robert, 41, 200, 348, 531.
Davis, Samuel (see Davies), 63, 200, 202, 311, 323, 380, 396, 428, 531, 532, 646.
Davis, Thomas (see Davies), 24, 66, 104, 201, 377, 397, 402, 532, 622.
Davis (Daves), William (see Davies), 22, 49, 51, 100, 101, 198, 201, 277, 278, 399, 576, 580, 595, 607, 646, 651, 655.
Davis, Zachariah, 32.
Davison, John (see Dawson), 202.
Davitt, George, 356.
Davoir, Cornelius, 105.
Davy, Edward, 199.
Daw, Edward, 342.
Daw (Dawe), George, 340, 360, 627.
Dawer, James, 464.
Dawes, Richard, 575.

Dawkins, Charles, 101, 531.
Dawling (or Dowling), Thos., 70.
Daws, Thomas, 9.
Dawson, Andrew, 198.
Dawson, Benjamin, 602.
Dawson, George, 384, 385, 402.
Dawson, James, 104, 418, 469, 507, 532.
Dawson (Davison), John, 199, 202, 312, 334, 614.
Dawson, Joseph, 62, 199, 610.
Dawson, Nathl., 61.
Dawson, Peter, 422, 471.
Dawson, Ralph, 615.
Dawson, Robert, 645.
Dawson, Thomas, 407.
Dawson, William, 101, 395, 450, 497, 532.
Day, Francis, 201.
Day, George, 647.
Day, Jacob, 103.
Day, Jesse, 34.
Day, John, 102, 294, 320, 646.
Day, Nicholas, 58.
Day, Owen, 339.
Day, Robert, 39.
Day, Samuel, 34, 200.
Day, William, 441, 533, 572.
Dayley, John (see Dailey).
Dayley, Patrick (see Dailey).
Dayley, Peter, 38.
Dayly, James (see Daly), 101.
Daymond, George, 35.
D'Courcy (see De Courcy).
Deacon, John, 338.
Deacon, Pierce, 105, 351, 420, 470, 533.
Deacon (Deacons), William, 562, 598.
Deakins, Francis, 43, 48, 49, 50.
Deakins, John, 393, 446, 507, 531, 626.
Deakins, Leonard, 42, 43.
Deakins, Will., Jr., 43, 44.
Deal, Noble (see Dean), 102.
Deale, George, 50.
Deale, Henry, 407.
Deale (Deal, Date), Isaac (Isaack), 418, 467, 504, 532.
Deale, John, 39, 102.
Deale, Joseph, 34, 572.
Deam, Frederick, 304.
Dean (Deane), Charles, 368, 395, 451, 497, 532.
Dean, David, 600.
Dean, Edward, 102, 293.
Dean (Deane), Elijah (see Dee), 199, 531.
Dean, George, 103.
Dean (Deane), John (Major), 65, 103, 105, 198, 363, 378, 383, 397, 402, 407, 479, 519, 532, 616.

Dean, Noble (see Deal), 294.
Dean (Deane), Robert, 419, 467, 503, 532.
Dean (Deane), Rodger, 51, 202.
Dean, Thomas, 199.
Deane, Francis, 105.
Dearlove, James, 277.
Dearmond, Neal, 12.
Dearmott, John, 400.
Dearmott, Thos., 302.
Dease, Michael, 105, 415.
Deaver (Dever), Aquilla (see Diver), 103, 396, 512, 531.
Deaver, David, 400.
Deaver, John, 102.
Deaver, Michael, 20.
Deaver, Samuel, 407.
Deaver, William, 103, 531, 617.
Deavond (see Deavour).
Deavour, Misail, 369.
Deavour (Deavond), Thomas, 562, 598.
Debora (Debore), Jacobus, 102, 441.
Debrular, John, 105, 301.
Decamp, Henry, 72.
Decamp, Peter, 626.
Decker, Henry, 265.
Decorn (see Dacorne).
De Courcey, Wm., 606.
De Courcy (D'Courcy, Courcy), Edward (D.), 28, 616.
Dee (or Dean), Elijah, 199.
Deefhem (or Deefherr). Fredk., 328.
Deford, Charles, 66.
Deford, Jesse, 198.
Deford, John, 199.
Deford, Joseph, 199, 532.
Deford, William, 66, 654.
Degazoone, Peter, 355, 460, 491, 531.
Dehorty (see Daugherty).
Deilman, John (see Dilman), 652.
Deitch (Dych), John Bartholomew, 266.
Deiver (or Devier), Hugh, 56.
Dela Franey (Delafrany, Delefraney), John Baptis (John B.), 33, 200, 327.
Delahay, Henry, 371.
Delanaway, John (see Delany), 66, 201, 531.
Delanaway, Thos., 651.
Deland, Roger, 58.
Delany, Chas., 335.
Delany, Edward, 104.
Delany (Delaney), James, 278, 293.
Delany, John (see Dailey and Delanaway), 202, 358, 463, 498, 531.

Delany, Nicholas, 200, 304.
Delany, William, 568, 574.
De Laplan, De Segond, 592.
Delawter, Henry, 261.
Delefraney (see Dela Franey).
Deliazon, Peter, 104.
Delihay, William, 643.
Delisle, O., 615.
Dellen, Theobald, 278.
Dellin, Roger, 59.
Delon (or Dolon), Peter, 200.
Delong, Bartholomew, 656.
Deloray, Barth., 607.
Delozior (Delozier), William, 101, 331.
Delvin, Richard (see Dalvin), 396.
Demar, Francis, 358, 431, 496, 531.
Demay, John, 104.
Demby (Dimby), Richard, 372, 396.
Demkin, Wm. (see Dunkin), 360.
Dempsey (Demsey, Dimpsey, Dimsey), Luke, 103, 354, 436, 490, 531.
Denaho, John, 105.
Denbugh, Wm., 104.
Denby (Dunby), Richard, 455, 488, 532.
Denear, Francis, 101.
Deneley (see Donelly).
Denion, John (see Dennison), 495.
Denison (see Dennisson).
Denmass, Wm., 105.
Denn, Edward, 201.
Dennerivay, Wm., 305.
Denney, John, 62.
Dennis, Adkins, 372.
Dennis, Basil, 200.
Dennis, Dunnick (Dunick), 22, 102.
Dennis, Edward, 103.
Dennis, Henry, 105, 303, 350.
Dennis, Jesse, 30.
Dennis, John, 60, 61.
Dennis, Joseph, 607, 656.
Dennis, Paul (see Donovan), 101.
Dennis, Peter, 330.
Dennison, James, 103, 301, 533.
Dennison (Denison, Denion), John, 202, 310, 357, 495.
Dennison, Patrick, 105, 358, 460, 498, 532.
Dennison, William, 198.
Dennison (or Denison), Richard, 39.
Denniston, James, 105, 350.
Denny, Oliver, 393, 401, 452.
Denny, Peter, 101.

Denny, Robert (R., Lt., ——), 201, 364, 381, 392, 397, 398, 404, 420, 421, 427, 481, 483, 519, 616, 617, 627.
Denny (Denney), Samuel, 19, 202, 388, 531.
Denoone (Denoon), John, 201, 347, 439, 502, 531.
Denshon, James, 103.
Denson, Isaac, 190.
Denson, John, 446, 531.
Denston, John, 102.
Dent, George, 31, 102, 329.
Dent, George, of John, 31.
Dent, Hatch, 18, 101, 616.
Dent, John, 32, 102, 103, 532, 605, 661.
Dent, Samuel, 377, 407.
Dent, Walter, 399.
Denton, Edward, 33.
Denton, James, 103.
Denwood, Levin, 103, 202, 363, 380, 408, 483, 519.
Deoran, James, 278.
Derinton, Elisha, 601.
Derling, Robert, 319.
De Roachbroom (Derochbroom), John, 385, 407.
Derrington, Francis, 104.
Derrington, Willm., 354, 436, 489, 532.
Derry, Michal, 105.
Dervin (or Duvin), Wm. (see Devine), 420.
De Segond, Capt., 592.
Deshield, Benjamin, 28.
De Shields (Dushield), Frans., 565, 566, 568.
Desire (Dewire), James, 104, 623.
Deskey, John, 446.
Désormeaux (Desormaux), Baptiste, 312, 334.
Detrow, Jacob, 395.
De Vaubrunne (De Vauburn), Levache (Levacher), 364, 380, 481.
Devaun, James, 17, 100.
Deven, James (see Devin), 36.
Devenish, George, 202.
Devenport, Adam (see Davenport), 105.
Dever (see Deaver).
Deveraux (Deveraue, Deverix, Devericks), William, 426, 468, 504, 532.
Devereaux, Jno., 101.
Devereaux (Deveraux, Devereux, Deverex, Devericks), James, 24, 101, 201, 278, 348, 353, 440, 487, 531.
Devier (see Deiver).
Devin (see Deven), James, 102, 331.
Devine, Barney, 60.
Devine, Daniel, 341.
Devine, Dennis, 100, 432, 644.

680 *Index.*

Devine (Devin), William (see Dervin), 464, 500, 532.
Devinns, Emanl., 101.
Devire, Darby, 105.
Devitt (Devit), George, 202, 311, 389, 438, 492, 531.
Devitt, Valentine, 407, 653.
Devo, Buto (or Brito), 432, 532.
Devons, Charles, 375.
Devonshire, George, 341.
Devorah, Butes, 101.
Devorant (Durrant), John (see Durant), 312.
Devorix, Thomas, 66.
Dew, John, 36.
Dewall, Richard, 353, 487.
Dewell, Thomas, 100.
Dewes (Dews), Edwd., 340, 360.
Dewire (see Desire).
Dewist (De Wist, Dewiss), Francis, 105, 351, 352, 398, 420, 464, 500, 532.
Dicamon, Manl. 608.
Dice (see Dyce).
Dice (or Dues), James, 190.
Dick——, ——, 566.
Dick, Hart., 277, 564.
Dick, John, 70.
Dick, Negro, 385.
Dick, Peter, 72.
Dickason, Wm., 200.
Dicke, Daniel, 656.
Dickenson, Thos., 405, 466.
Dickerson, Solomon, 42.
Dickerson, Thomas, 502.
Dickerson, Wm., 462.
Dickeson, John, 199.
Dickeson, Thomas, 532.
Dickett, Jno., 278.
Dickinson, William, 378.
Dickman, Wm., 305.
Dicks, George, 278.
Dicks, Jno., 51, 378, 407.
Dickson, Henry (see Dixon), 330.
Dickson, James, 70.
Dickson, John (see Dixon), 311, 656.
Dickson, Richard (see Dixon), 453.
Digman, Peter (see Sigman), 51.
Digman, Willm., 23.
Dignam, Christn., 100.
Dill, John, 18.
Dillon, James, 201.
Dillon (Dillen, Dilling), Jeremiah (Jerremiah), 307, 402, 416.
Dillon (Dillin), William, 102, 298, 359, 429, 531.
Dilman, John (see Deilman), 407.
Dimby (see Demby).
Dimond, Charles, 67, 199.
Dimpsey (Dimsey) (see Dempsey).

Dinet, Daniel, 27.
Dingle, William, 27, 643.
Diragin (or Duregin), John, 69.
Disheroon, Thos., 202.
Disman, Dennis, 394.
Disney, Ezekiel, 606, 656.
Disney, James, 15, 38, 41.
Disney, Richard, Jr., 41.
Diver, Aquilla (see Deaver), 430.
Divers, William, 51.
Dixon, Ellis, 33.
Dixon, George, 102, 354, 437, 480, 531.
Dixon (Dickson), Henry (Hanry), 101, 330, 359, 531.
Dixon (Dickson, Dixson, Dyxson), John (see Hickson), 101, 201, 202, 278, 311, 432, 503, 656.
Dixon, Joseph, 639.
Dixon (Dickson), Richard, 201, 278, 393, 453, 493, 532.
Dixon, Samuel, 318.
Dixon, Solomon, 384, 407.
Dixon, William, 49, 201, 414, 579, 583, 614.
Dixson, Jacob, 32.
Dixson (Dyxson), John (see Dixon), 432, 503.
Dixson, Thomas, 63.
Diz, George, 393.
Doblin, Edward, 190.
Dobson, Henry (Capt., Major), 73, 200, 346, 363, 370, 480, 518.
Dobson, Isaac, 388.
Dobson, John, 25, 383, 397, 402, 459, 532, 600.
Dobson, Joseph, 375.
Dobson, Samuel (see Dodson), 407.
Dobson, William, 407, 653.
Dochterman, Michael, 263.
Dodd, James, 202, 325.
Dodson, John, 101, 313.
Dodson, Michael, 46, 104.
Dodson, Samuel (see Dobson), 653.
Dodson (Doddson), William, 202, 309, 326.
Dogan (see Dugan).
Dogherty, Neil, 43.
Doherty, Arthur, 104.
Doherty (Doherty), Barney (see Dougherty).
Doherty, Jesse (see Dority), 101.
Doice, Dennis, 305.
Dolan, Dennis, 416.
Dolby (see Dalby).
Dolcy, Matthew, 532.
Doling, Barnabas, 415.
Dollison, James, 103, 297.
Dolly, James, 28.
Dolon (see Delon).
Dolton, Jacob, 267.

Dolton (Daulton) Peter, 57, 102.
Doltrey, Jesse, 317.
Dolvin, Richard (see Dalvin), 372, 454, 485, 532.
Dominick, Benja., 200, 348, 533.
Dominick (Dominic), Edward, 342, 461, 507, 531.
Dommit, William, 103.
Don——, Patrick, 653.
Donack, John, 45.
Donaghey, Arthur, 319.
Donahue (see Donohou).
Donald, George, 278.
Donaldson, John, 23.
Donaldson, Phil., 102.
Donaldson, Samuel, 22.
Donaldson, Thomas, 22.
Donaldson, Wm., 202, 618.
Donans, Dennis, 626.
Donavin, John (see Donovan), 607, 656.
Doncan (see Duncan and Dunkin).
Doncaster, James, 342.
Done, James, 21.
Donent, John, 202.
Donlon, Thedy, 653.
Donlon (Donlan), Timothy, 397, 402.
Donnald (Donnold), John, 419, 470.
Donnally (Dannally, Dannaly, Donoly), Edward, 63, 592, 593, 594.
Donnally, Patrick (see Donnelly), 200, 201.
Donnalson (Donoldson), Wm., 307.
Donnaly, Jas. (see Donnelly), 294.
Donnavan (Donavan) (see Donovan).
Donnelly (Donelly, Daniel,) Benj., 468, 504, 532.
Donnelly (Donelly), Caleb (see Donnolly), 200, 348.
Donnelly, James (see Donnaly), 294.
Donnelly (Donneley, Danelly, Deneley), Patrick (Pattrick, —) (see Donnally, 46, 362, 378, 407, 647.
Donnelly, Timothy, 459.
Donnoho (see Donoho).
Donnoliton, William, 31.
Donnolly (Donoly), Caleb (Calab) (see Donnelly, 63, 414.
Donnovin (see Donovan).
Donnowin (see Donovan).
Donogan, James, 532.
Donoghue (see Donohou).
Donoho (Donohoo, Donnoho), Joseph, 335, 357, 446, 495, 531.
Donoho, Wm., 397, 459.
Donohou, Bartho. (see Donohue), 570.

Donohou (Donoghue, Donahue), Danl. (Da—), 564, 567, 569.
Donohue (Donohou), Bartholomew, 52, 570.
Donolan, Thomas, 12.
Donoldson (see Donnalson).
Donoly, Edward (see Donnally), 63.
Donovan (Donnowin), Daniel, 65, 200, 304.
Donovan (Dunavan), James, 334, 335.
Donovan, Jeremh., 100.
Donovan (Donnavan, Donavin, Dunnevan), John, 58, 104, 277, 414, 531, 607, 656.
Donovan (or Dennis), Paul, 101.
Donovan (Donnavan, Donavan), Peter, 56, 102, 290.
Donovan (Donavan), Richard, 59, 75, 200, 518.
Donovan (Donnavan, Donnovin, Dunnavin), Timothy, 565, 567, 570, 574, 583.
Donovan (Donavan), William, 201, 202.
Doogan, Abraham (Abram, Ebram) (see Dugan).
Doogan, James, 63.
Dooley (Douly), William (see Duley), 562, 598.
Dorah (see Doron).
Doran, Barnaba, 104.
Doran (Doren), Michael, 199, 340, 360.
Doran, P., 153.
Doran, Patrick, 60, 200, 347, 355, 441, 531.
Doran, Peter, 491.
Dorch, William (see Dortch), 432, 509, 531.
Doren, James, 599.
Dorgin, John, 68.
Dorhorty, Francis, 104.
Doring, Michael, 394.
Doring, Mitchal, 627.
Dority, Jesse (see Doherty), 318.
Dorman, Major, 407.
Dorman, Thomas, 202, 311.
Dorman, William, 69.
Doron, Dineas (or Dorah, Dinnis), 268.
Dorough, John (see Darrough), 348.
Dorsey, Basil (Bassell, Basil J.), 422, 467, 503, 532.
Dorsey, Charles, 40, 105.
Dorsey, Col., 320.
Dorsey, Daniel, 38.
Dorsey, Edwd., 369.
Dorsey, Ely (Elie), 21, 102, 616.
Dorsey, Henry, 407.

Dorsey, John, 39, 199.
Dorsey, John Hammond, 393, 401, 450.
Dorsey, John Worthington, 38, 39.
Dorsey, Joseph, 656.
Dorsey, Joshua, 103.
Dorsey, Larkin, 18.
Dorsey, Levin (Leven, Leaven), 59, 200, 569.
Dorsey, Martin, 70, 277.
Dorsey, Nathan, 607.
Dorsey, Nicholas, 104.
Dorsey, Richard (Capt.), 18, 365, 477, 568, 573, 574, 575, 578, 581, 618, 656.
Dorsey, Stephen, 54.
Dorsey, Thomas, 41.
Dorsey, Vachel, 41.
Dortch, William (see Dorch), 101.
Dorton, William, 377.
Dotton, Peter, 300.
Dotts, George, 72.
Douch, William, 277.
Dougan, Abraham (see Dugan).
Dougherty (Dougharty, Doherty, Dohorty), Barnaba (Barnaby, Barns, Barney), 199, 393, 451, 507, 532, 623.
Dougherty (Dougherly), Dennis, 305.
Dougherty, Edmund (see Daugharty), 531.
Dougherty, Edward, 105.
Dougherty, John, 105, 423, 471.
Dougherty, Michael (see Daugherty), 200, 304, 422, 471.
Douglas, Danl., 401.
Douglass (Douglas), Archibald, 606, 656.
Douglass (Doyglass), Igns., 5, 100.
Douglass (Duglas), James, 104, 334, 335.
Douglass (Doughlas), William, 105, 335, 398, 456, 656.
Douly (see Dooley).
Doun, James, 277.
Dove, John, 202, 397, 514, 515, 516, 533.
Dove, Willm., Jr., 39.
Dowden, James, 105, 351, 352, 420, 465, 500, 532.
Dowdle, William, 587, 588, 589, 590.
Dowen, Nicholas, 105.
Dowes William, 102.
Dowlen, James, 391.
Dowlin, Roger, 349.
Dowling, Geo., 15.
Dowling, James, 101, 201.
Dowling, John, 277.
Dowling, Roger, 199.

Dowling, Thos. (see Dawling), 70.
Downed, Sammerset, 429.
Downes, Acquilla, 66.
Downes (Downs), Dennis, 343, 394, 445.
Downes, Edward, 645.
Downes, Henry, 68.
Downes, James, 101.
Downes (Downs), Lodman, 66, 198.
Downes (Downs), Michael, 394, 448, 453.
Downes (Downs), Richard, 202, 341, 342, 445, 533.
Downes (Downs), William, 104, 415, 454, 509, 531.
Downey (Downy), Alex., 199, 352, 434, 532.
Downey (or Dawney), Bartholomew, 57.
Downey, Cornelius, 72, 202.
Downey, Dennis, 103, 199.
Downey, Fredk. (see Tawney), 266.
Downey (Downy), John, 60, 103, 199, 352, 433, 531.
Downey, Pat., 63.
Downey, Peter Equed (see Equidowney), 455.
Downing, Deweast, 26, 643
Downing, Francis, 43.
Downing, James, 32, 615.
Downing, John, 38.
Downing, Nathaniel, 6, 100.
Downing, Saml., 101.
Downs, Bartholomew, 60.
Downs, Ignatius, 329.
Dowse, John, 642.
Doyal (Doyall) (see Doyle).
Doyer, Peter, 103.
Doyglass (see Douglass).
Doyle, Capt., 509.
Doyle, Dennis, 53.
Doyle (Doyl), Hugh, 201, 306.
Doyle (or Doyne), Jacob, 532.
Doyle (Doyl), James, 199, 352, 433, 531.
Doyle, John, 201.
Doyle (Doyal), Martin, 101, 330.
Doyle, Richard, 12.
Doyle (Doyl, Doyall), Thomas, 64, 104, 531.
Doyne, Jacob, 392, 429, 448, 509, 532.
Dozens, Isaac, 59.
Dozens, Jacob, 59.
Dozens, Wm. Gray, 59.
Draden, James, 336.
Drake, Richard, 101.
Drake, Robert, 44.
Draper, John (see Drapier), 102, 294.
Draper, Thomas, 103.
Draper, William, 43.
Drapier, John (see Draper), 322.

Dretch, John, 203.
Drew, Lieut., 601.
Drewitt, William, 53.
Driscoll, Jeremiah (see Driskill), 532.
Drishell, Jeremiah, 104.
Driskell, Dennis, 21.
Driskill (Driskell, Driscoll), Jeremiah, 68, 474, 511, 532, 605.
Driskill, John, 656.
Driskill, Timothy, 58.
Driver, James, 201, 383, 397, 402, 462, 491, 532.
Driver, John, 103, 295.
Drome, Wm., 46.
Drown, Thomas, 37.
Drowns, Robert, 105.
Drudge (Drudges), Thomas, 104, 430, 511, 531.
Drudo (or Dudderow), Jacob (see Dudderow), 497.
Druly, Samuel, 335.
Drury, John, 104.
Drury, John Barton, 330.
Drury (Drurey), Joseph, 102, 331.
Drury, Robt. B., 102.
Drury, Thomas, 277.
Ducasy, John, 278.
Ducater, Jno., 103.
Ducey, William, 101.
Dudderow (Dudderro, Duddera, Drudo, Tuddero), Jacob, 261, 450, 497, 532.
Dudley, Joseph, 102.
Dudley, William, 66.
Due, James, 353, 394, 463, 487, 532.
Dueberry, Joseph, 649.
Duel, Charles, 101.
Dues (see Dice).
Duff, Thomas (see Dusft), 343.
Duffee (see Duffey).
Duffey, Alex., 607.
Duffey (Duffee), Francis, 394, 445, 532.
Duffey (Duffy), John, 62, 202, 305, 311.
Duffey (Duffy, Duffee), Michael, 104, 562, 661, 623.
Duffey (Duffy, Duffee), Terrence, 200, 312, 381, 393, 445, 506, 532.
Duffey (Duffee), Thomas, 397, 402, 407, 458, 506, 532.
Duffield, William, 647.
Dufft (see Dusft).
Dugan (Doogan, Dougan, Dogan), Abraham (Abram, Ebram), 396, 405, 455, 498, 532.
Dugan, Danl., 101.
Dugan, Edward, 200.
Dugan, John, 562, 598.
Dugan (Duggan), Paul, 104, 562, 600.

Dugan, William, 65.
Duggins, Henry, 32.
Duglas (see Douglass).
Duhague, John, 199, 435, 485, 531.
Duis (see Dyers).
Dulany, Daniel, 342.
Dulany, Edward, 58.
Dulany, James, 102, 339.
Duley, Nathan (see Duling), 102, 293.
Duley, Saml., 200.
Duley (Duly), William (see Dooley), 59, 201, 306, 562.
Duling, Delahay, 24.
Duling, John, 370.
Duling, Nathan (see Duley), 24, 102.
Dullis, Charles, 45.
Duly (see Duley).
Dumatt, Edward, 50.
Dun (see Dunn).
Dunavan, James (see Donovan), 334.
Dunbar, Joseph, 607, 656.
Dunbar, Saml., 200.
Dunby, Richard (see Denby), 455, 532.
Duncan (Doncan), Daniel, 396, 454.
Duncan (Dunken, Dunkin), George, 342, 355, 441, 491, 532.
Duncan (Dunken, Dunkin, Doncan), Isaac, 69, 426, 465, 501, 532.
Duncan (Dunkin), James, 51, 203, 264, 598.
Duncan, Jessee, 202.
Duncan (Dunkin), John, 46, 102, 300.
Duncan (Dunken, Dunkin), Robert, 202, 311, 356, 380, 438, 493, 531.
Duncaster, John, 329.
Dunham, Aquilla, 649.
Dunkin (Doncan, Demkin), William, 360, 395.
Dunkle, Mathias, 264.
Dunn, Anthony, 64.
Dunn, Dennis, 101.
Dunn, James, Jr., 64.
Dunn, John, 9, 26, 278, 339, 643.
Dunn (Dun), Patrick, 199, 575, 581.
Dunn, Thomas, 103.
Dunn, William, 407, 414, 417, 467, 504, 532, 615, 652.
Dunnagan (Dunnegan, Dunnigan), John (see Dunnevan), 104, 457, 486.
Dunnavin (see Donovan).
Dunnevan, John (see Donovan), 58, 104.
Dunning, Dennis, 101, 431, 501, 531.
Dunning, James, 376, 407.

Dunnington (Dunington), Francis, 333, 437, 511, 531.
Dunnington, Hezekiah, 31.
Dunnington, Jer., 104.
Dunnington (Dunington), Wm., 108, 104, 296.
Dunster (Danster), John, 104, 619.
Dunster, Peter, 200.
Dunsyre, William, 52.
Duply, Col., 576.
Dupre, John, 333.
Durant (Durrant, Devorant), John, 312, 394, 453.
Durbin (Durbinn), John, 105, 598.
Durdin, Thomas, 656.
Duregin (see Diragin).
Durgan, Anthony, 200, 326.
Durgan, James, 199.
Durgan, Patrick, 199.
Durham, William, 59, 200, 348, 414.
Durnor, Thomas, 105.
Durough, John (see Darrough), 440.
Durrant (Devorant), John (see Durant), 312.
Dustt (or Dufft), Thomas (see Duff), 59.
Dushield (see De Shields).
Dusky, Jonathn., 102.
Dutch, Mathias (see Dytch), 199.
Dutterer, John, 47.
Dutton, George, 103.
Dutton, Notley, 100, 101.
Dutton, Thomas, 101, 331, 533.
Duvall, Benj., 36, 200, 382, 407.
Duvall, Edward (———), 102, 481, 616.
Duvall, G., 642, 644.
Duvall (Duvaull), George, 103, 297, 335.
Duvall, Isaac, 102, 296, 362, 378, 519.
Duvall, Joseph, 101, 572.
Duvall, Richard, 200, 349, 407, 440, 531.
Duvall, Samuel, 101, 407.
Duvall, William, 34, 35.
Duvin (see Dervin).
Dwer, William, 278.
Dwigens, Daniel, 14.
Dwigens, Samuel, 14.
Dwire, James, 562.
Dwyer, Darby, 415.
Dwyer, John, 46.
Dwyer (Dwier), Thomas, 13, 105, 415.
Dyace (see Dyce).
Dyal, David, 31.
Dyal, John, 198.
Dyar (see Dyer).
Dyce (Dyace, Dice), Geo., 352, 435, 532.
Dych (Dyche) (see Deitch, Dytch and Dytche).

Dycus, John, 416.
Dye, Benjamin, 51.
Dye, William, 104, 514.
Dyer, Edward (Lt.), 101, 326, 363, 379, 470, 480, 483, 518.
Dyer, George, 328, 443, 513, 532.
Dyer (Dyar), James, 103, 203, 267, 321, 330, 360, 463, 475, 512, 531, 532, 562.
Dyer (Dyar, Dyre), John, 103, 354, 437, 489, 531, 661.
Dyer, Jonathan, 100.
Dyer, Thomas, 101.
Dyer (Dyar), Walter, 35, 103, 363, 365, 380, 476, 480, 501, 519.
Dyer, Wm., 615.
Dyers (or Duis), George, 199.
Dyes, Anthony, 615.
Dyke, Wm., 420.
Dyre (see Dyer).
Dyson, Thos. A. (Thomas), 462, 476, 480, 519.
Dyson, Thos. Andrew, 32.
Dytch, George, 653.
Dytch (Dyche), Matthias (Mathias) (see Dutch), 353, 393, 439, 488, 531.
Dytch (Dych), William, 395, 454.
Dytche (Dyche) Peter, 105, 302.

Eabbs, Emanuel, 396, 455, 533.
Each, Adam, 407.
Eades, Samuel, 64, 646.
Eades, Thomas (see Eddis), 107.
Eadlin (see Edelen and Edelin).
Eagle (Eagill), William, 385, 425, 468, 505, 533.
Eagon (Eagen, Egan), Patrick, 204, 304, 347, 440.
Eakins, Archd., 107.
Eakins, Solomon, 107.
Eamick, Peter, 415.
Earle, Samuel, 65, 645.
Earls, Richard, 107.
Early, Benja., 204.
Earp, Petticoat, 39.
Eashom, Daniel, 372.
Easley, Richard, 371.
Easom, Bartholm. (see Essom), 106.
Easom, Joseph (see Eshome), 106.
Eassen, John, 318.
Easter, Nichs., 204.
Easton, John, 107, 415.
Eaton, Richard, 203, 610, 611, 612, 613.
Eaton, Robert, 395, 421, 451.
Eaton, William, 58, 107.

Ebbs (see Eabbs).
Eccleston, Jarvis, 203, 352, 434, 533.
Eccleston, John (Capt.), 25, 106, 293, 362, 378, 476, 477, 520, 619.
Eck, Adam, 653.
Eckhart, Michael, 594.
Eckister, Thos., 340.
Ecloes, John, 608.
Ecort, Godfrey, 107.
Eddis, Thomas (see Eades), 415.
Eddleman, Michl. (see Edelman), 204.
Eddy, James, 106, 294, 321.
Eddy, Jona., 649.
Edelen, Chris., 73.
Edelen (Eadlin), Edward, 6, 106.
Edelen, Leonard, 36.
Edelen, Richard B., 35.
Edelin, Bartholomew, 43.
Edelin, Basil, 107.
Edelin (Edelen), Clement, 6, 106.
Edelin (Edelen), George, 36, 107.
Edelin, Henry, 107.
Edelin (Eadlin), John, 8, 106.
Edelman, Michael (see Eddleman), 50.
Edes, Edward, 396.
Edes, James, 598.
Edge, Peter, 407, 653.
Edge, Wm., 40.
Edgell, Walter, 385.
Edgerly, Edward (Capt.), 13, 106, 364, 381, 481, 520.
Edgerly, Wm., 203.
Edilen, Franis, 32.
Edison, Thomas, 72.
Edmiston, Samuel, 355, 362, 378, 476, 478, 520.
Edmondson, Archibald, 33.
Edmondson, Sam. (———), 74, 203.
Edmondson, Thomas, 42.
Edmondstone, Geo., 641.
Edmonson, Ninian, 382.
Edmonston, Alexander, 59.
Edmonston, Thomas, 42.
Edwards, Barton, 339.
Edwards, Burton, 203.
Edwards, Edward, 17, 106, 425, 473.
Edwards (Edward), Heathcoat (Hethcoat, Heithcote, Hethesale, Heath C.), 397, 402, 459, 533.
Edwards, Jesse, 33.
Edwards, John, 106, 460, 507, 515, 533, 534, 641.
Edwards, Samuel, 204, 323.
Edwards, Stratton (Struton), 384, 408.
Edwards, Thomas, 107, 353, 456, 485, 533.
Edwards, Wm., 278.
Edwill, John, 581.

Edwis, Richard, 278.
Eggleston, Jos., 588.
Eggman, Jacob, 261.
Eiginor, Benedict, 50.
Eissell (see Eyssell).
Elbert, John L., 482, 483, 520.
Elbon, Mathew, 106.
Elbon, Nathanl., 106.
Elbon, Reubin, 372.
Elbon (Elbom), William, 372, 450.
Elburn, William, 395.
Elcott, John, 488.
Elder, Hugh, 49.
Elexson, Charles, 61.
Eley, David, 47.
Elfry, Godtrey, 203.
Elgin, Harrison, 377, 407.
Elgin, Hezekiah, 377, 408.
Elgin, Richard, 32.
Elgin, Samuel, 31.
Eliason, John, 70.
Elins, George, 533.
Eliott (see Elliott).
Elkins (Elkins), William, 344, 356, 452, 493, 533.
Elkison, William, 388.
Ellas, George, 375.
Elleary (or Hilleary), John (see Hillary), 203.
Ellensworth, Nehemiah, 294.
Ellery, Dennis, 203.
Ellery, John (see Hillary), 348.
Ellicot, Joseph (see Elliott), 533.
Ellicot, Thomas (see Elliott), 533.
Ellicott (Ellicot) (see Elliott), Edward, 106, 500, 533.
Ellicott, Nicholas (see Elliott), 533.
Elliot, Hooper, 27, 644.
Elliott (Ellit), Benja., 49, 204, 266, 323, 416.
Elliott, Edward (see Ellicott), 317, 432.
Elliott, James, 309, 581.
Elliott (Elliot, Eliot), John, 203, 348, 354, 399, 425, 440, 474, 533.
Elliott (Eliott), Joseph (see Ellicot), 13, 66, 203, 347, 353, 440, 489, 645.
Elliott, Mark, 407.
Elliott (Elliot), Nicholas (see Ellicott), 396, 455, 485.
Elliott, Robert, 107.
Elliott, Samuel, 107, 640.
Elliott (Elliotte, Elliot, Eliott, Ellitt), Thomas (see Ellicot), 106, 107, 300, 352, 377, 397, 456, 459, 485, 489, 533.
Elliott, William, 368.
Ellis, Barnard, 106.
Ellis, Benjamin, 38.

Ellis, Brion, 204.
Ellis, John, 49, 107.
Ellis, Joshua, 30.
Ellis, Michael, 106, 533.
Ellis, Richard, 203.
Ellis, Robert, 24, 106.
Ellis (Elliss), Thomas, 107, 204, 342, 345, 355, 492, 533.
Ellis, William, 107, 533, 564, 567, 570.
Ellison, Richard, 204.
Ellison, Thomas (see Allison), 465, 501, 533, 534.
Ellit (Ellitt (see Elliott).
Elkins (see Elkins).
Ellsperger, Wolfgn. (see Ettsperger), 204.
Ellwood (Elwood), Richd., 16, 107, 415.
Elms, George, 30, 203, 469, 510.
Elsing, Paul, 204.
Elson, John, 7.
Eltham, John, 106, 313.
Elvin, John, 204.
Elwood, John, 42.
Elwood, Richard F., 61.
Ely, Thos., 400.
Ely, William, 661.
Emanuel, Peters, 107.
Emerick, Peter (see Hemerick), 218, 262.
Emersly, John (see Hammersly), 268.
Emerton (Emmerton), Henry, 385, 408.
Emmes, Henry, 395.
Emmitt, David, 63.
Emmitt, John, 63.
Emory, Gideon, 203, 645.
Emory (Emmory), John, 23, 106.
Emory, Richard, 203, 645.
Emory, Samuel, 67.
Emory, Thomas Lane, 65, 645.
Emory, William, 67.
Emory, William Wilson, 645.
Empson, John, 68.
Emrich, Joseph, 50.
Engellee (or Angel), Peter, 204.
England, Benja., 204, 263.
England, Wm. (see Ingle), 107.
Engle (Engel), Bartle (Bartel), 204, 261, 262.
English, Danl., 278.
English, Isaac, 340.
English, James, 107.
English, John, 416.
English, Robert, 51.
English, Samuel, 107, 204, 620.
English, Thomas, 615.
English, William (see Inglis and Ingles), 107, 278, 416.
Engram (see Ingram).

Ennis, Enoch, 355, 441, 492, 533.
Ennis (Ennes), George (see Inness), 106, 330.
Ennis, John (see Innis), 355, 441, 491, 533.
Ennis, Leonard, 443, 510, 533.
Ennis, Thomas (see Innis), 107.
Ennis, Wm., 30.
Enniss, Henry, 449.
Enright (see Enwright).
Ensey, Jas., 204.
Ensley (Ensly), Francis (see Insley), 510, 533.
Ensor, Augusteen H., 61.
Enwright (Enright), John, 9, 106, 317, 319.
Eove (or Cove), John, 51.
Equidowney (Equidoroney, Equedoroney, Quidowney, Wedoney, Downey), Peter, 393, 401, 455, 485, 533.
Eppinstall (Eppinstoole), Jno., 395.
Erlinger, Stephen (see Allinger), 428, 475.
Ernest, Christian, 423, 471.
Ervin, Abraham (see Ervin), 106, 641.
Ervine, David, 278.
Ervine, James (see Erwin), 533.
Erving, Edward (see Irvin), 354.
Erwin, James (see Irvine and Ervine), 353, 393, 447, 488.
Eshome, Josh. (see Isham and Easom), 310.
Essom (Esom, Easom, Eshum), Bartholomew, 106, 356, 443, 494, 533.
Estep, Alexander, 42, 203.
Estep, Joseph, 42.
Estup, James, 46.
Etheridge, Jno., 203.
Etherington, John, 61.
Etnier, John (see Itnier), 204, 265.
Etter, Jacob, 204, 265.
Ettleman, George, 46.
Ettsperger, Wilfgang (see Ellsperger), 265.
Ettzinger, Wolfgang, 265.
Eubanks, Thomas (see Ewbanks), 408.
Evans, Alexander, 31.
Evans, Benja., 203, 324.
Evans, Capt., 75.
Evans, David, 305.
Evans (Evins), Edward, 107, 340, 353, 354, 393, 437, 457, 486, 490, 533, 661.
Evans, Elijah, 301, 350, 365, 520.
Evans, Ewill, 393.
Evans, Griffith, 400, 649.

Evans, Henry (see Evis), 55, 445, 495.
Evans, Hooper, 70.
Evans, James, 41, 302, 396, 455, 485, 533.
Evans, Jesse, 31.
Evans, John, 44, 107, 203, 204, 576, 580, 582, 583.
Evans, Mcl., 534.
Evans (Evins), Peregrine (Perry), 24, 106, 467, 503, 533.
Evans, Richard, 203.
Evans, Robert, 62, 656.
Evans, Samuel, 73, 382, 394, 416, 460, 496, 533.
Evans (Evins), Thomas, 107, 203, 278, 295, 336, 358, 427, 432, 436, 497, 509, 533, 562.
Evans, Walter, 402, 458.
Evans (Evins), William, 8, 34, 106, 107, 203, 346, 457, 506, 533, 661.
Evans, Zachariah, 44.
Evauns, George, 10.
Everett, Elihu, 408.
Everett (Everit), Elisha, 8, 106.
Everett (Everit, Everitt), Richard, 33, 204, 327.
Everett, Thomas, 33.
Everett, Willm., 40.
Everitt, Benjamin, 63.
Everitt, John, 40.
Everitt, Joseph, 106.
Everley, Leonard, 261.
Everly, Adam, 18.
Evins (see Evans).
Evis, Henry (see Evans), 495, 533.
Evitt, Henry, 393.
Ewbanks, Jona., 203.
Ewbanks, Richd., 203, 612.
Ewbanks (Eubanks), Thos., 408, 611, 613.
Ewens, John, 372.
Ewing, James (——), 106, 362, 378, 426, 481, 482, 483, 520, 627.
Ewing, James, 106, 362, 378, 426, 481, 483, 520, 627.
Ewing, Nathaniel, 13, 106.
Ewing, Samuel, 106.
Ewing, Thomas, 11, 30, 54.
Eyen, Frederick, 583.
Fyles, Samuel, 107, 414.
Eyre, John, 107, 414.
Eyssell (Eissell), John, 204, 266.

F——, George, 461.
Fagan, Charles, 110.
Fahay, David, 53.
Fain, Michael, 109.
Fair, John, 595.
Fairbairn, Wm. (see Fairburn), 617.
Fairbank, James, 68.

Fairbanks, Johns, 205.
Fairbourn, William (see Fairburn), 535.
Fairbrother, Francis, 16, 108, 358, 432, 497, 534.
Fairbrother, Thos., 41.
Fairburn (Fairburne, Fairbourn, Fairbairn), William, 109, 296, 460, 535, 617.
Fairfield, Thomas, 206.
Fairweather, John, 423, 466, 502, 535.
Falcon, Berkit, 70.
Falconer, Abraham, 63, 64.
Falconer, James, 606.
Fall, Patrick, 656.
Falling (Folling, Fallen, Foldier), John, 340, 389, 437, 497, 535.
Fane, Patk. (see Farn), 295.
Fangler, George, 328.
Fanis (see Faris).
Fannell (see Fennell).
Fanner, Mathias (see Funner), 617.
Fanner, William, 51.
Fanning, Thomas, 572, 575, 580, 583, 647.
Fanslar, Henry, 46.
Fantz, Jacob, 261.
Farber, Jacob, 261.
Farado (see Fardo).
Farden (see Farding).
Farding, Aaron (see Farthing), 408.
Farding (Farden), John, 109, 329.
Fardo (Farado), Absalom (Absolum, Absolam), 207, 311, 356, 390, 438, 493, 534.
Fardo, Wm. L., 111.
Farence (Tarance), Owen, 109, 170.
Farewell, Nicholas, 24.
Farguson (see Ferguson).
Faris (or Fanis), John, 612.
Farmer, John, 111.
Farmer, Nathl., 109.
Farmer, Samuel, 109, 334, 518.
Farmer, Thomas, 372.
Farn, Patrick (see Fane), 110.
Farr, Nicholas (see Carr), 408, 509, 535.
Farraby (Ferraby, Feraby, Ferreby), Richard, 110, 353, 396, 456, 486, 534.
Farrajara, John, 656.
Farral, Bryan, 573.
Farran, John, 207.
Farrance, Nichs., 206.
Farrand, Patk. (see Farren), 109.
Farrara (Farara), Emanuel, 340, 354, 435, 489, 534.
Farrel, Frances, 62.

Farrell (Farrill), Jas. (see Ferrell), 109, 110, 444, 494, 534.
Farrell, Jereh. (see Ferrell), 515.
Farrell (Farrol), John (see Harrell), 207, 336, 534.
Farrell, Peter, 535.
Farrell, Robert (see Ferrell), 444, 535.
Farrell, Walter (see Ferrall), 653.
Farrell, William (see Ferrell), 205, 534.
Farren, Patk. (see Farrand), 26, 642.
Farrill, James (see Farrell), 109.
Farrill, Thomas (see Ferrell), 109.
Farris, Francis, 279.
Farrol (see Farrell).
Farrow, Saml. (see Furrow), 612, 613.
Farrowfield, John, 205.
Farthing (Farding), Aaron, 408, 653.
Farthing, Robt., 279.
Farwell, James, 279, 509.
Faucett (Fawcitt), John (see Fossett), 398, 402.
Faulkner, Amos, 108.
Faulkner, Hynson, 387, 408.
Faulkner, Isaac, 387, 408.
Faulkner, Levy, 387.
Faup, Benja., 206.
Fawcitt (see Faucett).
Fawlit, Jos., 626.
Fear, Ignatius, 656.
Febiger, Lt. Col., 300.
Fehus, George, 408.
Feely (Freely), Chas., 51, 205.
Feely (Freely), Willm., 206, 279, 648.
Feeter, Abraham, 328.
Feilson, James, 326.
Feimley, Thos., 434.
Felick, Thomas, 67.
Fell (Fells), Christopher, 52, 109.
Fell, Edward, 110.
Felmott (Felmot, Filmot), Dorus (Doras, Dorest), 207, 391, 534.
Felson, Samuel (see Filson), 308.
Felton, Thomas, 206, 382.
Fenesick, Patrick, 620.
Fenitree, Thos., 618.
Fenly (or Finley), Thomas, 45.
Fennel, James, 416.
Fennell (Fennel, Fennile, Finnell), Edward, 208, 310, 326, 621.
Fennell (Fennel), John, 208, 266, 395, 448, 501, 535.

Fennell (Fennil), Stephen (Steaven), 342, 355, 394, 460, 491, 535, 569, 574, 618, 627.
Fenton, Charles, 41.
Fenton, Cornelius, 656.
Fenwick, Francis, 109.
Fenwick, Ign., 30.
Fenwick, Richard, 111, 396, 456, 535, 656.
Ferguson, Alex., 111.
Ferguson, Andw., 15.
Ferguson (Fergusson), Daniel, 50, 646.
Ferguson (Furganson), David, 40.
Ferguson (Farguson, Furguson), James, 68, 111, 205, 301.
Ferguson (Fergusson, Furguson), John, 50, 109, 207, 474, 534, 616.
Ferguson, Robert, 24, 108.
Ferguson (Forgeson), Wm., 58, 313.
Fergusson (see Ferguson).
Fernan, Dennis, 208.
Fernandez (Fernandis), James, 5, 108, 616.
Fernand (Ferneen, Fernen), Andrew (see Fernand), 109, 430, 535.
Ferns, Henry, 395, 448.
Ferraby (Feraby, Ferreby), Richard (see Farraby), 110, 456, 486.
Ferrall, Jeremiah (see Ferrell).
Ferrall (Ferral), John (see Ferrell).
Ferrall, Robert (see Ferrell).
Ferrall (Ferrill, Ferroll), Walter (see Farrell), 308, 402, 462, 487, 535.
Ferrell, James (see Farrell), 110, 294, 357.
Ferrell (Ferrall), Jeremiah (see Farrell), 42, 272, 279, 599.
Ferrell (Ferrel, Ferrall, Ferral, Ferril), John (see Farrell), 42, 49, 110, 311, 430, 512.
Ferrell, Richard, 32.
Ferrell (Ferrall, Ferroll), Robert (see Farrell), 342, 505, 617.
Ferrell, Thomas (see Farrill), 294, 322.
Ferrell (Ferroll), William (see Farrell), 352, 433.
Ferren, Philip, 109.
Ferrence, Henry, 323, 451.
Ferrill (Ferroll, Ferrol), Joseph, 312, 341, 395.
Ferrill, Walter (see Ferrall).
Ferrins, Henry, 208, 262, 267.

Ferroll (Ferrol) (see Ferrell, Ferrall, Ferrill).
Fervott, Peter, 347.
Fetcher (see Fletcher).
Fetteridge, Danl. (see McPatridge), 393.
Fettie, Abraham, 261.
Fevott (Furwott), Jno. Peter, 206, 414.
Ffooks, Charles, 70.
Fiche, Jno., 328.
Fickle, Benja. (Lt.), 207, 306, 315, 326, 364, 365, 381, 426, 476, 481, 520.
Fickle, Isaac, 408.
Fiddeman, Philip, 68, 69.
Fiegley, George, 51.
Fiegley, Peter, 51.
Fields, Charles, 408.
Fields (Field), George, 110, 297, 335, 356, 392, 452, 492.
Fields, John, 30, 329.
Fields, Joseph, 110, 330.
Fields, Michael, 205, 330.
Fields, Wm., 421.
Figgen, Francis, 641.
Fighter, George, 408.
Filbert, Joseph, 206.
Files, Thomas, 30.
Filler, Andrew (see Miller), 263.
Filler, Fredk., 208, 264.
Filleston (Filliston, Filleson, Findleston, Findleson, Finlason, Finleyson), George, 108, 423, 468, 505, 534, 617, 661.
Filley, William, 110.
Fillson, James, 207.
Filmot (see Felmott).
Filson (Fillson, Felson, Philson), Samuel, 207, 308, 315, 356, 389, 393, 437, 492, 534.
Filter, Frederick, 265.
Finacy, John, 206, 325.
Finacy, William, 206, 325.
Fincey (?), Jno., 415.
Finch, David, 208.
Finch, George, 108, 408, 641.
Finch, Joseph, 50, 207.
Fincham, Edward, 397, 400, 402, 459, 488, 535.
Findleston (Findleson, Finleyson), George (see Filleston), 423, 617, 661.
Findley, George (see Finley), 645.
Findley, John (see Finley), 645.
Fine, Peter, 47.
Finely, Coleman, 110.
Finlason, George (see Filleston), 108.
Finlay, George (see Finley), 305, 448, 506, 535.
Finley (Finly), Ebenezer, 365, 477, 573, 579.

Finley (Finlay, Findley), George, 205, 372, 395, 448, 506, 535, 645.
Finley (Findley), John, 64, 645.
Finley, Peter, 266, 269, 517.
Finleyson (see Findleston).
Finlow, Daniel, 206.
Finn (Firm), Bartholomew, 10, 60.
Finnch, John, 401.
Finnegan, Paddy, 111.
Finnell (see Fennell).
Finoughty, Thomas, 205.
Finton, Abram., 206.
Fipps (see Phipps).
Firm, Bartho. (see Finn), 60.
Firnano, Manl., 608.
Firth (Fyrth), Robert, 111, 351, 352, 397, 420, 464, 499, 535.
Fischer, Adam, 47, 73.
Fischer, Michael, 615.
Fish, Thomas, 51.
Fisher, Abram., 207.
Fisher, Balsor, 264.
Fisher, Danl., 51, 279.
Fisher, Henry, 45, 207, 208, 262, 267, 320, 358, 368, 395, 416, 447, 452, 499, 508, 534, 535.
Fisher, Jacob, 19.
Fisher, James, 368, 395, 416, 475.
Fisher, John, 36, 387.
Fisher, Joseph, 58, 110, 397, 462, 535.
Fisher, Philip, 208, 262, 264, 265, 344, 437, 506, 534, 630.
Fisher, Saml., 426, 468, 504, 535.
Fisher, Thomas, 14, 340.
Fisher, William, 108, 534.
Fishwater, Ben., 108.
Fister, Henry, 182, 261.
Fitcham, Edward, 405.
Fitcher, Geo. Lodo, 653.
Fite, James (see Slite), 250.
Fitgency, John, 369.
Fitspartrick, Nathan, 58.
Fitzburn, James, 279.
Fitzgerald (Fitzjarrald), Benja. (B.), 42, 207, 389, 396, 463, 506, 534.
Fitzgerald (Fitzgarral), Charles, 346, 355, 441, 492, 535.
Fitzgerald, Clement, 408.
Fitzgerald, Henry, 208.
Fitzgerald (Fitz Gerald), James, 63, 109, 110, 294, 343, 344, 534, 622.
Fitzgerald, Jeremiah (Jery), 207, 392, 442, 535.
Fitzgerald (Fitzgerrald, Fitzjarrold), John, 32, 111, 408, 415, 572, 573, 576, 580, 583, 648.

Fitzgerald (Fitzgerrald, Fitzjarld), Michael, 207, 311, 562.
Fitzgerald (Fitzjarold), Nicholas, 207, 391, 421, 472, 534.
Fitzgerald, Thomas, 205.
Fitzgerald, Timothy, 206, 348, 414.
Fitzgerald (Fitzgarral), William, 207, 346, 355, 441, 492, 535.
Fitz Gerrald (see Fitzgerald).
Fitzhugh, Peregrine, 616.
Fitzjarld (see Fitzgerald).
Fitzjarold, ——, 392.
Fitzjarold, Nichls. (see Fitzgerald).
Fitzjarrald (Fitzjarrold) (see Fitzgerald).
Fitz Jeffrys, Aaron, 656.
Fitzpatrick, Bars., 206.
Fitzpatrick, Bryan, 110.
Fitzpatrick, David, 68.
Fitzpatrick, Jno., 573.
Fitzpatrick, Lawrence (Laurence), 109, 294, 327, 642.
Fitzpatrick, Philip, 208, 266, 325, 357, 443, 494, 535.
Fitzpatrick, Wm., 68.
Fitzsimmons, Henry, 108.
Fitzsimmons, Thomas, 37, 206.
Flack, George (see Fleck).
Flack, James, 206, 328, 347, 445, 535.
Flack, Philip, 47, 51.
Flaharty, James, 110.
Flaharty, Stephen (see Flubarty), 208, 389.
Flaherty, Stephen (see Flubarty), 334.
Flaid, James, 279.
Flan, Anthony, 340.
Flanagan (Flannigan), Dennis, 457, 505, 534, 572, 617.
Flanagan (Flannagan), John, 293, 395, 453, 656.
Flanagan, Wm., 109, 110, 296.
Flannagan (Flanegan), Henry, 109, 339, 617.
Flannagan, John (see Flanagan), 656.
Flannery (Flanery), Christ., 110, 415.
Flannigan, Richd., 207.
Flanning, John, 208.
Flash, Lewis, 419, 464, 500, 535.
Flat, John, 388.
Flechinger, Michael, 408, 653.
Fleck, George (see Flack), 395.
Fleck, John (see Flick), 208.

Fleehearty (see Fluharty).
Fleeton, William, 109.
Fleetwood, Anthony, 70.
Fleming, James, 611.
Fleming (Flemming), John, 10, 24, 108, 279, 656.
Fleming (Fliming, Flemon), Patrick, 208, 265, 393, 452, 515.
Fleming (Flimming), Richard, 109, 581.
Fleming (Flemming), Thos., 111, 351, 352, 397, 420, 470, 509, 535.
Fleming (Flemming), William, 606, 656.
Flemon (see Fleming).
Fletcher (Fetcher), Benj., 383, 408.
Fletcher, Godfrey, 468.
Fletcher, John, 640.
Fletcher, Martin, 46.
Fletcher, Peter, 427, 473.
Fletcher, Philip, 46, 207, 306.
Fletcher, Richard, 45, 207.
Fletcher, Samuel, 323.
Flick, George, 50, 206.
Flick (Fleck, Fliet), John, 208, 264, 265.
Flimming (Fliming) (see Fleming).
Flinn (Flin), Edward (see Flynn), 26, 642.
Flinn (Flynn), Fredk., 110, 415, 467, 503, 534.
Flinn, Pharo, 335.
Flinn, Thomas, 111.
Flint, James, 108.
Flint, John, 10.
Flint, Thomas, 615.
Floharty (see Fluharty).
Floid (see Floyd).
Flood, Andrew, 393, 452.
Flood, James, 598.
Flood, Thomps., 601.
Flora (Flori), Jacob (see Flowers), 108, 358, 432, 497, 534, 641.
Florence, Lewis, 109.
Flowers, Edward, 205, 534.
Flowers (Flower), Jacob (see Flora), 394, 402, 415, 653.
Flowers, John, 395, 450.
Flowers, Lambert, 646.
Floyd, Daniel, 14.
Floyd, Elijah, 14.
Floyd, John, 14, 279.
Floyd, Jonathan, 67.
Floyd (Floid), Joseph, 205, 279, 342.
Floyd, Moses, 14.
Floyd, Saml., 279.
Fluart, Massy, 598.
Fluharty (Flaharty, Flaherty, Fleehearty, Floharty), Stephen, 19, 108, 208, 334, 356, 389, 437, 492, 534.
Flurry, Edward, 331.

Flynn, Bryan, 205.
Flynn (Flinn, Flin), Edward, 26, 108, 642.
Flynn, Fredk. (see Flinn), 415.
Foalks, John (see Folks).
Foard (see Ford).
Fogely, Chr., 51.
Foggitt (see Frogget).
Fogle, Henry, 72.
Fogle, John, 264.
Fogler, Simon, 264.
Fogwell, George, 207.
Foisdell (see Fosdale).
Folden, John, 358.
Foldier, John (see Falling), 497.
Folger, Robert, 369, 395, 468, 505, 535.
Folks (Foalks), John, 572, 576.
Follet (Folliot), Benjamin, 111, 534.
Follet (Folliot, Foliott), John, 208, 262, 395, 447.
Follett (Follet, Follitt, Folliott), Joseph, 111, 319, 393, 456, 535.
Follin, Kimbral, 70.
Folling (see Falling).
Foloue, Dennis, 606.
Forbes, John (Lieut.), 31, 32.
Forbes, William, 564, 568, 570, 574.
Forbey, Wm., 294, 323.
Forbus, John, 109, 295.
Force, Joseph, 206.
Forcbano, John, 602.
Ford, Archd., 108.
Ford, Ash, 205.
Ford (Foard), Benjamin (Col.), 7, 205, 364, 380, 402, 481, 520.
Ford, Edward, 639.
Ford (Foard), George, 65, 205, 206, 354, 436, 489, 535.
Ford (Foard), Hezekiah, 108, 362, 365, 378, 435, 476, 478, 520.
Ford, James, 576.
Ford (Foard), John, 69, 108, 111, 206, 279, 301.
Ford, Joseph, 17, 108, 313.
Ford, Notly, 35.
Ford, Robert, 18, 110.
Ford, Thomas, 375.
Ford (Foard), William, 61, 206, 408, 565.
Foreacres, Joseph, 66.
Foreman, Perry, 205.
Foreman, William (see Forman), 65, 205, 534.
Forester, G. W., 646.
Forgeson (see Ferguson).
Ferguson, Thomas, 10.
Forly, William, 109.
Forman, David, 604.
Forman, Jacob, 108.

Forman, Willm. (see Foreman), 375, 393, 433, 510.
Forney, James, 208, 265.
Fornivall (see Furnival).
Forough (see Furrow).
Forquer, William, 653.
Forreignner (see Furrener).
Forrell (see Torrell).
Forrest, Uriah (——), 20, 30, 109, 362, 378, 520, 628.
Forrester, Alex., 565, 567, 570, 574.
Forrester (Forester), Cornelius, 565, 566, 568, 574, 618.
Forrester, John, 565, 566, 569.
Forson, George, 205.
Forsyth, John, 111.
Forsythe, Jacob, 51.
Fort, Christopher, 648.
Fortune (Fourtune), William, 207, 309, 325.
Fosdale (Foysdale, Foisdell, Foysdoyle), Stafford, 111, 352, 396, 434, 534.
Fosh, James, 39, 110.
Fosney, David, 328.
Fossett (Fosset, Faucett, Fawcitt), John, 398, 402, 462, 487, 535.
Fossett (Fosset), Robert, 111, 606.
Foster, James, 110, 298, 330, 534, 619.
Foster, John, 47.
Foster, Jonathan, 206, 392, 416.
Foster (Forster), Mark, 205, 434, 508, 534.
Foster, Moses, 207, 308, 320, 356, 391, 439, 493, 534.
Foster (Forster), Nathan, 371, 408, 515.
Foster, Nathaniel, 205.
Foster (Forster), Rigby, 204, 358, 433, 497, 534.
Foster, Robert, 564.
Foster, Stephen, 205.
Foster, Thomas, 602.
Foster, Wm., 65, 69, 204, 602, 656.
Fouler (see Fowler).
Foumel, William, 108.
Fountain, Massy, 69.
Fountain, Peter, 111, 534.
Fountain, William, 205.
Fourtune (see Fortune).
Fouts, Jacob, 205.
Fowee, Jacob, 264.
Fowke, Gerard, 31.
Fowke, Richard, 31.
Fowler (Fouler), Henry, 108, 331.
Fowler, James, 110.
Fowler, John, 109, 207, 385.
Fowler, Jonathan, 108, 305, 358, 432, 534, 497.

Fowler, Joseph, 108, 313, 396, 432, 402, 534, 656.
Fowler, Patrick, 56.
Fowler, Saml., 319, 368.
Fowler, Thomas, 50.
Fowler, William, 108.
Fox, Anthony, 206.
Fox, Balser, 111, 336.
Fox, Henry, 72.
Fox, Jas., 570.
Fox, John, 110, 207, 307, 318.
Fox, Michael, 72.
Fox, Thomas, 52, 342.
Foxall, Daniel (or David) (see Foxwell), 535.
Foxall, Thos., 397, 402, 459, 488, 535.
Foxwell, Adam (Adams), 383, 408.
Foxwell, Charles, 27, 108, 294, 643.
Foxwell (Foxall), Daniel, 402, 487, 535.
Foxwell (Foxall), David, 383, 398, 402, 535.
Foy, John, 111.
Foysdoyle (Foysdale) (see Fosdale).
Fraim, John, 110.
Fraizer (see Frazier).
Frampton, Robt., 371.
France, Christian, 50.
France, Nicholas, 50.
France, Peter, 111.
Frances (see Francis).
Franceway, John (see Fransway), 313, 656.
Francher, Barnett, 335.
Francis (Frances), Alexander, 110, 296, 357, 430, 496, 534.
Francis, John, 451, 512, 515, 535.
Francis, Lewis, 319.
Francis, Peter, 428, 473.
Francois, John (see Fransway), 108, 436.
Franken, John, 263.
Franklin, Edwd., 109, 623.
Franklin, Francis, 109.
Franklin, John, 22, 31, 208, 408, 535, 653.
Franklin, Richd., 423, 471, 507, 535.
Franklin, Thos., 108, 330.
Franklin, William (William R., William Robertson), 31, 110, 333, 430, 508, 534.
Frankline, William, 40.
Fransway (Franceway, Fransey, Francois), John, 108, 313, 354, 395, 436, 489, 534, 656.
Frantz, Abraham (Abram), 208, 265.
Fraser, James (see Frazier), 30.
Fraser, William (see Frazier), 382.

Frasier (see Frazier).
Frawney, John, 335, 355, 443, 491, 535.
Frazier, Capt., 615.
Frazier, Henry, 394, 408, 468, 504, 535.
Frazier, Hobart, 108.
Frazier (Fraizer, Fraser), James, 39, 70, 612, 613.
Frazier, John, 402, 612, 615.
Frazier, Levin, 23.
Frazier, Philip, 423, 471.
Frazier, Richard, 25, 644.
Frazier, Samuel, 598.
Frazier (Frasier), Thomas, 387, 408.
Frazier, William (see Fraser), 23, 110, 204, 402, 428, 473, 612, 613, 615.
Fream, William, 408, 653.
Frederick, Bennet, 109.
Frederick, John, 402, 416, 653.
Free, George, 46.
Free, Nicholas, 451, 508, 535.
Freeland (Freeman), John, 204, 205.
Freeland, Nazreth, 64.
Freeland, Salethiel, 646.
Freely, Charles (see Feely), 205.
Freely, William (see Feely), 206.
Freeman, Abraham, 646.
Freeman, Edward, 13, 60, 343, 344, 457.
Freeman, Francis, 45, 109, 355, 442, 492, 534.
Freeman, Isaac, 646.
Freeman, Jacob, 46, 108.
Freeman, Jeremiah, 206.
Freeman, John (see Freeland), 22, 204, 342.
Freeman (Freemane), Richard, 110, 467, 534.
Freeman, Thomas, 42.
Fremly (Frimley, Frumley), Thomas, 205, 352, 535.
Freemoult, Robert, 116, 623.
Freind, Charles, 46.
Fre-Ladner, John, 340.
Fren, Andrew, 207.
French, James, 398, 405, 535.
French, Jeremiah, 355, 442, 492, 535.
French, John, 111.
French, Martin, 108.
French, Peter, 393, 401, 450, 535.
French, Randolph (Rudolph), 109, 329.
French, Stephen, 109, 329.
French, William, 370, 587, 588.
Fresh, Stephen, 108, 330, 358, 432, 406, 534.

Freshwater, Thomas, 645.
Frewen, Richard, 110.
Frey (Fry), Bernard (Barnard), 208, 263, 264.
Frey (Frye), Nicholas, 261, 266.
Freymiller (Frymiller), Jacob, 208, 265.
Friar, Jaby., 602.
Fricker, John, 109, 294, 322.
Friend (Frend), Cornish, 385, 397, 405, 459.
Friend, Daniel, 330.
Friend, James, 204.
Friend, Tobias, 264.
Frimley (see Fremly).
Frisby, William, 110.
Frogget (Froggat, Foggitt), Richard, 207, 311, 378, 408.
From, William, 72.
Fromee (see Froume).
Froshour, Adam, 261.
Frost, James, 279.
Frost, John, 41.
Frost, Silas, 393.
Frost, Silvester, 206.
Froume (Fromee), John, 69, 279.
Froward (see Howard).
Frumantle, Francis, 51.
Frumley (see Fremly).
Fry, Bernard (see Frey), 264.
Fry, Peter, 388.
Fryback, George, 42.
Fryback, John, 42.
Frye, Nicholas (see Frey), 261.
Frymiller, Jacob (see Freymiller), 208, 265.
Fubbard, Francis, 207.
Fuhrman, Danl., 263.
Fulfit, John, 401.
Fulford (Fullford), John (Capt.), 49, 356, 302, 454, 493, 535, 570, 572.
Fulham (Fullam, Fullim), Charles, 208, 262, 267, 320, 355, 395, 460, 490, 535.
Fulham (Fullham), John (see Fullam), 352, 485, 534.
Fullam (Fullim), Charles (see Fulham), 262, 395.
Fullam (Fullum), George, 53, 267, 305.
Fullam (Fullom), John (see Fulham), 205, 434.
Fullam, Michael, 206, 324.
Fuller, John, 335.
Fuller, William, 109, 206, 333, 349, 414.
Fulsom, John, 109, 446.
Fulsome, Jeremiah, 49.
Fulton, Alexander, 14, 108.
Fulton, James P., 408.
Fulton, William, 661.

Funner (Fummer), John M. (John Mths.), 207, 391, 475, 534.
Funner (Fanner), Matthias, 505, 617.
Furguson (Furganson) (see Ferguson).
Furlong, Benjamin, 52.
Furner (Furnor), Edward (see Furrener), 61, 109.
Furnier, James, 264.
Furnival (Furnivall, Furnavil, Fornivall), Alex. (Capt.), 563, 568, 572, 573, 618.
Furnor (see Furner).
Furrener (Forreignner), Edward (see Furner), 354, 449, 490, 534.
Furrough (see Furrow).
Furroughs (see Furrow).
Furrow (Forough, Furroughs), Jesse, 339, 393, 446.
Furrow (Furrough), Saml. (see Farrow), 346, 366, 416.
Furwott (see Fevott).
Fyrth, Robert (see Firth), 351.

Gaad, Robert, 209.
Gable, Jno., 328.
Gadd, Thomas, 280, 342, 355, 443, 491, 536.
Gadden, Richard, 359.
Gadden, Rich. E. (see Gatton), 30.
Gaddis, William, 60.
Gadrick, Philip, 114.
Gae, Richard, 356.
Gaggen (Gagan, Gagging), James, 607, 656.
Gaggen, William, 606, 656.
Gahagan, James, 210.
Gahort, Jacob, 211.
Gaiffin, Michael, 115.
Gailand, Gilbert, 112.
Gainer (see Gainor).
Gainer, Jno., 114.
Gainer, Robert, 30.
Gaines, Thomas, 26.
Gainford, Mathias, 116.
Gainor (Gainer, Gaynor), Hugh, 52, 115, 353, 457, 480, 536.
Gainsford, Michl., 414.
Gaither (Gater), Benjamin, 357, 394, 445, 495, 537.
Gaither, Greenbury, 42, 44.
Gaither, Henry (Capt.), 7, 111, 293, 341, 364, 380, 476, 480, 520.
Gaither, John, 42.
Gaither, Joseph, 656.
Gaither, Nicholas, 44.
Gaither, Silvester, 314.
Gaither, Thos., 41.
Gale, Capt., 578.
Gale, G., 618.

Gale, John, 113, 293, 364, 380, 476, 481, 520, 616.
Gallagan, Jno., 280.
Gallaspie, John, 280.
Gallaway, Joseph, 112.
Galliher, John, 210.
Gallinough, Edward, 62.
Gallion, Nathan, 400.
Gallispie, William (see Gillaspy), 537.
Gallop, Oliver, 646.
Galloway, Charles, 113.
Galloway, Hugh (see Galway), 112.
Galloway, James, 113.
Galloway, Marshall, 114, 537.
Gallworth, Peter, 7.
Galvin, David, 55.
Galvin, John, 313.
Galway, Hugh (see Galloway), 15.
Galway, Jno., 15.
Galwith, John, 40.
Galworth, Gabl., 113.
Gamble (Gambell), Abraham, 210, 435, 505, 536, 617, 630.
Gamble, Richardson, 27, 644.
Gamble, William, 115, 116.
Gambler, Michael (see Cambier and Ramler), 264, 336.
Gambrel, Gideon, 612, 613.
Game, Ephraim (see Ganes), 339.
Game, Jacob (see Games), 444.
Games, Absolam, 33.
Games, Francis, 210, 327.
Games (Game), Jacob, 444, 494, 537.
Games, Robert, 34.
Gandy, Jacob, 211, 306, 310, 325.
Ganes, Ephraim (see Game), 450.
Ganina, Abm. (see Garsene), 112.
Gannan, William, 209.
Ganney, Joseph, 615.
Gannon, John, 280.
Gannon, Perry, 69.
Gantley, Wm., 455.
Gantner (Gentner), Adam, 212, 261, 262.
Garceny (see Garsene).
Garcy, Saml., 390.
Gardener, William (see Gardner), 33.
Garder (see Gardner).
Gardiner, Alexd., 115.
Gardiner, George (see Gardner), 311.
Gardiner, James (see Gardner), 11.
Gardiner, John (see Gardner), 112.
Gardiner, John G., 331.

Gardiner, Luke, 33, 564, 566, 568.
Gardiner (Gardner), Peter, 40.
Gardiner, Richard, 30, 113, 114.
Gardner (Garner), Clement, 656.
Gardner (Garder, Gardners), George (see Gardiner), 60, 211, 322, 400, 416.
Gardner, Jacob, 18.
Gardner, James (see Gardiner), 416.
Gardner, John (see Gardiner), 40, 279, 464.
Gardner, Peter (see Gardiner), 40.
Gardner, Thomas, 656.
Gardner, William (see Gardener), 210, 327.
Gardners (see Gardner).
Garey, George, 68, 208.
Garey, John (see Garvey), 656.
Garish, Edward (see Garrish).
Garish, William, 113.
Garland (Gavland), Benj., 64, 646.
Garland, Gilbert, 7.
Garland, James, 280.
Garner, Abel, 113, 383, 408.
Garner, Clement (see Gardner), 656.
Garner, David, 345.
Garner, Edward, 51.
Garner, Henry, 113.
Garner, Mathew, G, 112.
Garner, Thomas, 112.
Garnett (Garnet), Andrew, 112, 356, 443, 494, 536.
Garnett, Benja., 210, 364, 380.
Garnett, Francis, 114.
Garnett, Pero, 210.
Garoughty, Edmund, 26, 643.
Garreguies, John, 343.
Garrehan, James, 210.
Garrett, Alex., 422, 471.
Garrett, Enoch, 200.
Garrett (Garrott), John, 25, 60, 114, 295.
Garrett, Leonard, 114.
Garrett (Garrott), William, 57, 61, 209.
Garrick, John, 424.
Garrish (Garish, Gearish), Edward, 210, 475, 536.
Garrish, Francis, 116, 414.
Garrison (Garritson), David, 563, 566, 568.
Garrity, Jno., 573.
Garrott, John (see Garrett), 25.
Garrott, William (see Garrett), 61.

Garsene (Gaseney, Garceny, Garsener), Abraham (see Ganina), 331, 358, 432, 496, 536.
Garten, William, 42.
Garth, James, 115, 536, 617, 630.
Garton, James, 112.
Gartrell, Charles, 42.
Gartrell, Joseph, 42.
Garvey, John (see Garey), 606.
Garvey, William, 112, 380.
Garvin, John, 115.
Garvis (see Jarvis).
Gaseney (see Garsene).
Gash, Godfrey, 640.
Gash, William, 60, 114, 400.
Gaskin, John, 44.
Gaskin, Wm., 211.
Gassaway, Henry, 113, 115, 364, 380, 476, 479, 481, 520.
Gassaway, John, 38, 113, 363, 379, 476, 479, 520, 639.
Gassaway, Lt., 503.
Gassaway, Nicholas, 16, 111, 114, 295, 357, 363, 379, 429, 476, 479, 520.
Gatchel, Elisha, 647.
Gater (see Gaither).
Gates, Gen., 349.
Gates, Henry, 24.
Gates, Leonard, 112, 330.
Gates, William, 112, 115, 331, 333, 430, 511, 536.
Gath, James, 457, 506.
Gatreen, John, 280.
Gatrell, Stephen, 42.
Gattau, Richard (see Gatton), 112.
Gatting (Gathing), Robert, 334.
Gatton, Azariah, 408.
Gatton (Gattin, Gadden), Richard E. (see Gattau), 30, 331.
Gatton (Gatten, Gattin, Gatting), Sylvester, 112, 331, 418, 465, 501, 536, 617.
Gauff, James, 43.
Gauff, John Baptis (see Gough), 43.
Gaugh, Thomas, 31.
Gaul, Richard, 212, 266, 322.
Gault, James, 116.
Gauser (see Gillon).
Gavin (Gavan, Gavon), Francis, 212, 265, 387, 402.
Gavin, Michl., 114.
Gavland (see Garland).
Gay, Robert, 646.
Gaynor, Hugh (see Gainor), 457, 486.
Gearey (see Geary).
Gearish (see Garrish).
Gearrish, Sampson, 211.

Geary, Richard, 114.
Geary (Gearey, Gerry), Samuel, 211, 408, 536.
Gee, George, 112, 279.
Gee, John, 395, 452, 497, 537.
Gee (Jee), Joseph, 39, 112.
Gee, Richard, 211, 391, 438, 493, 536.
Geehan (Guhan), John, 42.
Geerhert, Jacob, 328.
Geeting, John, 209.
Geffers (see Jeffers).
Geier, Joseph, 434.
Gellard, John, 615.
Gelon, John, 209.
Gemmeson, Richard (see Jamison), 342.
Gentile (Gentle), George, 49.
Gentile (Gentle), Stephen, 49, 408.
Gentils, John, 115.
Gentle (see Gentile).
Gentner (see Gantner).
Geoghegan (Georgehagan), John, 111, 210.
Geohagan (Georghegan), Anthony, 114, 354, 435, 489, 536.
George, Bennet, 395, 537.
George, Charles, 601.
George, Edward, 15, 114.
George, Indian, 336.
George, James, 209.
George, Joshua (Capt.), 61, 62.
George, Southard (Southern, Southy), 398, 462, 487, 537.
George, William, 210, 348, 398, 439, 537, 617.
Georgehagan (see Geoghegan).
Georghegan, Anthy. (see Geohagan).
Georghegan, Basil, 52.
German, John (see Jerman), 471.
German, Thomas, 210.
Germier, Abel, 70.
Germing, Wm., 116.
Gerock, Samuel, 182, 262, 572.
Gerrish, John, 19.
Gerry (see Geary).
Gest, Joseph, 581.
Getcomb, John, 115.
Getig (Getting), George, 212, 265.
Ghiselin (Ghirelin), John (Capt.), 44, 46, 210, 326, 620.
Giant, Isaac, 59.
Giant, Stephen, 65.
Giant, William, 65.
Gibbons, Edward, 607, 656.
Gibbons, John, 324.
Gibbons, William, 211.
Gibbs, Caleb, 605.
Gibbs, John, 280.

Gibhart, George, 314.
Gibney, David, 111.
Gibney, Simon, 63, 280.
Gibson, Francis, 648.
Gibson, Jacob, 421, 472, 645.
Gibson, Jas., 15.
Gibson, John, 114, 116, 209, 210, 297, 483, 536, 647.
Gibson, Jonathan (———), 67, 74, 208, 351, 364, 380, 480, 518, 645.
Gibson, Joseph, 115.
Gibson, Joshua, 656.
Gibson, Woolman, of John, 67.
Giddings, John, 40.
Giddy, Peter, 40.
Gieser, Mathias, 264.
Giffard (see Gilford).
Gilbert, Benj., 335, 443, 507, 536.
Gilbert, Henry, 606.
Gilbert, Michael, 59.
Gilbert, Thomas, 606.
Gilby, Henry, 208, 352, 433, 536, 656.
Gilby, Thomas, 656.
Gild (Guild), Whittington, 426, 466, 502, 537.
Gilder, Daniel, 601.
Giles, John, 113.
Giles, Maj., 446.
Giles, Samuel, 24, 112.
Gilford (Giffard), James, 606, 656.
Gilham (Gillham), Thos. (see Gilliam), 330, 433, 537.
Gilhampton, Robert, 58, 59, 115, 537.
Gill, John, 56, 114, 115, 210.
Gill, Jonathan, 576, 580, 583.
Gill, Thomas, 45, 314.
Gill, William, 209, 280.
Gillam (Gillum), John, 49.
Gillam, Thomas (see Gilliam).
Gillard, Thomas, 626.
Gillaspy, William (see Gallispie), 602.
Gillen (Gilling), Thomas (see Gillon), 208, 536, 605.
Gillham (see Gilham).
Gilliam (Gillam, Gillum, Gillsim), Thomas (see Gilham and Hillum), 49, 352, 377, 408.
Gilligan, John, 211.
Gillin, James, 416.
Gilling (see Gillen).
Gillis, James, 590.
Gillis, Joseph, 408.
Gillis, Thomas, 656.
Gillis, William, 408.
Gillispie, Richard, 345.
Gillon (Gauser), Thomas (see Gillen), 462, 499.

Gills, John, 113.
Gillsim (see Gillum).
Gillum, John (see Gillam).
Gillum (Gillsim), Thomas (see Gilliam), 377, 408.
Gilmore, James, 472, 505, 537.
Gilmore, Paul, 420, 470.
Gilmore (Gilmour), William, 45, 211.
Gilpin, Benjamin, 408, 594.
Gilpin, Henry, 426, 473.
Gilpin, Ignatious, 35, 114.
Gilpin, William, 35, 113.
Gilword, George, 627.
Gim (Negro), 38.
Gingle, George, 408.
Ginnivan, Jno., 573.
Girdler, Charles, 336, 352, 434, 485, 537.
Girte, Chrisr., 280.
Gisinger, John, 47.
Gist, John, 306, 520, 600.
Gist, Joseph, 581.
Gist, M., 58, 565, 644.
Gist, Mordecai (Col. Gen.), 29, 114, 457, 518, 600, 652.
Gist, Nathl. (Col.), 585, 599, 600.
Githin, Robt., 280.
Gittin, George, 263.
Gittin, Jacob, 263.
Gittin, Peter, 264.
Gittings, Thomas, 42.
Given, John, 536.
Givens, Ezekiel, 211.
Giveny, David, 18.
Gladman, Mich., 39.
Gladson, William, 113.
Glann, Saml., 280.
Glascow, Adam, 74.
Glascow (Glasco, Glascoe), William (see Glasgow).
Glasgow, Samuel, 11, 112.
Glasgow, Walter, 32, 113, 279.
Glasgow (Glassgow, Glasgoe, Glascow, Glascoe, Glasco), William, 114, 295, 330, 376, 408, 536.
Glashen, Hendry, 112.
Glass, Andrew, 116.
Glass, Anthony, 116.
Glass, George, 647.
Glaswey, Pat., 115.
Glatz, John, 19.
Glaudstone, Nathl., 209.
Glaver, Wm., 451.
Glaze, James, 49.
Glaze, Nathaniel, 50.
Gleen, John, 372.
Gleeson (Glessin), Thomas, 573, 579, 582, 584.
Glenmore, James, 421.
Glenn, James, 280.
Glenn, Thos., 418.
Glessin (see Gleeson).
Glinn, J. Thos., 469.
Glinn, James (see Glynn), 116.

Glory (Glorey, Gloury), William, 43, 115, 343, 357, 394, 445, 495, 536, 626.
Glover, Thomas, 112, 432, 511, 536.
Glover, William, 14, 341, 494, 537, 575, 581.
Glyn, Joseph, 59.
Glynn (Glinn), James, 116, 415.
Gnatzinger (see Gratsinger).
Goady, William, 209.
Goald (see Gould).
Goaley (see Goley).
Goar (see Gore).
Gobble, Christeen, 46.
Gobble, George, 46.
Godart (Godthart), Edward Barton (Barton), 113, 329.
Goddard (Goddart), John (see Gothard), 115, 430, 512, 536.
Godfrey, Edmund, 305.
Godfrey, Jno., 116.
Godfrey, Thomas, 60, 115.
Godfrey (Goodfrey), Wm., 211, 305.
Godman, Samuel (Capt.), 38, 115, 303, 619.
Godman, Wm., 563, 566, 508.
Godthart (see Godart).
Godwin, John, 66, 645.
Goff, Charles (see Gough), 537.
Goff, Richard, 116, 414.
Goffer, Richard, 335.
Gohegan (Gohogan) (see Geohagan).
Gold, ——— (see Gould, James), 74.
Gold, Samuel, 333.
Gold, William (see Gould).
Goldby, John, 209.
Golden, Eccabut, 449.
Goldsborough (Goldsbury), Charles, 115, 357, 430, 496, 536.
Goldsborough, Greenbury, 67, 68, 371.
Goldsborough (Gouldsborou, Goldsbury, Gouldsburry), Henry (———), 114, 115, 298, 329, 536.
Goldsborough (Goldsbury), John, 115, 383, 415, 631, 656.
Goldsborough, William (———), 67, 476, 480, 520.
Goldsbury, Chas. (see Goldsborough).
Goldsbury (Gouldsbury), Henry (see Goldsborough).
Goldsbury, John (see Goldsborough).

Goldsbury, Mark, 576, 580, 582, 583.
Goldsbury, Nicholas, 384.
Goldsbury, Stephen, 656.
Goldsmith, Notley, 114, 329.
Goldsmith (Gouldsmith), Thomas, 15, 54, 570.
Goley (Goaley), Thomas, 31.
Gollicor (Gollier), John, 115, 318.
Gollihigh, Wm., 112.
Gombare, John, 47, 630.
Gonsac, Jacob, 608.
Good, Jacob, 44, 46.
Good, John, 18.
Goodall, Elias, 115.
Goodburn, Francis, 209.
Goodchild, Wm., 279.
Goodeberger, Adam, 327.
Goodey (see Goody).
Goodfrey (see Godfrey).
Goodson, Wm., 55.
Goodwin, Edward, 43.
Goodwin, Henry, 211.
Goodwin, James, 114, 279, 537.
Goody (Goodey), Lambert, 395, 451, 490, 537.
Goody (Goodey), William, 395, 416, 451.
Goodyer, Edward, 113.
Goold (see Gould).
Goomes, Emanuel, 331.
Goosetree (Goostree), Absalom (Absolom), 333, 408.
Gooster, Reuben, 113, 536.
Gordey, Joshua, 641.
Gordon (Gordan, Gorden), Archibald, 587, 589.
Gordon, Charles, 397, 460.
Gordon, George, 112, 313, 603.
Gordon, Isaac, 656.
Gordon, James, 54.
Gordon (Gordan, Gorden), John, 12, 114, 116, 210, 296, 351, 352, 354, 398, 400, 420, 436, 470, 489, 508, 536, 581, 589.
Gordon (Gordan, Gorden), Joseph, 211, 391, 536.
Gordon, Joshua, 328.
Gordon, Peter, 211.
Gordon, Robert, 648.
Gordon, Sergt., 319, 320.
Gordon (Gorden), Thomas, 15, 37, 112, 113, 115, 370, 393, 428, 429, 449, 474, 601.
Gordon (Gordan, Jordon), William (see Jordan), 114.
Gore (Goar, Gorr), Andrew, 266, 270, 517.
Gore, George, 612.
Gore, Thos., 335.
Gorman, Hugh, 114.

Gorman (Gormon), John, 43, 66, 112, 116, 208, 280, 354, 393, 398, 422, 450, 490, 536, 564, 566, 569, 651.
Gormely, Joseph, 280.
Gorr (see Gore).
Gorrell, Abm., 114.
Gorsuch (Gossage), Thos., 114, 357, 429, 496, 536.
Gory, Daniel, 211.
Gosgraves, Thomas, 209.
Goslin, Samuel, 12.
Gosnell, Saml., 111.
Gossage (see Gorsuch).
Gothard, John (see Goddard), 397, 402.
Gothard, Thomas, 209.
Gother, John, 208, 434, 537.
Goud, Lt. (see Gould, James), 482.
Gouger, Joseph, 113.
Gough, Baptist (Baptis) (see Gauff), 384, 408.
Gough, Charles (see Goff), 112, 384, 408.
Gough, John Sparks, 408.
Gould, Edward, 212.
Gould (Gold), James (—) (see Goud), 66, 74, 208, 363, 379, 520.
Gould (Goold, Goald, Gold), William, 113, 293, 357, 443, 494, 536.
Gouldsborou (Gouldsburry) (see Goldsborough).
Gouldsmith (see Goldsmith).
Gouldsparks, Jas. (see Sparks), 210
Goutee, Wm. G., 70.
Gow, William, 209.
Gowarn, Brian, 116.
Gowers, Robert, 73.
Gownan, Michl., 621.
Grace, Aaron, 400.
Grace, Jesse, 114, 297, 475, 636.
Grace, John, 280.
Grace, Nathaniel, 615.
Grace, Richard, 21, 113.
Grace, William, 63, 113, 279, 372.
Gradey (Grady), William, 65.
Graff, Peter, 261.
Grafton, Wm., 400.
Graham, Alexr., 280.
Graham, George, 408.
Graham, John, 211, 393, 420, 450, 490, 537.
Graham, Moses, 210, 348, 354, 440, 489, 536.
Graham (Grahame), Philip, 381, 394, 458, 607, 537.
Grainger, Thos., 574.
Graitwood, John, 41.
Grames, John, 40.
Grammer, Fredk., 581.
Gramoth (see Gromath), 518.

Granada (Granade), John, 280, 626.
Granger, Samuel, 6.
Grant, ——, 602.
Grant, David, 344.
Grant (Grantt), James, 115, 279, 334.
Grant (Grantt), John, 8, 51, 211, 307, 314, 606, 656.
Grant, Marmaduke, 663, 566, 568.
Grant, Richard, 114.
Grant, Samuel, 113.
Grant, Thomas, 408, 417.
Grant, William, 386, 397, 405, 459, 537, 575, 581.
Grantham, Henry, 210, 322.
Grantham, William, 606, 656.
Grary, James (see Greavy), 475.
Grason, George, 614.
Grass, Jacob, 264.
Gratage, John, 601.
Gratsinger (Gnatzinger), John, 116, 351, 537.
Gravels, Benj., 318.
Graves, Isaac (see Greaves), 396, 536.
Graves, James, 114, 329.
Graves, John, 30.
Graves, Jonas, 209, 434.
Graves, Moses, 209.
Gravey (see Greavy).
Gray, Benjamin, 7, 111, 313, 396, 432, 511, 535.
Gray, George, 31, 34.
Gray, Jacob, 112.
Gray, James (see Grey), 113, 115, 116, 208, 353, 457, 486, 536.
Gray, James Woolford (James W., W. James, ——), 70, 74, 208, 354, 363, 379, 383, 450, 476, 480, 484, 489, 520.
Gray, Jesse, 23.
Gray, John, 25, 209, 372, 423, 465, 500, 537.
Gray, Joseph (see Grey), 113, 280, 293, 641.
Gray, Richard, 33, 113, 314.
Gray, Robert, 115, 415.
Gray, Samuel, 340, 354, 394, 449, 489, 537.
Gray, Thomas, 33, 115, 280, 460, 537.
Gray, Vincent, 405, 537.
Gray, William, 209, 280, 427, 473, 646, 651.
Gray, Wilson, 31, 603.
Gray, Zacha., 9.
Graybill (Graybell), Philip, 182, 265.
Grayham, Thomas, 26, 643.
Grayson, Col. William, 599, 601, 603, 634.
Greaden, Robert, 210.
Gready (see Gradey).
Greathouse, Jacob, 264.

Greaves, Absalom, 33, 210.
Greaves (Grieves, Graves), Isaac, 210, 349, 357, 396, 440, 494, 536.
Greaves, James Hudson, 66.
Greavy (Gravey), James (see Grary), 508, 637.
Greechbaum, Phillip, 264.
Greedy, James, 646.
Greegsby (see Gregsby).
Green, Able, 648.
Green, Amos, 7, 112, 358, 431, 496, 535.
Green, Benj., 331.
Green, Charles, 6.
Green, Christopher, 651.
Green, Clement, 408, 595.
Green, Cuthbert, 211.
Green, David (see Greene), 43, 211, 341.
Green, Edward, 6.
Green, George, 211.
Green, Henry (see Greene), 113, 443, 494, 536.
Green, Isaac, 114, 470, 536.
Green, James (see Greene), 51, 115, 397, 422, 607, 656.
Green, John (see Greene), 68, 111, 112, 116, 417, 426, 428, 461, 473, 504, 511, 536.
Green, Joseph, 16, 211.
Green, Nathan, 43.
Green, Peter, 651.
Green, R., 117.
Green, Richard, 112, 372, 396.
Green, Robert, 211, 310, 341.
Green, Samuel, 66, 112, 211, 331, 459, 536.
Green, Smart, 397.
Green, Solomon, 396, 455, 485, 537.
Green, Thomas, 606.
Green, William, 68, 111, 629.
Greenage, Benj., 375, 408.
Greenage, William (see Grenage).
Greenard (Grinard, Grinnard), Paul, 211, 353, 440, 488, 536.
Greene, David (see Green), 518.
Greene, Henry (see Graves), 357.
Greene, James (see Green), 415.
Greene, John (see Green), 536.
Greene (Green), Maj. Genl., 477, 478, 479, 588.
Greenfield, Wm. T. (or F.), 38.
Greenhill, William, 60.
Greenbugh, Jonathan, 368.
Greenland, Richd., 400.
Greenwalt, James, 112.
Greenwell, Jesse, 115.
Greenwell, John, 384, 408.

Greenwell, Robert, 114, 329.
Greenwell, Stephen, 329.
Greenwich, Thos., 621.
Greenwood, James (see Wood), 210, 347, 350, 439, 491, 536.
Greenwood, John, 383, 408, 425, 467, 503, 537, 643.
Greenwood, Joseph, 63.
Greenwood, Michl., 280.
Greenwood, Milburn, 210.
Greenwood, Philip, 72.
Greenwood, William, 67, 209.
Greer, James, 33, 607, 656.
Greer (Greir), Joseph, 366, 506, 537, 634.
Greer, Moses, 607, 656.
Greer (Greor), Smart, 459, 488, 537.
Gregory, Benja., 210.
Gregory, Jacob, 336.
Gregory, James, 210.
Gregory, John, 338, 357, 444, 494, 537.
Gregory, Saml., 280.
Gregory, Robert, 58, 115.
Gregory, William, 114.
Gregsby (Greegsby), Wilkinson (Wilkerson), 338, 366.
Greir (see Greer).
Grenage (Greenage), William, 209, 537.
Grenewald, Jacob, 19.
Greor (see Greer).
Grey, James (see Gray), 53.
Grey, Joseph (see Gray), 58.
Greyer, Lawrence, 39.
Grice (see Kruise).
Gridley (Gridler), Martin, 210, 325.
Grieg, Harvy, 211.
Grieves, Isaac (see Greaves), 357, 440.
Griffey (see Griffith).
Griffin, Amos (see Griffith), 459, 498.
Griffin, Charles, 6.
Griffin, Daniel (see Griffith), 305.
Griffin, Darby, 279.
Griffin, Elisha, 209.
Griffin, Ignatius, 384, 576.
Griffin, James, 52.
Griffin, John, 113.
Griffin (Griffen), Luke (see Griffith), 402, 460.
Griffin, Mark (Mack), 113, 536, 622.
Griffin, Michl., 415.
Griffin, Moses, 209.
Griffin, Nathan (Nathl.), 113, 536, 622.
Griffin (Griffen), Thomas, 52, 601.
Griffin, William, 112, 331, 464, 536, 617.
Griffis, John, 369.

Griffith, Amos (see Griffin), 383, 398, 402, 537.
Griffith (Griffiths), Charles, 45, 114, 425, 429, 466, 501, 537.
Griffith, Danl. (see Griffin), 211.
Griffith, Dennis, 42, 43.
Griffith, George, 53, 115.
Griffith, Greenbury, 53.
Griffith, James, 53, 111, 387, 408.
Griffith, John, 42.
Griffith, Luke (see Griffin), 397, 402.
Griffith, Matthew, 66.
Griffith, Michael, 421, 472.
Griffith, Moses, 402.
Griffith, Nathan, 53.
Griffith, Nicholas, 53.
Griffith, Philip, 302.
Griffith, Richard, 211.
Griffith, Samuel, 114, 209, 319, 435.
Griffith (Griffey), Stephen, 210, 304.
Griffith, Thomas, 279, 651.
Griffith, William, 408.
Griffith, Zadock, 45.
Griffiths, Chas. (see Griffith), 425.
Griffiths, John, 114.
Grilliot, Jos., 280.
Grim, Alex., 515.
Grimes, Anthony, 55.
Grimes, David, 116.
Grimes, Greenbury, 408.
Grimes, John, 33, 67.
Grimes, Nathl., 41.
Grimes, Terrence, 55.
Grimes, William, 12, 41, 573, 579, 582, 584.
Grimfeild, Henry, 608.
Grinall, Thomas, 41.
Grindage, James, 209.
Grinnard (Grinard), Paul (see Greenard), 211, 440, 536.
Grinnel, Stephen, 113.
Grishill, Jno., 113.
Gritchard, Thos., 423, 471.
Gromath (Gramoth, Grommet), Jacob, 261, 365, 518.
Groome (Groom), Charles, 576, 580, 581, 582, 583.
Grooms, Emanuel, 112.
Groop (Grupp), John, 212, 265.
Grose, Henry, 47.
Grosh, Adam (Capt.), 44, 211, 326, 621.
Grosh (Crush), Michael, 212, 263, 537.
Grosman, Sol., 280.
Grove, David, 56.
Grover, l. Mason, 111.
Grover, John, 210, 314, 327.
Grover, Samuel, 38.
Groves, James, 56.

Groves, William, 342, 357, 444, 495, 536.
Growley, Michael, 266.
Grunby, John, 211.
Grunlin (see Quinlin).
Grupp (see Groop).
Grymes, Stephen, 41.
Guantley, Wm., 306.
Guarn, Hugh, 115.
Gudgeon, William, 372, 395, 433, 501, 537.
Guhan (see Geehan).
Guibard, Thomas, 113.
Guice (see Guise).
Guild (see Gild).
Guilman, Saml., 336.
Guise (Guize, Guice), John, 211, 309.
Guist, George, 280.
Guize (see Guise).
Guggon (see Gudgeon).
Gullehan, John, 656.
Gullion, Jeremh., 116.
Gullion, John, 116.
Gully, John, 209.
Gumey, John, 280.
Gummy, Peter, 115.
Gunby, John (Col.), 20, 320, 321, 363, 378, 461, 476, 478, 483, 520, 621, 629, 641, 642.
Gundun, Benj., 319.
Gurney (Gumey), Jno., 280.
Guthrey, Wm., 116.
Guthry, William, 116.
Gutrick, William, 112.
Gutro, Martin, 564, 566, 569.
Gwin, Hugh, 57.
Gwin, Thomas, 33.
Gwinn (Gwin, Gwyne), John, 116, 353, 456, 486.
Gwynn, James, 111.

Hack, Daniel (see Heck), 653.
Hackethorn, Michael, 18.
Hackett (Hacket), James, 74, 121.
Hackett, John, 123, 318, 470, 623.
Hackett (Hecket, Hockett), Jonathan, 218, 264, 336, 416.
Hackett, Joshua, 120.
Hackett, Richard, 55.
Hadan (Hadin), George, 214, 539.
Hadan (Haden, Haiden, Haidon), John (see Haydon), 358, 380, 438, 498, 539.
Haddaway, Oakley, 68, 74, 609, 610.
Haddaway, Thomas Lambden, 68.
Haddaway, Wm., 387.
Hadder (Hader), Nebemiah, 430, 499, 539.
Haden (Hadin) (see Hadan).

Hadley, Samuel, 375, 409.
Haffley, Stephen, 652.
Haflegh, Peter, 328.
Hagan, Andw., 123.
Hagan (Hagans), Charles, 603, 657.
Hagan (Hogan), James, 506, 539, 606, 657.
Hagan (Hagon), Leonard, 43, 217, 341, 390, 439, 539.
Hagan, Michael, 49, 409.
Hagan, Nicholas, 377.
Hagan (Hagen), Ralph, 395, 537.
Hagan, Raphael, 118, 331, 471.
Hagan, Roger (see Hogan), 423.
Hagan, Walter, 217, 341, 390, 438, 512, 539.
Hagans (see Hagan).
Hagarthy, Andrew, 214.
Hagarthy, Dennis, 121.
Hagarthy (Hagerty, Hegerty) (see Hoggart), George, 119, 294, 322, 538.
Hagarthy (Hagarty), Paul, 8, 117, 630.
Hagen (see Hagan).
Hager, John, 51.
Hager, Wm. J., 30.
Hagerty (see Hagarthy).
Haggarty, Nic., 125.
Haggerty, Peter, 281.
Hagon (see Hagan).
Hahn, Peter, 263.
Haidon (Haiden) (see Hadan).
Haifley, Jacob, 327.
Haig, Jno. (see Hauge), 648.
Hailey, Caleb, 443, 541.
Hailey (Haly), Daniel, 213, 293.
Hailey (Hayley), John, 120, 207.
Hailey, Michael, 214.
Hailey (Haley), Thomas, 53, 124, 282.
Hain, Henry, 218, 261.
Haines, John (see Haynes).
Haines (Hains), Peter, 51, 124.
Hains (see Haynes).
Hair, Jas. (see Hare).
Hair (Haires), Robert, 122, 299, 343.
Haire (see Hare).
Hairs (see Haynes).
Haislip (Haislope), John Boucher (see Haslip), 333, 359, 430, 520, 538.
Haislip, Richard (see Haslip), 358, 448, 498.
Haislope (see Haislip).
Haisty (Heasty), James (see Hasty), 215, 325.
Hale, John, 606.
Hale, Michael, 45.
Hale, Thomas, 117, 426.

Hale, William, 27, 644.
Hales, Chas., 340.
Hales, James, 395.
Haley, Thomas (see Hailey), 53.
Haley (Halley), William, 215, 601, 646.
Halfpenny, Andrew, 212.
Halfpenny, Isaac, 125.
Halfpenny, Mark, 39.
Halfpenny, Thomas, 217, 266, 320.
Halkerson, John, 20.
Halkerston (Halkerson, Hatkerston), Robert, 120, 364, 380, 476, 481, 502, 520.
Hall, Aquilla, 59.
Hall, Arthur, 34.
Hall, Capt., 399.
Hall, Charles, 425, 473.
Hall, Daniel, 217, 391, 438, 541.
Hall, Elisha, 117.
Hall, Elihu, 62, 364, 520, 616.
Hall, Frederick, 120, 122, 333.
Hall, George, 119, 293.
Hall, Henry, 41.
Hall, Isaac, 52.
Hall, James (see Hill), 21, 212, 393, 408.
Hall, John, 119, 124, 213, 214, 215, 324, 354, 414, 440, 488, 539, 563, 565, 567, 568.
Hall, John Beedle, 59.
Hall, John Emory, 66, 645.
Hall, Joseph, 118, 216, 305, 358, 431, 496, 539.
Hall, Josias Carvel, 41, 59, 122, 300, 365, 520.
Hall, Nathl., 41.
Hall, Peter, 21.
Hall, Philip, 21.
Hall, Richard, 121, 298, 329, 357, 430, 496, 538.
Hall, Sam., 125.
Hall, Stephen, 657.
Hall, Thomas, 23, 216, 340, 408, 465, 500, 540, 651.
Hall, Tobias, 124, 281.
Hall, William, 61, 120, 122, 123, 215, 319, 335, 387, 408, 648, 657.
Haller, Fredk. Wm., 217, 265.
Halley (see Haley).
Hallin, William, 583.
Halloran (Halloron, Halloren, Halleron), James, 398, 403, 462, 540.
Halluran, Thomas, 63.
Hals, John, 124.
Halsey (Holsey), John, 10, 117.
Haltham, Joseph, 61.
Haly, Daniel (see Hailey).
Haly, Oliver, 657.

Index. 691

Ham, James, 216.
Hambleton, Charles, 657.
Hambleton, James (see Hamilton).
Hambleton, John (see Hamilton).
Hambleton, Samuel (see Hamilton).
Hambright, Fredk., 641.
Hame, Richard, 327.
Hamelton (see Hamilton).
Hamilton, Alex., 340.
Hamilton, Anthony, 261.
Hamilton, Edward, 409, 479, 482, 520.
Hamilton (Hamillton, Hamiltone, Hamelton), Geo. (Ensign), 10, 11, 61, 63, 117, 118, 124, 213, 356, 364, 380, 394, 452, 476, 480, 493, 518, 539.
Hamilton (Hambleton), James, 66, 653.
Hamilton (Hambleton), John, 53, 63, 121, 122, 281, 314, 320, 340, 345, 354, 362, 378, 383, 409, 435, 478, 482, 489, 520, 538, 627.
Hamilton, John Agner (John A., J. A., ——), 123, 363, 379, 418, 422, 427, 480, 483, 520.
Hamilton, Mathew, 214.
Hamilton, Robert, 281.
Hamilton (Hamiltone, Hamelton, Hambleton), Samuel, 6, 9, 34, 46, 117, 215, 333, 345, 357, 360, 430, 496, 518, 539.
Hamilton (Hamelton), Thomas, 11, 16, 117, 282.
Hamilton (Hamelton), William, 120, 333, 340, 394, 403, 429, 448, 541, 653.
Hammer (Hommer), Jacob, 261, 325.
Hammer, Peter, 344.
Hammer, Tobias, 46.
Hammersly, John (see Ammersley and Emersly), 321, 517.
Hammersly (Amersly), Jno. W., 217.
Hammon, Michael, 388.
Hammond, Andrew, 39.
Hammond, Charles, 653.
Hammond (Hammon), Edward, 217, 357, 430, 496, 539.
Hammond, James, 579, 583.
Hammond, Joseph, 120.
Hammond (Hammon), Peter, 397, 405, 541.
Hammond, Thomas, 39, 381, 394, 463, 509, 540.
Hammond (Hammon, Hamon), William, 64, 216, 308, 322.

Hampton (Hamston, Harnston), William (see Humpton), 217, 317, 390, 438, 512, 540.
Hamson, Elisha, 518.
Hamston (see Hampton).
Hamthon, Thomas, 213.
Hanagan, Charles, 214.
Hanagan, Patk. (see Hannagan).
Hanaman, Henry, 385.
Hanan (see Hannon).
Hanasy (see Hennessy).
Hancock (or Henwick), Elie, 408.
Hancock, John, 431, 508, 539.
Hancock, Stephen (Steven), 359, 396, 449, 504, 540, 581.
Hancock, Willm., 394, 448.
Hand, Thomas, 215, 345, 423, 428, 471.
Hand, William, 429, 509, 541.
Handlen, John, 565, 570, 574.
Handley (Handly), Handy, 368, 392, 429, 448.
Handley, James, 213.
Handley, John, 335.
Handley, Matthew, 70.
Handley (Handly), Philip, 124, 607.
Handley (Handly), Thos., 122, 372.
Hands, Chas., 651.
Handy, George, 69, 74, 212, 281.
Handy, Joseph, 610.
Handy, Levin (——), 68, 69, 74, 212, 520.
Handy, William, 372.
Hanee, Kinsey, 42.
Hanes (see Haynes).
Haney (Heney), Barney (Barna.), 59, 120, 468, 505, 538.
Haney, Dr., 445.
Haney, James, 27, 644.
Haney, John, 12, 294, 357, 443, 494, 538.
Haney, Michael (see Henny), 125.
Haney, William, 388, 408.
Haney, Zadock (see Harvey), 359.
Hangin, Peter, 326.
Haninghouse, Dedrick (see Henninghouse, Frederick), 218.
Hanington (see Harrington).
Hanlon, John, 567.
Hanna (see Hannah).
Hannagan (Hannagin), Brian, 116, 120.
Hannagan, Jno., 282.
Hannagan (Hanagan, Hennigan), Patrick, 217, 309.
Hannah (Hanna), Jas., 56.

Hannah (Hanna), Jno., 125, 422.
Hannah, Miles, 281.
Hannah (Hanna, Mannah), Robert, 66, 212, 648.
Hannen (Hanan, Hennen, Haynon), Thomas, 11, 117, 344, 369.
Hannon (Hanan), Henry, 35, 117.
Hannon, John, 118, 395, 452, 513, 541.
Hannon, Patrick, 215.
Hannon, Walter Warren, 377, 409.
Hansfield, George, 213.
Hansford, William, 125.
Hanson, Anthony, 606.
Hanson, Christian (see Hinson), 422, 471.
Hanson, George, 386.
Hanson, Isaac, 58, 122, 481, 483, 520.
Hanson, John, 657.
Hanson, Peter Contee, 48.
Hanson, Rezin (Reason, Reson), 215, 325, 414.
Hanson, Robt., 118, 282.
Hanson, Samuel, 5, 31, 117, 281, 330, 364, 381, 425, 476, 481, 520.
Hanson, Thomas, 31.
Hanson, William, 31, 460, 476, 481, 520.
Harbert (Harbest), Thos., 657.
Harbert, William (see Hurburt).
Harbeson, Rob., 125.
Harbeson, Wm., 125.
Harbest (see Harbert).
Harbin, Josh., 49.
Harbough, John (see Auber), 653.
Hardacre, William, 382.
Hardcastle, Peter (Lt.), 23, 216, 364, 380, 478, 518.
Hardcastle, Saml., 419, 469.
Hardekin (see Hardikin).
Harden (see Harding).
Hardenstein, Jacob, 265.
Hardesty, Peter, 50.
Hardesty, Thomas, 33, 34.
Hardie, James (see Hartie), 36, 120.
Hardikin (Hardiken, Hardekin), Edward, 27, 118, 293, 643.
Hardikin, Matthew, 25.
Hardin (see Harding).
Harding, A., 118.
Harding (Harden), Daniel, 122, 398, 462.
Harding (Harden, Hardin), Edward, 42, 69, 281.
Harding, Garah, 45.
Harding (Harden, Hardin), John (see Hardman), 42, 118, 119, 121, 299, 331.
Harding, Josiah, 5.
Harding, Richard, 657.

Harding, Robt., 117.
Harding (Hardin), Thomas, 123, 425, 429, 467, 503, 541.
Hardman, Frederick, 72.
Hardman, Henry (see Hartman), 48, 51, 217, 363, 379, 476, 479, 520, 616, 653.
Hardman, John (see Harding), 119, 121, 518.
Hardman, Michael (see Hartman), 267, 320, 354, 447.
Hardy, Andrew, 19.
Hardy (Hardey), Elias, 121, 359, 538.
Hardy, George, 118.
Hardy (Hardey), Isaac, 51, 282.
Hardy, John, 615.
Hardy, Kinsey, 408.
Hardy, Peter, 615.
Hardy, Thos. Dent, 116.
Hare (Haire, Hair), James, 120, 443, 538.
Hare, John, 539.
Hare, Thomas, 215.
Harey, Richard (see Harvey), 408.
Hargadine (Hargedine), John, 66, 214, 645.
Hargeroder (Hargrader, Hergeroder, Hergood), Henry, 266, 270, 517.
Hargraves, Dennis, 116.
Hargreaves, Dyonisius, 18.
Harkenson, Josiah, 124.
Harley, Edward, 121, 298, 329, 384, 538.
Harley (Horley), Henry, 121, 320, 538.
Harley, Jeremh., 123.
Harley (Hearley), John, 217, 265.
Harley, Philip, 640.
Harling, Cornelius, 49, 579, 584.
Harman, Jacob, 19.
Harman (Harmar, Harmer), Lazarous (Lazarus, Lar.), 356, 442, 493, 539.
Harmer, James, 294.
Harmer (or Hamer), John, 657.
Harmer (Harmor), Joseph, 119, 324.
Harmer (Harmar), Lazarus (see Harman).
Harmon, Geo., 282.
Harmon, John, 416.
Harmon, Midleton, 372.
Harmon, Robert, 414.
Harmony, George, 264.
Harmor (see Harmer).
Harness, Daniel, 465, 501, 540.
Harnsbury (Hornsbury, Hoursbury), Nathl. Robt., 370, 392, 448.
Harnston (see Hampton).

692   Index.

Harp, Reice, 122.
Harper, Anthony, 213.
Harper, Daniel, 657.
Harper (Harpur), Francis, 121, 299.
Harper, Henry, 383, 409.
Harper, Hezekiah, 213.
Harper, John, 17.
Harper, Joseph, 383, 398, 403, 409, 422, 462, 506, 540.
Harper, Nathan, 335, 460, 509, 539.
Harper, Richard, 119, 213, 294, 537.
Harper, Samuel, 357, 430, 496, 539.
Harper, Stephen, 44, 121.
Harper, William, 119, 294, 383, 397, 403, 409, 462, 484, 487, 540.
Harpham (Harpin), Robert, 124, 319, 464, 499, 538, 610.
Harrell (Horrell), John (see Farrell), 118, 358, 431, 498, 539.
Harriman, David, 58.
Harriman, William, 52.
Harring (see Heron).
Harrington, Henry, 70.
Harrington (Herrington, Hanington), Levin, 118, 383, 403, 465, 501, 540.
Harrington, Nathan, 24, 212.
Harrington (Herrington), Peter, 377, 378.
Harrington (Herrington, Hanington), Richard, 118, 383, 402, 466, 502, 540.
Harrington (Herrington, Horrington), William, 118, 317, 358, 383, 431, 496, 537.
Harris, Arthur, 214, 363, 379, 476, 479, 520.
Harris, Austin, 504.
Harris (Harriss), Benton, 339, 431, 617.
Harris, Burton, 541.
Harris, Daniel, 428.
Harris, Ezekiel, 647.
Harris, Henry, 372, 395, 449, 517, 541.
Harris (Harriss), James, 67, 120, 340, 344, 357, 375, 408, 432, 445, 495, 539, 645, 648.
Harris, Jesse, 647.
Harris (Harriss), John, 212, 372, 375, 395, 396, 434, 455, 485, 505, 538, 540, 639, 647.
Harris, Joseph, 122, 213.
Harris (Harriss), Josiah, 121, 295, 359, 538.
Harris, Perry, 213.
Harris, Richard, 123, 333.

Harris, Robert, 73, 214, 304, 648.
Harris, Silvester, 118.
Harris (Harriss), Solomon, 24, 68, 119, 293.
Harris (Harriss), Thomas, 122, 124, 302, 375, 395, 416, 465, 501, 538, 645.
Harris, Walter, 282.
Harris (Harriss), William, 37, 121, 214, 281, 332, 333, 348, 419, 428, 439, 467, 511, 538, 539, 541, 600, 657.
Harris, Zekiel, 572.
Harrison, Benjamin, 541.
Harrison, Charles (Col.), 575, 578, 596.
Harrison, Elisha, 481, 483.
Harrison, George, 33.
Harrison, John, 46, 212, 371.
Harrison, Jos., 120, 299.
Harrison, Kinsey, 124.
Harrison, Perry, 644.
Harrison, Richard, 41, 61, 215.
Harrison, Robert, 70, 615, 651.
Harrison, Samuel, 394, 448, 540.
Harrison, Stephen, 68, 281.
Harrison, Thomas, 27, 31, 45, 119, 281, 335, 359, 461, 512, 538, 540, 603, 643.
Harrison (Harrisson), William, 28, 31, 216, 382, 387, 392, 395, 422, 429, 449, 471, 497, 540.
Harriss, Edward, 645.
Harrod, Henry, 400.
Harrod, John, 117.
Harrod, Thomas, 59.
Harry (or Narry), Martain, 328.
Harry, Thomas, 118.
Harst (Hearse), Jacob, 214, 304.
Hart, Chr., 51.
Hart (Heart), John, 49, 215, 270, 272, 294, 516.
Hart, Joseph, 215.
Hart, Michael, 58.
Hart, Richard, 213, 214.
Hart, Thomas, 27, 119, 644.
Hart, (Heart), William, 13, 59, 118, 121, 124, 281, 350, 422, 471.
Hart, Zacha., 120.
Hartenstein, Jacob, 265.
Hartford, John, 340.
Hartie, James (see Hardie), 657.
Hartley, John, 213.
Hartley, Robert, 216.
Hartley, Thomas (Col.), 272, 327, 598, 599.
Hartley, Walter, 600.
Hartlove, John, 117.
Hartly, Michael, 328.

Hartman, Henry (see Hardman), 265.
Hartman (Hatman), Michael (see Hardman), 217, 271, 489, 540.
Hartman, William, 452, 490, 540.
Hartness, Robt., 264.
Hartsell (see Hartzell).
Hartshorn, George, 386.
Hartshorne (Hartshorn), John, 74, 123, 363, 379, 424, 480, 483, 520.
Hartshorne, Jonathan, 408.
Hartsoke, Peter, 653.
Harty (Hearty), Frederick, 217, 309, 326, 356, 390, 438, 493, 539.
Hartzell (Hartsell), Geo., 270, 271, 516.
Harvey, Benjamin, 33.
Harvey (Harvy), Charles, 39, 123, 353, 456, 486, 538.
Harvey (Hurvy), James, 42, 216, 282, 336.
Harvey, John, 342.
Harvey, Joshua, 587.
Harvey (Hervey), Phineas (Phinehas), 62, 422, 470.
Harvey (Harey), Richard, 124, 408.
Harvey, Robert, 11.
Harvey, William, 215.
Harvey (Haney), Zadock, 69, 213, 359, 538, 611, 613.
Harvie, Edward, 601.
Harvy, David, 73.
Harwood, Clement, 393.
Harwood, John C., 446, 506, 540.
Harwood, Nathl., 213.
Harwood, Richd., 40, 41, 575, 581.
Harwood, Thomas, 15, 117.
Haseligh, Jacob, 217.
Haselip, Richard B. (see Haslip), 540.
Hasil (see Hazle).
Hasley, Stephen, 408.
Haslip, John (see Haislip), 122.
Haslip (Haselip, Haislip, Hazlip, Hazelip, Haylip), Richard (Richard B.), 217, 266, 320, 358, 392, 448, 498, 540, 581.
Haslip, William, 120.
Hasselback, Nicholas, 50.
Hasser, John, 118.
Hassett, William, 59.
Hasson, Benj., 647.
Hasson, James, 647.
Hasty, James (see Haisty), 606.
Hatchcraft (see Hutchcraft).
Hatchen, John, 31.
Hatcher, Igns., 119.
Hatfied, Edward, 123.
Hatfield, Edward, 121.
Hatfield, John, 218, 265.

Hatkerston (see Halkerston).
Hatman (see Hartman).
Hatten, Bassil, 35.
Hatten (Hatton), David, 393, 450, 497, 540.
Hatton, John (see Heaton), 14, 124.
Hatton, Josiah, 10.
Hatton, Thomas, 123, 415.
Hatwell, Henry, 215.
Haufman (see Hoofman).
Hauge, John (see Haig), 282.
Haun, Michael, 20.
Hauseigger (Husacker, Hussecker), Nicholas, 181, 261, 262.
Hausman (Houseman, Housman), Conrad, 218, 261, 262.
Hausman, Michael, 270, 271, 516.
Havard, William, 657.
Havclay, Peter, 46.
Haven, James, 69.
Haver, Jacob, 265.
Haverin, Peter, 282.
Havers, John, 118, 313, 657.
Havey (see Heavey).
Hawbacker, George, 182.
Hawes, John, 540.
Hawk, Geo. Mich., 47.
Hawk, Henry, 261.
Hawke (Hawk), Michael, 575, 580, 582, 583.
Hawkes, Thos., 421, 472.
Hawkins, Edward, 340, 344.
Hawkins, Henry, 478, 501, 518.
Hawkins, J., 32.
Hawkins, James, 213, 606, 621, 657.
Hawkins, John (——), 65, 74, 212, 362, 378, 518, 645.
Hawkins, Philip, 18, 119.
Hawkins, Thomas, 369, 370.
Hawley, William, 215, 282, 304.
Hawson, Thomas, 355, 441, 491, 540.
Hawthorn, Nathl., 392, 429.
Hay, John, 124, 281.
Hay, Patrick, 304.
Hay, Thomas (see Hayes), 391.
Hayard (see Hayward).
Haycock, John (see Hancock), 508.
Haycock, Solomon, 409.
Haydon, George, 433, 512.
Haydon, John (see Hadan), 121.
Hayes (Hays), James, 61, 345, 393, 403, 415, 455.
Hayes (Hays), John, 124, 281.
Hayes, Levi, 647.
Hayes (Hays), Levin, 122, 217, 309, 648.
Hayes, Luke, 120.

Index. 693

Hayes (Hays), Richard, 61, 383, 392, 409, 446, 494, 540.
Hayes (Hays, Hay), Thos., 73, 213, 216, 311, 391, 647, 648.
Hayes (Hays), Vachel, 120, 538.
Hayes (Hays), William, 27, 43, 214, 324, 345, 655.
Hayle, Anthony, 119.
Hayley (see Hailey).
Haylip, Richard (see Haslip), 320.
Haymond (Haymon), Owen, 42, 215.
Hayne (see Haynie).
Haynes (Haines, Hains, Hanes, Hairs), John, 122, 216, 305, 394, 448, 511, 653.
Haynes, Joseph, 281.
Haynes, Lawce., 282.
Haynie (Hayne), Ezekiel, 120, 362, 378, 482, 483, 520.
Haynon (see Hannen).
Hays, Alex., 125.
Hays, Bartholo. (Barthw. Cook), 119, 204.
Hays, Gabriel, 124.
Hays, James (see Hayes).
Hays, John (see Hayes).
Hays, Joseph, 602.
Hays, Levin (see Hayes).
Hays, Richard (see Hayes).
Hays, Thomas (see Hayes).
Hays, Vachel (see Hayes).
Hays, William (see Hayes).
Hayton, James, 598.
Hayward, John, 27, 643.
Hayward (Hayard), Matthew, 26, 643.
Hayward (Hayard), Thos., 22, 27, 119, 644.
Haywood, Thomas, 30.
Hazel, Caleb, 661.
Hazel, Jeremiah (see Hazle).
Hazel, Strutton, 43.
Hazell, Philip, 118.
Hazen, Col. Moses, 585, 597.
Hazelip, Richd. (see Haslip), 217.
Hazle (Hasil), Edward, 384, 408.
Hazle (Hazel), Jeremiah, 384, 409.
Hazledine, Francis, 24.
Hazlewood, Jacob, 120, 125.
Hazlewood, Thomas, 218, 267, 321.
Hazlip, Richard (see Haslip), 266.
Head, George, 216.
Head, John, 118, 356, 443, 494, 537, 576, 580, 582, 583.
Head, William, 120.
Heading, John, 217.

Headwood, John, 313.
Heaney, John, 119.
Heany, William, 575.
Heard (Herd, Hurd), Bennett, 44, 408, 428, 474.
Hearly (see Harley).
Hearn, Edward, 41.
Hearse (see Harst).
Heart, John (see Hart), 49.
Heart, William (see Hart), 281.
Hearty, Frederick (see Harty).
Hearty, Nichls., 391.
Heasty (see Haisty).
Heater, George, 44.
Heath, Charles, 214.
Heath, John, 282.
Heathman, George, 44.
Heaton, John (see Hatton), 414.
Heavey (Havey), Daniel, 576, 580, 583.
Hebb, Jesse, 117.
Hebb, Wm., 30.
Heberly, Fredk., 216.
Heck, Daniel (see Hack), 408.
Hecket, Jonathan (see Hackett), 264.
Hecketon (Hecketorn, Heckentom), Martin, 47, 408, 653.
Hedge, William, 123, 353, 458, 486, 540.
Hedgely, John, 340.
Hedges, Josiah, 72.
Heefner (see Heffner).
Heeter, Frederick, 47.
Hefferson (Heffernon), Robert, 25, 387.
Heffner (Heefner), Jacob, 218, 264, 265.
Heffner, John, 261.
Hegerty (see Hagerty).
Heidley, Henry, 221.
Heiggens (see Higgins).
Heisler (Heister), Nicholas, 216, 539.
Heldmole (see Hellmold).
Hellam, Thomas, 124.
Hellen, Basil, 33, 327.
Hellen, James, 33.
Hellen, John, 44, 48.
Heller, Frederick, 266.
Hellin, William, 583.
Hellman, Willm., 392.
Helm, Christian, 132.
Helmes, John, 116, 653.
Helmes, William, 510.
Helmn, Balss., 216.
Hellmold (Heldmole), George, 19, 117.
Helms, Geo., 124.
Helmsley, John, 330.
Helphery, Thos., 416.
Helter, Philip, 270, 516.
Heltinhead, Jno., 123.
Hemerick, Peter (see Emerick), 218.
Hemphill, Joseph, 586, 587.

Hemphill, Robert, 63.
Hempstone, Willm., 341.
Hemsley, William, 342, 375.
Hemstone, Matthias, 647.
Hendersides (see Henderson).
Henderson, Danl., 51, 216.
Henderson, David, 587, 589.
Henderson, Henry, 53.
Henderson, Isaac, 339, 395, 416, 431.
Henderson, John, 46, 282.
Henderson, Robert, 27.
Henderson (Hendersides), Wm., 425, 429, 472, 661.
Hendley (see Henley).
Hendricks (Henricks), Albert (see Hendrickson), 260, 268.
Hendrickson, Albert (see Hendricks), 325.
Hendrickson, Ephraim, 345.
Hendrickson (Henrickson), James, 565, 567, 574, 584.
Hendrickson, John, 47.
Hendry, Wm., 30.
Henessey (Hennisy), Jas., 294, 322.
Henesy, Edward (see Hennessy).
Henesy (Henecy), Peter, 349, 446.
Heney (see Haney).
Henis, James, 281.
Henley (Hendley), Wm., 66.
Henly, John, 441.
Henly, Roger, 119.
Hennen (see Hannen).
Hennes, John (see Hennis), 647.
Hennessy (Henesey, Henesy, Henesee, Henecy, Hanasy), Edward, 118, 314, 397, 403, 458, 487, 540, 584.
Hennessy, Michael, 397, 403.
Hennigan (see Hanagan).
Henninger, George, 409.
Henninghouse, Frederick (see Haninghouse, Dedrick), 261.
Hennis, John (see Hennes), 122.
Hennis, Joseph, 123.
Hennis, Samuel, 630.
Hennisy (see Henessey).
Hennsey, Jno., 282.
Henny, Michael (see Haney), 215.
Henrick, John (see Kendrick), 268.
Henricks (see Hendricks).
Henrickson, James (see Hendrickson).
Henrickson, Wm., 47.
Henry, Adam, 119, 293, 313.
Henry, Elias, 121, 209, 329.
Henry, Isaac, 400.
Henry, James (———), 63, 74, 646, 657.

Henry, John, 49.
Henry, Peter, 215.
Henry, William, 31, 64, 65, 645, 646.
Hensell (Hensil), George, 270, 272, 517.
Henwick (see Hancock).
Henwood, Robert, 595.
Herbert (Hubbard), Jeremiah, 384, 409.
Herbert, Jesse, 30.
Herbert, William, 125.
Herd, Bennett (see Heard).
Herd, Francis, 54.
Herey, Zadock, 614.
Hergeroder (Hergood) (see Hargeroder).
Hergrears, John, 615.
Heritage, Benjamin, 58.
Heritage, Thomas, 216.
Herlity, William, 593.
Herold, Joseph, 594.
Heron, Capt., 598.
Heron (Herron, Harring), John, 12, 116, 212, 218, 263, 644.
Herring (Herrin), Daniel, 387, 408.
Herring, Henry, 217, 261, 262.
Herring, Nathaniel, 63.
Herring, Wm. (see Herron), 64.
Herrington (see Harrington).
Herron, Charles, 282.
Herron, John (see Heron).
Herron, William (see Herring), 212.
Hervey (see Harvey).
Herwell, Thomas, 122.
Hesse, Jacob, 647.
Hessey, John H., 122.
Heveron, Peter, 72.
Hewer, Peter, 218, 262.
Hewey, John (see Hughey), 68.
Hewey, Phineas (see Harvey).
Hewin, John, 120.
Hewington, Th. (see Hovington), 515.
Hewit, Henry, 214.
Hewitt, Elijah, 282.
Hewitt (Huett, Huet, Huitt), James, 346, 355, 366, 461, 492, 539.
Hewitt (Hewit), Thomas, 575, 581.
Hewkill (see Huckell).
Hewlett (Hewlet), John (see Hullett), 216, 454, 493.
Hews (see Hughes and Kews).
Heyder, Willm., 8.
Heyser, Willm. (see Keyser), 263.
Heyton, William, 615.
Heywood, John, 19, 117.
Hicke, William, 42.

Hicken, John (see Hickens), 393.
Hickenbottom (Hininbottom), James, 387, 408.
Hickenbottom, Thos. (see Higgenbotham), 394.
Hickens, John (see Hicken), 517, 540.
Hickey (Hickie), Charles, 381, 394, 446, 515, 517, 541.
Hickey (Hicky), Francis, 118, 331.
Hickey, L., 137.
Hickey, Leonard, 33, 38, 117.
Hickey, Thomas, 123, 318.
Hickey, William, 282.
Hickie (see Hickey).
Hickins (Hickings), John, 342, 456, 502.
Hickinson, Wm., 576.
Hickman, Joshua, 408.
Hickman, Matthias, 73.
Hickory, Jno., 123.
Hicks, John, 394, 463, 510, 540.
Hicks, William, 355, 443, 491, 530.
Hicks, Zebedee, 648.
Hickson, John (see Dixon), 382.
Hicnarl, John, 608.
Hide (see Hyde).
Higdon, George, 214.
Higdon, John, 49, 504.
Higdon (Higden), Joseph, 409, 504.
Higdon, Thomas, 121, 205.
Higdon, Wm., 118.
Higgenbotham, Thos. (see Hickenbottom), 340.
Higgins, Daniel, 24, 281.
Higgins (Heiggens), Dennis, 116, 335.
Higgins, Henry, 24.
Higgins, James, 40.
Higgins, John, 340, 342, 415, 539.
Higgins, Major, 399.
Higgins, Richard (see Huggins), 388.
Higgins, Saml. (see Huggins), 214.
Higgins, Wm., 387.
Higgs, George, 331.
Higgs, Henry, 576, 580, 581, 583.
Higgs, Lazarus (Lazerous, Lazaris), 340, 350, 394, 437, 509, 539, 626.
Iligh, George, 657.
Higman, Edward, 54.
Higoon, William, 331.
Hiland, George, 334.
Hildebrand, Henry, 261.
Hildrop, John, 314.
Hile (see Hoyle).
Hill, Abner, 119.
Hill, Charles (see Hills), 347, 538.

Hill, Casimer (Casemar, Cosomer, Causamer), 19, 262, 267, 314.
Hill, Ebenezer, 216.
Hill, Edward (Edmund), 119, 329.
Hill, George, 45, 586, 587, 588.
Hill, Henry, 217, 341.
Hill, Isaac, 394, 452, 509, 533.
Hill, James (see Hall), 119, 214, 408, 538.
Hill, John, 217, 309, 325.
Hill, Philip, 356, 363, 379, 450, 476, 480, 520.
Hill, Richard, 119.
Hill, Thomas, 12, 54, 68, 70, 125, 351, 352, 376, 420, 470, 509, 540.
Hill, William, 64, 212, 352, 426, 434, 473, 539.
Hill, William Earl, 346.
Hill, Wm. Green (see Wm. Greenhill).
Hillam, John, 428, 474.
Hilland, Mark, 123.
Hillard, John, 603.
Hillary (Hilleary), John (see Elleary), 440, 539.
Hillary (Hilleary, Hillery), Rignal (Regnal), 117, 354, 363, 379, 450, 476, 480, 520, 616, 628.
Hillery, Thomas, 45.
Hillman, William, 212, 217, 293, 356, 442, 494, 539.
Hills, Charles (see Hill), 214, 321.
Hills, Edward, 281.
Hillum, Thomas (see Gilliam), 319.
Hillyer, W. P., 119.
Hilsby, Thos., 387.
Hilton, Benjamin, 213.
Hilton, James, 334.
Hilton, Samuel, 121.
Hilton, Truman, 7.
Hilton, William, 45.
Hiltrhimer, Francis (see Keltrimer), 640.
Hiltzhimer (or Kelsimer), Franz, 116.
Hind (Hindes) (see Hynes).
Hindman, Edward (Capt. C.), 23, 619, 621.
Hindman, James, 23, 212, 647.
Hindman, John, 212.
Hindmore, Richard, 30, 281.
Hindon, Philip, 44.
Hinds, Daniel, 47.
Hinds, Henry (see Hines).
Hinds, James, 35, 212.
Hinds, John (see Hynes).
Hinds, Lawrence (see Hines).
Hinds, Thos. (see Hines).
Hinds, Thos. G., 330.

Hindsley, Solomon, 213.
Hiner (see Hyner).
Hines (Hinds), Henry, 47, 121, 538.
Hines, Jacob (see Hynes).
Hines (Hinds, Hynds), Lawrence, 60, 401.
Hines, Michael, 122.
Hines, Peter, 121, 300.
Hines (Hinds), Thomas, 214, 621.
Hinkle (Hinkel), Philip, 267, 324.
Hinks, Edwd., 415.
Hinks, Thomas, 60, 122.
Hininbottom, James (see Hickenbottom), 387.
Hinley, George, 58.
Hinon, Nichs., 123.
Hinson, Christopher (see Hanson), 465, 501, 541.
Hinths, Edward, 366.
Hinton, John, 648.
Hinton, Lovely (or Lovedy), 40.
Hioms, Fredk. (see Iams), 395.
Hipkins, John (see Hopkins), 58.
Hipsley, Jos., 123.
Hipwells, Benj., 3rd, 54.
Hired, ——, 11.
Hirsh, Jacob, 51.
Hislup, Kendall, 22.
Hitchcock, Asell, 60.
Hitchcock, Asell, Jr. (Azabel), 50, 60.
Hitchcox, Wm., 601.
Hite, John, 20.
Hitland, Henry, 123.
Hoarn (see Horn).
Hobb, John (see Hobbs), 339.
Hobbee (Hobee), Thomas, 213, 214.
Hobbins, Moses, 50.
Hobbs, John (see Hobb), 69, 214.
Hobbs, Joseph, 40.
Hobbs, Robert, 385.
Hobbs, Thomas, 119.
Hobbs, William, 60.
Hobee (see Hobbee).
Hobson, Richard, 325.
Hochshield (Hoshield), John, 218, 262.
Hockett (see Hackett).
Hockey (see Nockey).
Hodge, Philip, 27, 643.
Hodges, Gyks, 648.
Hodges, John, 124, 415.
Hodges, Richard, 215.
Hodgkins (Hodgskins, Hodskin), Samuel, 32, 60, 400.
Hodgson (Hodgdon), John, 214, 281.
Hodgson, Richard, 63.
Hodibuck, Conrad, 119.
Hodskin (see Hodgkins).
Hodson, Edward, 26, 643.

Hodson, Hooper (see Hudson), 25.
Hoffman, Jacob, 265.
Hoffman (Hoofman), John, 19, 281.
Hoey (see Hoy).
Hogan, James (see Hagan), 657.
Hogan, Richd., 420.
Hogan (Hagan, Hogans), Roger, 124, 423, 464, 500, 540.
Hoge, James, 6.
Hogg, James, 117, 640.
Hoggart (Hoggert), George (see Hagarthy), 421, 472.
Hoggins, John, 35.
Hoggins (Hogins, Hoggin), Richard (see Huggins), 351, 397, 502.
Hogins, Jere., 408.
Hogshield, Justimus, 261.
Hoharo, William, 572.
Hohne, Christopher, 575, 581.
Hoina, John, 471.
Hois, Thomas, 281.
Holbrook (see Holebrooke).
Holden, Habikuk (Habycuck), 216, 304.
Holden (Houlden), John (see Holder).
Holden, Jos., 123.
Holden, Kemp (see Holder).
Holden, Thomas, 215.
Holder, James, 641.
Holder (Houlder, Holden, Houlden), John, 64, 118, 120, 212, 293, 294, 320, 392, 512, 538, 641.
Holder (Holden), Kemp, 118, 293, 425, 466, 502, 541.
Holdine, Benjamin, 67.
Holding, John, 66.
Holding, William, 66, 645.
Holdman (Holoman), Daniel, 405, 464, 499, 540.
Holdson (see Holson and Holston).
Holdup, Thomas, 267, 321.
Holebrooke, Edward, 53.
Holebrooke (Holbrook), James, 121, 207.
Holeston, William, 119.
Holiday (see Holliday).
Hollahy, Peter, 450.
Holladay (see Holliday).
Holland, Basil, 20.
Holland, Benjamin, 44.
Holland, Charles, 400.
Holland, Daniel, 122, 335.
Holland, Edward, 355, 441, 491, 539, 575.
Holland, Francis, 74, 125.
Holland, Gabriel, 214, 321.
Holland, Isaac, 417, 467, 504, 541, 575.
Holland, Jacob, 8.

Index. 695

Holland, John, 30, 67, 212, 213, 314, 375, 408.
Holland, Thomas, 12, 122.
Holland, William, 43, 118, 418, 466, 502, 541.
Holliday, George, 45, 119, 314, 446.
Holliday (Holiday, Hollyday, Holloday, Hollady), John, 214, 281, 348, 353, 416, 440, 488, 538, 619, 622.
Holliday (Hollyday), Isaac, 123, 457, 486, 538.
Holliday, William, 41.
Hollings, William, 45.
Hollingsworth, William, 375.
Hollis, Pompey, 397, 403, 459, 511, 540.
Holloday (see Holliday).
Hollon, Reson, 42.
Holloren (Halloran) (see Halloran).
Holloway, John, 120, 217.
Holloway, William, 121.
Hollyday, Clement, 48, 49, 212.
Hollyday, Isaac (see Holliday).
Hollyday, John (see Holliday).
Hollyday, Robt., 215.
Hollyday, Thos., 215.
Hollowhurn, Peter, 395.
Holmes (Homes), James, 352, 434, 540, 600.
Holmes (Homes), John, 121, 298, 329, 538, 617.
Holmes, Solo., 610.
Holmes, Thomas, 66, 119.
Holmes (Holms), William, 14, 117.
Holms, Abraham, 62.
Holoman (see Holdman).
Holsey (see Halsey).
Holson (Holdson), Edward, 66, 217.
Holston (Holdson), John, 395, 450, 541.
Holston, Robert, 23.
Holt, Jas., 610.
Holt, John, 387, 409.
Holt, Leonard, 355, 393, 441, 491, 540.
Holt, William, 121, 217, 329, 463.
Holton, George, 395, 448, 506, 540.
Holton (Houlton), John, 563, 566, 568.
Holtz, Jacob, 45.
Holtzman, Henry, 216, 322, 408, 653.
Homersly, Nathan, 429.
Homes (see Holmes).
Hommer, Jacob (see Hammer), 325.
Homs, Henry, 296.
Honee, James Walter, 340.
Hood, Edward, 120.

Hood, James, 122, 124.
Hood, John (see Wood), 39, 50, 52, 120, 122, 336, 434, 485, 538, 539.
Hood, Joseph, 602.
Hood, Richard, 52, 121.
Hoofman (Haulman), Andrew, 370, 396.
Hoofman, John (see Hoffman).
Hook, Joseph, 217, 266.
Hooke, John Snowden, 49.
Hoole, Joseph, 120.
Hooper, Abram, 120, 215.
Hooper, Abraham, 304, 409.
Hooper, E. William, 212.
Hooper, Ezekiel, 70.
Hooper, Foster, 383, 403.
Hooper, Henry, 340, 377.
Hooper, Jacob, 53.
Hooper, Jeremh., 123.
Hooper, John, 17, 70.
Hooper, Robert, 216.
Hooper (Hoopper), Thos., 70, 334, 425, 429, 474, 626.
Hoops, Adam (———), 123, 135, 363, 379, 479, 520.
Hoover (Hover), Danl., 388, 408.
Hoover, George, 261.
Hoover, Jacob, 218, 265.
Hoover, Peter, 218, 261.
Hope, Ralph, 458, 486, 539.
Hope, Robert, 606, 657.
Hope, William, 355, 441, 491, 540.
Hoperly, Frederick, 304.
Hopewell, Jno., 120.
Hopewell, Thomas, 601, 657.
Hopewell, William, 69.
Hopkins, A. H., 117.
Hopkins, David, 588.
Hopkins, Francis, 121, 295, 354, 436, 480, 538.
Hopkins, James, 598.
Hopkins, John (see Hipkins), 24, 118, 216, 281, 308.
Hopkins, Joseph, 387.
Hopkins, Richard, 60, 267, 370, 648.
Hopkins, Robert, 387.
Hopkins, Roger, 657.
Hopkins, Samuel, 69.
Hopkins, Thomas, 214.
Hopkins, William, 18, 42, 217, 621.
Hopper, John, 41.
Hoppes, Joseph, 35.
Hopson, John, 6.
Hopwood, John, 303.
Horam (see Oram).
Horan (see Horn).
Horine, Jacob, 46.
Horley (see Harley).
Horn, John, 216.
Horn (Horan, Hoarn), Patrick, 214.
Horn, Thomas, 369.
Horne, George, 408.

Horner, Charles, 383, 398, 403, 409, 462.
Horner, George, 640.
Horner, Robert, 120, 281.
Horney, John, 213.
Horney, Philem., 610.
Horney, Solomon, 68.
Horney, Thomas, 213.
Horney, William, 213, 352, 434, 538.
Horns (see Homs).
Hornsbury, Robt. (see Harnsbury), 392.
Horrell (see Harrell).
Horrill, Jas., 117.
Horrington (see Harrington).
Horsefield, James, 294.
Horsefield (Horsfield), Jos., 119, 323, 444, 495, 538.
Horsefield (Horsfield), Luke, 120, 294, 323.
Horsfield, Thomas, 124, 350.
Hoshield (see Hochshield).
Horson, Thomas, 7, 116.
Horton, A., 600, 651.
Hose, Jacob, 218, 263, 264.
Hosel, John, 52.
Hosier, Joshua, 657.
Hosier, William, 69.
Hoskins, Charles, 49.
Hoskins, George, 49.
Hoskins, John, 121.
Hoskins, Joseph, 388, 408.
Hoskins, Randolph (Randal, Rand.), 118, 331, 359, 453, 539.
Hoskins, Zepheniah, 121, 330.
Hoskinson, Archibald, 42.
Hosler (Hoster), Jacob, 50, 216.
Hossilton, Edward, 72.
Hoster (see Hosler).
Hottenstein, Samuel, 321.
Hottfield, John, 264.
Hottle, Jacob, 282.
Hough, John, 121, 281.
Houghton, Benj., 419, 469.
Houks, Mathias, 51.
Houlden (see Holden).
Houlder (see Holder).
Hoult, Thomas, 593.
Houlton (see Holton).
Hoursbury, Nathan (see Harnsbury), 448.
House, William, 44, 614, 615.
Housely (Housley, Hously), John, 215, 348, 446, 500, 538.
Houseman (Housman), Conrad (see Hausman).
Houseman (Howsman), Thomas, 117, 465, 500, 541.
Housley (Owsley), William, 49, 215.
Hously, Rhody, 9.
Houspan, Jno. C., 122.
Houston, James, 314.

Houston, John, 21.
Houston, Thomas, 653.
Hover (see Hoover).
Hovington, Thomas (see Hewington, 217, 359.
How, Daniel (see Howe).
How, George (see Howe).
How, John (see Howe).
How, Robert, 58.
Howard, Austin, 30, 121, 298, 329, 354, 436, 490, 538.
Howard, Benja., 117.
Howard, Burgess, 16.
Howard, Charles, 122, 515.
Howard, Charles Wallace, 642.
Howard, Clement, 51.
Howard, Cornelius, 538.
Howard, Ignatius (Ignatious), 35, 384, 409.
Howard, James, 38, 52, 118.
Howard, John, 119, 121, 314, 350, 538, 562, 564, 566, 568, 574, 583, 587, 603, 617, 661.
Howard, J. B., 124.
Howard, John E., 52, 53, 122, 363, 378, 478, 481, 483, 520.
Howard, Joseph, 65, 116.
Howard, Leonard (see Boward), 119, 330.
Howard, Peregrine (Perrygreen, Peregrim), 122, 298, 357, 430, 496, 538.
Howard, Peter, 441, 492, 539.
Howard, Roger, 34.
Howard (or Froward), Simon, 60.
Howard, Stephen, 118.
Howard, Thomas, 117, 121, 606, 657.
Howard, William, 30, 121, 216, 607, 657.
Howby, Dennis, 117.
Howe (How), Daniel, 125, 350, 352, 397, 417, 420, 465, 500, 540.
Howe (How), George, 51, 216, 308.
Howe, James, 215.
Howe (How), John, 124, 301.
Howe, Walter, 116, 354, 435, 489, 539.
Howe, William, 60, 123, 510, 538.
Howe, Wm. Robt., 326.
Howell, John, 118, 119, 123, 281, 538.
Howell, Joseph (J.), 268, 271, 272, 477, 483, 583, 584.
Howell, Thomas, 26, 119, 216.
Hower, George, 47, 216.
Howley, Dennis, 16.
Hown, Joseph, 58.
Howsman (see Houseman).

696 Index.

Hoy (Hoye), Cephas, 16, 117.
Hoy, Dorset, 16.
Hoy, Joseph, 53.
Hoy, Patrick, 216.
Hoy (Hoey), Peter, 43.
Hoy (Hoye), Thomas, 217, 539.
Hoyle (Hile, Stoyle), Conrod, 218, 251, 264, 265.
Hubbard, Charles, 119.
Hubbard, Hanson, 117.
Hubbard, Jere. (see Herbert), 409.
Hubbard (Hubbert), Job, 377, 378, 400.
Hubbard, Wm., 70.
Hubley, ——, 270.
Hubley, Bernard, 182.
Hubley, George, 182.
Huckell (Huskill, Hugill, Hewkill), Joseph, 119, 357, 444, 495, 538.
Huddleston, Th., 123.
Hudson, Asariah, 214.
Hudson, George, 328, 377, 400.
Hudson (Hutson), Hooper (see Hodson), 385, 409.
Hudson (Hutson), James, 45, 393, 401, 451, 468, 499, 505, 540, 541.
Hudson (Hutson), John, 120, 215, 385, 393, 397, 401, 451, 458, 499, 540, 541, 615.
Hudson, Joseph, 427, 474.
Hudson, Richard, 33.
Hudson (Hutson), Robert, 124, 335, 414.
Hudson, Solomon, 214.
Hudson (Hutson), Thomas, 118, 203, 331.
Hudson (Hutson), William, 123, 385, 657.
Hueston (see Huston).
Huett (Huet, Huitt), Jas. (see Hewitt), 346, 355, 461.
Huffington, John, 383, 402.
Huffman, Henry, 47.
Hugg, Wm., 500.
Huggard, William, 607, 657.
Huggins (Hoggins, Hogins, Roggin), Richard (see Higgius), 351, 397, 466, 502, 540.
Huggins, Samuel (see Higgins), 618.
Huggins, William, 657.
Hughes (Hughs), Alex., 339, 394, 452.
Hughes, Andrew (A.), 24, 106, 117, 118, 647.
Hughes, Evin, 61.
Hughes, Henry, 117, 119, 341, 396, 452, 626.
Hughes, Jacob, 281.
Hughes (Hughs), James, 121, 218, 416.

Hughes (Hughs), John, 10, 24, 30, 64, 69, 117, 119, 120, 281, 313, 331, 333, 335, 394, 434, 512, 537.
Hughes (Hughs), Lawrence, 26, 119, 642.
Hughes (Hughs), Michael, 676, 584.
Hughes (Hughs), Samuel, 119, 121, 295, 538, 541, 620.
Hughes, Thomas, 63, 213, 281.
Hughes (Hews), William (see Kews), 118, 409, 432, 539.
Hughey, John (see Hewey), 213.
Hughey, Jona., 213.
Hughmore, John, 267.
Hughs, Alex. (see Hughes).
Hughs, Christr., 600.
Hughs, James (see Hughes).
Hughs, John (see Hughes).
Hughs, Lawrence (see Hughes).
Hughs, Michael (see Hughes).
Hughs, Samuel (see Hughes).
Hughston (see Hustone).
Hugill (see Huckell).
Hugou (Hugon), Thomas B. (B. Thomas), 212, 364, 378, 381, 422, 477, 482, 518.
Huitt (see Huett).
Hukell (Mahill), Robt., 397.
Hukell, Robt. (see Mahill), 397.
Hukill (Hukins), Abiah, 586, 587, 589.
Hukill (Hukell), Daniel, 424, 466, 503, 541.
Hukill, John, 424, 467, 503, 541.
Hukins, Abiah (see Hukill).
Hukins, John, 213.
Hukins, Joseph, 61.
Hulett (Hulet) (see Hullett).
Huling, Michael, 266.
Huling, Thos., 117.
Hull, Casimer, 217.
Hull, John, 213, 352, 433, 485, 538.
Hull, Nathaniel, 124, 538.
Hull, William, 123.
Hullet, William, 216.
Hullett (Hulett, Hulet, Hewlett), John, 216, 281, 311, 356, 392, 454, 493, 539.
Hulsman, Henry, 47.
Hum, Daniel, 125.
Humberry, And., 416.
Humhey, John, 24.
Humman, Peter, 415.

Humphreys (Humphrys, Humphries), James, 369, 396, 454, 485, 540.
Humphreys, Lewis, 657.
Humphreys (Humphrys), Thos., 217, 281.
Humphreys, Wm., 41.
Humpton, Wm. (see Hampton), 118.
Hundle (see Hurdle).
Hungerford, John, 33.
Hunt, Charles, 41, 281.
Hunt, Gilbert, 653.
Hunt, Gladden, 32.
Hunt, Jacob, 217, 309, 326, 390, 438, 511, 539.
Hunt, James, 118, 331, 418, 466, 501, 540.
Hunt, John, 282, 618.
Hunt, John Stone, 376, 539.
Hunt, Thomas, 217, 623.
Hunter, James, 408.
Hunter, Nathl., 282.
Hunter, Thomas, 118, 640.
Hunter, William, 64, 409, 426, 466, 502, 541, 653.
Huntington, John, 377.
Hurburt (Hurbert), Francis, 607, 657.
Hurbert (Harbert), William, 606, 657.
Hurd (see Heard).
Hurdle, James, 10.
Hurdle (Hundle), John, 359.
Hurdle, Lawrence, 42, 216, 390, 398, 438, 541.
Hurdle, Robt., 282.
Hurley (Hurly), Daniel, 424, 472.
Hurley, Denniss, 63.
Hurley, James, 59.
Hurley (Hurly), John, 37, 50, 61, 282, 345, 352, 396, 454, 485, 540.
Hurley, Josiah, 213.
Hurley (Hurly), William, 217, 341, 390, 442, 506, 539, 632.
Hurn, Henry, 125.
Hursk (see Husk).
Hurst, Cuthbert (Catwood), 657.
Hurst, John, 608.
Hurst, Phineas (Pinchas), 121, 298, 330.
Hurst, Samuel, 378, 393, 400, 451, 494, 540.
Hurt, James, 646.
Hurt, John, 646.
Hurvy (see Harvey).
Hus, Hans, 581.
Husacker (see Hauseigger).
Husey, James, 120.
Husk (Hursk), John, 425, 429, 474.
Huskill (see Huckell).
Husler, William, 61.
Hussa, James, 61.
Hussecker (see Hauseigger).

Husselton, John, 65.
Hussey, Saml., 212, 394.
Huston (Hueston, Hustons), Philip, 335, 396, 454, 506, 539.
Hustone (Hughston), Jacob, 26, 119, 642.
Hutcheson, William (see Hutchinson), 36, 540.
Hutchings, Herculus (see Hutchins).
Hutchings, Stephen, 33.
Hutchingson (see Atchison).
Hutchins, Caleb, 217.
Hutchins, Clement, 33.
Hutchins (Hutchings), Herculus, 468, 504, 541.
Hutchins, Zachariah, 11.
Hutchinson, John, 45.
Hutchinson, Nicholas, 215, 334.
Hutchinson, R. G., 117.
Hutchinson, Saml., 117, 382.
Hutchinson (Hutcheson), William (see Atchison), 36, 465, 501, 540.
Hutchcraft, James, 45, 216.
Hutchcraft, Jos., 310.
Hutchcraft (Hutchcroft, Hutchcrofft, Hatchcraft), Thomas, 217, 262, 267, 323, 353, 394, 448, 488, 540.
Hutchman, Wm., 424.
Hutin (see Hutton).
Hutson, Hooper (see Hudson).
Hutson, Hugh, 648.
Hutson, James (see Hudson).
Hutson, John (see Hudson).
Hutson, Robert (see Hudson).
Hutson, Thomas (see Hudson).
Hutson, Seth, 372.
Hutson, Wm. (see Hudson).
Hutt, Elijah, 303, 454, 507, 539.
Hutton, James, 579, 582, 583.
Hutton (Hutin), Lance (Laurence), 18, 118.
Hutton, William, 216, 308, 579, 583.
Huxter, David, 375.
Huxter, Sahret, 375.
Hyatt, Ely, 30.
Hyatt, George, 265, 270, 516.
Hyde (Hide), John, 123, 353, 456, 486, 538.
Hyde, William, 53, 59.
Hyland, John, 646.
Hynds (see Hines).
Hyndson, Anthony, 657.

Hyner, Joseph, 124, 272, 515, 599.
Hyner (Hiner), Nicholas, 395, 452, 493, 540.
Hynes, Andrew, 74, 75, 214, 303.
Hynes (Hind), Isaac, 124, 303, 318.
Hynes (Hines, Hindes), Jacob, 124, 318, 538.
Hynes (Hinds), John, 118, 331.
Hynes, Martin, 58.
Hynson, Wm., 64.
Hyringer, George, 653.

Iden, John, 51.
Iiames, Thomas, 126.
Iiams (Iams), Frederick (see Ilioms and Jams), 508, 542.
Iiams (Iams), John (see Irons), 126, 571.
Ijams, Henry, 515.
Ijams, Vachel, 409.
Imfeld, John, 261.
Imperfect Names, 22, 27, 297, 324, 325, 342, 566, 567, 576, 646.
Impy, Michael, 219.
Inch, John, 128.
Ingle, William (see England), 107, 353, 457, 486.
Inglehart, Ensign, 300.
Ingles, William (see English), 542.
Ingleton, Thomas, 125.
Inglis, Wm. (see English), 462.
Ingram, Abraham, 218.
Ingram, Edward, 70.
Ingram, James, 70.
Ingram (Engram), William, 203, 219.
Inness, George (see Ennis), 328.
Innis, John (see Ennis), 126.
Innis, Thomas (see Ennis), 128.
Insley, Francis (see Irsley and Ensley), 383, 409.
Insley, Joseph, 70, 383, 409.
Insley, Robert, 126.
Insly, David, 126.
Insly, John, 126.
Insly, Naboth, 126.
Ire, Frederick, 661.
Ireland, George, 33, 219.
Ireland, Henry, 41.
Ireland, John, 579, 582, 584.
Irissler, Jacob, 647.
Irons, Chas., 646.
Irons (Iron), John (see Iiams), 126, 128, 302, 358, 432, 497, 542.
Irsley, Francis (see Insley), 425, 472.

Irvin (Irvine, Irwine), Abraham (Abram) (see Ervin), 126, 357, 444, 495, 542.
Irvin (Irvine), Edward (see Erving), 126, 436, 490, 541.
Irvin, Mathias, 127.
Irvine, James (see Erwin), 541.
Irwine (see Irvin).
Isaacs, Isaac, 128.
Isaacs, James, 443, 542, 661.
Isaacs (Isaacks), Joseph, 394, 433, 513, 542.
Isabel (Issabel), Robert, 126, 542.
Isable, Richard, 293.
Isham (Ishome), Joshua (see Eshome), 220, 380.
Isingminger, Philip, 261.
Isleck, Pascho (Pasco), 369, 409.
Islman, Michl., 128.
Issabel (see Isabel).
Itnier, John (see Etnier), 264.
Ives, Lucas, 334, 394.
Ives, Walter, 22.
Ivory, Charles, 318.
Ivory, Patrick, 11, 125.

Jack, James, 564, 567, 570.
Jackell, Michael, 270, 516.
Jackquelin (Jackelen), Francis, 607, 657.
Jacks, Richard, 128, 414, 417.
Jackson, Abednigo, 63, 126, 329.
Jackson, Alex., 10.
Jackson, Anthony, 128, 340.
Jackson, Christopher, 645.
Jackson, Edward, 398, 403, 409, 462, 508, 542.
Jackson, George, 14.
Jackson, Jacob, 612, 613.
Jackson, James, 126, 343, 358, 381, 393, 394, 444, 490, 541, 626.
Jackson, John, 10, 65, 125, 128, 219, 220, 345, 348, 355, 409, 432, 496, 542, 645.
Jackson, Joseph, 24, 67.
Jackson, Peter, 424, 466, 502, 542.
Jackson, Rengard, 55.
Jackson, Richard, 305.
Jackson, Thomas, 67, 125, 385, 650.
Jackson, William, 127.
Jacob, Jesse (see Jacobs).
Jacob, Philip, 46.
Jacob, Zacha. (see Jacobs).
Jacobs, ——, 378, 379.
Jacobs, George, 219, 363, 520.
Jacobs, Henry, 126, 355, 463, 491, 541.

Jacobs, J., 349.
Jacobs (Jacob), Jesse, 219, 347, 353, 439, 487, 542, 616.
Jacobs, John, 74, 611, 613.
Jacobs, Jno. J. (J.), 219, 303, 349, 362.
Jacobs, Joseph, 41.
Jacobs, Levin, 610.
Jacobs, Robinson, 128.
Jacobs, William, 45.
Jacobs (Jacob), Zachariah, 125, 127, 541.
Jacoe, John, 603.
Jacoe, William, 603.
Jacquett (Jacquet, Jaques, Taquet), Danl. (Jno. Danl.), 220, 263, 264.
Jadwin, Barth., 385.
James, Francis, 128.
James, Isaac, 563.
James, John, 36, 125, 127, 220.
James, Joshua, 648.
James, Philip, 335.
James, Thomas, 60, 220, 260, 376, 394, 397, 416, 617.
James, Walter, 127.
James, William, 41, 128, 219, 575, 581.
Jameson, Adam (see Jamison), 128, 426, 483.
Jameson, John (see Jamison), 647.
Jameson, William, 647.
Jamieson, Adam (see Jamison), 457, 486.
Jamison, Adam (Lt.) (see Jameson, Jamieson and Jenison), 353, 364, 381, 445, 482, 520.
Jamison, Claudius, 60.
Jamison, John (see Jameson), 127.
Jamison, Richd. (see Gemmeson), 394.
Jams, Frederick (see Iiams, 450.
Jannett (see Jennett).
Jaques (see Jacquett).
Jaraliman, John, 61.
Jarboe, James, 35.
Jarboe (Jarber), Peter, 364, 409.
Jarboe, Robert, 384, 409.
Jarhoe, Thomas, 329.
Jarman, Abraham, 55.
Jarman, George, 23.
Jarman, Robert, 22.
Jarman, Willm., 21.
Jarmy (Jarmey), William, 128, 351.
Jarrett, James, 415.
Jarvis, Cato, 220.
Jarvis (Jervais), Daniel, 357, 446, 495, 542.
Jarvis, Jacob, 40.
Jarvis (Jerviss, Garvis), John, 314, 354, 436, 490, 542, 574.

Jarvis, Solomon, 21.
Jarvus (or Jervis), Willis, 69.
Jasper, John, 16, 125.
Javins (Javers), Daniel, 219, 349, 542.
Jeams, Walter, 127.
Jeans, John, 50.
Jeans (Jeanes), Joseph, 128, 350, 458, 508, 542.
Jeckett, William, 125.
Jee (see Gee).
Jefferies, David, 128.
Jefferies, Jacob (see Jeffers), 372, 395.
Jefferies (Jeffries), Wm. (see Jeffers), 392, 416, 618.
Jeffers, Bazil, 651.
Jeffers, Elias, 67, 651.
Jeffers, Jacob (see Jefferies), 24, 126, 450, 490, 542.
Jeffers (or Geffers), John (see Jeffreys), 651.
Jeffers, Peter, 24, 126.
Jeffers, Reuben, 24, 126.
Jeffers, Richard, 218, 416.
Jeffers, Thomas, 127.
Jeffers, William (see Jefferies), 218.
Jefferson (Jeffirson), Edard, 41, 118, 126, 576.
Jefferson, Jestinian, 409.
Jefferson, Wm., 345.
Jeffreys, John (see Jeffers), 58.
Jeffries, Wm. (see Jefferies), 618.
Jellom, John (see Yellum), 618.
Jenings, Charles, 328.
Jenings, George (see Jennings).
Jenings, Richard (see Jennings).
Jenison, Adam (see Jamison), 541.
Jenison (or Jimson), John, 41.
Jenkerson, Edward, 37.
Jenkins, Bazil, 10.
Jenkins (Jinkins), Chas., 66, 282.
Jenkins (Jinkings), Edward, 43, 125, 400, 594.
Jenkins, Francis, 219.
Jenkins (Jinkens), George, 35, 125.
Jenkins, Isaac, 126, 423, 472.
Jenkins, Jason, 125.
Jenkins, Jehu, 219.
Jenkins, John, 317.
Jenkins, Joseph, 126, 128, 218, 354, 400, 436, 489, 541.
Jenkins, Joseph Jason, 6.
Jenkins (Jinkins), Philip, 8, 125, 409.

698 *Index.*

Jenkins, Richard, 127, 319, 623.
Jenkins, Samuel, 218, 371.
Jenkins, Thomas, 35, 125, 220.
Jenkins (Jinkins), William, 24, 126, 282, 314, 341, 358, 444, 498, 542.
Jennett, Green, 657.
Jennett (or Jannett), Peter, 57.
Jennings (Jenings, Jinnings, Jurnings), George, 345, 352, 434, 485, 542.
Jennings, John, 384, 403.
Jennings (Jenings), Richard, 423, 465, 501, 542.
Jennings, Willm., 126, 314.
Jerbo, William, 44.
Jerman, John (see German), 375.
Jerrial, John, 657.
Jerriott, James, 128.
Jervais, Daniel (see Jarvis), 357.
Jervis, Willis (see Jarvus).
Jerviss, John (see Jarvis).
Jessup, John, 416.
Jessup (Jesap), Thomas, 128, 318.
Jester (or Tester), Aaron, 385, 403, 406.
Jester, Francis, 22.
Jewell, George, 385.
Jimson (see Jenison).
Jinkens (Jinkins, Jinkings) (see Jenkins).
Jinnings (see Jennings).
Joace, William (see Joice), 128.
Joel, John, 126, 294.
Johes (see Jones).
John, Cuthbert (see Jones), 298.
John, Thomas, 449, 542.
Johns, Aquilla, 657.
Johns, Benj., 327.
Johns, David, 330.
Johns, James, 127, 220, 297, 309.
Johns, John, 220.
Johns, Nathan, 400.
Johns, Richd., 400.
Johns, Thomas, 396, 490.
Johnson, Abram, 128, 219.
Johnson, Archibald (see Johnston), 126, 358, 393, 497, 541.
Johnson, Baker, 46, 344.
Johnson, Barnard (Barney), 127, 298.
Johnson, Benedict, 579, 582, 583.
Johnson, Benjamin (see Johnston), 34, 127, 295, 397, 409, 436, 541.
Johnson, Benj. Calbert, 376.
Johnson, David (see Johnston), 469.
Johnson, Edwd., 60.

Johnson, Edwd. Wm., 64.
Johnson, Frederick, 383, 409.
Johnson, George, 219.
Johnson, Gerrard, 32.
Johnson, Henry, 127, 575, 581.
Johnson, Hewit, 331.
Johnson, Horsford, 657.
Johnson, Isaac (see Johnston), 59, 420, 464, 542.
Johnson, Jacob, 31, 218, 603.
Johnson, James (see Johnston), 35, 40, 220, 262, 323.
Johnson, Jesse, 405.
Johnson, John (see Johnston and Jonson), 14, 126, 128, 218, 219, 310, 318, 327, 340, 372, 394, 421, 462, 503, 541, 542, 587, 647, 657.
Johnson, Jno. M., 128.
Johnson, Joseph (see Johnston), 21, 30, 128, 353, 400, 457, 486, 541.
Johnson, Josiah (Lt.), 63, 65, 74, 218.
Johnson, Levi, 383.
Johnson, Littleton, 21.
Johnson, Mason, 219.
Johnson, Matthew, 32, 331.
Johnson, Miles, 128.
Johnson, Nelson (Nellson), 376, 409.
Johnson, Nicholas (Nichols, Nickolas), 219, 270, 271, 282, 516.
Johnson, Richard, 8, 41, 127, 615.
Johnson (Joshson), Robert, 126, 219, 294, 383, 403, 409, 467, 503, 541, 542, 653.
Johnson, Simon, 220, 321.
Johnson, Thomas (Governor) (see Johnston), 30, 58, 218, 335, 603, 615, 650.
Johnson, Vincent, 125.
Johnson, William (see Johnston and Jonson), 16, 30, 32, 125, 126, 220, 322, 341, 422, 464, 499, 515, 542, 575, 581, 646, 647.
Johnston, Archibald (see Johnson), 452.
Johnston, Benjm. (see Johnson), 511.
Johnston, David (see Johnson), 418.
Johnston, Francis, 576, 580, 583.
Johnston, Isaac (see Johnson), 499.
Johnston, James (see Johnson), 220, 267, 447, 601.
Johnston, John (see Johnson), 282, 302, 434, 473, 510, 627.

Johnston, Joseph (see Johnson), 330.
Johnston, Saml., 601.
Johnston, Thomas (see Johnson), 219.
Johnston, William (see Johnson), 74, 266, 420, 471, 542, 576, 648.
Joice, Edward, 600.
Joice (Joyce, Joace, Joiel), William, 125, 128, 320, 335, 358, 432, 497, 541, 542.
Joiner, James, 614.
Jonas (see Jones).
Jones, ——, 74, 273, 567.
Jones (Jonas), Aaron, 126, 218, 352, 433, 542.
Jones, Ambrose, 602.
Jones, Aquila Lee, 59.
Jones, Benjamin, 35, 41, 65, 218, 219, 565, 567, 569, 573, 626.
Jones, Charles, 10, 30, 65, 220, 266, 323, 354, 392, 447, 488, 542, 615.
Jones, Cotter (Cutler), 425, 473, 510, 542.
Jones (John), Cuthbert, 127, 298, 384, 409.
Jones, David, 46, 126, 313, 383, 541.
Jones, Dennis, 220.
Jones, Edward, 9, 68, 282.
Jones, George, 387, 397, 458, 488, 542, 602.
Jones, Hanbury, 39.
Jones, Henry, 49, 315, 234.
Jones, Isaac, 39, 40, 41, 126, 369, 382.
Jones, Jacob, 218.
Jones, James, 24, 126, 127, 219, 220, 295, 382, 394, 498, 542.
Jones, Jerry, 18.
Jones, Job, 127.
Jones, John, 45, 70, 126, 127, 219, 220, 305, 322, 330, 340, 342, 366, 368, 381, 391, 392, 394, 437, 452, 461, 467, 493, 503, 542, 608, 616, 627.
Jones, John Courts, 48, 220, 364, 380, 476, 480, 520.
Jones, John Morgan, 21.
Jones, Jonathan, 47.
Jones, Joseph, 126, 127, 128, 319, 358, 421, 444, 472, 499, 541, 606, 657.
Jones, Joshua, 128.
Jones, Lewis, 126, 127.
Jones, Livie, 51.
Jones, Michael, 400.
Jones, Nathan, 657.
Jones, Nathl., 345.
Jones, Nealy (Neilee, Neelee, Neile), 126, 469, 510, 541.
Jones, Nelce, 398, 627.
Jones, Peter, 340.

Jones, Philip, 127, 564, 569, 579, 583, 584.
Jones, Reese, 59.
Jones, Richard, 38, 41, 127, 219, 381, 395, 399.
Jones (Johes), Robert, 393, 400, 401, 416, 421, 472.
Jones, Samuel, 5, 31, 127, 128, 220, 311, 319, 325, 409, 415.
Jones, Solomon, 70.
Jones, Thomas, 13, 51, 52, 53, 58, 60, 65, 70, 127, 218, 219, 335, 344, 354, 371, 394, 396, 398, 409, 421, 436, 447, 453, 455, 485, 488, 489, 541, 542.
Jones, William, 21, 39, 63, 65, 125, 127, 220, 297, 308, 325, 335, 338, 355, 357, 366, 370, 372, 385, 403, 442, 446, 492, 495, 515, 542, 575, 642.
Jonson, ——, Mister, 614.
Jonson, John (see Johnson), 67.
Jonson, William (see Johnson), 63.
Jordan (Jordon), James, 30, 51, 343, 648.
Jordan, Jesse, 30.
Jordan (Jordon, Jorden, Jordine, Jourdan), John, 13, 125, 128, 218, 350, 363, 369, 379, 394, 427, 455, 469, 542, 657.
Jordan, Richard, 648.
Jordan, Samuel, 30, 657.
Jordan, Thomas, 31, 341.
Jordan (Jordon), William (see Gordon), 56, 114, 282, 299, 648.
Jordon, James (see Jordan).
Jordon (Jorden, Jourdan), Jeremiah, 593, 657.
Jordon, John (see Jordan).
Jordon (Jourdan), Justian (Justinian, Jestenian), 127, 298.
Jordon, William (see Jordan).
Joseph, John, 128, 282.
Joshson (see Johnson).
Jourdan (Jeremiah) (see Jordon and Jorden).
Journey, Sabrit, 399.
Joy, Caleb, 27, 643.
Joyce, William (see Joice), 125, 335.
Joyse, Thomas, 218.
Judah, Wm., 573.
Judd, Wm., 400.
Judges, William, 606, 657.
Jump, Elijah, 368.
Jurnings (see Jennings).
Justice, Charles, 220.
Justice, Peter, 646.
Justice, William, 398, 403, 462, 542.

Index. 699

Kach, John, 221.
Kagen, Henry, 58.
Kahill (Kahil), Nathaniel, 384, 409.
Kahoe, John, 317.
Kain (Kaine), see Cain.
Kallenberger, Chr., 47.
Kallenberger, Frederick, 47.
Kamble, Stephen (see Kimble), 543.
Kanahan, John (see Canahan), 69.
Kann, John, 131.
Kaports (see Keeport).
Karney (see Carney).
Karns (see Kearns).
Karr (see Carr).
Kasler, John, 19.
Kattakan, Joseph, 221.
Kaufman (Kauffman, Caufman, Coffman), Jacob, 198, 223, 266, 322, 395, 517.
Kaugh (see Keough).
Kautz, Philip (see Kuntz), 265.
Keach, Ebenezer, 220.
Keadle, Thos., 382.
Keain, David, 646.
Kean, Danl., 131.
Kean, James, 131.
Kearnes (see Kearns).
Kearns (Karns), Benjamin (see Carnes), 355, 441, 491, 543.
Kearns, Christn., 262.
Kearns (Karns, Kerns, Carnes, Carns), Francis, 223, 266, 324, 354, 394, 447, 488, 543.
Kearns (Kearnes, Karnes, Karns), James, 129, 221, 304, 419, 470.
Kearns (Kearnes), Thomas, 221, 349, 440.
Kearse, James, 387.
Kearsey (Kearsy) (see Kersey).
Kearshner (see Kershner).
Keath, Andrew (see Keith), 648.
Keats, Thomas, 131.
Keay (see Key).
Kebler (see Kibler).
Keech, James, 32.
Keech (Keetch, Keitch), John, 389, 396, 453.
Keech, Saml., 129.
Keech, Walter, 443, 506, 543.
Keefe (Keeff), Thomas, 222, 391.
Keegan (Kiggan), John, 130, 296.
Keeland (Keiland, Keland, Keelan, Kelam), James, 45, 222, 307, 358, 438, 499, 543.
Keemer, John, 44.

Keen, Charles, 66.
Keen, John (see Keene).
Keen, Michael (see Keene).
Keen, Richard, 321.
Keen, William, 222.
Keenan, Larrons, 58.
Keene (Keen), Jobn, 129, 645.
Keene (Keen), Michael, 468, 504, 543.
Keene, Samuel Y., 478, 520.
Keene, Thomas, 70.
Keener, Barney, 305.
Keener, John, 262.
Keener, Lawrce., 129.
Keephart (Keepheart, Kephart, Kiphart, Kipart), Adam, 129, 314, 357, 444, 495, 543.
Keephart (Kipheart, Kephard, Kepphard), George, 19, 223, 262, 267.
Keeport (Kaports), Geo. P. (George) (see Keepott and Vreeports), 182, 262.
Keepott, George (see Keeport, Geo. P.), 563.
Kees (Keys), Charles, 269, 270, 271, 272, 517.
Kees, Matthias, 335.
Keeson, Jacob, 387.
Keetch (see Keech).
Keeth, John, 581.
Keetley (see Keitley).
Keiff, Patk., 283.
Keil, George O. (see O'Keil), 400.
Keintz (see Kintz).
Keiland (see Keeland).
Keiser (see Keyser).
Keitch, Daniel, 375.
Keitch, John (see Keech).
Keith, Andrew (see Keath), 572.
Keith, Daniel, 598, 661.
Keith, Duncan, 130, 295.
Keith, John, 575, 581.
Keitley (Keetley), Francis (see Kitely), 222, 309.
Kelam, James (see Keeland), 45.
Keland (see Keeland).
Kelby (Kilby), Thomas (see Kelly), 129, 294.
Keleher (see Kelleher).
Kellar, John, 47.
Kellee, Joseph, 338.
Kelleher (Keleher, Kelliher), Henry, 563, 566, 568, 574.
Keller, Adam, 46.
Keller, Fredk., 18.
Keller, George, 345.
Keller, Jacob, 307.
Kelley, Charles, 52, 59.
Kelley, Francis (see Keitley), 309.
Kelley, Gordon, 602.
Kelley, George (see Kelly).
Kelley, Hugh (see Kelly).
Kelley, James (see Kelly).

Kelley, Matthew (see Kelly).
Kelley, Owen, 602.
Kelley, Patrick (see Kelly).
Kelley, Thomas (see Kelly), 58, 294, 334.
Kelley, Timothy (see Kelly), 601.
Kelliher (see Kelleher).
Kellinough (Killinough), William, 27, 643.
Kellis, Dennis, 17.
Kellow (Kello, Killow), William, 129, 331, 543.
Kelly, Barnaby, 344.
Kelly, Benj., 9.
Kelly, Daniel, 222.
Kelly, David (see Relly), 220, 505, 543, 618.
Kelly, Dennis, 129, 431, 508, 542.
Kelly, Edward, 131, 221, 387, 409.
Kelly (Kelley), George, 45, 130, 222, 283, 311, 343.
Kelly (Kelley), Hugh, 26, 129, 130, 294, 334, 643.
Kelly, Jacob, 462, 507, 543.
Kelly (Kelley, Killey), James, 14, 70, 129, 130, 131, 222, 283, 305, 334, 335, 346, 354, 359, 382, 387, 389, 409, 435, 468, 489, 505, 543, 640, 661.
Kelly, John, 58, 129, 130, 283, 386, 409, 607.
Kelly (Kelley), Matthew, 130, 131, 392, 465, 501, 543, 569, 574, 627.
Kelly, Michael, 130.
Kelly (Kelley), Patrick, 130, 221, 222, 329, 340, 452.
Kelly, Richard, 130.
Kelly, Roger, 67.
Kelly (Kelley), Thomas (see Kelby), 58, 221, 222, 294, 312, 334, 403.
Kelly (Kelley), Timothy, 601, 607.
Kelly, William, 129, 221, 283, 433.
Kelner, John, 428, 474.
Kelsey, Joseph, 334.
Kelsimer, Franz (see Hiltzhimer), 116.
Kelson, George, 221, 440, 485, 543.
Keltrimer, Francis (see Hiltrhimer), 129.
Kelty, George, 463, 543.
Kelty, William (see Kilty).
Kelvin, George, 352.
Kemmel (see Kimmel).
Kemmer, Danl., 328.
Kemp, Capt., 386.
Kemp, James, 59, 131.
Kemp, John, 67.
Kemp, Robt., 371.
Kemp, Wilhelm, 270.

Kemp, William, 270, 517.
Kemper, Thomas (see Camper), 283.
Kempton, Thos., 283.
Kendall, Sam., 180.
Kendercline (Kenderdine), John, 573, 657.
Kendrick, James, 371.
Kendrick, John (see Henrick), 222, 266, 325.
Kenedy, Michl., 130.
Kenly, Richard, 400.
Kennady, Robt., 283.
Kennady, Tho. (see Kennedy), 129.
Kennard, Richard, 63.
Kennear, John, 336.
Kenneday, John (see Connady), 45.
Kennedy, David, 131, 598.
Kennedy, James, 131, 414.
Kennedy, Michael, 130.
Kennedy, Samuel, 220, 618.
Kennedy (Kennady, Cannady, Canady, Canada), Thomas, 129, 130, 222, 357, 430, 496, 529.
Kennedy, Timothy, 572.
Kennedy, William, 130, 221, 300, 325.
Kenney (see Kenny).
Kennick (Kinnick), William, 17, 221.
Kenniford, Robert, 66.
Kenny (Kenney, Kinney), John, 130, 222, 336.
Kenny, Joseph, 602.
Kenny (Kenney), Thomas, 52, 130.
Kenny (Kenney), William, 24, 222, 334.
Kent, Gideon, 581.
Kent, Henry, 592, 593.
Kent, Isaac, 409, 425, 467, 503, 543.
Kent, James, 65, 644, 645.
Kent, John, 645, 650.
Kent, Stephen, 220.
Kent, Wm., 422, 471.
Kentz, Jacob (see Kuntz), 223.
Keough (Kaugh), William, 221, 308, 464.
Kephard (Kepphard) (see Keephart).
Kephart, Adam (see Keephart).
Kephart (Kipheart), Martin, 19, 129.
Keplinger (Kepplinger), Christian (Chresn., Christopher), 222, 267, 324.
Kerbey, Richard, 30.
Kerby, Anthony, 370.
Kerby, John (see Kirby), 15, 387.
Kerby, Joseph, 384.
Kerby, Nathaniel, 221.
Kerby, Patk. (see Kirby).
Kern, Jacob, 47.
Kern, Philip, 19.

Index

Kernall (Kernal), Wm., 130, 431.
Kernam (see Kernan).
Kernan, Barna., 129.
Kernan, Martin, 221.
Kernan (Kernon, Kernam), Michael, 221, 328, 543.
Kerney, William, 51.
Kernon (see Kernan).
Kerns, Francis (see Kearns).
Kerns (Kearns), Jacob, 266.
Keron, John, 27.
Kerr, James, 615.
Kerr, John, 357, 581.
Kerr, Robt., 131.
Kerrick, Benj. H., 358, 439, 497, 543.
Kerrick, Joseph (see Carrick), 221, 439, 543.
Kerns, Robert (see Carnes), 630.
Kerny, Edward (see Carney), 50.
Kersey, Archibald, 393, 451.
Kersey, Brian, 129.
Kersey, Daniel, 129, 293.
Kersey (Kearsy, Kearsey), Edward, 52, 221, 355, 446, 492, 543.
Kersey (or Cearsey), Jas. (see Corsey), 66.
Kersey, Leven, 44.
Kershner, John, 328.
Kershner (Kearshner), Michael, 223, 265.
Kerven, Andrew, 383.
Kettle, Abraham, 223, 262, 353, 395, 448, 488, 543.
Kettle, Daniel, 223, 353, 448, 488, 543.
Kettle, Thomas, 469, 505.
Kettle, Thomas Gibson, 409.
Kettle, Thomas P., 543.
Kews (or Hews), Wm., 432.
Key (or Keay), Daniel, 57.
Key, John Ross, 28.
Key, Patt. (see Keys), 312.
Keyes (see Keys).
Keymer, William, 623.
Keys, Charles (see Kees), 270.
Keys, James, 400.
Keys (Key), Patrick, 222, 312.
Keys (Keyes), Thos., 425, 474.
Keyser (Kiser), Jacob, 223, 394, 447, 543.
Keyser (Keiser), Mathias, 222, 265.
Keyser, Nicholas, 266, 270, 517.
Keyser, William (see Heyser), 182, 263.
Keysey, Jno., 305.
Kibler (Kebler, Kibber), John, 222, 264, 265.
Kibley, Joseph, 409.

Kidd, John, 5, 131, 353, 456, 486, 543.
Kiding, Ludowick, 50.
Kidney, Michael, 220.
Kidwell, Benj., 130, 296.
Kidwell, Elijah, 35.
Kidwell, Ezekiel, 419, 470.
Kidwell, James, 35.
Kidwell, Matthew, 331.
Kiezer, Martin, 49.
Kiggan (see Keegan).
Kilby (see Kelby).
Kildare, John, 303, 455.
Kildee, Jas., 360.
Kildray, John, 340.
Killegan, James, 129, 461, 543.
Killey (see Kelly).
Killgrest, Andrew, 602.
Killing, Jno., 283.
Killinough (see Kellinough).
Killman, Edward, 129, 543.
Killow (see Kellow).
Killpin (see Calpin).
Killyham, Bradley, 305.
Kilty, James, 350.
Kilty (Kelty), John (J., Lieut.), 38, 40, 130, 616.
Kilty (Kelty), William, 220, 364, 380, 481, 483, 520, 621.
Kimble (Kimbal, Kimboll), Josias, 131, 302.
Kimble, Stephen (see Kamble), 130, 393, 452.
Kimmel (Kemmel), Thos. (see Campbell), 266.
Kimplin, William, 642.
Kincaid (Kinkead, Kinard), John, 220, 587, 588, 500.
Kincaid (Kincade, Cinquaid, Cincuid), Peter, 220, 306, 475, 543, 621.
Kinchley, Morgan, 222.
Kindle, Stephen, 64.
Kindle, William, 222, 301, 543.
King, Adam, 34, 129.
King, Charles, 221, 377, 409.
King, Daniel, 340, 344.
King, Francis, 221, 304, 414.
King, George, 129, 294.
King, Henry, 130, 330.
King, Isaac, 129, 290.
King, James, 131, 300.
King, Jeremiah, 130, 330.
King, Jesse (Jessey), 398, 626.
King, John, 34, 131, 222, 319, 327, 344, 353, 382, 384, 391, 396, 400, 455, 486, 543, 572.
King, Levin, 220.
King, Matthew, 46.
King, Mathias, 261.
King, Philip, 8, 129, 641.
King, Thomas, 41, 129, 382, 437, 502, 542, 617, 647.

King, William, 56, 131, 283, 461, 511, 543, 606, 617, 657.
Kingors, William, 602.
Kingston, George, 49, 283.
Kinkead (see Kincaid).
Kinnahan, John (see Canahan, 221.
Kinnard, Benjamin, 409.
Kinnard, James, 371.
Kinnard, Nathaniel, 63, 65.
Kinnard, Wm., 65.
Kinney (see Kenny).
Kinnick, Richard, 33.
Kinnick, William (see Kennick), 17.
Kinnimon, Philip, 67.
Kinsey, David, 129.
Kinsey (Kinsee, Kinser), George, 222, 310, 325, 344.
Kinsey, Samuel, 222.
Kinsey, Thomas, 658.
Kinstry, Frederick, 388.
Kintare (see Kittare).
Kintz (Keintz), Jacob, 265.
Kiphart (Kipart, Kipheart) (see Keephart).
Kirhy (Kerhy), John, 15, 129, 387, 615.
Kirby (Kerby), Patk., 131, 302.
Kirgery, Christiain, 328.
Kirk (Koik), Benj. H., 221, 304.
Kirk, Daniel, 658.
Kirk, David, 70.
Kirk, Edward, 131, 350, 352, 397, 420, 465, 500, 543.
Kirk, Ensign, 602.
Kirk, James, 14, 344, 393, 429, 466, 502, 543.
Kirk, John, 51, 601.
Kirk, Joseph, 61, 304.
Kirk, Thomas, Jr., 45.
Kirk, William, 130.
Kirkpatrick, William (see Patrick, Wm. Kirk), 384, 409.
Kirshaw, William, 221, 327.
Kisby (Kisbey), Richard, 44, 342, 355, 446, 491, 543.
Kiser (see Keyser and Kizer).
Kisk, James, 416.
Kite, William, 62.
Kitely (Keitley, Keetley), Francis, 50, 222, 309, 311, 391, 543.
Kittare (or Kintare), Peter, 601.
Kizer (or Kiser), Valentine, 58.
Klein, Frederick, 595.
Klein, Gottlieb, 261.
Kline, Jacob, 223, 264, 265.
Kline (Klein, Cline), John, 222, 261, 262.

Kline, Peter, 19.
Knap, Nero, 409.
Knapp, Thomas, 67.
Knave (Nave), Henry, 50, 221, 235.
Kneary, Lorentz, 265.
Knight, David, 131, 302.
Knight, George, 129.
Knight, Isaac, 221.
Knight, Jacob, 52, 129, 294, 323, 357, 394, 444, 494, 543.
Knight, John, 131, 606, 658.
Knight, Nehemiah, 641.
Knight, Philip, 397, 403.
Knight, Thomas, 130, 299, 344.
Knight, William, 67.
Knighton, John, 399.
Knighton, William, 602.
Knimptum, Thomas, 65.
Knock, Daniel, 63.
Knock (Knoc), John (see Knox), 40, 543.
Knock, Nathl., 646.
Knot, Nathaniel (see Nott), 543.
Knott, George, 9.
Knott, Ign., 30.
Knott (Knot), James (see Nott), 129, 355, 452, 491, 543.
Knott, Jeremh., 129.
Knotts, William, 66.
Knowell, John, 409.
Knowland, Lucas, 221.
Knowland, Michael (see Noland), 222.
Knowlar, Thomas, 43.
Knowles, William, 600.
Knox (or Nox), James, 307.
Knox, John (see Knock), 130, 222, 356, 463, 493, 543.
Knox, T. (Gen., M. G.), 575, 577.
Koefflich, Jacob, 263.
Koik (see Kirk).
Koons, Peter (see Kuntz), 223.
Koontz, Philip (see Kuntz), 653.
Korer, Henry, 405.
Korer, Martin, 405.
Kotz (Kottz), Jacob, 182, 263.
Koy (see McCoy).
Kraft (Krofft, Croft), William, 108, 266, 268.
Kries (Kruise), Peter, 222, 263.
Kuhnes, Henry, 648.
Kumius (Cunius, Cunnius), William, 266, 270, 517.
Kuntz (Kentz), Jacob, 223, 261.
Kuntz (Koons, Coons), Peter, 223, 261, 262, 395.
Kuntz (Koontz), Philip (see Kautz), 222, 653.

Index. 701

Kuny (Coony, Cooney, Coomy), John, 344, 514, 508.
Kurk, Samuel, 6.
Kurtz, Jacob, 261.

Laceman, Lodwick, 409.
Lacey, Daniel, 53, 335.
Lacey, John, 136.
Lacey, Stephen, 133.
Laci, Peter, 626.
Lacklin, Lenard, 34.
Lacy, Thomas, 60.
Ladder, John, 225.
Laffy, Thomas, 14.
Lago (see Leago).
Lahnnum, Kirney, 486.
Laigg, Edward (see Legg), 442.
Laighton, William, 14.
Laine, Bartley (see Lane).
Laine, Levin (see Lane).
Laine, Richard (see Lane).
Laine, Solomon, 133.
Laiswell, Andrew, 602.
Lake, William, 135.
Lakin, Basil, 388.
Lam, Thomas, 405.
Lamal (or Lamie), William, 135.
Lamar (Lemar), William, 50, 224, 362, 378, 388, 392, 421, 480, 481, 483, 521.
Lamb, Francis, 65.
Lamb, James, 13.
Lamb, John, 572.
Lamb, Joshua, 15, 132.
Lamb, Luke, 21.
Lambart, Samuel, 573.
Lambden, Wm., 387.
Lambert (Lamberts), Christopher, 398, 433, 505, 544, 630.
Lambert, George, 601.
Lamboth, Henry, 40.
Lamie (see Lamal).
Lamond, John, 607.
Lampert, John, 344.
Lanahan (Lenehan, Leneham), Darby (see Linian), 439, 513, 544.
Lancaster, Henry, 344.
Lancaster, John, 284.
Lancaster, Samuel, 410.
Lanchaster, Jeremiah, 61.
Land, Jas., 284.
Land, Richard, 133.
Land, William, 132, 658.
Landenberger, John, 182.
Landers (Launders), Roger (see Sanders), 294, 321, 357, 394, 444, 494, 544.
Lane (Laine), Bartholw. (Bartley), 133, 294.
Lane, Henry, 270, 271, 303, 517.
Lane (Laine), Levin, 70, 133.
Lane, Morris (or Mores), 70.

Lane (Laine), Richard, 65, 393, 442.
Lane, Thomas, 38, 385, 403, 460.
Lane, William, 387.
Lang, Francis, 355, 441, 491, 544.
Langford, Elizaha, 132.
Langle (see Langrale).
Langley (Langly), John, 72, 327.
Langley (Langly), William (see Longley), 41, 131.
Langly, James (see Longley), 333.
Langrale (Langle), Levin, 606, 658.
Langrell, Asquith, 133.
Langrell (Langrel, Langrill), Timothy, 383, 398, 403, 458, 487, 545.
Langton, John, 44.
Lanham, Eli, 35.
Lanham, Elias, 35.
Lanham, Henry, 8.
Lanham, Hillary, 424, 472.
Lanham, Jno., 131.
Lanham, John D., 8.
Lanham, Kinsey, 458, 544.
Lanham, Nehemiah, 136, 351, 397.
Lanham, Richard, 132.
Lanham, William, 43.
Lankford, Elijah, 293.
Lann, Thomas, 37.
Lansdale, Isaac, 39.
Lansdale, Thomas, 52, 53, 135, 362, 378, 379, 470, 482, 521.
Lantz, Martin, 225, 265.
Lappin (Lappine, Lapine, Lapping), Paul, 336, 352, 434, 485, 544.
Laramore (see Larramore).
Larance, John (see Laurence), 335.
Larantz, Fredk. (see Lorentz, Ferdinand), 225.
Laravier, Jean, 313.
Lard, William, 225.
Larey, Daniel (see Larry), 134.
Larey, William (see Larry), 66.
Larimore, David, 130.
Larkin, Anthony, 284.
Larkins (Larkan), Dennis, 606, 658.
Larmore, Thomas (see Larramore), 225, 354, 447.
Larner, John, 134.
Larose, John, 416.
Larramore (Larrymore, Laramore, Larmore), Thomas, 225, 354, 392, 447, 488, 544, 581.
Larrey, Wm. (see Leary).
Larry (Larey), Daniel (see Leary), 134, 305.

Larry (Larey), William (see Leary), 66, 225, 376, 645.
Larrymor, Samuel, 388.
Laruden, Thomas, 610.
Larymore (see Larramore).
Lash, George (see Lesh), 458.
Lasher, John (see Lashyear), 132.
Lashley, John (see Lesley), 463, 545.
Lashyear (or Layzare), John (see Lasher), 42.
Lassell, Alex., 133.
Lastly, Joseph, 283.
Latham, Aaron, 61, 409.
Latham (Laythrum), Silvester, 61, 283.
Latten, Thomas, 41.
Lattimore, Jno., 649.
Lattimore, Wm., 648.
Lattlemore, Anda., 283.
Laughlain (or Laughlanhon), Peter, 70.
Laukin, John, 224.
Lauglane (or MacLaughlin), Mark (see McLaughlin), 133.
Launders, Geo., 133.
Launders, John (see Saunders), 244.
Launders, Roger (see Landers).
Laurence, Adam, 63.
Laurence (Larance), John (see Lawrence), 66, 335.
Laurence, Peter (see Lawrence).
Laurence, Wm. (see Lawrence).
Lavely (Leavley), Jacob, 41, 135.
Lavender, Jno., 134.
Lavender, Thos., 299.
Lavigne, Michael, 333.
Lavington (see Leverton).
Lavy, John, 40.
Law, Joseph, 342.
Lawers (Lowers, Loyers), Henry (see Sowers), 358, 463, 406.
Lawler, David, 133, 134, 621.
Lawler, James, 283.
Lawler, John, 133, 135.
Lawler (Loller), Michael, 134, 357, 430, 496, 544.
Lawless, John, 224.
Lawless, Peter, 16.
Lawrence, David, 223.
Lawrence, James, 33, 52, 66, 135, 223, 327, 396.
Lawrence (Laurence), Jno., 66, 283, 335.
Lawrence, Joshua, 132, 658.
Lawrence, Levin, 224, 571.
Lawrence (Laurence), Peter, 576, 580, 582, 583.

Lawrence (Laurence), William, 58, 223, 417, 469, 509, 545.
Lawrenson, James, 61.
Lawrey, Galfried, 225.
Laws, George, 133, 544.
Laws, Henry, 544.
Laws, William, 133, 357, 444, 495, 544.
Lawsin, Robt., 305.
Lawson, James, 572.
Lawson, Michael, 132, 331.
Lawson, Ralph, 225.
Lawyer (Lawyers), Thos., 428, 474.
Lay, John, 35.
Layard, George, 136.
Laylan, Wm., 427.
Layland, Wm., 421, 472.
Layman, Garliner, 134.
Layman, Jeremh., 134.
Layman, William, 32, 132.
Laythrum, Sylvester (see Latham), 283.
Layton, Jehu, 223.
Layton, John, 427.
Layzare (see Lashyear).
Layzer, Adam, 224.
Lazenby, Alexander, 42.
Lazenby, Henry, 42.
Lazenby (Lessenby), William John, 387, 409.
Leadbourn (Leadburn, Leadbarn), George, 10, 132, 313.
Leach, James, 134.
Leach, Samuel, 31.
Leaf, Robert, 131.
Leago (Lego, Lago), Chas., 225, 268, 398, 448, 500, 544.
Leagor (Leagar), Thos., 426, 473.
Leakins (Leakin), William, 225, 390, 438, 493, 544.
Leamon, William, 135.
Leary (Larry, Larey), Daniel, 134, 135, 305, 319.
Leary, Dennis, 545.
Leary, Michael, 135.
Leary, Momus, 394.
Leary (Larry, Larrey, Larey), William, 66, 225, 312, 334, 376, 403, 645.
Leason, John, 40.
Leath (Lieth), Alexander, 225, 400.
Leath, John, 410.
Leather, John, 261.
Leatherman, Michael, 388, 409.
Leavley, Jacob (see Lavely), 135.
Lecrosse, John, 225.
Ledenham, Nathl., 223.
Lee, Benjamin, 342.
Lee (or Leigh), Christopher, 658.
Lee, Dudley, 224, 325, 345, 354, 436, 490, 544.

Index.

Lee (or See), Ephraim, 61.
Lee, Fergus, 53.
Lee, Henry (Capt., Major, Lieut.-Col., Col.), 585, 586, 587, 588, 589, 590, 592.
Lee, James, 345.
Lee, Jeremiah, 223, 224.
Lee, John, 134, 299, 305, 354, 426, 436, 441, 473, 489, 544.
Lee, Joseph, 134, 225, 312, 334.
Lee, Parker, 135.
Lee, Thomas, 225, 283.
Lee, Thomas Sim, 332, 339, 386, 399.
Lee, Timothy, 225.
Lee (Leigh), William, 26, 133, 319, 355, 397, 405, 409, 444, 459, 492, 507, 544, 545, 643, 611, 613, 658.
Leech, Charles, 16, 38.
Leedy, Abraham, 328.
Leeke (Leek), Henry, 7, 131.
Leeson, William, 14.
Legg, Arthur, 42.
Legg, Edward (see Laigg), 342, 545.
Legg, Robert, 342, 470, 611, 544.
Legg, Samuel, 67.
Lego (see Leago).
Lehea, William, 224.
Leigh, Christopher (see Lee), 658.
Leigh, William (see Lee), 658.
Leister (see Lester).
Leitch, Jeremiah, 382, 648.
Leitch, William, 44.
Leithauser (Lighthauser, Leithusier), George, 225, 265.
Lemar (see Lamar).
Lemmon (Lemon), Barney, 430, 510, 544.
Lemmon, Gerbiner, 299, 329.
Lemmon (Lemon), John, 563, 607, 658.
Lemon, Archibald, 61.
Lemon, Francis, 646.
Lemon, Patk., 136, 302.
Lendall, Thomas, 23.
Lenegen, John, 653.
Lenehan (Leneham) (see Lanahan).
Lennox (Lenox), John, 52, 135, 414.
Lentarage (see Lintridge).
Leonard, Adam, 224.
Leonard, George Rex, 9.
Leonard, Hugh, 134.
Leonard, James, 133.
Leonard, John Rex, 10.
Leonard, Joseph, 370.
Leonard, Robert, 225.
Lesache, Robert, 9.

Leseh, George, 397.
Leseland (Lislend), Wm., 312, 334.
Lesh (Lash), George, 458, 653.
Lesley (Lesslie, Lestley), John (see Lashley), 387, 396, 453, 485, 544.
Lessenby (see Lazenby).
Lester, John, 136, 414.
Lester (Lesster, Leister, Liester, Lister), Joshua, 225, 356, 391, 438, 492, 544, 581.
Lestley (see Lesley).
Letchworth, Jos., 284.
Letman, John, 382, 409.
Letman (Lettman), William, 133, 544.
Lett (Litt), Daniel, 224, 325.
Lett, James, 314.
Lett, Rosalius, 314.
Lettman (see Letman).
Letzinger (see Litzinger).
Leury, John, 658.
Levasche (Levash), John, 616, 628.
Levermore, Peter, 283.
Leverton (Lavington), Garey (George), 385, 409.
Leverton, John Foster, 24.
Levi (Levie), Alexander, 135, 355, 460, 491, 544.
Levingston, Henry, 133.
Levingston, Robert (see Livingston), 583.
Leviston (see Livistone).
Levy, David, 263, 270.
Levy, Jacob, 270.
Levy, Nicholas, 517.
Levy, Samuel, 41.
Lewden, Wm., 341.
Lewellin, Charles, 30.
Lewes, James, 284.
Lewin, John, 343, 354, 436, 490, 544, 600.
Lewis, Anthony, 405.
Lewis, Basil, 225.
Lewis, Benjamin, 7, 131.
Lewis, Charles, 134.
Lewis, Daniel, 42.
Lewis, Edward, 135.
Lewis, Enoch, 284.
Lewis, Howell, 573.
Lewis, Isaac, 67, 409.
Lewis, Jesse, 575, 581.
Lewis, Job, 53.
Lewis, Jonathan, 132, 320, 453, 505, 643.
Lewis, Joseph (Ensign), 52, 59, 132, 135, 395, 450, 509, 544, 562, 647.
Lewis, Lawrence, 136.
Lewis, Lewis, 136.
Lewis, Nicholas, 134.
Lewis, Richard, 49, 223, 283, 572, 583.
Lewis, Samuel, 63.
Lewis, Thomas, 134, 431, 544.

Lewis, William, 49, 224, 225, 263, 264, 270, 284, 388, 410.
Lewitz, Anthony, 403.
Lewton, Thomas, 134.
Licety (?), John, 414.
Lickliter, Peter, 72.
Lichte, Christn., 263.
Liedy, Simon, 388.
Lieser, Adam, 264.
Liester (see Lester).
Lieth, Alexander (see Leath), 225.
Lieuty, John, 135.
Life, Robert, 225.
Ligamire, Jacob, 653.
Lighter, Peter, 328.
Lightfoot, Thomas, 43.
Lighthauser (see Leithauser).
Lilburn (or Lilbon), Walter, 658.
Liles, Thomas, 25.
Lilly, Robert, 224.
Lilly (Lilley), William, 133, 135, 300, 357, 430, 496.
Limebarker, William, 52.
Limes (see Lines).
Lincey (see Linsey).
Linch (see Lynch).
Lincoln, Genl., 467.
Lincoln (Linken), John, 224, 348, 440, 511, 544.
Linday (see Linsey).
Lindenberger, John, 262.
Linder, Jacob, 51.
Linder, Nathaniel, 50.
Lindiff, John, 59, 135, 335.
Lindington, Peter, 132.
Lindsay, Andrew Ross, 5.
Lindsay, James (see Linley), 133.
Lindsay (Lindsey, Linsey, Linday), John, 7, 41, 51, 135, 457, 544, 617.
Lindsay (Lindsay, Linsday, Linsey, Lincey), Theophilus (Theophilus, Theops.), 132, 356, 392, 452, 492, 544.
Lines (Limes), Nicholas (Nickolas), 270, 271, 517.
Linex, James, 323.
Lingan, James (James M.), 365, 521, 616.
Lingan, Thomas, 52.
Lingard, Nehemiah, 378, 410, 451, 494, 645.
Lingist (see Longest).
Lingo, Thomas, 225.
Lingrell, Nehemiah, 397.
Linian, Darby (see Lanahan), 224.
Link, John, 72.
Linken (see Lincoln).
Linkenfetter, Ulrich, 263.
Linkins, Wm., 356.
Linley, James (see Lindsay), 136.

Linn (see Lynn).
Linnington, John, 410.
Linsday (see Lindsay).
Linsey, Daniel, 62.
Linsey (Linday), John (see Lindsay), 41, 457, 644, 617.
Linsey (Linday), Oliver (—liver), 72, 224, 304.
Linsey (Lincey), Theophilus (see Lindsay), 356, 452.
Linthicum, Aquila, 309.
Linthicum, Francis, 224.
Linton (Lynton), George, 340, 394, 453, 505, 544.
Lintridge (Lentarage), Samuel, 49, 224, 324.
Lion, Leonard, 11.
Lions, William (see Lyons), 135.
Lipscomb, James, 623.
Lisby, Kilman, 33.
Lislend (see Leseland).
Lister, Charles, 136.
Lister, Joshua (see Lester), 225, 581.
Litsinger (see Litzinger).
Litt (see Lett).
Little, John, 658.
Little, Richard, 132.
Little, Robert, 64.
Little, Walter, 443.
Little (Lytle), William, 12, 343, 393, 450, 489, 544, 545.
Littles, Geo., 646.
Litzinger (Litsinger, Littsinger, Letzinger), George, 563, 566, 568, 574.
Litzinger, William, 266.
Livingston (Levingston), Robert, 580, 583.
Livistone (Leviston), John, 136, 302.
Lloyd, Andrew, 416.
Lloyd (Loyd), John, 600, 645, 650.
Lloyd, Joseph, 223.
Lloyd, Michael, 132, 357, 444, 494, 543.
Lloyd, Richard, 445.
Lloyd, Thomas, 135, 284.
Loaness (Lonass, Lownas), John, 397, 405, 459, 545.
Loar, Peter, 50.
Loar, Philip, 50.
Locher (see Locker).
Lochlin, Michael, 225.
Lock, George, 224.
Lock, John, 47, 602.
Lock (Locke), William, 16, 132, 344, 346.
Locker (Locher), Frederick, 225, 264, 265.
Locker, James, 35.
Locker, Jesse, 397, 405, 465, 501, 545.
Locker (Lockyer), Philip, 34, 410.
Locker, Shedereck, 49.

Index. 703

Lockerman (Loockerman), Thos. Wyer (Thos. Wynn), 68, 69.
Lockett, Richd. (see Sockett), 283.
Lockhart, James, 602.
Lockhart, Jno., 136.
Lockwood, Stephen, 284.
Lockyer, Philip (see Locker), 410.
Loclen, John W., 390.
Lodgeade, Marthew, 42.
Lodwick, Chezloe, 474.
Loe, Andrew, 47.
Loe, Henry, 223.
Loffman (Lofman, Loftman, Loftsman), Benjamin, 223, 342, 352, 434, 544.
Logan, Charles, 131.
Logan, Jessy, 649.
Logan, William, 59.
Logie (Logey), James, 39, 134.
Lohra (see Lorah).
Lokerias, Frederick (see Zacharius), 325.
Loller (see Lawler).
Lomax, John, 132, 544.
Lomax, Theophilus (see Lowmuth), 223, 545.
Lonass, John (see Loaness), 459, 545.
London, John, 136.
London, William (see Louden), 132.
Lone, Isaac, 22.
Loney, John, 59.
Long, Chris., 284.
Long, Elisha, 372.
Long, Jacob, 50, 410.
Long, James, 647.
Long, John, 60, 388, 418, 468, 504, 545.
Long, Jonathan, 409.
Long, Joseph, 30, 224, 349, 358, 440, 493, 544.
Long, Patrick, 615.
Long, Solomon, 21, 132.
Long, Thomas, 132, 134, 375, 397, 403, 458, 487, 545.
Long, William, 35.
Longdon (Longden), Joseph, 224, 326.
Longdon, Thomas, 135, 414.
Longest (Longist, Lingist), Daniel, 134, 621, 623.
Longfellow, Andw., 225.
Longfellow, Arnold, 375, 410.
Longfellow, Gideon, 385, 400.
Longfellow, Thos., 224.
Longist (see Longest).
Longley, James (see Langly), 224.
Longley, William (see Langley), 2.
Longly, Edward, 35.
Longwill, Robert, 62.

Loockerman (see Lockerman).
Looney, Thomas, 134.
Lorah (Lora, Lohra), John (see O'Hara), 38, 182, 266, 641.
Lorantz (see Lorentz).
Lord, Andrew, 223, 359, 392.
Lord, Henry, 133, 223.
Lord, James, 339.
Lord, Levi, 355, 441, 491, 544.
Lord, Levin, 133.
Lorentz, Ferdinand (see Larantz, Fredk.), 265.
Lorentz (Lorantz), Wendel (Vendel), 225, 265.
Losada, Benito, 615.
Loud, Charles, 58.
Loud, George, 224.
Louden, William (see London), 45.
Loure, Gotfried, 263.
Loux, George, 324.
Love, Charles, 417, 464, 500, 545.
Love, David, 225, 389, 421, 437, 501, 544.
Love, John, 57, 133, 224, 290, 349, 354, 436, 489, 544.
Love, Robert, 645.
Love, Thomas, 43.
Love, William, 224.
Loveday, John, 225, 356, 389, 438, 493, 544.
Loveday, Thomas, 135, 420, 472, 545.
Loveden, John, 341.
Lovelass, Barton, 40.
Loveless, Charles, 49.
Loveless, Elisha (see Lovless), 132.
Loveless, James, 423.
Lovelet, Benja., 133.
Lovelin, William, 377, 410.
Lovely (Loveley), Joshua, 580, 583.
Lovely, Thomas, 136, 301, 350.
Lovely, Wm., 410.
Lovett, Charles, 58.
Lovett, Joseph, 600.
Lovitt (Lovet), William, 43, 369.
Lovless (see Loveless), 331.
Lovless, William, 331.
Lovley (see Lovely).
Low, Edward, 59.
Low, Gasper, 615.
Low, Jacob (see Lowe).
Low, James (see Lowe).
Low, Levi, 648.
Low, William (see Lowe).
Lowden, Michael, 131.
Lowe, Bazil, 594.
Lowe, Dennis, 594.
Lowe (Low), Jacob, 225, 261, 544.

Lowe (Low), James, 15, 35, 132.
Lowe, John, 133, 423, 465, 501, 545.
Lowe, John F., 293, 476.
Lowe, John Hawkins, 34.
Lowe, John T. (John G., John F.), 358, 362, 378, 448, 476, 478, 518.
Lowe, J. Tolson, 132.
Lowe, Nathan, 35.
Lowe, Nicholas, 382.
Lowe, Rezin, 424, 472.
Lowe, Richd., 8, 132.
Lowe (Low), William, 224, 611, 613, 615.
Lowers (or Sowers), Henry (see Lawers), 358.
Lowery (see Lowry).
Lowes, Henry, 134.
Lowman, James, 595.
Lowmuth (or Lowmuch), Theophilius (see Lomax), 65.
Lownas, John (see Loaness), 405.
Lowndes, Christopher, 332.
Lowny, David, 615.
Lowrey, Christn., 283.
Lowry (Lowrey), James, 223, 392, 429, 475, 511, 545.
Lowry (Lowrie, Lowrey), John, 14, 44, 223, 225, 376, 544, 617, 634, 661.
Lowry, William, 44, 343.
Lowther, James, 45, 224.
Loyal, John, 658.
Loyce, Peter, 224.
Loyd, Edward, 66.
Loyd, John (see Lloyd).
Loyder, Isaac, 427.
Loyers (see Lawers).
Luairn, Lewis, 319.
Lucas, Barton, 9, 333.
Lucas, Basil, 133.
Lucas (or Luckas), Charles, 49.
Lucas, James, 133, 135.
Lucas, John, 133, 135, 223, 353, 414, 433, 446, 487, 544.
Lucas (Luckas), William, 49, 132, 444, 544.
Lucast, Peter, 134.
Luckas (see Lucas).
Lucket, William, 49.
Luckett (Lucket), David, 132, 363, 365, 380, 476, 480, 521.
Luckett, Francis Ware, 6, 132.
Luckett, Henry, 32.
Luckett, Ignatius, 31.
Luckett (Luckitt), Samuel, 6, 132.
Luckett (Lucket), Thos. H., 365, 521, 616.
Ludford, Henry, 135.
Ludwick, Leonard, 225, 261, 262.

Luff, Jno., 134.
Luff, Thos., 134, 298.
Luffer, John, 132, 432.
Lugard, William, 13.
Lukart, Fredk., 284.
Luke, Folius, 658.
Lumley, Thomas, 24.
Lunceford, Edmond, 368.
Lund, Willm., 313.
Lunderkin (or Lundergin), Richard, 68.
Lunn, John, 136, 415.
Lunn, Nehemiah, 53.
Lusby, Edwd., 581.
Lusby, Henry, 658.
Lusby, Robert, 575, 581.
Lusby, Samuel, 581.
Lusby, Thomas, 581.
Lusby, Vincent, 41.
Luton, Joseph (see Newton), 235.
Lux, Robert, 658.
Lyan (see Lyon).
Lyday, Simon, 409.
Lyles, Henry (———), 133, 363, 380, 521.
Lyles, James, 381, 394, 453.
Lyles, Zachariah, 133, 545.
Lynch, Barney, 133.
Lynch (Linch), Daniel, 136, 643.
Lynch, Hugh, 52, 135.
Lynch, James, 393, 451.
Lynch (Linch), John (Capt., ———), 15, 25, 63, 70, 71, 74, 132, 133, 134, 135, 223, 293, 301, 303, 344, 353, 358, 364, 380, 393, 450, 457, 480, 481, 483, 486, 497, 521, 544, 577, 632.
Lynch, Patrick, 225, 307, 311, 515.
Lynch, Robert, 135, 457.
Lynch, Saml., 397.
Lynch, Timothy, 393.
Lynch (Linch), William, 46, 133, 300, 396, 430, 511, 544.
Lynes, William, 372.
Lynn (Linn), David (D., Capt.), 48, 50, 225, 310, 364, 380, 401, 402, 403, 404, 428, 480, 483, 521.
Lynn, Henry, 395, 398.
Lynn (Linn), John (Lt.), 224, 346, 364, 381, 427, 439, 476, 481, 482, 508, 520, 627.
Lynn, Thomas, 134.
Lynn (Linn), Valentine, 19, 131.
Lynn, William, 19.
Lynton (see Linton).
Lyon (Lyan), Isaac, 134, 295, 330.
Lyon (Lyons), Jacob, 133, 562, 621, 623.
Lyon, John (see Lyons), 60, 223.

Lyons, Elijah, 383, 425, 464.
Lyons, Jacob (see Lyon), 562, 623.
Lyons, John (see Lyon), 409.
Lyons, William (see Lions), 135, 326, 396.
Lysought, Jno., 283.
Lytle, William (see Little), 343, 393, 489, 661.

Macall (McCaul), William, 137, 545.
Macam (see Macum).
Macatee, Leonard (see McAtee), 46.
Macatee, Walter, 36.
Maccan, Thomas (see McCann), 32.
Macceney (McSeney), Jacob, 39.
Macclane (see McClain).
Maccubbin, Zachariah, 52.
Macdaniel, John, 35.
MacDonald, Bartholemew, 39.
Machall (see Mackall).
Machenheimer, John, 265.
Mackabee (see Mockbee).
Mackall, Benjamin, 33, 34, 327.
Mackall (Machall), Thos., 267, 268.
Mackanary, Simon, 340.
Mackay, Alex. (see Mackey), 515.
Mackay, John (see McCoy), 335.
Mackee (see Mackey).
Mackeman, Lodowick, 327.
Mackey (Mackay), Alex., 396, 515.
Mackey (Mackee, Makee), Henry, 44, 314.
Mackey (McKey), Jacob, 139, 330.
Mackey (McKey, McKay), Jno. Alex. (see McCoy, John), 230, 347, 415.
Mackey, Thomas, 136, 141, 300.
Mackey (McKey), William, 62, 226.
Maclamar (see McNamara).
Maclamary, Timothy, 43.
MacLaughlin, Mack (see Lauglane).
Macnamara, ——, 661.
Macnamara (see McNamara).
Macrell (Makrell), Thos., 322, 416.
Macum (Macam), John, 233, 515.
Madan, William, 465, 501.
Madcafe, Willm., 581.
Madcalf, Bennett, 51.
Madden, Christopher, 144, 318.
Madden, Martin, 403.

Madden, Michael, 394, 600.
Madden, William, 426, 548, 648.
Maddin (Madding), Nathan, 24, 226.
Maddin, Nathl., 233.
Maddin, Thomas, 342.
Madding, John, 44.
Madding, Nathan (see Maddin).
Madding, Sampson, 227.
Maddox, Aaron, 32.
Maddox (Maddux), Allison, 376, 410.
Maddox (Maddux), George, 377, 410.
Maddox, Ignatius, 49.
Maddox (Madox, Maddux), John, 30, 384, 410, 658.
Maddox, Noah, 31.
Maddox, Notley, 140, 284.
Maddox, Samuel, 31.
Maddox, Walter, 231.
Maddux (Mattock), Wm., 394, 416.
Madern, Adam, 322.
Madkin, John, 410.
Madox (see Maddox).
Maffitt, James, 345.
Magauran (MaGauran, McGauran), Francis, 353, 447, 487, 548, 568, 570.
Magee, Chas. (see McGee).
Magee, John (see McGee).
Magee, Josiah, 226.
Magee, Reuben, 22.
Magee, Wm., 298.
Magen, Henry, 577.
Maginnis (see McGinnis).
Maglamary (Meglamery), Edwd., 22, 140.
Maglin (see McGlin).
Maglocklin (see McLaughlin).
Magness, Wm., 284.
Magragh (Magraugh, Magraw) (see McGraw).
Magruder, Alex. Howard, 34, 38.
Magruder, Enoch, 145.
Magson (see Mayson).
Maguire (see McGuire).
Mahaney, James (see Mahoncy).
Mahaney (Mahany, Mahanny), Thomas (see Mahoney), 52, 228, 231, 349.
Mahawney (see Mahoney).
Mahew, Saml., 423, 471.
Mahew, Thomas (see Mayhew).
Mahill (see Hukell).
Mahoney, Charles, 43.
Mahoney, Clemt., 138.
Mahoney (Mchoney), Daniel, 231, 410, 658.
Mahoney (Mahony, Mahawney), Edwd., 230, 395, 449, 503, 547.
Mahoney (Mehaney, Mahaney), Jas., 56, 231.

Mahoney, Jno., 572.
Mahoney, Michael, 231.
Mahoney, Patrick, 232.
Mahoney, Saml., 231.
Mahoney, Smith, 330.
Mahoney, Stephen, 62.
Mahoney (Mahony, Mahaney, Mahany, Mahanny), Thomas, 52, 228, 231, 262, 267, 268, 315, 349, 548, 564, 566.
Mahoney, Wm., 345.
Mahony, Florence, 53.
Mahony, Timothy, 53.
Mahood, Jno., 140.
Mahorn, —— (see Monghon).
Mahorn, Patrick (see Mayhorne).
Mahugh (Mayhugh), Jonathan (see Mayhew), 142, 296, 466, 510, 546.
Mails, John, 232.
Main, David, 141.
Main, Henry, 285.
Mains, Francis, 145.
Mains, George, 145.
Maires, Saml., 141.
Mais, Wm. (see Mays), 334.
Major, Wm., 400.
Majors (Major), Charles, 232, 618.
Majors, John, 17, 137, 545.
Makee (see Mackey).
Makin (see McMaken).
Makrell (see Macrell).
Malachi, Daniel, 410.
Malady, John (see Mallady), 267, 321, 394, 447.
Malcomb, Tho., 137.
Malcolm, Thomas, 285.
Malcolm, William, 604.
Malcom, John, 515.
Malcome, Hugh, 230.
Malinia, William, 266.
Mallady, —— (see Malady), 262.
Mallen (Mallon), Andrew (see Mullen), 306, 391.
Mallimore, Jno., 305.
Mallon (see Mallen).
Mallone, And. (see Malone).
Mallone, Patk. (see Mellon), 392.
Malloon, Thomas (see Malone), 44.
Mallows, Robert, 143.
Malm, Andrew, 232.
Malom (see Malone).
Malone (Mallone), Andrew (see Mullen), 138, 405.
Malone, Conner, 144.
Malone, Hugh, 231.
Malone, John, 26, 140, 327, 643.
Malone (Malom, Mulloon), Thomas, 44, 67.
Maloney, James, 232.
Maloney, Thomas, 232, 307, 549.

Maloney (Melony), Wm., 25, 227.
Maloy, Barnabas, 415.
Maloy, Barney, 26, 139, 642.
Maloy (Meloy), Michael, 56, 139.
Maloy (Mulloy), Roger, 338, 366.
Malsny, William, 285.
Man, Robert, 14.
Man, Thomas, 327.
Man, William (see Mann).
Managa (Manage, Managee), James, 233, 358, 390, 463, 499, 546.
Mandwell (Mandewitt), Philip, 142, 296.
Manfield, Robt., 141.
Mangers, Nicholas (Lieut., Capt.), 141, 364, 380, 478, 479, 521.
Manham (Maning) (see Manning).
Manly, John, 587, 588.
Manly, Thomas, 586.
Manly (Manley), William, 355, 366, 400, 492, 547.
Mann, Daniel, 395, 458, 487, 548.
Mann, Jesse, 227.
Mann (Man, Mans), William, 27, 63, 70, 139, 232, 293, 356, 390, 439, 493, 545, 546, 643.
Mannah (see Hannah).
Mannan, Dennias, 648.
Mannan (Manyan), Patrick, 232, 307.
Manning (Maning, Manham), Abraham, 394, 453, 510, 548.
Manning, Hy., 140.
Manning, John, 385.
Manning, Joseph, 31.
Manning, Wm., 140.
Mans, William (see Mann), 232.
Mansell, James, 139.
Mansell (Mansel, Mansal), Richd., 58, 143, 415.
Mansfield, George, 228.
Mansfield (Mansfeld), Henry, 355, 366, 461, 491, 547.
Mansfield, James, 61, 140.
Mansfield, John, 67, 356.
Mansfield, William, 396, 416, 454, 508, 548.
Manspiker, Henry, 410.
Mantle (Mauntle, Montle, Mondle), George, 228, 348, 354, 439, 488, 546.
Mantle, John, 37, 229, 333, 347, 439, 512, 546.
Mantle, Serjt., 332.
Mantz, Peter, 44, 47, 48.
Manwaring, Chs., 143.
Manyan, Patrick (see Mannan), 232, 307.

Marbury (Marbery, Marborough), Joseph (Capt., J.), 5, 140, 223, 333, 351, 363, 379, 476, 480, 518, 621.
Marbury, Luke, 616.
March, Charles, 562, 598.
Marchmont, William, 21.
Mardary, William, 371.
Marfee, Michael (see Murphy), 284.
Marhay, Dennis, 42.
Mark, Robert, 41.
Markel, Adam, 263.
Markell, John, 229.
Markey, William, 226.
Markland, Edward, 387.
Marks, John, 143.
Markwell (Markwelch), Wm., 145, 303, 618.
Marlon, John, 145.
Marlow, Butler, 140, 382, 410.
Marlow (Marlowe), John, 35.
Marlow, Middleton (Middlen), 8, 136.
Marlow, Randolph, 38.
Marlow, Saml., 139.
Marlow, Thomas D., 34.
Marlow, William, 145, 351, 352, 381, 394, 397, 417, 420, 453, 501, 548.
Marolf, Rudolph, 262.
Maroney (Marony), David, 565, 566, 569, 574.
Maroney (Meroney), Philip, 44, 45.
Marquay, Ephraim, 68.
Marquay, Thomas, 68.
Marquis (Marquess, Marques), William, 33, 231, 272, 515, 599.
Marr, David, 61, 227.
Marr, John, 640.
Marr, Nicholas, 640.
Marr, Orrell (or Oriel), 40.
Marr, Paul, 230, 325.
Marr, William, 410, 640.
Marrah, Morriss, 65.
Marriott, Caleb, 581.
Marriott, William, 53.
Marrough, James (see Morrow), 227.
Marsh, Benjamin (see Mash), 137, 320, 395, 452, 548.
Marsh, Thomas, 284.
Marshall, Ben, 599.
Marshall, Edwd., 30, 41, 143.
Marshall, Ephraim, 425, 472.
Marshall, Isaac, 372.
Marshall, John, 32, 45, 229, 230, 304, 348.
Marshall, Peter, 70.
Marshall, Richard, 34.
Marshall, Robert, 229, 304.
Marshall, Thomas, 70.

Marshall, William, 138, 228, 372, 468, 504, 546, 617.
Martin, Charles, 285.
Martin, Danl., 296.
Martin (or Martain), Edward, 62.
Martin, George, 69, 410.
Martin, Henry, 24, 234, 285.
Martin, Hezek., 136.
Martin, Hugh, 563, 566, 569.
Martin, Ignatius, 32, 137.
Martin, Jacob, 46.
Martin, James, 51, 284.
Martin, John, 26, 47, 49, 139, 143, 231, 293, 294, 333, 349, 475, 505, 545, 546, 617, 644.
Martin, John of Dorset, 27.
Martin, John Selby, 69.
Martin, Joseph, 140, 388, 446.
Martin, Leonard, 331.
Martin, Lewis, 341.
Martin, Lond., 138.
Martin, Michael, 52, 141, 228, 297.
Martin, Pacel, 19.
Martin, Phil., 141.
Martin, Robt., 138.
Martin, Saml., 350.
Martin, Terrence, 12.
Martin, Thomas, 30, 285.
Martin, William, 11, 229, 284, 347, 336, 396, 431, 547.
Martindale, John, 137, 330, 357, 431, 496, 545, 629.
Martindale, Perdue, 23.
Martindale, William, 23.
Martuson, Philip, 579.
Maruny, John, 601.
Marwood, Andrew, 145, 335, 415.
Mash (Massh), Benjm. (see Marsh), 356, 403.
Maslin, ——, 74.
Mason, Abel, 607, 658.
Mason, Alex., 647.
Mason, Arthur, 227, 285.
Mason, Bennet, 21.
Mason, Caleb, 138, 140, 518.
Mason (alias Woodyard), Colvert, 428, 475, 561.
Mason, Issachar (Issacher, Isaccher), 355, 441, 491, 547.
Mason, James, 22, 139, 140, 357, 444, 494, 545.
Mason, John, 142, 227, 228.
Mason, Nathaniel, 594.
Mason, Matthew, 645.
Mason (Mayson), Thomas (Ensign, Capt.), 12, 68, 74, 136, 232, 305, 363, 379, 390, 441, 479, 521, 645.
Mason (Masson), Willm., 340, 393, 416, 627.
Masseck, Charles, 503.
Massenbach, Felix Lewis, Baron, 570.
Massey, Henry Lee, 658.

Massey, Hezekiah, 403, 410, 464, 547.
Massey, Jesse, 227.
Massey, John, 646.
Massey, William, 285.
Massh (see Mash).
Masson, Wm. (see Mason), 627.
Massy, Danl. Toas, 64.
Massy, Enoch, 646.
Masters, John, 35.
Masters, Watterly (Walterly), 607, 658.
Masters, William, 285.
Masterson, John, 25, 138.
Masterson, Phillip, 573, 582, 584.
Mate, John, 595.
Mathews, Daniel (see Matthews), 626.
Mathews, James (see Matthews), 60, 233.
Mathews, John (see Matthews), 143, 601.
Mathews, Jos. (see Matthews), 137.
Mathews, Richd., 233.
Mathews, Robert (see Matthews), 228, 322.
Mathews, Thomas (see Matthews), 230.
Mathews, William (see Matthews), 140, 143, 230, 231, 548.
Mathias (Mathies), James, 144, 564, 566, 569, 574.
Mathias, John, 546.
Matkins, John, 383.
Mattanly (see Mattingly).
Mattehannan, Wm., 141.
Matthews (Mathews), Daniel, 51, 626.
Matthews, Francis, 393, 456.
Matthews, Geo., 142.
Matthews, Henry, 458.
Matthews (Mathews), Jas., 12, 60, 233.
Matthews (Mathews), John, 142, 143, 396, 443, 455, 505, 545, 547, 658.
Matthews (Mathews), Joseph, 16, 137.
Matthews (Mathews), Robert, 228, 322, 349, 546.
Matthews, Saml., 139.
Matthew (Mathews), Thos., 139, 230, 314, 342, 385, 396, 454, 455, 487, 507, 547, 548.
Matthews (Mathews), William, 140, 143, 230, 231, 357, 423, 446, 468, 495, 504, 546, 548, 606, 641, 658.
Mattingby (see Mattingly).
Mattingley, Thos., 139, 330.
Mattingly, Chs., 142.
Mattingly (Mattingley), Igns. (ignatious), 384, 410.

Mattingly (Mattingley, Mattanly, Mattingby), Joseph, 16, 136, 234, 341, 389, 438, 512, 546.
Mattingly (Mattingley), Philip, 139, 330.
Mattinly, Edward, 30.
Mattinson, Danl., 143.
Matthiot, John, 410.
Mattock, Willm. (see Maddux), 416.
Mattox, Charles, 41.
Mattox, Cornelius, 39.
Mattrit, Adam, 266.
Matwell, John, 472.
Maulden, Henry, 61.
Mauledge, Samuel, 410.
Maunders, Thomas, 229.
Maunsel, Wm., 234.
Mauntle (see Mantle).
Maxfield, Jon., 389.
Maxwell, James, 74, 230, 347, 439, 504, 546.
Maxwell, John, 229, 233, 304, 424, 428, 439, 493, 546, 615.
Maxwell, Richd., 144, 319.
Maxwell, Wm., 140.
May, Dennis, 18, 137.
May, Francis, 284.
May, George, 67, 230, 328.
May, Hugh, 63.
May, John, 231, 349, 581.
May, Joseph, 142.
May, Peter, 284.
May, Richard, 138, 331.
Maybury (Mayberry), Benja., 231, 345.
Mayers, Christian (see Myers).
Mayers, Christopher (see Myers, Christian), 365.
Mayher, Pat., 418.
Mayhew, Bryan, 38.
Mayhew (Mayhugh, Mahugh), Jonathan, 142, 296, 466, 510, 546.
Mayhew (Mahew), Thomas, 137, 142, 331.
Mayhew, William, 38.
Mayhorne (Mayhorn, Mahorn), Patrick (see Monghon), 409, 509, 564.
Mayhugh (see Mayhew).
Maynadier, Hy., 137.
Maynard, James P., 575, 581.
Maynard, John, 45.
Maynard, Peter, 139.
Maynor (Mayner), Peter, 580, 582, 583, 584.
Mays, James, 60.
Mays, Thomas, 16, 39, 41.
Mays, William (see Mais), 600.
Mayson (Magson), Duke (Mard.), 141, 300.
Mayson, Thomas (see Mason), 645.
McAdams, Alexd., 145.

McAdams, John, 139, 293, 313, 658.
McAdams, Robt., 601.
McAffee, John, 403.
McAllen, Joseph, 45.
McAllester (McCollester), Joel (Toal), 59, 142.
McAllister (McCallister), Archd. (———), 136, 364, 381.
McAndrew, Pat., 138.
McAnt (see McCant).
McAntee (see McAtlee).
McAtee, John, 329.
McAtee, Leond. (Leod.) (see Macatee), 141, 329.
McAtee, Thomas, 141.
McAtlee (McAntee, McItee), Joseph, 343, 447, 486, 547, 627.
McAttee, Saml., 145.
McAvoy, Nicholas, 55.
McAway, Chas., 143.
McAway (McCaway), Christopher (see McWay), 458, 486, 546.
McAway, Henry, 414.
McAway, Stephen, 144.
McAway, Thomas, 144.
McBride, James, 226, 330.
McBride (McBryde), John, 145, 301, 350, 352, 397, 420, 470, 511, 548.
McBride, Thomas, 342.
McBruff (see McKouff).
McCabe, James, 315.
McCabe, John, 19.
McCain, ———, 136.
McCaleb (McCalleb), Patrick, 229, 304.
McCaliff (see McCauliff).
McCalister (see McCallister).
McCall (McCaull), Benjamin), 417, 466, 602, 548.
McCall, Hugh, 70.
McCall, John, 393, 401, 451, 497, 547.
McCall, William, 317.
McCalleb (see McCaleb).
McCalley, John, 142, 329.
McCallister, Arch. (see McAllister).
McCallister (McCallester, McCalister, McCollester, McCollester), Joseph, 140, 425, 429, 468, 505, 549.
McCalmont (McCallmont), James, 139, 620.
McCallo, George, 590.
McCallo, Thomas, 599.
McCanh, Jos., 140.
McCann (McCan), Francis, 376, 394, 403, 459, 488, 547.
McCann (McCan, McKann), John, 54, 141, 145, 295, 350, 358, 403, 498, 546.
McCann, Marmaduke, 410.

McCann (McCan), Michael, 229, 304, 347, 353, 439, 487, 546.
McCann, Patrick, 145, 302.
McCann, Thomas (see Maccan), 70.
McCant (McAnt), Jos., 32, 284.
McCarlin (see McCaslin).
McCarren (McCarnan), Barney, 334, 335.
McCarson, Jno., 285.
McCartin, Wm., 41.
McCartney (McKarteney), Edwd., 142, 329.
McCartny, Jere., 145.
McCartny, Peter, 145.
McCarty, Danl., 285.
McCarty, Dennis, 515, 517.
McCarty, Florence, 285, 658.
McCarty (McCartey), Jas., 137, 144, 410, 661.
McCarty, Jere., 143.
McCarty, Jesse (Jessy), 137, 305, 342, 627.
McCarty, Thomas, 227, 285.
McCarty (McKarty), Timothy (Thimothy), 139, 294, 322.
McCarty, Wm., 142.
McCasker, Michael, 62.
McCaslin (McCarlin), Nicholas, 427.
McCatchen, Forrest, 327.
McCaul (see Macall).
McCauley, George, 547.
McCauley, Thomas, 41, 547.
McCauley, Zachariah, 41.
McCauliff (McCaliff), John, 396, 454, 485, 548.
McCaull (see McCall).
McCaulley, William, 12.
McCaw (see McCoy).
McCaway (see McAway).
McCay, Henry, 139.
McCay, John (see McCoy), 141, 335, 434, 436, 546.
McCernon, Thomas, 546.
McClain (McLain, McLean), Arthur, 234, 388, 437, 505, 547.
McClain (McLane, McLean), Enoch, 233, 388, 469, 500, 546.
McClain (McClean, McLane), Hugh, 15, 137, 632.
McClain (McLean), James, 336, 345.
McClain (McClaine, McLain, McLane), John, 14, 37, 137, 227, 313, 393, 401, 452, 501, 548.
McClain, John (of Harford), 14.
McClain (McClaine, McLain, McLane), Joseph, 46, 393, 398, 451.
McClame (see McClane).
McCland, Robert, 321.

McClane, Francis, 343.
McClane, Simon, 61.
McClane (or McClame), William, 46.
McClannon (see McClelland).
McClary (see McClary).
McClarty, George, 285.
McClary (McClarey, McCleary), Basset (Bassett, Bassel), 61, 140, 392, 462.
McClary, John, 45.
McClary (McCleary), Robert, 424, 468, 504, 548.
McClean, Hugh (see McClain).
McClean, Lackn., 145.
McCleary (see McClary).
McCleery, Patrick, 231.
McClelland, George, 647.
McClelland, Nathl., 646.
McClelland (McCleland, McClenan, McClannon), Robert, 30, 658.
McClintock, John, 62.
McClockling (see McLaughlin).
McCloud, Edwd., 232.
McCloud, Hugh, 142, 284.
McColgain, John, 598.
McColla, John, 588.
McCollester, Jas., 25.
McCollester, Toal (see McAllester, Joel).
McCollister (McCollester) (see McCallister).
McColloch, John, 234.
McCollum, Daniel, 464, 548.
McCollum (McCullam), David, 418, 500.
McColough (see McCullough).
McComas, Saml., 401.
McConakin (see McConnican).
McConaughey, Alex., 639.
McCone, Thomas, 226.
McConikin (see McConnakin).
McConn, James, 615
McConnakin (McConneken, McConikin), John, 67, 139, 294.
McConnel, Stephen, 62.
McConnell, John, 229.
McConnell, Matthew, 410.
McConnell (McConnel), Samuel, 230, 347, 547.
McConnican, Daniel, 64.
McConnican (McConnikin, McConakin), Elias, 66.
McCoole, John, 61.
McCord, Saml., 145.
McCorgan, David, 263.
McCormick, Andrew, 233.
McCormick (McCormack), Dennis, 579, 583.
McCormick, John, 21, 138, 144, 431.
McCormick, Mathew, 140.
McCormick, Richd., 137.

McCormick (McCormack), Thos., 144, 318.
McCoune, John, 342.
McCowan, John (see McGowan), 445.
McCowan, Neal (see McOwen), 398, 455.
McCoy (McKoy, Mackey, Mackay), Alex. (see McCoy, John), 136, 396, 403, 422, 470, 515.
McCoy, Eneas, 145.
McCoy, George, 658.
McCoy (McKoy, McCaw, Koy), Hugh, 138, 266, 268, 323.
McCoy, James, 45, 230.
McCoy (McKoy, McKay, McCay, McKey, Mackay), John (see McCoy, Alex. and Mackey, Jno. Alex.), 30, 61, 137, 141, 227, 285, 286, 335, 352, 364, 380, 394, 434, 436, 481, 483, 485, 518, 546, 548.
McCoy (McKoy, McKay), William, 139, 294, 321.
McCracken (McCrackin, McCracking), James, 587, 588.
McCracken, Joseph, 46.
McCrackin, Isaac, 74, 229.
McCracking, Samuel, 26, 642.
McCray, Henry, 229.
McCray, James, 410, 421, 472.
McCreary, Angus, 400.
McCreary (McCrery), John 45, 229.
McCreary, Thos., 145.
McCubbin, Samuel, 14.
McCullam (see McCollum).
McCullim, Thos., 328.
McCulloch, David (see McCullough), 334.
McCulloch, James, 43.
McCulloch, Lewis (see McCullough), 234, 473.
McCulloch (McCullogh), Wm., 145, 302.
McCullogh (see McCulloch).
McCullough (McCulloch), David, 334, 648.
McCullough (McCulloch, McColough, McCuttough), Lewis, 234, 426, 473, 510, 549.
McCullough, Saml., 230.
McCummert, Michl., 142.
McCune, Andrew, 343.
McCurdey, Daniel, 61.
McCurdey, David, 61.
McCurdey (McCurdy), John, 61, 140.
McCure, Neal, 305.
McCuttough (see McCullough).
McDad, Philip, 594.
McDanald (see McDonald).

Index.   707

McDaniel, Anguish (see McDonnold), 226.
McDaniel, Elisha, 141.
McDaniel, James, 377, 397, 398.
McDaniel, John, 226, 345, 398, 414, 581, 599.
McDaniel, Richard, 24.
McDaniel, Roger, 136.
McDaniel, Thomas, 52, 59, 143, 336.
McDaniell, William, 14, 33.
McDaniell, Wm., 2nd, 14.
McDannell, Joseph, 319.
McDavid, John, 43.
McDearmett, John, 58.
McDeed, James, 43.
McDermot, Michael, 226.
McDermot, Owen, 143.
McDermot, Tho., 141.
McDevitt, Michael, 426, 473.
McDoal, James, 387.
McDole (see McDowell).
McDonah, Michl., 142.
McDonal (see McDonald).
McDonald, Alex., 139, 294.
McDonald, Allen, 230.
McDonald, Arch., 141.
McDonald, Charles, 227, 377, 410.
McDonald, Danl., 227.
McDonald (McDonnald), George, 45, 72, 232, 419, 470, 598.
McDonald (McDonnald, McDonnold, McDanald, McDonnall, McDonnel, McDonal), James, 234, 286, 312, 326, 334, 343, 390, 410, 414, 416, 438, 463, 507, 547, 581, 595, 605, 607.
McDonald (McDonnald, McDonold, McDonal, McDonnell), John, 37, 145, 228, 231, 233, 286, 314, 343, 359, 393, 410, 416, 418, 423, 431, 464, 471, 499, 512, 547, 548, 601, 623.
McDonald, Joseph, 144, 414.
McDonald, Martin, 229, 284.
McDonald (McDonnold), Michael, 233, 311, 315.
McDonald, Patk., 56, 345.
McDonald, Philip, 393, 401, 451.
McDonald, Richard, 468, 505, 549.
McDonald, Robert, 45, 232, 607, 658.
McDonald, Stephn., 138.
McDonald, Thos., 285, 414.
McDonald, Wm., 285, 336.
McDonald, Wm. D., 142.
McDonall, Jonathan, 46.
McDonnagh (McDonehough), John, 230, 325.

McDonnald, Elisha, 309.
McDonnall, James (see McDonald), 581.
McDonnel, James (see McDonald), 390.
McDonnell, John (see McDonald), 601.
McDonnold, Anguish (see McDaniel), 65.
McDono, Bartholony, 340.
McDonough, Patrick, 428, 474.
McDonough, Thos., 285.
McDonough, Wm., 136.
McDougle (McDugle), John, 139, 294.
McDowell (McDole), Hugh, 564, 567, 570, 574, 579, 583, 584, 618, 647.
McDowell, Matthew, 647.
McDowell, Thomas, 424, 467, 503, 548.
McDugle (see McDougle).
McElhaney, Mathw., 648.
McElroy, John, 418, 421, 469, 472, 510, 548.
McEntire (see McIntire).
McEvoy, Patk., 265.
McFadden (McFaddon, McFadon), Isaac, 417, 467, 503, 548.
McFadden (McFadon), Jas., 365, 477, 565, 568, 575, 580.
McFaddon (McFadon), John, 14, 230.
McFaden, Patrick, 62.
McFadgin, Abram., 231.
McFading, Edward, 25.
McFall, James (see McFaul).
McFall, John, 53.
McFarlane, Alex., 142.
McFarlen (McFarrin), Jas., 139, 294.
McFarlin, Charles, 227.
McFarlin, John, 423, 471.
McFarlin, Nicholas, 474.
McFaron, Wm., 336.
McFarren, Walter, 145.
McFarrin (see McFarlen).
McFaul (McFall), James, 233, 305.
McFee, Malcolm, 53.
McGahan, Henry, 61.
McGain, Pat., 143.
McGarey, Alex., 315.
McGarey, Henry, 653.
McGauran (see Magauran).
McGaw, James, 400.
McGaw, John, 400.
McGaw (McGeaugh), Nichs., 57, 285.
McGee, Hugh, 141.
McGee (Magee), Charles, 141, 298, 329, 354, 435, 490, 545.
McGee (Magee), John, 139, 314.
McGee, Thomas, 598, 661.

McGee, William, 141, 329, 354, 435, 489.
McGenalty, Pat., 415.
McGill, James, 17, 340, 607, 658.
McGill, Thomas, 410.
M'Giney, Danl., 610.
McGinney, Solomon, 227.
McGinnis, Andrew, 338.
McGinnis (Maginnis), John, 342, 461, 507, 547.
McGinnis, Robt., 284.
McGinnis, William, 11, 134.
McGinty, Pat., 144.
McGlachlan (see McLaughlin).
McGlamory, Elijah, 410.
McGlamory, John, 410.
McGlaskey, Philip, 396.
McGlaughian (see McLaughlin).
McGlaughland, J., 145.
McGlaughlin (see McLaughlin).
McGlenn (see McGlin).
McGlin (Maglin, McGlenn), John, 395, 452, 463, 548.
McGlochlin (McGlocklain) (see McLaughlin).
McGloghian, Chas., 577.
McGlouchlin (McGloughlin) (see McLaughlin).
McGowan, Ben., 145.
McGowan, John (see McCowan), 646.
McGowen, James, 583.
McGowen, Wm., 602.
McGower, Michael, 547.
McGrary (see McGreary).
McGraw (Magraw) Christopher), 441, 506, 545.
McGraw (Magraw, Magraugh), James, 139, 314, 410, 645.
McGraw (Megraw, Magragh), John, 70, 139, 294, 321.
McGraw, Leonard, 410.
McGraw, Levin, 383, 410.
McGraw (McGrough), Stephen, 266, 268, 321, 548.
McGreagor (McGreger), William, 14, 346.
McGreary (McGrary), Alex., 233, 310.
McGregor (McGrigger), Alexander, 422, 466, 502, 548.
McGrough (see McGraw).
McGuffin, Daniel, 647.
McGuire, Conrad, 606.
McGuire (McQuire), Daniel, 232, 305.
McGuire, Hugh, 377.
McGuire (McGwire, McGwin), James, 141, 515, 615.
McGuire (Maguire, McGuyar), John, 70, 141, 232, 342, 521.

McGuire, Michael, 141, 360, 475, 548, 562.
McGuire (Maguire), Nicholas, 410, 652.
McGuire, Pat., 145.
McGuire (Maguire, McGwire), Peter (Pett.), 234, 340, 341, 356, 438, 493, 546, 581.
McGuire, Philemon, 284.
McGuire (Maguire, McGuyer), Thomas, 12, 51, 232, 306.
McGurck, James, 231.
McGurrow, Francis, 394.
McGuyar, John (see McGuire), 70.
McGuyer, Thomas (see McGuire), 51.
McGwin (see McGwire).
McGwire (McGwin), James (see McGuire), 615.
McGwire, Pett. (see McGuire).
McHaffe, Benj., 546.
McHalsey (or Halfey), Benj., 226.
McHandy, Thomas, 439, 548.
McHannah, John, 66.
McHendricks, James, 139.
McHenry, Arthur, 21.
McHugh, Matthew, 600.
McIlvaine, Benjamin, 410.
McIntire, Alexr., 284.
McIntire, Daniel, 46, 52, 143, 415.
McIntire (McIntier, McEntire), James, 662, 598.
McIntire, Patric, 46.
McIntosh (McIntoch), George, 41, 143.
McIntosh, John, 227.
McIntyre, John, 606.
McItee (see McAtlee).
McKann, John (see McCann), 145, 350.
McKarteney (see McCartney).
McKarty (see McCarty).
McKay, Daniel, 9.
McKay, Isaac, 227.
McKay, John (see McCoy), 30, 227, 352, 394, 485.
McKay, John Alex. (see Mackey), 230.
McKay, William (see McCoy), 45.
McKean, Levin, 140.
McKean, MacNal., 137.
McKeel, Charles, 14.
McKeel, Thomas, 13, 136.
McKenley (see McKinley).
McKenney, John (see McKenny), 33, 139, 320.
McKennie, John (see McKenny), 607.
McKenny, James, 230, 327.
McKenny (McKenney, McKennie, McKinney), John, 33, 51, 63, 69, 139, 232, 294, 320, 340, 607.

McKenny, Lawr., 145.
McKenny, Robt., 142.
McKenny (McKinney), Roderick (see McKinsey), 145, 350, 397, 420.
McKensey, Wm. (see McKinsey), 136.
McKensie (see McKinsey).
McKensley, Charles, 336.
McKenzie, Aaron, 369.
McKenzie, Brice, 143.
McKenzie, Edward, 12.
McKernal, Thomas, 227.
McKew, Thomas, 144.
McKey, Jacob (see Mackey), 330.
McKey, John (see McCoy), 286.
McKey, John Alex. (see Mackey), 347.
McKey, William (see Mackey), 226.
McKibbin, James, 647.
McKim, Benjamin, 141, 410.
McKindly, Wm., 229.
McKinley, Archibald, 230.
McKinley, Hugh, 25.
McKinley (McKenley), James, 144, 319.
McKinney, John (see McKenny), 63, 69, 232, 294, 340.
McKinney, Roderick (see McKenny), 350.
McKinnis, Dennis, 602.
McKinny, Felix, 145.
McKinsey, Jesse, 392, 448, 507, 547.
McKinsey, John, 285.
McKinsey (McKinsay), Joshua, 264, 267, 321, 353, 392, 447, 488, 548.
McKinsey, Moses, 264, 267, 321, 353, 392, 447, 488, 548.
McKinsey, Patrick, 392, 453, 508, 548.
McKinsey (McKinsie, McKinney, McKenny), Roderick, 145, 350, 352, 397, 420, 465, 501, 547.
McKinsey (McKinsie, McKinsy, McKinzie, McKensie), Thomas, 145, 228, 350, 352, 420, 464, 500, 548.
McKinsey (McKensey), Wm., 17, 136, 227.
McKinzie, James, 45.
McKinzie, Thomas (see McKinsey).
McKirk, Benja., 229.
McKnabb (see McNabb).
McKnight, James, 59.
McKnight (McNight), John, 145, 353, 456, 486, 547.
McKnight, Michael, 403, 459.
McKouff (or McBruff), Thomas, 398.

McKoy, Alexander (see McCoy), 136.
McKoy, Hugh (see McCoy), 266.
McKoy, John (see McCoy), 30.
McKoy, Thomas, 50.
McKoy, Wm. (see McCoy), 294.
McLain (McLean), Arthur (see McClain), 233, 388, 547.
McLain, John (see McLane), 452.
McLain, Joseph (see McLane), 451.
McLain, Thomas, 53.
McLamar (Maclamar), Darby (see McNamara), 432, 496.
McLamar, Timothy, 141, 342, 547.
McLane, Capt., 585, 599.
McLane (McLean), Enoch (see McClain), 233, 388, 546.
McLane, Hugh (see McClain), 137.
McLane (McLain), John (see McClain), 137, 227, 313, 393, 452.
McLane (McLain), Jos. (see McClain), 393, 451.
McLaughlin, Barney, 53.
McLaughlin (McLochlin, McGlachlan, Maglocklin), Cornelius, 144, 318, 430, 545.
McLaughlin (McGlaughlan, McGlochlin), Hugh, 230, 388, 410, 602.
McLaughlin, James, 335.
McLaughlin (McGlaughlin, McGlochlin, McClockling), John, 11, 233, 305, 328, 546.
McLaughlin (McLaughlan, McGlocklain), Mark (see Lauglane), 142, 296, 658.
McLaughlin, Nichs., 140, 299.
McLaughlin, Philip, 285.
McLaughlin (McLaughlan, McLochlin, McGlaughlin, McGloughlin, McGlouchlin, Maglocklin), William, 12, 138, 230, 358, 445, 498, 545.
McLean, Arthur (see McLane), 234, 388.
McLean, Enoch (see McLane), 388.
McLean, James (see McClain), 345.
McLeland, Bennett, 330.
McLemarc, Wm. Cooke, 228.
McLenchey (see McLiney).
McLcod, Robert, 46, 228.
McLiney (or McLenchey), James, 228.

McLochlin, Cornelius (see McLaughlin).
McLochlin, Michl., 311.
McLochlin, Wm. (see McLaughlin).
McLone, James, 144.
McMachen, Peter, 145.
McMackin, Matthew (see McMahon), 359.
McMahon, Peter, 145.
McMahon, Benj., 647.
McMahon, Francis, 285.
McMahon, John, 53, 285.
McMahon (McMahone), Matthew (see McMackin), 573, 616.
McMahon, Morris, 344, 345.
McMahon, Timothy, 140, 454, 510, 548.
McMahone, Andrew, 341.
McMahone, Mathew (see McMahon).
McMaken (or Makin), James, 54.
McManis (McMannis), Barney (see McManus), 233, 305.
McManis, Henry, 228, 324.
McManis, Thomas, 231.
McManus (McManis, McMannis), Barny (Barney), 233, 305, 607.
McMasters, Michael, 602.
McMellon, Samuel, 11.
McMellon, William (see McMullen), 11.
McMillan (McMillen, McMillion), Hugh, 60, 144, 353, 456, 485, 546.
McMillion, Wm., 142.
McMullen (McMullon, McMullain), Alexander, 564, 567, 569, 574, 615.
McMullen (McMullin, McMellon), James, 11, 141, 231.
McMullen, Timo. (see McMahon), 140.
McMullin, Danl., 230.
McMullon (see McMullen).
McMunn, Alex., 640.
McMurray, Jeremh., 233.
McNabb (McKnabb), Chas., 233, 325, 356, 380, 396, 437, 492, 546.
McNabb, James, 401.
McNaiton, Wm., 229.
McNally (McNalley, McNaley, McNelly, McNellcy), John, 233, 308, 321, 301, 403, 493, 546.
McNamara, Benja., 137.
McNamara (McNamarra, Macnamara, McNemar, McLamar, Maclamar), Darby (Darley), 137, 312, 317, 358, 432, 496, 545.
McNamara (McNamarr), George, 24, 61.
McNamara, Jas., 437.

McNamara (McNamarra), Joseph, 343, 396, 455, 511, 547.
McNamara, Nicholas, 549.
McNamara (McNamarra), William, 327, 573.
McNash, Mathw., 284.
McNaughton, Peter, 18, 138, 357, 396, 626.
McNeal (McNeall), John (see McNiel), 143, 396, 454, 494, 547.
McNeal (McNeale, McNeil), William, 230, 325, 347, 441, 502, 547.
McNealis Charles, 606, 658.
McNear, Arch., 60.
McNear (McNier), Thos., 575, 581.
McNeil, Wm. (see McNeal), 347.
McNeile, Michael, 60.
McNelly (McNelley) (see McNally).
McNemar (see McNamara).
McNemara, Timy., 297.
McNemera, Pat., 138.
McNess, George, 410.
McNeue, Wm., 428.
McNew, Moses, 8, 137.
McNiel, John (see McNeal), 388.
McNier, John, 581.
McNier, Thos. (see McNear).
McNight (see McKnight).
McNorton (McNortin), Peter, 431, 495, 545.
McNorton, Willm., 40, 140.
McOwen, Neal (see McCowan), 401.
McPatridge, Danl. (see Fetteridge), 416.
McPherson, A., 140.
McPherson, John, 6.
McPherson, Mark (M.), 7, 137, 353, 363, 379, 456, 476, 479, 483, 521.
McPherson, Samuel (——), 5, 137, 356, 357, 364, 379, 380, 443, 479, 494, 521.
McPherson, William, 18, 381, 394, 450, 400, 548.
McQuality, James, 69.
McQuay, Martin, 228.
McQuay, Thomas, 226.
McQue, John, 21.
McQuinney (McQuinny), Thomas, 464, 500, 548.
McQuire (see McGuire).
McRea, John, 455.
McScney (see Maccency).
McSwain, Samuel, 34.
McTier, Daniel, 40.
McVay (McVey), David, 233, 392.
McVay, James, 145.
McWay, Chrisr. (see McAway), 353.
McWilliams, Wm., 61, 227.

Index. 709

Mead, James, 23, 139, 226, 469, 506, 546.
Mead (Moad, Mode), William, 233, 391, 473, 511, 546.
Meadows (Meddis, Medes, Middis), David, 383, 397, 403, 405, 410, 459, 490, 547.
Meadows, William, 58.
Meagher, Peter, 67.
Meakins, Bennet (Brannick, Binneck, Birnnick), 424, 464, 500, 548.
Means, Daniel, 46.
Mearick, Chas., 467.
Mears, John, 67.
Meason (see Mason).
Mec, Thomas, 549.
Meconican (see McConnican).
Medcalf (Metcalf), John, 139, 330.
Medcalf, Richd., 138.
Medcalf, Robert, 139, 313.
Meddis, Medes (see Meadows).
Medler, Boston (Bosston), 231, 356, 437, 492, 546.
Medler, Jacob, 231.
Medley, Enoch, 658.
Medley, Thomas, 228.
Medlicutt (Middlecut), James, 61, 140.
Meeds, Walter, 645.
Meek, Francis, 231.
Meek, Jesse, 137.
Meek (Mick, Meeks), John, 15, 234, 334, 391, 443, 505, 546, 630.
Meek, Johns, 369.
Meeke, Richard, 377.
Meekins, Robert, 383, 410.
Meeks, John (see Meek), 391.
Meeks, Robert, 65.
Meeks, Thomas, 228.
Meeks, William, 65.
Mefford, John (see Mifford), 653.
Mefford, William, 325.
Meglamery (see Maglamary).
Megraw (see McGraw).
Mehaney (Mehoney) (see Mahoney).
Melles, William, 226.
Mellon (Mellan, Mullone), Patrick (see Mullen), 336, 392, 405.
Mellone, William, 228.
Melony (Mullowny), Darby, 35, 608.
Melony (Molony), John, 41, 305.
Melony, William (see Maloney), 25.
Meloy, James, 53.
Meloy, Michael (see Maloy).
Melton, Chas., 601.

Melton, James, 30.
Melville (see Melvin).
Melvin (Melville), Aliard (Alyard, Alyand, Aliad), 397, 403, 459, 487, 547.
Melvin, Peter, 139, 357, 444, 495, 548.
Menchen (Menchon, Menchim), Humphrey (Humphry, Humpry), 40, 143, 546.
Menitry, Gueld'd (see Minitree), 138.
Menix, Charles, 72.
Menson, Richard, 328.
Mentges (Minges), Chrisn., 26, 139.
Menton, Danl., 141.
Meradith (see Meredith).
Mercer, Jno. (see Merser, Jno. Caspar), 141.
Mercer, Julius, 333.
Mercer, Stephen, 658.
Merchant, Joseph, 24.
Meredith (Meradith), James, 66, 285, 650.
Meredith, John, 67.
Meredith (Meridith, Meradith), Thomas, 66.
Merfey, Danl. (see Murphy), 46.
Merican, Edwd., 144.
Meridith (see Meredith).
Merino, Charles, 143.
Merl, Wm., 622.
Meroney, Henry, 45.
Meroney, Philip (see Maroney).
Merrick, John, 387, 410.
Merrick, William (Wm. L.), 410, 611, 613.
Merriken, Joshua, 39.
Merrill, Thomas, 69.
Merritt, Ronsey, 602.
Merritt (Merrit), Wm., 232, 305.
Merry, John, 282, 395.
Merryfield (Meryfield), Josiah, 228, 285.
Merryman, John, 419.
Merryman, Luke, 302, 448, 494, 548.
Merser, Jno. Casper (see Mercer, Jno.), 336.
Meryfield, Josiah (see Merryfield), 285.
Mesler (Mushter), Lawrence (Laurence), 417, 464, 499, 548.
Messar, John (see Messer), 233.
Messeck (Missick), Charles, 425, 549.
Messer (Messar), John, 233, 427, 474.
Messersmith, Wm., 50.
Metcalf (see Medcalf).
Metheny, Luke, 601.
Metts (Mitz), Chr. (Chris.), 51, 285.

Mettz, John, 264.
Meyer, John (see Myer), 410.
Meyers (see Myers).
Michael, Conrod, 327.
Michael, Henry, 234, 264, 265.
Michael, John, 234, 264.
Michael, Robt., 459.
Michall, Perry, 33.
Mick, John (see Meek), 234, 334, 443, 505, 546.
Middis (see Meadows).
Middlecut, James (see Medlicutt), 61.
Middleton, Henry, 52.
Middleton, Jas., 420, 422, 470.
Middleton, William, 645.
Mie, Thomas, 140.
Mielberger (see Millberger).
Miely, Jacob, 234.
Miers, Christopher (see Myers).
Miers, William, 368, 646.
Mifford, Jacob, 421, 466, 502, 548.
Mifford (Mefford, Mofford, Millford), John, 403, 415, 417, 653.
Mignot, George, 615.
Milburn (Milburne, Milbourne), Nicholas, 228, 347, 353, 440, 487, 547.
Mildorph (Mildurph), John A. (John), 397, 403, 415.
Miles, Edward, 377.
Miles, Fredk. (Frederick C.), 19, 140, 545.
Miles, Henry, 32.
Miles, Henry of Joseph, 32.
Miles, Jacob, 35.
Miles, James, 35.
Miles, John, 39, 60, 138, 144, 228, 400, 414, 493.
Miles, Joshua, 59, 60, 228, 231.
Miles, Murphey, 232.
Miles, Nicholas, 377, 410.
Miles, Richard, 393, 416.
Miles, Thomas, 226.
Miles, Walter (see Mills), 138, 512, 545.
Miles, William, 40, 60.
Mileter (Millater, Mittater), Patk., 140, 299.
Miley, Jacob, 266.
Millar, Andrew (see Miller), 36.
Millar, James (see Miller).
Millar, Peter, 52.
Millard, Thomas, 41, 284.
Millater (see Mileter).
Millberger (Millburger, Mielberger), Henry, 265, 270, 517.
Miller, Abraham, 51, 267, 324.
Miller, Adam, 388.

Miller (Millar), Andrew (see Filler), 36, 328, 437.
Miller, Anthony, 261, 266, 270, 517.
Miller, Benj., 41.
Miller, David, 145.
Miller, George, 263, 264, 410, 467, 503, 549, 599, 653.
Miller, Henry, 18, 46, 228.
Miller, Jacob, 35, 138, 234, 261, 262, 263, 266, 331.
Miller, Jacob, Jr., 234, 262.
Miller (Millar), James, 19, 139, 314, 649.
Miller, John, 23, 35, 45, 58, 138, 142, 144, 234, 261, 263, 269, 270, 284, 410, 428, 474, 517, 646, 653.
Miller, John Christr., 511, 547.
Miller, Joseph, 231, 305.
Miller, Joshua, 231.
Miller, Josiah, 137.
Miller, Josias, 6.
Miller, Ludwick, 602.
Miller, Michael, 19, 137, 358, 432, 496, 545.
Miller, Philip, 233, 265, 658.
Miller, Thomas, 233, 305, 601.
Miller, William (see Millions), 143, 284, 658.
Millet, George, 138.
Millford (see Mifford).
Millington, Allemby, 368, 385.
Millington, John (see Willington), 24.
Million, John, 284.
Millions, Wm. (see Miller), 143.
Millner (see Milner).
Mills, Benjm., 230.
Mills, Capt., 417.
Mills, Edward, 226.
Mills, Jacob, 49.
Mills, John, 8, 38, 62, 67, 136, 142, 226, 234, 339, 345, 352, 390, 429, 434, 438, 493, 512, 546, 547.
Mills, John Bapt., 331, 333.
Mills, Jonathan, 356, 658.
Mills, Martin, 431.
Mills, Walter (see Miles), 431.
Mills, William, 47, 70.
Mills, Zachariah, 398, 446, 498, 548.
Millstead, Jonathan, 139, 432.
Millston, Barker, 137.
Milner (Millner), Francis, 13, 58.
Milstead, John, 359, 396, 549.
Milstead, Thomas, 31.
Minetree (see Minitree).

Minges, Chris. (see Mentges), 26.
Mingo, Jos., 141.
Minie (see Minor).
Miniky (Minike), Guilford (Gilford, Giffard) (see Minitree), 455, 505, 545.
Mining, John, 59.
Minisham, Morris, 602.
Minitree (Minetree, Menitry), Gilferd (Gifford, Gueld'd) (see Miniky), 32, 138, 313.
Minitree, Paul, 32.
Minn, John, 231.
Minner (see Minor).
Minney, John, 58.
Minning, Jno., 141, 296.
Minor, John, 647.
Minor (Minner, Minie), Levin (Leven), 385, 410.
Miorley, Dennis, 228.
Mire (see Myre).
Misbett, Richard (see Nesbitt), 324.
Missell (Misseral), John, 511, 549.
Missett, Lawrence, 284.
Missick, Chas. (see Messick), 425.
Missick, Lawrence, 284.
Mitchel, Saml., 227.
Mitchell, Aaron (see Newberry), 383, 397, 403, 458, 484, 487, 547.
Mitchell, Andrew, 61.
Mitchell, Charles, 36.
Mitchell, Conrad, 145.
Mitchell, Edward, 36.
Mitchell (Mitchel), Francis, 17, 136, 232, 309, 618.
Mitchell, Henry, 138.
Mitchell, Igns., 137.
Mitchell, Isaac, 467, 503, 549.
Mitchell, James, 7, 136.
Mitchell (Mitchel), John (Capt.), 5, 70, 136, 137, 229, 286, 346, 364, 370, 380, 382, 458, 476, 480, 521, 602, 615, 641.
Mitchell, Levin, 140.
Mitchell, Miles, 42.
Mitchell, Nathan, 36.
Mitchell, Nathl., 366.
Mitchell (Mitchel), Richard, 140, 335, 358, 441, 498, 545.
Mitchell (Mitchel), Robert, 397, 400, 403, 488, 547, 563, 567, 570, 674.
Mitchell, Thomas, 35.
Mitchell, William, 142, 342, 354, 436, 489, 546, 603.
Mittag, Fredk., 261.
Mittater (see Mileter).
Mitz, Chris. (see Metts), 285.
Moad, William (see Mead), 233, 511, 546.

Mobberly, Thos. (see Mobley), 382.
Mober, Ludwick, 46.
Mobley, Thomas (see Mobberly), 142.
Mockbee (Mackabee), Alexander, 43.
Mockbee, Joseph, 382.
Mockbee, Wm., 139.
Mockbee, Zephaniah, 49.
Mode, Willm. (see Mead), 391.
Moffitt (Moffatt), Thomas, 57, 370, 410.
Mofford (see Mifford).
Mohan, Patk., 142.
Moire, Peter, 137.
Moland, James, 285, 341.
Moland (Moulan), Richard, 229, 304.
Molen (Molling), Vincent, 398, 403, 416.
Moles, Wm., 30.
Mollihan (see Molohon).
Molling (see Molen).
Molnix, William (see Mullinoux), 321.
Molohon (Mollihan), Patrick, 357, 430, 496, 548.
Molohon, Wm., 140.
Molony (see Melony).
Monahan, Thos., 400.
Monarch (Monark), Edward, 384, 410.
Monday, John, 602.
Mondis (see Mundus).
Mondle (see Mantle).
Money, Isaac, 51.
Money, Patrick (see Mooney), 46.
Money, Samuel, 61, 646.
Mong, Adam, 230.
Mong, Richard, 229.
Mongaul (Mongoal), Fredk., 234, 263.
Monghon (or Mahorn), ———, 142.
Monghon, Pat. (see Mayhorne), 142.
Mongoal (see Mongaul).
Montgomery, Joseph, 13.
Monk, William, 190, 231.
Monks (Munks), James, 228, 414.
Monks, Michael, 319.
Monro (Nunro, Munrow) Barney (Barny), 233, 391, 442.
Monro, John, 233.
Monroe, Danl., 136.
Monroe, Finley, 285.
Montgomery, Alex., 144, 405, 415.
Montgomery, Ignatius, 377, 410.
Montgomery, James, 32.
Montgomery, John, 658.
Montle (see Mantle).
Moody, Benj., 647.
Moody, Levi (or Levy), 369, 392, 452, 548, 602.

Mooney (Money), Patrick, 46, 230, 232, 307.
Mooney, William, 227.
Moor (see Moore).
Moore (More), Andrew, 233, 391, 546.
Moore, Asa, 475, 507.
Moore (More), Benjamin, 66, 228, 620.
Moore, Capt., 601.
Moore, Charles, 24, 293.
Moore, Daniel, 72.
Moore, Francis, 138.
Moore, Hezekiah, 138, 424, 472.
Moore, Hugh, 53, 322.
Moore, Isom, 475, 507, 549.
Moore, James, 60, 583.
Moore (More, Moor), John, 30, 51, 231, 232, 265, 270, 284, 311, 338, 342, 354, 355, 366, 390, 395, 435, 441, 443, 450, 466, 489, 491, 502, 506, 510, 517, 546, 547, 548, 626, 653, 658.
Moore (Moor), Joseph, 51, 330.
Moore, Leonard, 34.
Moore, Matthew, 52, 142, 143, 298, 353, 354, 437, 457, 486, 489, 546.
Moore, Nicholas Ruxton, 568, 570.
Moore, Peter, 317.
Moore, Reubin, 139, 293.
Moore, Richd., 140.
Moore, Robert, 227, 648.
Moore, Smith (Ensign), 74, 227.
Moore (More, Moor), Thos., 330, 607, 611, 613, 658.
Moore, William (see More), 70, 139, 230, 285, 293, 355, 357, 398, 410, 441, 444, 445, 491, 494, 495, 545, 546, 616, 653.
Moore, Zachariah, 423, 472, 509, 549.
Moore, Zedekiah, 363, 365, 379, 441, 479, 521.
Moorecraft (Moreeraft), Wm., 285, 394, 458.
Mooren (see Moran).
Moores, James R., 659.
Moorhead, Capt., 604.
Mooring, William (see Moran), 233.
Moorman, Thos., 231.
Moppes, Fredk., 263.
Morain, Jno. (see Moran), 140.
Moran, Azell, 138.
Moran (Mooren), Benj., 304, 349, 440, 546.
Moran, Edmond, 229.
Moran, Edward, 518.
Moran (Morain, Morant, Murrant), John, 140, 305, 397, 424, 445, 462, 549.

Moran (Moren), Patrick, 229, 334.
Moran (Moren, Morrane, Moring, Mooring), William, 70, 229, 233, 285, 305, 348, 414.
Morant, John (see Moran), 462.
More, Andrew (see Moore).
More, Benj. (see Moore).
More, John (see Moore).
More, Thomas (see Moore), 330.
More, William (see Moore), 139.
Morecraft (see Moorecraft).
Moree, James, 572, 577, 580, 582.
Moree, Robert, 572.
Morelache, Moses, 410.
Morelake (Morleck), Moses, 383, 397, 403, 410, 415.
Moreland, Henry, 226.
Moren, Patrick (see Moran), 229.
Moren (Morrane), William (see Moran), 70, 229.
Moreton, Joshua, 143.
Morfitt, George, 41.
Morgan, Benja., 229, 330.
Morgan, Daniel, 300.
Morgan, David, 365, 521.
Morgan, Edwd., 649.
Morgan, Jacob, 383.
Morgan, James, 23.
Morgan, Jeremiah, 142, 329.
Morgan, John, 40, 145, 387.
Morgan, Johnson (Johnsey), 139, 294, 320.
Morgan, Matthew, 647.
Morgan (Morgon), Richard, 51, 141, 229, 285, 304.
Morgan, Robert, 74.
Morgan, Thomas, 227, 410.
Morgan, William, 66, 226, 645, 651.
Moring (Mooring), Wm. (see Moran), 233, 305.
Morland, Philip, 331.
Morleck (see Morelake).
Morolf, Rudolph, 47.
Morrane (see Moran).
Morrindon, Michael, 227.
Morriner, George, 19.
Morris, Cornelius, 69, 234, 341, 390.
Morris, Edward, 59.
Morris, Evan, 72, 233, 315.
Morris, James, 230, 387, 410, 418, 428, 469, 474, 510, 548, 653.
Morris (Morriss), John, 23, 33, 59, 141, 142, 295, 299, 329, 397, 400, 403, 410, 462, 487, 545, 547, 653.
Morris, Jonathan (Capt.), 48, 232, 305, 326, 363, 378, 479, 521, 621.
Morris, Joseph, 64.
Morris, Levi, 22.
Morris, Michael, 59, 141.

Index. 711

Morris (Morriss), Neal (Neale, Nell), 356, 438, 493, 546.
Morris, Richard, 30.
Morris, Samuel, 35, 233, 309, 325.
Morris, Thomas, 141.
Morris, William, 144, 606, 658.
Morrison, David, 647.
Morrison, George, 51, 232.
Morrison, James, 422, 470.
Morrison, John, 139, 330, 395, 450, 512, 545.
Morrison, Michael, 61.
Morrison, Wm., 137, 629.
Morriss (see Morris).
Morrow, James (see Marrough), 647.
Morrow, John (see Murrough), 15.
Morrow, Robert, 11, 52, 53.
Morrow, Wm., 141.
Morsell, John, 285.
Mortimer, John, 233.
Morton, Archl., 144.
Morton, Benja., 285.
Morton, James, 140, 300.
Morton, Jos., 145.
Morton, Vachel, 143.
Mortt, John, 72.
Moseley, Joseph, 423, 472.
Mosen (see Moser).
Moser, Cruise, 138.
Moser (Nuser), Francis, 410, 653.
Moser (Mosen), Jacob, 264, 267, 322.
Moser (or Mouser), Ludwick, 72.
Moser, Michael, 261, 262, 410, 653.
Moses, Francis, 228.
Moses, Jacob, 142, 284, 296, 358, 436, 499, 546, 548.
Moss, Joseph, 61.
Moss, Nathan, 369.
Moss, Nicholas, 294.
Moss, Richard, 369.
Moss, Richardson, 642.
Moss, Thomas, 41.
Mouer (or Mourrer), John, 47.
Moulan (see Moland).
Mount, William, 388.
Mountgomery, George, 32.
Mourrer (see Mouer).
Mouser (see Moser).
Mowberry, George, 284.
Mowen, Jno., 51.
Moxey, Gregory, 140.
Moxley, Daniel, 49.
Moxley, John, 49.
Moylan, ———, 272.
Moylan, Stephen, 599.
Moyland, Dennis, 142, 300.
Moyer, (see Myers).
Moyston, Edward, 41, 143.
Mubary, Alexander, 305.

Muckleroy, Robert, 647.
Mud, Edwd., 475.
Mud, William, 36.
Mudd, Benjamin, 32.
Mudd, Bennett, 138, 331, 393, 549.
Mudd, Henry, 31, 140.
Mudd, Hezekiah, 377, 410.
Mudd, Jeremiah, 461, 511, 547, 629.
Mudd, John, 32.
Mudd, Martin, 137.
Mudd, Richard, 136, 137, 331, 545.
Mudd, Thomas, 137.
Mugg, John, 18.
Muir, Francis, 606.
Muirett (Muiret, Murritt), Charles, 577, 580, 582, 583.
Mulcahy, Daniel, 64.
Muldrob, Robert, 228.
Mulholland (Mullholland, Mulhulland), Arthur, 139, 294, 323.
Mullan, Edward, 38.
Mullen (Mullane, Malone, Mallone), Andrew, 138, 398, 403, 405.
Mullen, Dennis, 233.
Mullen, Michael (see Mullin), 19, 59, 233.
Mullen (Mullin), Patrick (see Mellon), 231, 401, 414.
Mullen (Mullens), Timothy, 142, 515.
Mullen, William, 647.
Mullens (see Mullen).
Muller, Joseph, 53.
Mullet, William, 232.
Mullholland (see Mulholland).
Mullican, Lewis, 44.
Mullihan, Archibald, 50.
Mullikin, Capt., 399.
Mullin, Michael (see Mullen), 70.
Mullin, Patrick (see Mullen).
Mullings, James, 326.
Mullinoux (Molnix), Wm., 284, 321.
Mullins, Jonathan, 62.
Mullowny, Darby (see Melony), 35.
Mulloy, Martin, 598.
Mulloy, Roger (see Maloy), 338.
Muma (see Mumma).
Mumford, Chs., 141.
Mumford, James, 372.
Mumford (Munford), John, 509, 549.
Mumford, Robt., 143.
Mumma (Mummaw, Mummard), Christian, 267, 268, 324.
Mumma (Muma), David, 265, 268.

Mummart (Mummert, Mummard), William, 234, 266, 321.
Mummaw (see Mumma).
Mummer, Michael, 297.
Mummert (see Mummart).
Munay (see Murray).
Munday, Jas., 649.
Mundus (Mondis), Michael, 369, 396.
Munford, John (see Mumford), 549.
Munford, Peter, 345.
Munks (see Monks).
Munn, Jas., 51.
Munro (see Monro).
Munroe, Alex., 603.
Munroe, Hugh, 13.
Munrow (see Monro).
Munson, Capt., 598.
Murdoch (Murdock), Benja., 232, 305.
Murdoch, George, 631.
Murdoch, Josias, 25.
Murdoch (Murdock), William (Lt.), 231, 363, 365, 379, 479.
Murdock, Benja. (see Murdoch).
Murdock, John, 43.
Mure, Thomas, 410.
Murley, Dennis, 434.
Murnet, Michl., 142.
Murphey, Darby, 53.
Murphey, David, 143.
Murphey, Hezekiah, 410.
Murphey, Joah, 59.
Murphy, Anthony, 139, 572, 648.
Murphy, Charles, 141, 299, 354, 450, 490, 545.
Murphy (Murphey), Cornelius, 13, 143, 457.
Murphy (Murphey, Merfey), Daniel, 46, 50, 141, 397, 403, 459, 487, 547.
Murphy (Murphey), Edward, 16, 55, 227.
Murphy, George, 70.
Murphy, Hugh, 230.
Murphy (Murphey), James, 9, 17, 70, 138, 139, 226, 266, 284, 293, 303, 305, 321, 417, 547, 624, 632, 639.
Murphy (Murphey), John, 10, 25, 26, 53, 140, 143, 144, 226, 227, 318, 334, 415, 642.
Murphy (Murphey), Joseph, 234, 334, 475, 510, 546.
Murphy, Martin, 421.
Murphy (Murphey, Marfee), Michael, 139, 145, 233, 284, 305.
Murphy, Miles, 307.
Murphy, Morgan, 606, 658.
Murphy (Murphey), Patrick, 44, 45, 143, 144, 232, 307, 335, 414.
Murphy, Richard, 342.

Murphy, Samuel, 658.
Murphy (Murphey), Thos., 53, 66, 143, 226, 228, 285, 340, 353, 457, 486, 546.
Murphy (Murphey), Timothy, 144, 415, 565, 567, 570, 574.
Murphy (Murphey), William, 43, 227, 230, 340, 383, 403, 410, 612, 661.
Murrant, John (see Moran), 397.
Murray, Alexander, 13, 137.
Murray, Daniel, 575, 581.
Murray (Murry), Edward, 232, 307.
Murray (Murrey), James, 141, 227, 331, 339, 418, 421, 469, 472.
Murray (Murrey, Murry), John, 58, 142, 144, 231, 426, 451, 473, 500, 547, 623.
Murray, Laurence, 231.
Murray (Murry), Matthew, 12, 137, 226, 606, 658.
Murray, Matthias, 410, 595.
Murray (or Munay), Rich., 615.
Murray, Thomas, 9, 229.
Murray, Thompson (Thomson), 234, 341.
Murray, Valentine, 299, 545.
Murray, William, 227.
Murrey, James (see Murray), 331.
Murrey (Murry), John (see Murray), 58, 144.
Murritt (see Muirett).
Murrough, John (see Morrow), 232.
Murry (see Murray).
Muschett, John, 629.
Muse, Thom., 70.
Muse, Walker (Walter), 13, 136, 363, 379, 476, 479, 499, 521, 616, 639.
Muser (see Moser).
Mushler (see Musler).
Mushter (see Mesler).
Musler (Mussler, Mushler), Adam, 266, 268, 321, 369, 395, 447, 507, 547.
Mustersbaugh, Philip, 387.
Mustin, Richard, 144.
Mutton, James, 640.
Myer, Henry, 47.
Myer, Jacob (see Myers).
Myer (Meyer), John (see Myers, John George), 45, 410.
Myer, Philip (see Myers).
Myers, Adam, 230, 573.
Myers (Meyers, Mayers), Christian, 182, 266, 270, 271, 365, 390, 521.
Myers (Miers, Mayers), Christopher, 232, 365, 546.
Myers, Francis, 264.

Myers (Meyers, Myirs, Moyer), Frederick (see Myre), 397, 405, 458.
Myers (Myer), George, 265.
Myers (Myer), Jacob, 265, 268, 269, 270, 317, 358, 460, 498, 547.
Myers, John George (see Myer, John), 232.
Myers, Lawrence, 47, 521.
Myers (Myer), Philip, 410, 653.
Myers, Robert, 580, 582, 583.
Myhan, Denniss, 572.
Myirs (see Myers).
Myre (Mire), Frederick (see Myers), 19, 137.
Myre, Peter, 20.
Myss, Nicholas (see Ticc), 320.

Nabb, Charles, 235, 375, 397, 404, 458, 486, 549.
Nabb, Elisha, 67.
Nabb, Joseph, 234, 352, 433, 549.
Nabb (Nab), Richard, 66, 234, 646.
Nabers (see Neighbours).
Nable, Leonard, 468, 504, 550.
Nable (Nabell), Richard, 423, 471.
Nagill (or Nagale), Michael, 658.
Nagle, Richard, 411, 653.
Nagle, William (see Neagle), 15.
Nail, David, 47.
Nailor, Alex. (see Naylor).
Nailor, Isaac, 148.
Nailor, Joshua (see Naylor), 147.
Nailor, Nicholas (see Naylor), 19.
Nailor (or Nalor), Thomas, 72.
Nailor, William, 234, 358, 432, 497, 549.
Nally, John McA., 356.
Narry, Martain (see Harry), 328.
Nary (see Neary).
Nash, Bernard, 6, 146.
Nash, Christopher, 508.
Nash, Chrisn., 147.
Nash, Edward, 235.
Nash, Joseph, 235.
Nash, Thomas, 235, 327, 658.
Nason, Saml., 147.
Nave (see Knave).
Nave (Neave), John, 462, 487, 549, 653.
Navey, John, 549.
Navey, Matthew, 383, 411.
Navy, James, 416.
Navy, William, 612, 613.
Naylor (Nailor), Alexr., 18, 146.

Naylor, George, 38.
Naylor, Joshua (see Nailor), 16, 147.
Naylor (Nailor), Nicholas, 19, 146.
Nayry (see Neary).
Nayse, Richard, 235.
Neagle, James, 235, 343, 440.
Neagle (Neigle), Morris (Morrice), 147, 286, 475, 512, 549.
Neagle (Nagle), William, 15, 146.
Neal, Chr., 51.
Neal (Neale, Neil), Daniel, 573, 579, 582, 584.
Neal, Elijah, 392.
Neal (Neale, Neil), John, 6, 53, 146, 286, 314.
Neal (Neale, Neall), Joseph, 148, 351, 352, 387, 398, 429, 465, 549.
Neal, St. Leger, 416.
Neale, Danl. (see Neal).
Neale, Henry, 25.
Neale (Neil), James, 336, 469, 579, 584.
Neale, John (see Neal), 146, 314.
Neale, Joseph (see Neal).
Neale (Neall, Neil), Thomas, 146, 317, 394, 550.
Neale, William, 377, 411.
Neall, Bennett, 45.
Neall, Charles, 146.
Neary (Nary, Nayry), John, 7, 146, 313, 396, 454, 512.
Neav—, John, 653.
Neave, John (see Nave), 653.
Need (or Neet), George, 72.
Needham, Michael, 411.
Needham, Wm. (William A.), 147, 355, 396, 456, 490, 549.
Needles, ———, 74.
Needles, John, 60.
Needs, James, 345, 396.
Neeley, Mathew, 640.
Neet (see Need).
Neguire, Peter, 503.
Neighbours, James, 612, 613.
Neighbours (Nabers), John, 235, 341, 438, 506, 549.
Neighbours, Joseph, 345.
Neighbours, Levi, 611.
Neigle (see Neagle).
Neil (see Neal and Neale).
Neilson, Alex., 575.
Neilson, Richard (see Nelson).
Neilson, Thomas (see Nelson).
Nelson, James, 22, 60.

Nelson, John (———), 31, 146, 147, 235, 362, 378, 397, 404, 411, 424, 459, 474, 489, 521, 549.
Nelson, Penner, 31.
Nelson (Neilson), Richard, 147, 549.
Nelson, Robert, 8.
Nelson, Roger, 364, 365, 381, 421.
Nelson (Neilson), Thomas, 565, 566, 569, 574.
Nesbit, Thomas, 650.
Nesbitt (Nisbett), Richard (see Misbett), 146, 294.
Nest, George, 26.
Neswangher (see Newsanger).
Netsley, John, 47.
Nevell, Robt., 234.
Nevill, Philip, 146.
Neville (Nevill), Samuel, 235, 510.
Neville, John, 65.
Nevin (Neven), Daniel, 606, 659.
Nevin, Mays, 577.
Nevin (Neving), William, 235, 266, 323.
Nevitt (Nevit, Nevet), John, 235, 268, 353, 433, 448, 488, 549.
Newberry, Aaron (see Mitchell), 383.
Newberry, John, 377, 429.
Newberry, Joseph, 376.
Newberry (Newbury) William, 392, 401, 448.
Newcomb (Newcome), Robert, 67, 147, 234.
Newell, David, 63, 67.
Newell, James, 501, 549.
Newell, John, 67.
Newell, Thomas, 647.
Newell, William, 235, 387.
Newgin (see Nugent).
Newland, John, 334.
Newland, Thos. (see Noland), 415.
Newman, Basil, 550.
Newman, Danl., 422, 471.
Newman, Freeman, 563, 567, 570, 574.
Newman, George, 35.
Newman, Jesse, 234.
Newman, John, 51, 235, 325, 396, 454.
Newman, Thomas, 23, 508, 550.
Newman, William, 234.
Newnam, Joseph, 67.
Newnam, Risdon, 67.
Newnan, Wm., 146.
Newsanger (or Neswangher), John, 47.
Newsom, Joseph, 646.
Newthall, Thos., 286.
Newton, Basil (Bazil), 34, 235, 420, 465, 501.
Newton, Henry, 34.

Newton (Nuton), John, 40, 369, 392, 446, 453, 499, 507, 549.
Newton (Luton), Joseph, 235, 384.
Newton, Levin, 372.
Newton, Thomas, 147.
Newton (Nuton), William, 146, 203, 355, 394, 461, 491, 549.
Newton, Zachariah, 384, 410.
Newvall, Wm., 305.
Niblett (Niblet), William, 235, 356, 391, 438, 494, 549.
Nicholas, Col., 300.
Nicholas, John, 235.
Nicholas, Joshua, 615.
Nicholason, William, 41.
Nicholasson, Richard, 42.
Nicholl (see Nichols).
Nicholls, Becket, 146.
Nicholls, John Haymond, 44.
Nichols, Ace, 411.
Nichols (Nicholl), Archibald, 147, 415.
Nichols (Nicholls), Asabel (Easy, Sael), 147, 320, 549.
Nichols (Nicholls), Edward, 147, 414.
Nichols (Nicholls), Isaac, 398, 462, 498, 549.
Nichols (Nicholls), John, 42, 235.
Nichols, John Mc., 235.
Nichols (Nicholls), Joseph, 147, 415.
Nichols, Josh., 341.
Nichols (Nicholls), Nicholas, 234, 515, 618.
Nichols (or Nickols), Ninion, 45.
Nichols (Nicholls), Thomas, 42, 235.
Nichols (Nicholl), Walter, 44, 650.
Nichols, William, 41, 572.
Nicholson, Alex., 606, 659.
Nicholson, Anthy., 147.
Nicholson, Emanuel, 70.
Nicholson, Geo., 147.
Nicholson (Nickleson), Henry, 146, 314, 355, 441, 491, 549.
Nicholson, James, 659.
Nicholson, John (Mr.), 23, 234, 260, 272, 353, 393, 422, 448, 468, 487, 504, 514, 549, 550, 633, 659.
Nicholson, Nicholas, 146, 395, 452, 512, 549.
Nicholson (Nickleson), Stephen, 146, 318, 420, 466, 502, 549.
Nicholson, Zacha., 14.
Nick (see Nicks).
Nickleson (see Nicholson).
Nickols (see Nichols).

Nicks, John, 235.
Nicks (Nick), William, 235, 311, 322.
Nicodemus, Frederick, 73.
Nicola, Lewis, 622, 623, 624.
Nicols, Robert, 581.
Niember (Nienbar), Thos. (see Wember), 21, 146.
Night, Peter, 648.
Night, Thomas, 344.
Night, Wm., 60.
Nilghbours, Thos., 387.
Ninor, Christr., 388.
Nisbet, Barney, 147.
Nisbett (see Nesbitt).
Nisbit, Charles, 147.
Nithington, Jere., 146.
Nivin, Patk., 286.
Nixon, Robert, 286.
Nixon, William, 12, 146.
Noaksworth, John, 286.
Noble, Francis, 27, 643.
Noble, John, 27, 146, 396, 644.
Noble, Martin, 146.
Noble, William, 146, 339.
Nockey (or Hockey), Christian, 328.
Nogle, Philip, 388.
Noice, Jno. (see Noyes), 305.
Noice, Richard, 51, 305.
Noland (Nolan, Nolen, Nolland, Nulan, Nowland), John, 61, 146, 456, 508, 549, 623, 646, 647.
Noland, Matthias, 368.
Noland (Nowland), Michael (see Knowland), 235, 549.
Noland (Nolan, Nowlan), Patrick, 8, 146, 147, 461, 549, 648.
Noland (Nowland, Nowlan), Thomas (see Newland), 18, 42, 70, 147.
Noles, Michel, 335.
Nolstone, Alexander, 59.
Nonan, William, 147.
Norman, Joseph, 427, 473.
Norman, Basil (Bazel), 235, 390, 439, 512, 549.
Norman, Richard, 286.
Norman, Thomas, 63, 286.
Norris, Arnold, 384, 410.
Norris, Benj., 46, 148.
Norris (Norriss), Daniel, 26, 386, 411, 642.
Norris, Henry, 384, 411.
Norris, Jacob, 235, 364, 381, 479, 521.
Norris, James, 59.
Norris, John, 6, 147, 330, 384, 400, 411.
Norris, Matthew, 424, 472.
Norris, Philip, 147.
Norris, Thomas, 5.
Norris, William, 321, 418, 648.
Norriss, Mark, 36.

North, Jacob, 68, 234.
North, James, 342.
North, Samuel, 27, 643.
North, Wm., 641.
Northerafft, Edward, 43.
Norton, David, 600.
Norton, George, 146.
Norton, John, 235.
Norton, Lawrence, 147.
Norton, Patrick, 60.
Norwood, Edward, 38, 147.
Norwood, Joseph, 387.
Norwood, Philip, 53.
Notaire, Michael, 32.
Nott, James (see Knott), 392.
Nott, Nathanl. (see Knot), 147.
Nottingham, John, 17.
Notts, John, 286.
Nowell, James, 235, 327, 348, 440.
Nowell, Willm., 40.
Nowels, Joseph, 68.
Nowlan, Patrick (see Noland).
Nowlan, Thomas (see Nowland), 18.
Nowland, Gilbert, 61.
Nowland, James, 147, 414.
Nowland (Nulan), John (see Noland), 61, 146, 623, 646.
Nowland, Michael (see Noland), 235.
Nowland (Nowlan), Thos. (see Noland), 18, 42, 70.
Nowles, Edward, 50.
Nowles, James, 50.
Nowry, Anthony, 314.
Noyes (Noice), John, 53, 305.
Noyes, Willm., 15, 146.
Nubry, Thos., 70.
Nugent (Nujant, Newgin), Patrick, 53, 147, 418, 460.
Nulan (see Noland).
Nunan, John, 147.
Nurse, Willm., 601.
Nuton (see Newton).
Nutt (Nut), George, 146, 643.
Nuttall, Joseph, 147.
Nuth, Thos., 340.

Oakley, Elijah, 398, 429, 461, 550.
Oakley, Elisha, 508.
Oar, John (see Orr), 286.
Oaram (see Oram).
Oard, Peter, 35.
Oaster (see Oyster).
Obalam, George, 46.
O'Boyle (see Boyles).
O'Branan, Timothy, 236.
O'Brian (Obrian) (see O'Bryan).
O'Brien, Daniel, 58.
Obrien, James (see O'Bryan), 602.
Obrion, Christr., 601.

O'Brion, John (see O'Bryan).
O'Bryan, Dennis, 475, 510, 550.
O'Bryan (O'Brian, Obrien), James, 324, 334, 343, 344, 355, 602.
O'Bryan (O'Brion), John, 24, 46, 148, 341, 390, 550, 562.
O'Bryan, Joseph, 236, 411.
O'Bryan (O'Brian), Michael, 575, 580, 582, 583.
O'Bryan (O'Brian, Obrian), Phillip (Philip), 572, 576, 580, 582, 583.
O'Bryan, M. Thos. (see O'Bryon, Thos. Meredith), 236.
O'Bryon, Thos. Meredith (see O'Bryan, M. Thos.), 66.
O'Connell, Wm., 148.
O'Conner, Dennis, 149.
O'Conner, Michael, 39, 573.
O'Connor (O'Conner), John, 397, 402, 450.
O'Daniel, Richard, 43.
Odle, Rigden, 411.
O'Donald (O'Donnald), Roger, 564, 569, 616.
O'Donnally, Thos. (or Tiny.), 149.
O'Donnell (O'Donel), John, 60, 573.
Ofalvey (Ofarling), Patk., 314.
O'Ferrell (O'Farol), Michael, 579, 584.
Offield (Ofield), John, 18, 148, 344, 400.
Offutt, Nathaniel, 411.
O'Furra, Jesse, 626.
Ogden, Andrew, 35.
Ogden, James, 148.
Ogden, John, 411, 653.
Ogelsby (Ogilsby) (see Oglesby).
Ogle, James, 653.
Ogle, Robt., 60.
Ogleby, James, 52, 58.
Oglesby (Ogelsby, Ogilsby), Charles, 236, 386, 411.
Oglesby, Robert, 601.
Oglevie (Oglevee), John, 71, 646, 647.
O'Hara, Arthur, 236.
O'Hara, George, 149.
O'Hara, James, 661.
O'Hara, John (see Lorah), 236.
O'Hara (O'Harra), Patrick, 149, 350.
O'Hara (O'Harra, O'Harr), William, 70, 286.
O'Hario, Dennis, 39.
O'Harr (see O'Hara).
O'Keiff, Constantine, 149.

O'Keil (O'Kell), George (or Keil, Geo. O.), 400, 411.
Okey, John, 286.
O'Lary, James, 12.
Older, George, 37.
Oldfield, Henry, 68.
Oldham, Danl., 415.
Oldham, Edward, 52, 58, 149, 364, 380, 476, 481, 521.
Oldstone, Edward, 236.
O'Legg, Vachel, 11.
Olingan (Olinger), Stephen, 5, 11, 550.
Oliphant (Olephant), Thomas, 236, 618.
Olive, James, 37.
Oliver, Daniel, 340.
Oliver, Griffin (or Griffith), 66.
Oliver (Olliver), John, 236, 311, 342.
Oliver, Nicholas, 148.
Oliver, William, 50, 377, 411.
Olvie, Thomas, 300.
O'Mullen (O'Mullan), Patrick, 236, 304.
O'Nail, Felix, 346.
O'Neal (O'Neall, Oneal), Danl., 398, 612, 616.
O'Neal (O'Neil), Darden, 426, 473.
Oneal (O'Neil), Hugh, 53, 149.
O'Neal (O'Neale, Oneill), John, 12, 59, 148, 401, 411, 653.
Oneal, Luke, 601.
O'Neal (O'Neale), Patrick, 236, 305.
O'Neale, Charles, 16, 56.
O'Neale, John (see O'Neal).
O'Neale, Nathaniel, 17.
O'Neale, Patrick (see O'Neal).
O'Neil (Oneil, Oneill) (see O'Neal, Oneal).
O'Neill, Joseph, 302.
Onerah, Christopher, 342.
—— oney, 567.
Onians (see Onions).
Onion, Charles, 369.
Onion, William, 399.
Onions (Onians), John, 354, 305, 450, 490, 550.
Onnell (Onnel), Christopr. (see Arnold), 80, 149.
Onsborn (see Osborn).
Onstrutt, George, 411.
O'Ph——, Stephen, 236.
O'Quin, Richard, 236, 267.
O'Quinn, Daniel, 149, 353, 457, 486, 550.
Oram, Andrew, 68.
Oram, Cooper, 148.
Oram (Oaram), John, 52, 149.
Oram, Peter, 236.

Index

Oram (Horam), Samuel, 124, 149, 550.
Oram, Spedden, 610.
Orber, John (see Auber), 572.
Orbough (Osbough), Francis (see Osburne), 418, 469.
Orchard, William, 236.
Orde, William, 35.
Ore, Marane, 340.
Orendorff (Orendorf, Orndorff), Christian (Capt.), 48, 50, 362, 378, 448, 477, 480, 521, 616.
Orm, Moses, 148.
Orm, William, 148.
Orme, Charles (see Ormes), 236.
Orme, Col., 341.
Orme, Joseph, 16, 148.
Orme, Nathan, 42.
Orme, Samuel Taylor, 42.
Ormer (see Ormes).
Ormes (Orms, Orme, Ormer), Charles, 354, 360, 463, 490, 550.
Ormond, Abel, 260.
Ormond, William, 148, 286.
Orndorff (see Orendorff).
Orr (Oar), John, 286, 649.
Orrell, Darden (Dorden), 468, 504, 550.
Orrell, James, 23.
Orridge, George, 340.
Orum, Henry, 601.
Ortner, Jacob, 594.
Osban (Osband), John (see Osborn), 236, 431, 497.
Osborn (Osborne, Onsborn), Elisha, 421, 472, 509, 550.
Osborn (Osburn, Osban, Osband), John, 236, 357, 431, 497, 550.
Osborn (Osborne, Osbourn, Osburn, Ozbon, Ozbun), William, 54, 67, 68, 148, 236.
Osborne, Luke, 395.
Osbough (see Orbough).
Osburn (or Ozenburn), Benjamin, 49.
Osburn, John (see Osborn).
Osburn, William (see Osborn), 67.
Osburne, Francis (see Orbough), 8.
Osburne, Samuel, 375.
Osmond, John, 148.
Osten (Ostin, Ostend, Oyster, Oaster), Henry (see Austin), 148, 294, 321, 461, 495, 550.
Oster, John, 328.
Oster, Peter, 328.
Ostin (see Osten).
Ostrow, William, 148.
Ostwabt, Henry, 334.
Othoson, Garrett, 61.

Outerbridge, Leonard, 148, 550.
Outerbridge, Stephen, 236.
Outhouse, Peter, 334, 389, 439, 499, 550.
Overcreek, Joseph, 148, 418, 469, 511, 550, 617.
Overfelt, Matbias, 47.
Overman, John, 392, 401.
Owen, Maj., 342.
Owen, Thomas, 36, 50.
Owens (Owings), Arthur, 148, 299.
Owens (Owings), Jacob, 579, 584.
Owens (Owings), James, 149, 236, 352, 433, 550.
Owens (Owings), Jeremiah, 10, 455.
Owens, John (see Owings), 148, 286, 619.
Owens (Owins, Owings), Joseph, 148, 331, 377, 586, 587.
Owens, Paris (Parris), 425, 429, 466, 502, 550.
Owens, Patrick, 388.
Owens, Samuel (see Owings), 293, 359, 550.
Owens, Stephen, 236, 348, 440, 504, 550.
Owens (Owins), Thomas, 62, 383, 411, 586.
Owens, William, 236.
Owings, Arthur (see Owens).
Owings, Jacob (see Owens).
Owings, James (see Owens).
Owings, Jeremiah (see Owens).
Owings, John (see Owens), 10, 148.
Owings, Joseph (see Owens).
Owings, Roddey, 10.
Owings, Roger, 502, 593.
Owings, Samuel (see Owens), 22, 148, 330.
Owsley (see Housley).
Oyster (Oaster, Ostend), Henry (see Osten), 148, 294, 321.
Ozbon (see Osborn), 67, 68.
Ozbun (see Osborn), 67, 68.
Ozburn, Thomas, 32.
Ozenburn (see Osburn).
Ozier, Joshua, 606.
Ozmond, Thomas, 371.

Paca, Aquila, 59.
Pack, James, 238, 321.
Pack, William, 44.
Packman, Peter, 608.
Paddison, William, 607.
Page, George, 287.
Page, John, 153, 318, 415.
Page, Richard, 41.
Paget, Moses, 16.

Pagett (Paggat), Joseph, 342, 376.
Paggatt, Benj., 38.
Pagram (see Pegrim).
Pain, Barnard (see Payne).
Pain, Edward, 50.
Pain, George (see Payne).
Pain, Igns. (see Payne).
Pain, John (see Payne).
Paine, Anthy., 153.
Paine, George (see Payne).
Paine, Jerem., 150.
Paine, John (see Payne).
Paine, Robert, 287.
Paine, William (see Payne).
Painter (see Bender).
Palfrey, Edward, 53.
Pallet, James, 150.
Palmer, Anthy., 149.
Palmer, Jacob, 154, 351.
Palmer, Michael, 238.
Palmer (Parmer), Nathl., 239, 311.
Palmer (Palmore, Parramore), Samuel, 238, 425, 467, 551.
Palmer (Parmer), Thomas (see Parramore), 152, 659.
Palmore (Parramore), Charles, 425, 466, 503, 551.
Palmore (Parramore), Saml. (see Palmer), 425, 467.
Palmour, Willm., 369.
Pane (see Payne).
Pannell (see Pinnall).
Paplow (see Peplow).
Pardo, Benjamin, 411.
Parfit (Parfoot), Thomas, 67, 287.
Park, Andw., 646.
Park, John, 343, 344.
Parker, Charles, 294.
Parker, Danl., 152.
Parker, George, 39, 154, 351, 352, 397, 475, 511, 550.
Parker, Gerrard (Jerrold), 153, 318.
Parker, Jesse, 69.
Parker, John, 151, 239, 294, 320.
Parker, Paul, 31.
Parker, Robert, 575.
Parker, Samuel F., 577.
Parker, William, 230.
Parkes, William, 66.
Parkfield, Wm., 237.
Parkinson (Pirkinson), John, 72, 149.
Parkinson (Perkinson, Pirkinson), Thomas, 72, 411, 653.
Parks, John, 308, 404.
Parmer, Nathl. (see Palmer).
Parmer, Thomas (see Palmer), 152.
Parr, William, 12, 149.

Parraclift, John, 318.
Parramore, Charles (see Palmore).
Parramore, Saml. (see Palmore).
Parramore (Parrumore), Thomas (see Palmer), 287, 641.
Parran, Benjamin, 33.
Parran (Parren), Thomas, 238, 239, 518.
Parrett (Parratt, Parriott), William, 39, 152.
Parriott, Is., 152.
Parriott, Wm. (see Parrett), 152.
Parris, John, 239.
Parrish, Edward, 52, 53, 153.
Parrot, Cbrisr., 150.
Parrott, George, 68.
Parrott (Parrot), John, 68, 603.
Parrott, Lilah, 69.
Parrs, Robert, 303.
Parrumore, Thos. (see Parramore), 287.
Parry, John, 152.
Parsley, Edwd., 151.
Parsley, Thomas, 61.
Parson, Robert, 72.
Parsons, Jeremiah, 331.
Parsons, John, 238, 312, 334.
Parsons, William, 150, 238, 313, 659.
Partner, Geo., 420.
Partridge, Samuel, 39.
Partus, Wm., 606.
Pascall, Peter, 287.
Pascoe (see Pasgrove).
Pasgrove (Pascoe), John, 127, 152.
Paskie, Capt., 484.
Pasterfield, Thomas, 239.
Patman, Benj., 576, 577.
Paton, John (see Patten), 152.
Patrick, George, 152, 299, 464, 512, 550.
Patrick, John, 647, 649.
Patrick, William, 50.
Patrick, Wm. Kirk (see Kirkpatrick, William), 648.
Pattan, Thomas, 41.
Patten (or Tatten), John (see Paton), 65.
Pattern, William (see Pattron), 414.
Patterson, Hezekiah, 331.
Patterson, John, 59, 62, 336, 345, 453.
Patterson, Levin, 287.
Patterson, Perry, 330.
Patterson (Peterson), Peter, 287, 327.
Patterson, Robert, 153, 318.

Index.

Patterson (Pattison), Thomas, 32, 394, 404, 445, 495, 551.
Patterson, William, 61, 153, 465, 500, 551.
Pattington, George, 53.
Pattison (see Patterson).
Patton, John, 151, 599.
Pattron (Pattern), William, 238, 414.
Patty, Orrise, 55.
Paul, Edward, 425, 466.
Paul, John, 422.
Paul, Lewis Griffith, 287.
Paul, Thomas, 237.
Paul, William, 287, 387, 397, 459, 488, 551.
Paulton, Hugh, 52.
Paupin, James, 336.
Paxman (Poxman), John, 397, 404, 460.
Payne (Pain, Pane), Barney (Barnard), 151, 329, 384, 411.
Payne (Paine, Pain, Peign), George, 149, 239, 309, 326.
Payne (Pain), Ignatious, 384, 411.
Payne (Paine, Pain), John, 150, 237, 287, 579, 583, 649.
Payne, Samuel, 287.
Payne (Paine), William, 287, 400, 411.
Peace, John, 239, 551.
Peach, William, 58, 153.
Peacock, Neal (Neale), 239, 307, 354, 390, 436, 489, 551.
Peacock, Robert, 286.
Peacock, Samuel, 60.
Peacock, Thomas, 239, 389, 516, 517, 551.
Peak (or Speake), Lewis, 49.
Peake (Peak, Peeke), Nathan, 10, 149, 313, 432, 550.
Peale, James, 15, 149, 318.
Peany (Penney), John (see Punney), 151, 443, 507, 550.
Pearce (Pearse, Pierce), Aquilla (Equilla), 151, 314, 357, 443, 494, 550.
Pearce (Pierce), Daniel, 151, 318, 388.
Pearce, Ezekiel, 149, 640.
Pearce (Pierce), George, 237, 358, 463, 497, 551.
Pearce, Gregry, 62.
Pearce, Hugh, 387, 411.
Pearce, Israel, 399.
Pearce (Pierce), John, 63, 149, 237, 386, 411.
Pearce (Pierce), Joshua, 45, 149, 354, 436, 490, 551.
Pearce, William, 10.
Pearson, Dennis, 330.
Pearson, Edward, 31, 151.

Pearson, John, 564, 566, 568, 574, 584.
Pearson, Matthew, 599.
Pearson, Thomas, 564, 567, 570, 574.
Peck, Joshua, 152.
Peck, Nathl., 149.
Pecker (Perker), Nicholas, 427, 474.
Pecker, William, 353, 457, 486, 551.
Peeke (see Peake).
Peen (see Penn).
Peggs, Henry, 286.
Pegman, Edward, 46.
Pegrim (Pagram), William, 151, 552, 617.
Peign (see Payne).
Peiken (or Pictern), Philip, 59.
Pelly, James, 44.
Pemberton, John, 61.
Pemwick, Jona., 295.
Pendall, John, 401.
Pendar (Pinder), John, 239, 396, 456.
Pendell (see Pindell).
Pender (Pendor), Thomas, 342, 355, 460, 491, 551.
Penderberry (Pendleberry), Marmd., 152, 297.
Pendergast (Pendergrast), John, 152, 296.
Pendergast (Pendergrast), William, 237, 363, 365, 379, 476, 480, 521.
Pendleberry (see Penderberry).
Pendor (see Pender).
Penewell, Elias, 372.
Penfold, George, 375, 411.
Penman, James, 334.
Penn, Benjamin, 41.
Penn, Jacob, 8.
Penn, John, 70, 150, 153, 331.
Penn (Pinn), Michael, 239, 334, 391.
Penn (or Peen), Shadrech, 42.
Penn, Stephen, 150, 331.
Pennerwell (see Pennywell).
Penney, John (see Peany), 151.
Pennifield (Pennefield, Pennyfield), Thomas, 342, 355, 460, 491, 551, 626.
Penington, Benedict, 646.
Pennington, Charles, 369.
Pennington, Elijah, 581.
Pennington, George, 237.
Pennington, James, 615.
Pennington, John, 151, 152, 316, 422, 470, 516.
Pennington, Robert, 237, 435, 551, 617.
Pennock, Jona. (see Pinnuch), 152.
Pennox, Isaac, 238, 287.

Pennuwell (see Pennywell).
Penny, James, 35.
Penny, Joseph, 43.
Pennyfield (see Pennifield).
Pennywell (Pennuwell, Pennerwell), Charles, 150, 151, 293.
Pennywell, Radcliffe, 239.
Penroad, Peter, 46.
Penson (see Benson).
Peny, William, 238.
Peplow (Paplow), Richd., 397, 416.
Pepper, Elijah, 239, 356, 390, 438, 493, 551.
Pepper, Josep, 152.
Pepple, Philip, 46.
Percival, Samuel, 18.
Perdue, Willm., 581.
Peres, Anthony, 659.
Perker, Nichs. (see Pecker), 427.
Perkins, Isaac, 63, 64.
Perkins, John, 387, 411.
Perkins, Richd., 423, 471.
Perkins, Thomas, 8.
Perkins, William, 562, 598.
Perkinson (see Parkinson).
Perkle, Jacob, 150.
Perrell, Richard, 601.
Perrie (see Perry).
Perrin, Philip, 152, 299.
Perry, Aaron, 388, 393, 404, 451.
Perry, Charles, 151.
Perry, Elias, 8.
Perry, Francis, 153.
Perry, Henry, 611, 613.
Perry, James, 8, 647.
Perry (Perrie), John, 150, 238, 331, 341.
Perry, Samuel, 552.
Perry (Perrie), Simon, 150, 330, 432, 499, 550, 629.
Perry, Thomas, 32, 450, 490, 551, 611, 613.
Peterson (see Patterson).
Petcock, Moses, 39.
Petegrew, Wm., 646.
Peterkin, Philip, 152.
Peters, Gabriel, 237, 551.
Peters, John, 615.
Peters, Joseph, 151, 237, 621.
Peters, Matthew, 66.
Peters, Nicholas, 659.
Peters, William, 152, 287, 430, 512, 550.
Petmore, Richd., 152.
Petterfer, William, 153.
Pettit (Petit), Thomas, 398, 510, 552.
Petty, Francis, 18.
Pew, Humphrey (see Pugh), 151.
Phap, Benjamin, 238.
Pharow, Benj., 64.
Phearson (see Pherson).
Pheasant (Pheasent), Samuel, 153, 551.

Phelan, John, 271, 272.
Phelean, Peter, 37.
Phelps, Benj., 41, 150, 318.
Phelps, John, 15.
Phelps, William, 39, 581.
Pherson (Phearson), Joseph, 150, 356, 392, 452, 492, 551.
Pherson, William, 150, 356, 463, 496, 550.
Philbert, Joseph, 32, 238, 331, 347, 359.
Philip (see Philips).
Philips, Abram, 287.
Philips (Phillips), David, 55, 151, 300.
Philips, Elijah, 237.
Philips (Phillips), George, 154, 239, 391, 516, 551.
Philips (Phillips), Henry, 151, 329, 360, 421, 472, 550.
Philips, Jacob, 237.
Philips (Phillips), James, 37, 343, 453, 508, 551.
Philips (Phillips, Philops), John, 31, 63, 64, 67, 149, 151, 152, 237, 314, 341, 417, 468, 505, 551, 565, 567, 569, 647.
Philips, Jonas, 583.
Philips (Phillips), Lambert, 342, 355, 460, 491, 551.
Philips, Patrick, 641.
Philips (Phillips), Samuel, 238, 414.
Philips, Stephen, 237.
Philips, Thos., 417.
Philips (Phillips, Philip), William, 149, 150, 151, 238, 287, 294, 321.
Phill, Samuel, 615.
Phillips, Nathan, 63.
Phillips, Paul, 369.
Phillips, Solomon, 66.
Phillipshill, Chas., 646.
Philops (see Philips).
Philpot, Bryan, 17.
Philpot, Charles, 239, 310.
Philpot, Charles Thomas, 49.
Philpot, Thomas, 411.
Philpot, Warran, 45.
Philson, Saml. (see Filson), 393.
Phinnimore, John, 52.
Phipher, Martain (see Pifer), 328.
Phipps (Phips, Fipps), Thomas, 109, 151, 551.
Pickard, John, 152.
Picker, William, 153.
Pickering (or Pickorine), Edward, 66.
Pickering, John (see Pickeron), 342, 550.
Pickering, Peter, 610.
Pickeron, John (see Pickering), 151, 293, 517.
Pickorine (see Pickering).

716   *Index.*

Pickrell, Richard, 35.
Pickron, Lewis, 70.
Pictern (see Peiken).
Pierce, Aquilla (see Pearce), 151, 357, 494, 550.
Pierce, Danl. (see Pearce), 151.
Pierce, Edward, 154.
Pierce, George (see Pearce), 237, 551.
Pierce, John (see Pearce), 237.
Pierce, Joshua (see Pearce), 354, 490, 551.
Pierce, Saml., 238.
Piercy (Piercey), William, 606, 659.
Pifer, Martin (see Phipher), 264.
Pigman, John, 287.
Pike, Hutchen, 153.
Pike, James, 150, 153.
Pike, John, 153, 414, 659.
Pike, Thomas, 152.
Pike, William, 152, 239, 384, 411.
Pilkerton (Pilkington, Pilkinton, Pilkoston), Michael, 237, 354, 393, 450, 490, 551.
Pinckley, Michael, 239.
Pinctly, John, 239.
Pindall, Nicks., 149.
Pindell (Pindle), Philip, 37, 238.
Pindell (Pendell), Richard, 152, 362, 378, 476, 478, 521.
Pinder, John (see Pendar), 239, 396.
Pindle (see Pindell).
Pine, Fredk., 568, 569, 574.
Pines, Lawrence, 468, 504, 551.
Pinfield (Pinkfield), Wm., 618, 651.
Pinfold, Thos., 393.
Pingston (Pinkston), Thomas, 338, 360, 415.
Pinkely, Nicholas, 50.
Pinkfield, Wm. (see Pinfield), 618.
Pinkney, Jona., 581.
Pinks, Jas., 154.
Pinkston, Thos. (see Pingston), 415.
Pinn (see Penn).
Pinnall (or Pannell), Joseph, 47.
Pinnox (see Pennox).
Pinnock, Jona. (see Pennock), 152.
Pinter, Thomas, 411.
Piper, Joseph, 238.
Pirkins, Joseph, 14.
Pirkinson (see Parkinson).
Pitcher, Thomas, 50.
Pitman, John, 152.

Pitsland, Richard, 565, 567, 569, 574.
Pitts, William, 24, 150, 287, 396.
Plant, John, 6, 149.
Platford, Edward, 411.
Plowman, James, 371.
Plowman, Philemon, 287.
Plumary, John, 442.
Plumley (Plumly), George, 345, 464, 551.
Plumley (Plumly), Jacob, 18, 287.
Plummer, Cupit (or Cupid), 151, 318, 550.
Plummer, George, 47.
Plummer, Obediah, 151, 318, 550.
Plummer, Solomon, 371.
Plunket, Daviot, 639.
Poague (Pogue, Poogue), Joseph, 577, 580, 581, 583.
Poe, John, 54.
Pointer, William, 240, 264, 416.
Points, Joseph, 446.
Poke, William, 239.
Poland (Polland, Poling), William, 49, 150, 330, 358, 432, 496, 550, 572, 659.
Pole, Lodwick, 404, 653.
Polehouse (Polhouse), Thomas (——), 239, 261, 262, 267, 324, 393, 552.
Polemus, Joseph, 623.
Poling (Polland) (see Poland).
Pollard, Kinsey, 151.
Pollard, William, 239, 647.
Polston, Emanuel, 153.
Polston, Joseph (see Ralston), 411.
Pomairol, Antoine, 313.
Pome, Barthw., 238.
Poneston, Robert, 562.
Poney, Edward, 237.
Poney, George, 371.
Poogue (see Poague).
Pool, James (see Poole).
Pool, Peter, 603.
Poole, Benja., 152.
Poole (Pool) James, 237, 427, 485, 502, 551.
Poor, Philip, 237.
Poore, John, 618.
Pope, Col., 302, 303.
Pope, James, 16, 150, 152, 661.
Pope, John, 419, 464, 500, 551.
Pope, William, 266, 323.
Popham, Capt., 508.
Popham, Benjamin, 411, 417.
Popham, Francis, 584.
Popham, Samuel, 153, 577.
Porter, Alexander, 372.
Porter, Andrew (——), 61, 62, 74.

Porter, Charles, 60, 149, 239.
Porter, John, 239.
Porter, Nathan, 610.
Porter, Philemon, 24, 150.
Porter, Robert, 240, 266, 322.
Porter, Thomas, 326, 357, 394, 446, 495, 551, 627.
Porter, William, 396, 454, 551, 607, 650.
Porterfield, Josiah, 647.
Porters, William, 237.
Portland, James, 369.
Poscy, Belain, 31, 32.
Posey, Benja. (see Postin), 149.
Posey, Bennet, 150, 331.
Posey, Francis, 331.
Poscy, James, 149.
Posey, Roger, 376, 411.
Posey, St. Larence, 32.
Posey, Thomas, 32.
Posey, Zachariah, 377, 411.
Postin, Benjamin (see Posey), 32.
Pote, Michael, 51.
Potster, Peter, 287.
Pott, Thos. (see Potts), 463.
Potter, Andrew, 419, 469.
Potter, Anthony, 55.
Potter, John, 286.
Potter, Thomas, 578, 582, 584.
Potter, William, 368, 394, 452, 484, 492, 551.
Potter, Zabdiel, 68.
Potts (Pott), Thomas, 143, 153, 368, 394, 463.
Poulain, Germain, 313.
Pound, Edward, 287.
Pound, John, 238, 414.
Pounder, Richard, 68, 237.
Powell, Giles, 340.
Powell (Powel), Henry, 39, 610, 612, 613.
Powell, James, 237, 306.
Powell (Powel), John, 14, 51, 149, 152, 153, 237, 239, 394, 416.
Powell, Joseph, 150, 317.
Powell, Levi, 372.
Powell, Peter, 153, 319.
Powell, Samuel, 626.
Powell, William, 68, 151, 425, 429, 465, 501, 551, 572.
Power, John, 563, 566, 569, 574, 606, 659.
Power, Joshua, 603.
Power, Samuel (see Powers), 153, 301.
Power, Thomas (see Powers), 642.
Power, Walter, 35.
Powers, Charles, 237.
Powers, Jesse, 393, 445, 511, 551.

Powers, Saml. (see Power), 418, 469.
Powers, Thomas (see Power), 150.
Powlet, Severn, 659.
Poxman (see Paxman).
Prall (Praul), Edward, 150, 362, 378, 431, 477, 482, 521, 616.
Prangley, William, 239, 323, 391.
Prarey, John, 286.
Prater (Preator), William, 394, 445, 508, 551.
Prather, Zachariah, 151, 446.
Pratt, Edward, 11.
Pratt, Jno., 287.
Pratt, Solomon, 645.
Pratt, William, 151, 384, 411.
Pratten, John, 340.
Praul (see Prall).
Preator (see Prater).
Preist (see Priest).
Preston, Andrew, 151, 294, 323.
Preston, Grafton, 60, 153.
Preston, Saml., 152.
Preston (Priston), Stephen, 51, 152, 296, 432, 509, 550, 617.
Preston, Thomas, 239, 304.
Preston, William, 13, 60, 72, 647.
Prew, William, 659.
Prewitt (Prewit) (see Pruet).
Price, Andrew, 69.
Price, Benj. (B., Capt.), 150, 355, 363, 379, 452, 480, 482, 484, 490, 521.
Price, Charles, 610, 611, 613.
Price, Daniel, 153.
Price (Pryse), Edward, 11, 140, 575.
Price, Ephraim, 61.
Price, George, 52, 612, 613.
Price, Henry, 659.
Price, James, 239, 371.
Price, James Kimble, 61.
Price, Jesse, 63.
Price, John, 12, 30, 150, 152, 237, 593, 608.
Price, Jonathan, 26, 643.
Price, Levin, 287.
Price, Nathan, 400, 404, 458, 486.
Price, Nathaniel, 398, 458, 551.
Price, Nicholas, 237.
Price, Noble, 61.
Price, Richard, 396, 463.
Price, Robert, 239, 305.
Price, Samuel, 19.
Price, Solomon, 66.
Price, Stephen (Stephen R.), 238, 304, 358, 439, 497, 551.

Index. 717

Price, Thomas (Col.), 5, 28, 41, 150, 152, 238, 293, 294, 299, 320, 321, 327, 363, 379, 447, 479, 521, 573.
Price, William, 33, 46, 55, 66, 151, 152, 300, 651.
Prichard, James (see Pritchard).
Prichard, Levin, 27, 643.
Priday (see Pryday).
Priest, John, 150.
Priest (Preist), William, 401, 506, 551.
Priestley, David, 24.
Prigg, Charles, 152.
Prigg, Edward, 400.
Primer, Henry, 286.
Primrose, David, 606, 659.
Prince, William, 607, 650.
Pringle, John, 150.
Pringle, Thomas, 153.
Pringle, Wm., 442.
Prior (Pryor), Benjamin, 331, 357, 431, 496, 551, 593.
Prior (Pryor), John, 153, 415.
Prior, William, 153, 550.
Priston (see Preston).
Pritchard, Arthur (see Pritchet), 425, 474.
Pritchard, Charles, 11.
Pritchard (Prichard), James, 151, 293.
Pritchard, Jno., 429.
Pritchard, Sam. (see Pritchet), 153.
Pritchard, Wm. (see Pritchett), 154, 302.
Pritchet, Arthur (see Pritchard), 552.
Pritchet, Saml. (see Pritchard), 67.
Pritchett, Henry, 70.
Pritchett, Peter, 287.
Pritchett, Wm. (see Pritchard), 383, 572.
Procter, George, 70.
Procter, Joshua, 270, 517.
Proctor (Procter), Charles, 150, 331.
Proctor, Daniel, 237.
Proctor (Prockter), James, 508, 551.
Proctor (Procter) Joseph, 265, 510, 551.
Proctor, Henry, 377, 411.
Proctor, John, 237.
Proctor (Procter, Proektor), Richard, 152, 357, 430, 496, 550.
Proctor (Procter), Thomas, 55, 239, 266, 411, 552.
Proctor (Procter), Walter, 150, 331.
Proctor (Procter), William, 378, 383, 411.
Pronso, Jacob, 411.
Proser, Danl., 154.
Prouce, John, 385.

Prout, John, 33, 579, 582, 584.
Prudent, Thomas, 153, 415.
Pruet (Pruit, Prewitt, Prewit), Walter, 397, 404, 458.
Pruett, William, 648.
Prutzman, Nathl., 388.
Pry, Capt., 598.
Pryday (Priday), John, 70, 237.
Pryor, Benj. (see Prior), 331.
Pryor, Jno. (see Prior), 415.
Pryse, Edward (see Price), 575.
Pugh, Hugh, 12.
Pugh (Pew), Humphrey, 151, 411.
Pugh, Thomas, 239.
Pulaski, Count (Gen.), 591, 592, 593, 594, 624.
Pully, Joseph, 418, 469.
Pumphry, John, 239, 305.
Punney John (see Peany), 65.
Punny, Thomas, 64.
Puntany, Edward, 52.
Purcell, Francis, 392, 448.
Purcell (Pursell), William, 152, 457, 512, 550.
Purchase (Purchace, Purchass), William, 151, 357, 444, 495, 550.
Purdell, Robert, 313.
Purden, Joseph, 646.
Purdy (Purdie), Edward, 40, 152, 238, 333, 347, 414.
Purdy, Henry (Henery), 238, 333, 340, 439, 512, 551.
Purdy, John, 21, 150, 151, 238, 333, 348, 430, 500, 551.
Purdy, Joseph (P. Joseph), 237, 469, 510, 551.
Purly, Francis, 510.
Purnell, Lambert, 23.
Purnell (Purnal), Samuel, 42, 239.
Purnell, Stephen, 153.
Purnell, Zadok, 21.
Pursell (see Purcell).
Pursley, Francis, 551.
Purtle, John, 13.
Purtle (Turtle), Robert, 151, 330.

Qu——, John, 653.
Qua (see Quay).
Quail, Thomas, 62.
Quain, John, 240.
Qualls, Whorton, 31.
Quarey, Elisha, 34.
Quarney (Querney), Lawrence), 7, 154.
Quay (Qua), James, 56, 154, 313, 659.
Quay (or Qua), Saml., 55.

Queah (Queake), Menasses (Manasses), 411, 653.
Queen, Jno., 154.
Queener, John, 411.
Queer (see Quier).
Querney (see Quarney).
Quick, John, 154, 355, 441, 490, 552.
Quidowney (see Equidowney).
Quier (Queer), Henry, 240, 264, 265.
Quiggins, Henry, 154.
Quiggins, John, 154.
Quigley, James, 62.
Quigley, Patk., 15.
Quin, Jno. (see Quinn).
Quin, Richard, 321.
Quine, Benjamin, 52.
Quinland, Jas., 154.
Quinley, Levin, 240, 308.
Quinlin (Grunlin), Cornelius, 212, 206.
Quinn, Barney, 504, 506, 509.
Quinn (Quin), John, 573, 584.
Quinn (Quynn), Joseph, 154, 319, 437, 506, 552, 661.
Quinn (Quynn), Patrick, 154, 302, 350, 397, 420, 465, 500, 552.
Quinney, Thos., 422.
Quinton, Dixon, 21.
Quinton (Quintum), William, 240, 341, 342, 356, 390, 438, 493, 552.
Quixall, Thomas, 287.
Quynn, Francis, 45.
Quynn, Joseph (see Quinn). 154, 319.
Quynn, Patrick (see Quinn), 420, 552.
Quynn, Timothy, 240.

Rach (Rack), Patrick, 26, 643.
Radery, John (see Radley), 554.
Radford, William, 606.
Radley (Radery, Rodery), John, 8, 159, 516, 554.
Rady, James (see Ready), 155.
Rady, Laurence (see Ready), 155.
Rae, Barny, 157.
Ragan, Darby, 242.
Ragan (Ragen), James (see Rogan), 64, 158.
Ragan, Morris, 157.
Ragan, Roderick, 659.
Raidy, Edmd., 288.
Raidy, James (see Ready), 49.
Railey (see Reily).
Rain, Barnet, 648.
Rains, Adam, 157, 552.
Rains, Henry, 602.

Rains, James, 602.
Raison (Raisin, Rasin, Reason), William, 240, 241, 355, 362, 365, 378, 431, 476, 478, 521.
Rakes, Wm., 371.
Raleigh (Raley), Walter (see Rieley), 49.
Ralph, William (see Rolph), 241.
Ralston (Balston), Joseph (see Polston), 241, 349.
Ramden (see Ramsey).
Ramler, Michl. (see Gambler), 416.
Ramon, Joseph, 615.
Ramsay, John, Jr., 33.
Ramsey, Charles, 242.
Ramsey (Ramsden, Ramden), Henry, 158, 353, 457, 486, 552.
Ramsey, Nathanial, 13, 157, 359, 365, 521, 616, 639.
Ramsey, Thomas, 73, 75, 647.
R——an, John, 297.
Randall, David, 156, 327.
Randall (Randle), John (J.), 50, 269, 270.
Randall (Randle), Thomas, 573, 579, 583, 584.
Randall, Wm., 443.
Randalls (Randles), Tobias (Tobyas), 418, 469.
Rankin (Rankins), Daniel, 8, 154.
Rankin, Robert, 241, 617.
Rankins, Daniel (see Rankin), 8.
Rankins, Wm., 159.
Ranson (Ransom), John, 396, 401, 456, 500, 553.
Ranter, James, 17.
Ranter, John, 382.
Rashe (Rash), John, 18, 154.
Rasin (see Raison).
Ratagan (see Rattican).
Ratcliff, Robt., 156.
Ratcliff, Townley, 31.
Ratcliffe (Ratcliff), John, 575, 580, 583.
Ratcliffe, Richard, 375.
Ratherford (see Rutherford).
Ratiken (see Rattican).
Ratrey (or Ratsey), Alex., 602.
Rattican (Battican), James, 241, 304.
Rattican (Ratagan, Ratiken), Peter, 242, 400, 411.
Raullings (see Rawlings).
Rauside, Andrew (see Rereside), 493.
Raven, Patrick (see Rawen), 294.
Ravenscroft, Francis, 601.
Raver, Christr., 243, 265.
Rawdon, Daniel, 582, 584.

Rawen (Rawn, Raven), Patrick (see Rowan), 156, 294, 322.
Rawlings, Aaron, 445, 501, 553.
Rawlings (Rollings), Benjamin, 38, 241, 331.
Rawlings, Bennet, 552.
Rawlings (Rollins), Elias, 376, 411.
Rawlings, Elijah, 38.
Rawlings (Rawlins), Isaac, 365, 477, 570.
Rawlings, Jacob, 53, 158.
Rawlings, John, 38.
Rawlings (Raullings), Jonathan, 156, 575, 581.
Rawlings, Moses (Col.), 77, 300, 327.
Rawlings, Nevitt, 38.
Rawlings, Richard, 16.
Rawlings (Rollins, Rowlins), Solomon, 72, 241, 304, 411, 653.
Rawlings, William, 579, 582, 583.
Rawn (see Rawen).
Ray, Basil, 37.
Ray, Benjamin, 411.
Ray, David, 158.
Ray, James, 24, 156.
Ray, Jesse, 575, 581.
Ray, John (see Reah), 42, 68.
Ray (Rhea), Joseph, 46, 156, 355, 442, 491, 552.
Ray, Robert, 62.
Ray, Samuel, 10, 155.
Ray, William (see Rea), 14, 40, 68, 240, 288.
Raybert, Chs. (or Chrisr.), 243.
Raynard, Francis, 473.
Raynard, Jno. C., 158.
Rayne, William, 241.
Raynolds (see Reynolds).
Raynor (Rayner, Reynor), Christopher (Christian), 423, 429, 471, 503, 553.
Rea, William (see Ray), 288.
Reach (see Roach).
Read, Alex., 648.
Read, Christopher (see Reed), 242.
Read, Francis (see Reed), 369.
Read, George, 11.
Read, James (Jas. Thos.) (see Reed), 156, 243, 294, 308.
Read, John (see Reed), 154, 156.
Read, Joseph, 26, 643.
Read, Matthew, 648.
Read, Obediah, 156, 293.
Read, Peregrine (see Reed), 411.
Read, Philip (see Reed), 363.

Read, Thos. (see Reed), 646.
Read, William (see Reed), 156, 243, 564, 569.
Reader (see Reeder).
Reading, Henry (see Reddine and Beading), 353.
Reading, John (see Beaden), 158.
Reading, Patrick (see Reding), 394, 454.
Readon, Patk., 157.
Ready (Rady), James (see Raidy), 155, 659.
Ready (Rady), Lawrence, 155, 659.
Ready, Michael (see Reidy), 288.
Reagon, Bartho., 602.
Reah, John (see Ray), 288.
Realley, Dennis, 47.
Ream, Fredk., 336.
Reancifer, John, 240.
Rear, William, 41.
Reardon, John (see Reordon), 241, 304.
Rearside (see Rereside).
Reason, Jacob, 241.
Reason, James, 242.
Reason, John, 242.
Reason, William (see Raison), 241.
Reaves (Beaves), Noah, 60, 242.
Reaves, Richd., 426.
Redding (Reading, Reeding, Riding), Henry, 158, 353, 457, 486, 552.
Redding (Ridding), William, 158, 298.
Redding, Thomas, 240.
Reddish (Riddish), Joseph, 610, 615.
Reddley (see Ridley).
Redenour (Ridenhour), John, 47, 261.
Redgrave, Robt., 335.
Redgrave, Sampson, 646.
Rediew, Joseph, 66.
Reding (Reading), Patrick, 335, 394, 454.
Redington, John, 70.
Redman, Elisha, 578, 582, 584.
Redman, John, 584.
Redman, Michael, 553.
Redman, Thomas, 159, 552, 579, 583.
Redweads, Jos., 288.
Reec (see Reese).
Reed (Ried), Benj., 398, 404, 462.
Reed, Casper, 388.
Reed (Read), Christopher, 242, 553, 618, 632.
Reed (Read), Francis, 369, 393, 451, 490, 553.
Reed (Read), James, 13, 66, 156, 157, 243, 294, 308.
Reed, Jeremiah, 446.

Reed (Read, Reid), John, 69, 74, 154, 156, 159, 419, 464, 499, 553, 641.
Reed, Patrick, 12, 453.
Reed (Read), Peregrine, 386, 411.
Reed (Read, Ried), Philip, 65, 240, 363, 379, 478, 482, 521.
Reed (Read), Thomas, 154, 640, 646.
Reed (Read), William (—m), 156, 243, 311, 564, 566, 569, 574.
Reeder, Hezekiah, 156.
Reeder (Reader), John, 354, 366, 393, 450, 489, 553.
Reeding, Henry (see Redding), 486.
Reedy, Edward, 53.
Reedy, Thomas, 158.
Reenals, Waitman, 601.
Rees, George, 563, 567, 570.
Rees, Henry (see Reese), 508, 563, 567.
Reese (Rees, Reec), Henry (Henery), 154, 243, 390, 393, 461, 508, 552, 563, 567.
Reese, James, 428.
Reese, John, 421.
Reese, Levi (Levy), 346, 366.
Reeter, Elias, 328.
Reevenach, Philip, 263.
Reever, Stuffle, 264.
Reeves, John, 288.
Reeves, Jos., 288.
Reevin, Stephen, 288.
Reewark, Jas. (see Ruark), 157.
Regele (Regle), Christopher), 265.
Regliman (Regalman, Riggleman), George, 243, 264, 265.
Reich, Henry (see Ritch), 72.
Reid, John (see Reed), 419.
Reidy, Michael (see Ready), 288.
Reidy, William, 157.
Reiley (Riley), Edward, 462, 511, 553.
Reiley, John (see Riley), 334.
Reiley (Rylie), Nicholas, 55.
Reiley (Reilley), Patrick (Partrick) (see Riley), 355, 438, 461, 491, 506.
Reiley (Reily, Riley, Riely, Roiley), William, 52, 53, 158, 288, 352, 362, 378, 433, 477, 482, 521, 615.
Reilly, Bernard (see Riely).
Reilly, John (see Riley), 416.

Reily (Rieley, Railey), Bennit, 579, 582, 584.
Reily, James (see Riley), 552.
Reily, John (see Riley), 240.
Reily, Miles, 288.
Reily, Patrick (see Riley), 268, 553.
Reily, William (see Reiley), 53, 288, 378.
Reinhart (see Rinehart).
Reitz, Conrad, 263.
Relahan (Retahan), Jno. (see Callahan), 157.
Reland, Mathew, 288.
Relly, David (see Kelly), 453.
Remsburg, Henry, 20.
Renalds (see Reynolds).
Renark, James (see Ruark), 299.
Rench, John, 48.
Renhard (see Rinehart).
Rentford, Henry, 606, 659.
Reordon, John (see Reardon), 241.
Rereside (Rearside, Reveside, Rauside), Andrew, 395, 454, 493, 553.
Reston (see Riston).
Reswick (see Riswick).
Retahan (see Callahan).
Revell (Revle) Randall (Randle), 156, 293.
Revelle (Revel), Chas., 346, 366.
Revelly (Revelley, Reveley, Revely), Francis (Frances, ——), 157, 358, 363, 379, 454, 476, 477, 480, 497, 521, 639.
Reves, Enos, 646.
Reveside (see Rereside).
Revle (see Revell).
Reybold, Jacob, 366, 521.
Reyley (see Riley).
Reynald, Tobias, 158.
Reynol, Christopher, 661.
Reynolds, Abraham, 372, 396, 450.
Reynolds, Benedict, 158, 159, 552.
Reynolds, Charles, 156, 342, 553.
Reynolds, Charles Maccubin, 42.
Reynolds, Francis, 242, 305, 392, 426.
Reynolds, George, 50.
Reynolds (Raynolds), Jas., 155, 241, 372, 396, 433, 449, 508, 511, 552, 553, 615.
Reynolds (Raynolds), John, 43, 48, 50, 68, 155, 242, 572, 577, 580, 583, 615, 648.
Reynolds, Richard, 158.
Reynolds, Robert, 70, 155.

Index. 719

Reynolds (Roynorld, Renalds), Thomas, 41, 240, 241, 335, 344, 418, 423, 469.
Reynolds, William, 41, 242.
Reynor, Christian (see Raynor, Christopher), 423, 471.
Rhea, Joseph (see Ray), 355, 491, 552.
Rhoades (see Rhodes).
Rhoads, Benj., 60.
Rhoads, John, 577.
Rhoads, Thos., 400.
Rhoads, Wm. (see Rhodes).
Rhodes, Elisha, 45.
Rhodes, George, 421, 472.
Rhodes, Jacob, 45.
Rhodes (Rhoades, Roads), Jeremiah, 157, 298, 330, 359, 456, 552.
Rhodes (Rhoads, Roads), William, 158, 346, 415.
Rhydmyer, Michael, 447, 510, 553.
Rian, William (see Ryan), 600.
Rice, ———, 270.
Rice, Benjn., 653.
Rice, George, 46.
Rice (Reec), Henry (see Reese), 461.
Rice, Isaac, 19.
Rice, James, 566, 568.
Rice, Robert, 242, 349, 552.
Rice, Simon, 651.
Rice, Thomas, 33.
Rice, William (see Rue), 56, 182, 242, 347, 357, 445, 465, 495, 552.
Rich, Samuel, 288, 319.
Rich, Vilet, 411.
Richard (see Rinehart).
Richards, ———, 431.
Richards, Clement, 411.
Richards (Rickords), John, 40, 157, 243, 266, 323, 333.
Richards, Paul, 157, 396, 512, 552.
Richards, Peter, 394, 433, 564, 566, 568, 574.
Richards, Samuel, 411.
Richards, Stephen, 241.
Richards, Thomas, 156, 314.
Richards, Wm., 159.
Richardson, Alexander, 659.
Richardson, Charles, 69, 240.
Richardson, Daniel, 24, 156.
Richardson, Edward, 156, 157, 430, 552.
Richardson, Elisha, 17, 155.
Richardson, George, 288, 317.
Richardson, Jacob, 646.
Richardson, Jas., 335.
Richardson, John, 7, 44, 157, 242, 366, 468, 504, 552, 565, 646.

Richardson, Jonathan, 63, 411.
Richardson, Jos., 68.
Richardson, Matthew, 646.
Richardson, Robert, 158, 552.
Richardson, Samuel, 51, 336, 352, 434, 485, 553, 598.
Richardson, Thomas, 241, 353, 398, 427, 462, 465, 487, 501, 552, 553, 612, 613, 617.
Richardson, William (Col.), 47, 61, 68, 74, 157, 240, 360, 411, 459, 553, 573, 586, 621, 626, 650, 653.
Richee (see Ritchee).
Richey (Richy), Willm., 156, 294, 320.
Richie, John (see Ritchee).
Richie, Peter, 329.
Richmond, Christopher (C., Lt.), 5, 155, 269, 271, 272, 363, 379, 478, 479, 516, 517, 521, 584, 590.
Richmond, Nathl., 288.
Richy (see Richey).
Rick, John, 265.
Rickenbaugh, Martin, 51.
Rickets, Andrew, 243.
Rickets, John (see Ricketts).
Rickets, Nicholas (see Ricketts).
Rickets, Robert, 44.
Ricketts (Rickets), John, 63, 155.
Ricketts (Rickets), Nicholas, 365, 477, 566, 568, 573, 579.
Ricketts, Richard, 41.
Ricketts, Vincent, 155.
Ricketts, William, 288.
Ricknagle, George, 243.
Rickords, John (see Richards), 40.
Rid, James, 574.
Ridd, John, 293.
Ridding (see Redding).
Riddish (see Reddish).
Riddle, Charles, 553.
Ridenhour, Bernhard (see Ridenour).
Ridenhour, John (see Redenour).
Ridenour (Ridenhour), Barnard, 267, 324.
Ridenour (Ridingour), Jacob, 46, 328.
Rider, Adam, 439, 507, 553.
Rider, James, 156.
Rider (Ryder), William, 243, 266, 323, 354, 395, 447, 488, 553.
Ridgaway, James, 70.
Ridge, William, 325, 411, 653.

Ridgely (Ridgly), Bazil (Basil), 8, 155.
Ridgely, Fredk., 288.
Ridgely, Henry, 5, 39, 41, 157.
Ridgely, Nicholas, 17.
Ridgely, Revely, 158.
Ridgely, Saml., 157.
Ridgely, William, 9, 155.
Ridgely, Zephaniah, 411.
Ridgeway, ———, 74.
Ridgway, William, 39.
Ridiford, Thomas, 64.
Riding, Henry (see Redding), 158.
Riding, John, 414.
Ridingour (see Ridenour).
Ridley (Reddley), Drew (Drue), 241, 321.
Ried, Benj. (see Reed).
Ried, Philip (see Reed), 240.
Rief, Danl., 305.
Rieley, Bennit (see Reily).
Rieley, John (see Riley), 12, 58.
Riely, Barney, 51, 242.
Riely (Reilly), Bernard, 243, 416.
Riely, Charles, 155.
Riely, Conrad, 243.
Riely, Edward (see Riley), 553.
Riely, James (see Riley), 157, 159.
Riely, John (see Riley), 155, 157, 158, 159, 243.
Riely (Riney), Jonathan, 156, 330.
Riely, Patrick (see Riley), 155, 241, 242, 552.
Riely (Raley, Raleigh), Walter, 49, 242.
Riely, William (see Reiley).
Rigan, John, 428, 474.
Rigbey, Joseph, 60.
Rigby, William, 241.
Rigden, James, 648.
Rigdon, John, 159.
Rigg, Charles (see Riggs), 155.
Rigg, George (see Riggs), 156.
Riggin, Charles, 31.
Riggin (Riggan), Timothy, 156, 293.
Riggleman (see Regliman).
Riggnagle, Jacob, 262.
Riggs, Andrew, 156, 552.
Riggs (Rigg), Charles, 155, 615.
Riggs (Rigg), George, 156, 444, 553.
Riggs, John, 242, 243, 334, 389, 435, 506, 552.
Riggs, William, 243.
Right, Elijah (see Wright), 411.
Right, Stephen, 62.

Rightmyer (Right Myer) (see Ritmier).
Rignall (or Rignell), Jacob, 72.
Rigney, Michl., 158.
Riley (Reiley, Riely), Edward, 397, 462, 511, 553.
Riley (Railey), Hugh, 288, 327.
Riley (Reily, Riely, Reyley), James, 64, 157, 159, 296, 313, 552.
Riley (Reiley, Reilley, Reily, Rieley, Riely), John, 12, 58, 155, 157, 158, 159, 240, 243, 334, 335, 350, 368, 397, 404, 416, 417.
Riley, Lawrence, 313.
Riley (Rily), Michael, 44, 659.
Riley (Reiley, Reily, Reilley, Riely, Reyley, Ryley), Patrick, 51, 155, 241, 242, 288, 306, 321, 335, 350, 390, 438, 461, 491, 506, 552, 553.
Riley, Tim., 659.
Riley, William (see Reiley), 52.
Rily, Michael (see Riley).
Rily, Zachariah, 43.
Rim, Nicholas, 53.
Rimington, John, 243.
Rine, Patrick (see Ryan), 49.
Rinehart (Renbard, Binehart, Richard), Andrew, 187, 242, 326.
Rinehart (Reinhart), Simon, 266.
Riney, Jonathan, 156, 330.
Ring, Jno., 569.
Ringer, Andrew, 47, 242, 310.
Ringer, Jacob, 72.
Ringer, John, 261.
Ringfield, James, 305.
Ringgold, James, 18.
Ringrose, James, 158, 288.
Rinker, Edward, 601.
Rinker, Jesse, 601.
Rippath, William, 31.
Risden, Zadock (see Riston), 465, 500, 553.
Rismel, George, 51.
Riston (Reston), Zadock (see Risden), 382, 411.
Riswick (Risswick, Reswick), Joseph (see Beswick), 156, 330, 384, 411.
Ritch, Henry (see Reich), 405.
Ritchee (Richee, Richie), John, 69, 240.
Ritchie, Benjamin, 317.
Ritchie, Matthew, 18, 154.
Ritchie, Robert, 15.
Rite, John (see Wright), 45.

Index.

Ritmier (Ritmire, Rightmyer, Right Myer), Michl., 243, 268, 395.
Ritter, William, 182, 262.
Rittlemeyer, George, 243, 265.
Rivers, Richard, 468, 504, 553.
Roach (Roche), Bartholomew, 422, 471.
Roach, Charles, 69.
Roach, George, 465.
Roach, James, 241.
Roach (Reach), John (see Rock), 58, 243, 260, 324, 358, 394, 498, 447, 553.
Roads, Jeremiah (see Rhodes).
Roads, Thos., 648.
Roads, William (see Rhodes).
Roan, Edward (see Rowan), 467, 503.
Roan, Joseph, 22.
Roan, Paul (Pauli) (see Rowan), 356, 553.
Roans (Rones), Samuel, 26, 156, 293, 642.
Robarts (see Roberts).
Robb, John, 157, 300.
Robbins (see Robins).
Robbs, Alex., 69.
Roberson, Charles (see Robertson), 155.
Roberson, David (see Robinson), 156.
Roberson, George, 23.
Roberson, Thomas (see Robinson), 157.
Roberts, Archibald, 411, 653.
Roberts, Basil, 341.
Roberts, Benjamin, 64, 74.
Roberts, Edward, 158, 358, 436, 498, 552, 575, 581.
Roberts, Henry, 40, 288, 335.
Roberts, Horatio, 243, 341, 553.
Roberts, John, 60, 157, 297, 344.
Roberts, Joseph, 158, 319, 457, 512, 552.
Roberts, Nathan, 44.
Roberts, Richard, 155, 317.
Roberts, Thomas, 13, 70, 156, 315, 606, 656.
Roberts (Robarts), William, 36, 40, 155, 317, 318, 358, 383, 405, 411, 463, 498, 552.
Roberts, Zacha., 155.
Robertson, Alex., 396.
Robertson (Roberson), Charles, 155, 330.
Robertson, Edward, 261, 411.
Robertson, George, 659.
Robertson, Isaac, 242.
Robertson, John, 33, 46, 156, 158, 264, 288, 295, 359, 601.
Robertson, Lambert, 156.
Robertson, Michl., 155.
Robertson, Robert, 242, 392, 416, 429.
Robertson, Saml., 241.
Robertson, Thomas (see Robinson), 155, 618.
Robertson, William (see Robinson), 32, 157, 405, 575, 581, 659.
Robertson, Zachariah, 394, 452.
Robeson (see Robertson).
Robey, Acton, 331.
Robey, John (see Roby, 392.
Robey, Joseph, 155.
Robey, Richard, 377.
Robins (Robbins), John, 342, 357, 444, 494, 553, 615.
Robinson, Alexander, 447, 507, 553.
Robinson, Andrew (——rew), 243, 262.
Robinson, Charles, 411, 432, 499, 552.
Robinson (Robson, Roberson), David, 156, 340, 610.
Robinson, Daniel, 647.
Robinson, Edward, 243, 262, 653.
Robinson, Elisha, 346.
Robinson, George, 41, 647.
Robinson, Henry, 590.
Robinson, Hugh, 158.
Robinson, James, 24, 67, 334, 340.
Robinson, John, 155, 328, 345, 552, 615.
Robinson, Jonathan, 7.
Robinson, Joseph, 387.
Robinson, Lambert, 24.
Robinson, Nathl., 156.
Robinson, Patrick, 39, 62.
Robinson, Peter, 158.
Robinson, Petter, 577.
Robinson, Richard, 41.
Robinson, Robert, 381, 387, 648.
Robinson (Robison, Roberson, Robertson), Thomas, 16, 51, 52, 157, 297, 317, 565, 566, 508, 574.
Robinson (Robeson, Robertson), William, 32, 59, 67, 157, 405, 475, 513, 553, 575, 581, 626, 645, 659.
Robinson, Zachariah, 494, 553.
Robison, Thos. (see Robinson), 51.
Robson, David (see Robinson).
Robson, Joseph, 644.
Roby (Robey), John, 155, 392.
Roby, Thomas, 36.
Roche, Barthw. (see Roach), 422.
Roche, Thomas, 288.
Rochester, Abram., 241.
Rochford, Edward, 243.
Rock, Edward, 157.
Rock, John (see Roach), 157, 159, 243, 288, 298, 329, 552.
Rock, Oliver, 157.
Rock, William, 30, 157, 298, 329, 552.
Rockhold (Rockhole), Asel (Hasael) (see Rockwell), 242, 348, 440.
Rockhold, T——, 288.
Rockwell, Asell (see Rockhold), 60.
Rodden, Daniel, 572, 579, 618.
Roderberk, John, 288.
Rodes, Nicholas, 647, 648.
Rodgers, Elisha, 71, 647.
Rodgers, John (see Rogers), 57, 464, 553.
Rodgers, William (see Rogers), 475, 512.
Rodery, John (see Radley), 8.
Rodness, Joseph, 66.
Roduger, Emanuel, 615.
Rodwell (Rodwall), Godfrey, 242, 304.
Roe (Rowe), James, 158, 426, 473, 509, 553.
Roe, Manna, 59.
Roe, Obediah, 243.
Roe, Thomas, 651.
Roe, William (see Boe), 242, 393, 414, 451, 645, 650.
Rogan, James (see Ragan), 14.
Rogers, Francis, 394, 442, 603.
Rogers (Rodgers), John, 57, 60, 268, 419, 464, 500, 553, 659.
Rogers, Joseph, 158.
Rogers, Joshua, 335.
Rogers, Michael, 241, 349, 414.
Rogers, Robert, 240.
Rogers (Rodgers), William, 66, 70, 154, 475, 512, 552.
Rohrbach (Rohhbaugh), Adam, 265.
Rohrer, Martin, 397.
Roiley, William (see Reiley), 615.
Roland, Patk., 157, 300.
Rolinson (or Rolingson), Thomas, 68.
Rollings, Benjamin (see Rawlings), 331.
Rollings, Isaac, 331.
Rollings, Richard (see Rollins), 58.
Rollins, Chs., 155.
Rollins, Elias (see Rawlings), 411.
Rollins (Rollings), Richard, 58, 293.
Rollins, Solomon (see Rawlings), 364.
Rollison, John, 63.
Rolls, Richard, 156.
Rolls, William (see Rowles).
Rolph, John, 64, 66.
Rolph, Thomas, 64, 66.
Rolph, William (see Ralph), 66, 592, 593.
Rolwagen, Frederick, 182.
Roly, Silvester, 156.
Romills (Rumwill), John, 366, 510, 553.
Rommelsem (Rummelson), William, 243, 265.
Rone (see Stone).
Ronenberger (Runenberger, Runnenberg, Ronemberger), Chas. (Christopher), 243, 358, 447, 497, 553.
Rones (see Roans).
Roney, Hugh, 427, 473, 509, 553.
Roney, James, 564, 569.
Roof, Peter, 159.
Rook, Michael (see Rorke), 460.
Rooker, James, 288.
Rooks, John (see Rork), 288.
Roper, Edward, 581.
Rorer, Henry, 397.
Rorer, Jacob, 328.
Rork, John (see Rooks), 242.
Rorke, Michl. (see Rook), 159.
Rosah, Martin, 460.
Rose, Edward, 636.
Rose, Isaac, 159, 301.
Rose, James, 150, 474, 511, 553.
Rose, Joseph, 383, 411, 425, 467, 563, 553.
Rose, William, 155, 396, 439, 487, 553.
Ross, Alexander, 242, 356, 389, 438, 492, 552.
Ross, Bathw., 240.
Ross, George, 411, 659.
Ross, Henry (see Russ), 396.
Ross (Rosse), John, 19, 65, 158, 334, 518, 619.
Ross, Joseph, 44.
Ross, Levin, 383, 411.
Ross, Nathan, 368, 396, 607, 659.
Ross, Nathaniel, 454, 553.
Ross, Reuben (Ruben), 159, 301.
Ross, Robert, 14.
Ross, Robinson (Robertson), 339, 358, 430, 498, 553.

Index. 721

Ross, Thomas, 241, 435.
Ross, William, 620.
Rosse, John (see Ross), 65.
Rosstell, Joseph, 243.
Roster, Thomas, 288.
Roster, William, 240.
Rothe, John, 264.
Rotherford, John, 242.
Rouerie, Marquis De La (see Col. Armand), 593.
Rough, Peter, 328.
Rouse (Rowse), Thomas, 364, 381, 476, 481, 503, 616.
Row, John (see Rowe), 18, 243, 336.
Rowan (Roan, Rone), Edward (see Stone), 418, 467, 503, 553.
Rowan, John, 18.
Rowan (Roan), Paul (Paull), 356, 493, 553.
Rowan (Rowing, Rowin), Patrick (see Rawen), 72, 357, 446, 495, 553.
Rowe, James (see Roe), 158, 473.
Rowe, John (see Row), 659.
Rowe, Robert, 155, 156.
Rowe, William, 157.
Rowell, William, 242.
Rowen, Christopher, 241.
Rowen, George, 607, 695.
Rowin (Rowing) (see Rowan).
Rowland, Henry, 159, 302.
Rowland, Jacob, 242, 288, 349, 440.
Rowland, William, 158.
Rowlands, Thomas, 267, 325.
Rowles (Rolls), William, 154, 158, 552.
Rowlings, Benedict, 158.
Rowlins, Solomon (see Rawlings), 72.
Rown, Thomas, 521.
Rownds (Rowns), James, 606, 659.
Rowley, John, 158.
Rowse (see Rouse).
Rowwen, Timothy, 454.
Roxburgh, Alexander (Major), 9, 154, 243, 365, 380, 390, 417, 421, 476, 480, 518.
Roynorld (see Reynolds).
Royston (Roystan), James, 576, 580, 582, 583.
Ruark (Ruarck, Reewark, Renark), James, 157, 299, 339, 358, 436, 498, 552.
Ruarke, Robert, 26, 643.
Rude, Andrew, 388.
Rudolph, Charles, 451.
Rudolph, Jacob, 159.
Rudolph, John, 586.
Rudolph, Michael, 586, 587, 588, 589.
Rudolph, Tobias, 589.

Rudreick, Mathew, 47.
Rue, William (see Rice), 157, 465, 501, 553.
Rugles, William, 388.
Rumbald, John, 338.
Rumble, William, 612, 613.
Rumfeld (Rumfell), Henry, 243, 265.
Rumford, William, 241.
Rummelson (see Rommelsen).
Rumsey, Charles, 62, 63, 647.
Rumwill, John (see Romills), 366.
Runenberger (see Ronenberger).
Runien, Henry, 156.
Runnenberg, Chas. (see Ronenberger), 358.
Ruppert, Jacob, 243, 266.
Russ, Adam, 72.
Russ, Henry (see Ross), 400.
Russell, Andrew, 340, 354, 437, 490, 553.
Russell, Aron, 243.
Russell, Henry, 155, 330.
Russell, James, 392.
Russell (Russel), John, 8, 159, 388.
Russell, Nichs., 159.
Russell, Philip, 375.
Russell, Thomas, 157, 297.
Russill, Abraham, 35.
Russum, Edward, 615.
Russum, Robert, 645.
Rutherford, Alex., 434, 499, 553.
Rutherford (Ratherford), Allener (Alliner), 336, 345.
Rutherford, Jas., 288.
Rutledge, Christopher, 62, 586, 587, 589.
Rutledge, Joshua, 364, 365, 380, 476, 481, 502, 521.
Rutledge, Wm., 60.
Rutlidge, Stephen, 51.
Rutter, Moses, 58.
Rutter, Thomas, 58, 157, 335.
Ryall, John, 241.
Ryan, Anthony, 16, 155.
Ryan (Ryon), George, 338, 366.
Ryan, Gilbert, 240.
Ryan (Ryon), Hugh, 241, 327.
Ryan, Jacob, 41.
Ryan (Ryant), James, 57, 58, 66, 159, 240, 288, 334, 554.
Ryan (Ryon), John, 24, 42, 59, 69, 156, 288, 340, 356, 382, 394, 438, 493, 553, 562, 598.
Ryan, Matthew, 155, 156.
Ryan, Michael, 154, 241.
Ryan, Nathan, 41, 157, 297.

Ryan (Ryon, Rine, Wryon), Patrick, 49, 243, 309, 320.
Ryan, Peter, 510, 554.
Ryan, Robert, 240.
Ryan, Timothy, 288.
Ryan (Rian), William, 54, 600.
Ryant, James (see Ryan), 58.
Ryder (see Rider).
Ryland, John, 61.
Ryland, Nicholas, 593.
Rylie (see Reiley).
Rylet, Edward, 344.
Ryley, Pat. (see Riley), 51.
Ryley, Silvester, 293.
Ryon, George (see Ryan), 366.
Ryon, Hugh (see Ryan), 327.
Ryon, John (see Ryan), 382, 394.
Ryon, Patk. (see Ryan), 309.
Ryon, Thomas, 335.

Sabolle, Joseph, 333.
Sadler, Humphy, 164.
Sadler, John, 167.
Sadler (Saddler), Saml. (S.), 572, 626.
Sadler, Thomas, 382, 412.
Saffell, Joshua, 9.
Saffle, Charles, 44.
Saftly, Henry, 50.
Sailor (Sealors), Alex., 250, 264.
Sails (Sales), Gabriel, 163, 340.
St. Clair (Sinclair), William, 244, 352, 433, 554.
Saint Tee, Valentine (or Tee, Valentine St.), 342.
Salbott, William, 166.
Sale, John, 601.
Salegh, Nichs., 249.
Sales (see Sails).
Sally, Wm. (see Selley), 41.
Salmon, Edward, 45.
Salmon, John (see Sammon), 554.
Salsbury, Thomas, 160, 330.
Sammon (Salmon), John, 162, 293, 357, 446, 484, 495, 554.
Sampson, John, 344.
Sampson (Samson, Sanson), Luke, 249, 356, 438, 493, 556, 630.
Sampson, Richard, 24, 161, 289.
Samuel, William, 245, 621.
Samuels, John, 68, 244.
Sandall (Sandle), John, 573, 579, 583.
Sanders, Aaron, 67.
Sanders Capt., 399.
Sanders, Bennit (see Saunders), 331.

Sanders, Daniel (see Saunders), 247.
Sanders, Enoch, 30.
Sanders, James (see Saunders), 162, 294.
Sanders, John (see Saunders), 33, 163, 164, 295, 300.
Sanders, John F. K., 36.
Sanders, Joseph, 649.
Sanders, Joshua (see Saunders), 167.
Sanders, Roger (see Landers), 544.
Sanders, Spencer (see Saunders), 161, 293.
Sanders, Thomas (see Saunders), 36, 160, 293, 629.
Sanders, Wm. (see Saunders), 70.
Sandlant, William, 57.
Sandle (see Sandall).
Sands, John, 575, 581, 647.
Sands, Thomas, 50.
Sands, Willm., 15.
Sanky, John, 250.
Sanquehart, Peter, 333.
Sansberry, Richd., 39, 165.
Sanson (see Sampson).
Sanxton, George, 68.
Sapington, Hartley, 64.
Sapington, James (see Sappington), 63.
Sapington, Thos. (see Sappington), 646.
Sapp, Robert, 9, 159, 327.
Sapp (Sap), Shadrach (Shadrick), 372, 395.
Sappington (Sapington), James, 63, 393, 401, 508, 556.
Sappington, Richard, 518.
Sappington (Sapington), Thomas, 163, 164, 245, 246, 289, 335, 433, 554, 646.
Sara, Dominick, 626.
Sargood, John, 249.
Sarjeant, Richard, Jr., 49.
Sarjent (see Sergeant).
Sarmer, Lynn, 606.
Sasser, Thos. Wm., 38.
Sasser, William, 38.
Satchell, James, 245.
Satchwell, Thomas, 249.
Satterfield, Wm., 248.
Saund, Thomas, 290.
Saunders (Sanders), Bennett (Bennit), 161, 331.
Saunders (Sanders), Daniel, 66, 247.
Saunders, George, 245, 358, 434, 499, 555.
Saunders (Sanders), James, 64, 102, 294, 416.
Saunders (Sanders, Lounders), John, 33, 102, 163, 164, 244, 295, 300, 344, 562, 572, 577, 623.
Saunders (Sanders), Joshua, 167, 301.

Saunders, Robert, 163.
Saunders (Sanders), Spencer, 27, 161, 293, 644.
Saunders (Sanders), Thos., 27, 36, 160, 163, 293, 554, 617, 629, 643.
Saunders (Sanders), William, 59, 70, 244.
Savage, William H., 462, 567.
Savere, Vachel, 68.
Savin, Edward, 61.
Savory, Joseph, 335.
Savoy (Savory), Philip, 160, 314, 354, 394, 451, 490, 556.
Sawyer, George, 334.
Sax, Henry, 411.
Sax, Richard, 290.
Sax, William (see Sykes), 358, 496.
Saxey, Geo., 289.
Sayers, James (see Sears), 297.
Saylers, William, 58.
Sayres (see Sears).
Scaggs, Christopher, 653.
Scaggs (Skaggs), William, 45, 446, 653.
Scalls (or Sealls), Alex., 416.
Scantlin (Scantlum), Edward, 395, 449.
Scantling, Thomas, 164.
Scarborough, Samuel, 400.
Scarriat, Thomas, 167.
Scary, Martin, 60.
Scego (see Seego).
Schaeffer, Adam (see Shaffer), 263.
Schaeffer, George, 182.
Schea (Seea), John, 606.
Schean, Danl. (see Shahan), 162, 314.
Schean, James (see Shehan), 162.
Schesler, George, 263.
Schevel, John (see Shovell), 315.
Schivener (see Scrivenor).
Schley (Shley, Shly, Sly), John, 564, 566, 568, 574, 618.
Schooling, William, 53.
Schorcht, John, 263.
Schrawder (Shrawder), Philip (———), 182, 264, 270.
Schreier (Shrayer), Mathias, 250, 263.
Schütz (Shutz), Jacob, 250, 263.
Schwager, John, 623.
Schwidzer, Fredrik (see Switzer), 264.
Scofield, William, 249.
Scondrick (see Scoudrick).
Scone (Scoone), Charles, 64, 659.
Scone, George (see Stone), 65, 244, 433, 557, 617.

Scoot (see Scott).
Scott, Absalom, 372, 396.
Scott, Alexr., 39, 165.
Scott, Benjamin, 73, 246, 304.
Scott, Charles, 64, 161, 162, 293, 330, 358, 431, 498, 554.
Scott, Edward, 294.
Scott, Gen., 301.
Scott, Henry, 572.
Scott (Scoot), Isaac, 162, 294, 339.
Scott, James, 31, 246, 249, 343, 396, 422, 437, 557, 565, 568, 661.
Scott, John, 165, 298, 317, 333, 389, 435, 492, 554, 615.
Scott, John Day, 15.
Scott, Joseph, 167.
Scott, Joshua, 161.
Scott, Levi, 458, 511, 555.
Scott, Michael, 428, 474.
Scott, Moses (Mores), 607, 659.
Scott, Patrick, 45, 249, 311.
Scott, Peter, 343.
Scott, Reuben, 577, 580, 582, 583.
Scott, Robert, 412.
Scott, Robert S., 61.
Scott, Samuel, 366, 412, 446, 502, 555.
Scott, Solo., 651.
Scott, Thomas, 9.
Scott (Scoot), William, 165, 289, 327, 404, 412, 645.
Scotton, Richd., 422, 471.
Scoudrick (Scondrick), Charles, 244, 557.
Scoudrick (Seondrick), Thomas, 69, 244, 556.
Scriables (Scraher), Jeremh., 164, 329.
Scribner (see Scriviner).
Scrivenor (Scrivner), Charles, 66, 645.
Scrivenor (Schivenor), Jacob, 419, 470.
Scrivenor, Robert (see Scriviner).
Scriviner (Scrivner, Souvener, Sherivenor), John, 40, 160, 317.
Scriviner (Scrivener, Scrivenor, Scrivner, Scribner), Robert, 67, 162, 314, 356, 392, 445, 494, 554.
Scroggy, Francis, 166, 415.
Scudder, Jesse, 246.
Scybert, Geo. (see Sybert).
Scybert, Nicholas, 42, 44.
Seabrooke (Seebrucks), Richard, 412, 653.
Seaburn, Peter, 50.
Seagreave, Patrick, 659.
Sealls (see Scalls).

Sealors, Alexander (see Sailor), 250.
Sears (Sayers), James, 164, 297, 581.
Sears, John (J., Lt.), 162, 163, 364, 369, 381, 402, 403, 404, 424, 476, 482, 522.
Sears (Sayres), Noah, 163, 357, 430, 497, 554.
Sears, William, 61.
Sebree (or Sibra), Spencer, 70.
Seburn, John, 248.
Second, George, 632.
See (see Lee).
Seea (see Schea).
Seebrucks (see Seabrooke).
Seego (Scego, Sergo), Thos., 467, 503, 557.
Seemore (Seemer) (see Seymore).
Seeney, Samuel, 645.
Segman (see Sigman).
Sehom, John, 45.
Selas, Andrew, 251.
Selby, James, 22.
Selby, Jesse, 21.
Selby, John Smith, 15.
Selby, Nichs., 369.
Self, John, 50, 165.
Selister (Silister), Anthony, 565, 567, 570.
Sellers (or Sellors), Robert, 72.
Selley (Solley), Wm. (see Sally), 424, 472.
Sellinger (see Sullinger).
Sellman, Jonathan (Capt.), 39, 106, 362, 378, 429, 462, 477, 478, 482, 521.
Sellman, John, 580.
Sellors (see Sellers).
Selly, John, 58.
Selwood (see Silwood).
Semms (see Simms).
Semore (see Seymore).
Senah (Sena), William, 465, 501, 557.
Sency, William, 659.
Seney, John, 65, 66.
Sengo, James, 428.
Senior, John (see Senner), 329.
Senner, John (see Senior), 162.
Seondrick (see Scoudrick).
Serell (see Sevell).
Sergeant (Sarjent), Thos., 162, 294.
Sergeant, William, 159.
Sergo (see Seego).
Series, John, 247.
Serjeant, George, 72.
Sermon, Leonard, 659.
Serverson, Benjamin, 61.
Seth, Charles, 651.
Seth, Jacob, 67, 244, 651.
Seth, William, 594.
Settlemeyer (Settlemires), Chr. (Christn.), 250, 263.

Sevell (or Serell), Daniel, 64.
Sevell, William (see Sevill).
Seveny, James, 248.
Sevill (Sevell, Sivill), William (see Sewell and Civill), 66, 245, 352.
Sevink (see Swink).
Sewall, Chas. (see Sewell), 36.
Sewall, Clement, 160.
Sewall, James (see Sewell).
Sewall, John (see Sewell).
Seward, David, 160.
Sewell (Sewall, Sewele, Sowall), Chas., 36, 39, 166.
Sewell (Sewall, Suel), James, 247, 349, 440, 498, 555.
Sewell (Sewall), John, 67, 166, 249, 306, 325, 387, 427, 464.
Sewell (Sewull), Joseph, 68, 615.
Sewell, Thos., 646.
Sewell (Sewel, Sevill, Sevell, Sivill), William (see Civill), 17, 66, 160, 245, 246, 352, 557, 615.
Seymore (Semore, Seemore, Seemer), Christopher, 343, 354, 436, 489, 555.
Shaaff, Arthur, 575, 581.
Shaaff, John T., 575, 581.
Shackler, Fredk., 328.
Shade, Jacob, 47.
Shadley (see Shanley).
Shadwick, William, 167.
Shafer, Adam (see Shaffer), 168.
Shafer, John (see Shaffer), 467.
Shaffer (Schaeffer), Adam (see Shafer), 251, 263.
Shaffer (Shafer, Sheffer, Shefer, Shefar, Shiffer), John, 250, 265, 404, 412, 467, 503, 555, 653.
Shahan (see Shehan).
Shame, Joseph, 47.
Shanahan, Elliott, 610.
Shandley (see Shanley).
Shane, Arthur (see Shean), 57.
Shane, Henry, 60.
Shane, James (see Shehan), 444, 506, 554.
Shank, John, 45.
Shanks, Alex., 30.
Shanks, John, 461, 506, 555.
Shanks (Shink), Joseph, 164, 329.
Shanks, Matthew, 30.
Shanks, Robert, 30.
Shanley (Shandley, Shadley), Jacob, 58, 249, 305, 623.

Index. 723

Shannen, Thomas (see Channon), 10.
Shannon, Patrick, 602.
Sharer, Michael, 246, 290.
Shark, John, 250.
Sharon, Frederick, 245.
Sharp (Sharpe), Henry, 161, 293.
Sharp, Joseph, 418, 469.
Sharp, Peter, 606, 659.
Sharp (Sharpe), William, 69, 245, 359, 554.
Sharpless, Robert, 246, 347, 439, 492, 555, 617, 632.
Sharpt (or Tharp), Danl., 245.
Shate, Adam (see Sheets), 344.
Shatz (see Shotz).
Shaughness (Shockness, Shoughnesey), Patrick (P——k, ——), 565, 567, 569, 574.
Shaver, Andrew, 249.
Shaver, George, 388.
Shaver, John, 248.
Shaver, Peter, 249.
Shaw, Alexander, 160, 640.
Shaw, Basil, 167, 350, 352, 397, 420, 460, 509, 556.
Shaw, Benj., 376, 453.
Shaw, Charles, 382.
Shaw, Dennis, 244.
Shaw, Henry, 336.
Shaw, John, 6, 70, 160, 248, 661.
Shaw, William, 168.
Shawhane, John, 68.
Shawnesey, Timothy, 58.
Shea, Daniel, 159.
Shea, Dennis, 603.
Sheafer, Christn., 261.
Sheafer, Jacob, 261.
Shean (Sheain), Arthur (see Shane), 57, 166.
Shean, Dennis, 248.
Shean, James (see Shehan), 630.
Shean (Sheehan), Patrick, 58, 165, 246, 323.
Shean (Sheehan), Timothy, 58, 165, 415.
Shears, Thomas, 342.
Sheavers, Danl., 245.
Shebrick (or Shelrick) (see Shoebrook).
Shedbolt, Wm., 40.
Shee, Murphy (Murphey), 417, 462, 487, 556, 653.
Sheehan, Patrick (see Shean), 58.
Sheehan, Timothy (see Shean), 58.
Sheehee (see Shehee).
Sheeke, Richard, 6.
Sheekels (Shukels, Shockles), John, 42, 393.
Sheekels (or Shukels), Thomas, 42.
Sheerlock, Salathiel, 249.
Sheese, Peter, 264.

Sheets, Adam (see Shate), 334.
Sheets, Jacob, 420.
Sheets, Thos., 472.
Sheffer (Shefer, Shefar) (see Shaffer).
Shehan (Shahan, Schean), Daniel, 45, 162, 314.
Shehan (Shehon, Schean, Shean, Shane), James, 162, 294, 324, 444, 506, 554, 630.
Shehan, Jeremiah, 336.
Shehawn, Jos., 70.
Shehee (Shehey, Sheehee), Edward, 246, 349, 446.
Shehee, Potter, 383.
Shehern, Miles, 27, 643.
Shehon (see Shehan).
Shell, Richard (see Stull), 164, 289, 296.
Shelly, John, 290.
Shelman, John, 47.
Shelmerdine, Stephen, 53, 166.
Shelrick (see Shebrick).
Shelton, Jno., 290.
Shenin, Thos., 611.
Shenk, John, 47.
Shepard, Francis (see Sherhard), 160.
Shephard, Jona. (see Shepherd), 167, 303.
Shephardson (Sheppardson), John, 423, 471.
Shepherd, Abraham, 616.
Shepherd, Henry, 336, 615.
Shepherd (Sheppard, Shepperd), James, 372, 395, 416, 453, 509, 555.
Shepherd (Shipperd), John, 412, 611, 613.
Shepherd (Shephard, Sheppard, Shepperd), Jonathan, 167, 303, 351, 397.
Shepherd, Nathaniel, 41.
Sheppard, James (see Shepherd), 395.
Sheppard, Jona. (see Shepherd), 397.
Sheppardson (see Shephardson).
Sheppart, Thomas, 44.
Shepperd, James (see Shepherd), 372, 416.
Shepperd, Jona. (see Shepherd), 303.
Sherburn, Luke Matthew, 6.
Shercliff (see Shircliff).
Sheredine, Upton, 73.
Sherhard, Francis (see Shepard), 6.
Sheridan (Sheriden), Bartholomew, 163, 598.
Sheridan (Sherridan), James, 163, 623.
Sheridan, John, 161.
Sheridan (Sheriden, Sheredan, Sheredin), Thomas, 160, 392, 401, 439, 509, 556.

Sherivenor (see Scriviner).
Sherren, James (J——), 27, 643.
Sherry, William, 289.
Sherwood, Charles, 371, 412.
Sherwood, Hugh, 68, 245.
Sherwood, John, 35, 67.
Sherwood, Nicholas, 610.
Shields, James, 68, 602.
Shields, John, 400, 427, 473.
Shields (Shiels), Patrick, 63, 404.
Shields, William, 67, 68, 289.
Shiercliff (Shutliff, Shirtley), Joseph, 36, 634.
Shiffer, John (see Shaffer), 404, 412, 653.
Shine (or Shrine), Adam (see Strine), 412.
Shingleborrough (Singleborough), George, 423, 471.
Shink, Joseph (see Shanks), 164.
Shipley, John, 58.
Shipley, Robert, 21, 161, 443, 556.
Shipley, Samuel, 247.
Shipperd (see Shepherd).
Shircliff, Thos., 30.
Shircliff (Shercliff), William, 34, 36, 166.
Shire, Nicholas, 600.
Shirkey, Chas., 345.
Shirley, Bennet, 355, 442, 491, 555.
Shirley, George, 164, 329.
Shirley, John, 345.
Shirley, William, 355, 442, 491, 556.
Shirtley (see Shiercliff).
Shirwin, Charles, 160.
Shively, John, 250, 266, 321, 447.
Shley (Shly), John (see Schley).
Shley, Paul, 51.
Shlife (Slife), John, 250, 265.
Shobrook (see Shoebrook).
Shock, Chris., 328.
Shockey (Shockee, Shokey, Stockee), Abraham (Abram), 290, 393, 445, 557.
Shockles (see Sheekels).
Shockley, John, 21.
Shocknesey, Thos., 168.
Shockness (see Shaughness).
Shoebrook (Shebrick, Shelrick), Edward, 426, 468, 504, 557.
Shoebrook (Shobrook, Strobrook), Philip, 162, 294, 313.

Shoemaker, Frederick (S. Fredk., ——k) (see Shoemaker, Samuel F.), 250, 262, 267.
Shoemaker, Herbert, 45.
Shoemaker, Jacob (Jacob R.), 167, 518.
Shoemaker, John, 264.
Shoemaker, Michael, 248, 250, 261, 262, 348.
Shoemaker, Peter, 249, 308, 322.
Shoemaker (Shomaker), Samuel F. (Saml.) (see Shoemaker, Frederick), 395, 447, 497, 556.
Shókey (see Shockey).
Sholly, Luke, 328.
Shoman, John, 405.
Shomig, Jasper, 595.
Shopper, Philip, 261.
Short, Christopher, 606, 659.
Short, Edward, 164.
Short, James, 249, 309, 310.
Short, Jonathan, 469, 556, 586, 590.
Short, Richard, 44.
Shorter, Roger, 245, 352, 434, 554.
Shortwell, Thomas, 454.
Shotten (Shottin), James, 161, 163, 443.
Shotter, Valentine, 261.
Shotz (Shotts, Shatz), John, 250, 261, 262.
Shoudon, Thomas, 289.
Shoughnesey (see Shaughness).
Shoulder, Nicholas, 248.
Shout, J. (see McKean, MacMal.), 137.
Shove, John, 245.
Shovell (Shovel, Schevel), John (see Chivel), 162, 294, 315, 446, 506, 554, 630.
Shrake (see Shrike).
Shrantz, George, 261.
Shrawder (see Schrawder).
Shrayer (see Schreier).
Shrayock (see Shryock).
Shriber, Jno., 328.
Shrike (Shriek, Shrake, Shrink), Andrew, 564, 567, 569, 573, 579, 584.
Shrine (see Shine).
Shrink, Andrew (see Shrike), 573, 579, 584.
Shriock (see Shryock).
Shriver, George, 270, 271, 517.
Shroop, Philip, 260.
Shrover, Peter, 270, 517.
Shryock, Henry, 51.
Shryock (Shriock, Shrayock), John, 250, 265.
Shubut, Christr., 340.
Shugar (Sugars), William, 35, 165, 296.

Index.

Slmgart, Martin, 182, 266, 365, 518.
Shugart (Shugert, Sugars), Peter, 247, 347, 439.
Shukels (see Sheekels).
Shukland, Joseph (see Strickland), 327.
Shuler, Andrew, 267, 322.
Shull, William, 602.
Shulmear, Peter, 167.
Shultz, John, 270, 517.
Shultz, Valentine, 270, 271, 517.
Shutliff (see Shiercliff).
Shutz (see Schütz).
Sibra (see Sebree).
Sicard, Anthy., 289.
Sickle (Syckle), Charles, 357, 383, 398, 404, 446, 495, 555.
Sickley, John, 336.
Sides, Christian, 264.
Sidney (Sidner), Joseph, 245, 434, 485, 556.
Siegfried, George, 47.
Sifer (see Sypher).
Sifton, Willm., 581.
Siggond, Capt., 593, 624.
Sigman (Segman), Peter (see Digman), 266, 270, 517.
Sikes (see Sykes).
Silister (see Selister).
Silk, James, 400, 412, 468, 504, 557.
Silk, Samuel, 394, 454, 557.
Silk (Silkes), William (see Sykes), 163, 432.
Sill, John, 46.
Sillman (see Sellman).
Sillivan (Sillivant) (see Sullivan).
Sillwood (see Silwood).
Silman (see Sellman).
Silver, George, 250, 268, 395, 447, 508, 556.
Silver, James, 72, 166, 457.
Silvester, Thomas, 245.
Silvey, Jacob, 290.
Silvor, Samuel, 45.
Silwood (Sillwood, Selwood), William, 251, 353, 447, 487, 556.
Sim, Jos., 38.
Sim (Sims), Patk., 7, 160.
Simister (Sinester), Thomas, 248, 347, 414.
Simkins, William, 247.
Simmes, James (see Simms), 169, 167, 364, 380.
Simmes, Jesse (see Simms), 165, 333.
Simmon (or Simon), Adam, 72.
Simmond, Wm. Fitz, 290.
Simmonds, Christr., 66.
Simmonds (Simonds), Thos., 419, 470.

Simmonds (Simonds), William, 393, 451, 508, 555.
Simmons, Aaron, 359, 603.
Simmons, Daniel, 160, 317.
Simmons, Geo., 39.
Simmons (Simonds, Symonds), James, 34, 572, 580, 582, 583.
Simmons, John, 32, 166, 167, 412, 414.
Simmons, Nathaniel, 33.
Simmons, Noble, 246.
Simmons (Simmonds, Simonds), Thomas, 67, 166, 305, 344, 419, 470.
Simmons (Simmonds, Simonds), Wm., 39, 335, 393, 451, 508, 555.
Simms, Alexcious, 42.
Simms, Charles, 640.
Simms, Edward, 161.
Simms, Ignatius (Ign.), 30, 160.
Simms (Simmes), James (see Sims), 169, 165, 167, 248, 364, 389, 518.
Simms (Simmes, Semmes), Jesse, 165, 333, 429, 506, 554.
Simms, Joseph, 31.
Simms, Roger, 36.
Simms, Thomas, 166.
Simon (see Simmon).
Simonds (Symonds), James (see Simmons), 580, 582, 583.
Simonds, Thos. (see Simmons).
Simonds, William (see Simmons).
Simons, Lawrence, 615.
Simpkins (Symkins), Charles, 248, 307, 356, 389, 439, 493, 555.
Simpkins, Thomas, 8.
Simpson, Alex., 647.
Simpson, Benj., 606, 659.
Simpson, Charles, 163.
Simpson, Greenbury, 36.
Simpson, Henry, 615.
Simpson, Lawrence (Laurence), 376, 396, 433, 463, 490, 511, 556.
Simpson, Luke, 300.
Simpson, Thomas, 5, 36, 169, 345.
Simpson, Thos., Jr., 36.
Sims, Andrew Green, 5.
Sims, James (see Simms), 5, 6.
Sims, Patrick (see Sim), 7.
Simson, James, 335.
Simson, William, 336.
Sinclair, Edward, 639.
Sinclair, William (see St. Clair).
Sinester (see Simister).
Singleborough (see Shingleborrough).
Sinklair, Andrew, 166.
Sinnett, Bryan, 23, 161.

Sinnett, Nicholas, 245.
Sinnett, Samuel, 63.
Sinnott, Barnaba, 645.
Sipher, Matthias (see Cyphert), 392.
Sissill, Joshua, 35.
Sitzler (Sitsler, Sitzley), Philip (———), 563, 567, 509.
Sivill (see Sevill).
Sizland (Sizeland), William, 250, 557.
Skaggs (see Scaggs).
Skel, Mathw., 648.
Skelly (Skally), Danl., 40, 166.
Skelly, John, 412.
Skepper, Isaac, 163.
Skepper, John (see Skipper).
Skerrett (Skerret, Skerritt), Clement, 365, 477, 575, 577.
Skerving (Skirvins), Chas. (Ensign), 439, 478.
Skiffington (Skivington), Mathew (Mathias, Math.), 52, 165, 415.
Skiffington, Roger, 161, 313, 660.
Skiles, Ephraim, 51.
Skinner, Arthur, 33.
Skinner, Daniel, 423, 472.
Skinner, Francis, 660.
Skinner, Frederick, 33.
Skinner, James John (Lt. ———), 74, 248, 362, 369, 378, 446, 506, 521, 572.
Skinner, Robert, 27, 161, 298, 644.
Skinner, Thomas, 67, 244.
Skipper (Skepper), John, 6, 160.
Skipper, William, 8, 160.
Skirvins (see Skerving).
Skivington (see Skiffington).
Skly, Randall (Randel), 422, 471.
Slack, Henry, 575, 580, 582, 583.
Slack, John, 40, 160, 577, 580, 582, 583.
Slackhouse (see Stackhouse).
Slade, John, 163, 164.
Slade, Thomas, 353, 457, 486, 554.
Slagel, John, 46.
Slately, Michael, 247.
Slater, Barthw., 249.
Slatry, Thomas, 60.
Slaughter, James Macy, 66.
Slaughter, Philip, 244.
Slaymaker, John, 660.
Slender, Christopher, 261.
Slick, William, 72.
Slife (see Shlife).
Slight, John, 416.
Slite (or Fite), James (see Stite), 250.

Sloan, John, 404.
Slocum (Slocome), Solomon), 162, 290.
Slone, Charles, 162, 322.
Sloop, John (see Stoops), 247.
Sloop, Joseph, 247, 348, 358, 440, 498, 555.
Slreiter, Joseph, 250.
Slups, Stephen (see Stubbs), 305.
Sly, John (see Schley).
Sly, William, 249, 555, 617.
Slye, Robert, 167.
Slyser, Jno. (see Stricer), 305.
Smadern (Smatter), John, 267, 321.
Small, Ephraim, 67.
Small, Jonathan, 67, 245, 289.
Smallwood, Bayne, 31, 35.
Smallwood, John, 358, 375, 396, 424, 442, 450, 500, 513, 555.
Smallwood, Ledstone, 35.
Smallwood, Walter Bean, 382, 392, 429, 440, 488, 556.
Smallwood, William (Gen., Brig. Gen.), 5, 20, 349, 366, 390, 425, 428, 467, 503, 522, 557, 581, 621, 634, 653.
Smart, Jonas, 39.
Smart, Richard, 164, 330.
Smatter (see Smadern).
Smee, Thomas, 162, 461, 617.
Smeltzer, Adam, 261.
Smeth (see Smith).
Smetherest (see Smothers).
Smith, Abram, 23.
Smith, Adam, 70, 182, 263, 343.
Smith, Alban, 6.
Smith, Alexander (see Smith, Dr.), 267, 323, 366, 476, 478, 518.
Smith, Alex. Lawson, 290, 300, 301, 362.
Smith, Alvin, 159.
Smith, Anthony, 161, 162, 554.
Smith, Aquilla (Aquila, Acquila), 249, 311, 324, 391, 555.
Smith, Bagwell, 289.
Smith, Bazil, 607.
Smith, Benjamin, 246, 392, 394, 415, 452, 507, 555.
Smith, Capt., 444, 621.
Smith, Charles, 5, 47, 160.
Smith, Christian, 45, 72, 250.
Smith, Christopher, 354, 392, 447, 489, 556.
Smith, Conrad (Conrod), 353, 457, 486, 554.

Smith, Daniel (see Smyth), 165, 250, 358, 389, 435, 437, 497, 505, 554, 555, 632.
Smith, David, 54, 554, 641.
Smith, Dinish, 62.
Smith, Dr. (see Smith, Alexander and Wm. J.), 457.
Smith, Edward, 6, 52, 165, 329, 344, 616.
Smith, Edward B., 35.
Smith, Edward Miles, 32, 164, 362, 378, 437, 478, 521.
Smith, Eli, 44.
Smith, Elias, 247, 354, 414, 463, 488, 556.
Smith, Elijah, 167, 353, 417, 457, 486, 554.
Smith, Emory, 412.
Smith, Everheart, 264.
Smith, Frederick, 307, 417, 462, 557.
Smith, Gilbert, 653.
Smith, Henry, 45, 47, 162, 165, 250, 261, 266, 268, 293, 575, 581.
Smith, Humphy., 167.
Smith, Ignatius (or Ignatious), 397, 412, 458, 556.
Smith, Isaac, 65, 248.
Smith, J., 581.
Smith, Jacob, 262, 270, 517.
Smith, James, 10, 56, 60, 61, 62, 160, 162, 163, 165, 166, 245, 248, 250, 264, 266, 267, 270, 293, 323, 346, 355, 365, 375, 382, 390, 394, 416, 421, 438, 443, 449, 461, 477, 492, 506, 517, 554, 555, 557, 575, 577, 578, 607, 617, 630, 660, 661.
Smith (Smyth, Smithley), John, 6, 11, 15, 24, 40, 43, 44, 46, 47, 52, 54, 56, 57, 58, 59, 62, 61, 66, 72, 160, 161, 162, 163, 164, 165, 166, 167, 245, 246, 247, 248, 249, 250, 251, 263, 264, 265, 266, 280, 290, 307, 315, 326, 327, 334, 335, 336, 342, 352, 363, 364, 379, 380, 382, 385, 391, 396, 412, 419, 428, 429, 433, 449, 453, 476, 477, 481, 482, 493, 503, 504, 521, 522, 554, 555, 556, 557, 562, 579, 584, 615, 616, 645, 648.
Smith, John Addison, 660.
Smith, Jonathan, 244.
Smith, Jonn, 648.
Smith, Joseph, 50, 51, 57, 59, 66, 72, 159, 160, 165, 265, 270, 289, 317, 330, 336, 366, 517, 522, 556, 572, 593, 600, 602, 606, 617, 660.

Smith, Joshua, 165.
Smith, Josiah, 557.
Smith, Josias, 164, 331.
Smith, Labs C., 166.
Smith, Leonard, 32, 164, 435, 506, 555.
Smith, Levi (Levy), 162, 244, 314, 352, 433, 554.
Smith, Levin (Levine), 165, 331.
Smith, Lodwick (Lodowk.), 388, 412.
Smith, Martin, 336.
Smith, Mathias, 250, 266, 323.
Smith, Matthew, 165, 331.
Smith, Michael, 63, 250, 267, 323, 354, 369, 393, 394, 448, 458, 488, 507, 556, 600.
Smith, Nathan (Nath.), 60, 167, 314, 364, 380, 385, 411, 481, 518.
Smith, Nathaniel, 161, 563, 565, 568, 570.
Smith, Nicholas, 386.
Smith, Patrick, 342, 627.
Smith, Peter, 12, 159, 305, 357, 431, 495, 554.
Smith (Smithly), Philip, 72, 250.
Smith, Reubin, 167, 358, 456, 498, 554.
Smith, Richard, 7, 32, 58, 73, 159, 385, 387, 412, 441, 500, 555, 612, 647.
Smith, Robert, 28, 133, 162, 163, 250, 266, 293, 323, 397, 404, 415, 416, 516, 577, 580, 582, 583.
Smith, Rowland, 265.
Smith, Samuel (Col.), 17, 18, 51, 164, 165, 314, 317, 392, 429, 640.
Smith, Thomas, 6, 47, 51, 166, 167, 246, 247, 289, 290, 301, 325, 340, 343, 349, 366, 383, 397, 404, 414, 440, 462, 499, 507, 554, 555, 556, 564, 567, 569, 574, 577, 580, 582, 588.
Smith, Valentine, 12, 160, 562, 623, 661.
Smith (Smyth), William, 19, 24, 26, 64, 150, 160, 163, 165, 166, 168, 246, 247, 248, 249, 280, 313, 314, 327, 335, 340, 345, 392, 397, 308, 400, 405, 418, 420, 449, 456, 464, 500, 512, 554, 556, 557, 598, 626, 643, 647.
Smith, Wm. J. (see Smith, Dr.), 518.
Smith, Winstone, 60.
Smitherd, John, 250.
Smithly (Smithley) John (see Smith), 251, 264, 265.

Smithly, Philip (see Smith), 250, 265.
Smock, Kendall, 22.
Smook (see Snook).
Smoot, John, 7.
Smoot (Smoote), Matthew, 377, 412.
Smoot, Thomas, 163.
Smoot (Smoote), William, 5, 150, 161, 162, 363, 379, 443, 479, 522.
Smothers (Smetherest), Robert, 53, 166.
Smulling, Randall, 21.
Smyley, John, 607.
Smyth, Daniel (see Smith), 53, 244.
Smyth, John (see Smith), 289, 290, 453.
Smyth, Joseph, 66, 290.
Smyth, Matthew, 64.
Smyth, Thomas, 18, 63, 64, 244.
Smyth, Wm. (see Smith), 335, 456.
Snead, Thomas, 601.
Snelling (Snilling), John, 161, 359, 554.
Snider, Casper, 328.
Snider (Snyder), Felix (Feolix), 336, 393.
Snider (Snyder), John, 47, 251, 261, 262, 336, 630, 640.
Snider, Willm., 261.
Snilling (see Snelling).
Snodey, Matthew, 59.
Snook (Snooks, Smook), Richard, 23, 161, 280.
Snow, Charles, 162, 317.
Snow, William, 335, 341, 437.
Snowdeigel (see Snowdenge).
Snowden, Cato, 397, 458, 487, 556.
Snowden, Ned, 412.
Snowden, William, 509, 557.
Snowdenge (or Snowdeigel), Peter, 47.
Snyder, Feolix (see Snider), 393.
Snyder, Frederick, 388, 336, 412.
Snyder, John (see Snider), 640.
Soap, Jno., 289.
Sockett, Richd. (see Lockett), 289.
Sohan, William, 607, 660.
Sollars, Jacob, 30.
Sollars, Robert, 40.
Sollers, Frederick, 250, 266.
Sollers, John, 38.
Sollers, Thos., 334, 335.
Sollers, William, 53, 165, 412.
Solley (see Selley).
Sollinder (see Sullender).
Sollovan (see Sullivan).

Solomon, David, 247.
Solomon, Exicael, 305.
Solomon, James, 603.
Solomon, Samuel, 42, 290.
Somervill, Alexander, 33, 34.
Somerville, George, 598.
Somerville (Somervill, Somervile, Sumervill, Summerville), James, 33, 34, 246, 349, 364, 381, 420, 481, 483, 521, 627.
Sommers, Jacob, 660.
Sommers, John (see Summers), 357, 610, 660.
Sothoren, Anthy., 289.
Souder, Adam, 653.
Sours, Michael (see Sowers), 439, 511, 555.
South, Alexander, 160, 317.
Southall, Joseph, 260, 354, 437, 489, 556.
Southard, Isaac, 27, 643.
Souther, Pheltr., 313.
Souther, Valenn., 161.
Souther, William, 412.
Southerland, Alex., 162.
Southerland, David, 290.
Southerland (Sutherland), Willm. (see Summerland), 160, 313.
Souvener (see Scriviner).
Sowall (see Sewell).
Sowden, Wm. (see Sowder), 474.
Sowder (Sowden), Wm., 428, 474.
Sowers (Sours), Michael, 248, 439, 511, 555.
Sowers, Henry (see Lowers), 358.
Spalding (Spaldin), Aaron, 161, 356, 462, 494, 554.
Spalding, Edward, 30.
Spalding, George, 164, 329.
Spalding, Henry, 162.
Spalding, William, 36, 161, 164, 329, 330.
Sparks (Sparkes), James Gould, 66, 645.
Sparks, Nimrod, 412.
Sparks, Richard, 39.
Sparrow, Alexander, 50, 246.
Speak, Andrew, 47.
Speak, Thomas, 164.
Speake (Speak), George, 31, 603.
Speake, Hezekiah, 49, 603.
Speake, Joseph, 248.
Speake, Lewis (see Peak), 49.
Speake (Speak), Nathan (Nathaniel), 246, 325, 440, 556.
Speake, William, 603.
Spears, John (see Spires), 451.
Speck, Henry, 262.
Speck, William, 266.
Spedden, Edward, 611, 613.

Spedden (Speddin, Spedding, Speden), Levin (Capt.), 611, 613, 614.
Spedding, Robert, 610.
Spence, John, 289.
Spencer, Augusteen, 63.
Spencer, Benj., 564, 567.
Spencer, Charles, 615.
Spencer, Col., 585.
Spencer, George, 247.
Spencer, Humphrey (Humphry), 24, 161, 289, 356, 441, 494, 654.
Spencer, James, 615.
Spencer, John, 66, 338.
Spencer, Jos., 161.
Spencer, Joseph H., 557.
Spencer, Oliver, 604.
Spencer, Richd., 387.
Spencer, Robt., 649.
Spencer, Samuel, 27, 644.
Spencer, Tamlin, 575.
Spencer, William, 165.
Spengle (Spengel, Spengell), Henry, 266, 270, 517.
Spesser, Nichl., 328.
Spicer, John, 162.
Spicer, Levin, 161, 293.
Spicer, William, 369.
Spicknall, Mathew, 161.
Spigman, John, 249.
Spilcey, Darbey, 577.
Spillard (Spilliard, Spilliards), Mathew (Matth.), 159, 167, 415.
Spillard, Matthias, 335.
Spindilow, Negro, 387.
Spindles, Richard, 602.
Spinknall, Robert, 33.
Spinks, Rawleyh (Rawling), 579.
Spires (Spyers, Spears), John, 382, 393, 451, 494, 555.
Spires (Spyers), Richard, 394, 453, 493, 555.
Spitsfathom, John, 601.
Splavin, Timothy, 159.
Splise, Peter, 51.
Sponk, Jacob, 247.
Sponsellor, John, 600.
Spottswood, Alexander, 604.
Spoutman, Francis, 247.
Spragu (Spraggs), John, 164, 329.
Spraigh (see Spray).
Sprangle, Peter, 423, 471.
Spratbrow, Wm., 244.
Spratt, Daniel, 660.
Spray (Spraigh), John, 162, 294, 321.
Sprigg, Samuel, 51.
Sprigg, Thomas, 73, 166, 336, 647.
Springer, John, 72.
Sprink, Andrew, 582.
Sprot, Wm., 646.
Spry, Joseph, 163.
Spry, William, 66.

Spunogle, Geo., 46.
Spurrier, Edward, 7, 39, 41, 166, 318, 319, 363, 379, 480, 482, 502, 522.
Spycer, Samuel, 43.
Spyers, Jno. (see Spires).
Spyers, Richard (see Spires).
Spyers, William, 246, 304.
Spyker, Benjamin, 42, 43, 248.
Spykes, William, 160.
Squible (Squib), John, 606, 660.
Stableford, Taylor, 244.
Stacey (Stacy), Robert, 166, 318, 457.
Stack, Elisha, 383.
Stackhouse (Slackhouse), John, 248, 348, 440, 500, 555.
Stackpole, Jas., 168.
Stacks, John, 168, 350.
Stacy (see Stacey).
Stafford, John, 167, 361.
Staid, Thomas, 167.
Stainger (see Stringer).
Stainton (see Stanton).
Stalcob, Henry, 247.
Stalion (see Stallings).
Stalker, William, 586, 583.
Stallings (Stallions), Abraham), 249, 306, 316, 323, 389, 437, 506, 555.
Stallings, Jacob, 164.
Stallings, Thomas, 161, 164, 246.
Stallings (or Stalion), William, 49.
Stallions (see Stallings).
Stalter (see Statler).
Standfield, Richard, 371.
Standley, Jacob, 557.
Standley, John (see Stanley).
Standley, Michael (see Stanley).
Standley, Roger, 163.
Standley, Salady (Selladay) (see Stanley).
Standley, William (see Stanley).
Stanford, Samuel, 70.
Stanley (Stanly), Christ. (Christr.), 47, 256.
Stanley (Standley), John, 579, 583.
Stanley (Standley), Michael, 43, 247, 349, 414, 424, 465, 501, 555.
Stanley (Standley, Standly), Salady (Selladay), 383, 404, 412, 465, 501, 556.
Stanley, Thomas, 47, 164, 584.
Stanley (Standley, Standly), William, 163, 368, 394, 449, 497, 556.
Stanton, Alexander, 606, 660.

Stanton, John, 250, 266, 314, 322, 354, 447, 488, 556.
Stanton (Stainton), Matthew, 163, 396, 455.
Stapleford, Henry, 24.
Stapleford (Staplefort), Joseph, 27, 644.
Stapleton (Stepleton), Richard, 249, 305.
Stapples, John, 575.
Starkey, John, 372, 396, 449, 508, 555.
Starr, Obediah, 412.
Starr, William, 168.
Start, John, 68.
Start, Moses, 244.
Start, Richard, 387, 412.
Start, Thomas, 24.
Statia, Robert, 581.
Statler (Stalter), Henry, 251, 264, 265.
Stauffer, George (——), 250, 265, 269, 270.
Staunton, Peter, 290.
Stead, William, 167.
Stean, William, 647.
Stedds (Stids), Richard, 166, 619.
Steel (Steele), Alexander, 381, 394, 445.
Steel, Capt., 599.
Steel, Elisha, 160.
Steel (Steele), James (see Still), 73, 334.
Steel (Steele), John (see Still), 49, 66, 314, 412, 426, 473, 595.
Steel, Joseph, 165, 648.
Steem, George, 445, 499, 555.
Steenson, John, 166.
Steers, John, 290.
Stein, Frederick, 315, 694.
Stein, Jacob, 263.
Stennett (see Stinnett).
Stephens (Stevens), Daniel, 426, 464, 508, 556.
Stephens, Edward, 38.
Stephens, Hugh, 38.
Stephens, James, 427, 473.
Stephens, John (see Stevens), 168, 305, 397, 404, 459.
Stephens, Oliver, 306, 449, 512, 556.
Stephens (Stevens), Peter (Pett.), 250, 356, 389, 437, 492, 555.
Stephens, Thomas, 53.
Stephens, William (see Stevens), 246, 294.
Stephenson, Alexander (see Stevenson), 304, 347.
Stephenson, John (see Stevenson), 244, 297, 646.
Stephins (see Stevens).
Stepleton (see Stapleton).
Sterling, Alex., 334.

Sterling (Stirling), William, 345, 436, 507, 555.
Stern, George, 247.
Sterne, John, 166.
Sterrett (Sterritt), William, 9, 160.
Sterling, Isaac, 162.
Steuart (or Stuart), Andrew (see Stewart), 68.
Steuart, Benj. (see Steward), 333.
Steuart, Charles (see Stewart), 647.
Steuart (Stuart), Isaac, 31. 67.
Steuart, James (see Steward), 333.
Steuart (Steward), Joshua, 377, 412.
Steuart (or Stuart), Robert (see Stewart), 68.
Steuart, Wm. (see Steward), 74.
Steuart, William Veal, 647.
Stevens, Benjamin, 161, 293.
Stevens (Stephins), George, 200, 338, 366, 445.
Stevens, Daniel (see Stephens), 556.
Stevens, Jacob, 47.
Stevens, John (see Stephens), 28, 33, 249, 346, 383, 602.
Stevens, Levi, 161.
Stevens, Peter (see Stephens), 250.
Stevens, Robert, 244.
Stevens, Vachel (of Benj.), 41.
Stevens, William (see Stephens), 167, 318, 324.
Stevenson, Aaron, 370.
Stevenson, Absolam, 10.
Stevenson (Stephenson), Alexander, 246, 304, 347, 353, 439, 487, 555, 648.
Stevenson, ——, Capt., 77.
Stevenson, James, 647.
Stevenson (Stephenson), John, 52, 164, 244, 297, 646.
Stevenson, Robert, 56.
Stevenson, Steven, 321.
Stevenson, Thomas, 57, 59.
Stewad (see Steward).
Steward, Alex. (Elexander) (see Stewart), 456, 627.
Steward (Stuard, Steuart), Benjm., 333, 357, 430, 496, 556.
Steward, David (see Stewart), 412.
Steward, Ignatious (see Stuart), 412.
Steward (Stewad), James (see Stewart), 34, 347, 353, 394, 439, 488.

Index. 727

Steward (Stewart, Stuart), John (Col., Maj., ——), 25, 43, 161, 248, 363, 370, 378, 379, 396, 449, 477, 613.
Steward, Joseph, 8.
Steward, Joshua (see Steuart), 412.
Steward, William, 445, 556.
Stewart (Steward), Alexander (Elexander), 456, 506, 555, 627.
Stewart (Steuart, Stuart), Andrew, 68, 245, 554.
Stewart (Steuart), Charles, 289, 290, 575, 580, 582, 583, 647.
Stewart (Steward), David, 370, 412.
Stewart, David Murray, 383.
Stewart, Edward, 63.
Stewart (Stuart, Sturt), George, 40, 59, 328.
Stewart (Steuart, Stuart), James, 51, 167, 248, 333, 415, 453, 554, 555.
Stewart, John (see Stewart), 43, 248, 482.
Stewart, Richard, 166.
Stewart (Steuart, Stuart), Robert, 68, 166, 305, 415.
Stewart, Saml., 247.
Stewart (Stuart), Thomas, 43, 245, 249, 289, 648.
Stewart (Steuart, Stuart), William, 74, 75, 249, 342, 392, 397, 416, 508.
Stids (see Stedds).
Stiener, Michael (see Stoner), 261.
Stiles, James, 266.
Stiles, Solomon, 660.
Still, George, 339.
Still, James (see Steel), 165.
Still, John (see Steel), 165.
Stilley, Ephraim, 22.
Stillman, John, 583.
Stillwell, Jas., 516.
Stillwell, Obadiah, 159, 640.
Stinnett (Stennett), John, 383, 404.
Stinson, William, 244, 645.
Stirling, William (see Sterling), 507, 555.
Stite (Slite, Fite), James, 250, 322.
Stiteley, Frederick, 412, 652.
Stoaker, James, 168.
Stoakes, Peter, 244.
Stoaks, John, 163.
Stoaks, Patrick (see Stokes).
Stockee (see Shockey).
Stockett, Henry, 166.
Stockett, Thomas, 245.
Stockley, John, 250.
Stocton, John, 61, 62.

Stockwell, William, 642.
Stoddart (Stoddert, Stoddard), William (Wm. T., Wm. Trueman, Wm. P.), 246, 364, 380, 481, 483, 522.
Stoffel (Stoffell, Stoffee), Fredk., 395, 463, 556.
Stoffel (Stoffell, Stoffle, Stoffee), John, 395, 453, 503, 556.
Stogdon, Thomas, 50.
Stoker, Charles, 615.
Stokes, James, 653.
Stokes (Stoaks), Patrick, 41, 166.
Stokes, Thomas, 163, 554.
Stonbreak, Valen., 249.
Stone, Charles, 294.
Stone, Cuthbert, 250, 391, 442.
Stone (Rone), Edward (see Rowan), 418, 469.
Stone, Frederick, 267.
Stone, George (see Scone), 244.
Stone, John, 39, 162, 329.
Stone, John Hoskin (Col.), 5, 160, 317, 376, 628, 629.
Stone, Joseph, 162, 329.
Stone, Richard, 10.
Stone, Thomas, 34, 40.
Stonebreaker, Adam, 251, 264.
Stonehouse, John, 573.
Stonehunt, Jno., 394.
Stonely, James (see Stovely), 414.
Stoner, Abraham, 419, 470.
Stoner, George, 47.
Stoner, Jno., 51.
Stoner, Michael (see Stiener), 251, 262.
Stoner, Samuel, 40.
Stonestreet, Butler Edelen, 35.
Stonestreet, William, 247, 349, 353, 440, 488, 555.
Stooncloser, Francis Anthony, 335.
Stoops, Andrew, 248.
Stoops, Benj., 646.
Stoops, John (see Sloop), 646.
Storm (Storam, Storrom, Storum, Storrum), Jacob, 51, 248, 306.
Story, Ephraim Wyn, 645.
Story, Robert, 290.
Stottlemeir, Davall, 18.
Stouder (Studer), Philip (see Strider), 250, 261.
Stout, John, 267, 323.
Stovely, James (see Stonely), 167.
Stover, Nicholas, 270, 272, 517.
Stowie, Jacob, 53.
Stoyle, Conrad (see Hoyle), 251.

Straam (Stroam, Strome), Henry, 250, 264.
Straights (see Streights).
Strap, Jacob (see Stroup), 160.
Stratford, Valentine, 60.
Stratton, Mack, 290.
Straup (see Stroup).
Strayly, Wentle, 264.
Street (Streett), George, 166, 414.
Street, James, 166.
Street, Samuel, 166, 475, 499, 556.
Streets, Robert (see Streights), 357, 495, 555.
Streets, Willm., 23.
Streib, David, 263.
Streights, Robert (see Streets), 335, 446.
Stricer (Striser, Slyser), John (see Stricker), 47, 305, 311.
Strickenburgh (Strikeingburg), Andw. John (Johnandrew), 63, 244.
Stricker, George, 18, 181.
Stricker, John (see Stricer), 249, 266.
Strickland, James, 602.
Strickland, Jos. (see Shukland), 162.
Strider, Philip (see Stouder), 262.
Strikeingburg (see Strickenburgh).
Strine (Shrine, Shine), Adam, 412, 653.
Stringer (Stainger), Forts (Fortunatus), 163, 299.
Stringer, Joseph, 164.
Striser, John (see Stricer), 47.
Striter, Jacob, 265.
Stroam (see Straam).
Strobrook (see Shoebrook).
Strome (see Straam).
Strong, Abram, 607, 660.
Strong, Charles, 70.
Strong, John, 164.
Strong, Nathan, 400.
Stroud (Strowd), William, 164, 299.
Stroup (Straup, Strap), Jacob, 57, 160.
Strum, Israel, 319.
Stuard (see Steward).
Stuart, Andrew (see Steuart).
Stuart, George (see Stewart), 328.
Stuart, Isaac (see Steuart).
Stuart (Steward), Ignatius, 377, 412.
Stuart, James (see Stewart), 415.
Stuart, John (see Steward), 427, 474, 611.
Stuart, Robert (see Steuart).

Stuart, Thomas (see Stewart), 289.
Stuart, William (see Stewart), 416.
Stubbs, Stephen (see Slups), 70.
Studdlemier, George, 261.
Studer (see Stouder).
Stuffle, Fettea, 46.
Stull, Daniel, 48, 248.
Stull, Richd. (see Shell), 296.
Stumm, George, 347.
Sturgis, Richard, 372.
Sturgis (Sturges, Sturgess), Thomas, 244, 424, 472, 509, 557.
Sturt, George (see Stewart), 40.
Such, George, 168.
Sucksberry, Joseph, 341.
Suffolk, Richard, 164, 295.
Suel (see Sewell)
Sugars, Peter (see Shugart), 347.
Sugars, William (see Shugar), 165, 296.
Suit, John Dent (John), 384, 412.
Suit (or Sute), Thomas, 32.
Suite (Suit), Edward, 163, 441, 556.
Suite (Suit, Sute), Jesse, 161, 392, 475, 509, 554.
Sulivan (Sulivain), James (see Sullivan), 27, 644.
Sulivan, Philip (see Sullivan).
Sulivan, Timothy, 600.
Sullavin (Sulivane) (see Sullivan).
Sullender (Sullener, Sollinder), Godfrey, 383, 397, 404, 415.
Sullinger (Sellinger), Daniel, 425, 429, 474, 505, 557.
Sullivan, Bright, 660.
Sullivan, Cornelius, 305.
Sullivan, Darby, 245.
Sullivan, Elijah, 464, 513, 556.
Sullivan, Elisha, 427.
Sullivan (Sullavin, Sulivan, Sulivain), James, 27, 164, 244, 343, 436, 505, 555, 644.
Sullivan (Swillivan), Jeremiah, 54, 340, 453, 512, 516, 555, 572.
Sullivan (Sillivan), John, 65, 160, 248, 289, 318, 400, 575, 619.
Sullivan, Lawrence, 247.
Sullivan, Mark, 163.
Sullivan (Sullavin), Nathaniel, 343, 436.
Sullivan, Owen, 290.
Sullivan, Patrick, 164, 395.
Sullivan, Perry (Perrigrine), 245, 352, 433, 554.

Sullivan (Sulivan, Sulivane), Philip, 49, 248, 341, 392, 438.
Sullivan (Sulivane, Sullivant, Sollovan), Solomon, 385, 465, 466, 501, 555.
Sullivan (Swillivan), Thomas, 54, 165, 249, 290.
Sullivan (Sillivant, Swillivan), William, 55, 67, 244, 358, 434, 497, 554.
Sullivane, Michael, 615.
Sullivant (see Sullivan).
Sumers (see Summers).
Sumervill (see Somerville).
Summerland, Wm. (see Southerland), 370.
Summers (Sommers), John, 246, 266, 347, 357, 445, 484, 495, 555, 610, 660.
Summers (Sumers), Obadiah (Oha., Obediah), 10, 133, 162, 163, 641.
Summers, Solomon, 245, 352, 434, 554.
Summers, Thomas, 162, 294, 360, 475, 499, 556.
Summers, William, 647.
Summerville (see Somerville).
Surkey, Peter, 395.
Surton, Robert, 246.
Sute (see Suit, Suite).
Sutherland, Walter, 32.
Sutherland, Wm. (see Southerland), 160.
Sutton, Abram, 244, 280, 587.
Sutton, Benjamin, 606, 660.
Sutton, Charles, 577, 580, 582, 583.
Sutton, Edward, 164.
Sutton, Henry, 70.
Sutton, Jacob, 607, 660.
Sutton, Martin, 602.
Sutton, Richard, 280, 606, 660.
Sutton, William, 647.
Swails (Swales), John, 427, 465, 501, 557.
Swails (Swailes, Swales), Robert, 165, 320, 660.
Swain, John, 164, 245, 280.
Swain, Richard, 248, 306.
Swain, Thomas, 382.
Swainey, Roger, 290.
Swan, Saml., 626.
Swaney, James, 162.
Swann (Swan), Alexander, 31, 163.
Swann, Barton, 160.
Swann, Basil, 32, 163, 280.
Swann, James, Jr., 32.
Swann (Swan), John, 17, 70, 164.
Swann (Swan), Leonard, 164, 206, 350, 554.
Swann (Swan), William, 165, 333, 420, 615.

Swann, Zeph., 32.
Swannick (Swanwick). Thomas, 249, 325.
Swanton, Peter, 246, 304.
Swanwick (see Swannick).
Swany, Thomas, 244.
Swartz, Christopher Godfrey, 182.
Swartz, Grodfried, 595.
Swartzell, Henry, 290.
Sweeney, John, 25.
Sweeney, Richd., 161.
Sweeny, Bryan, 70.
Sweeny, Edward, 289.
Sweiney, Charles, 58.
Sweney, ———, 399
Sweney, Notley, 309.
Sweney, Owen, 247.
Swepston, John, 601.
Swift, David, 245.
Swift, Gideon, 244.
Swift, John, 246.
Swillivan (see Sullivan).
Swine (see Swain).
Swiney, Dennis, 167.
Swink (Sevink), Abraham, 247, 349.
Switzer (Schwidger), Fredk., 251, 264.
Syass, James, 412.
Sybert (or Scybert), Geor., 44.
Sybert, Peter, 328.
Syble, Henry, 575.
Syckle (see Sickle).
Sydey, Adam, 328.
Sykes (Sikes, Sax), Willm. (see Silk), 313, 358, 406, 554.
Sylvester, Claudius, 66.
Sylvester, Job, 342, 355, 442, 492, 555.
Symkins (see Simpkins).
Symonds (see Simmons).
Sypher (Sifer), John (see Cypher), 300, 325.

T———, Henry, 462.
Tabbs, Barton, 252.
Tabbs, H. (Dr.), 291, 621.
Tabbs, Moses, 30.
Tabler, Jacob, 261.
Taft, Joseph, 251.
Taggart, Danl., 291.
Taggart, John, 252.
Talbot, Benjamin R., 53.
Talbot (or Talbort), Notley, 49.
Talbott (Talbot), Coxon, 7, 168.
Talbott, Elisha, 572.
Talbott, John, 53, 70.
Talbott (Talbot), Richard, 38, 39.
Talbott, William (see Tolbott), 290.
Talburt, Benjamin, 35.
Talburt, Osburn, 35.
Talen, Joseph, 63.
Tall (Toll), Anthony, 377, 378, 412.

Tallawer (see Tollaver).
Tallon, Thomas, 57.
Tally (see Tulley).
Talor (see Taylor)
Tame, Edward, 317.
Tamlane (see Tomlin).
Tancard, Thomas, 252.
Tanckard, Wm., 253.
Taney, Charles (see Tawney), 412.
Tannahill, Zacha., 9.
Tannehill (Tannahill), Adamson (A.), 301, 350, 365, 522.
Tannehill (Tannihill), James, 45, 382.
Tannehill, Josiah, 172.
Tanner, Edward, 393, 404, 450, 498, 558.
Tanner, James, 69.
Tanner, John, 251.
Tanner, Joseph, 71, 647.
Tanner, Thomas, 253, 311, 395, 558.
Tapler, John, 60.
Taquet (see Jacquett).
Tarance (see Farence).
Tarbutton, William, 375.
Tarings, Jno., 306.
Tarleton, Jeremha., 160.
Tarman, Benjamin, 326.
Tarman (Tawman), Henry, 170, 394.
Tarman, Richard, 412.
Tarr, Thomas, 66, 412.
Tarr, William, 24, 645.
Tarrance, William, 10.
Tarry, James (see Terry), 170.
Tasco (Tascow, Tasko), Richard, 295, 354, 486, 489, 557.
Tasker, Benjamin, 331.
Tasker, Richard, 170.
Tate, George, 423, 465, 501, 558.
Tate, James, 602.
Tate, John, 169.
Tate, John West, 342.
Tate, Timothy, 53.
Tatten (see Patten).
Tawman, Henry (see Tarman), 170.
Tawney (Taney), Charles, 384, 412.
Tawney (Downey), Frederick, 253, 266, 270, 517.
Tawney, Ralph, 463.
Tawson, James, 290.
Tayler, James (see Taylor).
Tayler, John (see Taylor), 169.
Tayler, Robert (see Taylor), 335.
Tayler, Solomon (see Taylor), 40.
Tayler, Willm. (see Taylor).
Taylor, Alex., 265.
Taylor, Amatio, 50.
Taylor, Aquilla, 168, 640.

Taylor, Belitha, 21.
Taylor, Benjamin, 252, 304, 349, 414.
Taylor, Capt., 598.
Taylor, Chas. Philpott, 45.
Taylor, Edward, 66, 169, 627, 645.
Taylor, Elisha, 641.
Taylor, Ezekiel, 456.
Taylor, Francis, 396, 454, 485, 558.
Taylor, George, 252, 348, 354, 440, 488, 558.
Taylor, Griffith, 170, 435.
Taylor, Jacob, 412.
Taylor (Tayler), James, 19, 168, 252, 377, 383, 412, 577, 603.
Taylor, Jason, 412.
Taylor (Tayler, Talor), John, 20, 35, 43, 66, 168, 169, 170, 171, 253, 331, 357, 397, 404, 415, 444, 459, 495, 498, 557, 572, 622, 649.
Taylor (or Talor), Joseph, 32.
Taylor, Joshua, 251, 433.
Taylor, Kendal, 372.
Taylor, Knotliff, 53.
Taylor, Lodowk., 18, 168.
Taylor, Marlow, 61, 646.
Taylor, Peter, 25, 643.
Taylor, Richard, 253, 341, 360, 389, 412, 438, 489, 558.
Taylor (Tayler), Robert, 170, 171, 252, 335, 347, 398, 430, 439, 499, 558, 627.
Taylor, Samuel, 42, 253, 389, 558.
Taylor, Simon, 308.
Taylor (Tayler), Solomon, 21, 40.
Taylor, Snowden, 41, 169.
Taylor, Thomas, 30, 169, 170, 252, 294, 297, 412.
Taylor, William, 168, 169, 171, 251, 252, 253, 262, 305, 318, 351, 356, 372, 391, 395, 420, 438, 450, 451, 494, 507, 508, 557, 558, 575, 581.
Taymon, Benja., 252.
Taymon, John, 399.
Teadly (see Tidley).
Teague, Laban, 22.
Teakle, Benj., 67.
Teams, Peter, 594.
Teanneclift, William, 38.
Tear, James, 30.
Tearn, Joseph, 30.
Tearnan (Ternan, Turnon), Dennis, 253, 341, 617.
Teat, Nathan, 335.
Teban, Peter, 558.
Tedford, John, 170, 593.
Todre, Reuben, 336.
Tee, Valentine Saint (Saint Tee, Valentine), 342.

Teener, Henry, 47.
Teeter, Jacob, 51.
Teeter, John, 51.
Telson (see Tolson).
Temblin (see Timblin).
Temple, Willm., 15.
Tenfield (T—ield), Richd., 170, 297.
Tenkins, Samuel, 587.
Tennaly, George, 47.
Tennant, James, 412.
Tennis (Tennes), Abraham, 13, 53.
Tennison, Jesse, 30.
Ternan (see Tearnan).
Terney, Dennis, 558.
Terrett (Terrot), William, 251, 342, 435.
Terrier, Charles, 251.
Terring, Wm. M., 172.
Terrot (see Terrett).
Terry (Tarry), James, 170, 300, 305, 453, 505, 558.
Terry, Joseph, 61.
Test, John, 45, 46.
Tester, Aaron (see Jester), 406.
Thackarel (Thackerel), Rezin, 168, 317.
Tharlkill, Robert, 331.
Tharp, Jacob, 169, 293.
Tharp, Danl. (see Sharpt), 245.
Thatcher, David, 24, 169.
Theston, Thos., 340.
Thom, John (see Thorn), 651.
Thom, William, 26, 642.
Thomas, Allen, 251.
Thomas, Anthony, 46.
Thomas, Beal, 386, 412.
Thomas, Caleb, 376.
Thomas, David (——vid), 565, 566, 569.
Thomas, Edward, 67, 650.
Thomas, Ellis, 69.
Thomas, Evan, 401, 464, 490, 558.
Thomas, George, 6, 168, 252, 387, 619.
Thomas, Giles, 442, 508, 558.
Thomas, Henry, 387.
Thomas, Hezeka, 169.
Thomas, Isaac, 251.
Thomas James, 50, 170, 298, 319, 329, 345, 354, 357, 431, 400, 406, 557, 558.
Thomas, John, 41, 67, 69, 171, 252, 317, 348, 358, 372, 396, 439, 455, 512, 558, 612, 613, 615, 645.
Thomas, John Allen, 25.
Thomas, John Germain (John Jerman), 586, 587.
Thomas, Joseph, 69, 169.
Thomas, Levi, 607.
Thomas, Levin, 378, 393, 412, 450, 507, 558.

Thomas, Michael, 64, 291.
Thomas, Nath., 572.
Thomas, P., 653.
Thomas, Richard, 251.
Thomas, Robert, 69.
Thomas, Samuel, 12, 74.
Thomas, Samuel Wright, 65, 645.
Thomas, Stanhope, 169.
Thomas, Starling, 387, 412.
Thomas, Thomas, 170, 171, 357, 430, 496, 558.
Thomas, William, 168, 327, 607.
Thomason, Ezekiel, 253.
Thompson (Thomson), Alex., 581, 647, 648.
Thompson, Andrew, 647.
Thompson (Thomson),, Athanatus (Athantius, Athas.), 170, 298, 329.
Thompson, Bartholomew, 169, 358, 412, 498, 557.
Thompson, Benjamin (see Thomson), 169, 251, 416, 473, 509, 558, 607.
Thompson, Bennet (Bennitt), 169, 427, 473.
Thompson, Bernard, 594.
Thompson, Charles (see Thomson), 169, 335.
Thompson, Col., 327.
Thompson, Cornelius, 251, 352, 434, 485, 557.
Thompson (Thomson), Francis, 8, 168, 313, 359, 432, 512, 558.
Thompson, George, 660.
Thompson, Henry, 251.
Thompson, Ignats., 170.
Thompson (Thomson), James, 6, 50, 168, 290, 412, 423, 472, 601.
Thompson (Thomson), Jeremiah, 253, 304.
Thompson, Jesse, 579, 582, 583.
Thompson (Thomson), John, 52, 171, 252, 253, 301, 394, 395, 401, 404, 448, 452, 488, 558, 575, 581, 660.
Thompson, John Baptist (John Battis), 44, 46.
Thompson, John D., 61, 62.
Thompson (Thomson), Joseph, 32, 171, 333, 430, 558.
Thompson, Lambert, 169, 314, 357, 444, 495, 557.
Thompson, Nathl., 49, 169, 252, 300.
Thompson (Thomson), Richard, 31, 168, 331.
Thompson, Robert, 564, 566, 568, 574.
Thompson, Samuel, 6, 168, 331, 563, 566, 568, 574, 587, 647.

Thompson (Thomson), Thomas, 169, 172, 294, 305, 333, 339, 430, 509, 557.
Thompson, William, 50, 169, 253.
Thomson, Alex. (see Thompson), 648.
Thomson, Athantius (see Thompson), 298.
Thomson, Barthola. (see Thompson), 169.
Thomson, Benj. (see Thompson), 330.
Thomson, Charles (see Thompson), 168, 171.
Thomson, Francis (see Thompson), 168.
Thomson, James (see Thompson), 168.
Thomson, Jerimiah (see Thompson), 304.
Thomson, John (see Thompson), 171.
Thompson, Joseph (see Thompson), 171.
Thomson, Richd. (see Thompson), 168.
Thomson, Thos. (see Thompson), 305.
Thorn (Thom), John, 67, 651.
Thornbourgh, Francis, 50.
Thornby, Joseph, 171.
Thornton, Harry, 291.
Thoroughgood (Thoroungood), Jno., 169, 415.
Thoupe, Richard, 253.
Thrift, Wm. Peregr., 646.
Thruston, Charles M., 599.
Tiarny (Torny), Patrick, 56, 290.
Tibbett, Henry, 427, 473.
Tibbles, Robert, 170.
Tibbs, John, 62.
Tibby, John, 68.
Tice, Nicholas (see Myss), 47.
Tidings (see Tydings).
Tidley (Teadly), Edward, 252, 347.
Tilley (Tilly), Zachariah, 9, 382, 412.
Timhlin (Timhen, Timlon, Timly, Temblin), John, 253, 267, 321, 326, 558.
Tindell (Tindel, Tindale), Samuel, 517, 558, 617.
T—ield, Richd. (see Tenfield), 297.
Tigner, James, 393, 451, 400, 558.
Tigner, Teagle, 393.
Tignor, William, 608.
Tiler, Edward, 169.
Tilghman, James, 387.
Tillard, Edward, 38, 39, 40, 252, 365, 522, 616.
Tillard, Froggitt, 63.
Tillard, James, 629.
Tillert, Samuel, 170.

Tillotson, Thomas, 645.
Tillotson, William, 646.
Tillwood, Wm., 397, 404, 416.
Tilyard, Wm., 647.
Timmons, Ambrose, 60.
Timmons, Philemon, 383.
Timmons, William, 168.
Timmons, Zadock, 22.
Timms, Edward, 168, 557.
Timms, Joseph, 31, 168.
Tindar, Mather, 608.
Tinsley, John, 601.
Tipling, Isaac, 171.
Tippet (Tippits, Tippitts), Peter, 170, 296, 557.
Tippett (Tippet), Henry, 509, 558.
Tippett (Tippet), Notley, 168, 320, 432, 500, 557, 593.
Tipton, Francis, 291.
Tiser, James, 171, 318.
Tite, James, 253, 447, 558.
Tobiry, Thomas, 47.
Todd (Tood), Benjamin, 171, 319, 568.
Todd, George, 400.
Todd, James, 24.
Todd, Levean, 20.
Todd, Richard, 393, 416.
Todd, Thomas, 571.
Todd, William, 325.
Toland (Towland), William, 169, 355, 461, 492, 557.
Tolbott, Wm. (see Talbott), 340.
Tolgan, Robert, 451.
Toll (see Tall).
Tollaver (Tallawer), Willm., 315.
Tolson, Benj., 67.
Tolson, George, 65.
Tolson (Telson), William, 476, 481.
Tom (see Tomm).
Tombleson (see Tomlinson and Tumbleson).
Tomey, Jas., 268.
Tomkins, Silus, 50.
Tomlin (or Tamlane), Grove, 49.
Tomlin (Tomling), Hugh, 7, 168.
Tomlinson (Tombleson), George, 423, 472, 601.
Tomlinson, Grove, 412.
Tomlinson (Tombleson), Zadock (Zadoch), 253, 309, 325.
Tomm (Tom), Henry, 264, 618.
Tompson, Lawce., 171.
Tompson, Smith, 602.
Tongue, Richard, 45.
Tongue, Robert, 253.
Tongue, Thomas, 370.
Tood (see Todd).
Toof (see Tuff).

Index

Toole (Tool), James, 52, 54, 56, 57, 66, 522.
Toole, John, 60, 345, 398, 404.
Toole (Tool), Robert (Ro———), 563, 567, 569.
Toole, Thomas, 170.
Tooloe, Dennis, 600.
Toomey, John (see Toomy), 251.
Toomy, Dennis, 253.
Toomy, John (see Toomey), 11, 600.
Tootal, Col., 443, 472.
Tootwiler (see Tutwiller).
Topet Robert, 660.
Tophouse, Thomas, 40.
Toplin, John, 341.
Topping, Peter, 171, 318, 353, 456, 486, 557.
Tordine, John, 473.
Torny, Patk. (see Tiarny), 290.
Torrell (or Forrell), Stephen, 58.
Torrey, John, 422, 471.
Tossuir, Clement, 607.
Touchstone (Tuchstone, Tuhton), Christopher 252, 349, 558.
Toughman, John, 46.
Toulson, John, 345.
Tower, John, 62.
Tower, Negroe, 400.
Towers, Henry, 299.
Towland (see Toland).
Towlin, John, 587.
Townley, Henry, 170, 356, 452, 493, 557.
Townsend (Townshend) Allen (Allin), 371, 394, 463, 509, 558.
Townsend, George, 370, 412.
Townsend, James, 642.
Townsend (Townshend), William, 171, 253, 391, 516, 558.
Townshend, Aaron, 253.
Townshend, Allen (see Townsend).
Townshend, Benja., 251.
Townshend, James, 253.
Townshend, Joseph, 253.
Townshend, Wm. (see Townsend).
Towson, William, 335, 522.
Towzey, Thomas, 168.
Trace, William, 46.
Tracey, Charles, 171.
Tracey, Thomas, 171.
Tracy, Philip, 49.
Tracy, William, 291.
Tragasskiss (Tregashes), Jacob, 170, 298, 660.
Trail, Archibald, 43.
Trail, Nathan, 44.
Trainer, Patrick, 252, 323, 620.
Trainer, Simon, 606, 660.

Traisey, Edward, 52.
Trammell (Tramel, Tramell, Trammel, Trammill, Tramnile), Dennis (Dinnis), 338, 359, 395, 450, 511, 557.
Traner, John, 608.
Traut, Henry, 263.
Travers, Joseph, 70.
Traverse, John (see Traviss), 465, 500, 558.
Travis, Andrew, 393.
Traviss (Treviss, Trevis, Traverse), John, 171, 351, 352, 420, 465, 500, 558.
Tree, Thomas, 171.
Tregashes, Jacob (see Tragasskiss), 660.
Trego, James, 169, 294.
Trego (Tregoe), Roger, 377, 378.
Trendall, Michael, 253.
Trene, James, 648.
Tress, Peter, 171.
Tressel, Goodhert, 328.
Treviss (Trevis), John (see Travisa), 171, 351, 420.
Trew, Thomas, 342.
Trice, George, 424, 465, 500, 558.
Trigg (Trig), Samuel, 170, 431, 558.
Triplett, Ensign, 603.
Trisner, John, 630.
Troth, Wm., Jr., 387.
Trott (Trot), William, 606, 660.
Trotten (Trotter), Lowden (Loudon), 171, 350.
Trotter, Loudon (see Trotten), 350.
Trout, Edward, 42.
Troxel (Troxal), Abraham, 51, 328.
Troxel, Jno., 51.
Troy, John, 171, 567.
Troy, Jeremiah, 412.
Troy, Timothy, 336.
Truck (Trucks) (see Trux).
True, Samuel, 334, 626.
Truelock, Henry, Jr., 65.
Trueman (Truman), Alexander (Capt.), 34, 38, 252, 327, 363, 368, 369, 370, 378, 402, 417, 439, 479, 522.
Trueman (Truman), John, 170, 298, 320, 363, 378, 478, 522, 627.
Trugard, William, 592, 593.
Truitt, George, 22.
Truitt, James, 21.
Truitt, Samuel, 22.
Trusky, Samuel, 171.
Truss, Wm., 400.
Trust, Peter, 171, 303.
Trusty (Trustee), John, 171, 335, 557.
Trux (Truck), John, 253, 263.

Trux (or Trucks), Peter, 72.
Trux, Willm., 263.
Tryall, Edward, 645.
Tryar, And., 172.
Tuchstone (see Touchstone).
Tucker, Alexander, 42.
Tucker, Anthony, 251, 558.
Tucker, Benj., 42.
Tucker, George, 412, 504.
Tucker, Henry, 404, 443, 558.
Tucker, Jacob, 383, 412.
Tucker (Tuckker), John, 33, 42, 168, 253, 341, 342, 432, 508, 557.
Tucker, Joseph, 572.
Tucker, Nathaniel, 66, 645.
Tucker, Thomas, 170.
Tucker, William, 168, 346.
Tuddero, Jacob (see Dudderow), 261.
Tuder, John, 52.
Tuell (Tuel), Wm., 35, 634.
Tuff (Toof), John, 252, 322, 622.
Tugby, John, 291.
Tuhton (see Touchstone).
Tull, John, 169, 641.
Tull, Solomon, 641.
Tulley, David, 63.
Tulley (Tully), John, 428, 429, 474.
Tulley (Tully, Tally), Jno. Davies (John D.), 394, 449, 490, 558.
Tullis, Litchfield, 251.
Tullock, William, 251.
Tumbleson (or Tombleson), Thomas, 72.
Tumbleston (Tumblestone, Tumberson), Evan (Evans), 171, 353, 458, 486, 557.
Tune, Robert, 19.
Tunstill, John, 345.
Turbott, John, 170, 296.
Turley, Dennis, 12.
Turnbridge, Saml., 252.
Turnbull, C. George, 660.
Turnbull, John, 601.
Turner, Abram, 169, 320.
Turner, Charles, 640.
Turner, Daniel, 63.
Turner, George, 372.
Turner, Henry, 204.
Turner, John, 43, 69, 170, 251, 253, 308, 320, 394, 419, 431, 448, 467, 500, 503, 557, 558, 564, 566, 569, 574, 584.
Turner, Joseph, 66, 394, 463.
Turner, Leonard, 171, 450.
Turner, Matthew, 304.
Turner, Nathl., 252.
Turner, Richard, 170, 252, 298, 615.
Turner, Samson, 171.

Turner, Samuel, 633.
Turner, Solomon, 253, 311, 314, 391, 412, 558, 653.
Turner, Thomas, 168, 171, 415.
Turner (Turnor), William, 169, 382, 394, 453.
Turner, Zachariah, 40.
Turnon (see Tearnan).
Turnstil, John, 626.
Turtle, Robert (see Purtle), 330.
Tutton (Tuten, Tutone), William, 169, 314, 623.
Tutwiler (Tootwiler), Jonathan, 253, 306.
Tuyger, Danl., 252.
Twinch, George, 172, 350, 352, 420, 470, 511, 558.
Twinch, Thomas, 510, 558.
Twiner, John, 47, 322, 356, 390, 438, 493, 558.
Twiner, Spintlo, 251.
Twining (Twineing), Nathaniel, 59, 171.
Twyford, Wm., 170.
Tyack, Thomas, 578, 583, 584.
Tyce, Henry, 328.
Tycont, Francis, 508.
Tydings (Tidings), Caleb, 171, 370, 412.
Tylea, Benjamin, 251.
Tyler, Elijah (see Tylor).
Tyler, John, 336.
Tyler, Littleton, 660.
Tyler, Richard, 382.
Tyler, Robert Bradley, 412.
Tyler, Saumel, 634, 635.
Tylor (or Tyler), Elijah, 69.
Tylor, Solomon, 26, 643.
Tyndall, Samuel, 661.
Tyser, Jacob, 328.
Tyser, Thomas, 32.

Ulence, Michael, 57.
Ulrich, Anthony, 505.
Uncles, Benja., 172.
Underhill, James, 308, 404, 416.
Underwood, John, 419, 470.
Urey, James, 27, 644.
Urquhart, Andw., 172.
Usher, John, 291, 400.
Utie, Wm., 424.

Vaine (Vain, Vane), John, 69, 424, 429, 465, 501, 550.
Vaine, Thomas, 69.
Valentine, George, 388, 412.
Valiant, Aaron (see Vallient, Ansell), 412.
Valiant (Vallient), John, 254, 606.
Valiant (Valient), Jonathan, 24, 172.
Vallent, Bennet, 425, 474.
Valient, Jonathan (see Valiant), 172.

Index. 731

Valient, William, 383.
Valliant, James, 254.
Valliant, Joseph, 613, 615.
Vallient, Ansell (see Valiant, Aaron), 385.
Vallient, John (see Valiant), 254.
Vallow (Varlow), John, 254, 434, 511, 559.
Vaubrunn, Levachee, 483.
Vandyke (Vandike), William, 56, 291.
Vane (see Vaine).
Van Ness, George, 377.
Vansant, Benj., 646.
Vansant, Christr., 646.
Vansant, Garret, 646.
Vansant, Geo., 646.
Vansant (Vanzant, Van Zandt), John, 53, 172, 457, 506, 559, 646, 661.
Vansickle, Gilbert, 660.
Vantier (Vantire, Vautier, Votier), Daniel, 172, 294, 324, 442.
Vanzant (Van Zandt), John (see Vansant), 53, 457, 506, 559, 661.
Vanzant, Joshua, 64.
Varlow, John (see Vallow), 559.
Varlow, Stephen, 172, 445, 511, 559.
Vatchle, John, 254.
Vaughan, Abraham, 660.
Vaughan, Cornelius, 254, 266, 323, 353, 395, 447, 488, 559.
Vaughan, James, 46.
Vaughan (Vaun), John, 576, 580, 582, 583, 607, 660.
Vaughan, Sherwood, 601.
Vaughan, William, 172, 559.
Vaun (see Vaughan).
Vautier, Daniel (see Vantier), 172.
Veach, John, 8.
Veal, James, 418.
Veatch, Abram, 254.
Veatch, Jacob, 43.
Veatch, William, 49.
Veazey, James, 587.
Veazey, Joseph, 61.
Veazey (Vezey), Levi, 11, 63.
Veazey, Noble, 61.
Veazey, William, 61.
Veazy, Edward, 28.
Vergen, John, 172.
Vermillion, Ben., 8.
Vermillion, Samuel, 7, 172, 463, 497, 559.
Vernon, George, 340, 559.
Vezey (see Veazey).
Vieeman, Richard, 305.
Vickers, Edward, 342, 358, 446, 498, 559.
Vickers, John, 172.
Videon, John, 564, 566, 569.

Viebler, John, 268.
Vincent (Vinson), Aaron, 383, 412.
Vincent, Benjamin, 254.
Vincent (Vinson), John, 35, 70, 172, 559.
Vincent, William, 254, 266, 323.
Vinestreet, Jno., 291.
Vinson, Aaron (see Vincent).
Vinson, John (see Vincent), 35, 70.
Visinger, Ludwick (see Wesinger), 261.
Votier, Daniel (see Vantier), 442.
Vreeportz, Geo. P. (see Keeport), 626.
Vycall (see Wykell).

Wachtel, John, 261, 263.
Waddle (Waddell), James, 336, 393, 416.
Waddle, Robert, 69.
Wade, Augustin, 292.
Wade, Edmund, 177.
Wade, Edward, 177, 297, 393, 447, 475, 512, 559, 605.
Wade, George, 35, 180.
Wade, Henry, 35.
Wade, James, 176.
Wade (Waid), John (——), 50, 258, 262, 267, 322, 353, 394, 447, 471, 487, 559.
Wade, Lanct., 173.
Wade, Richard, 10.
Wade, William, 573.
Wade, Zacharias Meek, 35.
Waggoner, Adam, 72.
Waggoner, Christian, 652.
Waggoner, Christopher, 259, 265, 412.
Waggoner, John, 72.
Waggoner, Joseph, 292.
Waggoner, Wilmington, 153.
Wagner, Henry, 264.
Wagner (Wagoner), Jacob, 250, 263.
Wagner, Stuffle, 264.
Wagoner, Jacob (see Wagner), 259.
Wagoner, Peter, 47.
Waid (see Wade).
Wailes (see Wales).
Wailey, Benj., 648.
Waite (Wait, Wate), Thomas, 176, 357, 444, 494, 559.
Wake, Richard, 175.
Waker, Edward, 44.
Walace, Whittington, 70.
Waldman (see Waltman).
Waldon, James, 335.
Waldon, John, 267.
Waldron (Waldrum, Walldram), Joseph, 179, 318, 415.

Wales (Wailes), Edward Lloyd (Edward L., Edward), 16, 187, 256.
Wales, William, 385.
Walker, Charles, 258, 651.
Walker, Chr., 51.
Walker, Edward, 174, 256, 257.
Walker, George, 331.
Walker, Gideon, 336, 369.
Walker, James, 58.
Walker, John, 8, 50, 59, 173, 174, 177, 179, 259, 358, 366, 394, 396, 418, 436, 447, 460, 498, 500, 503, 559, 560, 561.
Walker, Jonathan, 59.
Walker, Michal, 69.
Walker, Robert, 176, 442, 510, 559.
Walker, Samuel, 256, 660.
Walker, Thomas, 174, 606, 615, 660.
Walker, William, 43, 50, 69, 173, 291, 345, 382, 464.
Walkletts, Peter, 340.
Wall, David, 175.
Wall, Edward, 598.
Wall, Jesse, 175.
Wall, John, 620.
Wall, Patk., 174.
Wall, William, 175.
Wallace, Alex., 376, 419, 470.
Wallace, Charles, 5.
Wallace, David, 615.
Wallace, Herbert Alex., 648.
Wallace, Hugh, 14, 173.
Wallace, James, 63, 586.
Wallace, John (see Wallis), 36, 412.
Wallace, Michael, 5, 173.
Wallace, William (see Wallis), 66, 648.
Wallace, Zepheniah, 648.
Walldram (see Waldron).
Wallenberg, F., 180.
Waller, John, 57, 260, 294, 464, 512, 559.
Waller, Richard, 335.
Wallingsfort, James, 178, 369.
Wallis, John (see Wallace), 255.
Wallis, Richard, 291.
Wallis, Thomas, 42, 175.
Wallis, Wm. (see Wallace), 51.
Walls, George, 33, 412.
Walls, John, Jr., 64.
Walls, M. Alex., 254.
Walls, Richard, 334.
Walls, Sutton, 176.
Walls, Thos., 338.
Walls, William, 33, 64.
Walmsley (or Walmley), Robert, 61.
Walpole (Watpole), Joseph, 606.

Walsh, David (see Welch), 255, 564, 566, 574.
Walsh (Welsh), Edmund (Edward), 564, 567, 569, 573.
Walsh, James (see Welch), 577, 580.
Walsh, Nicholas (see Welch), 420.
Walsh, Patrick (see Welch), 18.
Walsh, Thomas (see Welch), 8.
Walten (see Walton).
Waltenback, Teeter, 50.
Walter, Edward, 394, 458, 561.
Walter, Levin, 660.
Walter, Mathew, 258.
Walters, Jacob, 66.
Walters (or Watters), John, 57.
Walters, Levi, 49.
Waltman (Waldman), Michael, 258, 358, 390, 436, 498, 560, 630.
Walton (Walten), John, 321, 341, 345.
Walts, Peter, 47.
Waltz, Michael, 8.
Walworth, Henry, 5.
Walworth, Hugh, 26, 70.
Wapels (or Waple), William, 31.
Ward, Benjamin, 395, 448, 506, 561.
Ward, Charles, 601.
Ward, Francis, 52.
Ward, George, 173, 330, 559.
Ward, Ignatius, 173.
Ward, James, 600.
Ward, John, 6, 51, 412, 423, 486, 660.
Ward, Joseph, 419, 465, 500, 561.
Ward, Lancelot, 331.
Ward, Mathew, 254.
Ward, Peter, 176, 335.
Ward, Philemon, 68.
Ward, Philip, 388.
Ward, Thomas, 58, 59, 173, 257, 305, 331.
Ward, William, 255, 256, 257.
Ward, Zachariah, 46, 256.
Warder, Jesse, 376, 413.
Warder (Warden), James, 134, 178.
Warden, James (see Warder), 178.
Ware, Francis, 20, 331, 376, 435, 476, 482, 522.
Ware, Hugh, 466, 502, 561.
Ware, John, 178.
Warfield, John, 254.
Warfield, Walter (W.), 173, 175, 363, 379, 476, 479, 522, 619, 620.
Waring, Basil, 450, 476, 480, 522.

Index.

Warlough, John, 175.
Warman, Stephen, 44.
Warman, Thomas, 616.
Warner, Arbukle, 254.
Warner, Benjn., 9.
Warner, George, 427, 473.
Warner, John, 68, 257.
Warner, Samuel, 35, 257.
Warner (Worner), William, 254, 615.
Warren, Hambleton, 24.
Warren, John (see Worren), 67, 254.
Warren, Thomas, 28.
Warrent, James, 257.
Warrick, Andrew, 12.
Warrier (see Warrior).
Warrin, William (see Warring), 331.
Warring, Basil (see Waring).
Warring (Warrin), William (see Worren), 177, 331.
Warrington, James, 377, 412.
Warrior (Warrier, Woriew), Daniel, 255, 322, 353, 439, 487, 500.
Wart, John, 46.
Warwick, James, 41, 179.
Warwick, Wm., 179.
Wary, David, 649.
Washington, Genl., 337, 366, 582, 591, 593, 596, 604, 623, 652.
Washington, Willm., 603.
Wastfalling, Danl., 258.
Wate (see Waite).
Waters, Abraham, 255.
Waters, Dyer, 423, 472.
Waters, James, 422, 471.
Waters, Jediah, 376.
Waters, John, 41, 256.
Waters, Nathan, 42.
Waters, Richard (R.), 173, 174, 363, 379, 425, 480, 483, 522.
Waters, Wevour, 42.
Waters, York, 175, 559.
Wathan, Francis (see Watkin), 32.
Wathan, Francis, of Barton, 32.
Wathen, Baker, 32.
Wathen, Barton, 376, 412.
Wathen (Watkin), Ign., 30.
Wathen (Watkin), John C., 30.
Wathington (see Worthington).
Watkin, Fran. (see Wathan), 30.
Watkin, Ign. (see Wathen).
Watkin, John C. (see Wathen).
Watkins, Capt., 399.
Watkins, Charles, 39.

Watkins John (J.), 21, 23, 26, 41, 383, 397, 404, 459, 511, 561.
Watkins, Gassaway (Gazaway), 7, 41, 257, 310, 364, 381, 480, 483, 522.
Watkins, James, 177.
Watkins, Leonard, 9, 172, 256.
Watkins, Martin, 261.
Watkins, Nicholas, 16, 17, 173.
Watkins, Peter, 176.
Watkins, Solomon, 257.
Watkins, Stephen, 41, 178.
Watkins, Thomas, 571.
Watkins, William, 176, 340, 426, 428, 460, 408, 502, 504, 560, 561.
Watpole (see Walpole).
Watson, Abraham (Abram), 180, 301.
Watson, George, 334, 561.
Watson, James, 256, 648, 660.
Watson, John, 38, 387, 419.
Watson, Solomon, 344.
Watson, Thomas, 53, 70, 176, 178, 297, 402, 500, 560, 600.
Watson, Walter, 338, 366, 442, 511, 560.
Watters (see Walters).
Watts, James, 24, 180.
Watts, John, 41.
Watts, Richard, 11, 173, 201.
Watts, Samuel, 41.
Watts, Solomon, 255.
Watts, William, 16, 25, 476, 480, 522.
Wattson (Watson), 291.
Waylon, Dennis, 324.
Wayman, Hezekiah, 575, 581.
Waymore, Thomas, 174.
Wayton, John, 176.
Waytts (see Wyatts).
Weaden (see Weedon).
Weagle, George (see Weefield), 258.
Weakley, James, 49.
Weakley (or Weaklin), Richard, 30.
Weakling, Alexander, 32.
Wearver (see Weaver).
Weatherly, Richd. Trane, 641.
Weathersby, Jas., 176.
Weathersby, Thos., 176.
Weatherholt (Weatherhold), Adam, 397, 406, 416.
Weaver (Wearver), Anthony, 345, 352, 434, 561.
Weaver, Capt., 327.
Weaver, Jacob, 261, 388.
Weaver, John, 613.
Weaver, Michael, 259, 264, 265.
Weaver, Peter, 46.

Webb, Banks, 338, 366, 396, 432, 500, 560.
Webb, John, 69, 176, 259, 291, 391.
Webb, Joseph, 41, 179.
Webb, William, 257.
Webber, George, 292.
Webber, William, 291.
Webster, John, 178, 415.
Webster, Thomas, 37, 174, 294.
Wedding, John, 177, 331.
Weden (see Weedon).
Wedge, Anthony, 342.
Wedge, Jono., 34.
Wedge, Samuel, 258, 334, 356, 463, 493, 560.
Wedge, William, 258, 311, 315, 391, 560.
Wedon, Joseph, 317.
Wedoney, Peter (see Equidowney), 491.
Weed, Edward (see Wade), 605.
Weeden, Henry (see Weedon).
Weeden (or Wheeden), Jesse, 30.
Weeden, Jonathan (see Weedon).
Weedon (Weeden), Henry, 16, 651.
Weedon (Weeden, Weaden, Weden), Jonathan, 38, 180, 350, 399, 417, 420, 469, 409, 559.
Weedon, John, 66.
Weedon, Thomas, 16.
Weefield, George (see Weagle), 602.
Weegul (Weeguel), John, 267, 268.
Weeks, Benjamin, 258.
Weems, David, 412.
Weems, James, 327.
Weems, Thos., 320.
Weer, Hugh, 424.
Weger (Weiger), Frederick, 265, 270, 517.
Weidman, John, 182.
Weiger, Frederick, 270, 517.
Weigle, Joseph, 321.
Weirey (Wierey, Wiery, Wirey), Michael, 257, 348, 358, 440, 498, 560.
Weirich, Christian, 50.
Weirich, Nicholas, 50.
Weiser, Benjamin, 182.
Weisong, Jacob, 50.
Welast, John, 412.
Welch (Welsh, Walsh), David, 255, 256, 335, 564, 566, 560, 574, 579, 582, 584.
Welch, Edward, 24.
Welch (Welsh) Garrett (Garrard), 393, 429, 449, 497, 561.
Welch, George (see Welsh), 173, 331.

Welch (Walsh), James (see Welsh), 294, 321, 577, 580, 581, 582, 583, 647.
Welch, John (see Welsh), 174, 179, 254, 300, 357, 416, 429, 443, 465, 494, 500, 561.
Welch, Joseph, 52, 178.
Welch, Mark, 257.
Welch (Walsh), Nicholas, 292, 352, 420, 440, 500, 559.
Welch (Walsh), Patk. (see Welsh), 18, 176.
Welch (Welsh), Philip, 397, 404, 561.
Welch (Walsh), Thomas (see Welsh), 8, 175, 178, 291.
Welch, William (see Welsh), 256, 304, 600.
Weller, John, 263.
Weller, Philip, 10, 173.
Wellman, Jacob, 173.
Wellman, William, 173.
Wells, Danl., 575, 581.
Wells, Edmund, 176.
Wells, Humphrey, 397, 404, 458, 510, 561.
Wells, James, 13, 53.
Wells, Jeremiah, 399.
Wells, John, 34, 41, 66, 177, 178, 344, 348, 354, 436, 490, 500, 572.
Wells, Martin, 175, 327.
Wells, Nathan, 40.
Wells, Richard, 45, 66.
Wells, Robert, 50.
Wells, Valentine, 257.
Wells, Willm., 30.
Welper, David (see Woelpper), 182.
Welsh, Abraham, 416.
Welsh, David (see Welch), 256, 560, 579.
Welsh, Edmund (see Walsh), 569.
Welsh, Francis, 575, 581.
Welsh, Garrett (see Welch), 393.
Welsh, George (see Welch), 397, 416.
Welsh, James (see Welch), 175, 335.
Welsh, John (see Welch), 26, 51, 177, 178, 392, 414, 423, 559, 575, 643.
Welsh, John Peirce, 51.
Welsh, Joseph (see Welch), 52.
Welsh, Patrick (see Welch), 53, 254, 292.
Welsh, Philip (see Welch), 397, 404.
Welsh, Robert, 40.
Welsh, Thomas (see Welch), 59.
Welsh, William (see Welch), 256, 397.
Welstead, William, 173.

Index. 733

Welstet (see Wetstet).
Weltner, Ludwick (Ludewick, Lodwick), 181, 262, 264, 266, 365, 522, 620.
Welty, John, 258, 266, 395.
Wember (Wimber), Thos. (see Niember), 355, 461, 491, 559.
Wesinger (Witsinger, Visinger), Ludwick, 259, 261, 262.
West, Alexander, 174, 341, 432, 559.
West, Fredk., 178.
West, James, 370, 392, 461, 507, 561.
West, John, 38, 174, 340, 341, 342, 355, 460, 491, 560.
West, John T., 460, 486, 559.
West, Jona., 400.
West, Joseph, 602.
West, Luke, 52.
West, Osborn, 44.
West, Shadrick, 653.
West, Stephen, 49, 50.
West, Thomas, 51.
West, William, 177, 294, 295, 462, 500.
Westbay, Robert, 641.
Westfield, Capt., 327.
Westlick, Wm., 311.
Weston, Joseph, 52.
Weston, Thomas, 39, 173, 317, 437.
Westwood, Williams, 256, 347.
Wetheral Samuel, 344.
Wetstet (or Welstet), William, 641.
Weyant (or Wicant), Jacob, 72.
Whailing (see Whaling).
Whaland (Whalin, Whaling, Whelan), Laurence (Lawrence D.), 256, 258, 322, 442.
Whaland, Owen, 64.
Whaland (Wheland, Wheylin, Whaling), William, 395, 452, 493, 559.
Whaley, Thos., 426, 473.
Whaley, Zadock (Zadoch, Zedekiah, Zedk.), 258, 356, 389, 438, 492, 561.
Whalin (see Whaland).
Whaling (Whailing), James, 577, 580, 582, 583.
Whaling, Lawrence (see Whaland), 258.
Whaling, William (see Whaland), 493.
Whalor, Ignatius Mitchell (see Wheeler), 257.
Wharton, Revel, 660.
Wharton, William, 258.
Whatmore, Robert, 258.
Whaylay (see Whaley).

Whealand (see Wheland).
Whealin (see Whelen).
Wheatcock, Joseph, 608.
Wheatley (Wheatly), Edward (Edmund), 427, 473, 510, 561.
Wheatley, George, 258.
Wheatley (Wheatly), John, 175, 329.
Wheatley, Silvester (or Sylvester), 175, 329, 561.
Wheatley (Wheatly), William, 6, 173, 174, 294, 559.
Wheatly, Henry, 174.
Wheatly, Samuel, 6, 173.
Wheeden (see Weeden).
Wheelan, Martin, 172, 641.
Wheelar, Charles (see Wheeler).
Wheelar, Ephraim, 26, 643.
Wheelar, Hezekiah, 368.
Wheelen, Christopher, 45.
Wheelen, Richard (see Whelen).
Wheeler (Wheelor), Basil, 331, 423, 471.
Wheeler, Benjamin, 660.
Wheeler (Wheelor, Wheelar), Charles, 385, 397, 404, 416, 463, 488, 560.
Wheeler (Whalor), Igns. (Ignatius Mitchell), 257, 389.
Wheeler, James, 179, 415.
Wheeler (Wheelor), John, 378, 413, 572, 583, 612, 613, 615.
Wheeler, John Hanson, 42.
Wheeler (Wheelor), Nathaniel, 174, 461, 617, 634.
Wheeler, Philip, 255.
Wheeler (Wheelor), Richard, 443, 506, 560.
Wheeler, Samuel, 42, 45.
Wheeler, William, 174, 340.
Wheelor, Thomas, 257.
Wheelton, Daniel, 23.
Wheelton, Joshua, 22.
Whelan, Laurence D. (see Whaland), 256.
Wheland, Geo., 179.
Wheland (Whealand), Jno., 179, 342.
Wheland, Willm. (see Whaland), 395.
Whelen (Whealin, Wheelen), Richard, 12, 173, 573.
Whelcy (see Whaley).
Wheylin (see Whaland).
Whight, Tarance, 178.
Whiley, Richard (see Wiley), 342.
Whilmon, Jno., 180.
Whipple, William, 258, 516.
Whips, Benj., 40.
Whireley, David (see Wirley), 180.

Whitaker (Whittaker, Whitticer, Whitekar), Francis, 174, 176, 297, 341.
Whitaker (Whitticar), William (see Whittico), 375, 404.
Whit, William, 322.
Whitchocks, Ezekiel, 378.
Whitcomb, John, 461, 492, 560.
Whitcomb (Whitcombe), Notley, 176, 359, 376, 396, 413, 433, 509, 560.
Whitcomb, Thos. (see Whittaker), 176.
White, Andrew, 313.
White, Benj., 660.
White, Capt., 589, 598.
White, Charles, 51, 342, 355, 442, 492, 561.
White, Daniel, 601.
White (Whyte), David, 564, 567, 570, 574, 584.
White, Edward, 30, 175, 314, 445, 516, 598.
White, Gregory, 648.
White, Henry, 413, 653.
White, James, 41, 174, 180, 258, 344, 390, 437, 511, 560, 627, 632.
White, James (of J.), 22.
White, James, of Wm., 22.
White, John, 35, 38, 40, 50, 52, 72, 177, 180, 292, 206, 344, 383, 413, 424, 466, 503, 561, 583, 615.
White, John Oldham, 401.
White, Jonathan, 172, 174, 331, 559, 573, 582, 617, 634.
White, Joseph, 255, 396, 454, 508, 561.
White, Jos. Wood (Wood, Jos.), 60, 292.
White, Leonard, 38.
White, Lewis, 393, 406, 416.
White, ——nee. 430.
White, Nicholas, 47.
White, Patrick, 46.
White, Peter, 258, 660.
White, Richard, 16, 516.
White, Samuel, 39, 66, 387, 645.
White, Samuel Beall, 42, 178, 437, 560, 632.
White, Thomas, 16, 46, 257, 466, 502, 561.
White, Walter, 73, 647.
White, William, 38, 267.
White, Zephaniah, 573.
Whitecotton, James, 179.
Whiteflatt, Joseph, 56.
Whitehead, Thomas, 382.
Whitehook, Ezekiel, 413.
Whitehouse, Joseph, 179, 319, 457.
Whitehouse, Samuel, 179, 386.
Whitekar (see Whitaker).

Whiteley (Whitely), William, 33, 177, 206, 346, 368, 384, 385.
Whiteman (Witeman), Conrod, 63, 255.
Whiticoe (see Whittico).
Whitman, Henry, 292.
Whitmore, Stephen, 177.
Whitmore, Wm., 394.
Whittaker, Francis (see Whitaker).
Whittaker (or Whitcomb), Thos., 176.
Whitticar (Whitticer) (see Whitaker).
Whittico (Whitticoe, Whiteco, Whiticoe), William (see Whitaker), 397, 404, 459, 488, 561.
Whittington, Benja., 255.
Whittington, Joseph, 255.
Whittle, Robert, 177, 295.
Whittocks, William, 387.
Whittom, Wm., 574.
Whyte (see White).
Wicant (see Weyant).
Wice, Peter, 256.
Wickert (Wickurt), Michael (Melchor), 388, 412.
Wickes, Richard, 645.
Wicks, Danl., 51.
Wier, Francis, 31.
Wierey (Wiery) (see Weirey).
Wiggins (Wigans), James, 179, 415.
Wilbey, John, 314.
Wilcox (Willcox), James, 177, 295.
Wilcoxen, John, 42.
Willcoxon, Thomas, 35.
Wild, James, 177.
Wild, Thomas, 418.
Wilder, Henry, 177.
Wilderman, Jacob, 52, 178.
Wildman, Edward (see Wilmon), 176.
Wildman, William, 258.
Wiley (Willey), John, 7, 70, 463, 496, 561.
Wiley (Whiley), Richard, 342, 355, 460, 492, 560.
Wilhelm, George, 259, 264.
Wilhite, Fredk., 261.
Wilhite, John, 653.
Wilk, Benj., 304.
Wilkerson, Geo., 292.
Wilkerson, John (see Wilkinson), 179, 352.
Wilkerson, Saml. (see Wilkinson).
Wilkes, Charles, 291.
Wilkes (Wilks) Joseph, 565, 567, 569, 573, 626.
Wilkeson (see Wilkinson).
Wilkie, Capt., 599.
Wilkins, Daniel, 427, 408, 504, 561.
Wilkins, John, 565, 566, 569, 574.
Wilkins, Thomas, 50.

Wilkinson (Wilkerson, Wilkeson), John, 175, 179, 255, 352, 433, 500, 561.
Wilkinson, Joseph, 33, 34.
Wilkinson, Richard, 564, 567, 569, 574, 617, 661.
Wilkinson (or Wilkerson), Saml., 651.
Wilkinson (Wilkeson), William, 177, 350, 560.
Wilkinson, Young, 365, 477, 506, 508, 573, 579.
Wilks (see Wilkes).
Willard, John, 400, 412.
Willby, William (see Willoughby).
Willcox (see Wilcox).
Willen, Charles, 412.
Willen, John (see Willing), 383.
Willen, William (see Willing), 340.
Willett (Willet), Charles, 376, 395, 450, 561.
Willey, John (see Wiley), 7, 496.
William, Jeriah (see Williams, Jeremiah), 353.
Williams, Alexr., 180.
Williams, Andrew, 180, 675, 581.
Williams, Basill, 51.
Williams, Benjamin, 257, 258, 347, 353, 350, 396, 437, 439, 455, 487, 492, 498, 559, 560, 561.
Williams, Cassitee (Caste), 70, 175.
Williams, Chaney, 41.
Williams, Charles, 59, 178, 309, 394, 448, 509, 560.
Williams, Culmore, 20.
Williams, Daniel, 258, 395, 447, 508, 559.
Williams, David, 174, 176, 201, 293, 559.
Williams, Edward, 27, 67, 643.
Williams, Eliot, 647.
Williams, Elisha, 42, 257.
Williams, Francis, 60, 334, 600.
Williams, Gabriel, 30, 258, 369, 396, 442, 508, 560.
Williams, George, 292, 383, 397, 404, 460, 490, 560.
Williams, Hazle, 601.
Williams, Henry, 251, 372, 396, 454, 498, 559.
Williams, Isiah, 370.
Williams, James, 49, 63, 64, 66, 255, 292, 385, 404, 413, 422, 465, 501, 561.
Williams, Jarvis, 179, 319, 457, 561.
Williams (William), Jeremiah (Jeriah), 176, 179, 353, 457, 486, 560.

Williams, John, 21, 23, 32, 35, 49, 63, 66, 173, 175, 177, 178, 179, 254, 257, 291, 292, 297, 313, 317, 318, 319, 33., 334, 357, 422, 426, 430, 406, 473, 475, 496, 502, 559, 560, 561, 575, 581, 602, 660.
Williams, Jno., Jr., 173.
Williams, Joseph, 36, 41, 47, 259, 266.
Williams, Laurance, 51.
Williams, Lilburn (Lilbourne, L.), 25, 318, 363, 379, 424, 425, 486, 482, 522.
Williams, Marshall, 660.
Williams, Mathw., 328.
Williams, Morgan, 292.
Williams, Moses, 343.
Williams, Nathan (Lieut.), 48, 51, 256, 292, 620.
Williams, Osborn (Osburn), 176, 295.
Williams, Otho Holland (Otho H., O. H., Otho, Col.), 28, 77, 255, 321, 349, 362, 368, 378, 444, 522, 616, 619, 620, 630.
Williams, Richd., 404.
Williams, Simon, 255.
Williams, Sullivan, 174.
Williams, Thomas, 15, 22, 41, 173, 178, 179, 254, 255, 256, 292, 324, 414, 572, 579, 583, 584, 634.
Williams, William, 40, 41, 170, 415, 641.
Williams, Zephaniah, 177, 329.
Williamson, Alexander, 175, 327.
Williamson, Ben., 292.
Williamson, Charles, 327.
Williamson, Daniel, 586.
Williamson, Gen., 477.
Williamson, Jeremiah, 400.
Williamson, Robt., 178.
Williamson, Thos., 178, 336.
Willin, John (see Willing), 395, 396, 397, 404.
Willin, William (see Willing), 69.
Willing (Willings), Evan (Evans), 424, 429, 467, 503, 561.
Willing (Willin, Willen), John, 383, 395, 396, 397, 404, 458, 496, 559, 561.
Willing, Littleton, 174.
Willing, Thomas, 173.
Willing (Willin, Willen, Willion), William, 69, 176, 340, 500.
Willing, Zacha., 10.
Willingham, John Bapt., 177, 329.
Willings (see Willing).
Willington, John (see Millington), 292.

Willion, William (see Willing), 500.
Willis, Andrew, 69, 254.
Willis, Daniel, 68, 254, 395, 449, 499, 560, 617.
Willis, Henry, 69.
Willis, Jarvis, 254.
Willis, John, 179, 256, 383, 396, 413, 456, 510, 559, 502, 603.
Willkird, Wm., 617.
Willman (see Wilman).
Willmott (see Wilmot).
Willon, David (see Wilton), 342.
Willoughby (Willoby, Willowby, Willby), William, 254, 387, 612, 613.
Wills, George, 175.
Wills, James, 13.
Wills, John, 58, 415, 617.
Willsdaugh, Henry, 265.
Willshire, John, 179.
Willshire, Samuel (see Wiltshire), 173.
Willson, Benjamin (see Wilson).
Willson, Edward, 58.
Willyard, Henry, 180.
Wilman (Willman), John, 466, 502, 561, 646.
Wilmington, Joseph, 179, 415.
Wilmon, Edward (see Wildman), 31.
Wilmore, John, 417, 469, 561.
Wilmot (Wilmott), Frederick, 176, 357, 431, 497, 559.
Wilmot (Wilmott, Willmott), Robert, 365, 477, 572, 579, 607.
Wilmot (Wilmott), William (Capt.), 52, 176, 296, 297, 363, 379, 456, 479, 485, 522.
Wilson, Acquila, 412.
Wilson, Barney (Barnaby, Barnard), 177, 178, 357, 430, 496, 560.
Wilson (Willson), Benjamin, 55, 562, 598.
Wilson, Daniel, 61, 175, 258.
Wilson, David, 255, 352, 434, 560.
Wilson, Gabril, 53.
Wilson (Willson), George, 255, 516, 560, 611, 613.
Wilson (Willson), Isaac, 58, 59.
Wilson (Willson), James, 43, 59, 64, 175, 176, 257, 297, 338, 344, 357, 372, 395, 416, 444, 450, 495, 508, 559, 560, 602, 627, 646.

Wilson (Willson), John, 35, 43, 172, 178, 254, 292, 297, 302, 319, 328, 393, 398, 401, 422, 424, 425, 426, 428, 448, 467, 472, 473, 488, 503, 560, 561, 607, 646, 660.
Wilson, John Fred., 172.
Wilson, Joseph, 601.
Wilson, Joseph Crawford, 413.
Wilson, Kilbreth (Helbraith), 180, 351.
Wilson, Mathew, 41, 292.
Wilson, Nathan, 43.
Wilson, Nathaniel, 33, 34.
Wilson (Willson), Obed, 42, 43.
Wilson, Richd., 292.
Wilson, Robert, 43.
Wilson, Samuel, 335, 441, 561, 667, 661.
Wilson (Wilsen), Thomas, 422, 471, 570.
Wilson, Tobias, 53, 178, 413.
Wilson, White, 53.
Wilson (Willson), William, 33, 70, 175, 177, 180, 258, 296, 343, 344, 351, 352, 372, 395, 420, 450, 463, 560, 561, 646.
Wilson, Zachariah, 382.
Wilstock (Witstock), Henry, 258, 265, 392, 448.
Wilthon, William, 584.
Wiltner (see Weltner).
Wilton, David (see Willon), 396.
Wilton, Jno., 291.
Wiltshier, Wm., 64.
Wiltshire, Jonathan, 294, 313.
Wiltshire (Willshire), Samuel, 12, 176.
Wiltz, Benja., 256.
Wimber (see Wember).
Wimberry, Thos., 175.
Wimer, John, 46.
Wimseld, James, 329.
Wimsott (see Winsett).
Winchester, George, 478, 522, 600.
Winchester, James (J., ——), 357, 358, 363, 379, 452, 478, 481, 482, 495, 522.
Windal (see Windle).
Winder, Henry, 425.
Winder, Levin, 13, 172, 364, 380, 476, 478, 522, 639.
Windgate (see Wingate).
Windham, George, 177, 297, 560.
Windham (Wyndham), Thomas, 173, 427, 431, 409, 559.
Windham, William, 49.
Windberry, George, 177.

Index. 735

Windle (Windal), Jonathan, 256, 348, 560.
Windley, Benja., 178.
Windley, John, 178.
Windom, George, 648.
Windom, Thomas, 10.
Windows, Henry, 407, 503, 561.
Windsor (Winser), Samuel Queen (Saml. Q.), 572, 648.
Winfrey, Aaron, 343, 617.
Wingate (Windgate), Andw., 175, 559.
Wingate, Thos., 380, 437.
Wink, Jacob, 259, 203.
Winkfield, James, 257.
Winn, John, 176, 601.
Winnaker, B., 180.
Winser (see Windsor)
Winset, Raphl., 174.
Winsett, James, 175.
Winsett (Winsott), Joseph, 384, 412.
Winslow, Jno., 395.
Winstandley, Henry, 68.
Winstandley, William, 68.
Winstanley (Winstanly), Francis, 178, 257.
Winstanley, John, 404.
Winstanly, Francis (see Winstanley), 178.
Winterbottom, Danl., 387.
Winterbottom, John (see Winterhurn), 255.
Winterburn, John (see Winterhottom), 300.
Wintz, George, 261.
Wire, James, 176.
Wirey (see Weirey).
Wirley (Whireley), David, 180, 328.
Wise, George, 264.
Wise, James, 64.
Wise, John, 454.
Wise, Lewis, 52.
Wise, Thomas, 44, 173, 175, 330, 384, 412.
Wisely, Benja., 174.
Wiseman, Thomas, 12, 173.
Wisenthal, Chas. Frederick, 20.
Wiser (Wizer), Michael, 258, 560.
Wisham, John, 588.
Witcomb (see Whitcomb).
Witeman, Conrod (see Whiteman), 255.
Withers (Witgurs), James, 292, 648.
Witner, William, 19.
Witsinger, Ludk. (see Wesinger), 259.
Witstock (see Wilstock).
Wizer (see Wiser).
Woelpper, David (see Welper), 182.
Woler, John, 323.
Wolf, Andrew, 47.
Wolf, Mathias, 50.

Wolf (Woolf), Peter, 256, 620.
Wolf, Samuel, 600.
Wolfe, Godfrey, 417.
Wolfred, Thomas, 322.
Wolgamot, David, 328.
Woller (or Wooler), Lodwick, 72.
Wolters, Ephriam (see Wootters), 258.
Woltmon, Nicholas, 258.
Wolveram, Fredk., 418, 469.
Wood, Aaron, 44.
Wood, Dorsey, 177, 319.
Wood, Gerard (Gerrard), 376, 479, 482, 522.
Wood, Henry, 33, 581.
Wood, Jacob, 179.
Wood, James, 179, 335, 358, 382, 395, 413, 448, 457, 498, 510, 560, 561.
Wood, James Green (see Greenwood), 64.
Wood, Jeremiah, 34, 412.
Wood, (Woods, Whood), John (see Hood), 10, 175, 176, 177, 292, 295, 300, 326, 435.
Wood, John Wilder, 32.
Wood, Joseph, 45, 48, 257.
Wood, Lenard, 42.
Wood, Richard, 26.
Wood, Robertson (Roberson, Robinson), 52, 178, 456, 510, 560.
Wood, Samuel, 370.
Wood, Thomas, 30, 42, 175, 176, 178, 372, 382, 396, 413, 428, 455, 458, 461, 472, 485, 499, 503, 509, 559, 560, 561, 509, 617.
Wood, William, 40, 173, 179, 257, 305, 615.
Woodall, John, 64.
Woodam, Robert, 256.
Woodard (see Woodward).
Woodburn (Woodbarn), Jonathan, 175, 329.
Woodburn, William, 33.
Wooden, John, 345.
Woodfind, Thos., 254.
Woodford, Gen., 302.
Woodland, James, 646.
Woodland, Rhode, 355, 442, 491, 560.
Woodland, Thomas, 304.
Woodley, Jonathan, 177.
Woodman, Jno., 180.
Woodringer, Daniel, 413.
Woods, Benjamin, 660.
Woods, David, 256.
Woods, James, 257.
Woods, John (see Wood), 293.
Woods, Jonathan, 67.
Woods, Joseph, 256, 304.
Woods, William, 24.
Woods, Zadock, 254, 618.
Woodthey, John, 177.
Woodward, Benedict, 9.

Woodward (Woodyard), Calvert (Colvert) (see Mason), 428, 475, 561.
Woodward, James, 412, 627.
Woodward (Woodard), Jesse (Jessee), 43, 173, 331.
Woodward, John, 175.
Woodward, Richard, 202.
Woodward, Wm., 368.
Woodyard (see Woodward).
Woolcott, William, 255, 435.
Woolcutt, John, 68.
Wooler (see Woller).
Woolf (see Wolf).
Woolfit, John, 581.
Woolford, James, 266.
Woolford, Michael, 176, 297, 354, 436, 400, 559.
Woolford, Thomas (Lieut. Col.), 25, 28, 174, 259, 364, 380, 480, 483, 522, 559, 620, 642, 644.
Woolford, William (W. ———), 25, 174, 340, 362, 378, 479, 522.
Wooling, Mason, 256.
Wooling, Richard, 256.
Woolmore, Godfrey, 60.
Woolsey, Wm., 563.
Wootters (Wolters), Ephm., 258, 308.
Word (see Wort).
Worder, John, 31.
Woriew (see Warrior).
Work, Alexander, 62.
Workman, Samuel, 19.
Worner, Solomon, 254.
Worner, William (see Warner), 254.
Worrell, Edward, 64.
Worren, William (see Warrin), 34.
Worren, John (see Warren), 35.
Worring, John, 174.
Worthington (Wathington), Wm., 340, 344.
Worthington, Benjamin, 24, 174, 202, 468, 505, 561.
Wort (or Word), Richard, 177.
Worslick, William, 258.
Worsley, John, 341.
Woster (Woter), John, 601.
Woulds, James, 254.
Wright, Absolum, 257, 354, 439, 488, 500.
Wright, Alexander, 14, 173.
Wright, Benjamin, 256, 331, 412, 428, 475.
Wright, Bozely, 7.
Wright, Charles, 291.
Wright, Constantine, 339.
Wright, Coursey, 255.
Wright, Danl., 291.
Wright, Edward, 12, 178, 257, 311, 457, 486, 560, 645.

Wright (Right), Elijah, 388, 411.
Wright George, 10.
Wright, James, 58, 256, 292, 376, 413, 647.
Wright, Jesse, 22, 174, 355, 412, 491, 559.
Wright (Wrighte), John (see Rite), 174, 178, 291, 294, 395, 463, 494, 511, 561, 606, 660, 661.
Wright, Joseph, 66, 645.
Wright, Nathan, 26, 174, 203, 303, 380, 426, 476, 480, 522, 643.
Wright, Nathanl., 254, 650.
Wright, Randall, 327.
Wright, Richard, 176.
Wright, Robert, 422, 471, 510, 561, 645, 651.
Wright, Samuel, 175, 250, 377, 448, 561, 616.
Wright, Samuel Turbutt (Samuel T.), 28, 522, 616.
Wright, Thomas, 65, 176, 257, 388, 412, 621.
Wright, William, 60, 175, 176, 255, 400.
Wrightson, Thomas, 370.
Wrinsile, Jesse, 427.
Write, Solomon, 35.
Wroth, Ishmael, 372.
Wroth, James, 61.
Wryon (see Ryan).
Wyatts (Waytts), Thomas, 340.
Wycoff, Saml., 388.
Wykell (or Vycall), Adam, 257.
Wyndham (see Windham).
Wynn, Wm. Smallwood, 35.
Wyonge, Philip, 50.

Yakely (Yeakly), Michael, 260, 264.
Yarnall, Benjamin, 55, 180.
Yater, Jacob, 53.
Yater (Yeator), Joseph, 16, 180.
Yates, James, 180, 330.
Yates, John, 43, 259.
Yates, Richard, 180, 661.
Yates (Yeats), Robert, 259, 310.
Yates (Yeates), Thomas, 52, 58, 413, 573, 618.
Yates, Vachel, 606, 661.
Yaulet, Samuel, 47.
Yeakly (see Yakely).
Yeast, Jacob, 307, 406, 459, 508, 562.
Yeater, Andrew, 18.
Yeates, Benjamin, 413, 653.
Yeates, Thomas (see Yates), 413.
Yeaton, John, 615.
Yeator (see Yater).
Yeats (see Yates).
Yeiser, Frederick, 182.

Yellum (Jellom), Jno., 572, 618.
Yewell, Christopher, 66, 645.
Yewell, C. Solomon, 259.
Yewell, John, 66.
Yewell, Thomas, 66, 342.
Yewling, Michael, 270, 517.
Yockley, Michael, 265.
Yoe, Joseph, 259.
Yoe, Robert, 259.
Yoe, Thomas, 259, 292, 651.
York, Thomas, 573.
York, William, 259.

Yost, George, 259.
Young, Balser, 388.
Young, Benja., 180.
Young, Daniel, 259, 327.
Young (Younge), David, 576, 580, 582, 583.
Young, Edward, 53.
Young, George, 34, 595.
Young, Godfrey (Godhed), 259, 264, 340, 562, 623.
Young, Henry, 18, 52, 250, 324, 475, 510, 562, 653.
Young, Isaac, 394, 452, 507, 562.

Young, James, 52, 54, 55, 57.
Young, John, 38, 180, 259, 319, 345, 347, 393, 396, 451, 457, 507, 562.
Young, Luke, 615.
Young, Peter, 180, 413.
Young, Robert, 646.
Young, Samuel, 250, 347, 353, 395, 439, 487, 562.
Young, Thomas, 259, 618.
Young, William, 74, 259, 390, 413, 438.
Younger, Frogget, 64.

Younger, George, 72, 259.
Younger, John, 33.
Younger, Thomas, 59.
Younger, Tiller, 887.

Zacharius (Lokerias), Fredk., 260, 300, 325.
Zarrell, Charles, 265.
Ziegler, Henry, 261.
Ziegler (Zeigler), John, 270, 517.
Zimmerman, John, 260, 261, 262.
Zimmerman, Tobias, 607.

www.ingramcontent.com/pod-product-compliance
Lightning Source LLC
Chambersburg PA
CBHW031537300426
44111CB00006BA/87